BIG IDEAS
MATH.

INTEGRATED
MATHEMATICS III

Ron Larson
Laurie Boswell

◆ **BIG IDEAS**
LEARNING ®

Erie, Pennsylvania
BigIdeasLearning.com

Big Ideas Learning, LLC
1762 Norcross Road
Erie, PA 16510-3838
USA

For product information and customer support, contact Big Ideas Learning
at **1-877-552-7766** or visit us at ***BigIdeasLearning.com***.

Cover Image
Jason Winter/Shutterstock.com, © Abidal | Dreamstime.com

Printed in the U.S.A.

ISBN 13: 978-1-68033-087-8
ISBN 10: 1-68033-087-X

3 4 5 6 7 8 9 10 WEB 19 18 17 16

Authors

Ron Larson, Ph.D., is well known as the lead author of a comprehensive program for mathematics that spans middle school, high school, and college courses. He holds the distinction of Professor Emeritus from Penn State Erie, The Behrend College, where he taught for nearly 40 years. He received his Ph.D. in mathematics from the University of Colorado. Dr. Larson's numerous professional activities keep him actively involved in the mathematics education community and allow him to fully understand the needs of students, teachers, supervisors, and administrators.

Ron Larson

Laurie Boswell, Ed.D., is the Head of School and a mathematics teacher at the Riverside School in Lyndonville, Vermont. Dr. Boswell is a recipient of the Presidential Award for Excellence in Mathematics Teaching and has taught mathematics to students at all levels, from elementary through college. Dr. Boswell was a Tandy Technology Scholar and served on the NCTM Board of Directors from 2002 to 2005. She currently serves on the board of NCSM and is a popular national speaker.

Laurie Boswell

Dr. Ron Larson and **Dr. Laurie Boswell** began writing together in 1992. Since that time, they have authored over two dozen textbooks. In their collaboration, Ron is primarily responsible for the student edition while Laurie is primarily responsible for the teaching edition.

For the Student

Welcome to *Big Ideas Math Integrated Mathematics III*. From start to finish, this program was designed with you, the learner, in mind.

As you work through the chapters in your Integrated Mathematics III course, you will be encouraged to think and to make conjectures while you persevere through challenging problems and exercises. You will make errors—and that is ok! Learning and understanding occur when you make errors and push through mental roadblocks to comprehend and solve new and challenging problems.

In this program, you will also be required to explain your thinking and your analysis of diverse problems and exercises. You will master content through engaging explorations that will provide deeper understanding, concise stepped-out examples and rich thought-provoking exercises. Being actively involved in learning will help you develop mathematical reasoning and use it to solve math problems and work through other everyday challenges. We wish you the best of luck as you explore Integrated Mathematics III. We are excited to be a part of your preparation for the challenges you will face in the remainder of your high school career and beyond.

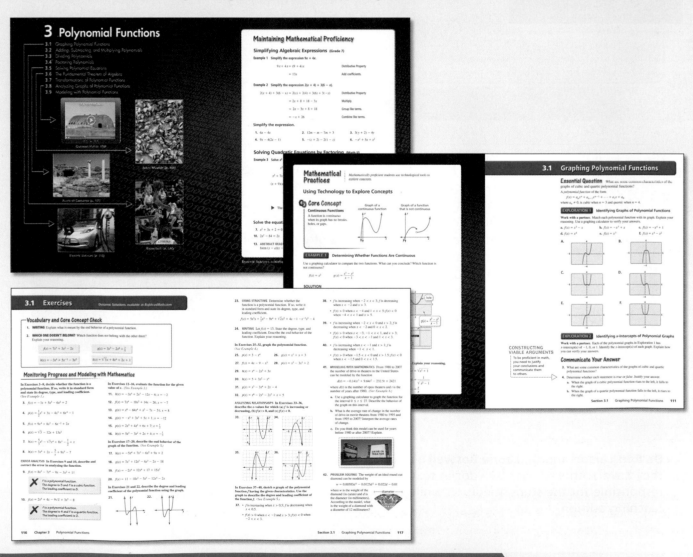

Big Ideas Math High School Research

Big Ideas Math Integrated Mathematics I, II, and III is a research-based program providing a rigorous, focused, and coherent curriculum for high school students. Ron Larson and Laurie Boswell utilized their expertise as well as the body of knowledge collected by additional expert mathematicians and researchers to develop each course.

The pedagogical approach to this program follows the best practices outlined in the most prominent and widely-accepted educational research and standards, including:

Achieve, ACT, and The College Board

Adding It Up: Helping Children Learn Mathematics
National Research Council ©2001

Common Core State Standards for Mathematics
National Governors Association Center for Best Practices and the Council of Chief State School Officers ©2010

Curriculum Focal Points and the *Principles and Standards for School Mathematics* ©2000
National Council of Teachers of Mathematics (NCTM)

Project Based Learning
The Buck Institute

Rigor/Relevance Framework™
International Center for Leadership in Education

Universal Design for Learning Guidelines
CAST ©2011

Big Ideas Math would like to express our gratitude to the mathematics education and instruction experts who served as consultants during the writing of *Big Ideas Math Integrated Mathematics I, II,* and *III*. Their input was an invaluable asset during the development of this program.

Kristen Karbon
Curriculum and Assessment Coordinator
Troy School District
Troy, Michigan

Jean Carwin
Math Specialist/TOSA
Snohomish School District
Snohomish, Washington

Carolyn Briles
Performance Tasks Consultant
Mathematics Teacher, Loudoun County Public Schools
Leesburg, Virginia

Bonnie Spence
Differentiated Instruction Consultant
Mathematics Lecturer, The University of Montana
Missoula, Montana

Connie Schrock, Ph.D.
Performance Tasks Consultant
Mathematics Professor, Emporia State University
Emporia, Kansas

We would also like to thank all of our reviewers who took the time to provide feedback during the final development phases. For a complete list of the *Big Ideas Math* program reviewers, please visit *www.BigIdeasLearning.com*.

Mathematical Practices

Make sense of problems and persevere in solving them.
- *Essential Questions* help students focus on core concepts as they analyze and work through each *Exploration*.
- Section opening *Explorations* allow students to struggle with new mathematical concepts and explain their reasoning in the *Communicate Your Answer* questions.

Reason abstractly and quantitatively.
- *Reasoning, Critical Thinking, Abstract Reasoning,* and *Problem Solving* exercises challenge students to apply their acquired knowledge and reasoning skills to solve each problem.
- *Thought Provoking* exercises test the reasoning skills of students as they analyze and interpret perplexing scenarios.

Construct viable arguments and critique the reasoning of others.
- Students must justify their responses to each *Essential Question* in the *Communicate Your Answer* questions at the end of each *Exploration* set.
- Students are asked to construct arguments and critique the reasoning of others in specialized exercises, including *Making an Argument, How Do You See It?, Drawing Conclusions, Reasoning, Error Analysis, Problem Solving,* and *Writing*.

Model with mathematics.
- Real-life scenarios are utilized in *Explorations, Examples, Exercises,* and *Assessments* so students have opportunities to apply the mathematical concepts they have learned to realistic situations.
- *Modeling with Mathematics* exercises allow students to interpret a problem in the context of a real-life situation, often utilizing tables, graphs, visual representations, and formulas.

Use appropriate tools strategically.
- Students are provided opportunities for selecting and utilizing the appropriate mathematical tool in *Using Tools* exercises. Students work with graphing calculators, dynamic geometry software, models, and more.
- A variety of tool papers and manipulatives are available for students to use in problems as strategically appropriate.

Attend to precision.
- *Vocabulary and Core Concept Check* exercises require students to use clear, precise mathematical language in their solutions and explanations.
- The many opportunities for cooperative learning in this program, including working with partners for each *Exploration*, support precise, explicit mathematical communication.

Look for and make use of structure.
- *Using Structure* exercises provide students with the opportunity to explore patterns and structure in mathematics.
- Students analyze structure in problems through *Justifying Steps* and *Analyzing Equations* exercises.

Look for and express regularity in repeated reasoning.
- Students are continually encouraged to evaluate the reasonableness of their solutions and their steps in the problem-solving process.
- Stepped-out *Examples* encourage students to maintain oversight of their problem-solving process and pay attention to the relevant details in each step.

Course Overview

Big Ideas Math Integrated Mathematics I, II, and *III* were developed using the consistent, dependable learning and instructional theory that have become synonymous with *Big Ideas Math*. Students will gain a deeper understanding of mathematics by narrowing their focus to fewer topics at each grade level. They will also master content through inductive reasoning opportunities, engaging explorations, concise stepped-out examples, and rich thought-provoking exercises.

The research-based curriculum features a continual development of concepts that have been previously taught while integrating algebra, geometry, probability, and statistics topics throughout each course.

In *Integrated Mathematics I*, students will study linear and exponential equations and functions. Students will use linear regression and perform data analysis. They will also learn about geometry topics such as simple proofs, congruence, and transformations.

Integrated Mathematics II expands into quadratic, absolute value, and other functions. Students will also explore polynomial equations and factoring, and probability and its applications. Coverage of geometry topics extends to polygon relationships, proofs, similarity, trigonometry, circles, and three-dimensional figures.

In *Integrated Mathematics III*, students will expand their understanding of area and volume with geometric modeling, which students will apply throughout the course as they learn new types of functions. Students will study polynomial, radical, logarithmic, rational, and trigonometric functions. They will also learn how visual displays and statistics relate to different types of data and probability distributions.

Geometric Modeling

See the Big Idea
Analyze the population density in various parts of Los Angeles—as viewed from an observation point high in the hills of Santa Monica.

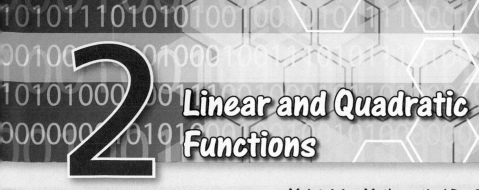

2 Linear and Quadratic Functions

See the Big Idea
Analyze the trajectory of a dirt bike after it
is launched off a ramp.

3 Polynomial Functions

See the Big Idea
Discover how Quonset Huts (and the related Nissen Huts) were utilized in World War II.

4 Rational Exponents and Radical Functions

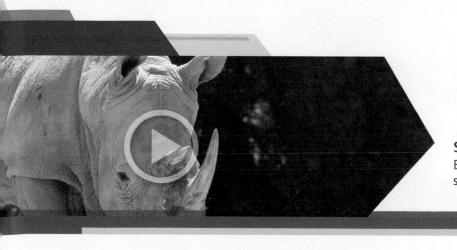

See the Big Idea
Explore heartbeat rates and life
spans for different animals.

5 Exponential and Logarithmic Functions

See the Big Idea
Explore how the USDA uses Newton's Law of Cooling to develop safe cooking regulations using rules based on time and temperature.

6 Rational Functions

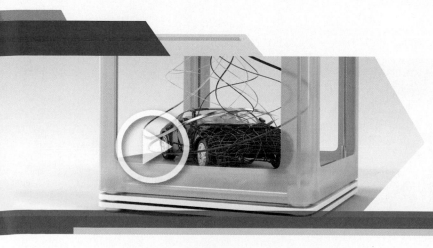

See the Big Idea
Analyze how 3-D printing compares economically
with traditional manufacturing.

7 Sequences and Series

See the Big Idea
Go on a field trip with the Friends of the LA River to explore the river's ecology.

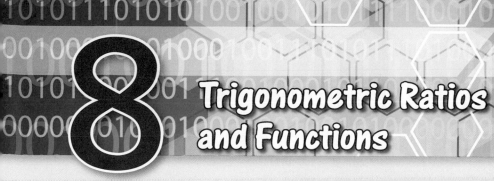

8 Trigonometric Ratios and Functions

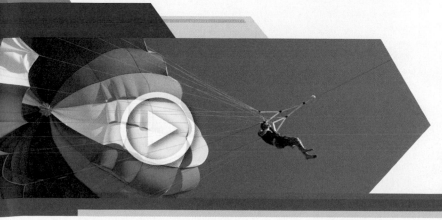

See the Big Idea
Join us as we find out just how high
a parasailer can go.

9 Trigonometric Identities and Formulas

See the Big Idea

Discover how the patterns made by your footsteps can reveal the efficiency in your stride.

10 Data Analysis and Statistics

See the Big Idea
Learn what kind of damage actually occurs after a volcanic eruption and how the information is collected.

How to Use Your Math Book

Get ready for each chapter by **Maintaining Mathematical Proficiency** and reviewing the **Mathematical Practices**. Begin each section by working through the EXPLORATIONS to **Communicate Your Answer** to the **Essential Question**. Each **Lesson** will explain **What You Will Learn** through EXAMPLES, **Core Concepts**, and **Core Vocabulary**. Answer the **Monitoring Progress** questions as you work through each lesson. Look for STUDY TIPS, COMMON ERRORS, and suggestions for looking at a problem ANOTHER WAY throughout the lessons. Take note of CONNECTIONS TO ALGEBRA and CONNECTIONS TO GEOMETRY which will inform you that the current concept can be applied to other topics throughout the program. We will also provide you with guidance for accurate mathematical READING and concept details you should REMEMBER.

Sharpen your newly acquired skills with **Exercises** at the end of every section. Halfway through each chapter you will be asked **What Did You Learn?** and you can use the Mid-Chapter **Quiz** to check your progress. You can also use the **Chapter Review** and **Chapter Test** to review and assess yourself after you have completed a chapter.

Apply what you learned in each chapter to a **Performance Task** and build your confidence for taking standardized tests with each chapter's **Cumulative Assessment**. For extra practice in any chapter, use your *Online Resources*, *Skills Review Handbook*, or your *Student Journal*.

1 Geometric Modeling

Silo *(p. 27)*

Sawmill *(p. 20)*

Road Salt *(p. 12)*

SEE the Big Idea

Population Density *(p. 4)*

Corral *(p. 5)*

Maintaining Mathematical Proficiency

Finding Areas of Two-Dimensional Figures

Example 1 Find the area of the circle or regular polygon.

a.

14.8 m

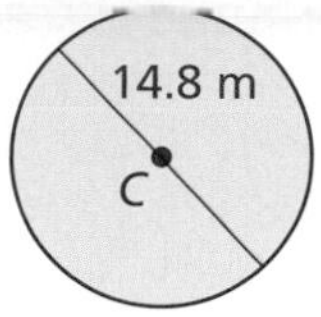

C

$A = \pi r^2$ Write area formula.

$= \pi \cdot (7.4)^2$ Substitute.

$= 54.76\pi$ Simplify.

≈ 172.03 Use a calculator.

▶ The area is about 172.03 square meters.

b.

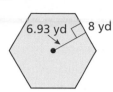
6.93 yd   8 yd

$A = \dfrac{1}{2} a \cdot ns$

$= \dfrac{1}{2}(6.93) \cdot (6)(8)$

$= 3.465 \cdot 48$

$= 166.32$

▶ The area is 166.32 square yards.

Find the indicated measure.

1. area of a circle with (a) a radius of 9.2 centimeters and (b) a diameter of 50.5 inches

2. area of a regular octagon with a perimeter of 80 feet and an apothem of 12.07 feet

Finding Surface Areas and Volumes of Three-Dimensional Figures

Example 2 Find the surface area and volume of the right cone.

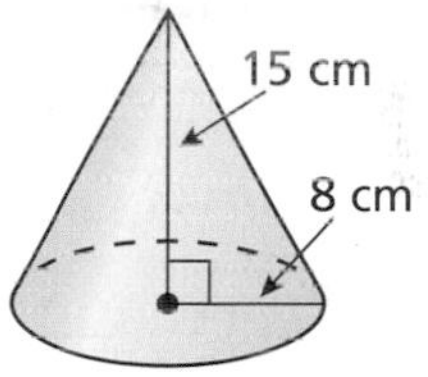

Using the Pythagorean Theorem, you can determine that the slant height ℓ is 17 centimeters.

15 cm

8 cm

Surface area

$S = \pi r^2 + \pi r \ell$ Write formula.

$= \pi(8)^2 + \pi(8)(17)$ Substitute.

$= 200\pi \approx 628.32$ Simplify.

Volume

$V = \dfrac{1}{3}\pi r^2 h$

$= \dfrac{1}{3}\pi(8)^2(15)$

$= 320\pi \approx 1005.31$

▶ The surface area is 200π, or about 628.32 square centimeters and the volume is 320π, or about 1005.31 cubic centimeters.

Find the surface area and volume of the solid.

3.

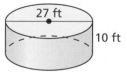
27 ft

10 ft

4.

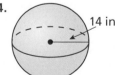
14 in.

5.

24 m

14 m

6. **ABSTRACT REASONING** A sphere with radius r fits perfectly inside a rectangular box. Can you determine the volume of the box? Explain your reasoning.

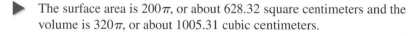

Mathematical Practices

Mathematically proficient students try simpler forms of the original problem.

Solving a Simpler Form of a Problem

⑤ Core Concept

Composite Figures and Area

A **composite figure** is a figure that consists of triangles, squares, rectangles, and other two-dimensional figures. To find the area of a composite figure, separate it into figures with areas you know how to find. Then find the sum of the areas of those figures.

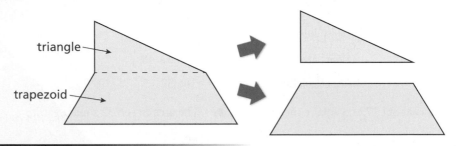

triangle

trapezoid

EXAMPLE 1 **Finding the Area of a Composite Figure**

Find the area of the composite figure.

SOLUTION

The figure consists of a parallelogram and a rectangle.

10.2 cm

11.7 cm

23.1 cm

Area of parallelogram	**Area of rectangle**
$A = bh$	$A = \ell w$
$= (23.1)(10.2)$	$= (23.1)(11.7)$
$= 235.62$	$= 270.27$

▶ The area of the figure is $235.62 + 270.27 = 505.89$ square centimeters.

Monitoring Progress

Find the area of the composite figure.

1.

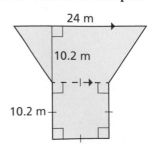

24 m

10.2 m

10.2 m

2.

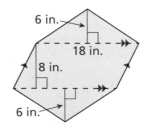

6 in.

18 in.

8 in.

6 in.

3.

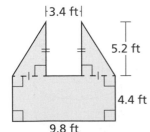

3.4 ft

5.2 ft

4.4 ft

9.8 ft

4. The concept above also applies when finding the surface area or volume of a composite solid. Why do you need to be careful when finding the surface area of a composite solid?

1.1 Modeling with Area

Essential Question How can you use the population and area of a region to describe how densely the region is populated?

EXPLORATION 1 Exploring Population and Area

Work with a partner. Use the Internet to find the population and land area of each county in California. Then find the number of people per square mile for each county.

a. Mendocino County

b. Lake County

c. Yolo County

d. Napa County

e. Sonoma County

f. Marin County

EXPLORATION 2 Analyzing Population and Area

Work with a partner. The six counties in Exploration 1 appear on a map as shown.

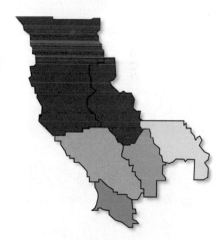

a. Without calculating, how would you expect the number of people per square mile in the entire 6-county region to compare to the values for each individual county in Exploration 1?

b. Use the populations and land areas in Exploration 1 to justify your answer in part (a).

MODELING WITH MATHEMATICS

To be proficient in math, you need to interpret mathematical results in real-life contexts.

Communicate Your Answer

3. How can you use the population and area of a region to describe how densely the region is populated?

4. Find the population and land area of the county in which you live. How densely populated is your county compared to the counties in Exploration 1?

5. In Exploration 1, the two northern counties are less densely populated than the other four. What factors do you think might influence how densely a region is populated?

What You Will Learn

▶ Use area formulas to solve problems.
▶ Use surface area formulas to solve problems.

Core Vocabulary

population density, *p. 4*

Previous
perimeter
area
surface area

Using Area Formulas

The **population density** of a city, county, or state is a measure of how many people live within a given area.

$$\text{Population density} = \frac{\text{number of people}}{\text{area of land}}$$

Population density is usually given in terms of square miles but can be expressed using other units, such as city blocks.

EXAMPLE 1   Finding a Population Density

The state of Nevada has a population of about 2.7 million people. Find the population density in people per square mile.

SOLUTION

Step 1 Find the area of Nevada. It is approximately shaped like a trapezoid. Use the formula for the area of a trapezoid to estimate the area of Nevada.

$$A = \frac{1}{2}h(b_1 + b_2) = \frac{1}{2}(320)(200 + 490) = 110{,}400 \text{ mi}^2$$

Step 2 Find the population density.

$$\text{Population density} = \frac{\text{number of people}}{\text{area of land}} = \frac{2{,}700{,}000}{110{,}400} \approx 24$$

▶ The population density is about 24 people per square mile.

EXAMPLE 2   Using the Formula for Population Density

A circular region has a population of about 430,000 people and a population density of about 5475 people per square mile. Find the radius of the region.

SOLUTION

Use the formula for population density. Let *r* represent the radius of the region.

$\text{Population density} = \dfrac{\text{number of people}}{\text{area of land}}$	Formula for population density
$5475 = \dfrac{430{,}000}{\pi r^2}$	Substitute.
$5475\pi r^2 = 430{,}000$	Multiply each side by πr^2.
$r^2 = \dfrac{430{,}000}{5475\pi}$	Divide each side by 5475π.
$r = \sqrt{\dfrac{430{,}000}{5475\pi}}$	Take the positive square root of each side.
$r \approx 5$	Use a calculator.

REMEMBER
You can solve quadratic equations of the form $x^2 = d$ by taking the square root of each side.

▶ The radius of the region is about 5 miles.

EXAMPLE 3   Using an Area Formula

You are designing a rectangular corral. A barn will form one side of the corral. The corral is to have an area of 450 square meters, but you want to minimize the amount of fencing that you need for the three sides of the corral not against the barn. This will include an opening that is 3 meters wide where a gate will be placed. How many meters of fencing do you need to build the corral?

SOLUTION

Step 1   Use what you know about the area and perimeter of the corral to find an expression that represents the perimeter of the three sides that need fencing.

The area A of a corral of length ℓ and width w is $A = \ell w$. So, $450 = \ell w$. Solving for ℓ gives $\ell = \dfrac{450}{w}$.

To minimize the amount of fencing you need, let a longer side of the corral be against the barn. So, the expression $2w + \ell$ represents the perimeter of the three sides that need fencing. Using substitution, this expression can be rewritten as $2w + \dfrac{450}{w}$.

Step 2   Use the *table* feature of a graphing calculator to create a table of values to find the width w that minimizes the value of $2w + \dfrac{450}{w}$. You may need to decrease the increment for the independent variable, as shown.

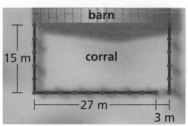

Increment of 4

X	Y1
4	120.5
8	72.25
12	61.5
16	60.125
20	62.5
24	66.75
28	72.071

X=16

Increment of 0.5

X	Y1
13.5	60.333
14	60.143
14.5	60.034
15	60
15.5	60.032
16	60.125
16.5	60.273

X=15

The width that minimizes the value of $2w + \dfrac{450}{w}$ is 15 meters. So, the length of the corral is $\ell = \dfrac{450}{w} = \dfrac{450}{15} = 30$ meters.

Step 3   Sketch a diagram of the corral that includes the gate opening, as shown.

barn

15 m   corral

27 m

3 m

USING TECHNOLOGY

In the first table, *y*-values decrease and then increase. Scrolling through *x*-values greater than 28 shows that *y*-values continue to increase. So, the minimum occurs near $x = 16$.

▶ So, you need $2w + \ell - 3 = 2(15) + 30 - 3 = 57$ meters of fencing.

Monitoring Progress   Help in English and Spanish at *BigIdeasMath.com*

1. About 58,000 people live in a circular region with a 2-mile radius. Find the population density in people per square mile.

2. A circular region has a population of about 175,000 people and a population density of about 1318 people per square mile. Find the radius of the region.

3. **WHAT IF?** You want the corral to have an area of 800 square meters. How many meters of fencing do you need?

Using Surface Area Formulas

EXAMPLE 4 **Using a Surface Area Formula**

A manufacturer designs the bearing shown. To prevent corrosion, the manufacturer coats each bearing with an anticorrosive grease.

2.5 mm

20 mm

a. A smaller bearing has linear dimensions that are one-half the dimensions of the bearing shown. Does the smaller bearing require one-half of the amount of grease that is used to coat the larger bearing? Explain.

b. A smaller bearing has the same radius and a height that is one-half the height of the bearing shown. Is one-half of the amount of anticorrosive grease used to coat the larger bearing enough to coat this bearing? Explain.

SOLUTION

The bearing is cylindrical. So, use the formula for the surface area of a cylinder to compare the bearings.

a.

	Larger bearing	Smaller bearing
Dimensions	$r = 2.5$ mm, $h = 20$ mm	$r = 1.25$ mm, $h = 10$ mm
Surface area	$S = 2\pi r^2 + 2\pi rh$ $= 2\pi(2.5)^2 + 2\pi(2.5)(20)$ $= 112.5\pi$ mm^2	$S = 2\pi r^2 + 2\pi rh$ $= 2\pi(1.25)^2 + 2\pi(1.25)(10)$ $= 28.125\pi$ mm^2

The surface area of the smaller bearing is $\dfrac{28.125\pi}{112.5\pi} = \dfrac{1}{4}$ times the surface area of the larger bearing.

▶ No, the smaller bearing requires only $\dfrac{1}{4}$ of the amount of grease that is used to coat the larger bearing.

b. The smaller bearing has a radius of 2.5 millimeters and a height of 10 millimeters. Its surface area is

$$S = 2\pi(2.5)^2 + 2\pi(2.5)(10)$$

$$= 62.5\pi \text{ mm}^2.$$

So, the surface area of the smaller bearing is $\dfrac{62.5\pi}{112.5\pi} = \dfrac{5}{9}$ times the surface area of the larger bearing.

▶ No, because $\dfrac{5}{9} > \dfrac{1}{2}$, one-half of the amount of anticorrosive grease used to coat the larger bearing is not enough to coat the smaller bearing.

ANALYZING MATHEMATICAL RELATIONSHIPS

Notice that while the surface area does not scale by a factor of $\dfrac{1}{2}$, the lateral surface area does scale by a factor of

$$\dfrac{2\pi(2.5)(10)}{2\pi(2.5)(20)} = \dfrac{50\pi}{100\pi} = \dfrac{1}{2}.$$

Monitoring Progress   Help in English and Spanish at *BigIdeasMath.com*

4. A manufacturer designs the bearing shown. To prevent corrosion, the manufacturer coats each bearing with an anticorrosive grease. Does a bearing with a diameter that is $\dfrac{3}{2}$ times the diameter of the given bearing need $\dfrac{3}{2}$ times the amount of grease to coat it? Explain.

├— 12 mm —┤

1.1 Exercises

Dynamic Solutions available at *BigIdeasMath.com*

Vocabulary and Core Concept Check

1. **WRITING** Explain, in your own words, the difference between the population of a state and the population density of a state.

2. **WHICH ONE DOESN'T BELONG?** Which expression does *not* belong with the other three? Explain your reasoning.

| bears per square mile | video gamers per city | people per square kilometer | trees per acre |

Monitoring Progress and Modeling with Mathematics

In Exercises 3–8, find the indicated measure. (*See Example 1.*)

3. The state of Kansas has a population of about 2.85 million people. Find the population density in people per square mile.

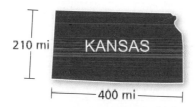

4. About 210,000 people live in a circular region with a 12-mile radius. Find the population density in people per square mile.

5. About 650,000 people live in a circular region with a 6-mile radius. Find the population density in people per square mile.

6. Yellowstone National Park has an area of about 2.22 million acres. The table shows the estimated park populations for several animals. Find the population density in animals per acre for each animal.

Animal	Grizzly bear	Elk	Mule deer	Bighorn sheep
Population	445	20,000	2400	260

7. A circular region with a 4-mile radius has a population density of 6366 people per square mile. Find the number of people who live in the region.

8. Central Park in New York City is rectangular with a length of 2.5 miles and a width of 0.5 mile. During an afternoon, its population density is about 15 people per acre. Find the number of people in the park that afternoon. One acre is equal to $\frac{1}{640}$ square mile.

9. **PROBLEM SOLVING** About 79,000 people live in a circular region with a population density of about 513 people per square mile. Find the radius of the region. (*See Example 2.*)

10. **PROBLEM SOLVING** About 1.15 million people live in a circular region with a population density of about 18,075 people per square kilometer. Find the radius of the region.

11. **ERROR ANALYSIS** Describe and correct the error in finding the number of people who live in a circular region with a 7.5-mile diameter and a population density of 1550 people per square mile.

$$1550 = \frac{x}{\pi \cdot 7.5^2}$$
$$1550 = \frac{x}{56.25\pi}$$
$$273,908 \approx x$$

The number of people who live in the region is about 273,908.

12. **HOW DO YOU SEE IT?** The two islands shown below with the given areas have the same population. Which has the greater population density? Explain.

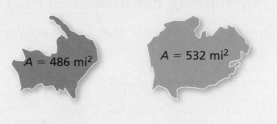

$A = 486 \text{ mi}^2$

$A = 532 \text{ mi}^2$

13. MODELING WITH MATHEMATICS A soccer field of length ℓ and width w has a perimeter of 320 yards. *(See Example 3.)*

   a. Write an expression that represents the area of the soccer field in terms of ℓ.

   b. Use your expression from part (a) to determine the dimensions of the field that maximize the area. What do you notice?

14. MODELING WITH MATHEMATICS You are using a 9-inch paint roller to paint a wall of your bedroom. The roller has a diameter of $1\frac{5}{8}$ inches and a nap thickness of $\frac{1}{4}$ inch, as shown. The *nap* is the fuzzy material on the surface of the roller.

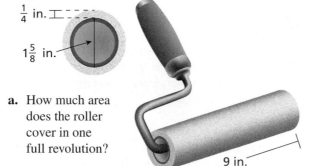

$\frac{1}{4}$ in.

$1\frac{5}{8}$ in.

9 in.

   a. How much area does the roller cover in one full revolution?

   b. The wall is 8 feet high. Painting vertically, you start at the bottom of the wall and make 8 full revolutions with the roller. Are you more than halfway up the wall? Justify your answer.

   c. A 3-inch roller has the same diameter and nap thickness as the roller above. How much area does this roller cover in one full revolution? How does this compare to the area in part (a)?

In Exercises 15 and 16, describe how the change affects the surface area of the right prism or right cylinder.

15. doubling all the linear dimensions

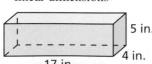

5 in.

4 in.

17 in.

16. tripling the radius

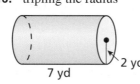

7 yd

2 yd

17. MODELING WITH MATHEMATICS A playground ball with a 16-inch diameter has a rubber coating on its surface. *(See Example 4.)*

   a. Does a ball with a diameter that is $\frac{1}{4}$ times the diameter of the given ball need $\frac{1}{4}$ times the amount of rubber coating? Explain.

   b. What is the radius of a ball that uses one-half of the amount of rubber coating used to cover the 16-inch ball?

18. MODELING WITH MATHEMATICS A cylindrical swimming pool has a diameter of 24 feet and a height of 4 feet. A smaller pool with the same height has a diameter of 12 feet. A vinyl liner covers the bottom and side of each pool.

   a. Does the smaller pool require one-half of the amount of vinyl liner that is used to cover the larger pool? Explain. If not, estimate the diameter of the cylindrical swimming pool that uses one-half of the amount of vinyl liner used to cover the larger pool. Assume the height of the pool is 4 feet.

   b. To install the vinyl liner, it costs $1.95 per square foot. You have $1000 in your budget to spend on the liner installation. What is the largest pool you can get without going over your liner budget? Assume the height of the pool is 4 feet.

19. MAKING AN ARGUMENT You ask your friend which U.S. states have the greatest population densities. Your friend says it must be California and Texas because they have the greatest populations. Is your friend correct? Explain.

20. THOUGHT PROVOKING Give an example from your everyday life of an object whose surface area changes. Sketch the object and determine what geometric shape can model it. Estimate the dimensions of the object before and after the change and explain how the surface area is affected.

Maintaining Mathematical Proficiency Reviewing what you learned in previous grades and lessons

Evaluate the expression when $x = -4$ and $y = 3$. *(Skills Review Handbook)*

21. $2x^2 + 5y^2$ **22.** $\frac{1}{3}(8xy - y^2)$ **23.** $-x^2 + 6x + 11y$ **24.** $-5(y + x^3 + 10)$

Find the volume of the solid. *(Skills Review Handbook)*

25.

4 ft   18.5 ft

26.

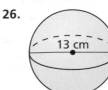

13 cm

27.

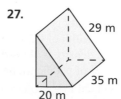

29 m

35 m

20 m

1.2 Modeling with Volume

Essential Question How can you use the mass and volume of an object to describe the density of the object?

EXPLORATION 1 **Finding Densities**

Work with a partner. Approximate the volume of each object whose mass is given. Then find the mass per unit of volume, or *density*, of each object.

a. Brick: 2.3 kg

5.7 cm

20 cm   10 cm

b. Log: 18.1 kg

44 cm

28 cm

c. Golf ball: 45.9 g

43 mm

d. Cork: 2.6 g

3 cm

3 cm

1.5 cm

CONSTRUCTING VIABLE ARGUMENTS

To be proficient in math, you need to justify your conclusions and communicate them to others.

EXPLORATION 2 **Analyzing Densities**

Work with a partner. The objects in Exploration 1 with a density greater than 1 gram per cubic centimeter will sink in water. The objects with a density less than 1 gram per cubic centimeter will float in water. You place each object in Exploration 1 in a bucket of water.

a. Which object(s) sink? float? Justify your answer.

b. Would your answers in part (a) change when each object is cut in half and placed in water? Explain your reasoning.

c. You dissolve enough salt in a bucket of water to cause one of the sunken objects to float. Which object is it and why do you think this happens?

Communicate Your Answer

3. How can you use the mass and volume of an object to describe the density of the object?

4. Use the Internet or some other reference to research the densities of water, mineral oil, and beeswax. You combine these substances in a bucket. How do you think the liquids interact? Where would the beeswax settle?

What You Will Learn

▶ Use volume formulas to find densities.
▶ Use volume formulas to solve problems.

Using Volume Formulas to Find Densities

Density is the amount of matter that an object has in a given unit of volume. The density of an object is calculated by dividing its mass by its volume.

$$\text{Density} = \frac{\text{Mass}}{\text{Volume}}$$

Different materials have different densities, so density can be used to distinguish between materials that look similar. For example, table salt and sugar look alike. However, table salt has a density of 2.16 grams per cubic centimeter, while sugar has a density of 1.58 grams per cubic centimeter.

EXAMPLE 1   Using the Formula for Density

The diagram shows the dimensions of a standard gold bar at Fort Knox. Gold has a density of 19.3 grams per cubic centimeter. Find the mass of a standard gold bar to the nearest gram.

1.75 in.

7 in.

3.625 in.

SOLUTION

Step 1 Convert the dimensions to centimeters using 1 inch = 2.54 centimeters.

Length $7 \text{ in.} \cdot \dfrac{2.54 \text{ cm}}{1 \text{ in.}} = 17.78 \text{ cm}$

Width $3.625 \text{ in.} \cdot \dfrac{2.54 \text{ cm}}{1 \text{ in.}} = 9.2075 \text{ cm}$

Height $1.75 \text{ in.} \cdot \dfrac{2.54 \text{ cm}}{1 \text{ in.}} = 4.445 \text{ cm}$

Step 2 Find the volume.

The area of a base is $B = 17.78(9.2075) = 163.70935 \text{ cm}^2$ and the height is $h = 4.445$ cm.

$$V = Bh = 163.70935(4.445) \approx 727.69 \text{ cm}^3$$

Step 3 Let x represent the mass in grams. Substitute the values for the volume and the density in the formula for density and solve for x.

$\text{Density} = \dfrac{\text{Mass}}{\text{Volume}}$	Formula for density
$19.3 \approx \dfrac{x}{727.69}$	Substitute.
$14{,}044 \approx x$	Multiply each side by 727.69.

▶ The mass of a standard gold bar is about 14,044 grams.

Monitoring Progress Help in English and Spanish at *BigIdeasMath.com*

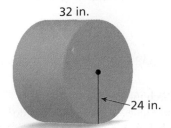

32 in.

24 in.

1. The diagram shows the dimensions of a concrete cylinder. Concrete has a density of 2.3 grams per cubic centimeter. Find the mass of the concrete cylinder to the nearest gram.

Using Volume Formulas

EXAMPLE 2 **Using a Volume Formula**

A tree harvester is often interested in the volume of a tree's trunk because most of the wood volume is located there. A tree harvester estimates the trunk of a sequoia tree to have a height of about 50 meters and a base diameter of about 0.8 meter.

a. The wood of a sequoia tree has a density of about 450 kilograms per cubic meter. Find the mass of the trunk to the nearest kilogram.

b. Each year, the tree trunk forms new cells that arrange themselves in concentric circles called *growth rings*. These rings indicate how much wood the tree produces annually. The harvester estimates that the trunk will put on a growth ring of about 1 centimeter thick and its height will increase by about 0.25 meter this year. How many cubic meters of wood does the tree trunk produce after one year? If the tree grows at a constant rate for the next five years, will it produce the same amount of wood each year? Explain.

SOLUTION

a. To estimate the volume of the tree trunk, assume that the trunk is cylindrical. So, the volume of the trunk is

$$V = \pi r^2 h = \pi(0.4)^2(50) = 8\pi \approx 25.13 \text{ m}^3.$$

Let x represent the mass in kilograms. Substitute the values for the volume and the density in the formula for density and solve for x.

$\text{Density} = \dfrac{\text{Mass}}{\text{Volume}}$	Formula for density
$450 \approx \dfrac{x}{25.13}$	Substitute.
$11{,}309 \approx x$	Multiply each side by 25.13.

▶ The mass of the trunk is about 11,309 kilograms.

COMMON ERROR

Because 1 cm = 0.01 m, the trunk will have a diameter of
0.8 + 0.01 + 0.01 = 0.82 m for Year 1.

b. Make a table that shows the trunk dimensions and volume for five years.

Year	1	2	3	4	5
Height (meters)	50.25	50.5	50.75	51	51.25
Base radius (meters)	0.41	0.42	0.43	0.44	0.45
Volume (cubic meters)	26.54	27.99	29.48	31.02	32.60

+ 1.45   + 1.49   + 1.54   + 1.58

▶ The tree will produce about 26.54 − 25.13 = 1.41 cubic meters of wood after one year. The tree will not produce the same amount of wood each year for five years because the differences between the volumes from year to year are increasing.

Monitoring Progress Help in English and Spanish at *BigIdeasMath.com*

2. **WHAT IF?** The tree harvester makes the same growth estimates for the trunk of a sequoia tree that has a height of about 40 meters and a base diameter of about 0.75 meter. (a) Find the mass of the trunk to the nearest kilogram. (b) How many cubic meters of wood will the trunk gain after four years?

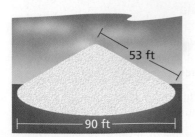

EXAMPLE 3   **Using a Volume Formula**

Before a winter storm, a pile of road salt has the dimensions shown. After the storm, the linear dimensions of the pile are one-half of the original dimensions.

a. How does this change affect the volume of the pile?

b. A *lane mile* is an area of pavement that is one mile long and one lane wide. During the storm, about 400 pounds of road salt was used for every lane mile. Estimate the number of lane miles that were covered with road salt during the storm. A cubic foot of road salt weighs about 80 pounds.

SOLUTION

a. The pile of road salt is approximately shaped like a cone. Use the Pythagorean Theorem to find the height h. Then use the formula for the volume of a cone to find the volume of the pile before and after the storm.

$$c^2 = a^2 + b^2 \qquad \text{Pythagorean Theorem}$$
$$53^2 = h^2 + 45^2 \qquad \text{Substitute.}$$
$$2809 = h^2 + 2025 \qquad \text{Multiply.}$$
$$784 = h^2 \qquad \text{Subtract 2025 from each side.}$$
$$28 = h \qquad \text{Find the positive square root.}$$

ANALYZING MATHEMATICAL RELATIONSHIPS

Notice that when all the linear dimensions are multiplied by k, the volume is multiplied by k^3.

	Before winter storm	**After winter storm**
Dimensions	$r = 45$ ft, $h = 28$ ft	$r = 22.5$ ft, $h = 14$ ft
Volume	$V = \dfrac{1}{3}\pi r^2 h$ $= \dfrac{1}{3}\pi(45)^2(28)$ $= 18{,}900\pi$ ft^3	$V = \dfrac{1}{3}\pi r^2 h$ $= \dfrac{1}{3}\pi(22.5)^2(14)$ $= 2362.5\pi$ ft^3

▶ The volume of the pile after the winter storm is $\dfrac{2362.5\pi}{18{,}900\pi} = \dfrac{1}{8}$ times the original volume.

b. During the storm, $18{,}900\pi - 2362.5\pi = 16{,}537.5\pi$ cubic feet of road salt was used. Use conversions to find the number of lane miles covered with road salt during the storm.

Pounds of road salt used: $16{,}537.5\pi \text{ ft}^3 \cdot \dfrac{80 \text{ lb}}{1 \text{ ft}^3} = 1{,}323{,}000\pi$ lb

Lane miles covered: $1{,}323{,}000\pi \text{ lb} \cdot \dfrac{1 \text{ lane mile}}{400 \text{ lb}} \approx 10{,}390.82$ lane miles

▶ So, about 10,400 lane miles were covered with road salt during the storm.

Monitoring Progress Help in English and Spanish at *BigIdeasMath.com*

3. In Example 3, the department of transportation pays about $31.50 for each ton of road salt. How much does the original pile of road salt cost?

4. WHAT IF? After a storm, the linear dimensions of the pile are $\frac{1}{4}$ of the original dimensions. (a) How does this change affect the volume of the pile? (b) Estimate the number of lane miles that were covered with road salt during the storm.

Vocabulary and Core Concept Check

1. **VOCABULARY** What do you obtain when you multiply an object's density by its volume?

2. **DIFFERENT WORDS, SAME QUESTION** Which is different? Find "both" answers.

   | What is the mass per unit of volume? | What is the mass in kilograms? |

   | What is the mass divided by the volume? | What is the density? |

Tourmaline

Mass = 6.2 g
Volume = 2 cm³

Monitoring Progress and Modeling with Mathematics

3. **PROBLEM SOLVING** A piece of copper with a volume of 8.25 cubic centimeters has a mass of 73.92 grams. A piece of iron with a volume of 5 cubic centimeters has a mass of 39.35 grams. Which metal has the greater density?

copper

iron

4. **PROBLEM SOLVING** The United States has minted one-dollar silver coins called the American Eagle Silver Bullion Coin since 1986. Each coin has a diameter of 40.6 millimeters and is 2.98 millimeters thick. The density of silver is 10.5 grams per cubic centimeter. What is the mass of an American Eagle Silver Bullion Coin to the nearest gram? *(See Example 1.)*

5. **ERROR ANALYSIS** Describe and correct the error in finding the density of an object that has a mass of 24 grams and a volume of 28.3 cubic centimeters.

    density $= \dfrac{28.3}{24} \approx 1.18$

   So, the density is about 1.18 cubic centimeters per gram.

6. **PROBLEM SOLVING** The height of a tree trunk is 20 meters and the base diameter is 0.5 meter. *(See Example 2.)*

   a. The wood has a density of 380 kilograms per cubic meter. Find the mass of the trunk to the nearest kilogram.

   b. The trunk puts on a growth ring of 4 millimeters and its height increases by 0.2 meter this year. How many cubic meters of wood does the tree trunk produce? The tree grows at a constant rate for the next five years. Does the tree produce the same amount of wood each year? Explain.

In Exercises 7 and 8, describe how the change affects the volume of the prism or pyramid.

7. tripling all the linear dimensions

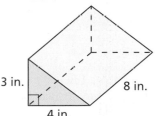

3 in.
8 in.
4 in.

8. multiplying the height by $\frac{3}{2}$

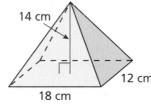

14 cm
18 cm
12 cm

9. **PROBLEM SOLVING** A conical pile of road salt has a diameter of 112 feet and a slant height of 65 feet. After a storm, the linear dimensions of the pile are $\frac{1}{3}$ of the original dimensions. *(See Example 3.)*

   a. How does this change affect the volume of the pile?

   b. During the storm, 350 pounds of road salt was used for every lane mile. Estimate the number of lane miles that were covered with salt. How many lane miles can be covered with the remaining salt? A cubic foot of road salt weighs about 80 pounds.

10. HOW DO YOU SEE IT? The two stone blocks shown below with the given densities have the same volume. Which block has a greater mass? Explain.

Granite: 2.7 g/cm³   Sandstone: 2.3 g/cm³

11. MODELING WITH MATHEMATICS A pool in the shape of a rectangular prism is 6 meters long and 3 meters wide. The water in the pool is 1 meter deep.

  a. The density of water is about 1 gram per cubic centimeter. Find the number of kilograms of water in the pool.

  b. You add 6000 kilograms of water to the pool. What is the depth of the water in the pool?

12. MODELING WITH MATHEMATICS A British thermal unit (Btu) is the amount of heat needed to raise the temperature of 1 pound of liquid water by 1°F. There are about 1000 Btu per cubic foot of natural gas and about 140,000 Btu per gallon of heating oil.

  a. In 2010, electricity-generating power plants paid $5.27 per 1000 cubic feet of natural gas and $56.35 per 42-gallon barrel of heating oil. Express the cost of each fuel in dollars per million Btu.

  b. The tank shown can be used to store heating oil. Write a formula for the volume of the tank.

  c. You pay $3.75 per gallon of heating oil to fill a new tank in which r is 1 foot. Compare your cost for heating oil in dollars per million Btu to a power plant's cost in part (a). How many Btu can be produced from a full tank of heating oil?

13. MAKING AN ARGUMENT As ocean depth increases, water molecules become closer together due in part to decreasing temperatures. Your friend says that the density of water increases as depth increases. Is your friend correct? Explain.

14. THOUGHT PROVOKING You place two cans of regular soda and two cans of diet soda in a container full of water. The two regular cans sink, but the two diet cans float.

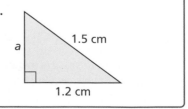

Use the Internet to research the contents of regular soda and diet soda. Then make a conjecture about why the diet cans float, but the regular cans sink. Include a discussion of *density* and *buoyancy* in your explanation.

15. MODELING WITH MATHEMATICS Links of a chain are made from cylindrical metal rods with a diameter of 6 millimeters. The density of the metal is about 8 grams per cubic centimeter.

  a. To approximate the length of a rod used to make a link, should you use the perimeter around the inside of the link? the outside? the average of these perimeters? Explain your reasoning. Then approximate the mass of a chain with 100 links.

  b. Approximate the length of a taut chain with 100 links. Explain your procedure.

Maintaining Mathematical Proficiency
Reviewing what you learned in previous grades and lessons

Find the missing length of the triangle. *(Skills Review Handbook)*

16.

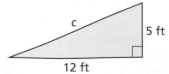

c   5 ft

12 ft

17.

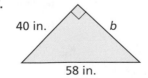

40 in.   *b*

58 in.

18.

a   1.5 cm

1.2 cm

1.1–1.2 What Did You Learn?

Core Vocabulary

population density, *p. 4*   density, *p. 10*

Core Concepts

Section 1.1
Finding a Population Density, *p. 4*

Section 1.2
Finding a Density, *p. 10*

Mathematical Practices

1. In Exercise 17(b) on page 8, explain the steps you used to find the radius of the ball.

2. You have a classmate who is confused about the difference between the mass of an object and the weight of an object in Exercise 4 on page 13. What resources can you use to help your friend figure it out?

3. In Exercise 7 on page 13, explain why the given change results in a volume that is 27 times the original volume.

Taking Control of Your Class Time

1. Sit where you can easily see and hear the teacher, and the teacher can see you.
2. Pay attention to what the teacher says about math, not just what is written on the board.
3. Ask a question if the teacher is moving through the material too fast.
4. Try to memorize new information while learning it.
5. Ask for clarification if you do not understand something.
6. Think as intensely as if you were going to take a quiz on the material at the end of class.
7. Volunteer when the teacher asks for someone to go up to the board.
8. At the end of class, identify concepts or problems for which you still need clarification.
9. Use the tutorials at *BigIdeasMath.com* for additional help.

STUDY SKILLS

1. The state of Wyoming has a population of about 564,000 people. The population density of the state is about 2.16 people per square kilometer. Find the width of Wyoming. *(Section 1.1)*

Wyoming

579 km

2. A circular region with a 3-mile radius has a population density of about 6195 people per square mile. Find the number of people who live in the region. *(Section 1.1)*

Describe how the change affects the surface area of the right cylinder or right cone. *(Section 1.1)*

3. multiplying all the linear dimensions by $\frac{1}{3}$

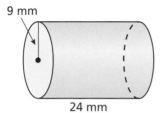

9 mm

24 mm

4. doubling the radius

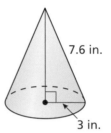

7.6 in.

3 in.

Describe how the change affects the volume of the prism or pyramid. *(Section 1.2)*

5. tripling the base and the height of the triangular bases

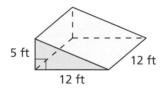

5 ft

12 ft

12 ft

6. multiplying all the linear dimensions by $\frac{1}{4}$

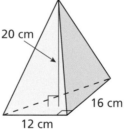

20 cm

16 cm

12 cm

7. You make the ball of aluminum foil shown. *(Section 1.1 and Section 1.2)*

   a. You add foil to the ball so its diameter is $\frac{3}{2}$ times the original diameter. How does this change affect the surface area and volume of the ball?

   b. Aluminum foil has a density of about 2.7 grams per cubic centimeter. Find the mass of the ball before and after you add the foil.

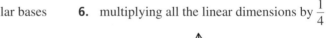

4 in.

8. An ice sculptor is carving the block of ice shown. *(Section 1.2)*

   a. The block has a mass of about 745 kilograms. Find the density of the block of ice. Is it greater than the density of water? Explain. The density of water is about 1 gram per cubic centimeter.

   b. Another rectangular block of ice has a mass of about 298 kilograms. Give two possible sets of dimensions for the block of ice.

80 cm

125 cm   80 cm

Essential Question How can you use a piece of food to create a real-life cross section?

Imagine cutting through a piece of food. The intersection formed by the cut you make and the piece of food is called a **cross section**. The shape of the cross section depends on the angle of the cut you make.

EXPLORATION 1 Describing Cross Sections

Work with a partner. Describe the shapes of the cross sections that are formed by making cuts into each given food so that it is separated into two congruent parts.

a. wheel of cheese

b. watermelon

c. stick of butter

d. cucumber

EXPLORATION 2 Forming Cross Sections

Work with a partner. Describe how you can slice the portion of cheese so that the cross section formed is the given shape.

a. triangle

b. rectangle

c. trapezoid

ATTENDING TO PRECISION

To be proficient in math, you need to communicate precisely with others.

Communicate Your Answer

3. How can you use a piece of food to create a real-life cross section?

4. Is there more than one way to slice the portion of cheese in Exploration 2 to form a triangular cross section? Explain. Use drawings to support your answer.

What You Will Learn

▶ Describe cross sections.

▶ Draw cross sections.

▶ Solve real-life problems involving cross sections.

Core Vocabulary

cross section, *p. 18*

Previous
plane
Pythagorean Theorem
square root

Describing Cross Sections

Imagine a plane slicing through a solid. The intersection of the plane and the solid is called a **cross section**. For example, three different cross sections of a cube are shown below.

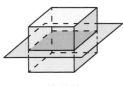

square   rectangle   triangle

STUDY TIP

To help you better visualize a cross section, rotate the solid mentally so you are looking directly at the cross section.

EXAMPLE 1 Describing Cross Sections

Describe the shape formed by the intersection of the plane and the solid.

a.    **b.**   **c.**

d.   **e.**   **f.**

SOLUTION

a. The cross section is a hexagon.   **b.** The cross section is a triangle.

c. The cross section is a rectangle.   **d.** The cross section is a circle.

e. The cross section is a circle.   **f.** The cross section is a trapezoid.

Monitoring Progress 🔊 Help in English and Spanish at *BigIdeasMath.com*

Describe the shape formed by the intersection of the plane and the solid.

1.   **2.**   **3.**

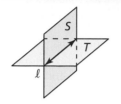
Drawing Cross Sections

The Plane Intersection Postulate states that if two planes intersect, then their intersection is a line. This postulate can help you when drawing a cross section.

EXAMPLE 2   Drawing a Cross Section

Draw the cross section formed by a plane parallel to the base that intersects the red line segment drawn on the square pyramid. What is the shape of the cross section?

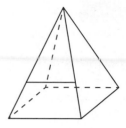

SOLUTION

Step 1 Visualize a horizontal plane parallel to the base that intersects the lateral face and passes through the red line segment.

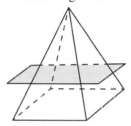

Step 2 The horizontal plane is parallel to the base of the pyramid. So, draw each pair of parallel line segments where the plane intersects the lateral faces of the pyramid.

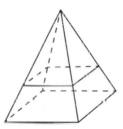

Step 3 Shade the cross section.

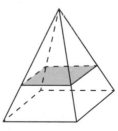

▶ The cross section is a square.

Monitoring Progress Help in English and Spanish at *BigIdeasMath.com*

4. **WHAT IF?** Draw the cross section formed by a plane perpendicular to the base that intersects the vertex of the square pyramid in Example 2. What is the shape of the cross section?

5. **REASONING** Describe how a plane can intersect the pyramid in Example 2 so that it forms a cross section that is (a) a trapezoid and (b) a line segment.

Solving Real-Life Problems

EXAMPLE 3 **Solving a Real-Life Problem**

A machine at a sawmill cuts a 4-inch by 4-inch piece of wood lengthwise along its diagonal, as shown. Find the perimeter and area of the cross section formed by the cut.

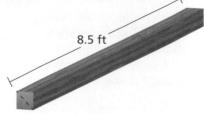

8.5 ft

SOLUTION

1. **Understand the Problem** You know that the piece of wood is shaped like a rectangular prism with a length of 8.5 feet and a width and height of 4 inches. You are asked to calculate the perimeter and area of the cross section formed when an 8.5-foot cut is made along its diagonal.

2. **Make a Plan** Determine the shape and the dimensions of the cross section. Then use the dimensions to calculate the perimeter and area of the cross section.

3. **Solve the Problem** Draw a diagram of the cross section. It is a rectangle with a length of 8.5 feet, or 102 inches.

Use the Pythagorean Theorem to find its width. The length and width of the end of the piece of wood is 4 inches.

$c^2 = a^2 + b^2$	Pythagorean Theorem
$c^2 = 4^2 + 4^2$	Substitute.
$c^2 = 16 + 16$	Multiply.
$c^2 = 32$	Add.
$c = \sqrt{32}$	Find the positive square root.
$c = 4\sqrt{2}$	Simplify.

The width of the rectangular cross section is $4\sqrt{2}$ inches.

Perimeter of cross section	**Area of cross section**
$P = 2\ell + 2w$	$A = \ell w$
$= 2(102) + 2(4\sqrt{2})$	$= 102 \cdot 4\sqrt{2}$
$= 204 + 8\sqrt{2}$	$= 408\sqrt{2}$
≈ 215.31	≈ 577

▶ The perimeter of the cross section is about 215.31 inches and the area of the cross section is about 577 square inches.

4. **Look Back** You can use estimation to check that your answer is reasonable. The length of the rectangular cross section is about 9 feet and its width is about 0.5 foot.

Perimeter of cross section: $P = 2\ell + 2w = 2(9) + 2(0.5) = 19$ ft $= 228$ in. ✔

Area of cross section: $A = \ell w = 9 \cdot 0.5 = 4.5$ ft$^2 = 648$ in.^{2} ✔

Monitoring Progress Help in English and Spanish at *BigIdeasMath.com*

6. A 6-inch by 6-inch piece of wood that is 10.25 feet long is cut lengthwise along its diagonal. Find the perimeter and area of the cross section formed by the cut.

Vocabulary and Core Concept Check

1. **COMPLETE THE SENTENCE** The intersection of a plane and a solid is called a _____.

2. **WRITING** Can a plane intersect a rectangular prism and form a cross section that is a circle? Explain.

Monitoring Progress and Modeling with Mathematics

In Exercises 3–6, describe the shape formed by the intersection of the plane and the solid. *(See Example 1.)*

3.
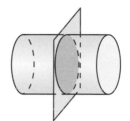

4.
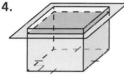

5.

6.
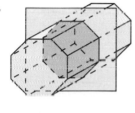

In Exercises 7–10, draw the cross section formed by the described plane that intersects the red line segment drawn on the solid. What is the shape of the cross section? *(See Example 2.)*

7. plane is perpendicular to base

8. plane is parallel to base

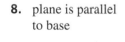

9. plane is parallel to bottom face

10. plane is perpendicular to bottom face

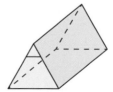
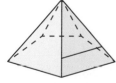

11. **ERROR ANALYSIS** Describe and correct the error in describing the shape formed by the intersection of the plane and the regular hexagonal prism.

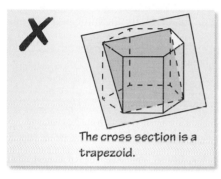

The cross section is a trapezoid.

12. **OPEN-ENDED** Give an example of a solid from which a triangular, hexagonal, and trapezoidal cross section can be formed.

In Exercises 13–18, draw the cross section formed by a vertical plane that divides the solid into two congruent parts. Is there more than one way to use a vertical plane to divide the figure into two congruent parts? If so, does the cross section change? Explain.

13.
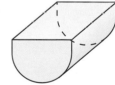

14.
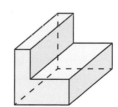

15.
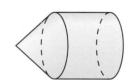

16.

17.
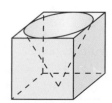

18.
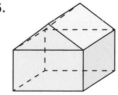

19. PROBLEM SOLVING You cut the cake vertically to make two congruent parts. *(See Example 3.)*

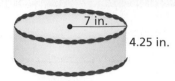

7 in.

4.25 in.

   a. Find the perimeter and area of the cross section formed by the cut.

   b. Find the surface area of the cake that is not frosted before the cut. How does the unfrosted surface area change after the cut?

   c. Can the cake be cut another way to make two congruent parts? If so, find the perimeter and area of the cross section formed by the cut.

20. PROBLEM SOLVING A mason uses a concrete saw to cut the block along the indicated diagonal.

   a. Identify the solids formed by the cut.

   b. Find the perimeter and area of the cross section formed by the cut.

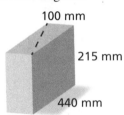

100 mm

215 mm

440 mm

   c. The block has a density of about 0.002 gram per cubic millimeter. Find the mass of the block to the nearest gram.

21. PROBLEM SOLVING Use the figure shown.

   a. One of the hexagonal pipes is cut vertically so that it is divided into two congruent parts. Draw two possible cross sections.

   b. How many different ways can a pipe be cut lengthwise to form two congruent parts? Explain.

22. PROBLEM SOLVING A regular octagonal pyramid is intersected by a plane perpendicular to its base. The plane passes through its vertex so it is divided into two congruent parts. Draw the cross section. Is there more than one way to divide the pyramid into two congruent parts? If so, does the shape of the cross section change? Explain.

23. MAKING AN ARGUMENT Your friend says that any plane that intersects a sphere forms a circular cross section. Is your friend correct? Explain.

24. HOW DO YOU SEE IT? Draw a plane that intersects the cube to form the given cross section.

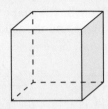

   a. isosceles triangle   **b.** equilateral triangle

   c. scalene triangle   **d.** parallelogram

   e. pentagon   **f.** hexagon

25. REASONING A plane intersects a sphere 7 meters from the center of the sphere. The radius of the sphere is 25 meters. Draw a diagram to represent this situation. Then find the area of the cross section to the nearest tenth.

26. THOUGHT PROVOKING Describe a solid that can be intersected by a plane to form the cross section shown. Explain how you form the cross section.

Maintaining Mathematical Proficiency   Reviewing what you learned in previous grades and lessons

Tell how many lines of symmetry the figure has. *(Skills Review Handbook)*

27.

28.

29.

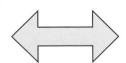

30.

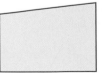

Graph the inequality in a coordinate plane. *(Skills Review Handbook)*

31. $x > 0$ **32.** $x \le \frac{1}{2}$ **33.** $y \ge 0$ **34.** $y < -2.5$

1.4 Solids of Revolution

Essential Question How can you create a solid of revolution?

A **solid of revolution** is a three-dimensional figure that is formed by rotating a two-dimensional shape around an axis.

EXPLORATION 1 Creating Solids of Revolution

Work with a partner. Tape the 5-inch side of a 3-inch by 5-inch index card to a pencil, as shown.

a. Rotate the pencil. What type of solid is produced by the rotating index card? What are its dimensions?

b. Tape the 3-inch side of the index card to the pencil. Rotate the pencil. What type of solid is produced by the rotating index card? What are its dimensions?

c. Do the solids in parts (a) and (b) have the same surface area? the same volume? Justify your answers.

d. Cut the index card in half along its diagonal. Tape the 5-inch leg of the triangle formed to a pencil. Rotate the pencil. What type of solid is produced? What are its dimensions?

e. Tape the 3-inch leg to a pencil. Rotate the pencil. What type of solid is produced? What are its dimensions?

f. Do the solids in parts (d) and (e) have the same surface area? the same volume? Justify your answers.

3 in.

5 in.

3 in.

5 in.

USING TOOLS STRATEGICALLY
To be proficient in math, you need to use appropriate tools strategically, including real objects.

EXPLORATION 2 Creating Solids of Revolution

Work with a partner. Tape the straight side of a protractor, similar to the one at the left, to a pencil, as shown.

a. Rotate the pencil. What type of solid is produced by the rotating protractor? What are its dimensions?

b. Find the surface area and volume of the solid produced in part (a).

c. Tape the straight side of a protractor, similar to the one at the right, to a pencil, as shown. Rotate the pencil. Is the solid produced by this rotating protractor different from the solid in part (a)? Explain. Draw a diagram to support your answer.

d. Describe a method you might use to approximate the volume of the solid in part (c).

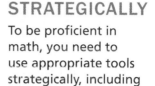

Communicate Your Answer

3. How can you create a solid of revolution?

4. Give some examples of real-life objects that are solids of revolution.

Core Vocabulary

solid of revolution, *p. 24*
axis of revolution, *p. 24*

Previous
surface area
volume

What You Will Learn

▶ Sketch and describe solids of revolution.

▶ Find surface areas and volumes of solids of revolution.

▶ Form solids of revolution in the coordinate plane.

Sketching and Describing Solids of Revolution

A **solid of revolution** is a three-dimensional figure that is formed by rotating a two-dimensional shape around an axis. The line around which the shape is rotated is called the **axis of revolution**.

For example, when you rotate a rectangle around a line that contains one of its sides, the solid of revolution that is produced is a cylinder.

EXAMPLE 1 **Sketching and Describing Solids of Revolution**

Sketch the solid produced by rotating the figure around the given axis. Then identify and describe the solid.

a.
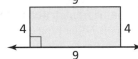

b.
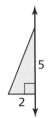

SOLUTION

a.
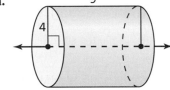

▶ The solid is a cylinder with a height of 9 units and a base radius of 4 units.

b.

▶ The solid is a cone with a height of 5 units and a base radius of 2 units.

Monitoring Progress 🔊 Help in English and Spanish at *BigIdeasMath.com*

Sketch the solid produced by rotating the figure around the given axis. Then identify and describe the solid.

1.
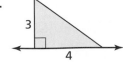

2.
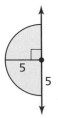

EXAMPLE 2 Sketching a Two-Dimensional Shape and Axis

Most vases are solids of revolution. Sketch a two-dimensional shape and an axis of revolution that forms the vase shown.

SOLUTION

The two-dimesional shape should match the outline of one side of the vase.

Monitoring Progress Help in English and Spanish at *BigIdeasMath.com*

3. Sketch a two-dimensional shape and an axis of revolution that forms the bird bath shown.

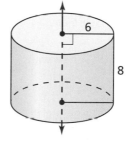

Finding Surface Areas and Volumes of Solids of Revolution

EXAMPLE 3 Finding the Surface Area and Volume of a Solid of Revolution

Sketch and describe the solid produced by rotating the figure around the given axis. Then find its surface area and volume.

SOLUTION

The solid is a cylinder with a height of 8 units and a base radius of 6 units.

Surface area: $S = 2\pi r^2 + 2\pi rh = 2\pi(6)^2 + 2\pi(6)(8) = 168\pi \approx 527.79$

Volume: $V = \pi r^2 h = \pi(6)^2(8) = 288\pi \approx 904.78$

▶ The cylinder has a surface area of about 527.79 square units and a volume of about 904.78 cubic units.

Monitoring Progress Help in English and Spanish at *BigIdeasMath.com*

4. Sketch and describe the solid produced by rotating the figure around the given axis. Then find its surface area and volume.

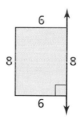

Forming Solids of Revolution in the Coordinate Plane

EXAMPLE 4 Forming a Solid of Revolution

Sketch and describe the solid that is produced when the region enclosed by $y = 0$, $y = x$, and $x = 5$ is rotated around the y-axis. Then find the volume of the solid.

SOLUTION

Step 1 Graph each equation and determine the region that will be rotated around the y-axis.

Step 2 Reflect the region in the y-axis.

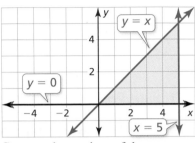

Step 3 Connect the vertices of the triangles using curved lines.

Step 4 The composite solid consists of a cylinder with a cone removed.

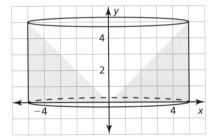
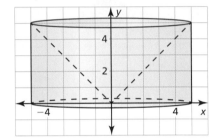

Step 5 Find the volume of the composite solid. The cylinder and the cone both have a height of 5 units and a base radius of 5 units.

Volume of solid	=	Volume of cylinder	−	Volume of cone

$$= \pi r^2 h - \frac{1}{3}\pi r^2 h \qquad \text{Write formulas.}$$

$$= \pi \cdot 5^2 \cdot 5 - \frac{1}{3}\pi \cdot 5^2 \cdot 5 \qquad \text{Substitute.}$$

$$= 125\pi - \frac{125}{3}\pi \qquad \text{Simplify.}$$

$$= \frac{250}{3}\pi \qquad \text{Subtract.}$$

$$\approx 261.80 \qquad \text{Use a calculator.}$$

▶ The volume of the solid is $\frac{250}{3}\pi$, or about 261.80 cubic units.

Monitoring Progress Help in English and Spanish at *BigIdeasMath.com*

5. **WHAT IF?** Does the solid change when the region is rotated around the x-axis? Explain.

6. Sketch and describe the solid that is produced when the region enclosed by $x = 0$, $y = -x$, and $y = -3$ is rotated around the x-axis. Then find the volume of the solid.

Vocabulary and Core Concept Check

1. **COMPLETE THE SENTENCE** When you rotate a square around a line that contains one of its sides, the solid of revolution that is produced is a _____.

2. **WHICH ONE DOESN'T BELONG?** Which object does *not* belong with the other three? Explain your reasoning.

Monitoring Progress and Modeling with Mathematics

In Exercises 3–6, sketch the solid produced by rotating the figure around the given axis. Then identify and describe the solid. *(See Example 1.)*

3.
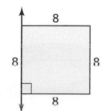

4.
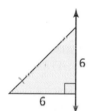

5.
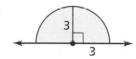

6.
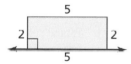

7. **ERROR ANALYSIS** Describe and correct the error in identifying and describing the solid produced by rotating the figure around the given axis.

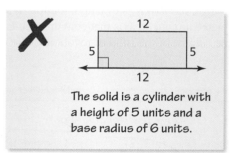

The solid is a cylinder with a height of 5 units and a base radius of 6 units.

8. **REASONING** Can you form any solid by rotating a two-dimensional figure around an axis? Explain.

In Exercises 9–12, sketch the solid of revolution. Then identify and describe the solid.

9. a square with side length 4 rotated around one side

10. a rectangle with length 6 and width 3 rotated around one of its shorter sides

11. a right triangle with legs of lengths 6 and 9 rotated around its longer leg

12. a semicircle with radius 10 rotated around its diameter

In Exercises 13–16, sketch a two-dimensional shape and an axis of revolution that forms the object shown. *(See Example 2.)*

13.

14.

15.

16.

In Exercises 17–22, sketch and describe the solid produced by rotating the figure around the given axis. Then find its surface area and volume. *(See Example 3.)*

17.

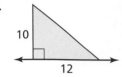
10
12

18.
6.8
6.1
6.1
6.8

19.

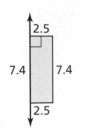
2.5
7.4
7.4
2.5

20.

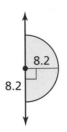
8.2
8.2

21.

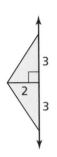
3
2
3

22.
4
8
11
4
5

In Exercises 23–26, sketch and describe the solid that is produced when the region enclosed by the given equations is rotated around the given axis. Then find the volume of the solid. *(See Example 4.)*

23. $x = 0$, $y = 0$, $y = x + 3$; x-axis

24. $x = 0$, $y = 0$, $y = -2x + 5$; y-axis

25. $x = 3$, $y = 0$, $y = \frac{1}{2}x$; y-axis

26. $x = -4$, $y = 0$, $y = x$; x-axis

27. MAKING AN ARGUMENT Your friend says when you rotate the figure shown around either the x-axis or the y-axis, the resulting solid is a sphere. Is your friend correct? Explain.

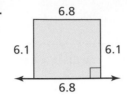

28. HOW DO YOU SEE IT? The figure shows the graph of a function f on an interval $[a, b]$. Sketch the solid produced when the region enclosed by the graph of f and the equations $x = a$, $x = b$, and $y = 0$ is rotated around the x-axis.

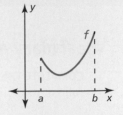

29. CRITICAL THINKING A right triangle has sides with lengths 15, 20, and 25, as shown. Describe the three solids formed when the triangle is rotated around each of its sides. Then find the volumes of the solids. Give your answers in terms of π.

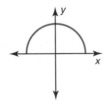
15
20
25

30. THOUGHT PROVOKING Write a system of equations whose enclosed region, when rotated around the x-axis or y-axis, produces the same solid with the same dimensions.

31. REASONING The solid shown is a type of *torus*.

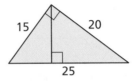

a. Sketch a two-dimensional shape and an axis of revolution that forms the torus.

b. Which solid can you use to "construct" a torus similar to the one above? Explain, in your words, how to manipulate the solid to form the torus. You can think of the surface of the solid you choose as being stretchable.

32. CRITICAL THINKING A 30°-30°-120° isosceles triangle has two legs of length 4 units. When it is rotated around an axis that contains one leg, what is the volume of the solid of revolution?

Maintaining Mathematical Proficiency
Reviewing what you learned in previous grades and lessons

Determine whether the ordered pair is a solution of the equation. *(Skills Review Handbook)*

33. $f(x) = 8x - 3$; $(-5, -37)$

34. $h(x) = 2x^2 - 7x - 1$; $(3, 2)$

35. $n(x) = -5x^2 - 4x$; $(1.5, -17.25)$

36. $p(x) = |6x + 5|$; $(-1, 11)$

37. A circular region has a population of about 2.5 million people and a population density of about 9824 people per square mile. Find the radius of the region. *(Section 1.1)*

Core Vocabulary

cross section, *p. 18*   solid of revolution, *p. 24*   axis of revolution, *p. 24*

Core Concepts

Section 1.3

Cross Section of a Solid, *p. 18*   Drawing a Cross Section, *p. 19*

Section 1.4

Solids of Revolution, *p. 24*   Surface Area and Volume of a   Solids of Revolution
                                        Solid of Revolution, *p. 25*   in the Coordinate Plane, *p. 26*

Mathematical Practices

1. What question(s) can you ask your friend to help her understand the error in the statement she made in Exercise 23 on page 22?

2. Describe the given information in Exercise 25 on page 22 and your plan for finding the solution.

3. Describe the overall step-by-step process you used to solve Exercise 32 on page 28.

Performance Task:

Population Density

Population density is a measure of how many people live within a given area. Locations of new schools are decided using geometric models based on population density. How can these models help officials draw new attendance boundaries when the schools are built?

To explore the answer to this question and more, check out the Performance Task and Real-Life STEM video at *BigIdeasMath.com*.

1.1 Modeling with Area *(pp. 3–8)*

About 210,000 people live in a circular region with a 4.5-mile radius. Find the population density in people per square mile.

Step 1 Find the area of the region.

$$A = \pi r^2 = \pi \cdot (4.5)^2 = 20.25\pi \text{ mi}^2$$

Step 2 Find the population density.

$$\text{Population density} = \frac{\text{number of people}}{\text{area of land}} = \frac{210,000}{20.25\pi} \approx 3301$$

▶ The population density is about 3301 people per square mile.

1. About 1.75 million people live in a circular region with a 15-mile diameter. Find the population density in people per square mile.

2. A circular region has a population of about 15,500 people and a population density of about 775 people per square kilometer. Find the radius of the region.

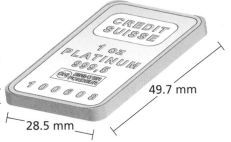

3. A furniture designer applies a thin glaze to the entire marble stool. How much of that amount is needed for a stool whose linear dimensions are

   a. $\frac{7}{8}$ times the dimensions of the given stool?

   b. $\frac{5}{4}$ times the dimensions of the given stool?

1.2 Modeling with Volume *(pp. 9–14)*

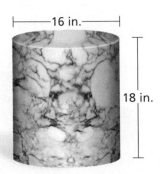

The diagram shows the dimensions of a bar of platinum. Platinum has a density of 21.4 grams per cubic centimeter. Find the mass of the bar to the nearest gram.

Step 1 Convert the dimensions to centimeters using 1 millimeter = 0.1 centimeter.

   Length 4.97 cm   **Width** 2.85 cm   **Height** 0.34 cm

Step 2 Find the volume.

$$V = Bh = 4.97(2.85)(0.34) = 4.81593 \text{ cm}^3$$

Step 3 Let x represent the mass in grams. Substitute the values for the volume and the density in the formula for density and solve for x.

$\text{Density} = \dfrac{\text{Mass}}{\text{Volume}}$	Formula for density
$21.4 = \dfrac{x}{4.81593}$	Substitute.
$103 \approx x$	Multiply each side by 4.81593.

▶ The mass of the bar of platinum is about 103 grams.

4. A bar of platinum has a mass of about 1000 grams. It has a width of 51 millimeters and a height of 9.7 millimeters. Find the length of the bar to the nearest millimeter.

Describe how the change affects the volume of the platinum bar in the example.

5. double the height

6. double the length and width

7. multiply the length by $\frac{1}{3}$

8. A part for a toy train is made by drilling a hole that has a diameter of 0.6 centimeter through a wooden ball that has a diameter of 4 centimeters.

    a. Estimate the volume of the wooden ball after the hole is made. Explain your reasoning.

    b. Do the surface area and volume of the wooden ball decrease after the hole is made? Explain.

1.3   Cross Sections of Solids   *(pp. 17–22)*

Describe the shape formed by the intersection of the plane and the solid.

▶   The cross section is a triangle.

Describe the shape formed by the intersection of the plane and the solid.

9.

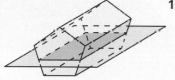

10.

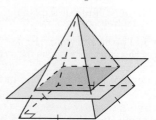

11.

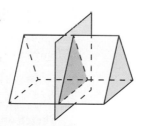

Draw the cross section formed by the described plane that intersects the red line segment drawn on the solid. What is the shape of the cross section?

12. plane is parallel to base

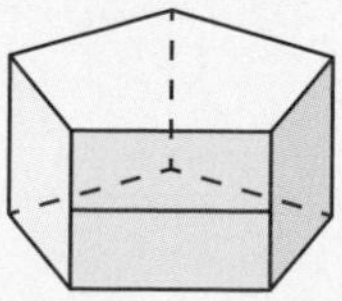

13. plane is parallel to bottom face

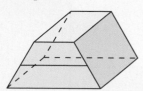

14. Describe and draw two cross sections that can be formed by a plane intersecting the solid in Exercise 12. The shapes of the cross sections should be different than the shape of the cross section in Exercise 12.

1.4   **Solids of Revolution**   *(pp. 23–28)*

a. Sketch the solid produced by rotating the figure around the given axis. Then identify and describe the solid.

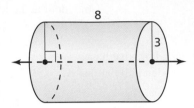

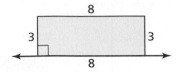

▶ The solid is a cylinder with a height of 8 units and a base radius of 3 units.

b. Sketch and describe the solid that is produced when the region enclosed by $y = 0$, $x = 0$, and $y = -x + 4$ is rotated around the *y*-axis. Then find the volume of the solid.

Step 1   Graph each equation and determine the region that will be rotated around the *y*-axis.

Step 2   Reflect the region in the *y*-axis.

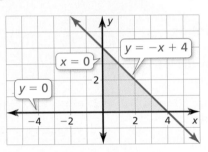

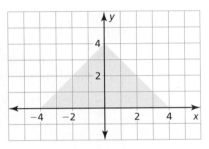

Step 3   Connect the vertices of the triangles using curved lines. The solid is a cone with a height of 4 units and a base radius of 4 units.

Step 4   Find the volume of the cone.

$$V = \frac{1}{3}\pi r^2 h = \frac{1}{3}\pi \cdot 4^2 \cdot 4 = \frac{64}{3}\pi \approx 67.02$$

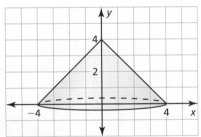

▶ The volume of the cone is $\frac{64}{3}\pi$, or about 67.02 cubic units.

Sketch and describe the solid produced by rotating the figure around the given axis. Then find its surface area and volume.

15.

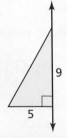

16.

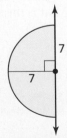

17.

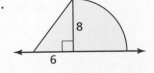

18.   Sketch and describe the solid that is produced when the region enclosed by $y = 0$, $y = x$, and $x = 2$ is rotated around the *y*-axis. Then find the volume of the solid.

1 Chapter Test

1. The island shown has a population of 12,175 people. Find the population density in people per square kilometer.

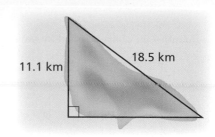

2. You slice the bagel shown in half horizontally to split with your friend. Describe the shape of the cross section you make. What does the cross section look like if you cut the bagel in half vertically?

Sketch and describe the solid produced by rotating the figure around the given axis. Then find its surface area and volume.

3.

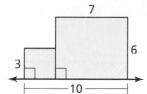

4.

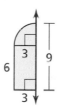

Describe how the change affects the surface area of the regular pyramid or right cone.

5. tripling all the linear dimensions

6. multiplying all the linear dimensions by $\frac{2}{3}$

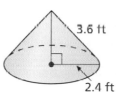

7. The candle has a mass of 1200 grams.

   a. What is the density of the candle wax in grams per cubic centimeter?

   b. After three hours of burning, the height of the candle is about 8.3 inches. How does this change affect the surface area and volume of the candle?

   c. How much mass, to the nearest gram, did the candle lose after 3 hours of burning? If this rate remains constant, estimate the number of hours of burning time the candle will have.

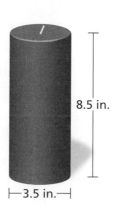

8. Sketch a two-dimensional shape and an axis of revolution that forms the water container shown.

9. A circular region with a 3-mile radius has a population density of about 1000 people per square mile. Find the number of people who live in the region.

10. Sketch and describe the solid that is produced when the region enclosed by $y = 0$, $y = -x + 8$, $x = 0$, and $x = 5$ is rotated around the y-axis. Then find the volume of the solid.

1. Identify the shape formed by the intersection of the plane and the solid.

   a.

   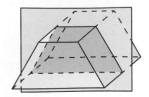

   b.

   c.

   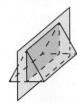

2. About 19,400 people live in a circular region with a 5-mile radius. Find the population density in people per square mile.

3. What is the volume of the solid that is produced when the region enclosed by $y = 0$, $y = 3.5$, $x = 0$, and $x = 8$ is rotated around the x-axis?

   A about 87.96 cubic units

   B about 307.88 cubic units

   C about 703.72 cubic units

   D about 1231.5 cubic units

4. You are vacationing at the cottage shown and after arriving, realize that you need to increase the inside air temperature. To raise the temperature to your desired level, you need 7 Btu per cubic foot. How many Btu do you need to raise the temperature of the cottage?

   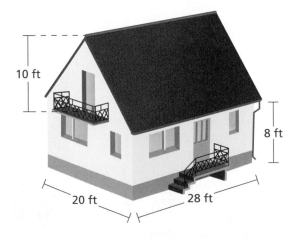

   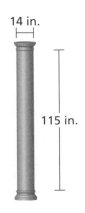

5. Marble has a density of 2.56 grams per cubic centimeter. What is the mass of the cylindrical portion of the marble pillar shown to the nearest kilogram?

6. The regular decagonal pyramid shown is intersected by a plane perpendicular to its base. The plane passes through its vertex so it is divided into two congruent parts. What is the shape of the cross section?

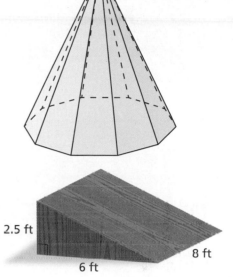

(A) triangle

(B) rectangle

(C) trapezoid

(D) decagon

7. You design the ramp shown. The outer surface of the ramp, including the bottom, is covered with plywood. Your friend wants to double the base and height of the triangular sides of your ramp. Your friend claims that the new ramp will use no more than twice the amount of plywood as your ramp. Do you support your friend's claim? Explain your reasoning.

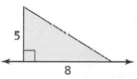

2.5 ft

6 ft

8 ft

8. Which figure has the greatest volume when it is rotated around the given axis?

(A)

5

8

(B)

6

4

6

(C)

3.8

3.8

(D)

6

3.4   3.4

6

9. A silo similar to the one shown has a height of 60 feet and a diameter of 18 feet. It is filled with grain to a height of about 30 feet. How many bushels of grain are currently in the silo? One bushel of grain is about 1.25 cubic feet.

2 Linear and Quadratic Functions

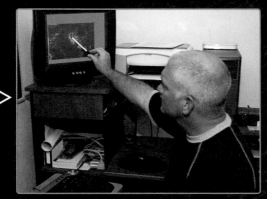

Meteorologist *(p. 93)*

Kangaroo *(p. 79)*

SEE the Big Idea

Dirt Bike *(p. 43)*

Soccer *(p. 89)*

Prom *(p. 57)*

Maintaining Mathematical Proficiency

Evaluating Expressions

Example 1 Evaluate the expression $36 \div (3^2 \times 2) - 3$.

$$36 \div (3^2 \times 2) - 3 = 36 \div (9 \times 2) - 3 \qquad \text{Evaluate the power within parentheses.}$$
$$= 36 \div 18 - 3 \qquad \text{Multiply within parentheses.}$$
$$= 2 - 3 \qquad \text{Divide.}$$
$$= -1 \qquad \text{Subtract.}$$

Evaluate.

1. $5 \cdot 2^3 + 7$

2. $4 - 2(3 + 2)^2$

3. $48 \div 4^2 + \frac{3}{5}$

4. $50 \div 5^2 \cdot 2$

5. $\frac{1}{2}(2^2 + 22)$

6. $\frac{1}{6}(6 + 18) - 2^2$

Transformations of Figures

Example 2 Reflect the black rectangle in the *x*-axis. Then translate the new rectangle 5 units to the left and 1 unit down.

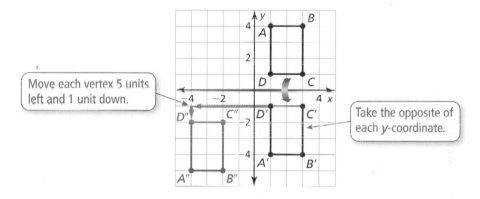

Move each vertex 5 units left and 1 unit down.

Take the opposite of each *y*-coordinate.

Graph the transformation of the figure.

7. Translate the rectangle 1 unit right and 4 units up.

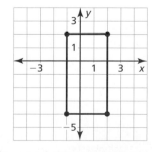

8. Reflect the triangle in the *y*-axis. Then translate 2 units left.

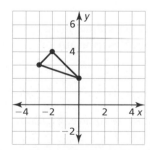

9. Translate the trapezoid 3 units down. Then reflect in the *x*-axis.

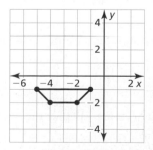

10. ABSTRACT REASONING Give an example to show why the order of operations is important when evaluating a numerical expression. Is the order of transformations of figures important? Justify your answer.

Mathematical Practices

Mathematically proficient students use technological tools to explore concepts.

Using a Graphing Calculator

Core Concept

Standard and Square Viewing Windows

A typical screen on a graphing calculator has a height-to-width ratio of 2 to 3. This means that when you view a graph using the *standard viewing window* of -10 to 10 (on each axis), the graph will not be shown in its true perspective.

```
WINDOW
Xmin=-10
Xmax=10
Xscl=1
Ymin=-10
Ymax=10
Yscl=1
```

This is the standard viewing window.

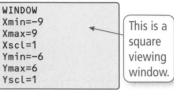

To view a graph in its true perspective, you need to change to a *square viewing window*, where the tick marks on the x-axis are spaced the same as the tick marks on the y-axis.

```
WINDOW
Xmin=-9
Xmax=9
Xscl=1
Ymin=-6
Ymax=6
Yscl=1
```

This is a square viewing window.

EXAMPLE 1 Using a Graphing Calculator

Use a graphing calculator to graph $y = |x| - 3$.

SOLUTION

In the standard viewing window, notice that the tick marks on the y-axis are closer together than those on the x-axis. This implies that the graph is not shown in its true perspective.

This is the graph in the standard viewing window.

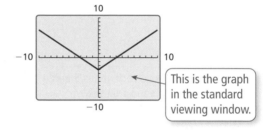

In a square viewing window, notice that the tick marks on both axes have the same spacing. This implies that the graph is shown in its true perspective.

This is the graph in a square viewing window.

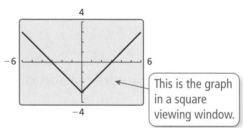

Monitoring Progress

Use a graphing calculator to graph the equation using the standard viewing window and a square viewing window. Describe any differences in the graphs.

1. $y = 2x - 3$ **2.** $y = -x + 1$ **3.** $y = -|x - 4|$

4. $y = |x + 2|$ **5.** $y = x^2 - 2$ **6.** $y = -x^2 + 1$

Determine whether the viewing window is square. Explain.

7. $-8 \leq x \leq 8,\ -2 \leq y \leq 8$ **8.** $-7 \leq x \leq 8,\ -2 \leq y \leq 8$

9. $-6 \leq x \leq 9,\ -2 \leq y \leq 8$ **10.** $-2 \leq x \leq 2,\ -3 \leq y \leq 3$

11. $-4 \leq x \leq 5,\ -3 \leq y \leq 3$ **12.** $-4 \leq x \leq 4,\ -3 \leq y \leq 3$

2.1 Parent Functions and Transformations

Essential Question What are the characteristics of some of the basic parent functions?

EXPLORATION 1 Identifying Basic Parent Functions

Work with a partner. Graphs of four basic parent functions are shown below. Classify each function as *linear*, *absolute value*, *quadratic*, or *exponential*. Justify your reasoning.

> **JUSTIFYING CONCLUSIONS**
> To be proficient in math, you need to justify your conclusions and communicate them clearly to others.

a.
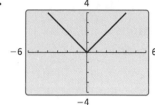

b.
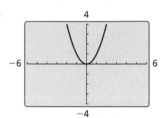

c.
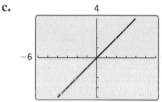

d.
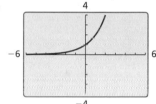

EXPLORATION 2 Identifying Basic Parent Functions

Work with a partner. Graphs of four basic parent functions that you will study later in this course are shown below. Classify each function as *square root*, *cube root*, *cubic*, or *reciprocal*. Justify your reasoning.

a.
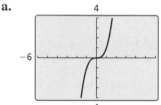

b.
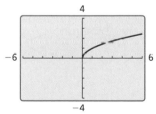

c.
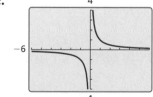

d.
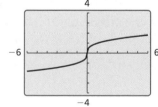

Communicate Your Answer

3. What are the characteristics of some of the basic parent functions?

4. Write an equation for each function whose graph is shown in Exploration 1. Then use a graphing calculator to verify that your equations are correct.

What You Will Learn

▶ Identify families of functions.

▶ Describe transformations of parent functions.

▶ Describe combinations of transformations.

Core Vocabulary

parent function, *p. 40*
transformation, *p. 41*
translation, *p. 41*
reflection, *p. 41*
vertical stretch, *p. 42*
vertical shrink, *p. 42*

Previous
function
domain
range
slope
scatter plot

Identifying Function Families

Functions that belong to the same *family* share key characteristics. The **parent function** is the most basic function in a family. Functions in the same family are *transformations* of their parent function.

Core Concept

Parent Functions

Family	Constant	Linear	Absolute Value	Quadratic
Rule	$f(x) = 1$	$f(x) = x$	$f(x) = \lvert x \rvert$	$f(x) = x^2$
Graph	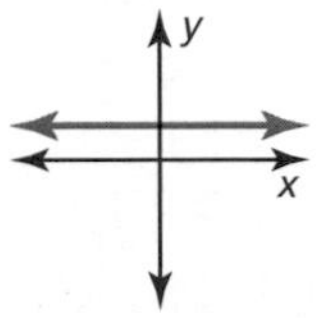	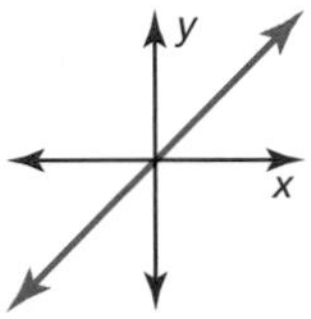	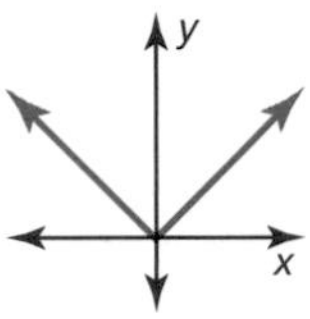	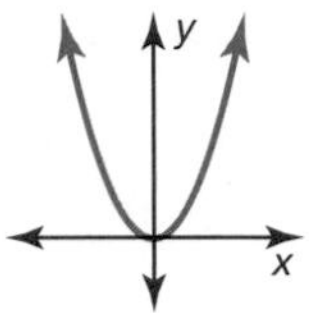
Domain	All real numbers	All real numbers	All real numbers	All real numbers
Range	$y = 1$	All real numbers	$y \geq 0$	$y \geq 0$

LOOKING FOR STRUCTURE

You can also use function rules to identify functions. The only variable term in *f* is an $\lvert x \rvert$-term, so it is an absolute value function.

EXAMPLE 1   Identifying a Function Family

Identify the function family to which *f* belongs. Compare the graph of *f* to the graph of its parent function.

SOLUTION

The graph of *f* is V-shaped, so *f* is an absolute value function.

The graph is shifted up and is narrower than the graph of the parent absolute value function. The domain of each function is all real numbers, but the range of *f* is $y \geq 1$ and the range of the parent absolute value function is $y \geq 0$.

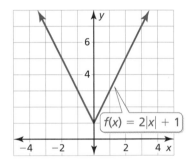

$f(x) = 2\lvert x \rvert + 1$

Monitoring Progress Help in English and Spanish at *BigIdeasMath.com*

1. Identify the function family to which *g* belongs. Compare the graph of *g* to the graph of its parent function.

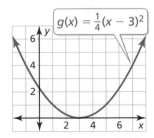

$g(x) = \frac{1}{4}(x - 3)^2$

Describing Transformations

A **transformation** changes the size, shape, position, or orientation of a graph. A **translation** is a transformation that shifts a graph horizontally and/or vertically but does not change its size, shape, or orientation.

REMEMBER

The slope-intercept form of a linear equation is $y = mx + b$, where m is the slope and b is the y-intercept.

EXAMPLE 2   Graphing and Describing Translations

Graph $g(x) = x - 4$ and its parent function. Then describe the transformation.

SOLUTION

The function g is a linear function with a slope of 1 and a y-intercept of -4. So, draw a line through the point $(0, -4)$ with a slope of 1.

The graph of g is 4 units below the graph of the parent linear function f.

▶ So, the graph of $g(x) = x - 4$ is a vertical translation 4 units down of the graph of the parent linear function.

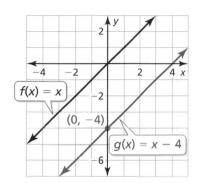

A **reflection** is a transformation that flips a graph over a line called the *line of reflection*. A reflected point is the same distance from the line of reflection as the original point but on the opposite side of the line.

EXAMPLE 3   Graphing and Describing Reflections

Graph $p(x) = -x^2$ and its parent function. Then describe the transformation.

SOLUTION

The function p is a quadratic function. Use a table of values to graph each function.

REMEMBER

The function $p(x) = -x^2$ is written in *function notation*, where $p(x)$ is another name for y.

x	$y = x^2$	$y = -x^2$
-2	4	-4
-1	1	-1
0	0	0
1	1	-1
2	4	-4

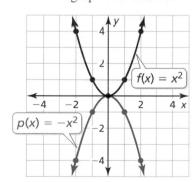

The graph of p is the graph of the parent function flipped over the x-axis.

▶ So, the graph of $p(x) = -x^2$ is a reflection in the x-axis of the graph of the parent quadratic function.

Monitoring Progress Help in English and Spanish at *BigIdeasMath.com*

Graph the function and its parent function. Then describe the transformation.

2. $g(x) = x + 3$ **3.** $h(x) = (x - 2)^2$ **4.** $n(x) = -|x|$

Another way to transform the graph of a function is to multiply all of the y-coordinates by the same positive factor (other than 1). When the factor is greater than 1, the transformation is a **vertical stretch**. When the factor is greater than 0 and less than 1, it is a **vertical shrink**.

EXAMPLE 4   Graphing and Describing Stretches and Shrinks

Graph each function and its parent function. Then describe the transformation.

a. $g(x) = 2|x|$ **b.** $h(x) = \frac{1}{2}x^2$

SOLUTION

a. The function g is an absolute value function. Use a table of values to graph the functions.

x	$y = |x|$	$y = 2|x|$
-2	2	4
-1	1	2
0	0	0
1	1	2
2	2	4

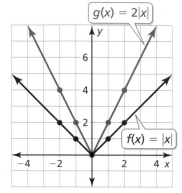

REASONING ABSTRACTLY

To visualize a vertical stretch, imagine *pulling* the points away from the x-axis.

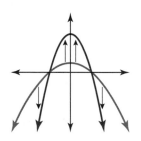

To visualize a vertical shrink, imagine *pushing* the points toward the x-axis.

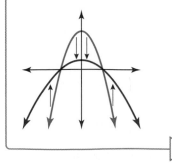

The y-coordinate of each point on g is two times the y-coordinate of the corresponding point on the parent function.

▶ So, the graph of $g(x) = 2|x|$ is a vertical stretch of the graph of the parent absolute value function.

b. The function h is a quadratic function. Use a table of values to graph the functions.

x	$y = x^2$	$y = \frac{1}{2}x^2$
-2	4	2
-1	1	$\frac{1}{2}$
0	0	0
1	1	$\frac{1}{2}$
2	4	2

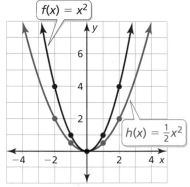

The y-coordinate of each point on h is one-half of the y-coordinate of the corresponding point on the parent function.

▶ So, the graph of $h(x) = \frac{1}{2}x^2$ is a vertical shrink of the graph of the parent quadratic function.

Monitoring Progress Help in English and Spanish at *BigIdeasMath.com*

Graph the function and its parent function. Then describe the transformation.

5. $g(x) = 3x$ **6.** $h(x) = \frac{3}{2}x^2$ **7.** $c(x) = 0.2|x|$

Combinations of Transformations

You can use more than one transformation to change the graph of a function.

EXAMPLE 5 **Describing Combinations of Transformations**

Use a graphing calculator to graph $g(x) = -|x + 5| - 3$ and its parent function. Then describe the transformations.

SOLUTION

The function g is an absolute value function.

▶ The graph shows that $g(x) = -|x + 5| - 3$ is a reflection in the x-axis followed by a translation 5 units left and 3 units down of the graph of the parent absolute value function.

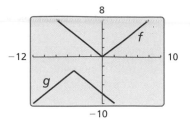

EXAMPLE 6 **Modeling with Mathematics**

Time (seconds), x	Height (feet), y
0	8
0.5	20
1	24
1.5	20
2	8

The table shows the height y of a dirt bike x seconds after jumping off a ramp. What type of function can you use to model the data? Estimate the height after 1.75 seconds.

SOLUTION

1. **Understand the Problem** You are asked to identify the type of function that can model the table of values and then to find the height at a specific time.

2. **Make a Plan** Create a scatter plot of the data. Then use the relationship shown in the scatter plot to estimate the height after 1.75 seconds.

3. **Solve the Problem** Create a scatter plot.

   The data appear to lie on a curve that resembles a quadratic function. Sketch the curve.

   ▶ So, you can model the data with a quadratic function. The graph shows that the height is about 15 feet after 1.75 seconds.

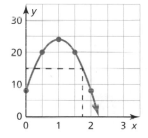

4. **Look Back** To check that your solution is reasonable, analyze the values in the table. Notice that the heights decrease after 1 second. Because 1.75 is between 1.5 and 2, the height must be between 20 feet and 8 feet.

$$8 < 15 < 20 ✓$$

Monitoring Progress   Help in English and Spanish at *BigIdeasMath.com*

Use a graphing calculator to graph the function and its parent function. Then describe the transformations.

8. $h(x) = -\frac{1}{4}x + 5$ **9.** $d(x) = 3(x - 5)^2 - 1$

10. The table shows the amount of fuel in a chainsaw over time. What type of function can you use to model the data? When will the tank be empty?

Time (minutes), x	0	10	20	30	40
Fuel remaining (fluid ounces), y	15	12	9	6	3

Vocabulary and Core Concept Check

1. **COMPLETE THE SENTENCE** The function $f(x) = x^2$ is the _____ of $f(x) = 2x^2 - 3$.

2. **DIFFERENT WORDS, SAME QUESTION** Which is different? Find "both" answers.

What are the vertices of the figure after a reflection in the *x*-axis, followed by a translation 2 units right?

What are the vertices of the figure after a translation 6 units up and 2 units right?

What are the vertices of the figure after a translation 2 units right, followed by a reflection in the *x*-axis?

What are the vertices of the figure after a translation 6 units up, followed by a reflection in the *x*-axis?

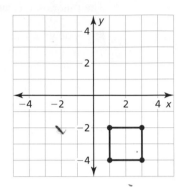

Monitoring Progress and Modeling with Mathematics

In Exercises 3–6, identify the function family to which *f* belongs. Compare the graph of *f* to the graph of its parent function. *(See Example 1.)*

3.

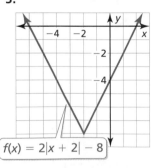

$f(x) = 2|x + 2| - 8$

4.

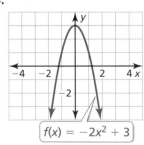

$f(x) = -2x^2 + 3$

5.

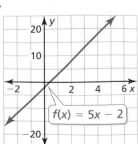

$f(x) = 5x - 2$

6.

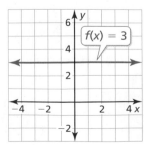

$f(x) = 3$

7. **MODELING WITH MATHEMATICS** At 8:00 A.M., the temperature is 43°F. The temperature increases 2°F each hour for the next 7 hours. Graph the temperatures over time *t* (*t* = 0 represents 8:00 A.M.). What type of function can you use to model the data? Explain.

8. **MODELING WITH MATHEMATICS** You purchase a car from a dealership for $10,000. The trade-in value of the car each year after the purchase is given by the function $f(x) = 10,000 - 250x^2$. Identify the function family to which *f* belongs.

In Exercises 9–18, graph the function and its parent function. Then describe the transformation. *(See Examples 2 and 3.)*

9. $g(x) = x + 4$

10. $f(x) = x - 6$

11. $f(x) = x^2 - 1$

12. $h(x) = (x + 4)^2$

13. $g(x) = |x - 5|$

14. $f(x) = 4 + |x|$

15. $h(x) = -x^2$

16. $g(x) = -x$

17. $f(x) = 3$

18. $f(x) = -2$

In Exercises 19–26, graph the function and its parent function. Then describe the transformation. (*See Example 4.*)

19. $f(x) = \frac{1}{3}x$

20. $g(x) = 4x$

21. $f(x) = 2x^2$

22. $h(x) = \frac{1}{3}x^2$

23. $h(x) = \frac{3}{4}x$

24. $g(x) = \frac{4}{3}x$

25. $h(x) = 3|x|$

26. $f(x) = \frac{1}{2}|x|$

In Exercises 27–34, use a graphing calculator to graph the function and its parent function. Then describe the transformations. (*See Example 5.*)

27. $f(x) = 3x + 2$

28. $h(x) = -x + 5$

29. $h(x) = -3|x| - 1$

30. $f(x) = \frac{3}{4}|x| + 1$

31. $g(x) = \frac{1}{2}x^2 - 6$

32. $f(x) = 4x^2 - 3$

33. $f(x) = -(x + 3)^2 + \frac{1}{4}$

34. $g(x) = -|x - 1| - \frac{1}{2}$

ERROR ANALYSIS In Exercises 35 and 36, identify and correct the error in describing the transformation of the parent function.

35.
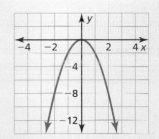

The graph is a reflection in the x-axis and a vertical shrink of the parent quadratic function.

36.
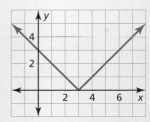

The graph is a translation 3 units right of the parent absolute value function, so the function is $f(x) = |x + 3|$.

MATHEMATICAL CONNECTIONS In Exercises 37 and 38, find the coordinates of the figure after the transformation.

37. Translate 2 units down.

38. Reflect in the x-axis.

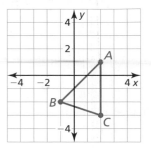
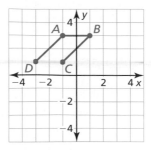

USING TOOLS In Exercises 39–44, identify the function family and describe the domain and range. Use a graphing calculator to verify your answer.

39. $g(x) = |x + 2| - 1$

40. $h(x) = |x - 3| + 2$

41. $g(x) = 3x + 4$

42. $f(x) = -4x + 11$

43. $f(x) = 5x^2 - 2$

44. $f(x) = -2x^2 + 6$

45. **MODELING WITH MATHEMATICS** The table shows the speeds of a car as it travels through an intersection with a stop sign. What type of function can you use to model the data? Estimate the speed of the car when it is 20 yards past the intersection. (*See Example 6.*)

Displacement from sign (yards), x	Speed (miles per hour), y
−100	40
−50	20
−10	4
0	0
10	4
50	20
100	40

46. **THOUGHT PROVOKING** In the same coordinate plane, sketch the graph of the parent quadratic function and the graph of a quadratic function that has no x-intercepts. Describe the transformation(s) of the parent function.

47. **USING STRUCTURE** Graph the functions $f(x) = |x - 4|$ and $g(x) = |x| - 4$. Are they equivalent? Explain.

48. HOW DO YOU SEE IT? Consider the graphs of f, g, and h.

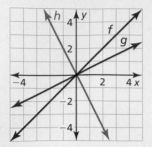

a. Does the graph of g represent a vertical stretch or a vertical shrink of the graph of f? Explain your reasoning.

b. Describe how to transform the graph of f to obtain the graph of h.

49. MAKING AN ARGUMENT Your friend says two different translations of the graph of the parent linear function can result in the graph of $f(x) = x - 2$. Is your friend correct? Explain.

50. DRAWING CONCLUSIONS A person swims at a constant speed of 1 meter per second. What type of function can be used to model the distance the swimmer travels? If the person has a 10-meter head start, what type of transformation does this represent? Explain.

51. PROBLEM SOLVING You are playing basketball with your friends. The height (in feet) of the ball above the ground t seconds after a shot is released from your hand is modeled by the function $f(t) = -16t^2 + 32t + 5.2$.

a. Without graphing, identify the type of function that models the height of the basketball.

b. What is the value of t when the ball is released from your hand? Explain your reasoning.

c. How many feet above the ground is the ball when it is released from your hand? Explain.

52. MODELING WITH MATHEMATICS The table shows the battery lives of a computer over time. What type of function can you use to model the data? Interpret the meaning of the x-intercept in this situation.

Time (hours), x	Battery life remaining, y
1	80%
3	40%
5	0%
6	20%
8	60%

53. REASONING Compare each function with its parent function. State whether it contains a *horizontal translation*, *vertical translation*, *both*, or *neither*. Explain your reasoning.

a. $f(x) = 2|x| - 3$ b. $f(x) = (x - 8)^2$

c. $f(x) = |x + 2| + 4$ d. $f(x) = 4x^2$

54. CRITICAL THINKING Use the values -1, 0, 1, and 2 in the correct box so the graph of each function intersects the x-axis. Explain your reasoning.

a. $f(x) = 3x^{\boxed{}} + 1$ b. $f(x) = |2x - 6| - \boxed{}$

c. $f(x) = \boxed{}x^2 + 1$ d. $f(x) = \boxed{}$

Maintaining Mathematical Proficiency
Reviewing what you learned in previous grades and lessons

Determine whether the ordered pair is a solution of the equation. *(Skills Review Handbook)*

55. $f(x) = |x + 2|; (1, -3)$ **56.** $f(x) = |x| - 3; (-2, -5)$

57. $f(x) = x - 3; (5, 2)$ **58.** $f(x) = x - 4; (12, 8)$

Find the x-intercept and the y-intercept of the graph of the equation. *(Skills Review Handbook)*

59. $y = x$ **60.** $y = x + 2$

61. $3x + y = 1$ **62.** $x - 2y = 8$

Transformations of Linear and Absolute Value Functions

Essential Question How do the graphs of $y = f(x) + k$, $y = f(x - h)$, and $y = -f(x)$ compare to the graph of the parent function f?

EXPLORATION 1 — Transformations of the Parent Absolute Value Function

Work with a partner. Compare the graph of the function

$$y = |x| + k \qquad \text{Transformation}$$

to the graph of the parent function

$$f(x) = |x|. \qquad \text{Parent function}$$

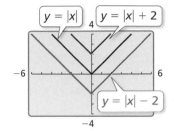

EXPLORATION 2 — Transformations of the Parent Absolute Value Function

Work with a partner. Compare the graph of the function

$$y = |x - h| \qquad \text{Transformation}$$

to the graph of the parent function

$$f(x) = |x|. \qquad \text{Parent function}$$

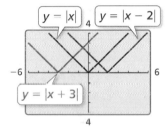

EXPLORATION 3 — Transformation of the Parent Absolute Value Function

Work with a partner. Compare the graph of the function

$$y = -|x| \qquad \text{Transformation}$$

to the graph of the parent function

$$f(x) = |x|. \qquad \text{Parent function}$$

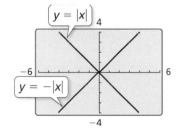

Communicate Your Answer

4. How do the graphs of $y = f(x) + k$, $y = f(x - h)$, and $y = -f(x)$ compare to the graph of the parent function f?

5. Compare the graph of each function to the graph of its parent function f. Use a graphing calculator to verify your answers are correct.

   a. $y = 2^x - 4$ b. $y = 2^{x+4}$ c. $y = -2^x$

   d. $y = x^2 + 1$ e. $y = (x - 1)^2$ f. $y = -x^2$

What You Will Learn

▶ Write functions representing translations and reflections.

▶ Write functions representing stretches and shrinks.

▶ Write functions representing combinations of transformations.

Translations and Reflections

You can use function notation to represent transformations of graphs of functions.

🜨 Core Concept

Horizontal Translations

The graph of $y = f(x - h)$ is a horizontal translation of the graph of $y = f(x)$, where $h \neq 0$.

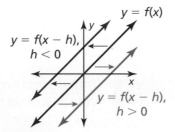

Subtracting h from the **inputs** before evaluating the function shifts the graph left when $h < 0$ and right when $h > 0$.

Vertical Translations

The graph of $y = f(x) + k$ is a vertical translation of the graph of $y = f(x)$, where $k \neq 0$.

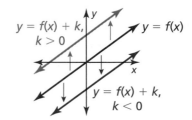

Adding k to the **outputs** shifts the graph down when $k < 0$ and up when $k > 0$.

EXAMPLE 1   Writing Translations of Functions

Let $f(x) = 2x + 1$.

a. Write a function g whose graph is a translation 3 units down of the graph of f.

b. Write a function h whose graph is a translation 2 units to the left of the graph of f.

SOLUTION

a. A translation 3 units down is a vertical translation that adds -3 to each output value.

$$g(x) = f(x) + (-3) \qquad \text{Add } -3 \text{ to the output.}$$
$$= 2x + 1 + (-3) \qquad \text{Substitute } 2x + 1 \text{ for } f(x).$$
$$= 2x - 2 \qquad \text{Simplify.}$$

▶ The translated function is $g(x) = 2x - 2$.

b. A translation 2 units to the left is a horizontal translation that subtracts -2 from each input value.

$$h(x) = f(x - (-2)) \qquad \text{Subtract } -2 \text{ from the input.}$$
$$= f(x + 2) \qquad \text{Add the opposite.}$$
$$= 2(x + 2) + 1 \qquad \text{Replace } x \text{ with } x + 2 \text{ in } f(x).$$
$$= 2x + 5 \qquad \text{Simplify.}$$

▶ The translated function is $h(x) = 2x + 5$.

Check

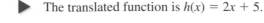

⑤ Core Concept

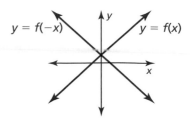

Reflections in the *x*-Axis

The graph of $y = -f(x)$ is a reflection in the *x*-axis of the graph of $y = f(x)$.

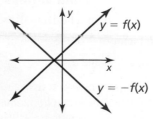

Multiplying the **outputs** by -1 changes their signs.

Reflections in the *y*-Axis

The graph of $y = f(-x)$ is a reflection in the *y*-axis of the graph of $y = f(x)$.

Multiplying the **inputs** by -1 changes their signs.

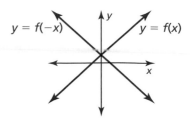

EXAMPLE 2   **Writing Reflections of Functions**

Let $f(x) = |x + 3| + 1$.

a. Write a function g whose graph is a reflection in the *x*-axis of the graph of f.

b. Write a function h whose graph is a reflection in the *y*-axis of the graph of f.

SOLUTION

a. A reflection in the *x*-axis changes the sign of each output value.

$$g(x) = -f(x) \qquad \text{Multiply the output by } -1.$$
$$= -\left(|x + 3| + 1\right) \qquad \text{Substitute } |x + 3| + 1 \text{ for } f(x).$$
$$= -|x + 3| - 1 \qquad \text{Distributive Property}$$

▶ The reflected function is $g(x) = -|x + 3| - 1$.

b. A reflection in the *y*-axis changes the sign of each input value.

$$h(x) = f(-x) \qquad \text{Multiply the input by } -1.$$
$$= |-x + 3| + 1 \qquad \text{Replace } x \text{ with } -x \text{ in } f(x).$$
$$= |-(x - 3)| + 1 \qquad \text{Factor out } -1.$$
$$= |-1| \cdot |x - 3| + 1 \qquad \text{Product Property of Absolute Value}$$
$$= |x - 3| + 1 \qquad \text{Simplify.}$$

▶ The reflected function is $h(x) = |x - 3| + 1$.

Check

Monitoring Progress   🔊 Help in English and Spanish at *BigIdeasMath.com*

Write a function g whose graph represents the indicated transformation of the graph of f. Use a graphing calculator to check your answer.

1. $f(x) = 3x$; translation 5 units up

2. $f(x) = |x| - 3$; translation 4 units to the right

3. $f(x) = -|x + 2| - 1$; reflection in the *x*-axis

4. $f(x) = \frac{1}{2}x + 1$; reflection in the *y*-axis

Stretches and Shrinks

In the previous section, you learned that vertical stretches and shrinks transform graphs. You can also use *horizontal* stretches and shrinks to transform graphs.

Core Concept

Horizontal Stretches and Shrinks

The graph of $y = f(ax)$ is a horizontal stretch or shrink by a factor of $\frac{1}{a}$ of the graph of $y = f(x)$, where $a > 0$ and $a \neq 1$.

Multiplying the **inputs** by a before evaluating the function stretches the graph horizontally (away from the y-axis) when $0 < a < 1$, and shrinks the graph horizontally (toward the y-axis) when $a > 1$.

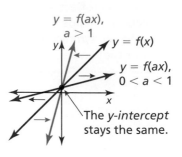

$y = f(ax)$, $a > 1$
$y = f(x)$
$y = f(ax)$, $0 < a < 1$
The *y-intercept* stays the same.

STUDY TIP

The graphs of $y = f(-ax)$ and $y = -a \cdot f(x)$ represent a stretch or shrink *and* a reflection in the x- or y-axis of the graph of $y = f(x)$.

Vertical Stretches and Shrinks

The graph of $y = a \cdot f(x)$ is a vertical stretch or shrink by a factor of a of the graph of $y = f(x)$, where $a > 0$ and $a \neq 1$.

Multiplying the **outputs** by a stretches the graph vertically (away from the x-axis) when $a > 1$, and shrinks the graph vertically (toward the x-axis) when $0 < a < 1$.

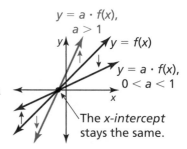

$y = a \cdot f(x)$, $a > 1$
$y = f(x)$
$y = a \cdot f(x)$, $0 < a < 1$
The *x-intercept* stays the same.

EXAMPLE 3   Writing Stretches and Shrinks of Functions

Let $f(x) = |x - 3| - 5$. Write (a) a function g whose graph is a horizontal shrink of the graph of f by a factor of $\frac{1}{3}$, and (b) a function h whose graph is a vertical stretch of the graph of f by a factor of 2.

SOLUTION

a. A horizontal shrink by a factor of $\frac{1}{3}$ multiplies each input value by 3.

$$g(x) = f(3x) \qquad \text{Multiply the input by 3.}$$
$$= |3x - 3| - 5 \qquad \text{Replace } x \text{ with } 3x \text{ in } f(x).$$

▶ The transformed function is $g(x) = |3x - 3| - 5$.

b. A vertical stretch by a factor of 2 multiplies each output value by 2.

$$h(x) = 2 \cdot f(x) \qquad \text{Multiply the output by 2.}$$
$$= 2 \cdot (|x - 3| - 5) \qquad \text{Substitute } |x - 3| - 5 \text{ for } f(x).$$
$$= 2|x - 3| - 10 \qquad \text{Distributive Property}$$

▶ The transformed function is $h(x) = 2|x - 3| - 10$.

Check

Monitoring Progress   <audio> Help in English and Spanish at *BigIdeasMath.com*

Write a function g whose graph represents the indicated transformation of the graph of f. Use a graphing calculator to check your answer.

5. $f(x) = 4x + 2$; horizontal stretch by a factor of 2

6. $f(x) = |x| - 3$; vertical shrink by a factor of $\frac{1}{3}$

Combinations of Transformations

You can write a function that represents a series of transformations on the graph of another function by applying the transformations one at a time in the stated order.

EXAMPLE 4   Combining Transformations

Let the graph of g be a vertical shrink by a factor of 0.25 followed by a translation 3 units up of the graph of $f(x) = x$. Write a rule for g.

SOLUTION

Check

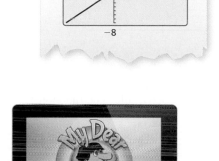

Step 1 First write a function h that represents the vertical shrink of f.

$$h(x) = 0.25 \cdot f(x) \qquad \text{Multiply the output by 0.25.}$$
$$= 0.25x \qquad \text{Substitute } x \text{ for } f(x).$$

Step 2 Then write a function g that represents the translation of h.

$$g(x) = h(x) + 3 \qquad \text{Add 3 to the output.}$$
$$= 0.25x + 3 \qquad \text{Substitute } 0.25x \text{ for } h(x).$$

▶ The transformed function is $g(x) = 0.25x + 3$.

EXAMPLE 5   Modeling with Mathematics

You design a computer game. Your revenue for x downloads is given by $f(x) = 2x$. Your profit is $50 less than 90% of the revenue for x downloads. Describe how to transform the graph of f to model the profit. What is your profit for 100 downloads?

SOLUTION

1. **Understand the Problem** You are given a function that represents your revenue and a verbal statement that represents your profit. You are asked to find the profit for 100 downloads.

2. **Make a Plan** Write a function p that represents your profit. Then use this function to find the profit for 100 downloads.

3. **Solve the Problem**   profit = 90% • revenue − 50

$$p(x) = 0.9 \cdot f(x) - 50$$

Vertical shrink by a factor of 0.9 ⎯⎯⎯⎯⎯⎯⎯⎯⎯ | ⎯⎯⎯⎯⎯⎯⎯ Translation 50 units down

$$= 0.9 \cdot 2x - 50 \qquad \text{Substitute } 2x \text{ for } f(x).$$
$$= 1.8x - 50 \qquad \text{Simplify.}$$

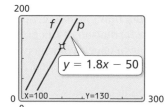

To find the profit for 100 downloads, evaluate p when $x = 100$.

$$p(100) = 1.8(100) - 50 = 130$$

▶ Your profit is $130 for 100 downloads.

4. **Look Back** The vertical shrink decreases the slope, and the translation shifts the graph 50 units down. So, the graph of p is below and not as steep as the graph of f.

Monitoring Progress Help in English and Spanish at *BigIdeasMath.com*

7. Let the graph of g be a translation 6 units down followed by a reflection in the x-axis of the graph of $f(x) = |x|$. Write a rule for g. Use a graphing calculator to check your answer.

8. **WHAT IF?** In Example 5, your revenue function is $f(x) = 3x$. How does this affect your profit for 100 downloads?

Vocabulary and Core Concept Check

1. **COMPLETE THE SENTENCE** The function $g(x) = |5x| - 4$ is a horizontal _____ of the function $f(x) = |x| - 4$.

2. **WHICH ONE DOESN'T BELONG?** Which transformation does *not* belong with the other three? Explain your reasoning.

Translate the graph of $f(x) = 2x + 3$ up 2 units.	Shrink the graph of $f(x) = x + 5$ horizontally by a factor of $\frac{1}{2}$.
Stretch the graph of $f(x) = x + 3$ vertically by a factor of 2.	Translate the graph of $f(x) = 2x + 3$ left 1 unit.

Monitoring Progress and Modeling with Mathematics

In Exercises 3–8, write a function g whose graph represents the indicated transformation of the graph of f. Use a graphing calculator to check your answer. *(See Example 1.)*

3. $f(x) = x - 5$; translation 4 units to the left

4. $f(x) = x + 2$; translation 2 units to the right

5. $f(x) = |4x + 3| + 2$; translation 2 units down

6. $f(x) = 2x - 9$; translation 6 units up

7. $f(x) = 4 - |x + 1|$ 8. $f(x) = |4x| + 5$

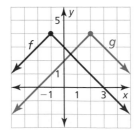
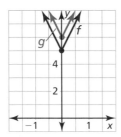

9. **WRITING** Describe two different translations of the graph of f that result in the graph of g.

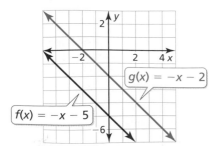

$g(x) = -x - 2$

$f(x) = -x - 5$

10. **PROBLEM SOLVING** You open a café. The function $f(x) = 4000x$ represents your expected net income (in dollars) after being open x weeks. Before you open, you incur an extra expense of $12,000. What transformation of f is necessary to model this situation? How many weeks will it take to pay off the extra expense?

In Exercises 11–16, write a function g whose graph represents the indicated transformation of the graph of f. Use a graphing calculator to check your answer. *(See Example 2.)*

11. $f(x) = -5x + 2$; reflection in the x-axis

12. $f(x) = \frac{1}{2}x - 3$; reflection in the x-axis

13. $f(x) = |6x| - 2$; reflection in the y-axis

14. $f(x) = |2x - 1| + 3$; reflection in the y-axis

15. $f(x) = -3 + |x - 11|$; reflection in the y-axis

16. $f(x) = -x + 1$; reflection in the y-axis

In Exercises 17–22, write a function g **whose graph represents the indicated transformation of the graph of** f. **Use a graphing calculator to check your answer.** (*See Example 3.*)

17. $f(x) = x + 2$; vertical stretch by a factor of 5

18. $f(x) = 2x + 6$; vertical shrink by a factor of $\frac{1}{2}$

19. $f(x) = |2x| + 4$; horizontal shrink by a factor of $\frac{1}{2}$

20. $f(x) = |x + 3|$; horizontal stretch by a factor of 4

21. $f(x) = -2|x - 4| + 2$

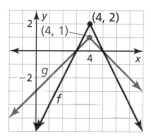

22. $f(x) = 6 - x$

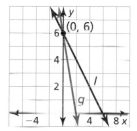

ANALYZING RELATIONSHIPS
In Exercises 23–26, match the graph of the transformation of f with the correct equation shown. Explain your reasoning.

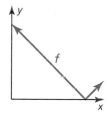

23.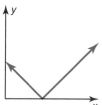

24.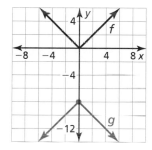

25.

26.

A. $y = 2f(x)$ **B.** $y = f(2x)$

C. $y = f(x + 2)$ **D.** $y = f(x) + 2$

In Exercises 27–32, write a function g **whose graph represents the indicated transformations of the graph of** f. (*See Example 4.*)

27. $f(x) = x$; vertical stretch by a factor of 2 followed by a translation 1 unit up

28. $f(x) = x$; translation 3 units down followed by a vertical shrink by a factor of $\frac{1}{3}$

29. $f(x) = |x|$; translation 2 units to the right followed by a horizontal stretch by a factor of 2

30. $f(x) = |x|$; reflection in the y-axis followed by a translation 3 units to the right

31. $f(x) = |x|$ **32.** $f(x) = |x|$

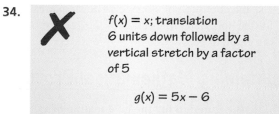

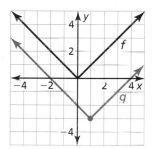

ERROR ANALYSIS In Exercises 33 and 34, identify and correct the error in writing the function g whose graph represents the indicated transformations of the graph of f.

33.

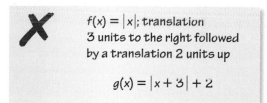

$f(x) = |x|$; translation 3 units to the right followed by a translation 2 units up

$g(x) = |x + 3| + 2$

34.

$f(x) = x$; translation 6 units down followed by a vertical stretch by a factor of 5

$g(x) = 5x - 6$

35. MAKING AN ARGUMENT Your friend claims that when writing a function whose graph represents a combination of transformations, the order is not important. Is your friend correct? Justify your answer.

36. MODELING WITH MATHEMATICS During a recent period of time, bookstore sales have been declining. The sales (in billions of dollars) can be modeled by the function $f(t) = -\frac{7}{5}t + 17.2$, where t is the number of years since 2006. Suppose sales decreased at twice the rate. How can you transform the graph of f to model the sales? Explain how the sales in 2010 are affected by this change. *(See Example 5.)*

MATHEMATICAL CONNECTIONS For Exercises 37–40, describe the transformation of the graph of f to the graph of g. Then find the area of the shaded triangle.

37. $f(x) = |x - 3|$

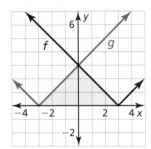

38. $f(x) = -|x| - 2$

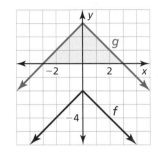

39. $f(x) = -x + 4$

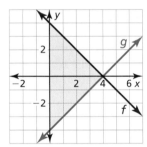

40. $f(x) = x - 5$

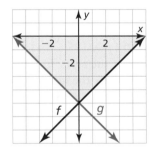

41. ABSTRACT REASONING The functions $f(x) = mx + b$ and $g(x) = mx + c$ represent two parallel lines.

    a. Write an expression for the vertical translation of the graph of f to the graph of g.

    b. Use the definition of slope to write an expression for the horizontal translation of the graph of f to the graph of g.

42. HOW DO YOU SEE IT? Consider the graph of $f(x) = mx + b$. Describe the effect each transformation has on the slope of the line and the intercepts of the graph.

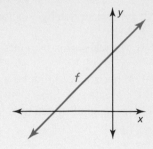

    a. Reflect the graph of f in the y-axis.

    b. Shrink the graph of f vertically by a factor of $\frac{1}{3}$.

    c. Stretch the graph of f horizontally by a factor of 2.

43. REASONING The graph of $g(x) = -4|x| + 2$ is a reflection in the x-axis, vertical stretch by a factor of 4, and a translation 2 units down of the graph of its parent function. Choose the correct order for the transformations of the graph of the parent function to obtain the graph of g. Explain your reasoning.

44. THOUGHT PROVOKING You are planning a cross-country bicycle trip of 4320 miles. Your distance d (in miles) from the halfway point can be modeled by $d = 72|x - 30|$, where x is the time (in days) and $x = 0$ represents June 1. Your plans are altered so that the model is now a right shift of the original model. Give an example of how this can happen. Sketch both the original model and the shifted model.

45. CRITICAL THINKING Use the correct value 0, -2, or 1 with a, b, and c so the graph of $g(x) = a|x - b| + c$ is a reflection in the x-axis followed by a translation one unit to the left and one unit up of the graph of $f(x) = 2|x - 2| + 1$. Explain your reasoning.

Maintaining Mathematical Proficiency
Reviewing what you learned in previous grades and lessons

Evaluate the function for the given value of x. *(Skills Review Handbook)*

46. $f(x) = x + 4; x = 3$

47. $f(x) = 4x - 1; x = -1$

48. $f(x) = -x + 3; x = 5$

49. $f(x) = -2x - 2; x = -1$

Create a scatter plot of the data. *(Skills Review Handbook)*

50.

x	8	10	11	12	15
f(x)	4	9	10	12	12

51.

x	2	5	6	10	13
f(x)	22	13	15	12	6

Essential Question
How can you use a linear function to model and analyze a real-life situation?

EXPLORATION 1 Modeling with a Linear Function

Work with a partner. A company purchases a copier for $12,000. The spreadsheet shows how the copier depreciates over an 8-year period.

a. Write a linear function to represent the value V of the copier as a function of the number t of years.

b. Sketch a graph of the function. Explain why this type of depreciation is called *straight line depreciation*.

MODELING WITH MATHEMATICS

To be proficient in math, you need to routinely interpret your results in the context of the situation.

c. Interpret the slope of the graph in the context of the problem.

	A	B
1	Year, *t*	Value, *V*
2	0	$12,000
3	1	$10,750
4	2	$9,500
5	3	$8,250
6	4	$7,000
7	5	$5,750
8	6	$4,500
9	7	$3,250
10	8	$2,000

EXPLORATION 2 Modeling with Linear Functions

Work with a partner. Match each description of the situation with its corresponding graph. Explain your reasoning.

a. A person gives $20 per week to a friend to repay a $200 loan.

b. An employee receives $12.50 per hour plus $2 for each unit produced per hour.

c. A sales representative receives $30 per day for food plus $0.565 for each mile driven.

d. A computer that was purchased for $750 depreciates $100 per year.

A.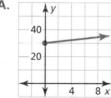

B.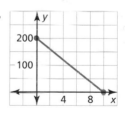

C.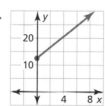

D.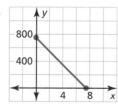

Communicate Your Answer

3. How can you use a linear function to model and analyze a real-life situation?

4. Use the Internet or some other reference to find a real-life example of straight line depreciation.

   a. Use a spreadsheet to show the depreciation.

   b. Write a function that models the depreciation.

   c. Sketch a graph of the function.

Core Vocabulary

line of fit, *p. 58*
line of best fit, *p. 59*
correlation coefficient, *p. 59*

Previous
slope
slope-intercept form
point-slope form
scatter plot

What You Will Learn

▶ Write equations of linear functions using points and slopes.
▶ Find lines of fit and lines of best fit.

Writing Linear Equations

Core Concept

Writing an Equation of a Line

Given slope m and y-intercept b   Use slope-intercept form:
$$y = mx + b$$

Given slope m and a point (x_1, y_1)   Use point-slope form:
$$y - y_1 = m(x - x_1)$$

Given points (x_1, y_1) and (x_2, y_2)   First use the slope formula to find m. Then use point-slope form with either given point.

EXAMPLE 1   **Writing a Linear Equation from a Graph**

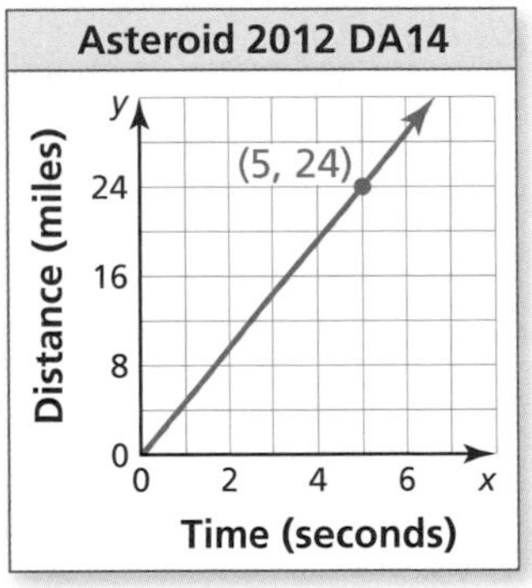

Asteroid 2012 DA14

(graph: Distance (miles) vs. Time (seconds), point (5, 24))

The graph shows the distance Asteroid 2012 DA14 travels in x seconds. Write an equation of the line and interpret the slope. The asteroid came within 17,200 miles of Earth in February, 2013. About how long does it take the asteroid to travel that distance?

SOLUTION

From the graph, you can see the slope is $m = \frac{24}{5} = 4.8$ and the y-intercept is $b = 0$. Use slope-intercept form to write an equation of the line.

$y = mx + b$ Slope-intercept form

$\quad = 4.8x + 0$ Substitute 4.8 for m and 0 for b.

The equation is $y = 4.8x$. The slope indicates that the asteroid travels 4.8 miles per second. Use the equation to find how long it takes the asteroid to travel 17,200 miles.

$17,200 = 4.8x$ Substitute 17,200 for y.

$3583 \approx x$ Divide each side by 4.8.

▶ Because there are 3600 seconds in 1 hour, it takes the asteroid about 1 hour to travel 17,200 miles.

REMEMBER

An equation of the form $y = mx$ indicates that x and y are in a proportional relationship.

Monitoring Progress 🔊 Help in English and Spanish at *BigIdeasMath.com*

1. The graph shows the remaining balance y on a car loan after making x monthly payments. Write an equation of the line and interpret the slope and y-intercept. What is the remaining balance after 36 payments?

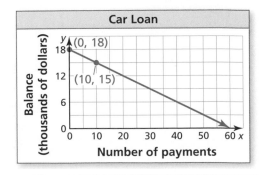

Car Loan

(graph: Balance (thousands of dollars) vs. Number of payments, points (0, 18) and (10, 15))

EXAMPLE 2   Modeling with Mathematics

Lakeside Inn	
Number of students, x	Total cost, y
100	$1500
125	$1800
150	$2100
175	$2400
200	$2700

Two prom venues charge a rental fee plus a fee per student. The table shows the total costs for different numbers of students at Lakeside Inn. The total cost y (in dollars) for x students at Sunview Resort is represented by the equation

$$y = 10x + 600.$$

Which venue charges less per student? How many students must attend for the total costs to be the same?

SOLUTION

1. **Understand the Problem** You are given an equation that represents the total cost at one venue and a table of values showing total costs at another venue. You need to compare the costs.

2. **Make a Plan** Write an equation that models the total cost at Lakeside Inn. Then compare the slopes to determine which venue charges less per student. Finally, equate the cost expressions and solve to determine the number of students for which the total costs are equal.

3. **Solve the Problem** First find the slope using any two points from the table. Use $(x_1, y_1) = (100, 1500)$ and $(x_2, y_2) = (125, 1800)$.

$$m = \frac{y_2 - y_1}{x_2 - x_1} = \frac{1800 - 1500}{125 - 100} = \frac{300}{25} = 12$$

Write an equation that represents the total cost at Lakeside Inn using the slope of 12 and a point from the table. Use $(x_1, y_1) = (100, 1500)$.

$y - y_1 = m(x - x_1)$	Point-slope form
$y - 1500 = 12(x - 100)$	Substitute for m, x_1, and y_1.
$y - 1500 = 12x - 1200$	Distributive Property
$y = 12x + 300$	Add 1500 to each side.

Equate the cost expressions and solve.

$10x + 600 = 12x + 300$	Set cost expressions equal.
$300 = 2x$	Combine like terms.
$150 = x$	Divide each side by 2.

▶ Comparing the slopes of the equations, Sunview Resort charges $10 per student, which is less than the $12 per student that Lakeside Inn charges. The total costs are the same for 150 students.

4. **Look Back** Notice that the table shows the total cost for 150 students at Lakeside Inn is $2100. To check that your solution is correct, verify that the total cost at Sunview Resort is also $2100 for 150 students.

$y = 10(150) + 600$	Substitute 150 for x.
$= 2100$ ✓	Simplify.

Check

Another way to check your solution is to graph each equation and find the point of intersection. The x-value of the point of intersection is 150.

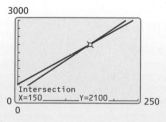

Monitoring Progress Help in English and Spanish at *BigIdeasMath.com*

2. **WHAT IF?** Maple Ridge charges a rental fee plus a $10 fee per student. The total cost is $1900 for 140 students. Describe the number of students that must attend for the total cost at Maple Ridge to be less than the total costs at the other two venues. Use a graph to justify your answer.

Finding Lines of Fit and Lines of Best Fit

Data do not always show an *exact* linear relationship. When the data in a scatter plot show an approximately linear relationship, you can model the data with a **line of fit**.

 **Core Concept**

Finding a Line of Fit

Step 1 Create a scatter plot of the data.

Step 2 Sketch the line that most closely appears to follow the trend given by the data points. There should be about as many points above the line as below it.

Step 3 Choose two points on the line and estimate the coordinates of each point. These points do not have to be original data points.

Step 4 Write an equation of the line that passes through the two points from Step 3. This equation is a model for the data.

EXAMPLE 3   Finding a Line of Fit

The table shows the femur lengths (in centimeters) and heights (in centimeters) of several people. Do the data show a linear relationship? If so, write an equation of a line of fit and use it to estimate the height of a person whose femur is 35 centimeters long.

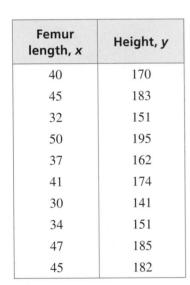

Femur length, x	Height, y
40	170
45	183
32	151
50	195
37	162
41	174
30	141
34	151
47	185
45	182

SOLUTION

Step 1 Create a scatter plot of the data. The data show a linear relationship.

Step 2 Sketch the line that most closely appears to fit the data. One possibility is shown.

Step 3 Choose two points on the line. For the line shown, you might choose (40, 170) and (50, 195).

Step 4 Write an equation of the line.

First, find the slope.

$$m = \frac{y_2 - y_1}{x_2 - x_1} = \frac{195 - 170}{50 - 40} = \frac{25}{10} = 2.5$$

Use point-slope form to write an equation. Use $(x_1, y_1) = (40, 170)$.

$y - y_1 = m(x - x_1)$	Point-slope form
$y - 170 = 2.5(x - 40)$	Substitute for m, x_1, and y_1.
$y - 170 = 2.5x - 100$	Distributive Property
$y = 2.5x + 70$	Add 170 to each side.

Use the equation to estimate the height of the person.

$y = 2.5(35) + 70$	Substitute 35 for x.
$= 157.5$	Simplify.

▶ The approximate height of a person with a 35-centimeter femur is 157.5 centimeters.

The **line of best fit** is the line that lies as close as possible to all of the data points. Many technology tools have a *linear regression* feature that you can use to find the line of best fit for a set of data.

The **correlation coefficient**, denoted by r, is a number from -1 to 1 that measures how well a line fits a set of data pairs (x, y). When r is near 1, the points lie close to a line with a positive slope. When r is near -1, the points lie close to a line with a negative slope. When r is near 0, the points do not lie close to any line.

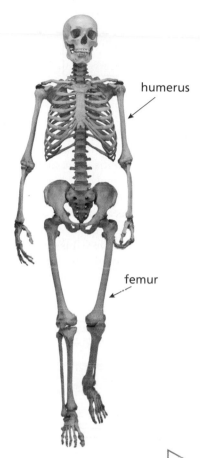

humerus

femur

ATTENDING TO PRECISION

Be sure to analyze the data values to help you select an appropriate viewing window for your graph.

EXAMPLE 4   Using a Graphing Calculator

Use the *linear regression* feature on a graphing calculator to find an equation of the line of best fit for the data in Example 3. Estimate the height of a person whose femur is 35 centimeters long. Compare this height to your estimate in Example 3.

SOLUTION

Step 1 Enter the data into two lists.

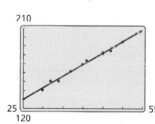

Step 2 Use the *linear regression* feature. The line of best fit is $y = 2.6x + 65$.

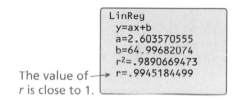

The value of r is close to 1.

Step 3 Graph the regression equation with the scatter plot.

Step 4 Use the *trace* feature to find the value of y when $x = 35$.

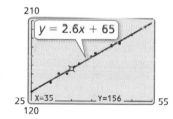

▶ The approximate height of a person with a 35-centimeter femur is 156 centimeters. This is less than the estimate found in Example 3.

Monitoring Progress Help in English and Spanish at *BigIdeasMath.com*

3. The table shows the humerus lengths (in centimeters) and heights (in centimeters) of several females.

Humerus length, x	33	25	22	30	28	32	26	27
Height, y	166	142	130	154	152	159	141	145

a. Do the data show a linear relationship? If so, write an equation of a line of fit and use it to estimate the height of a female whose humerus is 40 centimeters long.

b. Use the *linear regression* feature on a graphing calculator to find an equation of the line of best fit for the data. Estimate the height of a female whose humerus is 40 centimeters long. Compare this height to your estimate in part (a).

Vocabulary and Core Concept Check

1. **COMPLETE THE SENTENCE** The linear equation $y = \frac{1}{2}x + 3$ is written in _____ form.

2. **VOCABULARY** A line of best fit has a correlation coefficient of -0.98. What can you conclude about the slope of the line?

Monitoring Progress and Modeling with Mathematics

In Exercises 3–8, use the graph to write an equation of the line and interpret the slope. *(See Example 1.)*

3.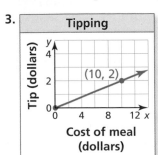

4.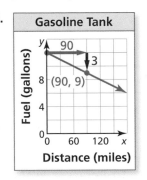

5.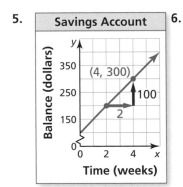

6.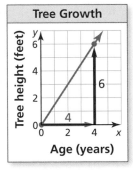

7.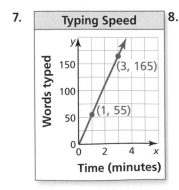

8.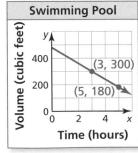

9. **MODELING WITH MATHEMATICS** Two newspapers charge a fee for placing an advertisement in their paper plus a fee based on the number of lines in the advertisement. The table shows the total costs for different length advertisements at the Daily Times. The total cost y (in dollars) for an advertisement that is x lines long at the Greenville Journal is represented by the equation $y = 2x + 20$. Which newspaper charges less per line? How many lines must be in an advertisement for the total costs to be the same? *(See Example 2.)*

Daily Times	
Number of lines, x	Total cost, y
4	27
5	30
6	33
7	36
8	39

10. **PROBLEM SOLVING** While on vacation in Canada, you notice that temperatures are reported in degrees Celsius. You know there is a linear relationship between Fahrenheit and Celsius, but you forget the formula. From science class, you remember the freezing point of water is 0°C or 32°F, and its boiling point is 100°C or 212°F.

   a. Write an equation that represents degrees Fahrenheit in terms of degrees Celsius.

   b. The temperature outside is 22°C. What is this temperature in degrees Fahrenheit?

   c. Rewrite your equation in part (a) to represent degrees Celsius in terms of degrees Fahrenheit.

   d. The temperature of the hotel pool water is 83°F. What is this temperature in degrees Celsius?

ERROR ANALYSIS In Exercises 11 and 12, describe and correct the error in interpreting the slope in the context of the situation.

11.

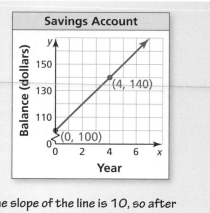

The slope of the line is 10, so after 7 years, the balance is $70.

12.

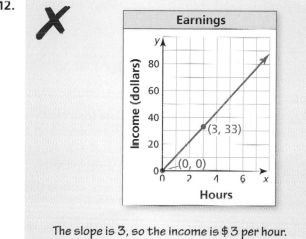

The slope is 3, so the income is $3 per hour.

In Exercises 13–16, determine whether the data show a linear relationship. If so, write an equation of a line of fit. Estimate y when x = 15 and explain its meaning in the context of the situation. *(See Example 3.)*

13.

Minutes walking, x	1	6	11	13	16
Calories burned, y	6	27	50	56	70

14.

Months, x	9	13	18	22	23
Hair length (in.), y	3	5	7	10	11

15.

Hours, x	3	7	9	17	20
Battery life (%), y	86	61	50	26	0

16.

Shoe size, x	6	8	8.5	10	13
Heart rate (bpm), y	112	94	100	132	87

17. **MODELING WITH MATHEMATICS** The data pairs (x, y) represent the average annual tuition y (in dollars) for public colleges in the United States x years after 2005. Use the *linear regression* feature on a graphing calculator to find an equation of the line of best fit. Estimate the average annual tuition in 2020. Interpret the slope and y-intercept in this situation. *(See Example 4.)*

(0, 11,386), (1, 11,731), (2, 11,848)

(3, 12,375), (4, 12,804), (5, 13,297)

18. **MODELING WITH MATHEMATICS** The table shows the numbers of tickets sold for a concert when different prices are charged. Write an equation of a line of fit for the data. Does it seem reasonable to use your model to predict the number of tickets sold when the ticket price is $85? Explain.

Ticket price (dollars), x	17	20	22	26
Tickets sold, y	450	423	400	395

USING TOOLS In Exercises 19–24, use the *linear regression* feature on a graphing calculator to find an equation of the line of best fit for the data. Find and interpret the correlation coefficient.

19.

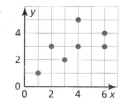

20.

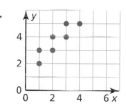

21.

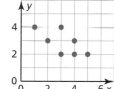

22.

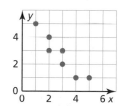

23.

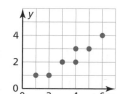

24.

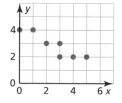

25. **OPEN-ENDED** Give two real-life quantities that have (a) a positive correlation, (b) a negative correlation, and (c) approximately no correlation. Explain.

26. HOW DO YOU SEE IT? You secure an interest-free loan to purchase a boat. You agree to make equal monthly payments for the next two years. The graph shows the amount of money you still owe.

Boat Loan

Loan balance (hundreds of dollars) vs *Time (months)*

a. What is the slope of the line? What does the slope represent?

b. What is the domain and range of the function? What does each represent?

c. How much do you still owe after making payments for 12 months?

27. MAKING AN ARGUMENT A set of data pairs has a correlation coefficient $r = 0.3$. Your friend says that because the correlation coefficient is positive, it is logical to use the line of best fit to make predictions. Is your friend correct? Explain your reasoning.

28. THOUGHT PROVOKING Points A and B lie on the line $y = -x + 4$. Choose coordinates for points A, B, and C where point C is the same distance from point A as it is from point B. Write equations for the lines connecting points A and C and points B and C.

29. ABSTRACT REASONING If x and y have a positive correlation, and y and z have a negative correlation, then what can you conclude about the correlation between x and z? Explain.

30. MATHEMATICAL CONNECTIONS Which equation has a graph that is a line passing through the point $(8, -5)$ and is perpendicular to the graph of $y = -4x + 1$?

Ⓐ $y = \frac{1}{4}x - 5$ Ⓑ $y = -4x + 27$

Ⓒ $y = -\frac{1}{4}x - 7$ Ⓓ $y = \frac{1}{4}x - 7$

31. PROBLEM SOLVING You are participating in an orienteering competition. The diagram shows the position of a river that cuts through the woods. You are currently 2 miles east and 1 mile north of your starting point, the origin. What is the shortest distance you must travel to reach the river?

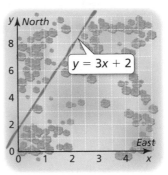

$y = 3x + 2$

32. ANALYZING RELATIONSHIPS Data from North American countries show a positive correlation between the number of personal computers per capita and the average life expectancy in the country.

a. Does a positive correlation make sense in this situation? Explain.

b. Is it reasonable to conclude that giving residents of a country personal computers will lengthen their lives? Explain.

Maintaining Mathematical Proficiency Reviewing what you learned in previous grades and lessons

Solve the system of linear equations in two variables by elimination or substitution.
(Skills Review Handbook)

33. $3x + y = 7$
$-2x - y = 9$

34. $4x + 3y = 2$
$2x - 3y = 1$

35. $2x + 2y = 3$
$x = 4y - 1$

36. $y = 1 + x$
$2x + y = -2$

37. $\frac{1}{2}x + 4y = 4$
$2x - y = 1$

38. $y = x - 4$
$4x + y = 26$

2.4 Solving Linear Systems

Essential Question
How can you determine the number of solutions of a linear system?

A linear system is *consistent* when it has at least one solution. A linear system is *inconsistent* when it has no solution.

EXPLORATION 1 **Recognizing Graphs of Linear Systems**

Work with a partner. Match each linear system with its corresponding graph. Explain your reasoning. Then classify the system as *consistent* or *inconsistent*.

a. $2x - 3y = 3$
$-4x + 6y = 6$

b. $2x - 3y = 3$
$x + 2y = 5$

c. $2x - 3y = 3$
$-4x + 6y = -6$

A. 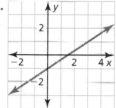 **B.** 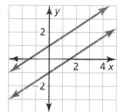 **C.**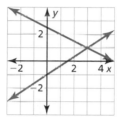

EXPLORATION 2 **Solving Systems of Linear Equations**

Work with a partner. Solve each linear system by substitution or elimination. Then use the graph of the system below to check your solution.

a. $2x + y = 5$
$x - y = 1$

b. $x + 3y = 1$
$-x + 2y = 4$

c. $x + y = 0$
$3x + 2y = 1$

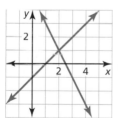 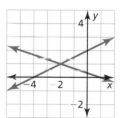 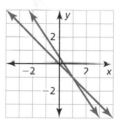

FINDING AN ENTRY POINT

To be proficient in math, you need to look for entry points to the solution of a problem.

Communicate Your Answer

3. How can you determine the number of solutions of a linear system?

4. Suppose you were given a system of *three* linear equations in *three* variables. Explain how you would approach solving such a system.

5. Apply your strategy in Question 4 to solve the linear system.

$$x + y + z = 1 \qquad \text{Equation 1}$$
$$x - y - z = 3 \qquad \text{Equation 2}$$
$$-x - y + z = -1 \qquad \text{Equation 3}$$

What You Will Learn

▶ Visualize solutions of systems of linear equations in three variables.

▶ Solve systems of linear equations in three variables algebraically.

▶ Solve real-life problems.

Visualizing Solutions of Systems

A **linear equation in three variables** x, y, and z is an equation of the form $ax + by + cz = d$, where a, b, and c are not all zero.

The following is an example of a **system of three linear equations** in three variables.

$$3x + 4y - 8z = -3 \qquad \text{Equation 1}$$

$$x + y + 5z = -12 \qquad \text{Equation 2}$$

$$4x - 2y + z = 10 \qquad \text{Equation 3}$$

A **solution** of such a system is an **ordered triple** (x, y, z) whose coordinates make each equation true.

The graph of a linear equation in three variables is a plane in three-dimensional space. The graphs of three such equations that form a system are three planes whose intersection determines the number of solutions of the system, as shown in the diagrams below.

Exactly One Solution
The planes intersect in a single point, which is the solution of the system.

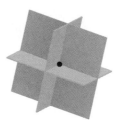

Infinitely Many Solutions
The planes intersect in a line. Every point on the line is a solution of the system.

The planes could also be the same plane. Every point in the plane is a solution of the system.

No Solution
There are no points in common with all three planes.

 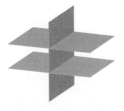 

Solving Systems of Equations Algebraically

The algebraic methods you used to solve systems of linear equations in two variables can be extended to solve a system of linear equations in three variables.

⑤ Core Concept

Solving a Three-Variable System

Step 1 Rewrite the linear system in three variables as a linear system in two variables by using the substitution or elimination method.

Step 2 Solve the new linear system for both of its variables.

Step 3 Substitute the values found in Step 2 into one of the original equations and solve for the remaining variable.

When you obtain a false equation, such as $0 = 1$, in any of the steps, the system has no solution.

When you do not obtain a false equation, but obtain an identity such as $0 = 0$, the system has infinitely many solutions.

LOOKING FOR STRUCTURE

The coefficient of -1 in Equation 3 makes y a convenient variable to eliminate.

EXAMPLE 1 Solving a Three-Variable System (One Solution)

Solve the system.

$$4x + 2y + 3z = 12 \qquad \text{Equation 1}$$
$$2x - 3y + 5z = -7 \qquad \text{Equation 2}$$
$$6x - y + 4z = -3 \qquad \text{Equation 3}$$

SOLUTION

Step 1 Rewrite the system as a linear system in *two* variables.

$$\begin{array}{l} 4x + 2y + 3z = 12 \\ \underline{12x - 2y + 8z = -6} \\ 16x \quad\quad + 11z = 6 \end{array}$$

Add 2 times Equation 3 to Equation 1 (to eliminate y).

New Equation 1

$$\begin{array}{l} 2x - 3y + 5z = -7 \\ \underline{18x + 3y - 12z = 9} \\ -16x \quad\quad - 7z = 2 \end{array}$$

Add -3 times Equation 3 to Equation 2 (to eliminate y).

New Equation 2

ANOTHER WAY

In Step 1, you could also eliminate x to get two equations in y and z, or you could eliminate z to get two equations in x and y.

Step 2 Solve the new linear system for both of its variables.

$$\begin{array}{l} 16x + 11z = 6 \\ \underline{-16x - 7z = 2} \\ \quad\quad\;\; 4z = 8 \end{array}$$

Add new Equation 1 and new Equation 2.

$$z = 2 \qquad \text{Solve for } z.$$
$$x = -1 \qquad \text{Substitute into new Equation 1 or 2 to find } x.$$

Step 3 Substitute $x = -1$ and $z = 2$ into an original equation and solve for y.

$$6x - y + 4z = -3 \qquad \text{Write original Equation 3.}$$
$$6(-1) - y + 4(2) = -3 \qquad \text{Substitute } -1 \text{ for } x \text{ and } 2 \text{ for } z.$$
$$y = 5 \qquad \text{Solve for } y.$$

▶ The solution is $x = -1$, $y = 5$, and $z = 2$, or the ordered triple $(-1, 5, 2)$. Check this solution in each of the original equations.

EXAMPLE 2 **Solving a Three-Variable System (No Solution)**

Solve the system.

$x + y + z = 2$	Equation 1
$5x + 5y + 5z = 3$	Equation 2
$4x + y - 3z = -6$	Equation 3

SOLUTION

Step 1 Rewrite the system as a linear system in *two* variables.

$$\begin{array}{r} -5x - 5y - 5z = -10 \\ 5x + 5y + 5z = 3 \\ \hline 0 = -7 \end{array}$$

Add -5 times Equation 1 to Equation 2.

▶ Because you obtain a false equation, the original system has no solution.

ANOTHER WAY

Subtracting Equation 2 from Equation 1 gives $z = 0$. After substituting 0 for z in each equation, you can see that each is equivalent to $y = x + 3$.

EXAMPLE 3 **Solving a Three-Variable System (Many Solutions)**

Solve the system.

$x - y + z = -3$	Equation 1
$x - y - z = -3$	Equation 2
$5x - 5y + z = -15$	Equation 3

SOLUTION

Step 1 Rewrite the system as a linear system in *two* variables.

$$\begin{array}{r} x - y + z = -3 \\ x - y - z = -3 \\ \hline 2x - 2y = -6 \end{array}$$

Add Equation 1 to Equation 2 (to eliminate z).

New Equation 2

$$\begin{array}{r} x - y - z = -3 \\ 5x - 5y + z = -15 \\ \hline 6x - 6y = -18 \end{array}$$

Add Equation 2 to Equation 3 (to eliminate z).

New Equation 3

Step 2 Solve the new linear system for both of its variables.

$$\begin{array}{r} -6x + 6y = 18 \\ 6x - 6y = -18 \\ \hline 0 = 0 \end{array}$$

Add -3 times new Equation 2 to new Equation 3.

Because you obtain the identity $0 = 0$, the system has infinitely many solutions.

Step 3 Describe the solutions of the system using an ordered triple. One way to do this is to solve new Equation 2 for y to obtain $y = x + 3$. Then substitute $x + 3$ for y in original Equation 1 to obtain $z = 0$.

▶ So, any ordered triple of the form $(x, x + 3, 0)$ is a solution of the system.

Monitoring Progress Help in English and Spanish at *BigIdeasMath.com*

Solve the system. Check your solution, if possible.

1. $x - 2y + z = -11$
$3x + 2y - z = 7$
$-x + 2y + 4z = -9$

2. $x + y - z = -1$
$4x + 4y - 4z = -2$
$3x + 2y + z = 0$

3. $x + y + z = 8$
$x - y + z = 8$
$2x + y + 2z = 16$

4. In Example 3, describe the solutions of the system using an ordered triple in terms of y.

Solving Real-Life Problems

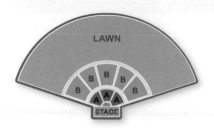
LAWN

EXAMPLE 4 Solving a Multi-Step Problem

An amphitheater charges $75 for each seat in Section A, $55 for each seat in Section B, and $30 for each lawn seat. There are three times as many seats in Section B as in Section A. The revenue from selling all 23,000 seats is $870,000. How many seats are in each section of the amphitheater?

SOLUTION

Step 1 Write a verbal model for the situation.

$$\boxed{\text{Number of seats in B, } y} = 3 \cdot \boxed{\text{Number of seats in A, } x}$$

$$\boxed{\text{Number of seats in A, } x} + \boxed{\text{Number of seats in B, } y} + \boxed{\text{Number of lawn seats, } z} = \boxed{\text{Total number of seats}}$$

$$75 \cdot \boxed{\text{Number of scats in A, } x} + 55 \cdot \boxed{\text{Number of seats in B, } y} + 30 \cdot \boxed{\text{Number of lawn seats, } z} = \boxed{\text{Total revenue}}$$

Step 2 Write a system of equations.

$y = 3x$	Equation 1
$x + y + z = 23{,}000$	Equation 2
$75x + 55y + 30z = 870{,}000$	Equation 3

Step 3 Rewrite the system in Step 2 as a linear system in *two* variables by substituting $3x$ for y in Equations 2 and 3.

$x + y + z = 23{,}000$	Write Equation 2.
$x + 3x + z = 23{,}000$	Substitute $3x$ for y.
$4x + z = 23{,}000$	New Equation 2
$75x + 55y + 30z = 870{,}000$	Write Equation 3.
$75x + 55(3x) + 30z = 870{,}000$	Substitute $3x$ for y.
$240x + 30z = 870{,}000$	New Equation 3

Step 4 Solve the new linear system for both of its variables.

$-120x - 30z = -690{,}000$	Add -30 times new Equation 2
$\underline{240x + 30z = 870{,}000}$	to new Equation 3.
$120x \qquad = 180{,}000$	
$x = 1500$	Solve for x.
$y = 4500$	Substitute into Equation 1 to find y.
$z = 17{,}000$	Substitute into Equation 2 to find z.

STUDY TIP

When substituting to find values of other variables, choose original or new equations that are easiest to use.

▶ The solution is $x = 1500$, $y = 4500$, and $z = 17{,}000$, or $(1500, 4500, 17{,}000)$. So, there are 1500 seats in Section A, 4500 seats in Section B, and 17,000 lawn seats.

Monitoring Progress Help in English and Spanish at *BigIdeasMath.com*

5. **WHAT IF?** On the first day, 10,000 tickets sold, generating $356,000 in revenue. The number of seats sold in Sections A and B are the same. How many lawn seats are still available?

Vocabulary and Core Concept Check

1. **VOCABULARY** The solution of a system of three linear equations is expressed as a(n) _____.

2. **WRITING** Explain how you know when a linear system in three variables has infinitely many solutions.

Monitoring Progress and Modeling with Mathematics

In Exercises 3–8, solve the system using the elimination method. *(See Example 1.)*

3. $x + y - 2z = 5$
   $-x + 2y + z = 2$
   $2x + 3y - z = 9$

4. $x + 4y - 6z = -1$
   $2x - y + 2z = -7$
   $-x + 2y - 4z = 5$

5. $2x + y - z = 9$
   $-x + 6y + 2z = -17$
   $5x + 7y + z = 4$

6. $3x + 2y - z = 8$
   $-3x + 4y + 5z = -14$
   $x - 3y + 4z = -14$

7. $2x + 2y + 5z = -1$
   $2x - y + z = 2$
   $2x + 4y - 3z = 14$

8. $3x + 2y - 3z = -2$
   $7x - 2y + 5z = -14$
   $2x + 4y + z = 6$

ERROR ANALYSIS In Exercises 9 and 10, describe and correct the error in the first step of solving the system of linear equations.

$$4x - y + 2z = -18$$
$$-x + 2y + z = 11$$
$$3x + 3y - 4z = 44$$

9. ✗
   $4x - y + 2z = -18$
   $\underline{-4x + 2y + z = 11}$
   $y + 3z = -7$

10. ✗
    $12x - 3y + 6z = -18$
    $\underline{3x + 3y - 4z = 44}$
    $15x + 2z = 26$

In Exercises 11–16, solve the system using the elimination method. *(See Examples 2 and 3.)*

11. $3x - y + 2z = 4$
    $6x - 2y + 4z = -8$
    $2x - y + 3z = 10$

12. $5x + y - z = 6$
    $x + y + z = 2$
    $12x + 4y = 10$

13. $x + 3y - z = 2$
    $x + y - z = 0$
    $3x + 2y - 3z = -1$

14. $x + 2y - z = 3$
    $-2x - y + z = -1$
    $6x - 3y - z = -7$

15. $x + 2y + 3z = 4$
    $-3x + 2y - z = 12$
    $-2x - 2y - 4z = -14$

16. $-2x - 3y + z = -6$
    $x + y - z = 5$
    $7x + 8y - 6z = 31$

17. **MODELING WITH MATHEMATICS** Three orders are placed at a pizza shop. Two small pizzas, a liter of soda, and a salad cost $14; one small pizza, a liter of soda, and three salads cost $15; and three small pizzas, a liter of soda, and two salads cost $22. How much does each item cost?

18. **MODELING WITH MATHEMATICS** Sam's Furniture Store places the following advertisement in the local newspaper. Write a system of equations for the three combinations of furniture. What is the price of each piece of furniture? Explain.

SALE SAM'S Furniture Store

$1300
Sofa and love seat

$1400
Sofa and two chairs

$1600
Sofa, love seat, and one chair

In Exercises 19–28, solve the system of linear equations using the substitution method. *(See Example 4.)*

19. $-2x + y + 6z = 1$
$3x + 2y + 5z = 16$
$7x + 3y - 4z = 11$

20. $x - 6y - 2z = -8$
$-x + 5y + 3z = 2$
$3x - 2y - 4z = 18$

21. $x + y + z = 4$
$5x + 5y + 5z = 12$
$x - 4y + z = 9$

22. $x + 2y = -1$
$-x + 3y + 2z = -4$
$-x + y - 4z = 10$

23. $2x - 3y + z = 10$
$y + 2z = 13$
$z = 5$

24. $x = 4$
$x + y = -6$
$4x - 3y + 2z = 26$

25. $x + y - z = 4$
$3x + 2y + 4z = 17$
$-x + 5y + z = 8$

26. $2x - y - z = 15$
$4x + 5y + 2z = 10$
$-x - 4y + 3z = -20$

27. $4x + y + 5z = 5$
$8x + 2y + 10z = 10$
$x - y - 2z = -2$

28. $x + 2y - z = 3$
$2x + 4y - 2z = 6$
$-x - 2y + z = -6$

29. PROBLEM SOLVING The number of left-handed people in the world is one-tenth the number of right-handed people. The percent of right-handed people is nine times the percent of left-handed people and ambidextrous people combined. What percent of people are ambidextrous?

30. MODELING WITH MATHEMATICS Use a system of linear equations to model the data in the following newspaper article. Solve the system to find how many athletes finished in each place.

Lawrence High prevailed in Saturday's track meet with the help of 20 individual-event placers earning a combined 68 points. A first-place finish earns 5 points, a second-place finish earns 3 points, and a third-place finish earns 1 point. Lawrence had a strong second-place showing, with as many second place finishers as first- and third-place finishers combined.

31. WRITING Explain when it might be more convenient to use the elimination method than the substitution method to solve a linear system. Give an example to support your claim.

32. REPEATED REASONING Using what you know about solving linear systems in two and three variables, plan a strategy for how you would solve a system that has *four* linear equations in *four* variables.

MATHEMATICAL CONNECTIONS In Exercises 33 and 34, write and use a linear system to answer the question.

33. The triangle has a perimeter of 65 feet. What are the lengths of sides ℓ, m, and n?

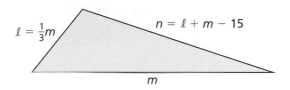

34. What are the measures of angles A, B, and C?

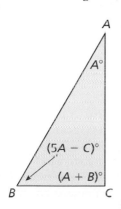

35. OPEN-ENDED Consider the system of linear equations below. Choose nonzero values for a, b, and c so the system satisfies the given condition. Explain your reasoning.

$$x + y + z = 2$$
$$ax + by + cz = 10$$
$$x - 2y + z = 4$$

a. The system has no solution.

b. The system has exactly one solution.

c. The system has infinitely many solutions.

36. MAKING AN ARGUMENT A linear system in three variables has no solution. Your friend concludes that it is not possible for two of the three equations to have any points in common. Is your friend correct? Explain your reasoning.

37. PROBLEM SOLVING A contractor is hired to build an apartment complex. Each 840-square-foot unit has a bedroom, kitchen, and bathroom. The bedroom will be the same size as the kitchen. The owner orders 980 square feet of tile to completely cover the floors of two kitchens and two bathrooms. Determine how many square feet of carpet is needed for each bedroom.

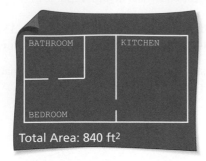

BATHROOM   KITCHEN

BEDROOM

Total Area: 840 ft²

38. THOUGHT PROVOKING Does the system of linear equations have more than one solution? Justify your answer.

$$4x + y + z = 0$$
$$2x + \tfrac{1}{2}y - 3z = 0$$
$$-x - \tfrac{1}{4}y - z = 0$$

39. PROBLEM SOLVING A florist must make 5 identical bridesmaid bouquets for a wedding. The budget is $160, and each bouquet must have 12 flowers. Roses cost $2.50 each, lilies cost $4 each, and irises cost $2 each. The florist wants twice as many roses as the other two types of flowers combined.

  a. Write a system of equations to represent this situation, assuming the florist plans to use the maximum budget.

  b. Solve the system to find how many of each type of flower should be in each bouquet.

  c. Suppose there is no limitation on the total cost of the bouquets. Does the problem still have exactly one solution? If so, find the solution. If not, give three possible solutions.

40. HOW DO YOU SEE IT? Determine whether the system of equations that represents the circles has *no solution*, *one solution*, or *infinitely many solutions*. Explain your reasoning.

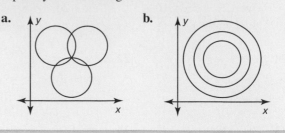

a.

b.

41. CRITICAL THINKING Find the values of a, b, and c so that the linear system shown has $(-1, 2, -3)$ as its only solution. Explain your reasoning.

$$x + 2y - 3z = a$$
$$-x - y + z = b$$
$$2x + 3y - 2z = c$$

42. ANALYZING RELATIONSHIPS Determine which arrangement(s) of the integers -5, 2, and 3 produce a solution of the linear system that consist of only integers. Justify your answer.

$$x - 3y + 6z = 21$$
$$\_\,x + \_\,y + \_\,z = -30$$
$$2x - 5y + 2z = -6$$

43. ABSTRACT REASONING Write a linear system to represent the first three pictures below. Use the system to determine how many tangerines are required to balance the apple in the fourth picture. *Note:* The first picture shows that one tangerine and one apple balance one grapefruit.

Maintaining Mathematical Proficiency
Reviewing what you learned in previous grades and lessons

Simplify. *(Skills Review Handbook)*

44. $(x - 2)^2$ **45.** $(3m + 1)^2$ **46.** $(2z - 5)^2$ **47.** $(4 - y)^2$

Write a function g described by the given transformation of $f(x) = |x| - 5$. *(Section 2.2)*

  48. translation 2 units to the left   **49.** reflection in the x-axis

  50. translation 4 units up   **51.** vertical stretch by a factor of 3

2.1–2.4   What Did You Learn?

Core Vocabulary

parent function, *p. 40*
transformation, *p. 41*
translation, *p. 41*
reflection, *p. 41*
vertical stretch, *p. 42*
vertical shrink, *p. 42*

line of fit, *p. 58*
line of best fit, *p. 59*
correlation coefficient, *p. 59*
linear equation in three variables,
 p. 64

system of three linear equations,
 p. 64
solution of a system of three linear
 equations, *p. 64*
ordered triple, *p. 64*

Core Concepts

Section 2.1

Parent Functions, *p. 40*

Describing Transformations, *p. 41*

Section 2.2

Horizontal Translations, *p. 48*
Vertical Translations, *p. 48*
Reflections in the *x*-Axis, *p. 49*

Reflections in the *y*-Axis, *p. 49*
Horizontal Stretches and Shrinks, *p. 50*
Vertical Stretches and Shrinks, *p. 50*

Section 2.3

Writing an Equation of a Line, *p. 56*

Finding a Line of Fit, *p. 58*

Section 2.4

Solving a Three-Variable System, *p. 65*

Mathematical Practices

1. Explain how you would round your answer in Exercise 10 on page 52 if the extra expense is $13,500.

2. Describe how you can write the equation of the line in Exercise 7 on page 60 using only one of the labeled points.

Using the Features of Your Textbook to Prepare for Quizzes and Tests

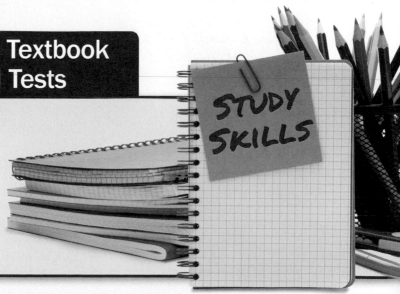

- Read and understand the core vocabulary and the contents of the Core Concept boxes.

- Review the Examples and the Monitoring Progress questions. Use the tutorials at *BigIdeasMath.com* for additional help.

- Review previously completed homework assignments.

Identify the function family to which g belongs. Compare the graph of the function to the graph of its parent function. *(Section 2.1)*

1.

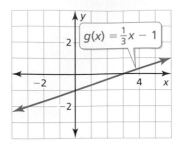

$g(x) = \frac{1}{3}x - 1$

2.

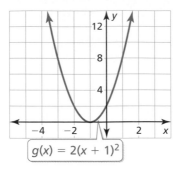

$g(x) = 2(x + 1)^2$

3.

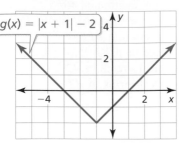

$g(x) = |x + 1| - 2$

Graph the function and its parent function. Then describe the transformation(s). *(Section 2.1)*

4. $f(x) = 3x$

5. $f(x) = -|x + 2| - 7$

6. $f(x) = \frac{1}{4}x^2 + 1$

Write a function g whose graph represents the indicated transformation(s) of the graph of f. *(Section 2.2)*

7. $f(x) = 2x + 1$; translation 3 units up

8. $f(x) = -3|x - 4|$; vertical shrink by a factor of $\frac{1}{2}$

9. $f(x) = |x|$; reflection in the *x*-axis and a vertical stretch by a factor of 4 followed by a translation 7 units down and 1 unit right

10. The total cost of an annual pass plus camping for *x* days in a National Park can be modeled by the function $f(x) = 20x + 80$. Senior citizens pay half of this price and receive an additional $30 discount. Describe how to transform the graph of *f* to model the total cost for a senior citizen. What is the total cost for a senior citizen to go camping for three days? *(Section 2.2)*

Write an equation of the line and interpret the slope and *y*-intercept. *(Section 2.3)*

11.

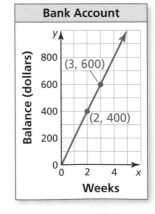

12.

13. A bakery sells doughnuts, muffins, and bagels. The bakery makes three times as many doughnuts as bagels. The bakery earns a total of $150 when all 130 baked items in stock are sold. How many of each item are in stock? Justify your answer. *(Section 2.4)*

Breakfast Specials

Doughnuts............ $1.00

Muffins $1.50

Bagels................... $1.20

Transformations of Quadratic Functions

Essential Question How do the constants a, h, and k affect the graph of the quadratic function $g(x) = a(x - h)^2 + k$?

The parent function of the quadratic family is $f(x) = x^2$. A transformation of the graph of the parent function is represented by the function $g(x) = a(x - h)^2 + k$, where $a \neq 0$.

EXPLORATION 1 Identifying Graphs of Quadratic Functions

Work with a partner. Match each quadratic function with its graph. Explain your reasoning. Then use a graphing calculator to verify that your answer is correct.

a. $g(x) = -(x - 2)^2$ **b.** $g(x) = (x - 2)^2 + 2$ **c.** $g(x) = -(x + 2)^2 - 2$

d. $g(x) = 0.5(x - 2)^2 - 2$ **e.** $g(x) = 2(x - 2)^2$ **f.** $g(x) = -(x + 2)^2 + 2$

A.
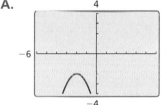

B.
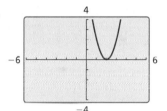

C.
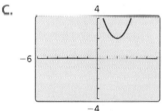

D.
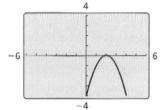

E.
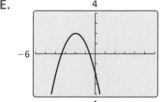

F.
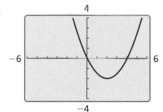

LOOKING FOR STRUCTURE

To be proficient in math, you need to look closely to discern a pattern or structure.

Communicate Your Answer

2. How do the constants a, h, and k affect the graph of the quadratic function $g(x) = a(x - h)^2 + k$?

3. Write the equation of the quadratic function whose graph is shown at the right. Explain your reasoning. Then use a graphing calculator to verify that your equation is correct.

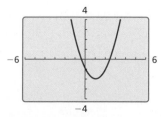

What You Will Learn

▶ Describe transformations of quadratic functions.

▶ Write transformations of quadratic functions.

Core Vocabulary

quadratic function, *p. 74*
parabola, *p. 74*
vertex of a parabola, *p. 76*
vertex form, *p. 76*

Previous
transformations

Describing Transformations of Quadratic Functions

A **quadratic function** is a function that can be written in the form $f(x) = a(x - h)^2 + k$, where $a \neq 0$. The U-shaped graph of a quadratic function is called a **parabola**.

In Section 2.1, you graphed quadratic functions using tables of values. You can also graph quadratic functions by applying transformations to the graph of the parent function $f(x) = x^2$.

🌀 Core Concept

Horizontal Translations

$f(x) = x^2$

$f(x - h) = (x - h)^2$

$y = (x - h)^2,$
$h < 0$

$y = x^2$

$y = (x - h)^2,$
$h > 0$

- shifts left when $h < 0$
- shifts right when $h > 0$

Vertical Translations

$f(x) = x^2$

$f(x) + k = x^2 + k$

$y = x^2 + k,$
$k > 0$

$y = x^2$

$y = x^2 + k,$
$k < 0$

- shifts down when $k < 0$
- shifts up when $k > 0$

EXAMPLE 1 **Translations of a Quadratic Function**

Describe the transformation of $f(x) = x^2$ represented by $g(x) = (x + 4)^2 - 1$. Then graph each function.

SOLUTION

Notice that the function is of the form $g(x) = (x - h)^2 + k$. Rewrite the function to identify h and k.

$$g(x) = (x - (-4))^2 + (-1)$$

$$\underset{h}{\uparrow}\underset{k}{\uparrow}$$

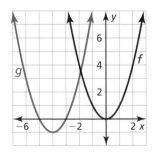

▶ Because $h = -4$ and $k = -1$, the graph of g is a translation 4 units left and 1 unit down of the graph of f.

Monitoring Progress Help in English and Spanish at *BigIdeasMath.com*

Describe the transformation of $f(x) = x^2$ represented by g. Then graph each function.

1. $g(x) = (x - 3)^2$ **2.** $g(x) = (x - 2)^2 - 2$ **3.** $g(x) = (x + 5)^2 + 1$

Core Concept

Reflections in the x-Axis	**Reflections in the y-Axis**
$f(x) = x^2$	$f(x) = x^2$
$-f(x) = -(x^2) = -x^2$	$f(-x) = (-x)^2 = x^2$
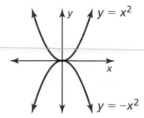	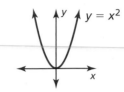
flips over the x-axis	$y = x^2$ is its own reflection in the y-axis.
Horizontal Stretches and Shrinks	**Vertical Stretches and Shrinks**
$f(x) = x^2$	$f(x) = x^2$
$f(ax) = (ax)^2$	$a \cdot f(x) = ax^2$
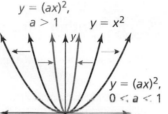	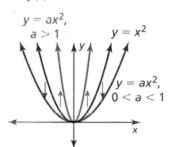
• horizontal stretch (away from y-axis) when $0 < a < 1$	• vertical stretch (away from x-axis) when $a > 1$
• horizontal shrink (toward y-axis) when $a > 1$	• vertical shrink (toward x-axis) when $0 < a < 1$

EXAMPLE 2   Transformations of Quadratic Functions

Describe the transformation of $f(x) = x^2$ represented by g. Then graph each function.

a. $g(x) = -\frac{1}{2}x^2$

b. $g(x) = (2x)^2 + 1$

LOOKING FOR STRUCTURE

In Example 2b, notice that $g(x) = 4x^2 + 1$. So, you can also describe the graph of g as a vertical stretch by a factor of 4 followed by a translation 1 unit up of the graph of f.

SOLUTION

a. Notice that the function is of the form $g(x) = -ax^2$, where $a = \frac{1}{2}$.

▶ So, the graph of g is a reflection in the x-axis and a vertical shrink by a factor of $\frac{1}{2}$ of the graph of f.

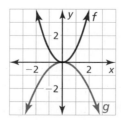

b. Notice that the function is of the form $g(x) = (ax)^2 + k$, where $a = 2$ and $k = 1$.

▶ So, the graph of g is a horizontal shrink by a factor of $\frac{1}{2}$ followed by a translation 1 unit up of the graph of f.

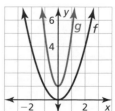

Describe the transformation of $f(x) = x^2$ represented by g. Then graph each function.

4. $g(x) = \left(\frac{1}{3}x\right)^2$ **5.** $g(x) = 3(x - 1)^2$ **6.** $g(x) = -(x + 3)^2 + 2$

Writing Transformations of Quadratic Functions

The lowest point on a parabola that opens up or the highest point on a parabola that opens down is the **vertex**. The **vertex form** of a quadratic function is $f(x) = a(x - h)^2 + k$, where $a \neq 0$ and the vertex is (h, k).

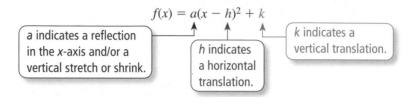

$$f(x) = a(x - h)^2 + k$$

| *a* indicates a reflection in the *x*-axis and/or a vertical stretch or shrink. | *h* indicates a horizontal translation. | *k* indicates a vertical translation. |

EXAMPLE 3 **Writing a Transformed Quadratic Function**

Let the graph of g be a vertical stretch by a factor of 2 and a reflection in the *x*-axis, followed by a translation 3 units down of the graph of $f(x) = x^2$. Write a rule for g and identify the vertex.

SOLUTION

Method 1 Identify how the transformations affect the constants in vertex form.

$$\left.\begin{array}{l}\text{reflection in } x\text{-axis}\\ \text{vertical stretch by 2}\end{array}\right\} a = -2$$

$$\text{translation 3 units down}\} \ k = -3$$

Write the transformed function.

$$g(x) = a(x - h)^2 + k \qquad \text{Vertex form of a quadratic function}$$
$$= -2(x - 0)^2 + (-3) \qquad \text{Substitute } -2 \text{ for } a, 0 \text{ for } h, \text{ and } -3 \text{ for } k.$$
$$= -2x^2 - 3 \qquad \text{Simplify.}$$

▶ The transformed function is $g(x) = -2x^2 - 3$. The vertex is $(0, -3)$.

Method 2 Begin with the parent function and apply the transformations one at a time in the stated order.

First write a function h that represents the reflection and vertical stretch of f.

$$h(x) = -2 \cdot f(x) \qquad \text{Multiply the output by } -2.$$
$$= -2x^2 \qquad \text{Substitute } x^2 \text{ for } f(x).$$

Then write a function g that represents the translation of h.

$$g(x) = h(x) - 3 \qquad \text{Subtract 3 from the output.}$$
$$= -2x^2 - 3 \qquad \text{Substitute } -2x^2 \text{ for } h(x).$$

▶ The transformed function is $g(x) = -2x^2 - 3$. The vertex is $(0, -3)$.

Check

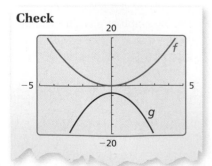

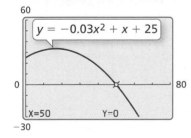

REMEMBER

To multiply two binomials, use the FOIL Method.

$$\text{(x + 1)(x + 2)} = x^2 + 2x + x + 2$$

First Inner
Outer Last

60

$$y = -0.03x^2 + x + 25$$

0 |_____| 80

X=50   Y=0

−30

EXAMPLE 4 **Writing a Transformed Quadratic Function**

Let the graph of g be a translation 3 units right and 2 units up, followed by a reflection in the y-axis of the graph of $f(x) = x^2 - 5x$. Write a rule for g.

SOLUTION

Step 1 First write a function h that represents the translation of f.

$h(x) = f(x - 3) + 2$	Subtract 3 from the input. Add 2 to the output.
$= (x - 3)^2 - 5(x - 3) + 2$	Replace x with $x - 3$ in $f(x)$.
$= x^2 - 11x + 26$	Simplify.

Step 2 Then write a function g that represents the reflection of h.

$g(x) = h(-x)$	Multiply the input by -1.
$= (-x)^2 - 11(-x) + 26$	Replace x with $-x$ in $h(x)$.
$= x^2 + 11x + 26$	Simplify.

EXAMPLE 5 **Modeling with Mathematics**

The height h (in feet) of water spraying from a fire hose can be modeled by $h(x) = -0.03x^2 + x + 25$, where x is the horizontal distance (in feet) from the fire truck. The crew raises the ladder so that the water hits the ground 10 feet farther from the fire truck. Write a function that models the new path of the water.

SOLUTION

1. **Understand the Problem** You are given a function that represents the path of water spraying from a fire hose. You are asked to write a function that represents the path of the water after the crew raises the ladder.

2. **Make a Plan** Analyze the graph of the function to determine the translation of the ladder that causes water to travel 10 feet farther. Then write the function.

3. **Solve the Problem** Use a graphing calculator to graph the original function.

   Because $h(50) = 0$, the water originally hits the ground 50 feet from the fire truck. The range of the function in this context does not include negative values. However, by observing that $h(60) = -23$, you can determine that a translation 23 units (feet) up causes the water to travel 10 feet farther from the fire truck.

$g(x) = h(x) + 23$	Add 23 to the output.
$= -0.03x^2 + x + 48$	Substitute for $h(x)$ and simplify.

   ▶ The new path of the water can be modeled by $g(x) = -0.03x^2 + x + 48$.

4. **Look Back** To check that your solution is correct, verify that $g(60) = 0$.

   $$g(60) = -0.03(60)^2 + 60 + 48 = -108 + 60 + 48 = 0 \checkmark$$

Monitoring Progress Help in English and Spanish at *BigIdeasMath.com*

7. Let the graph of g be a vertical shrink by a factor of $\frac{1}{2}$ followed by a translation 2 units up of the graph of $f(x) = x^2$. Write a rule for g and identify the vertex.

8. Let the graph of g be a translation 4 units left followed by a horizontal shrink by a factor of $\frac{1}{3}$ of the graph of $f(x) = x^2 + x$. Write a rule for g.

9. **WHAT IF?** In Example 5, the water hits the ground 10 feet closer to the fire truck after lowering the ladder. Write a function that models the new path of the water.

2.5 Exercises

Dynamic Solutions available at *BigIdeasMath.com*

Vocabulary and Core Concept Check

1. **COMPLETE THE SENTENCE** The graph of a quadratic function is called a(n) ________.

2. **VOCABULARY** Identify the vertex of the parabola given by $f(x) = (x + 2)^2 - 4$.

Monitoring Progress and Modeling with Mathematics

In Exercises 3–12, describe the transformation of $f(x) = x^2$ represented by g. Then graph each function. *(See Example 1.)*

3. $g(x) = x^2 - 3$
4. $g(x) = x^2 + 1$
5. $g(x) = (x + 2)^2$
6. $g(x) = (x - 4)^2$
7. $g(x) = (x - 1)^2$
8. $g(x) = (x + 3)^2$
9. $g(x) = (x + 6)^2 - 2$
10. $g(x) = (x - 9)^2 + 5$
11. $g(x) = (x - 7)^2 + 1$
12. $g(x) = (x + 10)^2 - 3$

ANALYZING RELATIONSHIPS **In Exercises 13–16, match the function with the correct transformation of the graph of f. Explain your reasoning.**

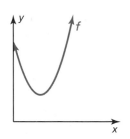

13. $y = f(x - 1)$
14. $y = f(x) + 1$
15. $y = f(x - 1) + 1$
16. $y = f(x + 1) - 1$

A.

B.

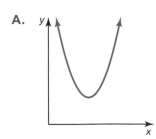

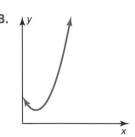

C.

D.

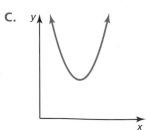

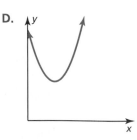

In Exercises 17–24, describe the transformation of $f(x) = x^2$ represented by g. Then graph each function. *(See Example 2.)*

17. $g(x) = -x^2$
18. $g(x) = (-x)^2$
19. $g(x) = 3x^2$
20. $g(x) = \frac{1}{3}x^2$
21. $g(x) = (2x)^2$
22. $g(x) = -(2x)^2$
23. $g(x) = \frac{1}{5}x^2 - 4$
24. $g(x) = \frac{1}{2}(x - 1)^2$

ERROR ANALYSIS **In Exercises 25 and 26, describe and correct the error in analyzing the graph of $f(x) = -6x^2 + 4$.**

25. ✗ The graph is a reflection in the y-axis and a vertical stretch by a factor of 6, followed by a translation 4 units up of the graph of the parent quadratic function.

26. ✗ The graph is a translation 4 units up, followed by a vertical stretch by a factor of 6 and a reflection in the x-axis of the graph of the parent quadratic function.

USING STRUCTURE **In Exercises 27–30, describe the transformation of the graph of the parent quadratic function. Then identify the vertex.**

27. $f(x) = 3(x + 2)^2 + 1$
28. $f(x) = -4(x + 1)^2 - 5$
29. $f(x) = -2x^2 + 5$
30. $f(x) = \frac{1}{2}(x - 1)^2$

In Exercises 31–34, write a rule for g described by the transformations of the graph of f. Then identify the vertex. *(See Examples 3 and 4.)*

31. $f(x) = x^2$; vertical stretch by a factor of 4 and a reflection in the x-axis, followed by a translation 2 units up

32. $f(x) = x^2$; vertical shrink by a factor of $\frac{1}{3}$ and a reflection in the y-axis, followed by a translation 3 units right

33. $f(x) = 8x^2 - 6$; horizontal stretch by a factor of 2 and a translation 2 units up, followed by a reflection in the y-axis

34. $f(x) = (x + 6)^2 + 3$; horizontal shrink by a factor of $\frac{1}{2}$ and a translation 1 unit down, followed by a reflection in the x-axis

USING TOOLS In Exercises 35–40, match the function with its graph. Explain your reasoning.

35. $g(x) = 2(x - 1)^2 - 2$ **36.** $g(x) = \frac{1}{2}(x + 1)^2 - 2$

37. $g(x) = -2(x - 1)^2 + 2$

38. $g(x) = 2(x + 1)^2 + 2$ **39.** $g(x) = -2(x + 1)^2 - 2$

40. $g(x) = 2(x - 1)^2 + 2$

A.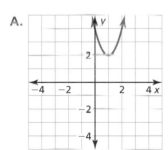

B.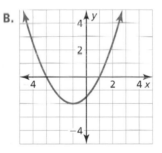

C.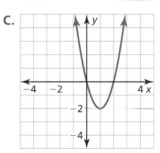

D.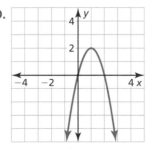

E.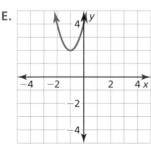

F.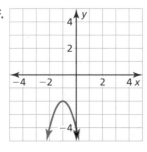

JUSTIFYING STEPS In Exercises 41 and 42, justify each step in writing a function g based on the transformations of $f(x) = 2x^2 + 6x$.

41. translation 6 units down followed by a reflection in the x-axis

$h(x) = f(x) - 6$

$\quad = 2x^2 + 6x - 6$

$g(x) = -h(x)$

$\quad = -(2x^2 + 6x - 6)$

$\quad = -2x^2 - 6x + 6$

42. reflection in the y-axis followed by a translation 4 units right

$h(x) = f(-x)$

$\quad = 2(-x)^2 + 6(-x)$

$\quad = 2x^2 - 6x$

$g(x) = h(x - 4)$

$\quad = 2(x - 4)^2 - 6(x - 4)$

$\quad = 2x^2 - 22x + 56$

43. MODELING WITH MATHEMATICS The function $h(x) = -0.03(x - 14)^2 + 6$ models the jump of a red kangaroo, where x is the horizontal distance traveled (in feet) and h(x) is the height (in feet). When the kangaroo jumps from a higher location, it lands 5 feet farther away. Write a function that models the second jump. *(See Example 5.)*

44. MODELING WITH MATHEMATICS The function $f(t) = -16t^2 + 10$ models the height (in feet) of an object t seconds after it is dropped from a height of 10 feet on Earth. The same object dropped from the same height on the moon is modeled by $g(t) = -\frac{8}{3}t^2 + 10$. Describe the transformation of the graph of f to obtain g. From what height must the object be dropped on the moon so it hits the ground at the same time as on Earth?

45. MODELING WITH MATHEMATICS Flying fish use their pectoral fins like airplane wings to glide through the air.

  a. Write an equation of the form $y = a(x - h)^2 + k$ with vertex $(33, 5)$ that models the flight path, assuming the fish leaves the water at $(0, 0)$.

  b. What are the domain and range of the function? What do they represent in this situation?

  c. Does the value of a change when the flight path has vertex $(30, 4)$? Justify your answer.

46. HOW DO YOU SEE IT? Describe the graph of g as a transformation of the graph of $f(x) = x^2$.

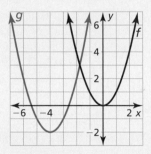

47. COMPARING METHODS Let the graph of g be a translation 3 units up and 1 unit right followed by a vertical stretch by a factor of 2 of the graph of $f(x) = x^2$.

  a. Identify the values of a, h, and k and use vertex form to write the transformed function.

  b. Use function notation to write the transformed function. Compare this function with your function in part (a).

  c. Suppose the vertical stretch was performed first, followed by the translations. Repeat parts (a) and (b).

  d. Which method do you prefer when writing a transformed function? Explain.

48. THOUGHT PROVOKING A jump on a pogo stick with a conventional spring can be modeled by $f(x) = -0.5(x - 6)^2 + 18$, where x is the horizontal distance (in inches) and $f(x)$ is the vertical distance (in inches). Write at least one transformation of the function and provide a possible reason for your transformation.

49. MATHEMATICAL CONNECTIONS The area of a circle depends on the radius, as shown in the graph. A circular earring with a radius of r millimeters has a circular hole with a radius of $\dfrac{3r}{4}$ millimeters. Describe a transformation of the graph below that models the area of the blue portion of the earring.

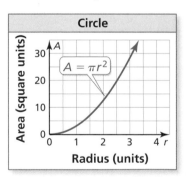

Circle

$A = \pi r^2$

Area (square units)

Radius (units)

Maintaining Mathematical Proficiency
Reviewing what you learned in previous grades and lessons

A line of symmetry for the figure is shown in red. Find the coordinates of point A.
(Skills Review Handbook)

50.

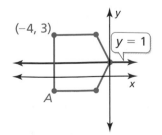

$(-4, 3)$

$y = 1$

A

51.

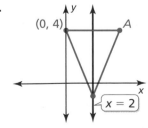

$(0, 4)$

A

$x = 2$

52.

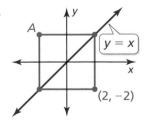

A

$y = x$

$(2, -2)$

2.6 Characteristics of Quadratic Functions

Essential Question What type of symmetry does the graph of $f(x) = a(x - h)^2 + k$ have and how can you describe this symmetry?

EXPLORATION 1   Parabolas and Symmetry

Work with a partner.

a. Complete the table. Then use the values in the table to sketch the graph of the function

$$f(x) = \tfrac{1}{2}x^2 - 2x - 2$$

on graph paper.

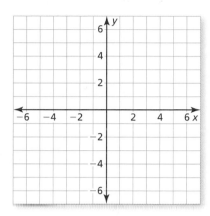

x	-2	-1	0	1	2
f(x)					

x	3	4	5	6
f(x)				

b. Use the results in part (a) to identify the vertex of the parabola.

c. Find a vertical line on your graph paper so that when you fold the paper, the left portion of the graph coincides with the right portion of the graph. What is the equation of this line? How does it relate to the vertex?

d. Show that the vertex form

$$f(x) = \tfrac{1}{2}(x - 2)^2 - 4$$

is equivalent to the function given in part (a).

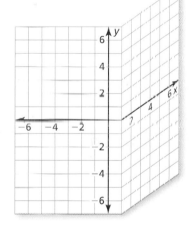

EXPLORATION 2   Parabolas and Symmetry

Work with a partner. Repeat Exploration 1 for the function given by

$$f(x) = -\tfrac{1}{3}x^2 + 2x + 3 = -\tfrac{1}{3}(x - 3)^2 + 6.$$

ATTENDING TO PRECISION

To be proficient in math, you need to use clear definitions in your reasoning and discussions with others.

Communicate Your Answer

3. What type of symmetry does the graph of $f(x) = a(x - h)^2 + k$ have and how can you describe this symmetry?

4. Describe the symmetry of each graph. Then use a graphing calculator to verify your answer.

   a. $f(x) = -(x - 1)^2 + 4$ b. $f(x) = (x + 1)^2 - 2$ c. $f(x) = 2(x - 3)^2 + 1$

   d. $f(x) = \tfrac{1}{2}(x + 2)^2$ e. $f(x) = -2x^2 + 3$ f. $f(x) = 3(x - 5)^2 + 2$

What You Will Learn

Core Vocabulary

axis of symmetry, *p. 82*
standard form, *p. 82*
minimum value, *p. 84*
maximum value, *p. 84*
intercept form, *p. 85*

Previous
x-intercept

▶ Explore properties of parabolas.
▶ Find maximum and minimum values of quadratic functions.
▶ Graph quadratic functions using *x*-intercepts.
▶ Rewrite equations.

Exploring Properties of Parabolas

An **axis of symmetry** is a line that divides a parabola into mirror images and passes through the vertex. Because the vertex of $f(x) = a(x - h)^2 + k$ is (h, k), the axis of symmetry is the vertical line $x = h$.

Previously, you used transformations to graph quadratic functions in vertex form. You can also use the axis of symmetry and the vertex to graph quadratic functions written in vertex form.

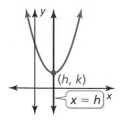

EXAMPLE 1 **Using Symmetry to Graph Quadratic Functions**

Graph $f(x) = -2(x + 3)^2 + 4$. Label the vertex and axis of symmetry.

SOLUTION

Step 1 Identify the constants $a = -2$, $h = -3$, and $k = 4$.

Step 2 Plot the vertex $(h, k) = (-3, 4)$ and draw the axis of symmetry $x = -3$.

Step 3 Evaluate the function for two values of x.

$$x = -2: f(-2) = -2(-2 + 3)^2 + 4 = 2$$
$$x = -1: f(-1) = -2(-1 + 3)^2 + 4 = -4$$

Plot the points $(-2, 2)$, $(-1, -4)$, and their reflections in the axis of symmetry.

Step 4 Draw a parabola through the plotted points.

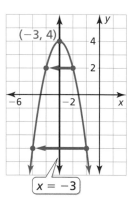

Quadratic functions can also be written in **standard form**, $f(x) = ax^2 + bx + c$, where $a \neq 0$. You can derive standard form by expanding vertex form.

$f(x) = a(x - h)^2 + k$	Vertex form
$f(x) = a(x^2 - 2hx + h^2) + k$	Expand $(x - h)^2$.
$f(x) = ax^2 - 2ahx + ah^2 + k$	Distributive Property
$f(x) = ax^2 + (-2ah)x + (ah^2 + k)$	Group like terms.
$f(x) = ax^2 + bx + c$	Let $b = -2ah$ and let $c = ah^2 + k$.

This allows you to make the following observations.

$a = a$: So, a has the same meaning in vertex form and standard form.

$b = -2ah$: Solve for h to obtain $h = -\dfrac{b}{2a}$. So, the axis of symmetry is $x = -\dfrac{b}{2a}$.

$c = ah^2 + k$: In vertex form $f(x) = a(x - h)^2 + k$, notice that $f(0) = ah^2 + k$. So, c is the y-intercept.

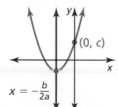

Core Concept

Properties of the Graph of $f(x) = ax^2 + bx + c$

$y = ax^2 + bx + c, a > 0$ $y = ax^2 + bx + c, a < 0$

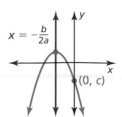

- The parabola opens up when $a > 0$ and opens down when $a < 0$.
- The graph is narrower than the graph of $f(x) = x^2$ when $|a| > 1$ and wider when $|a| < 1$.
- The axis of symmetry is $x = -\dfrac{b}{2a}$ and the vertex is $\left(-\dfrac{b}{2a}, f\left(-\dfrac{b}{2a}\right)\right)$.
- The y-intercept is c. So, the point $(0, c)$ is on the parabola.

EXAMPLE 2 Graphing a Quadratic Function in Standard Form

Graph $f(x) = 3x^2 - 6x + 1$. Label the vertex and axis of symmetry.

COMMON ERROR

Be sure to include the negative sign when writing the expression for the x-coordinate of the vertex.

SOLUTION

Step 1 Identify the coefficients $a = 3$, $b = -6$, and $c = 1$. Because $a > 0$, the parabola opens up.

Step 2 Find the vertex. First calculate the x-coordinate.

$$x = -\frac{b}{2a} = -\frac{-6}{2(3)} = 1$$

Then find the y-coordinate of the vertex.

$$f(1) = 3(1)^2 - 6(1) + 1 = -2$$

So, the vertex is $(1, -2)$. Plot this point.

Step 3 Draw the axis of symmetry $x = 1$.

Step 4 Identify the y-intercept c, which is 1. Plot the point $(0, 1)$ and its reflection in the axis of symmetry, $(2, 1)$.

Step 5 Evaluate the function for another value of x, such as $x = 3$.

$$f(3) = 3(3)^2 - 6(3) + 1 = 10$$

Plot the point $(3, 10)$ and its reflection in the axis of symmetry, $(-1, 10)$.

Step 6 Draw a parabola through the plotted points.

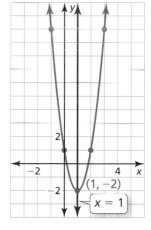

Monitoring Progress Help in English and Spanish at *BigIdeasMath.com*

Graph the function. Label the vertex and axis of symmetry.

1. $f(x) = -3(x + 1)^2$

2. $g(x) = 2(x - 2)^2 + 5$

3. $h(x) = x^2 + 2x - 1$

4. $p(x) = -2x^2 - 8x + 1$

Finding Maximum and Minimum Values

Because the vertex is the highest or lowest point on a parabola, its *y*-coordinate is the *maximum value* or *minimum value* of the function. The vertex lies on the axis of symmetry, so the function is *increasing* on one side of the axis of symmetry and *decreasing* on the other side.

🌀 Core Concept

Minimum and Maximum Values

For the quadratic function $f(x) = ax^2 + bx + c$, the *y*-coordinate of the vertex is the **minimum value** of the function when $a > 0$ and the **maximum value** when $a < 0$.

a > 0

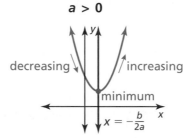

a < 0

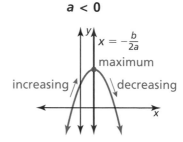

- Minimum value: $f\left(-\dfrac{b}{2a}\right)$

- Domain: All real numbers

- Range: $y \geq f\left(-\dfrac{b}{2a}\right)$

- Decreasing to the left of $x = -\dfrac{b}{2a}$

- Increasing to the right of $x = -\dfrac{b}{2a}$

- Maximum value: $f\left(-\dfrac{b}{2a}\right)$

- Domain: All real numbers

- Range: $y \leq f\left(-\dfrac{b}{2a}\right)$

- Increasing to the left of $x = -\dfrac{b}{2a}$

- Decreasing to the right of $x = -\dfrac{b}{2a}$

STUDY TIP

When a function f is written in vertex form, you can use $h = -\dfrac{b}{2a}$ and $k = f\left(-\dfrac{b}{2a}\right)$ to state the properties shown.

EXAMPLE 3 **Finding a Minimum or a Maximum Value**

Find the minimum value or maximum value of $f(x) = \frac{1}{2}x^2 - 2x - 1$. Describe the domain and range of the function, and where the function is increasing and decreasing.

SOLUTION

Identify the coefficients $a = \frac{1}{2}$, $b = -2$, and $c = -1$. Because $a > 0$, the parabola opens up and the function has a minimum value. To find the minimum value, calculate the coordinates of the vertex.

$$x = -\frac{b}{2a} = -\frac{-2}{2\left(\frac{1}{2}\right)} = 2 \quad \Rightarrow \quad f(2) = \frac{1}{2}(2)^2 - 2(2) - 1 = -3$$

▶ The minimum value is -3. So, the domain is all real numbers and the range is $y \geq -3$. The function is decreasing to the left of $x = 2$ and increasing to the right of $x = 2$.

Check

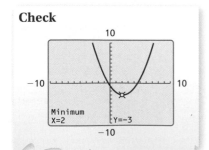

Monitoring Progress Help in English and Spanish at *BigIdeasMath.com*

5. Find the minimum value or maximum value of (a) $f(x) = 4x^2 + 16x - 3$ and (b) $h(x) = -x^2 + 5x + 9$. Describe the domain and range of each function, and where each function is increasing and decreasing.

Graphing Quadratic Functions Using *x*-Intercepts

When the graph of a quadratic function has at least one *x*-intercept, the function can be written in **intercept form**, $f(x) = a(x - p)(x - q)$, where $a \neq 0$.

Core Concept

Properties of the Graph of $f(x) = a(x - p)(x - q)$

- Because $f(p) = 0$ and $f(q) = 0$, p and q are the *x*-intercepts of the graph of the function.

- The axis of symmetry is halfway between $(p, 0)$ and $(q, 0)$. So, the axis of symmetry is $x = \dfrac{p + q}{2}$.

- The parabola opens up when $a > 0$ and opens down when $a < 0$.

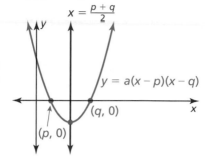

EXAMPLE 4 **Graphing a Quadratic Function in Intercept Form**

Graph $f(x) = -2(x + 3)(x - 1)$. Label the *x*-intercepts, vertex, and axis of symmetry.

SOLUTION

Step 1 Identify the *x*-intercepts. The *x*-intercepts are $p = -3$ and $q = 1$, so the parabola passes through the points $(-3, 0)$ and $(1, 0)$.

Step 2 Find the coordinates of the vertex.

$$x = \frac{p + q}{2} = \frac{-3 + 1}{2} = -1$$

$$f(-1) = -2(-1 + 3)(-1 - 1) = 8$$

So, the axis of symmetry is $x = -1$ and the vertex is $(-1, 8)$.

Step 3 Draw a parabola through the vertex and the points where the *x*-intercepts occur.

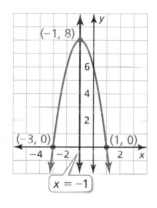

Check You can check your answer by generating a table of values for f on a graphing calculator.

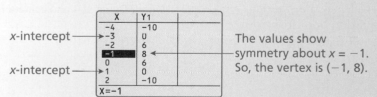

The values show symmetry about $x = -1$. So, the vertex is $(-1, 8)$.

Monitoring Progress   Help in English and Spanish at *BigIdeasMath.com*

Graph the function. Label the *x*-intercepts, vertex, and axis of symmetry.

6. $f(x) = -(x + 1)(x + 5)$

7. $g(x) = \frac{1}{4}(x - 6)(x - 2)$

Rewriting Equations

You can use completing the square to rewrite equations of the form

$$ax^2 + by^2 + cx + dy + e = 0$$

into forms that make it easier to identify characteristics of their graphs.

EXAMPLE 5 Rewriting Equations

Use completing the square to find the vertex of the parabola or the center and radius of the circle. Then graph the equation.

a. $-2x^2 + 8x - y + 7 = 0$ **b.** $x^2 + y^2 - 2x + 6y - 6 = 0$

SOLUTION

a. The equation has no y^2-term. So, isolate the x-terms and complete the square.

$-2x^2 + 8x = y - 7$	Isolate the x-terms.
$-2(x^2 - 4x) = y - 7$	Factor out -2 on the left side.
$-2(x^2 - 4x + 4) = y - 7 - 8$	Complete the square for $x^2 - 4x$.
$-2(x - 2)^2 + 15 = y$	Write in vertex form.

▶ The graph of the equation is a parabola with a vertex of $(2, 15)$.

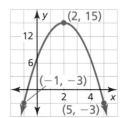

b. The equation has an x^2-term and a y^2-term. So, complete the square twice.

$x^2 + y^2 - 2x + 6y = 6$	Add 6 to each side.
$(x^2 - 2x) + (y^2 + 6y) = 6$	Group x-terms and y-terms.
$(x^2 - 2x + 1) + (y^2 + 6y + 9) = 6 + 1 + 9$	Complete the square for $x^2 - 2x$ and $y^2 + 6y$.
$(x - 1)^2 + (y + 3)^2 = 16$	Factor left side. Simplify right side.

▶ The graph of the equation is a circle with a radius of 4 and center $(1, -3)$.

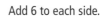

REMEMBER

To complete the square for an expression of the form $x^2 + bx$, add $\left(\dfrac{b}{2}\right)^2$ to the expression. In this example, you must also add $-2(4) = -8$ to the right side of the equation to preserve equality.

REMEMBER

Recall that the standard equation of a circle with center (h, k) and radius r is

$$(x - h)^2 + (y - k)^2 = r^2.$$

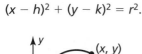

Monitoring Progress 🔊 Help in English and Spanish at *BigIdeasMath.com*

Use completing the square to find the vertex of the parabola or the center and radius of the circle. Then graph the equation.

8. $x^2 - 8x - y + 15 = 0$ **9.** $x^2 + y^2 + 2x - 8y - 8 = 0$

Vocabulary and Core Concept Check

1. **WRITING** Explain how to determine whether a quadratic function will have a minimum value or a maximum value.

2. **WHICH ONE DOESN'T BELONG?** The graph of which function does *not* belong with the other three? Explain.

$$f(x) = 3x^2 + 6x - 24$$

$$f(x) = 3x^2 + 24x - 6$$

$$f(x) = 3(x - 2)(x + 4)$$

$$f(x) = 3(x + 1)^2 - 27$$

Monitoring Progress and Modeling with Mathematics

In Exercises 3–14, graph the function. Label the vertex and axis of symmetry. *(See Example 1.)*

3. $f(x) = (x - 3)^2$

4. $h(x) = (x + 4)^2$

5. $g(x) = (x + 3)^2 + 5$

6. $y = (x - 7)^2 - 1$

7. $y = -4(x - 2)^2 + 4$

8. $g(x) = 2(x + 1)^2 - 3$

9. $f(x) = -2(x - 1)^2 - 5$

10. $h(x) = 4(x + 4)^2 + 6$

11. $y = -\frac{1}{4}(x + 2)^2 + 1$

12. $y = \frac{1}{2}(x - 3)^2 + 2$

13. $f(x) = 0.4(x - 1)^2$

14. $g(x) = 0.75x^2 - 5$

ANALYZING RELATIONSHIPS In Exercises 15–18, use the axis of symmetry to match the equation with its graph.

15. $y = 2(x - 3)^2 + 1$

16. $y = (x + 4)^2 - 2$

17. $y = \frac{1}{2}(x + 1)^2 + 3$

18. $y = (x - 2)^2 - 1$

A.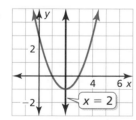

B.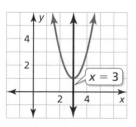

C.

D.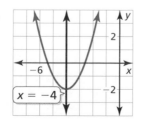

REASONING In Exercises 19 and 20, use the axis of symmetry to plot the reflection of each point and complete the parabola.

19.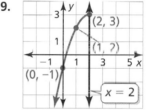

20.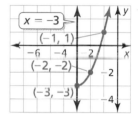

In Exercises 21–30, graph the function. Label the vertex and axis of symmetry. *(See Example 2.)*

21. $y = x^2 + 2x + 1$

22. $y = 3x^2 - 6x + 4$

23. $y = -4x^2 + 8x + 2$

24. $f(x) = -x^2 - 6x + 3$

25. $g(x) = -x^2 - 1$

26. $f(x) = 6x^2 - 5$

27. $g(x) = -1.5x^2 + 3x + 2$

28. $f(x) = 0.5x^2 + x - 3$

29. $y = \frac{3}{2}x^2 - 3x + 6$

30. $y = -\frac{5}{2}x^2 - 4x - 1$

31. **WRITING** Two quadratic functions have graphs with vertices $(2, 4)$ and $(2, -3)$. Explain why you can not use the axes of symmetry to distinguish between the two functions.

32. **WRITING** A quadratic function is increasing to the left of $x = 2$ and decreasing to the right of $x = 2$. Will the vertex be the highest or lowest point on the graph of the parabola? Explain.

ERROR ANALYSIS In Exercises 33 and 34, describe and correct the error in analyzing the graph of $y = 4x^2 + 24x - 7$.

33.
The x-coordinate of the vertex is
$$x = \frac{b}{2a} = \frac{24}{2(4)} = 3.$$

34.
The y-intercept of the graph is the value of c, which is 7.

MODELING WITH MATHEMATICS In Exercises 35 and 36, x is the horizontal distance (in feet) and y is the vertical distance (in feet). Find and interpret the coordinates of the vertex.

35. The path of a basketball thrown at an angle of 45° can be modeled by $y = -0.02x^2 + x + 6$.

36. The path of a shot put released at an angle of 35° can be modeled by $y = -0.01x^2 + 0.7x + 6$.

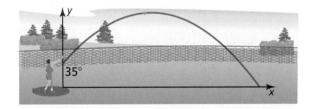

37. **ANALYZING EQUATIONS** The graph of which function has the same axis of symmetry as the graph of $y = x^2 + 2x + 2$?

Ⓐ $y = 2x^2 + 2x + 2$

Ⓑ $y = -3x^2 - 6x + 2$

Ⓒ $y = x^2 - 2x + 2$

Ⓓ $y = -5x^2 + 10x + 2$

38. **USING STRUCTURE** Which function represents the widest parabola? Explain your reasoning.

Ⓐ $y = 2(x + 3)^2$

Ⓑ $y = x^2 - 5$

Ⓒ $y = 0.5(x - 1)^2 + 1$

Ⓓ $y = -x^2 + 6$

In Exercises 39–48, find the minimum or maximum value of the function. Describe the domain and range of the function, and where the function is increasing and decreasing. *(See Example 3.)*

39. $y = 6x^2 - 1$

40. $y = 9x^2 + 7$

41. $y = -x^2 - 4x - 2$

42. $g(x) = -3x^2 - 6x + 5$

43. $f(x) = -2x^2 + 8x + 7$

44. $g(x) = 3x^2 + 18x - 5$

45. $h(x) = 2x^2 - 12x$

46. $h(x) = x^2 - 4x$

47. $y = \frac{1}{4}x^2 - 3x + 2$

48. $f(x) = \frac{3}{2}x^2 + 6x + 4$

49. **PROBLEM SOLVING** The path of a diver is modeled by the function $f(x) = -9x^2 + 9x + 1$, where $f(x)$ is the height of the diver (in meters) above the water and x is the horizontal distance (in meters) from the end of the diving board.

    a. What is the height of the diving board?

    b. What is the maximum height of the diver?

    c. Describe where the diver is ascending and where the diver is descending.

50. **PROBLEM SOLVING** The engine torque y (in foot-pounds) of one model of car is given by $y = -3.75x^2 + 23.2x + 38.8$, where x is the speed (in thousands of revolutions per minute) of the engine.

    a. Find the engine speed that maximizes torque. What is the maximum torque?

    b. Explain what happens to the engine torque as the speed of the engine increases.

MATHEMATICAL CONNECTIONS In Exercises 51 and 52, write an equation for the area of the figure. Then determine the maximum possible area of the figure.

51.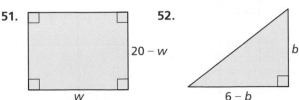
$20 - w$

w

52.
b

$6 - b$

In Exercises 53–60, graph the function. Label the
x-intercept(s), vertex, and axis of symmetry.
(See Example 4.)

53. $y = (x + 3)(x - 3)$ **54.** $y = (x + 1)(x - 3)$

55. $y = 3(x + 2)(x + 6)$ **56.** $f(x) = 2(x - 5)(x - 1)$

57. $g(x) = -x(x + 6)$ **58.** $y = -4x(x + 7)$

59. $f(x) = -2(x - 3)^2$ **60.** $y = 4(x - 7)^2$

USING TOOLS In Exercises 61–64, identify the
x-intercepts of the function and describe where the
graph is increasing and decreasing. Use a graphing
calculator to verify your answer.

61. $f(x) = \frac{1}{2}(x - 2)(x + 6)$

62. $y = \frac{3}{4}(x + 1)(x - 3)$

63. $g(x) = -4(x - 4)(x - 2)$

64. $h(x) = -5(x + 5)(x + 1)$

65. MODELING WITH MATHEMATICS A soccer player
kicks a ball downfield. The height of the ball increases
until it reaches a maximum
height of 8 yards, 20 yards
away from the player. A
second kick is modeled by
$y = x(0.4 - 0.008x)$. Which
kick travels farther before
hitting the ground? Which
kick travels higher?

66. MODELING WITH MATHEMATICS Although a football
field appears to be flat, some are actually shaped
like a parabola so that rain runs off to both sides.
The cross section of a field can be modeled by
$y = -0.000234x(x - 160)$, where *x* and *y* are
measured in feet. What is the width of the field? What
is the maximum height of the surface of the field?

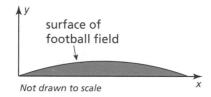

Not drawn to scale

67. OPEN-ENDED Write two different quadratic functions
in intercept form whose graphs have the axis of
symmetry $x = 3$.

68. USING STRUCTURE Write the quadratic function
$f(x) = x^2 + x - 12$ in intercept form. Graph the
function. Label the *x*-intercepts, *y*-intercept, vertex,
and axis of symmetry.

In Exercises 69–72, use completing the square to find
the vertex of the parabola or the center and radius of
the circle. Then graph the equation. *(See Example 5.)*

69. $3x^2 + 6x - y - 2 = 0$

70. $-2x^2 + 6x - 2y - 1 = 0$

71. $x^2 + y^2 + 12y - 13 = 0$

72. $4x^2 + 4y^2 - 24x - 24y - 9 = 0$

73. USING STRUCTURE Recall that the standard equation
of a parabola that opens right or left with vertex at
(h, k) is $x = \frac{1}{4p}(y - k)^2 + h$. Use completing the
square to find the focus, directrix, and vertex of
$y^2 - 4x - 8y + 20 = 0$. Then graph the equation.

74. REASONING Consider an equation of the form
$ax^2 + by^2 + cx + dy + e = 0$. What must be true
about the coefficients *a* and *b* for the graph of the
equation to be a parabola? a circle? Explain your
reasoning.

75. PROBLEM SOLVING An online music store sells about
4000 songs each day when it charges \$1 per song. For
each \$0.05 increase in price, about 80 fewer songs
per day are sold. Use the verbal model and quadratic
function to determine how much the store should
charge per song to maximize daily revenue.

Revenue (dollars)	=	Price (dollars/song)	·	Sales (songs)

$$R(x) \quad = \quad (1 + 0.05x) \quad \cdot \quad (4000 - 80x)$$

76. DRAWING CONCLUSIONS Compare the graphs of
the three quadratic functions. What do you notice?
Rewrite the functions *f* and *g* in standard form to
justify your answer.

$$f(x) = (x + 3)(x + 1)$$
$$g(x) = (x + 2)^2 - 1$$
$$h(x) = x^2 + 4x + 3$$

77. PROBLEM SOLVING A woodland jumping
mouse hops along a parabolic path given by
$y = -0.2x^2 + 1.3x$, where *x* is the mouse's horizontal
distance traveled (in feet) and *y* is the corresponding
height (in feet). Can the mouse jump over a fence that
is 3 feet high? Justify your answer.

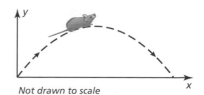

Not drawn to scale

78. HOW DO YOU SEE IT? Consider the graph of the function $f(x) = a(x - p)(x - q)$.

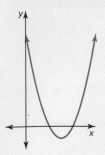

a. What does $f\left(\dfrac{p + q}{2}\right)$ represent in the graph?

b. If $a < 0$, how does your answer in part (a) change? Explain.

79. MODELING WITH MATHEMATICS The Gateshead Millennium Bridge spans the River Tyne. The arch of the bridge can be modeled by a parabola. The arch reaches a maximum height of 50 meters at a point roughly 63 meters across the river. Graph the curve of the arch. What are the domain and range? What do they represent in this situation?

80. THOUGHT PROVOKING You have 100 feet of fencing to enclose a rectangular garden. Draw three possible designs for the garden. Of these, which has the greatest area? Make a conjecture about the dimensions of the rectangular garden with the greatest possible area. Explain your reasoning.

81. MAKING AN ARGUMENT The point (1, 5) lies on the graph of a quadratic function with axis of symmetry $x = -1$. Your friend says the vertex could be the point (0, 5). Is your friend correct? Explain.

82. CRITICAL THINKING Find the y-intercept in terms of a, p, and q for the quadratic function $f(x) = a(x - p)(x - q)$.

83. MODELING WITH MATHEMATICS A kernel of popcorn contains water that expands when the kernel is heated, causing it to pop. The equations below represent the "popping volume" y (in cubic centimeters per gram) of popcorn with moisture content x (as a percent of the popcorn's weight).

Hot-air popping: $y = -0.761(x - 5.52)(x - 22.6)$

Hot-oil popping: $y = -0.652(x - 5.35)(x - 21.8)$

a. For hot-air popping, what moisture content maximizes popping volume? What is the maximum volume?

b. For hot-oil popping, what moisture content maximizes popping volume? What is the maximum volume?

c. Use a graphing calculator to graph both functions in the same coordinate plane. What are the domain and range of each function in this situation? Explain.

84. ABSTRACT REASONING A function is written in intercept form with $a > 0$. What happens to the vertex of the graph as a increases? as a approaches 0?

Maintaining Mathematical Proficiency
Reviewing what you learned in previous grades and lessons

Sketch the solid of revolution. Then identify and describe the solid. *(Section 1.4)*

85. a right triangle with legs of length 3 and 5 rotated around its shorter leg

86. a semicircle with radius 4 rotated around its diameter

Use a graphing calculator to find an equation for the line of best fit. *(Section 2.3)*

87.

x	0	3	6	7	11
y	4	9	24	29	46

88.

x	0	5	10	12	16
y	18	15	9	7	2

2.7 Modeling with Quadratic Functions

Essential Question How can you use a quadratic function to model a real-life situation?

EXPLORATION 1 Modeling with a Quadratic Function

Work with a partner. The graph shows a quadratic function of the form

$$P(t) = at^2 + bt + c$$

which approximates the yearly profits for a company, where $P(t)$ is the profit in year t.

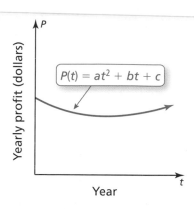

$P(t) = at^2 + bt + c$

a. Is the value of a positive, negative, or zero? Explain.

b. Write an expression in terms of a and b that represents the year t when the company made the least profit.

c. The company made the same yearly profits in 2004 and 2012. Estimate the year in which the company made the least profit.

d. Assume that the model is still valid today. Are the yearly profits currently increasing, decreasing, or constant? Explain.

EXPLORATION 2 Modeling with a Graphing Calculator

Work with a partner. The table shows the heights h (in feet) of a wrench t seconds after it has been dropped from a building under construction.

Time, t	0	1	2	3	4
Height, h	400	384	336	256	144

a. Use a graphing calculator to create a scatter plot of the data, as shown at the right. Explain why the data appear to fit a quadratic model.

b. Use the *quadratic regression* feature to find a quadratic model for the data.

MODELING WITH MATHEMATICS

To be proficient in math, you need to routinely interpret your results in the context of the situation.

c. Graph the quadratic function on the same screen as the scatter plot to verify that it fits the data.

d. When does the wrench hit the ground? Explain.

Communicate Your Answer

3. How can you use a quadratic function to model a real-life situation?

4. Use the Internet or some other reference to find examples of real-life situations that can be modeled by quadratic functions.

What You Will Learn

▶ Write equations of quadratic functions using vertices, points, and *x*-intercepts.

▶ Write quadratic equations to model data sets.

Writing Quadratic Equations

🅒 Core Concept

Writing Quadratic Equations

Given a point and the vertex (h, k)	Use vertex form: $$y = a(x - h)^2 + k$$
Given a point and *x*-intercepts p and q	Use intercept form: $$y = a(x - p)(x - q)$$
Given three points	Write and solve a system of three equations in three variables.

EXAMPLE 1   Writing an Equation Using a Vertex and a Point

The graph shows the parabolic path of a performer who is shot out of a cannon, where y is the height (in feet) and x is the horizontal distance traveled (in feet). Write an equation of the parabola. The performer lands in a net 90 feet from the cannon. What is the height of the net?

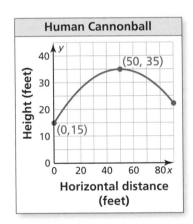

Human Cannonball

(50, 35)

(0, 15)

Height (feet)

Horizontal distance (feet)

SOLUTION

From the graph, you can see that the vertex (h, k) is (50, 35) and the parabola passes through the point (0, 15). Use the vertex and the point to solve for a in vertex form.

$y = a(x - h)^2 + k$	Vertex form
$15 = a(0 - 50)^2 + 35$	Substitute for h, k, x, and y.
$-20 = 2500a$	Simplify.
$-0.008 = a$	Divide each side by 2500.

Because $a = -0.008$, $h = 50$, and $k = 35$, the path can be modeled by the equation $y = -0.008(x - 50)^2 + 35$, where $0 \le x \le 90$. Find the height when $x = 90$.

$y = -0.008(90 - 50)^2 + 35$	Substitute 90 for x.
$= -0.008(1600) + 35$	Simplify.
$= 22.2$	Simplify.

▶ So, the height of the net is about 22 feet.

Monitoring Progress Help in English and Spanish at *BigIdeasMath.com*

1. **WHAT IF?** The vertex of the parabola is (50, 37.5). What is the height of the net?

2. Write an equation of the parabola that passes through the point $(-1, 2)$ and has vertex $(4, -9)$.

EXAMPLE 2 **Writing an Equation Using a Point and *x*-Intercepts**

A meteorologist creates a parabola to predict the temperature tomorrow, where *x* is the number of hours after midnight and *y* is the temperature (in degrees Celsius).

a. Write a function *f* that models the temperature over time. What is the coldest temperature?

b. What is the average rate of change in temperature over the interval in which the temperature is decreasing? increasing? Compare the average rates of change.

SOLUTION

a. The *x*-intercepts are 4 and 24 and the parabola passes through (0, 9.6). Use the *x*-intercepts and the point to solve for *a* in intercept form.

$y = a(x - p)(x - q)$	Intercept form
$9.6 = a(0 - 4)(0 - 24)$	Substitute for *p, q, x,* and *y*.
$9.6 = 96a$	Simplify.
$0.1 = a$	Divide each side by 96.

Because $a = 0.1$, $p = 4$, and $q = 24$, the temperature over time can be modeled by $f(x) = 0.1(x - 4)(x - 24)$, where $0 \le x \le 24$. The coldest temperature is the minimum value. So, find $f(x)$ when $x = \dfrac{4 + 24}{2} = 14$.

$f(14) = 0.1(14 - 4)(14 - 24)$	Substitute 14 for *x*.
$= -10$	Simplify.

▶ So, the coldest temperature is $-10°C$ at 14 hours after midnight, or 2 P.M.

b. The parabola opens up and the axis of symmetry is $x = 14$. So, the function is decreasing over the interval $0 < x < 14$ and increasing over the interval $14 < x < 24$.

Average rate of change over $0 < x < 14$:

$$\frac{f(14) - f(0)}{14 - 0} = \frac{-10 - 9.6}{14} = -1.4$$

Average rate of change over $14 < x < 24$:

$$\frac{f(24) - f(14)}{24 - 14} = \frac{0 - (-10)}{10} = 1$$

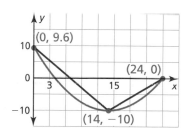

▶ Because $|-1.4| > |1|$, the average rate at which the temperature decreases from midnight to 2 P.M. is greater than the average rate at which it increases from 2 P.M. to midnight.

Temperature Forecast

REMEMBER

The average rate of change of a function *f* from x_1 to x_2 is the slope of the line connecting $(x_1, f(x_1))$ and $(x_2, f(x_2))$:

$$\frac{f(x_2) - f(x_1)}{x_2 - x_1}.$$

Monitoring Progress Help in English and Spanish at *BigIdeasMath.com*

3. **WHAT IF?** The *y*-intercept is 4.8. How does this change your answers in parts (a) and (b)?

4. Write an equation of the parabola that passes through the point (2, 5) and has *x*-intercepts −2 and 4.

Writing Equations to Model Data

When data have equally-spaced inputs, you can analyze patterns in the differences of the outputs to determine what type of function can be used to model the data. Linear data have constant *first differences*. Quadratic data have constant *second differences*.

EXAMPLE 3 Writing a Quadratic Equation Using Three Points

Time, t	Height, h
10	26,900
15	29,025
20	30,600
25	31,625
30	32,100
35	32,025
40	31,400

NASA can create a weightless environment by flying a plane in parabolic paths. The table shows heights h (in feet) of a plane t seconds after starting the flight path. Passengers experience a weightless environment above 30,800 feet. Write and solve an equation to approximate the period of weightlessness.

SOLUTION

Step 1 The input values are equally spaced. So, analyze the differences in the outputs to determine what type of function you can use to model the data.

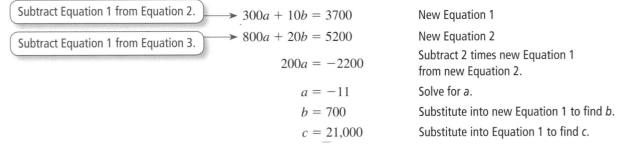

$h(10)$ $h(15)$ $h(20)$ $h(25)$ $h(30)$ $h(35)$ $h(40)$
26,900   29,025   30,600   31,625   32,100   32,025   31,400

first differences: 2125   1575   1025   475 -75 -625

second differences: -550 -550 -550 -550 -550

Because the second differences are constant, you can model the data with a quadratic function.

Step 2 Write a quadratic function of the form $h(t) = at^2 + bt + c$ that models the data. Use any three points (t, h) from the table to write a system of equations.

Use (10, 26,900): $100a + 10b + c = 26,900$	Equation 1
Use (20, 30,600): $400a + 20b + c = 30,600$	Equation 2
Use (30, 32,100): $900a + 30b + c = 32,100$	Equation 3

Use the elimination method to solve the system.

Subtract Equation 1 from Equation 2. → $300a + 10b = 3700$ New Equation 1

Subtract Equation 1 from Equation 3. → $800a + 20b = 5200$ New Equation 2

$200a = -2200$ Subtract 2 times new Equation 1 from new Equation 2.

$a = -11$ Solve for a.

$b = 700$ Substitute into new Equation 1 to find b.

$c = 21,000$ Substitute into Equation 1 to find c.

The data can be modeled by the function $h(t) = -11t^2 + 700t + 21,000$.

Step 3 To find the period of weightlessness, find the t-values for which $h(t) = 30,800$.

$30,800 = -11t^2 + 700t + 21,000$ Substitute 30,800 for $h(t)$.

$0 = -11t^2 + 700t - 9800$ Write in standard form.

$t = \dfrac{-700 \pm \sqrt{700^2 - 4(-11)(-9800)}}{2(-11)}$ Substitute -11 for a, 700 for b, and -9800 for c in the Quadratic Formula.

$t = \dfrac{-700 \pm \sqrt{58,800}}{-22}$ Simplify.

$t \approx 20.8$, or $t \approx 42.8$ Use a calculator.

> **REMEMBER**
> The Quadratic Formula,
> $$x = \frac{-b \pm \sqrt{b^2 - 4ac}}{2a},$$
> gives the solutions of $ax^2 + bx + c = 0$.

▶ The plane rises above 30,800 feet after 20.8 seconds and falls below 30,800 feet after 42.8 seconds. So, the period of weightlessness is $42.8 - 20.8 \approx 22$ seconds.

Real-life data that show a quadratic relationship usually do not have constant second differences because the data are not *exactly* quadratic. Relationships that are *approximately* quadratic have second differences that are relatively "close" in value. Many technology tools have a *quadratic regression* feature that you can use to find a quadratic function that best models a set of data.

EXAMPLE 4 **Using Quadratic Regression**

The table shows fuel efficiencies of a vehicle at different speeds. Write a function that models the data. Use the model to approximate the optimal driving speed.

SOLUTION

Because the x-values are not equally spaced, you cannot analyze the differences in the outputs. Use a graphing calculator to find a function that models the data.

Miles per hour, x	Miles per gallon, y
20	14.5
24	17.5
30	21.2
36	23.7
40	25.2
45	25.8
50	25.8
56	25.1
60	24.0
70	19.5

Step 1 Enter the data in a graphing calculator using two lists and create a scatter plot. The data show a quadratic relationship.

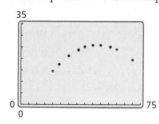

Step 2 Use the *quadratic regression* feature. A quadratic model that represents the data is $y = -0.014x^2 + 1.37x - 7.1$.

```
QuadReg
y=ax²+bx+c
a=-.014097349
b=1.366218867
c=-7.144052413
R²=.9992475882
```

Step 3 Graph the regression equation with the scatter plot.

In this context, the "optimal" driving speed is the speed at which the mileage per gallon is maximized. Using the *maximum* feature, you can see that the maximum mileage per gallon is about 26.4 miles per gallon when driving about 48.9 miles per hour.

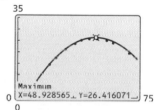

▶ So, the optimal driving speed is about 49 miles per hour.

Monitoring Progress  Help in English and Spanish at *BigIdeasMath.com*

5. Write an equation of the parabola that passes through the points $(-1, 4)$, $(0, 1)$, and $(2, 7)$.

6. The table shows the estimated profits y (in dollars) for a concert when the charge is x dollars per ticket. Write and solve an equation to determine what ticket prices result in profits above \$8000. What ticket price maximizes profit?

Ticket price, x	2	5	8	11	14	17
Profit, y	2600	6500	8600	8900	7400	4100

7. The table shows the results of an experiment testing the maximum weights y (in tons) supported by ice x inches thick. Write a function that models the data. How much weight can be supported by ice that is 22 inches thick?

Ice thickness, x	12	14	15	18	20	24	27
Maximum weight, y	3.4	7.6	10.0	18.3	25.0	40.6	54.3

Vocabulary and Core Concept Check

1. **WRITING** Explain when it is appropriate to use a quadratic model for a set of data.

2. **DIFFERENT WORDS, SAME QUESTION** Which is different? Find "both" answers.

What is the average rate of change over $0 \le x \le 2$?

What is the distance from $f(0)$ to $f(2)$?

What is the slope of the line segment?

What is $\dfrac{f(2) - f(0)}{2 - 0}$?

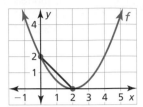

Monitoring Progress and Modeling with Mathematics

In Exercises 3–8, write an equation of the parabola in vertex form. *(See Example 1.)*

3.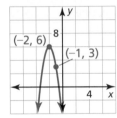

4.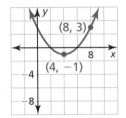

5. passes through $(13, 8)$ and has vertex $(3, 2)$

6. passes through $(-7, -15)$ and has vertex $(-5, 9)$

7. passes through $(0, -24)$ and has vertex $(-6, -12)$

8. passes through $(6, 35)$ and has vertex $(-1, 14)$

In Exercises 9–14, write an equation of the parabola in intercept form. *(See Example 2.)*

9.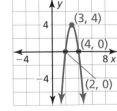

10.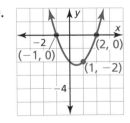

11. x-intercepts of 12 and -6; passes through $(14, 4)$

12. x-intercepts of 9 and 1; passes through $(0, -18)$

13. x-intercepts of -16 and -2; passes through $(-18, 72)$

14. x-intercepts of -7 and -3; passes through $(-2, 0.05)$

15. **WRITING** Explain when to use intercept form and when to use vertex form when writing an equation of a parabola.

16. **ANALYZING EQUATIONS** Which of the following equations represent the parabola?

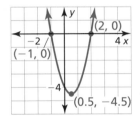

(A) $y = 2(x - 2)(x + 1)$

(B) $y = 2(x + 0.5)^2 - 4.5$

(C) $y = 2(x - 0.5)^2 - 4.5$

(D) $y = 2(x + 2)(x - 1)$

In Exercises 17–20, write an equation of the parabola in vertex form or intercept form.

17.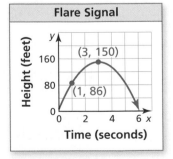

18.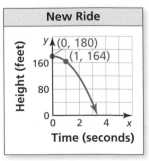

19.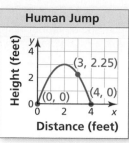

Human Jump

20.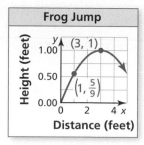

Frog Jump

24. MODELING WITH MATHEMATICS A baseball is thrown up in the air. The table shows the heights y (in feet) of the baseball after x seconds. Write and solve an equation to determine how long the ball is above 10 feet. How long is the ball in the air?

Time, x	0	2	4	6
Baseball height, y	6	22	22	6

21. ERROR ANALYSIS Describe and correct the error in writing an equation of the parabola.

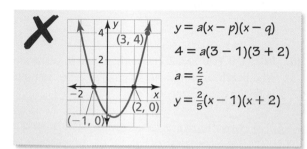

$y = a(x - p)(x - q)$

$4 = a(3 - 1)(3 + 2)$

$a = \dfrac{2}{5}$

$y = \dfrac{2}{5}(x - 1)(x + 2)$

25. COMPARING METHODS You use a system with three variables to find the equation of a parabola that passes through the points $(-8, 0)$, $(2, -20)$, and $(1, 0)$. Your friend uses intercept form to find the equation. Whose method is easier? Justify your answer.

26. MODELING WITH MATHEMATICS The table shows the distances y a motorcyclist is from home after x hours.

Time (hours), x	0	1	2	3
Distance (miles), y	0	45	90	135

22. MATHEMATICAL CONNECTIONS The area of a rectangle is modeled by the graph where y is the area (in square meters) and x is the width (in meters). Write an equation of the parabola. Find the dimensions and corresponding area of one possible rectangle. What dimensions result in the maximum area?

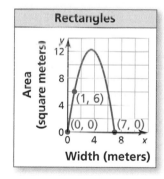

Rectangles

a. Determine what type of function you can use to model the data. Explain your reasoning.

b. Write and evaluate a function to determine the distance the motorcyclist is from home after 6 hours.

27. USING TOOLS The table shows the heights h (in feet) of a sponge t seconds after it was dropped by a window cleaner on top of a skyscraper. (*See Example 4.*)

Time, t	0	1	1.5	2.5	3
Height, h	280	264	244	180	136

a. Use a graphing calculator to create a scatter plot. Which better represents the data, a line or a parabola? Explain.

b. Use the *regression* feature of your calculator to find the model that best fits the data.

c. Use the model in part (b) to predict when the sponge will hit the ground.

d. Identify and interpret the domain and range in this situation.

23. MODELING WITH MATHEMATICS Every rope has a safe working load. A rope should not be used to lift a weight greater than its safe working load. The table shows the safe working loads S (in pounds) for ropes with circumference C (in inches). Write an equation for the safe working load for a rope. Find the safe working load for a rope that has a circumference of 10 inches. (*See Example 3.*)

Circumference, C	0	1	2	3
Safe working load, S	0	180	720	1620

28. MAKING AN ARGUMENT Your friend states that quadratic functions with the same x-intercepts have the same equations, vertex, and axis of symmetry. Is your friend correct? Explain your reasoning.

In Exercises 29–32, analyze the differences in the outputs to determine whether the data are *linear*, *quadratic*, or *neither*. Explain. If linear or quadratic, write an equation that fits the data.

29.

Price decrease (dollars), x	0	5	10	15	20
Revenue ($1000s), y	470	630	690	650	510

30.

Time (hours), x	0	1	2	3	4
Height (feet), y	40	42	44	46	48

31.

Time (hours), x	1	2	3	4	5
Population (hundreds), y	2	4	8	16	32

32.

Time (days), x	0	1	2	3	4
Height (feet), y	320	303	254	173	60

33. **PROBLEM SOLVING** The graph shows the number y of students absent from school due to the flu each day x.

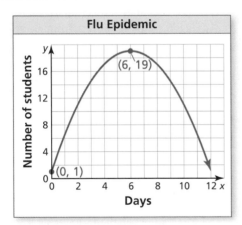

Flu Epidemic

a. Interpret the meaning of the vertex in this situation.

b. Write an equation for the parabola to predict the number of students absent on day 10.

c. Compare the average rates of change in the students with the flu from 0 to 6 days and 6 to 11 days.

34. **THOUGHT PROVOKING** Describe a real-life situation that can be modeled by a quadratic equation. Justify your answer.

35. **PROBLEM SOLVING** The table shows the heights y of a competitive water-skier x seconds after jumping off a ramp. Write a function that models the height of the water-skier over time. When is the water-skier 5 feet above the water? How long is the skier in the air?

Time (seconds), x	0	0.25	0.75	1	1.1
Height (feet), y	22	22.5	17.5	12	9.24

36. **HOW DO YOU SEE IT?** Use the graph to determine whether the average rate of change over each interval is *positive*, *negative*, or *zero*.

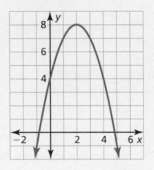

a. $0 \le x \le 2$ b. $2 \le x \le 5$

c. $2 \le x \le 4$ d. $0 \le x \le 4$

37. **REPEATED REASONING** The table shows the number of tiles in each figure. Verify that the data show a quadratic relationship. Predict the number of tiles in the 12th figure.

Figure 1   Figure 2   Figure 3   Figure 4

Figure	1	2	3	4
Number of Tiles	1	5	11	19

Maintaining Mathematical Proficiency
Reviewing what you learned in previous grades and lessons

Factor the trinomial. *(Skills Review Handbook)*

38. $x^2 + 4x + 3$ 39. $x^2 - 3x + 2$ 40. $3x^2 - 15x + 12$ 41. $5x^2 + 5x - 30$

Core Vocabulary

quadratic function, *p. 74*   vertex form, *p. 76*   minimum value, *p. 84*
parabola, *p. 74*   axis of symmetry, *p. 82*   maximum value, *p. 84*
vertex of a parabola, *p. 76*   standard form, *p. 82*   intercept form, *p. 85*

Core Concepts

Section 2.5

Horizontal Translations, *p. 74*   Reflections in the *y*-Axis, *p. 75*
Vertical Translations, *p. 74*   Horizontal Stretches and Shrinks, *p. 75*
Reflections in the *x*-Axis, *p. 75*   Vertical Stretches and Shrinks, *p. 75*

Section 2.6

Properties of the Graph of $f(x) = ax^2 + bx + c$,   Properties of the Graph of $f(x) = a(x - p)(x - q)$,
  p. 83   *p. 85*
Minimum and Maximum Values, *p. 84*

Section 2.7

Writing Quadratic Equations, *p. 92*   Writing Quadratic Equations to Model Data, *p. 94*

Mathematical Practices

1. Why does the height you found in Exercise 44 on page 79 make sense in the context of the situation?

2. How can you use technology to deepen your understanding of the concepts in Exercise 83 on page 90?

3. Describe how you were able to construct a viable argument in Exercise 28 on page 97.

Performance Task:

Changing the Course

Designers of motocross races use mathematics to create ramps and jumps for their courses. How could you modify their models so that riders will catch more air on your track?

To explore the answer to this question and more, check out the Performance Task and Real-Life STEM video at *BigIdeasMath.com*.

2.1 Parent Functions and Transformations (pp. 39–46)

Graph $g(x) = (x - 2)^2 + 1$ and its parent function. Then describe the transformation.

The function g is a quadratic function.

▶ The graph of g is a translation 2 units right and 1 unit up of the graph of the parent quadratic function.

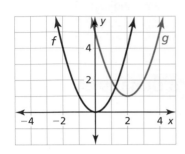

Graph the function and its parent function. Then describe the transformation.

1. $f(x) = x + 3$

2. $g(x) = |x| - 1$

3. $h(x) = \frac{1}{2}x^2$

4. $h(x) = 4$

5. $f(x) = -|x| - 3$

6. $g(x) = -3(x + 3)^2$

2.2 Transformations of Linear and Absolute Value Functions (pp. 47–54)

Let the graph of g be a translation 2 units to the right followed by a reflection in the y-axis of the graph of $f(x) = |x|$. Write a rule for g.

Step 1 First write a function h that represents the translation of f.

$$h(x) = f(x - 2) \qquad \text{Subtract 2 from the input.}$$
$$= |x - 2| \qquad \text{Replace } x \text{ with } x - 2 \text{ in } f(x).$$

Step 2 Then write a function g that represents the reflection of h.

$$g(x) = h(-x) \qquad \text{Multiply the input by } -1.$$
$$= |-x - 2| \qquad \text{Replace } x \text{ with } -x \text{ in } h(x).$$
$$= |-(x + 2)| \qquad \text{Factor out } -1.$$
$$= |-1| \cdot |x + 2| \qquad \text{Product Property of Absolute Value}$$
$$= |x + 2| \qquad \text{Simplify.}$$

▶ The transformed function is $g(x) = |x + 2|$.

Write a function g whose graph represents the indicated transformations of the graph of f. Use a graphing calculator to check your answer.

7. $f(x) = |x|$; reflection in the x-axis followed by a translation 4 units to the left

8. $f(x) = |x|$; vertical shrink by a factor of $\frac{1}{2}$ followed by a translation 2 units up

9. $f(x) = x$; translation 3 units down followed by a reflection in the y-axis

2.3 Modeling with Linear Functions (pp. 55–62)

The table shows the numbers of ice cream cones sold for different outside temperatures (in degrees Fahrenheit). Do the data show a linear relationship? If so, write an equation of a line of fit and use it to estimate how many ice cream cones are sold when the temperature is 60°F.

Temperature, x	53	62	70	82	90
Number of cones, y	90	105	117	131	147

Step 1 Create a scatter plot of the data. The data show a linear relationship.

Step 2 Sketch the line that appears to most closely fit the data. One possibility is shown.

Step 3 Choose two points on the line. For the line shown, you might choose (70, 117) and (90, 147).

Step 4 Write an equation of the line. First, find the slope.

$$m = \frac{y_2 - y_1}{x_2 - x_1} = \frac{147 - 117}{90 - 70} = \frac{30}{20} = 1.5$$

Use point-slope form to write an equation. Use $(x_1, y_1) = (70, 117)$.

$y - y_1 = m(x - x_1)$	Point-slope form
$y - 117 = 1.5(x - 70)$	Substitute for m, x_1, and y_1.
$y - 117 = 1.5x - 105$	Distributive Property
$y = 1.5x + 12$	Add 117 to each side.

Use the equation to estimate the number of ice cream cones sold.

$y = 1.5(60) + 12$	Substitute 60 for x.
$= 102$	Simplify.

▶ Approximately 102 ice cream cones are sold when the temperature is 60°F.

Write an equation of the line.

10. The table shows the total number y (in billions) of U.S. movie admissions each year for x years. Use a graphing calculator to find an equation of the line of best fit for the data.

Year, x	0	2	4	6	8	10
Admissions, y	1.24	1.26	1.39	1.47	1.49	1.57

11. You ride your bike and measure how far you travel. After 10 minutes, you travel 3.5 miles. After 30 minutes, you travel 10.5 miles. Write an equation to model your distance. How far can you ride your bike in 45 minutes?

Solve the system.

$$x - y + z = -3 \qquad \text{Equation 1}$$
$$2x - y + 5z = 4 \qquad \text{Equation 2}$$
$$4x + 2y - z = 2 \qquad \text{Equation 3}$$

Step 1 Rewrite the system as a linear system in two variables.

$$x - y + z = -3 \qquad \text{Add Equation 1 to}$$
$$\underline{4x + 2y - z = 2} \qquad \text{Equation 3 (to eliminate } z\text{).}$$
$$5x + y = -1 \qquad \text{New Equation 3}$$

$$-5x + 5y - 5z = 15 \qquad \text{Add } -5 \text{ times Equation 1 to}$$
$$\underline{2x - y + 5z = 4} \qquad \text{Equation 2 (to eliminate } z\text{).}$$
$$-3x + 4y = 19 \qquad \text{New Equation 2}$$

Step 2 Solve the new linear system for both of its variables.

$$-20x - 4y = 4 \qquad \text{Add } -4 \text{ times new Equation 3}$$
$$\underline{-3x + 4y = 19} \qquad \text{to new Equation 2.}$$
$$-23x = 23$$
$$x = -1 \qquad \text{Solve for } x.$$
$$y = 4 \qquad \text{Substitute into new Equation 2 or 3 to find } y.$$

Step 3 Substitute $x = -1$ and $y = 4$ into an original equation and solve for z.

$$x - y + z = -3 \qquad \text{Write original Equation 1.}$$
$$(-1) - 4 + z = -3 \qquad \text{Substitute } -1 \text{ for } x \text{ and } 4 \text{ for } y.$$
$$z = 2 \qquad \text{Solve for } z.$$

▶ The solution is $x = -1$, $y = 4$, and $z = 2$, or the ordered triple $(-1, 4, 2)$.

Solve the system. Check your solution, if possible.

12. $x + y + z = 3$
$-x + 3y + 2z = -8$
$x = 4z$

13. $2x - 5y - z = 17$
$x + y + 3z = 19$
$-4x + 6y + z = -20$

14. $x + y + z = 2$
$2x - 3y + z = 11$
$-3x + 2y - 2z = -13$

15. $x + 4y - 2z = 3$
$x + 3y + 7z = 1$
$2x + 9y - 13z = 2$

16. $x - y + 3z = 6$
$x - 2y = 5$
$2x - 2y + 5z = 9$

17. $x + 2z = 4$
$x + y + z = 6$
$3x + 3y + 4z = 28$

18. A school band performs a spring concert for a crowd of 600 people. The revenue for the concert is $3150. There are 150 more adults at the concert than students. How many of each type of ticket are sold?

BAND CONCERT

STUDENTS - $3   ADULTS - $7
CHILDREN UNDER 12 - $2

2.5 Transformations of Quadratic Functions *(pp. 73–80)*

Let the graph of g be a translation 1 unit left and 2 units up of the graph of $f(x) = x^2 + 1$. Write a rule for g.

$$g(x) = f(x - (-1)) + 2 \qquad \text{Subtract } -1 \text{ from the input. Add 2 to the output.}$$
$$= (x + 1)^2 + 1 + 2 \qquad \text{Replace } x \text{ with } x + 1 \text{ in } f(x).$$
$$= x^2 + 2x + 4 \qquad \text{Simplify.}$$

▶ The transformed function is $g(x) = x^2 + 2x + 4$.

Describe the transformation of $f(x) = x^2$ represented by g. Then graph each function.

19. $g(x) = (x + 4)^2$ **20.** $g(x) = (x - 7)^2 + 2$ **21.** $g(x) = -3(x + 2)^2 - 1$

Write a rule for g.

22. Let the graph of g be a horizontal shrink by a factor of $\frac{2}{3}$, followed by a translation 5 units left and 2 units down of the graph of $f(x) = x^2$.

23. Let the graph of g be a translation 2 units left and 3 units up, followed by a reflection in the y-axis of the graph of $f(x) = x^2 - 2x$.

2.6 Characteristics of Quadratic Functions *(pp. 81–90)*

Graph $f(x) = 2x^2 - 8x + 1$. Label the vertex and axis of symmetry.

Step 1 Identify the coefficients $a = 2$, $b = -8$, and $c = 1$.
Because $a > 0$, the parabola opens up.

Step 2 Find the vertex. First calculate the x-coordinate.

$$x = -\frac{b}{2a} = -\frac{-8}{2(2)} = 2$$

Then find the y-coordinate of the vertex.

$$f(2) = 2(2)^2 - 8(2) + 1 = -7$$

So, the vertex is $(2, -7)$. Plot this point.

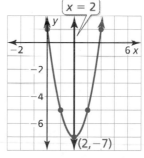

Step 3 Draw the axis of symmetry $x = 2$.

Step 4 Identify the y-intercept c, which is 1. Plot the point $(0, 1)$ and its reflection in the axis of symmetry, $(4, 1)$.

Step 5 Evaluate the function for another value of x, such as $x = 1$.

$$f(1) = 2(1)^2 - 8(1) + 1 = -5$$

Plot the point $(1, -5)$ and its reflection in the axis of symmetry, $(3, -5)$.

Step 6 Draw a parabola through the plotted points.

Graph the function. Label the vertex and axis of symmetry. Find the minimum or maximum value of f. Describe where the function is increasing and decreasing.

24. $f(x) = 3(x - 1)^2 - 4$ **25.** $g(x) = -2x^2 + 16x + 3$ **26.** $h(x) = (x - 3)(x + 7)$

2.7 **Modeling with Quadratic Functions** *(pp. 91–98)*

The graph shows the parabolic path of a stunt motorcyclist jumping off a ramp, where *y* is the height (in feet) and *x* is the horizontal distance traveled (in feet). Write an equation of the parabola. The motorcyclist lands on another ramp 160 feet from the first ramp. What is the height of the second ramp?

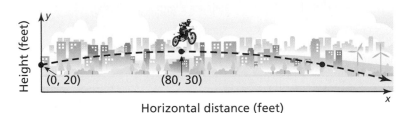

Height (feet)

(0, 20)   (80, 30)

Horizontal distance (feet)

Step 1 First write an equation of the parabola.

From the graph, you can see that the vertex (h, k) is (80, 30) and the parabola passes through the point (0, 20). Use the vertex and the point to solve for *a* in vertex form.

$$y = a(x - h)^2 + k \qquad \text{Vertex form}$$

$$20 = a(0 - 80)^2 + 30 \qquad \text{Substitute for } h, k, x, \text{ and } y.$$

$$-10 = 6400a \qquad \text{Simplify.}$$

$$-\frac{1}{640} = a \qquad \text{Divide each side by 6400.}$$

Because $a = -\dfrac{1}{640}$, $h = 80$, and $k = 30$, the path can be modeled by

$$y = -\frac{1}{640}(x - 80)^2 + 30, \text{ where } 0 \le x \le 160.$$

Step 2 Then find the height of the second ramp.

$$y = -\frac{1}{640}(160 - 80)^2 + 30 \qquad \text{Substitute 160 for } x.$$

$$= 20 \qquad \text{Simplify.}$$

▶ So, the height of the second ramp is 20 feet.

Write an equation of the parabola with the given characteristics.

27. passes through (1, 12) and has vertex (10, −4)

28. passes through (4, 3) and has *x*-intercepts of −1 and 5

29. passes through (−2, 7), (1, 10), and (2, 27)

30. The table shows the heights *y* of a dropped object after *x* seconds. Verify that the data show a quadratic relationship. Write a function that models the data. How long is the object in the air?

Time (seconds), *x*	0	0.5	1	1.5	2	2.5
Height (feet), *y*	150	146	134	114	86	50

Graph the function and its parent function. Then describe the transformation.

1. $f(x) = |x - 1|$

2. $f(x) = (3x)^2$

3. $f(x) = -\frac{1}{2}x - 4$

Match the transformation of $f(x) = x$ with its graph. Then write a rule for g.

4. $g(x) = 2f(x) + 3$

5. $g(x) = 3f(x) - 2$

6. $g(x) = -2f(x) - 3$

A.
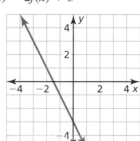

B.
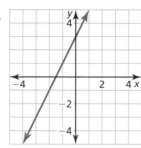

C.
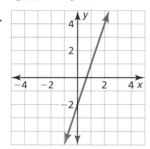

7. Graph $f(x) = 8x^2 - 4x + 3$. Label the vertex and axis of symmetry. Describe where the function is increasing and decreasing.

8. Let the graph of g be a translation 2 units left and 1 unit down, followed by a reflection in the y-axis of the graph of $f(x) = (2x + 1)^2 - 4$. Write a rule for g.

Write a linear function or a quadratic function that models the data.

9.

x	−2	−1	0	1	2
f(x)	1	3	7	11	15

10.

x	2	4	6	8	10
f(x)	0	−13	−34	−63	−100

Solve the system. Check your solution, if possible.

11. $-2x + y + 4z = 5$

$x + 3y - z = 2$

$4x + y - 6z = 11$

12. $y = \frac{1}{2}z$

$x + 2y + 5z = 2$

$3x + 6y - 3z = 9$

13. $x - y + 5z = 3$

$2x + 3y - z = 2$

$-4x - y - 9z = 8$

14. The graph of a quadratic function f has an axis of symmetry $x = 3$ and passes through the point $(0, 6)$. Find another point that lies on the parabola. Then write an equation of the parabola when the minimum value of f is -4.

15. A passenger on a stranded lifeboat shoots a distress flare into the air. The height (in feet) of the flare above the water is given by $f(t) = -16t(t - 8)$, where t is time (in seconds) since the flare was shot. The passenger shoots a second flare, whose path is modeled in the graph. Which flare travels higher? Which remains in the air longer? Justify your answer.

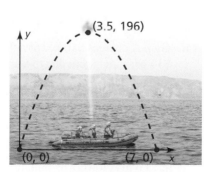

16. A surfboard shop sells 40 surfboards per month when it charges $500 per surfboard. Each time the shop decreases the price by $10, it sells 1 additional surfboard per month. How much should the shop charge per surfboard to maximize the amount of money earned? What is the maximum amount the shop can earn per month? Explain.

1. The function $g(x) = \frac{1}{2}|x - 4| + 4$ is a combination of transformations of $f(x) = |x|$. Which combinations describe the transformation from the graph of f to the graph of g?

   (A) translation 4 units right and vertical shrink by a factor of $\frac{1}{2}$, followed by a translation 4 units up

   (B) translation 4 units right and 4 units up, followed by a vertical shrink by a factor of $\frac{1}{2}$

   (C) vertical shrink by a factor of $\frac{1}{2}$, followed by a translation 4 units up and 4 units right

   (D) translation 4 units right and 8 units up, followed by a vertical shrink by a factor of $\frac{1}{2}$

2. Two balls are thrown in the air. The path of the first ball is represented in the graph. The second ball is released 1.5 feet higher than the first ball and after 3 seconds reaches its maximum height 5 feet lower than the first ball.

   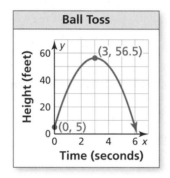

   a. Write an equation for the path of the second ball.

   b. Do the balls hit the ground at the same time? If so, how long are the balls in the air? If not, which ball hits the ground first? Explain your reasoning.

3. The paper clip is made from cylindrical metal wire with a diameter of 1 millimeter. The density of the metal is about 7.8 grams per cubic centimeter. Approximate the mass of the paper clip to the nearest gram. Explain your procedure.

   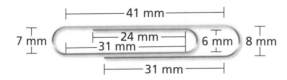

4. Gym A charges $10 per month plus an initiation fee of $100. Gym B charges $30 per month, but due to a special promotion, is not currently charging an initiation fee.

   a. Write an equation for each gym modeling the total cost y for a membership lasting x months.

   b. When is it more economical for a person to choose Gym A over Gym B?

   c. Gym A lowers its initiation fee to $25. Describe the transformation this change represents and how it affects your decision in part (b).

5. Let the graph of g be a translation 3 units right of the graph of f. The points $(-1, 6)$, $(3, 14)$, and $(6, 41)$ lie on the graph of f. Which points lie on the graph of g?

Ⓐ $(2, 6)$ Ⓑ $(2, 11)$ Ⓒ $(6, 14)$

Ⓓ $(6, 19)$ Ⓔ $(9, 41)$ Ⓕ $(9, 46)$

6. Draw a two-dimensional figure and an axis that produce a cylinder with a volume of 48π cubic feet when you rotate the figure around the axis.

7. You make DVDs of three types of shows: comedy, drama, and reality-based. An episode of a comedy lasts 30 minutes, while a drama and a reality-based episode each last 60 minutes. The DVDs can hold 360 minutes of programming.

   a. You completely fill a DVD with seven episodes and include twice as many episodes of a drama as a comedy. Create a system of equations that models the situation.

   b. How many episodes of each type of show are on the DVD in part (a)?

   c. You completely fill a second DVD with only six episodes. Do the two DVDs have a different number of comedies? dramas? reality-based episodes? Explain.

8. The graphs of f and g intersect at $(2, -2)$. Explain how you can use this point to find the solution of the equation $f(x) = g(x)$. Extend the tables to justify your answer.

x	f(x)
−5	−23
−4	−20
−3	−17
−2	−14

x	g(x)
−2	−18
−1	−14
0	−10
1	−6

9. You are building a rectangular deck against a house. You want the deck to have an area of 200 square feet. Draw a diagram of the deck including the location of the house that minimizes the amount of railing that you need to build for the three sides of the deck not against the house. Include a 4-foot-wide opening in the railing for stairs. How many feet of railing do you need?

10. Order the cross sections of the planes intersecting the rectangular prism from least area to greatest area. The length and width of the prism are equal.

   A.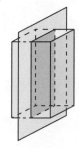

   B.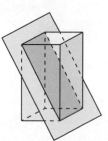

   C.

3 Polynomial Functions

SEE the Big Idea

Quonset Hut *(p. 174)*

Zebra Mussels *(p. 159)*

Ruins of Caesarea *(p. 151)*

Electric Vehicles *(p. 115)*

Basketball *(p. 134)*

Maintaining Mathematical Proficiency

Simplifying Algebraic Expressions (Grade 7)

Example 1 Simplify the expression $9x + 4x$.

$$9x + 4x = (9 + 4)x \qquad \text{Distributive Property}$$
$$= 13x \qquad \text{Add coefficients.}$$

Example 2 Simplify the expression $2(x + 4) + 3(6 - x)$.

$$2(x + 4) + 3(6 - x) = 2(x) + 2(4) + 3(6) + 3(-x) \qquad \text{Distributive Property}$$
$$= 2x + 8 + 18 - 3x \qquad \text{Multiply.}$$
$$= 2x - 3x + 8 + 18 \qquad \text{Group like terms.}$$
$$= -x + 26 \qquad \text{Combine like terms.}$$

Simplify the expression.

1. $6x - 4x$

2. $12m - m - 7m + 3$

3. $3(y + 2) - 4y$

4. $9x - 4(2x - 1)$

5. $-(z + 2) - 2(1 - z)$

6. $-x^2 + 5x + x^2$

Solving Quadratic Equations by Factoring (Math II)

Example 3 Solve $x^2 + 7x = 18$.

$$x^2 + 7x = 18 \qquad \text{Write equation.}$$
$$x^2 + 7x - 18 = 0 \qquad \text{Subtract 18 from each side.}$$
$$(x + 9)(x - 2) = 0 \qquad \text{Factor left side.}$$
$$x + 9 = 0 \quad or \quad x - 2 = 0 \qquad \text{Zero-Product Property}$$
$$x = -9 \quad or \quad x = 2 \qquad \text{Solve for } x.$$

▶ The solutions are $x = -9$ and $x = 2$.

Solve the equation by factoring.

7. $x^2 + 3x + 2 = 0$

8. $x^2 - 6x + 8 = 0$

9. $x^2 + 10x = -25$

10. $2x^2 - 84 = 2x$

11. $4x^2 = 12x - 9$

12. $8x - 3 = -3x^2$

13. ABSTRACT REASONING Explain how you can find the solutions of an equation of the form $(x - a)(x - b)(x - c) = 0$.

Mathematical Practices

Mathematically proficient students use technological tools to explore concepts.

Using Technology to Explore Concepts

Core Concept

Continuous Functions

A function is *continuous* when its graph has no breaks, holes, or gaps.

Graph of a continuous function

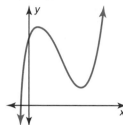

Graph of a function that is not continuous

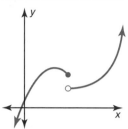

EXAMPLE 1   Determining Whether Functions Are Continuous

Use a graphing calculator to compare the two functions. What can you conclude? Which function is not continuous?

$$f(x) = x^2 \qquad g(x) = \frac{x^3 - x^2}{x - 1}$$

SOLUTION

The graphs appear to be identical, but g is not defined when $x = 1$. There is a *hole* in the graph of g at the point $(1, 1)$. Using the *table* feature of a graphing calculator, you obtain an error for $g(x)$ when $x = 1$. So, g is not continuous.

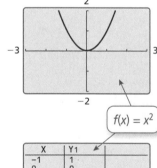

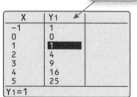

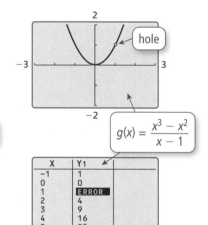

Monitoring Progress

Use a graphing calculator to determine whether the function is continuous. Explain your reasoning.

1. $f(x) = \dfrac{x^2 - x}{x}$

2. $f(x) = x^3 - 3$

3. $f(x) = \sqrt{x^2 + 1}$

4. $f(x) = |x + 2|$

5. $f(x) = \dfrac{1}{x}$

6. $f(x) = \dfrac{1}{\sqrt{x^2 - 1}}$

7. $f(x) = x$

8. $f(x) = 2x - 3$

9. $f(x) = \dfrac{x}{x}$

3.1 Graphing Polynomial Functions

Essential Question What are some common characteristics of the graphs of cubic and quartic polynomial functions?

A *polynomial function* of the form

$$f(x) = a_n x^n + a_{n-1}x^{n-1} + \cdots + a_1 x + a_0$$

where $a_n \neq 0$, is *cubic* when $n = 3$ and *quartic* when $n = 4$.

EXPLORATION 1 Identifying Graphs of Polynomial Functions

Work with a partner. Match each polynomial function with its graph. Explain your reasoning. Use a graphing calculator to verify your answers.

a. $f(x) = x^3 - x$ **b.** $f(x) = -x^3 + x$ **c.** $f(x) = -x^4 + 1$

d. $f(x) = x^4$ **e.** $f(x) = x^3$ **f.** $f(x) = x^4 - x^2$

A.
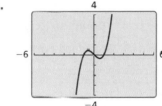

B.
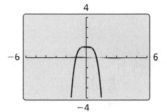

C.
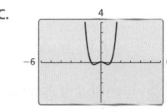

D.
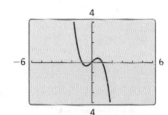

E.
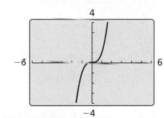

F.
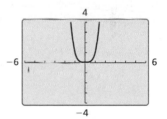

EXPLORATION 2 Identifying x-Intercepts of Polynomial Graphs

Work with a partner. Each of the polynomial graphs in Exploration 1 has x-intercept(s) of -1, 0, or 1. Identify the x-intercept(s) of each graph. Explain how you can verify your answers.

Communicate Your Answer

CONSTRUCTING VIABLE ARGUMENTS

To be proficient in math, you need to justify your conclusions and communicate them to others.

3. What are some common characteristics of the graphs of cubic and quartic polynomial functions?

4. Determine whether each statement is *true* or *false*. Justify your answer.

    a. When the graph of a cubic polynomial function rises to the left, it falls to the right.

    b. When the graph of a quartic polynomial function falls to the left, it rises to the right.

What You Will Learn

▶ Identify polynomial functions.

▶ Graph polynomial functions using tables and end behavior.

Polynomial Functions

Recall that a monomial is a number, a variable, or the product of a number and one or more variables with whole number exponents. A **polynomial** is a monomial or a sum of monomials. A **polynomial function** is a function of the form

$$f(x) = a_n x^n + a_{n-1} x^{n-1} + \cdots + a_1 x + a_0$$

where $a_n \neq 0$, the exponents are all whole numbers, and the coefficients are all real numbers. For this function, a_n is the leading coefficient, n is the degree, and a_0 is the constant term. A polynomial function is in *standard form* when its terms are written in descending order of exponents from left to right.

You are already familiar with some types of polynomial functions, such as linear and quadratic. Here is a summary of common types of polynomial functions.

	Common Polynomial Functions		
Degree	**Type**	**Standard Form**	**Example**
0	Constant	$f(x) = a_0$	$f(x) = -14$
1	Linear	$f(x) = a_1 x + a_0$	$f(x) = 5x - 7$
2	Quadratic	$f(x) = a_2 x^2 + a_1 x + a_0$	$f(x) = 2x^2 + x - 9$
3	Cubic	$f(x) = a_3 x^3 + a_2 x^2 + a_1 x + a_0$	$f(x) = x^3 - x^2 + 3x$
4	Quartic	$f(x) = a_4 x^4 + a_3 x^3 + a_2 x^2 + a_1 x + a_0$	$f(x) = x^4 + 2x - 1$

EXAMPLE 1 **Identifying Polynomial Functions**

Decide whether each function is a polynomial function. If so, write it in standard form and state its degree, type, and leading coefficient.

a. $f(x) = -2x^3 + 5x + 8$ **b.** $g(x) = -0.8x^3 + \sqrt{2}x^4 - 12$

c. $h(x) = -x^2 + 7x^{-1} + 4x$ **d.** $k(x) = x^2 + 3^x$

SOLUTION

a. The function is a polynomial function that is already written in standard form. It has degree 3 (cubic) and a leading coefficient of -2.

b. The function is a polynomial function written as $g(x) = \sqrt{2}x^4 - 0.8x^3 - 12$ in standard form. It has degree 4 (quartic) and a leading coefficient of $\sqrt{2}$.

c. The function is not a polynomial function because the term $7x^{-1}$ has an exponent that is not a whole number.

d. The function is not a polynomial function because the term 3^x does not have a variable base and an exponent that is a whole number.

Monitoring Progress Help in English and Spanish at *BigIdeasMath.com*

Decide whether the function is a polynomial function. If so, write it in standard form and state its degree, type, and leading coefficient.

  1. $f(x) = 7 - 1.6x^2 - 5x$ **2.** $p(x) = x + 2x^{-2} + 9.5$ **3.** $q(x) = x^3 - 6x + 3x^4$

EXAMPLE 2   **Evaluating a Polynomial Function**

Evaluate $f(x) = 2x^4 - 8x^2 + 5x - 7$ when $x = 3$.

SOLUTION

$$f(x) = 2x^4 - 8x^2 + 5x - 7 \qquad \text{Write original equation.}$$
$$f(3) = 2(3)^4 - 8(3)^2 + 5(3) - 7 \qquad \text{Substitute 3 for } x.$$
$$= 162 - 72 + 15 - 7 \qquad \text{Evaluate powers and multiply.}$$
$$= 98 \qquad \text{Simplify.}$$

The **end behavior** of a function's graph is the behavior of the graph as x approaches positive infinity $(+\infty)$ or negative infinity $(-\infty)$. For the graph of a polynomial function, the end behavior is determined by the function's degree and the sign of its leading coefficient.

Core Concept

READING

The expression "$x \to +\infty$" is read as "x approaches positive infinity."

End Behavior of Polynomial Functions

Degree: odd
Leading coefficient: positive

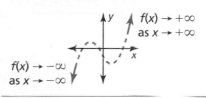

Degree: odd
Leading coefficient: negative

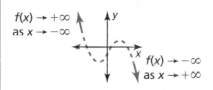

Degree: even
Leading coefficient: positive

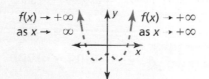

Degree: even
Leading coefficient: negative

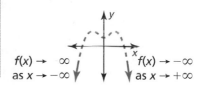

EXAMPLE 3   **Describing End Behavior**

Describe the end behavior of the graph of $f(x) = -0.5x^4 + 2.5x^2 + x - 1$.

Check

SOLUTION

The function has degree 4 and leading coefficient -0.5. Because the degree is even and the leading coefficient is negative, $f(x) \to -\infty$ as $x \to -\infty$ and $f(x) \to -\infty$ as $x \to +\infty$. Check this by graphing the function on a graphing calculator, as shown.

Monitoring Progress   🔊 Help in English and Spanish at *BigIdeasMath.com*

Evaluate the function for the given value of x.

4. $f(x) = -x^3 + 3x^2 + 9;\ x = 4$

5. $f(x) = 3x^5 - x^4 - 6x + 10;\ x = -2$

6. Describe the end behavior of the graph of $f(x) = 0.25x^3 - x^2 - 1$.

Graphing Polynomial Functions

To graph a polynomial function, first plot points to determine the shape of the graph's middle portion. Then connect the points with a smooth continuous curve and use what you know about end behavior to sketch the graph.

EXAMPLE 4   Graphing Polynomial Functions

Graph (a) $f(x) = -x^3 + x^2 + 3x - 3$ and (b) $f(x) = x^4 - x^3 - 4x^2 + 4$.

SOLUTION

a. To graph the function, make a table of values and plot the corresponding points. Connect the points with a smooth curve and check the end behavior.

x	−2	−1	0	1	2
f(x)	3	−4	−3	0	−1

The degree is odd and the leading coefficient is negative. So, $f(x) \to +\infty$ as $x \to -\infty$ and $f(x) \to -\infty$ as $x \to +\infty$.

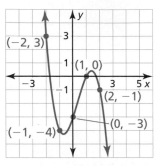

b. To graph the function, make a table of values and plot the corresponding points. Connect the points with a smooth curve and check the end behavior.

x	−2	−1	0	1	2
f(x)	12	2	4	0	−4

The degree is even and the leading coefficient is positive. So, $f(x) \to +\infty$ as $x \to -\infty$ and $f(x) \to +\infty$ as $x \to +\infty$.

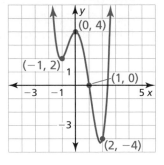

EXAMPLE 5   Sketching a Graph

Sketch a graph of the polynomial function f having these characteristics.

- f is increasing when $x < 0$ and $x > 4$.
- f is decreasing when $0 < x < 4$.
- $f(x) > 0$ when $-2 < x < 3$ and $x > 5$.
- $f(x) < 0$ when $x < -2$ and $3 < x < 5$.

Use the graph to describe the degree and leading coefficient of f.

SOLUTION

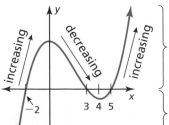

The graph is above the x-axis when $f(x) > 0$.

The graph is below the x-axis when $f(x) < 0$.

▶   From the graph, $f(x) \to -\infty$ as $x \to -\infty$ and $f(x) \to +\infty$ as $x \to +\infty$. So, the degree is odd and the leading coefficient is positive.

EXAMPLE 6   **Solving a Real-Life Problem**

The estimated number V (in thousands) of electric vehicles in use in the United States can be modeled by the polynomial function

$$V(t) = 0.151280t^3 - 3.28234t^2 + 23.7565t - 2.041$$

where t represents the year, with $t = 1$ corresponding to 2001.

a. Use a graphing calculator to graph the function for the interval $1 \le t \le 10$. Describe the behavior of the graph on this interval.

b. What was the average rate of change in the number of electric vehicles in use from 2001 to 2010?

c. Do you think this model can be used for years before 2001 or after 2010? Explain your reasoning.

SOLUTION

a. Using a graphing calculator and a viewing window of $1 \le x \le 10$ and $0 \le y \le 65$, you obtain the graph shown.

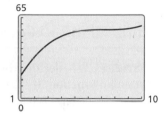

> From 2001 to 2004, the numbers of electric vehicles in use increased. Around 2005, the growth in the numbers in use slowed and started to level off. Then the numbers in use started to increase again in 2009 and 2010.

b. The years 2001 and 2010 correspond to $t = 1$ and $t = 10$.

Average rate of change over $1 \le t \le 10$:

$$\frac{V(10) - V(1)}{10 - 1} = \frac{58.57 - 18.58444}{9} \approx 4.443$$

> The average rate of change from 2001 to 2010 is about 4.4 thousand electric vehicles per year.

c. Because the degree is odd and the leading coefficient is positive, $V(t) \to -\infty$ as $t \to -\infty$ and $V(t) \to +\infty$ as $t \to +\infty$. The end behavior indicates that the model has unlimited growth as t increases. While the model may be valid for a few years after 2010, in the long run, unlimited growth is not reasonable. Notice in 2000 that $V(0) = -2.041$. Because negative values of $V(t)$ do not make sense given the context (electric vehicles in use), the model should not be used for years before 2001.

Monitoring Progress Help in English and Spanish at *BigIdeasMath.com*

Graph the polynomial function.

7. $f(x) = x^4 + x^2 - 3$

8. $f(x) = 4 - x^3$

9. $f(x) = x^3 - x^2 + x - 1$

10. Sketch a graph of the polynomial function f having these characteristics.

- f is decreasing when $x < -1.5$ and $x > 2.5$; f is increasing when $-1.5 < x < 2.5$.
- $f(x) > 0$ when $x < -3$ and $1 < x < 4$; $f(x) < 0$ when $-3 < x < 1$ and $x > 4$.

Use the graph to describe the degree and leading coefficient of f.

11. **WHAT IF?** Repeat Example 6 using the alternative model for electric vehicles of

$$V(t) = -0.0290900t^4 + 0.791260t^3 - 7.96583t^2 + 36.5561t - 12.025.$$

Vocabulary and Core Concept Check

1. **WRITING** Explain what is meant by the end behavior of a polynomial function.

2. **WHICH ONE DOESN'T BELONG?** Which function does *not* belong with the other three? Explain your reasoning.

$$f(x) = 7x^5 + 3x^2 - 2x$$

$$g(x) = 3x^3 - 2x^8 + \frac{3}{4}$$

$$h(x) = -3x^4 + 5x^{-1} - 3x^2$$

$$k(x) = \sqrt{3}x + 8x^4 + 2x + 1$$

Monitoring Progress and Modeling with Mathematics

In Exercises 3–8, decide whether the function is a polynomial function. If so, write it in standard form and state its degree, type, and leading coefficient. *(See Example 1.)*

3. $f(x) = -3x + 5x^3 - 6x^2 + 2$

4. $p(x) = \frac{1}{2}x^2 + 3x - 4x^3 + 6x^4 - 1$

5. $f(x) = 9x^4 + 8x^3 - 6x^{-2} + 2x$

6. $g(x) = \sqrt{3} - 12x + 13x^2$

7. $h(x) = \frac{5}{3}x^2 - \sqrt{7}x^4 + 8x^3 - \frac{1}{2} + x$

8. $h(x) = 3x^4 + 2x - \frac{5}{x} + 9x^3 - 7$

ERROR ANALYSIS In Exercises 9 and 10, describe and correct the error in analyzing the function.

9. $f(x) = 8x^3 - 7x^4 - 9x - 3x^2 + 11$

> *f* is a polynomial function.
> The degree is 3 and *f* is a cubic function.
> The leading coefficient is 8.

10. $f(x) = 2x^4 + 4x - 9\sqrt{x} + 3x^2 - 8$

> *f* is a polynomial function.
> The degree is 4 and *f* is a quartic function.
> The leading coefficient is 2.

In Exercises 11–16, evaluate the function for the given value of *x*. *(See Example 2.)*

11. $h(x) = -3x^4 + 2x^3 - 12x - 6; x = -2$

12. $f(x) = 7x^4 - 10x^2 + 14x - 26; x = -7$

13. $g(x) = x^6 - 64x^4 + x^2 - 7x - 51; x = 8$

14. $g(x) = -x^3 + 3x^2 + 5x + 1; x = -12$

15. $p(x) = 2x^3 + 4x^2 + 6x + 7; x = \frac{1}{2}$

16. $h(x) = 5x^3 - 3x^2 + 2x + 4; x = -\frac{1}{3}$

In Exercises 17–20, describe the end behavior of the graph of the function. *(See Example 3.)*

17. $h(x) = -5x^4 + 7x^3 - 6x^2 + 9x + 2$

18. $g(x) = 7x^7 + 12x^5 - 6x^3 - 2x - 18$

19. $f(x) = -2x^4 + 12x^8 + 17 + 15x^2$

20. $f(x) = 11 - 18x^2 - 5x^5 - 12x^4 - 2x$

In Exercises 21 and 22, describe the degree and leading coefficient of the polynomial function using the graph.

21.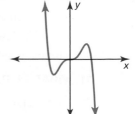

22.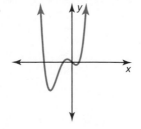

23. USING STRUCTURE Determine whether the function is a polynomial function. If so, write it in standard form and state its degree, type, and leading coefficient.

$$f(x) = 5x^3x + \tfrac{5}{2}x^3 - 9x^4 + \sqrt{2}x^2 + 4x - 1 - x^{-5}x^5 - 4$$

24. WRITING Let $f(x) = 13$. State the degree, type, and leading coefficient. Describe the end behavior of the function. Explain your reasoning.

In Exercises 25–32, graph the polynomial function. (*See Example 4.*)

25. $p(x) = 3 - x^4$ **26.** $g(x) = x^3 + x + 3$

27. $f(x) = 4x - 9 - x^3$ **28.** $p(x) = x^5 - 3x^3 + 2$

29. $h(x) = x^4 - 2x^3 + 3x$

30. $h(x) - 5 + 3x^2 - x^4$

31. $g(x) = x^5 - 3x^4 + 2x - 4$

32. $p(x) = x^6 - 2x^5 - 2x^3 + x + 5$

ANALYZING RELATIONSHIPS In Exercises 33–36, describe the x-values for which (a) f is increasing or decreasing, (b) $f(x) > 0$, and (c) $f(x) < 0$.

33.

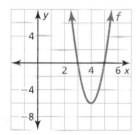

34.

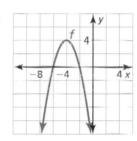

35.

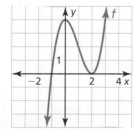

36.

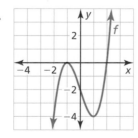

In Exercises 37–40, sketch a graph of the polynomial function f having the given characteristics. Use the graph to describe the degree and leading coefficient of the function f. (*See Example 5.*)

37. • f is increasing when $x > 0.5$; f is decreasing when $x < 0.5$.

     • $f(x) > 0$ when $x < -2$ and $x > 3$; $f(x) < 0$ when $-2 < x < 3$.

38. • f is increasing when $-2 < x < 3$; f is decreasing when $x < -2$ and $x > 3$.

     • $f(x) > 0$ when $x < -4$ and $1 < x < 5$; $f(x) < 0$ when $-4 < x < 1$ and $x > 5$.

39. • f is increasing when $-2 < x < 0$ and $x > 2$; f is decreasing when $x < -2$ and $0 < x < 2$.

     • $f(x) > 0$ when $x < -3$, $-1 < x < 1$, and $x > 3$; $f(x) < 0$ when $-3 < x < -1$ and $1 < x < 3$.

40. • f is increasing when $x < -1$ and $x > 1$; f is decreasing when $-1 < x < 1$.

     • $f(x) > 0$ when $-1.5 < x < 0$ and $x > 1.5$; $f(x) < 0$ when $x < -1.5$ and $0 < x < 1.5$.

41. MODELING WITH MATHEMATICS From 1980 to 2007 the number of drive-in theaters in the United States can be modeled by the function

$$d(t) = -0.141t^3 + 9.64t^2 - 232.5t + 2421$$

where $d(t)$ is the number of open theaters and t is the number of years after 1980. (*See Example 6.*)

a. Use a graphing calculator to graph the function for the interval $0 \le t < 27$. Describe the behavior of the graph on this interval.

b. What is the average rate of change in the number of drive-in movie theaters from 1980 to 1995 and from 1995 to 2007? Interpret the average rates of change.

c. Do you think this model can be used for years before 1980 or after 2007? Explain.

42. PROBLEM SOLVING The weight of an ideal round-cut diamond can be modeled by

$$w = 0.00583d^3 - 0.0125d^2 + 0.022d - 0.01$$

where w is the weight of the diamond (in carats) and d is the diameter (in millimeters). According to the model, what is the weight of a diamond with a diameter of 12 millimeters?

43. ABSTRACT REASONING Suppose $f(x) \to \infty$ as $x \to -\infty$ and $f(x) \to -\infty$ as $x \to \infty$. Describe the end behavior of $g(x) = -f(x)$. Justify your answer.

44. THOUGHT PROVOKING Write an even degree polynomial function such that the end behavior of f is given by $f(x) \to -\infty$ as $x \to -\infty$ and $f(x) \to -\infty$ as $x \to \infty$. Justify your answer by drawing the graph of your function.

45. USING TOOLS In Section 1.2 Exercise 12, the function $V = 4r^3(\pi + 4)$ represents the volume V of the tank. Use a graphing calculator to graph the function. Estimate the percent change in volume when r increases from 1 foot to 1 foot 1 inch. Is the percent change greater than you expected? Explain.

46. MAKING AN ARGUMENT Your friend uses the table to speculate that the function f is an even degree polynomial and the function g is an odd degree polynomial. Is your friend correct? Explain your reasoning.

x	f(x)	g(x)
−8	4113	497
−2	21	5
0	1	1
2	13	−3
8	4081	−495

47. DRAWING CONCLUSIONS The graph of a function is symmetric with respect to the y-axis if for each point (a, b) on the graph, $(-a, b)$ is also a point on the graph. The graph of a function is symmetric with respect to the origin if for each point (a, b) on the graph, $(-a, -b)$ is also a point on the graph.

 a. Use a graphing calculator to graph the function $y = x^n$ when $n = 1, 2, 3, 4, 5,$ and 6. In each case, identify the symmetry of the graph.

 b. Predict what symmetry the graphs of $y = x^{10}$ and $y = x^{11}$ each have. Explain your reasoning and then confirm your predictions by graphing.

48. HOW DO YOU SEE IT? The graph of a polynomial function is shown.

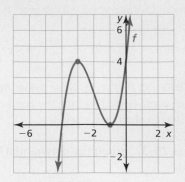

 a. Describe the degree and leading coefficient of f.

 b. Describe the intervals where the function is increasing and decreasing.

 c. What is the constant term of the polynomial function?

49. REASONING A cubic polynomial function f has a leading coefficient of 2 and a constant term of -5. When $f(1) = 0$ and $f(2) = 3$, what is $f(-5)$? Explain your reasoning.

50. CRITICAL THINKING The weight y (in pounds) of a rainbow trout can be modeled by $y = 0.000304x^3$, where x is the length (in inches) of the trout.

 a. Write a function that relates the weight y and length x of a rainbow trout when y is measured in kilograms and x is measured in centimeters. Use the fact that 1 kilogram ≈ 2.20 pounds and 1 centimeter ≈ 0.394 inch.

 b. Graph the original function and the function from part (a) in the same coordinate plane. What type of transformation can you apply to the graph of $y = 0.000304x^3$ to produce the graph from part (a)?

Maintaining Mathematical Proficiency
Reviewing what you learned in previous grades and lessons

Simplify the expression. *(Skills Review Handbook)*

51. $xy + x^2 + 2xy + y^2 - 3x^2$

52. $2h^3g + 3hg^3 + 7h^2g^2 + 5h^3g + 2hg^3$

53. $-wk + 3kz - 2kw + 9zk - kw$

54. $a^2(m - 7a^3) - m(a^2 - 10)$

55. $3x(xy - 4) + 3(4xy + 3) - xy(x^2y - 1)$

56. $cv(9 - 3c) + 2c(v - 4c) + 6c$

3.2 Adding, Subtracting, and Multiplying Polynomials

Essential Question How can you cube a binomial?

EXPLORATION 1   Cubing Binomials

Work with a partner. Find each product. Show your steps.

a. $(x + 1)^3 = (x + 1)(x + 1)^2$ Rewrite as a product of first and second powers.

     $= (x + 1)$ ▭   Multiply second power.

     $=$ ▭   Multiply binomial and trinomial.

     $=$ ▭   Write in standard form, $ax^3 + bx^2 + cx + d$.

b. $(a + b)^3 = (a + b)(a + b)^2$ Rewrite as a product of first and second powers.

     $= (a + b)$ ▭   Multiply second power.

     $=$ ▭   Multiply binomial and trinomial.

     $=$ ▭   Write in standard form.

c. $(x - 1)^3 = (x - 1)(x - 1)^2$ Rewrite as a product of first and second powers.

     $= (x - 1)$ ▭   Multiply second power.

     $=$ ▭   Multiply binomial and trinomial.

     $=$ ▭   Write in standard form.

d. $(a - b)^3 = (a - b)(a - b)^2$ Rewrite as a product of first and second powers.

     $= (a - b)$ ▭   Multiply second power.

     $=$ ▭   Multiply binomial and trinomial.

     $=$ ▭   Write in standard form.

LOOKING FOR STRUCTURE

To be proficient in math, you need to look closely to discern a pattern or structure.

EXPLORATION 2   Generalizing Patterns for Cubing a Binomial

Work with a partner.

a. Use the results of Exploration 1 to describe a pattern for the coefficients of the terms when you expand the cube of a binomial. How is your pattern related to Pascal's Triangle, shown at the right?

b. Use the results of Exploration 1 to describe a pattern for the exponents of the terms in the expansion of a cube of a binomial.

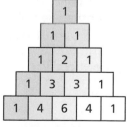

c. Explain how you can use the patterns you described in parts (a) and (b) to find the product $(2x - 3)^3$. Then find this product.

Communicate Your Answer

3. How can you cube a binomial?

4. Find each product.

     a. $(x + 2)^3$ **b.** $(x - 2)^3$ **c.** $(2x - 3)^3$

     d. $(x - 3)^3$ **e.** $(-2x + 3)^3$ **f.** $(3x - 5)^3$

3.2 Lesson

Core Vocabulary

Pascal's Triangle, *p. 123*
Binomial Theorem, *p. 124*

Previous
like terms
identity

What You Will Learn

▶ Add and subtract polynomials.
▶ Multiply polynomials.
▶ Use Pascal's Triangle and the Binomial Theorem to expand binomials.

Adding and Subtracting Polynomials

Recall that the set of integers is *closed* under addition and subtraction because every sum or difference results in an integer. To add or subtract polynomials, you add or subtract the coefficients of like terms. Because adding or subtracting polynomials results in a polynomial, the set of polynomials is closed under addition and subtraction.

EXAMPLE 1   Adding Polynomials Vertically and Horizontally

a. Add $3x^3 + 2x^2 - x - 7$ and $x^3 - 10x^2 + 8$ in a vertical format.

b. Add $9y^3 + 3y^2 - 2y + 1$ and $-5y^2 + y - 4$ in a horizontal format.

SOLUTION

a.
$$
\begin{array}{r}
3x^3 + 2x^2 - x - 7 \\
+ \quad x^3 - 10x^2 \quad\ + 8 \\
\hline
4x^3 - 8x^2 - x + 1
\end{array}
$$

b. $(9y^3 + 3y^2 - 2y + 1) + (-5y^2 + y - 4) = 9y^3 + 3y^2 - 5y^2 - 2y + y + 1 - 4$
$$= 9y^3 - 2y^2 - y - 3$$

To subtract one polynomial from another, add the opposite. To do this, change the sign of each term of the subtracted polynomial and then add the resulting like terms.

COMMON ERROR

A common mistake is to forget to change signs correctly when subtracting one polynomial from another. Be sure to add the opposite of *every* term of the subtracted polynomial.

EXAMPLE 2   Subtracting Polynomials Vertically and Horizontally

a. Subtract $2x^3 + 6x^2 - x + 1$ from $8x^3 - 3x^2 - 2x + 9$ in a vertical format.

b. Subtract $3z^2 + z - 4$ from $2z^2 + 3z$ in a horizontal format.

SOLUTION

a. Align like terms, then add the opposite of the subtracted polynomial.
$$
\begin{array}{r}
8x^3 - 3x^2 - 2x + 9 \\
- (2x^3 + 6x^2 - \ x + 1)
\end{array}
\quad\Longrightarrow\quad
\begin{array}{r}
8x^3 - 3x^2 - 2x + 9 \\
+ \quad -2x^3 - 6x^2 + \ x - 1 \\
\hline
6x^3 - 9x^2 - \ x + 8
\end{array}
$$

b. Write the opposite of the subtracted polynomial, then add like terms.
$$(2z^2 + 3z) - (3z^2 + z - 4) = 2z^2 + 3z - 3z^2 - z + 4$$
$$= -z^2 + 2z + 4$$

Monitoring Progress Help in English and Spanish at *BigIdeasMath.com*

Find the sum or difference.

1. $(2x^2 - 6x + 5) + (7x^2 - x - 9)$

2. $(3t^3 + 8t^2 - t - 4) - (5t^3 - t^2 + 17)$

Multiplying Polynomials

To multiply two polynomials, you multiply each term of the first polynomial by each term of the second polynomial. As with addition and subtraction, the set of polynomials is closed under multiplication.

EXAMPLE 3   Multiplying Polynomials Vertically and Horizontally

a. Multiply $-x^2 + 2x + 4$ and $x - 3$ in a vertical format.

b. Multiply $y + 5$ and $3y^2 - 2y + 2$ in a horizontal format.

SOLUTION

a.

$$
\begin{array}{r}
-x^2 + 2x + 4 \\
\times \quad\quad\quad x - 3 \\
\hline
3x^2 - 6x - 12 \\
-x^3 + 2x^2 + 4x \quad\quad\quad \\
\hline
-x^3 + 5x^2 - 2x - 12
\end{array}
$$

       Multiply $-x^2 + 2x + 4$ by -3.

       Multiply $-x^2 + 2x + 4$ by x.

       Combine like terms.

b.

$$
\begin{aligned}
(y + 5)(3y^2 - 2y + 2) &= (y + 5)3y^2 - (y + 5)2y + (y + 5)2 \\
&= 3y^3 + 15y^2 - 2y^2 - 10y + 2y + 10 \\
&= 3y^3 + 13y^2 - 8y + 10
\end{aligned}
$$

REMEMBER

Product of Powers Property

$a^m \cdot a^n = a^{m+n}$

a is a real number and m and n are integers.

EXAMPLE 4   Multiplying Three Binomials

Multiply $x - 1$, $x + 4$, and $x + 5$ in a horizontal format.

SOLUTION

$$
\begin{aligned}
(x - 1)(x + 4)(x + 5) &= (x^2 + 3x - 4)(x + 5) \\
&= (x^2 + 3x - 4)x + (x^2 + 3x - 4)5 \\
&= x^3 + 3x^2 - 4x + 5x^2 + 15x - 20 \\
&= x^3 + 8x^2 + 11x - 20
\end{aligned}
$$

Some binomial products occur so frequently that it is worth memorizing their patterns. You can verify these polynomial identities by multiplying.

COMMON ERROR

In general,
$$(a \pm b)^2 \neq a^2 \pm b^2$$
and
$$(a \pm b)^3 \neq a^3 \pm b^3.$$

Core Concept

Special Product Patterns

Sum and Difference	**Example**
$(a + b)(a - b) = a^2 - b^2$	$(x + 3)(x - 3) = x^2 - 9$

Square of a Binomial	**Example**
$(a + b)^2 = a^2 + 2ab + b^2$	$(y + 4)^2 = y^2 + 8y + 16$
$(a - b)^2 = a^2 - 2ab + b^2$	$(2t - 5)^2 = 4t^2 - 20t + 25$

Cube of a Binomial	**Example**
$(a + b)^3 = a^3 + 3a^2b + 3ab^2 + b^3$	$(z + 3)^3 = z^3 + 9z^2 + 27z + 27$
$(a - b)^3 = a^3 - 3a^2b + 3ab^2 - b^3$	$(m - 2)^3 = m^3 - 6m^2 + 12m - 8$

EXAMPLE 5   **Proving a Polynomial Identity**

a. Prove the polynomial identity for the cube of a binomial representing a sum:
$(a + b)^3 = a^3 + 3a^2b + 3ab^2 + b^3$.

b. Use the cube of a binomial in part (a) to calculate 11^3.

SOLUTION

a. Expand and simplify the expression on the left side of the equation.

$$(a + b)^3 = (a + b)(a + b)(a + b)$$
$$= (a^2 + 2ab + b^2)(a + b)$$
$$= (a^2 + 2ab + b^2)a + (a^2 + 2ab + b^2)b$$
$$= a^3 + a^2b + 2a^2b + 2ab^2 + ab^2 + b^3$$
$$= a^3 + 3a^2b + 3ab^2 + b^3 \checkmark$$

▶ The simplified left side equals the right side of the original identity. So, the identity $(a + b)^3 = a^3 + 3a^2b + 3ab^2 + b^3$ is true.

b. To calculate 11^3 using the cube of a binomial, note that $11 = 10 + 1$.

$11^3 = (10 + 1)^3$	Write 11 as $10 + 1$.
$= 10^3 + 3(10)^2(1) + 3(10)(1)^2 + 1^3$	Cube of a binomial
$= 1000 + 300 + 30 + 1$	Expand.
$= 1331$	Simplify.

EXAMPLE 6   **Using Special Product Patterns**

Find each product.

a. $(4n + 5)(4n - 5)$ **b.** $(9y - 2)^2$ **c.** $(ab + 4)^3$

SOLUTION

a. $(4n + 5)(4n - 5) = (4n)^2 - 5^2$	Sum and difference
$= 16n^2 - 25$	Simplify.
b. $(9y - 2)^2 = (9y)^2 - 2(9y)(2) + 2^2$	Square of a binomial
$= 81y^2 - 36y + 4$	Simplify.
c. $(ab + 4)^3 = (ab)^3 + 3(ab)^2(4) + 3(ab)(4)^2 + 4^3$	Cube of a binomial
$= a^3b^3 + 12a^2b^2 + 48ab + 64$	Simplify.

REMEMBER

Power of a Product Property

$(ab)^m = a^m b^m$

a and *b* are real numbers and *m* is an integer.

Monitoring Progress Help in English and Spanish at *BigIdeasMath.com*

Find the product.

3. $(4x^2 + x - 5)(2x + 1)$ **4.** $(y - 2)(5y^2 + 3y - 1)$

5. $(m - 2)(m - 1)(m + 3)$ **6.** $(3t - 2)(3t + 2)$

7. $(5a + 2)^2$ **8.** $(xy - 3)^3$

9. (a) Prove the polynomial identity for the cube of a binomial representing a difference: $(a - b)^3 = a^3 - 3a^2b + 3ab^2 - b^3$.

(b) Use the cube of a binomial in part (a) to calculate 9^3.

Pascal's Triangle and the Binomial Theorem

Consider the expansion of the binomial $(a + b)^n$ for whole number values of n. When you arrange the coefficients of the variables in the expansion of $(a + b)^n$, you will see a special pattern called **Pascal's Triangle**. Pascal's Triangle is named after French mathematician Blaise Pascal (1623–1662).

Core Concept

Pascal's Triangle

In Pascal's Triangle, the first and last numbers in each row are 1. Every number other than 1 is the sum of the closest two numbers in the row directly above it. The numbers in Pascal's Triangle are the same numbers that are the coefficients of binomial expansions, as shown in the first six rows.

	n	$(a + b)^n$	Binomial Expansion	Pascal's Triangle
0th row	0	$(a + b)^0 =$	1	1
1st row	1	$(a + b)^1 =$	$1a + 1b$	1　1
2nd row	2	$(a + b)^2 =$	$1a^2 + 2ab + 1b^2$	1　2　1
3rd row	3	$(a + b)^3 =$	$1a^3 + 3a^2b + 3ab^2 + 1b^3$	1　3　3　1
4th row	4	$(a + b)^4 = 1a^4 + 4a^3b + 6a^2b^2 + 4ab^3 + 1b^4$		1　4　6　4　1
5th row	5	$(a + b)^5 = 1a^5 + 5a^4b + 10a^3b^2 + 10a^2b^3 + 5ab^4 + 1b^5$		1　5　10　10　5　1

In general, the nth row in Pascal's Triangle gives the coefficients of $(a + b)^n$. Here are some other observations about the expansion of $(a + b)^n$.

1. An expansion has $n + 1$ terms.

2. The power of a begins with n, decreases by 1 in each successive term, and ends with 0.

3. The power of b begins with 0, increases by 1 in each successive term, and ends with n.

4. The sum of the powers of each term is n.

EXAMPLE 7　Using Pascal's Triangle to Expand Binomials

Use Pascal's Triangle to expand (a) $(x - 2)^5$ and (b) $(3y + 1)^3$.

SOLUTION

a. The coefficients from the fifth row of Pascal's Triangle are 1, 5, 10, 10, 5, and 1.

$$(x - 2)^5 = 1x^5 + 5x^4(-2) + 10x^3(-2)^2 + 10x^2(-2)^3 + 5x(-2)^4 + 1(-2)^5$$
$$= x^5 - 10x^4 + 40x^3 - 80x^2 + 80x - 32$$

b. The coefficients from the third row of Pascal's Triangle are 1, 3, 3, and 1.

$$(3y + 1)^3 = 1(3y)^3 + 3(3y)^2(1) + 3(3y)(1)^2 + 1(1)^3$$
$$= 27y^3 + 27y^2 + 9y + 1$$

Monitoring Progress　🔊 Help in English and Spanish at *BigIdeasMath.com*

10. Use Pascal's Triangle to expand (a) $(z + 3)^4$ and (b) $(2t - 1)^5$.

The coefficients in the expansion of $(a + b)^n$ can also be represented using combinations.

n	Pascal's Triangle as Numbers	Pascal's Triangle as Combinations	Binomial Expansion
0th row	0	1	${}_0C_0$	$(a + b)^0 =$ 1
1st row	1	1 1	${}_1C_0$ ${}_1C_1$	$(a + b)^1 =$ $1a + 1b$
2nd row	2	1 2 1	${}_2C_0$ ${}_2C_1$ ${}_2C_2$	$(a + b)^2 =$ $1a^2 + 2ab + 1b^2$
3rd row	3	1 3 3 1	${}_3C_0$ ${}_3C_1$ ${}_3C_2$ ${}_3C_3$	$(a + b)^3 = 1a^3 + 3a^2b + 3ab^2 + 1b^3$

The results in the table are generalized in the **Binomial Theorem**.

Core Concept

The Binomial Theorem

For any positive integer n, the binomial expansion of $(a + b)^n$ is

$$(a + b)^n = {}_nC_0\, a^n b^0 + {}_nC_1\, a^{n-1} b^1 + {}_nC_2\, a^{n-2} b^2 + \cdots + {}_nC_n\, a^0 b^n.$$

Notice that each term in the expansion of $(a + b)^n$ has the form ${}_nC_r\, a^{n-r} b^r$, where r is an integer from 0 to n.

REMEMBER

A *combination* is a selection of objects in which order is not important. The number of combinations of n objects taken r at a time, where $r \le n$, is given by

$${}_nC_r = \frac{n!}{(n - r)! \cdot r!}.$$

EXAMPLE 8   Using the Binomial Theorem

a. Use the Binomial Theorem to write the expansion of $(x^2 + y)^3$.

b. Find the coefficient of x^4 in the expansion of $(3x + 2)^{10}$.

SOLUTION

a. $(x^2 + y)^3 = {}_3C_0(x^2)^3 y^0 + {}_3C_1(x^2)^2 y^1 + {}_3C_2(x^2)^1 y^2 + {}_3C_3(x^2)^0 y^3$

$\qquad\qquad = (1)(x^6)(1) + (3)(x^4)(y^1) + (3)(x^2)(y^2) + (1)(1)(y^3)$

$\qquad\qquad = x^6 + 3x^4 y + 3x^2 y^2 + y^3$

b. From the Binomial Theorem, you know

$$(3x + 2)^{10} = {}_{10}C_0(3x)^{10}(2)^0 + {}_{10}C_1(3x)^9(2)^1 + \cdots + {}_{10}C_{10}(3x)^0(2)^{10}.$$

Each term in the expansion has the form ${}_{10}C_r(3x)^{10-r}(2)^r$. The term containing x^4 occurs when $r = 6$.

$${}_{10}C_6(3x)^4(2)^6 = (210)(81x^4)(64) = 1{,}088{,}640x^4$$

▶ The coefficient of x^4 is 1,088,640.

Monitoring Progress 🔊 Help in English and Spanish at *BigIdeasMath.com*

11. Use the Binomial Theorem to write the expansion of (a) $(x + 3)^5$ and (b) $(2p - q)^4$.

12. Find the coefficient of x^5 in the expansion of $(x - 3)^7$.

13. Find the coefficient of x^3 in the expansion of $(2x + 5)^8$.

Vocabulary and Core Concept Check

1. **WRITING** Describe three different methods to expand $(x + 3)^3$.

2. **WRITING** Is $(a + b)(a - b) = a^2 - b^2$ an identity? Explain your reasoning.

Monitoring Progress and Modeling with Mathematics

In Exercises 3–8, find the sum. *(See Example 1.)*

3. $(3x^2 + 4x - 1) + (-2x^2 - 3x + 2)$

4. $(-5x^2 + 4x - 2) + (-8x^2 + 2x + 1)$

5. $(12x^5 - 3x^4 + 2x - 5) + (8x^4 - 3x^3 + 4x + 1)$

6. $(8x^4 + 2x^2 - 1) + (3x^3 - 5x^2 + 7x + 1)$

7. $(7x^6 + 2x^5 - 3x^2 + 9x) + (5x^5 + 8x^3 - 6x^2 + 2x - 5)$

8. $(9x^4 - 3x^3 + 4x^2 + 5x + 7) + (11x^4 - 4x^2 - 11x - 9)$

In Exercises 9–14, find the difference. *(See Example 2.)*

9. $(3x^3 - 2x^2 + 4x - 8) - (5x^3 + 12x^2 - 3x - 4)$

10. $(7x^4 - 9x^3 - 4x^2 + 5x + 6) - (2x^4 + 3x^3 - x^2 + x - 4)$

11. $(5x^6 - 2x^4 + 9x^3 + 2x - 4) - (7x^5 - 8x^4 + 2x - 11)$

12. $(4x^5 - 7x^3 - 9x^2 + 18) - (14x^5 - 8x^4 + 11x^2 + x)$

13. $(8x^5 + 6x^3 - 2x^2 + 10x) - (9x^5 - x^3 - 13x^2 + 4)$

14. $(11x^4 - 9x^2 + 3x + 11) - (2x^4 + 6x^3 + 2x - 9)$

15. **MODELING WITH MATHEMATICS** During a recent period of time, the numbers (in thousands) of males M and females F that attend degree-granting institutions in the United States can be modeled by

    $M = 19.7t^2 + 310.5t + 7539.6$
    $F = 28t^2 + 368t + 10127.8$

    where t is time in years. Write a polynomial to model the total number of people attending degree-granting institutions. Interpret its constant term.

16. **MODELING WITH MATHEMATICS** A farmer plants a garden that contains corn and pumpkins. The total area (in square feet) of the garden is modeled by the expression $2x^2 + 5x + 4$. The area of the corn is modeled by the expression $x^2 - 3x + 2$. Write an expression that models the area of the pumpkins.

In Exercises 17–24, find the product. *(See Example 3.)*

17. $7x^3(5x^2 + 3x + 1)$

18. $-4x^5(11x^3 + 2x^2 + 9x + 1)$

19. $(5x^2 - 4x + 6)(-2x + 3)$

20. $(-x - 3)(2x^2 + 5x + 8)$

21. $(x^2 - 2x - 4)(x^2 - 3x - 5)$

22. $(3x^2 + x - 2)(-4x^2 - 2x - 1)$

23. $(3x^3 - 9x + 7)(x^2 - 2x + 1)$

24. $(4x^2 - 8x - 2)(x^4 + 3x^2 + 4x)$

ERROR ANALYSIS In Exercises 25 and 26, describe and correct the error in performing the operation.

25.

✗ $(x^2 - 3x + 4) - (x^3 + 7x - 2)$
$= x^2 - 3x + 4 - x^3 + 7x - 2$
$= -x^3 + x^2 + 4x + 2$

26.

✗ $(2x - 7)^3 = (2x)^3 - 7^3$
$= 8x^3 - 343$

In Exercises 27–32, find the product of the binomials. *(See Example 4.)*

27. $(x - 3)(x + 2)(x + 4)$

28. $(x - 5)(x + 2)(x - 6)$

29. $(x - 2)(3x + 1)(4x - 3)$

30. $(2x + 5)(x - 2)(3x + 4)$

31. $(3x - 4)(5 - 2x)(4x + 1)$

32. $(4 - 5x)(1 - 2x)(3x + 2)$

33. **REASONING** Prove the polynomial identity $(a + b)(a - b) = a^2 - b^2$. Then give an example of two whole numbers greater than 10 that can be multiplied using mental math and the given identity. Justify your answers. *(See Example 5.)*

34. **NUMBER SENSE** You have been asked to order textbooks for your class. You need to order 29 textbooks that cost \$31 each. Explain how you can use the polynomial identity $(a + b)(a - b) = a^2 - b^2$ and mental math to find the total cost of the textbooks.

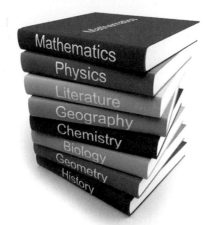

In Exercises 35–42, find the product. *(See Example 6.)*

35. $(x - 9)(x + 9)$

36. $(m + 6)^2$

37. $(3c - 5)^2$

38. $(2y - 5)(2y + 5)$

39. $(7h + 4)^2$

40. $(9g - 4)^2$

41. $(2k + 6)^3$

42. $(4n - 3)^3$

In Exercises 43–48, use Pascal's Triangle to expand the binomial. *(See Example 7.)*

43. $(2t + 4)^3$

44. $(6m + 2)^2$

45. $(2q - 3)^4$

46. $(g + 2)^5$

47. $(yz + 1)^5$

48. $(np - 1)^4$

In Exercises 49–52, find the *n*th row of Pascal's Triangle. Then expand the binomial.

49. $n = 6$; $(x + 3)^6$

50. $n = 7$; $(2s - t^4)^7$

51. $n = 9$; $(a + b^2)^9$

52. $n = 10$; $(y - 3z)^{10}$

53. **FINDING A PATTERN** What is the sum of the numbers in each of rows 0–4 of Pascal's Triangle? What is the sum of row *n*?

				1					Row 0
			1		1				Row 1
		1		2		1			Row 2
	1		3		3		1		Row 3
1		4		6		4		1	Row 4

1 5 10 10 5 1

54. **FINDING A PATTERN** Describe the pattern formed by the sums of the numbers along the diagonal segments of Pascal's Triangle. What is the name of this sequence of numbers?

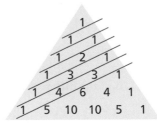

In Exercises 55–62, use the Binomial Theorem to write the binomial expansion. *(See Example 8a.)*

55. $(x + 2)^3$

56. $(c - 4)^5$

57. $(a + 3b)^4$

58. $(4p - q)^6$

59. $(w^3 - 3)^4$

60. $(2s^4 + 5)^5$

61. $(3u + v^2)^6$

62. $(x^3 - y^2)^4$

In Exercises 63–70, use the given value of *n* to find the coefficient of x^n in the expansion of the binomial. *(See Example 8b.)*

63. $(x - 2)^{10}$, $n = 5$

64. $(x - 3)^7$, $n = 4$

65. $(x^2 - 3)^8$, $n = 6$

66. $(3x + 2)^5$, $n = 3$

67. $(2x + 5)^{12}$, $n = 7$

68. $(3x - 1)^9$, $n = 2$

69. $\left(\frac{1}{2}x - 4\right)^{11}$, $n = 4$

70. $\left(\frac{1}{4}x + 6\right)^6$, $n = 3$

71. REASONING Write the eighth row of Pascal's Triangle as combinations and as numbers.

72. PROBLEM SOLVING The first four triangular numbers are 1, 3, 6, and 10.

  a. Use Pascal's Triangle to write the first four triangular numbers as combinations.

$$
\begin{array}{ccccccccccc}
 & & & & & 1 & & & & & \\
 & & & & 1 & & 1 & & & & \\
 & & & 1 & & 2 & & 1 & & & \\
 & & 1 & & 3 & & 3 & & 1 & & \\
 & 1 & & 4 & & 6 & & 4 & & 1 & \\
1 & & 5 & & 10 & & 10 & & 5 & & 1
\end{array}
$$

  b. Use your result from part (a) to write an explicit rule for the nth triangular number T_n.

NUMBER SENSE In Exercises 73–76, use the Binomial Theorem to approximate the quantity to the nearest thousandth. For example, in Exercise 73, use the expansion

$$(1.5)^6 = (1 + 0.5)^6$$

$$= 1 + 6(0.5) + 15(0.5)^2 \dots.$$

73. $(1.5)^6$ **74.** $(1.95)^7$

75. $(2.99)^8$ **76.** $(2.005)^9$

77. COMPARING METHODS Find the product of the expression $(a^2 + 4b^2)^2(3a^2 - b^2)^2$ using two different methods. Which method do you prefer? Explain.

78. THOUGHT PROVOKING Adjoin one or more polygons to the rectangle to form a single new polygon whose perimeter is double that of the rectangle. Find the perimeter of the new polygon.

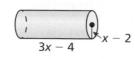

MATHEMATICAL CONNECTIONS In Exercises 79 and 80, write an expression for the volume of the figure as a polynomial in standard form.

79. $V = \ell w h$ **80.** $V = \pi r^2 h$

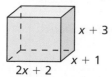
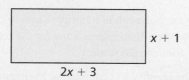

81. MODELING WITH MATHEMATICS Two people make three deposits into their bank accounts earning the same simple interest rate r.

Person A		Account No.
		2-5384100608
Date	Transaction	Amount
01/01/2012	Deposit	$2000.00
01/01/2013	Deposit	$3000.00
01/01/2014	Deposit	$1000.00

Person B		Account No.
		1-5233032905
Date	Transaction	Amount
01/01/2012	Deposit	$5000.00
01/01/2013	Deposit	$1000.00
01/01/2014	Deposit	$4000.00

Person A's account is worth

$$2000(1 + r)^3 + 3000(1 + r)^2 + 1000(1 + r)$$

on January 1, 2015.

  a. Write a polynomial for the value of Person B's account on January 1, 2015.

  b. Write the total value of the two accounts as a polynomial in standard form. Then interpret the coefficients of the polynomial.

  c. Suppose their interest rate is 0.05. What is the total value of the two accounts on January 1, 2015?

82. USING STRUCTURE Complete the table. What characteristic of Pascal's Triangle does the table illustrate?

n	r	$_nC_r$	$_nC_{n-r}$
3	1		
5	2		
7	4		
8	3		
10	6		
12	8		

83. BINOMIAL EXPERIMENT You roll a twelve-sided die 8 times. Let p be the probability of rolling a multiple of 3. Let q be the probability of rolling a number that is *not* a multiple of 3. The probability of rolling a multiple of 3 exactly k times in n rolls is

$$_nC_k \, p^k q^{n-k}.$$

Expand $\left(\frac{2}{3} + \frac{1}{3}\right)^8$ using the Binomial Theorem. Interpret each term in the context of the problem.

84. PROBLEM SOLVING The sphere is centered in the cube. Find an expression for the volume of the cube outside the sphere.

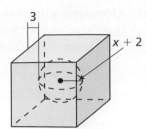

85. MAKING AN ARGUMENT Your friend claims the sum of two binomials is always a binomial and the product of two binomials is always a trinomial. Is your friend correct? Explain your reasoning.

86. HOW DO YOU SEE IT? You make a tin box by cutting x-inch-by-x-inch pieces of tin off the corners of a rectangle and folding up each side. The plan for your box is shown.

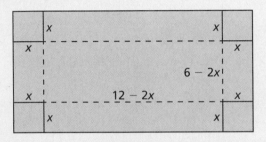

a. What are the dimensions of the original piece of tin?

b. Write a function that represents the volume of the box. Without multiplying, determine its degree.

USING TOOLS In Exercises 87–90, use a graphing calculator to make a conjecture about whether the two functions are equivalent. Explain your reasoning.

87. $f(x) = (2x - 3)^3$; $g(x) = 8x^3 - 36x^2 + 54x - 27$

88. $h(x) = (x + 2)^5$;
$k(x) = x^5 + 10x^4 + 40x^3 + 80x^2 + 64x$

89. $f(x) = (-x - 3)^4$;
$g(x) = x^4 + 12x^3 + 54x^2 + 108x + 80$

90. $f(x) = (-x + 5)^3$; $g(x) = -x^3 + 15x^2 - 75x + 125$

91. REWRITING EXPRESSIONS Expand the complex number (a) $(1 + i)^5$ and (b) $(3 - i)^6$. Simplify your results using the fact that i is defined as $i = \sqrt{-1}$.

92. ABSTRACT REASONING You are given the function $f(x) = (x + a)(x + b)(x + c)(x + d)$. When $f(x)$ is written in standard form, show that the coefficient of x^3 is the sum of a, b, c, and d, and the constant term is the product of a, b, c, and d.

93. DRAWING CONCLUSIONS Let $g(x) = 12x^4 + 8x + 9$ and $h(x) = 3x^5 + 2x^3 - 7x + 4$.

a. What is the degree of the polynomial $g(x) + h(x)$?

b. What is the degree of the polynomial $g(x) - h(x)$?

c. What is the degree of the polynomial $g(x) \cdot h(x)$?

d. In general, if $g(x)$ and $h(x)$ are polynomials such that $g(x)$ has degree m and $h(x)$ has degree n, and $m > n$, what are the degrees of $g(x) + h(x)$, $g(x) - h(x)$, and $g(x) \cdot h(x)$?

94. FINDING A PATTERN In this exercise, you will explore the sequence of square numbers. The first four square numbers are represented below.

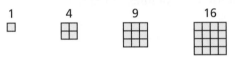

a. Find the differences between consecutive square numbers. Explain what you notice.

b. Show how the polynomial identity $(n + 1)^2 - n^2 = 2n + 1$ models the differences between square numbers.

c. Prove the polynomial identity in part (b).

95. CRITICAL THINKING Recall that a Pythagorean triple is a set of positive integers a, b, and c such that $a^2 + b^2 = c^2$. The numbers 3, 4, and 5 form a Pythagorean triple because $3^2 + 4^2 = 5^2$. You can use the polynomial identity $(x^2 - y^2)^2 + (2xy)^2 = (x^2 + y^2)^2$ to generate other Pythagorean triples.

a. Prove the polynomial identity is true by showing that the simplified expressions for the left and right sides are the same.

b. Use the identity to generate the Pythagorean triple when $x = 6$ and $y = 5$.

c. Verify that your answer in part (b) satisfies $a^2 + b^2 = c^2$.

Maintaining Mathematical Proficiency
Reviewing what you learned in previous grades and lessons

Perform the complex number operation. Write the answer in standard form. *(Skills Review Handbook)*

96. $(3 - 2i) + (5 + 9i)$

97. $(12 + 3i) - (7 - 8i)$

98. $(7i)(-3i)$

99. $(4 + i)(2 - i)$

3.3 Dividing Polynomials

Essential Question How can you use the factors of a cubic polynomial to solve a division problem involving the polynomial?

EXPLORATION 1 Dividing Polynomials

Work with a partner. Match each division statement with the graph of the related cubic polynomial $f(x)$. Explain your reasoning. Use a graphing calculator to verify your answers.

a. $\dfrac{f(x)}{x} = (x-1)(x+2)$ **b.** $\dfrac{f(x)}{x-1} = (x-1)(x+2)$

c. $\dfrac{f(x)}{x+1} = (x-1)(x+2)$ **d.** $\dfrac{f(x)}{x-2} = (x-1)(x+2)$

e. $\dfrac{f(x)}{x+2} = (x-1)(x+2)$ **f.** $\dfrac{f(x)}{x-3} = (x-1)(x+2)$

A.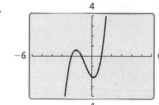

B.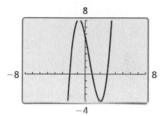

C.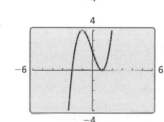

D.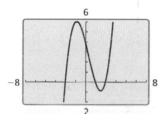

E.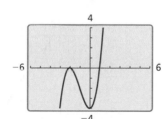

F.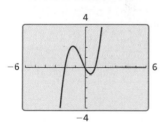

REASONING ABSTRACTLY

To be proficient in math, you need to understand a situation abstractly and represent it symbolically.

EXPLORATION 2 Dividing Polynomials

Work with a partner. Use the results of Exploration 1 to find each quotient. Write your answers in standard form. Check your answers by multiplying.

a. $(x^3 + x^2 - 2x) \div x$ **b.** $(x^3 - 3x + 2) \div (x-1)$

c. $(x^3 + 2x^2 - x - 2) \div (x+1)$ **d.** $(x^3 - x^2 - 4x + 4) \div (x-2)$

e. $(x^3 + 3x^2 - 4) \div (x+2)$ **f.** $(x^3 - 2x^2 - 5x + 6) \div (x-3)$

Communicate Your Answer

3. How can you use the factors of a cubic polynomial to solve a division problem involving the polynomial?

What You Will Learn

▶ Use long division to divide polynomials by other polynomials.

▶ Use synthetic division to divide polynomials by binomials of the form $x - k$.

▶ Use the Remainder Theorem.

Long Division of Polynomials

When you divide a polynomial $f(x)$ by a nonzero polynomial divisor $d(x)$, you get a quotient polynomial $q(x)$ and a remainder polynomial $r(x)$.

$$\frac{f(x)}{d(x)} = q(x) + \frac{r(x)}{d(x)}$$

The degree of the remainder must be less than the degree of the divisor. When the remainder is 0, the divisor *divides evenly* into the dividend. Also, the degree of the divisor is less than or equal to the degree of the dividend $f(x)$. One way to divide polynomials is called **polynomial long division**.

EXAMPLE 1   Using Polynomial Long Division

Divide $2x^4 + 3x^3 + 5x - 1$ by $x^2 + 3x + 2$.

SOLUTION

Write polynomial division in the same format you use when dividing numbers. Include a "0" as the coefficient of x^2 in the dividend. At each stage, divide the term with the highest power in what is left of the dividend by the first term of the divisor. This gives the next term of the quotient.

$$
\begin{array}{r}
2x^2 - 3x + 5 \quad \longleftarrow \text{quotient} \\
x^2 + 3x + 2 \overline{)\, 2x^4 + 3x^3 + 0x^2 + 5x - 1} \\
\underline{2x^4 + 6x^3 + 4x^2} \\
-3x^3 - 4x^2 + 5x \\
\underline{-3x^3 - 9x^2 - 6x} \\
5x^2 + 11x - 1 \\
\underline{5x^2 + 15x + 10} \\
-4x - 11 \quad \longleftarrow \text{remainder}
\end{array}
$$

Multiply divisor by $\frac{2x^4}{x^2} = 2x^2$.

Subtract. Bring down next term.

Multiply divisor by $\frac{-3x^3}{x^2} = -3x$.

Subtract. Bring down next term.

Multiply divisor by $\frac{5x^2}{x^2} = 5$.

▶ $\dfrac{2x^4 + 3x^3 + 5x - 1}{x^2 + 3x + 2} = 2x^2 - 3x + 5 + \dfrac{-4x - 11}{x^2 + 3x + 2}$

Check

You can check the result of a division problem by multiplying the quotient by the divisor and adding the remainder. The result should be the dividend.

$(2x^2 - 3x + 5)(x^2 + 3x + 2) + (-4x - 11)$

$= (2x^2)(x^2 + 3x + 2) - (3x)(x^2 + 3x + 2) + (5)(x^2 + 3x + 2) - 4x - 11$

$= 2x^4 + 6x^3 + 4x^2 - 3x^3 - 9x^2 - 6x + 5x^2 + 15x + 10 - 4x - 11$

$= 2x^4 + 3x^3 + 5x - 1$ ✓

Monitoring Progress 🔊 Help in English and Spanish at *BigIdeasMath.com*

Divide using polynomial long division.

1. $(x^3 - x^2 - 2x + 8) \div (x - 1)$ **2.** $(x^4 + 2x^2 - x + 5) \div (x^2 - x + 1)$

Synthetic Division

There is a shortcut for dividing polynomials by binomials of the form $x - k$. This shortcut is called **synthetic division**. This method is shown in the next example.

> ### EXAMPLE 2   Using Synthetic Division

Divide $-x^3 + 4x^2 + 9$ by $x - 3$.

SOLUTION

Step 1   Write the coefficients of the dividend in order of descending exponents. Include a "0" for the missing x-term. Because the divisor is $x - 3$, use $k = 3$. Write the k-value to the left of the vertical bar.

$$k\text{-value} \longrightarrow 3 \,|\, -1 \quad 4 \quad 0 \quad 9 \longleftarrow \text{coefficients of } -x^3 + 4x^2 + 9$$

Step 2   Bring down the leading coefficient. Multiply the leading coefficient by the k-value. Write the product under the second coefficient. Add.

$$
\begin{array}{r|rrrr}
3 & -1 & 4 & 0 & 9 \\
  &   & -3 & & \\
\hline
  & -1 & 1 & &
\end{array}
$$

Step 3   Multiply the previous sum by the k-value. Write the product under the third coefficient. Add. Repeat this process for the remaining coefficient. The first three numbers in the bottom row are the coefficients of the quotient, and the last number is the remainder.

$$
\begin{array}{r|rrrr}
3 & -1 & 4 & 0 & 9 \\
  &   & -3 & 3 & 9 \\
\hline
\text{coefficients of quotient} \longrightarrow & -1 & 1 & 3 & 18 \longleftarrow \text{remainder}
\end{array}
$$

▶ $\dfrac{-x^3 + 4x^2 + 9}{x - 3} = -x^2 + x + 3 + \dfrac{18}{x - 3}$

> ### EXAMPLE 3   Using Synthetic Division

Divide $3x^3 - 2x^2 + 2x - 5$ by $x + 1$.

SOLUTION

STUDY TIP

Note that dividing polynomials does not always result in a polynomial. This means that the set of polynomials is *not* closed under division.

Use synthetic division. Because the divisor is $x + 1 = x - (-1)$, $k = -1$.

$$
\begin{array}{r|rrrr}
-1 & 3 & -2 & 2 & -5 \\
   &   & -3 & 5 & -7 \\
\hline
   & 3 & -5 & 7 & -12
\end{array}
$$

▶ $\dfrac{3x^3 - 2x^2 + 2x - 5}{x + 1} = 3x^2 - 5x + 7 - \dfrac{12}{x + 1}$

Monitoring Progress Help in English and Spanish at *BigIdeasMath.com*

Divide using synthetic division.

3. $(x^3 - 3x^2 - 7x + 6) \div (x - 2)$ **4.** $(2x^3 - x - 7) \div (x + 3)$

The Remainder Theorem

The remainder in the synthetic division process has an important interpretation. When you divide a polynomial $f(x)$ by $d(x) = x - k$, the result is

$$\frac{f(x)}{d(x)} = q(x) + \frac{r(x)}{d(x)} \qquad\text{Polynomial division}$$

$$\frac{f(x)}{x - k} = q(x) + \frac{r(x)}{x - k} \qquad\text{Substitute } x - k \text{ for } d(x).$$

$$f(x) = (x - k)q(x) + r(x). \qquad\text{Multiply both sides by } x - k.$$

Because either $r(x) = 0$ *or* the degree of $r(x)$ is less than the degree of $x - k$, you know that $r(x)$ is a constant function. So, let $r(x) = r$, where r is a real number, and evaluate $f(x)$ when $x = k$.

$$f(k) = (k - k)q(k) + r \qquad\text{Substitute } k \text{ for } x \text{ and } r \text{ for } r(x).$$

$$f(k) = r \qquad\text{Simplify.}$$

This result is stated in the *Remainder Theorem*.

Core Concept

The Remainder Theorem

If a polynomial $f(x)$ is divided by $x - k$, then the remainder is $r = f(k)$.

The Remainder Theorem tells you that synthetic division can be used to evaluate a polynomial function. So, to evaluate $f(x)$ when $x = k$, divide $f(x)$ by $x - k$. The remainder will be $f(k)$.

EXAMPLE 4   **Evaluating a Polynomial**

Use synthetic division to evaluate $f(x) = 5x^3 - x^2 + 13x + 29$ when $x = -4$.

SOLUTION

```
-4 | 5    -1     13      29
   |      -20    84    -388
     5    -21    97    -359
```

▶ The remainder is -359. So, you can conclude from the Remainder Theorem that $f(-4) = -359$.

Check

Check this by substituting $x = -4$ in the original function.

$$f(-4) = 5(-4)^3 - (-4)^2 + 13(-4) + 29$$

$$= -320 - 16 - 52 + 29$$

$$= -359 \checkmark$$

Monitoring Progress   Help in English and Spanish at *BigIdeasMath.com*

Use synthetic division to evaluate the function for the indicated value of x.

5. $f(x) = 4x^2 - 10x - 21; x = 5$ **6.** $f(x) = 5x^4 + 2x^3 - 20x - 6; x = 2$

3.3 Exercises

Dynamic Solutions available at *BigIdeasMath.com*

Vocabulary and Core Concept Check

1. **WRITING** Explain the Remainder Theorem in your own words. Use an example in your explanation.

2. **VOCABULARY** What form must the divisor have to make synthetic division an appropriate method for dividing a polynomial? Provide examples to support your claim.

3. **VOCABULARY** Write the polynomial divisor, dividend, and quotient functions represented by the synthetic division shown at the right.

$$\begin{array}{r|rrrr} -3 & 1 & -2 & -9 & 18 \\ & & -3 & 15 & -18 \\ \hline & 1 & -5 & 6 & 0 \end{array}$$

4. **WRITING** Explain what the colored numbers represent in the synthetic division in Exercise 3.

Monitoring Progress and Modeling with Mathematics

In Exercises 5–10, divide using polynomial long division. *(See Example 1.)*

5. $(x^2 + x - 17) \div (x - 4)$

6. $(3x^2 - 14x - 5) \div (x - 5)$

7. $(x^3 + x^2 + x + 2) \div (x^2 - 1)$

8. $(7x^3 + x^2 + x) \div (x^2 + 1)$

9. $(5x^4 - 2x^3 - 7x^2 - 39) \div (x^2 + 2x - 4)$

10. $(4x^4 + 5x - 4) \div (x^2 - 3x - 2)$

In Exercises 11–18, divide using synthetic division. *(See Examples 2 and 3.)*

11. $(x^2 + 8x + 1) \div (x - 4)$

12. $(4x^2 - 13x - 5) \div (x - 2)$

13. $(2x^2 - x + 7) \div (x + 5)$

14. $(x^3 - 4x + 6) \div (x + 3)$

15. $(x^2 + 9) \div (x - 3)$

16. $(3x^3 - 5x^2 - 2) \div (x - 1)$

17. $(x^4 - 5x^3 - 8x^2 + 13x - 12) \div (x - 6)$

18. $(x^4 + 4x^3 + 16x - 35) \div (x + 5)$

ANALYZING RELATIONSHIPS In Exercises 19–22, match the equivalent expressions. Justify your answers.

19. $(x^2 + x - 3) \div (x - 2)$

20. $(x^2 - x - 3) \div (x - 2)$

21. $(x^2 - x + 3) \div (x - 2)$

22. $(x^2 + x + 3) \div (x - 2)$

A. $x + 1 - \frac{1}{x - 2}$

B. $x + 3 + \frac{9}{x - 2}$

C. $x + 1 + \frac{5}{x - 2}$

D. $x + 3 + \frac{3}{x - 2}$

ERROR ANALYSIS In Exercises 23 and 24, describe and correct the error in using synthetic division to divide $x^3 - 5x + 3$ by $x - 2$.

23. ✗

$$\begin{array}{r|rrrr} 2 & 1 & 0 & -5 & 3 \\ & & 2 & 4 & -2 \\ \hline & 1 & 2 & -1 & 1 \end{array}$$

$$\frac{x^3 - 5x + 3}{x - 2} = x^3 + 2x^2 - x + 1$$

24. ✗

$$\begin{array}{r|rrr} 2 & 1 & -5 & 3 \\ & & 2 & -6 \\ \hline & 1 & -3 & -3 \end{array}$$

$$\frac{x^3 - 5x + 3}{x - 2} = x^2 - 3x - \frac{3}{x - 2}$$

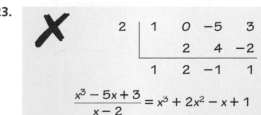

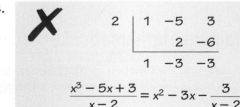

In Exercises 25–32, use synthetic division to evaluate the function for the indicated value of x. *(See Example 4.)*

25. $f(x) = -x^2 - 8x + 30; x = -1$

26. $f(x) = 3x^2 + 2x - 20; x = 3$

27. $f(x) = x^3 - 2x^2 + 4x + 3; x = 2$

28. $f(x) = x^3 + x^2 - 3x + 9; x = -4$

29. $f(x) = x^3 - 6x + 1; x = 6$

30. $f(x) = x^3 - 9x - 7; x = 10$

31. $f(x) = x^4 + 6x^2 - 7x + 1; x = 3$

32. $f(x) = -x^4 - x^3 - 2; x = 5$

33. **MAKING AN ARGUMENT** You use synthetic division to divide $f(x)$ by $(x - a)$ and find that the remainder equals 15. Your friend concludes that $f(15) = a$. Is your friend correct? Explain your reasoning.

34. **THOUGHT PROVOKING** A polygon has an area represented by $A = 4x^2 + 8x + 4$. The figure has at least one dimension equal to $2x + 2$. Draw the figure and label its dimensions.

35. **USING TOOLS** The total attendance A (in thousands) at NCAA women's basketball games and the number T of NCAA women's basketball teams over a period of time can be modeled by

$$A = -1.95x^3 + 70.1x^2 - 188x + 2150$$
$$T = 14.8x + 725$$

where x is in years and $0 < x < 18$. Write a function for the average attendance per team over this period of time.

36. **COMPARING METHODS** The profit P (in millions of dollars) for a DVD manufacturer can be modeled by $P = -6x^3 + 72x$, where x is the number (in millions) of DVDs produced. Use synthetic division to show that the company yields a profit of \$96 million when 2 million DVDs are produced. Is there an easier method? Explain.

37. **CRITICAL THINKING** What is the value of k such that $(x^3 - x^2 + kx - 30) \div (x - 5)$ has a remainder of zero?

Ⓐ -14 Ⓑ -2

Ⓒ 26 Ⓓ 32

38. **HOW DO YOU SEE IT?** The graph represents the polynomial function $f(x) = x^3 + 3x^2 - x - 3$.

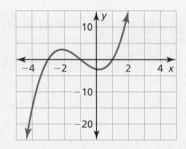

a. The expression $f(x) \div (x - k)$ has a remainder of -15. What is the value of k?

b. Use the graph to compare the remainders of $(x^3 + 3x^2 - x - 3) \div (x + 3)$ and $(x^3 + 3x^2 - x - 3) \div (x + 1)$.

39. **MATHEMATICAL CONNECTIONS** The volume V of the rectangular prism is given by $V = 2x^3 + 17x^2 + 46x + 40$. Find an expression for the missing dimension.

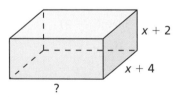

40. **USING STRUCTURE** You divide two polynomials and obtain the result $5x^2 - 13x + 47 - \dfrac{102}{x + 2}$. What is the dividend? How did you find it?

Maintaining Mathematical Proficiency   Reviewing what you learned in previous grades and lessons

Find the zero(s) of the function. *(Skills Review Handbook)*

41. $f(x) = x^2 - 6x + 9$

42. $g(x) = 3(x + 6)(x - 2)$

43. $g(x) = x^2 + 14x + 49$

44. $h(x) = 4x^2 + 36$

3.4 Factoring Polynomials

Essential Question How can you factor a polynomial?

EXPLORATION 1   Factoring Polynomials

Work with a partner. Match each polynomial equation with the graph of its related polynomial function. Use the x-intercepts of the graph to write each polynomial in factored form. Explain your reasoning.

a. $x^2 + 5x + 4 = 0$ **b.** $x^3 - 2x^2 - x + 2 = 0$

c. $x^3 + x^2 - 2x = 0$ **d.** $x^3 - x = 0$

e. $x^4 - 5x^2 + 4 = 0$ **f.** $x^4 - 2x^3 - x^2 + 2x = 0$

A.
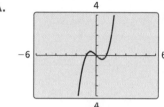

B.
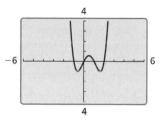

C.
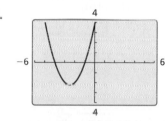

D.
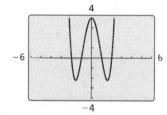

E.
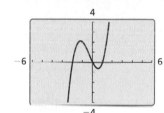

F.
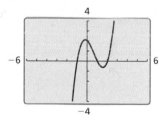

MAKING SENSE OF PROBLEMS

To be proficient in math, you need to check your answers to problems and continually ask yourself, "Does this make sense?"

EXPLORATION 2   Factoring Polynomials

Work with a partner. Use the x-intercepts of the graph of the polynomial function to write each polynomial in factored form. Explain your reasoning. Check your answers by multiplying.

a. $f(x) = x^2 - x - 2$ **b.** $f(x) = x^3 - x^2 - 2x$

c. $f(x) = x^3 - 2x^2 - 3x$ **d.** $f(x) = x^3 - 3x^2 - x + 3$

e. $f(x) = x^4 + 2x^3 - x^2 - 2x$ **f.** $f(x) = x^4 - 10x^2 + 9$

Communicate Your Answer

3. How can you factor a polynomial?

4. What information can you obtain about the graph of a polynomial function written in factored form?

3.4 Lesson

Core Vocabulary

factored completely, *p. 136*
factor by grouping, *p. 137*
quadratic form, *p. 137*

Previous
zero of a function
synthetic division

What You Will Learn

▶ Factor polynomials.
▶ Use the Factor Theorem.

Factoring Polynomials

Previously, you factored quadratic polynomials. You can also factor polynomials with degree greater than 2. Some of these polynomials can be *factored completely* using techniques you have previously learned. A factorable polynomial with integer coefficients is **factored completely** when it is written as a product of unfactorable polynomials with integer coefficients.

EXAMPLE 1   **Finding a Common Monomial Factor**

Factor each polynomial completely.

a. $x^3 - 4x^2 - 5x$ **b.** $3y^5 - 48y^3$ **c.** $5z^4 + 30z^3 + 45z^2$

SOLUTION

a. $x^3 - 4x^2 - 5x = x(x^2 - 4x - 5)$ Factor common monomial.

$= x(x - 5)(x + 1)$ Factor trinomial.

b. $3y^5 - 48y^3 = 3y^3(y^2 - 16)$ Factor common monomial.

$= 3y^3(y - 4)(y + 4)$ Difference of Two Squares Pattern

c. $5z^4 + 30z^3 + 45z^2 = 5z^2(z^2 + 6z + 9)$ Factor common monomial.

$= 5z^2(z + 3)^2$ Perfect Square Trinomial Pattern

Monitoring Progress Help in English and Spanish at *BigIdeasMath.com*

Factor the polynomial completely.

1. $x^3 - 7x^2 + 10x$ **2.** $3n^7 - 75n^5$ **3.** $8m^5 - 16m^4 + 8m^3$

In part (b) of Example 1, the special factoring pattern for the difference of two squares was used to factor the expression completely. There are also factoring patterns that you can use to factor the sum or difference of two *cubes*.

🌀 Core Concept

Special Factoring Patterns

Sum of Two Cubes   **Example**

$a^3 + b^3 = (a + b)(a^2 - ab + b^2)$ $64x^3 + 1 = (4x)^3 + 1^3$

$= (4x + 1)(16x^2 - 4x + 1)$

Difference of Two Cubes   **Example**

$a^3 - b^3 = (a - b)(a^2 + ab + b^2)$ $27x^3 - 8 = (3x)^3 - 2^3$

$= (3x - 2)(9x^2 + 6x + 4)$

EXAMPLE 2 Factoring the Sum or Difference of Two Cubes

Factor (a) $x^3 - 125$ and (b) $16s^5 + 54s^2$ completely.

SOLUTION

a. $x^3 - 125 = x^3 - 5^3$ Write as $a^3 - b^3$.

$= (x - 5)(x^2 + 5x + 25)$ Difference of Two Cubes Pattern

b. $16s^5 + 54s^2 = 2s^2(8s^3 + 27)$ Factor common monomial.

$= 2s^2[(2s)^3 + 3^3]$ Write $8s^3 + 27$ as $a^3 + b^3$.

$= 2s^2(2s + 3)(4s^2 - 6s + 9)$ Sum of Two Cubes Pattern

For some polynomials, you can **factor by grouping** pairs of terms that have a common monomial factor. The pattern for factoring by grouping is shown below.

$$ra + rb + sa + sb = r(a + b) + s(a + b)$$
$$= (r + s)(a + b)$$

EXAMPLE 3 Factoring by Grouping

Factor $z^3 + 5z^2 - 4z - 20$ completely.

SOLUTION

$z^3 + 5z^2 - 4z - 20 = z^2(z + 5) - 4(z + 5)$ Factor by grouping.

$= (z^2 - 4)(z + 5)$ Distributive Property

$= (z - 2)(z + 2)(z + 5)$ Difference of Two Squares Pattern

An expression of the form $au^2 + bu + c$, where u is an algebraic expression, is said to be in **quadratic form**. The factoring techniques you have studied can sometimes be used to factor such expressions.

LOOKING FOR STRUCTURE

The expression $16x^4 - 81$ is in quadratic form because it can be written as $u^2 - 81$ where $u = 4x^2$.

EXAMPLE 4 Factoring Polynomials in Quadratic Form

Factor (a) $16x^4 - 81$ and (b) $3p^8 + 15p^5 + 18p^2$ completely.

SOLUTION

a. $16x^4 - 81 = (4x^2)^2 - 9^2$ Write as $a^2 - b^2$.

$= (4x^2 + 9)(4x^2 - 9)$ Difference of Two Squares Pattern

$= (4x^2 + 9)(2x - 3)(2x + 3)$ Difference of Two Squares Pattern

b. $3p^8 + 15p^5 + 18p^2 = 3p^2(p^6 + 5p^3 + 6)$ Factor common monomial.

$= 3p^2(p^3 + 3)(p^3 + 2)$ Factor trinomial in quadratic form.

Monitoring Progress Help in English and Spanish at *BigIdeasMath.com*

Factor the polynomial completely.

4. $a^3 + 27$

5. $6z^5 - 750z^2$

6. $x^3 + 4x^2 - x - 4$

7. $3y^3 + y^2 + 9y + 3$

8. $-16n^4 + 625$

9. $5w^6 - 25w^4 + 30w^2$

The Factor Theorem

When dividing polynomials in the previous section, the examples had nonzero remainders. Suppose the remainder is 0 when a polynomial $f(x)$ is divided by $x - k$. Then,

$$\frac{f(x)}{x - k} = q(x) + \frac{0}{x - k} = q(x)$$

where $q(x)$ is the quotient polynomial. Therefore, $f(x) = (x - k) \cdot q(x)$, so that $x - k$ is a factor of $f(x)$. This result is summarized by the *Factor Theorem*, which is a special case of the Remainder Theorem.

READING

In other words, $x - k$ is a factor of $f(x)$ if and only if k is a zero of f.

Core Concept

The Factor Theorem

A polynomial $f(x)$ has a factor $x - k$ if and only if $f(k) = 0$.

STUDY TIP

In part (b), notice that direct substitution would have resulted in more difficult computations than synthetic division.

EXAMPLE 5   Determining Whether a Linear Binomial Is a Factor

Determine whether (a) $x - 2$ is a factor of $f(x) = x^2 + 2x - 4$ and (b) $x + 5$ is a factor of $f(x) = 3x^4 + 15x^3 - x^2 + 25$.

SOLUTION

a. Find $f(2)$ by direct substitution.

$$f(2) = 2^2 + 2(2) - 4$$
$$= 4 + 4 - 4$$
$$= 4$$

b. Find $f(-5)$ by synthetic division.

$$
\begin{array}{r|rrrrr}
-5 & 3 & 15 & -1 & 0 & 25 \\
   &   & -15 & 0 & 5 & -25 \\
\hline
   & 3 & 0 & -1 & 5 & 0 \\
\end{array}
$$

▶ Because $f(2) \neq 0$, the binomial $x - 2$ is not a factor of $f(x) = x^2 + 2x - 4$.

▶ Because $f(-5) = 0$, the binomial $x + 5$ is a factor of $f(x) = 3x^4 + 15x^3 - x^2 + 25$.

EXAMPLE 6   Factoring a Polynomial

Show that $x + 3$ is a factor of $f(x) = x^4 + 3x^3 - x - 3$. Then factor $f(x)$ completely.

SOLUTION

Show that $f(-3) = 0$ by synthetic division.

$$
\begin{array}{r|rrrrr}
-3 & 1 & 3 & 0 & -1 & -3 \\
   &   & -3 & 0 & 0 & 3 \\
\hline
   & 1 & 0 & 0 & -1 & 0 \\
\end{array}
$$

ANOTHER WAY

Notice that you can factor $f(x)$ by grouping.
$$f(x) = x^3(x + 3) - 1(x + 3)$$
$$= (x^3 - 1)(x + 3)$$
$$= (x + 3)(x - 1) \cdot$$
$$(x^2 + x + 1)$$

Because $f(-3) = 0$, you can conclude that $x + 3$ is a factor of $f(x)$ by the Factor Theorem. Use the result to write $f(x)$ as a product of two factors and then factor completely.

$$f(x) = x^4 + 3x^3 - x - 3 \qquad \text{Write original polynomial.}$$
$$= (x + 3)(x^3 - 1) \qquad \text{Write as a product of two factors.}$$
$$= (x + 3)(x - 1)(x^2 + x + 1) \qquad \text{Difference of Two Cubes Pattern}$$

Because the *x*-intercepts of the graph of a function are the zeros of the function, you can use the graph to approximate the zeros. You can check the approximations using the Factor Theorem.

EXAMPLE 7 **Real-Life Application**

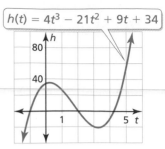
$h(t) = 4t^3 - 21t^2 + 9t + 34$

During the first 5 seconds of a roller coaster ride, the function $h(t) = 4t^3 - 21t^2 + 9t + 34$ represents the height *h* (in feet) of the roller coaster after *t* seconds. How long is the roller coaster at or below ground level in the first 5 seconds?

SOLUTION

1. **Understand the Problem** You are given a function rule that represents the height of a roller coaster. You are asked to determine how long the roller coaster is at or below ground during the first 5 seconds of the ride.

2. **Make a Plan** Use a graph to estimate the zeros of the function and check using the Factor Theorem. Then use the zeros to describe where the graph lies below the *t*-axis.

3. **Solve the Problem** From the graph, two of the zeros appear to be -1 and 2. The third zero is between 4 and 5.

   Step 1 Determine whether -1 is a zero using synthetic division.

$$
\begin{array}{r|rrrr}
-1 & 4 & -21 & 9 & 34 \\
   &   & -4 & 25 & -34 \\
\hline
   & 4 & -25 & 34 & 0
\end{array}
$$

   $h(-1) = 0$, so -1 is a zero of *h* and $t + 1$ is a factor of $h(t)$.

   Step 2 Determine whether 2 is a zero. If 2 is also a zero, then $t - 2$ is a factor of the resulting quotient polynomial. Check using synthetic division.

STUDY TIP
You could also check that 2 is a zero using the original function, but using the quotient polynomial helps you find the remaining factor.

$$
\begin{array}{r|rrr}
2 & 4 & -25 & 34 \\
  &   & 8   & -34 \\
\hline
  & 4 & -17 & 0
\end{array}
$$

   The remainder is 0, so $t - 2$ is a factor of $h(t)$ and 2 is a zero of *h*.

   So, $h(t) = (t + 1)(t - 2)(4t - 17)$. The factor $4t - 17$ indicates that the zero between 4 and 5 is $\frac{17}{4}$, or 4.25.

   ▶ The zeros are -1, 2, and 4.25. Only $t = 2$ and $t = 4.25$ occur in the first 5 seconds. The graph shows that the roller coaster is at or below ground level for $4.25 - 2 = 2.25$ seconds.

4. **Look Back** Use a table of values to verify the positive zeros and heights between the zeros.

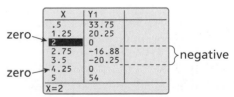

zero
zero
negative

X	Y1
.5	33.75
1.25	20.25
2	0
2.75	-16.88
3.5	-20.25
4.25	0
5	54

X=2

Monitoring Progress Help in English and Spanish at *BigIdeasMath.com*

10. Determine whether $x - 4$ is a factor of $f(x) = 2x^2 + 5x - 12$.

11. Show that $x - 6$ is a factor of $f(x) = x^3 - 5x^2 - 6x$. Then factor $f(x)$ completely.

12. In Example 7, does your answer change when you first determine whether 2 is a zero and then whether -1 is a zero? Justify your answer.

Vocabulary and Core Concept Check

1. **COMPLETE THE SENTENCE** The expression $9x^4 - 49$ is in _____ form because it can be written as $u^2 - 49$ where $u = $ _____.

2. **VOCABULARY** Explain when you should try factoring a polynomial by grouping.

3. **WRITING** How do you know when a polynomial is factored completely?

4. **WRITING** Explain the Factor Theorem and why it is useful.

Monitoring Progress and Modeling with Mathematics

In Exercises 5–12, factor the polynomial completely. *(See Example 1.)*

5. $x^3 - 2x^2 - 24x$

6. $4k^5 - 100k^3$

7. $3p^5 - 192p^3$

8. $2m^6 - 24m^5 + 64m^4$

9. $2q^4 + 9q^3 - 18q^2$

10. $3r^6 - 11r^5 - 20r^4$

11. $10w^{10} - 19w^9 + 6w^8$

12. $18v^9 + 33v^8 + 14v^7$

In Exercises 13–20, factor the polynomial completely. *(See Example 2.)*

13. $x^3 + 64$

14. $y^3 + 512$

15. $g^3 - 343$

16. $c^3 - 27$

17. $3h^9 - 192h^6$

18. $9n^6 - 6561n^3$

19. $16t^7 + 250t^4$

20. $135z^{11} - 1080z^8$

ERROR ANALYSIS In Exercises 21 and 22, describe and correct the error in factoring the polynomial.

21.

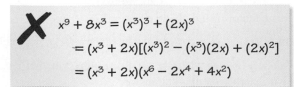

$$3x^3 + 27x = 3x(x^2 + 9)$$
$$= 3x(x + 3)(x - 3)$$

22.

$$x^9 + 8x^3 = (x^3)^3 + (2x)^3$$
$$= (x^3 + 2x)[(x^3)^2 - (x^3)(2x) + (2x)^2]$$
$$= (x^3 + 2x)(x^6 - 2x^4 + 4x^2)$$

In Exercises 23–30, factor the polynomial completely. *(See Example 3.)*

23. $y^3 - 5y^2 + 6y - 30$

24. $m^3 - m^2 + 7m - 7$

25. $3a^3 + 18a^2 + 8a + 48$

26. $2k^3 - 20k^2 + 5k - 50$

27. $x^3 - 8x^2 - 4x + 32$

28. $z^3 - 5z^2 - 9z + 45$

29. $4q^3 - 16q^2 - 9q + 36$

30. $16n^3 + 32n^2 - n - 2$

In Exercises 31–38, factor the polynomial completely. *(See Example 4.)*

31. $49k^4 - 9$

32. $4m^4 - 25$

33. $c^4 + 9c^2 + 20$

34. $y^4 - 3y^2 - 28$

35. $16z^4 - 81$

36. $81a^4 - 256$

37. $3r^8 + 3r^5 - 60r^2$

38. $4n^{12} - 32n^7 + 48n^2$

In Exercises 39–44, determine whether the binomial is a factor of $f(x)$. *(See Example 5.)*

39. $f(x) = 2x^3 + 5x^2 - 37x - 60; \ x - 4$

40. $f(x) = 3x^3 - 28x^2 + 29x + 140; \ x + 7$

41. $f(x) = 6x^5 - 15x^4 - 9x^3; \ x + 3$

42. $f(x) = 8x^5 - 58x^4 + 60x^3 + 140; \ x - 6$

43. $f(x) = 6x^4 - 6x^3 - 84x^2 + 144x; \ x + 4$

44. $f(x) = 48x^4 + 36x^3 - 138x^2 - 36x; \ x + 2$

In Exercises 45–50, show that the binomial is a factor of $f(x)$**. Then factor** $f(x)$ **completely.**
(See Example 6.)

45. $f(x) = x^3 - x^2 - 20x; \ x + 4$

46. $f(x) = x^3 - 5x^2 - 9x + 45; \ x - 5$

47. $f(x) = x^4 - 6x^3 - 8x + 48; \ x - 6$

48. $f(x) = x^4 + 4x^3 - 64x - 256; \ x + 4$

49. $f(x) = x^3 - 37x + 84; \ x + 7$

50. $f(x) = x^3 - x^2 - 24x - 36; \ x + 2$

ANALYZING RELATIONSHIPS In Exercises 51–54, match the function with the correct graph. Explain your reasoning.

51. $f(x) = (x - 2)(x - 3)(x + 1)$

52. $g(x) = x(x + 2)(x + 1)(x - 2)$

53. $h(x) = (x + 2)(x + 3)(x - 1)$

54. $k(x) = x(x - 2)(x - 1)(x + 2)$

A.
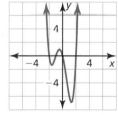

B.
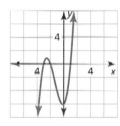

C.
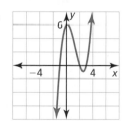

D.
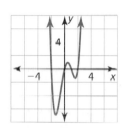

55. MODELING WITH MATHEMATICS The volume (in cubic inches) of a shipping box is modeled by $V = 2x^3 - 19x^2 + 39x$, where x is the length (in inches). Determine the values of x for which the model makes sense. Explain your reasoning. *(See Example 7.)*

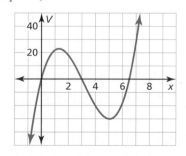

56. MODELING WITH MATHEMATICS The volume (in cubic inches) of a rectangular birdcage can be modeled by $V = 3x^3 - 17x^2 + 29x - 15$, where x is the length (in inches). Determine the values of x for which the model makes sense. Explain your reasoning.

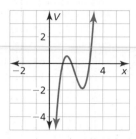

USING STRUCTURE In Exercises 57–64, use the method of your choice to factor the polynomial completely. Explain your reasoning.

57. $a^6 + a^5 - 30a^4$

58. $8m^3 - 343$

59. $z^3 - 7z^2 - 9z + 63$

60. $2p^8 - 12p^5 + 16p^2$

61. $64r^3 + 729$

62. $5x^5 - 10x^4 - 40x^3$

63. $16n^4 - 1$

64. $9k^3 - 24k^2 + 3k - 8$

65. REASONING Determine whether each polynomial is factored completely. If not, factor completely.

    a. $7z^4(2z^2 - z - 6)$

    b. $(2 - n)(n^2 + 6n)(3n - 11)$

    c. $3(4y - 5)(9y^2 - 6y - 4)$

66. PROBLEM SOLVING The profit P (in millions of dollars) for a T-shirt manufacturer can be modeled by $P = -x^3 + 4x^2 + x$, where x is the number (in millions) of T-shirts produced. Currently the company produces 4 million T-shirts and makes a profit of $4 million. What lesser number of T-shirts could the company produce and still make the same profit?

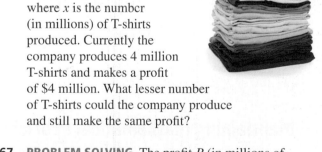

67. PROBLEM SOLVING The profit P (in millions of dollars) for a shoe manufacturer can be modeled by $P = -21x^3 + 46x$, where x is the number (in millions) of shoes produced. The company now produces 1 million shoes and makes a profit of $25 million, but it would like to cut back production. What lesser number of shoes could the company produce and still make the same profit?

68. THOUGHT PROVOKING Find a value of k such that $\dfrac{f(x)}{x-k}$ has a remainder of 0. Justify your answer.
$$f(x) = x^3 - 3x^2 - 4x$$

69. COMPARING METHODS You are taking a test where calculators are not permitted. One question asks you to evaluate $g(7)$ for the function $g(x) = x^3 - 7x^2 - 4x + 28$. You use the Factor Theorem and synthetic division and your friend uses direct substitution. Whose method do you prefer? Explain your reasoning.

70. MAKING AN ARGUMENT You divide $f(x)$ by $(x - a)$ and find that the remainder does not equal 0. Your friend concludes that $f(x)$ cannot be factored. Is your friend correct? Explain your reasoning.

71. CRITICAL THINKING What is the value of k such that $x - 7$ is a factor of $h(x) = 2x^3 - 13x^2 - kx + 105$? Justify your answer.

72. HOW DO YOU SEE IT? Use the graph to write an equation of the cubic function in factored form. Explain your reasoning.

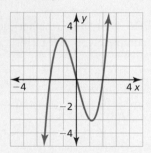

73. ABSTRACT REASONING Factor each polynomial completely.

  a. $7ac^2 + bc^2 - 7ad^2 - bd^2$

  b. $x^{2n} - 2x^n + 1$

  c. $a^5b^2 - a^2b^4 + 2a^4b - 2ab^3 + a^3 - b^2$

74. REASONING The graph of the function $f(x) = x^4 + 3x^3 + 2x^2 + x + 3$ is shown. Can you use the Factor Theorem to factor $f(x)$? Explain.

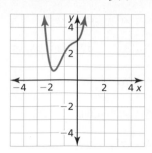

75. MATHEMATICAL CONNECTIONS The standard equation of an *ellipse* with center (h, k) is
$$\frac{(x - h)^2}{a^2} + \frac{(y - k)^2}{b^2} = 1.$$

  a. An equation of an ellipse is $3x^2 + y^2 - 6x = 9$. Rewrite the equation in standard form. Identify the center and then graph the ellipse.

  b. Repeat part (a) using the equation $x^2 + 2y^2 - 4y = 4$.

  c. Describe the graph of an ellipse.

76. CRITICAL THINKING Use the diagram to complete parts (a)–(c).

  a. Explain why $a^3 - b^3$ is equal to the sum of the volumes of the solids I, II, and III.

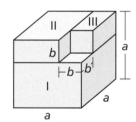

  b. Write an algebraic expression for the volume of each of the three solids. Leave your expressions in factored form.

  c. Use the results from part (a) and part (b) to derive the factoring pattern $a^3 - b^3$.

Maintaining Mathematical Proficiency
Reviewing what you learned in previous grades and lessons

Solve the quadratic equation by factoring. *(Skills Review Handbook)*

77. $x^2 - x - 30 = 0$

78. $2x^2 - 10x - 72 = 0$

79. $3x^2 - 11x + 10 = 0$

80. $9x^2 - 28x + 3 = 0$

Solve the quadratic equation by completing the square. *(Skills Review Handbook)*

81. $x^2 - 12x + 36 = 144$

82. $x^2 - 8x - 11 = 0$

83. $3x^2 + 30x + 63 = 0$

84. $4x^2 + 36x - 4 = 0$

3.1–3.4 What Did You Learn?

Core Vocabulary

Core Concepts

Section 3.1

Section 3.2

Section 3.3

Section 3.4

Mathematical Practices

1. Describe the entry points you used to analyze the function in Exercise 43 on page 118.

2. Describe how you maintained oversight in the process of factoring the polynomial in Exercise 49 on page 141.

Keeping Your Mind Focused

- When you sit down at your desk, review your notes from the last class.

- Repeat in your mind what you are writing in your notes.

- When a mathematical concept is particularly difficult, ask your teacher for another example.

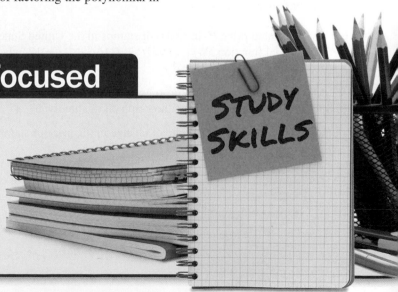

STUDY SKILLS

Decide whether the function is a polynomial function. If so, write it in standard form and state its degree, type, and leading coefficient. *(Section 3.1)*

1. $f(x) = 5 + 2x^2 - 3x^4 - 2x - x^3$

2. $g(x) = \frac{1}{4}x^3 + 2x - 3x^2 + 1$

3. $h(x) = 3 - 6x^3 + 4x^{-2} + 6x$

4. Describe the x-values for which (a) f is increasing or decreasing, (b) $f(x) > 0$, and (c) $f(x) < 0$. *(Section 3.1)*

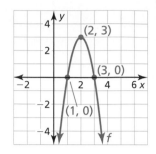

5. Write an expression for the area and perimeter for the figure shown. *(Section 3.2)*

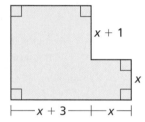

Perform the indicated operation. *(Section 3.2)*

6. $(7x^2 - 4) - (3x^2 - 5x + 1)$

7. $(x^2 - 3x + 2)(3x - 1)$

8. $(x - 1)(x + 3)(x - 4)$

9. Use Pascal's Triangle or the Binomial Theorem to expand $(x + 2)^5$. *(Section 3.2)*

10. Divide $4x^4 - 2x^3 + x^2 - 5x + 8$ by $x^2 - 2x - 1$. *(Section 3.3)*

Factor the polynomial completely. *(Section 3.4)*

11. $a^3 - 2a^2 - 8a$

12. $8m^3 + 27$

13. $z^3 + z^2 - 4z - 4$

14. $49b^4 - 64$

15. Show that $x + 5$ is a factor of $f(x) = x^3 - 2x^2 - 23x + 60$. Then factor $f(x)$ completely. *(Section 3.4)*

16. The estimated price P (in cents) of stamps in the United States can be modeled by the polynomial function $P(t) = 0.007t^3 - 0.16t^2 + 1t + 17$, where t represents the number of years since 1990. *(Section 3.1)*

    a. Use a graphing calculator to graph the function for the interval $0 \le t \le 20$. Describe the behavior of the graph on this interval.

    b. What was the average rate of change in the price of stamps from 1990 to 2010?

17. The volume V (in cubic feet) of a rectangular wooden crate is modeled by the function $V(x) = 2x^3 - 11x^2 + 12x$, where x is the width (in feet) of the crate. Determine the values of x for which the model makes sense. Explain your reasoning. *(Section 3.4)*

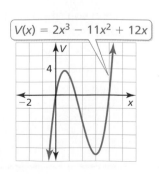

3.5 Solving Polynomial Equations

Essential Question How can you determine whether a polynomial equation has a repeated solution?

EXPLORATION 1 Cubic Equations and Repeated Solutions

Work with a partner. Some cubic equations have three distinct solutions. Others have repeated solutions. Match each cubic polynomial equation with the graph of its related polynomial function. Then solve each equation. For those equations that have repeated solutions, describe the behavior of the related function near the repeated zero using the graph or a table of values.

a. $x^3 - 6x^2 + 12x - 8 = 0$ **b.** $x^3 + 3x^2 + 3x + 1 = 0$

c. $x^3 - 3x + 2 = 0$ **d.** $x^3 + x^2 - 2x = 0$

e. $x^3 - 3x - 2 = 0$ **f.** $x^3 - 3x^2 + 2x = 0$

A.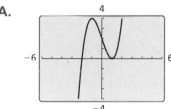

B.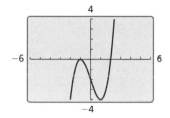

C.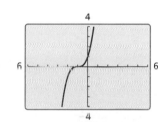

D.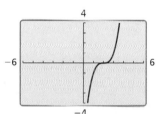

E.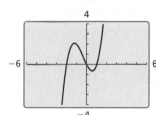

F.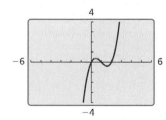

EXPLORATION 2 Quartic Equations and Repeated Solutions

Work with a partner. Determine whether each quartic equation has repeated solutions using the graph of the related quartic function or a table of values. Explain your reasoning. Then solve each equation.

a. $x^4 - 4x^3 + 5x^2 - 2x = 0$ **b.** $x^4 - 2x^3 - x^2 + 2x = 0$

c. $x^4 - 4x^3 + 4x^2 = 0$ **d.** $x^4 + 3x^3 = 0$

Communicate Your Answer

3. How can you determine whether a polynomial equation has a repeated solution?

4. Write a cubic or a quartic polynomial equation that is different from the equations in Explorations 1 and 2 and has a repeated solution.

Core Vocabulary

repeated solution, *p. 146*

Previous
roots of an equation
real numbers
conjugates

What You Will Learn

▶ Find solutions of polynomial equations and zeros of polynomial functions.
▶ Use the Rational Root Theorem.
▶ Use the Irrational Conjugates Theorem.

Finding Solutions and Zeros

You have used the Zero-Product Property to solve factorable quadratic equations. You can extend this technique to solve some higher-degree polynomial equations.

EXAMPLE 1 **Solving a Polynomial Equation by Factoring**

Solve $2x^3 - 12x^2 + 18x = 0$.

SOLUTION

$2x^3 - 12x^2 + 18x = 0$	Write the equation.
$2x(x^2 - 6x + 9) = 0$	Factor common monomial.
$2x(x - 3)^2 = 0$	Perfect Square Trinomial Pattern
$2x = 0$ or $(x - 3)^2 = 0$	Zero-Product Property
$x = 0$ or $x = 3$	Solve for *x*.

▶ The solutions, or roots, are $x = 0$ and $x = 3$.

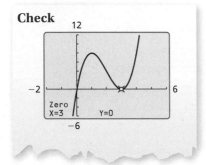

Check

In Example 1, the factor $x - 3$ appears more than once. This creates a **repeated solution** of $x = 3$. Note that the graph of the related function touches the *x*-axis (but does not cross the *x*-axis) at the repeated zero $x = 3$, and crosses the *x*-axis at the zero $x = 0$. This concept can be generalized as follows.

• When a factor $x - k$ of $f(x)$ is raised to an odd power, the graph of f *crosses* the *x*-axis at $x = k$.

• When a factor $x - k$ of $f(x)$ is raised to an even power, the graph of f *touches* the *x*-axis (but does not cross the *x*-axis) at $x = k$.

EXAMPLE 2 **Finding Zeros of a Polynomial Function**

Find the zeros of $f(x) = -2x^4 + 16x^2 - 32$. Then sketch a graph of the function.

SOLUTION

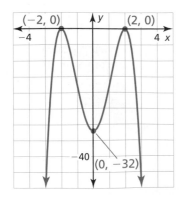

$0 = -2x^4 + 16x^2 - 32$	Set $f(x)$ equal to 0.
$0 = -2(x^4 - 8x^2 + 16)$	Factor out -2.
$0 = -2(x^2 - 4)(x^2 - 4)$	Factor trinomial in quadratic form.
$0 = -2(x + 2)(x - 2)(x + 2)(x - 2)$	Difference of Two Squares Pattern
$0 = -2(x + 2)^2(x - 2)^2$	Rewrite using exponents.

Because both factors $x + 2$ and $x - 2$ are raised to an even power, the graph of f touches the *x*-axis at the zeros $x = -2$ and $x = 2$.

By analyzing the original function, you can determine that the *y*-intercept is -32. Because the degree is even and the leading coefficient is negative, $f(x) \to -\infty$ as $x \to -\infty$ and $f(x) \to -\infty$ as $x \to +\infty$. Use these characteristics to sketch a graph of the function.

Solve the equation.

1. $4x^4 - 40x^2 + 36 = 0$ **2.** $2x^5 + 24x = 14x^3$

Find the zeros of the function. Then sketch a graph of the function.

3. $f(x) = 3x^4 - 6x^2 + 3$ **4.** $f(x) = x^3 + x^2 - 6x$

The Rational Root Theorem

The solutions of the equation $64x^3 + 152x^2 - 62x - 105 = 0$ are $-\frac{5}{2}$, $-\frac{3}{4}$, and $\frac{7}{8}$. Notice that the numerators (5, 3, and 7) of the zeros are factors of the constant term, -105. Also notice that the denominators (2, 4, and 8) are factors of the leading coefficient, 64. These observations are generalized by the *Rational Root Theorem*.

⑤ Core Concept

The Rational Root Theorem

If $f(x) = a_n x^n + \cdots + a_1 x + a_0$ has *integer* coefficients, then every rational solution of $f(x) = 0$ has the following form:

$$\frac{p}{q} = \frac{\text{factor of constant term } a_0}{\text{factor of leading coefficient } a_n}$$

STUDY TIP

Notice that you can use the Rational Root Theorem to list possible zeros of polynomial functions.

The Rational Root Theorem can be a starting point for finding solutions of polynomial equations. However, the theorem lists only *possible* solutions. In order to find the *actual* solutions, you must test values from the list of possible solutions.

EXAMPLE 3   **Using the Rational Root Theorem**

Find all real solutions of $x^3 - 8x^2 + 11x + 20 = 0$.

SOLUTION

The polynomial $f(x) = x^3 - 8x^2 + 11x + 20$ is not easily factorable. Begin by using the Rational Root Theorem.

ANOTHER WAY

You can use direct substitution to test possible solutions, but synthetic division helps you identify other factors of the polynomial.

Step 1   List the possible rational solutions. The leading coefficient of $f(x)$ is 1 and the constant term is 20. So, the possible rational solutions of $f(x) = 0$ are

$$x = \pm\frac{1}{1}, \pm\frac{2}{1}, \pm\frac{4}{1}, \pm\frac{5}{1}, \pm\frac{10}{1}, \pm\frac{20}{1}.$$

Step 2   Test possible solutions using synthetic division until a solution is found.

Test $x = 1$:

$$
\begin{array}{r|rrrr}
1 & 1 & -8 & 11 & 20 \\
  &   & 1 & -7 & 4 \\
\hline
  & 1 & -7 & 4 & 24
\end{array}
$$

$f(1) \neq 0$, so $x - 1$ is not a factor of $f(x)$.

Test $x = -1$:

$$
\begin{array}{r|rrrr}
-1 & 1 & -8 & 11 & 20 \\
   &   & -1 & 9 & -20 \\
\hline
   & 1 & -9 & 20 & 0
\end{array}
$$

$f(-1) = 0$, so $x + 1$ is a factor of $f(x)$.

Step 3   Factor completely using the result of the synthetic division.

$(x + 1)(x^2 - 9x + 20) = 0$ Write as a product of factors.

$(x + 1)(x - 4)(x - 5) = 0$ Factor the trinomial.

▶ So, the solutions are $x = -1$, $x = 4$, and $x = 5$.

In Example 3, the leading coefficient of the polynomial is 1. When the leading coefficient is not 1, the list of possible rational solutions or zeros can increase dramatically. In such cases, the search can be shortened by using a graph.

EXAMPLE 4   Finding Zeros of a Polynomial Function

Find all real zeros of $f(x) = 10x^4 - 11x^3 - 42x^2 + 7x + 12$.

SOLUTION

Step 1   List the possible rational zeros of f: $\pm\frac{1}{1}, \pm\frac{2}{1}, \pm\frac{3}{1}, \pm\frac{4}{1}, \pm\frac{6}{1}, \pm\frac{12}{1},$

$\pm\frac{1}{2}, \pm\frac{3}{2}, \pm\frac{1}{5}, \pm\frac{2}{5}, \pm\frac{3}{5}, \pm\frac{4}{5}, \pm\frac{6}{5}, \pm\frac{12}{5}, \pm\frac{1}{10}, \pm\frac{3}{10}$

Step 2   Choose reasonable values from the list above to test using the graph of the function. For f, the values

$x = -\frac{3}{2}, x = -\frac{1}{2}, x = \frac{3}{5},$ and $x = \frac{12}{5}$

are reasonable based on the graph shown at the right.

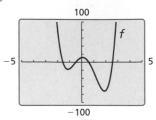

Step 3   Test the values using synthetic division until a zero is found.

$$
-\frac{3}{2} \begin{array}{|rrrrr} 10 & -11 & -42 & 7 & 12 \\ & -15 & 39 & \frac{9}{2} & -\frac{69}{4} \\ \hline 10 & -26 & -3 & \frac{23}{2} & -\frac{21}{4} \end{array}
$$

$$
-\frac{1}{2} \begin{array}{|rrrrr} 10 & -11 & -42 & 7 & 12 \\ & -5 & 8 & 17 & -12 \\ \hline 10 & -16 & -34 & 24 & 0 \end{array}
$$

$-\frac{1}{2}$ is a zero.

Step 4   Factor out a binomial using the result of the synthetic division.

$f(x) = \left(x + \frac{1}{2}\right)(10x^3 - 16x^2 - 34x + 24)$ Write as a product of factors.

$= \left(x + \frac{1}{2}\right)(2)(5x^3 - 8x^2 - 17x + 12)$ Factor 2 out of the second factor.

$= (2x + 1)(5x^3 - 8x^2 - 17x + 12)$ Multiply the first factor by 2.

Step 5   Repeat the steps above for $g(x) = 5x^3 - 8x^2 - 17x + 12$. Any zero of g will also be a zero of f. The possible rational zeros of g are:

$x = \pm1, \pm2, \pm3, \pm4, \pm6, \pm12, \pm\frac{1}{5}, \pm\frac{2}{5}, \pm\frac{3}{5}, \pm\frac{4}{5}, \pm\frac{6}{5}, \pm\frac{12}{5}$

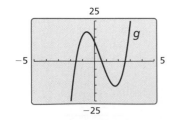

The graph of g shows that $\frac{3}{5}$ may be a zero. Synthetic division shows that $\frac{3}{5}$ is a zero and $g(x) = \left(x - \frac{3}{5}\right)(5x^2 - 5x - 20) = (5x - 3)(x^2 - x - 4)$. It follows that:

$f(x) = (2x + 1) \cdot g(x) = (2x + 1)(5x - 3)(x^2 - x - 4)$

Step 6   Find the remaining zeros of f by solving $x^2 - x - 4 = 0$.

$x = \dfrac{-(-1) \pm \sqrt{(-1)^2 - 4(1)(-4)}}{2(1)}$ Substitute 1 for a, -1 for b, and -4 for c in the Quadratic Formula.

$x = \dfrac{1 \pm \sqrt{17}}{2}$ Simplify.

▶   The real zeros of f are $-\frac{1}{2}, \frac{3}{5}, \frac{1 + \sqrt{17}}{2} \approx 2.56$, and $\frac{1 - \sqrt{17}}{2} \approx -1.56$.

5. Find all real solutions of $x^3 - 5x^2 - 2x + 24 = 0$.

6. Find all real zeros of $f(x) = 3x^4 - 2x^3 - 37x^2 + 24x + 12$.

The Irrational Conjugates Theorem

In Example 4, notice that the irrational zeros are *conjugates* of the form $a + \sqrt{b}$ and $a - \sqrt{b}$. This illustrates the theorem below.

Core Concept

The Irrational Conjugates Theorem

Let f be a polynomial function with rational coefficients, and let a and b be rational numbers such that $\sqrt{b}$ is irrational. If $a + \sqrt{b}$ is a zero of f, then $a - \sqrt{b}$ is also a zero of f.

EXAMPLE 5 Using Zeros to Write a Polynomial Function

Write a polynomial function f of least degree that has rational coefficients, a leading coefficient of 1, and the zeros 3 and $2 + \sqrt{5}$.

SOLUTION

Because the coefficients are rational and $2 + \sqrt{5}$ is a zero, $2 - \sqrt{5}$ must also be a zero by the Irrational Conjugates Theorem. Use the three zeros and the Factor Theorem to write $f(x)$ as a product of three factors.

$$f(x) = (x - 3)\left[x - (2 + \sqrt{5})\right]\left[x - (2 - \sqrt{5})\right] \qquad \text{Write } f(x) \text{ in factored form.}$$
$$= (x - 3)\left[(x - 2) - \sqrt{5}\right]\left[(x - 2) + \sqrt{5}\right] \qquad \text{Regroup terms.}$$
$$= (x - 3)\left[(x - 2)^2 - 5\right] \qquad \text{Multiply.}$$
$$= (x - 3)\left[(x^2 - 4x + 4) - 5\right] \qquad \text{Expand binomial.}$$
$$= (x - 3)(x^2 - 4x - 1) \qquad \text{Simplify.}$$
$$= x^3 - 4x^2 - x - 3x^2 + 12x + 3 \qquad \text{Multiply.}$$
$$= x^3 - 7x^2 + 11x + 3 \qquad \text{Combine like terms.}$$

Check

You can check this result by evaluating f at each of its three zeros.

$$f(3) = 3^3 - 7(3)^2 + 11(3) + 3 = 27 - 63 + 33 + 3 = 0 \checkmark$$
$$f(2 + \sqrt{5}) = (2 + \sqrt{5})^3 - 7(2 + \sqrt{5})^2 + 11(2 + \sqrt{5}) + 3$$
$$= 38 + 17\sqrt{5} - 63 - 28\sqrt{5} + 22 + 11\sqrt{5} + 3$$
$$= 0 \checkmark$$

Because $f(2 + \sqrt{5}) = 0$, by the Irrational Conjugates Theorem $f(2 - \sqrt{5}) = 0$. $\checkmark$

7. Write a polynomial function f of least degree that has rational coefficients, a leading coefficient of 1, and the zeros 4 and $1 - \sqrt{5}$.

Vocabulary and Core Concept Check

1. **COMPLETE THE SENTENCE** If a polynomial function f has integer coefficients, then every rational solution of $f(x) = 0$ has the form $\frac{p}{q}$, where p is a factor of the _____ and q is a factor of the _____.

2. **DIFFERENT WORDS, SAME QUESTION** Which is different? Find "both" answers.

   Find the y-intercept of the graph of $y = x^3 - 2x^2 - x + 2$.

   Find the x-intercepts of the graph of $y = x^3 - 2x^2 - x + 2$.

   Find all the real solutions of $x^3 - 2x^2 - x + 2 = 0$.

   Find the real zeros of $f(x) = x^3 - 2x^2 - x + 2$.

Monitoring Progress and Modeling with Mathematics

In Exercises 3–12, solve the equation. *(See Example 1.)*

3. $z^3 - z^2 - 12z = 0$

4. $a^3 - 4a^2 + 4a = 0$

5. $2x^4 - 4x^3 = -2x^2$

6. $v^3 - 2v^2 - 16v = -32$

7. $5w^3 = 50w$

8. $9m^5 = 27m^3$

9. $2c^4 - 6c^3 = 12c^2 - 36c$

10. $p^4 + 40 = 14p^2$

11. $12n^2 + 48n = -n^3 - 64$

12. $y^3 - 27 = 9y^2 - 27y$

In Exercises 13–20, find the zeros of the function. Then sketch a graph of the function. *(See Example 2.)*

13. $h(x) = x^4 + x^3 - 6x^2$

14. $f(x) = x^4 - 18x^2 + 81$

15. $p(x) = x^6 - 11x^5 + 30x^4$

16. $g(x) = -2x^5 + 2x^4 + 40x^3$

17. $g(x) = -4x^4 + 8x^3 + 60x^2$

18. $h(x) = -x^3 - 2x^2 + 15x$

19. $h(x) = -x^3 - x^2 + 9x + 9$

20. $p(x) = x^3 - 5x^2 - 4x + 20$

21. **USING EQUATIONS** According to the Rational Root Theorem, which is *not* a possible solution of the equation $2x^4 - 5x^3 + 10x^2 - 9 = 0$?

   Ⓐ -9 Ⓑ $-\frac{1}{2}$ Ⓒ $\frac{5}{2}$ Ⓓ 3

22. **USING EQUATIONS** According to the Rational Root Theorem, which is *not* a possible zero of the function $f(x) = 40x^5 - 42x^4 - 107x^3 + 107x^2 + 33x - 36$?

   Ⓐ $-\frac{2}{3}$ Ⓑ $-\frac{3}{8}$ Ⓒ $\frac{3}{4}$ Ⓓ $\frac{4}{5}$

ERROR ANALYSIS In Exercises 23 and 24, describe and correct the error in listing the possible rational zeros of the function.

23.

$f(x) = x^3 + 5x^2 - 9x - 45$

Possible rational zeros of f:
$1, 3, 5, 9, 15, 45$

24.

$f(x) = 3x^3 + 13x^2 - 41x + 8$

Possible rational zeros of f:
$\pm 1, \pm 3, \pm\frac{1}{2}, \pm\frac{1}{4}, \pm\frac{1}{8}, \pm\frac{3}{2}, \pm\frac{3}{4}, \pm\frac{3}{8}$

In Exercises 25–32, find all the real solutions of the equation. *(See Example 3.)*

25. $x^3 + x^2 - 17x + 15 = 0$

26. $x^3 - 2x^2 - 5x + 6 = 0$

27. $x^3 - 10x^2 + 19x + 30 = 0$

28. $x^3 + 4x^2 - 11x - 30 = 0$

29. $x^3 - 6x^2 - 7x + 60 = 0$

30. $x^3 - 16x^2 + 55x + 72 = 0$

31. $2x^3 - 3x^2 - 50x - 24 = 0$

32. $3x^3 + x^2 - 38x + 24 = 0$

In Exercises 33–38, find all the real zeros of the function. *(See Example 4.)*

33. $f(x) = x^3 - 2x^2 - 23x + 60$

34. $g(x) = x^3 - 28x - 48$

35. $h(x) = x^3 + 10x^2 + 31x + 30$

36. $f(x) = x^3 - 14x^2 + 55x - 42$

37. $p(x) = 2x^3 - x^2 - 27x + 36$

38. $g(x) = 3x^3 - 25x^2 + 58x - 40$

USING TOOLS In Exercises 39 and 40, use the graph to shorten the list of possible rational zeros of the function. Then find all real zeros of the function.

39. $f(x) = 4x^3 - 20x + 16$ 40. $f(x) = 4x^3 - 49x - 60$

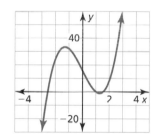
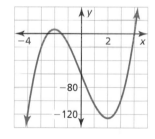

In Exercises 41–46, write a polynomial function f of least degree that has a leading coefficient of 1 and the given zeros. *(See Example 5.)*

41. $-2, 3, 6$

42. $-4, -2, 5$

43. $-2, 1 + \sqrt{7}$

44. $4, 6 - \sqrt{7}$

45. $-6, 0, 3 - \sqrt{5}$

46. $0, 5, -5 + \sqrt{8}$

47. **COMPARING METHODS** Solve the equation $x^3 - 4x^2 - 9x + 36 = 0$ using two different methods. Which method do you prefer? Explain your reasoning.

48. **REASONING** Is it possible for a cubic function to have more than three real zeros? Explain.

49. **PROBLEM SOLVING** At a factory, molten glass is poured into molds to make paperweights. Each mold is a rectangular prism with a height 3 centimeters greater than the length of each side of its square base. Each mold holds 112 cubic centimeters of glass. What are the dimensions of the mold?

50. **MATHEMATICAL CONNECTIONS** The volume of the cube shown is 8 cubic centimeters.

    a. Write a polynomial equation that you can use to find the value of x.

    b. Identify the possible rational solutions of the equation in part (a).

    c. Use synthetic division to find a rational solution of the equation. Show that no other real solutions exist.

    d. What are the dimensions of the cube?

51. **PROBLEM SOLVING** Archaeologists discovered a huge hydraulic concrete block at the ruins of Caesarea with a volume of 945 cubic meters. The block is x meters high by $12x - 15$ meters long by $12x - 21$ meters wide. What are the dimensions of the block?

52. **MAKING AN ARGUMENT** Your friend claims that when a polynomial function has a leading coefficient of 1 and the coefficients are all integers, every possible rational zero is an integer. Is your friend correct? Explain your reasoning.

53. **MODELING WITH MATHEMATICS** During a 10-year period, the amount (in millions of dollars) of athletic equipment E sold domestically can be modeled by $E(t) = -20t^3 + 252t^2 - 280t + 21{,}614$, where t is in years.

    a. Write a polynomial equation to find the year when about \$24,014,000,000 of athletic equipment is sold.

    b. List the possible whole-number solutions of the equation in part (a). Consider the domain when making your list of possible solutions.

    c. Use synthetic division to find when \$24,014,000,000 of athletic equipment is sold.

54. **THOUGHT PROVOKING** Write a third or fourth degree polynomial function that has zeros at $\pm\frac{3}{4}$. Justify your answer.

55. **MODELING WITH MATHEMATICS** You are designing a marble basin that will hold a fountain for a city park. The sides and bottom of the basin should be 1 foot thick. Its outer length should be twice its outer width and outer height. What should the outer dimensions of the basin be if it is to hold 36 cubic feet of water?

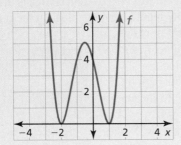

56. **HOW DO YOU SEE IT?** Use the information in the graph to answer the questions.

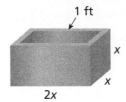

a. What are the real zeros of the function f?

b. Write an equation of the quartic function in factored form.

57. **REASONING** Determine the value of k for each equation so that the given x-value is a solution.

a. $x^3 - 6x^2 - 7x + k = 0$; $x = 4$

b. $2x^3 + 7x^2 - kx - 18 = 0$; $x = -6$

c. $kx^3 - 35x^2 + 19x + 30 = 0$; $x = 5$

58. **WRITING EQUATIONS** Write a polynomial function g of least degree that has rational coefficients, a leading coefficient of 1, and the zeros $-2 + \sqrt{7}$ and $3 + \sqrt{2}$.

In Exercises 59–62, solve $f(x) = g(x)$ by graphing and algebraic methods.

59. $f(x) = x^3 + x^2 - x - 1$; $g(x) = -x + 1$

60. $f(x) = x^4 - 5x^3 + 2x^2 + 8x$; $g(x) = -x^2 + 6x - 8$

61. $f(x) = x^3 - 4x^2 + 4x$; $g(x) = -2x + 4$

62. $f(x) = x^4 + 2x^3 - 11x^2 - 12x + 36$;
$g(x) = -x^2 - 6x - 9$

63. **MODELING WITH MATHEMATICS** You are building a pair of ramps for a loading platform. The left ramp is twice as long as the right ramp. If 150 cubic feet of concrete are used to build the ramps, what are the dimensions of each ramp?

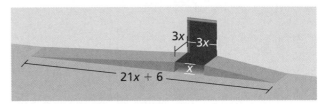

64. **MODELING WITH MATHEMATICS** Some ice sculptures are made by filling a mold and then freezing it. You are making an ice mold for a school dance. It is to be shaped like a pyramid with a height 1 foot greater than the length of each side of its square base. The volume of the ice sculpture is 4 cubic feet. What are the dimensions of the mold?

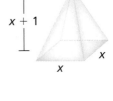

65. **ABSTRACT REASONING** Let a_n be the leading coefficient of a polynomial function f and a_0 be the constant term. If a_n has r factors and a_0 has s factors, what is the greatest number of possible rational zeros of f that can be generated by the Rational Zero Theorem? Explain your reasoning.

Maintaining Mathematical Proficiency
Reviewing what you learned in previous grades and lessons

Decide whether the function is a polynomial function. If so, write it in standard form and state its degree, type, and leading coefficient. *(Section 3.1)*

66. $h(x) = -3x^2 + 2x - 9 + \sqrt{4}x^3$

67. $g(x) = 2x^3 - 7x^2 - 3x^{-1} + x$

68. $f(x) = \frac{1}{3}x^2 + 2x^3 - 4x^4 - \sqrt{3}$

69. $p(x) = 2x - 5x^3 + 9x^2 + \sqrt[4]{x} + 1$

Find the zeros of the function. *(Skills Review Handbook)*

70. $f(x) = 7x^2 + 42$ 71. $g(x) = 9x^2 + 81$ 72. $h(x) = 5x^2 + 40$ 73. $f(x) = 8x^2 - 1$

Essential Question How can you determine whether a polynomial equation has imaginary solutions?

EXPLORATION 1 Cubic Equations and Imaginary Solutions

Work with a partner. Match each cubic polynomial equation with the graph of its related polynomial function. Then find *all* solutions. Make a conjecture about how you can use a graph or table of values to determine the number and types of solutions of a cubic polynomial equation.

a. $x^3 - 3x^2 + x + 5 = 0$

b. $x^3 - 2x^2 - x + 2 = 0$

c. $x^3 - x^2 - 4x + 4 = 0$

d. $x^3 + 5x^2 + 8x + 6 = 0$

e. $x^3 - 3x^2 + x - 3 = 0$

f. $x^3 - 3x^2 + 2x = 0$

A.
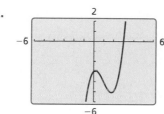

B.
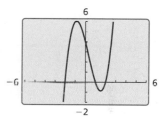

C.
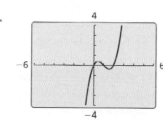

D.
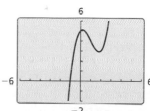

E.
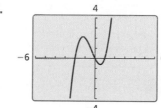

F.
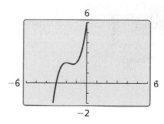

USING TOOLS STRATEGICALLY

To be proficient in math, you need to use technology to enable you to visualize results and explore consequences.

EXPLORATION 2 Quartic Equations and Imaginary Solutions

Work with a partner. Use the graph of the related quartic function, or a table of values, to determine whether each quartic equation has imaginary solutions. Explain your reasoning. Then find *all* solutions.

a. $x^4 - 2x^3 - x^2 + 2x = 0$

b. $x^4 - 1 = 0$

c. $x^4 + x^3 - x - 1 = 0$

d. $x^4 - 3x^3 + x^2 + 3x - 2 = 0$

Communicate Your Answer

3. How can you determine whether a polynomial equation has imaginary solutions?

4. Is it possible for a cubic equation to have three imaginary solutions? Explain your reasoning.

3.6 Lesson

Core Vocabulary

complex conjugates, *p. 155*

Previous
repeated solution
degree of a polynomial
solution of an equation
zero of a function
conjugates

What You Will Learn

▶ Use the Fundamental Theorem of Algebra.
▶ Find conjugate pairs of complex zeros of polynomial functions.
▶ Use Descartes's Rule of Signs.

The Fundamental Theorem of Algebra

The table shows several polynomial equations and their solutions, including repeated solutions. In the last equation, the repeated solution $x = -1$ is counted twice.

Equation	Degree	Solution(s)	Number of solutions
$2x - 1 = 0$	1	$\frac{1}{2}$	1
$x^2 + 2 = 0$	2	$\pm i\sqrt{2}$	2
$x^3 + x^2 - x - 1 = 0$	3	$-1, -1, 1$	3

In the table, note the relationship between the degree of the polynomial $f(x)$ and the number of solutions of $f(x) = 0$. This relationship is generalized by the *Fundamental Theorem of Algebra*.

Core Concept

The Fundamental Theorem of Algebra

Theorem   If $f(x)$ is a polynomial of degree n where $n > 0$, then the equation $f(x) = 0$ has at least one solution in the set of complex numbers.

Corollary   If $f(x)$ is a polynomial of degree n where $n > 0$, then the equation $f(x) = 0$ has exactly n solutions provided each solution repeated twice is counted as two solutions, each solution repeated three times is counted as three solutions, and so on.

STUDY TIP

The statements "the polynomial equation $f(x) = 0$ has exactly n solutions" and "the polynomial function f has exactly n zeros" are equivalent.

The corollary to the Fundamental Theorem of Algebra also means that an nth-degree polynomial function f has exactly n zeros.

EXAMPLE 1   Solving a Polynomial Equation

How many solutions does $x^4 + x^3 + 8x + 8 = 0$ have? Find all the solutions.

SOLUTION

Because $x^4 + x^3 + 8x + 8 = 0$ is a polynomial equation of degree 4, it has four solutions. Notice that you can use factoring by grouping to begin solving the equation.

$$(x^4 + x^3) + (8x + 8) = 0 \qquad \text{Group terms with common factors.}$$
$$x^3(x + 1) + 8(x + 1) = 0 \qquad \text{Factor out GCF of each pair of terms.}$$
$$(x + 1)(x^3 + 8) = 0 \qquad \text{Factor out } (x + 1).$$
$$(x + 1)(x + 2)(x^2 - 2x + 4) = 0 \qquad \text{Sum of Two Cubes Pattern}$$

The linear factors indicate that -2 and -1 are solutions. To find the remaining two solutions, solve $x^2 - 2x + 4 = 0$ by using the Quadratic Formula.

$$x = \frac{-(-2) \pm \sqrt{(-2)^2 - 4(1)(4)}}{2(1)} = 1 \pm i\sqrt{3}$$

▶ The solutions are $-2, -1, 1 - i\sqrt{3}$, and $1 + i\sqrt{3}$.

EXAMPLE 2   Finding the Zeros of a Polynomial Function

Find all zeros of $f(x) = x^5 + x^3 - 2x^2 - 12x - 8$.

SOLUTION

Step 1 Find the rational zeros of f. Because f is a polynomial function of degree 5, it has five zeros. The possible rational zeros are ± 1, ± 2, ± 4, and ± 8. Using synthetic division, you can determine that -1 is a zero repeated twice and 2 is also a zero.

Step 2 Write $f(x)$ in factored form. Dividing $f(x)$ by its known factors $x + 1$, $x + 1$, and $x - 2$ gives a quotient of $x^2 + 4$. So,

$$f(x) = (x + 1)^2(x - 2)(x^2 + 4).$$

Step 3 Find the complex zeros of f. Solving $x^2 + 4 = 0$, you get $x = \pm 2i$. This means $x^2 + 4 = (x + 2i)(x - 2i)$.

$$f(x) = (x + 1)^2(x - 2)(x + 2i)(x - 2i)$$

▶ From the factorization, there are five zeros. The zeros of f are

$$-1, -1, 2, -2i, \text{ and } 2i.$$

The graph of f and the real zeros are shown. Notice that only the *real* zeros appear as x-intercepts. Also, the graph of f touches the x-axis at the repeated zero $x = -1$ and crosses the x-axis at $x = 2$.

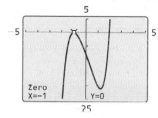
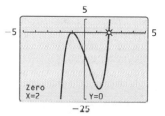

STUDY TIP

Notice that you can use imaginary numbers to write $(x^2 + 4)$ as $(x + 2i)(x - 2i)$. In general, $(a^2 + b^2) = (a + bi)(a - bi)$.

Monitoring Progress   Help in English and Spanish at *BigIdeasMath.com*

Identify the number of solutions of the polynomial equation. Then find all solutions of the equation.

1. $x^5 - 4x^3 - x^2 + 4 = 0$ **2.** $x^4 + 7x^2 - 144 = 0$

Find all zeros of the polynomial function.

3. $f(x) = x^3 + 7x^2 + 16x + 12$

4. $f(x) = x^5 - 3x^4 + 5x^3 - x^2 - 6x + 4$

Complex Conjugates

Pairs of complex numbers of the forms $a + bi$ and $a - bi$, where $b \neq 0$, are called **complex conjugates**. In Example 2, notice that the zeros $2i$ and $-2i$ are complex conjugates. This illustrates the next theorem.

 Core Concept

The Complex Conjugates Theorem

If f is a polynomial function with real coefficients, and $a + bi$ is an imaginary zero of f, then $a - bi$ is also a zero of f.

EXAMPLE 3 **Using Zeros to Write a Polynomial Function**

Write a polynomial function f of least degree that has rational coefficients, a leading coefficient of 1, and the zeros 2 and $3 + i$.

SOLUTION

Because the coefficients are rational and $3 + i$ is a zero, $3 - i$ must also be a zero by the Complex Conjugates Theorem. Use the three zeros and the Factor Theorem to write $f(x)$ as a product of three factors.

$$f(x) = (x - 2)[x - (3 + i)][x - (3 - i)] \qquad \text{Write } f(x) \text{ in factored form.}$$
$$= (x - 2)[(x - 3) - i][(x - 3) + i] \qquad \text{Regroup terms.}$$
$$= (x - 2)[(x - 3)^2 - i^2] \qquad \text{Multiply.}$$
$$= (x - 2)[(x^2 - 6x + 9) - (-1)] \qquad \text{Expand binomial and use } i^2 = -1.$$
$$= (x - 2)(x^2 - 6x + 10) \qquad \text{Simplify.}$$
$$= x^3 - 6x^2 + 10x - 2x^2 + 12x - 20 \qquad \text{Multiply.}$$
$$= x^3 - 8x^2 + 22x - 20 \qquad \text{Combine like terms.}$$

Check

You can check this result by evaluating f at each of its three zeros.

$$f(2) = (2)^3 - 8(2)^2 + 22(2) - 20 = 8 - 32 + 44 - 20 = 0 \ ✓$$

$$f(3 + i) = (3 + i)^3 - 8(3 + i)^2 + 22(3 + i) - 20$$
$$= 18 + 26i - 64 - 48i + 66 + 22i - 20$$
$$= 0 \ ✓$$

Because $f(3 + i) = 0$, by the Complex Conjugates Theorem $f(3 - i) = 0$. ✓

Monitoring Progress Help in English and Spanish at *BigIdeasMath.com*

Write a polynomial function f of least degree that has rational coefficients, a leading coefficient of 1, and the given zeros.

5. $-1, 4i$ **6.** $3, 1 + i\sqrt{5}$ **7.** $\sqrt{2}, 1 - 3i$ **8.** $2, 2i, 4 - \sqrt{6}$

Descartes's Rule of Signs

French mathematician René Descartes (1596–1650) found the following relationship between the coefficients of a polynomial function and the number of positive and negative zeros of the function.

Core Concept

Descartes's Rule of Signs

Let $f(x) = a_n x^n + a_{n-1} x^{n-1} + \cdots + a_2 x^2 + a_1 x + a_0$ be a polynomial function with real coefficients.

- The number of *positive real zeros* of f is equal to the number of changes in sign of the coefficients of $f(x)$ or is less than this by an even number.

- The number of *negative real zeros* of f is equal to the number of changes in sign of the coefficients of $f(-x)$ or is less than this by an even number.

EXAMPLE 4 Using Descartes's Rule of Signs

Determine the possible numbers of positive real zeros, negative real zeros, and imaginary zeros for $f(x) = x^6 - 2x^5 + 3x^4 - 10x^3 - 6x^2 - 8x - 8$.

SOLUTION

$$f(x) = x^6 - 2x^5 + 3x^4 - 10x^3 - 6x^2 - 8x - 8.$$

The coefficients in $f(x)$ have 3 sign changes, so f has 3 or 1 positive real zero(s).

$$f(-x) = (-x)^6 - 2(-x)^5 + 3(-x)^4 - 10(-x)^3 - 6(-x)^2 - 8(-x) - 8$$
$$= x^6 + 2x^5 + 3x^4 + 10x^3 - 6x^2 + 8x - 8$$

The coefficients in $f(-x)$ have 3 sign changes, so f has 3 or 1 negative zero(s).

▶ The possible numbers of zeros for f are summarized in the table below.

Positive real zeros	Negative real zeros	Imaginary zeros	Total zeros
3	3	0	6
3	1	2	6
1	3	2	6
1	1	4	6

EXAMPLE 5 Real-Life Application

A tachometer measures the speed (in revolutions per minute, or RPMs) at which an engine shaft rotates. For a certain boat, the speed x (in hundreds of RPMs) of the engine shaft and the speed s (in miles per hour) of the boat are modeled by

$$s(x) = 0.00547x^3 - 0.225x^2 + 3.62x - 11.0.$$

What is the tachometer reading when the boat travels 15 miles per hour?

SOLUTION

Substitute 15 for $s(x)$ in the function. You can rewrite the resulting equation as

$$0 = 0.00547x^3 - 0.225x^2 + 3.62x - 26.0.$$

The related function to this equation is $f(x) = 0.00547x^3 - 0.225x^2 + 3.62x - 26.0$. By Descartes's Rule of Signs, you know f has 3 or 1 positive real zero(s). In the context of speed, negative real zeros and imaginary zeros do not make sense, so you do not need to check for them. To approximate the positive real zeros of f, use a graphing calculator. From the graph, there is 1 real zero, $x \approx 19.9$.

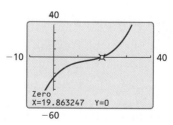

▶ The tachometer reading is about 1990 RPMs.

Monitoring Progress Help in English and Spanish at *BigIdeasMath.com*

Determine the possible numbers of positive real zeros, negative real zeros, and imaginary zeros for the function.

9. $f(x) = x^3 + 9x - 25$ **10.** $f(x) = 3x^4 - 7x^3 + x^2 - 13x + 8$

11. WHAT IF? In Example 5, what is the tachometer reading when the boat travels 20 miles per hour?

Vocabulary and Core Concept Check

1. **COMPLETE THE SENTENCE** The expressions $5 + i$ and $5 - i$ are _____.

2. **WRITING** How many solutions does the polynomial equation $(x + 8)^3(x - 1) = 0$ have? Explain.

Monitoring Progress and Modeling with Mathematics

In Exercises 3–8, identify the number of solutions of the polynomial equation. Then find all solutions of the equation. *(See Example 1.)*

3. $x^3 + 64 = 0$

4. $8y^4 - y = 0$

5. $t^6 - t^2 = 0$

6. $z^4 + 5z^2 - 14 = 0$

7. $s^5 - s^3 - s^2 + 1 = 0$

8. $x^3 - 3x^2 + 2x - 6 = 0$

In Exercises 9–16, find all zeros of the polynomial function. *(See Example 2.)*

9. $f(x) = x^4 - 6x^3 + 7x^2 + 6x - 8$

10. $f(x) = x^4 + 5x^3 - 7x^2 - 29x + 30$

11. $g(x) = x^4 - 9x^2 - 4x + 12$

12. $h(x) = x^3 + 5x^2 - 4x - 20$

13. $g(x) = x^4 + 4x^3 + 7x^2 + 16x + 12$

14. $h(x) = x^4 - x^3 + 7x^2 - 9x - 18$

15. $g(x) = x^5 + 3x^4 - 4x^3 - 2x^2 - 12x - 16$

16. $f(x) = x^5 - 20x^3 + 20x^2 - 21x + 20$

ANALYZING RELATIONSHIPS In Exercises 17–20, determine the number of imaginary zeros for the function with the given degree and graph. Explain your reasoning.

17. Degree: 4

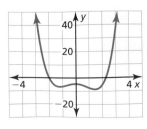

18. Degree: 5

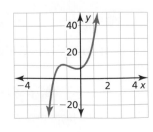

19. Degree: 2

20. Degree: 3

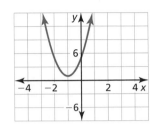

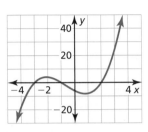

In Exercises 21–28, write a polynomial function f of least degree that has rational coefficients, a leading coefficient of 1, and the given zeros. *(See Example 3.)*

21. $-5, -1, 2$

22. $-2, 1, 3$

23. $3, 4 + i$

24. $2, 5 - i$

25. $4, -\sqrt{5}$

26. $3i, 2 - i$

27. $2, 1 + i, 2 - \sqrt{3}$

28. $3, 4 + 2i, 1 + \sqrt{7}$

ERROR ANALYSIS In Exercises 29 and 30, describe and correct the error in writing a polynomial function with rational coefficients and the given zero(s).

29. Zeros: $2, 1 + i$

$$
\begin{aligned}
f(x) &= (x - 2)[x - (1 + i)] \\
&= x(x - 1 - i) - 2(x - 1 - i) \\
&= x^2 - x - ix - 2x + 2 + 2i \\
&= x^2 - (3 + i)x + (2 + 2i)
\end{aligned}
$$

30. Zero: $2 + i$

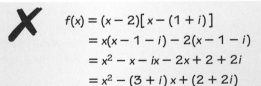

$$
\begin{aligned}
f(x) &= [x - (2 + i)][x + (2 + i)] \\
&= (x - 2 - i)(x + 2 + i) \\
&= x^2 + 2x + ix - 2x - 4 - 2i - ix - 2i - i^2 \\
&= x^2 - 4i - 3
\end{aligned}
$$

31. **OPEN-ENDED** Write a polynomial function of degree 6 with zeros 1, 2, and $-i$. Justify your answer.

32. **REASONING** Two zeros of $f(x) = x^3 - 6x^2 - 16x + 96$ are 4 and -4. Explain why the third zero must also be a real number.

In Exercises 33–40, determine the possible numbers of positive real zeros, negative real zeros, and imaginary zeros for the function. *(See Example 4.)*

33. $g(x) = x^4 - x^2 - 6$

34. $g(x) = -x^3 + 5x^2 + 12$

35. $g(x) = x^3 - 4x^2 + 8x + 7$

36. $g(x) = x^5 - 2x^3 - x^2 + 6$

37. $g(x) = x^5 - 3x^3 + 8x - 10$

38. $g(x) = x^5 + 7x^4 - 4x^3 - 3x^2 + 9x - 15$

39. $g(x) = x^6 + x^5 - 3x^4 + x^3 + 5x^2 + 9x - 18$

40. $g(x) = x^7 + 4x^4 - 10x + 25$

41. **REASONING** Which is *not* a possible classification of zeros for $f(x) = x^5 - 4x^3 + 6x^2 + 2x - 6$? Explain.

   Ⓐ three positive real zeros, two negative real zeros, and zero imaginary zeros

   Ⓑ three positive real zeros, zero negative real zeros, and two imaginary zeros

   Ⓒ one positive real zero, four negative real zeros, and zero imaginary zeros

   Ⓓ one positive real zero, two negative real zeros, and two imaginary zeros

42. **USING STRUCTURE** Use Descartes's Rule of Signs to determine which function has at least 1 positive real zero.

   Ⓐ $f(x) = x^4 + 2x^3 - 9x^2 - 2x + 8$

   Ⓑ $f(x) = x^4 + 4x^3 + 8x^2 + 16x + 16$

   Ⓒ $f(x) = -x^4 - 5x^2 - 4$

   Ⓓ $f(x) = x^4 + 4x^3 + 7x^2 + 12x + 12$

43. **MODELING WITH MATHEMATICS** From 1890 to 2000, the American Indian, Eskimo, and Aleut population P (in thousands) can be modeled by the function $P = 0.004t^3 - 0.24t^2 + 4.9t + 243$, where t is the number of years since 1890. In which year did the population first reach 722,000? *(See Example 5.)*

44. **MODELING WITH MATHEMATICS** Over a period of 14 years, the number N of inland lakes infested with zebra mussels in a certain state can be modeled by

$$N = -0.0284t^4 + 0.5937t^3 - 2.464t^2 + 8.33t - 2.5$$

where t is time (in years). In which year did the number of infested inland lakes first reach 120?

45. **MODELING WITH MATHEMATICS** For the 12 years that a grocery store has been open, its annual revenue R (in millions of dollars) can be modeled by the function

$$R = 0.0001(-t^4 + 12t^3 - 77t^2 + 600t + 13{,}650)$$

where t is the number of years since the store opened. In which year(s) was the revenue $1.5 million?

46. **MAKING AN ARGUMENT** Your friend claims that $2 - i$ is a complex zero of the polynomial function $f(x) = x^3 - 2x^2 + 2x + 5i$, but that its conjugate is *not* a zero. You claim that both $2 - i$ and its conjugate *must* be zeros by the Complex Conjugates Theorem. Who is correct? Justify your answer.

47. **MATHEMATICAL CONNECTIONS** A solid monument with the dimensions shown is to be built using 1000 cubic feet of marble. What is the value of x?

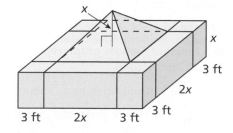

48. THOUGHT PROVOKING Write and graph a polynomial function of degree 5 that has all positive or negative real zeros. Label each x-intercept. Then write the function in standard form.

49. WRITING The graph of the constant polynomial function $f(x) = 2$ is a line that does not have any x-intercepts. Does the function contradict the Fundamental Theorem of Algebra? Explain.

50. HOW DO YOU SEE IT? The graph represents a polynomial function of degree 6.

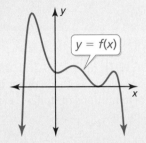

a. How many positive real zeros does the function have? negative real zeros? imaginary zeros?

b. Use Descartes's Rule of Signs and your answers in part (a) to describe the possible sign changes in the coefficients of $f(x)$.

51. FINDING A PATTERN Use a graphing calculator to graph the function $f(x) = (x + 3)^n$ for $n = 2, 3, 4, 5, 6,$ and 7.

a. Compare the graphs when n is even and n is odd.

b. Describe the behavior of the graph near the zero $x = -3$ as n increases.

c. Use your results from parts (a) and (b) to describe the behavior of the graph of $g(x) = (x - 4)^{20}$ near $x = 4$.

52. DRAWING CONCLUSIONS Find the zeros of each function.

$$f(x) = x^2 - 5x + 6$$
$$g(x) = x^3 - 7x + 6$$
$$h(x) = x^4 + 2x^3 + x^2 + 8x - 12$$
$$k(x) = x^5 - 3x^4 - 9x^3 + 25x^2 - 6x$$

a. Describe the relationship between the sum of the zeros of a polynomial function and the coefficients of the polynomial function.

b. Describe the relationship between the product of the zeros of a polynomial function and the coefficients of the polynomial function.

53. PROBLEM SOLVING You want to save money so you can buy a used car in four years. At the end of each summer, you deposit $1000 earned from summer jobs into your bank account. The table shows the value of your deposits over the four-year period. In the table, g is the growth factor $1 + r$, where r is the annual interest rate expressed as a decimal.

Deposit	Year 1	Year 2	Year 3	Year 4
1st Deposit	1000	1000g	1000g^2	1000g^3
2nd Deposit	–	1000		
3rd Deposit	–	–	1000	
4th Deposit	–	–	–	1000

a. Copy and complete the table.

b. Write a polynomial function that gives the value v of your account at the end of the fourth summer in terms of g.

c. You want to buy a car that costs about $4300. What growth factor do you need to obtain this amount? What annual interest rate do you need?

Maintaining Mathematical Proficiency
Reviewing what you learned in previous grades and lessons

Describe the transformation of $f(x) = x^2$ represented by g. Then graph each function. *(Section 2.5)*

54. $g(x) = -3x^2$

55. $g(x) = (x - 4)^2 + 6$

56. $g(x) = -(x - 1)^2$

57. $g(x) = 5(x + 4)^2$

Write a function g whose graph represents the indicated transformation of the graph of f. *(Sections 2.2 and 2.5)*

58. $f(x) = x$; vertical shrink by a factor of $\frac{1}{3}$ and a reflection in the y-axis

59. $f(x) = |x + 1| - 3$; horizontal stretch by a factor of 9

60. $f(x) = x^2$; reflection in the x-axis, followed by a translation 2 units right and 7 units up

3.7 Transformations of Polynomial Functions

Essential Question How can you transform the graph of a polynomial function?

EXPLORATION 1 **Transforming the Graph of a Cubic Function**

Work with a partner. The graph of the cubic function

$$f(x) = x^3$$

is shown. The graph of each cubic function g represents a transformation of the graph of f. Write a rule for g. Use a graphing calculator to verify your answers.

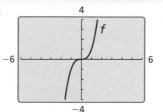

a.

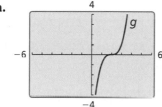

b.

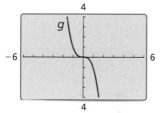

c.

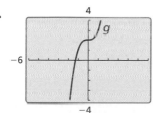

d.

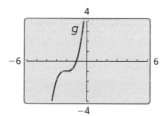

EXPLORATION 2 **Transforming the Graph of a Quartic Function**

Work with a partner. The graph of the quartic function

$$f(x) = x^4$$

is shown. The graph of each quartic function g represents a transformation of the graph of f. Write a rule for g. Use a graphing calculator to verify your answers.

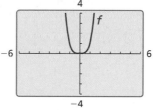

a.

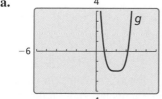

b.

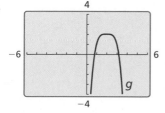

LOOKING FOR STRUCTURE

To be proficient in math, you need to see complicated things, such as some algebraic expressions, as being single objects or as being composed of several objects.

Communicate Your Answer

3. How can you transform the graph of a polynomial function?

4. Describe the transformation of $f(x) = x^4$ represented by $g(x) = (x + 1)^4 + 3$. Then graph g.

Section 3.7 Transformations of Polynomial Functions **161**

What You Will Learn

▶ Describe transformations of polynomial functions.

▶ Write transformations of polynomial functions.

Describing Transformations of Polynomial Functions

You can transform graphs of polynomial functions in the same way you transformed graphs of linear functions, absolute value functions, and quadratic functions. Examples of transformations of the graph of $f(x) = x^4$ are shown below.

Core Concept

Transformation	$f(x)$ Notation	Examples	
Horizontal Translation Graph shifts left or right.	$f(x - h)$	$g(x) = (x - 5)^4$	5 units right
		$g(x) = (x + 2)^4$	2 units left
Vertical Translation Graph shifts up or down.	$f(x) + k$	$g(x) = x^4 + 1$	1 unit up
		$g(x) = x^4 - 4$	4 units down
Reflection Graph flips over x- or y-axis.	$f(-x)$	$g(x) = (-x)^4 = x^4$	over y-axis
	$-f(x)$	$g(x) = -x^4$	over x-axis
Horizontal Stretch or Shrink Graph stretches away from or shrinks toward y-axis.	$f(ax)$	$g(x) = (2x)^4$	shrink by a factor of $\frac{1}{2}$
		$g(x) = \left(\frac{1}{2}x\right)^4$	stretch by a factor of 2
Vertical Stretch or Shrink Graph stretches away from or shrinks toward x-axis.	$a \cdot f(x)$	$g(x) = 8x^4$	stretch by a factor of 8
		$g(x) = \frac{1}{4}x^4$	shrink by a factor of $\frac{1}{4}$

EXAMPLE 1   Translating a Polynomial Function

Describe the transformation of $f(x) = x^3$ represented by $g(x) = (x + 5)^3 + 2$. Then graph each function.

SOLUTION

Notice that the function is of the form $g(x) = (x - h)^3 + k$. Rewrite the function to identify h and k.

$$g(x) = (x - (-5))^3 + 2$$

$$\qquad\qquad \uparrow h \qquad\quad \uparrow k$$

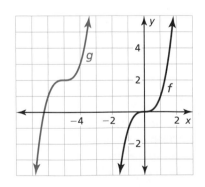

▶ Because $h = -5$ and $k = 2$, the graph of g is a translation 5 units left and 2 units up of the graph of f.

Monitoring Progress  Help in English and Spanish at *BigIdeasMath.com*

1. Describe the transformation of $f(x) = x^4$ represented by $g(x) = (x - 3)^4 - 1$. Then graph each function.

EXAMPLE 2   Transforming Polynomial Functions

Describe the transformation of f represented by g. Then graph each function.

a. $f(x) = x^4$, $g(x) = -\frac{1}{4}x^4$

b. $f(x) = x^5$, $g(x) = (2x)^5 - 3$

SOLUTION

a. Notice that the function is of the form $g(x) = -ax^4$, where $a = \frac{1}{4}$.

▶ So, the graph of g is a reflection in the x-axis and a vertical shrink by a factor of $\frac{1}{4}$ of the graph of f.

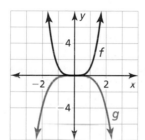

b. Notice that the function is of the form $g(x) = (ax)^5 + k$, where $a = 2$ and $k = -3$.

▶ So, the graph of g is a horizontal shrink by a factor of $\frac{1}{2}$ and a translation 3 units down of the graph of f.

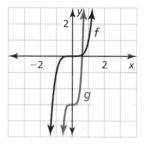

Monitoring Progress Help in English and Spanish at BigIdeasMath.com

2. Describe the transformation of $f(x) = x^3$ represented by $g(x) = 4(x + 2)^3$. Then graph each function.

Writing Transformations of Polynomial Functions

EXAMPLE 3   Writing Transformed Polynomial Functions

Let $f(x) = x^3 + x^2 + 1$. Write a rule for g and then graph each function. Describe the graph of g as a transformation of the graph of f.

a. $g(x) = f(-x)$

b. $g(x) = 3f(x)$

SOLUTION

a. $g(x) = f(-x)$

$\quad = (-x)^3 + (-x)^2 + 1$

$\quad = -x^3 + x^2 + 1$

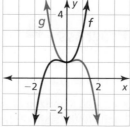

▶ The graph of g is a reflection in the y-axis of the graph of f.

b. $g(x) = 3f(x)$

$\quad = 3(x^3 + x^2 + 1)$

$\quad = 3x^3 + 3x^2 + 3$

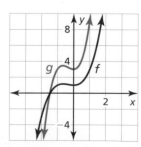

▶ The graph of g is a vertical stretch by a factor of 3 of the graph of f.

REMEMBER

Vertical stretches and shrinks do not change the x-intercept(s) of a graph. You can observe this using the graph in Example 3(b).

EXAMPLE 4   Writing a Transformed Polynomial Function

Let the graph of g be a vertical stretch by a factor of 2, followed by a translation 3 units up of the graph of $f(x) = x^4 - 2x^2$. Write a rule for g.

SOLUTION

Check

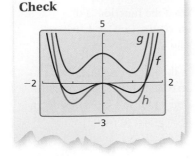

Step 1 First write a function h that represents the vertical stretch of f.

$$h(x) = 2 \cdot f(x) \qquad \text{Multiply the output by 2.}$$
$$= 2(x^4 - 2x^2) \qquad \text{Substitute } x^4 - 2x^2 \text{ for } f(x).$$
$$= 2x^4 - 4x^2 \qquad \text{Distributive Property}$$

Step 2 Then write a function g that represents the translation of h.

$$g(x) = h(x) + 3 \qquad \text{Add 3 to the output.}$$
$$= 2x^4 - 4x^2 + 3 \qquad \text{Substitute } 2x^4 - 4x^2 \text{ for } h(x).$$

▶ The transformed function is $g(x) = 2x^4 - 4x^2 + 3$.

EXAMPLE 5   Modeling with Mathematics

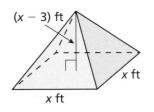
$(x - 3)$ ft
x ft
x ft

The function $V(x) = \frac{1}{3}x^3 - x^2$ represents the volume (in cubic feet) of the square pyramid shown. The function $W(x) = V(3x)$ represents the volume (in cubic feet) when x is measured in yards. Write a rule for W. Find and interpret $W(10)$.

SOLUTION

1. **Understand the Problem** You are given a function V whose inputs are in feet and whose outputs are in cubic feet. You are given another function W whose inputs are in yards and whose outputs are in cubic feet. The horizontal shrink shown by $W(x) = V(3x)$ makes sense because there are 3 feet in 1 yard. You are asked to write a rule for W and interpret the output for a given input.

2. **Make a Plan** Write the transformed function $W(x)$ and then find $W(10)$.

3. **Solve the Problem** $W(x) = V(3x)$

$$= \frac{1}{3}(3x)^3 - (3x)^2 \qquad \text{Replace } x \text{ with } 3x \text{ in } V(x).$$
$$= 9x^3 - 9x^2 \qquad \text{Simplify.}$$

Next, find $W(10)$.

$$W(10) = 9(10)^3 - 9(10)^2 = 9000 - 900 = 8100$$

▶ When x is 10 yards, the volume of the pyramid is 8100 cubic feet.

4. **Look Back** Because $W(10) = V(30)$, you can check that your solution is correct by verifying that $V(30) = 8100$.

$$V(30) = \frac{1}{3}(30)^3 - (30)^2 = 9000 - 900 = 8100 ✓$$

CONNECTIONS TO GEOMETRY

You can verify the function given in Example 5 using the formula for the volume of a pyramid you learned in a previous course.

$$V = \frac{1}{3}Bh$$
$$= \frac{1}{3}(x^2)(x - 3)$$
$$= \frac{1}{3}(x^3 - 3x^2)$$
$$= \frac{1}{3}x^3 - x^2$$

Monitoring Progress   🔊 Help in English and Spanish at *BigIdeasMath.com*

3. Let $f(x) = x^5 - 4x + 6$ and $g(x) = -f(x)$. Write a rule for g and then graph each function. Describe the graph of g as a transformation of the graph of f.

4. Let the graph of g be a horizontal stretch by a factor of 2, followed by a translation 3 units to the right of the graph of $f(x) = 8x^3 + 3$. Write a rule for g.

5. **WHAT IF?** In Example 5, the height of the pyramid is $6x$, and the volume (in cubic feet) is represented by $V(x) = 2x^3$. Write a rule for W. Find and interpret $W(7)$.

Vocabulary and Core Concept Check

1. **COMPLETE THE SENTENCE** The graph of $f(x) = (x + 2)^3$ is a _____ translation of the graph of $f(x) = x^3$.

2. **VOCABULARY** Describe how the vertex form of quadratic functions is similar to the form $f(x) = a(x - h)^3 + k$ for cubic functions.

Monitoring Progress and Modeling with Mathematics

In Exercises 3–6, describe the transformation of *f* represented by *g*. Then graph each function. *(See Example 1.)*

3. $f(x) = x^4$, $g(x) = x^4 + 3$

4. $f(x) = x^4$, $g(x) = (x - 5)^4$

5. $f(x) = x^5$, $g(x) = (x - 2)^5 - 1$

6. $f(x) = x^6$, $g(x) = (x + 1)^6 - 4$

ANALYZING RELATIONSHIPS In Exercises 7–10, match the function with the correct transformation of the graph of *f*. Explain your reasoning.

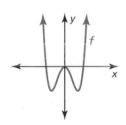

7. $y = f(x - 2)$

8. $y = f(x + 2) + 2$

9. $y = f(x - 2) + 2$

10. $y = f(x) - 2$

A.

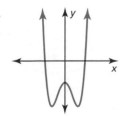

B.

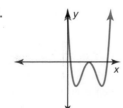

C.

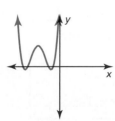

D.

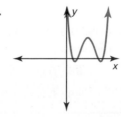

In Exercises 11–16, describe the transformation of *f* represented by *g*. Then graph each function. *(See Example 2.)*

11. $f(x) = x^4$, $g(x) = -2x^4$

12. $f(x) - x^6$, $g(x) = -3x^6$

13. $f(x) = x^3$, $g(x) = 5x^3 + 1$

14. $f(x) = x^4$, $g(x) = \frac{1}{2}x^4 + 1$

15. $f(x) = x^5$, $g(x) = \frac{3}{4}(x + 4)^5$

16. $f(x) - x^4$, $g(x) = (2x)^4 - 3$

In Exercises 17–20, write a rule for *g* and then graph each function. Describe the graph of *g* as a transformation of the graph of *f*. *(See Example 3.)*

17. $f(x) = x^4 + 1$, $g(x) = f(x + 2)$

18. $f(x) = x^5 - 2x + 3$, $g(x) = 3f(x)$

19. $f(x) = 2x^3 - 2x^2 + 6$, $g(x) = -\frac{1}{2}f(x)$

20. $f(x) = x^4 + x^3 - 1$, $g(x) = f(-x) - 5$

21. **ERROR ANALYSIS** Describe and correct the error in graphing the function $g(x) = (x + 2)^4 - 6$.

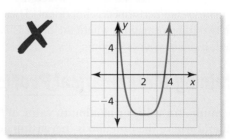

22. ERROR ANALYSIS Describe and correct the error in describing the transformation of the graph of $f(x) = x^5$ represented by the graph of $g(x) = (3x)^5 - 4$.

> The graph of g is a horizontal shrink by a factor of 3, followed by a translation 4 units down of the graph of f.

In Exercises 23–26, write a rule for g that represents the indicated transformations of the graph of f. (*See Example 4.*)

23. $f(x) = x^3 - 6$; translation 3 units left, followed by a reflection in the y-axis

24. $f(x) = x^4 + 2x + 6$; vertical stretch by a factor of 2, followed by a translation 4 units right

25. $f(x) = x^3 + 2x^2 - 9$; horizontal shrink by a factor of $\frac{1}{3}$ and a translation 2 units up, followed by a reflection in the x-axis

26. $f(x) = 2x^5 - x^3 + x^2 + 4$; reflection in the y-axis and a vertical stretch by a factor of 3, followed by a translation 1 unit down

27. MODELING WITH MATHEMATICS The volume V (in cubic feet) of the pyramid is given by $V(x) = x^3 - 4x$. The function $W(x) = V(3x)$ gives the volume (in cubic feet) of the pyramid when x is measured in yards. Write a rule for W. Find and interpret $W(5)$. (*See Example 5.*)

x ft

$(2x - 4)$ ft $(3x + 6)$ ft

28. MAKING AN ARGUMENT The volume of a cube with side length x is given by $V(x) = x^3$. Your friend claims that when you divide the volume in half, the volume decreases by a greater amount than when you divide each side length in half. Is your friend correct? Justify your answer.

29. OPEN-ENDED Describe two transformations of the graph of $f(x) = x^5$ where the order in which the transformations are performed is important. Then describe two transformations where the order is *not* important. Explain your reasoning.

30. THOUGHT PROVOKING Write and graph a transformation of the graph of $f(x) = x^5 - 3x^4 + 2x - 4$ that results in a graph with a y-intercept of -2.

31. PROBLEM SOLVING A portion of the path that a hummingbird flies while feeding can be modeled by the function

$$f(x) = -\frac{1}{5}x(x - 4)^2(x - 7), \ 0 \le x \le 7$$

where x is the horizontal distance (in meters) and $f(x)$ is the height (in meters). The hummingbird feeds each time it is at ground level.

a. At what distances does the hummingbird feed?

b. A second hummingbird feeds 2 meters farther away than the first hummingbird and flies twice as high. Write a function to model the path of the second hummingbird.

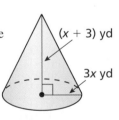

32. HOW DO YOU SEE IT? Determine the real zeros of each function. Then describe the transformation of the graph of f that results in the graph of g.

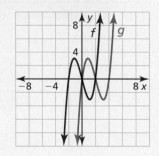

33. MATHEMATICAL CONNECTIONS Write a function V for the volume (in cubic yards) of the right circular cone shown. Then write a function W that gives the volume (in cubic yards) of the cone when x is measured in feet. Find and interpret $W(3)$.

$(x + 3)$ yd

$3x$ yd

Maintaining Mathematical Proficiency
Reviewing what you learned in previous grades and lessons

Find the minimum value or maximum value of the function. Describe the domain and range of the function, and where the function is increasing and decreasing. (*Section 2.6*)

34. $h(x) = (x + 5)^2 - 7$ **35.** $f(x) = 4 - x^2$ **36.** $f(x) = 3(x - 10)(x + 4)$

37. $g(x) = -(x + 2)(x + 8)$ **38.** $h(x) = \frac{1}{2}(x - 1)^2 - 3$ **39.** $f(x) = -2x^2 + 4x - 1$

Analyzing Graphs of Polynomial Functions

Essential Question   How many turning points can the graph of a polynomial function have?

A *turning point* of the graph of a polynomial function is a point on the graph at which the function changes from

- increasing to decreasing, or

- decreasing to increasing.

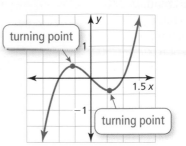

EXPLORATION 1   Approximating Turning Points

Work with a partner. Match each polynomial function with its graph. Explain your reasoning. Then use a graphing calculator to approximate the coordinates of the turning points of the graph of the function. Round your answers to the nearest hundredth.

a. $f(x) = 2x^2 + 3x - 4$

b. $f(x) = x^2 + 3x + 2$

c. $f(x) = x^3 - 2x^2 - x + 1$

d. $f(x) = -x^3 + 5x - 2$

e. $f(x) = x^4 - 3x^2 + 2x - 1$

f. $f(x) = -2x^5 - x^2 + 5x + 3$

A.

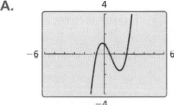

B.

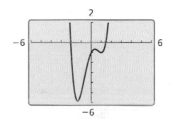

C.

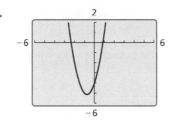

D.

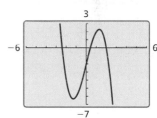

E.

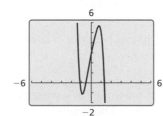

F.

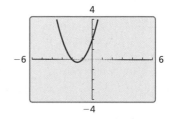

ATTENDING TO PRECISION

To be proficient in math, you need to express numerical answers with a degree of precision appropriate for the problem context.

Communicate Your Answer

2. How many turning points can the graph of a polynomial function have?

3. Is it possible to sketch the graph of a cubic polynomial function that has *no* turning points? Justify your answer.

What You Will Learn

▶ Use x-intercepts to graph polynomial functions.

▶ Use the Location Principle to identify zeros of polynomial functions.

▶ Find turning points and identify local maximums and local minimums of graphs of polynomial functions.

▶ Identify even and odd functions.

Graphing Polynomial Functions

In this chapter, you have learned that zeros, factors, solutions, and x-intercepts are closely related concepts. Here is a summary of these relationships.

⑤ Core Concept

Zeros, Factors, Solutions, and Intercepts

Let $f(x) = a_nx^n + a_{n-1}x^{n-1} + \cdots + a_1x + a_0$ be a polynomial function. The following statements are equivalent.

Zero: k is a zero of the polynomial function f.

Factor: $x - k$ is a factor of the polynomial $f(x)$.

Solution: k is a solution (or root) of the polynomial equation $f(x) = 0$.

x-Intercept: If k is a real number, then k is an x-intercept of the graph of the polynomial function f. The graph of f passes through $(k, 0)$.

EXAMPLE 1   Using x-Intercepts to Graph a Polynomial Function

Graph the function

$$f(x) = \tfrac{1}{6}(x + 3)(x - 2)^2.$$

SOLUTION

Step 1   Plot the x-intercepts. Because -3 and 2 are zeros of f, plot $(-3, 0)$ and $(2, 0)$.

Step 2   Plot points between and beyond the x-intercepts.

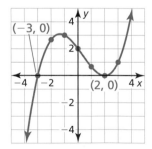

x	-2	-1	0	1	3
y	$\frac{8}{3}$	3	2	$\frac{2}{3}$	1

Step 3   Determine end behavior. Because $f(x)$ has three factors of the form $x - k$ and a constant factor of $\frac{1}{6}$, f is a cubic function with a positive leading coefficient. So, $f(x) \rightarrow -\infty$ as $x \rightarrow -\infty$ and $f(x) \rightarrow +\infty$ as $x \rightarrow +\infty$.

Step 4   Draw the graph so that it passes through the plotted points and has the appropriate end behavior.

Monitoring Progress   Help in English and Spanish at *BigIdeasMath.com*

Graph the function.

1. $f(x) = \tfrac{1}{2}(x + 1)(x - 4)^2$ **2.** $f(x) = \tfrac{1}{4}(x + 2)(x - 1)(x - 3)$

The Location Principle

You can use the *Location Principle* to help you find real zeros of polynomial functions.

Core Concept

The Location Principle

If f is a polynomial function, and a and b are two real numbers such that $f(a) < 0$ and $f(b) > 0$, then f has at least one real zero between a and b.

To use this principle to locate real zeros of a polynomial function, find a value a at which the polynomial function is negative and another value b at which the function is positive. You can conclude that the function has *at least* one real zero between a and b.

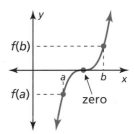

EXAMPLE 2   Locating Real Zeros of a Polynomial Function

Find all real zeros of

$$f(x) = 6x^3 + 5x^2 - 17x - 6.$$

SOLUTION

Step 1   Use a graphing calculator to make a table.

X	Y1
0	-6
1	-12
2	28
3	150
4	390
5	784
6	1368

X=1

Step 2   Use the Location Principle. From the table shown, you can see that $f(1) < 0$ and $f(2) > 0$. So, by the Location Principle, f has a zero between 1 and 2. Because f is a polynomial function of degree 3, it has three zeros. The only possible *rational* zero between 1 and 2 is $\frac{3}{2}$. Using synthetic division, you can confirm that $\frac{3}{2}$ is a zero.

Step 3   Write $f(x)$ in factored form. Dividing $f(x)$ by its known factor $x - \frac{3}{2}$ gives a quotient of $6x^2 + 14x + 4$. So, you can factor $f(x)$ as

$$f(x) = \left(x - \tfrac{3}{2}\right)(6x^2 + 14x + 4)$$

$$= 2\left(x - \tfrac{3}{2}\right)(3x^2 + 7x + 2)$$

$$= 2\left(x - \tfrac{3}{2}\right)(3x + 1)(x + 2).$$

Check

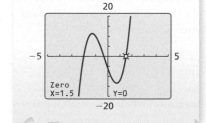

▶ From the factorization, there are three zeros. The zeros of f are

$$\tfrac{3}{2}, -\tfrac{1}{3}, \text{ and } -2.$$

Check this by graphing f.

Monitoring Progress   Help in English and Spanish at *BigIdeasMath.com*

3. Find all real zeros of $f(x) = 18x^3 + 21x^2 - 13x - 6.$

Turning Points

Another important characteristic of graphs of polynomial functions is that they have *turning points* corresponding to local maximum and minimum values.

- The *y*-coordinate of a turning point is a **local maximum** of the function when the point is higher than all nearby points.

- The *y*-coordinate of a turning point is a **local minimum** of the function when the point is lower than all nearby points.

The turning points of a graph help determine the intervals for which a function is increasing or decreasing. You can write these intervals using interval notation.

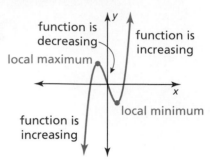

Core Concept

Turning Points of Polynomial Functions

1. The graph of every polynomial function of degree *n* has *at most n − 1* turning points.

2. If a polynomial function of degree *n* has *n* distinct real zeros, then its graph has *exactly n − 1* turning points.

EXAMPLE 3   **Finding Turning Points**

Graph each function. Identify the *x*-intercepts and the points where the local maximums and local minimums occur. Determine the intervals for which each function is increasing or decreasing.

a. $f(x) = x^3 - 3x^2 + 6$ **b.** $g(x) = x^4 - 6x^3 + 3x^2 + 10x - 3$

SOLUTION

a. Use a graphing calculator to graph the function. The graph of *f* has one *x*-intercept and two turning points. Use the graphing calculator's *zero, maximum,* and *minimum* features to approximate the coordinates of the points.

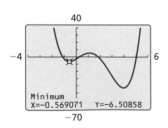

▶ The *x*-intercept of the graph is $x \approx -1.20$. The function has a local maximum at $(0, 6)$ and a local minimum at $(2, 2)$. The function is increasing when $x < 0$ and $x > 2$ and decreasing when $0 < x < 2$.

b. Use a graphing calculator to graph the function. The graph of *g* has four *x*-intercepts and three turning points. Use the graphing calculator's *zero, maximum,* and *minimum* features to approximate the coordinates of the points.

▶ The *x*-intercepts of the graph are $x \approx -1.14$, $x \approx 0.29$, $x \approx 1.82$, and $x \approx 5.03$. The function has a local maximum at $(1.11, 5.11)$ and local minimums at $(-0.57, -6.51)$ and $(3.96, -43.04)$. The function is increasing when $-0.57 < x < 1.11$ and $x > 3.96$ and decreasing when $x < -0.57$ and $1.11 < x < 3.96$.

Monitoring Progress Help in English and Spanish at *BigIdeasMath.com*

4. Graph $f(x) = 0.5x^3 + x^2 - x + 2$. Identify the *x*-intercepts and the points where the local maximums and local minimums occur. Determine the intervals for which the function is increasing or decreasing.

Even and Odd Functions

Core Concept

Even and Odd Functions

A function f is an **even function** when $f(-x) = f(x)$ for all x in its domain. The graph of an even function is *symmetric about the y-axis*.

A function f is an **odd function** when $f(-x) = -f(x)$ for all x in its domain. The graph of an odd function is *symmetric about the origin*. One way to recognize a graph that is symmetric about the origin is that it looks the same after a $180°$ rotation about the origin.

Even Function	Odd Function
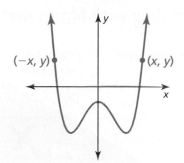	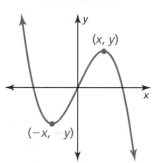

For an even function, if (x, y) is on the graph, then $(-x, y)$ is also on the graph.

For an odd function, if (x, y) is on the graph, then $(-x, -y)$ is also on the graph.

EXAMPLE 4   Identifying Even and Odd Functions

Determine whether each function is *even*, *odd*, or *neither*.

a. $f(x) = x^3 - 7x$ 　　　　**b.** $g(x) = x^4 + x^2 - 1$ 　　　　**c.** $h(x) = x^3 + 2$

SOLUTION

a. Replace x with $-x$ in the equation for f, and then simplify.

$$f(-x) = (-x)^3 - 7(-x) = -x^3 + 7x = -(x^3 - 7x) = -f(x)$$

▶　Because $f(-x) = -f(x)$, the function is odd.

b. Replace x with $-x$ in the equation for g, and then simplify.

$$g(-x) = (-x)^4 + (-x)^2 - 1 = x^4 + x^2 - 1 = g(x)$$

▶　Because $g(-x) = g(x)$, the function is even.

c. Replacing x with $-x$ in the equation for h produces

$$h(-x) = (-x)^3 + 2 = -x^3 + 2.$$

▶　Because $h(x) = x^3 + 2$ and $-h(x) = -x^3 - 2$, you can conclude that $h(-x) \neq h(x)$ and $h(-x) \neq -h(x)$. So, the function is neither even nor odd.

Monitoring Progress   Help in English and Spanish at *BigIdeasMath.com*

Determine whether the function is *even*, *odd*, or *neither*.

5. $f(x) = -x^2 + 5$ 　　　　**6.** $f(x) = x^4 - 5x^3$ 　　　　**7.** $f(x) = 2x^5$

Vocabulary and Core Concept Check

1. **COMPLETE THE SENTENCE** A local maximum or local minimum of a polynomial function occurs at a _____ point of the graph of the function.

2. **WRITING** Explain what a local maximum of a function is and how it may be different from the maximum value of the function.

Monitoring Progress and Modeling with Mathematics

ANALYZING RELATIONSHIPS In Exercises 3–6, match the function with its graph.

3. $f(x) = (x - 1)(x - 2)(x + 2)$

4. $h(x) = (x + 2)^2(x + 1)$

5. $g(x) = (x + 1)(x - 1)(x + 2)$

6. $f(x) = (x - 1)^2(x + 2)$

A.
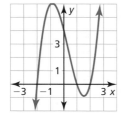

B.
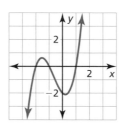

C.
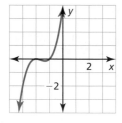

D.
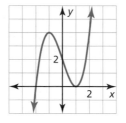

In Exercises 7–14, graph the function. *(See Example 1.)*

7. $f(x) = (x - 2)^2(x + 1)$

8. $f(x) = (x + 2)^2(x + 4)^2$

9. $h(x) = (x + 1)^2(x - 1)(x - 3)$

10. $g(x) = 4(x + 1)(x + 2)(x - 1)$

11. $h(x) = \frac{1}{3}(x - 5)(x + 2)(x - 3)$

12. $g(x) = \frac{1}{12}(x + 4)(x + 8)(x - 1)$

13. $h(x) = (x - 3)(x^2 + x + 1)$

14. $f(x) = (x - 4)(2x^2 - 2x + 1)$

ERROR ANALYSIS In Exercises 15 and 16, describe and correct the error in using factors to graph f.

15. $f(x) = (x + 2)(x - 1)^2$

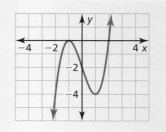

16. $f(x) = x^2(x - 3)^3$

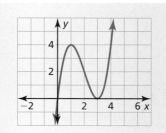

In Exercises 17–22, find all real zeros of the function. *(See Example 2.)*

17. $f(x) = x^3 - 4x^2 - x + 4$

18. $f(x) = x^3 - 3x^2 - 4x + 12$

19. $h(x) = 2x^3 + 7x^2 - 5x - 4$

20. $h(x) = 4x^3 - 2x^2 - 24x - 18$

21. $g(x) = 4x^3 + x^2 - 51x + 36$

22. $f(x) = 2x^3 - 3x^2 - 32x - 15$

In Exercises 23–30, graph the function. Identify the *x*-intercepts and the points where the local maximums and local minimums occur. Determine the intervals for which the function is increasing or decreasing. *(See Example 3.)*

23. $g(x) = 2x^3 + 8x^2 - 3$

24. $g(x) = -x^4 + 3x$

25. $h(x) = x^4 - 3x^2 + x$

26. $f(x) = x^5 - 4x^3 + x^2 + 2$

27. $f(x) = 0.5x^3 - 2x + 2.5$

28. $f(x) = 0.7x^4 - 3x^3 + 5x$

29. $h(x) = x^5 + 2x^2 - 17x - 4$

30. $g(x) = x^4 - 5x^3 + 2x^2 + x - 3$

In Exercises 31–36, estimate the coordinates of each turning point. State whether each corresponds to a local maximum or a local minimum. Then estimate the real zeros and find the least possible degree of the function.

31.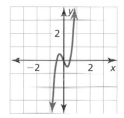

32.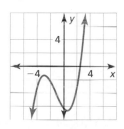

33.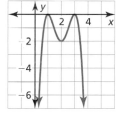

34.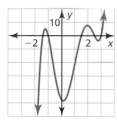

35.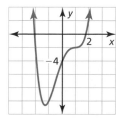

36.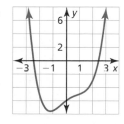

OPEN-ENDED In Exercises 37 and 38, sketch a graph of a polynomial function *f* having the given characteristics.

37. • The graph of *f* has *x*-intercepts at $x = -4$, $x = 0$, and $x = 2$.

   • *f* has a local maximum value when $x = 1$.

   • *f* has a local minimum value when $x = -2$.

38. • The graph of *f* has *x*-intercepts at $x = -3$, $x = 1$, and $x = 5$.

   • *f* has a local maximum value when $x = 1$.

   • *f* has a local minimum value when $x = -2$ and when $x = 4$.

In Exercises 39–46, determine whether the function is *even*, *odd*, or *neither*. *(See Example 4.)*

39. $h(x) = 4x^7$

40. $g(x) = -2x^6 + x^2$

41. $f(x) = x^4 + 3x^2 - 2$

42. $f(x) = x^5 + 3x^3 - x$

43. $g(x) = x^2 + 5x + 1$

44. $f(x) = -x^3 + 2x - 9$

45. $f(x) - x^4 - 12x^2$

46. $h(x) = x^5 + 3x^4$

47. **USING TOOLS** When a swimmer does the breaststroke, the function

$$S = -241t^7 + 1060t^6 - 1870t^5 + 1650t^4 - 737t^3 + 144t^2 - 2.43t$$

models the speed *S* (in meters per second) of the swimmer during one complete stroke, where *t* is the number of seconds since the start of the stroke and $0 \le t \le 1.22$. Use a graphing calculator to graph the function. At what time during the stroke is the swimmer traveling the fastest?

48. **USING TOOLS** During a recent period of time, the number *S* (in thousands) of students enrolled in public schools in a certain country can be modeled by $S = 1.64x^3 - 102x^2 + 1710x + 36,300$, where *x* is time (in years). Use a graphing calculator to graph the function for the interval $0 \le x \le 41$. Then describe how the public school enrollment changes over this period of time.

49. **WRITING** Why is the adjective *local*, used to describe the maximums and minimums of cubic functions, sometimes not required for quadratic functions?

50. HOW DO YOU SEE IT? The graph of a polynomial function is shown.

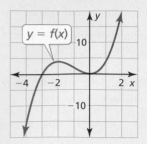

a. Find the zeros, local maximum, and local minimum values of the function.

b. Compare the x-intercepts of the graphs of $y = f(x)$ and $y = -f(x)$.

c. Compare the maximum and minimum values of the functions $y = f(x)$ and $y = -f(x)$.

51. MAKING AN ARGUMENT Your friend claims that the product of two odd functions is an odd function. Is your friend correct? Explain your reasoning.

52. MODELING WITH MATHEMATICS You are making a rectangular box out of a 16-inch-by-20-inch piece of cardboard. The box will be formed by making the cuts shown in the diagram and folding up the sides. You want the box to have the greatest volume possible.

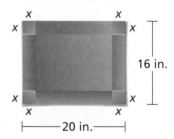

a. How long should you make the cuts?

b. What is the maximum volume?

c. What are the dimensions of the finished box?

53. PROBLEM SOLVING Quonset huts are temporary, all-purpose structures shaped like half-cylinders. You have 1100 square feet of material to build a quonset hut.

a. The surface area S of a quonset hut is given by $S = \pi r^2 + \pi r \ell$. Substitute 1100 for S and then write an expression for ℓ in terms of r.

b. The volume V of a quonset hut is given by $V = \frac{1}{2}\pi r^2 \ell$. Write an equation that gives V as a function in terms of r only.

c. Find the value of r that maximizes the volume of the hut.

54. THOUGHT PROVOKING Write and graph a polynomial function that has one real zero in each of the intervals $-2 < x < -1$, $0 < x < 1$, and $4 < x < 5$. Is there a maximum degree that such a polynomial function can have? Justify your answer.

55. MATHEMATICAL CONNECTIONS A cylinder is inscribed in a sphere of radius 8 inches. Write an equation for the volume of the cylinder as a function of h. Find the value of h that maximizes the volume of the inscribed cylinder. What is the maximum volume of the cylinder?

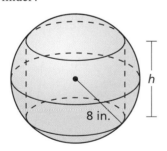

Maintaining Mathematical Proficiency
Reviewing what you learned in previous grades and lessons

State whether the table displays *linear data*, *quadratic data*, or *neither*. **Explain.** *(Section 2.7)*

56.

Months, x	0	1	2	3
Savings (dollars), y	100	150	200	250

57.

Time (seconds), x	0	1	2	3
Height (feet), y	300	284	236	156

3.9 Modeling with Polynomial Functions

Essential Question How can you find a polynomial model for real-life data?

EXPLORATION 1   Modeling Real-Life Data

Work with a partner. The distance a baseball travels after it is hit depends on the angle at which it was hit and the initial speed. The table shows the distances a baseball hit at an angle of 35° travels at various initial speeds.

Initial speed, x (miles per hour)	80	85	90	95	100	105	110	115
Distance, y (feet)	194	220	247	275	304	334	365	397

a. Recall that when data have equally-spaced x-values, you can analyze patterns in the differences of the y-values to determine what type of function can be used to model the data. If the first differences are constant, then the set of data fits a linear model. If the second differences are constant, then the set of data fits a quadratic model.

Find the first and second differences of the data. Are the data linear or quadratic? Explain your reasoning.

194   220   247   275   304   334   365   397

USING TOOLS STRATEGICALLY

To be proficient in math, you need to use technological tools to explore and deepen your understanding of concepts.

b. Use a graphing calculator to draw a scatter plot of the data. Do the data appear linear or quadratic? Use the *regression* feature of the graphing calculator to find a linear or quadratic model that best fits the data.

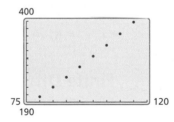

c. Use the model you found in part (b) to find the distance a baseball travels when it is hit at an angle of 35° and travels at an initial speed of 120 miles per hour.

d. According to the *Baseball Almanac*, "Any drive over 400 feet is noteworthy. A blow of 450 feet shows exceptional power, as the majority of major league players are unable to hit a ball that far. Anything in the 500-foot range is genuinely historic." Estimate the initial speed of a baseball that travels a distance of 500 feet.

Communicate Your Answer

2. How can you find a polynomial model for real-life data?

3. How well does the model you found in Exploration 1(b) fit the data? Do you think the model is valid for any initial speed? Explain your reasoning.

3.9 Lesson

Core Vocabulary
finite differences, *p. 176*

Previous
scatter plot

What You Will Learn

▶ Write polynomial functions for sets of points.
▶ Write polynomial functions using finite differences.
▶ Use technology to find models for data sets.

Writing Polynomial Functions for a Set of Points

You know that two points determine a line and three points not on a line determine a parabola. In Example 1, you will see that four points not on a line or a parabola determine the graph of a cubic function.

EXAMPLE 1 Writing a Cubic Function

Write the cubic function whose graph is shown.

SOLUTION

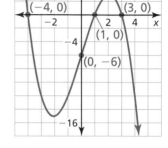

Step 1 Use the three *x*-intercepts to write the function in factored form.

$$f(x) = a(x + 4)(x - 1)(x - 3)$$

Step 2 Find the value of *a* by substituting the coordinates of the point $(0, -6)$.

$$-6 = a(0 + 4)(0 - 1)(0 - 3)$$
$$-6 = 12a$$
$$-\tfrac{1}{2} = a$$

Check

Check the end behavior of *f*. The degree of *f* is odd and $a < 0$. So, $f(x) \to +\infty$ as $x \to -\infty$ and $f(x) \to -\infty$ as $x \to +\infty$, which matches the graph. ✔

▶ The function is $f(x) = -\tfrac{1}{2}(x + 4)(x - 1)(x - 3)$.

Monitoring Progress Help in English and Spanish at *BigIdeasMath.com*

Write a cubic function whose graph passes through the given points.

1. $(-4, 0), (0, 10), (2, 0), (5, 0)$ **2.** $(-1, 0), (0, -12), (2, 0), (3, 0)$

Finite Differences

When the *x*-values in a data set are equally spaced, the differences of consecutive *y*-values are called **finite differences**. Recall from Section 2.7 that the first and second differences of $y = x^2$ are:

equally-spaced *x*-values

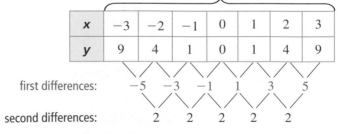

x	−3	−2	−1	0	1	2	3
y	9	4	1	0	1	4	9

first differences: −5 −3 −1 1 3 5

second differences: 2 2 2 2 2

Notice that $y = x^2$ has degree *two* and that the *second* differences are constant and nonzero. This illustrates the first of the two properties of finite differences shown on the next page.

Core Concept

Properties of Finite Differences

1. If a polynomial function $y = f(x)$ has degree n, then the nth differences of function values for equally-spaced x-values are nonzero and constant.

2. Conversely, if the nth differences of equally-spaced data are nonzero and constant, then the data can be represented by a polynomial function of degree n.

The second property of finite differences allows you to write a polynomial function that models a set of equally-spaced data.

EXAMPLE 2 Writing a Function Using Finite Differences

Use finite differences to determine the degree of the polynomial function that fits the data. Then use technology to find the polynomial function.

x	1	2	3	4	5	6	7
f(x)	1	4	10	20	35	56	84

SOLUTION

Step 1 Write the function values. Find the first differences by subtracting consecutive values. Then find the second differences by subtracting consecutive first differences. Continue until you obtain differences that are nonzero and constant.

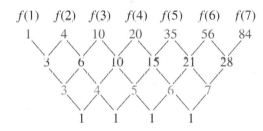

Write function values for equally-spaced x-values.

First differences

Second differences

Third differences

Because the third differences are nonzero and constant, you can model the data *exactly* with a cubic function.

Step 2 Enter the data into a graphing calculator and use cubic regression to obtain a polynomial function.

> Because $\frac{1}{6} \approx 0.1666666667$, $\frac{1}{2} = 0.5$, and $\frac{1}{3} \approx 0.333333333$, a polynomial function that fits the data exactly is
>
> $f(x) = \frac{1}{6}x^3 + \frac{1}{2}x^2 + \frac{1}{3}x.$

```
CubicReg
y=ax³+bx²+cx+d
a=.1666666667
b=.5
c=.3333333333
d=0
R²=1
```

Monitoring Progress   Help in English and Spanish at *BigIdeasMath.com*

3. Use finite differences to determine the degree of the polynomial function that fits the data. Then use technology to find the polynomial function.

x	−3	−2	−1	0	1	2
f(x)	6	15	22	21	6	−29

Finding Models Using Technology

In Examples 1 and 2, you found a cubic model that *exactly* fits a set of data. In many real-life situations, you cannot find models to fit data exactly. Despite this limitation, you can still use technology to approximate the data with a polynomial model, as shown in the next example.

EXAMPLE 3 **Real-Life Application**

The table shows the total U.S. biomass energy consumptions y (in trillions of British thermal units, or Btus) in the year t, where $t = 1$ corresponds to 2001. Find a polynomial model for the data. Use the model to estimate the total U.S. biomass energy consumption in 2013.

t	1	2	3	4	5	6
y	2622	2701	2807	3010	3117	3267

t	7	8	9	10	11	12
y	3493	3866	3951	4286	4421	4316

According to the U.S. Department of Energy, *biomass* includes "agricultural and forestry residues, municipal solid wastes, industrial wastes, and terrestrial and aquatic crops grown solely for energy purposes." Among the uses for biomass is production of electricity and liquid fuels such as ethanol.

SOLUTION

Step 1 Enter the data into a graphing calculator and make a scatter plot. The data suggest a cubic model.

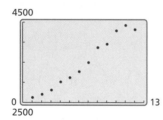

Step 2 Use the *cubic regression* feature. The polynomial model is

$$y = -2.545t^3 + 51.95t^2 - 118.1t + 2732.$$

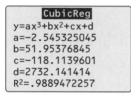

Step 3 Check the model by graphing it and the data in the same viewing window.

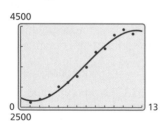

Step 4 Use the *trace* feature to estimate the value of the model when $t = 13$.

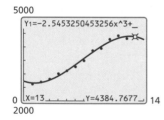

▶ The approximate total U.S. biomass energy consumption in 2013 was about 4385 trillion Btus.

Monitoring Progress Help in English and Spanish at *BigIdeasMath.com*

Use a graphing calculator to find a polynomial function that fits the data.

4.

x	1	2	3	4	5	6
y	5	13	17	11	11	56

5.

x	0	2	4	6	8	10
y	8	0	15	69	98	87

Vocabulary and Core Concept Check

1. **COMPLETE THE SENTENCE** When the *x*-values in a set of data are equally spaced, the differences of consecutive *y*-values are called _____.

2. **WRITING** Explain how you know when a set of data could be modeled by a cubic function.

Monitoring Progress and Modeling with Mathematics

In Exercises 3–6, write a cubic function whose graph is shown. *(See Example 1.)*

3.

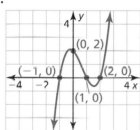

4.

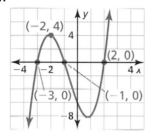

5.

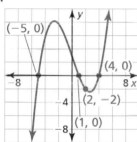

6.

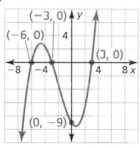

In Exercises 7–12, use finite differences to determine the degree of the polynomial function that fits the data. Then use technology to find the polynomial function. *(See Example 2.)*

7.

x	−6	−3	0	3	6	9
f(x)	−2	15	−4	49	282	803

8.

x	−1	0	1	2	3	4
f(x)	−14	−5	−2	7	34	91

9. $(-4, -317)$, $(-3, -37)$, $(-2, 21)$, $(-1, 7)$, $(0, -1)$, $(1, 3)$, $(2, -47)$, $(3, -289)$, $(4, -933)$

10. $(-6, 744)$, $(-4, 154)$, $(-2, 4)$, $(0, -6)$, $(2, 16)$, $(4, 154)$, $(6, 684)$, $(8, 2074)$, $(10, 4984)$

11. $(-2, 968)$, $(-1, 422)$, $(0, 142)$, $(1, 26)$, $(2, -4)$, $(3, -2)$, $(4, 2)$, $(5, 2)$, $(6, 16)$

12. $(1, 0)$, $(2, 6)$, $(3, 2)$, $(4, 6)$, $(5, 12)$, $(6, -10)$, $(7, -114)$, $(8, -378)$, $(9, -904)$

13. **ERROR ANALYSIS** Describe and correct the error in writing a cubic function whose graph passes through the given points.

> ✗ $(-6, 0)$, $(1, 0)$, $(3, 0)$, $(0, 54)$
> $54 = a(0 - 6)(0 + 1)(0 + 3)$
> $54 = -18a$
> $a = -3$
> $f(x) = -3(x - 6)(x + 1)(x + 3)$

14. **MODELING WITH MATHEMATICS** The dot patterns show pentagonal numbers. The number of dots in the *n*th pentagonal number is given by $f(n) = \frac{1}{2}n(3n - 1)$. Show that this function has constant second-order differences.

15. **OPEN-ENDED** Write three different cubic functions that pass through the points $(3, 0)$, $(4, 0)$, and $(2, 6)$. Justify your answers.

16. **MODELING WITH MATHEMATICS** The table shows the ages of cats and their corresponding ages in human years. Find a polynomial model for the data for the first 8 years of a cat's life. Use the model to estimate the age (in human years) of a cat that is 3 years old. *(See Example 3.)*

Age of cat, x	1	2	4	6	7	8
Human years, y	15	24	32	40	44	48

17. **MODELING WITH MATHEMATICS** The data in the table show the average speeds y (in miles per hour) of a pontoon boat for several different engine speeds x (in hundreds of revolutions per minute, or RPMs). Find a polynomial model for the data. Estimate the average speed of the pontoon boat when the engine speed is 2800 RPMs.

x	10	20	25	30	45	55
y	4.5	8.9	13.8	18.9	29.9	37.7

18. **HOW DO YOU SEE IT?** The graph shows typical speeds y (in feet per second) of a space shuttle x seconds after it is launched.

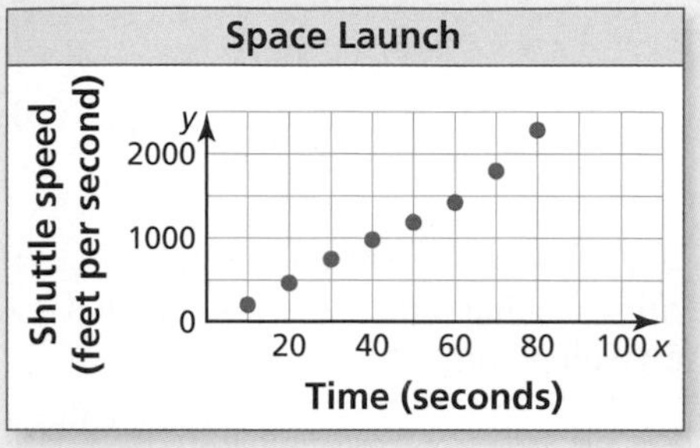

Space Launch

[Graph: Shuttle speed (feet per second) on y-axis from 0 to 2000; Time (seconds) on x-axis from 20 to 100; data points rising]

a. What type of polynomial function models the data? Explain.

b. Which nth-order finite difference should be constant for the function in part (a)? Explain.

19. **MATHEMATICAL CONNECTIONS** The table shows the number of diagonals for polygons with n sides. Find a polynomial function that fits the data. Determine the total number of diagonals in the decagon shown.

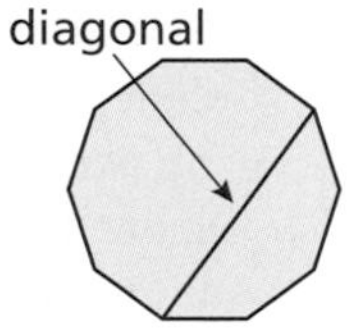

diagonal

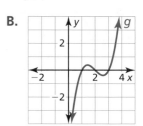

Number of sides, n	3	4	5	6	7	8
Number of diagonals, d	0	2	5	9	14	20

20. **MAKING AN ARGUMENT** Your friend states that it is not possible to determine the degree of a function given the first-order differences. Is your friend correct? Explain your reasoning.

21. **WRITING** Explain why you cannot always use finite differences to find a model for real-life data sets.

22. **THOUGHT PROVOKING** A, B, and C are zeros of a cubic polynomial function. Choose values for A, B, and C such that the distance from A to B is less than or equal to the distance from A to C. Then write the function using the A, B, and C values you chose.

23. **MULTIPLE REPRESENTATIONS** Order the polynomial functions according to their degree, from least to greatest.

A. $f(x) = -3x + 2x^2 + 1$

B. [Graph showing curve g with y-axis and x-axis, passing through origin area]

C.
x	−2	−1	0	1	2	3
h(x)	8	6	4	2	0	−2

D.
x	−2	−1	0	1	2	3
k(x)	25	6	7	4	−3	10

24. **ABSTRACT REASONING** Substitute the expressions $z, z + 1, z + 2, \ldots, z + 5$ for x in the function $f(x) = ax^3 + bx^2 + cx + d$ to generate six equally-spaced ordered pairs. Then show that the third-order differences are constant.

Maintaining Mathematical Proficiency
Reviewing what you learned in previous grades and lessons

Solve the equation using square roots. *(Skills Review Handbook)*

25. $x^2 - 6 = 30$

26. $5x^2 - 38 = 187$

27. $2(x - 3)^2 = 24$

28. $\frac{4}{3}(x + 5)^2 = 4$

Solve the equation using the Quadratic Formula. *(Skills Review Handbook)*

29. $2x^2 + 3x = 5$

30. $2x^2 + \frac{1}{2} = 2x$

31. $2x^2 + 3x = -3x^2 + 1$

32. $4x - 20 = x^2$

3.5–3.9   What Did You Learn?

Core Vocabulary

Core Concepts

Section 3.5

Section 3.6

Section 3.7

Section 3.8

Section 3.9

Mathematical Practices

1. Explain how understanding the Complex Conjugates Theorem allows you to construct your argument in Exercise 46 on page 159.

2. Describe how you use structure to accurately match each graph with its transformation in Exercises 7–10 on page 165.

Performance Task:

Quonset Huts

Over 153,000 Quonset huts were procured by the United States Navy during the 1940s. The most common huts were 20 feet wide and 48 feet long. How many different sizes of Quonset huts can you design that have approximately the same volume as this model? How do the surface areas of your new huts compare to the original model?

To explore the answers to these questions and more, check out the Performance Task and Real-Life STEM video at *BigIdeasMath.com*.

3.1 Graphing Polynomial Functions *(pp. 111–118)*

Graph $f(x) = x^3 + 3x^2 - 3x - 10$.

To graph the function, make a table of values and plot the corresponding points. Connect the points with a smooth curve and check the end behavior.

x	-3	-2	-1	0	1	2	3
$f(x)$	-1	0	-5	-10	-9	4	35

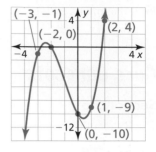

The degree is odd and the leading coefficient is positive.
So, $f(x) \to -\infty$ as $x \to -\infty$ and $f(x) \to +\infty$ as $x \to +\infty$.

Decide whether the function is a polynomial function. If so, write it in standard form and state its degree, type, and leading coefficient.

1. $h(x) = -x^3 + 2x^2 - 15x^7$

2. $p(x) = x^3 - 5x^{0.5} + 13x^2 + 8$

Graph the polynomial function.

3. $h(x) = x^2 + 6x^5 - 5$

4. $f(x) = 3x^4 - 5x^2 + 1$

5. $g(x) = -x^4 + x + 2$

3.2 Adding, Subtracting, and Multiplying Polynomials *(pp. 119–128)*

a. Multiply $(x - 2)$, $(x - 1)$, and $(x + 3)$ in a horizontal format.

$$(x - 2)(x - 1)(x + 3) = (x^2 - 3x + 2)(x + 3)$$
$$= (x^2 - 3x + 2)x + (x^2 - 3x + 2)3$$
$$= x^3 - 3x^2 + 2x + 3x^2 - 9x + 6$$
$$= x^3 - 7x + 6$$

b. Use Pascal's Triangle to expand $(4x + 2)^4$.

The coefficients from the fourth row of Pascal's Triangle are 1, 4, 6, 4, and 1.

$$(4x + 2)^4 = 1(4x)^4 + 4(4x)^3(2) + 6(4x)^2(2)^2 + 4(4x)(2)^3 + 1(2)^4$$
$$= 256x^4 + 512x^3 + 384x^2 + 128x + 16$$

Find the sum or difference.

6. $(4x^3 - 12x^2 - 5) - (-8x^2 + 4x + 3)$

7. $(x^4 + 3x^3 - x^2 + 6) + (2x^4 - 3x + 9)$

8. $(3x^2 + 9x + 13) - (x^2 - 2x + 12)$

Find the product.

9. $(2y^2 + 4y - 7)(y + 3)$

10. $(2m + n)^3$

11. $(s + 2)(s + 4)(s - 3)$

Use Pascal's Triangle or the Binomial Theorem to expand the binomial.

12. $(m + 4)^4$

13. $(3s + 2)^5$

14. $(z + 1)^6$

3.3 Dividing Polynomials *(pp. 129–134)*

Use synthetic division to evaluate $f(x) = -2x^3 + 4x^2 + 8x + 10$ **when** $x = -3$.

$$
\begin{array}{r|rrrr}
-3 & -2 & 4 & 8 & 10 \\
   &   & 6 & -30 & 66 \\
\hline
   & -2 & 10 & -22 & 76
\end{array}
$$

▶ The remainder is 76. So, you can conclude from the Remainder Theorem that $f(-3) = 76$. You can check this by substituting $x = -3$ in the original function.

> **Check**
>
> $$f(-3) = -2(-3)^3 + 4(-3)^2 + 8(-3) + 10$$
> $$= 54 + 36 - 24 + 10$$
> $$= 76 \checkmark$$

Divide using polynomial long division or synthetic division.

15. $(x^3 + x^2 + 3x - 4) \div (x^2 + 2x + 1)$

16. $(x^4 + 3x^3 - 4x^2 + 5x + 3) : (x^2 + x + 4)$

17. $(x^4 - x^2 - 7) \div (x + 4)$

18. Use synthetic division to evaluate $g(x) = 4x^3 + 2x^2 - 4$ when $x = 5$.

3.4 Factoring Polynomials *(pp. 135–142)*

a. Factor $x^4 + 8x$ **completely.**

$$x^4 + 8x = x(x^3 + 8)$$ Factor common monomial.

$$= x(x^3 + 2^3)$$ Write $x^3 + 8$ as $a^3 + b^3$.

$$= x(x + 2)(x^2 - 2x + 4)$$ Sum of Two Cubes Pattern

b. Determine whether $x + 4$ **is a factor of** $f(x) = x^5 + 4x^4 + 2x + 8$.

Find $f(-4)$ by synthetic division.

$$
\begin{array}{r|rrrrrr}
-4 & 1 & 4 & 0 & 0 & 2 & 8 \\
   &   & -4 & 0 & 0 & 0 & -8 \\
\hline
   & 1 & 0 & 0 & 0 & 2 & 0
\end{array}
$$

▶ Because $f(-4) = 0$, the binomial $x + 4$ is a factor of $f(x) = x^5 + 4x^4 + 2x + 8$.

Factor the polynomial completely.

19. $64x^3 - 8$ **20.** $2z^5 - 12z^3 + 10z$ **21.** $2a^3 - 7a^2 - 8a + 28$

22. Show that $x + 2$ is a factor of $f(x) = x^4 + 2x^3 - 27x - 54$. Then factor $f(x)$ completely.

3.5 **Solving Polynomial Equations** *(pp. 145–152)*

a. Find all real solutions of $x^3 + x^2 - 8x - 12 = 0$.

Step 1 List the possible rational solutions. The leading coefficient of the polynomial $f(x) = x^3 + x^2 - 8x - 12$ is 1, and the constant term is -12. So, the possible rational solutions of $f(x) = 0$ are

$$x = \pm\frac{1}{1}, \pm\frac{2}{1}, \pm\frac{3}{1}, \pm\frac{4}{1}, \pm\frac{6}{1}, \pm\frac{12}{1}.$$

Step 2 Test possible solutions using synthetic division until a solution is found.

$$
\begin{array}{r|rrrr}
2 & 1 & 1 & -8 & -12 \\
  &   & 2 & 6 & -4 \\
\hline
  & 1 & 3 & -2 & -16
\end{array}
\qquad\qquad
\begin{array}{r|rrrr}
-2 & 1 & 1 & -8 & -12 \\
   &   & -2 & 2 & 12 \\
\hline
   & 1 & -1 & -6 & 0
\end{array}
$$

$f(2) \neq 0$, so $x - 2$ is not a factor of $f(x)$. $f(-2) = 0$, so $x + 2$ is a factor of $f(x)$.

Step 3 Factor completely using the result of synthetic division.

$$
\begin{aligned}
(x + 2)(x^2 - x - 6) &= 0 &\qquad& \text{Write as a product of factors.} \\
(x + 2)(x + 2)(x - 3) &= 0 &\qquad& \text{Factor the trinomial.}
\end{aligned}
$$

▶ So, the solutions are $x = -2$ and $x = 3$.

b. Write a polynomial function f of least degree that has rational coefficients, a leading coefficient of 1, and the zeros -4 and $1 + \sqrt{2}$.

By the Irrational Conjugates Theorem, $1 - \sqrt{2}$ must also be a zero of f.

$$
\begin{aligned}
f(x) &= (x + 4)\left[x - (1 + \sqrt{2})\right]\left[x - (1 - \sqrt{2})\right] &\qquad& \text{Write } f(x) \text{ in factored form.} \\
&= (x + 4)\left[(x - 1) - \sqrt{2}\right]\left[(x - 1) + \sqrt{2}\right] &\qquad& \text{Regroup terms.} \\
&= (x + 4)\left[(x - 1)^2 - 2\right] &\qquad& \text{Multiply.} \\
&= (x + 4)\left[(x^2 - 2x + 1) - 2\right] &\qquad& \text{Expand binomial.} \\
&= (x + 4)(x^2 - 2x - 1) &\qquad& \text{Simplify.} \\
&= x^3 - 2x^2 - x + 4x^2 - 8x - 4 &\qquad& \text{Multiply.} \\
&= x^3 + 2x^2 - 9x - 4 &\qquad& \text{Combine like terms.}
\end{aligned}
$$

Find all real solutions of the equation.

23. $x^3 + 3x^2 - 10x - 24 = 0$

24. $x^3 + 5x^2 - 2x - 24 = 0$

Write a polynomial function f of least degree that has rational coefficients, a leading coefficient of 1, and the given zeros.

25. $1, 2 - \sqrt{3}$

26. $2, 3, \sqrt{5}$

27. $-2, 5, 3 + \sqrt{6}$

28. You use 240 cubic inches of clay to make a sculpture shaped as a rectangular prism. The width is 4 inches less than the length and the height is 2 inches more than three times the length. What are the dimensions of the sculpture? Justify your answer.

3.6 The Fundamental Theorem of Algebra (pp. 153–160)

Find all zeros of $f(x) = x^4 + 2x^3 + 6x^2 + 18x - 27$.

Step 1 Find the rational zeros of f. Because f is a polynomial function of degree 4, it has four zeros. The possible rational zeros are ± 1, ± 3, ± 9, and ± 27. Using synthetic division, you can determine that 1 is a zero and -3 is also a zero.

Step 2 Write $f(x)$ in factored form. Dividing $f(x)$ by its known factors $x - 1$ and $x + 3$ gives a quotient of $x^2 + 9$. So,

$$f(x) = (x - 1)(x + 3)(x^2 + 9).$$

Step 3 Find the complex zeros of f. Solving $x^2 + 9 = 0$, you get $x = \pm 3i$. This means $x^2 + 9 = (x + 3i)(x - 3i)$.

$$f(x) = (x - 1)(x + 3)(x + 3i)(x - 3i)$$

▶ From the factorization, there are four zeros. The zeros of f are 1, -3, $-3i$, and $3i$.

Write a polynomial function f of least degree that has rational coefficients, a leading coefficient of 1, and the given zeros.

29. $3, 1 + 2i$

30. $-1, 2, 4i$

31. $-5, -4, 1 - i\sqrt{3}$

Determine the possible numbers of positive real zeros, negative real zeros, and imaginary zeros for the function.

32. $f(x) = x^4 - 10x + 8$

33. $f(x) = -6x^4 - x^3 + 3x^2 + 2x + 18$

3.7 Transformations of Polynomial Functions (pp. 161–166)

Describe the transformation of $f(x) = x^3$ represented by $g(x) = (x - 6)^3 - 2$. Then graph each function.

Notice that the function is of the form $g(x) = (x - h)^3 + k$. Rewrite the function to identify h and k.

$$g(x) = (x - 6)^3 + (-2)$$

$\uparrow$ $\uparrow$
h k

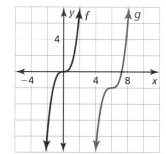

▶ Because $h = 6$ and $k = -2$, the graph of g is a translation 6 units right and 2 units down of the graph of f.

Describe the transformation of f represented by g. Then graph each function.

34. $f(x) = x^3, g(x) = (-x)^3 + 2$

35. $f(x) = x^4, g(x) = -(x + 9)^4$

Write a rule for g.

36. Let the graph of g be a horizontal stretch by a factor of 4, followed by a translation 3 units right and 5 units down of the graph of $f(x) = x^5 + 3x$.

37. Let the graph of g be a translation 5 units up, followed by a reflection in the y-axis of the graph of $f(x) = x^4 - 2x^3 - 12$.

3.8 Analyzing Graphs of Polynomial Functions (pp. 167–174)

Graph the function $f(x) = x(x + 2)(x - 2)$. Then estimate the points where the local maximums and local minimums occur.

Step 1 Plot the x-intercepts. Because -2, 0, and 2 are zeros of f, plot $(-2, 0)$, $(0, 0)$, and $(2, 0)$.

Step 2 Plot points between and beyond the x-intercepts.

x	−3	−2	−1	0	1	2	3
y	−15	0	3	0	−3	0	15

Step 3 Determine end behavior. Because $f(x)$ has three factors of the form $x - k$ and a constant factor of 1, f is a cubic function with a positive leading coefficient. So $f(x) \to -\infty$ as $x \to -\infty$ and $f(x) \to +\infty$ as $x \to +\infty$.

Step 4 Draw the graph so it passes through the plotted points and has the appropriate end behavior.

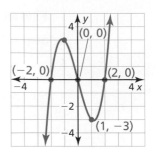

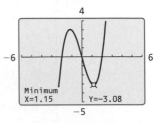

▶ The function has a local maximum at $(-1.15, 3.08)$ and a local minimum at $(1.15, -3.08)$.

Graph the function. Identify the x-intercepts and the points where the local maximums and local minimums occur. Determine the intervals for which the function is increasing or decreasing.

38. $f(x) = -2x^3 - 3x^2 - 1$ **39.** $f(x) = x^4 + 3x^3 - x^2 - 8x + 2$

Determine whether the function is *even*, *odd*, or *neither*.

40. $f(x) = 2x^3 + 3x$ **41.** $g(x) = 3x^2 - 7$ **42.** $h(x) = x^6 + 3x^5$

3.9 Modeling with Polynomial Functions (pp. 175–180)

Write the cubic function whose graph is shown.

Step 1 Use the three x-intercepts to write the function in factored form.

$$f(x) = a(x + 3)(x + 1)(x - 2)$$

Step 2 Find the value of a by substituting the coordinates of the point $(0, -12)$.

$$-12 = a(0 + 3)(0 + 1)(0 - 2)$$
$$-12 = -6a$$
$$2 = a$$

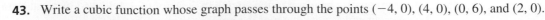

▶ The function is $f(x) = 2(x + 3)(x + 1)(x - 2)$.

43. Write a cubic function whose graph passes through the points $(-4, 0)$, $(4, 0)$, $(0, 6)$, and $(2, 0)$.

44. Use finite differences to determine the degree of the polynomial function that fits the data. Then use technology to find the polynomial function.

x	1	2	3	4	5	6	7
f(x)	−11	−24	−27	−8	45	144	301

Write a polynomial function f of least degree that has rational coefficients, a leading coefficient of 1, and the given zeros.

1. $3, 1 - \sqrt{2}$

2. $-2, 4, 3i$

Find the product or quotient.

3. $(x^6 - 4)(x^2 - 7x + 5)$

4. $(3x^4 - 2x^3 - x - 1) \div (x^2 - 2x + 1)$

5. $(2x^3 - 3x^2 + 5x - 1) \div (x + 2)$

6. $(2x + 3)^3$

7. The graphs of $f(x) = x^4$ and $g(x) = (x - 3)^4$ are shown.

   a. How many zeros does each function have? Explain.

   b. Describe the transformation of f represented by g.

   c. Determine the intervals for which the function g is increasing or decreasing.

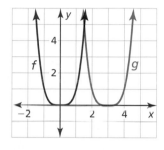

8. The volume V (in cubic feet) of an aquarium is modeled by the polynomial function $V(x) = x^3 + 2x^2 - 13x + 10$, where x is the length of the tank.

   a. Explain how you know $x = 4$ is *not* a possible rational zero.

   b. Show that $x - 1$ is a factor of $V(x)$. Then factor $V(x)$ completely.

   c. Find the dimensions of the aquarium shown.

Volume = 3 ft³

9. One special product pattern is $(a - b)^2 = a^2 - 2ab + b^2$. Using Pascal's Triangle to expand $(a - b)^2$ gives $1a^2 + 2a(-b) + 1(-b)^2$. Are the two expressions equivalent? Explain.

10. Can you use the synthetic division procedure that you learned in this chapter to divide *any* two polynomials? Explain.

11. Let T be the number (in thousands) of new truck sales. Let C be the number (in thousands) of new car sales. During a 10-year period, T and C can be modeled by the following equations where t is time (in years).

    $$T = 23t^4 - 330t^3 + 3500t^2 - 7500t + 9000$$

    $$C = 14t^4 - 330t^3 + 2400t^2 - 5900t + 8900$$

    a. Find a new model S for the total number of new vehicle sales.

    b. Is the function S *even*, *odd*, or *neither*? Explain your reasoning.

12. Your friend has started a golf caddy business. The table shows the profits p (in dollars) of the business in the first 5 months. Use finite differences to find a polynomial model for the data. Then use the model to predict the profit after 7 months.

Month, t	1	2	3	4	5
Profit, p	4	2	6	22	56

3 Cumulative Assessment

1. The synthetic division below represents $f(x) \div (x - 3)$. Choose a value for m so that $x - 3$ is a factor of $f(x)$. Justify your answer.

3	1	−3	m	3
		3	0	
	1	0		

−3	3
−2	2
−1	1

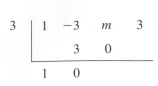

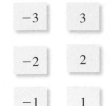

2. Analyze the graph of the polynomial function to determine the sign of the leading coefficient, the degree of the function, and the number of real zeros. Explain.

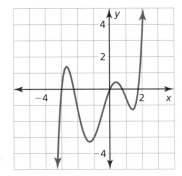

3. About 52,300 people live in a 3-kilometer radius of a city's center. Ten years ago, the population density in this region was about 1750 people per square kilometer. Which statement is *not* true?

Ⓐ The area of the region is 9π square kilometers.

Ⓑ The current population density is about 1850 people per square kilometer.

Ⓒ Ten years ago, there were about 49,480 people living in this region.

Ⓓ The current population density is less than it was 10 years ago.

4. A parabola passes through the point shown in the graph. The equation of the axis of symmetry is $x = -a$. Which of the given points could lie on the parabola? If the axis of symmetry was $x = a$, then which points could lie on the parabola? Explain your reasoning.

(1, 1)	(0, 1)	(−2, 1)
(−3, 1)	(−4, 1)	(−5, 1)

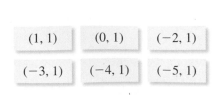

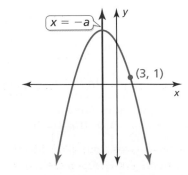

5. Select values for the function to model each transformation of the graph of $f(x) = x$.

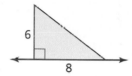

$$g(x) = \boxed{}\left(x - \boxed{}\right) + \boxed{}$$

   a. The graph is a translation 2 units up and 3 units left.

   b. The graph is a translation 2 units right and 3 units down.

   c. The graph is a vertical stretch by a factor of 2, followed by a translation 2 units up.

   d. The graph is a translation 3 units right and a vertical shrink by a factor of $\frac{1}{2}$, followed by a translation 4 units down.

6. Which description represents the solid produced by rotating the figure around the given axis?

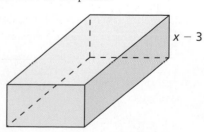

  Ⓐ cone with a height of 6 and a radius of 8

  Ⓑ cone with a height of 8 and a radius of 6

  Ⓒ pyramid with a height of 6 and a square base whose edge length is 8

  Ⓓ pyramid with a height of 8 and a square base whose edge length is 6

7. Classify each function as *even*, *odd*, or *neither*. Justify your answer.

   a. $f(x) = 3x^5$ **b.** $f(x) = 4x^3 + 8x$

   c. $f(x) = 3x^3 + 12x^2 + 1$ **d.** $f(x) = 2x^4$

   e. $f(x) = x^{11} - x^7$ **f.** $f(x) = 2x^8 + 4x^4 + x^2 - 5$

8. The volume of the rectangular prism shown is given by $V = 2x^3 + 7x^2 - 18x - 63$. Which polynomial represents the area of the base of the prism?

  Ⓐ $2x^2 + x - 21$

  Ⓑ $2x^2 + 21 - x$

  Ⓒ $13x + 21 + 2x^2$

  Ⓓ $2x^2 - 21 - 13x$

$x - 3$

9. The number R (in tens of thousands) of retirees receiving Social Security benefits is represented by the function

$$R = 0.286t^3 - 4.68t^2 + 8.8t + 403, \quad 0 \le t \le 10$$

where t represents the number of years since 2000. Identify any turning points on the given interval. What does a turning point represent in this situation?

4 Rational Exponents and Radical Functions

Hull Speed *(p. 238)*

SEE the Big Idea

White Rhino *(p. 228)*

Concert *(p. 224)*

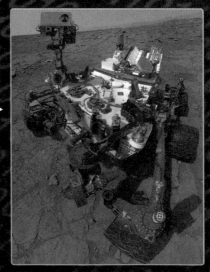

Mars Rover *(p. 210)*

Constellations *(p. 206)*

Maintaining Mathematical Proficiency

Properties of Integer Exponents

Example 1 Simplify the expression $\dfrac{x^5 \cdot x^2}{x^3}$.

$$\dfrac{x^5 \cdot x^2}{x^3} = \dfrac{x^{5+2}}{x^3}$$ Product of Powers Property

$$= \dfrac{x^7}{x^3}$$ Add exponents.

$$= x^{7-3}$$ Quotient of Powers Property

$$= x^4$$ Subtract exponents.

Example 2 Simplify the expression $\left(\dfrac{2s^3}{t}\right)^2$.

$$\left(\dfrac{2s^3}{t}\right)^2 = \dfrac{(2s^3)^2}{t^2}$$ Power of a Quotient Property

$$= \dfrac{2^2 \cdot (s^3)^2}{t^2}$$ Power of a Product Property

$$= \dfrac{4s^6}{t^2}$$ Power of a Power Property

Simplify the expression.

1. $y^6 \cdot y$

2. $\dfrac{n^4}{n^3}$

3. $\dfrac{x^5}{x^6 \cdot x^2}$

4. $\dfrac{x^6}{x^5} \cdot 3x^2$

5. $\left(\dfrac{4w^3}{2z^2}\right)^3$

6. $\left(\dfrac{m^7 \cdot m}{z^2 \cdot m^3}\right)^2$

Rewriting Literal Equations

Example 3 Solve the literal equation $-5y - 2x = 10$ for y.

$$-5y - 2x = 10$$ Write the equation.

$$-5y - 2x + 2x = 10 + 2x$$ Add $2x$ to each side.

$$-5y = 10 + 2x$$ Simplify.

$$\dfrac{-5y}{-5} = \dfrac{10 + 2x}{-5}$$ Divide each side by -5.

$$y = -2 - \dfrac{2}{5}x$$ Simplify.

Solve the literal equation for y.

7. $4x + y = 2$

8. $x - \dfrac{1}{3}y = -1$

9. $2y - 9 = 13x$

10. $2xy + 6y = 10$

11. $8x - 4xy = 3$

12. $6x + 7xy = 15$

13. **ABSTRACT REASONING** Is the order in which you apply properties of exponents important? Explain your reasoning.

Mathematical Practices

Mathematically proficient students express numerical answers precisely.

Using Technology to Evaluate Roots

⑤ Core Concept

Evaluating Roots with a Calculator

	Example
Square root:	$\sqrt{64} = 8$
Cube root:	$\sqrt[3]{64} = 4$
Fourth root:	$\sqrt[4]{256} = 4$
Fifth root:	$\sqrt[5]{32} = 2$

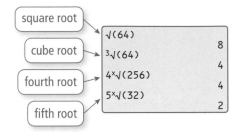

square root → √(64) 8
cube root → ³√(64) 4
fourth root → 4×√(256) 4
fifth root → 5×√(32) 2

EXAMPLE 1   Approximating Roots

Evaluate each root using a calculator. Round your answer to two decimal places.

a. $\sqrt{50}$ **b.** $\sqrt[3]{50}$ **c.** $\sqrt[4]{50}$ **d.** $\sqrt[5]{50}$

SOLUTION

a. $\sqrt{50} \approx 7.07$ Round down.

b. $\sqrt[3]{50} \approx 3.68$ Round down.

c. $\sqrt[4]{50} \approx 2.66$ Round up.

d. $\sqrt[5]{50} \approx 2.19$ Round up.

√(50)
     7.071067812
³√(50)
     3.684031499
4×√(50)
     2.659147948
5×√(50)
     2.186724148

Monitoring Progress

1. Use the Pythagorean Theorem to find the exact lengths of a, b, c, and d in the figure.

2. Use a calculator to approximate each length to the nearest tenth of an inch in Monitoring Progress Question 1.

3. Use a ruler to check the reasonableness of your answers in Monitoring Progress Question 2.

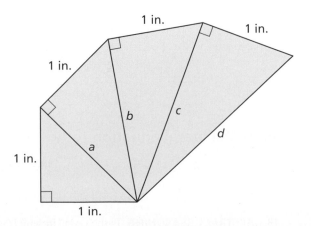

4.1 nth Roots and Rational Exponents

Essential Question How can you use a rational exponent to represent a power involving a radical?

Previously, you learned that the nth root of a can be represented as

$$\sqrt[n]{a} = a^{1/n} \qquad \text{Definition of rational exponent}$$

for any real number a and integer n greater than 1.

EXPLORATION 1 **Exploring the Definition of a Rational Exponent**

Work with a partner. Use a calculator to show that each statement is true.

a. $\sqrt{9} = 9^{1/2}$ b. $\sqrt{2} = 2^{1/2}$ c. $\sqrt[3]{8} = 8^{1/3}$

d. $\sqrt[3]{3} = 3^{1/3}$ e. $\sqrt[4]{16} = 16^{1/4}$ f. $\sqrt[4]{12} = 12^{1/4}$

CONSTRUCTING VIABLE ARGUMENTS

To be proficient in math, you need to understand and use stated definitions and previously established results.

EXPLORATION 2 **Writing Expressions in Rational Exponent Form**

Work with a partner. Use the definition of a rational exponent and the properties of exponents to write each expression as a base with a single rational exponent. Then use a calculator to evaluate each expression. Round your answer to two decimal places.

Sample

$$\left(\sqrt[3]{4}\right)^2 = (4^{1/3})^2$$

$$= 4^{2/3}$$

$$\approx 2.52$$

```
4^(2/3)
              2.5198421
```

a. $\left(\sqrt{5}\right)^3$ b. $\left(\sqrt[4]{4}\right)^2$ c. $\left(\sqrt[3]{9}\right)^2$

d. $\left(\sqrt[5]{10}\right)^4$ e. $\left(\sqrt{15}\right)^3$ f. $\left(\sqrt[3]{27}\right)^4$

EXPLORATION 3 **Writing Expressions in Radical Form**

Work with a partner. Use the properties of exponents and the definition of a rational exponent to write each expression as a radical raised to an exponent. Then use a calculator to evaluate each expression. Round your answer to two decimal places.

Sample $5^{2/3} = (5^{1/3})^2 = \left(\sqrt[3]{5}\right)^2 \approx 2.92$

a. $8^{2/3}$ b. $6^{5/2}$ c. $12^{3/4}$

d. $10^{3/2}$ e. $16^{3/2}$ f. $20^{6/5}$

Communicate Your Answer

4. How can you use a rational exponent to represent a power involving a radical?

5. Evaluate each expression *without* using a calculator. Explain your reasoning.

a. $4^{3/2}$ b. $32^{4/5}$ c. $625^{3/4}$

d. $49^{3/2}$ e. $125^{4/3}$ f. $100^{6/3}$

4.1 Lesson

Core Vocabulary

nth root of a, p. 194
index of a radical, p. 194

Previous
square root
cube root
exponent

What You Will Learn

▶ Find nth roots of numbers.

▶ Evaluate expressions with rational exponents.

▶ Solve equations using nth roots.

nth Roots

You can extend the concept of a square root to other types of roots. For example, 2 is a cube root of 8 because $2^3 = 8$. In general, for an integer n greater than 1, if $b^n = a$, then b is an **nth root of a**. An nth root of a is written as $\sqrt[n]{a}$, where n is the **index** of the radical.

You can also write an nth root of a as a power of a. If you assume the Power of a Power Property applies to rational exponents, then the following is true.

$$(a^{1/2})^2 = a^{(1/2) \cdot 2} = a^1 = a$$

$$(a^{1/3})^3 = a^{(1/3) \cdot 3} = a^1 = a$$

$$(a^{1/4})^4 = a^{(1/4) \cdot 4} = a^1 = a$$

Because $a^{1/2}$ is a number whose square is a, you can write $\sqrt{a} = a^{1/2}$. Similarly, $\sqrt[3]{a} = a^{1/3}$ and $\sqrt[4]{a} = a^{1/4}$. In general, $\sqrt[n]{a} = a^{1/n}$ for any integer n greater than 1.

UNDERSTANDING MATHEMATICAL TERMS

When n is even and $a > 0$, there are two real roots. The positive root is called the *principal root*.

Core Concept

Real nth Roots of a

Let n be an integer ($n > 1$) and let a be a real number.

n is an even integer.	**n is an odd integer.**
$a < 0$ No real nth roots	$a < 0$ One real nth root: $\sqrt[n]{a} = a^{1/n}$
$a = 0$ One real nth root: $\sqrt[n]{0} = 0$	$a = 0$ One real nth root: $\sqrt[n]{0} = 0$
$a > 0$ Two real nth roots: $\pm\sqrt[n]{a} = \pm a^{1/n}$	$a > 0$ One real nth root: $\sqrt[n]{a} = a^{1/n}$

EXAMPLE 1   Finding nth Roots

Find the indicated real nth root(s) of a.

a. $n = 3$, $a = -216$

b. $n = 4$, $a = 81$

SOLUTION

a. Because $n = 3$ is odd and $a = -216 < 0$, -216 has one real cube root.
Because $(-6)^3 = -216$, you can write $\sqrt[3]{-216} = -6$ or $(-216)^{1/3} = -6$.

b. Because $n = 4$ is even and $a = 81 > 0$, 81 has two real fourth roots.
Because $3^4 = 81$ and $(-3)^4 = 81$, you can write $\pm\sqrt[4]{81} = \pm 3$ or $\pm 81^{1/4} = \pm 3$.

Monitoring Progress Help in English and Spanish at *BigIdeasMath.com*

Find the indicated real nth root(s) of a.

1. $n = 4$, $a = 16$

2. $n = 2$, $a = -49$

3. $n = 3$, $a = -125$

4. $n = 5$, $a = 243$

Rational Exponents

A rational exponent does not have to be of the form $1/n$. Other rational numbers, such as $3/2$ and $-1/2$, can also be used as exponents. Two properties of rational exponents are shown below.

Core Concept

Rational Exponents

Let $a^{1/n}$ be an nth root of a, and let m be a positive integer.

$$a^{m/n} = (a^{1/n})^m = (\sqrt[n]{a})^m$$

$$a^{-m/n} = \frac{1}{a^{m/n}} = \frac{1}{(a^{1/n})^m} = \frac{1}{(\sqrt[n]{a})^m},\ a \neq 0$$

EXAMPLE 2   Evaluating Expressions with Rational Exponents

Evaluate each expression.

a. $16^{3/2}$ **b.** $32^{-3/5}$

SOLUTION

Rational Exponent Form	Radical Form
a. $16^{3/2} = (16^{1/2})^3 = 4^3 = 64$	$16^{3/2} = (\sqrt{16})^3 = 4^3 = 64$
b. $32^{-3/5} = \dfrac{1}{32^{3/5}} = \dfrac{1}{(32^{1/5})^3} = \dfrac{1}{2^3} = \dfrac{1}{8}$	$32^{-3/5} = \dfrac{1}{32^{3/5}} = \dfrac{1}{(\sqrt[5]{32})^3} = \dfrac{1}{2^3} = \dfrac{1}{8}$

When using a calculator to approximate an nth root, you may want to rewrite the nth root in rational exponent form.

EXAMPLE 3   Approximating Expressions with Rational Exponents

Evaluate each expression using a calculator. Round your answer to two decimal places.

a. $9^{1/5}$ **b.** $12^{3/8}$ **c.** $(\sqrt[4]{7})^3$

SOLUTION

a. $9^{1/5} \approx 1.55$

b. $12^{3/8} \approx 2.54$

c. Before evaluating $(\sqrt[4]{7})^3$, rewrite the expression in rational exponent form.

$$(\sqrt[4]{7})^3 = 7^{3/4} \approx 4.30$$

```
9^(1/5)
           1.551845574
12^(3/8)
           2.539176951
7^(3/4)
           4.303517071
```

Monitoring Progress Help in English and Spanish at *BigIdeasMath.com*

Evaluate the expression without using a calculator.

5. $4^{5/2}$ **6.** $9^{-1/2}$ **7.** $81^{3/4}$ **8.** $1^{7/8}$

Evaluate the expression using a calculator. Round your answer to two decimal places when appropriate.

9. $6^{2/5}$ **10.** $64^{-2/3}$ **11.** $(\sqrt[4]{16})^5$ **12.** $(\sqrt[3]{-30})^2$

Solving Equations Using *n*th Roots

To solve an equation of the form $u^n = d$, where u is an algebraic expression, take the *n*th root of each side.

EXAMPLE 4   Solving Equations Using *n*th Roots

Find the real solution(s) of (a) $4x^5 = 128$ and (b) $(x - 3)^4 = 21$.

SOLUTION

a. $4x^5 = 128$ Write original equation.

    $x^5 = 32$ Divide each side by 4.

    $x = \sqrt[5]{32}$ Take fifth root of each side.

    $x = 2$ Simplify.

▶ The solution is $x = 2$.

b. $(x - 3)^4 = 21$ Write original equation.

    $x - 3 = \pm\sqrt[4]{21}$ Take fourth root of each side.

       $x = 3 \pm \sqrt[4]{21}$ Add 3 to each side.

       $x = 3 + \sqrt[4]{21}$ or $x = 3 - \sqrt[4]{21}$ Write solutions separately.

       $x \approx 5.14$ or $x \approx 0.86$ Use a calculator.

▶ The solutions are $x \approx 5.14$ and $x \approx 0.86$.

EXAMPLE 5   Real-Life Application

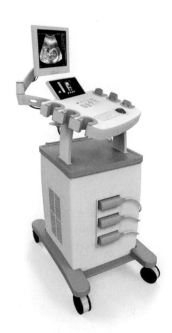

A hospital purchases an ultrasound machine for $50,000. The hospital expects the useful life of the machine to be 10 years, at which time its value will have depreciated to $8000. The hospital uses the declining balances method for depreciation, so the annual depreciation rate r (in decimal form) is given by the formula

$$r = 1 - \left(\frac{S}{C}\right)^{1/n}.$$

In the formula, n is the useful life of the item (in years), S is the salvage value (in dollars), and C is the original cost (in dollars). What annual depreciation rate did the hospital use?

SOLUTION

The useful life is 10 years, so $n = 10$. The machine depreciates to $8000, so $S = 8000$. The original cost is $50,000, so $C = 50,000$. So, the annual depreciation rate is

$$r = 1 - \left(\frac{S}{C}\right)^{1/n} = 1 - \left(\frac{8000}{50,000}\right)^{1/10} = 1 - \left(\frac{4}{25}\right)^{1/10} \approx 0.167.$$

▶ The annual depreciation rate is about 0.167, or 16.7%.

Monitoring Progress Help in English and Spanish at *BigIdeasMath.com*

Find the real solution(s) of the equation. Round your answer to two decimal places when appropriate.

13. $8x^3 = 64$ **14.** $\frac{1}{2}x^5 = 512$ **15.** $(x + 5)^4 = 16$ **16.** $(x - 2)^3 = -14$

17. WHAT IF? In Example 5, what is the annual depreciation rate when the salvage value is $6000?

Vocabulary and Core Concept Check

1. **VOCABULARY** Rewrite the expression $a^{-s/t}$ in radical form. Then state the index of the radical.

2. **COMPLETE THE SENTENCE** For an integer n greater than 1, if $b^n = a$, then b is a(n) _____ of a.

3. **WRITING** Explain how to use the sign of a to determine the number of real fourth roots of a and the number of real fifth roots of a.

4. **WHICH ONE DOESN'T BELONG?** Which expression does *not* belong with the other three? Explain your reasoning.

| $(a^{1/n})^m$ | $(\sqrt[n]{a})^m$ | $(\sqrt[m]{a})^{-n}$ | $a^{m/n}$ |

Monitoring Progress and Modeling with Mathematics

In Exercises 5–10, find the indicated real nth root(s) of a. *(See Example 1.)*

5. $n = 3, a = 8$

6. $n = 5, a = -1$

7. $n = 2, a = 0$

8. $n = 4, a = 256$

9. $n = 5, a = -32$

10. $n = 6, a = -729$

In Exercises 11–18, evaluate the expression without using a calculator. *(See Example 2.)*

11. $64^{1/6}$

12. $8^{1/3}$

13. $25^{3/2}$

14. $81^{3/4}$

15. $(-243)^{1/5}$

16. $(-64)^{4/3}$

17. $8^{-2/3}$

18. $16^{-7/4}$

ERROR ANALYSIS In Exercises 19 and 20, describe and correct the error in evaluating the expression.

19.
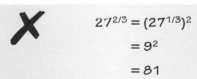

$$27^{2/3} = (27^{1/3})^2$$
$$= 9^2$$
$$= 81$$

20.

$$256^{4/3} = (\sqrt[4]{256})^3$$
$$= 4^3$$
$$= 64$$

USING STRUCTURE In Exercises 21–24, match the equivalent expressions. Explain your reasoning.

21. $(\sqrt[3]{5})^4$

22. $(\sqrt[4]{5})^3$

23. $\dfrac{1}{\sqrt[4]{5}}$

24. $-\sqrt[4]{5}$

A. $5^{-1/4}$

B. $5^{4/3}$

C. $-5^{1/4}$

D. $5^{3/4}$

In Exercises 25–32, evaluate the expression using a calculator. Round your answer to two decimal places when appropriate. *(See Example 3.)*

25. $\sqrt[5]{32,768}$

26. $\sqrt[7]{1695}$

27. $25^{-1/3}$

28. $85^{1/6}$

29. $20,736^{4/5}$

30. $86^{-5/6}$

31. $(\sqrt[4]{187})^3$

32. $(\sqrt[5]{-8})^8$

MATHEMATICAL CONNECTIONS In Exercises 33 and 34, find the radius of the figure with the given volume.

33. $V = 216 \text{ ft}^3$

34. $V = 1332 \text{ cm}^3$

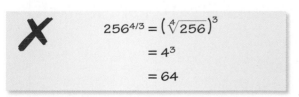
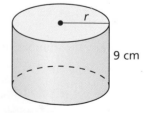

In Exercises 35–44, find the real solution(s) of the equation. Round your answer to two decimal places when appropriate. *(See Example 4.)*

35. $x^3 = 125$

36. $5x^3 = 1080$

37. $(x + 10)^5 = 70$

38. $(x - 5)^4 = 256$

39. $x^5 = -48$

40. $7x^4 = 56$

41. $x^6 + 36 = 100$

42. $x^3 + 40 = 25$

43. $\frac{1}{3}x^4 = 27$

44. $\frac{1}{6}x^3 = -36$

45. MODELING WITH MATHEMATICS When the average price of an item increases from p_1 to p_2 over a period of n years, the annual rate of inflation r (in decimal form) is given by $r = \left(\dfrac{p_2}{p_1}\right)^{1/n} - 1$. Find the rate of inflation for each item in the table. *(See Example 5.)*

Item	Price in 1913	Price in 2013
Potatoes (lb)	$0.016	$0.627
Ham (lb)	$0.251	$2.693
Eggs (dozen)	$0.373	$1.933

46. HOW DO YOU SEE IT? The graph of $y = x^n$ is shown in red. What can you conclude about the value of n? Determine the number of real nth roots of a. Explain your reasoning.

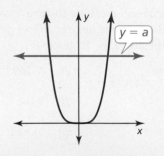

47. NUMBER SENSE Between which two consecutive integers does $\sqrt[4]{125}$ lie? Explain your reasoning.

48. THOUGHT PROVOKING In 1619, Johannes Kepler published his third law, which can be given by $d^3 = t^2$, where d is the mean distance (in astronomical units) of a planet from the Sun and t is the time (in years) it takes the planet to orbit the Sun. It takes Mars 1.88 years to orbit the Sun. Graph a possible location of Mars. Justify your answer. (The diagram shows the Sun at the origin of the xy-plane and a possible location of Earth.)

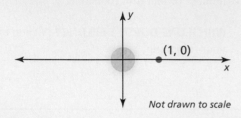

Not drawn to scale

49. PROBLEM SOLVING A *weir* is a dam that is built across a river to regulate the flow of water. The flow rate Q (in cubic feet per second) can be calculated using the formula $Q = 3.367\ell h^{3/2}$, where ℓ is the length (in feet) of the bottom of the spillway and h is the depth (in feet) of the water on the spillway. Determine the flow rate of a weir with a spillway that is 20 feet long and has a water depth of 5 feet.

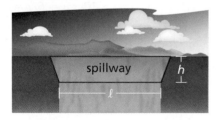

50. REPEATED REASONING The mass of the particles that a river can transport is proportional to the sixth power of the speed of the river. A certain river normally flows at a speed of 1 meter per second. What must its speed be in order to transport particles that are twice as massive as usual? 10 times as massive? 100 times as massive?

Maintaining Mathematical Proficiency
Reviewing what you learned in previous grades and lessons

Simplify the expression. Write your answer using only positive exponents. *(Skills Review Handbook)*

51. $5 \cdot 5^4$

52. $\dfrac{4^2}{4^7}$

53. $(z^2)^{-3}$

54. $\left(\dfrac{3x}{2}\right)^4$

Write the number in standard form. *(Skills Review Handbook)*

55. 5×10^3

56. 4×10^{-2}

57. 8.2×10^{-1}

58. 6.93×10^6

4.2 Properties of Rational Exponents and Radicals

Essential Question
How can you use properties of exponents to simplify products and quotients of radicals?

EXPLORATION 1 — Reviewing Properties of Exponents

Work with a partner. Let a and b be real numbers. Use the properties of exponents to complete each statement. Then match each completed statement with the property it illustrates.

Statement	Property
a. $a^{-2} = $ _____, $a \neq 0$	**A.** Product of Powers
b. $(ab)^4 = $ _____	**B.** Power of a Power
c. $(a^3)^4 = $ _____	**C.** Power of a Product
d. $a^3 \cdot a^4 = $ _____	**D.** Negative Exponent
e. $\left(\dfrac{a}{b}\right)^3 = $ _____, $b \neq 0$	**E.** Zero Exponent
f. $\dfrac{a^6}{a^2} = $ _____, $a \neq 0$	**F.** Quotient of Powers
g. $a^0 = $ _____, $a \neq 0$	**G.** Power of a Quotient

EXPLORATION 2 — Simplifying Expressions with Rational Exponents

Work with a partner. Show that you can apply the properties of integer exponents to rational exponents by simplifying each expression. Use a calculator to check your answers.

a. $5^{2/3} \cdot 5^{4/3}$ **b.** $3^{1/5} \cdot 3^{4/5}$ **c.** $(4^{2/3})^3$

d. $(10^{1/2})^4$ **e.** $\dfrac{8^{5/2}}{8^{1/2}}$ **f.** $\dfrac{7^{2/3}}{7^{5/3}}$

EXPLORATION 3 — Simplifying Products and Quotients of Radicals

Work with a partner. Use the properties of exponents to write each expression as a single radical. Then evaluate each expression. Use a calculator to check your answers.

a. $\sqrt{3} \cdot \sqrt{12}$ **b.** $\sqrt[3]{5} \cdot \sqrt[3]{25}$ **c.** $\sqrt[4]{27} \cdot \sqrt[4]{3}$

d. $\dfrac{\sqrt{98}}{\sqrt{2}}$ **e.** $\dfrac{\sqrt[4]{4}}{\sqrt[4]{1024}}$ **f.** $\dfrac{\sqrt[3]{625}}{\sqrt[3]{5}}$

Communicate Your Answer

4. How can you use properties of exponents to simplify products and quotients of radicals?

5. Simplify each expression.

a. $\sqrt{27} \cdot \sqrt{6}$ **b.** $\dfrac{\sqrt[3]{240}}{\sqrt[3]{15}}$ **c.** $(5^{1/2} \cdot 16^{1/4})^2$

USING TOOLS STRATEGICALLY

To be proficient in math, you need to consider the tools available to help you check your answers. For instance, the following calculator screen shows that $\sqrt[3]{4} \cdot \sqrt[3]{2}$ and $\sqrt[3]{8}$ are equivalent.

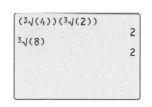

4.2 Lesson

Core Vocabulary

simplest form of a radical,
 p. 201
conjugate, p. 202
like radicals, p. 202

Previous
properties of integer
 exponents
rationalizing the
 denominator
absolute value

COMMON ERROR

When you multiply powers, *do not* multiply the exponents. For example, $3^2 \cdot 3^5 \neq 3^{10}$.

What You Will Learn

▶ Use properties of rational exponents to simplify expressions with rational exponents.

▶ Use properties of radicals to simplify and write radical expressions in simplest form.

Properties of Rational Exponents

The properties of integer exponents that you have previously learned can also be applied to rational exponents.

🌀 Core Concept

Properties of Rational Exponents

Let a and b be real numbers and let m and n be rational numbers, such that the quantities in each property are real numbers.

Property Name	Definition	Example
Product of Powers	$a^m \cdot a^n = a^{m+n}$	$5^{1/2} \cdot 5^{3/2} = 5^{(1/2+3/2)} = 5^2 = 25$
Power of a Power	$(a^m)^n = a^{mn}$	$(3^{5/2})^2 = 3^{(5/2 \cdot 2)} = 3^5 = 243$
Power of a Product	$(ab)^m = a^m b^m$	$(16 \cdot 9)^{1/2} = 16^{1/2} \cdot 9^{1/2} = 4 \cdot 3 = 12$
Negative Exponent	$a^{-m} = \dfrac{1}{a^m}, a \neq 0$	$36^{-1/2} = \dfrac{1}{36^{1/2}} = \dfrac{1}{6}$
Zero Exponent	$a^0 = 1, a \neq 0$	$213^0 = 1$
Quotient of Powers	$\dfrac{a^m}{a^n} = a^{m-n}, a \neq 0$	$\dfrac{4^{5/2}}{4^{1/2}} = 4^{(5/2-1/2)} = 4^2 = 16$
Power of a Quotient	$\left(\dfrac{a}{b}\right)^m = \dfrac{a^m}{b^m}, b \neq 0$	$\left(\dfrac{27}{64}\right)^{1/3} = \dfrac{27^{1/3}}{64^{1/3}} = \dfrac{3}{4}$

EXAMPLE 1 Using Properties of Exponents

Use the properties of rational exponents to simplify each expression.

a. $7^{1/4} \cdot 7^{1/2} = 7^{(1/4+1/2)} = 7^{3/4}$

b. $(6^{1/2} \cdot 4^{1/3})^2 = (6^{1/2})^2 \cdot (4^{1/3})^2 = 6^{(1/2 \cdot 2)} \cdot 4^{(1/3 \cdot 2)} = 6^1 \cdot 4^{2/3} = 6 \cdot 4^{2/3}$

c. $(4^5 \cdot 3^5)^{-1/5} = [(4 \cdot 3)^5]^{-1/5} = (12^5)^{-1/5} = 12^{[5 \cdot (-1/5)]} = 12^{-1} = \dfrac{1}{12}$

d. $\dfrac{5}{5^{1/3}} = \dfrac{5^1}{5^{1/3}} = 5^{(1-1/3)} = 5^{2/3}$

e. $\left(\dfrac{42^{1/3}}{6^{1/3}}\right)^2 = \left[\left(\dfrac{42}{6}\right)^{1/3}\right]^2 = (7^{1/3})^2 = 7^{(1/3 \cdot 2)} = 7^{2/3}$

Monitoring Progress Help in English and Spanish at *BigIdeasMath.com*

Simplify the expression.

1. $2^{3/4} \cdot 2^{1/2}$

2. $\dfrac{3}{3^{1/4}}$

3. $\left(\dfrac{20^{1/2}}{5^{1/2}}\right)^3$

4. $(5^{1/3} \cdot 7^{1/4})^3$

Simplifying Radical Expressions

The Power of a Product and Power of a Quotient properties can be expressed using radical notation when $m = 1/n$ for some integer n greater than 1.

Core Concept

Properties of Radicals

Let a and b be real numbers and let n be an integer greater than 1.

Property Name	Definition	Example
Product Property	$\sqrt[n]{a \cdot b} = \sqrt[n]{a} \cdot \sqrt[n]{b}$	$\sqrt[3]{4} \cdot \sqrt[3]{2} = \sqrt[3]{8} = 2$
Quotient Property	$\sqrt[n]{\dfrac{a}{b}} = \dfrac{\sqrt[n]{a}}{\sqrt[n]{b}}, b \neq 0$	$\dfrac{\sqrt[4]{162}}{\sqrt[4]{2}} = \sqrt[4]{\dfrac{162}{2}} = \sqrt[4]{81} = 3$

EXAMPLE 2 Using Properties of Radicals

Use the properties of radicals to simplify each expression.

a. $\sqrt[3]{12} \cdot \sqrt[3]{18} = \sqrt[3]{12 \cdot 18} = \sqrt[3]{216} = 6$ Product Property of Radicals

b. $\dfrac{\sqrt[4]{80}}{\sqrt[4]{5}} = \sqrt[4]{\dfrac{80}{5}} = \sqrt[4]{16} = 2$ Quotient Property of Radicals

An expression involving a radical with index n is in **simplest form** when these three conditions are met.

- No radicands have perfect nth powers as factors other than 1.
- No radicands contain fractions.
- No radicals appear in the denominator of a fraction.

To meet the last two conditions, rationalize the denominator by multiplying the expression by an appropriate form of 1 that eliminates the radical from the denominator.

EXAMPLE 3 Writing Radicals in Simplest Form

Write each expression in simplest form.

a. $\sqrt[3]{135}$ **b.** $\dfrac{\sqrt[5]{7}}{\sqrt[5]{8}}$

SOLUTION

a. $\sqrt[3]{135} = \sqrt[3]{27 \cdot 5}$ Factor out perfect cube.

$\phantom{\sqrt[3]{135}} = \sqrt[3]{27} \cdot \sqrt[3]{5}$ Product Property of Radicals

$\phantom{\sqrt[3]{135}} = 3\sqrt[3]{5}$ Simplify.

b. $\dfrac{\sqrt[5]{7}}{\sqrt[5]{8}} = \dfrac{\sqrt[5]{7}}{\sqrt[5]{8}} \cdot \dfrac{\sqrt[5]{4}}{\sqrt[5]{4}}$ Make the radicand in the denominator a perfect fifth power.

$\phantom{\dfrac{\sqrt[5]{7}}{\sqrt[5]{8}}} = \dfrac{\sqrt[5]{28}}{\sqrt[5]{32}}$ Product Property of Radicals

$\phantom{\dfrac{\sqrt[5]{7}}{\sqrt[5]{8}}} = \dfrac{\sqrt[5]{28}}{2}$ Simplify.

For a denominator that is a sum or difference involving square roots, multiply both the numerator and denominator by the **conjugate** of the denominator. The expressions

$$a\sqrt{b} + c\sqrt{d} \qquad \text{and} \qquad a\sqrt{b} - c\sqrt{d}$$

are conjugates of each other, where a, b, c, and d are rational numbers.

EXAMPLE 4 Writing a Radical Expression in Simplest Form

Write $\dfrac{1}{5 + \sqrt{3}}$ in simplest form.

SOLUTION

$$\frac{1}{5 + \sqrt{3}} = \frac{1}{5 + \sqrt{3}} \cdot \frac{5 - \sqrt{3}}{5 - \sqrt{3}} \qquad \text{The conjugate of } 5 + \sqrt{3} \text{ is } 5 - \sqrt{3}.$$

$$= \frac{1(5 - \sqrt{3})}{5^2 - (\sqrt{3})^2} \qquad \text{Sum and Difference Pattern}$$

$$= \frac{5 - \sqrt{3}}{22} \qquad \text{Simplify.}$$

Radical expressions with the same index and radicand are **like radicals**. To add or subtract like radicals, use the Distributive Property.

EXAMPLE 5 Adding and Subtracting Like Radicals and Roots

Simplify each expression.

a. $\sqrt[4]{10} + 7\sqrt[4]{10}$ **b.** $2(8^{1/5}) + 10(8^{1/5})$ **c.** $\sqrt[3]{54} - \sqrt[3]{2}$

SOLUTION

a. $\sqrt[4]{10} + 7\sqrt[4]{10} = (1 + 7)\sqrt[4]{10} = 8\sqrt[4]{10}$

b. $2(8^{1/5}) + 10(8^{1/5}) = (2 + 10)(8^{1/5}) = 12(8^{1/5})$

c. $\sqrt[3]{54} - \sqrt[3]{2} = \sqrt[3]{27} \cdot \sqrt[3]{2} - \sqrt[3]{2} = 3\sqrt[3]{2} - \sqrt[3]{2} = (3 - 1)\sqrt[3]{2} = 2\sqrt[3]{2}$

Monitoring Progress Help in English and Spanish at *BigIdeasMath.com*

Simplify the expression.

5. $\sqrt[4]{27} \cdot \sqrt[4]{3}$ **6.** $\dfrac{\sqrt[3]{250}}{\sqrt[3]{2}}$ **7.** $\sqrt[3]{104}$ **8.** $\sqrt[5]{\dfrac{3}{4}}$

9. $\dfrac{3}{6 - \sqrt{2}}$ **10.** $7\sqrt[5]{12} - \sqrt[5]{12}$ **11.** $4(9^{2/3}) + 8(9^{2/3})$ **12.** $\sqrt[3]{5} + \sqrt[3]{40}$

The properties of rational exponents and radicals can also be applied to expressions involving variables. Because a variable can be positive, negative, or zero, sometimes absolute value is needed when simplifying a variable expression.

	Rule	Example
When n is odd	$\sqrt[n]{x^n} = x$	$\sqrt[7]{5^7} = 5$ and $\sqrt[7]{(-5)^7} = -5$
When n is even	$\sqrt[n]{x^n} = |x|$	$\sqrt[4]{3^4} = 3$ and $\sqrt[4]{(-3)^4} = 3$

Absolute value is not needed when all variables are assumed to be positive.

EXAMPLE 6 Simplifying Variable Expressions

Simplify each expression.

a. $\sqrt[3]{64y^6}$

b. $\sqrt[4]{\dfrac{x^4}{y^8}}$

SOLUTION

a. $\sqrt[3]{64y^6} = \sqrt[3]{4^3(y^2)^3} = \sqrt[3]{4^3} \cdot \sqrt[3]{(y^2)^3} = 4y^2$

b. $\sqrt[4]{\dfrac{x^4}{y^8}} = \dfrac{\sqrt[4]{x^4}}{\sqrt[4]{y^8}} = \dfrac{\sqrt[4]{x^4}}{\sqrt[4]{(y^2)^4}} = \dfrac{|x|}{y^2}$

STUDY TIP

You do not need to take the absolute value of y because y is being squared.

EXAMPLE 7 Writing Variable Expressions in Simplest Form

Write each expression in simplest form. Assume all variables are positive.

a. $\sqrt[5]{4a^8b^{14}c^5}$

b. $\dfrac{x}{\sqrt[3]{y^8}}$

c. $\dfrac{14xy^{1/3}}{2x^{3/4}z^{-6}}$

SOLUTION

a. $\sqrt[5]{4a^8b^{14}c^5} = \sqrt[5]{4a^5a^3b^{10}b^4c^5}$ Factor out perfect fifth powers.

$= \sqrt[5]{a^5b^{10}c^5} \cdot \sqrt[5]{4a^3b^4}$ Product Property of Radicals

$= ab^2c\sqrt[5]{4a^3b^4}$ Simplify.

b. $\dfrac{x}{\sqrt[3]{y^8}} = \dfrac{x}{\sqrt[3]{y^8}} \cdot \dfrac{\sqrt[3]{y}}{\sqrt[3]{y}}$ Make denominator a perfect cube.

$= \dfrac{x\sqrt[3]{y}}{\sqrt[3]{y^9}}$ Product Property of Radicals

$= \dfrac{x\sqrt[3]{y}}{y^3}$ Simplify.

c. $\dfrac{14xy^{1/3}}{2x^{3/4}z^{-6}} = 7x^{(1-3/4)}y^{1/3}z^{-(-6)} = 7x^{1/4}y^{1/3}z^6$

COMMON ERROR

You must multiply both the numerator *and* denominator of the fraction by $\sqrt[3]{y}$ so that the value of the fraction does not change.

EXAMPLE 8 Adding and Subtracting Variable Expressions

Perform each indicated operation. Assume all variables are positive.

a. $5\sqrt{y} + 6\sqrt{y}$

b. $12\sqrt[3]{2z^5} - z\sqrt[3]{54z^2}$

SOLUTION

a. $5\sqrt{y} + 6\sqrt{y} = (5 + 6)\sqrt{y} = 11\sqrt{y}$

b. $12\sqrt[3]{2z^5} - z\sqrt[3]{54z^2} = 12z\sqrt[3]{2z^2} - 3z\sqrt[3]{2z^2} = (12z - 3z)\sqrt[3]{2z^2} = 9z\sqrt[3]{2z^2}$

Monitoring Progress 🔊 Help in English and Spanish at *BigIdeasMath.com*

Simplify the expression. Assume all variables are positive.

13. $\sqrt[3]{27q^9}$

14. $\sqrt[5]{\dfrac{x^{10}}{y^5}}$

15. $\dfrac{6xy^{3/4}}{3x^{1/2}y^{1/2}}$

16. $\sqrt{9w^5} - w\sqrt{w^3}$

Vocabulary and Core Concept Check

1. **WRITING** How do you know when a radical expression is in simplest form?

2. **WHICH ONE DOESN'T BELONG?** Which radical expression does *not* belong with the other three? Explain your reasoning.

$$\sqrt[3]{\frac{4}{5}} \qquad 2\sqrt{x} \qquad \sqrt[4]{11} \qquad 3\sqrt[5]{9x}$$

Monitoring Progress and Modeling with Mathematics

In Exercises 3–12, use the properties of rational exponents to simplify the expression. (*See Example 1.*)

3. $(9^2)^{1/3}$

4. $(12^2)^{1/4}$

5. $\dfrac{6}{6^{1/4}}$

6. $\dfrac{7}{7^{1/3}}$

7. $\left(\dfrac{8^4}{10^4}\right)^{-1/4}$

8. $\left(\dfrac{9^3}{6^3}\right)^{-1/3}$

9. $(3^{-2/3} \cdot 3^{1/3})^{-1}$

10. $(5^{1/2} \cdot 5^{-3/2})^{-1/4}$

11. $\dfrac{2^{2/3} \cdot 16^{2/3}}{4^{2/3}}$

12. $\dfrac{49^{3/8} \cdot 49^{7/8}}{7^{5/4}}$

In Exercises 13–20, use the properties of radicals to simplify the expression. (*See Example 2.*)

13. $\sqrt{2} \cdot \sqrt{72}$

14. $\sqrt[3]{16} \cdot \sqrt[3]{32}$

15. $\sqrt[4]{6} \cdot \sqrt[4]{8}$

16. $\sqrt[4]{8} \cdot \sqrt[4]{8}$

17. $\dfrac{\sqrt[5]{486}}{\sqrt[5]{2}}$

18. $\dfrac{\sqrt{2}}{\sqrt{32}}$

19. $\dfrac{\sqrt[3]{6} \cdot \sqrt[3]{72}}{\sqrt[3]{2}}$

20. $\dfrac{\sqrt[3]{3} \cdot \sqrt[3]{18}}{\sqrt[6]{2} \cdot \sqrt[6]{2}}$

In Exercises 21–28, write the expression in simplest form. (*See Example 3.*)

21. $\sqrt[4]{567}$

22. $\sqrt[5]{288}$

23. $\dfrac{\sqrt[3]{5}}{\sqrt[3]{4}}$

24. $\dfrac{\sqrt[4]{4}}{\sqrt[4]{27}}$

25. $\sqrt{\dfrac{3}{8}}$

26. $\sqrt[3]{\dfrac{7}{4}}$

27. $\sqrt[3]{\dfrac{64}{49}}$

28. $\sqrt[4]{\dfrac{1296}{25}}$

In Exercises 29–36, write the expression in simplest form. (*See Example 4.*)

29. $\dfrac{1}{1 + \sqrt{3}}$

30. $\dfrac{1}{2 + \sqrt{5}}$

31. $\dfrac{5}{3 - \sqrt{2}}$

32. $\dfrac{11}{9 - \sqrt{6}}$

33. $\dfrac{9}{\sqrt{3} + \sqrt{7}}$

34. $\dfrac{2}{\sqrt{8} + \sqrt{7}}$

35. $\dfrac{\sqrt{6}}{\sqrt{3} - \sqrt{5}}$

36. $\dfrac{\sqrt{7}}{\sqrt{10} - \sqrt{2}}$

In Exercises 37–46, simplify the expression. (*See Example 5.*)

37. $9\sqrt[3]{11} + 3\sqrt[3]{11}$

38. $8\sqrt[6]{5} - 12\sqrt[6]{5}$

39. $3(11^{1/4}) + 9(11^{1/4})$

40. $13(8^{3/4}) - 4(8^{3/4})$

41. $5\sqrt{12} - 19\sqrt{3}$

42. $27\sqrt{6} + 7\sqrt{150}$

43. $\sqrt[5]{224} + 3\sqrt[5]{7}$

44. $7\sqrt[3]{2} - \sqrt[3]{128}$

45. $5(24^{1/3}) - 4(3^{1/3})$

46. $5^{1/4} + 6(405^{1/4})$

47. **ERROR ANALYSIS** Describe and correct the error in simplifying the expression.

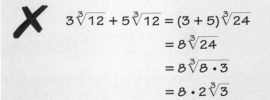

$$3\sqrt[3]{12} + 5\sqrt[3]{12} = (3 + 5)\sqrt[3]{24}$$
$$= 8\sqrt[3]{24}$$
$$= 8\sqrt[3]{8 \cdot 3}$$
$$= 8 \cdot 2\sqrt[3]{3}$$
$$= 16\sqrt[3]{3}$$

48. MULTIPLE REPRESENTATIONS Which radical expressions are like radicals?

Ⓐ $(5^{2/9})^{3/2}$

Ⓑ $\dfrac{5^3}{\left(\sqrt[3]{5}\right)^8}$

Ⓒ $\sqrt[3]{625}$

Ⓓ $\sqrt[3]{5145} - \sqrt[3]{875}$

Ⓔ $\sqrt[3]{5} + 3\sqrt[3]{5}$

Ⓕ $7\sqrt[4]{80} - 2\sqrt[4]{405}$

In Exercises 49–54, simplify the expression. (*See Example 6.*)

49. $\sqrt[4]{81y^8}$

50. $\sqrt[3]{64r^3t^6}$

51. $\sqrt[5]{\dfrac{m^{10}}{n^5}}$

52. $\sqrt[4]{\dfrac{k^{16}}{16z^4}}$

53. $\sqrt[6]{\dfrac{g^6h}{h^7}}$

54. $\sqrt[8]{\dfrac{n^{18}p^7}{n^2p^{-1}}}$

55. ERROR ANALYSIS Describe and correct the error in simplifying the expression.

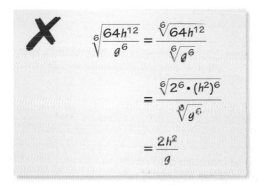

$$\sqrt[6]{\dfrac{64h^{12}}{g^6}} = \dfrac{\sqrt[6]{64h^{12}}}{\sqrt[6]{g^6}}$$

$$= \dfrac{\sqrt[6]{2^6 \cdot (h^2)^6}}{\sqrt[6]{g^6}}$$

$$= \dfrac{2h^2}{g}$$

56. OPEN-ENDED Write two variable expressions involving radicals, one that needs absolute value in simplifying and one that does not need absolute value. Justify your answers.

In Exercises 57–64, write the expression in simplest form. Assume all variables are positive. (*See Example 7.*)

57. $\sqrt{81a^7b^{12}c^9}$

58. $\sqrt[3]{125r^4s^9t^7}$

59. $\sqrt[5]{\dfrac{160m^6}{n^7}}$

60. $\sqrt[4]{\dfrac{405x^3y^3}{5x^{-1}y}}$

61. $\dfrac{\sqrt[3]{w} \cdot \sqrt{w^5}}{\sqrt{25w^{16}}}$

62. $\dfrac{\sqrt[4]{v^6}}{\sqrt[7]{v^5}}$

63. $\dfrac{18w^{1/3}v^{5/4}}{27w^{4/3}v^{1/2}}$

64. $\dfrac{7x^{-3/4}y^{5/2}z^{-2/3}}{56x^{-1/2}y^{1/4}}$

In Exercises 65–70, perform the indicated operation. Assume all variables are positive. (*See Example 8.*)

65. $12\sqrt[3]{y} + 9\sqrt[3]{y}$

66. $11\sqrt{2z} - 5\sqrt{2z}$

67. $3x^{7/2} - 5x^{7/2}$

68. $7\sqrt[3]{m^7} + 3m^{7/3}$

69. $\sqrt[4]{16w^{10}} + 2w\sqrt[4]{w^6}$

70. $(p^{1/2} \cdot p^{1/4}) - \sqrt[4]{16p^3}$

MATHEMATICAL CONNECTIONS In Exercises 71 and 72, find simplified expressions for the perimeter and area of the given figure.

71.

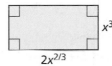

x^3

$2x^{2/3}$

72.

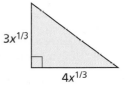

$3x^{1/3}$

$4x^{1/3}$

73. MODELING WITH MATHEMATICS The optimum diameter d (in millimeters) of the pinhole in a pinhole camera can be modeled by $d = 1.9[(5.5 \times 10^{-4})\ell]^{1/2}$, where ℓ is the length (in millimeters) of the camera box. Find the optimum pinhole diameter for a camera box with a length of 10 centimeters.

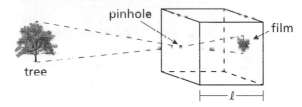

tree

pinhole

film

ℓ

74. MODELING WITH MATHEMATICS The surface area S (in square centimeters) of a mammal can be modeled by $S = km^{2/3}$, where m is the mass (in grams) of the mammal and k is a constant. The table shows the values of k for different mammals.

Mammal	Rabbit	Human	Bat
Value of k	9.75	11.0	57.5

a. Find the surface area of a bat whose mass is 32 grams.

b. Find the surface area of a rabbit whose mass is 3.4 kilograms (3.4×10^3 grams).

c. Which mammal has the greatest mass per square centimeter of surface area, the bat in part (a), the rabbit in part (b), or a human whose mass is 59 kilograms?

75. **MAKING AN ARGUMENT** Your friend claims it is not possible to simplify the expression $7\sqrt{11} - 9\sqrt{44}$ because it does not contain like radicals. Is your friend correct? Explain your reasoning.

76. **PROBLEM SOLVING** The apparent magnitude of a star is a number that indicates how faint the star is in relation to other stars. The expression $\dfrac{2.512^{m_1}}{2.512^{m_2}}$ tells how many times fainter a star with apparent magnitude m_1 is than a star with apparent magnitude m_2.

Star	Apparent magnitude	Constellation
Vega	0.03	Lyra
Altair	0.77	Aquila
Deneb	1.25	Cygnus

a. How many times fainter is Altair than Vega?

b. How many times fainter is Deneb than Altair?

c. How many times fainter is Deneb than Vega?

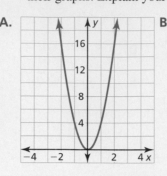

77. **CRITICAL THINKING** Find a radical expression for the perimeter of the triangle inscribed in the square shown. Simplify the expression.

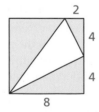

78. **HOW DO YOU SEE IT?** Without finding points, match the functions $f(x) = \sqrt{64x^2}$ and $g(x) = \sqrt[3]{64x^6}$ with their graphs. Explain your reasoning.

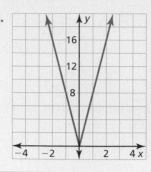

A.

B.

79. **REWRITING A FORMULA** You have filled two round balloons with water. One balloon contains twice as much water as the other balloon.

a. Solve the formula for the volume of a sphere, $V = \frac{4}{3}\pi r^3$, for r.

b. Substitute the expression for r from part (a) into the formula for the surface area of a sphere, $S = 4\pi r^2$. Simplify to show that $S = (4\pi)^{1/3}(3V)^{2/3}$.

c. Compare the surface areas of the two water balloons using the formula in part (b).

80. **THOUGHT PROVOKING** Determine whether the expressions $(x^2)^{1/6}$ and $(x^{1/6})^2$ are equivalent for all values of x.

81. **DRAWING CONCLUSIONS** Substitute different combinations of odd and even positive integers for m and n in the expression $\sqrt[n]{x^m}$. When you cannot assume x is positive, explain when absolute value is needed in simplifying the expression.

82. **REWRITING A FORMULA** Rewrite the formula in Exercise 74 so that one side is $\dfrac{m}{S}$. Use this formula to justify your answer in part (c).

Maintaining Mathematical Proficiency
Reviewing what you learned in previous grades and lessons

Graph the function. Label the vertex, axis of symmetry, and *x*-intercepts. *(Section 2.6)*

83. $g(x) = 6(x - 4)^2$

84. $h(x) = 2x(x - 3)$

85. $f(x) = x^2 + 2x + 5$

Write a rule for *g*. Describe the graph of *g* as a transformation of the graph of *f*. *(Section 3.7)*

86. $f(x) = x^4 - 3x^2 - 2x,\ g(x) = -f(x)$

87. $f(x) = x^3 - x,\ g(x) = f(x) - 3$

88. $f(x) = x^3 - 4,\ g(x) = f(x - 2)$

89. $f(x) = x^4 + 2x^3 - 4x^2,\ g(x) = f(2x)$

Essential Question How can you identify the domain and range of a radical function?

Identifying Graphs of Radical Functions

Work with a partner. Match each function with its graph. Explain your reasoning. Then identify the domain and range of each function.

a. $f(x) = \sqrt{x}$ **b.** $f(x) = \sqrt[3]{x}$ **c.** $f(x) = \sqrt[4]{x}$ **d.** $f(x) = \sqrt[5]{x}$

A.
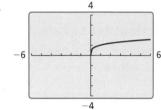

B.
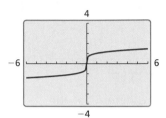

C.
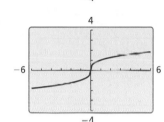

D.
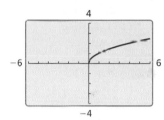

Identifying Graphs of Transformations

Work with a partner. Match each transformation of $f(x) = \sqrt{x}$ with its graph. Explain your reasoning. Then identify the domain and range of each function.

a. $g(x) = \sqrt{x + 2}$ **b.** $g(x) = \sqrt{x - 2}$ **c.** $g(x) = \sqrt{x + 2} - 2$ **d.** $g(x) = -\sqrt{x + 2}$

A.
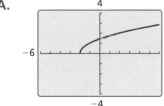

B.
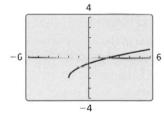

C.
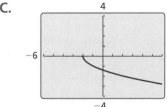

D.
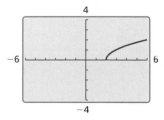

LOOKING FOR STRUCTURE

To be proficient in math, you need to look closely to discern a pattern or structure.

Communicate Your Answer

3. How can you identify the domain and range of a radical function?

4. Use the results of Exploration 1 to describe how the domain and range of a radical function are related to the index of the radical.

Core Vocabulary

radical function, *p. 208*

Previous
transformations
parabola
circle

What You Will Learn

▶ Graph radical functions.

▶ Write transformations of radical functions.

▶ Graph parabolas and circles.

Graphing Radical Functions

A **radical function** contains a radical expression with the independent variable in the radicand. When the radical is a square root, the function is called a *square root function*. When the radical is a cube root, the function is called a *cube root function*.

⑤ Core Concept

Parent Functions for Square Root and Cube Root Functions

The parent function for the family of square root functions is $f(x) = \sqrt{x}$.

The parent function for the family of cube root functions is $f(x) = \sqrt[3]{x}$.

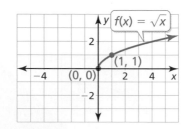

Domain: $x \geq 0$, Range: $y \geq 0$ Domain and range: All real numbers

STUDY TIP

A *power function* has the form $y = ax^b$, where a is a real number and b is a rational number. Notice that the parent square root function is a power function, where $a = 1$ and $b = \frac{1}{2}$.

EXAMPLE 1 **Graphing Radical Functions**

Graph each function. Identify the domain and range of each function.

a. $f(x) = \sqrt{\frac{1}{4}x}$

b. $g(x) = -3\sqrt[3]{x}$

LOOKING FOR STRUCTURE

Example 1(a) uses *x*-values that are multiples of 4 so that the radicand is an integer.

SOLUTION

a. Make a table of values and sketch the graph.

x	0	4	8	12	16
y	0	1	1.41	1.73	2

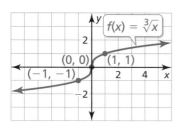

▶ The radicand of a square root must be nonnegative. So, the domain is $x \geq 0$. The range is $y \geq 0$.

b. Make a table of values and sketch the graph.

x	−2	−1	0	1	2
y	3.78	3	0	−3	−3.78

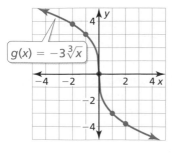

▶ The radicand of a cube root can be any real number. So, the domain and range are all real numbers.

In Example 1, notice that the graph of f is a horizontal stretch of the graph of the parent square root function. The graph of g is a vertical stretch and a reflection in the x-axis of the graph of the parent cube root function. You can transform graphs of radical functions in the same way you transformed graphs of functions previously.

Core Concept

Transformation	$f(x)$ Notation	Examples	
Horizontal Translation Graph shifts left or right.	$f(x - h)$	$g(x) = \sqrt{x - 2}$ $g(x) = \sqrt{x + 3}$	2 units right 3 units left
Vertical Translation Graph shifts up or down.	$f(x) + k$	$g(x) = \sqrt{x} + 7$ $g(x) = \sqrt{x} - 1$	7 units up 1 unit down
Reflection Graph flips over x- or y-axis.	$f(-x)$ $-f(x)$	$g(x) = \sqrt{-x}$ $g(x) = -\sqrt{x}$	in the y-axis in the x-axis
Horizontal Stretch or Shrink Graph stretches away from or shrinks toward y-axis.	$f(ax)$	$g(x) = \sqrt{3x}$ $g(x) = \sqrt{\frac{1}{2}x}$	shrink by a factor of $\frac{1}{3}$ stretch by a factor of 2
Vertical Stretch or Shrink Graph stretches away from or shrinks toward x-axis.	$a \cdot f(x)$	$g(x) = 4\sqrt{x}$ $g(x) = \frac{1}{5}\sqrt{x}$	stretch by a factor of 4 shrink by a factor of $\frac{1}{5}$

EXAMPLE 2   **Transforming Radical Functions**

Describe the transformation of f represented by g. Then graph each function.

a. $f(x) = \sqrt{x}, \; g(x) = \sqrt{x - 3} + 4$ **b.** $f(x) = \sqrt[3]{x}, \; g(x) = \sqrt[3]{-8x}$

LOOKING FOR STRUCTURE

In Example 2(b), you can use the Product Property of Radicals to write $g(x) = -2\sqrt[3]{x}$. So, you can also describe the graph of g as a vertical stretch by a factor of 2 and a reflection in the x-axis of the graph of f.

SOLUTION

a. Notice that the function is of the form $g(x) = \sqrt{x - h} + k$, where $h = 3$ and $k = 4$.

▶ So, the graph of g is a translation 3 units right and 4 units up of the graph of f.

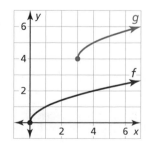

b. Notice that the function is of the form $g(x) = \sqrt[3]{ax}$, where $a = -8$.

▶ So, the graph of g is a horizontal shrink by a factor of $\frac{1}{8}$ and a reflection in the y-axis of the graph of f.

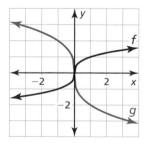

Monitoring Progress Help in English and Spanish at *BigIdeasMath.com*

1. Graph $g(x) = \sqrt{x + 1}$. Identify the domain and range of the function.

2. Describe the transformation of $f(x) = \sqrt[3]{x}$ represented by $g(x) = -\sqrt[3]{x} - 2$. Then graph each function.

Writing Transformations of Radical Functions

Modeling with Mathematics

The function $E(d) = 0.25\sqrt{d}$ approximates the number of seconds it takes a dropped object to fall d feet on Earth. The function $M(d) = 1.6 \cdot E(d)$ approximates the number of seconds it takes a dropped object to fall d feet on Mars. Write a rule for M. How long does it take a dropped object to fall 64 feet on Mars?

SOLUTION

1. **Understand the Problem** You are given a function that represents the number of seconds it takes a dropped object to fall d feet on Earth. You are asked to write a similar function for Mars and then evaluate the function for a given input.

2. **Make a Plan** Multiply $E(d)$ by 1.6 to write a rule for M. Then find $M(64)$.

3. **Solve the Problem**

$$M(d) = 1.6 \cdot E(d)$$
$$= 1.6 \cdot 0.25\sqrt{d} \qquad \text{Substitute } 0.25\sqrt{d} \text{ for } E(d).$$
$$= 0.4\sqrt{d} \qquad \text{Simplify.}$$

Self-Portrait of
NASA's Mars Rover Curiosity

Next, find $M(64)$.

$$M(64) = 0.4\sqrt{64} = 0.4(8) = 3.2$$

▶ It takes a dropped object about 3.2 seconds to fall 64 feet on Mars.

4. **Look Back** Use the original functions to check your solution.

$$E(64) = 0.25\sqrt{64} = 2 \qquad M(64) = 1.6 \cdot E(64) = 1.6 \cdot 2 = 3.2 \checkmark$$

Writing a Transformed Radical Function

Let the graph of g be a horizontal shrink by a factor of $\frac{1}{6}$ followed by a translation 3 units to the left of the graph of $f(x) = \sqrt[3]{x}$. Write a rule for g.

SOLUTION

Step 1 First write a function h that represents the horizontal shrink of f.

$$h(x) = f(6x) \qquad \text{Multiply the input by } 1 \div \frac{1}{6} = 6.$$
$$= \sqrt[3]{6x} \qquad \text{Replace } x \text{ with } 6x \text{ in } f(x).$$

Step 2 Then write a function g that represents the translation of h.

$$g(x) = h(x + 3) \qquad \text{Subtract } -3, \text{ or add 3, to the input.}$$
$$= \sqrt[3]{6(x + 3)} \qquad \text{Replace } x \text{ with } x + 3 \text{ in } h(x).$$
$$= \sqrt[3]{6x + 18} \qquad \text{Distributive Property}$$

Check

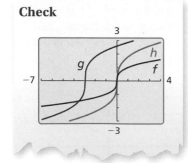

▶ The transformed function is $g(x) = \sqrt[3]{6x + 18}$.

Monitoring Progress Help in English and Spanish at *BigIdeasMath.com*

3. **WHAT IF?** In Example 3, the function $N(d) = 2.4 \cdot E(d)$ approximates the number of seconds it takes a dropped object to fall d feet on the Moon. Write a rule for N. How long does it take a dropped object to fall 25 feet on the Moon?

4. In Example 4, is the transformed function the same when you perform the translation followed by the horizontal shrink? Explain your reasoning.

Graphing Parabolas and Circles

To graph parabolas and circles using a graphing calculator, first solve their equations for y to obtain radical functions. Then graph the functions.

EXAMPLE 5 Graphing a Parabola (Horizontal Axis of Symmetry)

Use a graphing calculator to graph $\frac{1}{2}y^2 = x$. Identify the vertex and the direction that the parabola opens.

SOLUTION

Step 1 Solve for y.

$$\frac{1}{2}y^2 = x \qquad \text{Write the original equation.}$$

$$y^2 = 2x \qquad \text{Multiply each side by 2.}$$

$$y = \pm\sqrt{2x} \qquad \text{Take square root of each side.}$$

Step 2 Graph both radical functions.

$$y_1 = \sqrt{2x}$$

$$y_2 = -\sqrt{2x}$$

▶ The vertex is $(0, 0)$ and the parabola opens right.

EXAMPLE 6 Graphing a Circle

Use a graphing calculator to graph $x^2 + y^2 = 16$. Identify the center, radius, and intercepts.

SOLUTION

Step 1 Solve for y.

$$x^2 + y^2 = 16 \qquad \text{Write the original equation.}$$

$$y^2 = 16 - x^2 \qquad \text{Subtract } x^2 \text{ from each side.}$$

$$y = \pm\sqrt{16 - x^2} \qquad \text{Take square root of each side.}$$

Step 2 Graph both radical functions using a square viewing window.

$$y_1 = \sqrt{16 - x^2}$$

$$y_2 = -\sqrt{16 - x^2}$$

▶ The center is $(0, 0)$ and the radius is 4 units. The x-intercepts are ±4. The y-intercepts are also ±4.

Monitoring Progress   Help in English and Spanish at *BigIdeasMath.com*

5. Use a graphing calculator to graph $-4y^2 = x + 1$. Identify the vertex and the direction that the parabola opens.

6. Use a graphing calculator to graph $(x + 2)^2 + y^2 = 25$. Identify the center, radius, and intercepts.

Vocabulary and Core Concept Check

1. **COMPLETE THE SENTENCE** Square root functions and cube root functions are examples of _____ functions.

2. **COMPLETE THE SENTENCE** When graphing $y = a\sqrt[3]{x - h} + k$, translate the graph of $y = a\sqrt[3]{x}$ h units _____ and k units _____.

Monitoring Progress and Modeling with Mathematics

In Exercises 3–8, match the function with its graph.

3. $f(x) = \sqrt{x} + 3$

4. $h(x) = \sqrt{x} + 3$

5. $f(x) = \sqrt{x} - 3$

6. $g(x) = \sqrt{x} - 3$

7. $h(x) = \sqrt{x + 3} - 3$

8. $f(x) = \sqrt{x - 3} + 3$

A.
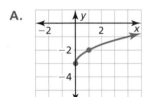

B.
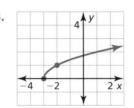

C.
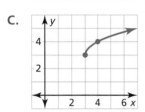

D.
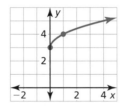

E.
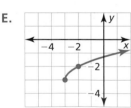

F.
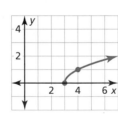

In Exercises 9–18, graph the function. Identify the domain and range of the function. *(See Example 1.)*

9. $h(x) = \sqrt{x} + 4$

10. $g(x) = \sqrt{x} - 5$

11. $g(x) = -\sqrt[3]{2x}$

12. $f(x) = \sqrt[3]{-5x}$

13. $g(x) = \frac{1}{5}\sqrt{x - 3}$

14. $f(x) = \frac{1}{2}\sqrt[3]{x + 6}$

15. $f(x) = (6x)^{1/2} + 3$

16. $g(x) = -3(x + 1)^{1/3}$

17. $h(x) = -\sqrt[4]{x}$

18. $h(x) = \sqrt[5]{2x}$

In Exercises 19–26, describe the transformation of f represented by g. Then graph each function. *(See Example 2.)*

19. $f(x) = \sqrt{x}, g(x) = \sqrt{x + 1} + 8$

20. $f(x) = \sqrt{x}, g(x) = 2\sqrt{x - 1}$

21. $f(x) = \sqrt[3]{x}, g(x) = -\sqrt[3]{x} - 1$

22. $f(x) = \sqrt[3]{x}, g(x) = \sqrt[3]{x + 4} - 5$

23. $f(x) = x^{1/2}, g(x) = \frac{1}{4}(-x)^{1/2}$

24. $f(x) = x^{1/3}, g(x) = \frac{1}{3}x^{1/3} + 6$

25. $f(x) = \sqrt[4]{x}, g(x) = 2\sqrt[4]{x + 5} - 4$

26. $f(x) = \sqrt[5]{x}, g(x) = \sqrt[5]{-32x} + 3$

27. **ERROR ANALYSIS** Describe and correct the error in graphing $f(x) = \sqrt{x - 2} - 2$.

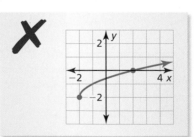

28. **ERROR ANALYSIS** Describe and correct the error in describing the transformation of the parent square root function represented by $g(x) = \sqrt{\frac{1}{2}x} + 3$.

> ✗ The graph of g is a horizontal shrink by a factor of $\frac{1}{2}$ and a translation 3 units up of the parent square root function.

USING TOOLS In Exercises 29–34, use a graphing calculator to graph the function. Then identify the domain and range of the function.

29. $g(x) = \sqrt{x^2 + x}$

30. $h(x) = \sqrt{x^2 - 2x}$

31. $f(x) = \sqrt[3]{x^2 + x}$

32. $f(x) = \sqrt[3]{3x^2 - x}$

33. $f(x) = \sqrt{2x^2 + x + 1}$

34. $h(x) = \sqrt[3]{\frac{1}{2}x^2 - 3x + 4}$

ABSTRACT REASONING In Exercises 35–38, complete the statement with *sometimes*, *always*, or *never*.

35. The domain of the function $y = a\sqrt{x}$ is _____ $x \geq 0$.

36. The range of the function $y = a\sqrt{x}$ is _____ $y \geq 0$.

37. The domain and range of the function $y = \sqrt[3]{x - h} + k$ are _____ all real numbers.

38. The domain of the function $y = a\sqrt{-x} + k$ is _____ $x \geq 0$.

39. **PROBLEM SOLVING** The distance (in miles) a pilot can see to the horizon can be approximated by $E(n) = 1.22\sqrt{n}$, where n is the plane's altitude (in feet above sea level) on Earth. The function $M(n) = 0.75E(n)$ approximates the distance a pilot can see to the horizon n feet above the surface of Mars. Write a rule for M. What is the distance a pilot can see to the horizon from an altitude of 10,000 feet above Mars? *(See Example 3.)*

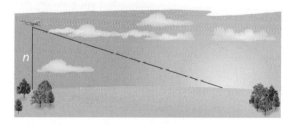

40. **MODELING WITH MATHEMATICS** The speed (in knots) of sound waves in air can be modeled by

$$v(K) = 643.855\sqrt{\frac{K}{273.15}}$$

where K is the air temperature (in kelvin). The speed (in meters per second) of sound waves in air can be modeled by

$$s(K) = \frac{v(K)}{1.944}.$$

Write a rule for s. What is the speed (in meters per second) of sound waves when the air temperature is 305 kelvin?

In Exercises 41–44, write a rule for g described by the transformations of the graph of f. *(See Example 4.)*

41. Let g be a vertical stretch by a factor of 2, followed by a translation 2 units up of the graph of $f(x) = \sqrt{x} + 3$.

42. Let g be a reflection in the y-axis, followed by a translation 1 unit right of the graph of $f(x) = 2\sqrt[3]{x} - 1$.

43. Let g be a horizontal shrink by a factor of $\frac{2}{3}$, followed by a translation 4 units left of the graph of $f(x) = \sqrt{6x}$.

44. Let g be a translation 1 unit down and 5 units right, followed by a reflection in the x-axis of the graph of $f(x) = -\frac{1}{2}\sqrt[4]{x} + \frac{3}{2}$.

In Exercises 45 and 46, write a rule for g.

45.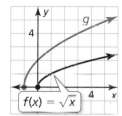

46.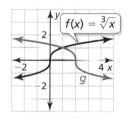

In Exercises 47–50, write a rule for g that represents the indicated transformation of the graph of f.

47. $f(x) = 2\sqrt{x}$, $g(x) = f(x + 3)$

48. $f(x) = \frac{1}{3}\sqrt{x} - 1$, $g(x) = -f(x) + 9$

49. $f(x) = -\sqrt{x^2 - 2}$, $g(x) = -2f(x + 5)$

50. $f(x) = \sqrt[3]{x^2 + 10x}$, $g(x) = \frac{1}{4}f(-x) + 6$

In Exercises 51–56, use a graphing calculator to graph the equation of the parabola. Identify the vertex and the direction that the parabola opens. *(See Example 5.)*

51. $\frac{1}{4}y^2 = x$

52. $3y^2 = x$

53. $-8y^2 + 2 = x$

54. $2y^2 = x - 4$

55. $x + 8 = \frac{1}{5}y^2$

56. $\frac{1}{2}x = y^2 - 4$

In Exercises 57–62, use a graphing calculator to graph the equation of the circle. Identify the center, radius, and intercepts. *(See Example 6.)*

57. $x^2 + y^2 = 9$

58. $x^2 + y^2 = 4$

59. $64 - (x - 1)^2 = y^2$

60. $1 - (y + 3)^2 = x^2$

61. $x^2 + y^2 + 12x - 13 = 0$

62. $x^2 + y^2 - 4x + 6y = -9$

63. MODELING WITH MATHEMATICS The *period* of a pendulum is the time the pendulum takes to complete one back-and-forth swing. The period T (in seconds) can be modeled by the function $T = 1.11\sqrt{\ell}$, where ℓ is the length (in feet) of the pendulum. Graph the function. Estimate the length of a pendulum with a period of 2 seconds. Explain your reasoning.

64. HOW DO YOU SEE IT? Does the graph represent a square root function or a cube root function? Explain. What are the domain and range of the function?

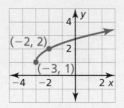

65. PROBLEM SOLVING For a drag race car with a total weight of 3500 pounds, the speed s (in miles per hour) at the end of a race can be modeled by $s = 14.8\sqrt[3]{p}$, where p is the power (in horsepower). Graph the function.

a. Determine the power of a 3500-pound car that reaches a speed of 200 miles per hour.

b. What is the average rate of change in speed as the power changes from 1000 horsepower to 1500 horsepower?

66. THOUGHT PROVOKING The graph of a radical function f passes through the points $(3, 1)$ and $(4, 0)$. Write two different functions that could represent $f(x + 2) + 1$. Explain.

67. MULTIPLE REPRESENTATIONS The terminal velocity v_t (in feet per second) of a skydiver who weighs 140 pounds is given by

$$v_t = 33.7\sqrt{\frac{140}{A}}$$

where A is the cross-sectional surface area (in square feet) of the skydiver. The table shows the terminal velocities (in feet per second) for various surface areas (in square feet) of a skydiver who weighs 165 pounds.

Cross-sectional surface area, A	Terminal velocity, v_t
1	432.9
3	249.9
5	193.6
7	163.6

a. Which skydiver has a greater terminal velocity for each value of A given in the table?

b. Describe how the different values of A given in the table relate to the possible positions of the falling skydiver.

68. MATHEMATICAL CONNECTIONS The surface area S of a right circular cone with a slant height of 1 unit is given by $S = \pi r + \pi r^2$, where r is the radius of the cone.

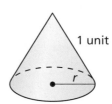

a. Use completing the square to show that

$$r = \frac{1}{\sqrt{\pi}}\sqrt{S + \frac{\pi}{4}} - \frac{1}{2}.$$

b. Graph the equation in part (a) using a graphing calculator. Then find the radius of a right circular cone with a slant height of 1 unit and a surface area of $\frac{3\pi}{4}$ square units.

Maintaining Mathematical Proficiency

Reviewing what you learned in previous grades and lessons

Solve the equation. Check your solutions. *(Skills Review Handbook)*

69. $|3x + 2| = 5$ **70.** $|4x + 9| = -7$ **71.** $|2x - 6| = |x|$ **72.** $|x + 8| = |2x + 2|$

Solve the inequality. Graph the solution on a number line. *(Skills Review Handbook)*

73. $4x - 4 > 8$ **74.** $-x + 7 \leq 4 - 2x$ **75.** $-3(x - 4) \geq 24$

4.1–4.3 What Did You Learn?

Core Vocabulary

*n*th root of *a*, *p. 194*
index of a radical, *p. 194*
simplest form of a radical, *p. 201*

conjugate, *p. 202*
like radicals, *p. 202*
radical function, *p. 208*

Core Concepts

Section 4.1

Real *n*th Roots of *a*, *p. 194*
Rational Exponents, *p. 195*

Section 4.2

Properties of Rational Exponents, *p. 200*
Properties of Radicals, *p. 201*

Section 4.3

Parent Functions for Square Root and Cube Root Functions, *p. 208*
Transformations of Radical Functions, *p. 209*

Mathematical Practices

1. How can you use definitions to explain your reasoning in Exercises 21–24 on page 197?

2. How did you use structure to solve Exercise 76 on page 206?

3. How can you check that your answer is reasonable in Exercise 39 on page 213?

4. How can you make sense of the terms of the surface area formula given in Exercise 68 on page 214?

Analyzing Your Errors

Application Errors

What Happens: You can do numerical problems, but you struggle with problems that have context.

How to Avoid This Error: Do not just mimic the steps of solving an application problem. Explain out loud what the question is asking and why you are doing each step. After solving the problem, ask yourself, "Does my solution make sense?"

STUDY SKILLS

Find the indicated real nth root(s) of a. *(Section 4.1)*

1. $n = 4, a = 81$

2. $n = 5, a = -1024$

3. Evaluate (a) $16^{3/4}$ and (b) $125^{2/3}$ without using a calculator. Explain your reasoning. *(Section 4.1)*

Find the real solution(s) of the equation. Round your answer to two decimal places when appropriate. *(Section 4.1)*

4. $2x^6 = 1458$

5. $(x + 6)^3 = 28$

Simplify the expression. *(Section 4.2)*

6. $\left(\dfrac{48^{1/4}}{6^{1/4}}\right)^6$

7. $\sqrt[4]{3} \cdot \sqrt[4]{432}$

8. $\dfrac{1}{3 + \sqrt{2}}$

9. $\sqrt[3]{16} - 5\sqrt[3]{2}$

10. Simplify $\sqrt[8]{x^9 y^8 z^{16}}$. *(Section 4.2)*

Write the expression in simplest form. Assume all variables are positive. *(Section 4.2)*

11. $\sqrt[3]{216p^9}$

12. $\dfrac{\sqrt[5]{32}}{\sqrt[5]{m^3}}$

13. $\sqrt[4]{n^4 q} + 7n\sqrt[4]{q}$

14. Graph $f(x) = 2\sqrt[3]{x} + 1$. Identify the domain and range of the function. *(Section 4.3)*

Describe the transformation of the graph of f represented by the graph of g. Then write a rule for g. *(Section 4.3)*

15. $f(x) = \sqrt{x}$

16. $f(x) = \sqrt[3]{x}$

17. $f(x) = \sqrt{x}$

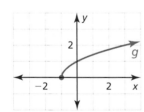

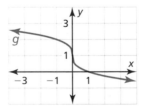

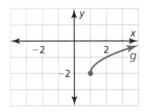

18. Use a graphing calculator to graph $x = 3y^2 - 6$. Identify the vertex and direction the parabola opens. *(Section 4.3)*

19. A jeweler is setting a stone cut in the shape of a regular octahedron. A regular octahedron is a solid with eight equilateral triangles as faces, as shown. The formula for the volume of the stone is $V = 0.47s^3$, where s is the side length (in millimeters) of an edge of the stone. The volume of the stone is 161 cubic millimeters. Find the length of an edge of the stone. *(Section 4.1)*

20. An investigator can determine how fast a car was traveling just prior to an accident using the model $s = 4\sqrt{d}$, where s is the speed (in miles per hour) of the car and d is the length (in feet) of the skid marks. Graph the model. The length of the skid marks of a car is 90 feet. Was the car traveling at the posted speed limit prior to the accident? Explain your reasoning. *(Section 4.3)*

4.4 Solving Radical Equations and Inequalities

Essential Question How can you solve a radical equation?

EXPLORATION 1 Solving Radical Equations

Work with a partner. Match each radical equation with the graph of its related radical function. Explain your reasoning. Then use the graph to solve the equation, if possible. Check your solutions.

a. $\sqrt{x-1} - 1 = 0$ **b.** $\sqrt{2x+2} - \sqrt{x+4} = 0$ **c.** $\sqrt{9-x^2} = 0$

d. $\sqrt{x+2} - x = 0$ **e.** $\sqrt{-x+2} - x = 0$ **f.** $\sqrt{3x^2+1} = 0$

A.
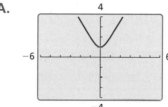

B.
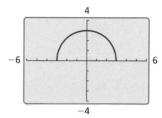

C.
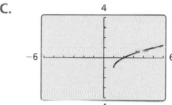

D.
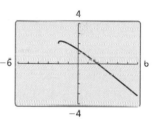

E.
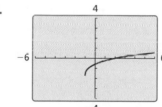

F.
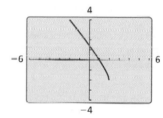

LOOKING FOR STRUCTURE

To be proficient in math, you need to look closely to discern a pattern or structure.

EXPLORATION 2 Solving Radical Equations

Work with a partner. Look back at the radical equations in Exploration 1. Suppose that you did not know how to solve the equations using a graphical approach.

a. Show how you could use a *numerical approach* to solve one of the equations. For instance, you might use a spreadsheet to create a table of values.

b. Show how you could use an *analytical approach* to solve one of the equations. For instance, look at the similarities between the equations in Exploration 1. What first step may be necessary so you could square each side to eliminate the radical(s)? How would you proceed to find the solution?

Communicate Your Answer

3. How can you solve a radical equation?

4. Would you prefer to use a graphical, numerical, or analytical approach to solve the given equation? Explain your reasoning. Then solve the equation.

$$\sqrt{x+3} - \sqrt{x-2} = 1$$

What You Will Learn

▶ Solve equations containing radicals and rational exponents.
▶ Solve radical inequalities.

Solving Equations

Equations with radicals that have variables in their radicands are called **radical equations**. An example of a radical equation is $2\sqrt{x+1} = 4$.

Core Concept

Solving Radical Equations

To solve a radical equation, follow these steps:

Step 1 Isolate the radical on one side of the equation, if necessary.

Step 2 Raise each side of the equation to the same exponent to eliminate the radical and obtain a linear, quadratic, or other polynomial equation.

Step 3 Solve the resulting equation using techniques you learned previously. Check your solution.

EXAMPLE 1 **Solving Radical Equations**

Solve (a) $2\sqrt{x+1} = 4$ and (b) $\sqrt[3]{2x-9} - 1 = 2$.

SOLUTION

a.

$2\sqrt{x+1} = 4$	Write the original equation.
$\sqrt{x+1} = 2$	Divide each side by 2.
$\left(\sqrt{x+1}\right)^2 = 2^2$	Square each side to eliminate the radical.
$x + 1 = 4$	Simplify.
$x = 3$	Subtract 1 from each side.

Check

$2\sqrt{3+1} \overset{?}{=} 4$
$2\sqrt{4} \overset{?}{=} 4$
$4 = 4$ ✓

▶ The solution is $x = 3$.

b.

$\sqrt[3]{2x-9} - 1 = 2$	Write the original equation.
$\sqrt[3]{2x-9} = 3$	Add 1 to each side.
$\left(\sqrt[3]{2x-9}\right)^3 = 3^3$	Cube each side to eliminate the radical.
$2x - 9 = 27$	Simplify.
$2x = 36$	Add 9 to each side.
$x = 18$	Divide each side by 2.

Check

$\sqrt[3]{2(18)-9} - 1 \overset{?}{=} 2$
$\sqrt[3]{27} - 1 \overset{?}{=} 2$
$2 = 2$ ✓

▶ The solution is $x = 18$.

Monitoring Progress Help in English and Spanish at *BigIdeasMath.com*

Solve the equation. Check your solution.

1. $\sqrt[3]{x} - 9 = -6$ **2.** $\sqrt{x+25} = 2$ **3.** $2\sqrt[3]{x-3} = 4$

EXAMPLE 2 Solving a Real-Life Problem

In a hurricane, the mean sustained wind velocity v (in meters per second) can be modeled by $v(p) = 6.3\sqrt{1013 - p}$, where p is the air pressure (in millibars) at the center of the hurricane. Estimate the air pressure at the center of the hurricane when the mean sustained wind velocity is 54.5 meters per second.

SOLUTION

$v(p) = 6.3\sqrt{1013 - p}$	Write the original function.
$54.5 = 6.3\sqrt{1013 - p}$	Substitute 54.5 for $v(p)$.
$8.65 \approx \sqrt{1013 - p}$	Divide each side by 6.3.
$8.65^2 \approx \left(\sqrt{1013 - p}\right)^2$	Square each side.
$74.8 \approx 1013 - p$	Simplify.
$-938.2 \approx -p$	Subtract 1013 from each side.
$938.2 \approx p$	Divide each side by -1.

▶ The air pressure at the center of the hurricane is about 938 millibars.

Monitoring Progress Help in English and Spanish at *BigIdeasMath.com*

4. WHAT IF? Estimate the air pressure at the center of the hurricane when the mean sustained wind velocity is 48.3 meters per second.

Raising each side of an equation to the same exponent may introduce solutions that are *not* solutions of the original equation. These solutions are called **extraneous solutions**. When you use this procedure, you should always check each apparent solution in the *original* equation.

EXAMPLE 3 Solving an Equation with an Extraneous Solution

Solve $x + 1 = \sqrt{7x + 15}$.

SOLUTION

$x + 1 = \sqrt{7x + 15}$	Write the original equation.
$(x + 1)^2 = \left(\sqrt{7x + 15}\right)^2$	Square each side.
$x^2 + 2x + 1 = 7x + 15$	Expand left side and simplify right side.
$x^2 - 5x - 14 = 0$	Write in standard form.
$(x - 7)(x + 2) = 0$	Factor.
$x - 7 = 0 \quad \text{or} \quad x + 2 = 0$	Zero-Product Property
$x = 7 \quad \text{or} \qquad x = -2$	Solve for x.

Check

$7 + 1 \overset{?}{=} \sqrt{7(7) + 15}$ $\qquad$ $-2 + 1 \overset{?}{=} \sqrt{7(-2) + 15}$

$8 \overset{?}{=} \sqrt{64}$ $\qquad\qquad\qquad$ $-1 \overset{?}{=} \sqrt{1}$

$8 = 8 \checkmark$ $\qquad\qquad\qquad\qquad$ $-1 \neq 1 \; ✗$

▶ The apparent solution $x = -2$ is extraneous. So, the only solution is $x = 7$.

ATTEND TO PRECISION

To understand how extraneous solutions can be introduced, consider the equation $\sqrt{x} = -3$. This equation has no real solution; however, you obtain $x = 9$ after squaring each side.

EXAMPLE 4   Solving an Equation with Two Radicals

Solve $\sqrt{x + 2} + 1 = \sqrt{3 - x}$.

SOLUTION

$\sqrt{x + 2} + 1 = \sqrt{3 - x}$	Write the original equation.
$\left(\sqrt{x + 2} + 1\right)^2 = \left(\sqrt{3 - x}\right)^2$	Square each side.
$x + 2 + 2\sqrt{x + 2} + 1 = 3 - x$	Expand left side and simplify right side.
$2\sqrt{x + 2} = -2x$	Isolate radical expression.
$\sqrt{x + 2} = -x$	Divide each side by 2.
$\left(\sqrt{x + 2}\right)^2 = (-x)^2$	Square each side.
$x + 2 = x^2$	Simplify.
$0 = x^2 - x - 2$	Write in standard form.
$0 = (x - 2)(x + 1)$	Factor.
$x - 2 = 0 \quad \text{or} \quad x + 1 = 0$	Zero-Product Property
$x = 2 \quad \text{or} \quad x = -1$	Solve for x.

ANOTHER METHOD

You can also graph each side of the equation and find the x-value where the graphs intersect.

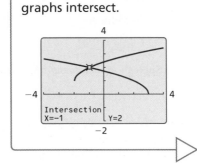

Check

$\sqrt{2 + 2} + 1 \overset{?}{=} \sqrt{3 - 2}$ $\sqrt{-1 + 2} + 1 \overset{?}{=} \sqrt{3 - (-1)}$

$\sqrt{4} + 1 \overset{?}{=} \sqrt{1}$ $\sqrt{1} + 1 \overset{?}{=} \sqrt{4}$

$3 \neq 1$ ✗ $2 = 2$ ✓

▶ The apparent solution $x = 2$ is extraneous. So, the only solution is $x = -1$.

Monitoring Progress   🔊 Help in English and Spanish at *BigIdeasMath.com*

Solve the equation. Check your solution(s).

5. $\sqrt{10x + 9} = x + 3$ **6.** $\sqrt{2x + 5} = \sqrt{x + 7}$ **7.** $\sqrt{x + 6} - 2 = \sqrt{x - 2}$

When an equation contains a power with a rational exponent, you can solve the equation using a procedure similar to the one for solving radical equations. In this case, you first isolate the power and then raise each side of the equation to the reciprocal of the rational exponent.

EXAMPLE 5   Solving an Equation with a Rational Exponent

Solve $(2x)^{3/4} + 2 = 10$.

SOLUTION

$(2x)^{3/4} + 2 = 10$	Write the original equation.
$(2x)^{3/4} = 8$	Subtract 2 from each side.
$\left[(2x)^{3/4}\right]^{4/3} = 8^{4/3}$	Raise each side to the four-thirds.
$2x = 16$	Simplify.
$x = 8$	Divide each side by 2.

Check

$(2 \cdot 8)^{3/4} + 2 \overset{?}{=} 10$

$16^{3/4} + 2 \overset{?}{=} 10$

$10 = 10$ ✓

▶ The solution is $x = 8$.

EXAMPLE 6   Solving an Equation with a Rational Exponent

Solve $(x + 30)^{1/2} = x$.

SOLUTION

Check $(6 + 30)^{1/2} \overset{?}{=} 6$

$36^{1/2} \overset{?}{=} 6$

$6 = 6$ ✓

$(-5 + 30)^{1/2} \overset{?}{=} -5$

$25^{1/2} \overset{?}{=} -5$

$5 \neq -5$ ✗

$(x + 30)^{1/2} = x$	Write the original equation.
$[(x + 30)^{1/2}]^2 = x^2$	Square each side.
$x + 30 = x^2$	Simplify.
$0 = x^2 - x - 30$	Write in standard form.
$0 = (x - 6)(x + 5)$	Factor.
$x - 6 = 0$ or $x + 5 = 0$	Zero-Product Property
$x = 6$ or $x = -5$	Solve for x.

▶ The apparent solution $x = -5$ is extraneous. So, the only solution is $x = 6$.

Monitoring Progress Help in English and Spanish at *BigIdeasMath.com*

Solve the equation. Check your solution(s).

8. $(3x)^{1/3} = -3$ **9.** $(x + 6)^{1/2} = x$ **10.** $(x + 2)^{3/4} = 8$

Solving Radical Inequalities

To solve a simple radical inequality of the form $\sqrt[n]{u} < d$, where u is an algebraic expression and d is a nonnegative number, raise each side to the exponent n. This procedure also works for $>$, $\leq$, and $\geq$. Be sure to consider the possible values of the radicand.

EXAMPLE 7   Solving a Radical Inequality

Solve $3\sqrt{x - 1} \leq 12$.

SOLUTION

Step 1   Solve for x.

$3\sqrt{x - 1} \leq 12$	Write the original inequality.
$\sqrt{x - 1} \leq 4$	Divide each side by 3.
$x - 1 \leq 16$	Square each side.
$x \leq 17$	Add 1 to each side.

Check

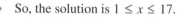

Step 2   Consider the radicand.

$x - 1 \geq 0$	The radicand cannot be negative.
$x \geq 1$	Add 1 to each side.

▶ So, the solution is $1 \leq x \leq 17$.

Monitoring Progress Help in English and Spanish at *BigIdeasMath.com*

11. Solve (a) $2\sqrt{x} - 3 \geq 3$ and (b) $4\sqrt[3]{x + 1} < 8$.

Vocabulary and Core Concept Check

1. **VOCABULARY** Is the equation $3x - \sqrt{2} = \sqrt{6}$ a radical equation? Explain your reasoning.

2. **WRITING** Explain the steps you should use to solve $\sqrt{x} + 10 < 15$.

Monitoring Progress and Modeling with Mathematics

In Exercises 3–12, solve the equation. Check your solution. *(See Example 1.)*

3. $\sqrt{5x + 1} = 6$ 4. $\sqrt{3x + 10} = 8$

5. $\sqrt[3]{x - 16} = 2$ 6. $\sqrt[3]{x} - 10 = -7$

7. $-2\sqrt{24x} + 13 = -11$

8. $8\sqrt[3]{10x} - 15 = 17$

9. $\frac{1}{5}\sqrt[3]{3x} + 10 = 8$ 10. $\sqrt{2x} - \frac{2}{3} = 0$

11. $2\sqrt[5]{x} + 7 = 15$ 12. $\sqrt[4]{4x} - 13 = -15$

13. **MODELING WITH MATHEMATICS** Biologists have discovered that the shoulder height h (in centimeters) of a male Asian elephant can be modeled by $h = 62.5\sqrt[3]{t} + 75.8$, where t is the age (in years) of the elephant. Determine the age of an elephant with a shoulder height of 250 centimeters. *(See Example 2.)*

14. **MODELING WITH MATHEMATICS** In an amusement park ride, a rider suspended by cables swings back and forth from a tower. The maximum speed v (in meters per second) of the rider can be approximated by $v = \sqrt{2gh}$, where h is the height (in meters) at the top of each swing and g is the acceleration due to gravity ($g \approx 9.8$ m/sec^2). Determine the height at the top of the swing of a rider whose maximum speed is 15 meters per second.

In Exercises 15–26, solve the equation. Check your solution(s). *(See Examples 3 and 4.)*

15. $x - 6 = \sqrt{3x}$ 16. $x - 10 = \sqrt{9x}$

17. $\sqrt{44 - 2x} = x - 10$ 18. $\sqrt{2x + 30} = x + 3$

19. $\sqrt[3]{8x^3 - 1} = 2x - 1$ 20. $\sqrt[4]{3 - 8x^2} = 2x$

21. $\sqrt{4x + 1} = \sqrt{x + 10}$ 22. $\sqrt{3x - 3} - \sqrt{x + 12} = 0$

23. $\sqrt[3]{2x - 5} - \sqrt[3]{8x + 1} = 0$

24. $\sqrt[3]{x + 5} = 2\sqrt[3]{2x + 6}$ 25. $\sqrt{3x - 8} + 1 = \sqrt{x + 5}$

26. $\sqrt{x + 2} = 2 - \sqrt{x}$

In Exercises 27–34, solve the equation. Check your solution(s). *(See Examples 5 and 6.)*

27. $2x^{2/3} = 8$ 28. $4x^{3/2} = 32$

29. $x^{1/4} + 3 = 0$ 30. $2x^{3/4} - 14 = 40$

31. $(x + 6)^{1/2} = x$ 32. $(5 - x)^{1/2} - 2x = 0$

33. $2(x + 11)^{1/2} = x + 3$ 34. $(5x^2 - 4)^{1/4} = x$

ERROR ANALYSIS In Exercises 35 and 36, describe and correct the error in solving the equation.

35.
$$\sqrt[3]{3x - 8} = 4$$
$$\left(\sqrt[3]{3x - 8}\right)^3 = 4$$
$$3x - 8 = 4$$
$$3x = 12$$
$$x = 4$$

36.
$$8x^{3/2} = 1000$$
$$8(x^{3/2})^{2/3} = 1000^{2/3}$$
$$8x = 100$$
$$x = \frac{25}{2}$$

In Exercises 37–44, solve the inequality. *(See Example 7.)*

37. $2\sqrt[3]{x} - 5 \geq 3$

38. $\sqrt[3]{x-4} \leq 5$

39. $4\sqrt{x-2} > 20$

40. $7\sqrt{x} + 1 < 9$

41. $2\sqrt{x} + 3 \leq 8$

42. $\sqrt[3]{x+7} \geq 3$

43. $-2\sqrt[3]{x+4} < 12$

44. $-0.25\sqrt{x} - 6 \leq -3$

45. **MODELING WITH MATHEMATICS** The length ℓ (in inches) of a standard nail can be modeled by $\ell = 54d^{3/2}$, where d is the diameter (in inches) of the nail. What is the diameter of a standard nail that is 3 inches long?

46. **DRAWING CONCLUSIONS** "Hang time" is the time you are suspended in the air during a jump. Your hang time t (in seconds) is given by the function $t = 0.5\sqrt{h}$, where h is the height (in feet) of the jump. Suppose a kangaroo and a snowboarder jump with the hang times shown.

$t = 0.81$

$t = 1.21$

a. Find the heights that the snowboarder and the kangaroo jump.

b. Double the hang times of the snowboarder and the kangaroo and calculate the corresponding heights of each jump.

c. When the hang time doubles, does the height of the jump double? Explain.

In Exercises 47–52, solve the nonlinear system. Justify your answer with a graph.

47. $y = \sqrt{x-3}$
$y = x - 3$

48. $y = \sqrt{4x+17}$
$y = x + 5$

49. $x^2 + y^2 = 4$
$y = x - 2$

50. $x^2 + y^2 = 25$
$y = -\frac{3}{4}x + \frac{25}{4}$

51. $x^2 + y^2 = 1$
$y = \frac{1}{2}x^2 - 1$

52. $x^2 + y^2 = 4$
$y^2 = x + 2$

53. **PROBLEM SOLVING** The speed s (in miles per hour) of a car can be given by $s = \sqrt{30fd}$, where f is the coefficient of friction and d is the stopping distance (in feet). The table shows the coefficient of friction for different surfaces.

Surface	Coefficient of friction, f
dry asphalt	0.75
wet asphalt	0.30
snow	0.30
ice	0.15

a. Compare the stopping distances of a car traveling 45 miles per hour on the surfaces given in the table.

b. You are driving 35 miles per hour on an icy road when a deer jumps in front of your car. How far away must you begin to brake to avoid hitting the deer? Justify your answer.

54. **MODELING WITH MATHEMATICS** The Beaufort wind scale was devised to measure wind speed. The Beaufort numbers B, which range from 0 to 12, can be modeled by $B = 1.69\sqrt{s + 4.25} - 3.55$, where s is the wind speed (in miles per hour).

Beaufort number	Force of wind
0	calm
3	gentle breeze
6	strong breeze
9	strong gale
12	hurricane

a. What is the wind speed for $B = 0$? $B = 3$?

b. Write an inequality that describes the range of wind speeds represented by the Beaufort model.

55. **REASONING** Solve the equation $x - 4 = \sqrt{2x}$. Then solve the equation $x - 4 = -\sqrt{2x}$.

a. How does changing $\sqrt{2x}$ to $-\sqrt{2x}$ change the solution(s) of the equation?

b. Justify your answer in part (a) using graphs.

56. **MAKING AN ARGUMENT** Your friend says it is impossible for a radical equation to have two extraneous solutions. Is your friend correct? Explain your reasoning.

57. USING STRUCTURE Explain how you know the radical equation $\sqrt{x + 4} = -5$ has no real solution without solving it.

58. HOW DO YOU SEE IT? Use the graph to find the solution of the equation $2\sqrt{x - 4} = -\sqrt{x - 1} + 4$. Explain your reasoning.

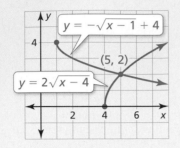

59. WRITING A company determines that the price p of a product can be modeled by $p = 70 - \sqrt{0.02x + 1}$, where x is the number of units of the product demanded per day. Describe the effect that raising the price has on the number of units demanded.

60. THOUGHT PROVOKING City officials rope off a circular area to prepare for a concert in the park. They estimate that each person occupies 6 square feet. Describe how you can use a radical inequality to determine the possible radius of the region when P people are expected to attend the concert.

61. MATHEMATICAL CONNECTIONS The Moeraki Boulders along the coast of New Zealand are stone spheres with radii of approximately 3 feet. A formula for the radius of a sphere is

$$r = \frac{1}{2}\sqrt{\frac{S}{\pi}}$$

where S is the surface area of the sphere. Find the surface area of a Moeraki Boulder.

62. PROBLEM SOLVING You are trying to determine the height of a truncated pyramid, which cannot be measured directly. The height h and slant height ℓ of the truncated pyramid are related by the formula below.

$$\ell = \sqrt{h^2 + \frac{1}{4}(b_2 - b_1)^2}$$

In the given formula, b_1 and b_2 are the side lengths of the upper and lower bases of the pyramid, respectively. When $\ell = 5$, $b_1 = 2$, and $b_2 = 4$, what is the height of the pyramid?

63. REWRITING A FORMULA A burning candle has a radius of r inches and was initially h_0 inches tall. After t minutes, the height of the candle has been reduced to h inches. These quantities are related by the formula

$$r = \sqrt{\frac{kt}{\pi(h_0 - h)}}$$

where k is a constant. Suppose the radius of a candle is 0.875 inch, its initial height is 6.5 inches, and $k = 0.04$.

a. Rewrite the formula, solving for h in terms of t.

b. Use your formula in part (a) to determine the height of the candle after it burns for 45 minutes.

Maintaining Mathematical Proficiency   Reviewing what you learned in previous grades and lessons

Perform the indicated operation.   *(Section 3.2 and Section 3.3)*

64. $(x^3 - 2x^2 + 3x + 1) + (x^4 - 7x)$ **65.** $(2x^5 + x^4 - 4x^2) - (x^5 - 3)$

66. $(x^3 + 2x^2 + 1)(x^2 + 5)$ **67.** $(x^4 + 2x^3 + 11x^2 + 14x - 16) \div (x + 2)$

Let $f(x) = x^3 - 4x^2 + 6$. Write a rule for g. Describe the graph of g as a transformation of the graph of f.   *(Section 3.7)*

68. $g(x) = f(-x) + 4$ **69.** $g(x) = \frac{1}{2}f(x) - 3$ **70.** $g(x) = -f(x - 1) + 6$

4.5 Performing Function Operations

Essential Question How can you use the graphs of two functions to sketch the graph of an arithmetic combination of the two functions?

Just as two real numbers can be combined by the operations of addition, subtraction, multiplication, and division to form other real numbers, two functions can be combined to form other functions. For example, the functions $f(x) = 2x - 3$ and $g(x) = x^2 - 1$ can be combined to form the sum, difference, product, or quotient of f and g.

$$f(x) + g(x) = (2x - 3) + (x^2 - 1) = x^2 + 2x - 4 \qquad \text{sum}$$

$$f(x) - g(x) = (2x - 3) - (x^2 - 1) = -x^2 + 2x - 2 \qquad \text{difference}$$

$$f(x) \cdot g(x) = (2x - 3)(x^2 - 1) = 2x^3 - 3x^2 - 2x + 3 \qquad \text{product}$$

$$\frac{f(x)}{g(x)} = \frac{2x - 3}{x^2 - 1} \qquad \text{quotient}$$

EXPLORATION 1 **Graphing the Sum of Two Functions**

Work with a partner. Use the graphs of f and g to sketch the graph of $f + g$. Explain your steps.

Sample Choose a point on the graph of g. Use a compass or a ruler to measure its distance above or below the x-axis. If above, add the distance to the y-coordinate of the point with the same x-coordinate on the graph of f. If below, subtract the distance. Plot the new point. Repeat this process for several points. Finally, draw a smooth curve through the new points to obtain the graph of $f + g$.

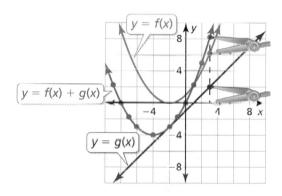

a.

b.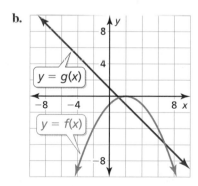

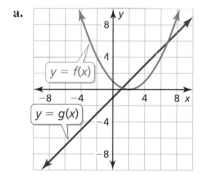

MAKING SENSE OF PROBLEMS

To be proficient in math, you need to check your answers to problems using a different method and continually ask yourself, "Does this make sense?"

Communicate Your Answer

2. How can you use the graphs of two functions to sketch the graph of an arithmetic combination of the two functions?

3. Check your answers in Exploration 1 by writing equations for f and g, adding the functions, and graphing the sum.

What You Will Learn

▶ Add, subtract, multiply, and divide functions.

Core Vocabulary

Previous
domain
scientific notation

Operations on Functions

You have learned how to add, subtract, multiply, and divide polynomial expressions. These operations can also be defined for functions.

⑤ Core Concept

Operations on Functions

Let f and g be any two functions. A new function can be defined by performing any of the four basic operations on f and g.

Operation	Definition	Example: $f(x) = 5x$, $g(x) = x + 2$
Addition	$(f + g)(x) = f(x) + g(x)$	$(f + g)(x) = 5x + (x + 2) = 6x + 2$
Subtraction	$(f - g)(x) = f(x) - g(x)$	$(f - g)(x) = 5x - (x + 2) = 4x - 2$
Multiplication	$(fg)(x) = f(x) \cdot g(x)$	$(fg)(x) = 5x(x + 2) = 5x^2 + 10x$
Division	$\left(\dfrac{f}{g}\right)(x) = \dfrac{f(x)}{g(x)}$	$\left(\dfrac{f}{g}\right)(x) = \dfrac{5x}{x + 2}$

The domains of the sum, difference, product, and quotient functions consist of the x-values that are in the domains of both f and g. Additionally, the domain of the quotient does not include x-values for which $g(x) = 0$.

EXAMPLE 1 **Adding Two Functions**

Let $f(x) = 3\sqrt{x}$ and $g(x) = -10\sqrt{x}$. Find $(f + g)(x)$ and state the domain. Then evaluate the sum when $x = 4$.

SOLUTION

$$(f + g)(x) = f(x) + g(x) = 3\sqrt{x} + (-10\sqrt{x}) = (3 - 10)\sqrt{x} = -7\sqrt{x}$$

The functions f and g each have the same domain: all nonnegative real numbers. So, the domain of $f + g$ also consists of all nonnegative real numbers. To evaluate $f + g$ when $x = 4$, you can use several methods. Here are two:

Method 1 Use an algebraic approach.

When $x = 4$, the value of the sum is

$$(f + g)(4) = -7\sqrt{4} = -14.$$

Method 2 Use a graphical approach.

Enter the functions $y_1 = 3\sqrt{x}$, $y_2 = -10\sqrt{x}$, and $y_3 = y_1 + y_2$ in a graphing calculator. Then graph y_3, the sum of the two functions. Use the *trace* feature to find the value of $f + g$ when $x = 4$. From the graph, $(f + g)(4) = -14$.

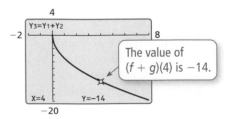

The value of $(f + g)(4)$ is -14.

EXAMPLE 2   **Subtracting Two Functions**

Let $f(x) = 3x^3 - 2x^2 + 5$ and $g(x) = x^3 - 3x^2 + 4x - 2$. Find $(f - g)(x)$ and state the domain. Then evaluate the difference when $x = -2$.

SOLUTION

$$(f - g)(x) = f(x) - g(x) = 3x^3 - 2x^2 + 5 - (x^3 - 3x^2 + 4x - 2) = 2x^3 + x^2 - 4x + 7$$

The functions f and g each have the same domain: all real numbers. So, the domain of $f - g$ also consists of all real numbers. When $x = -2$, the value of the difference is

$$(f - g)(-2) = 2(-2)^3 + (-2)^2 - 4(-2) + 7 = 3.$$

EXAMPLE 3   **Multiplying Two Functions**

Let $f(x) = x^2$ and $g(x) = \sqrt{x}$. Find $(fg)(x)$ and state the domain. Then evaluate the product when $x = 9$.

SOLUTION

$$(fg)(x) = f(x) \cdot g(x) = x^2(\sqrt{x}) = x^2(x^{1/2}) = x^{(2+1/2)} = x^{5/2}$$

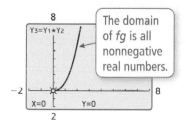

The domain of fg is all nonnegative real numbers.

The domain of f consists of all real numbers, and the domain of g consists of all nonnegative real numbers. So, the domain of fg consists of all nonnegative real numbers. To confirm this, enter the functions $y_1 = x^2$, $y_2 = \sqrt{x}$, and $y_3 = y_1 \cdot y_2$ in a graphing calculator. Then graph y_3, the product of the two functions. It appears from the graph that the domain of fg consists of all nonnegative real numbers. When $x = 9$, the value of the product is

$$(fg)(9) = 9^{5/2} = (9^{1/2})^5 = 3^5 = 243.$$

EXAMPLE 4   **Dividing Two Functions**

Let $f(x) = 6x$ and $g(x) = x^{3/4}$. Find $\left(\dfrac{f}{g}\right)(x)$ and state the domain. Then evaluate the quotient when $x = 16$.

SOLUTION

$$\left(\frac{f}{g}\right)(x) = \frac{f(x)}{g(x)} = \frac{6x}{x^{3/4}} = 6x^{(1-3/4)} = 6x^{1/4}$$

The domain of f consists of all real numbers, and the domain of g consists of all nonnegative real numbers. Because $g(0) = 0$, the domain of $\dfrac{f}{g}$ is restricted to all *positive* real numbers. When $x = 16$, the value of the quotient is

$$\left(\frac{f}{g}\right)(16) = 6(16)^{1/4} = 6(2^4)^{1/4} = 12.$$

ANOTHER WAY

In Example 4, you can also evaluate $\left(\dfrac{f}{g}\right)(16)$ as

$$\left(\frac{f}{g}\right)(16) = \frac{f(16)}{g(16)}$$

$$= \frac{6(16)}{(16)^{3/4}}$$

$$= \frac{96}{8}$$

$$= 12.$$

Monitoring Progress Help in English and Spanish at *BigIdeasMath.com*

1. Let $f(x) = -2x^{2/3}$ and $g(x) = 7x^{2/3}$. Find $(f + g)(x)$ and $(f - g)(x)$ and state the domain of each. Then evaluate $(f + g)(8)$ and $(f - g)(8)$.

2. Let $f(x) = 3x$ and $g(x) = x^{1/5}$. Find $(fg)(x)$ and $\left(\dfrac{f}{g}\right)(x)$ and state the domain of each. Then evaluate $(fg)(32)$ and $\left(\dfrac{f}{g}\right)(32)$.

EXAMPLE 5 Performing Function Operations Using Technology

Let $f(x) = \sqrt{x}$ and $g(x) = \sqrt{9 - x^2}$. Use a graphing calculator to evaluate $(f + g)(x)$, $(f - g)(x)$, $(fg)(x)$, and $\left(\dfrac{f}{g}\right)(x)$ when $x = 2$. Round your answers to two decimal places.

SOLUTION

Enter the functions $y_1 = \sqrt{x}$ and $y_2 = \sqrt{9 - x^2}$ in a graphing calculator. On the home screen, enter $y_1(2) + y_2(2)$. The first entry on the screen shows that $y_1(2) + y_2(2) \approx 3.65$, so $(f + g)(2) \approx 3.65$. Enter the other function operations as shown. Here are the results of the other function operations rounded to two decimal places:

```
Y1(2)+Y2(2)
              3.65028154
Y1(2)-Y2(2)
             -.8218544151
Y1(2)*Y2(2)
              3.16227766
Y1(2)/Y2(2)
               .632455532
```

$$(f - g)(2) \approx -0.82 \qquad (fg)(2) \approx 3.16 \qquad \left(\frac{f}{g}\right)(2) \approx 0.63$$

EXAMPLE 6 Solving a Real-Life Problem

For a white rhino, heart rate r (in beats per minute) and life span s (in minutes) are related to body mass m (in kilograms) by the functions

$$r(m) = 241m^{-0.25}$$

and

$$s(m) = (6 \times 10^6)m^{0.2}.$$

a. Find $(rs)(m)$.

b. Explain what $(rs)(m)$ represents.

SOLUTION

a. $(rs)(m) = r(m) \cdot s(m)$ Definition of multiplication

$\qquad\qquad\quad = 241m^{-0.25}[(6 \times 10^6)m^{0.2}]$ Write product of $r(m)$ and $s(m)$.

$\qquad\qquad\quad = 241(6 \times 10^6)m^{-0.25+0.2}$ Product of Powers Property

$\qquad\qquad\quad = (1446 \times 10^6)m^{-0.05}$ Simplify.

$\qquad\qquad\quad = (1.446 \times 10^9)m^{-0.05}$ Use scientific notation.

b. Multiplying heart rate by life span gives the total number of heartbeats over the lifetime of a white rhino with body mass m.

Monitoring Progress Help in English and Spanish at *BigIdeasMath.com*

3. Let $f(x) = 8x$ and $g(x) = 2x^{5/6}$. Use a graphing calculator to evaluate $(f + g)(x)$, $(f - g)(x)$, $(fg)(x)$, and $\left(\dfrac{f}{g}\right)(x)$ when $x = 5$. Round your answers to two decimal places.

4. In Example 5, explain why you can evaluate $(f + g)(3)$, $(f - g)(3)$, and $(fg)(3)$ but not $\left(\dfrac{f}{g}\right)(3)$.

5. Use the answer in Example 6(a) to find the total number of heartbeats over the lifetime of a white rhino when its body mass is 1.7×10^5 kilograms.

Vocabulary and Core Concept Check

1. **WRITING** Let f and g be any two functions. Describe how you can use f, g, and the four basic operations to create new functions.

2. **WRITING** What x-values are not included in the domain of the quotient of two functions?

Monitoring Progress and Modeling with Mathematics

In Exercises 3–6, find $(f + g)(x)$ and $(f - g)(x)$ and state the domain of each. Then evaluate $f + g$ and $f - g$ for the given value of x. *(See Examples 1 and 2.)*

3. $f(x) = -5\sqrt[4]{x},\ g(x) = 19\sqrt[4]{x};\ x = 16$

4. $f(x) = \sqrt[3]{2x},\ g(x) = -11\sqrt[3]{2x};\ x = -4$

5. $f(x) = 6x - 4x^2 - 7x^3,\ g(x) = 9x^2 - 5x;\ x = -1$

6. $f(x) = 11x + 2x^2,\ g(x) = -7x - 3x^2 + 4;\ x = 2$

In Exercises 7–12, find $(fg)(x)$ and $\left(\dfrac{f}{g}\right)(x)$ and state the domain of each. Then evaluate fg and $\dfrac{f}{g}$ for the given value of x. *(See Examples 3 and 4.)*

7. $f(x) = 2x^3,\ g(x) = \sqrt[3]{x};\ x = -27$

8. $f(x) = x^4,\ g(x) = 3\sqrt{x};\ x = 4$

9. $f(x) = 4x,\ g(x) = 9x^{1/2};\ x = 9$

10. $f(x) = 11x^3,\ g(x) = 7x^{7/3};\ x = -8$

11. $f(x) = 7x^{3/2},\ g(x) = -14x^{1/3};\ x = 64$

12. $f(x) = 4x^{5/4},\ g(x) = 2x^{1/2};\ x = 16$

USING TOOLS In Exercises 13–16, use a graphing calculator to evaluate $(f + g)(x)$, $(f - g)(x)$, $(fg)(x)$, and $\left(\dfrac{f}{g}\right)(x)$ when $x = 5$. Round your answers to two decimal places. *(See Example 5.)*

13. $f(x) = 4x^4;\ g(x) = 24x^{1/3}$

14. $f(x) = 7x^{5/3};\ g(x) = 49x^{2/3}$

15. $f(x) = -2x^{1/3};\ g(x) = 5x^{1/2}$

16. $f(x) = 4x^{1/2};\ g(x) = 6x^{3/4}$

ERROR ANALYSIS In Exercises 17 and 18, describe and correct the error in stating the domain.

17.
$f(x) = x^{1/2}$ and $g(x) = x^{3/2}$
The domain of fg is all real numbers.

18.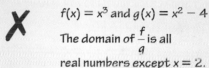
$f(x) = x^3$ and $g(x) = x^2 - 4$
The domain of $\dfrac{f}{g}$ is all real numbers except $x = 2$.

19. **MODELING WITH MATHEMATICS** From 1990 to 2010, the numbers (in millions) of female F and male M employees from the ages of 16 to 19 in the United States can be modeled by $F(t) = -0.007t^2 + 0.10t + 3.7$ and $M(t) = 0.0001t^3 - 0.009t^2 + 0.11t + 3.7$, where t is the number of years since 1990. *(See Example 6.)*

   a. Find $(F + M)(t)$.

   b. Explain what $(F + M)(t)$ represents.

20. **MODELING WITH MATHEMATICS** From 2005 to 2009, the numbers of cruise ship departures (in thousands) from around the world W and Florida F can be modeled by the equations

   $$W(t) = -5.8333t^3 + 17.43t^2 + 509.1t + 11496$$

   $$F(t) = 12.5t^3 - 60.29t^2 + 136.6t + 4881$$

   where t is the number of years since 2005.

   a. Find $(W - F)(t)$.

   b. Explain what $(W - F)(t)$ represents.

21. **MAKING AN ARGUMENT** Your friend claims that the addition of functions and the multiplication of functions are commutative. Is your friend correct? Explain your reasoning.

22. HOW DO YOU SEE IT? The graphs of the functions $f(x) = 3x^2 - 2x - 1$ and $g(x) = 3x + 4$ are shown. Which graph represents the function $f + g$? the function $f - g$? Explain your reasoning.

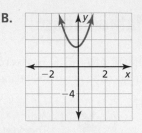

A.

B.

23. REASONING The table shows the outputs of the two functions f and g. Use the table to evaluate $(f + g)(3)$, $(f - g)(1)$, $(fg)(2)$, and $\left(\dfrac{f}{g}\right)(0)$.

x	0	1	2	3	4
f(x)	−2	−4	0	10	26
g(x)	−1	−3	−13	−31	−57

24. THOUGHT PROVOKING Is it possible to write two functions whose sum contains radicals, but whose product does not? Justify your answers.

25. MATHEMATICAL CONNECTIONS
A triangle is inscribed in a square, as shown. Write and simplify a function r in terms of x that represents the area of the shaded region.

26. REWRITING A FORMULA For a mammal that weighs w grams, the volume b (in milliliters) of air breathed in and the volume d (in milliliters) of "dead space" (the portion of the lungs not filled with air) can be modeled by

$$b(w) = 0.007w \text{ and } d(w) = 0.002w.$$

The breathing rate r (in breaths per minute) of a mammal that weighs w grams can be modeled by

$$r(w) = \frac{1.1w^{0.734}}{b(w) - d(w)}.$$

Simplify $r(w)$ and calculate the breathing rate for body weights of 6.5 grams, 300 grams, and 70,000 grams.

27. PROBLEM SOLVING A mathematician at a lake throws a tennis ball from point A along the water's edge to point B in the water, as shown. His dog, Elvis, first runs along the beach from point A to point D and then swims to fetch the ball at point B.

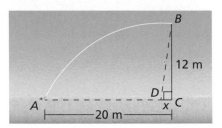

a. Elvis runs at a speed of about 6.4 meters per second. Write a function r in terms of x that represents the time he spends running from point A to point D. Elvis swims at a speed of about 0.9 meter per second. Write a function s in terms of x that represents the time he spends swimming from point D to point B.

b. Write a function t in terms of x that represents the total time Elvis spends traveling from point A to point D to point B.

c. Use a graphing calculator to graph t. Find the value of x that minimizes t. Explain the meaning of this value.

Maintaining Mathematical Proficiency
Reviewing what you learned in previous grades and lessons

Solve the literal equation for n. *(Skills Review Handbook)*

28. $3xn - 9 = 6y$

29. $5z = 7n + 8nz$

30. $3nb = 5n - 6z$

31. $\dfrac{3 + 4n}{n} = 7b$

Determine whether the relation is a function. Explain. *(Skills Review Handbook)*

32. $(3, 4), (4, 6), (1, 4), (2, -1)$

33. $(-1, 2), (3, 7), (0, 2), (-1, -1)$

34. $(1, 6), (7, -3), (4, 0), (3, 0)$

35. $(3, 8), (2, 5), (9, 5), (2, -3)$

4.6 Inverse of a Function

Essential Question How can you sketch the graph of the inverse of a function?

EXPLORATION 1 Graphing Functions and Their Inverses

Work with a partner. Each pair of functions are *inverses* of each other. Use a graphing calculator to graph f and g in the same viewing window. What do you notice about the graphs?

a. $f(x) = 4x + 3$

$g(x) = \dfrac{x - 3}{4}$

b. $f(x) = x^3 + 1$

$g(x) = \sqrt[3]{x - 1}$

c. $f(x) = \sqrt{x - 3}$

$g(x) = x^2 + 3, x \geq 0$

d. $f(x) = -\sqrt{x} + 2$

$g(x) = (2 - x)^2, x \leq 2$

EXPLORATION 2 Sketching Graphs of Inverse Functions

Work with a partner. Use the graph of f to sketch the graph of g, the inverse function of f, on the same set of coordinate axes. Explain your reasoning.

a.

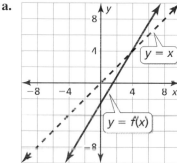

b.

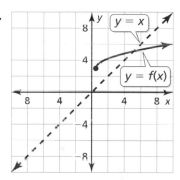

c.

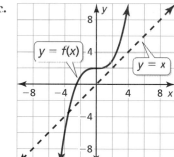

d.

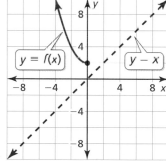

Communicate Your Answer

3. How can you sketch the graph of the inverse of a function?

4. In Exploration 1, what do you notice about the relationship between the equations of f and g? Use your answer to find g, the inverse function of

$$f(x) = 2x - 3.$$

Use a graph to check your answer.

What You Will Learn

▶ Explore inverses of functions.

▶ Find and verify inverses of nonlinear functions.

▶ Solve real-life problems using inverse functions.

Core Vocabulary

inverse functions, *p. 233*

Previous
input
output
inverse operations
reflection
line of reflection

Exploring Inverses of Functions

You have used given inputs to find corresponding outputs of $y = f(x)$ for various types of functions. You have also used given outputs to find corresponding inputs. Now you will solve equations of the form $y = f(x)$ for x to obtain a general formula for finding the input given a specific output of a function f.

EXAMPLE 1 **Writing a Formula for the Input of a Function**

Let $f(x) = 2x + 3$.

a. Solve $y = f(x)$ for x.

b. Find the input when the output is -7.

SOLUTION

a.
$y = 2x + 3$	Set y equal to $f(x)$.
$y - 3 = 2x$	Subtract 3 from each side.
$\dfrac{y - 3}{2} = x$	Divide each side by 2.

b. Find the input when $y = -7$.

$x = \dfrac{-7 - 3}{2}$	Substitute -7 for y.
$= \dfrac{-10}{2}$	Subtract.
$= -5$	Divide.

▶ So, the input is -5 when the output is -7.

Check

$f(-5) = 2(-5) + 3$
$= -10 + 3$
$= -7$ ✓

Monitoring Progress Help in English and Spanish at *BigIdeasMath.com*

Solve $y = f(x)$ for x. Then find the input(s) when the output is 2.

1. $f(x) = x - 2$ **2.** $f(x) = 2x^2$ **3.** $f(x) = -x^3 + 3$

In Example 1, notice the steps involved after substituting for x in $y = 2x + 3$ and after substituting for y in $x = \dfrac{y - 3}{2}$.

$y = 2x + 3$ $x = \dfrac{y - 3}{2}$

Step 1 Multiply by 2.   **Step 1** Subtract 3.

Step 2 Add 3.   **Step 2** Divide by 2.

inverse operations
in the reverse order

Notice that these steps *undo* each other. Functions that undo each other are called
inverse functions. In Example 1, you can use the equation solved for x to write the
inverse of f by switching the roles of x and y.

$$f(x) = 2x + 3 \quad \text{original function} \qquad g(x) = \frac{x - 3}{2} \quad \text{inverse function}$$

Because inverse functions interchange the input and output values of the original
function, the domain and range are also interchanged.

Original function: $f(x) = 2x + 3$

x	−2	−1	0	1	2
y	−1	1	3	5	7

Inverse function: $g(x) = \dfrac{x - 3}{2}$

x	−1	1	3	5	7
y	−2	−1	0	1	2

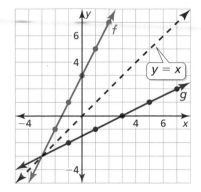

The graph of an inverse function is a *reflection* of the graph of the original function.
The *line of reflection* is $y = x$. To find the inverse of a function algebraically, switch
the roles of x and y, and then solve for y.

EXAMPLE 2 **Finding the Inverse of a Linear Function**

Find the inverse of $f(x) = 3x - 1$.

SOLUTION

Method 1 Use inverse operations in the reverse order.

$$f(x) = 3x - 1 \qquad \text{Multiply the input } x \text{ by 3 and then subtract 1}$$

To find the inverse, apply inverse operations in the reverse order.

$$g(x) = \frac{x + 1}{3} \qquad \text{Add 1 to the input } x \text{ and then divide by 3.}$$

▶ The inverse of f is $g(x) = \dfrac{x + 1}{3}$, or $g(x) = \dfrac{1}{3}x + \dfrac{1}{3}$.

Method 2 Set y equal to $f(x)$. Switch the roles of x and y and solve for y.

$$y = 3x - 1 \qquad \text{Set } y \text{ equal to } f(x).$$
$$x = 3y - 1 \qquad \text{Switch } x \text{ and } y.$$
$$x + 1 = 3y \qquad \text{Add 1 to each side.}$$
$$\frac{x + 1}{3} = y \qquad \text{Divide each side by 3.}$$

▶ The inverse of f is $g(x) = \dfrac{x + 1}{3}$, or $g(x) = \dfrac{1}{3}x + \dfrac{1}{3}$.

Check

The graph of g appears to be a
reflection of the graph of f in the
line $y = x$. ✓

Monitoring Progress ◗)) Help in English and Spanish at *BigIdeasMath.com*

Find the inverse of the function. Then graph the function and its inverse.

4. $f(x) = 2x$ **5.** $f(x) = -x + 1$ **6.** $f(x) = \frac{1}{3}x - 2$

Inverses of Nonlinear Functions

In the previous examples, the inverses of the linear functions were also functions. However, inverses are not always functions. The graphs of $f(x) = x^2$ and $f(x) = x^3$ are shown along with their reflections in the line $y = x$. Notice that the inverse of $f(x) = x^3$ is a function, but the inverse of $f(x) = x^2$ is *not* a function.

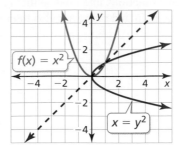
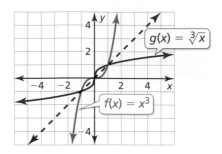

When the domain of $f(x) = x^2$ is *restricted* to only nonnegative real numbers, the inverse of f is a function.

EXAMPLE 3   **Finding the Inverse of a Quadratic Function**

Find the inverse of $f(x) = x^2$, $x \geq 0$. Then graph the function and its inverse.

SOLUTION

$$f(x) = x^2 \qquad \text{Write the original function.}$$

$$y = x^2 \qquad \text{Set } y \text{ equal to } f(x).$$

$$x = y^2 \qquad \text{Switch } x \text{ and } y.$$

$$\pm\sqrt{x} = y \qquad \text{Take square root of each side.}$$

STUDY TIP

If the domain of f were restricted to $x \leq 0$, then the inverse would be $g(x) = -\sqrt{x}$.

The domain of f is restricted to nonnegative values of x. So, the range of the inverse must also be restricted to nonnegative values.

▶ So, the inverse of f is $g(x) = \sqrt{x}$.

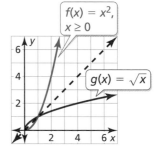

You can use the graph of a function f to determine whether the inverse of f is a function by applying the *horizontal line test*.

---

⑤ Core Concept

Horizontal Line Test

The inverse of a function f is also a function if and only if no horizontal line intersects the graph of f more than once.

Inverse is a function	Inverse is not a function

EXAMPLE 4   **Finding the Inverse of a Cubic Function**

Consider the function $f(x) = 2x^3 + 1$. Determine whether the inverse of f is a function. Then find the inverse.

SOLUTION

Graph the function f. Notice that no horizontal line intersects the graph more than once. So, the inverse of f is a function. Find the inverse.

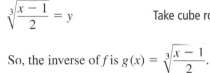

$$y = 2x^3 + 1 \qquad \text{Set } y \text{ equal to } f(x).$$

$$x = 2y^3 + 1 \qquad \text{Switch } x \text{ and } y.$$

$$x - 1 = 2y^3 \qquad \text{Subtract 1 from each side.}$$

$$\frac{x-1}{2} = y^3 \qquad \text{Divide each side by 2.}$$

$$\sqrt[3]{\frac{x-1}{2}} = y \qquad \text{Take cube root of each side.}$$

▶ So, the inverse of f is $g(x) = \sqrt[3]{\dfrac{x-1}{2}}$.

Check

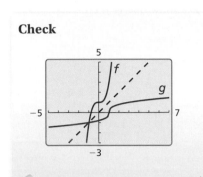

EXAMPLE 5   **Finding the Inverse of a Radical Function**

Consider the function $f(x) = 2\sqrt{x} - 3$. Determine whether the inverse of f is a function. Then find the inverse.

SOLUTION

Graph the function f. Notice that no horizontal line intersects the graph more than once. So, the inverse of f is a function. Find the inverse.

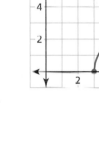

$$y = 2\sqrt{x} - 3 \qquad \text{Set } y \text{ equal to } f(x).$$

$$x = 2\sqrt{y} - 3 \qquad \text{Switch } x \text{ and } y.$$

$$x^2 = \left(2\sqrt{y} - 3\right)^2 \qquad \text{Square each side.}$$

$$x^2 = 4(y - 3) \qquad \text{Simplify.}$$

$$x^2 = 4y - 12 \qquad \text{Distributive Property}$$

$$x^2 + 12 = 4y \qquad \text{Add 12 to each side.}$$

$$\tfrac{1}{4}x^2 + 3 = y \qquad \text{Divide each side by 4.}$$

Check

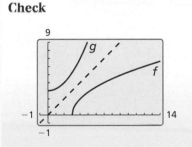

Because the range of f is $y \ge 0$, the domain of the inverse must be restricted to $x \ge 0$.

▶ So, the inverse of f is $g(x) = \tfrac{1}{4}x^2 + 3$, where $x \ge 0$.

Monitoring Progress Help in English and Spanish at *BigIdeasMath.com*

Find the inverse of the function. Then graph the function and its inverse.

7. $f(x) = -x^2, x \le 0$ **8.** $f(x) = -x^3 + 4$ **9.** $f(x) = \sqrt{x+2}$

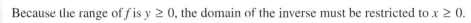

REASONING
ABSTRACTLY
Inverse functions *undo* each other. So, when you evaluate a function for a specific input, and then evaluate its inverse using the output, you obtain the original input.

Let f and g be inverse functions. If $f(a) = b$, then $g(b) = a$. So, in general,

$$f(g(x)) = x \quad \text{and} \quad g(f(x)) = x.$$

EXAMPLE 6 Verifying Functions Are Inverses

Verify that $f(x) = 3x - 1$ and $g(x) = \dfrac{x + 1}{3}$ are inverse functions.

SOLUTION

Step 1 Show that $f(g(x)) = x$.

$$f(g(x)) = f\left(\frac{x + 1}{3}\right)$$

$$= 3\left(\frac{x + 1}{3}\right) - 1$$

$$= x + 1 - 1$$

$$= x \ \checkmark$$

Step 2 Show that $g(f(x)) = x$.

$$g(f(x)) = g(3x - 1)$$

$$= \frac{3x - 1 + 1}{3}$$

$$= \frac{3x}{3}$$

$$= x \ \checkmark$$

Monitoring Progress Help in English and Spanish at *BigIdeasMath.com*

Determine whether the functions are inverse functions.

10. $f(x) = x + 5$, $g(x) = x - 5$

11. $f(x) = 8x^3$, $g(x) = \sqrt[3]{2x}$

Solving Real-Life Problems

In many real-life problems, formulas contain meaningful variables, such as the radius r in the formula for the surface area S of a sphere, $S = 4\pi r^2$. In this situation, switching the variables to find the inverse would create confusion by switching the meanings of S and r. So, when finding the inverse, solve for r without switching the variables.

EXAMPLE 7 Solving a Multi-Step Problem

Find the inverse of the function that represents the surface area of a sphere, $S = 4\pi r^2$. Then find the radius of a sphere that has a surface area of 100π square feet.

SOLUTION

Step 1 Find the inverse of the function.

$$S = 4\pi r^2$$

$$\frac{S}{4\pi} = r^2$$

$$\sqrt{\frac{S}{4\pi}} = r$$

The radius r must be positive, so disregard the negative square root.

Step 2 Evaluate the inverse when $S = 100\pi$.

$$r = \sqrt{\frac{100\pi}{4\pi}}$$

$$= \sqrt{25} = 5$$

▶ The radius of the sphere is 5 feet.

Monitoring Progress Help in English and Spanish at *BigIdeasMath.com*

12. The distance d (in meters) that a dropped object falls in t seconds on Earth is represented by $d = 4.9t^2$. Find the inverse of the function. How long does it take an object to fall 50 meters?

Vocabulary and Core Concept Check

1. **VOCABULARY** In your own words, state the definition of inverse functions.

2. **WRITING** Explain how to determine whether the inverse of a function is also a function.

3. **COMPLETE THE SENTENCE** Functions f and g are inverses of each other provided that $f(g(x)) = $ _____ and $g(f(x)) = $ _____.

4. **DIFFERENT WORDS, SAME QUESTION** Which is different? Find "both" answers.

Let $f(x) = 5x - 2$. Solve $y = f(x)$ for x and then switch the roles of x and y.	Write an equation that represents a reflection of the graph of $f(x) = 5x - 2$ in the x-axis.
Write an equation that represents a reflection of the graph of $f(x) = 5x - 2$ in the line $y = x$.	Find the inverse of $f(x) = 5x - 2$.

Monitoring Progress and Modeling with Mathematics

In Exercises 5–12, solve $y = f(x)$ for x. Then find the input(s) when the output is -3. *(See Example 1.)*

5. $f(x) = 3x + 5$

6. $f(x) = -7x - 2$

7. $f(x) = \frac{1}{2}x - 3$

8. $f(x) = -\frac{2}{3}x + 1$

9. $f(x) = 3x^3$

10. $f(x) = 2x^4 - 5$

11. $f(x) = (x - 2)^2 - 7$

12. $f(x) = (x - 5)^3 - 1$

In Exercises 13–20, find the inverse of the function. Then graph the function and its inverse. *(See Example 2.)*

13. $f(x) = 6x$

14. $f(x) = -3x$

15. $f(x) = -2x + 5$

16. $f(x) = 6x - 3$

17. $f(x) = -\frac{1}{2}x + 4$

18. $f(x) = \frac{1}{3}x - 1$

19. $f(x) = \frac{2}{3}x - \frac{1}{3}$

20. $f(x) = -\frac{4}{5}x + \frac{1}{5}$

21. **COMPARING METHODS** Find the inverse of the function $f(x) = -3x + 4$ by switching the roles of x and y and solving for y. Then find the inverse of the function f by using inverse operations in the reverse order. Which method do you prefer? Explain.

22. **REASONING** Determine whether each pair of functions f and g are inverses. Explain your reasoning.

   a.

x	-2	-1	0	1	2
f(x)	-2	1	4	7	10

x	-2	1	4	7	10
g(x)	-2	-1	0	1	2

   b.

x	2	3	4	5	6
f(x)	8	6	4	2	0

x	2	3	4	5	6
g(x)	-8	-6	-4	-2	0

   c.

x	-4	-2	0	2	4
f(x)	2	10	18	26	34

x	-4	-2	0	2	4
g(x)	$\frac{1}{2}$	$\frac{1}{10}$	$\frac{1}{18}$	$\frac{1}{26}$	$\frac{1}{34}$

In Exercises 23–28, find the inverse of the function. Then graph the function and its inverse. *(See Example 3.)*

23. $f(x) = 4x^2, x \leq 0$

24. $f(x) = 9x^2, x \leq 0$

25. $f(x) = (x - 3)^3$

26. $f(x) = (x + 4)^3$

27. $f(x) = 2x^4, x \geq 0$

28. $f(x) = -x^6, x \geq 0$

ERROR ANALYSIS In Exercises 29 and 30, describe and correct the error in finding the inverse of the function.

29.

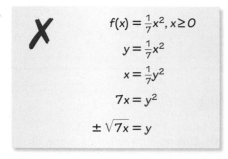

$$f(x) = -x + 3$$
$$y = -x + 3$$
$$-x = y + 3$$
$$-x - 3 = y$$

30.

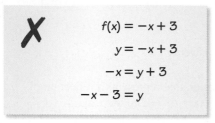

$$f(x) = \tfrac{1}{7}x^2, x \geq 0$$
$$y = \tfrac{1}{7}x^2$$
$$x = \tfrac{1}{7}y^2$$
$$7x = y^2$$
$$\pm\sqrt{7x} = y$$

USING TOOLS In Exercises 31–34, use the graph to determine whether the inverse of f is a function. Explain your reasoning.

31.

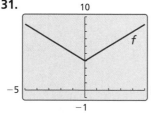

32.

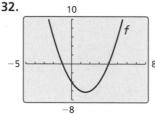

33.

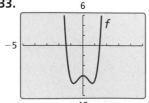

34.

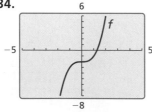

In Exercises 35–46, determine whether the inverse of f is a function. Then find the inverse.
(See Examples 4 and 5.)

35. $f(x) = x^3 - 1$

36. $f(x) = -x^3 + 3$

37. $f(x) = \sqrt{x + 4}$

38. $f(x) = \sqrt{x - 6}$

39. $f(x) = 2\sqrt[3]{x - 5}$

40. $f(x) = 2x^2 - 5$

41. $f(x) = x^4 + 2$

42. $f(x) = 2x^3 - 5$

43. $f(x) = 3\sqrt[3]{x + 1}$

44. $f(x) = -\sqrt[3]{\dfrac{2x + 4}{3}}$

45. $f(x) = \tfrac{1}{2}x^5$

46. $f(x) = -3\sqrt{\dfrac{4x - 7}{3}}$

47. WRITING EQUATIONS What is the inverse of the function whose graph is shown?

   Ⓐ $g(x) = \tfrac{3}{2}x - 6$

   Ⓑ $g(x) = \tfrac{3}{2}x + 6$

   Ⓒ $g(x) = \tfrac{2}{3}x - 6$

   Ⓓ $g(x) = \tfrac{2}{3}x + 12$

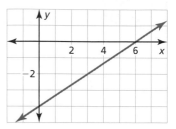

48. WRITING EQUATIONS What is the inverse of $f(x) = -\dfrac{1}{64}x^3?$

   Ⓐ $g(x) = -4x^3$ Ⓑ $g(x) = 4\sqrt[3]{x}$

   Ⓒ $g(x) = -4\sqrt[3]{x}$ Ⓓ $g(x) = \sqrt[3]{-4x}$

In Exercises 49–52, determine whether the functions are inverse functions. *(See Example 6.)*

49. $f(x) = 2x - 9, g(x) = \dfrac{x}{2} + 9$

50. $f(x) = \dfrac{x - 3}{4}, g(x) = 4x + 3$

51. $f(x) = \sqrt[5]{\dfrac{x + 9}{5}}, g(x) = 5x^5 - 9$

52. $f(x) = 7x^{3/2} - 4, g(x) = \left(\dfrac{x + 4}{7}\right)^{3/2}$

53. MODELING WITH MATHEMATICS The maximum hull speed v (in knots) of a boat with a displacement hull can be approximated by $v = 1.34\sqrt{\ell}$, where ℓ is the waterline length (in feet) of the boat. Find the inverse function. What waterline length is needed to achieve a maximum speed of 7.5 knots? *(See Example 7.)*

Waterline length

54. MODELING WITH MATHEMATICS Elastic bands can be used for exercising to provide a range of resistance. The resistance R (in pounds) of a band can be modeled by $R = \frac{3}{8}L - 5$, where L is the total length (in inches) of the stretched band. Find the inverse function. What length of the stretched band provides 19 pounds of resistance?

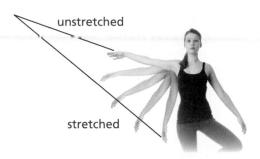

unstretched

stretched

ANALYZING RELATIONSHIPS In Exercises 55–58, match the graph of the function with the graph of its inverse.

55.

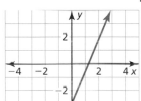

56.

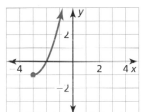

57.

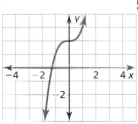

58.

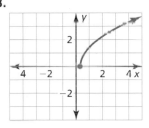

A.

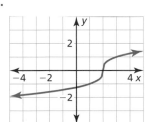

B.

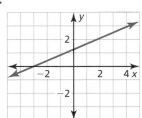

C.

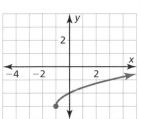

D.

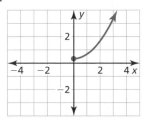

59. REASONING You and a friend are playing a number-guessing game. You ask your friend to think of a positive number, square the number, multiply the result by 2, and then add 3. Your friend's final answer is 53. What was the original number chosen? Justify your answer.

60. MAKING AN ARGUMENT Your friend claims that every quadratic function whose domain is restricted to nonnegative values has an inverse function. Is your friend correct? Explain your reasoning.

61. PROBLEM SOLVING When calibrating a spring scale, you need to know how far the spring stretches for various weights. Hooke's Law states that the length a spring stretches is proportional to the weight attached to it. A model for one scale is $\ell = 0.5w + 3$, where ℓ is the total length (in inches) of the stretched spring and w is the weight (in pounds) of the object.

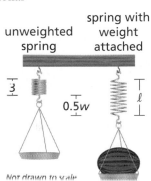

spring with
unweighted   weight
spring   attached

Not drawn to scale

a. Find the inverse function. Describe what it represents.

b. You place a melon on the scale, and the spring stretches to a total length of 5.5 inches. Determine the weight of the melon.

c. Verify that the function $\ell = 0.5w + 3$ and the inverse model in part (a) are inverse functions.

62. THOUGHT PROVOKING Do functions of the form $y = x^{m/n}$, where m and n are positive integers, have inverse functions? Justify your answer with examples.

63. PROBLEM SOLVING At the start of a dog sled race in Anchorage, Alaska, the temperature was 5°C. By the end of the race, the temperature was −10°C. The formula for converting temperatures from degrees Fahrenheit F to degrees Celsius C is $C = \frac{5}{9}(F - 32)$.

a. Find the inverse function. Describe what it represents.

b. Find the Fahrenheit temperatures at the start and end of the race.

c. Use a graphing calculator to graph the original function and its inverse. Find the temperature that is the same on both temperature scales.

64. PROBLEM SOLVING The surface area A (in square meters) of a person with a mass of 60 kilograms can be approximated by $A = 0.2195h^{0.3964}$, where h is the height (in centimeters) of the person.

   a. Find the inverse function. Then estimate the height of a 60-kilogram person who has a body surface area of 1.6 square meters.

   b. Verify that function A and the inverse model in part (a) are inverse functions.

USING STRUCTURE In Exercises 65–68, match the function with the graph of its inverse.

65. $f(x) = \sqrt[3]{x - 4}$

66. $f(x) = \sqrt[3]{x + 4}$

67. $f(x) = \sqrt{x + 1} - 3$

68. $f(x) = \sqrt{x - 1} + 3$

A.
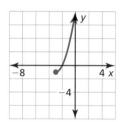

B.
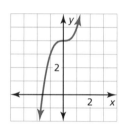

C.
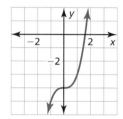

D.
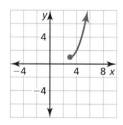

69. DRAWING CONCLUSIONS Determine whether the statement is *true* or *false*. Explain your reasoning.

   a. If $f(x) = x^n$ and n is a positive even integer, then the inverse of f is a function.

   b. If $f(x) = x^n$ and n is a positive odd integer, then the inverse of f is a function.

70. HOW DO YOU SEE IT? The graph of the function f is shown. Name three points that lie on the graph of the inverse of f. Explain your reasoning.

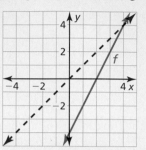

71. ABSTRACT REASONING Show that the inverse of any linear function $f(x) = mx + b$, where $m \neq 0$, is also a linear function. Identify the slope and y-intercept of the graph of the inverse function in terms of m and b.

72. CRITICAL THINKING Consider the function $f(x) = -x$.

   a. Graph $f(x) = -x$ and explain why it is its own inverse. Also, verify that $f(x) = -x$ is its own inverse algebraically.

   b. Graph other linear functions that are their own inverses. Write equations of the lines you graphed.

   c. Use your results from part (b) to write a general equation describing the family of linear functions that are their own inverses.

Maintaining Mathematical Proficiency
Reviewing what you learned in previous grades and lessons

Simplify the expression. Write your answer using only positive exponents. *(Skills Review Handbook)*

73. $(-3)^{-3}$

74. $2^3 \cdot 2^2$

75. $\dfrac{4^5}{4^3}$

76. $\left(\dfrac{2}{3}\right)^4$

Describe the x-values for which the function is increasing, decreasing, positive, and negative. *(Section 3.1)*

77.
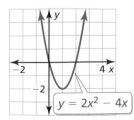
$y = 2x^2 - 4x$

78.
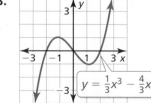
$y = \frac{1}{3}x^3 - \frac{4}{3}x$

79.
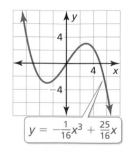
$y = -\frac{1}{16}x^3 + \frac{25}{16}x$

Core Vocabulary

radical equation, *p. 218*
extraneous solutions, *p. 219*
inverse functions, *p. 233*

Core Concepts

Section 4.4

Solving Radical Equations, *p. 218*
Solving Radical Inequalities, *p. 221*

Section 4.5

Operations on Functions, *p. 226*

Section 4.6

Exploring Inverses of Functions, *p. 232*
Inverses of Nonlinear Functions, *p. 234*
Horizontal Line Test, *p. 234*

Mathematical Practices

1. How did you find the endpoints of the range in part (b) of Exercise 54 on page 223?

2. How did you use structure in Exercise 57 on page 224?

3. How can you evaluate the reasonableness of the results in Exercise 27 on page 230?

4. How can you use a graphing calculator to check your answers in Exercises 49–52 on page 238?

Performance Task:

The Heartbeat Hypothesis

Biologists use mathematical functions to model characteristics of different species, such as heart rate, body mass, and life span. How can the functions be combined to tell us even more?

To explore the answer to this question and more, check out the Performance Task and Real-Life STEM video at *BigIdeasMath.com*.

4 Chapter Review

Dynamic Solutions available at *BigIdeasMath.com*

4.1 *n*th Roots and Rational Exponents *(pp. 193–198)*

a. Evaluate $8^{4/3}$ without using a calculator.

Rational Exponent Form	**Radical Form**
$8^{4/3} = (8^{1/3})^4 = 2^4 = 16$	$8^{4/3} = (\sqrt[3]{8})^4 = 2^4 = 16$

b. Find the real solution(s) of $x^4 - 45 = 580$.

$x^4 - 45 = 580$ Write original equation.

$x^4 = 625$ Add 45 to each side.

$x = \pm\sqrt[4]{625}$ Take fourth root of each side.

$x = 5$ or $x = -5$ Simplify.

▶ The solutions are $x = 5$ and $x = -5$.

Evaluate the expression without using a calculator.

1. $8^{7/3}$ **2.** $9^{5/2}$ **3.** $(-27)^{-2/3}$

Find the real solution(s) of the equation. Round your answer to two decimal places when appropriate.

4. $x^5 + 17 = 35$ **5.** $7x^3 = 189$ **6.** $(x + 8)^4 = 16$

4.2 Properties of Rational Exponents and Radicals *(pp. 199–206)*

a. Use the properties of rational exponents to simplify $\left(\dfrac{54^{1/3}}{2^{1/3}}\right)^4$.

$$\left(\frac{54^{1/3}}{2^{1/3}}\right)^4 = \left[\left(\frac{54}{2}\right)^{1/3}\right]^4 = (27^{1/3})^4 = 3^4 = 81$$

b. Write $\sqrt[4]{16x^{13}y^8z^7}$ in simplest form. Assume all variables are positive.

$\sqrt[4]{16x^{13}y^8z^7} = \sqrt[4]{16x^{12}xy^8z^4z^3}$ Factor out perfect fourth powers.

$= \sqrt[4]{16x^{12}y^8z^4} \cdot \sqrt[4]{xz^3}$ Product Property of Radicals

$= 2x^3y^2z\sqrt[4]{xz^3}$ Simplify.

Simplify the expression.

7. $\left(\dfrac{6^{1/5}}{6^{2/5}}\right)^3$ **8.** $\sqrt[4]{32} \cdot \sqrt[4]{8}$ **9.** $\dfrac{1}{2 - \sqrt[4]{9}}$

10. $4\sqrt[5]{8} + 3\sqrt[5]{8}$ **11.** $2\sqrt{48} - \sqrt{3}$ **12.** $(5^{2/3} \cdot 2^{3/2})^{1/2}$

Simplify the expression. Assume all variables are positive.

13. $\sqrt[3]{125z^9}$ **14.** $\dfrac{2^{1/4}z^{5/4}}{6z}$ **15.** $\sqrt{10z^5} - z^2\sqrt{40z}$

4.3 Graphing Radical Functions (pp. 207–214)

Describe the transformation of $f(x) = \sqrt{x}$ represented by $g(x) = 2\sqrt{x + 5}$. Then graph each function.

Notice that the function is of the form
$g(x) = a\sqrt{x - h}$, where $a = 2$ and $h = -5$.

▶ So, the graph of g is a vertical stretch
by a factor of 2 and a translation 5 units
left of the graph of f.

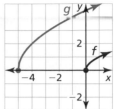

Describe the transformation of f represented by g. Then graph each function.

16. $f(x) = \sqrt{x}$, $g(x) = -2\sqrt{x}$

17. $f(x) = \sqrt[3]{x}$, $g(x) = \sqrt[3]{-x} - 6$

18. Let the graph of g be a reflection in the y-axis, followed by a translation 7 units to the right of the graph of $f(x) = \sqrt[3]{x}$. Write a rule for g.

19. Use a graphing calculator to graph $2y^2 = x - 8$. Identify the vertex and the direction that the parabola opens.

20. Use a graphing calculator to graph $x^2 + y^2 = 81$. Identify the center, radius, and the intercepts.

4.4 Solving Radical Equations and Inequalities (pp. 217–224)

Solve $6\sqrt{x + 2} < 18$.

Step 1 Solve for x.

$6\sqrt{x + 2} < 18$	Write the original inequality.
$\sqrt{x + 2} < 3$	Divide each side by 6.
$x + 2 < 9$	Square each side.
$x < 7$	Subtract 2 from each side.

Step 2 Consider the radicand.

$x + 2 \geq 0$	The radicand cannot be negative.
$x \geq -2$	Subtract 2 from each side.

Check

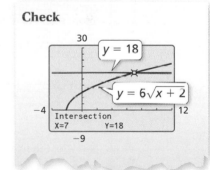

▶ So, the solution is $-2 \leq x < 7$.

Solve the equation. Check your solution(s).

21. $4\sqrt[3]{2x + 1} = 20$

22. $\sqrt{4x - 4} = \sqrt{5x - 1} - 1$

23. $(6x)^{2/3} = 36$

Solve the inequality.

24. $5\sqrt{x} + 2 > 17$

25. $2\sqrt{x - 8} < 24$

26. $7\sqrt[3]{x - 3} \geq 21$

27. In a tsunami, the wave speeds (in meters per second) can be modeled by $s(d) = \sqrt{9.8d}$, where d is the depth (in meters) of the water. Estimate the depth of the water when the wave speed is 200 meters per second.

4.5 Performing Function Operations (pp. 225–230)

Let $f(x) = 2x^{3/2}$ and $g(x) = x^{1/4}$. Find $\left(\dfrac{f}{g}\right)(x)$ and state the domain. Then evaluate the quotient when $x = 81$.

$$\left(\frac{f}{g}\right)(x) = \frac{f(x)}{g(x)} = \frac{2x^{3/2}}{x^{1/4}} = 2x^{(3/2-1/4)} = 2x^{5/4}$$

The functions f and g each have the same domain: all nonnegative real numbers. Because $g(0) = 0$, the domain of $\dfrac{f}{g}$ is restricted to all *positive* real numbers.

When $x = 81$, the value of the quotient is

$$\left(\frac{f}{g}\right)(81) = 2(81)^{5/4} = 2(81^{1/4})^5 = 2(3)^5 = 2(243) = 486.$$

28. Let $f(x) = 2\sqrt{3-x}$ and $g(x) = 4\sqrt[3]{3-x}$. Find $(fg)(x)$ and $\left(\dfrac{f}{g}\right)(x)$ and state the domain of each. Then evaluate $(fg)(2)$ and $\left(\dfrac{f}{g}\right)(2)$.

29. Let $f(x) = 3x^2 + 1$ and $g(x) = x + 4$. Find $(f+g)(x)$ and $(f-g)(x)$ and state the domain of each. Then evaluate $(f+g)(-5)$ and $(f-g)(-5)$.

4.6 Inverse of a Function (pp. 231–240)

Consider the function $f(x) = (x+5)^3$. Determine whether the inverse of f is a function. Then find the inverse.

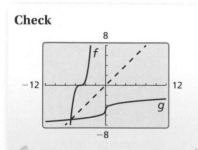

$f(x) = (x + 5)^3$

Graph the function f. Notice that no horizontal line intersects the graph more than once. So, the inverse of f is a function. Find the inverse.

$y = (x + 5)^3$	Set y equal to $f(x)$.
$x = (y + 5)^3$	Switch x and y.
$\sqrt[3]{x} = y + 5$	Take cube root of each side.
$\sqrt[3]{x} - 5 = y$	Subtract 5 from each side.

▶ So, the inverse of f is $g(x) = \sqrt[3]{x} - 5$.

Check

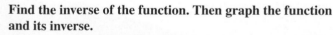

Find the inverse of the function. Then graph the function and its inverse.

30. $f(x) = -\dfrac{1}{2}x + 10$ **31.** $f(x) = x^2 + 8, x \geq 0$

32. $f(x) = -x^3 - 9$ **33.** $f(x) = 3\sqrt{x} + 5$

Determine whether the functions are inverse functions.

34. $f(x) = 4(x - 11)^2,\ g(x) = \dfrac{1}{4}(x + 11)^2$ **35.** $f(x) = -2x + 6,\ g(x) = -\dfrac{1}{2}x + 3$

36. On a certain day, the function that gives U.S. dollars in terms of British pounds is $d = 1.587p$, where d represents U.S. dollars and p represents British pounds. Find the inverse function. Then find the number of British pounds equivalent to 100 U.S. dollars.

4 Chapter Test

1. Solve the inequality $5\sqrt{x-3} - 2 \le 13$ and the equation $5\sqrt{x-3} - 2 = 13$. Describe the similarities and differences in solving radical equations and radical inequalities.

Describe the transformation of f represented by g. Then write a rule for g.

2. $f(x) = \sqrt{x}$

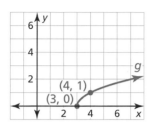

3. $f(x) = \sqrt[3]{x}$

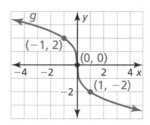

4. $f(x) = \sqrt[5]{x}$

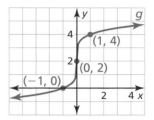

Simplify the expression. Explain your reasoning.

5. $64^{2/3}$

6. $(-27)^{5/3}$

7. $\sqrt[4]{48xy^{11}z^3}$

8. $\dfrac{\sqrt[3]{256}}{\sqrt[3]{32}}$

9. Write two functions whose graphs are translations of the graph of $y = \sqrt{x}$. The first function should have a domain of $x \ge 4$. The second function should have a range of $y \ge -2$.

10. In bowling, a handicap is a change in score to adjust for differences in the abilities of players. You belong to a bowling league in which your handicap h is determined using the formula $h = 0.9(200 - a)$, where a is your average score. Find the inverse of the model. Then find the average score for a bowler whose handicap is 36.

11. The basal metabolic rate of an animal is a measure of the amount of calories burned at rest for basic functioning. Kleiber's law states that an animal's basal metabolic rate R (in kilocalories per day) can be modeled by $R = 73.3w^{3/4}$, where w is the mass (in kilograms) of the animal. Find the basal metabolic rates of each animal in the table.

Animal	Mass (kilograms)
rabbit	2.5
sheep	50
human	70
lion	210

12. Let $f(x) = 6x^{3/5}$ and $g(x) = -x^{3/5}$. Find $(f + g)(x)$ and $(f - g)(x)$ and state the domain of each. Then evaluate $(f + g)(32)$ and $(f - g)(32)$.

13. Let $f(x) = \dfrac{1}{2}x^{3/4}$ and $g(x) = 8x$. Find $(fg)(x)$ and $\left(\dfrac{f}{g}\right)(x)$ and state the domain of each. Then evaluate $(fg)(16)$ and $\left(\dfrac{f}{g}\right)(16)$.

14. A football player jumps to catch a pass. The maximum height h (in feet) of the player above the ground is given by the function $h = \dfrac{1}{64}s^2$, where s is the initial speed (in feet per second) of the player. Find the inverse of the function. Use the inverse to find the initial speed of the player shown. Verify that the functions are inverse functions.

1. Identify three pairs of equivalent expressions. Assume all variables are positive. Justify your answer.

$$a \qquad a^{1/n} \qquad \sqrt[n]{a^n} \qquad a^{-1/n}$$

$$(\sqrt{a})^n \qquad \sqrt{a^n} \qquad \sqrt[n]{a} \qquad a^n$$

2. The graph represents the function $f(x) = \left(x - \boxed{}\right)^2 + \boxed{}$. Choose the correct values to complete the function.

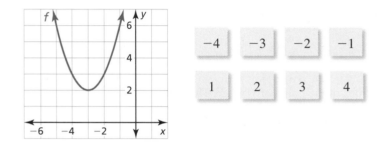

$$-4 \qquad -3 \qquad -2 \qquad -1$$

$$1 \qquad 2 \qquad 3 \qquad 4$$

3. In rowing, the boat speed s (in meters per second) can be modeled by $s = 4.62\sqrt[9]{n}$, where n is the number of rowers.

   a. Find the boat speeds for crews of 2 people, 4 people, and 8 people.

   b. Does the boat speed double when the number of rowers doubles? Explain.

   c. Find the time (in minutes) it takes each crew in part (a) to complete a 2000-meter race.

4. A polynomial function fits the data in the table. Use finite differences to find the degree of the function and complete the table. Explain your reasoning.

x	−4	−3	−2	−1	0	1	2	3
f(x)	28	2	−6	−2	8	18		

5. A city charges $3.70 per 100 cubic feet of water used.

   a. What is the cost of filling the pool to a depth of 3 feet?

   b. There are about 7.48 gallons in 1 cubic foot of water. Express the cost of water in dollars per 100 gallons.

   c. You add water to the 3-foot-deep pool in part (a) until the water is 1 meter deep. The density of water is about 1000 kilograms per cubic meter. What is the mass of the additional water?

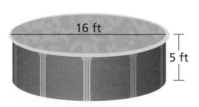

16 ft

5 ft

6. Which equations are represented by parabolas? Which equations are functions? Place check marks in the appropriate spaces. Explain your reasoning.

Equation	Parabola	Function
$y = (x + 3)^2$		
$x = 4y^2 - 2$		
$y = (x - 1)^{1/2} + 6$		
$y^2 = 10 - x^2$		

7. What is the solution of the inequality $2\sqrt{x + 3} - 1 < 3$?

  (A) $x < 1$

  (B) $-3 < x < 1$

  (C) $-3 \le x < 1$

  (D) $x \ge -3$

8. Which function does the graph represent? Explain your reasoning.

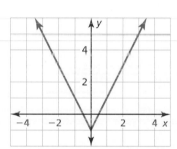

  (A) $y = -|2x| - 1$

  (B) $y = -2|x + 1|$

  (C) $y = |2x| - 1$

  (D) $y = 2|x + 1|$

9. Your friend releases a weather balloon 50 feet from you. The balloon rises vertically. When the balloon is at height h, the distance d between you and the balloon is given by $d = \sqrt{2500 + h^2}$, where h and d are measured in feet. Find the inverse of the function. What is the height of the balloon when the distance between you and the balloon is 100 feet?

10. The graphs of two functions f and g are shown. Are f and g inverse functions? Explain your reasoning.

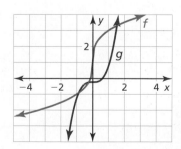

5 Exponential and Logarithmic Functions

Astronaut Health *(p. 295)*

SEE the Big Idea

Cooking *(p. 283)*

Recording Studio *(p. 278)*

Tornado Wind Speed *(p. 263)*

Tritium Decay *(p. 256)*

Maintaining Mathematical Proficiency

Using Exponents

Example 1 Evaluate $\left(-\dfrac{1}{3}\right)^4$.

$$\left(-\dfrac{1}{3}\right)^4 = \left(-\dfrac{1}{3}\right) \cdot \left(-\dfrac{1}{3}\right) \cdot \left(-\dfrac{1}{3}\right) \cdot \left(-\dfrac{1}{3}\right) \qquad \text{Rewrite } \left(-\dfrac{1}{3}\right)^4 \text{ as repeated multiplication.}$$

$$= \left(\dfrac{1}{9}\right) \cdot \left(-\dfrac{1}{3}\right) \cdot \left(-\dfrac{1}{3}\right) \qquad \text{Multiply.}$$

$$= \left(-\dfrac{1}{27}\right) \cdot \left(-\dfrac{1}{3}\right) \qquad \text{Multiply.}$$

$$= \dfrac{1}{81} \qquad \text{Multiply.}$$

Evaluate the expression.

1. $3 \cdot 2^4$

2. $(-2)^5$

3. $-\left(\dfrac{5}{6}\right)^2$

4. $\left(\dfrac{3}{4}\right)^3$

Graphing Exponential Growth and Decay Functions

Example 2 Tell whether (a) $y = 3^x$ and (b) $f(x) = 0.5^x$ represent *exponential growth* or *exponential decay*. Then graph each function.

a. Because the base, 3, is greater than 1, the function represents exponential growth. Use a table to graph the function.

x	-1	0	1	2
y	$\frac{1}{3}$	1	3	9

b. Because the base, 0.5, is less than 1, the function represents exponential decay. Use a table to graph the function.

x	-4	-2	0	2
y	16	4	1	0.25

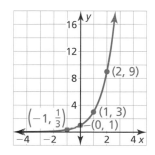

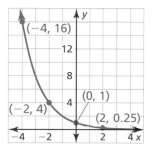

Tell whether the function represents *exponential growth* or *exponential decay*. Then graph the function.

5. $y = 2^x$

6. $f(x) = 1.5^x$

7. $g(x) = 0.9^x$

8. ABSTRACT REASONING Consider the expressions -4^n and $(-4)^n$, where n is an integer. For what values of n is each expression negative? positive? Explain your reasoning.

Mathematical Practices

Mathematically proficient students know when it is appropriate to use general methods and shortcuts.

Exponential Models

⑤ Core Concept

Consecutive Ratio Test for Exponential Models

Consider a table of values of the given form.

x	0	1	2	3	4	5	6	7	8	9
y	a_0	a_1	a_2	a_3	a_4	a_5	a_6	a_7	a_8	a_9

If the consecutive ratios of the *y*-values are all equal to a common value *r*, then *y* can be modeled by an exponential function. When $r > 1$, the model represents exponential *growth*.

$$r = \frac{a_{n+1}}{a_n} \qquad \text{Common ratio}$$

$$y = a_0 r^x \qquad \text{Exponential model}$$

EXAMPLE 1   Modeling Real-Life Data

The table shows the amount *A* (in dollars) in a savings account over time. Write a model for the amount in the account as a function of time *t* (in years). Then use the model to find the amount after 10 years.

Year, t	0	1	2	3	4	5
Amount, A	$1000	$1040	$1081.60	$1124.86	$1169.86	$1216.65

SOLUTION

Begin by determining whether the ratios of consecutive amounts are equal.

$$\frac{1040}{1000} = 1.04, \quad \frac{1081.60}{1040} = 1.04, \quad \frac{1124.86}{1081.60} \approx 1.04, \quad \frac{1169.86}{1124.86} \approx 1.04, \quad \frac{1216.65}{1169.86} \approx 1.04$$

The ratios of consecutive amounts are equal, so the amount *A* after *t* years can be modeled by

$$A = 1000(1.04)^t.$$

Using this model, the amount when $t = 10$ is $A = 1000(1.04)^{10} = \$1480.24$.

Monitoring Progress

Determine whether the data can be modeled by an exponential or linear function. Explain your reasoning. Then write the appropriate model and find *y* when *x* = 10.

1.

x	0	1	2	3	4
y	1	2	4	8	16

2.

x	0	1	2	3	4
y	0	4	8	12	16

3.

x	0	1	2	3	4
y	1	4	7	10	13

4.

x	0	1	2	3	4
y	1	3	9	27	81

5.1 The Natural Base e

Essential Question What is the natural base e?

So far in your study of mathematics, you have worked with special numbers such as π and i. Another special number is called the *natural base* and is denoted by e. The natural base e is irrational, so you cannot find its exact value.

EXPLORATION 1 Approximating the Natural Base e

Work with a partner. One way to approximate the natural base e is to approximate the sum

$$1 + \frac{1}{1} + \frac{1}{1 \cdot 2} + \frac{1}{1 \cdot 2 \cdot 3} + \frac{1}{1 \cdot 2 \cdot 3 \cdot 4} + \cdots.$$

Use a spreadsheet or a graphing calculator to approximate this sum. Explain the steps you used. How many decimal places did you use in your approximation?

EXPLORATION 2 Approximating the Natural Base e

Work with a partner. Another way to approximate the natural base e is to consider the expression

$$\left(1 + \frac{1}{x}\right)^x.$$

As x increases, the value of this expression approaches the value of e. Copy and complete the table. Then use the results in the table to approximate e. Compare this approximation to the one you obtained in Exploration 1.

x	10^1	10^2	10^3	10^4	10^5	10^6
$\left(1 + \frac{1}{x}\right)^x$						

EXPLORATION 3 Graphing a Natural Base Function

Work with a partner. Use your approximate value of e in Exploration 1 or 2 to complete the table. Then sketch the graph of the *natural base exponential function* $y = e^x$. You can use a graphing calculator and the e^x key to check your graph. What are the domain and range of $y = e^x$? Justify your answers.

x	-2	-1	0	1	2
$y = e^x$					

Communicate Your Answer

4. What is the natural base e?

5. Repeat Exploration 3 for the natural base exponential function $y = e^{-x}$. Then compare the graph of $y = e^x$ to the graph of $y = e^{-x}$.

6. The natural base e is used in a wide variety of real-life applications. Use the Internet or some other reference to research some of the real-life applications of e.

> ### USING TOOLS STRATEGICALLY
>
> To be proficient in math, you need to use technological tools to explore and deepen your understanding of concepts.

What You Will Learn

▶ Define and use the natural base e.
▶ Graph natural base functions.
▶ Solve real-life problems.

The Natural Base *e*

The history of mathematics is marked by the discovery of special numbers, such as π and i. Another special number is denoted by the letter e. The number is called the **natural base e**. The expression $\left(1 + \dfrac{1}{x}\right)^x$ approaches e as x increases, as shown in the graph and table.

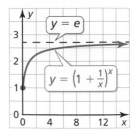

x	10^1	10^2	10^3	10^4	10^5	10^6
$\left(1 + \dfrac{1}{x}\right)^x$	2.59374	2.70481	2.71692	2.71815	2.71827	2.71828

Core Concept

The Natural Base *e*

The natural base e is irrational. It is defined as follows:

As x approaches $+\infty$, $\left(1 + \dfrac{1}{x}\right)^x$ approaches $e \approx 2.71828182846$.

EXAMPLE 1 **Simplifying Natural Base Expressions**

Simplify each expression.

a. $e^3 \cdot e^6$

b. $\dfrac{16e^5}{4e^4}$

c. $(3e^{-4x})^2$

SOLUTION

a. $e^3 \cdot e^6 = e^{3+6}$

$\qquad = e^9$

b. $\dfrac{16e^5}{4e^4} = 4e^{5-4}$

$\qquad = 4e$

c. $(3e^{-4x})^2 = 3^2(e^{-4x})^2$

$\qquad = 9e^{-8x}$

$\qquad = \dfrac{9}{e^{8x}}$

Monitoring Progress Help in English and Spanish at *BigIdeasMath.com*

Simplify the expression.

1. $e^7 \cdot e^4$

2. $\dfrac{24e^8}{8e^5}$

3. $(10e^{-3x})^3$

Graphing Natural Base Functions

⚙ Core Concept

Natural Base Functions

A function of the form $y = ae^{rx}$ is called a *natural base exponential function*.

- When $a > 0$ and $r > 0$, the function is an exponential growth function.

- When $a > 0$ and $r < 0$, the function is an exponential decay function.

The graphs of the basic functions $y = e^x$ and $y = e^{-x}$ are shown.

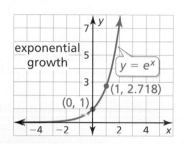

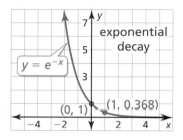

REMEMBER

An *asymptote* is a line that a graph approaches more and more closely. In the graphs of these natural base exponential functions, the line $y = 0$ is an asymptote.

EXAMPLE 2 Graphing Natural Base Functions

Tell whether each function represents *exponential growth* or *exponential decay*. Then graph the function.

a. $y = 3e^x$

b. $f(x) = e^{-0.5x}$

SOLUTION

a. Because $a = 3$ is positive and $r = 1$ is positive, the function is an exponential growth function. Use a table to graph the function.

x	-2	-1	0	1
y	0.41	1.10	3	8.15

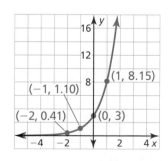

b. Because $a = 1$ is positive and $r = -0.5$ is negative, the function is an exponential decay function. Use a table to graph the function.

x	-4	-2	0	2
y	7.39	2.72	1	0.37

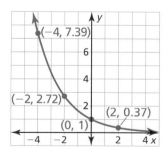

LOOKING FOR STRUCTURE

You can rewrite natural base exponential functions to find percent rates of change. In Example 2(b),

$$f(x) = e^{-0.5x}$$
$$= (e^{-0.5})^x$$
$$\approx (0.6065)^x$$
$$= (1 - 0.3935)^x.$$

So, the percent decrease is about 39.35%.

Monitoring Progress Help in English and Spanish at *BigIdeasMath.com*

Tell whether the function represents *exponential growth* or *exponential decay*. Then graph the function.

4. $y = \frac{1}{2}e^x$

5. $y = 4e^{-x}$

6. $f(x) = 2e^{2x}$

Solving Real-Life Problems

You have learned that the balance of an account earning compound interest is given by $A = P\left(1 + \dfrac{r}{n}\right)^{nt}$. As the frequency n of compounding approaches positive infinity, the compound interest formula approximates the following formula.

Core Concept

Continuously Compounded Interest

When interest is compounded *continuously*, the amount A in an account after t years is given by the formula

$$A = Pe^{rt}$$

where P is the principal and r is the annual interest rate expressed as a decimal.

EXAMPLE 3   **Modeling with Mathematics**

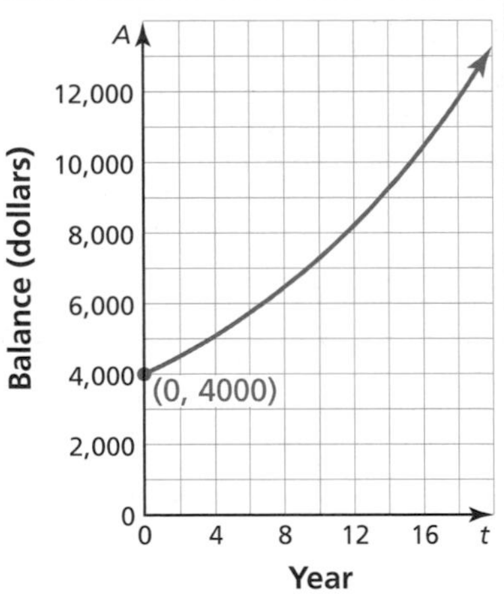

You and your friend each have accounts that earn annual interest compounded continuously. The balance A (in dollars) of your account after t years can be modeled by $A = 4500e^{0.04t}$. The graph shows the balance of your friend's account over time. Which account has a greater principal? Which has a greater balance after 10 years?

SOLUTION

Your Friend's Account

(graph: Balance (dollars) vs. Year, passing through $(0, 4000)$)

1. **Understand the Problem** You are given a graph and an equation that represent account balances. You are asked to identify the account with the greater principal and the account with the greater balance after 10 years.

2. **Make a Plan** Use the equation to find your principal and account balance after 10 years. Then compare these values to the graph of your friend's account.

3. **Solve the Problem** The equation $A = 4500e^{0.04t}$ is of the form $A = Pe^{rt}$, where $P = 4500$. So, your principal is \$4500. Your balance A when $t = 10$ is

$$A = 4500e^{0.04(10)} = \$6713.21.$$

Because the graph passes through $(0, 4000)$, your friend's principal is \$4000. The graph also shows that the balance is about \$7250 when $t = 10$.

▶ So, your account has a greater principal, but your friend's account has a greater balance after 10 years.

4. **Look Back** Because your friend's account has a lesser principal but a greater balance after 10 years, the average rate of change from $t = 0$ to $t = 10$ should be greater for your friend's account than for your account.

> **MAKING CONJECTURES**
>
> You can also use this reasoning to conclude that your friend's account has a greater annual interest rate than your account.

Your account: $\dfrac{A(10) - A(0)}{10 - 0} = \dfrac{6713.21 - 4500}{10} = 221.321$

Your friend's account: $\dfrac{A(10) - A(0)}{10 - 0} \approx \dfrac{7250 - 4000}{10} = 325$ ✔

Monitoring Progress  Help in English and Spanish at *BigIdeasMath.com*

7. You deposit \$4250 in an account that earns 5% annual interest compounded continuously. Compare the balance after 10 years with the accounts in Example 3.

Vocabulary and Core Concept Check

1. **VOCABULARY** What is the Euler number?

2. **WRITING** Tell whether the function $f(x) = \frac{1}{3}e^{4x}$ represents exponential growth or exponential decay. Explain.

Monitoring Progress and Modeling with Mathematics

In Exercises 3–12, simplify the expression. *(See Example 1.)*

3. $e^3 \cdot e^5$

4. $e^{-4} \cdot e^6$

5. $\dfrac{11e^9}{22e^{10}}$

6. $\dfrac{27e^7}{3e^4}$

7. $(5e^{7x})^4$

8. $(4e^{-2x})^3$

9. $\sqrt{9e^{6x}}$

10. $\sqrt[3]{8e^{12x}}$

11. $e^x \cdot e^{-6x} \cdot e^8$

12. $e^x \cdot e^4 \cdot e^{x+3}$

ERROR ANALYSIS In Exercises 13 and 14, describe and correct the error in simplifying the expression.

13.
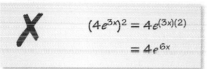
$$(4e^{3x})^2 = 4e^{(3x)(2)}$$
$$= 4e^{6x}$$

14.
$$\frac{e^{5x}}{e^{-2x}} = e^{5x-2x}$$
$$= e^{3x}$$

In Exercises 15–22, tell whether the function represents *exponential growth* or *exponential decay*. Then graph the function. *(See Example 2.)*

15. $y = e^{3x}$

16. $y = e^{-2x}$

17. $y = 2e^{-x}$

18. $y = 3e^{2x}$

19. $y = 0.5e^x$

20. $y = 0.25e^{-3x}$

21. $y = 0.4e^{-0.25x}$

22. $y = 0.6e^{0.5x}$

ANALYZING EQUATIONS In Exercises 23–26, match the function with its graph. Explain your reasoning.

23. $y = e^{2x}$

24. $y = e^{-2x}$

25. $y = 4e^{-0.5x}$

26. $y = 0.75e^x$

A.
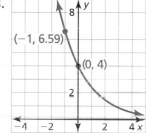

B.
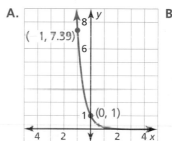

C.
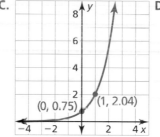

D.
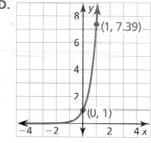

USING STRUCTURE In Exercises 27–30, use the properties of exponents to rewrite the function in the form $y = a(1 + r)^t$ or $y = a(1 - r)^t$. Then find the percent rate of change.

27. $y = e^{-0.25t}$

28. $y = e^{-0.75t}$

29. $y = 2e^{0.4t}$

30. $y = 0.5e^{0.8t}$

USING TOOLS In Exercises 31–34, use a table of values or a graphing calculator to graph the function. Then identify the domain and range.

31. $y = e^{x-2}$

32. $y = e^{x+1}$

33. $y = 2e^x + 1$

34. $y = 3e^x - 5$

35. **MODELING WITH MATHEMATICS** Investment accounts for a house and education earn annual interest compounded continuously. The balance H (in dollars) of the house fund after t years can be modeled by $H = 3224e^{0.05t}$. The graph shows the balance in the education fund over time. Which account has the greater principal? Which account has a greater balance after 10 years? *(See Example 3.)*

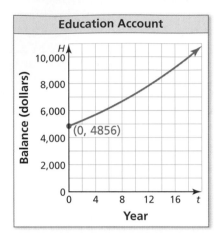

Education Account

36. **MODELING WITH MATHEMATICS** Tritium is an isotope of hydrogen that can be used to illuminate watches. Tritium and sodium-22 decay over time. In a sample of tritium, the amount y (in milligrams) remaining after t years is given by $y = 10e^{-0.0562t}$. The graph shows the amount of sodium-22 in a sample over time. Which sample started with a greater amount? Which has a greater amount after 10 years?

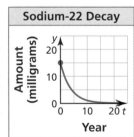

Sodium-22 Decay

37. **OPEN-ENDED** Find values of a, b, r, and q such that $f(x) = ae^{rx}$ and $g(x) = be^{qx}$ are exponential decay functions, but $\dfrac{f(x)}{g(x)}$ represents exponential growth.

38. **THOUGHT PROVOKING** Explain why $A = P\left(1 + \dfrac{r}{n}\right)^{nt}$ approximates $A = Pe^{rt}$ as n approaches positive infinity.

39. **WRITING** Can the natural base e be written as a ratio of two integers? Explain.

40. **MAKING AN ARGUMENT** Your friend evaluates $f(x) = e^{-x}$ when $x = 1000$ and concludes that the graph of $y = f(x)$ has an x-intercept at $(1000, 0)$. Is your friend correct? Explain your reasoning.

41. **DRAWING CONCLUSIONS** You invest \$2500 in an account to save for college. Account 1 pays 6% annual interest compounded quarterly. Account 2 pays 4% annual interest compounded continuously. Which account should you choose to obtain the greater amount in 10 years? Justify your answer.

42. **HOW DO YOU SEE IT?** Use the graph to complete each statement.

    a. $f(x)$ approaches ____ as x approaches $+\infty$.

    b. $f(x)$ approaches ____ as x approaches $-\infty$.

    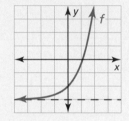

43. **PROBLEM SOLVING** The growth of *Mycobacterium tuberculosis* bacteria can be modeled by the function $N(t) = ae^{0.166t}$, where N is the number of cells after t hours and a is the number of cells when $t = 0$.

    a. At 1:00 P.M., there are 30 *M. tuberculosis* bacteria in a sample. Write a function that gives the number of bacteria after 1:00 P.M.

    b. Use a graphing calculator to graph the function in part (a).

    c. Describe how to find the number of cells in the sample at 3:45 P.M.

Maintaining Mathematical Proficiency
Reviewing what you learned in previous grades and lessons

Write the number in scientific notation. *(Skills Review Handbook)*

44. 0.006

45. 5000

46. 26,000,000

47. 0.000000047

Find the inverse of the function. Then graph the function and its inverse. *(Section 4.6)*

48. $y = 3x + 5$

49. $y = x^2 - 1, x \le 0$

50. $y = \sqrt{x + 6}$

51. $y = x^3 - 2$

Essential Question What are some of the characteristics of the graph of a logarithmic function?

Every exponential function of the form $f(x) = b^x$, where b is a positive real number other than 1, has an inverse function that you can denote by $g(x) = \log_b x$. This inverse function is called a *logarithmic function with base b*.

EXPLORATION 1   Rewriting Exponential Equations

Work with a partner. Find the value of x in each exponential equation. Explain your reasoning. Then use the value of x to rewrite the exponential equation in its equivalent logarithmic form, $x = \log_b y$.

a. $2^x = 8$ b. $3^x = 9$ c. $4^x = 2$

d. $5^x = 1$ e. $5^x = \frac{1}{5}$ f. $8^x = 4$

EXPLORATION 2   Graphing Exponential and Logarithmic Functions

Work with a partner. Complete each table for the given exponential function. Use the results to complete the table for the given logarithmic function. Explain your reasoning. Then sketch the graphs of f and g in the same coordinate plane.

a.

x	-2	-1	0	1	2
$f(x) = 2^x$					

x					
$g(x) = \log_2 x$	-2	-1	0	1	2

b.

x	-2	-1	0	1	2
$f(x) = 10^x$					

x					
$g(x) = \log_{10} x$	-2	-1	0	1	2

CONSTRUCTING VIABLE ARGUMENTS

To be proficient in math, you need to justify your conclusions and communicate them to others.

EXPLORATION 3   Characteristics of Graphs of Logarithmic Functions

Work with a partner. Use the graphs you sketched in Exploration 2 to determine the domain, range, x-intercept, and asymptote of the graph of $g(x) = \log_b x$, where b is a positive real number other than 1. Explain your reasoning.

Communicate Your Answer

4. What are some of the characteristics of the graph of a logarithmic function?

5. How can you use the graph of an exponential function to obtain the graph of a logarithmic function?

Core Vocabulary

logarithm of y with base b, *p. 258*
common logarithm, *p. 259*
natural logarithm, *p. 259*

Previous
inverse functions

What You Will Learn

▶ Define and evaluate logarithms.
▶ Use inverse properties of logarithmic and exponential functions.
▶ Graph logarithmic functions.

Logarithms

You know that $2^2 = 4$ and $2^3 = 8$. However, for what value of x does $2^x = 6$? Mathematicians define this x-value using a *logarithm* and write $x = \log_2 6$. The definition of a logarithm can be generalized as follows.

⑤ Core Concept

Definition of Logarithm with Base b

Let b and y be positive real numbers with $b \neq 1$. The **logarithm of y with base b** is denoted by $\log_b y$ and is defined as

$$\log_b y = x \qquad \text{if and only if} \qquad b^x = y.$$

The expression $\log_b y$ is read as "log base b of y."

This definition tells you that the equations $\log_b y = x$ and $b^x = y$ are equivalent. The first is in *logarithmic form*, and the second is in *exponential form*.

EXAMPLE 1 Rewriting Logarithmic Equations

Rewrite each equation in exponential form.

a. $\log_2 16 = 4$ **b.** $\log_4 1 = 0$ **c.** $\log_{12} 12 = 1$ **d.** $\log_{1/4} 4 = -1$

SOLUTION

Logarithmic Form	**Exponential Form**
a. $\log_2 16 = 4$	$2^4 = 16$
b. $\log_4 1 = 0$	$4^0 = 1$
c. $\log_{12} 12 = 1$	$12^1 = 12$
d. $\log_{1/4} 4 = -1$	$\left(\frac{1}{4}\right)^{-1} = 4$

EXAMPLE 2 Rewriting Exponential Equations

Rewrite each equation in logarithmic form.

a. $5^2 = 25$ **b.** $10^{-1} = 0.1$ **c.** $8^{2/3} = 4$ **d.** $6^{-3} = \frac{1}{216}$

SOLUTION

Exponential Form	**Logarithmic Form**
a. $5^2 = 25$	$\log_5 25 = 2$
b. $10^{-1} = 0.1$	$\log_{10} 0.1 = -1$
c. $8^{2/3} = 4$	$\log_8 4 = \frac{2}{3}$
d. $6^{-3} = \frac{1}{216}$	$\log_6 \frac{1}{216} = -3$

Parts (b) and (c) of Example 1 illustrate two special logarithm values that you should learn to recognize. Let b be a positive real number such that $b \neq 1$.

Logarithm of 1

$\log_b 1 = 0$ because $b^0 = 1$.

Logarithm of b with Base b

$\log_b b = 1$ because $b^1 = b$.

EXAMPLE 3 Evaluating Logarithmic Expressions

Evaluate each logarithm.

a. $\log_4 64$ **b.** $\log_5 0.2$ **c.** $\log_{1/5} 125$ **d.** $\log_{36} 6$

SOLUTION

To help you find the value of $\log_b y$, ask yourself what power of b gives you y.

a. What power of 4 gives you 64? $4^3 = 64$, so $\log_4 64 = 3$.

b. What power of 5 gives you 0.2? $5^{-1} = 0.2$, so $\log_5 0.2 = -1$.

c. What power of $\frac{1}{5}$ gives you 125? $\left(\frac{1}{5}\right)^{-3} = 125$, so $\log_{1/5} 125 = -3$.

d. What power of 36 gives you 6? $36^{1/2} = 6$, so $\log_{36} 6 = \frac{1}{2}$.

A **common logarithm** is a logarithm with base 10. It is denoted by $\log_{10}$ or simply by log. A **natural logarithm** is a logarithm with base e. It can be denoted by $\log_e$ but is usually denoted by ln.

Common Logarithm

$\log_{10} x = \log x$

Natural Logarithm

$\log_e x = \ln x$

EXAMPLE 4 Evaluating Common and Natural Logarithms

Evaluate (a) log 8 and (b) ln 0.3 using a calculator. Round your answer to three decimal places.

SOLUTION

Check

```
10^(0.903)
        7.99834255
e^(-1.204)
        .2999918414
```

Most calculators have keys for evaluating common and natural logarithms.

a. $\log 8 \approx 0.903$

b. $\ln 0.3 \approx -1.204$

Check your answers by rewriting each logarithm in exponential form and evaluating.

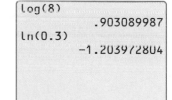

```
log(8)
        .903089987
ln(0.3)
       -1.203972804
```

Monitoring Progress Help in English and Spanish at *BigIdeasMath.com*

Rewrite the equation in exponential form.

1. $\log_3 81 = 4$ **2.** $\log_7 7 = 1$ **3.** $\log_{14} 1 = 0$ **4.** $\log_{1/2} 32 = -5$

Rewrite the equation in logarithmic form.

5. $7^2 = 49$ **6.** $50^0 = 1$ **7.** $4^{-1} = \frac{1}{4}$ **8.** $256^{1/8} = 2$

Evaluate the logarithm. If necessary, use a calculator and round your answer to three decimal places.

9. $\log_2 32$ **10.** $\log_{27} 3$ **11.** $\log 12$ **12.** $\ln 0.75$

Using Inverse Properties

By the definition of a logarithm, it follows that the logarithmic function $g(x) = \log_b x$ is the inverse of the exponential function $f(x) = b^x$. This means that

$$g(f(x)) = \log_b b^x = x \quad \text{and} \quad f(g(x)) = b^{\log_b x} = x.$$

In other words, exponential functions and logarithmic functions "undo" each other.

EXAMPLE 5   Using Inverse Properties

Simplify (a) $10^{\log 4}$ and (b) $\log_5 25^x$.

SOLUTION

a. $10^{\log 4} = 4$ $\qquad\qquad\qquad\qquad$ $b^{\log_b x} = x$

b. $\log_5 25^x = \log_5(5^2)^x$ $\qquad\qquad$ Express 25 as a power with base 5.

$\qquad\quad = \log_5 5^{2x}$ $\qquad\qquad\quad$ Power of a Power Property

$\qquad\quad = 2x$ $\qquad\qquad\qquad\quad$ $\log_b b^x = x$

EXAMPLE 6   Finding Inverse Functions

Find the inverse of each function.

a. $f(x) = 6^x$ $\qquad\qquad\qquad\qquad\qquad$ **b.** $y = \ln(x + 3)$

SOLUTION

a. From the definition of logarithm, the inverse of $f(x) = 6^x$ is $g(x) = \log_6 x$.

b. $\qquad y = \ln(x + 3)$ $\qquad\qquad$ Write original function.

$\qquad\quad x = \ln(y + 3)$ $\qquad\qquad$ Switch x and y.

$\qquad\quad e^x = y + 3$ $\qquad\qquad\quad$ Write in exponential form.

$\quad e^x - 3 = y$ $\qquad\qquad\qquad$ Subtract 3 from each side.

▶ The inverse of $y = \ln(x + 3)$ is $y = e^x - 3$.

Check

a. $f(g(x)) = 6^{\log_6 x} = x$ ✔ $\qquad\qquad$ **b.**

$\quad\; g(f(x)) = \log_6 6^x = x$ ✔

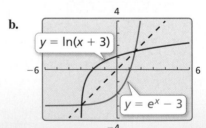

The graphs appear to be reflections of each other in the line $y = x$. ✔

Monitoring Progress Help in English and Spanish at *BigIdeasMath.com*

Simplify the expression.

13. $8^{\log_8 x}$ $\qquad$ **14.** $\log_7 7^{-3x}$ $\qquad$ **15.** $\log_2 64^x$ $\qquad$ **16.** $e^{\ln 20}$

17. Find the inverse of $y = 4^x$. $\qquad\qquad$ **18.** Find the inverse of $y = \ln(x - 5)$.

Graphing Logarithmic Functions

You can use the inverse relationship between exponential and logarithmic functions to graph logarithmic functions.

Core Concept

Parent Graphs for Logarithmic Functions

The graph of $f(x) = \log_b x$ is shown below for $b > 1$ and for $0 < b < 1$. Because $f(x) = \log_b x$ and $g(x) = b^x$ are inverse functions, the graph of $f(x) = \log_b x$ is the reflection of the graph of $g(x) = b^x$ in the line $y = x$.

Graph of $f(x) = \log_b x$ for $b > 1$ **Graph of $f(x) = \log_b x$ for $0 < b < 1$**

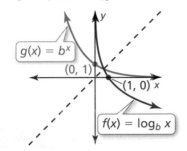

Note that the y-axis is a vertical asymptote of the graph of $f(x) = \log_b x$. The domain of $f(x) = \log_b x$ is $x > 0$, and the range is all real numbers.

EXAMPLE 7   Graphing a Logarithmic Function

Graph $f(x) = \log_3 x$.

SOLUTION

Step 1 Find the inverse of f. From the definition of logarithm, the inverse of $f(x) = \log_3 x$ is $g(x) = 3^x$.

Step 2 Make a table of values for $g(x) = 3^x$.

x	-2	-1	0	1	2
g(x)	$\frac{1}{9}$	$\frac{1}{3}$	1	3	9

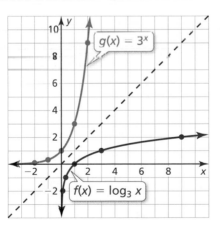

Step 3 Plot the points from the table and connect them with a smooth curve.

Step 4 Because $f(x) = \log_3 x$ and $g(x) = 3^x$ are inverse functions, the graph of f is obtained by reflecting the graph of g in the line $y = x$. To do this, reverse the coordinates of the points on g and plot these new points on the graph of f.

Monitoring Progress Help in English and Spanish at *BigIdeasMath.com*

Graph the function.

19. $y = \log_2 x$ **20.** $f(x) = \log_5 x$ **21.** $y = \log_{1/2} x$

Vocabulary and Core Concept Check

1. **COMPLETE THE SENTENCE** A logarithm with base 10 is called a(n) _____ logarithm.

2. **COMPLETE THE SENTENCE** The expression $\log_3 9$ is read as _____.

3. **WRITING** Describe the relationship between $y = 7^x$ and $y = \log_7 x$.

4. **DIFFERENT WORDS, SAME QUESTION** Which is different? Find "both" answers.

What power of 4 gives you 16?	What is log base 4 of 16?
Evaluate 4^2.	Evaluate $\log_4 16$.

Monitoring Progress and Modeling with Mathematics

In Exercises 5–10, rewrite the equation in exponential form. *(See Example 1.)*

5. $\log_3 9 = 2$

6. $\log_4 4 = 1$

7. $\log_6 1 = 0$

8. $\log_7 343 = 3$

9. $\log_{1/2} 16 = -4$

10. $\log_3 \frac{1}{3} = -1$

In Exercises 11–16, rewrite the equation in logarithmic form. *(See Example 2.)*

11. $6^2 = 36$

12. $12^0 = 1$

13. $16^{-1} = \frac{1}{16}$

14. $5^{-2} = \frac{1}{25}$

15. $125^{2/3} = 25$

16. $49^{1/2} = 7$

In Exercises 17–24, evaluate the logarithm. *(See Example 3.)*

17. $\log_3 81$

18. $\log_7 49$

19. $\log_3 3$

20. $\log_{1/2} 1$

21. $\log_5 \frac{1}{625}$

22. $\log_8 \frac{1}{512}$

23. $\log_4 0.25$

24. $\log_{10} 0.001$

25. **NUMBER SENSE** Order the logarithms from least value to greatest value.

$\log_5 23$	$\log_6 38$	$\log_7 8$	$\log_2 10$

26. **WRITING** Explain why the expressions $\log_2(-1)$ and $\log_1 1$ are not defined.

In Exercises 27–32, evaluate the logarithm using a calculator. Round your answer to three decimal places. *(See Example 4.)*

27. $\log 6$

28. $\ln 12$

29. $\ln \frac{1}{3}$

30. $\log \frac{2}{7}$

31. $3 \ln 0.5$

32. $\log 0.6 + 1$

33. **MODELING WITH MATHEMATICS** Skydivers use an instrument called an *altimeter* to track their altitude as they fall. The altimeter determines altitude by measuring air pressure. The altitude h (in meters) above sea level is related to the air pressure P (in pascals) by the function shown in the diagram. What is the altitude above sea level when the air pressure is 57,000 pascals?

$h = -8005 \ln \dfrac{P}{101,300}$

$h = 7438$ m
$P = 40,000$ Pa

$h = 3552$ m
$P = 65,000$ Pa

$h = ?$
$P = 57,000$ Pa

Not drawn to scale

34. **MODELING WITH MATHEMATICS** The pH value for a substance measures how acidic or alkaline the substance is. It is given by the formula pH = $-\log[\text{H}^+]$, where H^+ is the hydrogen ion concentration (in moles per liter). Find the pH of each substance.

a. baking soda: $[\text{H}^+] = 10^{-8}$ moles per liter

b. vinegar: $[\text{H}^+] = 10^{-3}$ moles per liter

In Exercises 35–40, simplify the expression.
(See Example 5.)

35. $7^{\log_7 x}$

36. $3^{\log_3 5x}$

37. $e^{\ln 4}$

38. $10^{\log 15}$

39. $\log_3 3^{2x}$

40. $\ln e^{x+1}$

41. ERROR ANALYSIS Describe and correct the error in rewriting $4^{-3} = \frac{1}{64}$ in logarithmic form.

 $\log_4 (-3) = \dfrac{1}{64}$

42. ERROR ANALYSIS Describe and correct the error in simplifying the expression $\log_4 64^x$.

$$\log_4 64^x = \log_4(16 \cdot 4^x)$$
$$= \log_4(4^2 \cdot 4^x)$$
$$= \log_4 4^{2+x}$$
$$= 2 + x$$

In Exercises 43–52, find the inverse of the function.
(See Example 6.)

43. $y = 0.3^x$

44. $y = 11^x$

45. $y = \log_2 x$

46. $y = \log_{1/5} x$

47. $y = \ln(x - 1)$

48. $y = \ln 2x$

49. $y = e^{3x}$

50. $y = e^{x-4}$

51. $y = 5^x - 9$

52. $y = 13 + \log x$

53. PROBLEM SOLVING The wind speed s (in miles per hour) near the center of a tornado can be modeled by $s = 93 \log d + 65$, where d is the distance (in miles) that the tornado travels.

  a. In 1925, a tornado traveled 220 miles through three states. Estimate the wind speed near the center of the tornado.

  b. Find the inverse of the given function. Describe what the inverse represents.

54. MODELING WITH MATHEMATICS The energy magnitude M of an earthquake can be modeled by $M = \frac{2}{3} \log E - 9.9$, where E is the amount of energy released (in ergs).

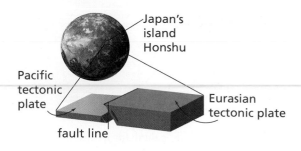

Japan's island Honshu

Pacific tectonic plate

Eurasian tectonic plate

fault line

  a. In 2011, a powerful earthquake in Japan, caused by the slippage of two tectonic plates along a fault, released 2.24×10^{28} ergs. What was the energy magnitude of the earthquake?

  b. Find the inverse of the given function. Describe what the inverse represents.

In Exercises 55–60, graph the function. *(See Example 7.)*

55. $y = \log_4 x$

56. $y = \log_6 x$

57. $y = \log_{1/3} x$

58. $y = \log_{1/4} x$

59. $y = \log_2 x - 1$

60. $y = \log_3(x + 2)$

USING TOOLS In Exercises 61–64, use a graphing calculator to graph the function. Determine the domain, range, and asymptote of the function.

61. $y = \log(x + 2)$

62. $y = -\ln x$

63. $y = \ln(-x)$

64. $y = 3 - \log x$

65. MAKING AN ARGUMENT Your friend states that every logarithmic function of the form $y = \log_b x$ will pass through the point $(1, 0)$. Is your friend correct? Explain your reasoning.

66. ANALYZING RELATIONSHIPS Rank the functions in order from the least average rate of change to the greatest average rate of change over the interval $1 \le x \le 10$.

  a. $y = \log_6 x$

  b. $y = \log_{3/5} x$

  c.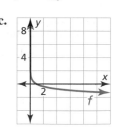

  d.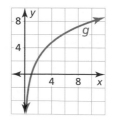

67. PROBLEM SOLVING Biologists have found that the length ℓ (in inches) of an alligator and its weight w (in pounds) are related by the function $\ell = 27.1 \ln w - 32.8$.

a. Use a graphing calculator to graph the function.

b. Use your graph to estimate the weight of an alligator that is 10 feet long.

c. Use the *zero* feature to find the x-intercept of the graph of the function. Does this x-value make sense in the context of the situation? Explain.

68. HOW DO YOU SEE IT? The figure shows the graphs of the two functions f and g.

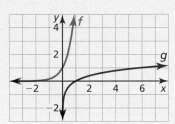

a. Compare the end behavior of the logarithmic function g to that of the exponential function f.

b. Determine whether the functions are inverse functions. Explain.

c. What is the base of each function? Explain.

69. PROBLEM SOLVING A study in Florida found that the number s of fish species in a pool or lake can be modeled by the function

$$s = 30.6 - 20.5 \log A + 3.8(\log A)^2$$

where A is the area (in square meters) of the pool or lake.

a. Use a graphing calculator to graph the function on the domain $200 \leq A \leq 35{,}000$.

b. Use your graph to estimate the number of species in a lake with an area of 30,000 square meters.

c. Use your graph to estimate the area of a lake that contains six species of fish.

d. Describe what happens to the number of fish species as the area of a pool or lake increases. Explain why your answer makes sense.

70. THOUGHT PROVOKING Write a logarithmic function that has an output of -4. Then sketch the graph of your function.

71. CRITICAL THINKING Evaluate each logarithm. (*Hint*: For each logarithm $\log_b x$, rewrite b and x as powers of the same base.)

a. $\log_{125} 25$ b. $\log_8 32$

c. $\log_{27} 81$ d. $\log_4 128$

Maintaining Mathematical Proficiency
Reviewing what you learned in previous grades and lessons

Let $f(x) = \sqrt[3]{x}$. Write a rule for g that represents the indicated transformation of the graph of f.
(Section 4.3)

72. $g(x) = -f(x)$ **73.** $g(x) = f\left(\frac{1}{2}x\right)$

74. $g(x) = f(-x) + 3$ **75.** $g(x) = f(x + 2)$

Identify the function family to which f belongs. Compare the graph of f to the graph of its parent function. *(Section 2.1)*

76. 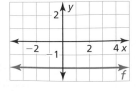   **77.** 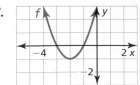   **78.**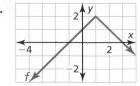

5.3 Transformations of Exponential and Logarithmic Functions

Essential Question How can you transform the graphs of exponential and logarithmic functions?

EXPLORATION 1 **Identifying Transformations**

Work with a partner. Each graph shown is a transformation of the parent function

$$f(x) = e^x \quad \text{or} \quad f(x) = \ln x.$$

Match each function with its graph. Explain your reasoning. Then describe the transformation of f represented by g.

a. $g(x) = e^{x+2} - 3$ **b.** $g(x) = -e^{x+2} + 1$ **c.** $g(x) = e^{x-2} - 1$

d. $g(x) = \ln(x + 2)$ **e.** $g(x) = 2 + \ln x$ **f.** $g(x) = 2 + \ln(-x)$

A.

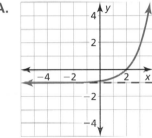

B.

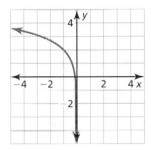

C.

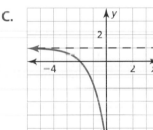

D.

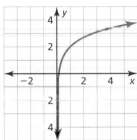

E.

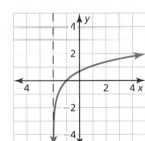

F.

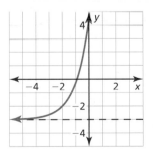

EXPLORATION 2 **Characteristics of Graphs**

REASONING QUANTITATIVELY

To be proficient in math, you need to make sense of quantities and their relationships in problem situations.

Work with a partner. Determine the domain, range, and asymptote of each function in Exploration 1. Justify your answers.

Communicate Your Answer

3. How can you transform the graphs of exponential and logarithmic functions?

4. Find the inverse of each function in Exploration 1. Then check your answer by using a graphing calculator to graph each function and its inverse in the same viewing window.

What You Will Learn

▶ Transform graphs of exponential functions.

▶ Transform graphs of logarithmic functions.

▶ Write transformations of graphs of exponential and logarithmic functions.

Transforming Graphs of Exponential Functions

You can transform graphs of exponential and logarithmic functions in the same way you transformed graphs of functions in previous chapters. Examples of transformations of the graph of $f(x) = 4^x$ are shown below.

⟳ Core Concept

Transformation	$f(x)$ Notation	Examples	
Horizontal Translation Graph shifts left or right.	$f(x - h)$	$g(x) = 4^{x-3}$	3 units right
		$g(x) = 4^{x+2}$	2 units left
Vertical Translation Graph shifts up or down.	$f(x) + k$	$g(x) = 4^x + 5$	5 units up
		$g(x) = 4^x - 1$	1 unit down
Reflection Graph flips over x- or y-axis.	$f(-x)$ $-f(x)$	$g(x) = 4^{-x}$	in the y-axis
		$g(x) = -4^x$	in the x-axis
Horizontal Stretch or Shrink Graph stretches away from or shrinks toward y-axis.	$f(ax)$	$g(x) = 4^{2x}$	shrink by a factor of $\frac{1}{2}$
		$g(x) = 4^{x/2}$	stretch by a factor of 2
Vertical Stretch or Shrink Graph stretches away from or shrinks toward x-axis.	$a \cdot f(x)$	$g(x) = 3(4^x)$	stretch by a factor of 3
		$g(x) = \frac{1}{4}(4^x)$	shrink by a factor of $\frac{1}{4}$

EXAMPLE 1   **Translating an Exponential Function**

Describe the transformation of $f(x) = \left(\dfrac{1}{2}\right)^x$ represented by $g(x) = \left(\dfrac{1}{2}\right)^x - 4$.

Then graph each function.

SOLUTION

Notice that the function is of the form $g(x) = \left(\dfrac{1}{2}\right)^x + k$.

STUDY TIP

Notice in the graph that the vertical translation also shifted the asymptote 4 units down, so the range of g is $y > -4$.

Rewrite the function to identify k.

$$g(x) = \left(\frac{1}{2}\right)^x + (-4)$$

$$\uparrow$$
$$k$$

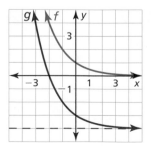

▶ Because $k = -4$, the graph of g is a translation 4 units down of the graph of f.

EXAMPLE 2 **Translating a Natural Base Exponential Function**

Describe the transformation of $f(x) = e^x$ represented by $g(x) = e^{x+3} + 2$. Then graph each function.

SOLUTION

STUDY TIP

Notice in the graph that the vertical translation also shifted the asymptote 2 units up, so the range of g is $y > 2$.

Notice that the function is of the form $g(x) = e^{x-h} + k$. Rewrite the function to identify h and k.

$$g(x) = e^{x-(-3)} + 2$$
$$\phantom{g(x) = e^{x-}}\uparrow \uparrow$$
$$\phantom{g(x) = e^{x-}}h k$$

▶ Because $h = -3$ and $k = 2$, the graph of g is a translation 3 units left and 2 units up of the graph of f.

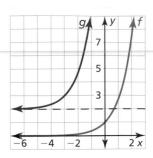

EXAMPLE 3 **Transforming Exponential Functions**

Describe the transformation of f represented by g. Then graph each function.

a. $f(x) = 3^x$, $g(x) = 3^{3x-5}$

b. $f(x) = e^{-x}$, $g(x) = -\frac{1}{8}e^{-x}$

LOOKING FOR STRUCTURE

In Example 3(a), the horizontal shrink follows the translation. In the function $h(x) = 3^{3(x-5)}$, the translation 5 units right follows the horizontal shrink by a factor of $\frac{1}{3}$.

SOLUTION

a. Notice that the function is of the form $g(x) = 3^{ax-h}$, where $a = 3$ and $h = 5$.

▶ So, the graph of g is a translation 5 units right, followed by a horizontal shrink by a factor of $\frac{1}{3}$ of the graph of f.

b. Notice that the function is of the form $g(x) = ae^{-x}$, where $a = -\frac{1}{8}$.

▶ So, the graph of g is a reflection in the x-axis and a vertical shrink by a factor of $\frac{1}{8}$ of the graph of f.

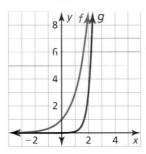

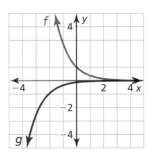

Monitoring Progress Help in English and Spanish at *BigIdeasMath.com*

Describe the transformation of f represented by g. Then graph each function.

1. $f(x) = 2^x$, $g(x) = 2^{x-3} + 1$

2. $f(x) = e^{-x}$, $g(x) = e^{-x} - 5$

3. $f(x) = 0.4^x$, $g(x) = 0.4^{-2x}$

4. $f(x) = e^x$, $g(x) = -e^{x+6}$

Transforming Graphs of Logarithmic Functions

Examples of transformations of the graph of $f(x) = \log x$ are shown below.

⑤ Core Concept

Transformation	$f(x)$ Notation	Examples	
Horizontal Translation Graph shifts left or right.	$f(x - h)$	$g(x) = \log(x - 4)$ $g(x) = \log(x + 7)$	4 units right 7 units left
Vertical Translation Graph shifts up or down.	$f(x) + k$	$g(x) = \log x + 3$ $g(x) = \log x - 1$	3 units up 1 unit down
Reflection Graph flips over x- or y-axis.	$f(-x)$ $-f(x)$	$g(x) = \log(-x)$ $g(x) = -\log x$	in the y-axis in the x-axis
Horizontal Stretch or Shrink Graph stretches away from or shrinks toward y-axis.	$f(ax)$	$g(x) = \log(4x)$ $g(x) = \log\left(\frac{1}{3}x\right)$	shrink by a factor of $\frac{1}{4}$ stretch by a factor of 3
Vertical Stretch or Shrink Graph stretches away from or shrinks toward x-axis.	$a \cdot f(x)$	$g(x) = 5 \log x$ $g(x) = \frac{2}{3} \log x$	stretch by a factor of 5 shrink by a factor of $\frac{2}{3}$

EXAMPLE 4 **Transforming Logarithmic Functions**

Describe the transformation of f represented by g. Then graph each function.

a. $f(x) = \log x$, $g(x) = \log\left(-\frac{1}{2}x\right)$ **b.** $f(x) = \log_{1/2} x$, $g(x) = 2 \log_{1/2}(x + 4)$

SOLUTION

a. Notice that the function is of the form $g(x) = \log(ax)$, where $a = -\frac{1}{2}$.

▶ So, the graph of g is a reflection in the y-axis and a horizontal stretch by a factor of 2 of the graph of f.

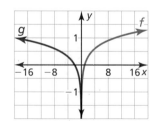

STUDY TIP

In Example 4(b), notice in the graph that the horizontal translation also shifted the asymptote 4 units left, so the domain of g is $x > -4$.

b. Notice that the function is of the form $g(x) = a \log_{1/2}(x - h)$, where $a = 2$ and $h = -4$.

▶ So, the graph of g is a horizontal translation 4 units left and a vertical stretch by a factor of 2 of the graph of f.

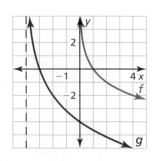

Describe the transformation of *f* represented by *g*. Then graph each function.

5. $f(x) = \log_2 x$, $g(x) = -3 \log_2 x$ **6.** $f(x) = \log_{1/4} x$, $g(x) = \log_{1/4}(4x) - 5$

Writing Transformations of Graphs of Functions

EXAMPLE 5   Writing a Transformed Exponential Function

Let the graph of *g* be a reflection in the *x*-axis followed by a translation 4 units right of the graph of $f(x) = 2^x$. Write a rule for *g*.

SOLUTION

Check

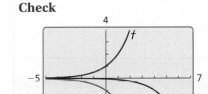

Step 1 First write a function *h* that represents the reflection of *f*.

     $h(x) = -f(x)$ Multiply the output by -1.

          $= -2^x$ Substitute 2^x for $f(x)$.

Step 2 Then write a function *g* that represents the translation of *h*.

     $g(x) = h(x - 4)$ Subtract 4 from the input.

          $= -2^{x-4}$ Replace *x* with $x - 4$ in $h(x)$.

▶ The transformed function is $g(x) = -2^{x-4}$.

EXAMPLE 6   Writing a Transformed Logarithmic Function

Let the graph of *g* be a translation 2 units up followed by a vertical stretch by a factor of 2 of the graph of $f(x) = \log_{1/3} x$. Write a rule for *g*.

SOLUTION

Check

Step 1 First write a function *h* that represents the translation of *f*.

     $h(x) = f(x) + 2$ Add 2 to the output.

        $= \log_{1/3} x + 2$ Substitute $\log_{1/3} x$ for $f(x)$.

Step 2 Then write a function *g* that represents the vertical stretch of *h*.

     $g(x) = 2 \cdot h(x)$ Multiply the output by 2.

        $= 2 \cdot (\log_{1/3} x + 2)$ Substitute $\log_{1/3} x + 2$ for $h(x)$.

        $= 2 \log_{1/3} x + 4$ Distributive Property

▶ The transformed function is $g(x) = 2 \log_{1/3} x + 4$.

Monitoring Progress Help in English and Spanish at *BigIdeasMath.com*

7. Let the graph of *g* be a horizontal stretch by a factor of 3, followed by a translation 2 units up of the graph of $f(x) = e^{-x}$. Write a rule for *g*.

8. Let the graph of *g* be a reflection in the *y*-axis, followed by a translation 4 units to the left of the graph of $f(x) = \log x$. Write a rule for *g*.

Vocabulary and Core Concept Check

1. **WRITING** Given the function $f(x) = ab^{x-h} + k$, describe the effects of a, h, and k on the graph of the function.

2. **COMPLETE THE SENTENCE** The graph of $g(x) = \log_4(-x)$ is a reflection in the _____ of the graph of $f(x) = \log_4 x$.

Monitoring Progress and Modeling with Mathematics

In Exercises 3–6, match the function with its graph. Explain your reasoning.

3. $f(x) = 2^{x+2} - 2$

4. $g(x) = 2^{x+2} + 2$

5. $h(x) = 2^{x-2} - 2$

6. $k(x) = 2^{x-2} + 2$

A.

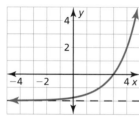

B.

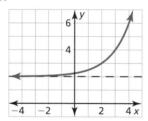

C.

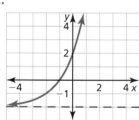

D.

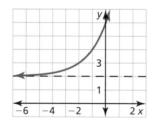

In Exercises 7–16, describe the transformation of f represented by g. Then graph each function. *(See Examples 1 and 2.)*

7. $f(x) = 3^x$, $g(x) = 3^x + 5$

8. $f(x) = 4^x$, $g(x) = 4^x - 8$

9. $f(x) = e^x$, $g(x) = e^x - 1$

10. $f(x) = e^x$, $g(x) = e^x + 4$

11. $f(x) = 2^x$, $g(x) = 2^{x-7}$

12. $f(x) = 5^x$, $g(x) = 5^{x+1}$

13. $f(x) = e^{-x}$, $g(x) = e^{-x} + 6$

14. $f(x) = e^{-x}$, $g(x) = e^{-x} - 9$

15. $f(x) = \left(\dfrac{1}{4}\right)^x$, $g(x) = \left(\dfrac{1}{4}\right)^{x-3} + 12$

16. $f(x) = \left(\dfrac{1}{3}\right)^x$, $g(x) = \left(\dfrac{1}{3}\right)^{x+2} - \dfrac{2}{3}$

In Exercises 17–24, describe the transformation of f represented by g. Then graph each function. *(See Example 3.)*

17. $f(x) = e^x$, $g(x) = e^{2x}$

18. $f(x) = e^x$, $g(x) = \dfrac{4}{3}e^x$

19. $f(x) = 2^x$, $g(x) = -2^{x-3}$

20. $f(x) = 4^x$, $g(x) = 4^{0.5x - 5}$

21. $f(x) = e^{-x}$, $g(x) = 3e^{-6x}$

22. $f(x) = e^{-x}$, $g(x) = e^{-5x} + 2$

23. $f(x) = \left(\dfrac{1}{2}\right)^x$, $g(x) = 6\left(\dfrac{1}{2}\right)^{x+5} - 2$

24. $f(x) = \left(\dfrac{3}{4}\right)^x$, $g(x) = -\left(\dfrac{3}{4}\right)^{x-7} + 1$

ERROR ANALYSIS In Exercises 25 and 26, describe and correct the error in graphing the function.

25. $f(x) = 2^x + 3$

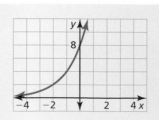

26. $f(x) = 3^{-x}$

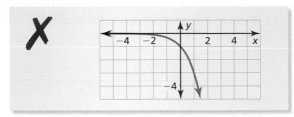

In Exercises 27–30, describe the transformation of f represented by g. Then graph each function. *(See Example 4.)*

27. $f(x) = \log_4 x$, $g(x) = 3 \log_4 x - 5$

28. $f(x) = \log_{1/3} x$, $g(x) = \log_{1/3}(-x) + 6$

29. $f(x) = \log_{1/5} x$, $g(x) = -\log_{1/5}(x - 7)$

30. $f(x) = \log_2 x$, $g(x) = \log_2(x + 2) - 3$

ANALYZING RELATIONSHIPS In Exercises 31–34, match the function with the correct transformation of the graph of f. Explain your reasoning.

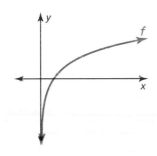

31. $y = f(x - 2)$ **32.** $y = f(x + 2)$

33. $y = 2f(x)$ **34.** $y = f(2x)$

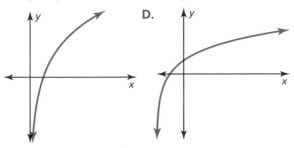

In Exercises 35–38, write a rule for g that represents the indicated transformations of the graph of f. *(See Example 5.)*

35. $f(x) = 5^x$; translation 2 units down, followed by a reflection in the y-axis

36. $f(x) = \left(\frac{2}{3}\right)^x$; reflection in the x-axis, followed by a vertical stretch by a factor of 6 and a translation 4 units left

37. $f(x) = e^x$; horizontal shrink by a factor of $\frac{1}{2}$, followed by a translation 5 units up

38. $f(x) = e^{-x}$; translation 4 units right and 1 unit down, followed by a vertical shrink by a factor of $\frac{1}{3}$

In Exercises 39–42, write a rule for g that represents the indicated transformation of the graph of f. *(See Example 6.)*

39. $f(x) = \log_6 x$; vertical stretch by a factor of 6, followed by a translation 5 units down

40. $f(x) = \log_5 x$; reflection in the x-axis, followed by a translation 9 units left

41. $f(x) = \log_{1/2} x$; translation 3 units left and 2 units up, followed by a reflection in the y-axis

42. $f(x) = \ln x$; translation 3 units right and 1 unit up, followed by a horizontal stretch by a factor of 8

JUSTIFYING STEPS In Exercises 43 and 44, justify each step in writing a rule for g that represents the indicated transformations of the graph of f.

43. $f(x) = \log_7 x$; reflection in the x-axis, followed by a translation 6 units down

$$h(x) = -f(x)$$
$$= -\log_7 x$$
$$g(x) = h(x) - 6$$
$$= -\log_7 x - 6$$

44. $f(x) = 8^x$; vertical stretch by a factor of 4, followed by a translation 1 unit up and 3 units left

$$h(x) = 4 \cdot f(x)$$
$$= 4 \cdot 8^x$$
$$g(x) = h(x + 3) + 1$$
$$= 4 \cdot 8^{x + 3} + 1$$

USING STRUCTURE In Exercises 45–48, describe the transformation of the graph of f represented by the graph of g. Then give an equation of the asymptote.

45. $f(x) = e^x$, $g(x) = e^x + 4$

46. $f(x) = 3^x$, $g(x) = 3^{x-9}$

47. $f(x) = \ln x$, $g(x) = \ln(x + 6)$

48. $f(x) = \log_{1/5} x$, $g(x) = \log_{1/5} x + 13$

49. MODELING WITH MATHEMATICS The slope S of a beach is related to the average diameter d (in millimeters) of the sand particles on the beach by the equation $S = 0.159 + 0.118 \log d$. Describe the transformation of $f(d) = \log d$ represented by S. Then use the function to determine the slope of a beach for each sand type below.

Sand particle	Diameter (mm), d
fine sand	0.125
medium sand	0.25
coarse sand	0.5
very coarse sand	1

50. HOW DO YOU SEE IT?
The graphs of $f(x) = b^x$ and $g(x) = \left(\dfrac{1}{b}\right)^x$ are shown for $b = 2$.

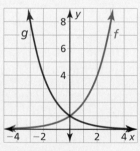

a. Use the graph to describe a transformation of the graph of f that results in the graph of g.

b. Does your answer in part (a) change when $0 < b < 1$? Explain.

51. MAKING AN ARGUMENT Your friend claims a single transformation of $f(x) = \log x$ can result in a function g whose graph never intersects the graph of f. Is your friend correct? Explain your reasoning.

52. THOUGHT PROVOKING Is it possible to transform the graph of $f(x) = e^x$ to obtain the graph of $g(x) = \ln x$? Explain your reasoning.

53. ABSTRACT REASONING Determine whether each statement is *always*, *sometimes*, or *never* true. Explain your reasoning.

a. A vertical translation of the graph of $f(x) = \log x$ changes the equation of the asymptote.

b. A vertical translation of the graph of $f(x) = e^x$ changes the equation of the asymptote.

c. A horizontal shrink of the graph of $f(x) = \log x$ does not change the domain.

d. The graph of $g(x) = ab^{x-h} + k$ does not intersect the x-axis.

54. PROBLEM SOLVING The amount P (in grams) of 100 grams of plutonium-239 that remains after t years can be modeled by $P = 100(0.99997)^t$.

a. Describe the domain and range of the function.

b. How much plutonium-239 is present after 12,000 years?

c. Describe the transformation of the function if the initial amount of plutonium-239 was 550 grams.

d. Does the transformation in part (c) affect the domain and range of the function? Explain your reasoning.

55. CRITICAL THINKING Consider the graph of the function $h(x) = e^{-x-2}$. Describe the transformation of the graph of $f(x) = e^{-x}$ represented by the graph of h. Then describe the transformation of the graph of $g(x) = e^x$ represented by the graph of h. Justify your answers.

56. OPEN-ENDED Write a function of the form $y = ab^{x-h} + k$ whose graph has a y-intercept of 5 and an asymptote of $y = 2$.

Maintaining Mathematical Proficiency
Reviewing what you learned in previous grades and lessons

Perform the indicated operation. *(Section 4.5)*

57. Let $f(x) = x^4$ and $g(x) = x^2$. Find $(fg)(x)$. Then evaluate the product when $x = 3$.

58. Let $f(x) = 4x^6$ and $g(x) = 2x^3$. Find $\left(\dfrac{f}{g}\right)(x)$. Then evaluate the quotient when $x = 5$.

59. Let $f(x) = 6x^3$ and $g(x) = 8x^3$. Find $(f + g)(x)$. Then evaluate the sum when $x = 2$.

60. Let $f(x) = 2x^2$ and $g(x) = 3x^2$. Find $(f - g)(x)$. Then evaluate the difference when $x = 6$.

5.1–5.3 What Did You Learn?

Core Vocabulary

Core Concepts

Section 5.1

Section 5.2

Section 5.3

Mathematical Practices

1. How can you justify your conclusions in Exercises 23–26 on page 255?

2. How did you monitor and evaluate your progress in Exercise 66 on page 263?

3. How can you check the reasonableness of your answers in Exercise 49 on page 272?

Forming a Weekly Study Group

STUDY SKILLS

- Select students who are just as dedicated to doing well in the math class as you are.

- Find a regular meeting place that has minimal distractions.

- Compare schedules and plan at least one time a week to meet, allowing at least 1.5 hours for study time.

5.1–5.3 Quiz

Tell whether the function represents *exponential growth* or *exponential decay*. Explain your reasoning. *(Section 5.1)*

1. $f(x) = 4e^{-x}$

2. $y = \frac{1}{2}e^{3x}$

3. $y = e^{0.6x}$

4. $f(x) = 5e^{-2x}$

Simplify the expression. *(Sections 5.1 and 5.2)*

5. $e^8 \cdot e^4$

6. $\dfrac{15e^3}{3e}$

7. $(5e^{4x})^3$

8. $e^{\ln 9}$

9. $\log_7 49^x$

10. $\log_3 81^{-2x}$

Rewrite the expression in exponential or logarithmic form. *(Section 5.2)*

11. $\log_4 1024 = 5$

12. $\log_{1/3} 27 = -3$

13. $7^4 = 2401$

14. $4^{-2} = 0.0625$

Evaluate the logarithm. If necessary, use a calculator and round your answer to three decimal places. *(Section 5.2)*

15. $\log 45$

16. $\ln 1.4$

17. $\log_2 32$

Graph the function and its inverse. *(Section 5.2)*

18. $f(x) = \left(\dfrac{1}{9}\right)^x$

19. $y = \ln(x - 7)$

20. $f(x) = \log_5(x + 1)$

The graph of *g* is a transformation of the graph of *f*. Write a rule for *g*. *(Section 5.3)*

21. $f(x) = \log_3 x$

22. $f(x) = 3^x$

23. $f(x) = \log_{1/2} x$

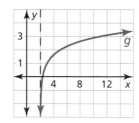
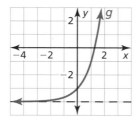
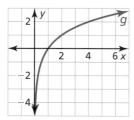

24. A local bank advertises two certificate of deposit (CD) accounts that you can use to save money and earn interest. The interest is compounded continuously for both accounts. *(Section 5.1)*

   a. You deposit the minimum required amounts in each CD account. How much money is in each account at the end of its term? How much interest does each account earn? Justify your answers.

   b. Describe the benefits and drawbacks of each account.

25. The Richter scale is used for measuring the magnitude of an earthquake. The Richter magnitude *R* is given by $R = 0.67 \ln E + 1.17$, where *E* is the energy (in kilowatt-hours) released by the earthquake. Graph the model. What is the Richter magnitude for an earthquake that releases 23,000 kilowatt-hours of energy? *(Section 5.3)*

5.4 Properties of Logarithms

Essential Question How can you use properties of exponents to derive properties of logarithms?

Let

$$x = \log_b m \qquad \text{and} \qquad y = \log_b n.$$

The corresponding exponential forms of these two equations are

$$b^x = m \qquad \text{and} \qquad b^y = n.$$

CONSTRUCTING
VIABLE ARGUMENTS

To be proficient in math, you need to understand and use stated assumptions, definitions, and previously established results.

EXPLORATION 1 Product Property of Logarithms

Work with a partner. To derive the Product Property, multiply m and n to obtain

$$mn = b^x b^y = b^{x+y}.$$

The corresponding logarithmic form of $mn = b^{x+y}$ is $\log_b mn = x + y$. So,

$$\log_b mn = \underline{\qquad\qquad}. \qquad \text{Product Property of Logarithms}$$

EXPLORATION 2 Quotient Property of Logarithms

Work with a partner. To derive the Quotient Property, divide m by n to obtain

$$\frac{m}{n} = \frac{b^x}{b^y} = b^{x-y}.$$

The corresponding logarithmic form of $\frac{m}{n} = b^{x-y}$ is $\log_b \frac{m}{n} = x - y$. So,

$$\log_b \frac{m}{n} = \underline{\qquad\qquad}. \qquad \text{Quotient Property of Logarithms}$$

EXPLORATION 3 Power Property of Logarithms

Work with a partner. To derive the Power Property, substitute b^x for m in the expression $\log_b m^n$, as follows.

$$\log_b m^n = \log_b (b^x)^n \qquad \text{Substitute } b^x \text{ for } m.$$
$$= \log_b b^{nx} \qquad \text{Power of a Power Property of Exponents}$$
$$= nx \qquad \text{Inverse Property of Logarithms}$$

So, substituting $\log_b m$ for x, you have

$$\log_b m^n = \underline{\qquad\qquad}. \qquad \text{Power Property of Logarithms}$$

Communicate Your Answer

4. How can you use properties of exponents to derive properties of logarithms?

5. Use the properties of logarithms that you derived in Explorations 1–3 to evaluate each logarithmic expression.

   a. $\log_4 16^3$

   b. $\log_3 81^{-3}$

   c. $\ln e^2 + \ln e^5$

   d. $2 \ln e^6 - \ln e^5$

   e. $\log_5 75 - \log_5 3$

   f. $\log_4 2 + \log_4 32$

What You Will Learn

▶ Use the properties of logarithms to evaluate logarithms.
▶ Use the properties of logarithms to expand or condense logarithmic expressions.
▶ Use the change-of-base formula to evaluate logarithms.

Properties of Logarithms

You know that the logarithmic function with base b is the inverse function of the exponential function with base b. Because of this relationship, it makes sense that logarithms have properties similar to properties of exponents.

⑤ Core Concept

Properties of Logarithms

Let b, m, and n be positive real numbers with $b \neq 1$.

Product Property $\log_b mn = \log_b m + \log_b n$

Quotient Property $\log_b \dfrac{m}{n} = \log_b m - \log_b n$

Power Property $\log_b m^n = n \log_b m$

STUDY TIP

These three properties of logarithms correspond to these three properties of exponents.

$a^m a^n = a^{m+n}$

$\dfrac{a^m}{a^n} = a^{m-n}$

$(a^m)^n = a^{mn}$

COMMON ERROR

Note that in general

$\log_b \dfrac{m}{n} \neq \dfrac{\log_b m}{\log_b n}$ and

$\log_b mn \neq (\log_b m)(\log_b n)$.

EXAMPLE 1   Using Properties of Logarithms

Use $\log_2 3 \approx 1.585$ and $\log_2 7 \approx 2.807$ to evaluate each logarithm.

a. $\log_2 \dfrac{3}{7}$ **b.** $\log_2 21$ **c.** $\log_2 49$

SOLUTION

a. $\log_2 \dfrac{3}{7} = \log_2 3 - \log_2 7$ Quotient Property

$\approx 1.585 - 2.807$ Use the given values of $\log_2 3$ and $\log_2 7$.

$= -1.222$ Subtract.

b. $\log_2 21 = \log_2 (3 \cdot 7)$ Write 21 as 3 • 7.

$= \log_2 3 + \log_2 7$ Product Property

$\approx 1.585 + 2.807$ Use the given values of $\log_2 3$ and $\log_2 7$.

$= 4.392$ Add.

c. $\log_2 49 = \log_2 7^2$ Write 49 as 7^2.

$= 2 \log_2 7$ Power Property

$\approx 2(2.807)$ Use the given value $\log_2 7$.

$= 5.614$ Multiply.

Monitoring Progress Help in English and Spanish at *BigIdeasMath.com*

Use $\log_6 5 \approx 0.898$ and $\log_6 8 \approx 1.161$ to evaluate the logarithm.

1. $\log_6 \dfrac{5}{8}$ **2.** $\log_6 40$ **3.** $\log_6 64$ **4.** $\log_6 125$

Rewriting Logarithmic Expressions

You can use the properties of logarithms to expand and condense logarithmic expressions.

EXAMPLE 2 **Expanding a Logarithmic Expression**

Expand $\ln \dfrac{5x^7}{y}$.

SOLUTION

$\ln \dfrac{5x^7}{y} = \ln 5x^7 - \ln y$	Quotient Property
$\quad\quad = \ln 5 + \ln x^7 - \ln y$	Product Property
$\quad\quad = \ln 5 + 7 \ln x - \ln y$	Power Property

EXAMPLE 3 **Condensing a Logarithmic Expression**

Condense $\log 9 + 3 \log 2 - \log 3$.

SOLUTION

$\log 9 + 3 \log 2 - \log 3 - \log 9 + \log 2^3 - \log 3$	Power Property
$\quad = \log(9 \cdot 2^3) - \log 3$	Product Property
$\quad - \log \dfrac{9 \cdot 2^3}{3}$	Quotient Property
$\quad = \log 24$	Simplify.

Monitoring Progress Help in English and Spanish at *BigIdeasMath.com*

Expand the logarithmic expression.

5. $\log_6 3x^4$

6. $\ln \dfrac{5}{12x}$

Condense the logarithmic expression.

7. $\log x - \log 9$

8. $\ln 4 + 3 \ln 3 - \ln 12$

Change-of-Base Formula

Logarithms with any base other than 10 or e can be written in terms of common or natural logarithms using the *change-of-base formula*. This allows you to evaluate any logarithm using a calculator.

Core Concept

Change-of-Base Formula

If a, b, and c are positive real numbers with $b \neq 1$ and $c \neq 1$, then

$$\log_c a = \frac{\log_b a}{\log_b c}.$$

In particular, $\log_c a = \dfrac{\log a}{\log c}$ and $\log_c a = \dfrac{\ln a}{\ln c}$.

ANOTHER WAY

In Example 4, $\log_3 8$ can be evaluated using natural logarithms.

$$\log_3 8 = \frac{\ln 8}{\ln 3} \approx 1.893$$

Notice that you get the same answer whether you use natural logarithms or common logarithms in the change-of-base formula.

EXAMPLE 4   **Changing a Base Using Common Logarithms**

Evaluate $\log_3 8$ using common logarithms.

SOLUTION

$$\log_3 8 = \frac{\log 8}{\log 3} \qquad\qquad \log_c a = \frac{\log a}{\log c}$$

$$\approx \frac{0.9031}{0.4771} \approx 1.893 \qquad \text{Use a calculator. Then divide.}$$

EXAMPLE 5   **Changing a Base Using Natural Logarithms**

Evaluate $\log_6 24$ using natural logarithms.

SOLUTION

$$\log_6 24 = \frac{\ln 24}{\ln 6} \qquad\qquad \log_c a = \frac{\ln a}{\ln c}$$

$$\approx \frac{3.1781}{1.7918} \approx 1.774 \qquad \text{Use a calculator. Then divide.}$$

EXAMPLE 6   **Solving a Real-Life Problem**

For a sound with intensity I (in watts per square meter), the loudness $L(I)$ of the sound (in decibels) is given by the function

$$L(I) = 10 \log \frac{I}{I_0}$$

where I_0 is the intensity of a barely audible sound (about 10^{-12} watts per square meter). An artist in a recording studio turns up the volume of a track so that the intensity of the sound doubles. By how many decibels does the loudness increase?

SOLUTION

Let I be the original intensity, so that $2I$ is the doubled intensity.

$$\begin{aligned}
\text{increase in loudness} &= L(2I) - L(I) && \text{Write an expression.}\\
&= 10 \log \frac{2I}{I_0} - 10 \log \frac{I}{I_0} && \text{Substitute.}\\
&= 10 \left(\log \frac{2I}{I_0} - \log \frac{I}{I_0} \right) && \text{Distributive Property}\\
&= 10 \left(\log 2 + \log \frac{I}{I_0} - \log \frac{I}{I_0} \right) && \text{Product Property}\\
&= 10 \log 2 && \text{Simplify.}
\end{aligned}$$

▶ The loudness increases by $10 \log 2$ decibels, or about 3 decibels.

Monitoring Progress Help in English and Spanish at *BigIdeasMath.com*

Use the change-of-base formula to evaluate the logarithm.

9. $\log_5 8$ **10.** $\log_8 14$ **11.** $\log_{26} 9$ **12.** $\log_{12} 30$

13. WHAT IF? In Example 6, the artist turns up the volume so that the intensity of the sound triples. By how many decibels does the loudness increase?

Vocabulary and Core Concept Check

1. **COMPLETE THE SENTENCE** To condense the expression $\log_3 2x + \log_3 y$, you need to use the _____ Property of Logarithms.

2. **WRITING** Describe two ways to evaluate $\log_7 12$ using a calculator.

Monitoring Progress and Modeling with Mathematics

In Exercises 3–8, use $\log_7 4 \approx 0.712$ and $\log_7 12 \approx 1.277$ to evaluate the logarithm. *(See Example 1.)*

3. $\log_7 3$

4. $\log_7 48$

5. $\log_7 16$

6. $\log_7 64$

7. $\log_7 \frac{1}{4}$

8. $\log_7 \frac{1}{3}$

In Exercises 9–12, match the expression with the logarithm that has the same value. Justify your answer.

9. $\log_3 6 - \log_3 2$ **A.** $\log_3 64$

10. $2 \log_3 6$ **B.** $\log_3 3$

11. $6 \log_3 2$ **C.** $\log_3 12$

12. $\log_3 6 + \log_3 2$ **D.** $\log_3 36$

In Exercises 13–20, expand the logarithmic expression. *(See Example 2.)*

13. $\log_3 4x$

14. $\log_8 3x$

15. $\log 10x^5$

16. $\ln 3x^4$

17. $\ln \dfrac{x}{3y}$

18. $\ln \dfrac{6x^2}{y^4}$

19. $\log_7 5\sqrt{x}$

20. $\log_5 \sqrt[3]{x^2 y}$

ERROR ANALYSIS In Exercises 21 and 22, describe and correct the error in expanding the logarithmic expression.

21.

$$\log_2 5x = (\log_2 5)(\log_2 x)$$

22.

$$\ln 8x^3 = 3 \ln 8 + \ln x$$

In Exercises 23–30, condense the logarithmic expression. *(See Example 3.)*

23. $\log_4 7 - \log_4 10$

24. $\ln 12 - \ln 4$

25. $6 \ln x + 4 \ln y$

26. $2 \log x + \log 11$

27. $\log_5 4 + \frac{1}{3} \log_5 x$

28. $6 \ln 2 - 4 \ln y$

29. $5 \ln 2 + 7 \ln x + 4 \ln y$

30. $\log_3 4 + 2 \log_3 \frac{1}{2} + \log_3 x$

31. **REASONING** Which of the following is *not* equivalent to $\log_5 \dfrac{y^4}{3x}$? Justify your answer.

  Ⓐ $4 \log_5 y - \log_5 3x$

  Ⓑ $4 \log_5 y - \log_5 3 + \log_5 x$

  Ⓒ $4 \log_5 y - \log_5 3 - \log_5 x$

  Ⓓ $\log_5 y^4 - \log_5 3 - \log_5 x$

32. **REASONING** Which of the following equations is correct? Justify your answer.

  Ⓐ $\log_7 x + 2 \log_7 y = \log_7(x + y^2)$

  Ⓑ $9 \log x - 2 \log y = \log \dfrac{x^9}{y^2}$

  Ⓒ $5 \log_4 x + 7 \log_2 y = \log_6 x^5 y^7$

  Ⓓ $\log_9 x - 5 \log_9 y = \log_9 \dfrac{x}{5y}$

In Exercises 33–40, use the change-of-base formula to evaluate the logarithm. *(See Examples 4 and 5.)*

33. $\log_4 7$

34. $\log_5 13$

35. $\log_9 15$

36. $\log_8 22$

37. $\log_6 17$

38. $\log_2 28$

39. $\log_7 \frac{3}{16}$

40. $\log_3 \frac{9}{40}$

41. **MAKING AN ARGUMENT** Your friend claims you can use the change-of-base formula to graph $y = \log_3 x$ using a graphing calculator. Is your friend correct? Explain your reasoning.

42. **HOW DO YOU SEE IT?** Use the graph to determine the value of $\dfrac{\log 8}{\log 2}$.

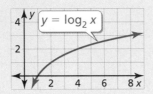

MODELING WITH MATHEMATICS In Exercises 43 and 44, use the function $L(I)$ given in Example 6.

43. The blue whale can produce sound with an intensity that is 1 million times greater than the intensity of the loudest sound a human can make. Find the difference in the decibel levels of the sounds made by a blue whale and a human. *(See Example 6.)*

44. The intensity of the sound of a certain television advertisement is 10 times greater than the intensity of the television program. By how many decibels does the loudness increase?

Intensity of Television Sound

During show: Intensity = I

During ad: Intensity = $10I$

45. **REWRITING A FORMULA** Under certain conditions, the wind speed s (in knots) at an altitude of h meters above a grassy plain can be modeled by the function

$$s(h) = 2 \ln 100h.$$

a. By what amount does the wind speed increase when the altitude doubles?

b. Show that the given function can be written in terms of common logarithms as

$$s(h) = \frac{2}{\log e}(\log h + 2).$$

46. **THOUGHT PROVOKING** Determine whether the formula

$$\log_b(M + N) = \log_b M + \log_b N$$

is true for all positive, real values of M, N, and b (with $b \neq 1$). Justify your answer.

47. **USING STRUCTURE** Use the properties of exponents to prove the change-of-base formula. (*Hint:* Let $x = \log_b a$, $y = \log_b c$, and $z = \log_c a$.)

48. **CRITICAL THINKING** Describe *three* ways to transform the graph of $f(x) = \log x$ to obtain the graph of $g(x) = \log 100x - 1$. Justify your answers.

Maintaining Mathematical Proficiency
Reviewing what you learned in previous grades and lessons

Solve the equation using any method. Explain your choice of method. *(Skills Review Handbook)*

49. $(x - 1)^2 = 9$

50. $x^2 - 4x + 6 = 2$

51. $x^2 + 6x = -7$

52. $\frac{1}{2}x^2 + 3x - 3 = 0$

Solve the inequality. Graph the solution. *(Skills Review Handbook)*

53. $2x - 3 < 5$

54. $4 - 8y \geq 12$

55. $\frac{n}{3} + 6 > 1$

56. $-\frac{2s}{5} \leq 8$

5.5 Solving Exponential and Logarithmic Equations

Essential Question

How can you solve exponential and logarithmic equations?

EXPLORATION 1 Solving Exponential and Logarithmic Equations

Work with a partner. Match each equation with the graph of its related system of equations. Explain your reasoning. Then use the graph to solve the equation.

a. $e^x = 2$

b. $\ln x = -1$

c. $2^x = 3^{-x}$

d. $\log_4 x = 1$

e. $\log_5 x = \frac{1}{2}$

f. $4^x = 2$

A.

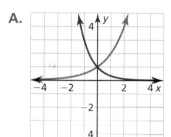

B.

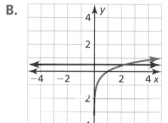

C.

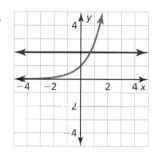

D.

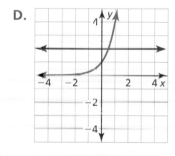

E.

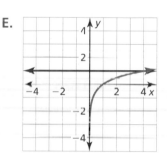

F.

MAKING SENSE OF PROBLEMS

To be proficient in math, you need to plan a solution pathway rather than simply jumping into a solution attempt.

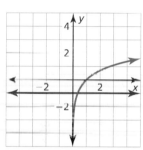

EXPLORATION 2 Solving Exponential and Logarithmic Equations

Work with a partner. Look back at the equations in Explorations 1(a) and 1(b). Suppose you want a more accurate way to solve the equations than using a graphical approach.

a. Show how you could use a *numerical approach* by creating a table. For instance, you might use a spreadsheet to solve the equations.

b. Show how you could use an *analytical approach*. For instance, you might try solving the equations by using the inverse properties of exponents and logarithms.

Communicate Your Answer

3. How can you solve exponential and logarithmic equations?

4. Solve each equation using any method. Explain your choice of method.

a. $16^x = 2$

b. $2^x = 4^{2x+1}$

c. $2^x = 3^{x+1}$

d. $\log x = \frac{1}{2}$

e. $\ln x = 2$

f. $\log_3 x = \frac{3}{2}$

Core Vocabulary

exponential equations, *p. 282*
logarithmic equations, *p. 283*

Previous
extraneous solution
inequality

What You Will Learn

▶ Solve exponential equations.
▶ Solve logarithmic equations.
▶ Solve exponential and logarithmic inequalities.

Solving Exponential Equations

Exponential equations are equations in which variable expressions occur as exponents. The result below is useful for solving certain exponential equations.

🌀 Core Concept

Property of Equality for Exponential Equations

Algebra If b is a positive real number other than 1, then $b^x = b^y$ if and only if $x = y$.

Example If $3^x = 3^5$, then $x = 5$. If $x = 5$, then $3^x = 3^5$.

The preceding property is useful for solving an exponential equation when each side of the equation uses the same base (or can be rewritten to use the same base). When it is not convenient to write each side of an exponential equation using the same base, you can try to solve the equation by taking a logarithm of each side.

EXAMPLE 1 Solving Exponential Equations

Solve each equation.

a. $100^x = \left(\dfrac{1}{10}\right)^{x-3}$

b. $2^x = 7$

SOLUTION

Check

$100^1 \stackrel{?}{=} \left(\dfrac{1}{10}\right)^{1-3}$

$100 \stackrel{?}{=} \left(\dfrac{1}{10}\right)^{-2}$

$100 = 100$ ✔

a.

$100^x = \left(\dfrac{1}{10}\right)^{x-3}$	Write original equation.
$(10^2)^x = (10^{-1})^{x-3}$	Rewrite 100 and $\dfrac{1}{10}$ as powers with base 10.
$10^{2x} = 10^{-x+3}$	Power of a Power Property
$2x = -x + 3$	Property of Equality for Exponential Equations
$x = 1$	Solve for x.

b.

$2^x = 7$	Write original equation.
$\log_2 2^x = \log_2 7$	Take $\log_2$ of each side.
$x = \log_2 7$	$\log_b b^x = x$
$x \approx 2.807$	Use a calculator.

Check

Enter $y = 2^x$ and $y = 7$ in a graphing calculator. Use the *intersect* feature to find the intersection point of the graphs. The graphs intersect at about (2.807, 7). So, the solution of $2^x = 7$ is about 2.807. ✔

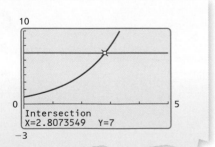

Notice that Newton's Law of Cooling models the temperature of a cooling body by adding a constant function, T_R, to a decaying exponential function, $(T_0 - T_R)e^{-rt}$.

An important application of exponential equations is *Newton's Law of Cooling*. This law states that for a cooling substance with initial temperature T_0, the temperature T after t minutes can be modeled by

$$T = (T_0 - T_R)e^{-rt} + T_R$$

where T_R is the surrounding temperature and r is the cooling rate of the substance.

EXAMPLE 2   Solving a Real-Life Problem

You are cooking *aleecha*, an Ethiopian stew. When you take it off the stove, its temperature is 212°F. The room temperature is 70°F, and the cooling rate of the stew is $r = 0.046$. How long will it take to cool the stew to a serving temperature of 100°F?

SOLUTION

Use Newton's Law of Cooling with $T = 100$, $T_0 = 212$, $T_R = 70$, and $r = 0.046$.

$T = (T_0 - T_R)e^{-rt} + T_R$	Newton's Law of Cooling
$100 = (212 - 70)e^{-0.046t} + 70$	Substitute for T, T_0, T_R, and r.
$30 = 142e^{-0.046t}$	Subtract 70 from each side.
$0.211 \approx e^{-0.046t}$	Divide each side by 142.
$\ln 0.211 \approx \ln e^{\,0.046t}$	Take natural log of each side.
$-1.556 \approx -0.046t$	$\ln e^x = \log_e e^x = x$
$33.8 \approx t$	Divide each side by -0.046.

▶ You should wait about 34 minutes before serving the stew.

Monitoring Progress Help in English and Spanish at *BigIdeasMath.com*

Solve the equation.

1. $2^x = 5$ **2.** $7^{9x} = 15$ **3.** $4e^{-0.3x} - 7 = 13$

4. WHAT IF? In Example 2, how long will it take to cool the stew to 100°F when the room temperature is 75°F?

Solving Logarithmic Equations

Logarithmic equations are equations that involve logarithms of variable expressions. You can use the next property to solve some types of logarithmic equations.

⟳ Core Concept

Property of Equality for Logarithmic Equations

Algebra If b, x, and y are positive real numbers with $b \neq 1$, then $\log_b x = \log_b y$ if and only if $x = y$.

Example If $\log_2 x = \log_2 7$, then $x = 7$. If $x = 7$, then $\log_2 x = \log_2 7$.

The preceding property implies that if you are given an equation $x = y$, then you can exponentiate each side to obtain an equation of the form $b^x = b^y$. This technique is useful for solving some logarithmic equations.

EXAMPLE 3 **Solving Logarithmic Equations**

Solve (a) $\ln(4x - 7) = \ln(x + 5)$ and (b) $\log_2(5x - 17) = 3$.

SOLUTION

a. $\ln(4x - 7) = \ln(x + 5)$ — Write original equation.

$4x - 7 = x + 5$ — Property of Equality for Logarithmic Equations

$3x - 7 = 5$ — Subtract x from each side.

$3x = 12$ — Add 7 to each side.

$x = 4$ — Divide each side by 3.

b. $\log_2(5x - 17) = 3$ — Write original equation.

$2^{\log_2(5x - 17)} = 2^3$ — Exponentiate each side using base 2.

$5x - 17 = 8$ — $b^{\log_b x} = x$

$5x = 25$ — Add 17 to each side.

$x = 5$ — Divide each side by 5.

Because the domain of a logarithmic function generally does not include all real numbers, be sure to check for extraneous solutions of logarithmic equations. You can do this algebraically or graphically.

Check

$\ln(4 \cdot 4 - 7) \overset{?}{=} \ln(4 + 5)$

$\ln(16 - 7) \overset{?}{=} \ln 9$

$\ln 9 = \ln 9$ ✓

Check

$\log_2(5 \cdot 5 - 17) \overset{?}{=} 3$

$\log_2(25 - 17) \overset{?}{=} 3$

$\log_2 8 \overset{?}{=} 3$

Because $2^3 = 8$, $\log_2 8 = 3$. ✓

EXAMPLE 4 **Solving a Logarithmic Equation**

Solve $\log 2x + \log(x - 5) = 2$.

SOLUTION

$\log 2x + \log(x - 5) = 2$ — Write original equation.

$\log[2x(x - 5)] = 2$ — Product Property of Logarithms

$10^{\log[2x(x - 5)]} = 10^2$ — Exponentiate each side using base 10.

$2x(x - 5) = 100$ — $b^{\log_b x} = x$

$2x^2 - 10x = 100$ — Distributive Property

$2x^2 - 10x - 100 = 0$ — Write in standard form.

$x^2 - 5x - 50 = 0$ — Divide each side by 2.

$(x - 10)(x + 5) = 0$ — Factor.

$x = 10$ or $x = -5$ — Zero-Product Property

▶ The apparent solution $x = -5$ is extraneous. So, the only solution is $x = 10$.

Check

$\log(2 \cdot 10) + \log(10 - 5) \overset{?}{=} 2$

$\log 20 + \log 5 \overset{?}{=} 2$

$\log 100 \overset{?}{=} 2$

$2 = 2$ ✓

$\log[2 \cdot (-5)] + \log(-5 - 5) \overset{?}{=} 2$

$\log(-10) + \log(-10) \overset{?}{=} 2$

Because $\log(-10)$ is not defined, -5 is not a solution. ✗

Monitoring Progress Help in English and Spanish at *BigIdeasMath.com*

Solve the equation. Check for extraneous solutions.

5. $\ln(7x - 4) = \ln(2x + 11)$

6. $\log_2(x - 6) = 5$

7. $\log 5x + \log(x - 1) = 2$

8. $\log_4(x + 12) + \log_4 x = 3$

Solving Exponential and Logarithmic Inequalities

Exponential inequalities are inequalities in which variable expressions occur as exponents, and *logarithmic inequalities* are inequalities that involve logarithms of variable expressions. To solve exponential and logarithmic inequalities algebraically, use these properties. Note that the properties are true for ≤ and ≥.

Exponential Property of Inequality: If b is a positive real number greater than 1, then $b^x > b^y$ if and only if $x > y$, and $b^x < b^y$ if and only if $x < y$.

Logarithmic Property of Inequality: If b, x, and y are positive real numbers with $b > 1$, then $\log_b x > \log_b y$ if and only if $x > y$, and $\log_b x < \log_b y$ if and only if $x < y$.

STUDY TIP

Be sure you understand that these properties of inequality are only true for values of $b > 1$.

You can also solve an inequality by taking a logarithm of each side or by exponentiating.

EXAMPLE 5 Solving an Exponential Inequality

Solve $3^x < 20$.

SOLUTION

$3^x < 20$	Write original inequality.
$\log_3 3^x < \log_3 20$	Take $\log_3$ of each side.
$x < \log_3 20$	$\log_b b^x = x$

▶ The solution is $x < \log_3 20$. Because $\log_3 20 \approx 2.727$, the approximate solution is $x < 2.727$.

EXAMPLE 6 Solving a Logarithmic Inequality

Solve $\log x \leq 2$.

SOLUTION

Method 1 Use an algebraic approach.

$\log x \leq 2$	Write original inequality.
$10^{\log_{10} x} \leq 10^2$	Exponentiate each side using base 10.
$x \leq 100$	$b^{\log_b x} = x$

▶ Because $\log x$ is only defined when $x > 0$, the solution is $0 < x \leq 100$.

Method 2 Use a graphical approach.

Graph $y = \log x$ and $y = 2$ in the same viewing window. Use the *intersect* feature to determine that the graphs intersect when $x = 100$. The graph of $y = \log x$ is on or below the graph of $y = 2$ when $0 < x \leq 100$.

▶ The solution is $0 < x \leq 100$.

Monitoring Progress Help in English and Spanish at *BigIdeasMath.com*

Solve the inequality.

9. $e^x < 2$ **10.** $10^{2x-6} > 3$ **11.** $\log x + 9 < 45$ **12.** $2 \ln x - 1 > 4$

Vocabulary and Core Concept Check

1. **COMPLETE THE SENTENCE** The equation $3^{x-1} = 34$ is an example of a(n) _____ equation.

2. **WRITING** Compare the methods for solving exponential and logarithmic equations.

3. **WRITING** When do logarithmic equations have extraneous solutions?

4. **COMPLETE THE SENTENCE** If b is a positive real number other than 1, then $b^x = b^y$ if and only if _____.

Monitoring Progress and Modeling with Mathematics

In Exercises 5–16, solve the equation. *(See Example 1.)*

5. $2^{3x+5} = 2^{1-x}$

6. $e^{2x} = e^{3x-1}$

7. $5^{x-3} = 25^{x-5}$

8. $6^{2x-6} = 36^{3x-5}$

9. $3^x = 7$

10. $10^x = 33$

11. $100^{5x+2} = \left(\dfrac{1}{10}\right)^{11-x}$

12. $512^{5x-1} = \left(\dfrac{1}{8}\right)^{-4-x}$

13. $5(7)^{5x} = 60$

14. $3(2)^{6x} = 99$

15. $3e^{4x} + 9 = 15$

16. $2e^{2x} - 7 = 5$

17. **MODELING WITH MATHEMATICS** The length ℓ (in centimeters) of a scalloped hammerhead shark can be modeled by the function

$$\ell = 266 - 219e^{-0.05t}$$

where t is the age (in years) of the shark. How old is a shark that is 175 centimeters long?

18. **MODELING WITH MATHEMATICS** One hundred grams of radium are stored in a container. The amount R (in grams) of radium present after t years can be modeled by $R = 100e^{-0.00043t}$. After how many years will only 5 grams of radium be present?

In Exercises 19 and 20, use Newton's Law of Cooling to solve the problem. *(See Example 2.)*

19. You are driving on a hot day when your car overheats and stops running. The car overheats at 280°F and can be driven again at 230°F. When it is 80°F outside, the cooling rate of the car is $r = 0.0058$. How long do you have to wait until you can continue driving?

20. You cook a turkey until the internal temperature reaches 180°F. The turkey is placed on the table until the internal temperature reaches 100°F and it can be carved. When the room temperature is 72°F, the cooling rate of the turkey is $r = 0.067$. How long do you have to wait until you can carve the turkey?

In Exercises 21–32, solve the equation. *(See Example 3.)*

21. $\ln(4x - 7) = \ln(x + 11)$

22. $\ln(2x - 4) = \ln(x + 6)$

23. $\log_2(3x - 4) = \log_2 5$

24. $\log(7x + 3) = \log 38$

25. $\log_2(4x + 8) = 5$

26. $\log_3(2x + 1) = 2$

27. $\log_7(4x + 9) = 2$

28. $\log_5(5x + 10) = 4$

29. $\log(12x - 9) = \log 3x$

30. $\log_6(5x + 9) = \log_6 6x$

31. $\log_2(x^2 - x - 6) = 2$

32. $\log_3(x^2 + 9x + 27) = 2$

In Exercises 33–40, solve the equation. Check for extraneous solutions. (*See Example 4.*)

33. $\log_2 x + \log_2(x - 2) = 3$

34. $\log_6 3x + \log_6(x - 1) = 3$

35. $\ln x + \ln(x + 3) = 4$

36. $\ln x + \ln(x - 2) = 5$

37. $\log_3 3x^2 + \log_3 3 = 2$

38. $\log_4(-x) + \log_4(x + 10) = 2$

39. $\log_3(x - 9) + \log_3(x - 3) = 2$

40. $\log_5(x + 4) + \log_5(x + 1) = 2$

ERROR ANALYSIS In Exercises 41 and 42, describe and correct the error in solving the equation.

41.

$$\log_3(5x - 1) = 4$$
$$3^{\log_3(5x - 1)} = 4^3$$
$$5x - 1 = 64$$
$$5x = 65$$
$$x = 13$$

42.

$$\log_4(x + 12) + \log_4 x = 3$$
$$\log_4[(x + 12)(x)] = 3$$
$$4^{\log_4[(x + 12)(x)]} = 4^3$$
$$(x + 12)(x) = 64$$
$$x^2 + 12x - 64 = 0$$
$$(x + 16)(x - 4) = 0$$
$$x = -16 \quad \text{or} \quad x = 4$$

43. **PROBLEM SOLVING** You deposit $100 in an account that pays 6% annual interest. How long will it take for the balance to reach $1000 for each frequency of compounding?

    a. annual   b. quarterly

    c. daily   d. continuously

44. **MODELING WITH MATHEMATICS** The *apparent magnitude* of a star is a measure of the brightness of the star as it appears to observers on Earth. The apparent magnitude M of the dimmest star that can be seen with a telescope is $M = 5 \log D + 2$, where D is the diameter (in millimeters) of the telescope's objective lens. What is the diameter of the objective lens of a telescope that can reveal stars with a magnitude of 12?

45. **ANALYZING RELATIONSHIPS** Approximate the solution of each equation using the graph.

    a. $1 - 5^{5 - x} = -9$ b. $\log_2 5x = 2$

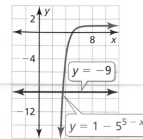 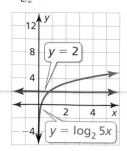

46. **MAKING AN ARGUMENT** Your friend states that a logarithmic equation cannot have a negative solution because logarithmic functions are not defined for negative numbers. Is your friend correct? Justify your answer.

In Exercises 47–54, solve the inequality. (*See Examples 5 and 6.*)

47. $9^x > 54$

48. $4^x \le 36$

49. $\ln x \ge 3$

50. $\log_4 x < 4$

51. $3^{4x - 5} < 8$

52. $e^{3x + 4} > 11$

53. $-3 \log_5 x + 6 \le 9$

54. $-4 \log_5 x - 5 \ge 3$

55. **COMPARING METHODS** Solve $\log_5 x < 2$ algebraically and graphically. Which method do you prefer? Explain your reasoning.

56. **PROBLEM SOLVING** You deposit $1000 in an account that pays 3.5% annual interest compounded monthly. When is your balance at least $1200? $3500?

57. **PROBLEM SOLVING** An investment that earns a rate of return r doubles in value in t years, where $t = \dfrac{\ln 2}{\ln(1 + r)}$ and r is expressed as a decimal. What rates of return will double the value of an investment in less than 10 years?

58. **PROBLEM SOLVING** Your family purchases a new car for $20,000. Its value decreases by 15% each year. During what interval does the car's value exceed $10,000?

USING TOOLS In Exercises 59–62, use a graphing calculator to solve the equation.

59. $\ln 2x = 3^{-x + 2}$

60. $\log x = 7^{-x}$

61. $\log x = 3^{x - 3}$

62. $\ln 2x = e^{x - 3}$

63. **REWRITING A FORMULA** A biologist can estimate the age of an African elephant by measuring the length of its footprint and using the equation $\ell = 45 - 25.7e^{-0.09a}$, where ℓ is the length (in centimeters) of the footprint and a is the age (in years).

36 cm
32 cm
28 cm
24 cm

  a. Rewrite the equation, solving for a in terms of ℓ.

  b. Use the equation in part (a) to find the ages of the elephants whose footprints are shown.

64. **HOW DO YOU SEE IT?** Use the graph to approximate the solution of the inequality $4 \ln x + 6 > 9$. Explain your reasoning.

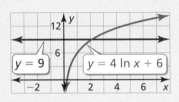

$y = 9$ $y = 4 \ln x + 6$

65. **OPEN-ENDED** Write an exponential equation that has a solution of $x = 4$. Then write a logarithmic equation that has a solution of $x = -3$.

66. **THOUGHT PROVOKING** Give examples of logarithmic or exponential equations that have one solution, two solutions, and no solutions.

CRITICAL THINKING In Exercises 67–72, solve the equation.

67. $2^{x+3} = 5^{3x-1}$ 68. $10^{3x-8} = 2^{5-x}$

69. $\log_3(x - 6) = \log_9 2x$

70. $\log_4 x = \log_8 4x$ 71. $2^{2x} - 12 \cdot 2^x + 32 = 0$

72. $5^{2x} + 20 \cdot 5^x - 125 = 0$

73. **WRITING** In Exercises 67–70, you solved exponential and logarithmic equations with different bases. Describe general methods for solving such equations.

74. **PROBLEM SOLVING** When X-rays of a fixed wavelength strike a material x centimeters thick, the intensity $I(x)$ of the X-rays transmitted through the material is given by $I(x) = I_0 e^{-\mu x}$, where I_0 is the initial intensity and μ is a value that depends on the type of material and the wavelength of the X-rays. The table shows the values of μ for various materials and X-rays of medium wavelength.

Material	Aluminum	Copper	Lead
Value of μ	0.43	3.2	43

  a. Find the thickness of aluminum shielding that reduces the intensity of X-rays to 30% of their initial intensity. (*Hint*: Find the value of x for which $I(x) = 0.3I_0$.)

  b. Repeat part (a) for the copper shielding.

  c. Repeat part (a) for the lead shielding.

  d. Your dentist puts a lead apron on you before taking X-rays of your teeth to protect you from harmful radiation. Based on your results from parts (a)–(c), explain why lead is a better material to use than aluminum or copper.

Maintaining Mathematical Proficiency   Reviewing what you learned in previous grades and lessons

Write an equation in point-slope form of the line that passes through the given point and has the given slope. *(Skills Review Handbook)*

75. $(1, -2); m = 4$ 76. $(3, 2); m = -2$

77. $(3, -8); m = -\frac{1}{3}$ 78. $(2, 5); m = 2$

Use finite differences to determine the degree of the polynomial function that fits the data. Then use technology to find the polynomial function. *(Section 3.9)*

79. $(-3, -50), (-2, -13), (-1, 0), (0, 1), (1, 2), (2, 15), (3, 52), (4, 125)$

80. $(-3, 139), (-2, 32), (-1, 1), (0, -2), (1, -1), (2, 4), (3, 37), (4, 146)$

81. $(-3, -327), (-2, -84), (-1, -17), (0, -6), (1, -3), (2, -32), (3, -189), (4, -642)$

Modeling with Exponential and Logarithmic Functions

Essential Question How can you recognize polynomial, exponential, and logarithmic models?

EXPLORATION 1 Recognizing Different Types of Models

Work with a partner. Match each type of model with the appropriate scatter plot. Use a regression program to find a model that fits the scatter plot.

a. linear (positive slope) **b.** linear (negative slope) **c.** quadratic

d. cubic **e.** exponential **f.** logarithmic

A.
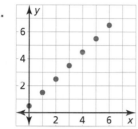

B.
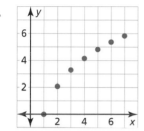

C.
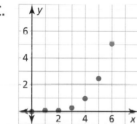

D.
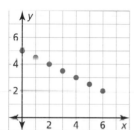

E.
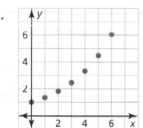

F.
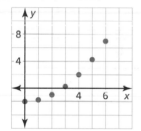

USING TOOLS STRATEGICALLY

To be proficient in math, you need to use technological tools to explore and deepen your understanding of concepts.

EXPLORATION 2 Exploring Gaussian and Logistic Models

Work with a partner. Two common types of functions that are related to exponential functions are given. Use a graphing calculator to graph each function. Then determine the domain, range, intercept, and asymptote(s) of the function.

a. Gaussian Function: $f(x) = e^{-x^2}$ **b.** Logistic Function: $f(x) = \dfrac{1}{1 + e^{-x}}$

Communicate Your Answer

3. How can you recognize polynomial, exponential, and logarithmic models?

4. Use the Internet or some other reference to find real-life data that can be modeled using one of the types given in Exploration 1. Create a table and a scatter plot of the data. Then use a regression program to find a model that fits the data.

5.6 Lesson

Core Vocabulary

Previous
finite differences
common ratio
point-slope form

What You Will Learn

▶ Classify data sets.

▶ Write exponential functions.

▶ Use technology to find exponential and logarithmic models.

Classifying Data

You have analyzed *finite differences* of data with equally-spaced inputs to determine what type of polynomial function can be used to model the data. For exponential data with equally-spaced inputs, the outputs are multiplied by a constant factor. So, consecutive outputs form a constant ratio.

EXAMPLE 1 **Classifying Data Sets**

Determine the type of function represented by each table.

a.

x	−2	−1	0	1	2	3	4
y	0.5	1	2	4	8	16	32

b.

x	−8	−6	−4	−2	0	2	4
y	−1	8	7	2	−1	4	23

SOLUTION

a. The inputs are equally spaced. Look for a pattern in the outputs.

x	−2	−1	0	1	2	3	4
y	0.5	1	2	4	8	16	32

×2 ×2 ×2 ×2 ×2 ×2

▶ As *x* increases by 1, *y* is multiplied by 2. So, the common ratio is 2, and the data represent an exponential function.

b. The inputs are equally spaced. The outputs do not have a common ratio. So, analyze the finite differences.

x	−8	−6	−4	−2	0	2	4
y	−1	8	7	2	−1	4	23

   9   −1   −5   −3   5   19   first differences

     −10 −4   2   8   14   second differences

       6   6   6   6   third differences

▶ The third differences are constant. So, the data represent a cubic function.

REMEMBER

First differences of linear functions are constant, second differences of quadratic functions are constant, and so on.

Monitoring Progress  Help in English and Spanish at *BigIdeasMath.com*

Determine the type of function represented by the table. Explain your reasoning.

1.

x	0	10	20	30
y	15	12	9	6

2.

x	0	2	4	6
y	27	9	3	1

Writing Exponential Functions

You know that two points determine a line. Similarly, two points determine an exponential curve.

EXAMPLE 2   **Writing an Exponential Function Using Two Points**

Write an exponential function $y = ab^x$ whose graph passes through $(1, 6)$ and $(3, 54)$.

SOLUTION

Step 1   Substitute the coordinates of the two given points into $y = ab^x$.

$$6 = ab^1 \qquad \text{Equation 1: Substitute 6 for } y \text{ and 1 for } x.$$

$$54 = ab^3 \qquad \text{Equation 2: Substitute 54 for } y \text{ and 3 for } x.$$

Step 2   Solve for a in Equation 1 to obtain $a = \dfrac{6}{b}$ and substitute this expression for a in Equation 2.

$$54 = \left(\frac{6}{b}\right)b^3 \qquad \text{Substitute } \frac{6}{b} \text{ for } a \text{ in Equation 2.}$$

$$54 = 6b^2 \qquad \text{Simplify.}$$

$$9 = b^2 \qquad \text{Divide each side by 6.}$$

$$3 = b \qquad \text{Take the positive square root because } b > 0.$$

REMEMBER

By the definition of an exponential function, you know that b must be positive.

Step 3   Determine that $a = \dfrac{6}{b} = \dfrac{6}{3} = 2$.

▶ So, the exponential function is $y = 2(3^x)$.

Data do not always show an *exact* exponential relationship. When the data in a scatter plot show an *approximately* exponential relationship, you can model the data with an exponential function.

EXAMPLE 3   **Finding an Exponential Model**

A store sells trampolines. The table shows the numbers y of trampolines sold during the xth year that the store has been open. Write a function that models the data.

Year, x	Number of trampolines, y
1	12
2	16
3	25
4	36
5	50
6	67
7	96

SOLUTION

Step 1   Make a scatter plot of the data. The data appear exponential.

Step 2   Choose any two points to write a model, such as $(1, 12)$ and $(4, 36)$. Substitute the coordinates of these two points into $y = ab^x$.

$$12 = ab^1$$

$$36 = ab^4$$

Solve for a in the first equation to obtain $a = \dfrac{12}{b}$. Substitute to obtain $b = \sqrt[3]{3} \approx 1.44$ and $a = \dfrac{12}{\sqrt[3]{3}} \approx 8.32$.

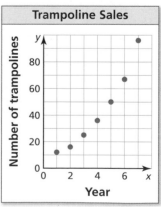

Trampoline Sales

▶ So, an exponential function that models the data is $y = 8.32(1.44)^x$.

A set of more than two points (x, y) fits an exponential pattern if and only if the set of transformed points $(x, \ln y)$ fits a linear pattern.

Graph of points (x, y)

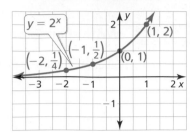

The graph is an exponential curve.

Graph of points $(x, \ln y)$

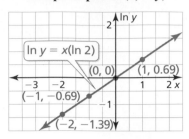

The graph is a line.

EXAMPLE 4 **Writing a Model Using Transformed Points**

Use the data from Example 3. Create a scatter plot of the data pairs $(x, \ln y)$ to show that an exponential model should be a good fit for the original data pairs (x, y). Then write an exponential model for the original data.

SOLUTION

Step 1 Create a table of data pairs $(x, \ln y)$.

x	1	2	3	4	5	6	7
ln y	2.48	2.77	3.22	3.58	3.91	4.20	4.56

LOOKING FOR STRUCTURE

Because the axes are x and $\ln y$, the point-slope form is rewritten as $\ln y - \ln y_1 = m(x - x_1)$. The slope of the line through $(1, 2.48)$ and $(7, 4.56)$ is

$$\frac{4.56 - 2.48}{7 - 1} \approx 0.35.$$

Step 2 Plot the transformed points as shown. The points lie close to a line, so an exponential model should be a good fit for the original data.

Step 3 Find an exponential model $y = ab^x$ by choosing any two points on the line, such as $(1, 2.48)$ and $(7, 4.56)$. Use these points to write an equation of the line. Then solve for y.

$$\ln y - 2.48 = 0.35(x - 1) \qquad \text{Equation of line}$$
$$\ln y = 0.35x + 2.13 \qquad \text{Simplify.}$$
$$y = e^{0.35x + 2.13} \qquad \text{Exponentiate each side using base } e.$$
$$y = e^{0.35x}(e^{2.13}) \qquad \text{Use properties of exponents.}$$
$$y = 8.41(1.42)^x \qquad \text{Simplify.}$$

▶ So, an exponential function that models the data is $y = 8.41(1.42)^x$.

Monitoring Progress Help in English and Spanish at *BigIdeasMath.com*

Write an exponential function $y = ab^x$ whose graph passes through the given points.

3. $(2, 12), (3, 24)$ **4.** $(1, 2), (3, 32)$ **5.** $(2, 16), (5, 2)$

6. WHAT IF? Repeat Examples 3 and 4 using the sales data from another store.

Year, x	1	2	3	4	5	6	7
Number of trampolines, y	15	23	40	52	80	105	140

Using Technology

You can use technology to find best-fit models for exponential and logarithmic data.

EXAMPLE 5   Finding an Exponential Model

Use a graphing calculator to find an exponential model for the data in Example 3. Then use this model and the models in Examples 3 and 4 to predict the number of trampolines sold in the eighth year. Compare the predictions.

SOLUTION

Enter the data into a graphing calculator and perform an exponential regression. The model is $y = 8.46(1.42)^x$.

Substitute $x = 8$ into each model to predict the number of trampolines sold in the eighth year.

```
ExpReg
 y=a*b^x
 a=8.457377971
 b=1.418848603
 r²=.9972445053
 r=.9986213023
```

$$\text{Example 3: } y = 8.32(1.44)^8 \approx 154$$

$$\text{Example 4: } y = 8.41(1.42)^8 \approx 139$$

$$\text{Regression model: } y = 8.46(1.42)^8 \approx 140$$

▶ The predictions are close for the regression model and the model in Example 4 that used transformed points. These predictions are less than the prediction for the model in Example 3.

EXAMPLE 6   Finding a Logarithmic Model

The atmospheric pressure decreases with increasing altitude. At sea level, the average air pressure is 1 atmosphere (1.033227 kilograms per square centimeter). The table shows the pressures p (in atmospheres) at selected altitudes h (in kilometers). Use a graphing calculator to find a logarithmic model of the form $h = a + b \ln p$ that represents the data. Estimate the altitude when the pressure is 0.75 atmosphere.

Air pressure, p	1	0.55	0.25	0.12	0.06	0.02
Altitude, h	0	5	10	15	20	25

SOLUTION

Enter the data into a graphing calculator and perform a logarithmic regression. The model is $h = 0.86 - 6.45 \ln p$.

Substitute $p = 0.75$ into the model to obtain

$$h = 0.86 - 6.45 \ln 0.75 \approx 2.7.$$

```
LnReg
 y=a+blnx
 a=.8626578705
 b=-6.447382985
 r²=.9925582287
 r=-.996272166
```

Weather balloons carry instruments that send back information such as wind speed, temperature, and air pressure.

▶ So, when the air pressure is 0.75 atmosphere, the altitude is about 2.7 kilometers.

Monitoring Progress Help in English and Spanish at *BigIdeasMath.com*

7. Use a graphing calculator to find an exponential model for the data in Monitoring Progress Question 6.

8. Use a graphing calculator to find a logarithmic model of the form $p = a + b \ln h$ for the data in Example 6. Explain why the result is an error message.

Vocabulary and Core Concept Check

1. **COMPLETE THE SENTENCE** Given a set of more than two data pairs (x, y), you can decide whether a(n) _____ function fits the data well by making a scatter plot of the points $(x, \ln y)$.

2. **WRITING** Given a table of values, explain how you can determine whether an exponential function is a good model for a set of data pairs (x, y).

Monitoring Progress and Modeling with Mathematics

In Exercises 3–6, determine the type of function represented by the table. Explain your reasoning. *(See Example 1.)*

3.
x	0	3	6	9	12	15
y	0.25	1	4	16	64	256

4.
x	−4	−3	−2	−1	0	1	2
y	16	8	4	2	1	$\frac{1}{2}$	$\frac{1}{4}$

5.
x	5	10	15	20	25	30
y	4	3	7	16	30	49

6.
x	−3	−1	1	3	5	7
y	61	5	5	13	−19	−139

In Exercises 7–16, write an exponential function $y = ab^x$ whose graph passes through the given points. *(See Example 2.)*

7. $(1, 3), (2, 12)$

8. $(2, 24), (3, 144)$

9. $(3, 1), (5, 4)$

10. $(3, 27), (5, 243)$

11. $(1, 2), (3, 50)$

12. $(1, 40), (3, 640)$

13. $(-1, 10), (4, 0.31)$

14. $(2, 6.4), (5, 409.6)$

15.
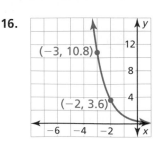

16.

ERROR ANALYSIS In Exercises 17 and 18, describe and correct the error in determining the type of function represented by the data.

17.
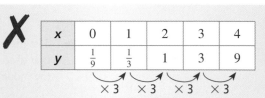

The outputs have a common ratio of 3, so the data represent a linear function.

18.
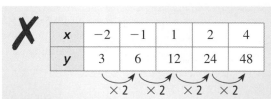

The outputs have a common ratio of 2, so the data represent an exponential function.

19. **MODELING WITH MATHEMATICS** A store sells motorized scooters. The table shows the numbers y of scooters sold during the xth year that the store has been open. Write a function that models the data. *(See Example 3.)*

x	y
1	9
2	14
3	19
4	25
5	37
6	53
7	71

20. **MODELING WITH MATHEMATICS** The table shows the numbers y of visits to a website during the xth month. Write a function that models the data. Then use your model to predict the number of visits after 1 year.

x	1	2	3	4	5	6	7
y	22	39	70	126	227	408	735

In Exercises 21–24, determine whether the data show an exponential relationship. Then write a function that models the data.

21.

x	1	6	11	16	21
y	12	28	76	190	450

22.

x	-3	-1	1	3	5
y	2	7	24	68	194

23.

x	0	10	20	30	40	50	60
y	66	58	48	42	31	26	21

24.

x	20	13	6	1	8	15
y	25	19	14	11	8	6

25. **MODELING WITH MATHEMATICS** Your visual near point is the closest point at which your eyes can see an object distinctly. The diagram shows the near point y (in centimeters) at age x (in years). Create a scatter plot of the data pairs $(x, \ln y)$ to show that an exponential model should be a good fit for the original data pairs (x, y). Then write an exponential model for the original data. *(See Example 4.)*

Visual Near Point Distances

Age 20
12 cm

Age 30
15 cm

Age 40
25 cm

Age 50
40 cm

Age 60
100 cm

26. **MODELING WITH MATHEMATICS** Use the data from Exercise 19. Create a scatter plot of the data pairs $(x, \ln y)$ to show that an exponential model should be a good fit for the original data pairs (x, y). Then write an exponential model for the original data.

In Exercises 27–30, create a scatter plot of the points $(x, \ln y)$ to determine whether an exponential model fits the data. If so, find an exponential model for the data.

27.

x	1	2	3	4	5
y	18	36	72	144	288

28.

x	1	4	7	10	13
y	3.3	10.1	30.6	92.7	280.9

29.

x	-13	-6	1	8	15
y	9.8	12.2	15.2	19	23.8

30.

x	-8	-5	-2	1	4
y	1.4	1.67	5.32	6.41	7.97

31. **USING TOOLS** Use a graphing calculator to find an exponential model for the data in Exercise 19. Then use the model to predict the number of motorized scooters sold in the tenth year. *(See Example 5.)*

32. **USING TOOLS** A doctor measures an astronaut's pulse rate y (in beats per minute) at various times x (in minutes) after the astronaut has finished exercising. The results are shown in the table. Use a graphing calculator to find an exponential model for the data. Then use the model to predict the astronaut's pulse rate after 16 minutes.

x	y
0	172
2	132
4	110
6	92
8	84
10	78
12	75

33. **USING TOOLS** An object at a temperature of 160°C is removed from a furnace and placed in a room at 20°C. The table shows the temperatures d (in degrees Celsius) at selected times t (in hours) after the object was removed from the furnace. Use a graphing calculator to find a logarithmic model of the form $t = a + b \ln d$ that represents the data. Estimate how long it takes for the object to cool to 50°C.
(*See Example 6.*)

d	160	90	56	38	29	24
t	0	1	2	3	4	5

34. **USING TOOLS** The f-stops on a camera control the amount of light that enters the camera. Let s be a measure of the amount of light that strikes the film and let f be the f-stop. The table shows several f-stops on a 35-millimeter camera. Use a graphing calculator to find a logarithmic model of the form $s = a + b \ln f$ that represents the data. Estimate the amount of light that strikes the film when $f = 5.657$.

f	s
1.414	1
2.000	2
2.828	3
4.000	4
11.314	7

35. **DRAWING CONCLUSIONS** The table shows the average weight (in kilograms) of an Atlantic cod that is x years old from the Gulf of Maine.

Age, x	1	2	3	4	5
Weight, y	0.751	1.079	1.702	2.198	3.438

a. Show that an exponential model fits the data. Then find an exponential model for the data.

b. By what percent does the weight of an Atlantic cod increase each year in this period of time? Explain.

36. **HOW DO YOU SEE IT?** The graph shows a set of data points $(x, \ln y)$. Do the data pairs (x, y) fit an exponential pattern? Explain your reasoning.

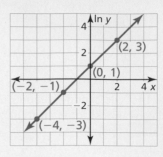

37. **MAKING AN ARGUMENT** Your friend says it is possible to find a logarithmic model of the form $d = a + b \ln t$ for the data in Exercise 33. Is your friend correct? Explain.

38. **THOUGHT PROVOKING** Is it possible to write y as an exponential function of x when p is positive? If so, write the function. If not, explain why not.

x	y
1	p
2	$2p$
3	$4p$
4	$8p$
5	$16p$

39. **CRITICAL THINKING** You plant a sunflower seedling in your garden. The height h (in centimeters) of the seedling after t weeks can be modeled by the *logistic function*
$$h(t) = \frac{256}{1 + 13e^{-0.65t}}.$$

a. Find the time it takes the sunflower seedling to reach a height of 200 centimeters.

b. Use a graphing calculator to graph the function. Interpret the meaning of the asymptote in the context of this situation.

Maintaining Mathematical Proficiency

Reviewing what you learned in previous grades and lessons

Tell whether x and y are in a proportional relationship. Explain your reasoning.
(*Skills Review Handbook*)

40. $y = \dfrac{x}{2}$

41. $y = 3x - 12$

42. $y = \dfrac{5}{x}$

43. $y = -2x$

Solve the proportion. (*Skills Review Handbook*)

44. $\dfrac{1}{2} = \dfrac{x}{4}$

45. $\dfrac{2}{3} = \dfrac{x}{9}$

46. $\dfrac{-1}{4} = \dfrac{3}{x}$

47. $\dfrac{5}{2} = \dfrac{-20}{x}$

5.4–5.6   What Did You Learn?

Core Vocabulary

exponential equations, *p. 282*
logarithmic equations, *p. 283*

Core Concepts

Section 5.4

Properties of Logarithms, *p. 276*
Change-of-Base Formula, *p. 277*

Section 5.5

Property of Equality for Exponential Equations, *p. 282*
Property of Equality for Logarithmic Equations, *p. 283*
Solving Exponential and Logarithmic Inequalities, *p. 285*

Section 5.6

Classifying Data, *p. 290*
Writing Exponential Functions, *p. 291*
Using Exponential and Logarithmic Regression, *p. 293*

Mathematical Practices

1. Explain how you used properties of logarithms to rewrite the function in part (b) of Exercise 45 on page 280.

2. How can you use cases to analyze the argument given in Exercise 46 on page 287?

Performance Task:

Preparing A Picnic

Is that picnic food safe to eat? That depends. At certain temperature ranges, some foods are breeding grounds for harmful bacteria. How can an exponential function help you prepare picnic food that is bacteria-free?

To explore the answers to these questions and more, check out the Performance Task and Real-Life STEM video at *BigIdeasMath.com*.

5 Chapter Review

Dynamic Solutions available at *BigIdeasMath.com*

5.1 The Natural Base *e* (pp. 251–256)

Tell whether $y = e^{0.5x}$ represents *exponential growth* or *exponential decay*. Then graph the function.

Because $a = 1$ is positive and $r = 0.5$ is positive, the function is an exponential growth function. Use a table to graph the function.

x	−2	0	2	4
y	0.37	1	2.72	7.39

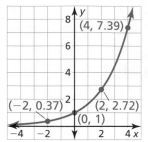

Simplify the expression.

1. $e^4 \cdot e^{11}$
2. $\dfrac{20e^3}{10e^6}$
3. $(-3e^{-5x})^2$

Tell whether the function represents *exponential growth* or *exponential decay*. Then graph the function.

4. $f(x) = \frac{1}{3}e^x$
5. $y = 6e^{-x}$
6. $y = 3e^{-0.75x}$

5.2 Logarithms and Logarithmic Functions (pp. 257–264)

Find the inverse of the function $y = \ln(x - 2)$.

$y = \ln(x - 2)$ — Write original function.

$x = \ln(y - 2)$ — Switch *x* and *y*.

$e^x = y - 2$ — Write in exponential form.

$e^x + 2 = y$ — Add 2 to each side.

▶ The inverse of $y = \ln(x - 2)$ is $y = e^x + 2$.

Check

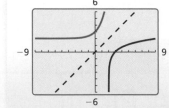

The graphs appear to be reflections of each other in the line $y = x$. ✓

Evaluate the logarithm.

7. $\log_2 8$
8. $\log_6 \frac{1}{36}$
9. $\log_5 1$

Find the inverse of the function.

10. $f(x) = 8^x$
11. $y = \ln(x - 4)$
12. $y = \log(x + 9)$
13. Graph $y = \log_2 x + 1$.

5.3 Transformations of Exponential and Logarithmic Functions *(pp. 265–272)*

Describe the transformation of $f(x) = \left(\frac{1}{3}\right)^x$ represented by $g(x) = \left(\frac{1}{3}\right)^{x-1} + 3$. Then graph each function.

Notice that the function is of the form $g(x) = \left(\frac{1}{3}\right)^{x-h} + k$, where $h = 1$ and $k = 3$.

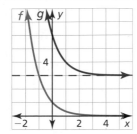

▶ So, the graph of g is a translation 1 unit right and 3 units up of the graph of f.

Describe the transformation of f represented by g. Then graph each function.

14. $f(x) = e^{-x}$, $g(x) = e^{-5x} - 8$

15. $f(x) = \log_4 x$, $g(x) = \frac{1}{2}\log_4(x + 5)$

Write a rule for g.

16. Let the graph of g be a vertical stretch by a factor of 3, followed by a translation 6 units left and 3 units up of the graph of $f(x) = e^x$.

17. Let the graph of g be a translation 2 units down, followed by a reflection in the y-axis of the graph of $f(x) = \log x$.

5.4 Properties of Logarithms *(pp. 275–280)*

a. Expand $\ln\dfrac{12x^5}{y}$.

$$\ln\frac{12x^5}{y} = \ln 12x^5 - \ln y \qquad \text{Quotient Property}$$

$$= \ln 12 + \ln x^5 - \ln y \qquad \text{Product Property}$$

$$= \ln 12 + 5\ln x - \ln y \qquad \text{Power Property}$$

b. Evaluate $\log_4 36$ using natural logarithms.

$$\log_4 36 = \frac{\ln 36}{\ln 4} \qquad\qquad \log_c a = \frac{\ln a}{\ln c}$$

$$\approx \frac{3.5835}{1.3863} \approx 2.585 \qquad \text{Use a calculator. Then divide.}$$

Expand or condense the logarithmic expression.

18. $\log_8 3xy$

19. $\log 10x^3y$

20. $\ln\dfrac{3y}{x^5}$

21. $3\log_7 4 + \log_7 6$

22. $\log_2 12 - 2\log_2 x$

23. $2\ln x + 5\ln 2 - \ln 8$

Use the change-of-base formula to evaluate the logarithm.

24. $\log_2 10$

25. $\log_7 9$

26. $\log_{23} 42$

5.5 Solving Exponential and Logarithmic Equations *(pp. 281–288)*

Solve $\ln(3x - 9) = \ln(2x + 6)$.

$\ln(3x - 9) = \ln(2x + 6)$	Write original equation.
$3x - 9 = 2x + 6$	Property of Equality for Logarithmic Equations
$x - 9 = 6$	Subtract 2x from each side.
$x = 15$	Add 9 to each side.

Check

$$\ln(3 \cdot 15 - 9) \stackrel{?}{=} \ln(2 \cdot 15 + 6)$$
$$\ln(45 - 9) \stackrel{?}{=} \ln(30 + 6)$$
$$\ln 36 = \ln 36 \ \checkmark$$

Solve the equation. Check for extraneous solutions.

27. $5^x = 8$

28. $\log_3(2x - 5) = 2$

29. $\ln x + \ln(x + 2) = 3$

Solve the inequality.

30. $6^x > 12$

31. $\ln x \le 9$

32. $e^{4x - 2} \ge 16$

5.6 Modeling with Exponential and Logarithmic Functions *(pp. 289–296)*

Write an exponential function $y = ab^x$ whose graph passes through (1, 3) and (4, 24).

Step 1 Substitute the coordinates of the two given points into $y = ab^x$.

$3 = ab^1$	Equation 1: Substitute 3 for y and 1 for x.
$24 = ab^4$	Equation 2: Substitute 24 for y and 4 for x.

Step 2 Solve for a in Equation 1 to obtain $a = \dfrac{3}{b}$ and substitute this expression for a in Equation 2.

$24 = \left(\dfrac{3}{b}\right)b^4$	Substitute $\dfrac{3}{b}$ for a in Equation 2.
$24 = 3b^3$	Simplify.
$8 = b^3$	Divide each side by 3.
$2 = b$	Take cube root of each side.

Step 3 Determine that $a = \dfrac{3}{b} = \dfrac{3}{2}$.

▶ So, the exponential function is $y = \dfrac{3}{2}(2^x)$.

Write an exponential function $y = ab^x$ whose graph passes through the given points.

33. (1, 12), (2, 24)

34. (3, 8), (5, 2)

35. (4, 25), (1, 0.2)

36. A shoe store sells a new type of basketball shoe. The table shows the pairs sold s over time t (in weeks). Use a graphing calculator to find a logarithmic model of the form $s = a + b \ln t$ that represents the data. Estimate how many pairs of shoes are sold after 6 weeks.

Week, t	1	3	5	7	9
Pairs sold, s	5	32	48	58	65

Graph the equation. State the domain, range, and asymptote.

1. $y = \frac{2}{3}e^x$

2. $y = \log_{1/5} x$

3. $y = 4e^{-2x}$

Describe the transformation of f represented by g. Then write a rule for g.

4. $f(x) = \log x$

5. $f(x) = e^x$

6. $f(x) = \left(\frac{1}{4}\right)^x$

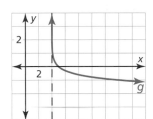

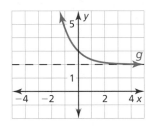

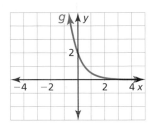

Use $\log_3 4 \approx 1.262$ and $\log_3 13 \approx 2.335$ to evaluate the logarithm.

7. $\log_3 52$

8. $\log_3 \frac{13}{9}$

9. $\log_3 16$

10. $\log_3 8 + \log_3 \frac{1}{2}$

11. Describe the similarities and differences in solving the equations $4^{5x-2} = 16$ and $\log_4(10x + 6) = 1$. Then solve each equation.

12. Without calculating, determine whether $\log_5 11$, $\dfrac{\log 11}{\log 5}$, and $\dfrac{\ln 11}{\ln 5}$ are equivalent expressions. Explain your reasoning.

13. The amount y of oil collected by a petroleum company drilling on the U.S. continental shelf can be modeled by $y = 12.263 \ln x - 45.381$, where y is measured in billions of barrels and x is the number of wells drilled. About how many barrels of oil would you expect to collect after drilling 1000 wells? Find the inverse function and describe what the inverse represents.

14. The percent L of surface light that filters down through bodies of water can be modeled by the exponential function $L(x) = 100e^{kx}$, where k is a measure of the murkiness of the water and x is the depth (in meters) below the surface.

   a. A recreational submersible is traveling in clear water with a k-value of about -0.02. Write a function that gives the percent of surface light that filters down through clear water as a function of depth.

   b. Tell whether your function in part (a) represents exponential growth or exponential decay. Explain your reasoning.

   c. Estimate the percent of surface light available at a depth of 40 meters.

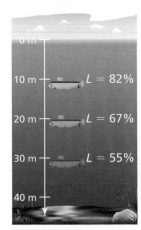

15. The table shows the values y (in dollars) of a new snowmobile after x years of ownership. Describe three different ways to find an exponential model that represents the data. Then write and use a model to find the year when the snowmobile is worth $2500.

Year, x	0	1	2	3	4
Value, y	4200	3780	3402	3061.80	2755.60

1. Select every value of b for the equation $y = b^x$ that could result in the graph shown.

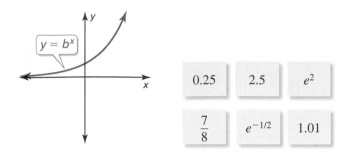

| 0.25 | 2.5 | e^2 |

| $\dfrac{7}{8}$ | $e^{-1/2}$ | 1.01 |

2. Your friend claims more interest is earned when an account pays interest compounded continuously than when it pays interest compounded daily. Do you agree with your friend? Justify your answer.

3. You are designing a picnic cooler with a length four times its width and height twice its width. The cooler has insulation that is 1 inch thick on each of the four sides and 2 inches thick on the top and bottom.

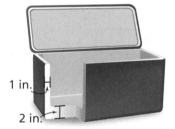

1 in.

2 in.

   a. Let x represent the width of the cooler. Write a polynomial function T that gives the volume of the rectangular prism formed by the outer surfaces of the cooler.

   b. Write a polynomial function C for the volume of the inside of the cooler.

   c. Let I be a polynomial function that represents the volume of the insulation. How is I related to T and C?

   d. Write I in standard form. What is the volume of the insulation when the width of the cooler is 8 inches?

4. What is the solution to the logarithmic inequality $-4 \log_2 x \geq -20$?

   Ⓐ $x \leq 32$

   Ⓑ $0 \leq x \leq 32$

   Ⓒ $0 < x \leq 32$

   Ⓓ $x \geq 32$

5. Describe the transformation of $f(x) = \log_2 x$ represented by the graph of g.

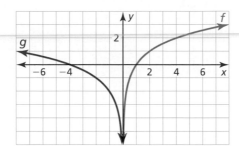

6. Let $f(x) = 2x^3 - 4x^2 + 8x - 1$, $g(x) = 2x - 3x^4 - 6x^3 + 5$, and $h(x) = -7 + x^2 + x$. Order the following functions from least degree to greatest degree.

   A. $f + g$

   B. hg

   C. $h - f$

   D. fh

7. Write an exponential model that represents each data set. Compare the two models.

   a.
   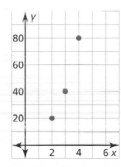

   b.

x	2	3	4	5	6
y	4.5	13.5	40.5	121.5	364.5

8. A binomial $(x - a)$ is a factor of a polynomial $f(x)$.

   a. Can you determine the value of $f(a)$? Explain your reasoning.

   b. Assume that $f(b) = 1$. Could $(x - b)$ be a factor of $f(x)$? Explain your reasoning.

9. At the annual pumpkin-tossing contest, contestants compete to see whose catapult will send pumpkins the longest distance. The table shows the horizontal distances y (in feet) a pumpkin travels when launched at different angles x (in degrees). Create a scatter plot of the data. Do the data show a linear, quadratic, or exponential relationship? Use technology to find a model for the data. Find the angle(s) at which a launched pumpkin travels 500 feet.

Angle (degrees), x	20	30	40	50	60	70
Distance (feet), y	372	462	509	501	437	323

6 Rational Functions

Cost of Fuel *(p. 345)*

Galapagos Penguin *(p. 330)*

Lightning Strike *(p. 319)*

SEE the Big Idea

3-D Printer *(p. 317)*

Volunteer Project *(p. 310)*

Maintaining Mathematical Proficiency

Adding and Subtracting Rational Numbers

Example 1 Find the sum $-\dfrac{3}{4} + \dfrac{1}{3}$.

$$-\frac{3}{4} + \frac{1}{3} = -\frac{9}{12} + \frac{4}{12}$$ Rewrite using the LCD (least common denominator).

$$= \frac{-9 + 4}{12}$$ Write the sum of the numerators over the common denominator.

$$= -\frac{5}{12}$$ Add.

Example 2 Find the difference $\dfrac{7}{8} - \left(-\dfrac{5}{8}\right)$.

$$\frac{7}{8} - \left(-\frac{5}{8}\right) = \frac{7}{8} + \frac{5}{8}$$ Add the opposite of $-\dfrac{5}{8}$.

$$= \frac{7 + 5}{8}$$ Write the sum of the numerators over the common denominator.

$$= \frac{12}{8}$$ Add.

$$= \frac{3}{2}, \text{ or } 1\frac{1}{2}$$ Simplify.

Evaluate.

1. $\dfrac{3}{5} + \dfrac{2}{3}$

2. $-\dfrac{4}{7} + \dfrac{1}{6}$

3. $\dfrac{7}{9} - \dfrac{4}{9}$

4. $\dfrac{5}{12} - \left(-\dfrac{1}{2}\right)$

5. $\dfrac{2}{7} + \dfrac{1}{7} - \dfrac{6}{7}$

6. $\dfrac{3}{10} - \dfrac{3}{4} + \dfrac{2}{5}$

Simplifying Complex Fractions

Example 3 Simplify $\dfrac{\frac{1}{2}}{\frac{4}{5}}$.

$$\frac{\frac{1}{2}}{\frac{4}{5}} = \frac{1}{2} \div \frac{4}{5}$$ Rewrite the quotient.

$$= \frac{1}{2} \cdot \frac{5}{4}$$ Multiply by the reciprocal of $\dfrac{4}{5}$.

$$= \frac{1 \cdot 5}{2 \cdot 4}$$ Multiply the numerators and denominators.

$$= \frac{5}{8}$$ Simplify.

Simplify.

7. $\dfrac{\frac{3}{8}}{\frac{5}{6}}$

8. $\dfrac{\frac{1}{4}}{-\frac{5}{7}}$

9. $\dfrac{\frac{2}{3}}{\frac{2}{3} + \frac{1}{4}}$

10. **ABSTRACT REASONING** For what value of x is the expression $\dfrac{1}{x}$ undefined? Explain your reasoning.

Mathematical Practices

Mathematically proficient students are careful about specifying units of measure and clarifying the relationship between quantities in a problem.

Specifying Units of Measure

◔ Core Concept

Converting Units of Measure

To convert from one unit of measure to another unit of measure, you can begin by writing the new units. Then multiply the old units by the appropriate conversion factors. For example, you can convert 60 miles per hour to feet per second as follows.

old units $\longrightarrow$ $\dfrac{60 \text{ mi}}{1 \text{ h}}$ $\qquad\qquad = \dfrac{? \text{ ft}}{1 \text{ sec}}$ $\longleftarrow$ new units

$$\frac{60 \text{ mi}}{1 \text{ h}} \cdot \frac{1 \text{ h}}{60 \text{ min}} \cdot \frac{1 \text{ min}}{60 \text{ sec}} \cdot \frac{5280 \text{ ft}}{1 \text{ mi}} = \frac{5280 \text{ ft}}{60 \text{ sec}}$$

$$= \frac{88 \text{ ft}}{1 \text{ sec}}$$

EXAMPLE 1   Converting Units of Measure

You are given two job offers. Which has the greater annual income?

• $45,000 per year

• $22 per hour

SOLUTION

One way to answer this question is to convert $22 per hour to dollars per year and then compare the two annual salaries. Assume there are 40 hours in a work week.

$\dfrac{22 \text{ dollars}}{1 \text{ h}} \qquad\qquad = \dfrac{? \text{ dollars}}{1 \text{ yr}}$ Write new units.

$\dfrac{22 \text{ dollars}}{1 \text{ h}} \cdot \dfrac{40 \text{ h}}{1 \text{ week}} \cdot \dfrac{52 \text{ weeks}}{1 \text{ yr}} = \dfrac{45,760 \text{ dollars}}{1 \text{ yr}}$ Multiply by conversion factors.

▶ The second offer has the greater annual salary.

Monitoring Progress

1. You drive a car at a speed of 60 miles per hour. What is the speed in meters per second?

2. A hose carries a pressure of 200 pounds per square inch. What is the pressure in kilograms per square centimeter?

3. A concrete truck pours concrete at the rate of 1 cubic yard per minute. What is the rate in cubic feet per hour?

4. Water in a pipe flows at a rate of 10 gallons per minute. What is the rate in liters per second?

6.1 Inverse Variation

Essential Question
How can you recognize when two quantities vary directly or inversely?

EXPLORATION 1 Recognizing Direct Variation

Work with a partner. You hang different weights from the same spring.

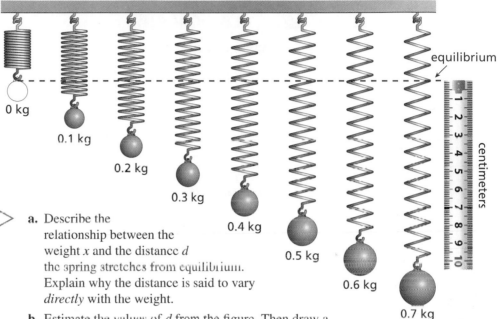

0 kg
0.1 kg
0.2 kg
0.3 kg
0.4 kg
0.5 kg
0.6 kg
0.7 kg

equilibrium
centimeters

a. Describe the relationship between the weight x and the distance d the spring stretches from equilibrium. Explain why the distance is said to vary *directly* with the weight.

b. Estimate the values of d from the figure. Then draw a scatter plot of the data. What are the characteristics of the graph?

c. Write an equation that represents d as a function of x.

d. In physics, the relationship between d and x is described by *Hooke's Law*. How would you describe Hooke's Law?

EXPLORATION 2 Recognizing Inverse Variation

Work with a partner. The table shows the length x (in inches) and the width y (in inches) of a rectangle. The area of each rectangle is 64 square inches.

x	y
1	
2	
4	
8	
16	
32	
64	

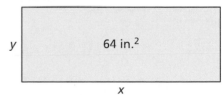

y 64 in.²

x

a. Copy and complete the table.

b. Describe the relationship between x and y. Explain why y is said to vary *inversely* with x.

c. Draw a scatter plot of the data. What are the characteristics of the graph?

d. Write an equation that represents y as a function of x.

Communicate Your Answer

3. How can you recognize when two quantities vary directly or inversely?

4. Does the flapping rate of the wings of a bird vary directly or inversely with the length of its wings? Explain your reasoning.

What You Will Learn

▶ Classify direct and inverse variation.

▶ Write inverse variation equations.

Core Vocabulary

inverse variation, *p. 308*
constant of variation, *p. 308*

Previous
direct variation
ratios

Classifying Direct and Inverse Variation

You have learned that two variables x and y show direct variation when $y = ax$ for some nonzero constant a. Another type of variation is called *inverse variation*.

🌀 Core Concept

Inverse Variation

Two variables x and y show **inverse variation** when they are related as follows:

$$y = \frac{a}{x}, a \neq 0$$

The constant a is the **constant of variation**, and y is said to *vary inversely* with x.

EXAMPLE 1   Classifying Equations

Tell whether x and y show *direct variation*, *inverse variation*, or *neither*.

a. $xy = 5$

b. $y = x - 4$

c. $\dfrac{y}{2} = x$

STUDY TIP

The equation in part (b) does not show direct variation because $y = x - 4$ is not of the form $y = ax$.

SOLUTION

Given Equation	Solved for y	Type of Variation
a. $xy = 5$	$y = \dfrac{5}{x}$	inverse
b. $y = x - 4$	$y = x - 4$	neither
c. $\dfrac{y}{2} = x$	$y = 2x$	direct

Monitoring Progress Help in English and Spanish at *BigIdeasMath.com*

Tell whether x and y show ***direct variation***, ***inverse variation***, or ***neither***.

1. $6x = y$

2. $xy = -0.25$

3. $y + x = 10$

The general equation $y = ax$ for direct variation can be rewritten as $\dfrac{y}{x} = a$. So, a set of data pairs (x, y) shows direct variation when the ratios $\dfrac{y}{x}$ are constant.

The general equation $y = \dfrac{a}{x}$ for inverse variation can be rewritten as $xy = a$. So, a set of data pairs (x, y) shows inverse variation when the products xy are constant.

EXAMPLE 2 **Classifying Data**

Tell whether x and y show *direct variation*, *inverse variation*, or *neither*.

a.

x	2	4	6	8
y	−12	−6	−4	−3

b.

x	1	2	3	4
y	2	4	8	16

SOLUTION

a. Find the products xy and ratios $\dfrac{y}{x}$.

xy	−24	−24	−24	−24	The products are constant.
$\dfrac{y}{x}$	$\dfrac{-12}{2} = -6$	$\dfrac{-6}{4} = -\dfrac{3}{2}$	$\dfrac{-4}{6} = -\dfrac{2}{3}$	$-\dfrac{3}{8}$	The ratios are not constant.

▶ So, x and y show inverse variation.

ANALYZING RELATIONSHIPS

In Example 2(b), notice in the original table that as x increases by 1, y is multiplied by 2. So, the data in the table represent an exponential function.

b. Find the products xy and ratios $\dfrac{y}{x}$.

xy	2	8	24	64	The products are not constant.
$\dfrac{y}{x}$	$\dfrac{2}{1} = 2$	$\dfrac{4}{2} = 2$	$\dfrac{8}{3}$	$\dfrac{16}{4} = 4$	The ratios are not constant.

▶ So, x and y show neither direct nor inverse variation.

Monitoring Progress Help in English and Spanish at *BigIdeasMath.com*

Tell whether x and y show *direct variation*, *inverse variation*, or *neither*.

4.

x	4	3	2	1
y	20	15	10	5

5.

x	1	2	3	4
y	60	30	20	15

Writing Inverse Variation Equations

EXAMPLE 3 **Writing an Inverse Variation Equation**

The variables x and y vary inversely, and $y = 4$ when $x = 3$. Write an equation that relates x and y. Then find y when $x = -2$.

SOLUTION

ANOTHER WAY

Because x and y vary inversely, you also know that the products xy are constant. This product equals the constant of variation a. So, you can quickly determine that $a = xy = 3(4) = 12$.

$y = \dfrac{a}{x}$ Write general equation for inverse variation.

$4 = \dfrac{a}{3}$ Substitute 4 for y and 3 for x.

$12 = a$ Multiply each side by 3.

▶ The inverse variation equation is $y = \dfrac{12}{x}$. When $x = -2$, $y = \dfrac{12}{-2} = -6$.

EXAMPLE 4   Modeling with Mathematics

The time *t* (in hours) that it takes a group of volunteers to build a playground varies inversely with the number *n* of volunteers. It takes a group of 10 volunteers 8 hours to build the playground.

- Make a table showing the time that it would take to build the playground when the number of volunteers is 15, 20, 25, and 30.

- What happens to the time it takes to build the playground as the number of volunteers increases?

SOLUTION

1. **Understand the Problem** You are given a description of two quantities that vary inversely and one pair of data values. You are asked to create a table that gives additional data pairs.

2. **Make a Plan** Use the time that it takes 10 volunteers to build the playground to find the constant of variation. Then write an inverse variation equation and substitute for the different numbers of volunteers to find the corresponding times.

3. **Solve the Problem**

$$t = \frac{a}{n}$$ Write general equation for inverse variation.

$$8 = \frac{a}{10}$$ Substitute 8 for *t* and 10 for *n*.

$$80 = a$$ Multiply each side by 10.

The inverse variation equation is $t = \dfrac{80}{n}$. Make a table of values.

n	15	20	25	30
t	$\frac{80}{15} = 5$ h 20 min	$\frac{80}{20} = 4$ h	$\frac{80}{25} = 3$ h 12 min	$\frac{80}{30} = 2$ h 40 min

▶ As the number of volunteers increases, the time it takes to build the playground decreases.

4. **Look Back** Because the time decreases as the number of volunteers increases, the time for 5 volunteers to build the playground should be greater than 8 hours.

$$t = \frac{80}{5} = 16 \text{ hours} \checkmark$$

LOOKING FOR A PATTERN

Notice that as the number of volunteers increases by 5, the time decreases by a lesser and lesser amount.

From *n* = 15 to *n* = 20, *t* decreases by 1 hour 20 minutes.

From *n* = 20 to *n* = 25, *t* decreases by 48 minutes.

From *n* = 25 to *n* = 30, *t* decreases by 32 minutes.

Monitoring Progress   Help in English and Spanish at *BigIdeasMath.com*

The variables *x* and *y* vary inversely. Use the given values to write an equation relating *x* and *y*. Then find *y* when *x* = 2.

6. *x* = 4, *y* = 5

7. *x* = 6, *y* = −1

8. $x = \frac{1}{2}, y = 16$

9. WHAT IF? In Example 4, it takes a group of 10 volunteers 12 hours to build the playground. How long would it take a group of 15 volunteers?

Vocabulary and Core Concept Check

1. **VOCABULARY** Explain how direct variation equations and inverse variation equations are different.

2. **DIFFERENT WORDS, SAME QUESTION** Which is different? Find "both" answers.

What is an inverse variation equation relating x and y with $a = 4$?	What is an equation for which the ratios $\frac{y}{x}$ are constant and $a = 4$?
What is an equation for which y varies inversely with x and $a = 4$?	What is an equation for which the products xy are constant and $a = 4$?

Monitoring Progress and Modeling with Mathematics

In Exercises 3–10, tell whether x and y show *direct variation*, *inverse variation*, or *neither*. *(See Example 1.)*

3. $y = \dfrac{2}{x}$

4. $xy = 12$

5. $\dfrac{y}{x} = 8$

6. $4x = y$

7. $y - x + 4$

8. $x + y = 6$

9. $8y = x$

10. $xy = \dfrac{1}{5}$

In Exercises 11–14, tell whether x and y show *direct variation*, *inverse variation*, or *neither*. *(See Example 2.)*

11.

x	12	18	23	29	34
y	132	198	253	319	374

12.

x	1.5	2.5	4	7.5	10
y	13.5	22.5	36	67.5	90

13.

x	4	6	8	8.4	12
y	21	14	10.5	10	7

14.

x	4	5	6.2	7	11
y	16	11	10	9	6

In Exercises 15–22, the variables x and y vary inversely. Use the given values to write an equation relating x and y. Then find y when $x = 3$. *(See Example 3.)*

15. $x = 5, y = -4$

16. $x = 1, y = 9$

17. $x = \quad 3, y = 8$

18. $x = 7, y = 2$

19. $x = \dfrac{3}{4}, y = 28$

20. $x = -4, y = -\dfrac{5}{4}$

21. $x - -12, y - -\dfrac{1}{6}$

22. $x = \dfrac{5}{3}, y = -7$

ERROR ANALYSIS In Exercises 23 and 24, the variables x and y vary inversely. Describe and correct the error in writing an equation relating x and y.

23. $x = 8, y = 5$

$$\cancel{\times} \quad \begin{aligned} y &= ax \\ 5 &= a(8) \\ \tfrac{5}{8} &= a \end{aligned}$$

So, $y = \dfrac{5}{8}x$.

24. $x = 5, y = 2$

$$\cancel{\times} \quad \begin{aligned} xy &= a \\ 5 \cdot 2 &= a \\ 10 &= a \end{aligned}$$

So, $y = 10x$.

25. MODELING WITH MATHEMATICS The number y of songs that can be stored on an MP3 player varies inversely with the average size x of a song. A certain MP3 player can store 2500 songs when the average size of a song is 4 megabytes (MB). *(See Example 4.)*

a. Make a table showing the numbers of songs that will fit on the MP3 player when the average size of a song is 2 MB, 2.5 MB, 3 MB, and 5 MB.

b. What happens to the number of songs as the average song size increases?

26. MODELING WITH MATHEMATICS When you stand on snow, the average pressure P (in pounds per square inch) that you exert on the snow varies inversely with the total area A (in square inches) of the soles of your footwear. Suppose the pressure is 0.43 pound per square inch when you wear the snowshoes shown. Write an equation that gives P as a function of A. Then find the pressure when you wear the boots shown.

Snowshoes:
$A = 360$ in.²

Boots:
$A = 60$ in.²

27. PROBLEM SOLVING Computer chips are etched onto silicon wafers. The table compares the area A (in square millimeters) of a computer chip with the number c of chips that can be obtained from a silicon wafer. Write a model that gives c as a function of A. Then predict the number of chips per wafer when the area of a chip is 81 square millimeters.

Area (mm²), A	58	62	66	70
Number of chips, c	448	424	392	376

28. HOW DO YOU SEE IT? Does the graph of f represent inverse variation or direct variation? Explain your reasoning.

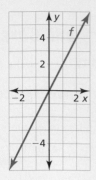

29. MAKING AN ARGUMENT You have enough money to buy 5 hats for $10 each or 10 hats for $5 each. Your friend says this situation represents inverse variation. Is your friend correct? Explain your reasoning.

30. THOUGHT PROVOKING The weight w (in pounds) of an object varies inversely with the square of the distance d (in miles) of the object from the center of Earth. At sea level (3978 miles from the center of the Earth), an astronaut weighs 210 pounds. How much does the astronaut weigh 200 miles above sea level?

31. OPEN-ENDED Describe a real-life situation that can be modeled by an inverse variation equation.

32. CRITICAL THINKING Suppose x varies inversely with y and y varies inversely with z. How does x vary with z? Justify your answer.

33. USING STRUCTURE To balance the board in the diagram, the distance (in feet) of each animal from the center of the board must vary inversely with its weight (in pounds). What is the distance of each animal from the fulcrum? Justify your answer.

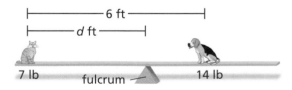

6 ft

d ft

7 lb   fulcrum   14 lb

Maintaining Mathematical Proficiency
Reviewing what you learned in previous grades and lessons

Divide. *(Section 3.3)*

34. $(x^2 + 2x - 99) \div (x + 11)$

35. $(3x^4 - 13x^2 - x^3 + 6x - 30) \div (3x^2 - x + 5)$

Graph the function. Then state the domain and range. *(Section 5.3)*

36. $f(x) = 5^x + 4$

37. $g(x) = e^{x-1}$

38. $y = \ln 3x - 6$

39. $h(x) = 2\ln(x + 9)$

6.2 Graphing Rational Functions

Essential Question
What are some of the characteristics of the graph of a rational function?

The parent function for rational functions with a linear numerator and a linear denominator is

$$f(x) = \frac{1}{x}. \qquad \text{Parent function}$$

The graph of this function, shown at the right, is a *hyperbola*.

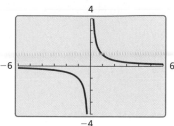

EXPLORATION 1 Identifying Graphs of Rational Functions

Work with a partner. Each function is a transformation of the graph of the parent function $f(x) = \frac{1}{x}$. Match the function with its graph. Explain your reasoning. Then describe the transformation.

a. $g(x) = \dfrac{1}{x - 1}$

b. $g(x) = \dfrac{-1}{x - 1}$

c. $g(x) = \dfrac{x + 1}{x - 1}$

d. $g(x) = \dfrac{x - 2}{x + 1}$

e. $g(x) = \dfrac{x}{x + 2}$

f. $g(x) = \dfrac{-x}{x + 2}$

A.
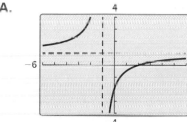

B.
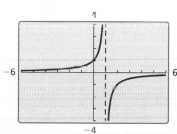

C.
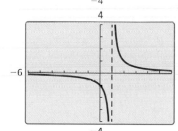

D.
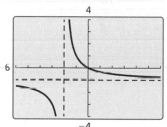

E.
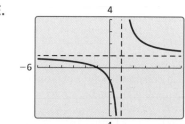

F.
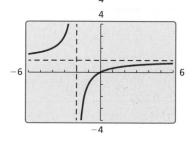

LOOKING FOR STRUCTURE

To be proficient in math, you need to look closely to discern a pattern or structure.

Communicate Your Answer

2. What are some of the characteristics of the graph of a rational function?

3. Determine the intercepts, asymptotes, domain, and range of the rational function $g(x) = \dfrac{x - a}{x - b}$.

What You Will Learn

▶ Graph simple rational functions.

▶ Translate simple rational functions.

▶ Graph other rational functions.

Graphing Simple Rational Functions

A **rational function** has the form $f(x) = \dfrac{p(x)}{q(x)}$, where $p(x)$ and $q(x)$ are polynomials and $q(x) \neq 0$. The inverse variation function $f(x) = \dfrac{a}{x}$ is a rational function. The graph of this function when $a = 1$ is shown below.

⑤ Core Concept

Parent Function for Simple Rational Functions

The graph of the parent function $f(x) = \dfrac{1}{x}$ is a *hyperbola*, which consists of two symmetrical parts called branches. The domain and range are all nonzero real numbers.

Any function of the form $g(x) = \dfrac{a}{x}$ ($a \neq 0$) has the same asymptotes, domain, and range as the function $f(x) = \dfrac{1}{x}$.

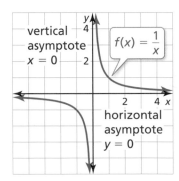

STUDY TIP

Notice that $\dfrac{1}{x} \to 0$ as $x \to \infty$ and as $x \to -\infty$. This explains why $y = 0$ is a horizontal asymptote of the graph of $f(x) = \dfrac{1}{x}$. You can also analyze y-values as x approaches 0 to see why $x = 0$ is a vertical asymptote.

EXAMPLE 1 **Graphing a Rational Function of the Form $y = \dfrac{a}{x}$**

Graph $g(x) = \dfrac{4}{x}$. Compare the graph with the graph of $f(x) = \dfrac{1}{x}$.

SOLUTION

Step 1 The function is of the form $g(x) = \dfrac{a}{x}$, so the asymptotes are $x = 0$ and $y = 0$. Draw the asymptotes.

Step 2 Make a table of values and plot the points. Include both positive and negative values of x.

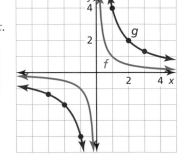

x	-3	-2	-1	1	2	3
y	$-\frac{4}{3}$	-2	-4	4	2	$\frac{4}{3}$

LOOKING FOR STRUCTURE

Because the function is of the form $g(x) = a \cdot f(x)$, where $a = 4$, the graph of g is a vertical stretch by a factor of 4 of the graph of f.

Step 3 Draw the two branches of the hyperbola so that they pass through the plotted points and approach the asymptotes.

▶ The graph of g lies farther from the axes than the graph of f. Both graphs lie in the first and third quadrants and have the same asymptotes, domain, and range.

Monitoring Progress Help in English and Spanish at *BigIdeasMath.com*

1. Graph $g(x) = \dfrac{-6}{x}$. Compare the graph with the graph of $f(x) = \dfrac{1}{x}$.

Translating Simple Rational Functions

⑤ Core Concept

Graphing Translations of Simple Rational Functions

To graph a rational function of the form $y = \dfrac{a}{x - h} + k$, follow these steps:

Step 1 Draw the asymptotes $x = h$ and $y = k$.

Step 2 Plot points to the left and to the right of the vertical asymptote.

Step 3 Draw the two branches of the hyperbola so that they pass through the plotted points and approach the asymptotes.

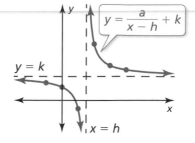

$$y = \dfrac{a}{x - h} + k$$

EXAMPLE 2 Graphing a Translation of a Rational Function

Graph $g(x) = \dfrac{-4}{x + 2} - 1$. State the domain and range.

SOLUTION

Step 1 Draw the asymptotes $x = -2$ and $y = -1$.

Step 2 Plot points to the left of the vertical asymptote, such as $(-3, 3)$, $(-4, 1)$, and $(-6, 0)$. Plot points to the right of the vertical asymptote, such as $(-1, -5)$, $(0, -3)$, and $(2, -2)$.

Step 3 Draw the two branches of the hyperbola so that they pass through the plotted points and approach the asymptotes.

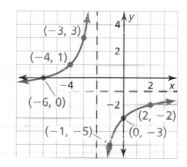

> The domain is all real numbers except -2 and the range is all real numbers except -1.

LOOKING FOR STRUCTURE

Let $f(x) = \dfrac{-4}{x}$. Notice that g is of the form $g(x) = f(x - h) + k$, where $h = -2$ and $k = -1$. So, the graph of g is a translation 2 units left and 1 unit down of the graph of f.

Monitoring Progress Help in English and Spanish at *BigIdeasMath.com*

Graph the function. State the domain and range.

2. $y = \dfrac{3}{x} - 2$

3. $y = \dfrac{-1}{x + 4}$

4. $y = \dfrac{1}{x - 1} + 5$

Graphing Other Rational Functions

All rational functions of the form $y = \dfrac{ax + b}{cx + d}$ also have graphs that are hyperbolas.

- The vertical asymptote of the graph is the line $x = -\dfrac{d}{c}$ because the function is undefined when the denominator $cx + d$ is zero.

- The horizontal asymptote is the line $y = \dfrac{a}{c}$.

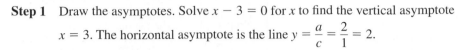

EXAMPLE 3 **Graphing a Rational Function of the Form** $y = \dfrac{ax + b}{cx + d}$

Graph $f(x) = \dfrac{2x + 1}{x - 3}$. State the domain and range.

SOLUTION

Step 1 Draw the asymptotes. Solve $x - 3 = 0$ for x to find the vertical asymptote $x = 3$. The horizontal asymptote is the line $y = \dfrac{a}{c} = \dfrac{2}{1} = 2$.

Step 2 Plot points to the left of the vertical asymptote, such as $(2, -5)$, $\left(0, -\frac{1}{3}\right)$, and $\left(-2, \frac{3}{5}\right)$. Plot points to the right of the vertical asymptote, such as $(4, 9)$, $\left(6, \frac{13}{3}\right)$, and $\left(8, \frac{17}{5}\right)$.

Step 3 Draw the two branches of the hyperbola so that they pass through the plotted points and approach the asymptotes.

▶ The domain is all real numbers except 3 and the range is all real numbers except 2.

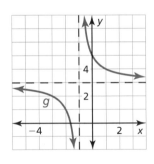

Rewriting a rational function may reveal properties of the function and its graph. For example, rewriting a rational function in the form $y = \dfrac{a}{x - h} + k$ reveals that it is a translation of $y = \dfrac{a}{x}$ with vertical asymptote $x = h$ and horizontal asymptote $y = k$.

EXAMPLE 4 **Rewriting and Graphing a Rational Function**

Rewrite $g(x) = \dfrac{3x + 5}{x + 1}$ in the form $g(x) = \dfrac{a}{x - h} + k$. Graph the function. Describe the graph of g as a transformation of the graph of $f(x) = \dfrac{a}{x}$.

ANOTHER WAY

You will use a different method to rewrite g in Example 5 of Lesson 6.4.

SOLUTION

Rewrite the function by using long division:

$$x + 1 \overline{\smash{)}\begin{array}{r} 3 \\ 3x + 5 \\ \underline{3x + 3} \\ 2 \end{array}}$$

▶ The rewritten function is $g(x) = \dfrac{2}{x + 1} + 3$.

The graph of g is a translation 1 unit left and 3 units up of the graph of $f(x) = \dfrac{2}{x}$.

Monitoring Progress Help in English and Spanish at *BigIdeasMath.com*

Graph the function. State the domain and range.

5. $f(x) = \dfrac{x - 1}{x + 3}$

6. $f(x) = \dfrac{2x + 1}{4x - 2}$

7. $f(x) = \dfrac{-3x + 2}{-x - 1}$

8. Rewrite $g(x) = \dfrac{2x + 3}{x + 1}$ in the form $g(x) = \dfrac{a}{x - h} + k$. Graph the function. Describe the graph of g as a transformation of the graph of $f(x) = \dfrac{a}{x}$.

EXAMPLE 5   **Modeling with Mathematics**

A 3-D printer builds up layers of materials to make three-dimensional models. Each deposited layer bonds to the layer below it. A company decides to make small display models of engine components using a 3-D printer. The printer costs $1000. The material for each model costs $50.

- Estimate how many models must be printed for the average cost per model to fall to $90.

- What happens to the average cost as more models are printed?

SOLUTION

1. **Understand the Problem** You are given the cost of a printer and the cost to create a model using the printer. You are asked to find the number of models for which the average cost falls to $90.

2. **Make a Plan** Write an equation that represents the average cost. Use a graphing calculator to estimate the number of models for which the average cost is about $90. Then analyze the horizontal asymptote of the graph to determine what happens to the average cost as more models are printed.

USING A GRAPHING CALCULATOR

Because the number of models and average cost cannot be negative, choose a viewing window in the first quadrant.

3. **Solve the Problem** Let c be the average cost (in dollars) and m be the number of models printed.

$$c = \frac{(\text{Unit cost})(\text{Number printed}) + (\text{Cost of printer})}{\text{Number printed}} = \frac{50m + 1000}{m}$$

Use a graphing calculator to graph the function.

▶ Using the *trace* feature, the average cost falls to $90 per model after about 25 models are printed. Because the horizontal asymptote is $c = 50$, the average cost approaches $50 as more models are printed.

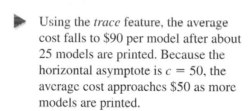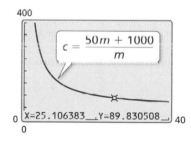

4. **Look Back** Use a graphing calculator to create tables of values for large values of m. The tables show that the average cost approaches $50 as more models are printed.

X	Y1	
0	ERROR	
50	70	
100	60	
150	56.667	
200	55	
250	54	
300	53.333	
X=0		

X	Y1	
0	ERROR	
10000	50.1	
20000	50.05	
30000	50.033	
40000	50.025	
50000	50.02	
60000	50.017	
X=0		

Monitoring Progress Help in English and Spanish at *BigIdeasMath.com*

9. **WHAT IF?** How do the answers in Example 5 change when the cost of the 3-D printer is $800?

Vocabulary and Core Concept Check

1. **COMPLETE THE SENTENCE** The function $y = \dfrac{7}{x + 4} + 3$ has a(n) _____ of all real numbers except 3 and a(n) _____ of all real numbers except -4.

2. **WRITING** Is $f(x) = \dfrac{-3x + 5}{2^x + 1}$ a rational function? Explain your reasoning.

Monitoring Progress and Modeling with Mathematics

In Exercises 3–10, graph the function. Compare the graph with the graph of $f(x) = \dfrac{1}{x}$. *(See Example 1.)*

3. $g(x) = \dfrac{3}{x}$

4. $g(x) = \dfrac{10}{x}$

5. $g(x) = \dfrac{-5}{x}$

6. $g(x) = \dfrac{-9}{x}$

7. $g(x) = \dfrac{15}{x}$

8. $g(x) = \dfrac{-12}{x}$

9. $g(x) = \dfrac{-0.5}{x}$

10. $g(x) = \dfrac{0.1}{x}$

In Exercises 11–18, graph the function. State the domain and range. *(See Example 2.)*

11. $g(x) = \dfrac{4}{x} + 3$

12. $y = \dfrac{2}{x} - 3$

13. $h(x) = \dfrac{6}{x - 1}$

14. $y = \dfrac{1}{x + 2}$

15. $h(x) = \dfrac{-3}{x + 2}$

16. $f(x) = \dfrac{-2}{x - 7}$

17. $g(x) = \dfrac{-3}{x - 4} - 1$

18. $y = \dfrac{10}{x + 7} - 5$

ERROR ANALYSIS In Exercises 19 and 20, describe and correct the error in graphing the rational function.

19. $y = \dfrac{-8}{x}$

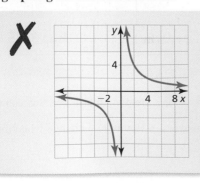

20. $y = \dfrac{2}{x - 1} - 2$

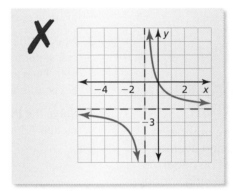

ANALYZING RELATIONSHIPS In Exercises 21–24, match the function with its graph. Explain your reasoning.

21. $g(x) = \dfrac{2}{x - 3} + 1$

22. $h(x) = \dfrac{2}{x + 3} + 1$

23. $f(x) = \dfrac{2}{x - 3} - 1$

24. $y = \dfrac{2}{x + 3} - 1$

A.

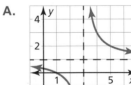

B.

C.

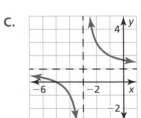

D.

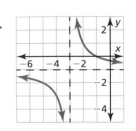

In Exercises 25–32, graph the function. State the domain and range. *(See Example 3.)*

25. $f(x) = \dfrac{x + 4}{x - 3}$

26. $y = \dfrac{x - 1}{x + 5}$

27. $y = \dfrac{x + 6}{4x - 8}$

28. $h(x) = \dfrac{8x + 3}{2x - 6}$

29. $f(x) = \dfrac{-5x + 2}{4x + 5}$

30. $g(x) = \dfrac{6x - 1}{3x - 1}$

31. $h(x) = \dfrac{-5x}{-2x - 3}$

32. $y = \dfrac{-2x + 3}{-x + 10}$

In Exercises 33–40, rewrite the function in the form $g(x) = \dfrac{a}{x - h} + k$. Graph the function. Describe the graph of g as a transformation of the graph of $f(x) = \dfrac{a}{x}$. *(See Example 4.)*

33. $g(x) = \dfrac{5x + 6}{x + 1}$

34. $g(x) = \dfrac{7x + 4}{x - 3}$

35. $g(x) = \dfrac{2x - 4}{x - 5}$

36. $g(x) = \dfrac{4x - 11}{x - 2}$

37. $g(x) = \dfrac{x + 18}{x - 6}$

38. $g(x) = \dfrac{x + 2}{x - 8}$

39. $g(x) = \dfrac{7x + 20}{x + 13}$

40. $g(x) = \dfrac{9x - 3}{x + 7}$

41. PROBLEM SOLVING Your school purchases a math software program. The program has an initial cost of $500 plus $20 for each student that uses the program. *(See Example 5.)*

    a. Estimate how many students must use the program for the average cost per student to fall to $30.

    b. What happens to the average cost as more students use the program?

42. PROBLEM SOLVING To join a rock climbing gym, you must pay an initial fee of $100 and a monthly fee of $59.

    a. Estimate how many months you must purchase a membership for the average cost per month to fall to $69.

    b. What happens to the average cost as the number of months that you are a member increases?

43. USING STRUCTURE What is the vertical asymptote of the graph of the function $y = \dfrac{2}{x + 4} + 7$?

    Ⓐ $x = -7$ Ⓑ $x = -4$

    Ⓒ $x = 4$ Ⓓ $x = 7$

44. REASONING What are the x-intercept(s) of the graph of the function $y = \dfrac{x - 5}{x^2 - 1}$?

    Ⓐ $1, -1$ Ⓑ 5

    Ⓒ 1 Ⓓ -5

45. USING TOOLS The time t (in seconds) it takes for sound to travel 1 kilometer can be modeled by

$$t = \dfrac{1000}{0.6T + 331}$$

where T is the air temperature (in degrees Celsius).

    a. You are 1 kilometer from a lightning strike. You hear the thunder 2.9 seconds later. Use a graph to find the approximate air temperature.

    b. Find the average rate of change in the time it takes sound to travel 1 kilometer as the air temperature increases from 0°C to 10°C.

46. MODELING WITH MATHEMATICS A business is studying the cost to remove a pollutant from the ground at its site. The function $y = \dfrac{15x}{1.1 - x}$ models the estimated cost y (in thousands of dollars) to remove x percent (expressed as a decimal) of the pollutant.

    a. Graph the function. Describe a reasonable domain and range.

    b. How much does it cost to remove 20% of the pollutant? 40% of the pollutant? 80% of the pollutant? Does doubling the percentage of the pollutant removed double the cost? Explain.

USING TOOLS In Exercises 47–50, use a graphing calculator to graph the function. Then determine whether the function is *even, odd,* or *neither.*

47. $h(x) = \dfrac{6}{x^2 + 1}$

48. $f(x) = \dfrac{2x^2}{x^2 - 9}$

49. $y = \dfrac{x^3}{3x^2 + x^4}$

50. $f(x) = \dfrac{4x^2}{2x^3 - x}$

51. MAKING AN ARGUMENT Your friend claims it is possible for a rational function to have two vertical asymptotes. Is your friend correct? Justify your answer.

52. HOW DO YOU SEE IT? Use the graph of f to determine the equations of the asymptotes. Explain.

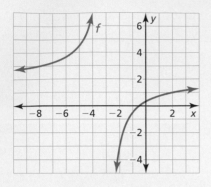

53. DRAWING CONCLUSIONS In what line(s) is the graph of $y = \dfrac{1}{x}$ symmetric? What does this symmetry tell you about the inverse of the function $f(x) = \dfrac{1}{x}$?

54. THOUGHT PROVOKING There are four basic types of conic sections: parabola, circle, ellipse, and hyperbola. Each of these can be represented by the intersection of a double-napped cone and a plane. The intersections for a parabola, circle, and ellipse are shown below. Sketch the intersection for a hyperbola.

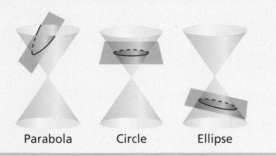

Parabola   Circle   Ellipse

55. REASONING The graph of the rational function f is a hyperbola. The asymptotes of the graph of f intersect at (3, 2). The point (2, 1) is on the graph. Find another point on the graph. Explain your reasoning.

56. ABSTRACT REASONING Describe the intervals where the graph of $y = \dfrac{a}{x}$ is increasing or decreasing when (a) $a > 0$ and (b) $a < 0$. Explain your reasoning.

57. PROBLEM SOLVING An Internet service provider charges a $50 installation fee and a monthly fee of $43. The table shows the average monthly costs y of a competing provider for x months of service. Under what conditions would a person choose one provider over the other? Explain your reasoning.

Months, x	Average monthly cost (dollars), y
6	$49.83
12	$46.92
18	$45.94
24	$45.45

58. MODELING WITH MATHEMATICS The Doppler effect occurs when the source of a sound is moving relative to a listener, so that the frequency f_ℓ (in hertz) heard by the listener is different from the frequency f_s (in hertz) at the source. In both equations below, r is the speed (in miles per hour) of the sound source.

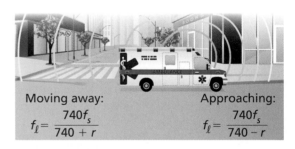

Moving away:
$$f_\ell = \frac{740 f_s}{740 + r}$$

Approaching:
$$f_\ell = \frac{740 f_s}{740 - r}$$

a. An ambulance siren has a frequency of 2000 hertz. Write two equations modeling the frequencies heard when the ambulance is approaching and when the ambulance is moving away.

b. Graph the equations in part (a) using the domain $0 \le r \le 60$.

c. For any speed r, how does the frequency heard for an approaching sound source compare with the frequency heard when the source moves away?

Maintaining Mathematical Proficiency
Reviewing what you learned in previous grades and lessons

Factor the polynomial. *(Skills Review Handbook)*

59. $4x^2 - 4x - 80$ **60.** $3x^2 - 3x - 6$ **61.** $2x^2 - 2x - 12$ **62.** $10x^2 + 31x - 14$

Simplify the expression. *(Section 4.2)*

63. $3^2 \cdot 3^4$ **64.** $2^{1/2} \cdot 2^{3/5}$ **65.** $\dfrac{6^{5/6}}{6^{1/6}}$ **66.** $\dfrac{6^8}{6^{10}}$

Core Vocabulary

inverse variation, *p. 308*
constant of variation, *p. 308*
rational function, *p. 314*

Core Concepts

Section 6.1

Inverse Variation, *p. 308*
Writing Inverse Variation Equations, *p. 309*

Section 6.2

Parent Function for Simple Rational Functions, *p. 314*
Graphing Translations of Simple Rational Functions, *p. 315*

Mathematical Practices

1. Explain the meaning of the given information in Exercise 25 on page 312.

2. How are you able to recognize whether the logic used in Exercise 29 on page 312 is correct or flawed?

3. How can you evaluate the reasonableness of your answer in part (b) of Exercise 41 on page 319?

4. How did the context allow you to determine a reasonable domain and range for the function in Exercise 46 on page 319?

Analyzing Your Errors

Study Errors

What Happens: You do not study the right material or you do not learn it well enough to remember it on a test without resources such as notes.

How to Avoid This Error: Take a practice test. Work with a study group. Discuss the topics on the test with your teacher. Do not try to learn a whole chapter's worth of material in one night.

STUDY SKILLS

Tell whether *x* and *y* show *direct variation*, *inverse variation*, or *neither*. Explain your reasoning. *(Section 6.1)*

1. $x + y = 7$

2. $\frac{2}{5}x = y$

3. $xy = 0.45$

4.

x	3	6	9	12
y	9	18	27	36

5.

x	1	2	3	4
y	−24	−12	−8	−6

6.

x	2	4	6	8
y	72	36	18	9

7. The variables *x* and *y* vary inversely, and $y = 10$ when $x = 5$. Write an equation that relates *x* and *y*. Then find *y* when $x = -2$. *(Section 6.1)*

Match the function with its graph. Explain your reasoning. *(Section 6.2)*

8. $f(x) = \dfrac{3}{x} + 2$

9. $y = \dfrac{-2}{x + 3} - 2$

10. $h(x) = \dfrac{2x + 2}{3x + 1}$

A.

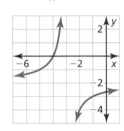

B.

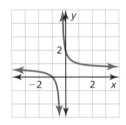

C.

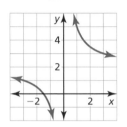

11. Rewrite $g(x) = \dfrac{2x + 9}{x + 8}$ in the form $g(x) = \dfrac{a}{x - h} + k$. Graph the function. Describe the graph of *g* as a transformation of the graph of $f(x) = \dfrac{a}{x}$. *(Section 6.2)*

12. The time *t* (in minutes) required to empty a tank varies inversely with the pumping rate *r* (in gallons per minute). The rate of a certain pump is 70 gallons per minute. It takes the pump 20 minutes to empty the tank. Complete the table for the times it takes the pump to empty a tank for the given pumping rates. *(Section 6.1)*

Pumping rate (gal/min)	Time (min)
50	
60	
65	
75	

13. A pitcher throws 16 strikes in the first 38 pitches. The table shows how a pitcher's strike percentage changes when the pitcher throws *x* consecutive strikes after the first 38 pitches. Write a rational function for the strike percentage in terms of *x*. Graph the function. How many consecutive strikes must the pitcher throw to reach a strike percentage of 0.60? *(Section 6.2)*

x	Total strikes	Total pitches	Strike percentage
0	16	38	0.42
5	21	43	0.49
10	26	48	0.54
x	x + 16	x + 38	

6.3 Multiplying and Dividing Rational Expressions

Essential Question How can you determine the excluded values in a product or quotient of two rational expressions?

You can multiply and divide rational expressions in much the same way that you multiply and divide fractions. Values that make the denominator of an expression zero are *excluded values*.

$$\frac{1}{\cancel{x}} \cdot \frac{\cancel{x}}{x + 1} = \frac{1}{x + 1}, x \neq 0 \qquad \text{Product of rational expressions}$$

$$\frac{1}{x} \div \frac{x}{x + 1} = \frac{1}{x} \cdot \frac{x + 1}{x} = \frac{x + 1}{x^2}, x \neq -1 \qquad \text{Quotient of rational expressions}$$

EXPLORATION 1   Multiplying and Dividing Rational Expressions

Work with a partner. Find the product or quotient of the two rational expressions. Then match the product or quotient with its excluded values. Explain your reasoning.

Product or Quotient

a. $\dfrac{1}{x - 1} \cdot \dfrac{x - 2}{x + 1} = \ $ ⬚

b. $\dfrac{1}{x - 1} \cdot \dfrac{-1}{x - 1} = \ $ ⬚

c. $\dfrac{1}{x - 2} \cdot \dfrac{x - 2}{x + 1} = \ $ ⬚

d. $\dfrac{x + 2}{x - 1} \cdot \dfrac{-x}{x + 2} = \ $ ⬚

e. $\dfrac{x}{x + 2} \div \dfrac{x + 1}{x + 2} = \ $ ⬚

f. $\dfrac{x}{x - 2} \div \dfrac{x + 1}{x} = \ $ ⬚

g. $\dfrac{x}{x + 2} \div \dfrac{x}{x - 1} = \ $ ⬚

h. $\dfrac{x + 2}{x} \div \dfrac{x + 1}{x - 1} = \ $ ⬚

Excluded Values

A.   1, 0, and 2

B. -2 and 1

C. -2, 0, and 1

D. -1 and 2

E. -1, 0, and 1

F. -1 and 1

G. -2 and -1

H.   1

To be proficient in math, you need to know and flexibly use different properties of operations and objects.

EXPLORATION 2   Writing a Product or Quotient

Work with a partner. Write a product or quotient of rational expressions that has the given excluded values. Justify your answer.

a. -1 b. -1 and 3   c. -1, 0, and 3

Communicate Your Answer

3. How can you determine the excluded values in a product or quotient of two rational expressions?

4. Is it possible for the product or quotient of two rational expressions to have *no* excluded values? Explain your reasoning. If it is possible, give an example.

Section 6.3   Multiplying and Dividing Rational Expressions   **323**

What You Will Learn

▶ Simplify rational expressions.

▶ Multiply rational expressions.

▶ Divide rational expressions.

Core Vocabulary

rational expression, *p. 324*
simplified form of a rational
   expression, *p. 324*

Previous
fractions
polynomials
domain
equivalent expressions
reciprocal

Simplifying Rational Expressions

A **rational expression** is a fraction whose numerator and denominator are nonzero polynomials. The *domain* of a rational expression excludes values that make the denominator zero. A rational expression is in **simplified form** when its numerator and denominator have no common factors (other than ± 1).

Core Concept

Simplifying Rational Expressions

Let a, b, and c be expressions with $b \neq 0$ and $c \neq 0$.

Property $\dfrac{a\cancel{c}}{b\cancel{c}} = \dfrac{a}{b}$ Divide out common factor c.

Examples $\dfrac{15}{65} = \dfrac{3 \cdot \cancel{5}}{13 \cdot \cancel{5}} = \dfrac{3}{13}$ Divide out common factor 5.

$\dfrac{4\cancel{(x+3)}}{(x+3)\cancel{(x+3)}} = \dfrac{4}{x+3}$ Divide out common factor $x + 3$.

STUDY TIP

Notice that you can divide out common factors in the second expression at the right. You cannot, however, divide out like terms in the third expression.

Simplifying a rational expression usually requires two steps. First, factor the numerator and denominator. Then, divide out any factors that are common to both the numerator and denominator. Here is an example:

$$\frac{x^2 + 7x}{x^2} = \frac{x(x + 7)}{x \cdot x} = \frac{x + 7}{x}$$

EXAMPLE 1   **Simplifying a Rational Expression**

Simplify $\dfrac{x^2 - 4x - 12}{x^2 - 4}$.

SOLUTION

COMMON ERROR

Do not divide out variable terms that are not factors.

$\dfrac{x - 6}{x - 2} \neq \dfrac{-6}{-2}$

$\dfrac{x^2 - 4x - 12}{x^2 - 4} = \dfrac{(x + 2)(x - 6)}{(x + 2)(x - 2)}$ Factor numerator and denominator.

$= \dfrac{\cancel{(x + 2)}(x - 6)}{\cancel{(x + 2)}(x - 2)}$ Divide out common factor.

$= \dfrac{x - 6}{x - 2}, \quad x \neq -2$ Simplified form

The original expression is undefined when $x = -2$. To make the original and simplified expressions equivalent, restrict the domain of the simplified expression by excluding $x = -2$. Both expressions are undefined when $x = 2$, so it is not necessary to list it.

Monitoring Progress   Help in English and Spanish at *BigIdeasMath.com*

Simplify the rational expression, if possible.

1. $\dfrac{2(x + 1)}{(x + 1)(x + 3)}$ 2. $\dfrac{x + 4}{x^2 - 16}$ 3. $\dfrac{4}{x(x + 2)}$ 4. $\dfrac{x^2 - 2x - 3}{x^2 - x - 6}$

Multiplying Rational Expressions

The rule for multiplying rational expressions is the same as the rule for multiplying numerical fractions: multiply numerators, multiply denominators, and write the new fraction in simplified form. Similar to rational numbers, rational expressions are closed under multiplication.

Core Concept

Multiplying Rational Expressions

Let a, b, c, and d be expressions with $b \neq 0$ and $d \neq 0$.

Property $\quad \dfrac{a}{b} \cdot \dfrac{c}{d} = \dfrac{ac}{bd} \qquad$ Simplify $\dfrac{ac}{bd}$ if possible.

Example $\quad \dfrac{5x^2}{2xy^2} \cdot \dfrac{6xy^3}{10y} = \dfrac{30x^3y^3}{20xy^3} = \dfrac{\cancel{10} \cdot 3 \cdot \cancel{x} \cdot x^2 \cdot \cancel{y^3}}{\cancel{10} \cdot 2 \cdot \cancel{x} \cdot \cancel{y^3}} = \dfrac{3x^2}{2}, \quad x \neq 0, y \neq 0$

ANOTHER WAY

In Example 2, you can first simplify each rational expression, then multiply, and finally simplify the result.

$\dfrac{8x^3y}{2xy^2} \cdot \dfrac{7x^4y^3}{4y}$

$= \dfrac{4x^2}{y} \cdot \dfrac{7x^4y^2}{4}$

$= \dfrac{\cancel{4} \cdot 7 \cdot x^6 \cdot \cancel{y} \cdot y}{\cancel{4} \cdot \cancel{y}}$

$= 7x^6y, \quad x \neq 0, y \neq 0$

EXAMPLE 2   **Multiplying Rational Expressions**

Find the product $\dfrac{8x^3y}{2xy^2} \cdot \dfrac{7x^4y^3}{4y}$.

SOLUTION

$\dfrac{8x^3y}{2xy^2} \cdot \dfrac{7x^4y^3}{4y} = \dfrac{56x^7y^4}{8xy^3}$ Multiply numerators and denominators.

$= \dfrac{\cancel{8} \cdot 7 \cdot \cancel{x} \cdot x^6 \cdot \cancel{y^3} \cdot y}{\cancel{8} \cdot \cancel{x} \cdot \cancel{y^3}}$ Factor and divide out common factors.

$= 7x^6y, \quad x \neq 0, y \neq 0$ Simplified form

EXAMPLE 3   **Multiplying Rational Expressions**

Find the product $\dfrac{3x - 3x^2}{x^2 + 4x - 5} \cdot \dfrac{x^2 + x - 20}{3x}$.

SOLUTION

$\dfrac{3x - 3x^2}{x^2 + 4x - 5} \cdot \dfrac{x^2 + x - 20}{3x} = \dfrac{3x(1 - x)}{(x - 1)(x + 5)} \cdot \dfrac{(x + 5)(x - 4)}{3x}$ Factor numerators and denominators.

$= \dfrac{3x(1 - x)(x + 5)(x - 4)}{(x - 1)(x + 5)(3x)}$ Multiply numerators and denominators.

$= \dfrac{3x(-1)(x - 1)(x + 5)(x - 4)}{(x - 1)(x + 5)(3x)}$ Rewrite $1 - x$ as $(-1)(x - 1)$.

$= \dfrac{\cancel{3x}(-1)\cancel{(x - 1)}\cancel{(x + 5)}(x - 4)}{\cancel{(x - 1)}\cancel{(x + 5)}\cancel{(3x)}}$ Divide out common factors.

$= -x + 4, \quad x \neq -5, x \neq 0, x \neq 1$ Simplified form

Check

X	Y1	Y2
-5	ERROR	9
-4	**8**	**8**
-3	7	7
-2	6	6
-1	5	5
0	ERROR	4
1	ERROR	3

X=-4

Check the simplified expression. Enter the original expression as y_1 and the simplified expression as y_2 in a graphing calculator. Then use the *table* feature to compare the values of the two expressions. The values of y_1 and y_2 are the same, except when $x = -5$, $x = 0$, and $x = 1$. So, when these values are excluded from the domain of the simplified expression, it is equivalent to the original expression.

EXAMPLE 4 **Multiplying a Rational Expression by a Polynomial**

Find the product $\dfrac{x+2}{x^3-27} \cdot (x^2 + 3x + 9)$.

SOLUTION

$$\dfrac{x+2}{x^3-27} \cdot (x^2 + 3x + 9) = \dfrac{x+2}{x^3-27} \cdot \dfrac{x^2+3x+9}{1} \qquad \text{Write polynomial as a rational expression.}$$

$$= \dfrac{(x+2)(x^2+3x+9)}{(x-3)(x^2+3x+9)} \qquad \text{Multiply. Factor denominator.}$$

$$= \dfrac{(x+2)\cancel{(x^2+3x+9)}}{(x-3)\cancel{(x^2+3x+9)}} \qquad \text{Divide out common factor.}$$

$$= \dfrac{x+2}{x-3} \qquad \text{Simplified form}$$

STUDY TIP

Notice that $x^2 + 3x + 9$ does not equal zero for any real value of x. So, no values must be excluded from the domain to make the simplified form equivalent to the original.

Monitoring Progress Help in English and Spanish at *BigIdeasMath.com*

Find the product.

5. $\dfrac{3x^5y^2}{8xy} \cdot \dfrac{6xy^2}{9x^3y}$

6. $\dfrac{2x^2-10x}{x^2-25} \cdot \dfrac{x+3}{2x^2}$

7. $\dfrac{x+5}{x^3-1} \cdot (x^2 + x + 1)$

Dividing Rational Expressions

To divide one rational expression by another, multiply the first rational expression by the reciprocal of the second rational expression. Rational expressions are closed under nonzero division.

Core Concept

Dividing Rational Expressions

Let a, b, c, and d be expressions with $b \ne 0$, $c \ne 0$, and $d \ne 0$.

Property $\dfrac{a}{b} \div \dfrac{c}{d} = \dfrac{a}{b} \cdot \dfrac{d}{c} = \dfrac{ad}{bc}$ Simplify $\dfrac{ad}{bc}$ if possible.

Example $\dfrac{7}{x+1} \div \dfrac{x+2}{2x-3} = \dfrac{7}{x+1} \cdot \dfrac{2x-3}{x+2} = \dfrac{7(2x-3)}{(x+1)(x+2)}, x \ne \dfrac{3}{2}$

EXAMPLE 5 **Dividing Rational Expressions**

Find the quotient $\dfrac{7x}{2x-10} \div \dfrac{x^2-6x}{x^2-11x+30}$.

SOLUTION

$$\dfrac{7x}{2x-10} \div \dfrac{x^2-6x}{x^2-11x+30} = \dfrac{7x}{2x-10} \cdot \dfrac{x^2-11x+30}{x^2-6x} \qquad \text{Multiply by reciprocal.}$$

$$= \dfrac{7x}{2(x-5)} \cdot \dfrac{(x-5)(x-6)}{x(x-6)} \qquad \text{Factor.}$$

$$= \dfrac{7x\cancel{(x-5)}\cancel{(x-6)}}{2\cancel{(x-5)}(x)\cancel{(x-6)}} \qquad \text{Multiply. Divide out common factors.}$$

$$= \dfrac{7}{2}, \quad x \ne 0, x \ne 5, x \ne 6 \qquad \text{Simplified form}$$

EXAMPLE 6 **Dividing a Rational Expression by a Polynomial**

Find the quotient $\dfrac{6x^2 + x - 15}{4x^2} \div (3x^2 + 5x)$.

SOLUTION

$$\dfrac{6x^2 + x - 15}{4x^2} \div (3x^2 + 5x) = \dfrac{6x^2 + x - 15}{4x^2} \cdot \dfrac{1}{3x^2 + 5x} \qquad \text{Multiply by reciprocal.}$$

$$= \dfrac{(3x + 5)(2x - 3)}{4x^2} \cdot \dfrac{1}{x(3x + 5)} \qquad \text{Factor.}$$

$$= \dfrac{\cancel{(3x + 5)}(2x - 3)}{4x^2(x)\cancel{(3x + 5)}} \qquad \begin{array}{l}\text{Multiply. Divide out}\\\text{common factor.}\end{array}$$

$$= \dfrac{2x - 3}{4x^3}, \quad x \neq -\dfrac{5}{3} \qquad \text{Simplified form}$$

EXAMPLE 7 **Solving a Real-Life Problem**

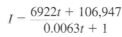

The total annual amount I (in millions of dollars) of personal income earned in Alabama and its annual population P (in millions) can be modeled by

$$I = \dfrac{6922t + 106{,}947}{0.0063t + 1}$$

and

$$P = 0.0343t + 4.432$$

where t represents the year, with $t = 1$ corresponding to 2001. Find a model M for the annual per capita income. (Per capita means per person.) Estimate the per capita income in 2010. (Assume $t > 0$.)

SOLUTION

To find a model M for the annual per capita income, divide the total amount I by the population P.

$$M = \dfrac{6922t + 106{,}947}{0.0063t + 1} \div (0.0343t + 4.432) \qquad \text{Divide } I \text{ by } P.$$

$$= \dfrac{6922t + 106{,}947}{0.0063t + 1} \cdot \dfrac{1}{0.0343t + 4.432} \qquad \text{Multiply by reciprocal.}$$

$$= \dfrac{6922t + 106{,}947}{(0.0063t + 1)(0.0343t + 4.432)} \qquad \text{Multiply.}$$

To estimate Alabama's per capita income in 2010, let $t = 10$ in the model.

$$M = \dfrac{6922 \cdot 10 + 106{,}947}{(0.0063 \cdot 10 + 1)(0.0343 \cdot 10 + 4.432)} \qquad \text{Substitute 10 for } t.$$

$$\approx 34{,}707 \qquad \text{Use a calculator.}$$

▶ In 2010, the per capita income in Alabama was about \$34,707.

Monitoring Progress Help in English and Spanish at *BigIdeasMath.com*

Find the quotient.

8. $\dfrac{4x}{5x - 20} \div \dfrac{x^2 - 2x}{x^2 - 6x + 8}$

9. $\dfrac{2x^2 + 3x - 5}{6x} \div (2x^2 + 5x)$

Vocabulary and Core Concept Check

1. **WRITING** Describe how to multiply and divide two rational expressions.

2. **WHICH ONE DOESN'T BELONG?** Which rational expression does *not* belong with the other three? Explain your reasoning.

$$\dfrac{x-4}{x^2} \qquad \dfrac{x^2+4x-12}{x^2+6x} \qquad \dfrac{9+x}{3x^2} \qquad \dfrac{x^2-x-12}{x^2-6x}$$

Monitoring Progress and Modeling with Mathematics

In Exercises 3–10, simplify the expression, if possible. *(See Example 1.)*

3. $\dfrac{2x^2}{3x^2-4x}$

4. $\dfrac{7x^3-x^2}{2x^3}$

5. $\dfrac{x^2-3x-18}{x^2-7x+6}$

6. $\dfrac{x^2+13x+36}{x^2-7x+10}$

7. $\dfrac{x^2+11x+18}{x^3+8}$

8. $\dfrac{x^2-7x+12}{x^3-27}$

9. $\dfrac{32x^4-50}{4x^3-12x^2-5x+15}$

10. $\dfrac{3x^3-3x^2+7x-7}{27x^4-147}$

In Exercises 11–20, find the product. *(See Examples 2, 3, and 4.)*

11. $\dfrac{4xy^3}{x^2y} \cdot \dfrac{y}{8x}$

12. $\dfrac{48x^5y^3}{y^4} \cdot \dfrac{x^2y}{6x^3y^2}$

13. $\dfrac{x^2(x-4)}{x-3} \cdot \dfrac{(x-3)(x+6)}{x^3}$

14. $\dfrac{x^3(x+5)}{x-9} \cdot \dfrac{(x-9)(x+8)}{3x^3}$

15. $\dfrac{x^2-3x}{x-2} \cdot \dfrac{x^2+x-6}{x}$

16. $\dfrac{x^2-4x}{x-1} \cdot \dfrac{x^2+3x-4}{2x}$

17. $\dfrac{x^2+3x-4}{x^2+4x+4} \cdot \dfrac{2x^2+4x}{x^2-4x+3}$

18. $\dfrac{x^2-x-6}{4x^3} \cdot \dfrac{2x^2+2x}{x^2+5x+6}$

19. $\dfrac{x^2+5x-36}{x^2-49} \cdot (x^2-11x+28)$

20. $\dfrac{x^2-x-12}{x^2-16} \cdot (x^2+2x-8)$

21. **ERROR ANALYSIS** Describe and correct the error in simplifying the rational expression.

$$\dfrac{x^2+\overset{2}{\cancel{16}}x+\overset{3}{\cancel{48}}}{x^2+\underset{1}{\cancel{8}}x+\underset{1}{\cancel{16}}} = \dfrac{x^2+2x+3}{x^2+x+1}$$

22. **ERROR ANALYSIS** Describe and correct the error in finding the product.

$$\dfrac{x^2-25}{3-x} \cdot \dfrac{x-3}{x+5} = \dfrac{(x+5)(x-5)}{3-x} \cdot \dfrac{x-3}{x+5}$$

$$= \dfrac{\cancel{(x+5)}(x-5)\cancel{(x-3)}}{\cancel{(3-x)}\cancel{(x+5)}}$$

$$= x-5, x \neq 3, x \neq -5$$

23. **USING STRUCTURE** Which rational expression is in simplified form?

   Ⓐ $\dfrac{x^2-x-6}{x^2+3x+2}$ Ⓑ $\dfrac{x^2+6x+8}{x^2+2x-3}$

   Ⓒ $\dfrac{x^2-6x+9}{x^2-2x-3}$ Ⓓ $\dfrac{x^2+3x-4}{x^2+x-2}$

24. **COMPARING METHODS** Find the product below by multiplying the numerators and denominators, then simplifying. Then find the product by simplifying each expression, then multiplying. Which method do you prefer? Explain.

$$\dfrac{4x^2y}{2x^3} \cdot \dfrac{12y^4}{24x^2}$$

25. WRITING Compare the function

$$f(x) = \frac{(3x - 7)(x + 6)}{(3x - 7)}$$ to the function $g(x) = x + 6$.

26. MODELING WITH MATHEMATICS Write a model in terms of x for the total area of the base of the building.

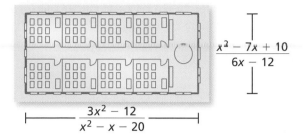

$$\frac{x^2 - 7x + 10}{6x - 12}$$

$$\frac{3x^2 - 12}{x^2 - x - 20}$$

In Exercises 27–34, find the quotient. (*See Examples 5 and 6.*)

27. $\dfrac{32x^3y}{y^8} \div \dfrac{y^7}{8x^4}$

28. $\dfrac{2xyz}{x^3z^3} \div \dfrac{6y^4}{2x^2z^2}$

29. $\dfrac{x^2 - x - 6}{2x^4} \div \dfrac{x + 2}{6x^3}$

30. $\dfrac{2x^2 - 12x}{x^2 - 7x + 6} \div \dfrac{2x}{3x - 3}$

31. $\dfrac{x^2 - x - 6}{x + 4} \div (x^2 - 6x + 9)$

32. $\dfrac{x^2 - 5x - 36}{x + 2} \div (x^2 - 18x + 81)$

33. $\dfrac{x^2 + 9x + 18}{x^2 + 6x + 8} \div \dfrac{x^2 - 3x - 18}{x^2 + 2x - 8}$

34. $\dfrac{x^2 - 3x - 40}{x^2 + 8x - 20} \div \dfrac{x^2 + 13x + 40}{x^2 + 12x + 20}$

In Exercises 35 and 36, use the following information.

Manufacturers often package products in a way that uses the least amount of material. One measure of the efficiency of a package is the ratio of its surface area S to its volume V. The smaller the ratio, the more efficient the packaging.

35. You are examining three cylindrical containers.

a. Write an expression for the efficiency ratio $\dfrac{S}{V}$ of a cylinder.

b. Find the efficiency ratio for each cylindrical can listed in the table. Rank the three cans according to efficiency.

	Soup	Coffee	Paint
Height, h	10.2 cm	15.9 cm	19.4 cm
Radius, r	3.4 cm	7.8 cm	8.4 cm

36. A popcorn company is designing a new tin with the same square base and twice the height of the old tin.

a. Write an expression for the efficiency ratio $\dfrac{S}{V}$ of each tin.

b. Did the company make a good decision by creating the new tin? Explain.

37. MODELING WITH MATHEMATICS The total amount I (in millions of dollars) of healthcare expenditures and the residential population P (in millions) in the United States can be modeled by

$$I = \frac{171{,}000t + 1{,}361{,}000}{1 + 0.018t} \quad \text{and}$$

$$P = 2.96t + 278.649$$

where t is the number of years since 2000. Find a model M for the annual healthcare expenditures per resident. Estimate the annual healthcare expenditures per resident in 2010. (*See Example 7.*)

38. MODELING WITH MATHEMATICS The total amount I (in millions of dollars) of school expenditures from prekindergarten to a college level and the enrollment P (in millions) in prekindergarten through college in the United States can be modeled by

$$I = \frac{17{,}913t + 709{,}569}{1 - 0.028t} \text{ and } P = 0.5906t + 70.219$$

where t is the number of years since 2001. Find a model M for the annual education expenditures per student. Estimate the annual education expenditures per student in 2009.

39. USING EQUATIONS Refer to the population model P in Exercise 37.

a. Interpret the meaning of the coefficient of t.

b. Interpret the meaning of the constant term.

40. HOW DO YOU SEE IT? Use the graphs of f and g to determine the excluded values of the functions $h(x) = (fg)(x)$ and $k(x) = \left(\dfrac{f}{g}\right)(x)$. Explain your reasoning.

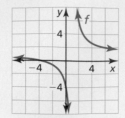 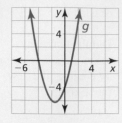

41. DRAWING CONCLUSIONS Complete the table for the function $y = \dfrac{x + 4}{x^2 - 16}$. Then use the *trace* feature of a graphing calculator to explain the behavior of the function at $x = -4$.

x	y
−3.5	
−3.8	
−3.9	
−4.1	
−4.2	

42. MAKING AN ARGUMENT You and your friend are asked to state the domain of the expression below.

$$\frac{x^2 + 6x - 27}{x^2 + 4x - 45}$$

Your friend claims the domain is all real numbers except 5. You claim the domain is all real numbers except −9 and 5. Who is correct? Explain.

43. MATHEMATICAL CONNECTIONS Find the ratio of the perimeter to the area of the triangle shown.

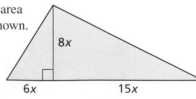

44. CRITICAL THINKING Find the expression that makes the following statement true. Assume $x \neq -2$ and $x \neq 5$.

$$\frac{x - 5}{x^2 + 2x - 35} \div \frac{\boxed{}}{x^2 - 3x - 10} = \frac{x + 2}{x + 7}$$

USING STRUCTURE In Exercises 45 and 46, perform the indicated operations.

45. $\dfrac{2x^2 + x - 15}{2x^2 - 11x - 21} \cdot (6x + 9) \div \dfrac{2x - 5}{3x - 21}$

46. $(x^3 + 8) \cdot \dfrac{x - 2}{x^2 - 2x + 4} \div \dfrac{x^2 - 4}{x - 6}$

47. REASONING Animals that live in temperatures several degrees colder than their bodies must avoid losing heat to survive. Animals can better conserve body heat as their surface area to volume ratios decrease. Find the surface area to volume ratio of each penguin shown by using cylinders to approximate their shapes. Which penguin is better equipped to live in a colder environment? Explain your reasoning.

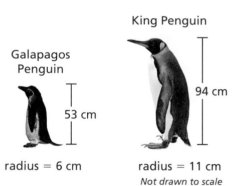

48. THOUGHT PROVOKING Is it possible to write two radical functions whose product when graphed is a parabola and whose quotient when graphed is a hyperbola? Justify your answer.

49. REASONING Find two rational functions f and g that have the stated product and quotient.

$$(fg)(x) = x^2, \quad \left(\frac{f}{g}\right)(x) = \frac{(x - 1)^2}{(x + 2)^2}$$

Maintaining Mathematical Proficiency
Reviewing what you learned in previous grades and lessons

Solve the equation. Check your solution. *(Skills Review Handbook)*

50. $\frac{1}{2}x + 4 = \frac{3}{2}x + 5$

51. $\frac{1}{3}x - 2 = \frac{3}{4}x$

52. $\frac{1}{4}x - \frac{3}{5} = \frac{9}{2}x - \frac{4}{5}$

53. $\frac{1}{2}x + \frac{1}{3} = \frac{3}{4}x - \frac{1}{5}$

Write the prime factorization of the number. If the number is prime, then write *prime*. *(Skills Review Handbook)*

54. 42

55. 91

56. 72

57. 79

6.4 Adding and Subtracting Rational Expressions

Essential Question How can you determine the domain of the sum or difference of two rational expressions?

You can add and subtract rational expressions in much the same way that you add and subtract fractions.

$$\frac{x}{x+1} + \frac{2}{x+1} = \frac{x+2}{x+1}$$ Sum of rational expressions

$$\frac{1}{x} - \frac{1}{2x} = \frac{2}{2x} - \frac{1}{2x} = \frac{1}{2x}$$ Difference of rational expressions

EXPLORATION 1 Adding and Subtracting Rational Expressions

Work with a partner. Find the sum or difference of the two rational expressions. Then match the sum or difference with its domain. Explain your reasoning.

Sum or Difference

a. $\dfrac{1}{x-1} + \dfrac{3}{x-1} =$

b. $\dfrac{1}{x-1} + \dfrac{1}{x} =$

c. $\dfrac{1}{x-2} + \dfrac{1}{2-x} =$

d. $\dfrac{1}{x-1} + \dfrac{-1}{x+1} =$

e. $\dfrac{x}{x+2} - \dfrac{x+1}{2+x} =$

f. $\dfrac{x}{x-2} - \dfrac{x+1}{x} =$

g. $\dfrac{x}{x+2} - \dfrac{x}{x-1} =$

h. $\dfrac{x+2}{x} - \dfrac{x+1}{x} =$

Domain

A. all real numbers except -2

B. all real numbers except -1 and 1

C. all real numbers except 1

D. all real numbers except 0

E. all real numbers except -2 and 1

F. all real numbers except 0 and 1

G. all real numbers except 2

H. all real numbers except 0 and 2

EXPLORATION 2 Writing a Sum or Difference

Work with a partner. Write a sum or difference of rational expressions that has the given domain. Justify your answer.

a. all real numbers except -1 **b.** all real numbers except -1 and 3

c. all real numbers except $-1, 0,$ and 3

CONSTRUCTING
VIABLE ARGUMENTS
To be proficient in math, you need to justify your conclusions and communicate them to others.

Communicate Your Answer

3. How can you determine the domain of the sum or difference of two rational expressions?

4. Your friend found a sum as follows. Describe and correct the error(s).

$$\frac{x}{x+4} + \frac{3}{x-4} = \frac{x+3}{2x}$$

What You Will Learn

▶ Add or subtract rational expressions.

▶ Rewrite rational functions.

▶ Simplify complex fractions.

Adding or Subtracting Rational Expressions

As with numerical fractions, the procedure used to add (or subtract) two rational expressions depends upon whether the expressions have like or unlike denominators. To add (or subtract) rational expressions with like denominators, simply add (or subtract) their numerators. Then place the result over the common denominator.

🔄 Core Concept

Adding or Subtracting with Like Denominators

Let a, b, and c be expressions with $c \neq 0$.

Addition

$$\frac{a}{c} + \frac{b}{c} = \frac{a+b}{c}$$

Subtraction

$$\frac{a}{c} - \frac{b}{c} = \frac{a-b}{c}$$

EXAMPLE 1 Adding or Subtracting with Like Denominators

a. $\dfrac{7}{4x} + \dfrac{3}{4x} = \dfrac{7+3}{4x} = \dfrac{10}{4x} = \dfrac{5}{2x}$ Add numerators and simplify.

b. $\dfrac{2x}{x+6} - \dfrac{5}{x+6} = \dfrac{2x-5}{x+6}$ Subtract numerators.

Monitoring Progress Help in English and Spanish at *BigIdeasMath.com*

Find the sum or difference.

1. $\dfrac{8}{12x} - \dfrac{5}{12x}$ **2.** $\dfrac{2}{3x^2} + \dfrac{1}{3x^2}$ **3.** $\dfrac{4x}{x-2} - \dfrac{x}{x-2}$ **4.** $\dfrac{2x^2}{x^2+1} + \dfrac{2}{x^2+1}$

To add (or subtract) two rational expressions with *unlike* denominators, find a common denominator. Rewrite each rational expression using the common denominator. Then add (or subtract).

🔄 Core Concept

Adding or Subtracting with Unlike Denominators

Let a, b, c, and d be expressions with $c \neq 0$ and $d \neq 0$.

Addition

$$\frac{a}{c} + \frac{b}{d} = \frac{ad}{cd} + \frac{bc}{cd} = \frac{ad+bc}{cd}$$

Subtraction

$$\frac{a}{c} - \frac{b}{d} = \frac{ad}{cd} - \frac{bc}{cd} = \frac{ad-bc}{cd}$$

You can always find a common denominator of two rational expressions by multiplying the denominators, as shown above. However, when you use the least common denominator (LCD), which is the least common multiple (LCM) of the denominators, simplifying your answer may take fewer steps.

To find the LCM of two (or more) expressions, factor the expressions completely. The LCM is the product of the highest power of each factor that appears in any of the expressions.

EXAMPLE 2 **Finding a Least Common Multiple (LCM)**

Find the least common multiple of $4x^2 - 16$ and $6x^2 - 24x + 24$.

SOLUTION

Step 1 Factor each polynomial. Write numerical factors as products of primes.

$$4x^2 - 16 = 4(x^2 - 4) = (2^2)(x + 2)(x - 2)$$

$$6x^2 - 24x + 24 = 6(x^2 - 4x + 4) = (2)(3)(x - 2)^2$$

Step 2 The LCM is the product of the highest power of each factor that appears in either polynomial.

$$\text{LCM} = (2^2)(3)(x + 2)(x - 2)^2 = 12(x + 2)(x - 2)^2$$

EXAMPLE 3 **Adding with Unlike Denominators**

Find the sum $\dfrac{7}{9x^2} + \dfrac{x}{3x^2 + 3x}$.

SOLUTION

Method 1 Use the definition for adding rational expressions with unlike denominators.

$$\frac{7}{9x^2} + \frac{x}{3x^2 + 3x} = \frac{7(3x^2 + 3x) + x(9x^2)}{9x^2(3x^2 + 3x)} \qquad \frac{a}{c} + \frac{b}{d} = \frac{ad + bc}{cd}$$

$$= \frac{21x^2 + 21x + 9x^3}{9x^2(3x^2 + 3x)} \qquad \text{Distributive Property}$$

$$= \frac{3x(3x^2 + 7x + 7)}{9x^2(x + 1)(3x)} \qquad \text{Factor. Divide out common factors.}$$

$$= \frac{3x^2 + 7x + 7}{9x^2(x + 1)} \qquad \text{Simplify.}$$

Method 2 Find the LCD and then add. To find the LCD, factor each denominator and write each factor to the highest power that appears in either denominator. Note that $9x^2 = 3^2x^2$ and $3x^2 + 3x = 3x(x + 1)$, so the LCD is $9x^2(x + 1)$.

$$\frac{7}{9x^2} + \frac{x}{3x^2 + 3x} = \frac{7}{9x^2} + \frac{x}{3x(x + 1)} \qquad \begin{array}{l}\text{Factor second}\\\text{denominator.}\end{array}$$

$$= \frac{7}{9x^2} \cdot \frac{x + 1}{x + 1} + \frac{x}{3x(x + 1)} \cdot \frac{3x}{3x} \qquad \text{LCD is } 9x^2(x + 1).$$

$$= \frac{7x + 7}{9x^2(x + 1)} + \frac{3x^2}{9x^2(x + 1)} \qquad \text{Multiply.}$$

$$= \frac{3x^2 + 7x + 7}{9x^2(x + 1)} \qquad \text{Add numerators.}$$

Note in Examples 1 and 3 that when adding or subtracting rational expressions, the result is a rational expression. In general, similar to rational numbers, rational expressions are closed under addition and subtraction.

EXAMPLE 4 **Subtracting with Unlike Denominators**

Find the difference $\dfrac{x + 2}{2x - 2} - \dfrac{-2x - 1}{x^2 - 4x + 3}$.

SOLUTION

COMMON ERROR

When subtracting rational expressions, remember to distribute the negative sign to all the terms in the quantity that is being subtracted.

$$\dfrac{x + 2}{2x - 2} - \dfrac{-2x - 1}{x^2 - 4x + 3} = \dfrac{x + 2}{2(x - 1)} - \dfrac{-2x - 1}{(x - 1)(x - 3)}$$ Factor each denominator.

$$= \dfrac{x + 2}{2(x - 1)} \cdot \dfrac{x - 3}{x - 3} - \dfrac{-2x - 1}{(x - 1)(x - 3)} \cdot \dfrac{2}{2}$$ LCD is $2(x - 1)(x - 3)$.

$$= \dfrac{x^2 - x - 6}{2(x - 1)(x - 3)} - \dfrac{-4x - 2}{2(x - 1)(x - 3)}$$ Multiply.

$$= \dfrac{x^2 - x - 6 - (-4x - 2)}{2(x - 1)(x - 3)}$$ Subtract numerators.

$$= \dfrac{x^2 + 3x - 4}{2(x - 1)(x - 3)}$$ Simplify numerator.

$$= \dfrac{(x - 1)(x + 4)}{2(x - 1)(x - 3)}$$ Factor numerator. Divide out common factor.

$$= \dfrac{x + 4}{2(x - 3)}, x \neq -1$$ Simplify.

Monitoring Progress Help in English and Spanish at *BigIdeasMath.com*

5. Find the least common multiple of $5x^3$ and $10x^2 - 15x$.

Find the sum or difference.

6. $\dfrac{3}{4x} - \dfrac{1}{7}$

7. $\dfrac{1}{3x^2} + \dfrac{x}{9x^2 - 12}$

8. $\dfrac{x}{x^2 - x - 12} + \dfrac{5}{12x - 48}$

Rewriting Rational Functions

Rewriting a rational function may reveal properties of the function and its graph. In Example 4 of Section 6.2, you used long division to rewrite a rational function. In the next example, you will use inspection.

EXAMPLE 5 **Rewriting and Graphing a Rational Function**

Rewrite $g(x) = \dfrac{3x + 5}{x + 1}$ in the form $g(x) = \dfrac{a}{x - h} + k$. Graph the function. Describe the graph of g as a transformation of the graph of $f(x) = \dfrac{a}{x}$.

SOLUTION

Rewrite by inspection:

$$\dfrac{3x + 5}{x + 1} = \dfrac{3x + 3 + 2}{x + 1} = \dfrac{3(x + 1) + 2}{x + 1} = \dfrac{3(x + 1)}{x + 1} + \dfrac{2}{x + 1} = 3 + \dfrac{2}{x + 1}$$

▶ The rewritten function is $g(x) = \dfrac{2}{x + 1} + 3$. The graph of g is a translation 1 unit left and 3 units up of the graph of $f(x) = \dfrac{2}{x}$.

Monitoring Progress Help in English and Spanish at *BigIdeasMath.com*

9. Rewrite $g(x) = \dfrac{2x - 4}{x - 3}$ in the form $g(x) = \dfrac{a}{x - h} + k$. Graph the function. Describe the graph of g as a transformation of the graph of $f(x) = \dfrac{a}{x}$.

Complex Fractions

A **complex fraction** is a fraction that contains a fraction in its numerator or denominator. A complex fraction can be simplified using either of the methods below.

Core Concept

Simplifying Complex Fractions

Method 1   If necessary, simplify the numerator and denominator by writing each as a single fraction. Then divide by multiplying the numerator by the reciprocal of the denominator.

Method 2   Multiply the numerator and the denominator by the LCD of *every* fraction in the numerator and denominator. Then simplify.

EXAMPLE 6   Simplifying a Complex Fraction

Simplify $\dfrac{\dfrac{5}{x+4}}{\dfrac{1}{x+4}+\dfrac{2}{x}}$.

SOLUTION

Method 1 $\dfrac{\dfrac{5}{x+4}}{\dfrac{1}{x+4}+\dfrac{2}{x}} = \dfrac{\dfrac{5}{x+4}}{\dfrac{3x+8}{x(x+4)}}$ Add fractions in denominator.

$= \dfrac{5}{x+4} \cdot \dfrac{x(x+4)}{3x+8}$ Multiply by reciprocal.

$= \dfrac{5x\cancel{(x+4)}}{\cancel{(x+4)}(3x+8)}$ Divide out common factors.

$= \dfrac{5x}{3x+8}, x \neq -4, x \neq 0$ Simplify.

Method 2   The LCD of all the fractions in the numerator and denominator is $x(x+4)$.

$\dfrac{\dfrac{5}{x+4}}{\dfrac{1}{x+4}+\dfrac{2}{x}} = \dfrac{\dfrac{5}{x+4}}{\dfrac{1}{x+4}+\dfrac{2}{x}} \cdot \dfrac{x(x+4)}{x(x+4)}$ Multiply numerator and denominator by the LCD.

$= \dfrac{\dfrac{5}{\cancel{x+4}} \cdot x\cancel{(x+4)}}{\dfrac{1}{\cancel{x+4}} \cdot x\cancel{(x+4)} + \dfrac{2}{\cancel{x}} \cdot \cancel{x}(x+4)}$ Divide out common factors.

$= \dfrac{5x}{x+2(x+4)}$ Simplify.

$= \dfrac{5x}{3x+8}, x \neq -4, x \neq 0$ Simplify.

Monitoring Progress Help in English and Spanish at *BigIdeasMath.com*

Simplify the complex fraction.

10. $\dfrac{\dfrac{x}{6}-\dfrac{x}{3}}{\dfrac{x}{5}-\dfrac{7}{10}}$

11. $\dfrac{\dfrac{2}{x}-4}{\dfrac{2}{x}+3}$

12. $\dfrac{\dfrac{3}{x+5}}{\dfrac{2}{x-3}+\dfrac{1}{x+5}}$

Vocabulary and Core Concept Check

1. **COMPLETE THE SENTENCE** A fraction that contains a fraction in its numerator or denominator is called a(n) _____.

2. **WRITING** Explain how adding and subtracting rational expressions is similar to adding and subtracting numerical fractions.

Monitoring Progress and Modeling with Mathematics

In Exercises 3–8, find the sum or difference. *(See Example 1.)*

3. $\dfrac{15}{4x} + \dfrac{5}{4x}$

4. $\dfrac{x}{16x^2} - \dfrac{4}{16x^2}$

5. $\dfrac{9}{x+1} - \dfrac{2x}{x+1}$

6. $\dfrac{3x^2}{x-8} + \dfrac{6x}{x-8}$

7. $\dfrac{5x}{x+3} + \dfrac{15}{x+3}$

8. $\dfrac{4x^2}{2x-1} - \dfrac{1}{2x-1}$

In Exercises 9–16, find the least common multiple of the expressions. *(See Example 2.)*

9. $3x, 3(x-2)$

10. $2x^2, 4x+12$

11. $2x, 2x(x-5)$

12. $24x^2, 8x^2 - 16x$

13. $x^2 - 25, x - 5$

14. $9x^2 - 16, 3x^2 + x - 4$

15. $x^2 + 3x - 40, x - 8$

16. $x^2 - 2x - 63, x + 7$

ERROR ANALYSIS In Exercises 17 and 18, describe and correct the error in finding the sum.

17.

$$\boldsymbol{\times} \quad \dfrac{2}{5x} + \dfrac{4}{x^2} = \dfrac{2+4}{5x+x^2} = \dfrac{6}{x(5+x)}$$

18.

$$\boldsymbol{\times} \quad \dfrac{x}{x+2} + \dfrac{4}{x-5} = \dfrac{x+4}{(x+2)(x-5)}$$

In Exercises 19–26, find the sum or difference. *(See Examples 3 and 4.)*

19. $\dfrac{12}{5x} - \dfrac{7}{6x}$

20. $\dfrac{8}{3x^2} + \dfrac{5}{4x}$

21. $\dfrac{3}{x+4} - \dfrac{1}{x+6}$

22. $\dfrac{9}{x-3} + \dfrac{2x}{x+1}$

23. $\dfrac{12}{x^2+5x-24} + \dfrac{3}{x-3}$

24. $\dfrac{x^2-5}{x^2+5x-14} - \dfrac{x+3}{x+7}$

25. $\dfrac{x+2}{x-4} + \dfrac{2}{x} + \dfrac{5x}{3x-1}$

26. $\dfrac{x+3}{x^2-25} - \dfrac{x-1}{x-5} + \dfrac{3}{x+3}$

REASONING In Exercises 27 and 28, tell whether the statement is *always*, *sometimes*, or *never* true. Explain.

27. The LCD of two rational expressions is the product of the denominators.

28. The LCD of two rational expressions will have a degree greater than or equal to that of the denominator with the higher degree.

29. **ANALYZING EQUATIONS** How would you begin to rewrite the function $g(x) = \dfrac{4x+1}{x+2}$ to obtain the form $g(x) = \dfrac{a}{x-h} + k$?

   (A) $g(x) = \dfrac{4(x+2)-7}{x+2}$

   (B) $g(x) = \dfrac{4(x+2)+1}{x+2}$

   (C) $g(x) = \dfrac{(x+2)+(3x-1)}{x+2}$

   (D) $g(x) = \dfrac{4x+2-1}{x+2}$

30. **ANALYZING EQUATIONS** How would you begin to rewrite the function $g(x) = \dfrac{x}{x-5}$ to obtain the form $g(x) = \dfrac{a}{x-h} + k$?

   (A) $g(x) = \dfrac{x(x+5)(x-5)}{x-5}$

   (B) $g(x) = \dfrac{x-5+5}{x-5}$

   (C) $g(x) = \dfrac{x}{x-5+5}$

   (D) $g(x) = \dfrac{x}{x} - \dfrac{x}{5}$

In Exercises 31–38, rewrite the function in the form $g(x) = \dfrac{a}{x-h} + k$. **Graph the function. Describe the graph of g as a transformation of the graph of $f(x) = \dfrac{a}{x}$.**
(See Example 5.)

31. $g(x) = \dfrac{5x-7}{x-1}$

32. $g(x) = \dfrac{6x+4}{x+5}$

33. $g(x) = \dfrac{12x}{x-5}$

34. $g(x) = \dfrac{8x}{x+13}$

35. $g(x) = \dfrac{2x+3}{x}$

36. $g(x) = \dfrac{4x-6}{x}$

37. $g(x) = \dfrac{3x+11}{x-3}$

38. $g(x) = \dfrac{7x-9}{x+10}$

In Exercises 39–44, simplify the complex fraction.
(See Example 6.)

39. $\dfrac{\dfrac{x}{3}-6}{10+\dfrac{4}{x}}$

40. $\dfrac{15-\dfrac{2}{x}}{\dfrac{x}{5}+4}$

41. $\dfrac{\dfrac{1}{2x}-\dfrac{7}{8x-20}}{\dfrac{x}{2x-5}}$

42. $\dfrac{\dfrac{16}{x-2}}{\dfrac{4}{x+1}+\dfrac{6}{x}}$

43. $\dfrac{\dfrac{1}{3x^2-3}}{\dfrac{5}{x+1}-\dfrac{x+4}{x^2-3x-4}}$

44. $\dfrac{\dfrac{3}{x-2}-\dfrac{6}{x^2}-4}{\dfrac{3}{x+2}+\dfrac{1}{x-2}}$

45. PROBLEM SOLVING The total time T (in hours) needed to fly from New York to Los Angeles and back can be modeled by the equation below, where d is the distance (in miles) each way, a is the average airplane speed (in miles per hour), and j is the average speed (in miles per hour) of the jet stream. Simplify the equation. Then find the total time it takes to fly 2468 miles when $a = 510$ miles per hour and $j = 115$ miles per hour.

$$T = \dfrac{d}{a-j} + \dfrac{d}{a+j}$$

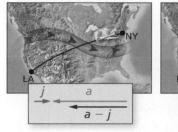
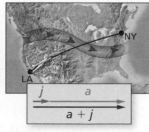

46. REWRITING A FORMULA The total resistance R_t of two resistors in a parallel circuit with resistances R_1 and R_2 (in ohms) is given by the equation shown. Simplify the complex fraction. Then find the total resistance when $R_1 = 2000$ ohms and $R_2 = 5600$ ohms.

$$R_t = \dfrac{1}{\dfrac{1}{R_1}+\dfrac{1}{R_2}}$$

47. PROBLEM SOLVING You plan a trip that involves a 40-mile bus ride and a train ride. The entire trip is 140 miles. The time (in hours) the bus travels is $y_1 = \dfrac{40}{x}$, where x is the average speed (in miles per hour) of the bus. The time (in hours) the train travels is $y_2 = \dfrac{100}{x+30}$. Write and simplify a model that shows the total time y of the trip.

48. PROBLEM SOLVING You participate in a sprint triathlon that involves swimming, bicycling, and running. The table shows the distances (in miles) and your average speed for each portion of the race.

	Distance (miles)	Speed (miles per hour)
Swimming	0.5	r
Bicycling	22	$15r$
Running	6	$r+5$

a. Write a model in simplified form for the total time (in hours) it takes to complete the race.

b. How long does it take to complete the race if you can swim at an average speed of 2 miles per hour? Justify your answer.

49. MAKING AN ARGUMENT Your friend claims that the least common multiple of two numbers is always greater than each of the numbers. Is your friend correct? Justify your answer.

50. HOW DO YOU SEE IT?

Use the graph of the function $f(x) = \dfrac{a}{x - h} + k$ to determine the values of h and k.

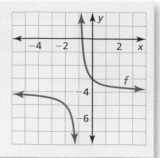

51. REWRITING A FORMULA You borrow P dollars to buy a car and agree to repay the loan over t years at a monthly interest rate of i (expressed as a decimal). Your monthly payment M is given by either formula below.

$$M = \frac{Pi}{1 - \left(\dfrac{1}{1 + i}\right)^{12t}} \quad \text{or} \quad M = \frac{Pi(1 + i)^{12t}}{(1 + i)^{12t} - 1}$$

a. Show that the formulas are equivalent by simplifying the first formula.

b. Find your monthly payment when you borrow $15,500 at a monthly interest rate of 0.5% and repay the loan over 4 years.

52. THOUGHT PROVOKING Is it possible to write two rational functions whose sum is a quadratic function? Justify your answer.

53. USING TOOLS Use technology to rewrite the function $g(x) = \dfrac{(97.6)(0.024) + x(0.003)}{12.2 + x}$ in the form $g(x) = \dfrac{a}{x - h} + k$. Describe the graph of g as a transformation of the graph of $f(x) = \dfrac{a}{x}$.

54. MATHEMATICAL CONNECTIONS Find an expression for the surface area of the box.

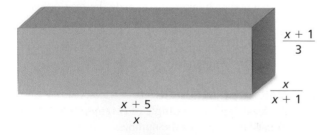

55. PROBLEM SOLVING You are hired to wash the new cars at a car dealership with two other employees. You take an average of 40 minutes to wash a car ($R_1 = 1/40$ car per minute). The second employee washes a car in x minutes. The third employee washes a car in $x + 10$ minutes.

a. Write a single expression R for the combined rate of cars washed per minute by the group.

b. Evaluate your expression in part (a) when the second employee washes a car in 35 minutes. How many cars per hour does this represent? Explain your reasoning.

56. USING TOOLS The expression $2w + \dfrac{450}{w}$ models the perimeter of the corral in Section 1.1 Example 3. Find the sum of the terms. Then use a graph to justify the value of w found in the example. How is the graph different from previous graphs of rational functions?

57. MODELING WITH MATHEMATICS The amount A (in milligrams) of aspirin in a person's bloodstream can be modeled by

$$A = \frac{391t^2 + 0.112}{0.218t^4 + 0.991t^2 + 1}$$

where t is the time (in hours) after one dose is taken.

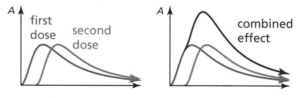

a. A second dose is taken 1 hour after the first dose. Write an equation to model the amount of the second dose in the bloodstream.

b. Write a model for the *total* amount of aspirin in the bloodstream after the second dose is taken.

58. FINDING A PATTERN Find the next two expressions in the pattern shown. Then simplify all five expressions. What value do the expressions approach?

$$1 + \cfrac{1}{2 + \cfrac{1}{2}}, \; 1 + \cfrac{1}{2 + \cfrac{1}{2 + \cfrac{1}{2}}}, \; 1 + \cfrac{1}{2 + \cfrac{1}{2 + \cfrac{1}{2 + \cfrac{1}{2}}}}, \ldots$$

Maintaining Mathematical Proficiency

Reviewing what you learned in previous grades and lessons

Solve $f(x) = g(x)$ by graphing and algebraic methods. *(Section 3.5)*

59. $f(x) = 2x^3 + 5$
$\quad\;\; g(x) = x^3 - 3$

60. $f(x) = x^3 + x^2$
$\quad\;\; g(x) = 9x + 9$

61. $f(x) = x^4 - 3x^2 + 2$
$\quad\;\; g(x) = x^2 + 2$

6.5 Solving Rational Equations

Essential Question How can you solve a rational equation?

EXPLORATION 1 **Solving Rational Equations**

Work with a partner. Match each equation with the graph of its related system of equations. Explain your reasoning. Then use the graph to solve the equation.

a. $\dfrac{2}{x-1} = 1$

b. $\dfrac{2}{x-2} = 2$

c. $\dfrac{-x-1}{x-3} = x+1$

d. $\dfrac{2}{x-1} = x$

e. $\dfrac{1}{x} = \dfrac{-1}{x-2}$

f. $\dfrac{1}{x} = x^2$

A.
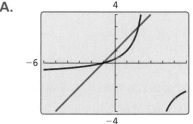

B.
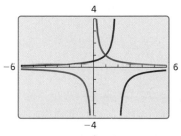

C.
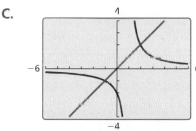

D.
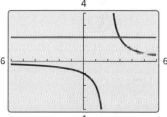

E.
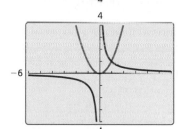

F.
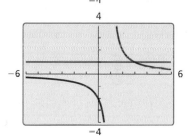

MAKING SENSE OF PROBLEMS

To be proficient in math, you need to plan a solution pathway rather than simply jumping into a solution attempt.

EXPLORATION 2 **Solving Rational Equations**

Work with a partner. Look back at the equations in Explorations 1(d) and 1(e). Suppose you want a more accurate way to solve the equations than using a graphical approach.

a. Show how you could use a *numerical approach* by creating a table. For instance, you might use a spreadsheet to solve the equations.

b. Show how you could use an *analytical approach*. For instance, you might use the method you used to solve proportions.

Communicate Your Answer

3. How can you solve a rational equation?

4. Use the method in either Exploration 1 or 2 to solve each equation.

a. $\dfrac{x+1}{x-1} = \dfrac{x-1}{x+1}$

b. $\dfrac{1}{x+1} = \dfrac{1}{x^2+1}$

c. $\dfrac{1}{x^2-1} = \dfrac{1}{x-1}$

What You Will Learn

▶ Solve rational equations by cross multiplying.

▶ Solve rational equations by using the least common denominator.

▶ Use inverses of functions.

Solving by Cross Multiplying

You can use **cross multiplying** to solve a rational equation when each side of the equation is a single rational expression.

EXAMPLE 1   Solving a Rational Equation by Cross Multiplying

Solve $\dfrac{3}{x+1} = \dfrac{9}{4x+5}$.

SOLUTION

$$\dfrac{3}{x+1} = \dfrac{9}{4x+5} \qquad \text{Write original equation.}$$

$$3(4x+5) = 9(x+1) \qquad \text{Cross multiply.}$$

$$12x + 15 = 9x + 9 \qquad \text{Distributive Property}$$

$$3x + 15 = 9 \qquad \text{Subtract } 9x \text{ from each side.}$$

$$3x = -6 \qquad \text{Subtract 15 from each side.}$$

$$x = -2 \qquad \text{Divide each side by 3.}$$

▶ The solution is $x = -2$. Check this in the original equation.

Check

$$\dfrac{3}{-2+1} \overset{?}{=} \dfrac{9}{4(-2)+5}$$

$$\dfrac{3}{-1} \overset{?}{=} \dfrac{9}{-3}$$

$$-3 = -3 \checkmark$$

EXAMPLE 2   Writing and Using a Rational Model

An *alloy* is formed by mixing two or more metals. Sterling silver is an alloy composed of 92.5% silver and 7.5% copper by weight. You have 15 ounces of 800 grade silver, which is 80% silver and 20% copper by weight. How much pure silver should you mix with the 800 grade silver to make sterling silver?

SOLUTION

$$\text{percent of copper in mixture} = \dfrac{\text{weight of copper in mixture}}{\text{total weight of mixture}}$$

$$\dfrac{7.5}{100} = \dfrac{(0.2)(15)}{15+x} \qquad x \text{ is the amount of silver added.}$$

$$7.5(15+x) = 100(0.2)(15) \qquad \text{Cross multiply.}$$

$$112.5 + 7.5x = 300 \qquad \text{Simplify.}$$

$$7.5x = 187.5 \qquad \text{Subtract 112.5 from each side.}$$

$$x = 25 \qquad \text{Divide each side by 7.5.}$$

▶ You should mix 25 ounces of pure silver with the 15 ounces of 800 grade silver.

Monitoring Progress Help in English and Spanish at *BigIdeasMath.com*

Solve the equation by cross multiplying. Check your solution(s).

1. $\dfrac{3}{5x} = \dfrac{2}{x-7}$

2. $\dfrac{-4}{x+3} = \dfrac{5}{x-3}$

3. $\dfrac{1}{2x+5} = \dfrac{x}{11x+8}$

Solving by Using the Least Common Denominator

When a rational equation is not expressed as a proportion, you can solve it by multiplying each side of the equation by the least common denominator of the rational expressions.

EXAMPLE 3   Solving Rational Equations by Using the LCD

Solve each equation.

a. $\dfrac{5}{x} + \dfrac{7}{4} = -\dfrac{9}{x}$

b. $1 - \dfrac{8}{x-5} = \dfrac{3}{x}$

SOLUTION

a.

$\dfrac{5}{x} + \dfrac{7}{4} = -\dfrac{9}{x}$	Write original equation.
$4x\left(\dfrac{5}{x} + \dfrac{7}{4}\right) = 4x\left(-\dfrac{9}{x}\right)$	Multiply each side by the LCD, $4x$.
$20 + 7x = -36$	Simplify.
$7x = 56$	Subtract 20 from each side.
$x = 8$	Divide each side by 7.

▶ The solution is $x = -8$. Check this in the original equation.

Check

$\dfrac{5}{-8} + \dfrac{7}{4} \overset{?}{=} -\dfrac{9}{-8}$

$-\dfrac{5}{8} + \dfrac{14}{8} \overset{?}{=} \dfrac{9}{8}$

$\dfrac{9}{8} = \dfrac{9}{8}$ ✓

b.

$1 - \dfrac{8}{x-5} = \dfrac{3}{x}$	Write original equation.
$x(x-5)\left(1 - \dfrac{8}{x-5}\right) = x(x-5) \cdot \dfrac{3}{x}$	Multiply each side by the LCD, $x(x-5)$.
$x(x-5) - 8x = 3(x-5)$	Simplify
$x^2 - 5x - 8x = 3x - 15$	Distributive Property
$x^2 - 16x + 15 = 0$	Write in standard form.
$(x-1)(x-15) = 0$	Factor.
$x = 1 \quad \text{or} \quad x = 15$	Zero-Product Property

▶ The solutions are $x = 1$ and $x = 15$. Check these in the original equation.

Check

$1 - \dfrac{8}{1-5} \overset{?}{=} \dfrac{3}{1}$	Substitute for x.	$1 - \dfrac{8}{15-5} \overset{?}{=} \dfrac{3}{15}$
$1 + 2 \overset{?}{=} 3$	Simplify.	$1 - \dfrac{4}{5} \overset{?}{=} \dfrac{1}{5}$
$3 = 3$ ✓		$\dfrac{1}{5} = \dfrac{1}{5}$ ✓

Monitoring Progress Help in English and Spanish at *BigIdeasMath.com*

Solve the equation by using the LCD. Check your solution(s).

4. $\dfrac{15}{x} + \dfrac{4}{5} = \dfrac{7}{x}$

5. $\dfrac{3x}{x+1} - \dfrac{5}{2x} = \dfrac{3}{2x}$

6. $\dfrac{4x+1}{x+1} = \dfrac{12}{x^2-1} + 3$

When solving a rational equation, you may obtain solutions that are extraneous.
Be sure to check for extraneous solutions by checking your solutions in the
original equation.

EXAMPLE 4   **Solving an Equation with an Extraneous Solution**

Solve $\dfrac{6}{x-3} = \dfrac{8x^2}{x^2-9} - \dfrac{4x}{x+3}$.

SOLUTION

Write each denominator in factored form. The LCD is $(x+3)(x-3)$.

$$\frac{6}{x-3} = \frac{8x^2}{(x+3)(x-3)} - \frac{4x}{x+3}$$

$$(x+3)(x-3) \cdot \frac{6}{x-3} = (x+3)(x-3) \cdot \frac{8x^2}{(x+3)(x-3)} - (x+3)(x-3) \cdot \frac{4x}{x+3}$$

$$6(x+3) = 8x^2 - 4x(x-3)$$

$$6x + 18 = 8x^2 - 4x^2 + 12x$$

$$0 = 4x^2 + 6x - 18$$

$$0 = 2x^2 + 3x - 9$$

$$0 = (2x-3)(x+3)$$

$$2x - 3 = 0 \quad \text{or} \quad x + 3 = 0$$

$$x = \frac{3}{2} \quad \text{or} \quad x = -3$$

Check

Check $x = \dfrac{3}{2}$:

$$\frac{6}{\frac{3}{2}-3} \stackrel{?}{=} \frac{8\left(\frac{3}{2}\right)^2}{\left(\frac{3}{2}\right)^2-9} - \frac{4\left(\frac{3}{2}\right)}{\frac{3}{2}+3}$$

$$\frac{6}{-\frac{3}{2}} \stackrel{?}{=} \frac{18}{-\frac{27}{4}} - \frac{6}{\frac{9}{2}}$$

$$-4 \stackrel{?}{=} -\frac{8}{3} - \frac{4}{3}$$

$$-4 = -4 \checkmark$$

Check $x = -3$:

$$\frac{6}{-3-3} \stackrel{?}{=} \frac{8(-3)^2}{(-3)^2-9} - \frac{4(-3)}{-3+3}$$

$$\frac{6}{-6} \stackrel{?}{=} \frac{72}{0} - \frac{-12}{0} \quad ✗$$

Division by zero is undefined.

ANOTHER WAY

You can also graph each
side of the equation and
find the x-value where the
graphs intersect.

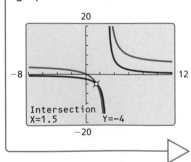

▶ The apparent solution $x = -3$ is extraneous. So, the only solution is $x = \dfrac{3}{2}$.

Monitoring Progress 🔊 Help in English and Spanish at *BigIdeasMath.com*

Solve the equation. Check your solution(s).

7. $\dfrac{9}{x-2} + \dfrac{6x}{x+2} = \dfrac{9x^2}{x^2-4}$

8. $\dfrac{7}{x-1} - 5 = \dfrac{6}{x^2-1}$

Using Inverses of Functions

EXAMPLE 5 **Finding the Inverse of a Rational Function**

Consider the function $f(x) = \dfrac{2}{x+3}$. Determine whether the inverse of f is a function. Then find the inverse.

SOLUTION

Graph the function f. Notice that no horizontal line intersects the graph more than once. So, the inverse of f is a function. Find the inverse.

Check

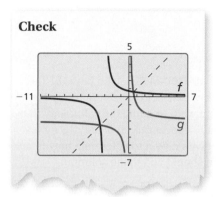

$$y = \frac{2}{x+3} \qquad \text{Set } y \text{ equal to } f(x).$$

$$x = \frac{2}{y+3} \qquad \text{Switch } x \text{ and } y.$$

$$x(y+3) = 2 \qquad \text{Cross multiply.}$$

$$y + 3 = \frac{2}{x} \qquad \text{Divide each side by } x.$$

$$y = \frac{2}{x} - 3 \qquad \text{Subtract 3 from each side.}$$

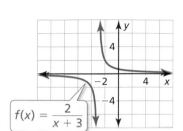

$f(x) = \dfrac{2}{x+3}$

▶ So, the inverse of f is $g(x) = \dfrac{2}{x} - 3$.

EXAMPLE 6 **Solving a Real-Life Problem**

REMEMBER

In part (b), the variables are meaningful. Switching them to find the inverse would create confusion. So, solve for m without switching variables.

In Section 6.2 Example 5, you wrote the function $c = \dfrac{50m + 1000}{m}$, which represents the average cost c (in dollars) of making m models using a 3-D printer. Find how many models must be printed for the average cost per model to fall to $90 by (a) solving an equation, and (b) using the inverse of the function.

SOLUTION

a. Substitute 90 for c and solve by cross multiplying.

$$90 = \frac{50m + 1000}{m}$$

$$90m = 50m + 1000$$

$$40m = 1000$$

$$m = 25$$

b. Solve the equation for m.

$$c = \frac{50m + 1000}{m}$$

$$c = 50 + \frac{1000}{m}$$

$$c - 50 = \frac{1000}{m}$$

$$m = \frac{1000}{c - 50}$$

When $c = 90$, $m = \dfrac{1000}{90 - 50} = 25$.

▶ So, the average cost falls to $90 per model after 25 models are printed.

Monitoring Progress Help in English and Spanish at *BigIdeasMath.com*

9. Consider the function $f(x) = \dfrac{1}{x} - 2$. Determine whether the inverse of f is a function. Then find the inverse.

10. WHAT IF? How do the answers in Example 6 change when $c = \dfrac{50m + 800}{m}$?

Vocabulary and Core Concept Check

1. **WRITING** When can you solve a rational equation by cross multiplying? Explain.

2. **WRITING** A student solves the equation $\dfrac{4}{x-3} = \dfrac{x}{x-3}$ and obtains the solutions 3 and 4. Are either of these extraneous solutions? Explain.

Monitoring Progress and Modeling with Mathematics

In Exercises 3–10, solve the equation by cross multiplying. Check your solution(s). *(See Example 1.)*

3. $\dfrac{4}{2x} = \dfrac{5}{x+6}$

4. $\dfrac{9}{3x} = \dfrac{4}{x+2}$

5. $\dfrac{6}{x-1} = \dfrac{9}{x+1}$

6. $\dfrac{8}{3x-2} = \dfrac{2}{x-1}$

7. $\dfrac{x}{2x+7} = \dfrac{x-5}{x-1}$

8. $\dfrac{-2}{x-1} = \dfrac{x-8}{x+1}$

9. $\dfrac{x^2-3}{x+2} = \dfrac{x-3}{2}$

10. $\dfrac{-1}{x-3} = \dfrac{x-4}{x^2-27}$

11. **USING EQUATIONS** So far in your volleyball practice, you have put into play 37 of the 44 serves you have attempted. Solve the equation $\dfrac{90}{100} = \dfrac{37+x}{44+x}$ to find the number of consecutive serves you need to put into play in order to raise your serve percentage to 90%.

12. **USING EQUATIONS** So far this baseball season, you have 12 hits out of 60 times at-bat. Solve the equation $0.360 = \dfrac{12+x}{60+x}$ to find the number of consecutive hits you need to raise your batting average to 0.360.

13. **MODELING WITH MATHEMATICS** Brass is an alloy composed of 55% copper and 45% zinc by weight. You have 25 ounces of copper. How many ounces of zinc do you need to make brass? *(See Example 2.)*

14. **MODELING WITH MATHEMATICS** You have 0.2 liter of an acid solution whose acid concentration is 16 moles per liter. You want to dilute the solution with water so that its acid concentration is only 12 moles per liter. Use the given model to determine how many liters of water you should add to the solution.

Concentration of new solution	$=$	$\dfrac{\text{Concentration of original solution} \cdot \text{Volume of original solution}}{\text{Volume of original solution} + \text{Volume of water added}}$

USING STRUCTURE In Exercises 15–18, identify the LCD of the rational expressions in the equation.

15. $\dfrac{x}{x+3} + \dfrac{1}{x} = \dfrac{3}{x}$

16. $\dfrac{5x}{x-1} - \dfrac{7}{x} = \dfrac{9}{x}$

17. $\dfrac{2}{x+1} + \dfrac{x}{x+4} = \dfrac{1}{2}$

18. $\dfrac{4}{x+9} + \dfrac{3x}{2x-1} = \dfrac{10}{3}$

In Exercises 19–30, solve the equation by using the LCD. Check your solution(s). *(See Examples 3 and 4.)*

19. $\dfrac{3}{2} + \dfrac{1}{x} = 2$

20. $\dfrac{2}{3x} + \dfrac{1}{6} = \dfrac{4}{3x}$

21. $\dfrac{x-3}{x-4} + 4 = \dfrac{3x}{x}$

22. $\dfrac{2}{x-3} + \dfrac{1}{x} = \dfrac{x-1}{x-3}$

23. $\dfrac{6x}{x+4} + 4 = \dfrac{2x+2}{x-1}$

24. $\dfrac{10}{x} + 3 = \dfrac{x+9}{x-4}$

25. $\dfrac{18}{x^2-3x} - \dfrac{6}{x-3} = \dfrac{5}{x}$

26. $\dfrac{10}{x^2-2x} + \dfrac{4}{x} = \dfrac{5}{x-2}$

27. $\dfrac{x+1}{x+6} + \dfrac{1}{x} = \dfrac{2x+1}{x+6}$

28. $\dfrac{x+3}{x-3} + \dfrac{x}{x-5} = \dfrac{x+5}{x-5}$

29. $\dfrac{5}{x} - 2 = \dfrac{2}{x+3}$

30. $\dfrac{5}{x^2+x-6} = 2 + \dfrac{x-3}{x-2}$

ERROR ANALYSIS In Exercises 31 and 32, describe and correct the error in the first step of solving the equation.

31.

✗
$$\frac{5}{3x} + \frac{2}{x^2} = 1$$

$$3x^3 \cdot \frac{5}{3x} + 3x^3 \cdot \frac{2}{x^2} = 1$$

32.

✗
$$\frac{7x+1}{2x+5} + 4 = \frac{10x-3}{3x}$$

$$(2x+5)3x \cdot \frac{7x+1}{2x+5} + 4 = \frac{10x-3}{3x} \cdot (2x+5)3x$$

33. **PROBLEM SOLVING** You can paint a room in 8 hours. Working together, you and your friend can paint the room in just 5 hours.

   a. Let t be the time (in hours) your friend would take to paint the room when working alone. Copy and complete the table.
   (*Hint*: (Work done) = (Work rate) × (Time))

	Work rate	Time	Work done
You	$\frac{1 \text{ room}}{8 \text{ hours}}$	5 hours	
Friend		5 hours	

   b. Explain what the sum of the expressions represents in the last column. Write and solve an equation to find how long your friend would take to paint the room when working alone.

34. **PROBLEM SOLVING** You can clean a park in 2 hours. Working together, you and your friend can clean the park in just 1.2 hours.

   a. Let t be the time (in hours) your friend would take to clean the park when working alone. Copy and complete the table.
   (*Hint*: (Work done) = (Work rate) × (Time))

	Work rate	Time	Work done
You	$\frac{1 \text{ park}}{2 \text{ hours}}$	1.2 hours	
Friend		1.2 hours	

   b. Explain what the sum of the expressions represents in the last column. Write and solve an equation to find how long your friend would take to clean the park when working alone.

35. **OPEN-ENDED** Give an example of a rational equation that you would solve using cross multiplication and one that you would solve using the LCD. Explain your reasoning.

36. **OPEN-ENDED** Describe a real-life situation that can be modeled by a rational equation. Justify your answer.

In Exercises 37–44, determine whether the inverse of f is a function. Then find the inverse. (*See Example 5.*)

37. $f(x) = \dfrac{2}{x-4}$

38. $f(x) = \dfrac{7}{x+6}$

39. $f(x) = \dfrac{3}{x} - 2$

40. $f(x) = \dfrac{5}{x} - 6$

41. $f(x) = \dfrac{4}{11-2x}$

42. $f(x) = \dfrac{8}{9+5x}$

43. $f(x) = \dfrac{1}{x^2} + 4$

44. $f(x) = \dfrac{1}{x^4} - 7$

45. **PROBLEM SOLVING** The recommended percent p (in decimal form) of nitrogen (by volume) in the air that a diver breathes is given by $p = \dfrac{105.07}{d+33}$, where d is the depth (in feet) of the diver. Find the depth when the air contains 47% recommended nitrogen by (a) solving an equation, and (b) using the inverse of the function. (*See Example 6.*)

46. **PROBLEM SOLVING** The cost of fueling your car for 1 year can be calculated using this equation:

$$\text{Fuel cost for 1 year} = \frac{\text{Miles driven} \cdot \text{Price per gallon of fuel}}{\text{Fuel-efficiency rate}}$$

Last year you drove 9000 miles, paid $3.24 per gallon of gasoline, and spent a total of $1389 on gasoline. Find the fuel-efficiency rate of your car by (a) solving an equation, and (b) using the inverse of the function.

USING TOOLS In Exercises 47–50, use a graphing calculator to solve the equation $f(x) = g(x)$.

47. $f(x) = \dfrac{2}{3x}$, $g(x) = x$

48. $f(x) = -\dfrac{3}{5x}$, $g(x) = -x$

49. $f(x) = \dfrac{1}{x} + 1$, $g(x) = x^2$

50. $f(x) = \dfrac{2}{x} + 1$, $g(x) = x^2 + 1$

51. MATHEMATICAL CONNECTIONS *Golden rectangles* are rectangles for which the ratio of the width w to the length ℓ is equal to the ratio of ℓ to $\ell + w$. The ratio of the length to the width for these rectangles is called the golden ratio. Find the value of the golden ratio using a rectangle with a width of 1 unit.

w

ℓ

52. HOW DO YOU SEE IT? Use the graph to identify the solution(s) of the rational equation $\dfrac{4(x-1)}{x-1} = \dfrac{2x-2}{x+1}$. Explain your reasoning.

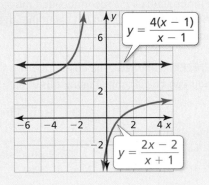

$y = \dfrac{4(x-1)}{x-1}$

$y = \dfrac{2x-2}{x+1}$

USING STRUCTURE In Exercises 53 and 54, find the inverse of the function. (*Hint:* Try rewriting the function by using either inspection or long division.)

53. $f(x) = \dfrac{3x+1}{x-4}$

54. $f(x) = \dfrac{4x-7}{2x+3}$

55. ABSTRACT REASONING Find the inverse of rational functions of the form $y = \dfrac{ax+b}{cx+d}$. Verify your answer is correct by using it to find the inverses in Exercises 53 and 54.

56. THOUGHT PROVOKING Is it possible to write a rational equation that has the following number of solutions? Justify your answers.

a. no solution
b. exactly one solution
c. exactly two solutions
d. infinitely many solutions

57. CRITICAL THINKING Let a be a nonzero real number. Tell whether each statement is *always true*, *sometimes true*, or *never true*. Explain your reasoning.

a. For the equation $\dfrac{1}{x-a} = \dfrac{x}{x-a}$, $x = a$ is an extraneous solution.

b. The equation $\dfrac{3}{x-a} = \dfrac{x}{x-a}$ has exactly one solution.

c. The equation $\dfrac{1}{x-a} = \dfrac{2}{x+a} + \dfrac{2a}{x^2-a^2}$ has no solution.

58. MAKING AN ARGUMENT Your friend claims that it is not possible for a rational equation of the form $\dfrac{x-a}{b} = \dfrac{x-c}{d}$, where $b \neq 0$ and $d \neq 0$, to have extraneous solutions. Is your friend correct? Explain your reasoning.

Maintaining Mathematical Proficiency
Reviewing what you learned in previous grades and lessons

Is the domain discrete or continuous? Explain. Graph the function using its domain.
(Skills Review Handbook)

59. The linear function $y = 0.25x$ represents the amount of money y (in dollars) of x quarters in your pocket. You have a maximum of eight quarters in your pocket.

60. A store sells broccoli for \$2 per pound. The total cost t of the broccoli is a function of the number of pounds p you buy.

Evaluate the function for the given value of x. *(Section 3.1)*

61. $f(x) = x^3 - 2x + 7$; $x = -2$

62. $g(x) = -2x^4 + 7x^3 + x - 2$; $x = 3$

63. $h(x) = -x^3 + 3x^2 + 5x$; $x = 3$

64. $k(x) = -2x^3 - 4x^2 + 12x - 5$; $x = -5$

Core Vocabulary

rational expression, *p. 324*
simplified form of a rational expression, *p. 324*

complex fraction, *p. 335*
cross multiplying, *p. 340*

Core Concepts

Section 6.3

Simplifying Rational Expressions, *p. 324*
Dividing Rational Expressions, *p. 326*

Multiplying Rational Expressions, *p. 325*

Section 6.4

Adding or Subtracting with Like Denominators, *p. 332*
Adding or Subtracting with Unlike Denominators, *p. 332*
Simplifying Complex Fractions, *p. 335*

Section 6.5

Solving Rational Equations by Cross Multiplying, *p. 340*
Solving Rational Equations by Using the Least Common Denominator, *p. 341*
Using Inverses of Functions, *p. 343*

Mathematical Practices

1. In Exercise 37 on page 329, what type of equation did you expect to get as your solution? Explain why this type of equation is appropriate in the context of this situation.

2. Write a simpler problem that is similar to Exercise 44 on page 330. Describe how to use the simpler problem to gain insight into the solution of the more complicated problem in Exercise 44.

3. In Exercise 58 on page 338, what conjecture did you make about the value the given expressions were approaching? What logical progression led you to determine whether your conjecture was correct?

4. Compare the methods for solving Exercise 45 on page 345. Be sure to discuss the similarities and differences between the methods as precisely as possible.

Performance Task:

The Price Is Right

Rational functions can model key economic information for businesses. In manufacturing, start-up costs can be high because of the equipment required to make a product. Rational functions can model these costs as well as the profit. How can rational functions help manufacturers set the right price for their product?

To explore the answer to this question and more, check out the Performance Task and Real-Life STEM video at *BigIdeasMath.com*.

6.1 Inverse Variation *(pp. 307–312)*

The variables x and y vary inversely, and $y = 12$ when $x = 3$. Write an equation that relates x and y. Then find y when $x = -4$.

$y = \dfrac{a}{x}$ Write general equation for inverse variation.

$12 = \dfrac{a}{3}$ Substitute 12 for *y* and 3 for *x*.

$36 = a$ Multiply each side by 3.

▶ The inverse variation equation is $y = \dfrac{36}{x}$. When $x = -4$, $y = \dfrac{36}{-4} = -9$.

Tell whether *x* and *y* show *direct variation*, *inverse variation*, or *neither*.

1. $xy = 5$ **2.** $5y = 6x$ **3.** $15 = \dfrac{x}{y}$ **4.** $y - 3 = 2x$

5.

x	7	11	15	20
y	35	55	75	100

6.

x	5	8	10	20
y	6.4	4	3.2	1.6

The variables *x* and *y* vary inversely. Use the given values to write an equation relating *x* and *y*. Then find *y* when $x = -3$.

7. $x = 1, y = 5$ **8.** $x = -4, y = -6$ **9.** $x = \dfrac{5}{2}, y = 18$ **10.** $x = -12, y = \dfrac{2}{3}$

6.2 Graphing Rational Functions *(pp. 313–320)*

Graph $y = \dfrac{2x + 5}{x - 1}$. State the domain and range.

Step 1 Draw the asymptotes. Solve $x - 1 = 0$ for x to find the vertical asymptote $x = 1$. The horizontal asymptote is the line $y = \dfrac{a}{c} = \dfrac{2}{1} = 2$.

Step 2 Plot points to the left of the vertical asymptote, such as $\left(-2, -\dfrac{1}{3}\right), \left(-1, -\dfrac{3}{2}\right)$, and $(0, -5)$. Plot points to the right of the vertical asymptote, such as $\left(3, \dfrac{11}{2}\right), \left(5, \dfrac{15}{4}\right)$, and $\left(7, \dfrac{19}{6}\right)$.

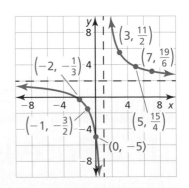

Step 3 Draw the two branches of the hyperbola so that they pass through the plotted points and approach the asymptotes.

▶ The domain is all real numbers except 1 and the range is all real numbers except 2.

Graph the function. State the domain and range.

11. $y = \dfrac{4}{x - 3}$ **12.** $y = \dfrac{1}{x + 5} + 2$ **13.** $f(x) = \dfrac{3x - 2}{x - 4}$

6.3 Multiplying and Dividing Rational Expressions *(pp. 323–330)*

Find the quotient $\dfrac{3x + 27}{6x - 48} \div \dfrac{x^2 + 9x}{x^2 - 4x - 32}$.

$$\dfrac{3x + 27}{6x - 48} \div \dfrac{x^2 + 9x}{x^2 - 4x - 32} = \dfrac{3x + 27}{6x - 48} \cdot \dfrac{x^2 - 4x - 32}{x^2 + 9x}$$ Multiply by reciprocal.

$$= \dfrac{3(x + 9)}{6(x - 8)} \cdot \dfrac{(x + 4)(x - 8)}{x(x + 9)}$$ Factor.

$$= \dfrac{3(x + 9)(x + 4)(x - 8)}{2(3)(x - 8)(x)(x + 9)}$$ Multiply. Divide out common factors.

$$= \dfrac{x + 4}{2x}, \; x \neq 8, x \neq -9, x \neq -4$$ Simplified form

Find the product or quotient.

14. $\dfrac{80x^4}{y^3} \cdot \dfrac{xy}{5x^2}$

15. $\dfrac{x - 3}{2x - 8} \cdot \dfrac{6x^2 - 96}{x^2 - 9}$

16. $\dfrac{16x^2 - 8x + 1}{x^3 - 7x^2 + 12x} \div \dfrac{20x^2 - 5x}{15x^3}$

17. $\dfrac{x^2 - 13x + 40}{x^2 - 2x - 15} \div (x^2 - 5x - 24)$

6.4 Adding and Subtracting Rational Expressions *(pp. 331–338)*

Find the sum $\dfrac{x}{6x + 24} + \dfrac{x + 2}{x^2 + 9x + 20}$.

$$\dfrac{x}{6x + 24} + \dfrac{x + 2}{x^2 + 9x + 20} = \dfrac{x}{6(x + 4)} + \dfrac{x + 2}{(x + 4)(x + 5)}$$ Factor each denominator.

$$= \dfrac{x}{6(x + 4)} \cdot \dfrac{x + 5}{x + 5} + \dfrac{x + 2}{(x + 4)(x + 5)} \cdot \dfrac{6}{6}$$ LCD is $6(x + 4)(x + 5)$.

$$= \dfrac{x^2 + 5x}{6(x + 4)(x + 5)} + \dfrac{6x + 12}{6(x + 4)(x + 5)}$$ Multiply.

$$= \dfrac{x^2 + 11x + 12}{6(x + 4)(x + 5)}$$ Add numerators.

Find the sum or difference.

18. $\dfrac{5}{6(x + 3)} + \dfrac{x + 4}{2x}$

19. $\dfrac{5x}{x + 8} + \dfrac{4x - 9}{x^2 + 5x - 24}$

20. $\dfrac{x + 2}{x^2 + 4x + 3} - \dfrac{5x}{x^2 - 9}$

Rewrite the function in the form $g(x) = \dfrac{a}{x - h} + k$. Graph the function. Describe the graph of g as a transformation of the graph of $f(x) = \dfrac{a}{x}$.

21. $g(x) = \dfrac{5x + 1}{x - 3}$

22. $g(x) = \dfrac{4x + 2}{x + 7}$

23. $g(x) = \dfrac{9x - 10}{x - 1}$

24. Let f be the focal length of a thin camera lens, p be the distance between the lens and an object being photographed, and q be the distance between the lens and the film. For the photograph to be in focus, the variables should satisfy the lens equation to the right. Simplify the complex fraction.

$$f = \dfrac{1}{\dfrac{1}{p} + \dfrac{1}{q}}$$

Solve $\dfrac{-4}{x+3} = \dfrac{x-1}{x+3} + \dfrac{x}{x-4}$.

The LCD is $(x+3)(x-4)$.

$$\frac{-4}{x+3} = \frac{x-1}{x+3} + \frac{x}{x-4}$$

$$(x+3)(x-4) \cdot \frac{-4}{x+3} = (x+3)(x-4) \cdot \frac{x-1}{x+3} + (x+3)(x-4) \cdot \frac{x}{x-4}$$

$$-4(x-4) = (x-1)(x-4) + x(x+3)$$

$$-4x + 16 = x^2 - 5x + 4 + x^2 + 3x$$

$$0 = 2x^2 + 2x - 12$$

$$0 = x^2 + x - 6$$

$$0 = (x+3)(x-2)$$

$$x + 3 = 0 \quad \text{or} \quad x - 2 = 0$$

$$x = -3 \quad \text{or} \quad x = 2$$

Check

Check $x = -3$:

$$\frac{-4}{-3+3} \overset{?}{=} \frac{-3-1}{-3+3} + \frac{-3}{-3-4}$$

$$\frac{-4}{0} \overset{?}{=} \frac{-4}{0} + \frac{-3}{-7} \quad \textbf{X}$$

Division by zero is undefined.

Check $x = 2$:

$$\frac{-4}{2+3} \overset{?}{=} \frac{2-1}{2+3} + \frac{2}{2-4}$$

$$\frac{-4}{5} \overset{?}{=} \frac{1}{5} + \frac{2}{-2}$$

$$\frac{-4}{5} = \frac{-4}{5} \quad \checkmark$$

▶ The apparent solution $x = -3$ is extraneous. So, the only solution is $x = 2$.

Solve the equation. Check your solution(s).

25. $\dfrac{5}{x} = \dfrac{7}{x+2}$

26. $\dfrac{8(x-1)}{x^2-4} = \dfrac{4}{x+2}$

27. $\dfrac{2(x+7)}{x+4} - 2 = \dfrac{2x+20}{2x+8}$

Determine whether the inverse of f is a function. Then find the inverse.

28. $f(x) = \dfrac{3}{x+6}$

29. $f(x) = \dfrac{10}{x-7}$

30. $f(x) = \dfrac{1}{x} + 8$

31. At a bowling alley, shoe rentals cost \$3 and each game costs \$4. The average cost c (in dollars) of bowling n games is given by $c = \dfrac{4n+3}{n}$. Find how many games you must bowl for the average cost to fall to \$4.75 by (a) solving an equation, and (b) using the inverse of a function.

The variables x and y vary inversely. Use the given values to write an equation relating x and y. Then find y when $x = 4$.

1. $x = 5, y = 2$

2. $x = -4, y = \frac{7}{2}$

3. $x = \frac{3}{4}, y = \frac{5}{8}$

The graph shows the function $y = \dfrac{1}{x - h} + k$. Determine whether the value of each constant h and k is *positive*, *negative*, or *zero*. Explain your reasoning.

4.

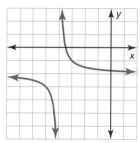

5.

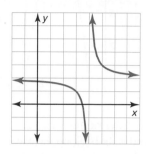

6.

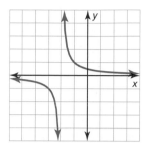

Perform the indicated operation.

7. $\dfrac{3x^2 y}{4x^3 y^5} \div \dfrac{6y^2}{2xy^3}$

8. $\dfrac{3x}{x^2 + x - 12} - \dfrac{6}{x + 4}$

9. $\dfrac{x^2 - 3x - 4}{x^2 - 3x - 18} \cdot \dfrac{x - 6}{x + 1}$

10. $\dfrac{4}{x + 5} + \dfrac{2x}{x^2 - 25}$

11. Let $g(x) = \dfrac{(x + 3)(x - 2)}{x + 3}$. Simplify $g(x)$. Determine whether the graph of $f(x) = x - 2$ and the graph of g are different. Explain your reasoning.

12. You start a small beekeeping business. Your initial costs are $500 for equipment and bees. You estimate it will cost $1.25 per pound to collect, clean, bottle, and label the honey. How many pounds of honey must you produce before your average cost per pound is $1.79? Justify your answer.

13. You can use a simple lever to lift a 300-pound rock. The force F (in foot-pounds) needed to lift the rock is inversely related to the distance d (in feet) from the pivot point of the lever. To lift the rock, you need 60 pounds of force applied to a lever with a distance of 10 feet from the pivot point. What force is needed when you increase the distance to 15 feet from the pivot point? Justify your answer.

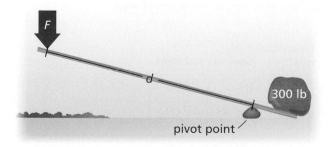

14. Three tennis balls fit tightly in a can as shown.

  a. Write an expression for the height h of the can in terms of its radius r. Then rewrite the formula for the volume of a cylinder in terms of r only.

  b. Find the percent of the can's volume that is *not* occupied by tennis balls.

1. Which of the following functions are shown in the graph? Select all that apply. Justify your answers.

   (A) $y = -2x^2 + 12x - 10$

   (B) $y = x^2 - 6x + 13$

   (C) $y = -2(x - 3)^2 + 8$

   (D) $y = -(x - 1)(x - 5)$

   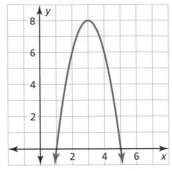

2. You step onto an escalator and begin descending. After riding for 12 feet, you realize that you dropped your keys on the upper floor and walk back up the escalator to retrieve them. The total time T of your trip down and up the escalator is given by

$$T = \frac{12}{s} + \frac{12}{w - s}$$

   where s is the speed of the escalator and w is your walking speed. The trip took 9 seconds, and you walk at a speed of 6 feet per second. Find two possible speeds of the escalator.

3. The graph of a rational function has asymptotes that intersect at the point (4, 3). Choose the correct values to complete the equation of the function. Then graph the function.

12	-3

   $$y = \frac{\boxed{}\, x + 6}{\boxed{}\, x + \boxed{}}$$

9	-6

3	-12

4. The tables below give the amounts A (in dollars) of money in two different bank accounts after t years.

Checking Account			
t	1	2	3	4
A	5000	5110	5220	5330

Savings Account			
t	0	1	2	3
A	5000	5100	5202	5306.04

   a. Determine the type of function represented by the data in each table.

   b. Which account has a greater initial balance? Explain your reasoning.

   c. Which account has a greater value after 10 years? after 15 years? Justify your answers.

5. Order the expressions from least to greatest. Justify your answer.

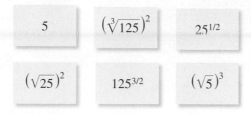

6. You claim it is possible to create a function from the given values that has an axis of symmetry of $x = 2$. Your friend claims it is possible to create a function that has an axis of symmetry of $x = -2$. What values can you use to support your claim? What values support your friend's claim?

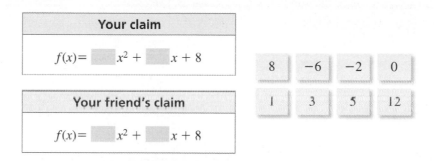

Your claim
$f(x) = \underline{\hspace{0.5cm}} x^2 + \underline{\hspace{0.5cm}} x + 8$

8	−6	−2	0
1	3	5	12

Your friend's claim
$f(x) = \underline{\hspace{0.5cm}} x^2 + \underline{\hspace{0.5cm}} x + 8$

7. Choose the correct relationship among the variables in the table. Justify your answer by writing an equation that relates p, q, and r.

p	−12	3	30	−1.5
q	20	1	−82	4
r	16	−10	−8	0.5

(A) The variable p varies directly with the difference of q and r.

(B) The variable r varies inversely with the difference of p and q.

(C) The variable q varies inversely with the sum of p and r.

(D) The variable p varies directly with the sum of q and r.

8. You have taken five quizzes in your history class, and your average score is 83 points. You think you can score 95 points on each remaining quiz. How many quizzes do you need to take to raise your average quiz score to 90 points? Justify your answer.

7 Sequences and Series

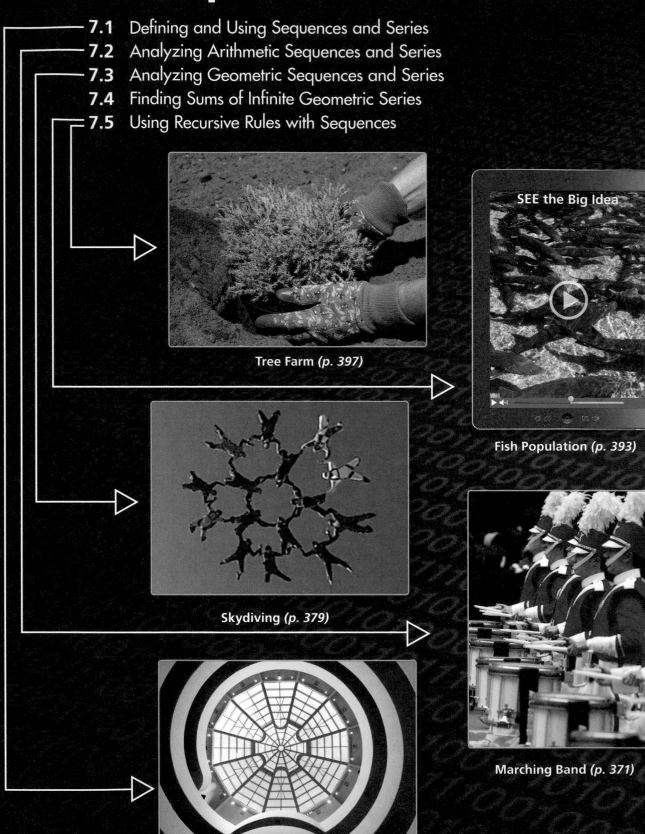

Tree Farm *(p. 397)*

SEE the Big Idea

Fish Population *(p. 393)*

Skydiving *(p. 379)*

Marching Band *(p. 371)*

Museum Skylight *(p. 364)*

Maintaining Mathematical Proficiency

Evaluating Functions

Example 1 Evaluate the function $y = 2x^2 - 10$ for the values $x = 0, 1, 2, 3,$ and 4.

Input, x	$2x^2 - 10$	Output, y
0	$2(0)^2 - 10$	-10
1	$2(1)^2 - 10$	-8
2	$2(2)^2 - 10$	-2
3	$2(3)^2 - 10$	8
4	$2(4)^2 - 10$	22

Copy and complete the table to evaluate the function.

1. $y = 3 - 2^x$

x	y
1	
2	
3	

2. $y = 5x^2 + 1$

x	y
2	
3	
4	

3. $y = -4x + 24$

x	y
5	
10	
15	

Solving Equations

Example 2 Solve the equation $45 = 5(3)^x$.

$$45 = 5(3)^x \qquad \text{Write original equation.}$$

$$\frac{45}{5} = \frac{5(3)^x}{5} \qquad \text{Divide each side by 5.}$$

$$9 = 3^x \qquad \text{Simplify.}$$

$$\log_3 9 = \log_3 3^x \qquad \text{Take } \log_3 \text{ of each side.}$$

$$2 = x \qquad \text{Simplify.}$$

Solve the equation. Check your solution(s).

4. $7x + 3 = 31$

5. $\dfrac{1}{16} = 4\left(\dfrac{1}{2}\right)^x$

6. $216 = 3(x + 6)$

7. $2^x + 16 = 144$

8. $\dfrac{1}{4}x - 8 = 17$

9. $8\left(\dfrac{3}{4}\right)^x = \dfrac{27}{8}$

10. ABSTRACT REASONING The graph of the exponential decay function $f(x) - b^x$ has an asymptote $y = 0$. How is the graph of f different from a scatter plot consisting of the points $(1, b^1), (2, b^1 + b^2), (3, b^1 + b^2 + b^3), \ldots$? How is the graph of f similar?

Mathematical Practices

Mathematically proficient students consider the available tools when solving a mathematical problem.

Using Appropriate Tools Strategically

Core Concept

Using a Spreadsheet

To use a spreadsheet, it is common to write one cell as a function of another cell. For instance, in the spreadsheet shown, the cells in column A starting with cell A2 contain functions of the cell in the preceding row. Also, the cells in column B contain functions of the cells in the same row in column A.

A2 = A1+1

B1 = 2*A1−2

	A	B
1	1	0
2	2	2
3	3	4
4	4	6
5	5	8
6	6	10
7	7	12
8	8	14

EXAMPLE 1   Using a Spreadsheet

You deposit $1000 in stocks that earn 15% interest compounded annually. Use a spreadsheet to find the balance at the end of each year for 8 years. Describe the type of growth.

SOLUTION

You can enter the given information into a spreadsheet and generate the graph shown. From the formula in the spreadsheet, you can see that the growth pattern is exponential. The graph also appears to be exponential.

	A	B
1	Year	Balance
2	0	$1000.00
3	1	$1150.00
4	2	$1322.50
5	3	$1520.88
6	4	$1749.01
7	5	$2011.36
8	6	$2313.06
9	7	$2660.02
10	8	$3059.02

B3 = B2*1.15

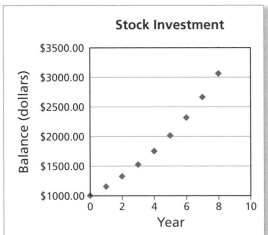

Monitoring Progress

Use a spreadsheet to help you answer the question.

1. A pilot flies a plane at a speed of 500 miles per hour for 4 hours. Find the total distance flown at 30-minute intervals. Describe the pattern.

2. A population of 60 rabbits increases by 25% each year for 8 years. Find the population at the end of each year. Describe the type of growth.

3. An endangered population has 500 members. The population declines by 10% each decade for 80 years. Find the population at the end of each decade. Describe the type of decline.

4. The top eight runners finishing a race receive cash prizes. First place receives $200, second place receives $175, third place receives $150, and so on. Find the fifth through eighth place prizes. Describe the type of decline.

7.1 Defining and Using Sequences and Series

Essential Question How can you write a rule for the nth term of a sequence?

A **sequence** is an ordered list of numbers. There can be a limited number or an infinite number of *terms* of a sequence.

$$a_1, a_2, a_3, a_4, \ldots, a_n, \ldots \qquad \text{Terms of a sequence}$$

Here is an example.

$$1, 4, 7, 10, \ldots, 3n - 2, \ldots$$

CONSTRUCTING VIABLE ARGUMENTS

To be proficient in math, you need to reason inductively about data.

EXPLORATION 1   Writing Rules for Sequences

Work with a partner. Match each sequence with its graph. The horizontal axes represent n, the position of each term in the sequence. Then write a rule for the nth term of the sequence, and use the rule to find a_{10}.

a. $1, 2.5, 4, 5.5, 7, \ldots$ **b.** $8, 6.5, 5, 3.5, 2, \ldots$ **c.** $\dfrac{1}{4}, \dfrac{4}{4}, \dfrac{9}{4}, \dfrac{16}{4}, \dfrac{25}{4}, \ldots$

d. $\dfrac{25}{4}, \dfrac{16}{4}, \dfrac{9}{4}, \dfrac{4}{4}, \dfrac{1}{4}, \ldots$ **e.** $\dfrac{1}{2}, 1, 2, 4, 8, \ldots$ **f.** $8, 4, 2, 1, \dfrac{1}{2}, \ldots$

A.
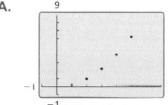

B.
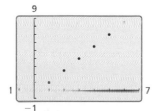

C.
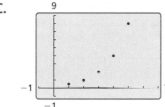

D.
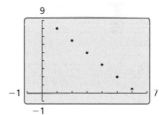

E.
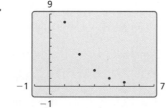

F.
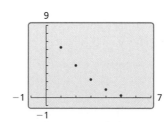

Communicate Your Answer

2. How can you write a rule for the nth term of a sequence?

3. What do you notice about the relationship between the terms in (a) an arithmetic sequence and (b) a geometric sequence? Justify your answers.

Core Vocabulary

sequence, *p. 358*
terms of a sequence, *p. 358*
series, *p. 360*
summation notation, *p. 360*
sigma notation, *p. 360*

Previous
domain
range

What You Will Learn

▶ Use sequence notation to write terms of sequences.

▶ Write a rule for the *n*th term of a sequence.

▶ Sum the terms of a sequence to obtain a series and use summation notation.

Writing Terms of Sequences

💿 Core Concept

Sequences

A **sequence** is an ordered list of numbers. A *finite sequence* is a function that has a limited number of terms and whose domain is the finite set $\{1, 2, 3, \ldots, n\}$. The values in the range are called the **terms** of the sequence.

Domain: 1   2   3   4   . . .   *n*   Relative position of each term

Range: a_1 a_2 a_3 a_4 . . . a_n Terms of the sequence

An *infinite sequence* is a function that continues without stopping and whose domain is the set of positive integers. Here are examples of a finite sequence and an infinite sequence.

Finite sequence: 2, 4, 6, 8   **Infinite sequence:**   2, 4, 6, 8, . . .

A sequence can be specified by an equation, or *rule*. For example, both sequences above can be described by the rule $a_n = 2n$ or $f(n) = 2n$.

The domain of a sequence may begin with 0 instead of 1. When this is the case, the domain of a finite sequence is the set $\{0, 1, 2, 3, \ldots, n\}$ and the domain of an infinite sequence becomes the set of nonnegative integers. Unless otherwise indicated, assume the domain of a sequence begins with 1.

EXAMPLE 1   **Writing the Terms of Sequences**

Write the first six terms of (a) $a_n = 2n + 5$ and (b) $f(n) = (-3)^{n-1}$.

SOLUTION

a. $a_1 = 2(1) + 5 = 7$ 1st term   b. $f(1) = (-3)^{1-1} = 1$

$a_2 = 2(2) + 5 = 9$ 2nd term $f(2) = (-3)^{2-1} = -3$

$a_3 = 2(3) + 5 = 11$ 3rd term $f(3) = (-3)^{3-1} = 9$

$a_4 = 2(4) + 5 = 13$ 4th term $f(4) = (-3)^{4-1} = -27$

$a_5 = 2(5) + 5 = 15$ 5th term $f(5) = (-3)^{5-1} = 81$

$a_6 = 2(6) + 5 = 17$ 6th term $f(6) = (-3)^{6-1} = -243$

Monitoring Progress   Help in English and Spanish at *BigIdeasMath.com*

Write the first six terms of the sequence.

1. $a_n = n + 4$ **2.** $f(n) = (-2)^{n-1}$ **3.** $a_n = \dfrac{n}{n+1}$

Writing Rules for Sequences

When the terms of a sequence have a recognizable pattern, you may be able to write a rule for the nth term of the sequence.

STUDY TIP

When you are given only the first several terms of a sequence, there may be more than one rule for the nth term. For instance, the sequence 2, 4, 8, . . . can be given by $a_n = 2^n$ or $a_n = n^2 - n + 2$.

EXAMPLE 2   Writing Rules for Sequences

Describe the pattern, write the next term, and write a rule for the nth term of the sequences (a) $-1, -8, -27, -64, \ldots$ and (b) $0, 2, 6, 12, \ldots$.

SOLUTION

a. You can write the terms as $(-1)^3, (-2)^3, (-3)^3, (-4)^3, \ldots$. The next term is $a_5 = (-5)^3 = -125$. A rule for the nth term is $a_n = (-n)^3$.

b. You can write the terms as $0(1), 1(2), 2(3), 3(4), \ldots$. The next term is $f(5) = 4(5) = 20$. A rule for the nth term is $f(n) = (n-1)n$.

To graph a sequence, let the horizontal axis represent the position numbers (the domain) and the vertical axis represent the terms (the range).

EXAMPLE 3   Solving a Real-Life Problem

You work in a grocery store and are stacking apples in the shape of a square pyramid with seven layers. Write a rule for the number of apples in each layer. Then graph the sequence.

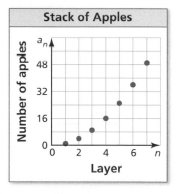

first layer

SOLUTION

Step 1 Make a table showing the number of fruit in the first three layers. Let a_n represent the number of apples in layer n.

Layer, n	1	2	3
Number of apples, a_n	$1 = 1^2$	$4 = 2^2$	$9 = 3^2$

COMMON ERROR

Although the plotted points in Example 3 follow a curve, do not draw the curve because the sequence is defined only for integer values of n, specifically $n = 1, 2, 3, 4, 5, 6,$ and 7.

Step 2 Write a rule for the number of apples in each layer. From the table, you can see that $a_n = n^2$.

Step 3 Plot the points $(1, 1), (2, 4), (3, 9), (4, 16), (5, 25), (6, 36),$ and $(7, 49)$. The graph is shown at the right.

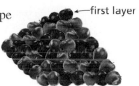

Stack of Apples

Monitoring Progress Help in English and Spanish at *BigIdeasMath.com*

Describe the pattern, write the next term, graph the first five terms, and write a rule for the nth term of the sequence.

4. $3, 5, 7, 9, \ldots$

5. $3, 8, 15, 24, \ldots$

6. $1, -2, 4, -8, \ldots$

7. $2, 5, 10, 17, \ldots$

8. WHAT IF? In Example 3, suppose there are nine layers of apples. How many apples are in the ninth layer?

Writing Rules for Series

Core Concept

Series and Summation Notation

When the terms of a sequence are added together, the resulting expression is a **series**. A series can be finite or infinite.

Finite series: $2 + 4 + 6 + 8$

Infinite series: $2 + 4 + 6 + 8 + \cdots$

You can use **summation notation** to write a series. For example, the two series above can be written in summation notation as follows:

Finite series: $2 + 4 + 6 + 8 = \displaystyle\sum_{i=1}^{4} 2i$

Infinite series: $2 + 4 + 6 + 8 + \cdots = \displaystyle\sum_{i=1}^{\infty} 2i$

For both series, the *index of summation* is i and the *lower limit of summation* is 1. The *upper limit of summation* is 4 for the finite series and ∞ (infinity) for the infinite series. Summation notation is also called **sigma notation** because it uses the uppercase Greek letter *sigma*, written Σ.

READING

When written in summation notation, this series is read as "the sum of 2*i* for values of *i* from 1 to 4."

EXAMPLE 4 Writing Series Using Summation Notation

Write each series using summation notation.

a. $25 + 50 + 75 + \cdots + 250$

b. $\dfrac{1}{2} + \dfrac{2}{3} + \dfrac{3}{4} + \dfrac{4}{5} + \cdots$

SOLUTION

a. Notice that the first term is $25(1)$, the second is $25(2)$, the third is $25(3)$, and the last is $25(10)$. So, the terms of the series can be written as:

$a_i = 25i$, where $i = 1, 2, 3, \ldots, 10$

The lower limit of summation is 1 and the upper limit of summation is 10.

▶ The summation notation for the series is $\displaystyle\sum_{i=1}^{10} 25i$.

b. Notice that for each term, the denominator of the fraction is 1 more than the numerator. So, the terms of the series can be written as:

$a_i = \dfrac{i}{i+1}$, where $i = 1, 2, 3, 4, \ldots$

The lower limit of summation is 1 and the upper limit of summation is infinity.

▶ The summation notation for the series is $\displaystyle\sum_{i=1}^{\infty} \dfrac{i}{i+1}$.

Monitoring Progress ◄)) Help in English and Spanish at *BigIdeasMath.com*

Write the series using summation notation.

9. $5 + 10 + 15 + \cdots + 100$

10. $\dfrac{1}{2} + \dfrac{4}{5} + \dfrac{9}{10} + \dfrac{16}{17} + \cdots$

11. $6 + 36 + 216 + 1296 + \cdots$

12. $5 + 6 + 7 + \cdots + 12$

The index of summation for a series does not have to be i—any letter can be used. Also, the index does not have to begin at 1. For instance, the index begins at 4 in the next example.

COMMON ERROR

Be sure to use the correct lower and upper limits of summation when finding the sum of a series.

EXAMPLE 5 Finding the Sum of a Series

Find the sum $\displaystyle\sum_{k=4}^{8}(3 + k^2)$.

SOLUTION

$$\sum_{k=4}^{8}(3 + k^2) = (3 + 4^2) + (3 + 5^2) + (3 + 6^2) + (3 + 7^2) + (3 + 8^2)$$

$$= 19 + 28 + 39 + 52 + 67$$

$$= 205$$

For series with many terms, finding the sum by adding the terms can be tedious. Below are formulas you can use to find the sums of three special types of series.

Core Concept

Formulas for Special Series

Sum of n terms of 1: $\displaystyle\sum_{i=1}^{n}1 = n$

Sum of first n positive integers: $\displaystyle\sum_{i=1}^{n}i = \frac{n(n+1)}{2}$

Sum of squares of first n positive integers: $\displaystyle\sum_{i=1}^{n}i^2 = \frac{n(n+1)(2n+1)}{6}$

EXAMPLE 6 Using a Formula for a Sum

How many apples are in the stack in Example 3?

SOLUTION

From Example 3, you know that the ith term of the series is given by $a_i = i^2$, where $i = 1, 2, 3, \ldots, 7$. Using summation notation and the third formula listed above, you can find the total number of apples as follows:

$$1^2 + 2^2 + \cdots + 7^2 = \sum_{i=1}^{7}i^2 = \frac{7(7+1)(2 \cdot 7 + 1)}{6} = \frac{7(8)(15)}{6} = 140$$

▶ There are 140 apples in the stack. Check this by adding the number of apples in each of the seven layers.

Monitoring Progress 🔊 Help in English and Spanish at *BigIdeasMath.com*

Find the sum.

13. $\displaystyle\sum_{i=1}^{5}8i$

14. $\displaystyle\sum_{k=3}^{7}(k^2 - 1)$

15. $\displaystyle\sum_{i=1}^{34}1$

16. $\displaystyle\sum_{k=1}^{6}k$

17. WHAT IF? Suppose there are nine layers in the apple stack in Example 3. How many apples are in the stack?

Vocabulary and Core Concept Check

1. **VOCABULARY** What is another name for summation notation?

2. **COMPLETE THE SENTENCE** In a sequence, the numbers are called _____ of the sequence.

3. **WRITING** Compare sequences and series.

4. **WHICH ONE DOESN'T BELONG?** Which does *not* belong with the other three? Explain your reasoning.

$$\sum_{i=1}^{6} i^2 \qquad 91 \qquad 1 + 4 + 9 + 16 + 25 + 36 \qquad \sum_{i=0}^{5} i^2$$

Monitoring Progress and Modeling with Mathematics

In Exercises 5–14, write the first six terms of the sequence. *(See Example 1.)*

5. $a_n = n + 2$

6. $a_n = 6 - n$

7. $a_n = n^2$

8. $f(n) = n^3 + 2$

9. $f(n) = 4^{n-1}$

10. $a_n = -n^2$

11. $a_n = n^2 - 5$

12. $a_n = (n + 3)^2$

13. $f(n) = \dfrac{2n}{n + 2}$

14. $f(n) = \dfrac{n}{2n - 1}$

In Exercises 15–26, describe the pattern, write the next term, and write a rule for the *n*th term of the sequence. *(See Example 2.)*

15. $1, 6, 11, 16, \ldots$

16. $1, 2, 4, 8, \ldots$

17. $3.1, 3.8, 4.5, 5.2, \ldots$

18. $9, 16.8, 24.6, 32.4, \ldots$

19. $5.8, 4.2, 2.6, 1, -0.6 \ldots$

20. $-4, 8, -12, 16, \ldots$

21. $\frac{1}{4}, \frac{2}{4}, \frac{3}{4}, \frac{4}{4}, \ldots$

22. $\frac{1}{10}, \frac{3}{20}, \frac{5}{30}, \frac{7}{40}, \ldots$

23. $\frac{2}{3}, \frac{2}{6}, \frac{2}{9}, \frac{2}{12}, \ldots$

24. $\frac{2}{3}, \frac{4}{4}, \frac{6}{5}, \frac{8}{6}, \ldots$

25. $2, 9, 28, 65, \ldots$

26. $1.2, 4.2, 9.2, 16.2, \ldots$

27. **FINDING A PATTERN** Which rule gives the total number of squares in the *n*th figure of the pattern shown? Justify your answer.

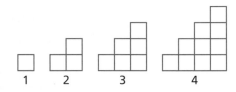

(A) $a_n = 3n - 3$ (B) $a_n = 4n - 5$

(C) $a_n = n$ (D) $a_n = \dfrac{n(n + 1)}{2}$

28. **FINDING A PATTERN** Which rule gives the total number of green squares in the *n*th figure of the pattern shown? Justify your answer.

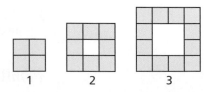

(A) $a_n = n^2 - 1$ (B) $a_n = \dfrac{n^2}{2}$

(C) $a_n = 4n$ (D) $a_n = 2n + 1$

29. **MODELING WITH MATHEMATICS** Rectangular tables are placed together along their short edges, as shown in the diagram. Write a rule for the number of people that can be seated around n tables arranged in this manner. Then graph the sequence. *(See Example 3.)*

30. **MODELING WITH MATHEMATICS** An employee at a construction company earns $33,000 for the first year of employment. Employees at the company receive raises of $2400 each year. Write a rule for the salary of the employee each year. Then graph the sequence.

In Exercises 31–38, write the series using summation notation. *(See Example 4.)*

31. $7 + 10 + 13 + 16 + 19$

32. $5 + 11 + 17 + 23 + 29$

33. $4 + 7 + 12 + 19 + \cdots$

34. $-1 + 2 + 7 + 14 + \cdots$

35. $\frac{1}{3} + \frac{1}{9} + \frac{1}{27} + \frac{1}{81} + \cdots$

36. $\frac{1}{4} + \frac{2}{5} + \frac{3}{6} + \frac{4}{7} + \cdots$

37. $-3 + 4 - 5 + 6 - 7$

38. $-2 + 4 - 8 + 16 - 32$

In Exercises 39–50, find the sum. *(See Examples 5 and 6.)*

39. $\sum_{i=1}^{6} 2i$

40. $\sum_{i=1}^{5} 7i$

41. $\sum_{n=0}^{4} n^3$

42. $\sum_{k=1}^{4} 3k^2$

43. $\sum_{k=3}^{6} (5k - 2)$

44. $\sum_{n=1}^{5} (n^2 - 1)$

45. $\sum_{i=2}^{8} \frac{2}{i}$

46. $\sum_{k=4}^{6} \frac{k}{k + 1}$

47. $\sum_{i=1}^{35} 1$

48. $\sum_{n=1}^{16} n$

49. $\sum_{i=10}^{25} i$

50. $\sum_{n=1}^{18} n^2$

ERROR ANALYSIS In Exercises 51 and 52, describe and correct the error in finding the sum of the series.

51.

✗ $\sum_{n=1}^{10} (3n - 5) = -2 + 1 + 4 + 7 + 10$
$= 20$

52.

✗ $\sum_{i=2}^{4} i^2 = \frac{4(4 + 1)(2 \cdot 4 + 1)}{6}$
$= \frac{180}{6}$
$= 30$

53. **PROBLEM SOLVING** You want to save $500 for a school trip. You begin by saving a penny on the first day. You save an additional penny each day after that. For example, you will save two pennies on the second day, three pennies on the third day, and so on.

   a. How much money will you have saved after 100 days?

   b. Use a series to determine how many days it takes you to save $500.

54. **MODELING WITH MATHEMATICS** You begin an exercise program. The first week you do 25 push-ups. Each week you do 10 more push-ups than the previous week. How many push-ups will you do in the ninth week? Justify your answer.

55. **MODELING WITH MATHEMATICS** For a display at a sports store, you are stacking soccer balls in a pyramid whose base is an equilateral triangle with five layers. Write a rule for the number of soccer balls in each layer. Then graph the sequence.

← first layer

56. HOW DO YOU SEE IT? Use the diagram to determine the sum of the series. Explain your reasoning.

$$1+3+5+7+9+\cdots+(2n-1) = ?$$

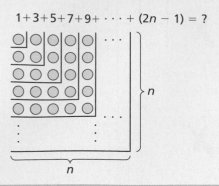

57. MAKING AN ARGUMENT You use a calculator to evaluate $\sum\limits_{i=3}^{1659} i$ because the lower limit of summation is 3, not 1. Your friend claims there is a way to use the formula for the sum of the first n positive integers. Is your friend correct? Explain.

58. MATHEMATICAL CONNECTIONS A *regular* polygon has equal angle measures and equal side lengths. For a regular n-sided polygon ($n \geq 3$), the measure a_n of an interior angle is given by $a_n = \dfrac{180(n-2)}{n}$.

 a. Write the first five terms of the sequence.

 b. Write a rule for the sequence giving the sum T_n of the measures of the interior angles in each regular n-sided polygon.

 c. Use your rule in part (b) to find the sum of the interior angle measures in the Guggenheim Museum skylight, which is a regular dodecagon.

Guggenheim Museum Skylight

59. USING STRUCTURE Determine whether each statement is true. If so, provide a proof. If not, provide a counterexample.

 a. $\sum\limits_{i=1}^{n} ca_i = c \sum\limits_{i=1}^{n} a_i$

 b. $\sum\limits_{i=1}^{n} (a_i + b_i) = \sum\limits_{i=1}^{n} a_i + \sum\limits_{i=1}^{n} b_i$

 c. $\sum\limits_{i=1}^{n} a_i b_i = \sum\limits_{i=1}^{n} a_i \sum\limits_{i=1}^{n} b_i$

 d. $\sum\limits_{i=1}^{n} (a_i)^c = \left(\sum\limits_{i=1}^{n} a_i\right)^c$

60. THOUGHT PROVOKING In this section, you learned the following formulas.

$$\sum\limits_{i=1}^{n} 1 = n$$

$$\sum\limits_{i=1}^{n} i = \frac{n(n+1)}{2}$$

$$\sum\limits_{i=1}^{n} i^2 = \frac{n(n+1)(2n+1)}{6}$$

Write a formula for the sum of the cubes of the first n positive integers.

61. MODELING WITH MATHEMATICS In the puzzle called the Tower of Hanoi, the object is to use a series of moves to take the rings from one peg and stack them in order on another peg. A move consists of moving exactly one ring, and no ring may be placed on top of a smaller ring. The minimum number a_n of moves required to move n rings is 1 for 1 ring, 3 for 2 rings, 7 for 3 rings, 15 for 4 rings, and 31 for 5 rings.

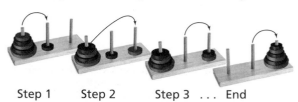

Step 1   Step 2   Step 3 ... End

 a. Write a rule for the sequence.

 b. What is the minimum number of moves required to move 6 rings? 7 rings? 8 rings?

Maintaining Mathematical Proficiency
Reviewing what you learned in previous grades and lessons

Solve the system. Check your solution. *(Section 2.4)*

62. $2x - y - 3z = 6$
$x + y + 4z = -1$
$3x - 2z = 8$

63. $2x - 2y + z = 5$
$-2x + 3y + 2z = -1$
$x - 4y + 5z = 4$

64. $2x - 3y + z = 4$
$x - 2z = 1$
$y + z = 2$

Analyzing Arithmetic Sequences and Series

Essential Question How can you recognize an arithmetic sequence from its graph?

In an **arithmetic sequence**, the difference of consecutive terms, called the *common difference*, is constant. For example, in the arithmetic sequence 1, 4, 7, 10, . . . , the common difference is 3.

EXPLORATION 1 **Recognizing Graphs of Arithmetic Sequences**

Work with a partner. Determine whether each graph shows an arithmetic sequence. If it does, then write a rule for the nth term of the sequence, and use a spreadsheet to find the sum of the first 20 terms. What do you notice about the graph of an arithmetic sequence?

a.
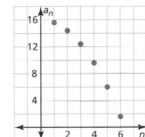

b.
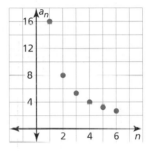

c.
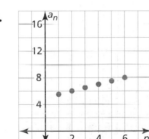

d.
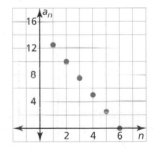

EXPLORATION 2 **Finding the Sum of an Arithmetic Sequence**

REASONING ABSTRACTLY

To be proficient in math, you need to make sense of quantities and their relationships in problem situations.

Work with a partner. A teacher of German mathematician Carl Friedrich Gauss (1777–1855) asked him to find the sum of all the whole numbers from 1 through 100. To the astonishment of his teacher, Gauss came up with the answer after only a few moments. Here is what Gauss did:

$$
\begin{array}{ccccccccc}
1 & + & 2 & + & 3 & + & \cdots & + & 100 \\
100 & + & 99 & + & 98 & + & \cdots & + & 1 \\
\hline
101 & + & 101 & + & 101 & + & \cdots & + & 101
\end{array}
\qquad \frac{100 \times 101}{2} = 5050
$$

Explain Gauss's thought process. Then write a formula for the sum S_n of the first n terms of an arithmetic sequence. Verify your formula by finding the sums of the first 20 terms of the arithmetic sequences in Exploration 1. Compare your answers to those you obtained using a spreadsheet.

Communicate Your Answer

3. How can you recognize an arithmetic sequence from its graph?

4. Find the sum of the terms of each arithmetic sequence.

    a. 1, 4, 7, 10, . . . , 301   **b.** 1, 2, 3, 4, . . . , 1000   **c.** 2, 4, 6, 8, . . . , 800

Core Vocabulary

arithmetic sequence, *p. 366*
common difference, *p. 366*
arithmetic series, *p. 368*

Previous
linear function
mean

What You Will Learn

▶ Identify arithmetic sequences.
▶ Write rules for arithmetic sequences.
▶ Find sums of finite arithmetic series.

Identifying Arithmetic Sequences

In an **arithmetic sequence**, the difference of consecutive terms is constant. This constant difference is called the **common difference** and is denoted by d.

EXAMPLE 1 **Identifying Arithmetic Sequences**

Tell whether each sequence is arithmetic.

a. $-9, -2, 5, 12, 19, \ldots$ **b.** $23, 15, 9, 5, 3, \ldots$

SOLUTION

Find the differences of consecutive terms.

a. $a_2 - a_1 = -2 - (-9) = 7$

$a_3 - a_2 = 5 - (-2) = 7$

$a_4 - a_3 = 12 - 5 = 7$

$a_5 - a_4 = 19 - 12 = 7$

▶ Each difference is 7, so the sequence is arithmetic.

b. $a_2 - a_1 = 15 - 23 = -8$

$a_3 - a_2 = 9 - 15 = -6$

$a_4 - a_3 = 5 - 9 = -4$

$a_5 - a_4 = 3 - 5 = -2$

▶ The differences are not constant, so the sequence is not arithmetic.

Monitoring Progress Help in English and Spanish at *BigIdeasMath.com*

Tell whether the sequence is arithmetic. Explain your reasoning.

1. $2, 5, 8, 11, 14, \ldots$ **2.** $15, 9, 3, -3, -9, \ldots$ **3.** $8, 4, 2, 1, \frac{1}{2}, \ldots$

Writing Rules for Arithmetic Sequences

⟳ Core Concept

Rule for an Arithmetic Sequence

Algebra   The nth term of an arithmetic sequence with first term a_1 and common difference d is given by:

$$a_n = a_1 + (n-1)d$$

Example   The nth term of an arithmetic sequence with a first term of 3 and a common difference of 2 is given by:

$$a_n = 3 + (n-1)2, \text{ or } a_n = 2n + 1$$

EXAMPLE 2 Writing a Rule for the nth Term

Write a rule for the nth term of each sequence. Then find a_{15}.

a. 3, 8, 13, 18, . . .   **b.** 55, 47, 39, 31, . . .

SOLUTION

COMMON ERROR

In the general rule for an arithmetic sequence, note that the common difference d is multiplied by $n - 1$, not n.

a. The sequence is arithmetic with first term $a_1 = 3$, and common difference $d = 8 - 3 = 5$. So, a rule for the nth term is

$$a_n = a_1 + (n - 1)d \qquad \text{Write general rule.}$$
$$= 3 + (n - 1)5 \qquad \text{Substitute 3 for } a_1 \text{ and 5 for } d.$$
$$= 5n - 2. \qquad \text{Simplify.}$$

▶ A rule is $a_n = 5n - 2$, and the 15th term is $a_{15} = 5(15) - 2 = 73$.

b. The sequence is arithmetic with first term $a_1 = 55$, and common difference $d = 47 - 55 = -8$. So, a rule for the nth term is

$$a_n = a_1 + (n - 1)d \qquad \text{Write general rule.}$$
$$= 55 + (n - 1)(-8) \qquad \text{Substitute 55 for } a_1 \text{ and } -8 \text{ for } d.$$
$$= -8n + 63. \qquad \text{Simplify.}$$

▶ A rule is $a_n = -8n + 63$, and the 15th term is $a_{15} = -8(15) + 63 = -57$.

Monitoring Progress Help in English and Spanish at *BigIdeasMath.com*

4. Write a rule for the nth term of the sequence 7, 11, 15, 19, ... Then find a_{15}.

EXAMPLE 3 Writing a Rule Given a Term and Common Difference

One term of an arithmetic sequence is $a_{19} = -45$. The common difference is $d = -3$. Write a rule for the nth term. Then graph the first six terms of the sequence.

SOLUTION

Step 1 Use the general rule to find the first term.

$$a_n = a_1 + (n - 1)d \qquad \text{Write general rule.}$$
$$a_{19} = a_1 + (19 - 1)d \qquad \text{Substitute 19 for } n.$$
$$-45 = a_1 + 18(-3) \qquad \text{Substitute } -45 \text{ for } a_{19} \text{ and } -3 \text{ for } d.$$
$$9 = a_1 \qquad \text{Solve for } a_1.$$

ANALYZING RELATIONSHIPS

Notice that the points lie on a line. This is true for any arithmetic sequence. So, an arithmetic sequence is a linear function whose domain is a subset of the integers. You can also use function notation to write sequences:

$$f(n) = -3n + 12.$$

Step 2 Write a rule for the nth term.

$$a_n = a_1 + (n - 1)d \qquad \text{Write general rule.}$$
$$= 9 + (n - 1)(-3) \qquad \text{Substitute 9 for } a_1 \text{ and } -3 \text{ for } d.$$
$$= -3n + 12. \qquad \text{Simplify.}$$

Step 3 Use the rule to create a table of values for the sequence. Then plot the points.

n	1	2	3	4	5	6
a_n	9	6	3	0	-3	-6

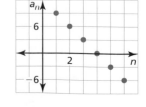

EXAMPLE 4   **Writing a Rule Given Two Terms**

Two terms of an arithmetic sequence are $a_7 = 17$ and $a_{26} = 93$. Write a rule for the nth term.

SOLUTION

Step 1   Write a system of equations using $a_n = a_1 + (n - 1)d$. Substitute 26 for n to write Equation 1. Substitute 7 for n to write Equation 2.

$$a_{26} = a_1 + (26 - 1)d \quad \Rightarrow \quad 93 = a_1 + 25d \qquad \text{Equation 1}$$

$$a_7 = a_1 + (7 - 1)d \quad \Rightarrow \quad \underline{17 = a_1 + \ 6d} \qquad \text{Equation 2}$$

Step 2   Solve the system.

$$76 = \quad\ \ 19d \qquad \text{Subtract.}$$

$$4 = d \qquad \text{Solve for } d.$$

$$93 = a_1 + 25(4) \qquad \text{Substitute for } d \text{ in Equation 1.}$$

$$-7 = a_1 \qquad \text{Solve for } a_1.$$

Step 3   Write a rule for a_n.

$$\begin{aligned} a_n &= a_1 + (n - 1)d & \text{Write general rule.} \\ &= -7 + (n - 1)4 & \text{Substitute for } a_1 \text{ and } d. \\ &= 4n - 11 & \text{Simplify.} \end{aligned}$$

Check

Use the rule to verify that the 7th term is 17 and the 26th term is 93.

$a_7 = 4(7) - 11 = 17$ ✔

$a_{26} = 4(26) - 11 = 93$ ✔

Monitoring Progress   Help in English and Spanish at *BigIdeasMath.com*

Write a rule for the nth term of the sequence. Then graph the first six terms of the sequence.

5. $a_{11} = 50, d = 7$

6. $a_7 = 71, a_{16} = 26$

Finding Sums of Finite Arithmetic Series

The expression formed by adding the terms of an arithmetic sequence is called an **arithmetic series**. The sum of the first n terms of an arithmetic series is denoted by S_n. To find a rule for S_n, you can write S_n in two different ways and add the results.

$$S_n = a_1 \qquad\ + (a_1 + d) \ + (a_1 + 2d) + \cdots + a_n$$

$$\underline{S_n = a_n \qquad\ + (a_n - d) \ + (a_n - 2d) + \cdots + a_1}$$

$$2S_n = \underbrace{(a_1 + a_n) + (a_1 + a_n) + (a_1 + a_n) \ + \cdots + (a_1 + a_n)}$$

$(a_1 + a_n)$ is added n times.

You can conclude that $2S_n = n(a_1 + a_n)$, which leads to the following result.

🌀 Core Concept

The Sum of a Finite Arithmetic Series

The sum of the first n terms of an arithmetic series is

$$S_n = n\left(\frac{a_1 + a_n}{2}\right).$$

In words, S_n is the mean of the first and nth terms, multiplied by the number of terms.

| | EXAMPLE 5 | Finding the Sum of an Arithmetic Series |

Find the sum $\displaystyle\sum_{i=1}^{20}(3i + 7)$.

SOLUTION

Step 1 Find the first and last terms.

$$a_1 = 3(1) + 7 = 10 \qquad \text{Identify first term.}$$

$$a_{20} = 3(20) + 7 = 67 \qquad \text{Identify last term.}$$

Step 2 Find the sum.

$$S_{20} = 20\left(\frac{a_1 + a_{20}}{2}\right) \qquad \text{Write rule for } S_{20}.$$

$$= 20\left(\frac{10 + 67}{2}\right) \qquad \text{Substitute 10 for } a_1 \text{ and 67 for } a_{20}.$$

$$= 770 \qquad \text{Simplify.}$$

STUDY TIP

This sum is actually a *partial* sum. You cannot find the complete sum of an infinite arithmetic series because its terms continue indefinitely.

| | EXAMPLE 6 | Solving a Real-Life Problem |

You are making a house of cards similar to the one shown.

a. Write a rule for the number of cards in the *n*th row when the top row is row 1.

b. How many cards do you need to make a house of cards with 12 rows?

first row

SOLUTION

a. Starting with the top row, the number of cards in the rows are 3, 6, 9, 12, ... These numbers form an arithmetic sequence with a first term of 3 and a common difference of 3. So, a rule for the sequence is:

$$a_n = a_1 + (n - 1)d \qquad \text{Write general rule.}$$

$$= 3 + (n - 1)(3) \qquad \text{Substitute 3 for } a_1 \text{ and 3 for } d.$$

$$= 3n \qquad \text{Simplify.}$$

b. Find the sum of an arithmetic series with first term $a_1 = 3$ and last term $a_{12} = 3(12) = 36$.

$$S_{12} = 12\left(\frac{a_1 + a_{12}}{2}\right) = 12\left(\frac{3 + 36}{2}\right) = 234$$

▶ So, you need 234 cards to make a house of cards with 12 rows.

Check

Use a graphing calculator to check the sum.

```
sum(seq(3X,X,1,1
2))
              234
```

Monitoring Progress Help in English and Spanish at *BigIdeasMath.com*

Find the sum.

7. $\displaystyle\sum_{i=1}^{10}9i$

8. $\displaystyle\sum_{k=1}^{12}(7k + 2)$

9. $\displaystyle\sum_{n=1}^{20}(-4n + 6)$

10. WHAT IF? In Example 6, how many cards do you need to make a house of cards with eight rows?

Vocabulary and Core Concept Check

1. **COMPLETE THE SENTENCE** The constant difference between consecutive terms of an arithmetic sequence is called the _____.

2. **DIFFERENT WORDS, SAME QUESTION** Which is different? Find "both" answers.

> What sequence consists of all the positive odd numbers?

> What sequence starts with 1 and has a common difference of 2?

> What sequence has an nth term of $a_n = 1 + (n - 1)2$?

> What sequence has an nth term of $a_n = 2n + 1$?

Monitoring Progress and Modeling with Mathematics

In Exercises 3–10, tell whether the sequence is arithmetic. Explain your reasoning. *(See Example 1.)*

3. $1, -1, -3, -5, -7, \ldots$ 4. $12, 6, 0, -6, -12, \ldots$

5. $5, 8, 13, 20, 29, \ldots$ 6. $3, 5, 9, 15, 23, \ldots$

7. $36, 18, 9, \frac{9}{2}, \frac{9}{4}, \ldots$ 8. $81, 27, 9, 3, 1, \ldots$

9. $\frac{1}{2}, \frac{3}{4}, 1, \frac{5}{4}, \frac{3}{2}, \ldots$ 10. $\frac{1}{6}, \frac{1}{2}, \frac{5}{6}, \frac{7}{6}, \frac{3}{2}, \ldots$

11. **WRITING EQUATIONS** Write a rule for the arithmetic sequence with the given description.

    a. The first term is -3 and each term is 6 less than the previous term.

    b. The first term is 7 and each term is 5 more than the previous term.

12. **WRITING** Compare the terms of an arithmetic sequence when $d > 0$ to when $d < 0$.

In Exercises 13–20, write a rule for the nth term of the sequence. Then find a_{20}. *(See Example 2.)*

13. $12, 20, 28, 36, \ldots$ 14. $7, 12, 17, 22, \ldots$

15. $51, 48, 45, 42, \ldots$ 16. $86, 79, 72, 65, \ldots$

17. $-1, -\frac{1}{3}, \frac{1}{3}, 1, \ldots$ 18. $-2, -\frac{5}{4}, -\frac{1}{2}, \frac{1}{4}, \ldots$

19. $2.3, 1.5, 0.7, -0.1, \ldots$ 20. $11.7, 10.8, 9.9, 9, \ldots$

ERROR ANALYSIS In Exercises 21 and 22, describe and correct the error in writing a rule for the nth term of the arithmetic sequence $22, 9, -4, -17, -30, \ldots$.

21.

> Use $a_1 = 22$ and $d = -13$.
> $a_n = a_1 + nd$
> $a_n = 22 + n(-13)$
> $a_n = 22 - 13n$

22.

> The first term is 22 and the common difference is -13.
> $a_n = -13 + (n - 1)(22)$
> $a_n = -35 + 22n$

In Exercises 23–28, write a rule for the nth term of the sequence. Then graph the first six terms of the sequence. *(See Example 3.)*

23. $a_{11} = 43, d = 5$ 24. $a_{13} = 42, d = 4$

25. $a_{20} = -27, d = -2$ 26. $a_{15} = -35, d = -3$

27. $a_{17} = -5, d = -\frac{1}{2}$ 28. $a_{21} = -25, d = -\frac{3}{2}$

29. **USING EQUATIONS** One term of an arithmetic sequence is $a_8 = -13$. The common difference is -8. What is a rule for the nth term of the sequence?

    (A) $a_n = 51 + 8n$ (B) $a_n = 35 + 8n$

    (C) $a_n = 51 - 8n$ (D) $a_n = 35 - 8n$

30. FINDING A PATTERN One term of an arithmetic sequence is $a_{12} = 43$. The common difference is 6. What is another term of the sequence?

    (A) $a_3 = -11$ **(B)** $a_4 = -53$

    (C) $a_5 = 13$ **(D)** $a_6 = -47$

In Exercises 31–38, write a rule for the nth term of the arithmetic sequence. *(See Example 4.)*

31. $a_5 = 41,\ a_{10} = 96$

32. $a_7 = 58,\ a_{11} = 94$

33. $a_6 = -8,\ a_{15} = -62$

34. $a_8 = -15,\ a_{17} = -78$

35. $a_{18} = -59,\ a_{21} = -71$

36. $a_{12} = -38,\ a_{19} = -73$

37. $a_8 = 12,\ a_{16} = 22$

38. $a_{12} = 9,\ a_{27} = 15$

WRITING EQUATIONS In Exercises 39–44, write a rule for the sequence with the given terms.

39.
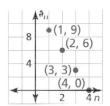

40.
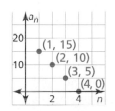

41.
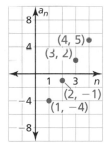

42.
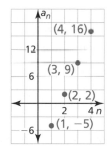

43.

n	4	5	6	7	8
a_n	25	29	33	37	41

44.

n	4	5	6	7	8
a_n	31	39	47	55	63

45. WRITING Compare the graph of $a_n = 3n + 1$, where n is a positive integer, with the graph of $f(x) = 3x + 1$, where x is a real number.

46. DRAWING CONCLUSIONS Describe how doubling each term in an arithmetic sequence changes the common difference of the sequence. Justify your answer.

In Exercises 47–52, find the sum. *(See Example 5.)*

47. $\displaystyle\sum_{i=1}^{20}(2i - 3)$ **48.** $\displaystyle\sum_{i=1}^{26}(4i + 7)$

49. $\displaystyle\sum_{i=1}^{33}(6 - 2i)$ **50.** $\displaystyle\sum_{i=1}^{31}(-3 - 4i)$

51. $\displaystyle\sum_{i=1}^{41}(-2.3 + 0.1i)$ **52.** $\displaystyle\sum_{i=1}^{39}(-4.1 + 0.4i)$

NUMBER SENSE In Exercises 53 and 54, find the sum of the arithmetic sequence.

53. The first 19 terms of the sequence $9, 2, -5, -12, \ldots$.

54. The first 22 terms of the sequence $17, 9, 1, -7, \ldots$.

55. MODELING WITH MATHEMATICS A marching band is arranged in rows. The first row has three band members, and each row after the first has two more band members than the row before it. *(See Example 6.)*

    a. Write a rule for the number of band members in the nth row.

    b. How many band members are in a formation with seven rows?

56. MODELING WITH MATHEMATICS Domestic bees make their honeycomb by starting with a single hexagonal cell, then forming ring after ring of hexagonal cells around the initial cell, as shown. The number of cells in successive rings forms an arithmetic sequence.

Initial   1 ring   2 rings
cell

    a. Write a rule for the number of cells in the nth ring.

    b. How many cells are in the honeycomb after the ninth ring is formed?

57. MATHEMATICAL CONNECTIONS A quilt is made up of strips of cloth, starting with an inner square surrounded by rectangles to form successively larger squares. The inner square and all rectangles have a width of 1 foot. Write an expression using summation notation that gives the sum of the areas of all the strips of cloth used to make the quilt shown. Then evaluate the expression.

58. HOW DO YOU SEE IT? Which graph(s) represents an arithmetic sequence? Explain your reasoning.

a.
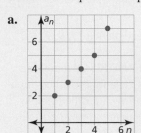

b.
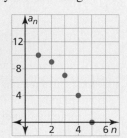

c.
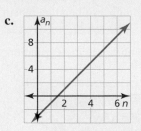

d.
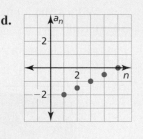

59. MAKING AN ARGUMENT Your friend believes the sum of a series doubles when the common difference of an arithmetic series is doubled and the first term and number of terms in the series remain unchanged. Is your friend correct? Explain your reasoning.

60. THOUGHT PROVOKING In number theory, the *Dirichlet Prime Number Theorem* states that if a and b are relatively prime, then the arithmetic sequence

$$a, a + b, a + 2b, a + 3b, \ldots$$

contains infinitely many prime numbers. Find the first 10 primes in the sequence when $a = 3$ and $b = 4$.

61. REASONING Find the sum of the positive odd integers less than 300. Explain your reasoning.

62. USING EQUATIONS Find the value of n.

a. $\displaystyle\sum_{i=1}^{n}(3i + 5) = 544$ b. $\displaystyle\sum_{i=1}^{n}(-4i - 1) = -1127$

c. $\displaystyle\sum_{i=5}^{n}(7 + 12i) = 455$ d. $\displaystyle\sum_{i=3}^{n}(-3 - 4i) = -507$

63. ABSTRACT REASONING A theater has n rows of seats, and each row has d more seats than the row in front of it. There are x seats in the last (nth) row and a total of y seats in the entire theater. How many seats are in the front row of the theater? Write your answer in terms of n, x, and y.

64. CRITICAL THINKING The expressions $3 - x$, x, and $1 - 3x$ are the first three terms in an arithmetic sequence. Find the value of x and the next term in the sequence.

65. CRITICAL THINKING One of the major sources of our knowledge of Egyptian mathematics is the Ahmes papyrus, which is a scroll copied in 1650 B.C. by an Egyptian scribe. The following problem is from the Ahmes papyrus.

> *Divide 10 hekats of barley among 10 men so that the common difference is $\frac{1}{8}$ of a hekat of barley.*

Use what you know about arithmetic sequences and series to determine what portion of a hekat each man should receive.

Maintaining Mathematical Proficiency
Reviewing what you learned in previous grades and lessons

Simplify the expression. *(Section 4.2)*

66. $\dfrac{7}{7^{1/3}}$

67. $\dfrac{3^{-2}}{3^{-4}}$

68. $\left(\dfrac{9}{49}\right)^{1/2}$

69. $(5^{1/2} \cdot 5^{1/4})$

Tell whether the function represents *exponential growth* or *exponential decay*. Then graph the function. *(Section 5.1)*

70. $y = 2e^x$ **71.** $y = e^{-3x}$ **72.** $y = 3e^{-x}$ **73.** $y = e^{0.25x}$

Analyzing Geometric Sequences and Series

Essential Question How can you recognize a geometric sequence from its graph?

In a **geometric sequence**, the ratio of any term to the previous term, called the *common ratio*, is constant. For example, in the geometric sequence $1, 2, 4, 8, \ldots$, the common ratio is 2.

EXPLORATION 1 Recognizing Graphs of Geometric Sequences

Work with a partner. Determine whether each graph shows a geometric sequence. If it does, then write a rule for the nth term of the sequence and use a spreadsheet to find the sum of the first 20 terms. What do you notice about the graph of a geometric sequence?

a.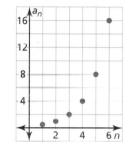

b.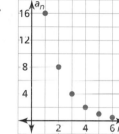

c.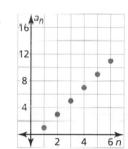

d.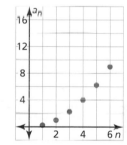

EXPLORATION 2 Finding the Sum of a Geometric Sequence

LOOKING FOR REGULARITY IN REPEATED REASONING

To be proficient in math, you need to notice when calculations are repeated, and look both for general methods and for shortcuts.

Work with a partner. You can write the nth term of a geometric sequence with first term a_1 and common ratio r as

$$a_n = a_1 r^{n-1}.$$

So, you can write the sum S_n of the first n terms of a geometric sequence as

$$S_n = a_1 + a_1 r + a_1 r^2 + a_1 r^3 + \cdots + a_1 r^{n-1}.$$

Rewrite this formula by finding the difference $S_n - rS_n$ and solving for S_n. Then verify your rewritten formula by finding the sums of the first 20 terms of the geometric sequences in Exploration 1. Compare your answers to those you obtained using a spreadsheet.

Communicate Your Answer

3. How can you recognize a geometric sequence from its graph?

4. Find the sum of the terms of each geometric sequence.

    a. $1, 2, 4, 8, \ldots, 8192$ **b.** $0.1, 0.01, 0.001, 0.0001, \ldots, 10^{-10}$

Core Vocabulary

geometric sequence, *p. 374*
common ratio, *p. 374*
geometric series, *p. 376*

Previous
exponential function
properties of exponents

What You Will Learn

▶ Identify geometric sequences.
▶ Write rules for geometric sequences.
▶ Find sums of finite geometric series.

Identifying Geometric Sequences

In a **geometric sequence**, the ratio of any term to the previous term is constant. This constant ratio is called the **common ratio** and is denoted by r.

EXAMPLE 1 Identifying Geometric Sequences

Tell whether each sequence is geometric.

a. 6, 12, 20, 30, 42, . . .

b. 256, 64, 16, 4, 1, . . .

SOLUTION

Find the ratios of consecutive terms.

a. $\dfrac{a_2}{a_1} = \dfrac{12}{6} = 2 \qquad \dfrac{a_3}{a_2} = \dfrac{20}{12} = \dfrac{5}{3} \qquad \dfrac{a_4}{a_3} = \dfrac{30}{20} = \dfrac{3}{2} \qquad \dfrac{a_5}{a_4} = \dfrac{42}{30} = \dfrac{7}{5}$

▶ The ratios are not constant, so the sequence is not geometric.

b. $\dfrac{a_2}{a_1} = \dfrac{64}{256} = \dfrac{1}{4} \qquad \dfrac{a_3}{a_2} = \dfrac{16}{64} = \dfrac{1}{4} \qquad \dfrac{a_4}{a_3} = \dfrac{4}{16} = \dfrac{1}{4} \qquad \dfrac{a_5}{a_4} = \dfrac{1}{4}$

▶ Each ratio is $\frac{1}{4}$, so the sequence is geometric.

Monitoring Progress Help in English and Spanish at *BigIdeasMath.com*

Tell whether the sequence is geometric. Explain your reasoning.

1. 27, 9, 3, 1, $\dfrac{1}{3}$, . . .   **2.** 2, 6, 24, 120, 720, . . .   **3.** $-1, 2, -4, 8, -16, . . .$

Writing Rules for Geometric Sequences

Core Concept

Rule for a Geometric Sequence

Algebra The nth term of a geometric sequence with first term a_1 and common ratio r is given by:

$$a_n = a_1 r^{n-1}$$

Example The nth term of a geometric sequence with a first term of 2 and a common ratio of 3 is given by:

$$a_n = 2(3)^{n-1}$$

EXAMPLE 2 — Writing a Rule for the nth Term

Write a rule for the nth term of each sequence. Then find a_8.

a. 5, 15, 45, 135, . . .

b. 88, −44, 22, −11, . . .

SOLUTION

COMMON ERROR

In the general rule for a geometric sequence, note that the exponent is $n - 1$, not n.

a. The sequence is geometric with first term $a_1 = 5$ and common ratio $r = \frac{15}{5} = 3$.

So, a rule for the nth term is

$$a_n = a_1 r^{n-1} \qquad \text{Write general rule.}$$
$$= 5(3)^{n-1}. \qquad \text{Substitute 5 for } a_1 \text{ and 3 for } r.$$

▶ A rule is $a_n = 5(3)^{n-1}$, and the 8th term is $a_8 = 5(3)^{8-1} = 10{,}935$.

b. The sequence is geometric with first term $a_1 = 88$ and common ratio $r = \frac{-44}{88} = -\frac{1}{2}$. So, a rule for the nth term is

$$a_n = a_1 r^{n-1} \qquad \text{Write general rule.}$$
$$= 88\left(-\frac{1}{2}\right)^{n-1}. \qquad \text{Substitute 88 for } a_1 \text{ and } -\frac{1}{2} \text{ for } r.$$

▶ A rule is $a_n = 88\left(-\frac{1}{2}\right)^{n-1}$, and the 8th term is $a_8 = 88\left(-\frac{1}{2}\right)^{8-1} = -\frac{11}{16}$.

Monitoring Progress 🔊 Help in English and Spanish at *BigIdeasMath.com*

4. Write a rule for the nth term of the sequence 3, 15, 75, 375, ... Then find a_9.

EXAMPLE 3 — Writing a Rule Given a Term and Common Ratio

One term of a geometric sequence is $a_4 = 12$. The common ratio is $r = 2$. Write a rule for the nth term. Then graph the first six terms of the sequence.

SOLUTION

Step 1 Use the general rule to find the first term.

$$a_n = a_1 r^{n-1} \qquad \text{Write general rule.}$$
$$a_4 = a_1 r^{4-1} \qquad \text{Substitute 4 for } n.$$
$$12 = a_1(2)^3 \qquad \text{Substitute 12 for } a_4 \text{ and 2 for } r.$$
$$1.5 = a_1 \qquad \text{Solve for } a_1.$$

Step 2 Write a rule for the nth term.

$$a_n = a_1 r^{n-1} \qquad \text{Write general rule.}$$
$$= 1.5(2)^{n-1} \qquad \text{Substitute 1.5 for } a_1 \text{ and 2 for } r.$$

ANALYZING RELATIONSHIPS

Notice that the points lie on an exponential curve because consecutive terms change by equal factors. So, a geometric sequence in which $r > 0$ and $r \neq 1$ is an exponential function whose domain is a subset of the integers.

Step 3 Use the rule to create a table of values for the sequence. Then plot the points.

n	1	2	3	4	5	6
a_n	1.5	3	6	12	24	48

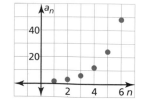

EXAMPLE 4 **Writing a Rule Given Two Terms**

Two terms of a geometric sequence are $a_2 = 12$ and $a_5 = -768$. Write a rule for the nth term.

SOLUTION

Step 1 Write a system of equations using $a_n = a_1 r^{n-1}$. Substitute 2 for n to write Equation 1. Substitute 5 for n to write Equation 2.

$$a_2 = a_1 r^{2-1} \quad \Longrightarrow \quad 12 = a_1 r \qquad \text{Equation 1}$$

$$a_5 = a_1 r^{5-1} \quad \Longrightarrow \quad -768 = a_1 r^4 \qquad \text{Equation 2}$$

Step 2 Solve the system.

$$\frac{12}{r} = a_1 \qquad \text{Solve Equation 1 for } a_1.$$

$$-768 = \frac{12}{r}(r^4) \qquad \text{Substitute for } a_1 \text{ in Equation 2.}$$

$$-768 = 12r^3 \qquad \text{Simplify.}$$

$$-4 = r \qquad \text{Solve for } r.$$

$$12 = a_1(-4) \qquad \text{Substitute for } r \text{ in Equation 1.}$$

$$-3 = a_1 \qquad \text{Solve for } a_1.$$

Step 3 Write a rule for a_n.

$$a_n = a_1 r^{n-1} \qquad \text{Write general rule.}$$

$$= -3(-4)^{n-1} \qquad \text{Substitute for } a_1 \text{ and } r.$$

Check

Use the rule to verify that the 2nd term is 12 and the 5th term is -768.

$$a_2 = -3(-4)^{2-1}$$

$$= -3(-4)$$

$$= 12 \checkmark$$

$$a_5 = -3(-4)^{5-1}$$

$$= -3(256)$$

$$= -768 \checkmark$$

Monitoring Progress Help in English and Spanish at *BigIdeasMath.com*

Write a rule for the nth term of the sequence. Then graph the first six terms of the sequence.

5. $a_6 = -96, r = -2$

6. $a_2 = 12, a_4 = 3$

Finding Sums of Finite Geometric Series

The expression formed by adding the terms of a geometric sequence is called a **geometric series**. The sum of the first n terms of a geometric series is denoted by S_n. You can develop a rule for S_n as follows.

$$S_n = a_1 + a_1 r + a_1 r^2 + a_1 r^3 + \cdots + a_1 r^{n-1}$$

$$\underline{-rS_n = \qquad - a_1 r - a_1 r^2 - a_1 r^3 - \cdots - a_1 r^{n-1} - a_1 r^n}$$

$$S_n - rS_n = a_1 + 0 + 0 + 0 + \cdots + 0 \qquad - a_1 r^n$$

$$S_n(1 - r) = a_1(1 - r^n)$$

When $r \neq 1$, you can divide each side of this equation by $1 - r$ to obtain the following rule for S_n.

⑤ Core Concept

The Sum of a Finite Geometric Series

The sum of the first n terms of a geometric series with common ratio $r \neq 1$ is

$$S_n = a_1\left(\frac{1 - r^n}{1 - r}\right).$$

EXAMPLE 5   Finding the Sum of a Geometric Series

Find the sum $\sum_{k=1}^{10} 4(3)^{k-1}$.

SOLUTION

Step 1   Find the first term and the common ratio.

$$a_1 = 4(3)^{1-1} = 4 \qquad \text{Identify first term.}$$

$$r = 3 \qquad \text{Identify common ratio.}$$

Step 2   Find the sum.

$$S_{10} = a_1\left(\frac{1-r^{10}}{1-r}\right) \qquad \text{Write rule for } S_{10}.$$

$$= 4\left(\frac{1-3^{10}}{1-3}\right) \qquad \text{Substitute 4 for } a_1 \text{ and 3 for } r.$$

$$= 118{,}096 \qquad \text{Simplify.}$$

Check

Use a graphing calculator to check the sum.

```
sum(seq(4*3^(X-1
),X,1,10))
            118096
```

EXAMPLE 6   Solving a Real-Life Problem

You can calculate the monthly payment M (in dollars) for a loan using the formula

$$M = \frac{L}{\sum_{k=1}^{t}\left(\dfrac{1}{1+i}\right)^{k}}$$

where L is the loan amount (in dollars), i is the monthly interest rate (in decimal form), and t is the term (in months). Calculate the monthly payment on a 5-year loan for $20,000 with an annual interest rate of 6%.

SOLUTION

Step 1   Substitute for L, i, and t. The loan amount is $L = 20{,}000$, the monthly interest rate is $i = \dfrac{0.06}{12} = 0.005$, and the term is $t = 5(12) = 60$.

$$M = \frac{20{,}000}{\sum_{k=1}^{60}\left(\dfrac{1}{1+0.005}\right)^{k}}$$

USING TECHNOLOGY

Storing the value of $\dfrac{1}{1.005}$ helps minimize mistakes and also assures an accurate answer. Rounding this value to 0.995 results in a monthly payment of $386.94.

Step 2   Notice that the denominator is a geometric series with first term $\dfrac{1}{1.005}$ and common ratio $\dfrac{1}{1.005}$. Use a calculator to find the monthly payment.

```
1/1.005→R
         .9950248756
R((1-R^60)/(1-R)
)
         51.72556075
20000/Ans
         386.6560306
```

▶ So, the monthly payment is $386.66.

Monitoring Progress Help in English and Spanish at *BigIdeasMath.com*

Find the sum.

7. $\sum_{k=1}^{8} 5^{k-1}$

8. $\sum_{i=1}^{12} 6(-2)^{i-1}$

9. $\sum_{t=1}^{7} -16(0.5)^{t-1}$

10. WHAT IF? In Example 6, how does the monthly payment change when the annual interest rate is 5%?

Vocabulary and Core Concept Check

1. **COMPLETE THE SENTENCE** The constant ratio of consecutive terms in a geometric sequence is called the _____.

2. **WRITING** How can you determine whether a sequence is geometric from its graph?

3. **COMPLETE THE SENTENCE** The nth term of a geometric sequence has the form $a_n = $ _____.

4. **VOCABULARY** State the rule for the sum of the first n terms of a geometric series.

Monitoring Progress and Modeling with Mathematics

In Exercises 5–12, tell whether the sequence is geometric. Explain your reasoning. *(See Example 1.)*

5. $96, 48, 24, 12, 6, \ldots$ 6. $729, 243, 81, 27, 9, \ldots$

7. $2, 4, 6, 8, 10, \ldots$ 8. $5, 20, 35, 50, 65, \ldots$

9. $0.2, 3.2, -12.8, 51.2, -204.8, \ldots$

10. $0.3, -1.5, 7.5, -37.5, 187.5, \ldots$

11. $\dfrac{1}{2}, \dfrac{1}{6}, \dfrac{1}{18}, \dfrac{1}{54}, \dfrac{1}{162}, \ldots$

12. $\dfrac{1}{4}, \dfrac{1}{16}, \dfrac{1}{64}, \dfrac{1}{256}, \dfrac{1}{1024}, \ldots$

13. **WRITING EQUATIONS** Write a rule for the geometric sequence with the given description.

   a. The first term is -3, and each term is 5 times the previous term.

   b. The first term is 72, and each term is $\frac{1}{3}$ times the previous term.

14. **WRITING** Compare the terms of a geometric sequence when $r > 1$ to when $0 < r < 1$.

In Exercises 15–22, write a rule for the nth term of the sequence. Then find a_7. *(See Example 2.)*

15. $4, 20, 100, 500, \ldots$ 16. $6, 24, 96, 384, \ldots$

17. $112, 56, 28, 14, \ldots$ 18. $375, 75, 15, 3, \ldots$

19. $4, 6, 9, \frac{27}{2}, \ldots$ 20. $2, \frac{3}{2}, \frac{9}{8}, \frac{27}{32}, \ldots$

21. $1.3, -3.9, 11.7, -35.1, \ldots$

22. $1.5, -7.5, 37.5, -187.5, \ldots$

In Exercises 23–30, write a rule for the nth term of the sequence. Then graph the first six terms of the sequence. *(See Example 3.)*

23. $a_3 = 4, r = 2$ 24. $a_3 = 27, r = 3$

25. $a_2 = 30, r = \frac{1}{2}$ 26. $a_2 = 64, r = \frac{1}{4}$

27. $a_4 = -192, r = 4$ 28. $a_4 = -500, r = 5$

29. $a_5 = 3, r = -\frac{1}{3}$ 30. $a_5 = 1, r = -\frac{1}{5}$

ERROR ANALYSIS In Exercises 31 and 32, describe and correct the error in writing a rule for the nth term of the geometric sequence for which $a_2 = 48$ and $r = 6$.

31.

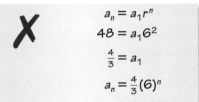

$$a_n = a_1 r^n$$
$$48 = a_1 6^2$$
$$\frac{4}{3} = a_1$$
$$a_n = \frac{4}{3}(6)^n$$

32.

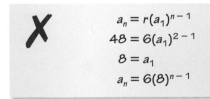

$$a_n = r(a_1)^{n-1}$$
$$48 = 6(a_1)^{2-1}$$
$$8 = a_1$$
$$a_n = 6(8)^{n-1}$$

In Exercises 33–40, write a rule for the nth term of the geometric sequence. *(See Example 4.)*

33. $a_2 = 28, a_5 = 1792$ 34. $a_1 = 11, a_4 = 88$

35. $a_1 = -6, a_5 = -486$ 36. $a_2 = -10, a_6 = -6250$

37. $a_2 = 64, a_4 = 1$ 38. $a_1 = 1, a_2 = 49$

39. $a_2 = -72, a_6 = -\frac{1}{18}$ 40. $a_2 = -48, a_5 = \frac{3}{4}$

WRITING EQUATIONS In Exercises 41–46, write a rule for the sequence with the given terms.

41.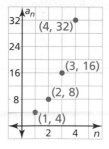

32 (4, 32)
24
16 (3, 16)
8 (2, 8)
(1, 4)
2   4   n

42.

128 (4, 135)
96
64
(3, 45)
32 (1, 5)
(2, 15)
2   4 n

43.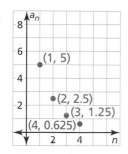

8
6
(1, 5)
4
2 (2, 2.5)
(3, 1.25)
(4, 0.625)
2   4   n

44.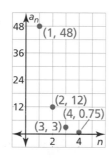

48 (1, 48)
36
24
12 (2, 12)
(4, 0.75)
(3, 3)
2   4   n

45.

n	2	3	4	5	6
a_n	-12	24	-48	96	-192

46.

n	2	3	4	5	6
a_n	21	63	-189	567	-1701

In Exercises 47–52, find the sum. *(See Example 5.)*

47. $\sum_{i=1}^{9} 6(7)^{i-1}$

48. $\sum_{i=1}^{10} 7(4)^{i-1}$

49. $\sum_{i=1}^{10} 4\left(\frac{3}{4}\right)^{i-1}$

50. $\sum_{i=1}^{8} 5\left(\frac{1}{3}\right)^{i-1}$

51. $\sum_{i=0}^{8} 8\left(-\frac{2}{3}\right)^{i}$

52. $\sum_{i=0}^{9} 9\left(-\frac{3}{4}\right)^{i}$

NUMBER SENSE In Exercises 53 and 54, find the sum.

53. The first 8 terms of the geometric sequence
$-12, -48, -192, -768, \ldots$.

54. The first 9 terms of the geometric sequence
$-14, -42, -126, -378, \ldots$.

55. **WRITING** Compare the graph of $a_n = 5(3)^{n-1}$, where n is a positive integer, to the graph of $f(x) = 5 \cdot 3^{x-1}$, where x is a real number.

56. **ABSTRACT REASONING** Use the rule for the sum of a finite geometric series to write each polynomial as a rational expression.

a. $1 + x + x^2 + x^3 + x^4$

b. $3x + 6x^3 + 12x^5 + 24x^7$

MODELING WITH MATHEMATICS In Exercises 57 and 58, use the monthly payment formula given in Example 6.

57. You are buying a new car. You take out a 5-year loan for $15,000. The annual interest rate of the loan is 4%. Calculate the monthly payment. *(See Example 6.)*

58. You are buying a new house. You take out a 30-year mortgage for $200,000. The annual interest rate of the loan is 4.5%. Calculate the monthly payment.

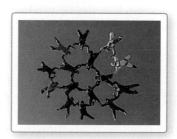

59. **MODELING WITH MATHEMATICS** A regional soccer tournament has 64 participating teams. In the first round of the tournament, 32 games are played. In each successive round, the number of games decreases by a factor of $\frac{1}{2}$.

a. Write a rule for the number of games played in the nth round. For what values of n does the rule make sense? Explain.

b. Find the total number of games played in the regional soccer tournament.

60. **MODELING WITH MATHEMATICS** In a skydiving formation with R rings, each ring after the first has twice as many skydivers as the preceding ring. The formation for $R = 2$ is shown.

a. Let a_n be the number of skydivers in the nth ring. Write a rule for a_n.

b. Find the total number of skydivers when there are four rings.

61. PROBLEM SOLVING The *Sierpinski carpet* is a fractal created using squares. The process involves removing smaller squares from larger squares. First, divide a large square into nine congruent squares. Then remove the center square. Repeat these steps for each smaller square, as shown below. Assume that each side of the initial square is 1 unit long.

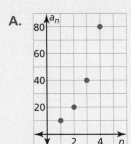

Stage 1   Stage 2   Stage 3

a. Let a_n be the total number of squares removed at the nth stage. Write a rule for a_n. Then find the total number of squares removed through Stage 8.

b. Let b_n be the remaining area of the original square after the nth stage. Write a rule for b_n. Then find the remaining area of the original square after Stage 12.

62. HOW DO YOU SEE IT? Match each sequence with its graph. Explain your reasoning.

a. $a_n = 10\left(\dfrac{1}{2}\right)^{n-1}$ b. $a_n = 10(2)^{n-1}$

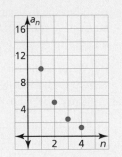

A.   B.

63. CRITICAL THINKING On January 1, you deposit $2000 in a retirement account that pays 5% annual interest. You make this deposit each January 1 for the next 30 years. How much money do you have in your account immediately after you make your last deposit?

64. THOUGHT PROVOKING The first four iterations of the fractal called the *Koch snowflake* are shown below. Find the perimeter and area of each iteration. Do the perimeters and areas form geometric sequences? Explain your reasoning.

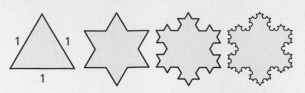

65. MAKING AN ARGUMENT You and your friend are comparing two loan options for a $165,000 house. Loan 1 is a 15-year loan with an annual interest rate of 3%. Loan 2 is a 30-year loan with an annual interest rate of 4%. Your friend claims the total amount repaid over the loan will be less for Loan 2. Is your friend correct? Justify your answer.

66. CRITICAL THINKING Let L be the amount of a loan (in dollars), i be the monthly interest rate (in decimal form), t be the term (in months), and M be the monthly payment (in dollars).

a. When making monthly payments, you are paying the loan amount plus the interest the loan gathers each month. For a 1-month loan, $t = 1$, the equation for repayment is $L(1 + i) - M = 0$. For a 2-month loan, $t = 2$, the equation is $[L(1 + i) - M](1 + i) - M = 0$. Solve both of these repayment equations for L.

b. Use the pattern in the equations you solved in part (a) to write a repayment equation for a t-month loan. (*Hint*: L is equal to M times a geometric series.) Then solve the equation for M.

c. Use the rule for the sum of a finite geometric series to show that the formula in part (b) is equivalent to

$$M = L\left(\dfrac{i}{1 - (1 + i)^{-t}}\right).$$

Use this formula to check your answers in Exercises 57 and 58.

Maintaining Mathematical Proficiency

Reviewing what you learned in previous grades and lessons

Graph the function. State the domain and range. *(Section 6.2)*

67. $f(x) = \dfrac{1}{x - 3}$

68. $g(x) = \dfrac{2}{x} + 3$

69. $h(x) = \dfrac{1}{x - 2} + 1$

70. $p(x) = \dfrac{3}{x + 1} - 2$

380   Chapter 7   Sequences and Series

7.1–7.3 What Did You Learn?

Core Vocabulary

Core Concepts

Section 7.1

Section 7.2

Section 7.3

Mathematical Practices

1. Explain how viewing each arrangement as individual tables can be helpful in Exercise 29 on page 363.

2. How can you use tools to find the sum of the arithmetic series in Exercises 53 and 54 on page 371?

3. How did understanding the domain of each function help you to compare the graphs in Exercise 55 on page 379?

Keeping Your Mind Focused

- Before doing homework, review the concept boxes and examples. Talk through the examples out loud.

- Complete homework as though you were also preparing for a quiz. Memorize the different types of problems, formulas, rules, and so on.

STUDY SKILLS

Describe the pattern, write the next term, and write a rule for the *n*th term of the sequence. *(Section 7.1)*

1. $1, 7, 13, 19, \ldots$

2. $-5, 10, -15, 20, \ldots$

3. $\dfrac{1}{20}, \dfrac{2}{30}, \dfrac{3}{40}, \dfrac{4}{50}, \ldots$

Write the series using summation notation. Then find the sum of the series. *(Section 7.1)*

4. $1 + 2 + 3 + 4 + \cdots + 15$

5. $0 + \dfrac{1}{2} + \dfrac{2}{3} + \dfrac{3}{4} + \cdots + \dfrac{7}{8}$

6. $9 + 16 + 25 + \cdots + 100$

Write a rule for the *n*th term of the sequence. *(Sections 7.2 and 7.3)*

7.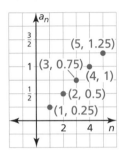

8.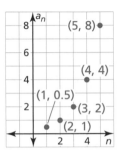

9.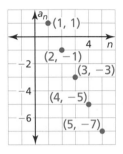

Tell whether the sequence is *arithmetic*, *geometric*, or *neither*. Write a rule for the *n*th term of the sequence. Then find a_9. *(Sections 7.2 and 7.3)*

10. $13, 6, -1, -8, \ldots$

11. $\dfrac{1}{2}, \dfrac{1}{3}, \dfrac{1}{4}, \dfrac{1}{5}, \ldots$

12. $1, -3, 9, -27, \ldots$

13. One term of an arithmetic sequence is $a_{12} = 19$. The common difference is $d = 7$. Write a rule for the *n*th term. Then graph the first six terms of the sequence. *(Section 7.2)*

14. Two terms of a geometric sequence are $a_6 = -50$ and $a_9 = -6250$. Write a rule for the *n*th term. *(Section 7.3)*

Find the sum. *(Sections 7.2 and 7.3)*

15. $\displaystyle\sum_{n=1}^{9} (3n + 5)$

16. $\displaystyle\sum_{k=1}^{5} 11(-3)^{k-2}$

17. $\displaystyle\sum_{i=1}^{12} -4\left(\dfrac{1}{2}\right)^{i+3}$

18. Pieces of chalk are stacked in a pile. Part of the pile is shown. The bottom row has 15 pieces of chalk, and the top row has 6 pieces of chalk. Each row has one less piece of chalk than the row below it. How many pieces of chalk are in the pile? *(Section 7.2)*

19. You accept a job as an environmental engineer that pays a salary of $45,000 in the first year. After the first year, your salary increases by 3.5% per year. *(Section 7.3)*

   a. Write a rule giving your salary a_n for your *n*th year of employment.

   b. What will your salary be during your fifth year of employment?

   c. You work 10 years for the company. What are your total earnings? Justify your answer.

7.4 Finding Sums of Infinite Geometric Series

Essential Question How can you find the sum of an infinite geometric series?

EXPLORATION 1 Finding Sums of Infinite Geometric Series

Work with a partner. Enter each geometric series in a spreadsheet. Then use the spreadsheet to determine whether the infinite geometric series has a finite sum. If it does, find the sum. Explain your reasoning. (The figure shows a partially completed spreadsheet for part (a).)

a. $1 + \dfrac{1}{2} + \dfrac{1}{4} + \dfrac{1}{8} + \dfrac{1}{16} + \cdots$

b. $1 + \dfrac{1}{3} + \dfrac{1}{9} + \dfrac{1}{27} + \dfrac{1}{81} + \cdots$

c. $1 + \dfrac{3}{2} + \dfrac{9}{4} + \dfrac{27}{8} + \dfrac{81}{16} + \cdots$

d. $1 + \dfrac{5}{4} + \dfrac{25}{16} + \dfrac{125}{64} + \dfrac{625}{256} + \cdots$

e. $1 + \dfrac{4}{5} + \dfrac{16}{25} + \dfrac{64}{125} + \dfrac{256}{625} + \cdots$

f. $1 + \dfrac{9}{10} + \dfrac{81}{100} + \dfrac{729}{1000} + \dfrac{6561}{10,000} + \cdots$

	A	B
1	1	1
2	2	0.5
3	3	0.25
4	4	0.125
5	5	0.0625
6	6	0.03125
7	7	
8	8	
9	9	
10	10	
11	11	
12	12	
13	13	
14	14	
15	15	
16	Sum	

EXPLORATION 2 Writing a Conjecture

Work with a partner. Look back at the infinite geometric series in Exploration 1. Write a conjecture about how you can determine whether the infinite geometric series

$$u_1 + u_1 r + u_1 r^2 + u_1 r^3 + \cdots$$

has a finite sum.

EXPLORATION 3 Writing a Formula

Work with a partner. In Lesson 7.3, you learned that the sum of the first n terms of a geometric series with first term a_1 and common ratio $r \neq 1$ is

$$S_n = a_1 \left(\dfrac{1 - r^n}{1 - r} \right).$$

When an infinite geometric series has a finite sum, what happens to r^n as n increases? Explain your reasoning. Write a formula to find the sum of an infinite geometric series. Then verify your formula by checking the sums you obtained in Exploration 1.

Communicate Your Answer

4. How can you find the sum of an infinite geometric series?

5. Find the sum of each infinite geometric series, if it exists.

a. $1 + 0.1 + 0.01 + 0.001 + 0.0001 + \cdots$ **b.** $2 + \dfrac{4}{3} + \dfrac{8}{9} + \dfrac{16}{27} + \dfrac{32}{81} + \cdots$

Core Vocabulary

partial sum, *p. 384*

Previous
repeating decimal
fraction in simplest form
rational number

What You Will Learn

▶ Find partial sums of infinite geometric series.

▶ Find sums of infinite geometric series.

Partial Sums of Infinite Geometric Series

The sum S_n of the first n terms of an infinite series is called a **partial sum**. The partial sums of an infinite geometric series may approach a limiting value.

> **EXAMPLE 1   Finding Partial Sums**

Consider the infinite geometric series

$$\frac{1}{2} + \frac{1}{4} + \frac{1}{8} + \frac{1}{16} + \frac{1}{32} + \cdots .$$

Find and graph the partial sums S_n for $n = 1, 2, 3, 4,$ and 5. Then describe what happens to S_n as n increases.

SOLUTION

Step 1   Find the partial sums.

$$S_1 = \frac{1}{2} = 0.5$$

$$S_2 = \frac{1}{2} + \frac{1}{4} = 0.75$$

$$S_3 = \frac{1}{2} + \frac{1}{4} + \frac{1}{8} \approx 0.88$$

$$S_4 = \frac{1}{2} + \frac{1}{4} + \frac{1}{8} + \frac{1}{16} \approx 0.94$$

$$S_5 = \frac{1}{2} + \frac{1}{4} + \frac{1}{8} + \frac{1}{16} + \frac{1}{32} \approx 0.97$$

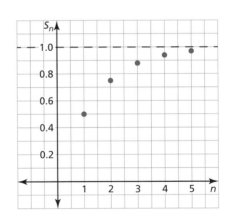

Step 2   Plot the points $(1, 0.5)$, $(2, 0.75)$, $(3, 0.88)$, $(4, 0.94)$, and $(5, 0.97)$. The graph is shown at the right.

▶ From the graph, S_n appears to approach 1 as n increases.

Sums of Infinite Geometric Series

In Example 1, you can understand why S_n approaches 1 as n increases by considering the rule for the sum of a finite geometric series.

$$S_n = a_1 \left(\frac{1 - r^n}{1 - r} \right) = \frac{1}{2} \left(\frac{1 - \left(\frac{1}{2} \right)^n}{1 - \frac{1}{2}} \right) = 1 - \left(\frac{1}{2} \right)^n$$

As n increases, $\left(\frac{1}{2} \right)^n$ approaches 0, so S_n approaches 1. Therefore, 1 is defined to be the sum of the infinite geometric series in Example 1. More generally, as n increases for *any* infinite geometric series with common ratio r between -1 and 1, the value of S_n approaches

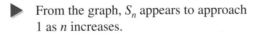

$$S_n = a_1 \left(\frac{1 - r^n}{1 - r} \right) \approx a_1 \left(\frac{1 - 0}{1 - r} \right) = \frac{a_1}{1 - r}.$$

⑤ Core Concept

The Sum of an Infinite Geometric Series

The sum of an infinite geometric series with first term a_1 and common ratio r is given by

$$S = \frac{a_1}{1 - r}$$

provided $|r| < 1$. If $|r| \geq 1$, then the series has no sum.

UNDERSTANDING MATHEMATICAL TERMS

Even though a geometric series with a common ratio of $|r| < 1$ has *infinitely* many terms, the series has a *finite* sum.

EXAMPLE 2 **Finding Sums of Infinite Geometric Series**

Find the sum of each infinite geometric series, if it exists.

a. $\displaystyle\sum_{i=1}^{\infty} 3(0.7)^{i-1}$ **b.** $1 + 3 + 9 + 27 + \cdots$ **c.** $1 - \dfrac{3}{4} + \dfrac{9}{16} - \dfrac{27}{64} + \cdots$

SOLUTION

a. For this series, $a_1 = 3(0.7)^{1-1} = 3$ and $r = 0.7$. The sum of the series is

$$S = \frac{a_1}{1 - r} \qquad \text{Formula for sum of an infinite geometric series}$$

$$= \frac{3}{1 - 0.7} \qquad \text{Substitute 3 for } a_1 \text{ and 0.7 for } r.$$

$$= 10. \qquad \text{Simplify.}$$

b. For this series, $a_1 = 1$ and $a_2 = 3$. So, the common ratio is $r = \dfrac{3}{1} = 3$.

Because $|3| \geq 1$, the sum does not exist.

c. For this series, $a_1 = 1$ and $a_2 = -\dfrac{3}{4}$. So, the common ratio is

$$r = \frac{-\dfrac{3}{4}}{1} = -\frac{3}{4}.$$

The sum of the series is

$$S = \frac{a_1}{1 - r} \qquad \text{Formula for sum of an infinite geometric series}$$

$$= \frac{1}{1 - \left(-\dfrac{3}{4}\right)} \qquad \text{Substitute 1 for } a_1 \text{ and } -\dfrac{3}{4} \text{ for } r.$$

$$= \frac{4}{7}. \qquad \text{Simplify.}$$

STUDY TIP

For the geometric series in part (b), the graph of the partial sums S_n for $n = 1, 2, 3, 4, 5,$ and 6 are shown. From the graph, it appears that as n increases, the partial sums do not approach a fixed number.

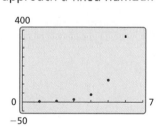

Monitoring Progress Help in English and Spanish at *BigIdeasMath.com*

1. Consider the infinite geometric series

$$\frac{2}{5} + \frac{4}{25} + \frac{8}{125} + \frac{16}{1625} + \frac{32}{3125} + \cdots.$$

Find and graph the partial sums S_n for $n = 1, 2, 3, 4,$ and 5. Then describe what happens to S_n as n increases.

Find the sum of the infinite geometric series, if it exists.

2. $\displaystyle\sum_{n=1}^{\infty} \left(-\frac{1}{2}\right)^{n-1}$ **3.** $\displaystyle\sum_{n=1}^{\infty} 3\left(\frac{5}{4}\right)^{n-1}$ **4.** $3 + \dfrac{3}{4} + \dfrac{3}{16} + \dfrac{3}{64} + \cdots$

EXAMPLE 3 Solving a Real-Life Problem

A pendulum that is released to swing freely travels 18 inches on the first swing. On each successive swing, the pendulum travels 80% of the distance of the previous swing. What is the total distance the pendulum swings?

18   18(0.8)   18(0.8)^2 18(0.8)^3

SOLUTION

The total distance traveled by the pendulum is given by the infinite geometric series

$$18 + 18(0.8) + 18(0.8)^2 + 18(0.8)^3 + \cdots .$$

For this series, $a_1 = 18$ and $r = 0.8$. The sum of the series is

$$S = \frac{a_1}{1 - r}$$ Formula for sum of an infinite geometric series

$$= \frac{18}{1 - 0.8}$$ Substitute 18 for a_1 and 0.8 for r.

$$= 90.$$ Simplify.

▶ The pendulum travels a total distance of 90 inches, or 7.5 feet.

EXAMPLE 4 Writing a Repeating Decimal as a Fraction

Write 0.242424 . . . as a fraction in simplest form.

SOLUTION

Write the repeating decimal as an infinite geometric series.

$$0.242424 \ldots = 0.24 + 0.0024 + 0.000024 + 0.00000024 + \cdots$$

For this series, $a_1 = 0.24$ and $r = \dfrac{0.0024}{0.24} = 0.01$. Next, write the sum of the series.

$$S = \frac{a_1}{1 - r}$$ Formula for sum of an infinite geometric series

$$= \frac{0.24}{1 - 0.01}$$ Substitute 0.24 for a_1 and 0.01 for r.

$$= \frac{0.24}{0.99}$$ Simplify.

$$= \frac{24}{99}$$ Write as a quotient of integers.

$$= \frac{8}{33}$$ Simplify.

> **REMEMBER**
>
> Because a repeating decimal is a rational number, it can be written as $\dfrac{a}{b}$, where a and b are integers and $b \neq 0$.

Monitoring Progress Help in English and Spanish at *BigIdeasMath.com*

5. **WHAT IF?** In Example 3, suppose the pendulum travels 10 inches on its first swing. What is the total distance the pendulum swings?

Write the repeating decimal as a fraction in simplest form.

6. 0.555 . . .   7. 0.727272 . . .   8. 0.131313 . . .

Vocabulary and Core Concept Check

1. **COMPLETE THE SENTENCE** The sum S_n of the first n terms of an infinite series is called a(n) _____.

2. **WRITING** Explain how to tell whether the series $\sum\limits_{i=1}^{\infty} a_1 r^{i-1}$ has a sum.

Monitoring Progress and Modeling with Mathematics

In Exercises 3–6, consider the infinite geometric series. Find and graph the partial sums S_n for $n = 1, 2, 3, 4,$ and 5. Then describe what happens to S_n as n increases. *(See Example 1.)*

3. $\dfrac{1}{2} + \dfrac{1}{6} + \dfrac{1}{18} + \dfrac{1}{54} + \dfrac{1}{162} + \cdots$

4. $\dfrac{2}{3} + \dfrac{1}{3} + \dfrac{1}{6} + \dfrac{1}{12} + \dfrac{1}{24} + \cdots$

5. $4 + \dfrac{12}{5} + \dfrac{36}{25} + \dfrac{108}{125} + \dfrac{324}{625} + \cdots$

6. $2 + \dfrac{2}{6} + \dfrac{2}{36} + \dfrac{2}{216} + \dfrac{2}{1296} + \cdots$

In Exercises 7–14, find the sum of the infinite geometric series, if it exists. *(See Example 2.)*

7. $\sum\limits_{n=1}^{\infty} 8\left(\dfrac{1}{5}\right)^{n-1}$

8. $\sum\limits_{k=1}^{\infty} -6\left(\dfrac{3}{2}\right)^{k-1}$

9. $\sum\limits_{k=1}^{\infty} \dfrac{11}{3}\left(\dfrac{3}{8}\right)^{k-1}$

10. $\sum\limits_{i=1}^{\infty} \dfrac{2}{5}\left(\dfrac{5}{3}\right)^{i-1}$

11. $2 + \dfrac{6}{4} + \dfrac{18}{16} + \dfrac{54}{64} + \cdots$

12. $-5 - 2 - \dfrac{4}{5} - \dfrac{8}{25} - \cdots$

13. $3 + \dfrac{5}{2} + \dfrac{25}{12} + \dfrac{125}{72} + \cdots$

14. $\dfrac{1}{2} - \dfrac{5}{3} + \dfrac{50}{9} - \dfrac{500}{27} + \cdots$

ERROR ANALYSIS In Exercises 15 and 16, describe and correct the error in finding the sum of the infinite geometric series.

15. $\sum\limits_{n=1}^{\infty} \left(\dfrac{7}{2}\right)^{n-1}$

For this series, $a_1 = 1$ and $r = \dfrac{7}{2}$.

$S = \dfrac{a_1}{1-r} = \dfrac{1}{1 - \dfrac{7}{2}} = \dfrac{1}{-\dfrac{5}{2}} = -\dfrac{2}{5}$

16. $4 + \dfrac{8}{3} + \dfrac{16}{9} + \dfrac{32}{27} + \cdots$

For this series, $a_1 = 4$ and $r = \dfrac{4}{\frac{8}{3}} = \dfrac{3}{2}$.

Because $\left|\dfrac{3}{2}\right| > 1$, the series has no sum.

17. **MODELING WITH MATHEMATICS** You push your younger cousin on a tire swing one time and then allow your cousin to swing freely. On the first swing, your cousin travels a distance of 14 feet. On each successive swing, your cousin travels 75% of the distance of the previous swing. What is the total distance your cousin swings? *(See Example 3.)*

14   14(0.75)   14(0.75)²

18. **MODELING WITH MATHEMATICS** A company had a profit of $350,000 in its first year. Since then, the company's profit has decreased by 12% per year. Assuming this trend continues, what is the total profit the company can make over the course of its lifetime? Justify your answer.

In Exercises 19–24, write the repeating decimal as a fraction in simplest form. *(See Example 4.)*

19. $0.222\ldots$

20. $0.444\ldots$

21. $0.161616\ldots$

22. $0.625625625\ldots$

23. $32.323232\ldots$

24. $130.130130130\ldots$

25. **OPEN-ENDED** Write two infinite geometric series that each have a sum of 6. Justify your answers.

26. HOW DO YOU SEE IT?
The graph shows the partial sums of the geometric series $a_1 + a_2 + a_3 + a_4 + \cdots$.

What is the value of $\sum\limits_{n=1}^{\infty} a_n$? Explain.

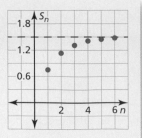

27. MODELING WITH MATHEMATICS A radio station has a daily contest in which a random listener is asked a trivia question. On the first day, the station gives $500 to the first listener who answers correctly. On each successive day, the winner receives 90% of the winnings from the previous day. What is the total amount of prize money the radio station gives away during the contest?

28. THOUGHT PROVOKING Archimedes used the sum of a geometric series to compute the area enclosed by a parabola and a straight line. In "Quadrature of the Parabola," he proved that the area of the region is $\frac{4}{3}$ the area of the inscribed triangle. The first term of the series for the parabola below is represented by the area of the blue triangle and the second term is represented by the area of the red triangles. Use Archimedes' result to find the area of the region. Then write the area as the sum of an infinite geometric series.

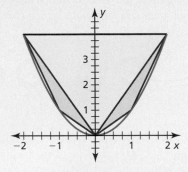

29. DRAWING CONCLUSIONS Can a person running at 20 feet per second ever catch up to a tortoise that runs 10 feet per second when the tortoise has a 20-foot head start? The Greek mathematician Zeno said no. He reasoned as follows:

The person will keep halving the distance but will never catch up to the tortoise.

Looking at the race as Zeno did, the distances and the times it takes the person to run those distances both form infinite geometric series. Using the table, show that both series have finite sums. Does the person catch up to the tortoise? Justify your answer.

Distance (ft)	20	10	5	2.5	. . .
Time (sec)	1	0.5	0.25	0.125	. . .

30. MAKING AN ARGUMENT Your friend claims that 0.999 . . . is equal to 1. Is your friend correct? Justify your answer.

31. CRITICAL THINKING The *Sierpinski triangle* is a fractal created using equilateral triangles. The process involves removing smaller triangles from larger triangles by joining the midpoints of the sides of the larger triangles as shown. Assume that the initial triangle has an area of 1 square foot.

Stage 1   Stage 2   Stage 3

a. Let a_n be the total area of all the triangles that are removed at Stage n. Write a rule for a_n.

b. Find $\sum\limits_{n=1}^{\infty} a_n$. Interpret your answer in the context of this situation.

Maintaining Mathematical Proficiency
Reviewing what you learned in previous grades and lessons

Determine the type of function represented by the table. *(Section 5.6)*

32.

x	−3	−2	−1	0	1
y	0.5	1.5	4.5	13.5	40.5

33.

x	0	4	8	12	16
y	−7	−1	2	2	−1

Determine whether the sequence is *arithmetic*, *geometric*, or *neither*. *(Sections 7.2 and 7.3)*

34. $-7, -1, 5, 11, 17, \ldots$

35. $0, -1, -3, -7, -15, \ldots$

36. $13.5, 40.5, 121.5, 364.5, \ldots$

7.5 Using Recursive Rules with Sequences

Essential Question How can you define a sequence recursively?

A **recursive rule** gives the beginning term(s) of a sequence and a *recursive equation* that tells how a_n is related to one or more preceding terms.

EXPLORATION 1 Evaluating a Recursive Rule

Work with a partner. Use each recursive rule and a spreadsheet to write the first six terms of the sequence. Classify the sequence as arithmetic, geometric, or neither. Explain your reasoning. (The figure shows a partially completed spreadsheet for part (a).)

a. $a_1 = 7, a_n = a_{n-1} + 3$

b. $a_1 = 5, a_n = a_{n-1} - 2$

c. $a_1 = 1, a_n = 2a_{n-1}$

d. $a_1 = 1, a_n = \frac{1}{2}(a_{n-1})^2$

e. $a_1 = 3, a_n = a_{n-1} + 1$

f. $a_1 = 4, a_n = \frac{1}{2}a_{n-1} - 1$

g. $a_1 = 4, a_n = \frac{1}{2}a_{n-1}$

h. $a_1 = 4, a_2 = 5, a_n = a_{n-1} + a_{n-2}$

	A	B
1	n	nth Term
2	1	7
3	2	10
4	3	
5	4	
6	5	
7	6	

B2+3

ATTENDING TO PRECISION

To be proficient in math, you need to communicate precisely to others.

EXPLORATION 2 Writing a Recursive Rule

Work with a partner. Write a recursive rule for the sequence. Explain your reasoning.

a. 3, 6, 9, 12, 15, 18, . . .

b. 18, 14, 10, 6, 2, −2, . . .

c. 3, 6, 12, 24, 48, 96, . . .

d. 128, 64, 32, 16, 8, 4, . . .

e. 5, 5, 5, 5, 5, 5, . . .

f. 1, 1, 2, 3, 5, 8, . . .

EXPLORATION 3 Writing a Recursive Rule

Work with a partner. Write a recursive rule for the sequence whose graph is shown.

a.

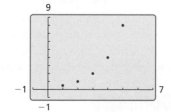

b.

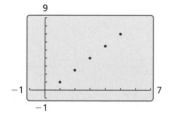

Communicate Your Answer

4. How can you define a sequence recursively?

5. Write a recursive rule that is different from those in Explorations 1–3. Write the first six terms of the sequence. Then graph the sequence and classify it as arithmetic, geometric, or neither.

What You Will Learn

▶ Evaluate recursive rules for sequences.

▶ Write recursive rules for sequences.

▶ Translate between recursive and explicit rules for sequences.

▶ Use recursive rules to solve real-life problems.

Evaluating Recursive Rules

So far in this chapter, you have worked with explicit rules for the nth term of a sequence, such as $a_n = 3n - 2$ and $a_n = 7(0.5)^n$. An **explicit rule** gives a_n as a function of the term's position number n in the sequence.

In this section, you will learn another way to define a sequence—by a *recursive rule*. A **recursive rule** gives the beginning term(s) of a sequence and a *recursive equation* that tells how a_n is related to one or more preceding terms.

EXAMPLE 1   Evaluating Recursive Rules

Write the first six terms of each sequence.

a. $a_0 = 1, a_n = a_{n-1} + 4$ **b.** $f(1) = 1, f(n) = 3 \cdot f(n-1)$

SOLUTION

a. $a_0 = 1$	1st term	**b.** $f(1) = 1$
$a_1 = a_0 + 4 = 1 + 4 = 5$	2nd term	$f(2) = 3 \cdot f(1) = 3(1) = 3$
$a_2 = a_1 + 4 = 5 + 4 = 9$	3rd term	$f(3) = 3 \cdot f(2) = 3(3) = 9$
$a_3 = a_2 + 4 = 9 + 4 = 13$	4th term	$f(4) = 3 \cdot f(3) = 3(9) = 27$
$a_4 = a_3 + 4 = 13 + 4 = 17$	5th term	$f(5) = 3 \cdot f(4) = 3(27) = 81$
$a_5 = a_4 + 4 = 17 + 4 = 21$	6th term	$f(6) = 3 \cdot f(5) = 3(81) = 243$

Monitoring Progress Help in English and Spanish at *BigIdeasMath.com*

Write the first six terms of the sequence.

1. $a_1 = 3, a_n = a_{n-1} - 7$ **2.** $a_0 = 162, a_n = 0.5a_{n-1}$

3. $f(0) = 1, f(n) = f(n-1) + n$ **4.** $a_1 = 4, a_n = 2a_{n-1} - 1$

Writing Recursive Rules

In part (a) of Example 1, the *differences* of consecutive terms of the sequence are constant, so the sequence is arithmetic. In part (b), the *ratios* of consecutive terms are constant, so the sequence is geometric. In general, rules for arithmetic and geometric sequences can be written recursively as follows.

🎴 Core Concept

Recursive Equations for Arithmetic and Geometric Sequences
Arithmetic Sequence

$a_n = a_{n-1} + d$, where d is the common difference

Geometric Sequence

$a_n = r \cdot a_{n-1}$, where r is the common ratio

EXAMPLE 2 Writing Recursive Rules

Write a recursive rule for (a) 3, 13, 23, 33, 43, . . . and (b) 16, 40, 100, 250, 625, ...

SOLUTION

Use a table to organize the terms and find the pattern.

a.

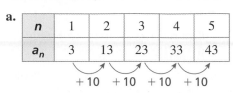

n	1	2	3	4	5
a_n	3	13	23	33	43

+10 +10 +10 +10

COMMON ERROR

A recursive *equation* for a sequence does not include the initial term. To write a recursive *rule* for a sequence, the initial term(s) must be included.

The sequence is arithmetic with first term $a_1 = 3$ and common difference $d = 10$.

$$a_n = a_{n-1} + d \qquad \text{Recursive equation for arithmetic sequence}$$
$$= a_{n-1} + 10 \qquad \text{Substitute 10 for } d.$$

▶ A recursive rule for the sequence is $a_1 = 3$, $a_n = a_{n-1} + 10$.

b.

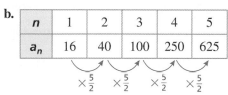

n	1	2	3	4	5
a_n	16	40	100	250	625

$\times \frac{5}{2}$ $\times \frac{5}{2}$ $\times \frac{5}{2}$ $\times \frac{5}{2}$

The sequence is geometric with first term $a_1 = 16$ and common ratio $r = \frac{5}{2}$.

$$a_n = r \cdot a_{n-1} \qquad \text{Recursive equation for geometric sequence}$$
$$= \frac{5}{2}a_{n-1} \qquad \text{Substitute } \frac{5}{2} \text{ for } r.$$

▶ A recursive rule for the sequence is $a_1 = 16$, $a_n = \frac{5}{2}a_{n-1}$.

EXAMPLE 3 Writing Recursive Rules

STUDY TIP

The sequence in part (a) of Example 3 is called the *Fibonacci sequence*. The sequence in part (b) lists *factorial numbers*.

Write a recursive rule for each sequence.

a. 1, 1, 2, 3, 5, . . . **b.** 1, 1, 2, 6, 24, . . .

SOLUTION

a. The terms have neither a common difference nor a common ratio. Beginning with the third term in the sequence, each term is the sum of the two previous terms.

▶ A recursive rule for the sequence is $a_1 = 1$, $a_2 = 1$, $a_n = a_{n-2} + a_{n-1}$.

b. The terms have neither a common difference nor a common ratio. Denote the first term by $a_0 = 1$. Note that $a_1 = 1 = 1 \cdot a_0$, $a_2 = 2 = 2 \cdot a_1$, $a_3 = 6 = 3 \cdot a_2$, and so on.

▶ A recursive rule for the sequence is $a_0 = 1$, $a_n = n \cdot a_{n-1}$.

Monitoring Progress Help in English and Spanish at *BigIdeasMath.com*

Write a recursive rule for the sequence.

5. 2, 14, 98, 686, 4802, . . . **6.** 19, 13, 7, 1, −5, . . .

7. 11, 22, 33, 44, 55, . . . **8.** 1, 2, 2, 4, 8, 32, . . .

Translating Between Recursive and Explicit Rules

EXAMPLE 4 **Translating from Explicit Rules to Recursive Rules**

Write a recursive rule for (a) $a_n = -6 + 8n$ and (b) $a_n = -3\left(\frac{1}{2}\right)^{n-1}$.

SOLUTION

a. The explicit rule represents an arithmetic sequence with first term
$a_1 = -6 + 8(1) = 2$ and common difference $d = 8$.

$a_n = a_{n-1} + d$	Recursive equation for arithmetic sequence
$a_n = a_{n-1} + 8$	Substitute 8 for d.

▶ A recursive rule for the sequence is $a_1 = 2, a_n = a_{n-1} + 8$.

b. The explicit rule represents a geometric sequence with first term $a_1 = -3\left(\frac{1}{2}\right)^0 = -3$
and common ratio $r = \frac{1}{2}$.

$a_n = r \cdot a_{n-1}$	Recursive equation for geometric sequence
$a_n = \frac{1}{2}a_{n-1}$	Substitute $\frac{1}{2}$ for r.

▶ A recursive rule for the sequence is $a_1 = -3, a_n = \frac{1}{2}a_{n-1}$.

EXAMPLE 5 **Translating from Recursive Rules to Explicit Rules**

Write an explicit rule for each sequence.

a. $a_1 = -5, a_n = a_{n-1} - 2$ **b.** $a_1 = 10, a_n = 2a_{n-1}$

SOLUTION

a. The recursive rule represents an arithmetic sequence with first term $a_1 = -5$ and
common difference $d = -2$.

$a_n = a_1 + (n - 1)d$	Explicit rule for arithmetic sequence
$a_n = -5 + (n - 1)(-2)$	Substitute -5 for a_1 and -2 for d.
$a_n = -3 - 2n$	Simplify.

▶ An explicit rule for the sequence is $a_n = -3 - 2n$.

b. The recursive rule represents a geometric sequence with first term $a_1 = 10$ and
common ratio $r = 2$.

$a_n = a_1 r^{n-1}$	Explicit rule for geometric sequence
$a_n = 10(2)^{n-1}$	Substitute 10 for a_1 and 2 for r.

▶ An explicit rule for the sequence is $a_n = 10(2)^{n-1}$.

Monitoring Progress Help in English and Spanish at *BigIdeasMath.com*

Write a recursive rule for the sequence.

9. $a_n = 17 - 4n$ **10.** $a_n = 16(3)^{n-1}$

Write an explicit rule for the sequence.

11. $a_1 = -12, a_n = a_{n-1} + 16$ **12.** $a_1 = 2, a_n = -6a_{n-1}$

Solving Real-Life Problems

EXAMPLE 6 Solving a Real-Life Problem

A lake initially contains 5200 fish. Each year, the population declines 30% due to fishing and other causes, so the lake is restocked with 400 fish.

a. Write a recursive rule for the number a_n of fish at the start of the nth year.

b. Find the number of fish at the start of the fifth year.

c. Describe what happens to the population of fish over time.

SOLUTION

a. The initial value is 5200. Because the population declines 30% each year, 70% of the fish remain in the lake from one year to the next. Also, 400 fish are added each year. Here is a verbal model for the recursive equation.

Fish at start of year n	$= 0.7 \cdot$	Fish at start of year $n - 1$	$+$	New fish added

$$a_n \qquad = 0.7 \cdot \qquad a_{n-1} \qquad + \qquad 400$$

▶ A recursive rule is $a_1 = 5200$, $a_n = (0.7)a_{n-1} + 400$.

b. To find the number of fish at the start of the fifth year, enter 5200 (the value of a_1) into a graphing calculator. Then enter the rule

$$.7 \times \text{Ans} + 400$$

to find a_2. Press the *enter* button three more times to find $a_5 \approx 2262$.

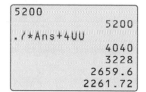

```
5200
            5200
.7*Ans+400
            4040
            3228
          2659.6
         2261.72
```

▶ There are about 2262 fish in the lake at the start of the fifth year.

c. To describe what happens to the population of fish over time, continue pressing *enter* on the calculator. The screen at the right shows the fish populations for years 44 to 50. Observe that the population of fish approaches 1333.

```
1333.334178
1333.333924
1333.333747
1333.333623
1333.333536
1333.333475
1333.333433
```

▶ Over time, the population of fish in the lake stabilizes at about 1333 fish.

Check

Set a graphing calculator to *sequence* and *dot* modes. Graph the sequence and use the *trace* feature. From the graph, it appears the sequence approaches 1333.

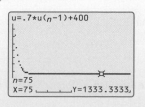

```
u=.7*u(n-1)+400




n=75
X=75          Y=1333.3333
```

Monitoring Progress Help in English and Spanish at *BigIdeasMath.com*

13. **WHAT IF?** In Example 6, suppose 75% of the fish remain each year. What happens to the population of fish over time?

EXAMPLE 7 **Modeling with Mathematics**

You borrow $150,000 at 6% annual interest compounded monthly for 30 years. The monthly payment is $899.33.

- Find the balance after the third payment.

- Due to rounding in the calculations, the last payment is often different from the original payment. Find the amount of the last payment.

REMEMBER

In Section 7.3, you used a formula involving a geometric series to calculate the monthly payment for a similar loan.

SOLUTION

1. **Understand the Problem** You are given the conditions of a loan. You are asked to find the balance after the third payment and the amount of the last payment.

2. **Make a Plan** Because the balance after each payment depends on the balance after the previous payment, write a recursive rule that gives the balance after each payment. Then use a spreadsheet to find the balance after each payment, rounded to the nearest cent.

3. **Solve the Problem** Because the monthly interest rate is $\dfrac{0.06}{12} = 0.005$, the balance increases by a factor of 1.005 each month, and then the payment of $899.33 is subtracted.

$$\boxed{\begin{array}{c}\text{Balance after}\\\text{payment}\end{array}} = 1.005 \cdot \boxed{\begin{array}{c}\text{Balance before}\\\text{payment}\end{array}} - \boxed{\text{Payment}}$$

$$a_n = 1.005 \cdot a_{n-1} - 899.33$$

Use a spreadsheet and the recursive rule to find the balance after the third payment and after the 359th payment.

	A	B
1	Payment number	Balance after payment
2	1	149850.67
3	2	149700.59
4	3	149549.76

B2 =Round(1.005*150000−899.33, 2)
B3 =Round(1.005*B2−899.33, 2)

358	357	2667.38
359	358	1781.39
360	359	890.97

B360 =Round(1.005*B359−899.33, 2)

▶ The balance after the third payment is $149,549.76. The balance after the 359th payment is $890.97, so the final payment is 1.005(890.97) = $895.42.

4. **Look Back** By continuing the spreadsheet for the 360th payment using the original monthly payment of $899.33, the balance is −3.91.

361	360	−3.91

B361 =Round(1.005*B360−899.33, 2)

This shows an overpayment of $3.91. So, it is reasonable that the last payment is $899.33 − $3.91 = $895.42.

Monitoring Progress  Help in English and Spanish at *BigIdeasMath.com*

14. **WHAT IF?** How do the answers in Example 7 change when the annual interest rate is 7.5% and the monthly payment is $1048.82?

Vocabulary and Core Concept Check

1. **COMPLETE THE SENTENCE** A recursive _____ tells how the nth term of a sequence is related to one or more preceding terms.

2. **WRITING** Explain the difference between an explicit rule and a recursive rule for a sequence.

Monitoring Progress and Modeling with Mathematics

In Exercises 3–10, write the first six terms of the sequence. *(See Example 1.)*

3. $a_1 = 1$
   $a_n = a_{n-1} + 3$

4. $a_1 = 1$
   $a_n = a_{n-1} - 5$

5. $f(0) = 4$
   $f(n) = 2f(n-1)$

6. $f(0) = 10$
   $f(n) = \frac{1}{2}f(n-1)$

7. $a_1 = 2$
   $a_n = (a_{n-1})^2 + 1$

8. $a_1 = 1$
   $a_n = (a_{n-1})^2 - 10$

9. $f(0) = 2, f(1) = 4$
   $f(n) = f(n-1) - f(n-2)$

10. $f(1) = 2, f(2) = 3$
    $f(n) = f(n-1) \cdot f(n-2)$

In Exercises 11–22, write a recursive rule for the sequence. *(See Examples 2 and 3.)*

11. $21, 14, 7, 0, -7, \ldots$

12. $54, 43, 32, 21, 10, \ldots$

13. $3, 12, 48, 192, 768, \ldots$

14. $4, -12, 36, -108, \ldots$

15. $44, 11, \frac{11}{4}, \frac{11}{16}, \frac{11}{64}, \ldots$

16. $1, 8, 15, 22, 29, \ldots$

17. $2, 5, 10, 50, 500, \ldots$

18. $3, 5, 15, 75, 1125, \ldots$

19. $1, 4, 5, 9, 14, \ldots$

20. $16, 9, 7, 2, 5, \ldots$

21. $6, 12, 36, 144, 720, \ldots$

22. $-3, -1, 2, 6, 11, \ldots$

In Exercises 23–26, write a recursive rule for the sequence shown in the graph.

23.
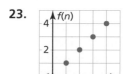

24.
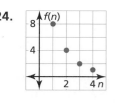

25.

26.

ERROR ANALYSIS In Exercises 27 and 28, describe and correct the error in writing a recursive rule for the sequence $5, 2, 3, -1, 4, \ldots$.

27.

   Beginning with the third term in the sequence, each term a_n equals $a_{n-2} - a_{n-1}$. So, a recursive rule is given by
   $$a_n = a_{n-2} - a_{n-1}.$$

28.

   Beginning with the second term in the sequence, each term a_n equals $a_{n-1} - 3$. So, a recursive rule is given by
   $$a_1 = 5, a_n = a_{n-1} - 3.$$

In Exercises 29–38, write a recursive rule for the sequence. *(See Example 4.)*

29. $a_n = 3 + 4n$

30. $a_n = -2 - 8n$

31. $a_n = 12 - 10n$

32. $a_n = 9 - 5n$

33. $a_n = 12(11)^{n-1}$

34. $a_n = -7(6)^{n-1}$

35. $a_n = 2.5 - 0.6n$

36. $a_n = -1.4 + 0.5n$

37. $a_n = -\frac{1}{2}\left(\frac{1}{4}\right)^{n-1}$

38. $a_n = \frac{1}{4}(5)^{n-1}$

39. REWRITING A FORMULA You have saved $82 to buy a bicycle. You save an additional $30 each month. The explicit rule $a_n = 30n + 82$ gives the amount saved after n months. Write a recursive rule for the amount you have saved n months from now.

40. REWRITING A FORMULA Your salary is given by the explicit rule $a_n = 35{,}000(1.04)^{n-1}$, where n is the number of years you have worked. Write a recursive rule for your salary.

In Exercises 41–48, write an explicit rule for the sequence. *(See Example 5.)*

41. $a_1 = 3, a_n = a_{n-1} - 6$ **42.** $a_1 = 16, a_n = a_{n-1} + 7$

43. $a_1 = -2, a_n = 3a_{n-1}$ **44.** $a_1 = 13, a_n = 4a_{n-1}$

45. $a_1 = -12, a_n = a_{n-1} + 9.1$

46. $a_1 = -4, a_n = 0.65a_{n-1}$

47. $a_1 = 5, a_n = a_{n-1} - \frac{1}{3}$ **48.** $a_1 = -5, a_n = \frac{1}{4}a_{n-1}$

49. REWRITING A FORMULA A grocery store arranges cans in a pyramid-shaped display with 20 cans in the bottom row and two fewer cans in each subsequent row going up. The number of cans in each row is represented by the recursive rule $a_1 = 20$, $a_n = a_{n-1} - 2$. Write an explicit rule for the number of cans in row n.

50. REWRITING A FORMULA The value of a car is given by the recursive rule $a_1 = 25{,}600, a_n = 0.86a_{n-1}$, where n is the number of years since the car was new. Write an explicit rule for the value of the car after n years.

51. USING STRUCTURE What is the 1000th term of the sequence whose first term is $a_1 = 4$ and whose nth term is $a_n = a_{n-1} + 6$? Justify your answer.

   Ⓐ 4006   Ⓑ 5998

   Ⓒ 1010   Ⓓ 10,000

52. USING STRUCTURE What is the 873rd term of the sequence whose first term is $a_1 = 0.01$ and whose nth term is $a_n = 1.01a_{n-1}$? Justify your answer.

   Ⓐ 58.65   Ⓑ 8.73

   Ⓒ 1.08   Ⓓ 586,459.38

53. PROBLEM SOLVING An online music service initially has 50,000 members. Each year, the company loses 20% of its current members and gains 5000 new members. *(See Example 6.)*

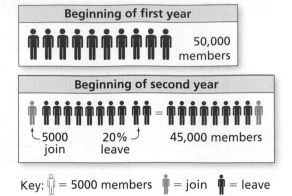

Key:

a. Write a recursive rule for the number a_n of members at the start of the nth year.

b. Find the number of members at the start of the fifth year.

c. Describe what happens to the number of members over time.

54. PROBLEM SOLVING You add chlorine to a swimming pool. You add 34 ounces of chlorine the first week and 16 ounces every week thereafter. Each week, 40% of the chlorine in the pool evaporates.

34 oz of chlorine are added   16 oz of chlorine are added

40% of chlorine has evaporated

First week   **Each successive week**

a. Write a recursive rule for the amount of chlorine in the pool at the start of the nth week.

b. Find the amount of chlorine in the pool at the start of the third week.

c. Describe what happens to the amount of chlorine in the pool over time.

55. OPEN-ENDED Give an example of a real-life situation which you can represent with a recursive rule that does not approach a limit. Write a recursive rule that represents the situation.

56. OPEN-ENDED Give an example of a sequence in which each term after the third term is a function of the three terms preceding it. Write a recursive rule for the sequence and find its first eight terms.

57. MODELING WITH MATHEMATICS You borrow $2000 at 9% annual interest compounded monthly for 2 years. The monthly payment is $91.37. *(See Example 7.)*

   a. Find the balance after the fifth payment.

   b. Find the amount of the last payment.

58. MODELING WITH MATHEMATICS You borrow $10,000 to build an extra bedroom onto your house. The loan is secured for 7 years at an annual interest rate of 11.5%. The monthly payment is $173.86.

   a. Find the balance after the fourth payment.

   b. Find the amount of the last payment.

59. COMPARING METHODS In 1202, the mathematician Leonardo Fibonacci wrote *Liber Abaci,* in which he proposed the following rabbit problem:

   Begin with a pair of newborn rabbits. When a pair of rabbits is two months old, the rabbits begin producing a new pair of rabbits each month. Assume none of the rabbits die.

Month	1	2	3	4	5	6
Pairs at start of month	1	1	2	3	5	8

   This problem produces a sequence called the Fibonacci sequence, which has both a recursive formula and an explicit formula as follows.

   Recursive: $a_1 = 1, a_2 = 1, a_n = a_{n-2} + a_{n-1}$

   Explicit: $f_n = \dfrac{1}{\sqrt{5}}\left(\dfrac{1+\sqrt{5}}{2}\right)^n - \dfrac{1}{\sqrt{5}}\left(\dfrac{1-\sqrt{5}}{2}\right)^n, n \geq 1$

   Use each formula to determine how many rabbits there will be after one year. Justify your answers.

60. USING TOOLS A town library initially has 54,000 books in its collection. Each year, 2% of the books are lost or discarded. The library can afford to purchase 1150 new books each year.

   a. Write a recursive rule for the number a_n of books in the library at the beginning of the nth year.

   b. Use the *sequence* mode and the *dot* mode of a graphing calculator to graph the sequence. What happens to the number of books in the library over time? Explain.

61. DRAWING CONCLUSIONS A tree farm initially has 9000 trees. Each year, 10% of the trees are harvested and 800 seedlings are planted.

   a. Write a recursive rule for the number of trees on the tree farm at the beginning of the nth year.

   b. What happens to the number of trees after an extended period of time?

62. DRAWING CONCLUSIONS You sprain your ankle and your doctor prescribes 325 milligrams of an anti-inflammatory drug every 8 hours for 10 days. Sixty percent of the drug is removed from the bloodstream every 8 hours.

   a. Write a recursive rule for the amount of the drug in the bloodstream after n doses.

   b. The value that a drug level approaches after an extended period of time is called the *maintenance level.* What is the maintenance level of this drug given the prescribed dosage?

   c. How does doubling the dosage affect the maintenance level of the drug? Justify your answer.

63. FINDING A PATTERN A fractal tree starts with a single branch (the trunk). At each stage, each new branch from the previous stage grows two more branches, as shown.

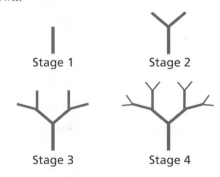

   a. List the number of new branches in each of the first seven stages. What type of sequence do these numbers form?

   b. Write an explicit rule and a recursive rule for the sequence in part (a).

64. THOUGHT PROVOKING Let $a_1 = 34$. Then write the terms of the sequence until you discover a pattern.

$$a_{n+1} = \begin{cases} \frac{1}{2}a_n, & \text{if } a_n \text{ is even} \\ 3a_n + 1, & \text{if } a_n \text{ is odd} \end{cases}$$

Do the same for $a_1 = 25$. What can you conclude?

65. MODELING WITH MATHEMATICS You make a $500 down payment on a $3500 diamond ring. You borrow the remaining balance at 10% annual interest compounded monthly. The monthly payment is $213.59. How long does it take to pay back the loan? What is the amount of the last payment? Justify your answers.

66. HOW DO YOU SEE IT? The graph shows the first six terms of the sequence $a_1 = p$, $a_n = ra_{n-1}$.

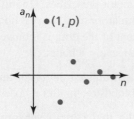

a. Describe what happens to the values in the sequence as n increases.

b. Describe the set of possible values for r. Explain your reasoning.

67. REASONING The rule for a recursive sequence is as follows.

$$f(1) = 3, f(2) = 10$$
$$f(n) = 4 + 2f(n-1) - f(n-2)$$

a. Write the first five terms of the sequence.

b. Use finite differences to find a pattern. What type of relationship do the terms of the sequence show?

c. Write an explicit rule for the sequence.

68. MAKING AN ARGUMENT Your friend says it is impossible to write a recursive rule for a sequence that is neither arithmetic nor geometric. Is your friend correct? Justify your answer.

69. CRITICAL THINKING The first four triangular numbers T_n and the first four square numbers S_n are represented by the points in each diagram.

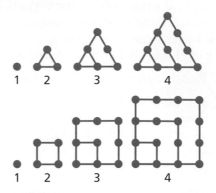

a. Write an explicit rule for each sequence.

b. Write a recursive rule for each sequence.

c. Write a rule for the square numbers in terms of the triangular numbers. Draw diagrams to explain why this rule is true.

70. CRITICAL THINKING You are saving money for retirement. You plan to withdraw $30,000 at the beginning of each year for 20 years after you retire. Based on the type of investment you are making, you can expect to earn an annual return of 8% on your savings after you retire.

a. Let a_n be your balance n years after retiring. Write a recursive equation that shows how a_n is related to a_{n-1}.

b. Solve the equation from part (a) for a_{n-1}. Find a_0, the minimum amount of money you should have in your account when you retire. (*Hint:* Let $a_{20} = 0$.)

Maintaining Mathematical Proficiency Reviewing what you learned in previous grades and lessons

Solve the equation. Check your solution. *(Section 4.4)*

71. $\sqrt{x} + 2 = 7$

72. $2\sqrt{x} - 5 = 15$

73. $\sqrt[3]{x} + 16 = 19$

74. $2\sqrt[3]{x} - 13 = -5$

The variables x and y vary inversely. Use the given values to write an equation relating x and y. Then find y when $x = 4$. *(Section 6.1)*

75. $x = 2, y = 9$

76. $x = -4, y = 3$

77. $x = 10, y = 32$

Core Vocabulary

partial sum, *p. 384*
explicit rule, *p. 390*
recursive rule, *p. 390*

Core Concepts

Section 7.4

Partial Sums of Infinite Geometric Series, *p. 384*
The Sum of an Infinite Geometric Series, *p. 385*

Section 7.5

Evaluating Recursive Rules, *p. 390*
Recursive Equations for Arithmetic and Geometric Sequences, *p. 390*
Translating Between Recursive and Explicit Rules, *p. 392*

Mathematical Practices

1. Describe how labeling the axes in Exercises 3–6 on page 387 clarifies the relationship between the quantities in the problems.

2. What logical progression of arguments can you use to determine whether the statement in Exercise 30 on page 388 is true?

3. Describe how the structure of the equation presented in Exercise 40 on page 396 allows you to determine the starting salary and the raise you receive each year.

4. Does the recursive rule in Exercise 61 on page 397 make sense when $n = 5$? Explain your reasoning.

Performance Task:

Wildlife Conservation

Recursive sequences can be used to model population growth. Their patterns give critical information to wildlife conservationists who work to increase numbers of native species in their natural habitats. How can these sequences prevent species from becoming endangered?

To explore the answer to this question and more, check out the Performance Task and Real-Life STEM video at *BigIdeasMath.com*.

7.1 Defining and Using Sequences and Series (pp. 357–364)

Find the sum $\displaystyle\sum_{i=1}^{4}(i^2 - 3)$.

$$\sum_{i=1}^{4}(i^2 - 3) = (1^2 - 3) + (2^2 - 3) + (3^2 - 3) + (4^2 - 3)$$

$$= -2 + 1 + 6 + 13$$

$$= 18$$

1. Describe the pattern shown in the figure. Then write a rule for the nth layer of the figure, where $n = 1$ represents the top layer.

Write the series using summation notation.

2. $7 + 10 + 13 + \cdots + 40$

3. $0 + 2 + 6 + 12 + \cdots$

Find the sum.

4. $\displaystyle\sum_{i=2}^{7}(9 - i^3)$

5. $\displaystyle\sum_{i=1}^{46}i$

6. $\displaystyle\sum_{i=1}^{12}i^2$

7. $\displaystyle\sum_{i=1}^{5}\frac{3 + i}{2}$

7.2 Analyzing Arithmetic Sequences and Series (pp. 365–372)

Write a rule for the nth term of the sequence 9, 14, 19, 24, ... Then find a_{14}.

The sequence is arithmetic with first term $a_1 = 9$ and common difference $d = 14 - 9 = 5$. So, a rule for the nth term is

$a_n = a_1 + (n - 1)d$ Write general rule.

$= 9 + (n - 1)5$ Substitute 9 for a_1 and 5 for d.

$= 5n + 4.$ Simplify.

▶ A rule is $a_n = 5n + 4$, and the 14th term is $a_{14} = 5(14) + 4 = 74$.

8. Tell whether the sequence 12, 4, −4, −12, −20, . . . is arithmetic. Explain your reasoning.

Write a rule for the nth term of the arithmetic sequence. Then graph the first six terms of the sequence.

9. 2, 8, 14, 20, . . .

10. $a_{14} = 42, d = 3$

11. $a_6 = -12, a_{12} = -36$

12. Find the sum $\displaystyle\sum_{i=1}^{36}(2 + 3i)$.

13. You take a job with a starting salary of $37,000. Your employer offers you an annual raise of $1500 for the next 6 years. Write a rule for your salary in the nth year. What are your total earnings in 6 years?

Find the sum $\sum_{i=1}^{8} 6(3)^{i-1}$.

Step 1 Find the first term and the common ratio.

$$a_1 = 6(3)^{1-1} = 6 \qquad \text{Identify first term.}$$

$$r = 3 \qquad \text{Identify common ratio.}$$

Step 2 Find the sum.

$$S_8 = a_1\left(\frac{1 - r^8}{1 - r}\right) \qquad \text{Write rule for } S_8.$$

$$= 6\left(\frac{1 - 3^8}{1 - 3}\right) \qquad \text{Substitute 6 for } a_1 \text{ and 3 for } r.$$

$$= 19{,}680 \qquad \text{Simplify.}$$

14. Tell whether the sequence 7, 14, 28, 56, 112, . . . is geometric. Explain your reasoning.

Write a rule for the nth term of the geometric sequence. Then graph the first six terms of the sequence.

15. $25, 10, 4, \dfrac{8}{5}, \ldots$

16. $a_5 = 162, r = -3$

17. $a_3 = 16, a_5 = 256$

18. Find the sum $\sum_{i=1}^{9} 5(-2)^{i-1}$.

Find the sum of the series $\sum_{i=1}^{\infty} \left(\dfrac{4}{5}\right)^{i-1}$, if it exists.

For this series, $a_1 = 1$ and $r = \dfrac{4}{5}$. Because $\left|\dfrac{4}{5}\right| < 1$, the sum of the series exists.

The sum of the series is

$$S = \frac{a_1}{1 - r} \qquad \text{Formula for the sum of an infinite geometric series}$$

$$= \frac{1}{1 - \dfrac{4}{5}} \qquad \text{Substitute 1 for } a_1 \text{ and } \dfrac{4}{5} \text{ for } r.$$

$$= 5. \qquad \text{Simplify.}$$

19. Consider the infinite geometric series $1, -\dfrac{1}{4}, \dfrac{1}{16}, -\dfrac{1}{64}, \dfrac{1}{256}, \ldots$ Find and graph the partial sums S_n for $n = 1, 2, 3, 4,$ and 5. Then describe what happens to S_n as n increases.

20. Find the sum of the infinite geometric series $-2 + \dfrac{1}{2} - \dfrac{1}{8} + \dfrac{1}{32} + \cdots$, if it exists.

21. Write the repeating decimal $0.1212\ldots$ as a fraction in simplest form.

a. Write the first six terms of the sequence $a_0 = 46$, $a_n = a_{n-1} - 8$.

$a_0 = 46$	1st term
$a_1 = a_0 - 8 = 46 - 8 = 38$	2nd term
$a_2 = a_1 - 8 = 38 - 8 = 30$	3rd term
$a_3 = a_2 - 8 = 30 - 8 = 22$	4th term
$a_4 = a_3 - 8 = 22 - 8 = 14$	5th term
$a_5 = a_4 - 8 = 14 - 8 = 6$	6th term

b. Write a recursive rule for the sequence 6, 10, 14, 18, 22, ...

Use a table to organize the terms and find the pattern.

n	1	2	3	4	5
a_n	6	10	14	18	22

$$+4 \quad +4 \quad +4 \quad +4$$

The sequence is arithmetic with the first term $a_1 = 6$ and common difference $d = 4$.

$a_n = a_{n-1} + d$	Recursive equation for arithmetic sequence
$= a_{n-1} + 4$	Substitute 4 for d.

▶ A recursive rule for the sequence is $a_1 = 6$, $a_n = a_{n-1} + 4$.

Write the first six terms of the sequence.

22. $a_1 = 7$, $a_n = a_{n-1} + 11$ **23.** $a_1 = 6$, $a_n = 4a_{n-1}$ **24.** $f(0) = 4$, $f(n) = f(n-1) + 2n$

Write a recursive rule for the sequence.

25. $9, 6, 4, \dfrac{8}{3}, \dfrac{16}{9}, \ldots$ **26.** $2, 2, 4, 12, 48, \ldots$ **27.** $7, 3, 4, -1, 5, \ldots$

28. Write a recursive rule for $a_n = 105\left(\dfrac{3}{5}\right)^{n-1}$.

Write an explicit rule for the sequence.

29. $a_1 = -4$, $a_n = a_{n-1} + 26$ **30.** $a_1 = 8$, $a_n = -5a_{n-1}$ **31.** $a_1 = 26$, $a_n = \dfrac{2}{5}a_{n-1}$

32. A town's population increases at a rate of about 4% per year. In 2010, the town had a population of 11,120. Write a recursive rule for the population P_n of the town in year n. Let $n = 1$ represent 2010.

33. The numbers 1, 6, 15, 28, . . . are called hexagonal numbers because they represent the number of dots used to make hexagons, as shown. Write a recursive rule for the nth hexagonal number.

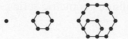

Find the sum.

1. $\displaystyle\sum_{i=1}^{24}(6i-13)$

2. $\displaystyle\sum_{n=1}^{16}n^2$

3. $\displaystyle\sum_{k=1}^{\infty}2(0.8)^{k-1}$

4. $\displaystyle\sum_{i=1}^{6}4(-3)^{i-1}$

Determine whether the graph represents an *arithmetic sequence*, *geometric sequence*, or *neither*. Explain your reasoning. Then write a rule for the *n*th term.

5.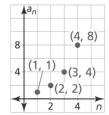

6.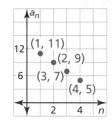

7.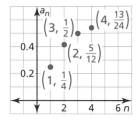

Write a recursive rule for the sequence. Then find a_9.

8. $a_1=32,\ r=\frac{1}{2}$

9. $a_n=2+7n$

10. $2, 0, -3, -7, -12, \ldots$

11. Write a recursive rule for the sequence $5, -20, 80, -320, 1280, \ldots$. Then write an explicit rule for the sequence using your recursive rule.

12. The numbers a, b, and c are the first three terms of an arithmetic sequence. Is b half of the sum of a and c? Explain your reasoning.

13. Use the pattern of checkerboard quilts shown.

$n=1,\ a_n=1$ $n=2,\ a_n=2$ $n=3,\ a_n=5$ $n=4,\ a_n=8$

  a. What does n represent for each quilt? What does a_n represent?

  b. Make a table that shows n and a_n for $n=1, 2, 3, 4, 5, 6, 7,$ and 8.

  c. Use the rule $a_n=\dfrac{n^2}{2}+\dfrac{1}{4}[1-(-1)^n]$ to find a_n for $n=1, 2, 3, 4, 5, 6, 7,$ and 8. Compare these values to those in your table in part (b). What can you conclude? Explain.

14. During a baseball season, a company pledges to donate $5000 to a charity plus $100 for each home run hit by the local team. Does this situation represent a sequence or a series? Explain your reasoning.

15. The length ℓ_1 of the first loop of a spring is 16 inches. The length ℓ_2 of the second loop is 0.9 times the length of the first loop. The length ℓ_3 of the third loop is 0.9 times the length of the second loop, and so on. Suppose the spring has infinitely many loops, would its length be finite or infinite? Explain. Find the length of the spring, if possible.

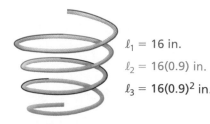

$\ell_1=16$ in.

$\ell_2=16(0.9)$ in.

$\ell_3=16(0.9)^2$ in.

1. The frequencies (in hertz) of the notes on a piano form a geometric sequence. The frequencies of G (labeled 8) and A (labeled 10) are shown in the diagram. What is the approximate frequency of E flat (labeled 4)?

   (A) 247 Hz

   (B) 311 Hz

   (C) 330 Hz

   (D) 554 Hz

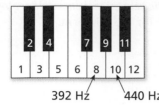

   392 Hz   440 Hz

2. You take out a loan for $16,000 with an interest rate of 0.75% per month. At the end of each month, you make a payment of $300.

   a. Write a recursive rule for the balance a_n of the loan at the beginning of the nth month.

   b. How much do you owe at the beginning of the 18th month?

   c. How long will it take to pay off the loan?

   d. If you pay $350 instead of $300 each month, how long will it take to pay off the loan? How much money will you save? Explain.

3. The table shows that the force F (in pounds) needed to loosen a certain bolt with a wrench depends on the length ℓ (in inches) of the wrench's handle. Write an equation that relates ℓ and F. Describe the relationship.

Length, ℓ	4	6	10	12
Force, F	375	250	150	125

4. Order the functions from the least average rate of change to the greatest average rate of change on the interval $1 \le x \le 4$. Justify your answers.

   A. $f(x) = 4\sqrt{x} + 2$

   B. x and y vary inversely, and $y = 2$ when $x = 5$.

   C.
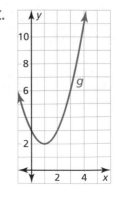

   D.

x	y
1	−4
2	−1
3	2
4	5

5. A running track is shaped like a rectangle with two semicircular ends, as shown. The track has 8 lanes that are each 1.22 meters wide. The lanes are numbered from 1 to 8 starting from the inside lane. The distance from the center of a semicircle to the inside of a lane is called the curve radius of that lane. The curve radius of lane 1 is 36.5 meters, as shown in the figure.

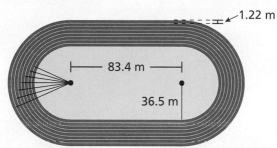

Not drawn to scale

   a. Is the sequence formed by the curve radii arithmetic, geometric, or neither? Explain.

   b. Write a rule for the sequence formed by the curve radii.

   c. World records must be set on tracks that have a curve radius of at most 50 meters in the outside lane. Does the track shown meet the requirement? Explain.

6. Order the sums from least to greatest. Justify your answer.

$$\sum_{k=2}^{10}(k^2-2)$$

$$\sum_{i=1}^{10}(5i+8)$$

$$\sum_{k=1}^{\infty}\frac{21}{2}\left(\frac{7}{8}\right)^{k-1}$$

$$\sum_{i=1}^{12}-8\left(\frac{1}{2}\right)^{i-1}$$

$$\sum_{n=1}^{\infty}60(0.25)^{n-1}$$

$$\sum_{t=1}^{5}2(4)^{t-1}$$

7. The diagram shows the bounce heights of a basketball and a baseball dropped from a height of 10 feet. On each bounce, the basketball bounces to 36% of its previous height, and the baseball bounces to 30% of its previous height. About how much greater is the total distance traveled by the basketball than the total distance traveled by the baseball?

    (A) 1.34 feet   (B) 2.00 feet

    (C) 2.68 feet   (D) 5.63 feet

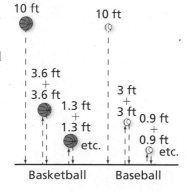

8. A semicircle with a diameter of 1.5 units is rotated around its diameter. What is the volume of the solid of revolution that is formed?

    (A) about 1.77 cubic units   (B) about 7.07 cubic units

    (C) about 14.14 cubic units   (D) about 28.27 cubic units

8 Trigonometric Ratios and Functions

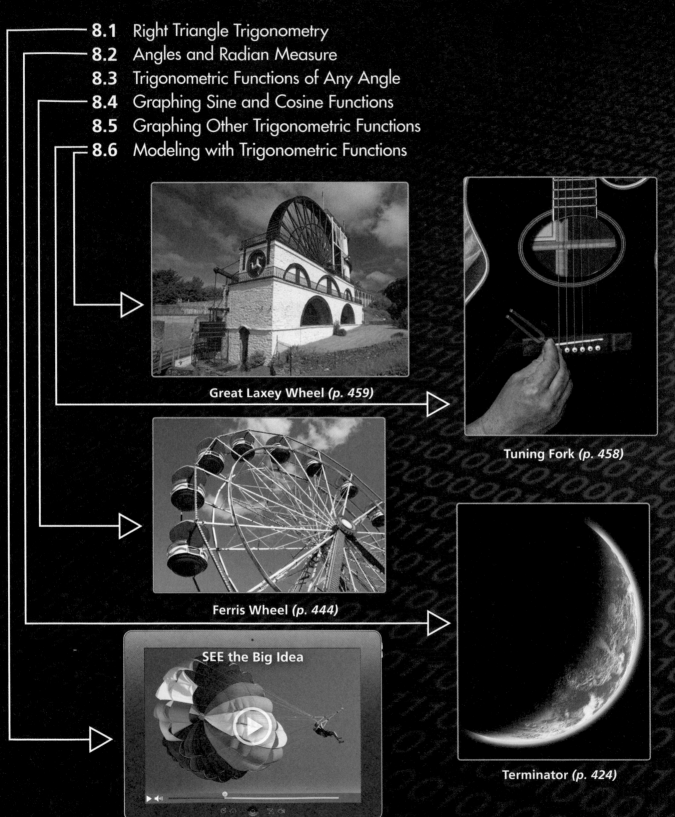

Great Laxey Wheel *(p. 459)*

Tuning Fork *(p. 458)*

Ferris Wheel *(p. 444)*

SEE the Big Idea

Terminator *(p. 424)*

Parasailing *(p. 413)*

Maintaining Mathematical Proficiency

Using *x*-Intercepts to Graph Functions

Example 1 Graph the function $f(x) = \frac{1}{2}(x - 1)(x - 5)^2$.

Step 1 Plot the *x*-intercepts. Because 1 and 5 are zeros of *f*, plot (1, 0) and (5, 0).

Step 2 Plot points between and beyond the *x*-intercepts.

x	0	2	3	4	6
y	$-\frac{25}{2}$	$\frac{9}{2}$	4	$\frac{3}{2}$	$\frac{5}{2}$

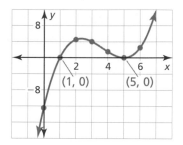

Step 3 Determine end behavior. Because $f(x)$ has three factors of the form $x - k$ and a constant factor of $\frac{1}{2}$, *f* is a cubic function with a positive leading coefficient. So, $f(x) \to -\infty$ as $x \to -\infty$ and $f(x) \to +\infty$ as $x \to +\infty$.

Step 4 Draw the graph so that it passes through the plotted points and has the appropriate end behavior.

Graph the function.

1. $f(x) = (x + 3)(x + 1)(x - 2)$ **2.** $f(x) = -\frac{1}{4}x(x + 4)(x - 3)$ **3.** $f(x) = (x + 2)^2(x - 1)^2$

Pythagorean Theorem

Example 2 Find the missing side length of the triangle.

10 cm
26 cm *b*

$a^2 + b^2 = c^2$	Write the Pythagorean Theorem.
$10^2 + b^2 = 26^2$	Substitute 10 for *a* and 26 for *c*.
$100 + b^2 = 676$	Evaluate powers.
$b^2 = 576$	Subtract 100 from each side.
$b = 24$	Take positive square root of each side.

▶ So, the length is 24 centimeters.

Find the missing side length of the triangle.

4.
12 m *c*
5 m

5.
a 35 km
21 km

6.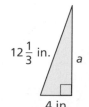
$12\frac{1}{3}$ in. *a*
4 in.

7.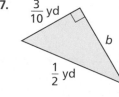
$\frac{3}{10}$ yd *b*
$\frac{1}{2}$ yd

8. **ABSTRACT REASONING** The line segments connecting the points (x_1, y_1), (x_2, y_1), and (x_2, y_2) form a triangle. Is the triangle a right triangle? Justify your answer.

Mathematical Practices

Mathematically proficient students reason quantitatively by creating valid representations of problems.

Reasoning Abstractly and Quantitatively

🔄 Core Concept

The Unit Circle

The **unit circle** is a circle in the coordinate plane. Its center is at the origin, and it has a radius of 1 unit. The equation of the unit circle is

$$x^2 + y^2 = 1.$$ Equation of unit circle

As the point (x, y) starts at $(1, 0)$ and moves counterclockwise around the unit circle, the angle θ (the Greek letter *theta*) moves from $0°$ through $360°$.

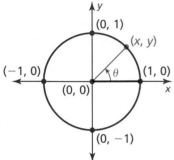

EXAMPLE 1   Finding Coordinates of a Point on the Unit Circle

Find the exact coordinates of the point (x, y) on the unit circle.

SOLUTION

Because $\theta = 45°$, (x, y) lies on the line $y = x$.

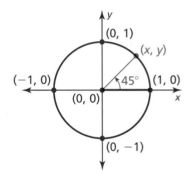

$x^2 + y^2 = 1$	Write equation of unit circle.
$x^2 + x^2 = 1$	Substitute x for y.
$2x^2 = 1$	Add like terms.
$x^2 = \dfrac{1}{2}$	Divide each side by 2.
$x = \dfrac{1}{\sqrt{2}}$	Take positive square root of each side.

▶ The coordinates of (x, y) are $\left(\dfrac{1}{\sqrt{2}}, \dfrac{1}{\sqrt{2}}\right)$, or $\left(\dfrac{\sqrt{2}}{2}, \dfrac{\sqrt{2}}{2}\right)$.

Monitoring Progress

Find the exact coordinates of the point (x, y) on the unit circle.

1.
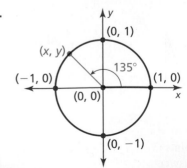

2.
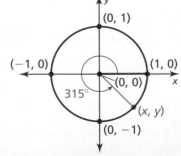

3.
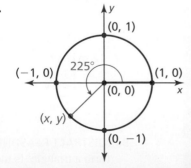

8.1 Right Triangle Trigonometry

Essential Question   How can you find a trigonometric function of an acute angle θ?

Consider one of the acute angles θ of a right triangle.
Ratios of a right triangle's side lengths are used to
define the six *trigonometric functions*, as shown.

Sine $\sin \theta = \dfrac{\text{opp.}}{\text{hyp.}}$ **Cosine** $\cos \theta = \dfrac{\text{adj.}}{\text{hyp.}}$

Tangent $\tan \theta = \dfrac{\text{opp.}}{\text{adj.}}$ **Cotangent** $\cot \theta = \dfrac{\text{adj.}}{\text{opp.}}$

Secant $\sec \theta = \dfrac{\text{hyp.}}{\text{adj.}}$ **Cosecant** $\csc \theta = \dfrac{\text{hyp.}}{\text{opp.}}$

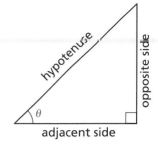

EXPLORATION 1   Trigonometric Functions of Special Angles

Work with a partner. Find the exact values of the sine, cosine, and tangent functions
for the angles 30°, 45°, and 60° in the right triangles shown.

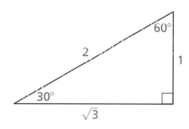

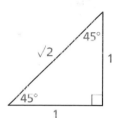

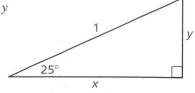

**CONSTRUCTING
VIABLE ARGUMENTS**

To be proficient in
math, you need to
understand and use stated
assumptions, definitions,
and previously established
results in constructing
arguments.

EXPLORATION 2   Exploring Trigonometric Identities

Work with a partner.

Use the definitions of the trigonometric functions to explain why each *trigonometric
identity* is true.

a. $\sin \theta = \cos(90° - \theta)$

b. $\cos \theta = \sin(90° - \theta)$

c. $\sin \theta = \dfrac{1}{\csc \theta}$

d. $\tan \theta = \dfrac{1}{\cot \theta}$

Use the definitions of the trigonometric functions to complete each trigonometric
identity.

e. $(\sin \theta)^2 + (\cos \theta)^2 = \underline{\quad\quad}$

f. $(\sec \theta)^2 - (\tan \theta)^2 = \underline{\quad\quad}$

Communicate Your Answer

3. How can you find a trigonometric function of an acute angle θ?

4. Use a calculator to find the lengths x and y
of the legs of the right triangle shown.

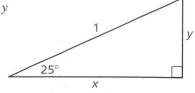

What You Will Learn

▶ Evaluate trigonometric functions of acute angles.
▶ Find unknown side lengths and angle measures of right triangles.
▶ Use trigonometric functions to solve real-life problems.

The Six Trigonometric Functions

Consider a right triangle that has an acute angle θ (the Greek letter *theta*). The three sides of the triangle are the *hypotenuse*, the side *opposite* θ, and the side *adjacent* to θ.

Ratios of a right triangle's side lengths are used to define the six trigonometric functions: **sine, cosine, tangent, cosecant, secant,** and **cotangent**. These six functions are abbreviated sin, cos, tan, csc, sec, and cot, respectively.

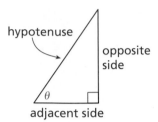

Core Concept

Right Triangle Definitions of Trigonometric Functions

Let θ be an acute angle of a right triangle. The six trigonometric functions of θ are defined as shown.

$$\sin \theta = \frac{\text{opposite}}{\text{hypotenuse}} \qquad \cos \theta = \frac{\text{adjacent}}{\text{hypotenuse}} \qquad \tan \theta = \frac{\text{opposite}}{\text{adjacent}}$$

$$\csc \theta = \frac{\text{hypotenuse}}{\text{opposite}} \qquad \sec \theta = \frac{\text{hypotenuse}}{\text{adjacent}} \qquad \cot \theta = \frac{\text{adjacent}}{\text{opposite}}$$

The abbreviations *opp.*, *adj.*, and *hyp.* are often used to represent the side lengths of the right triangle. Note that the ratios in the second row are reciprocals of the ratios in the first row.

$$\csc \theta = \frac{1}{\sin \theta} \qquad \sec \theta = \frac{1}{\cos \theta} \qquad \cot \theta = \frac{1}{\tan \theta}$$

EXAMPLE 1 Evaluating Trigonometric Functions

Evaluate the six trigonometric functions of the angle θ.

SOLUTION

From the Pythagorean Theorem, the length of the hypotenuse is

$$\text{hyp.} = \sqrt{5^2 + 12^2}$$

$$= \sqrt{169}$$

$$= 13.$$

Using adj. = 5, opp. = 12, and hyp. = 13, the values of the six trigonometric functions of θ are:

$$\sin \theta = \frac{\text{opp.}}{\text{hyp.}} \, \frac{12}{13} \qquad \cos \theta = \frac{\text{adj.}}{\text{hyp.}} \, \frac{5}{13} \qquad \tan \theta = \frac{\text{opp.}}{\text{adj.}} = \frac{12}{5}$$

$$\csc \theta = \frac{\text{hyp.}}{\text{opp.}} = \frac{13}{12} \qquad \sec \theta = \frac{\text{hyp.}}{\text{adj.}} = \frac{13}{5} \qquad \cot \theta = \frac{\text{adj.}}{\text{opp.}} = \frac{5}{12}$$

EXAMPLE 2 **Evaluating Trigonometric Functions**

In a right triangle, θ is an acute angle and $\sin \theta = \frac{4}{7}$. Evaluate the other five trigonometric functions of θ.

SOLUTION

Step 1 Draw a right triangle with acute angle θ such that the leg opposite θ has length 4 and the hypotenuse has length 7.

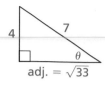

Step 2 Find the length of the adjacent side. By the Pythagorean Theorem, the length of the other leg is

$$\text{adj.} = \sqrt{7^2 - 4^2} = \sqrt{33}.$$

Step 3 Find the values of the remaining five trigonometric functions.

Because $\sin \theta = \frac{4}{7}$, $\csc \theta = \dfrac{\text{hyp.}}{\text{opp.}} = \frac{7}{4}$. The other values are:

$$\cos \theta = \frac{\text{adj.}}{\text{hyp.}} = \frac{\sqrt{33}}{7} \qquad\qquad \tan \theta = \frac{\text{opp.}}{\text{adj.}} = \frac{4}{\sqrt{33}} = \frac{4\sqrt{33}}{33}$$

$$\sec \theta = \frac{\text{hyp.}}{\text{adj.}} = \frac{7}{\sqrt{33}} = \frac{7\sqrt{33}}{33} \qquad \cot \theta = \frac{\text{adj.}}{\text{opp.}} = \frac{\sqrt{33}}{4}$$

Monitoring Progress Help in English and Spanish at *BigIdeasMath.com*

Evaluate the six trigonometric functions of the angle θ.

1.

2.

3.

4. In a right triangle, θ is an acute angle and $\cos \theta = \frac{7}{10}$. Evaluate the other five trigonometric functions of θ.

The angles 30°, 45°, and 60° occur frequently in trigonometry. You can use the trigonometric values for these angles to find unknown side lengths in special right triangles.

Core Concept

Trigonometric Values for Special Angles

The table gives the values of the six trigonometric functions for the angles 30°, 45°, and 60°. You can obtain these values from the triangles shown.

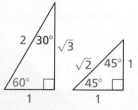

θ	$\sin \theta$	$\cos \theta$	$\tan \theta$	$\csc \theta$	$\sec \theta$	$\cot \theta$
30°	$\dfrac{1}{2}$	$\dfrac{\sqrt{3}}{2}$	$\dfrac{\sqrt{3}}{3}$	2	$\dfrac{2\sqrt{3}}{3}$	$\sqrt{3}$
45°	$\dfrac{\sqrt{2}}{2}$	$\dfrac{\sqrt{2}}{2}$	1	$\sqrt{2}$	$\sqrt{2}$	1
60°	$\dfrac{\sqrt{3}}{2}$	$\dfrac{1}{2}$	$\sqrt{3}$	$\dfrac{2\sqrt{3}}{3}$	2	$\dfrac{\sqrt{3}}{3}$

Finding Side Lengths and Angle Measures

EXAMPLE 3 Finding an Unknown Side Length

Find the value of *x* for the right triangle.

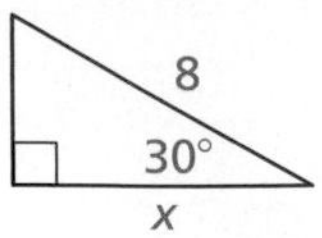

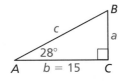

SOLUTION

Write an equation using a trigonometric function that involves the ratio of *x* and 8. Solve the equation for *x*.

$$\cos 30° = \frac{\text{adj.}}{\text{hyp.}}$$ Write trigonometric equation.

$$\frac{\sqrt{3}}{2} = \frac{x}{8}$$ Substitute.

$$4\sqrt{3} = x$$ Multiply each side by 8.

▶ The length of the side is $x = 4\sqrt{3} \approx 6.93$.

Finding all unknown side lengths and angle measures of a triangle is called *solving the triangle*. Solving right triangles that have acute angles other than 30°, 45°, and 60° may require the use of a calculator. Be sure the calculator is set in *degree* mode.

EXAMPLE 4 Using a Calculator to Solve a Right Triangle

Solve △*ABC*.

SOLUTION

Because the triangle is a right triangle, *A* and *B* are complementary angles. So, $B = 90° − 28° = 62°$.

Next, write two equations using trigonometric functions, one that involves the ratio of *a* and 15, and one that involves the ratio of *c* and 15. Solve the first equation for *a* and the second equation for *c*.

$$\tan 28° = \frac{\text{opp.}}{\text{adj.}}$$ Write trigonometric equation. $$\sec 28° = \frac{\text{hyp.}}{\text{adj.}}$$

$$\tan 28° = \frac{a}{15}$$ Substitute. $$\sec 28° = \frac{c}{15}$$

$$15(\tan 28°) = a$$ Solve for the variable. $$15\left(\frac{1}{\cos 28°}\right) = c$$

$$7.98 \approx a$$ Use a calculator. $$16.99 \approx c$$

▶ So, $B = 62°$, $a \approx 7.98$, and $c \approx 16.99$.

Monitoring Progress Help in English and Spanish at *BigIdeasMath.com*

READING

Throughout this book, a capital letter is used to denote both an angle of a triangle and its measure. The same letter in lowercase is used to denote the length of the side opposite that angle.

5. Find the value of *x* for the right triangle shown.

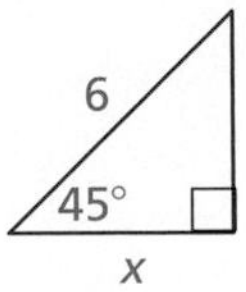

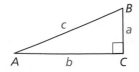

Solve △*ABC* using the diagram at the left and the given measurements.

6. $B = 45°$, $c = 5$

7. $A = 32°$, $b = 10$

8. $A = 71°$, $c = 20$

9. $B = 60°$, $a = 7$

Solving Real-Life Problems

EXAMPLE 5 **Using Indirect Measurement**

FINDING AN ENTRY POINT

The tangent function is used to find the unknown distance because it involves the ratio of *x* and 2.

You are hiking near a canyon. While standing at *A*, you measure an angle of 90° between *B* and *C*, as shown. You then walk to *B* and measure an angle of 76° between *A* and *C*. The distance between *A* and *B* is about 2 miles. How wide is the canyon between *A* and *C*?

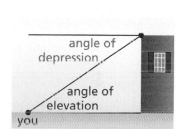

SOLUTION

$$\tan 76° = \frac{x}{2} \qquad \text{Write trigonometric equation.}$$

$$2(\tan 76°) = x \qquad \text{Multiply each side by 2.}$$

$$8.0 \approx x \qquad \text{Use a calculator.}$$

▶ The width is about 8.0 miles.

If you look at a point above you, such as the top of a building, the angle that your line of sight makes with a line parallel to the ground is called the *angle of elevation*. At the top of the building, the angle between a line parallel to the ground and your line of sight is called the *angle of depression*. These two angles have the same measure.

EXAMPLE 6 **Using an Angle of Elevation**

A parasailer is attached to a boat with a rope that is 72 feet long. The angle of elevation from the boat to the parasailer is 28°. Estimate the parasailer's height above the boat.

SOLUTION

Step 1 Draw a diagram that represents the situation.

Step 2 Write and solve an equation to find the height *h*.

$$\sin 28° = \frac{h}{72} \qquad \text{Write trigonometric equation.}$$

$$72(\sin 28°) = h \qquad \text{Multiply each side by 72.}$$

$$33.8 \approx h \qquad \text{Use a calculator.}$$

▶ The height of the parasailer above the boat is about 33.8 feet.

Monitoring Progress Help in English and Spanish at *BigIdeasMath.com*

10. In Example 5, find the distance between *B* and *C*.

11. **WHAT IF?** In Example 6, estimate the height of the parasailer above the boat when the angle of elevation is 38°.

Vocabulary and Core Concept Check

1. **COMPLETE THE SENTENCE** In a right triangle, the two trigonometric functions of θ that are defined using the lengths of the hypotenuse and the side adjacent to θ are _____ and _____.

2. **VOCABULARY** Compare an angle of elevation to an angle of depression.

3. **WRITING** Explain what it means to solve a right triangle.

4. **DIFFERENT WORDS, SAME QUESTION** Which is different? Find "both" answers.

| What is the cosecant of θ? |
| What is $\dfrac{1}{\sin \theta}$? |
| What is the ratio of the side opposite θ to the hypotenuse? |
| What is the ratio of the hypotenuse to the side opposite θ? |

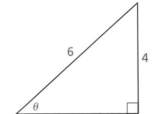

Monitoring Progress and Modeling with Mathematics

In Exercises 5–10, evaluate the six trigonometric functions of the angle θ. *(See Example 1.)*

5.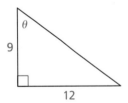

6.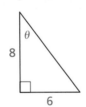

7.

8.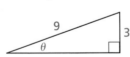

9.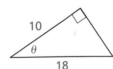

10.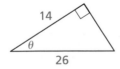

11. **REASONING** Let θ be an acute angle of a right triangle. Use the two trigonometric functions $\tan \theta = \dfrac{4}{9}$ and $\sec \theta = \dfrac{\sqrt{97}}{9}$ to sketch and label the right triangle. Then evaluate the other four trigonometric functions of θ.

12. **ANALYZING RELATIONSHIPS** Evaluate the six trigonometric functions of the angle $90° - \theta$ in Exercises 5–10. Describe the relationships you notice.

In Exercises 13–18, let θ be an acute angle of a right triangle. Evaluate the other five trigonometric functions of θ. *(See Example 2.)*

13. $\sin \theta = \dfrac{7}{11}$

14. $\cos \theta = \dfrac{5}{12}$

15. $\tan \theta = \dfrac{7}{6}$

16. $\csc \theta = \dfrac{15}{8}$

17. $\sec \theta = \dfrac{14}{9}$

18. $\cot \theta = \dfrac{16}{11}$

19. **ERROR ANALYSIS** Describe and correct the error in finding $\sin \theta$ of the triangle below.

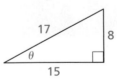

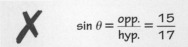

20. ERROR ANALYSIS Describe and correct the error in finding csc θ, given that θ is an acute angle of a right triangle and cos $\theta = \frac{7}{11}$.

 $\csc \theta = \frac{1}{\cos \theta} = \frac{11}{7}$

In Exercises 21–26, find the value of x for the right triangle. *(See Example 3.)*

21.

9
60°
x

22.

6
60°
x

23.

30°
12
x

24.
30°
13
x

25.

8
45° x

26.

7
45° x

USING TOOLS In Exercises 27–32, evaluate the trigonometric function using a calculator. Round your answer to four decimal places.

27. cos 14°

28. tan 31°

29. csc 59°

30. sin 23°

31. cot 6°

32. sec 11°

In Exercises 33–40, solve $\triangle ABC$ using the diagram and the given measurements. *(See Example 4.)*

A
b c
C a B

33. $B = 36°, a = 23$

34. $A = 27°, b = 9$

35. $A = 55°, a = 17$

36. $B = 16°, b = 14$

37. $A = 43°, b = 31$

38. $B = 31°, a = 23$

39. $B = 72°, c = 12.8$

40. $A = 64°, a = 7.4$

41. MODELING WITH MATHEMATICS To measure the width of a river, you plant a stake on one side of the river, directly across from a boulder. You then walk 100 meters to the right of the stake and measure a 79° angle between the stake and the boulder. What is the width w of the river? *(See Example 5.)*

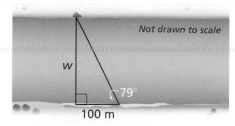
Not drawn to scale
w
79°
100 m

42. MODELING WITH MATHEMATICS Katoomba Scenic Railway in Australia is the steepest railway in the world. The railway makes an angle of about 52° with the ground. The railway extends horizontally about 458 feet. What is the height of the railway at its highest point?

43. MODELING WITH MATHEMATICS A person whose eye level is 1.5 meters above the ground is standing 75 meters from the base of the Jin Mao Building in Shanghai, China. The person estimates the angle of elevation to the top of the building is about 80°. What is the approximate height of the building? *(See Example 6.)*

44. MODELING WITH MATHEMATICS The Duquesne Incline in Pittsburgh, Pennsylvania, has an angle of elevation of 30°. The track has a length of about 800 feet. Find the height of the incline at its highest point.

45. MODELING WITH MATHEMATICS You are standing on the Grand View Terrace viewing platform at Mount Rushmore, 1000 feet from the base of the monument.

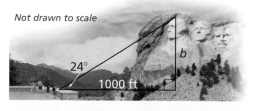
Not drawn to scale
24°
1000 ft
b

a. You look up at the top of Mount Rushmore at an angle of 24°. How high is the top of the monument from where you are standing? Assume your eye level is 5.5 feet above the platform.

b. The elevation of the Grand View Terrace is 5280 feet. Use your answer in part (a) to find the elevation of the top of Mount Rushmore.

46. WRITING Write a real-life problem that can be solved using a right triangle. Then solve your problem.

47. MATHEMATICAL CONNECTIONS The Tropic of Cancer is the circle of latitude farthest north of the equator where the Sun can appear directly overhead. It lies 23.5° north of the equator, as shown.

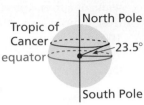

a. Find the circumference of the Tropic of Cancer using 3960 miles as the approximate radius of Earth.

b. What is the distance between two points on the Tropic of Cancer that lie directly across from each other?

48. HOW DO YOU SEE IT? Use the figure to answer each question.

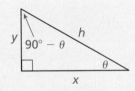

a. Which side is adjacent to θ?

b. Which side is opposite of θ?

c. Does $\cos \theta = \sin(90° - \theta)$? Explain.

49. PROBLEM SOLVING A passenger in an airplane sees two towns directly to the left of the plane.

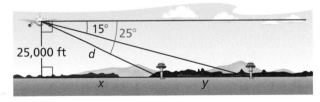

a. What is the distance d from the airplane to the first town?

b. What is the horizontal distance x from the airplane to the first town?

c. What is the distance y between the two towns? Explain the process you used to find your answer.

50. PROBLEM SOLVING You measure the angle of elevation from the ground to the top of a building as 32°. When you move 50 meters closer to the building, the angle of elevation is 53°. What is the height of the building?

51. MAKING AN ARGUMENT Your friend claims it is possible to draw a right triangle so the values of the cosine function of the acute angles are equal. Is your friend correct? Explain your reasoning.

52. THOUGHT PROVOKING Consider a semicircle with a radius of 1 unit, as shown below. Write the values of the six trigonometric functions of the angle θ. Explain your reasoning.

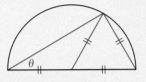

53. CRITICAL THINKING A procedure for approximating π based on the work of Archimedes is to inscribe a regular hexagon in a circle.

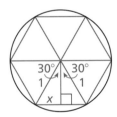

a. Use the diagram to solve for x. What is the perimeter of the hexagon?

b. Show that a regular n-sided polygon inscribed in a circle of radius 1 has a perimeter of
$$2n \cdot \sin\left(\frac{180}{n}\right)°.$$

c. Use the result from part (b) to find an expression in terms of n that approximates π. Then evaluate the expression when $n = 50$.

Maintaining Mathematical Proficiency Reviewing what you learned in previous grades and lessons

Write the repeating decimal as a fraction in simplest form. *(Section 7.4)*

54. $0.777\ldots$ **55.** $0.575757\ldots$ **56.** $0.345345345\ldots$ **57.** $112.112112112\ldots$

Find the circumference and area of the circle with the given radius or diameter.
(Skills Review Handbook)

58. $r = 6$ centimeters   **59.** $r = 11$ inches   **60.** $d = 14$ feet

8.2   Angles and Radian Measure

Essential Question   How can you find the measure of an angle in radians?

Let the vertex of an angle be at the origin, with one side of the angle on the positive *x*-axis. The *radian measure* of the angle is a measure of the intercepted arc length on a circle of radius 1. To convert between degree and radian measure, use the fact that

$$\frac{\pi \text{ radians}}{180°} = 1.$$

EXPLORATION 1   **Writing Radian Measures of Angles**

Work with a partner. Write the radian measure of each angle with the given degree measure. Explain your reasoning.

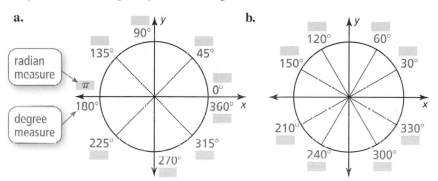

EXPLORATION 2   **Writing Degree Measures of Angles**

Work with a partner. Write the degree measure of each angle with the given radian measure. Explain your reasoning.

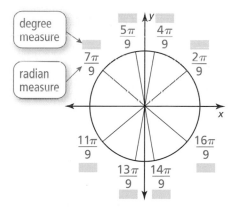

REASONING ABSTRACTLY

To be proficient in math, you need to make sense of quantities and their relationships in problem situations.

Communicate Your Answer

3. How can you find the measure of an angle in radians?

4. The figure shows an angle whose measure is 30 radians. What is the measure of the angle in degrees? How many times greater is 30 radians than 30 degrees? Justify your answers.

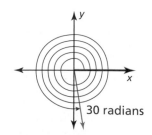

30 radians

What You Will Learn

▶ Draw angles in standard position.

▶ Find coterminal angles.

▶ Use radian measure.

Core Vocabulary

initial side, *p. 418*
terminal side, *p. 418*
standard position, *p. 418*
coterminal, *p. 419*
radian, *p. 419*
sector, *p. 420*
central angle, *p. 420*

Previous
radius of a circle
circumference of a circle

Drawing Angles in Standard Position

In this lesson, you will expand your study of angles to include angles with measures that can be any real numbers.

Core Concept

Angles in Standard Position

In a coordinate plane, an angle can be formed by fixing one ray, called the **initial side**, and rotating the other ray, called the **terminal side**, about the vertex.

An angle is in **standard position** when its vertex is at the origin and its initial side lies on the positive *x*-axis.

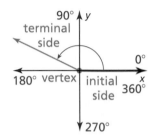

The measure of an angle is positive when the rotation of its terminal side is counterclockwise and negative when the rotation is clockwise. The terminal side of an angle can rotate more than 360°.

EXAMPLE 1 **Drawing Angles in Standard Position**

Draw an angle with the given measure in standard position.

a. 240°   **b.** 500°   **c.** −50°

SOLUTION

a. Because 240° is 60° more than 180°, the terminal side is 60° counterclockwise past the negative *x*-axis.

b. Because 500° is 140° more than 360°, the terminal side makes one complete rotation 360° counterclockwise plus 140° more.

c. Because −50° is negative, the terminal side is 50° clockwise from the positive *x*-axis.

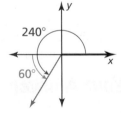

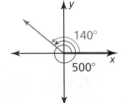

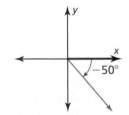

Monitoring Progress Help in English and Spanish at *BigIdeasMath.com*

Draw an angle with the given measure in standard position.

1. 65°   **2.** 300°   **3.** −120°   **4.** −450°

Finding Coterminal Angles

In Example 1(b), the angles 500° and 140° are **coterminal** because their terminal sides coincide. An angle coterminal with a given angle can be found by adding or subtracting multiples of 360°.

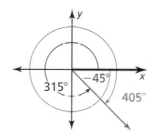

STUDY TIP

If two angles differ by a multiple of 360°, then the angles are coterminal.

EXAMPLE 2 Finding Coterminal Angles

Find one positive angle and one negative angle that are coterminal with (a) −45° and (b) 395°.

SOLUTION

There are many such angles, depending on what multiple of 360° is added or subtracted.

a. −45° + 360° = 315°
−45° − 360° = −405°

b. 395° − 360° = 35°
395° − 2(360°) = −325°

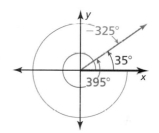

Monitoring Progress 🔊 Help in English and Spanish at *BigIdeasMath.com*

Find one positive angle and one negative angle that are coterminal with the given angle.

5. 80°   **6.** 230°   **7.** 740°   **8.** −135°

Using Radian Measure

STUDY TIP

Notice that 1 radian is approximately equal to 57.3°.

$180° = \pi$ radians

$\dfrac{180°}{\pi} = 1$ radian

$57.3° \approx 1$ radian

Angles can also be measured in *radians*. To define a radian, consider a circle with radius r centered at the origin, as shown. One **radian** is the measure of an angle in standard position whose terminal side intercepts an arc of length r.

Because the circumference of a circle is $2\pi r$, there are 2π radians in a full circle. So, degree measure and radian measure are related by the equation $360° = 2\pi$ radians, or $180° = \pi$ radians.

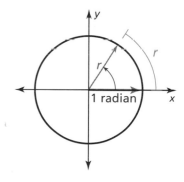

🌀 Core Concept

Converting Between Degrees and Radians

Degrees to radians

Multiply degree measure by

$$\frac{\pi \text{ radians}}{180°}.$$

Radians to degrees

Multiply radian measure by

$$\frac{180°}{\pi \text{ radians}}.$$

EXAMPLE 3   **Convert Between Degrees and Radians**

Convert the degree measure to radians or the radian measure to degrees.

a. $120°$ **b.** $-\dfrac{\pi}{12}$

SOLUTION

> **READING**
>
> The unit "radians" is often omitted. For instance, the measure $-\dfrac{\pi}{12}$ radians may be written simply as $-\dfrac{\pi}{12}$.

a. $120° = 120 \text{ degrees}\left(\dfrac{\pi \text{ radians}}{180 \text{ degrees}}\right)$

$\qquad = \dfrac{2\pi}{3}$

b. $-\dfrac{\pi}{12} = \left(-\dfrac{\pi}{12}\text{ radians}\right)\left(\dfrac{180°}{\pi \text{ radians}}\right)$

$\qquad = -15°$

Concept Summary

Degree and Radian Measures of Special Angles

The diagram shows equivalent degree and radian measures for special angles from $0°$ to $360°$ (0 radians to 2π radians).

You may find it helpful to memorize the equivalent degree and radian measures of special angles in the first quadrant and for $90° = \dfrac{\pi}{2}$ radians. All other special angles shown are multiples of these angles.

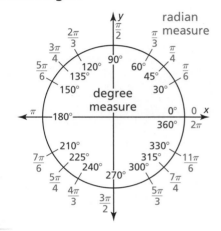

Monitoring Progress   Help in English and Spanish at *BigIdeasMath.com*

Convert the degree measure to radians or the radian measure to degrees.

9. $135°$ **10.** $-40°$ **11.** $\dfrac{5\pi}{4}$ **12.** -6.28

A **sector** is a region of a circle that is bounded by two radii and an arc of the circle. The **central angle** θ of a sector is the angle formed by the two radii. There are simple formulas for the arc length and area of a sector when the central angle is measured in radians.

Core Concept

Arc Length and Area of a Sector

The arc length s and area A of a sector with radius r and central angle θ (measured in radians) are as follows.

Arc length: $s = r\theta$

Area: $A = \dfrac{1}{2}r^2\theta$

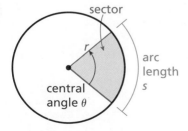

EXAMPLE 4 **Modeling with Mathematics**

A softball field forms a sector with the dimensions shown. Find the length of the outfield fence and the area of the field.

SOLUTION

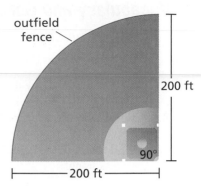

1. **Understand the Problem** You are given the dimensions of a softball field. You are asked to find the length of the outfield fence and the area of the field.

2. **Make a Plan** Find the measure of the central angle in radians. Then use the arc length and area of a sector formulas.

3. **Solve the Problem**

Step 1 Convert the measure of the central angle to radians.

$$90° = 90 \text{ degrees}\left(\frac{\pi \text{ radians}}{180 \text{ degrees}}\right)$$

$$= \frac{\pi}{2} \text{ radians}$$

COMMON ERROR

You must write the measure of an angle in radians when using these formulas for the arc length and area of a sector.

Step 2 Find the arc length and the area of the sector.

Arc length: $s = r\theta$	Area: $A = \frac{1}{2}r^2\theta$
$= 200\left(\frac{\pi}{2}\right)$	$= \frac{1}{2}(200)^2\left(\frac{\pi}{2}\right)$
$= 100\pi$	$= 10,000\pi$
≈ 314	$\approx 31,416$

ANOTHER WAY

Because the central angle is 90°, the sector represents $\frac{1}{4}$ of a circle with a radius of 200 feet. So,

$s = \frac{1}{4} \cdot 2\pi r$

$= \frac{1}{4} \cdot 2\pi(200)$

$= 100\pi$

and

$A = \frac{1}{4} \cdot \pi r^2$

$= \frac{1}{4} \cdot \pi(200)^2$

$= 10,000\pi.$

▶ The length of the outfield fence is about 314 feet. The area of the field is about 31,416 square feet.

4. **Look Back** To check the area of the field, consider the square formed using the two 200-foot sides.

By drawing the diagonal, you can see that the area of the field is less than the area of the square but greater than one-half of the area of the square.

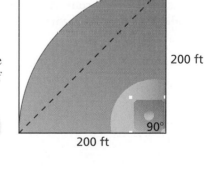

$\frac{1}{2} \cdot$ (area of square)   area of square

$$\frac{1}{2}(200)^2 \overset{?}{<} 31,416 \overset{?}{<} 200^2$$

$$20,000 < 31,416 < 40,000 \checkmark$$

Monitoring Progress 🔊 Help in English and Spanish at *BigIdeasMath.com*

13. **WHAT IF?** In Example 4, the outfield fence is 220 feet from home plate. Estimate the length of the outfield fence and the area of the field.

8.2 Exercises

Dynamic Solutions available at *BigIdeasMath.com*

Vocabulary and Core Concept Check

1. **COMPLETE THE SENTENCE** An angle is in standard position when its vertex is at the __________ and its __________ lies on the positive x-axis.

2. **WRITING** Explain how the sign of an angle measure determines its direction of rotation.

3. **VOCABULARY** In your own words, define a radian.

4. **WHICH ONE DOESN'T BELONG?** Which angle does *not* belong with the other three? Explain your reasoning.

$-90°$	$450°$	$90°$	$-270°$

Monitoring Progress and Modeling with Mathematics

In Exercises 5–8, draw an angle with the given measure in standard position. *(See Example 1.)*

5. $110°$

6. $450°$

7. $-900°$

8. $-10°$

In Exercises 9–12, find one positive angle and one negative angle that are coterminal with the given angle. *(See Example 2.)*

9. $70°$

10. $255°$

11. $-125°$

12. $-800°$

In Exercises 13–20, convert the degree measure to radians or the radian measure to degrees. *(See Example 3.)*

13. $40°$

14. $315°$

15. $-260°$

16. $-500°$

17. $\frac{\pi}{9}$

18. $\frac{3\pi}{4}$

19. -5

20. 12

21. **WRITING** The terminal side of an angle in standard position rotates one-sixth of a revolution counterclockwise from the positive x-axis. Describe how to find the measure of the angle in both degree and radian measures.

22. **OPEN-ENDED** Using radian measure, give one positive angle and one negative angle that are coterminal with the angle shown. Justify your answers.

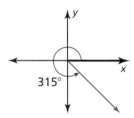

ANALYZING RELATIONSHIPS In Exercises 23–26, match the angle measure with the angle.

23. $600°$

24. $-\frac{9\pi}{4}$

25. $\frac{5\pi}{6}$

26. $-240°$

A.

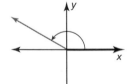

B.

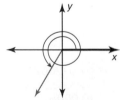

C.

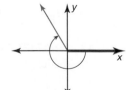

D.

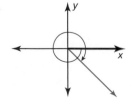

27. MODELING WITH MATHEMATICS The observation deck of a building forms a sector with the dimensions shown. Find the length of the safety rail and the area of the deck. *(See Example 4.)*

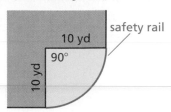

28. MODELING WITH MATHEMATICS In the men's shot put event at the 2012 Summer Olympic Games, the length of the winning shot was 21.89 meters. A shot put must land within a sector having a central angle of 34.92° to be considered fair.

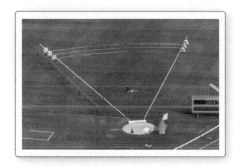

a. The officials draw an arc across the fair landing area, marking the farthest throw. Find the length of the arc.

b. All fair throws in the 2012 Olympics landed within a sector bounded by the arc in part (a). What is the area of this sector?

29. ERROR ANALYSIS Describe and correct the error in converting the degree measure to radians.

$$24° = 24 \text{ degrees} \left(\frac{180 \text{ degrees}}{\pi \text{ radians}} \right)$$

$$= \frac{4320}{\pi} \text{ radians}$$

$$\approx 1375.1 \text{ radians}$$

30. ERROR ANALYSIS Describe and correct the error in finding the area of a sector with a radius of 6 centimeters and a central angle of 40°.

$$A = \frac{1}{2}(6)^2(40) = 720 \text{ cm}^2$$

31. PROBLEM SOLVING When a CD player reads information from the outer edge of a CD, the CD spins about 200 revolutions per minute. At that speed, through what angle does a point on the CD spin in one minute? Give your answer in both degree and radian measures.

32. PROBLEM SOLVING You work every Saturday from 9:00 A.M. to 5:00 P.M. Draw a diagram that shows the rotation completed by the hour hand of a clock during this time. Find the measure of the angle generated by the hour hand in both degrees and radians. Compare this angle with the angle generated by the minute hand from 9:00 A.M. to 5:00 P.M.

USING TOOLS In Exercises 33–38, use a calculator to evaluate the trigonometric function.

33. $\cos \dfrac{4\pi}{3}$

34. $\sin \dfrac{7\pi}{8}$

35. $\csc \dfrac{10\pi}{11}$

36. $\cot \left(-\dfrac{6\pi}{5} \right)$

37. $\cot(-14)$

38. $\cos 6$

39. MODELING WITH MATHEMATICS The rear windshield wiper of a car rotates 120°, as shown. Find the area cleared by the wiper.

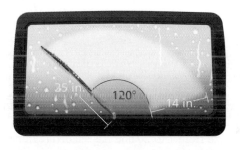

40. MODELING WITH MATHEMATICS A scientist performed an experiment to study the effects of gravitational force on humans. In order for humans to experience twice Earth's gravity, they were placed in a centrifuge 58 feet long and spun at a rate of about 15 revolutions per minute.

a. Through how many radians did the people rotate each second?

b. Find the length of the arc through which the people rotated each second.

41. REASONING In astronomy, the *terminator* is the day-night line on a planet that divides the planet into daytime and nighttime regions. The terminator moves across the surface of a planet as the planet rotates. It takes about 4 hours for Earth's terminator to move across the continental United States. Through what angle has Earth rotated during this time? Give your answer in both degree and radian measures.

42. HOW DO YOU SEE IT? Use the graph to find the measure of θ. Explain your reasoning.

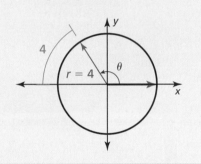

43. MODELING WITH MATHEMATICS A dartboard is divided into 20 sectors. Each sector is worth a point value from 1 to 20 and has shaded regions that double or triple this value. A sector is shown below. Find the areas of the entire sector, the double region, and the triple region.

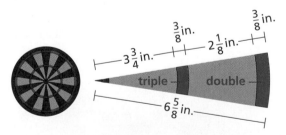

44. THOUGHT PROVOKING π is an irrational number, which means that it cannot be written as the ratio of two whole numbers. π can, however, be written exactly as a *continued fraction*, as follows.

$$3 + \cfrac{1}{7 + \cfrac{1}{15 + \cfrac{1}{1 + \cfrac{1}{292 + \cfrac{1}{1 + \cfrac{1}{1 + \cfrac{1}{1 + \cdots}}}}}}}$$

Show how to use this continued fraction to obtain a decimal approximation for π.

45. MAKING AN ARGUMENT Your friend claims that when the arc length of a sector equals the radius, the area can be given by $A = \dfrac{s^2}{2}$. Is your friend correct? Explain.

46. PROBLEM SOLVING A spiral staircase has 15 steps. Each step is a sector with a radius of 42 inches and a central angle of $\dfrac{\pi}{8}$.

a. What is the length of the arc formed by the outer edge of a step?

b. Through what angle would you rotate by climbing the stairs?

c. How many square inches of carpeting would you need to cover the 15 steps?

47. MULTIPLE REPRESENTATIONS There are 60 *minutes* in 1 degree of arc, and 60 *seconds* in 1 minute of arc. The notation $50° \, 30' \, 10''$ represents an angle with a measure of 50 degrees, 30 minutes, and 10 seconds.

a. Write the angle measure $70.55°$ using the notation above.

b. Write the angle measure $110° \, 45' \, 30''$ to the nearest hundredth of a degree. Justify your answer.

Maintaining Mathematical Proficiency
Reviewing what you learned in previous grades and lessons

Find the distance between the two points. *(Skills Review Handbook)*

48. $(1, 4), (3, 6)$ **49.** $(-7, -13), (10, 8)$ **50.** $(2, 12), (8, -5)$ **51.** $(4, 16), (-1, 34)$

52. What is the volume of the solid that is produced when the region enclosed by $y = 0$, $x = 0$, and $y = -\dfrac{1}{3}x + 3$ is rotated about (a) the x-axis and (b) the y-axis? *(Section 1.4)*

Trigonometric Functions of Any Angle

Essential Question How can you use the unit circle to define the trigonometric functions of any angle?

Let θ be an angle in standard position with (x, y) a point on the terminal side of θ and $r = \sqrt{x^2 + y^2} \neq 0$. The six trigonometric functions of θ are defined as shown.

$$\sin \theta = \frac{y}{r} \qquad\qquad \csc \theta = \frac{r}{y}, y \neq 0$$

$$\cos \theta = \frac{x}{r} \qquad\qquad \sec \theta = \frac{r}{x}, x \neq 0$$

$$\tan \theta = \frac{y}{x}, x \neq 0 \qquad \cot \theta = \frac{x}{y}, y \neq 0$$

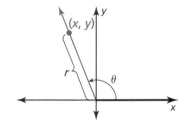

EXPLORATION 1 Writing Trigonometric Functions

Work with a partner. Find the sine, cosine, and tangent of the angle θ in standard position whose terminal side intersects the unit circle at the point (x, y) shown.

a. $\left(\frac{-1}{2}, \frac{\sqrt{3}}{2}\right)$

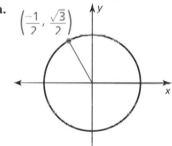

b. $\left(\frac{-1}{\sqrt{2}}, \frac{1}{\sqrt{2}}\right)$

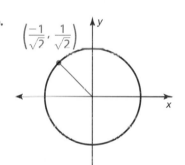

c. $(0, -1)$

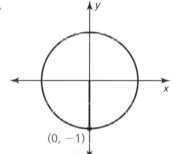

d. $\left(\frac{1}{2}, \frac{-\sqrt{3}}{2}\right)$

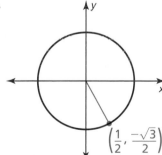

e. $\left(\frac{1}{\sqrt{2}}, \frac{-1}{\sqrt{2}}\right)$

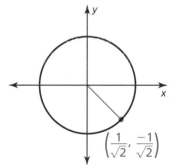

f. $(-1, 0)$

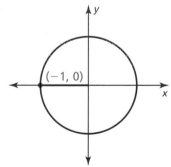

CONSTRUCTING VIABLE ARGUMENTS

To be proficient in math, you need to understand and use stated assumptions, definitions, and previously established results.

Communicate Your Answer

2. How can you use the unit circle to define the trigonometric functions of any angle?

3. For which angles are each function undefined? Explain your reasoning.

    a. tangent   b. cotangent   c. secant   d. cosecant

Core Vocabulary

unit circle, *p. 427*
quadrantal angle, *p. 427*
reference angle, *p. 428*

Previous
circle
radius
Pythagorean Theorem

What You Will Learn

▶ Evaluate trigonometric functions of any angle.
▶ Find and use reference angles to evaluate trigonometric functions.

Trigonometric Functions of Any Angle

You can generalize the right-triangle definitions of trigonometric functions so that they apply to any angle in standard position.

🅢 Core Concept

General Definitions of Trigonometric Functions

Let θ be an angle in standard position, and let (x, y) be the point where the terminal side of θ intersects the circle $x^2 + y^2 = r^2$. The six trigonometric functions of θ are defined as shown.

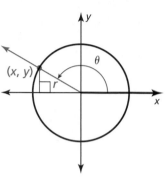

$$\sin \theta = \frac{y}{r} \qquad \csc \theta = \frac{r}{y}, y \neq 0$$

$$\cos \theta = \frac{x}{r} \qquad \sec \theta = \frac{r}{x}, x \neq 0$$

$$\tan \theta = \frac{y}{x}, x \neq 0 \qquad \cot \theta = \frac{x}{y}, y \neq 0$$

These functions are sometimes called *circular functions*.

EXAMPLE 1 **Evaluating Trigonometric Functions Given a Point**

Let $(-4, 3)$ be a point on the terminal side of an angle θ in standard position. Evaluate the six trigonometric functions of θ.

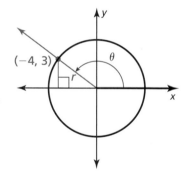

SOLUTION

Use the Pythagorean Theorem to find the length of r.

$$r = \sqrt{x^2 + y^2}$$

$$= \sqrt{(-4)^2 + 3^2}$$

$$= \sqrt{25}$$

$$= 5$$

Using $x = -4$, $y = 3$, and $r = 5$, the values of the six trigonometric functions of θ are:

$$\sin \theta = \frac{y}{r} = \frac{3}{5} \qquad \csc \theta = \frac{r}{y} = \frac{5}{3}$$

$$\cos \theta = \frac{x}{r} = -\frac{4}{5} \qquad \sec \theta = \frac{r}{x} = -\frac{5}{4}$$

$$\tan \theta = \frac{y}{x} = -\frac{3}{4} \qquad \cot \theta = \frac{x}{y} = -\frac{4}{3}$$

🌀 Core Concept

The Unit Circle

The circle $x^2 + y^2 = 1$, which has center $(0, 0)$ and radius 1, is called the **unit circle**. The values of $\sin \theta$ and $\cos \theta$ are simply the y-coordinate and x-coordinate, respectively, of the point where the terminal side of θ intersects the unit circle.

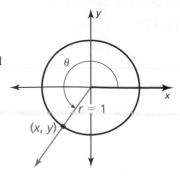

$$\sin \theta = \frac{y}{r} = \frac{y}{1} = y$$

$$\cos \theta = \frac{x}{r} = \frac{x}{1} = x$$

ANOTHER WAY

The general circle $x^2 + y^2 = r^2$ can also be used to find the six trigonometric functions of θ. The terminal side of θ intersects the circle at $(0, -r)$. So,

$$\sin \theta = \frac{y}{r} = \frac{-r}{r} = -1.$$

The other functions can be evaluated similarly.

It is convenient to use the unit circle to find trigonometric functions of **quadrantal angles**. A quadrantal angle is an angle in standard position whose terminal side lies on an axis. The measure of a quadrantal angle is always a multiple of 90°, or $\frac{\pi}{2}$ radians.

EXAMPLE 2   Using the Unit Circle

Use the unit circle to evaluate the six trigonometric functions of $\theta = 270°$.

SOLUTION

Step 1   Draw a unit circle with the angle $\theta = 270°$ in standard position.

Step 2   Identify the point where the terminal side of θ intersects the unit circle. The terminal side of θ intersects the unit circle at $(0, -1)$.

Step 3   Find the values of the six trigonometric functions. Let $x = 0$ and $y = -1$ to evaluate the trigonometric functions.

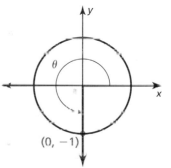

$$\sin \theta = \frac{y}{r} = \frac{-1}{1} = -1 \qquad\qquad \csc \theta = \frac{r}{y} = \frac{1}{-1} = -1$$

$$\cos \theta = \frac{x}{r} = \frac{0}{1} = 0 \qquad\qquad \sec \theta = \frac{r}{x} = \frac{1}{0} \;\; \text{undefined}$$

$$\tan \theta = \frac{y}{x} = \frac{-1}{0} \;\; \text{undefined} \qquad\qquad \cot \theta = \frac{x}{y} = \frac{0}{-1} = 0$$

Monitoring Progress Help in English and Spanish at *BigIdeasMath.com*

Evaluate the six trigonometric functions of θ.

1.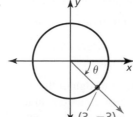
$(3, -3)$

2. $(-8, 15)$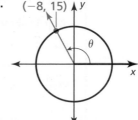

3.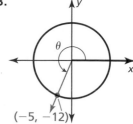
$(-5, -12)$

4. Use the unit circle to evaluate the six trigonometric functions of $\theta = 180°$.

Reference Angles

READING

The symbol θ' is read as "theta prime."

Core Concept

Reference Angle Relationships

Let θ be an angle in standard position. The **reference angle** for θ is the acute angle θ' formed by the terminal side of θ and the x-axis. The relationship between θ and θ' is shown below for nonquadrantal angles θ such that $90° < \theta < 360°$ or, in radians, $\dfrac{\pi}{2} < \theta < 2\pi$.

Quadrant II   **Quadrant III**   **Quadrant IV**

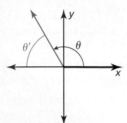   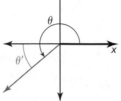   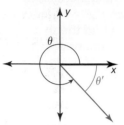

Degrees: $\theta' = 180° - \theta$ Degrees: $\theta' = \theta - 180°$ Degrees: $\theta' = 360° - \theta$

Radians: $\theta' = \pi - \theta$ Radians: $\theta' = \theta - \pi$ Radians: $\theta' = 2\pi - \theta$

EXAMPLE 3   **Finding Reference Angles**

Find the reference angle θ' for (a) $\theta = \dfrac{5\pi}{3}$ and (b) $\theta = -130°$.

SOLUTION

a. The terminal side of θ lies in Quadrant IV. So,

$\theta' = 2\pi - \dfrac{5\pi}{3} = \dfrac{\pi}{3}$. The figure at the right shows

$\theta = \dfrac{5\pi}{3}$ and $\theta' = \dfrac{\pi}{3}$.

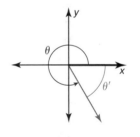

b. Note that θ is coterminal with 230°, whose terminal side lies in Quadrant III. So, $\theta' = 230° - 180° = 50°$. The figure at the left shows $\theta = -130°$ and $\theta' = 50°$.

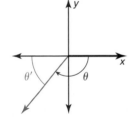

Reference angles allow you to evaluate a trigonometric function for any angle θ. The sign of the trigonometric function value depends on the quadrant in which θ lies.

Core Concept

Evaluating Trigonometric Functions

Use these steps to evaluate a trigonometric function for any angle θ:

Step 1   Find the reference angle θ'.

Step 2   Evaluate the trigonometric function for θ'.

Step 3   Determine the sign of the trigonometric function value from the quadrant in which θ lies.

Signs of Function Values

Quadrant II	Quadrant I
$\sin\theta,\ \csc\theta : +$	$\sin\theta,\ \csc\theta : +$
$\cos\theta,\ \sec\theta : -$	$\cos\theta,\ \sec\theta : +$
$\tan\theta,\ \cot\theta : -$	$\tan\theta,\ \cot\theta : +$
Quadrant III	Quadrant IV
$\sin\theta,\ \csc\theta : -$	$\sin\theta,\ \csc\theta : -$
$\cos\theta,\ \sec\theta : -$	$\cos\theta,\ \sec\theta : +$
$\tan\theta,\ \cot\theta : +$	$\tan\theta,\ \cot\theta : -$

EXAMPLE 4 Using Reference Angles to Evaluate Functions

Evaluate (a) $\tan(-240°)$ and (b) $\csc \dfrac{17\pi}{6}$.

SOLUTION

a. The angle $-240°$ is coterminal with $120°$. The reference angle is $\theta' = 180° - 120° = 60°$. The tangent function is negative in Quadrant II, so

$$\tan(-240°) = -\tan 60° = -\sqrt{3}.$$

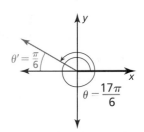

b. The angle $\dfrac{17\pi}{6}$ is coterminal with $\dfrac{5\pi}{6}$. The reference angle is

$$\theta' = \pi - \frac{5\pi}{6} = \frac{\pi}{6}.$$

The cosecant function is positive in Quadrant II, so

$$\csc \frac{17\pi}{6} = \csc \frac{\pi}{6} = 2.$$

INTERPRETING MODELS

This model neglects air resistance and assumes that the projectile's starting and ending heights are the same.

EXAMPLE 5 Solving a Real-Life Problem

The horizontal distance d (in feet) traveled by a projectile launched at an angle θ and with an initial speed v (in feet per second) is given by

$$d = \frac{v^2}{32} \sin 2\theta. \qquad \text{Model for horizontal distance}$$

Estimate the horizontal distance traveled by a golf ball that is hit at an angle of $50°$ with an initial speed of 105 feet per second.

SOLUTION

Note that the golf ball is launched at an angle of $\theta = 50°$ with initial speed of $v = 105$ feet per second.

$$d = \frac{v^2}{32} \sin 2\theta \qquad \text{Write model for horizontal distance.}$$

$$- \frac{105^2}{32} \sin(2 \cdot 50°) \qquad \text{Substitute 105 for } v \text{ and } 50° \text{ for } \theta.$$

$$\approx 339 \qquad \text{Use a calculator.}$$

▶ The golf ball travels a horizontal distance of about 339 feet.

Monitoring Progress Help in English and Spanish at *BigIdeasMath.com*

Sketch the angle. Then find its reference angle.

5. $210°$ **6.** $-260°$ **7.** $\dfrac{-7\pi}{9}$ **8.** $\dfrac{15\pi}{4}$

Evaluate the function without using a calculator.

9. $\cos(-210°)$ **10.** $\sec \dfrac{11\pi}{4}$

11. Use the model given in Example 5 to estimate the horizontal distance traveled by a track and field long jumper who jumps at an angle of $20°$ and with an initial speed of 27 feet per second.

Vocabulary and Core Concept Check

1. **COMPLETE THE SENTENCE** A(n) _____ is an angle in standard position whose terminal side lies on an axis.

2. **WRITING** Given an angle θ in standard position with its terminal side in Quadrant III, explain how you can use a reference angle to find cos θ.

Monitoring Progress and Modeling with Mathematics

In Exercises 3–8, evaluate the six trigonometric functions of θ. *(See Example 1.)*

3.

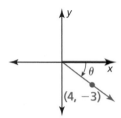
$(4, -3)$

4.

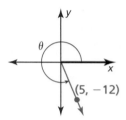
$(5, -12)$

5.

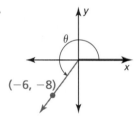
$(-6, -8)$

6.

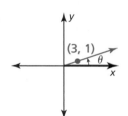
$(3, 1)$

7.

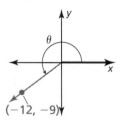
$(-12, -9)$

8.

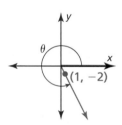
$(1, -2)$

In Exercises 9–14, use the unit circle to evaluate the six trigonometric functions of θ. *(See Example 2.)*

9. $\theta = 0°$

10. $\theta = 540°$

11. $\theta = \dfrac{\pi}{2}$

12. $\theta = \dfrac{7\pi}{2}$

13. $\theta = -270°$

14. $\theta = -2\pi$

In Exercises 15–22, sketch the angle. Then find its reference angle. *(See Example 3.)*

15. $-100°$

16. $150°$

17. $320°$

18. $-370°$

19. $\dfrac{23\pi}{4}$

20. $\dfrac{8\pi}{3}$

21. $-\dfrac{5\pi}{6}$

22. $-\dfrac{13\pi}{6}$

23. **ERROR ANALYSIS** Let $(-3, 2)$ be a point on the terminal side of an angle θ in standard position. Describe and correct the error in finding tan θ.

  $\tan \theta = \dfrac{x}{y} = -\dfrac{3}{2}$

24. **ERROR ANALYSIS** Describe and correct the error in finding a reference angle θ' for $\theta = 650°$.

θ is coterminal with $290°$, whose terminal side lies in Quadrant IV.

So, $\theta' = 290° - 270° = 20°$.

In Exercises 25–32, evaluate the function without using a calculator. *(See Example 4.)*

25. $\sec 135°$

26. $\tan 240°$

27. $\sin(-150°)$

28. $\csc(-420°)$

29. $\tan\left(-\dfrac{3\pi}{4}\right)$

30. $\cot\left(\dfrac{-8\pi}{3}\right)$

31. $\cos \dfrac{7\pi}{4}$

32. $\sec \dfrac{11\pi}{6}$

In Exercises 33–36, use the model for horizontal distance given in Example 5.

33. You kick a football at an angle of 60° with an initial speed of 49 feet per second. Estimate the horizontal distance traveled by the football. *(See Example 5.)*

34. The "frogbot" is a robot designed for exploring rough terrain on other planets. It can jump at a 45° angle with an initial speed of 14 feet per second. Estimate the horizontal distance the frogbot can jump on Earth.

35. At what speed must the in-line skater launch himself off the ramp in order to land on the other side of the ramp?

36. To win a javelin throwing competition, your last throw must travel a horizontal distance of at least 100 feet. You release the javelin at a 40° angle with an initial speed of 71 feet per second. Do you win the competition? Justify your answer.

37. MODELING WITH MATHEMATICS A rock climber is using a rock climbing treadmill that is 10 feet long. The climber begins by lying horizontally on the treadmill, which is then rotated about its midpoint by 110° so that the rock climber is climbing toward the top. If the midpoint of the treadmill is 6 feet above the ground, how high above the ground is the top of the treadmill?

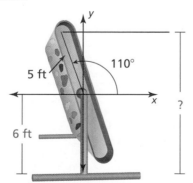

38. REASONING A Ferris wheel has a radius of 75 feet. You board a car at the bottom of the Ferris wheel, which is 10 feet above the ground, and rotate 255° counterclockwise before the ride temporarily stops. How high above the ground are you when the ride stops? If the radius of the Ferris wheel is doubled, is your height above the ground doubled? Explain your reasoning.

39. DRAWING CONCLUSIONS A sprinkler at ground level is used to water a garden. The water leaving the sprinkler has an initial speed of 25 feet per second.

a. Use the model for horizontal distance given in Example 5 to complete the table.

Angle of sprinkler, θ	Horizontal distance water travels, d
30°	
35°	
40°	
45°	
50°	
55°	
60°	

b. Which value of θ appears to maximize the horizontal distance traveled by the water? Use the model for horizontal distance and the unit circle to explain why your answer makes sense.

c. Compare the horizontal distance traveled by the water when $\theta = (45 - k)°$ with the distance when $\theta = (45 + k)°$, for $0 < k < 45$.

40. MODELING WITH MATHEMATICS Your school's marching band is performing at halftime during a football game. In the last formation, the band members form a circle 100 feet wide in the center of the field. You start at a point on the circle 100 feet from the goal line, march 300° around the circle, and then walk toward the goal line to exit the field. How far from the goal line are you at the point where you leave the circle?

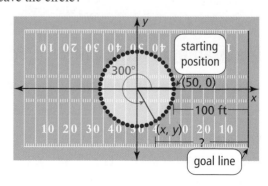

41. ANALYZING RELATIONSHIPS Use symmetry and the given information to label the coordinates of the other points corresponding to special angles on the unit circle.

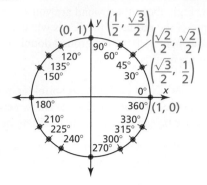

42. THOUGHT PROVOKING Use the interactive unit circle tool at *BigIdeasMath.com* to describe all values of θ for each situation.

  a. $\sin \theta > 0$, $\cos \theta < 0$, and $\tan \theta > 0$

  b. $\sin \theta > 0$, $\cos \theta < 0$, and $\tan \theta < 0$

43. CRITICAL THINKING Write $\tan \theta$ as the ratio of two other trigonometric functions. Use this ratio to explain why $\tan 90°$ is undefined but $\cot 90° = 0$.

44. HOW DO YOU SEE IT? Determine whether each of the six trigonometric functions of θ is *positive*, *negative*, or *zero*. Explain your reasoning.

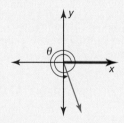

45. USING STRUCTURE A line with slope m passes through the origin. An angle θ in standard position has a terminal side that coincides with the line. Use a trigonometric function to relate the slope of the line to the angle.

46. MAKING AN ARGUMENT Your friend claims that the only solution to the trigonometric equation $\tan \theta = \sqrt{3}$ is $\theta = 60°$. Is your friend correct? Explain your reasoning.

47. PROBLEM SOLVING When two atoms in a molecule are bonded to a common atom, chemists are interested in both the bond angle and the lengths of the bonds. An ozone molecule is made up of two oxygen atoms bonded to a third oxygen atom, as shown.

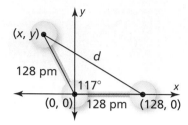

  a. In the diagram, coordinates are given in picometers (pm). (*Note*: 1 pm $= 10^{-12}$ m) Find the coordinates (x, y) of the center of the oxygen atom in Quadrant II.

  b. Find the distance d (in picometers) between the centers of the two unbonded oxygen atoms.

48. MATHEMATICAL CONNECTIONS The latitude of a point on Earth is the degree measure of the shortest arc from that point to the equator. For example, the latitude of point P in the diagram equals the degree measure of arc PE. At what latitude θ is the circumference of the circle of latitude at P half the distance around the equator?

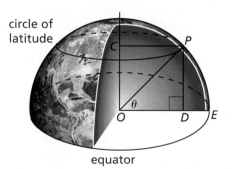

Maintaining Mathematical Proficiency *Reviewing what you learned in previous grades and lessons*

Find all real zeros of the polynomial function. *(Section 3.6)*

49. $f(x) = x^4 + 2x^3 + x^2 + 8x - 12$ **50.** $f(x) = x^5 + 4x^4 - 14x^3 - 14x^2 - 15x - 18$

Graph the function. *(Section 3.8)*

51. $f(x) = 2(x + 3)^2(x - 1)$ **52.** $f(x) = \frac{1}{3}(x - 4)(x + 5)(x + 9)$ **53.** $f(x) = x^2(x + 1)^3(x - 2)$

Core Vocabulary

sine, *p. 410*
cosine, *p. 410*
tangent, *p. 410*
cosecant, *p. 410*
secant, *p. 410*
cotangent, *p. 410*

initial side, *p. 418*
terminal side, *p. 418*
standard position, *p. 418*
coterminal, *p. 419*
radian, *p. 419*
sector, *p. 420*

central angle, *p. 420*
unit circle, *p. 427*
quadrantal angle, *p. 427*
reference angle, *p. 428*

Core Concepts

Section 8.1

Right Triangle Definitions of Trigonometric Functions, *p. 410*
Trigonometric Values for Special Angles, *p. 411*

Section 8.2

Angles in Standard Position, *p. 418*
Converting Between Degrees and Radians, *p. 419*

Degree and Radian Measures of Special Angles, *p. 420*
Arc Length and Area of a Sector, *p. 420*

Section 8.3

General Definitions of Trigonometric Functions, *p. 426*
The Unit Circle, *p. 427*

Reference Angle Relationships, *p. 428*
Evaluating Trigonometric Functions, *p. 428*

Mathematical Practices

1. How can you use a diagram to help you solve Exercise 50 on page 416?

2. Explain your plan for solving Exercise 40 on page 423.

3. Make a conjecture about the horizontal distances traveled in part (c) of Exercise 39 on page 431.

Form a Final Exam Study Group

Form a study group several weeks before the final exam. The intent of this group is to review what you have already learned while continuing to learn new material.

STUDY SKILLS

1. In a right triangle, θ is an acute angle and $\sin \theta = \frac{2}{7}$. Evaluate the other five trigonometric functions of θ. *(Section 8.1)*

Find the value of x for the right triangle. *(Section 8.1)*

2.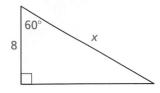

3.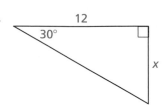

4.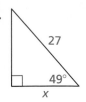

Draw an angle with the given measure in standard position. Then find one positive angle and one negative angle that are coterminal with the given angle. *(Section 8.2)*

5. $40°$

6. $\dfrac{5\pi}{6}$

7. $-960°$

Convert the degree measure to radians or the radian measure to degrees. *(Section 8.2)*

8. $\dfrac{3\pi}{10}$

9. $-60°$

10. $72°$

Evaluate the six trigonometric functions of θ. *(Section 8.3)*

11.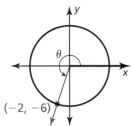

12.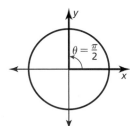

13.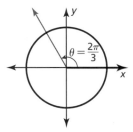

Sketch the angle. Then find its reference angle. *(Section 8.3)*

14. $315°$

15. $-\dfrac{2\pi}{3}$

16. $\dfrac{17\pi}{6}$

Evaluate the function without using a calculator. *(Section 8.3)*

17. $\cos \dfrac{4\pi}{3}$

18. $\sec(-330°)$

19. $\cot \dfrac{11\pi}{4}$

20. You are flying a kite at an angle of $70°$. You have let out a total of 400 feet of string and are holding the reel steady 4 feet above the ground. *(Section 8.1)*

    a. How high above the ground is the kite?

    b. A friend watching the kite estimates that the angle of elevation to the kite is $85°$. How far from your friend are you standing?

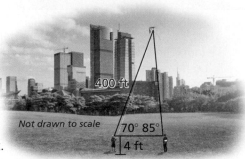

21. The top of the Space Needle in Seattle, Washington, is a revolving, circular restaurant. The restaurant has a radius of 47.25 feet and makes one complete revolution in about an hour. You have dinner at a window table from 7:00 P.M. to 8:55 P.M. Compare the distance you revolve with the distance of a person seated 5 feet away from the windows. *(Section 8.2)*

8.4 Graphing Sine and Cosine Functions

Essential Question What are the characteristics of the graphs of the sine and cosine functions?

EXPLORATION 1 Graphing the Sine Function

Work with a partner.

a. Complete the table for $y = \sin x$, where x is an angle measure in radians.

x	-2π	$-\dfrac{7\pi}{4}$	$-\dfrac{3\pi}{2}$	$-\dfrac{5\pi}{4}$	$-\pi$	$-\dfrac{3\pi}{4}$	$-\dfrac{\pi}{2}$	$-\dfrac{\pi}{4}$	0
$y = \sin x$									

x	$\dfrac{\pi}{4}$	$\dfrac{\pi}{2}$	$\dfrac{3\pi}{4}$	π	$\dfrac{5\pi}{4}$	$\dfrac{3\pi}{2}$	$\dfrac{7\pi}{4}$	2π	$\dfrac{9\pi}{4}$
$y = \sin x$									

b. Plot the points (x, y) from part (a). Draw a smooth curve through the points to sketch the graph of $y = \sin x$.

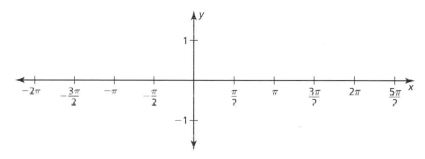

c. Use the graph to identify the x-intercepts, the x-values where the local maximums and minimums occur, and the intervals for which the function is increasing or decreasing over $-2\pi \le x \le 2\pi$. Is the sine function *even*, *odd*, or *neither*?

EXPLORATION 2 Graphing the Cosine Function

Work with a partner.

a. Complete a table for $y = \cos x$ using the same values of x as those used in Exploration 1.

b. Plot the points (x, y) from part (a) and sketch the graph of $y = \cos x$.

c. Use the graph to identify the x-intercepts, the x-values where the local maximums and minimums occur, and the intervals for which the function is increasing or decreasing over $-2\pi \le x \le 2\pi$. Is the cosine function *even*, *odd*, or *neither*?

LOOKING FOR STRUCTURE

To be proficient in math, you need to look closely to discern a pattern or structure.

Communicate Your Answer

3. What are the characteristics of the graphs of the sine and cosine functions?

4. Describe the end behavior of the graph of $y = \sin x$.

8.4 Lesson

Core Vocabulary

amplitude, *p. 436*
periodic function, *p. 436*
cycle, *p. 436*
period, *p. 436*
phase shift, *p. 438*
midline, *p. 438*

Previous
transformations
x-intercept
maximum value
minimum value

What You Will Learn

▶ Explore characteristics of sine and cosine functions.

▶ Stretch and shrink graphs of sine and cosine functions.

▶ Translate graphs of sine and cosine functions.

▶ Reflect graphs of sine and cosine functions.

Exploring Characteristics of Sine and Cosine Functions

In this lesson, you will learn to graph sine and cosine functions. The graphs of sine and cosine functions are related to the graphs of the parent functions $y = \sin x$ and $y = \cos x$, which are shown below.

x	-2π	$-\dfrac{3\pi}{2}$	$-\pi$	$-\dfrac{\pi}{2}$	0	$\dfrac{\pi}{2}$	π	$\dfrac{3\pi}{2}$	2π
$y = \sin x$	0	1	0	-1	0	1	0	-1	0
$y = \cos x$	1	0	-1	0	1	0	-1	0	1

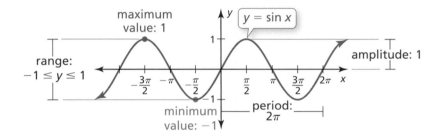

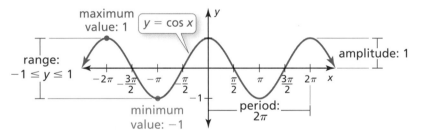

Core Concept

Characteristics of $y = \sin x$ and $y = \cos x$

- The domain of each function is all real numbers.

- The range of each function is $-1 \le y \le 1$. So, the minimum value of each function is -1 and the maximum value is 1.

- The **amplitude** of the graph of each function is one-half of the difference of the maximum value and the minimum value, or $\frac{1}{2}[1 - (-1)] = 1$.

- Each function is **periodic**, which means that its graph has a repeating pattern. The shortest repeating portion of the graph is called a **cycle**. The horizontal length of each cycle is called the **period**. Each graph shown above has a period of 2π.

- The *x*-intercepts for $y = \sin x$ occur when $x = 0, \pm\pi, \pm2\pi, \pm3\pi, \ldots$.

- The *x*-intercepts for $y = \cos x$ occur when $x = \pm\dfrac{\pi}{2}, \pm\dfrac{3\pi}{2}, \pm\dfrac{5\pi}{2}, \pm\dfrac{7\pi}{2}, \ldots$.

Stretching and Shrinking Sine and Cosine Functions

The graphs of $y = a \sin bx$ and $y = a \cos bx$ represent transformations of their parent functions. The value of a indicates a vertical stretch ($a > 1$) or a vertical shrink ($0 < a < 1$) and changes the amplitude of the graph. The value of b indicates a horizontal stretch ($0 < b < 1$) or a horizontal shrink ($b > 1$) and changes the period of the graph.

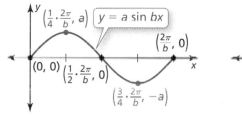

$$y = a \sin bx$$
$$y = a \cos bx$$

vertical stretch or shrink by a factor of a ⎯⎦   ⎣⎯ horizontal stretch or shrink by a factor of $\frac{1}{b}$

🌀 Core Concept

Amplitude and Period

The amplitude and period of the graphs of $y = a \sin bx$ and $y = a \cos bx$, where a and b are nonzero real numbers, are as follows:

$$\text{Amplitude} = |a| \qquad\qquad \text{Period} = \frac{2\pi}{|b|}$$

Each graph below shows five key points that partition the interval $0 \le x \le \frac{2\pi}{b}$ into four equal parts. You can use these points to sketch the graphs of $y = a \sin bx$ and $y = a \cos bx$. The x-intercepts, maximum, and minimum occur at these points.

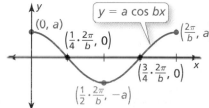

EXAMPLE 1   **Graphing a Sine Function**

Identify the amplitude and period of $g(x) = 4 \sin x$. Then graph the function and describe the graph of g as a transformation of the graph of $f(x) = \sin x$.

SOLUTION

The function is of the form $g(x) = a \sin bx$ where $a = 4$ and $b = 1$. So, the amplitude is $a = 4$ and the period is $\frac{2\pi}{b} = \frac{2\pi}{1} = 2\pi$.

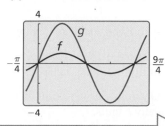

Intercepts: $(0, 0)$; $\left(\frac{1}{2} \cdot 2\pi, 0\right) = (\pi, 0)$; $(2\pi, 0)$

Maximum: $\left(\frac{1}{4} \cdot 2\pi, 4\right) = \left(\frac{\pi}{2}, 4\right)$

Minimum: $\left(\frac{3}{4} \cdot 2\pi, -4\right) = \left(\frac{3\pi}{2}, -4\right)$

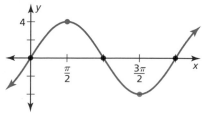

▶   The graph of g is a vertical stretch by a factor of 4 of the graph of f.

EXAMPLE 2 Graphing a Cosine Function

Identify the amplitude and period of $g(x) = \frac{1}{2}\cos 2\pi x$. Then graph the function and describe the graph of g as a transformation of the graph of $f(x) = \cos x$.

SOLUTION

The function is of the form $g(x) = a\cos bx$ where $a = \frac{1}{2}$ and $b = 2\pi$. So, the amplitude is $a = \frac{1}{2}$ and the period is $\frac{2\pi}{b} = \frac{2\pi}{2\pi} = 1$.

Intercepts: $\left(\frac{1}{4}\cdot 1, 0\right) = \left(\frac{1}{4}, 0\right); \left(\frac{3}{4}\cdot 1, 0\right) = \left(\frac{3}{4}, 0\right)$

Maximums: $\left(0, \frac{1}{2}\right); \left(1, \frac{1}{2}\right)$

Minimum: $\left(\frac{1}{2}\cdot 1, -\frac{1}{2}\right) = \left(\frac{1}{2}, -\frac{1}{2}\right)$

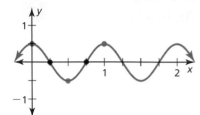

STUDY TIP

After you have drawn one complete cycle of the graph in Example 2 on the interval $0 \le x \le 1$, you can extend the graph by repeating the cycle as many times as desired to the left and right of $0 \le x \le 1$.

▶ The graph of g is a vertical shrink by a factor of $\frac{1}{2}$ and a horizontal shrink by a factor of $\frac{1}{2\pi}$ of the graph of f.

Monitoring Progress ◀)) Help in English and Spanish at *BigIdeasMath.com*

Identify the amplitude and period of the function. Then graph the function and describe the graph of g as a transformation of the graph of its parent function.

1. $g(x) = \frac{1}{4}\sin x$ 2. $g(x) = \cos 2x$ 3. $g(x) = 2\sin \pi x$ 4. $g(x) = \frac{1}{3}\cos \frac{1}{2}x$

REMEMBER

The graph of $y = f(x) + k$ is a vertical translation of the graph of $y = f(x)$.

The graph of $y = f(x - h)$ is a horizontal translation of the graph of $y = f(x)$.

Translating Sine and Cosine Functions

The graphs of $y = a\sin b(x - h) + k$ and $y = a\cos b(x - h) + k$ represent translations of $y = a\sin bx$ and $y = a\cos bx$. The value of k indicates a translation up ($k > 0$) or down ($k < 0$). The value of h indicates a translation left ($h < 0$) or right ($h > 0$). A horizontal translation of a periodic function is called a **phase shift**.

🌀 Core Concept

Graphing $y = a\sin b(x - h) + k$ and $y = a\cos b(x - h) + k$

To graph $y = a\sin b(x - h) + k$ or $y = a\cos b(x - h) + k$ where $a > 0$ and $b > 0$, follow these steps:

Step 1 Identify the amplitude a, the period $\frac{2\pi}{b}$, the horizontal shift h, and the vertical shift k of the graph.

Step 2 Draw the horizontal line $y = k$, called the **midline** of the graph.

Step 3 Find the five key points by translating the key points of $y = a\sin bx$ or $y = a\cos bx$ horizontally h units and vertically k units.

Step 4 Draw the graph through the five translated key points.

EXAMPLE 3 **Graphing a Vertical Translation**

Graph $g(x) = 2 \sin 4x + 3$.

SOLUTION

LOOKING FOR STRUCTURE

The graph of g is a translation 3 units up of the graph of $f(x) = 2 \sin 4x$. So, add 3 to the y-coordinates of the five key points of f.

Step 1 Identify the amplitude, period, horizontal shift, and vertical shift.

Amplitude: $a = 2$ Horizontal shift: $h = 0$

Period: $\dfrac{2\pi}{b} = \dfrac{2\pi}{4} = \dfrac{\pi}{2}$ Vertical shift: $k = 3$

Step 2 Draw the midline of the graph, $y = 3$.

Step 3 Find the five key points.

On $y = k$: $(0, 0 + 3) = (0, 3)$; $\left(\dfrac{\pi}{4}, 0 + 3\right) = \left(\dfrac{\pi}{4}, 3\right)$; $\left(\dfrac{\pi}{2}, 0 + 3\right) = \left(\dfrac{\pi}{2}, 3\right)$

Maximum: $\left(\dfrac{\pi}{8}, 2 + 3\right) = \left(\dfrac{\pi}{8}, 5\right)$

Minimum: $\left(\dfrac{3\pi}{8}, -2 + 3\right) - \left(\dfrac{3\pi}{8}, 1\right)$

Step 4 Draw the graph through the key points.

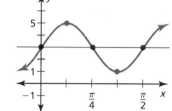

EXAMPLE 4 **Graphing a Horizontal Translation**

Graph $g(x) = 5 \cos \dfrac{1}{2}(x - 3\pi)$.

SOLUTION

LOOKING FOR STRUCTURE

The graph of g is a translation 3π units right of the graph of $f(x) = 5 \cos \frac{1}{2}x$. So, add 3π to the x-coordinates of the five key points of f.

Step 1 Identify the amplitude, period, horizontal shift, and vertical shift.

Amplitude: $a = 5$ Horizontal shift: $h = 3\pi$

Period: $\dfrac{2\pi}{b} = \dfrac{2\pi}{\dfrac{1}{2}} = 4\pi$ Vertical shift: $k = 0$

Step 2 Draw the midline of the graph. Because $k = 0$, the midline is the x-axis.

Step 3 Find the five key points.

On $y = k$: $(\pi + 3\pi, 0) = (4\pi, 0)$;
$(3\pi + 3\pi, 0) = (6\pi, 0)$

Maximums: $(0 + 3\pi, 5) = (3\pi, 5)$;
$(4\pi + 3\pi, 5) = (7\pi, 5)$

Minimum: $(2\pi + 3\pi, -5) = (5\pi, -5)$

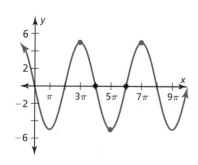

Step 4 Draw the graph through the key points.

Monitoring Progress   Help in English and Spanish at *BigIdeasMath.com*

Graph the function.

5. $g(x) = \cos x + 4$ **6.** $g(x) = \dfrac{1}{2} \sin\left(x - \dfrac{\pi}{2}\right)$ **7.** $g(x) = \sin(x + \pi) - 1$

Reflecting Sine and Cosine Functions

You have graphed functions of the form $y = a \sin b(x - h) + k$ and $y = a \cos b(x - h) + k$, where $a > 0$ and $b > 0$. To see what happens when $a < 0$, consider the graphs of $y = -\sin x$ and $y = -\cos x$.

REMEMBER

This result makes sense because the graph of $y = -f(x)$ is a reflection in the x-axis of the graph of $y = f(x)$.

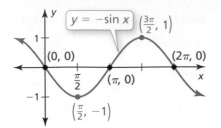
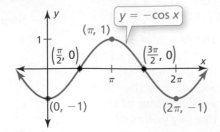

The graphs are reflections of the graphs of $y = \sin x$ and $y = \cos x$ in the x-axis. In general, when $a < 0$, the graphs of $y = a \sin b(x - h) + k$ and $y = a \cos b(x - h) + k$ are reflections of the graphs of $y = |a| \sin b(x - h) + k$ and $y = |a| \cos b(x - h) + k$, respectively, in the midline $y = k$.

EXAMPLE 5   **Graphing a Reflection**

Graph $g(x) = -2 \sin \dfrac{2}{3}\left(x - \dfrac{\pi}{2}\right)$.

SOLUTION

Step 1   Identify the amplitude, period, horizontal shift, and vertical shift.

Amplitude: $|a| = |-2| = 2$ Horizontal shift: $h = \dfrac{\pi}{2}$

Period: $\dfrac{2\pi}{b} = \dfrac{2\pi}{\frac{2}{3}} = 3\pi$ Vertical shift: $k = 0$

Step 2   Draw the midline of the graph. Because $k = 0$, the midline is the x-axis.

Step 3   Find the five key points of $f(x) = |-2| \sin \dfrac{2}{3}\left(x - \dfrac{\pi}{2}\right)$.

On $y = k$: $\left(0 + \dfrac{\pi}{2}, 0\right) = \left(\dfrac{\pi}{2}, 0\right)$; $\left(\dfrac{3\pi}{2} + \dfrac{\pi}{2}, 0\right) = (2\pi, 0)$; $\left(3\pi + \dfrac{\pi}{2}, 0\right) = \left(\dfrac{7\pi}{2}, 0\right)$

Maximum: $\left(\dfrac{3\pi}{4} + \dfrac{\pi}{2}, 2\right) = \left(\dfrac{5\pi}{4}, 2\right)$ Minimum: $\left(\dfrac{9\pi}{4} + \dfrac{\pi}{2}, -2\right) = \left(\dfrac{11\pi}{4}, -2\right)$

STUDY TIP

In Example 5, the maximum value and minimum value of f are the minimum value and maximum value, respectively, of g.

Step 4   Reflect the graph. Because $a < 0$, the graph is reflected in the midline $y = 0$. So, $\left(\dfrac{5\pi}{4}, 2\right)$ becomes $\left(\dfrac{5\pi}{4}, -2\right)$ and $\left(\dfrac{11\pi}{4}, -2\right)$ becomes $\left(\dfrac{11\pi}{4}, 2\right)$.

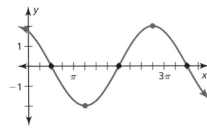

Step 5   Draw the graph through the key points.

Monitoring Progress Help in English and Spanish at *BigIdeasMath.com*

Graph the function.

8. $g(x) = -\cos\left(x + \dfrac{\pi}{2}\right)$ **9.** $g(x) = -3 \sin \dfrac{1}{2}x + 2$ **10.** $g(x) = -2 \cos 4x - 1$

Vocabulary and Core Concept Check

1. **COMPLETE THE SENTENCE** The shortest repeating portion of the graph of a periodic function is called a(n) _____.

2. **WRITING** Compare the amplitudes and periods of the functions $y = \frac{1}{2}\cos x$ and $y = 3\cos 2x$.

3. **VOCABULARY** What is a phase shift? Give an example of a sine function that has a phase shift.

4. **VOCABULARY** What is the midline of the graph of the function $y = 2 \sin 3(x + 1) - 2$?

Monitoring Progress and Modeling with Mathematics

USING STRUCTURE In Exercises 5–8, determine whether the graph represents a periodic function. If so, identify the period.

5.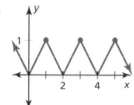

6.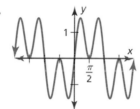

7.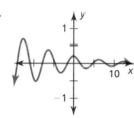

8.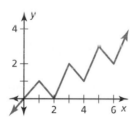

In Exercises 9–12, identify the amplitude and period of the graph of the function.

9.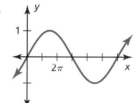

10.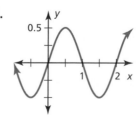

11.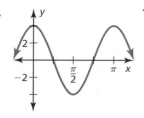

12.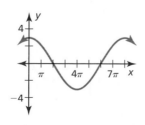

In Exercises 13–20, identify the amplitude and period of the function. Then graph the function and describe the graph of *g* as a transformation of the graph of its parent function. *(See Examples 1 and 2.)*

13. $g(x) = 3 \sin x$

14. $g(x) = 2 \sin x$

15. $g(x) = \cos 3x$

16. $g(x) = \cos 4x$

17. $g(x) = \sin 2\pi x$

18. $g(x) = 3 \sin 2x$

19. $g(x) = \frac{1}{4}\cos 4x$

20. $g(x) = \frac{1}{2}\cos 4\pi x$

21. **ANALYZING EQUATIONS** Which functions have an amplitude of 4 and a period of 2?

　Ⓐ $y = 4 \cos 2x$

　Ⓑ $y = -4 \sin \pi x$

　Ⓒ $y = 2 \sin 4x$

　Ⓓ $y = 4 \cos \pi x$

22. **WRITING EQUATIONS** Write an equation of the form $y = a \sin bx$, where $a > 0$ and $b > 0$, so that the graph has the given amplitude and period.

　a. amplitude: 1　　　　b. amplitude: 10
　　period: 5　　　　　　　period: 4

　c. amplitude: 2　　　　d. amplitude: $\frac{1}{2}$
　　period: 2π　　　　　　period: 3π

23. **MODELING WITH MATHEMATICS** The motion of a pendulum can be modeled by the function $d = 4 \cos 8\pi t$, where d is the horizontal displacement (in inches) of the pendulum relative to its position at rest and t is the time (in seconds). Find and interpret the period and amplitude in the context of this situation. Then graph the function.

24. MODELING WITH MATHEMATICS A buoy bobs up and down as waves go past. The vertical displacement y (in feet) of the buoy with respect to sea level can be modeled by $y = 1.75 \cos \frac{\pi}{3}t$, where t is the time (in seconds). Find and interpret the period and amplitude in the context of the problem. Then graph the function.

In Exercises 25–34, graph the function. (*See Examples 3 and 4.*)

25. $g(x) = \sin x + 2$

26. $g(x) = \cos x - 4$

27. $g(x) = \cos\left(x - \frac{\pi}{2}\right)$

28. $g(x) = \sin\left(x + \frac{\pi}{4}\right)$

29. $g(x) = 2 \cos x - 1$

30. $g(x) = 3 \sin x + 1$

31. $g(x) = \sin 2(x + \pi)$

32. $g(x) = \cos 2(x - \pi)$

33. $g(x) = \sin \frac{1}{2}(x + 2\pi) + 3$

34. $g(x) = \cos \frac{1}{2}(x - 3\pi) - 5$

35. ERROR ANALYSIS Describe and correct the error in finding the period of the function $y = \sin \frac{2}{3}x$.

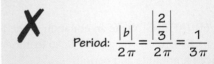

Period: $\dfrac{|b|}{2\pi} = \dfrac{\left|\frac{2}{3}\right|}{2\pi} = \dfrac{1}{3\pi}$

36. ERROR ANALYSIS Describe and correct the error in determining the point where the maximum value of the function $y = 2 \sin\left(x - \frac{\pi}{2}\right)$ occurs.

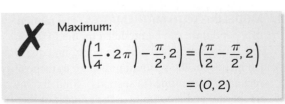

Maximum:

$\left(\left(\frac{1}{4} \cdot 2\pi\right) - \frac{\pi}{2}, 2\right) = \left(\frac{\pi}{2} - \frac{\pi}{2}, 2\right)$

$= (0, 2)$

USING STRUCTURE In Exercises 37–40, describe the transformation of the graph of f represented by the function g.

37. $f(x) = \cos x, \; g(x) = 2 \cos\left(x - \frac{\pi}{2}\right) + 1$

38. $f(x) = \sin x, \; g(x) = 3 \sin\left(x + \frac{\pi}{4}\right) - 2$

39. $f(x) = \sin x, \; g(x) = \sin 3(x + 3\pi) - 5$

40. $f(x) = \cos x, \; g(x) = \cos 6(x - \pi) + 9$

In Exercises 41–48, graph the function. (*See Example 5.*)

41. $g(x) = -\cos x + 3$

42. $g(x) = -\sin x - 5$

43. $g(x) = -\sin \frac{1}{2}x - 2$

44. $g(x) = -\cos 2x + 1$

45. $g(x) = -\sin(x - \pi) + 4$

46. $g(x) = -\cos(x + \pi) - 2$

47. $g(x) = -4 \cos\left(x + \frac{\pi}{4}\right) - 1$

48. $g(x) = -5 \sin\left(x - \frac{\pi}{2}\right) + 3$

49. USING EQUATIONS Which of the following is a point where the maximum value of the graph of $y = -4 \cos\left(x - \frac{\pi}{2}\right)$ occurs?

(A) $\left(-\frac{\pi}{2}, 4\right)$

(B) $\left(\frac{\pi}{2}, 4\right)$

(C) $(0, 4)$

(D) $(\pi, 4)$

50. ANALYZING RELATIONSHIPS Match each function with its graph. Explain your reasoning.

a. $y = 3 + \sin x$

b. $y = -3 + \cos x$

c. $y = \sin 2\left(x - \frac{\pi}{2}\right)$

d. $y = \cos 2\left(x - \frac{\pi}{2}\right)$

A.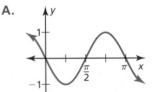

B.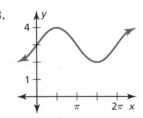

C.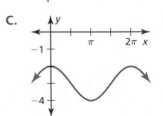

D.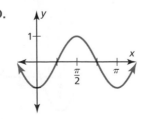

WRITING EQUATIONS In Exercises 51–54, write a rule for g that represents the indicated transformations of the graph of f.

51. $f(x) = 3 \sin x$; translation 2 units up and π units right

52. $f(x) = \cos 2\pi x$; translation 4 units down and 3 units left

53. $f(x) = \frac{1}{3} \cos \pi x$; translation 1 unit down, followed by a reflection in the line $y = -1$

54. $f(x) = \frac{1}{2} \sin 6x$; translation $\frac{3}{2}$ units down and 1 unit right, followed by a reflection in the line $y = -\frac{3}{2}$

55. MODELING WITH MATHEMATICS The height h (in feet) of a swing above the ground can be modeled by the function $h = -8 \cos \theta + 10$, where the pivot is 10 feet above the ground, the rope is 8 feet long, and θ is the angle (in degrees) that the rope makes with the vertical. Graph the function. What is the height of the swing when θ is 45°?

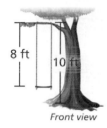

Front view

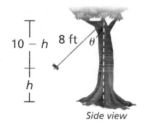

Side view

56. DRAWING A CONCLUSION In a particular region, the population L (in thousands) of lynx (the predator) and the population H (in thousands) of hares (the prey) can be modeled by the equations

$$L = 11.5 + 6.5 \sin \frac{\pi}{5} t$$

$$H = 27.5 + 17.5 \cos \frac{\pi}{5} t$$

where t is the time in years.

a. Determine the ratio of hares to lynx when $t = 0, 2.5, 5,$ and 7.5 years.

b. Use the figure to explain how the changes in the two populations appear to be related.

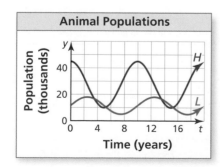

57. USING TOOLS The average wind speed s (in miles per hour) in the Boston Harbor can be approximated by

$$s = 3.38 \sin \frac{\pi}{180}(t + 3) + 11.6$$

where t is the time in days and $t = 0$ represents January 1. Use a graphing calculator to graph the function. On which days of the year is the average wind speed 10 miles per hour? Explain your reasoning.

58. USING TOOLS The water depth d (in feet) for the Bay of Fundy can be modeled by $d = 35 - 28 \cos \frac{\pi}{6.2} t$, where t is the time in hours and $t = 0$ represents midnight. Use a graphing calculator to graph the function. At what time(s) is the water depth 7 feet? Explain.

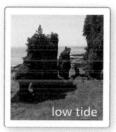

high tide | low tide

59. MULTIPLE REPRESENTATIONS Find the average rate of change of each function over the interval $0 < x < \pi$.

a. $y = 2 \cos x$

b.

x	0	$\frac{\pi}{2}$	π	$\frac{3\pi}{2}$	2π
$f(x) = -\cos x$	−1	0	1	0	−1

c.

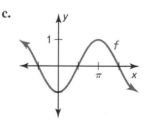

60. REASONING Consider the functions $y = \sin(-x)$ and $y = \cos(-x)$.

a. Construct a table of values for each equation using the quadrantal angles in the interval $-2\pi \le x \le 2\pi$.

b. Graph each function.

c. Describe the transformations of the graphs of the parent functions.

61. MODELING WITH MATHEMATICS You are riding a Ferris wheel that turns for 180 seconds. Your height h (in feet) above the ground at any time t (in seconds) can be modeled by the equation

$$h = 85 \sin \frac{\pi}{20}(t - 10) + 90.$$

a. Graph the function.

b. How many cycles does the Ferris wheel make in 180 seconds?

c. What are your maximum and minimum heights?

62. HOW DO YOU SEE IT? Use the graph to answer each question.

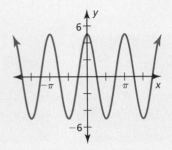

a. Does the graph represent a function of the form $f(x) = a \sin bx$ or $f(x) = a \cos bx$? Explain.

b. Identify the maximum value, minimum value, period, and amplitude of the function.

63. FINDING A PATTERN Write an expression in terms of the integer n that represents all the x-intercepts of the graph of the function $y = \cos 2x$. Justify your answer.

64. MAKING AN ARGUMENT Your friend states that for functions of the form $y = a \sin bx$ and $y = a \cos bx$, the values of a and b affect the x-intercepts of the graph of the function. Is your friend correct? Explain.

65. CRITICAL THINKING Describe a transformation of the graph of $f(x) = \sin x$ that results in the graph of $g(x) = \cos x$.

66. THOUGHT PROVOKING Use a graphing calculator to find a function of the form $y = \sin b_1 x + \cos b_2 x$ whose graph matches that shown below.

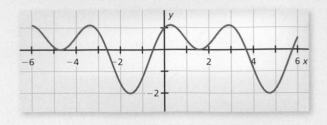

67. PROBLEM SOLVING For a person at rest, the blood pressure P (in millimeters of mercury) at time t (in seconds) is given by the function

$$P = 100 - 20 \cos \frac{8\pi}{3}t.$$

Graph the function. One cycle is equivalent to one heartbeat. What is the pulse rate (in heartbeats per minute) of the person?

68. PROBLEM SOLVING The motion of a spring can be modeled by $y = A \cos kt$, where y is the vertical displacement (in feet) of the spring relative to its position at rest, A is the initial displacement (in feet), k is a constant that measures the elasticity of the spring, and t is the time (in seconds).

a. You have a spring whose motion can be modeled by the function $y = 0.2 \cos 6t$. Find the initial displacement and the period of the spring. Then graph the function.

b. When a damping force is applied to the spring, the motion of the spring can be modeled by the function $y = 0.2e^{-4.5t} \cos 4t$. Graph this function. What effect does damping have on the motion?

Maintaining Mathematical Proficiency

Reviewing what you learned in previous grades and lessons

Simplify the rational expression, if possible. *(Section 6.3)*

69. $\dfrac{x^2 + x - 6}{x + 3}$

70. $\dfrac{x^3 - 2x^2 - 24x}{x^2 - 2x - 24}$

71. $\dfrac{x^2 - 4x - 5}{x^2 + 4x - 5}$

72. $\dfrac{x^2 - 16}{x^2 + x - 20}$

Find the least common multiple of the expressions. *(Section 6.4)*

73. $2x, 2(x - 5)$

74. $x^2 - 4, x + 2$

75. $x^2 + 8x + 12, x + 6$

8.5 Graphing Other Trigonometric Functions

Essential Question What are the characteristics of the graph of the tangent function?

EXPLORATION 1 Graphing the Tangent Function

Work with a partner.

a. Complete the table for $y = \tan x$, where x is an angle measure in radians.

x	$-\dfrac{\pi}{2}$	$-\dfrac{\pi}{3}$	$-\dfrac{\pi}{4}$	$-\dfrac{\pi}{6}$	0	$\dfrac{\pi}{6}$	$\dfrac{\pi}{4}$	$\dfrac{\pi}{3}$	$\dfrac{\pi}{2}$
$y = \tan x$									

x	$\dfrac{2\pi}{3}$	$\dfrac{3\pi}{4}$	$\dfrac{5\pi}{6}$	π	$\dfrac{7\pi}{6}$	$\dfrac{5\pi}{4}$	$\dfrac{4\pi}{3}$	$\dfrac{3\pi}{2}$	$\dfrac{5\pi}{3}$
$y = \tan x$									

b. The graph of $y = \tan x$ has vertical asymptotes at x-values where $\tan x$ is undefined. Plot the points (x, y) from part (a). Then use the asymptotes to sketch the graph of $y = \tan x$.

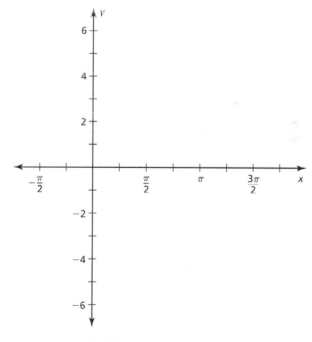

MAKING SENSE OF PROBLEMS

To be proficient in math, you need to consider analogous problems and try special cases of the original problem in order to gain insight into its solution.

c. For the graph of $y = \tan x$, identify the asymptotes, the x-intercepts, and the intervals for which the function is increasing or decreasing over $-\dfrac{\pi}{2} \le x \le \dfrac{3\pi}{2}$. Is the tangent function *even*, *odd*, or *neither*?

Communicate Your Answer

2. What are the characteristics of the graph of the tangent function?

3. Describe the asymptotes of the graph of $y = \cot x$ on the interval $-\dfrac{\pi}{2} < x < \dfrac{3\pi}{2}$.

Section 8.5 Graphing Other Trigonometric Functions **445**

What You Will Learn

▶ Explore characteristics of tangent and cotangent functions.

▶ Graph tangent and cotangent functions.

▶ Graph secant and cosecant functions.

Exploring Tangent and Cotangent Functions

The graphs of tangent and cotangent functions are related to the graphs of the parent functions $y = \tan x$ and $y = \cot x$, which are graphed below.

	← x approaches $-\dfrac{\pi}{2}$				x approaches $\dfrac{\pi}{2}$ →			
x	$-\dfrac{\pi}{2}$	-1.57	-1.5	$-\dfrac{\pi}{4}$	0	$\dfrac{\pi}{4}$	1.5	1.57	$\dfrac{\pi}{2}$
y = tan x	Undef.	-1256	-14.10	-1	0	1	14.10	1256	Undef.

← tan x approaches $-\infty$ ——— tan x approaches ∞ →

Because $\tan x = \dfrac{\sin x}{\cos x}$, $\tan x$ is undefined for *x*-values at which $\cos x = 0$, such as

$$x = \pm\frac{\pi}{2} \approx \pm 1.571.$$

The table indicates that the graph has asymptotes at these values. The table represents one cycle of the graph, so the period of the graph is π.

You can use a similar approach to graph $y = \cot x$. Because

$\cot x = \dfrac{\cos x}{\sin x}$, $\cot x$ is undefined for *x*-values at which $\sin x = 0$, which are multiples of π. The graph has asymptotes at these values. The period of the graph is also π.

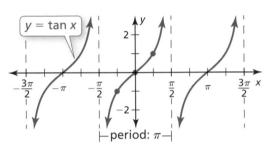

$y = \tan x$

period: π

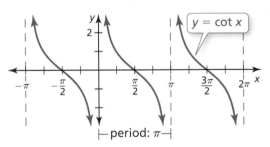

$y = \cot x$

period: π

🔄 Core Concept

Characteristics of y = tan x and y = cot x

The functions $y = \tan x$ and $y = \cot x$ have the following characteristics.

- The domain of $y = \tan x$ is all real numbers except odd multiples of $\dfrac{\pi}{2}$. At these *x*-values, the graph has vertical asymptotes.

- The domain of $y = \cot x$ is all real numbers except multiples of π. At these *x*-values, the graph has vertical asymptotes.

- The range of each function is all real numbers. So, the functions do not have maximum or minimum values, and the graphs do not have an amplitude.

- The period of each graph is π.

- The *x*-intercepts for $y = \tan x$ occur when $x = 0, \pm\pi, \pm 2\pi, \pm 3\pi, \ldots$.

- The *x*-intercepts for $y = \cot x$ occur when $x = \pm\dfrac{\pi}{2}, \pm\dfrac{3\pi}{2}, \pm\dfrac{5\pi}{2}, \pm\dfrac{7\pi}{2}, \ldots$.

STUDY TIP

Odd multiples of $\dfrac{\pi}{2}$ are values such as these:

$$\pm 1 \cdot \frac{\pi}{2} = \pm\frac{\pi}{2}$$

$$\pm 3 \cdot \frac{\pi}{2} = \pm\frac{3\pi}{2}$$

$$\pm 5 \cdot \frac{\pi}{2} = \pm\frac{5\pi}{2}$$

Graphing Tangent and Cotangent Functions

The graphs of $y = a \tan bx$ and $y = a \cot bx$ represent transformations of their parent functions. The value of a indicates a vertical stretch ($a > 1$) or a vertical shrink ($0 < a < 1$). The value of b indicates a horizontal stretch ($0 < b < 1$) or a horizontal shrink ($b > 1$) and changes the period of the graph.

Core Concept

Period and Vertical Asymptotes of $y = a \tan bx$ and $y = a \cot bx$

The period and vertical asymptotes of the graphs of $y = a \tan bx$ and $y = a \cot bx$, where a and b are nonzero real numbers, are as follows.

- The period of the graph of each function is $\dfrac{\pi}{|b|}$.

- The vertical asymptotes for $y = a \tan bx$ occur at odd multiples of $\dfrac{\pi}{2|b|}$.

- The vertical asymptotes for $y = a \cot bx$ occur at multiples of $\dfrac{\pi}{|b|}$.

Each graph below shows five key x-values that you can use to sketch the graphs of $y = a \tan bx$ and $y = a \cot bx$ for $a > 0$ and $b > 0$. These are the x-intercept, the x-values where the asymptotes occur, and the x-values halfway between the x-intercept and the asymptotes. At each halfway point, the value of the function is either a or $-a$.

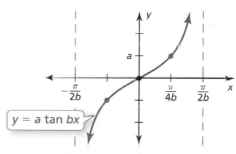

EXAMPLE 1   **Graphing a Tangent Function**

Graph one period of $g(x) = 2 \tan 3x$. Describe the graph of g as a transformation of the graph of $f(x) = \tan x$.

SOLUTION

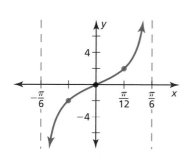

The function is of the form $g(x) = a \tan bx$ where $a = 2$ and $b = 3$. So, the period is $\dfrac{\pi}{|b|} = \dfrac{\pi}{3}$.

Intercept: $(0, 0)$

Asymptotes: $x = \dfrac{\pi}{2|b|} = \dfrac{\pi}{2(3)}$, or $x = \dfrac{\pi}{6}$; $x = -\dfrac{\pi}{2|b|} = -\dfrac{\pi}{2(3)}$, or $x = -\dfrac{\pi}{6}$

Halfway points: $\left(\dfrac{\pi}{4b}, a \right) = \left(\dfrac{\pi}{4(3)}, 2 \right) = \left(\dfrac{\pi}{12}, 2 \right)$;

$$\left(-\dfrac{\pi}{4b}, -a \right) = \left(-\dfrac{\pi}{4(3)}, -2 \right) = \left(-\dfrac{\pi}{12}, -2 \right)$$

▶ The graph of g is a vertical stretch by a factor of 2 and a horizontal shrink by a factor of $\frac{1}{3}$ of the graph of f.

EXAMPLE 2 **Graphing a Cotangent Function**

Graph one period of $g(x) = \cot \frac{1}{2}x$. Describe the graph of g as a transformation of the graph of $f(x) = \cot x$.

SOLUTION

The function is of the form $g(x) = a \cot bx$ where $a = 1$ and $b = \frac{1}{2}$. So, the period is $\frac{\pi}{|b|} = \frac{\pi}{\frac{1}{2}} = 2\pi$.

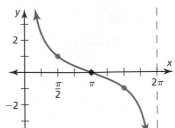

Intercept: $\left(\dfrac{\pi}{2b}, 0\right) = \left(\dfrac{\pi}{2\left(\frac{1}{2}\right)}, 0\right) = (\pi, 0)$

Asymptotes: $x = 0$; $x = \dfrac{\pi}{|b|} = \dfrac{\pi}{\frac{1}{2}}$, or $x = 2\pi$

Halfway points: $\left(\dfrac{\pi}{4b}, a\right) = \left(\dfrac{\pi}{4\left(\frac{1}{2}\right)}, 1\right) = \left(\dfrac{\pi}{2}, 1\right)$; $\left(\dfrac{3\pi}{4b}, -a\right) = \left(\dfrac{3\pi}{4\left(\frac{1}{2}\right)}, -1\right) = \left(\dfrac{3\pi}{2}, -1\right)$

▶ The graph of g is a horizontal stretch by a factor of 2 of the graph of f.

Monitoring Progress Help in English and Spanish at *BigIdeasMath.com*

Graph one period of the function. Describe the graph of g as a transformation of the graph of its parent function.

1. $g(x) = \tan 2x$ **2.** $g(x) = \frac{1}{3}\cot x$ **3.** $g(x) = 2\cot 4x$ **4.** $g(x) = 5\tan \pi x$

STUDY TIP

Because $\sec x = \dfrac{1}{\cos x}$, $\sec x$ is undefined for x-values at which $\cos x = 0$. The graph of $y = \sec x$ has vertical asymptotes at these x-values. You can use similar reasoning to understand the vertical asymptotes of the graph of $y = \csc x$.

Graphing Secant and Cosecant Functions

The graphs of secant and cosecant functions are related to the graphs of the parent functions $y = \sec x$ and $y = \csc x$, which are shown below.

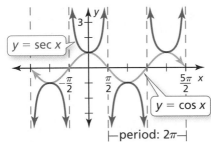

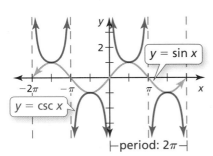

Core Concept

Characteristics of $y = \sec x$ and $y = \csc x$

The functions $y = \sec x$ and $y = \csc x$ have the following characteristics.

- The domain of $y = \sec x$ is all real numbers except odd multiples of $\frac{\pi}{2}$. At these x-values, the graph has vertical asymptotes.

- The domain of $y = \csc x$ is all real numbers except multiples of π. At these x-values, the graph has vertical asymptotes.

- The range of each function is $y \leq -1$ and $y \geq 1$. So, the graphs do not have an amplitude.

- The period of each graph is 2π.

To graph $y = a \sec bx$ or $y = a \csc bx$, first graph the function $y = a \cos bx$ or $y = a \sin bx$, respectively. Then use the asymptotes and several points to sketch a graph of the function. Notice that the value of b represents a horizontal stretch or shrink by a factor of $\frac{1}{b}$, so the period of $y = a \sec bx$ and $y = a \csc bx$ is $\frac{2\pi}{|b|}$.

EXAMPLE 3   Graphing a Secant Function

Graph one period of $g(x) = 2 \sec x$. Describe the graph of g as a transformation of the graph of $f(x) = \sec x$.

SOLUTION

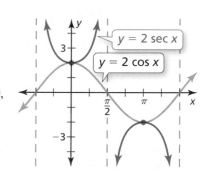

Step 1   Graph the function $y = 2 \cos x$.

The period is $\frac{2\pi}{1} = 2\pi$.

Step 2   Graph asymptotes of g. Because the asymptotes of g occur when $2 \cos x = 0$, graph $x = -\frac{\pi}{2}$, $x = \frac{\pi}{2}$, and $x = \frac{3\pi}{2}$.

Step 3   Plot points on g, such as $(0, 2)$ and $(\pi, -2)$. Then use the asymptotes to sketch the curve.

▶   The graph of g is a vertical stretch by a factor of 2 of the graph of f.

EXAMPLE 4   Graphing a Cosecant Function

Graph one period of $g(x) = \frac{1}{2} \csc \pi x$. Describe the graph of g as a transformation of the graph of $f(x) = \csc x$.

SOLUTION

Step 1   Graph the function $y = \frac{1}{2} \sin \pi x$. The period is $\frac{2\pi}{\pi} = 2$.

Step 2   Graph asymptotes of g. Because the asymptotes of g occur when $\frac{1}{2} \sin \pi x = 0$, graph $x = 0$, $x = 1$, and $x = 2$.

Step 3   Plot points on g, such as $\left(\frac{1}{2}, \frac{1}{2}\right)$ and $\left(\frac{3}{2}, -\frac{1}{2}\right)$. Then use the asymptotes to sketch the curve.

▶   The graph of g is a vertical shrink by a factor of $\frac{1}{2}$ and a horizontal shrink by a factor of $\frac{1}{\pi}$ of the graph of f.

LOOKING FOR A PATTERN

In Examples 3 and 4, notice that the plotted points are on both graphs. Also, these points represent a local maximum on one graph and a local minimum on the other graph.

Monitoring Progress   🔊 Help in English and Spanish at *BigIdeasMath.com*

Graph one period of the function. Describe the graph of g as a transformation of the graph of its parent function.

5. $g(x) = \csc 3x$ **6.** $g(x) = \frac{1}{2} \sec x$ **7.** $g(x) = 2 \csc 2x$ **8.** $g(x) = 2 \sec \pi x$

8.5 Exercises

Dynamic Solutions available at *BigIdeasMath.com*

Vocabulary and Core Concept Check

1. **WRITING** Explain why the graphs of the tangent, cotangent, secant, and cosecant functions do not have an amplitude.

2. **COMPLETE THE SENTENCE** The ______ and ______ functions are undefined for x-values at which $\sin x = 0$.

3. **COMPLETE THE SENTENCE** The period of the function $y = \sec x$ is _____, and the period of $y = \cot x$ is _____.

4. **WRITING** Explain how to graph a function of the form $y = a \sec bx$.

Monitoring Progress and Modeling with Mathematics

In Exercises 5–12, graph one period of the function. Describe the graph of g as a transformation of the graph of its parent function. *(See Examples 1 and 2.)*

5. $g(x) = 2 \tan x$
6. $g(x) = 3 \tan x$
7. $g(x) = \cot 3x$
8. $g(x) = \cot 2x$
9. $g(x) = 3 \cot \frac{1}{4}x$
10. $g(x) = 4 \cot \frac{1}{2}x$
11. $g(x) = \frac{1}{2} \tan \pi x$
12. $g(x) = \frac{1}{3} \tan 2\pi x$

13. **ERROR ANALYSIS** Describe and correct the error in finding the period of the function $y = \cot 3x$.

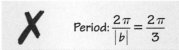

✗ Period: $\frac{2\pi}{|b|} = \frac{2\pi}{3}$

14. **ERROR ANALYSIS** Describe and correct the error in describing the transformation of $f(x) = \tan x$ represented by $g(x) = 2 \tan 5x$.

✗ A vertical stretch by a factor of 5 and a horizontal shrink by a factor of $\frac{1}{2}$.

15. **ANALYZING RELATIONSHIPS** Use the given graph to graph each function.

a. $f(x) = 3 \sec 2x$

b. $f(x) = 4 \csc 3x$

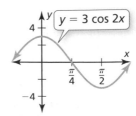

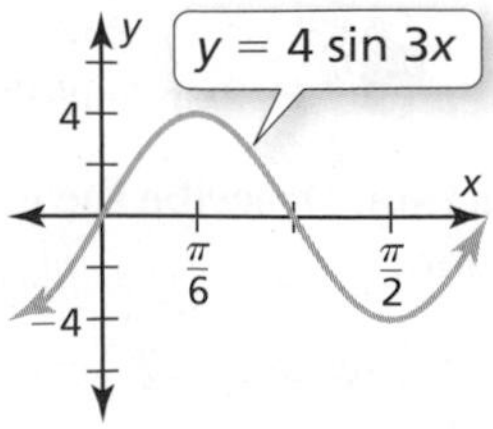

16. **USING EQUATIONS** Which of the following are asymptotes of the graph of $y = 3 \tan 4x$?

Ⓐ $x = \frac{\pi}{8}$

Ⓑ $x = \frac{\pi}{4}$

Ⓒ $x = 0$

Ⓓ $x = -\frac{5\pi}{8}$

In Exercises 17–24, graph one period of the function. Describe the graph of g as a transformation of the graph of its parent function. *(See Examples 3 and 4.)*

17. $g(x) = 3 \csc x$
18. $g(x) = 2 \csc x$
19. $g(x) = \sec 4x$
20. $g(x) = \sec 3x$
21. $g(x) = \frac{1}{2} \sec \pi x$
22. $g(x) = \frac{1}{4} \sec 2\pi x$
23. $g(x) = \csc \frac{\pi}{2}x$
24. $g(x) = \csc \frac{\pi}{4}x$

ATTENDING TO PRECISION In Exercises 25–28, use the graph to write a function of the form $y = a \tan bx$.

25.

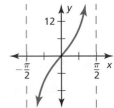

26.

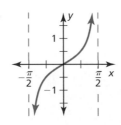

27.

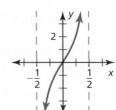

28.

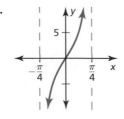

USING STRUCTURE In Exercises 29–34, match the equation with the correct graph. Explain your reasoning.

29. $g(x) = 4 \tan x$

30. $g(x) = 4 \cot x$

31. $g(x) = 4 \csc \pi x$

32. $g(x) = 4 \sec \pi x$

33. $g(x) = \sec 2x$

34. $g(x) = \csc 2x$

A.

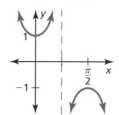

B.

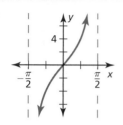

C.

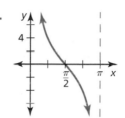

D.

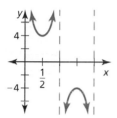

E.

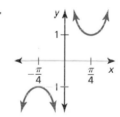

F.

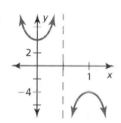

35. **WRITING** Explain why there is more than one tangent function whose graph passes through the origin and has asymptotes at $x = -\pi$ and $x = \pi$.

36. **USING EQUATIONS** Graph one period of each function. Describe the transformation of the graph of its parent function.

   a. $g(x) = \sec x + 3$ **b.** $g(x) = \csc x - 2$

   c. $g(x) = \cot(x - \pi)$ **d.** $g(x) = -\tan x$

WRITING EQUATIONS In Exercises 37–40, write a rule for g that represents the indicated transformation of the graph of f.

37. $f(x) = \cot 2x$; translation 3 units up and $\dfrac{\pi}{2}$ units left

38. $f(x) = 2 \tan x$; translation π units right, followed by a horizontal shrink by a factor of $\dfrac{1}{3}$

39. $f(x) = 5 \sec(x - \pi)$; translation 2 units down, followed by a reflection in the x-axis

40. $f(x) = 4 \csc x$; vertical stretch by a factor of 2 and a reflection in the x-axis

41. **MULTIPLE REPRESENTATIONS** Which function has a greater local maximum value? Which has a greater local minimum value? Explain.

   A. $f(x) = \frac{1}{4} \csc \pi x$ **B.**

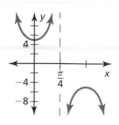

42. **ANALYZING RELATIONSHIPS** Order the functions from the least average rate of change to the greatest average rate of change over the interval $-\dfrac{\pi}{4} < x < \dfrac{\pi}{4}$.

   A.

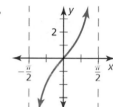

   B.

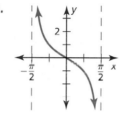

   C.

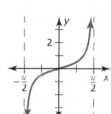

   D.

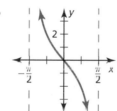

43. **REASONING** You are standing on a bridge 140 feet above the ground. You look down at a car traveling away from the underpass. The distance d (in feet) the car is from the base of the bridge can be modeled by $d = 140 \tan \theta$. Graph the function. Describe what happens to θ as d increases.

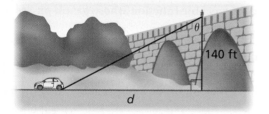

44. **USING TOOLS** You use a video camera to pan up the Statue of Liberty. The height h (in feet) of the part of the Statue of Liberty that can be seen through your video camera after t seconds can be modeled by $h = 100 \tan \dfrac{\pi}{36} t$. Graph the function using a graphing calculator. What viewing window did you use? Explain.

45. MODELING WITH MATHEMATICS You are standing 120 feet from the base of a 260-foot building. You watch your friend go down the side of the building in a glass elevator.

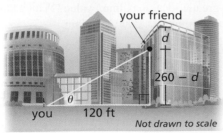

your friend

d

$260 - d$

θ

you   120 ft

Not drawn to scale

a. Write an equation that gives the distance d (in feet) your friend is from the top of the building as a function of the angle of elevation θ.

b. Graph the function found in part (a). Explain how the graph relates to this situation.

46. MODELING WITH MATHEMATICS You are standing 300 feet from the base of a 200-foot cliff. Your friend is rappelling down the cliff.

a. Write an equation that gives the distance d (in feet) your friend is from the top of the cliff as a function of the angle of elevation θ.

b. Graph the function found in part (a).

c. Use a graphing calculator to determine the angle of elevation when your friend has rappelled halfway down the cliff.

47. MAKING AN ARGUMENT Your friend states that it is not possible to write a cosecant function that has the same graph as $y = \sec x$. Is your friend correct? Explain your reasoning.

48. HOW DO YOU SEE IT? Use the graph to answer each question.

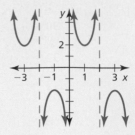

a. What is the period of the graph?

b. What is the range of the function?

c. Is the function of the form $f(x) = a \csc bx$ or $f(x) = a \sec bx$? Explain.

49. ABSTRACT REASONING Rewrite $a \sec bx$ in terms of $\cos bx$. Use your results to explain the relationship between the local maximums and minimums of the cosine and secant functions.

50. THOUGHT PROVOKING A trigonometric equation that is true for all values of the variable for which both sides of the equation are defined is called a *trigonometric identity*. Use a graphing calculator to graph the function

$$y = \frac{1}{2}\left(\tan \frac{x}{2} + \cot \frac{x}{2}\right).$$

Use your graph to write a trigonometric identity involving this function. Explain your reasoning.

51. CRITICAL THINKING Find a tangent function whose graph intersects the graph of $y = 2 + 2 \sin x$ only at the local minimums of the sine function.

Maintaining Mathematical Proficiency   Reviewing what you learned in previous grades and lessons

Write a cubic function whose graph passes through the given points. *(Section 3.9)*

52. $(-1, 0), (1, 0), (3, 0), (0, 3)$

53. $(-2, 0), (1, 0), (3, 0), (0, -6)$

54. $(-1, 0), (2, 0), (3, 0), (1, -2)$

55. $(-3, 0), (-1, 0), (3, 0), (-2, 1)$

Find the amplitude and period of the graph of the function. *(Section 8.4)*

56.

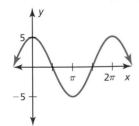

57.

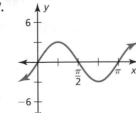

58.

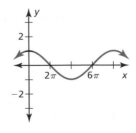

8.6 Modeling with Trigonometric Functions

Essential Question What are the characteristics of the real-life problems that can be modeled by trigonometric functions?

EXPLORATION 1 Modeling Electric Currents

Work with a partner. Find a sine function that models the electric current shown in each oscilloscope screen. State the amplitude and period of the graph.

a.
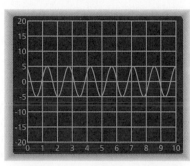

b.
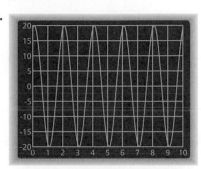

c.
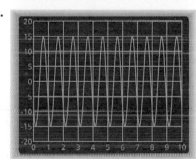

d.
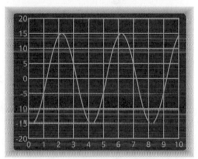

e.
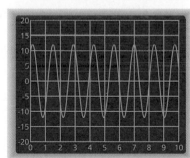

f.
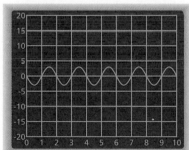

Communicate Your Answer

2. What are the characteristics of the real-life problems that can be modeled by trigonometric functions?

3. Use the Internet or some other reference to find examples of real-life situations that can be modeled by trigonometric functions.

frequency, *p. 454*
sinusoid, *p. 455*

Previous
amplitude
period
midline

What You Will Learn

▶ Interpret and use frequency.
▶ Write trigonometric functions.
▶ Use technology to find trigonometric models.

Frequency

The periodic nature of trigonometric functions makes them useful for modeling *oscillating* motions or repeating patterns that occur in real life. Some examples are sound waves, the motion of a pendulum, and temperature during the year. In such applications, the reciprocal of the period is called the **frequency**, which gives the number of cycles per unit of time.

EXAMPLE 1 Using Frequency

A sound consisting of a single frequency is called a *pure tone*. An audiometer produces pure tones to test a person's auditory functions. An audiometer produces a pure tone with a frequency *f* of 2000 hertz (cycles per second). The maximum pressure *P* produced from the pure tone is 2 millipascals. Write and graph a sine model that gives the pressure *P* as a function of the time *t* (in seconds).

SOLUTION

Step 1 Find the values of *a* and *b* in the model $P = a \sin bt$. The maximum pressure is 2, so $a = 2$. Use the frequency *f* to find *b*.

$$\text{frequency} = \frac{1}{\text{period}} \qquad \text{Write relationship involving frequency and period.}$$

$$2000 = \frac{b}{2\pi} \qquad \text{Substitute.}$$

$$4000\pi = b \qquad \text{Multiply each side by } 2\pi.$$

The pressure *P* as a function of time *t* is given by $P = 2 \sin 4000\pi t$.

Step 2 Graph the model. The amplitude is $a = 2$ and the period is

$$\frac{1}{f} = \frac{1}{2000}.$$

The key points are:

Intercepts: $(0, 0)$; $\left(\frac{1}{2} \cdot \frac{1}{2000}, 0\right) = \left(\frac{1}{4000}, 0\right)$; $\left(\frac{1}{2000}, 0\right)$

Maximum: $\left(\frac{1}{4} \cdot \frac{1}{2000}, 2\right) = \left(\frac{1}{8000}, 2\right)$

Minimum: $\left(\frac{3}{4} \cdot \frac{1}{2000}, -2\right) = \left(\frac{3}{8000}, -2\right)$

▶ The graph of $P = 2 \sin 4000\pi t$ is shown at the left.

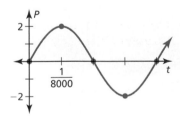

1. **WHAT IF?** In Example 1, how would the function change when the audiometer produced a pure tone with a frequency of 1000 hertz?

Writing Trigonometric Functions

Graphs of sine and cosine functions are called **sinusoids**. One method to write a sine or cosine function that models a sinusoid is to find the values of *a*, *b*, *h*, and *k* for

$$y = a \sin b(x - h) + k \qquad \text{or} \qquad y = a \cos b(x - h) + k$$

where $|a|$ is the amplitude, $\dfrac{2\pi}{b}$ is the period ($b > 0$), *h* is the horizontal shift, and *k* is the vertical shift.

EXAMPLE 2   Writing a Trigonometric Function

Write a function for the sinusoid shown.

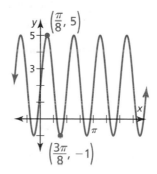

SOLUTION

Step 1 Find the maximum and minimum values. From the graph, the maximum value is 5 and the minimum value is -1.

Step 2 Identify the vertical shift, *k*. The value of *k* is the mean of the maximum and minimum values.

$$k = \frac{(\text{maximum value}) + (\text{minimum value})}{2} = \frac{5 + (-1)}{2} = \frac{4}{2} = 2$$

STUDY TIP

Because the graph repeats every $\dfrac{\pi}{2}$ units, the period is $\dfrac{\pi}{2}$.

Step 3 Decide whether the graph should be modeled by a sine or cosine function. Because the graph crosses the midline $y = 2$ on the *y*-axis, the graph is a sine curve with no horizontal shift. So, $h = 0$.

Step 4 Find the amplitude and period. The period is

$$\frac{\pi}{2} = \frac{2\pi}{b} \qquad \Longrightarrow \qquad b = 4.$$

The amplitude is

$$|a| = \frac{(\text{maximum value}) - (\text{minimum value})}{2} = \frac{5 - (-1)}{2} = \frac{6}{2} = 3.$$

The graph is not a reflection, so $a > 0$. Therefore, $a = 3$.

Check

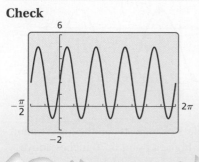

▶ The function is $y = 3 \sin 4x + 2$. Check this by graphing the function on a graphing calculator.

EXAMPLE 3 Modeling Circular Motion

Two people swing jump ropes, as shown in the diagram. The highest point of the middle of each rope is 75 inches above the ground, and the lowest point is 3 inches. The rope makes 2 revolutions per second. Write a model for the height h (in inches) of a rope as a function of the time t (in seconds) given that the rope is at its lowest point when $t = 0$.

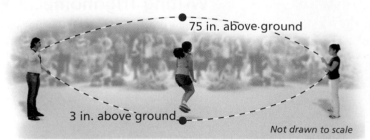

75 in. above ground

3 in. above ground

Not drawn to scale

SOLUTION

A rope oscillates between 3 inches and 75 inches above the ground. So, a sine or cosine function may be an appropriate model for the height over time.

Step 1 Identify the maximum and minimum values. The maximum height of a rope is 75 inches. The minimum height is 3 inches.

Step 2 Identify the vertical shift, k.

$$k = \frac{(\text{maximum value}) + (\text{minimum value})}{2} = \frac{75 + 3}{2} = 39$$

Step 3 Decide whether the height should be modeled by a sine or cosine function. When $t = 0$, the height is at its minimum. So, use a cosine function whose graph is a reflection in the x-axis with no horizontal shift ($h = 0$).

Step 4 Find the amplitude and period.

The amplitude is $|a| = \dfrac{(\text{maximum value}) - (\text{minimum value})}{2} = \dfrac{75 - 3}{2} = 36$.

Because the graph is a reflection in the x-axis, $a < 0$. So, $a = -36$. Because a rope is rotating at a rate of 2 revolutions per second, one revolution is completed in 0.5 second. So, the period is $\dfrac{2\pi}{b} = 0.5$, and $b = 4\pi$.

▶ A model for the height of a rope is $h(t) = -36 \cos 4\pi t + 39$.

> **Check**
>
> Use the *table* feature of a graphing calculator to check your model.
>
> | X | Y₁ | |
> |---|---|---|
> | 0 | 3 | |
> | .25 | 75 | |
> | .5 | 3 | 2 revolutions |
> | .75 | 75 | |
> | 1 | 3 | |
> | 1.25 | 75 | |
> | 1.5 | 3 | |
> | X=0 | | |

Monitoring Progress Help in English and Spanish at *BigIdeasMath.com*

Write a function for the sinusoid.

2.

(0, 2)

$\dfrac{2\pi}{3}$

$\left(\dfrac{\pi}{3}, -2\right)$

3.

$\left(\dfrac{1}{2}, 1\right)$

$\dfrac{1}{2}$ $\dfrac{3}{2}$ $\dfrac{5}{2}$

$\left(\dfrac{3}{2}, -3\right)$

4. WHAT IF? Describe how the model in Example 3 changes when the lowest point of a rope is 5 inches above the ground and the highest point is 70 inches above the ground.

Using Technology to Find Trigonometric Models

Another way to model sinusoids is to use a graphing calculator that has a sinusoidal regression feature.

EXAMPLE 4   **Using Sinusoidal Regression**

The table shows the numbers N of hours of daylight in Denver, Colorado, on the 15th day of each month, where $t = 1$ represents January. Write a model that gives N as a function of t and interpret the period of its graph.

t	1	2	3	4	5	6
N	9.68	10.75	11.93	13.27	14.38	14.98

t	7	8	9	10	11	12
N	14.70	13.73	12.45	11.17	9.98	9.38

SOLUTION

Step 1   Enter the data in a graphing calculator.

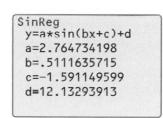

Step 2   Make a scatter plot.

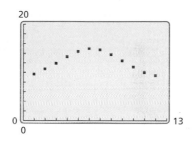

Step 3   The scatter plot appears sinusoidal. So, perform a sinusoidal regression.

Step 4   Graph the data and the model in the same viewing window.

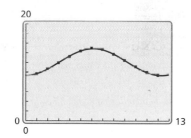

STUDY TIP

Notice that the *sinusoidal regression* feature finds a model of the form $y = a \sin(bx + c) + d$. This function has a period of $\dfrac{2\pi}{b}$ because it can be written as $y = a \sin b\left(x + \dfrac{c}{b}\right) + d$.

▶   The model appears to be a good fit. So, a model for the data is

$N = 2.76 \sin(0.511t - 1.59) + 12.1$. The period, $\dfrac{2\pi}{0.511} \approx 12$, makes sense

because there are 12 months in a year and you would expect this pattern to continue in following years.

Monitoring Progress Help in English and Spanish at *BigIdeasMath.com*

5. The table shows the average daily temperature T (in degrees Fahrenheit) for a city each month, where $m = 1$ represents January. Write a model that gives T as a function of m and interpret the period of its graph.

m	1	2	3	4	5	6	7	8	9	10	11	12
T	29	32	39	48	59	68	74	72	65	54	45	35

Vocabulary and Core Concept Check

1. **COMPLETE THE SENTENCE** Graphs of sine and cosine functions are called _____.

2. **WRITING** Describe how to find the frequency of the function whose graph is shown.

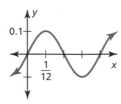

Monitoring Progress and Modeling with Mathematics

In Exercises 3–10, find the frequency of the function.

3. $y = \sin x$

4. $y = \sin 3x$

5. $y = \cos 4x + 2$

6. $y = -\cos 2x$

7. $y = \sin 3\pi x$

8. $y = \cos \dfrac{\pi x}{4}$

9. $y = \dfrac{1}{2} \cos 0.75x - 8$

10. $y = 3 \sin 0.2x + 6$

11. **MODELING WITH MATHEMATICS** The lowest frequency of sounds that can be heard by humans is 20 hertz. The maximum pressure P produced from a sound with a frequency of 20 hertz is 0.02 millipascal. Write and graph a sine model that gives the pressure P as a function of the time t (in seconds). *(See Example 1.)*

12. **MODELING WITH MATHEMATICS** A middle-A tuning fork vibrates with a frequency f of 440 hertz (cycles per second). You strike a middle-A tuning fork with a force that produces a maximum pressure of 5 pascals. Write and graph a sine model that gives the pressure P as a function of the time t (in seconds).

In Exercises 13–16, write a function for the sinusoid. *(See Example 2.)*

13.

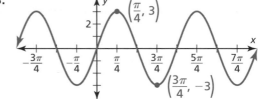

14.

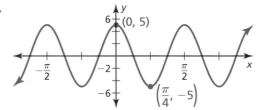

15.

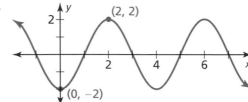

16.

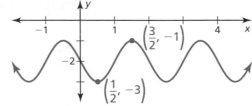

17. ERROR ANALYSIS Describe and correct the error in finding the amplitude of a sinusoid with a maximum point at (2, 10) and a minimum point at (4, −6).

✗ $|a| = \dfrac{(\text{maximum value}) + (\text{minimum value})}{2}$

$= \dfrac{10 - 6}{2}$

$= 2$

18. ERROR ANALYSIS Describe and correct the error in finding the vertical shift of a sinusoid with a maximum point at (3, −2) and a minimum point at (7, −8).

✗ $k = \dfrac{(\text{maximum value}) + (\text{minimum value})}{2}$

$= \dfrac{7 + 3}{2}$

$= 5$

19. MODELING WITH MATHEMATICS One of the largest sewing machines in the world has a *flywheel* (which turns as the machine sews) that is 5 feet in diameter. The highest point of the handle at the edge of the flywheel is 9 feet above the ground, and the lowest point is 4 feet. The wheel makes a complete turn every 2 seconds. Write a model for the height *h* (in feet) of the handle as a function of the time *t* (in seconds) given that the handle is at its lowest point when *t* = 0. *(See Example 3.)*

20. MODELING WITH MATHEMATICS The Great Laxey Wheel, located on the Isle of Man, is the largest working water wheel in the world. The highest point of a bucket on the wheel is 70.5 feet above the viewing platform, and the lowest point is 2 feet below the viewing platform. The wheel makes a complete turn every 24 seconds. Write a model for the height *h* (in feet) of the bucket as a function of time *t* (in seconds) given that the bucket is at its lowest point when *t* = 0.

USING TOOLS In Exercises 21 and 22, the time *t* is measured in months, where *t* = 1 represents January. Write a model that gives the average monthly high temperature *D* as a function of *t* and interpret the period of the graph. *(See Example 4.)*

21.

Air Temperatures in Apple Valley, CA					
t	1	2	3	4	5	6
D	60	63	69	75	85	94
t	7	8	9	10	11	12
D	99	99	93	81	69	60

22.

Water Temperatures at Miami Beach, FL					
t	1	2	3	4	5	6
D	71	73	75	78	81	85
t	7	8	9	10	11	12
D	86	85	84	81	76	73

23. MODELING WITH MATHEMATICS A circuit has an alternating voltage of 100 volts that peaks every 0.5 second. Write a sinusoidal model for the voltage *V* as a function of the time *t* (in seconds).

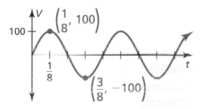

24. MULTIPLE REPRESENTATIONS The graph shows the average daily temperature of Lexington, Kentucky. The average daily temperature of Louisville, Kentucky, is modeled by $y = -22 \cos \dfrac{\pi}{6}t + 57$, where *y* is the temperature (in degrees Fahrenheit) and *t* is the number of months since January 1. Which city has the greater average daily temperature? Explain.

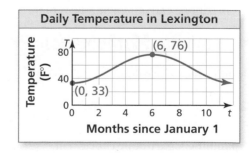

25. USING TOOLS The table shows the numbers of employees N (in thousands) at a sporting goods company each year for 11 years. The time t is measured in years, with $t = 1$ representing the first year.

t	1	2	3	4	5	6
N	20.8	22.7	24.6	23.2	20	17.5

t	7	8	9	10	11
N	16.7	17.8	21	22	24.1

a. Use sinusoidal regression to find a model that gives N as a function of t.

b. Predict the number of employees at the company in the 12th year.

26. THOUGHT PROVOKING The figure shows a tangent line drawn to the graph of the function $y = \sin x$. At several points on the graph, draw a tangent line to the graph and estimate its slope. Then plot the points (x, m), where m is the slope of the tangent line. What can you conclude?

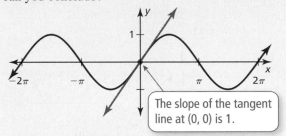

The slope of the tangent line at (0, 0) is 1.

27. REASONING Determine whether you would use a sine or cosine function to model each sinusoid with the y-intercept described. Explain your reasoning.

a. The y-intercept occurs at the maximum value of the function.

b. The y-intercept occurs at the minimum value of the function.

c. The y-intercept occurs halfway between the maximum and minimum values of the function.

28. HOW DO YOU SEE IT? What is the frequency of the function whose graph is shown? Explain.

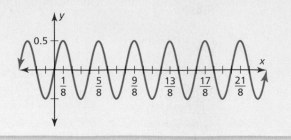

29. USING STRUCTURE During one cycle, a sinusoid has a minimum at $\left(\dfrac{\pi}{2}, 3\right)$ and a maximum at $\left(\dfrac{\pi}{4}, 8\right)$. Write a sine function *and* a cosine function for the sinusoid. Use a graphing calculator to verify that your answers are correct.

30. MAKING AN ARGUMENT Your friend claims that a function with a frequency of 2 has a greater period than a function with a frequency of $\frac{1}{2}$. Is your friend correct? Explain your reasoning.

31. PROBLEM SOLVING The low tide at a port is 3.5 feet and occurs at midnight. After 6 hours, the port is at high tide, which is 16.5 feet.

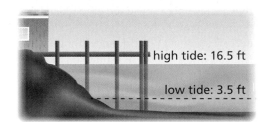

high tide: 16.5 ft

low tide: 3.5 ft

a. Write a sinusoidal model that gives the tide depth d (in feet) as a function of the time t (in hours). Let $t = 0$ represent midnight.

b. Find all the times when low and high tides occur in a 24-hour period.

c. Explain how the graph of the function you wrote in part (a) is related to a graph that shows the tide depth d at the port t hours after 3:00 A.M.

Maintaining Mathematical Proficiency
Reviewing what you learned in previous grades and lessons

Simplify the expression. *(Section 4.2)*

32. $\dfrac{17}{\sqrt{2}}$

33. $\dfrac{3}{\sqrt{6} - 2}$

34. $\dfrac{8}{\sqrt{10} + 3}$

35. $\dfrac{13}{\sqrt{3} + \sqrt{11}}$

Expand the logarithmic expression. *(Section 5.4)*

36. $\log_8 \dfrac{x}{7}$

37. $\ln 2x$

38. $\log_3 5x^3$

39. $\ln \dfrac{4x^6}{y}$

Core Vocabulary

amplitude, *p. 436*   phase shift, *p. 438*
periodic function, *p. 436*   midline, *p. 438*
cycle, *p. 436*   frequency, *p. 454*
period, *p. 436*   sinusoid, *p. 455*

Core Concepts

Section 8.4

Characteristics of $y = \sin x$ and $y = \cos x$, *p. 436*
Amplitude and Period, *p. 437*
Graphing $y = a \sin b(x - h) + k$ and $y = a \cos b(x - h) + k$, *p. 438*

Section 8.5

Characteristics of $y = \tan x$ and $y = \cot x$, *p. 446*
Period and Vertical Asymptotes of $y = a \tan bx$ and $y = a \cot bx$, *p. 447*
Characteristics of $y = \sec x$ and $y = \csc x$, *p. 448*

Section 8.6

Frequency, *p. 454*
Writing Trigonometric Functions, *p. 455*
Using Technology to Find Trigonometric Models, *p. 457*

Mathematical Practices

1. Explain why the quantities in part (a) of Exercise 56 on page 443 make sense in the context of the situation.

2. Explain why the relationship between θ and d makes sense in the context of the situation in Exercise 43 on page 451.

Performance Task:

Parasailing to Great Heights

The Federal Aviation Administration has set the maximum height for parasailing at 500 feet. How can trigonometry help you stay within that limit?

To explore the answer to this question and more, check out the Performance Task and Real-Life STEM video at *BigIdeasMath.com*.

8.1 Right Triangle Trigonometry *(pp. 409–416)*

Evaluate the six trigonometric functions of the angle θ.

From the Pythagorean Theorem, the length of the hypotenuse is

$$\text{hyp.} = \sqrt{6^2 + 8^2}$$
$$= \sqrt{100}$$
$$= 10.$$

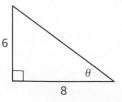

Using adj. = 8, opp. = 6, and hyp. = 10, the values of the six trigonometric functions of θ are:

$$\sin \theta = \frac{\text{opp.}}{\text{hyp.}} = \frac{6}{10} = \frac{3}{5} \qquad \cos \theta = \frac{\text{adj.}}{\text{hyp.}} = \frac{8}{10} = \frac{4}{5} \qquad \tan \theta = \frac{\text{opp.}}{\text{adj.}} = \frac{6}{8} = \frac{3}{4}$$

$$\csc \theta = \frac{\text{hyp.}}{\text{opp.}} = \frac{10}{6} = \frac{5}{3} \qquad \sec \theta = \frac{\text{hyp.}}{\text{adj.}} = \frac{10}{8} = \frac{5}{4} \qquad \cot \theta = \frac{\text{adj.}}{\text{opp.}} = \frac{8}{6} = \frac{4}{3}$$

1. In a right triangle, θ is an acute angle and $\cos \theta = \frac{6}{11}$. Evaluate the other five trigonometric functions of θ.

2. The shadow of a tree measures 25 feet from its base. The angle of elevation to the Sun is 31°. How tall is the tree?

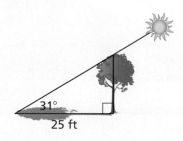

31°

25 ft

8.2 Angles and Radian Measure *(pp. 417–424)*

Convert the degree measure to radians or the radian measure to degrees.

a. 110°

b. $\dfrac{7\pi}{12}$

$$110° = 110 \text{ degrees} \left(\frac{\pi \text{ radians}}{180 \text{ degrees}} \right)$$

$$= \frac{11\pi}{18}$$

$$\frac{7\pi}{12} = \frac{7\pi}{12} \text{ radians} \left(\frac{180°}{\pi \text{ radians}} \right)$$

$$= 105°$$

3. Find one positive angle and one negative angle that are coterminal with 382°.

Convert the degree measure to radians or the radian measure to degrees.

4. 30°   **5.** 225°   **6.** $\dfrac{3\pi}{4}$ **7.** $\dfrac{5\pi}{3}$

8. A sprinkler system on a farm rotates 140° and sprays water up to 35 meters. Draw a diagram that shows the region that can be irrigated with the sprinkler. Then find the area of the region.

8.3 Trigonometric Functions of Any Angle *(pp. 425–432)*

Evaluate csc 210°.

The reference angle is $\theta' = 210° - 180° = 30°$. The cosecant function is negative in Quadrant III, so $\csc 210° = -\csc 30° = -2$.

Evaluate the six trigonometric functions of θ.

9.
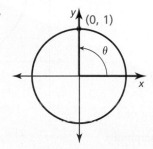

10.
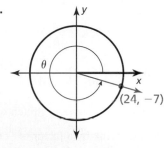

11.
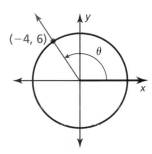

Evaluate the function without using a calculator.

12. $\tan 330°$

13. $\sec(-405°)$

14. $\sin \dfrac{13\pi}{6}$

15. $\sec \dfrac{11\pi}{3}$

8.4 Graphing Sine and Cosine Functions *(pp. 435–444)*

Identify the amplitude and period of $g(x) = \dfrac{1}{2} \sin 2x$. Then graph the function and describe the graph of g as a transformation of the graph of $f(x) = \sin x$.

The function is of the form $g(x) = a \sin bx$, where $a = \dfrac{1}{2}$ and $b = 2$. So, the amplitude is $a = \dfrac{1}{2}$ and the period is $\dfrac{2\pi}{b} = \dfrac{2\pi}{2} = \pi$.

Intercepts: $(0, 0)$; $\left(\dfrac{1}{2} \cdot \pi, 0\right) = \left(\dfrac{\pi}{2}, 0\right)$; $(\pi, 0)$

Maximum: $\left(\dfrac{1}{4} \cdot \pi, \dfrac{1}{2}\right) = \left(\dfrac{\pi}{4}, \dfrac{1}{2}\right)$

Minimum: $\left(\dfrac{3}{4} \cdot \pi, -\dfrac{1}{2}\right) = \left(\dfrac{3\pi}{4}, -\dfrac{1}{2}\right)$

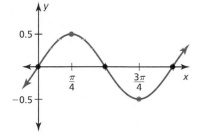

▶ The graph of g is a vertical shrink by a factor of $\dfrac{1}{2}$ and a horizontal shrink by a factor of $\dfrac{1}{2}$ of the graph of f.

Identify the amplitude and period of the function. Then graph the function and describe the graph of g as a transformation of the graph of the parent function.

16. $g(x) = 8 \cos x$

17. $g(x) = 6 \sin \pi x$

18. $g(x) = \dfrac{1}{4} \cos 4x$

Graph the function.

19. $g(x) = \cos(x + \pi) + 2$

20. $g(x) = -\sin x - 4$

21. $g(x) = 2 \sin\left(x + \dfrac{\pi}{2}\right)$

Graph one period of $g(x) = 7 \cot \pi x$. Describe the graph of g as a transformation of the graph of $f(x) = \cot x$.

The function is of the form $g(x) = a \cot bx$, where $a = 7$ and $b = \pi$. So, the period is $\dfrac{\pi}{|b|} = \dfrac{\pi}{\pi} = 1$.

Intercepts: $\left(\dfrac{\pi}{2b}, 0\right) = \left(\dfrac{\pi}{2\pi}, 0\right) = \left(\dfrac{1}{2}, 0\right)$

Asymptotes: $x = 0$; $x = \dfrac{\pi}{|b|} = \dfrac{\pi}{\pi}$, or $x = 1$

Halfway points: $\left(\dfrac{\pi}{4b}, a\right) = \left(\dfrac{1}{4}, 7\right)$; $\left(\dfrac{3\pi}{4b}, -a\right) = \left(\dfrac{3}{4}, -7\right)$

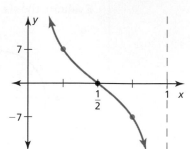

▶ The graph of g is a vertical stretch by a factor of 7 and a horizontal shrink by a factor of $\dfrac{1}{\pi}$ of the graph of f.

Graph one period of the function. Describe the graph of g as a transformation of the graph of its parent function.

22. $g(x) = 2 \cot x$ **23.** $g(x) = 4 \tan 3\pi x$ **24.** $g(x) = 5 \sec \pi x$ **25.** $g(x) = \dfrac{1}{2} \csc \dfrac{\pi}{4} x$

Write a function for the sinusoid shown.

Step 1 Find the maximum and minimum values. From the graph, the maximum value is 3 and the minimum value is -1.

Step 2 Identify the vertical shift: $k = \dfrac{3 + (-1)}{2} = \dfrac{2}{2} = 1$

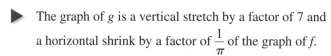

Step 3 Because the graph crosses the midline $y = 1$ on the y-axis and then decreases to its minimum value, the graph is a sine curve with a reflection in the x-axis and no horizontal shift. So, $h = 0$.

Step 4 Find the amplitude and period. The period is $\dfrac{2\pi}{3} = \dfrac{2\pi}{b}$. So, $b = 3$.

The amplitude is $|a| = \dfrac{(\text{maximum value}) - (\text{minimum value})}{2} = \dfrac{3 - (-1)}{2} = \dfrac{4}{2} = 2$.

Because the graph is a reflection in the x-axis, $a < 0$. So, $a = -2$.

▶ The function is $y = -2 \sin 3x + 1$.

Write a function for the sinusoid.

26.

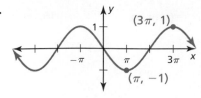

27.

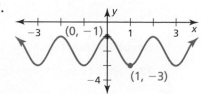

1. You put a reflector on a spoke of your bicycle wheel. The highest point of the reflector is 25 inches above the ground, and the lowest point is 2 inches. The reflector makes 1 revolution per second. Write a model for the height h (in inches) of a reflector as a function of time t (in seconds) given that the reflector is at its lowest point when $t = 0$.

2. Evaluate $\sec(-300°)$ without using a calculator.

Write a function for the sinusoid.

3.

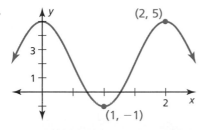

4.

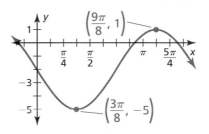

Graph the function. Then describe the graph of g as a transformation of the graph of its parent function.

5. $g(x) = -4 \tan 2x$

6. $g(x) = -2 \cos \frac{1}{3}x + 3$

7. $g(x) = 3 \csc \pi x$

Convert the degree measure to radians or the radian measure to degrees. Then find one positive angle and one negative angle that are coterminal with the given angle.

8. $-50°$

9. $\dfrac{4\pi}{5}$

10. $\dfrac{8\pi}{3}$

11. Find the arc length and area of a sector with radius $r = 13$ inches and central angle $\theta = 40°$.

Evaluate the six trigonometric functions of θ.

12.

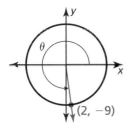

13.

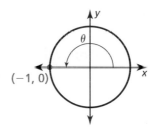

14. In which quadrant does the terminal side of θ lie when $\cos \theta < 0$ and $\tan \theta > 0$? Explain.

15. How tall is the building? Justify your answer.

16. The table shows the average daily high temperatures T (in degrees Fahrenheit) in Baltimore, Maryland, where $m = 1$ represents January. Write a model that gives T as a function of m and interpret the period of its graph.

m	1	2	3	4	5	6	7	8	9	10	11	12
T	41	45	54	65	74	83	87	85	78	67	56	45

1. Which statement describes the graph of $g(x) = \frac{1}{3} \cot 2\pi x$ as a transformation of the graph of $f(x) = \cot x$?

   (A) vertical shrink by a factor of $\frac{1}{3}$ and a horizontal shrink by a factor of $\frac{1}{2\pi}$

   (B) vertical shrink by a factor of $\frac{1}{3}$ and a horizontal shrink by a factor of 2π

   (C) vertical shrink by a factor of $\frac{1}{2\pi}$ and a horizontal shrink by a factor of $\frac{1}{3}$

   (D) vertical shrink by a factor of 2π and a horizontal shrink by a factor of $\frac{1}{3}$

2. Which rational expression represents the ratio of the perimeter to the area of the playground shown in the diagram?

   (A) $\frac{9}{7x}$

   (B) $\frac{11}{14x}$

   (C) $\frac{1}{x}$

   (D) $\frac{1}{2x}$

   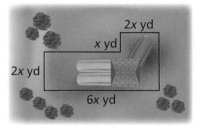

3. The chart shows the average monthly temperatures (in degrees Fahrenheit) and the gas usages (in cubic feet) of a household for 12 months.

January	February	March	April	May	June
32°F	21°F	15°F	22°F	35°F	49°F
20,000 ft³	27,000 ft³	23,000 ft³	22,000 ft³	21,000 ft³	14,000 ft³

July	August	September	October	November	December
62°F	78°F	71°F	63°F	55°F	40°F
8,000 ft³	9,000 ft³	13,000 ft³	15,000 ft³	19,000 ft³	23,000 ft³

   a. Use a graphing calculator to find trigonometric models for the average temperature y_1 as a function of time and the gas usage y_2 (in thousands of cubic feet) as a function of time. Let $t = 1$ represent January.

   b. Graph the two regression equations in the same coordinate plane on your graphing calculator. Describe the relationship between the graphs.

4. Evaluate each logarithm using $\log_2 5 \approx 2.322$ and $\log_2 3 \approx 1.585$, if necessary. Then order the logarithms by value from least to greatest.

   a. $\log 1000$

   b. $\log_2 15$

   c. $\ln e$

   d. $\log_2 9$

   e. $\log_2 \frac{5}{3}$

   f. $\log_2 1$

5. Which function is *not* represented by the graph?

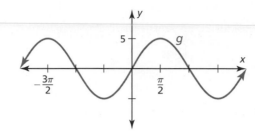

(A) $y = 5 \sin x$

(B) $y = 5 \cos\left(\dfrac{\pi}{2} - x\right)$

(C) $y = 5 \cos\left(x + \dfrac{\pi}{2}\right)$

(D) $y = -5 \sin(x + \pi)$

6. Complete each statement with $<$ or $>$ so that each statement is true.

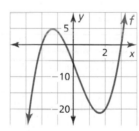

a. θ ⬚ 3 radians

b. $\tan \theta$ ⬚ 0

c. θ' ⬚ $45°$

7. Use the Rational Root Theorem and the graph to find all the real zeros of the function $f(x) = 2x^3 - x^2 - 13x - 6$.

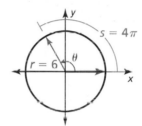

8. Your friend claims $-210°$ is coterminal with the angle $\dfrac{5\pi}{6}$. Is your friend correct? Explain your reasoning.

9. Company A and Company B offer the same starting annual salary of \$20,000. Company A gives a \$1000 raise each year. Company B gives a 4% raise each year.

a. Write rules giving the salaries a_n and b_n for your nth year of employment at Company A and Company B, respectively. Tell whether the sequence represented by each rule is *arithmetic*, *geometric*, or *neither*.

b. Graph each sequence in the same coordinate plane.

c. Under what conditions would you choose to work for Company B?

d. After 20 years of employment, compare your total earnings.

9 Trigonometric Identities and Formulas

Zip Line *(p. 497)*

SEE the Big Idea

Step Angle *(p. 495)*

Observation Deck *(p. 491)*

Leaning Tower of Pisa *(p. 491)*

Sundial *(p. 476)*

Maintaining Mathematical Proficiency

Solving Proportions

Example 1   Solve $\dfrac{6}{2x + 7} = \dfrac{15}{26}$.

$$\dfrac{6}{2x + 7} = \dfrac{15}{26} \qquad \text{Write the proportion.}$$

$$6 \cdot 26 = (2x + 7) \cdot 15 \qquad \text{Cross Products Property}$$

$$156 = 30x + 105 \qquad \text{Multiply.}$$

$$1.7 = x \qquad \text{Solve for } x.$$

Solve the proportion.

1. $\dfrac{3x - 5}{10} = \dfrac{13}{25}$

2. $\dfrac{9}{32} = \dfrac{1 + 5x}{8}$

3. $\dfrac{4}{21} = \dfrac{16}{8x + 7}$

4. $\dfrac{5}{18 - 6x} = \dfrac{2}{11}$

5. $\dfrac{18}{x} = \dfrac{x}{2}$

6. $\dfrac{x}{10} = \dfrac{40}{x}$

Solving Right Triangles

Example 2   Solve $\triangle ABC$.

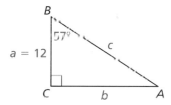

Because the triangle is a right triangle, A and B are complementary angles. So, $A = 90° - 57° = 33°$.

Write two equations, one that involves the ratio of b and 12, and one that involves the ratio of c and 12. Solve the first equation for b and the second equation for c.

$\tan 57° = \dfrac{\text{opp.}}{\text{adj.}}$	Write trigonometric equation.	$\sec 57° = \dfrac{\text{hyp.}}{\text{adj.}}$
$\tan 57° = \dfrac{b}{12}$	Substitute.	$\sec 57° = \dfrac{c}{12}$
$12(\tan 57°) = b$	Solve for the variable.	$12\left(\dfrac{1}{\cos 57°}\right) = c$
$18.48 \approx b$	Use a calculator.	$22.03 \approx c$

▶ So, $A = 33°$, $b \approx 18.48$, and $c \approx 22.03$.

Solve $\triangle ABC$ using the diagram and the given measurements.

7. $B = 73°$, $c = 9$

8. $B = 35°$, $a = 12$

9. $A = 42°$, $c = 16$

10. $A = 29°$, $b = 40.5$

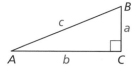

11. ABSTRACT REASONING You know that $\tan A = \dfrac{x}{y}$ in a right triangle. Can you determine the value of $\sec A$ without finding the angle measure of A? Explain.

Mathematical Practices

Mathematically proficient students use technology tools to explore concepts.

Using a Graphing Calculator

⑤ Core Concept

Using Graphs to Find Trigonometric Identities

A trigonometric equation that is true for all values of the variable for which both sides of the equation are defined is called a **trigonometric identity**. You can use graphs of trigonometric functions to help you write and verify trigonometric identities. For example, knowing whether a trigonometric function is *even* or *odd* can help you write a trigonometric identity.

Recall that a function f is an *even function* when $f(-x) = f(x)$ for all x in its domain. The graph of an even function is *symmetric about the y-axis*. A function f is an *odd function* when $f(-x) = -f(x)$ for all x in its domain. The graph of an odd function is *symmetric about the origin*.

EXAMPLE 1 **Writing a Trigonometric Identity**

Use a graphing calculator to graph $f(x) = \cos x$. Determine whether f is *even* or *odd* and then use the corresponding definition to write a trigonometric identity.

SOLUTION

Graph the function. Notice that the graph appears to be symmetric about the y-axis. Use a table of values to confirm this symmetry.

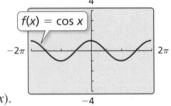

Because the graph is symmetric about the y-axis, f is even, meaning that $f(-x) = f(x)$. Use this equation to write an identity.

$f(-x) = f(x)$ Definition of an even function

$\cos(-x) = \cos x$ Substitute using $f(x) = \cos x$.

Notice that you can confirm your identity by observing that the graphs of $y = \cos(-x)$ and $y = \cos x$ coincide.

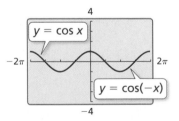

▶ So, $f(x) = \cos x$ is an even function and $\cos(-x) = \cos x$.

Monitoring Progress

Use a graphing calculator to graph the function. Determine whether the function is *even* or *odd* and then use the corresponding definition to write a trigonometric identity.

1. $f(x) = \sin x$ 2. $f(x) = \tan x$ 3. $f(x) = \sec x$

4. Use a graphing calculator to graph $f(x) = \sin^2 x + \cos^2 x$. What do you notice? Use your observation to write a trigonometric identity.

Essential Question How can you verify a trigonometric identity?

EXPLORATION 1 **Writing a Trigonometric Identity**

Work with a partner. In the figure, (x, y) is on a circle of radius c with center at the origin.

a. Write an equation that relates a, b, and c.

b. Write expressions for the sine and cosine ratios of angle θ.

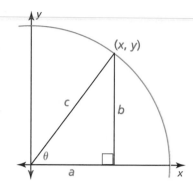

c. Use the results from parts (a) and (b) to find the sum of $\sin^2 \theta$ and $\cos^2 \theta$.

d. Use a table to verify that the identity you wrote in part (c) is valid for angles in each of the four quadrants.

e. The trigonometric identity you derived in part (c) is called a *Pythagorean identity*. There are two other Pythagorean identities. Divide each side of the identity in part (c) by $\cos^2 \theta$ and simplify. Divide each side of the identity in part (c) by $\sin^2 \theta$ and simplify.

REASONING ABSTRACTLY

To be proficient in math, you need to know and flexibly use different properties of operations and objects.

EXPLORATION 2 **Writing Cofunction Identities**

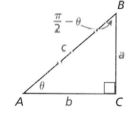

Work with a partner. Use the figure at the left. Recall that the two acute angles of a right triangle are complementary. Given the radian measure of one of the acute angles of a right triangle is θ, the measure of the other must be $\dfrac{\pi}{2} - \theta$.

a. Write expressions for the six trigonometric functions of the angle θ and of the angle $\dfrac{\pi}{2} - \theta$.

b. Which expressions in part (a) are equivalent? Use the results to write trigonometric identities for the six trigonometric functions of the angle $\dfrac{\pi}{2} - \theta$.

EXPLORATION 3 **Writing Negative Angle Identities**

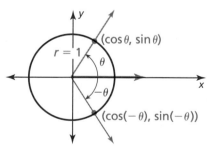

Work with a partner. Use the figure at the left.

a. Describe the transformation of the point $(\cos \theta, \sin \theta)$ that results from replacing θ with $-\theta$. Explain your reasoning.

b. Use the coordinate rule for the transformation you described in part (a) to write trigonometric identities for $\cos(-\theta)$ and $\sin(-\theta)$.

c. Use the results of part (b) to write trigonometric identities for the remaining four trigonometric functions of the angle $-\theta$.

Communicate Your Answer

4. How can you verify a trigonometric identity?

5. Is $\sin \theta = \cos \theta$ a trigonometric identity? Explain your reasoning.

What You Will Learn

▶ Use trigonometric identities to evaluate trigonometric functions and simplify trigonometric expressions.

▶ Verify trigonometric identities.

Using Trigonometric Identities

Recall that when an angle θ is in standard position with its terminal side intersecting the unit circle at (x, y), then $x = \cos\theta$ and $y = \sin\theta$. Because (x, y) is on a circle centered at the origin with radius 1, it follows that

$$x^2 + y^2 = 1$$

and

$$\cos^2\theta + \sin^2\theta = 1.$$

STUDY TIP

Note that $\sin^2\theta$ represents $(\sin\theta)^2$ and $\cos^2\theta$ represents $(\cos\theta)^2$.

The equation $\cos^2\theta + \sin^2\theta = 1$ is true for any value of θ. A trigonometric equation that is true for all values of the variable for which both sides of the equation are defined is called a **trigonometric identity**. In Section 8.1, you used reciprocal identities to find the values of the cosecant, secant, and cotangent functions. These and other fundamental trigonometric identities are listed below.

Core Concept

Fundamental Trigonometric Identities

Reciprocal Identities

$$\sin\theta = \frac{1}{\csc\theta} \qquad \cos\theta = \frac{1}{\sec\theta} \qquad \tan\theta = \frac{1}{\cot\theta}$$

$$\csc\theta = \frac{1}{\sin\theta} \qquad \sec\theta = \frac{1}{\cos\theta} \qquad \cot\theta = \frac{1}{\tan\theta}$$

Tangent and Cotangent Identities

$$\tan\theta = \frac{\sin\theta}{\cos\theta} \qquad \cot\theta = \frac{\cos\theta}{\sin\theta}$$

Pythagorean Identities

$$\sin^2\theta + \cos^2\theta = 1 \qquad 1 + \tan^2\theta = \sec^2\theta \qquad 1 + \cot^2\theta = \csc^2\theta$$

Cofunction Identities

$$\sin\!\left(\frac{\pi}{2} - \theta\right) = \cos\theta \qquad \cos\!\left(\frac{\pi}{2} - \theta\right) = \sin\theta \qquad \tan\!\left(\frac{\pi}{2} - \theta\right) = \cot\theta$$

$$\csc\!\left(\frac{\pi}{2} - \theta\right) = \sec\theta \qquad \sec\!\left(\frac{\pi}{2} - \theta\right) = \csc\theta \qquad \cot\!\left(\frac{\pi}{2} - \theta\right) = \tan\theta$$

Negative Angle Identities

$$\sin(-\theta) = -\sin\theta \qquad \cos(-\theta) = \cos\theta \qquad \tan(-\theta) = -\tan\theta$$

$$\csc(-\theta) = -\csc\theta \qquad \sec(-\theta) = \sec\theta \qquad \cot(-\theta) = -\cot\theta$$

EXAMPLE 1 Finding Trigonometric Values

Given that $\sin \theta = \dfrac{4}{5}$ and $\dfrac{\pi}{2} < \theta < \pi$, find the values of the other five trigonometric functions of θ.

SOLUTION

Step 1 Find $\cos \theta$.

$$\sin^2 \theta + \cos^2 \theta = 1 \qquad \text{Write Pythagorean identity.}$$

$$\left(\dfrac{4}{5}\right)^2 + \cos^2 \theta = 1 \qquad \text{Substitute } \dfrac{4}{5} \text{ for } \sin \theta.$$

$$\cos^2 \theta = 1 - \left(\dfrac{4}{5}\right)^2 \qquad \text{Subtract } \left(\dfrac{4}{5}\right)^2 \text{ from each side.}$$

$$\cos^2 \theta = \dfrac{9}{25} \qquad \text{Simplify.}$$

$$\cos \theta = \pm\dfrac{3}{5} \qquad \text{Take square root of each side.}$$

$$\cos \theta - \dfrac{3}{5} \qquad \text{Because } \theta \text{ is in Quadrant II, } \cos \theta \text{ is negative.}$$

Step 2 Find the values of the other four trigonometric functions of θ using the values of $\sin \theta$ and $\cos \theta$.

$$\tan \theta = \dfrac{\sin \theta}{\cos \theta} = \dfrac{\frac{4}{5}}{-\frac{3}{5}} = -\dfrac{4}{3} \qquad \cot \theta = \dfrac{\cos \theta}{\sin \theta} = \dfrac{-\frac{3}{5}}{\frac{4}{5}} = -\dfrac{3}{4}$$

$$\csc \theta = \dfrac{1}{\sin \theta} = \dfrac{1}{\frac{4}{5}} = \dfrac{5}{4} \qquad \sec \theta = \dfrac{1}{\cos \theta} = \dfrac{1}{\frac{3}{5}} = -\dfrac{5}{3}$$

EXAMPLE 2 Simplifying Trigonometric Expressions

Simplify (a) $\tan\left(\dfrac{\pi}{2} - \theta\right)\sin \theta$ and (b) $\sec \theta \tan^2 \theta + \sec \theta$.

SOLUTION

a. $\tan\left(\dfrac{\pi}{2} - \theta\right)\sin \theta = \cot \theta \sin \theta$ ⟶ Cofunction identity

$= \left(\dfrac{\cos \theta}{\sin \theta}\right)(\sin \theta)$ ⟶ Cotangent identity

$= \cos \theta$ ⟶ Simplify.

b. $\sec \theta \tan^2 \theta + \sec \theta = \sec \theta(\sec^2 \theta - 1) + \sec \theta$ ⟶ Pythagorean identity

$= \sec^3 \theta - \sec \theta + \sec \theta$ ⟶ Distributive Property

$= \sec^3 \theta$ ⟶ Simplify.

Monitoring Progress Help in English and Spanish at *BigIdeasMath.com*

1. Given that $\cos \theta = \dfrac{1}{6}$ and $0 < \theta < \dfrac{\pi}{2}$, find the values of the other five trigonometric functions of θ.

Simplify the expression.

2. $\sin x \cot x \sec x$

3. $\cos \theta - \cos \theta \sin^2 \theta$

4. $\dfrac{\sec^2 x - \tan^2 x}{\cos(-x)\tan x}$

Verifying Trigonometric Identities

You can use the fundamental identities you have already learned to verify new trigonometric identities. When verifying an identity, begin with the expression on one side. Use algebra and trigonometric properties to manipulate the expression until it is identical to the other side.

EXAMPLE 3 Verifying a Trigonometric Identity

Verify the identity $\dfrac{\sec^2 \theta - 1}{\sec^2 \theta} = \sin^2 \theta$.

SOLUTION

$$\frac{\sec^2 \theta - 1}{\sec^2 \theta} = \frac{\sec^2 \theta}{\sec^2 \theta} - \frac{1}{\sec^2 \theta} \qquad \text{Write as separate fractions.}$$

$$= 1 - \left(\frac{1}{\sec \theta}\right)^2 \qquad \text{Simplify.}$$

$$= 1 - \cos^2 \theta \qquad \text{Reciprocal identity}$$

$$= \sin^2 \theta \qquad \text{Pythagorean identity}$$

Notice that verifying an identity is not the same as solving an equation. When verifying an identity, you cannot assume that the two sides of the equation are equal because you are trying to verify that they are equal. So, you cannot use any properties of equality, such as adding the same quantity to each side of the equation.

EXAMPLE 4 Verifying a Trigonometric Identity

Verify the identity $\sec x + \tan x = \dfrac{\cos x}{1 - \sin x}$.

LOOKING FOR STRUCTURE

To verify the identity, you must introduce $1 - \sin x$ into the denominator. Multiply the numerator and the denominator by $1 - \sin x$ so you get an equivalent expression.

SOLUTION

$$\sec x + \tan x = \frac{1}{\cos x} + \tan x \qquad \text{Reciprocal identity}$$

$$= \frac{1}{\cos x} + \frac{\sin x}{\cos x} \qquad \text{Tangent identity}$$

$$= \frac{1 + \sin x}{\cos x} \qquad \text{Add fractions.}$$

$$= \frac{1 + \sin x}{\cos x} \cdot \frac{1 - \sin x}{1 - \sin x} \qquad \text{Multiply by } \frac{1 - \sin x}{1 - \sin x}.$$

$$= \frac{1 - \sin^2 x}{\cos x(1 - \sin x)} \qquad \text{Simplify numerator.}$$

$$= \frac{\cos^2 x}{\cos x(1 - \sin x)} \qquad \text{Pythagorean identity}$$

$$= \frac{\cos x}{1 - \sin x} \qquad \text{Simplify.}$$

Monitoring Progress Help in English and Spanish at *BigIdeasMath.com*

Verify the identity.

5. $\cos \theta \cot\left(\dfrac{\pi}{2} - \theta\right) = \sin \theta$

6. $\dfrac{\csc^2 x - \cot^2 x}{\cos x \tan(-x)} = -\csc x$

7. $\csc^2 x(1 - \sin^2 x) = \cot^2 x$

8. $(\tan^2 x + 1)(\cos^2 x - 1) = -\tan^2 x$

Vocabulary and Core Concept Check

1. **WRITING** Describe the difference between a trigonometric identity and a trigonometric equation.

2. **WHICH ONE DOESN'T BELONG?** Which trigonometric expression does *not* belong with the other three? Explain your reasoning.

$$\cos\left(\frac{\pi}{2} - \theta\right)$$ $$\sin(-\theta)$$ $$\cos(-\theta)\tan\theta$$ $$\frac{1}{\csc\theta}$$

Monitoring Progress and Modeling with Mathematics

In Exercises 3–10, find the values of the other five trigonometric functions of θ. *(See Example 1.)*

3. $\sin\theta = \dfrac{1}{3}, 0 < \theta < \dfrac{\pi}{2}$

4. $\sin\theta = -\dfrac{7}{10}, \pi < \theta < \dfrac{3\pi}{2}$

5. $\tan\theta = -\dfrac{3}{7}, \dfrac{\pi}{2} < \theta < \pi$

6. $\cot\theta = -\dfrac{2}{5}, \dfrac{\pi}{2} < \theta < \pi$

7. $\cos\theta = -\dfrac{5}{6}, \pi < \theta < \dfrac{3\pi}{2}$

8. $\sec\theta = \dfrac{9}{4}, \dfrac{3\pi}{2} < \theta < 2\pi$

9. $\cot\theta = -3, \dfrac{3\pi}{2} < \theta < 2\pi$

10. $\csc\theta = -\dfrac{5}{3}, \pi < \theta < \dfrac{3\pi}{2}$

In Exercises 11–22, simplify the expression. *(See Example 2.)*

11. $\sin x \cot x$

12. $\cos\theta(1 + \tan^2\theta)$

13. $\dfrac{\sin(-\theta)}{\cos(-\theta)}$

14. $\dfrac{\cos^2 x}{\cot^2 x}$

15. $\dfrac{\sin x + \cos x}{1 - \tan(-x)}$

16. $\sin\left(\dfrac{\pi}{2} - \theta\right)\sec\theta$

17. $\cot(-x)\csc\left(\dfrac{\pi}{2} - x\right)$

18. $\cos\theta\sec(-\theta)$

19. $\dfrac{\csc^2 x - \cot^2 x}{\sin(-x)\cot x}$

20. $\dfrac{\cos^2 x \tan^2(-x) - 1}{\cos^2 x}$

21. $\dfrac{\cos\left(\dfrac{\pi}{2} - \theta\right)}{\csc\theta} + \cos^2\theta$

22. $\dfrac{\sec x \sin x + \cos\left(\dfrac{\pi}{2} - x\right)}{1 + \sec x}$

23. **ERROR ANALYSIS** Describe and correct the error in simplifying the expression.

> ✗ $1 - \sin^2\theta = 1 - (1 + \cos^2\theta)$
> $= 1 - 1 - \cos^2\theta$
> $= -\cos^2\theta$

24. **REASONING** Explain how you can use a graphing calculator to determine which of the six trigonometric functions is equal to $\cot x \cos x + \sin x$.

In Exercises 25–34, verify the identity. *(See Examples 3 and 4.)*

25. $\sin x \csc x = 1$

26. $\tan\theta \csc\theta \cos\theta = 1$

27. $\cos\left(\dfrac{\pi}{2} - x\right)\cot x = \cos x$

28. $\tan x + \tan\left(\dfrac{\pi}{2} - x\right) = \csc x \sec x$

29. $\dfrac{\cos\left(\dfrac{\pi}{2} - \theta\right) + 1}{1 - \sin(-\theta)} = 1$

30. $\dfrac{\sin^2(-x)}{\tan^2 x} = \cos^2 x$

31. $\dfrac{1 + \cos x}{\sin x} + \dfrac{\sin x}{1 + \cos x} = 2\csc x$

32. $\dfrac{\sin x}{1 - \cos(-x)} = \csc x + \cot x$

33. $\dfrac{2\sin\theta + \csc(-\theta)}{1 - \cot^2\theta} = \sin\theta$

34. $\dfrac{2\cos\theta - \sec(-\theta)}{1 - \tan^2\theta} = \cos\theta$

35. **USING STRUCTURE** A function f is *odd* when $f(-x) = -f(x)$. A function f is *even* when $f(-x) = f(x)$. Which of the six trigonometric functions are odd? Which are even? Justify your answers using identities and graphs.

36. **ANALYZING RELATIONSHIPS** As the value of $\cos \theta$ increases, what happens to the value of $\sec \theta$? Explain your reasoning.

37. **MAKING AN ARGUMENT** Your friend simplifies an expression and obtains $\sec x \tan x - \sin x$. You simplify the same expression and obtain $\sin x \tan^2 x$. Are your answers equivalent? Justify your answer.

38. **HOW DO YOU SEE IT?** The figure shows the unit circle and the angle θ.

    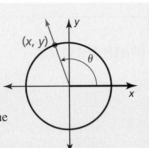

    a. Is $\sin \theta$ positive or negative? $\cos \theta$? $\tan \theta$?

    b. In what quadrant does the terminal side of $-\theta$ lie?

    c. Is $\sin(-\theta)$ positive or negative? $\cos(-\theta)$? $\tan(-\theta)$?

39. **MODELING WITH MATHEMATICS** A vertical *gnomon* (the part of a sundial that projects a shadow) has height h. The length s of the shadow cast by the gnomon when the angle of the Sun above the horizon is θ can be modeled by the equation below. Show that the equation below is equivalent to $s = h \cot \theta$.

    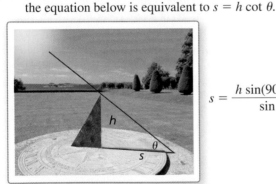

    $$s = \frac{h \sin(90° - \theta)}{\sin \theta}$$

40. **THOUGHT PROVOKING** Explain how you can use a trigonometric identity to find all the values of x for which $\sin x = \cos x$.

41. **DRAWING CONCLUSIONS** *Static friction* is the amount of force necessary to keep a stationary object on a flat surface from moving. Suppose a book weighing W pounds is lying on a ramp inclined at an angle θ. The coefficient of static friction u for the book can be found using the equation $uW \cos \theta = W \sin \theta$.

    a. Solve the equation for u and simplify the result.

    b. Use the equation from part (a) to determine what happens to the value of u as the angle θ increases from $0°$ to $90°$.

42. **PROBLEM SOLVING** When light traveling in a medium (such as air) strikes the surface of a second medium (such as water) at an angle θ_1, the light begins to travel at a different angle θ_2. This change of direction is defined by Snell's law, $n_1 \sin \theta_1 = n_2 \sin \theta_2$, where n_1 and n_2 are the *indices of refraction* for the two mediums. Snell's law can be derived from the equation

    $$\frac{n_1}{\sqrt{\cot^2 \theta_1 + 1}} = \frac{n_2}{\sqrt{\cot^2 \theta_2 + 1}}.$$

    a. Simplify the equation to derive Snell's law.

    b. What is the value of n_1 when $\theta_1 = 55°$, $\theta_2 = 35°$, and $n_2 = 2$?

    c. If $\theta_1 = \theta_2$, then what must be true about the values of n_1 and n_2? Explain when this situation would occur.

43. **WRITING** Explain how transformations of the graph of the parent function $f(x) = \sin x$ support the cofunction identity $\sin\left(\dfrac{\pi}{2} - \theta\right) = \cos \theta$.

44. **USING STRUCTURE** Verify each identity.

    a. $\ln|\sec \theta| = -\ln|\cos \theta|$

    b. $\ln|\tan \theta| = \ln|\sin \theta| - \ln|\cos \theta|$

Maintaining Mathematical Proficiency
Reviewing what you learned in previous grades and lessons

Evaluate the function without using a calculator. *(Section 8.3)*

45. $\sin(-210°)$

46. $\tan \dfrac{4\pi}{3}$

47. $\csc 135°$

48. $\cos\left(-\dfrac{13\pi}{6}\right)$

49. Describe the transformation of the graph of $f(x) = \sin x$ represented by the function $g(x) = 3 \sin 4x - 1$. *(Section 8.4)*

9.2 Using Sum and Difference Formulas

Essential Question How can you evaluate trigonometric functions of the sum or difference of two angles?

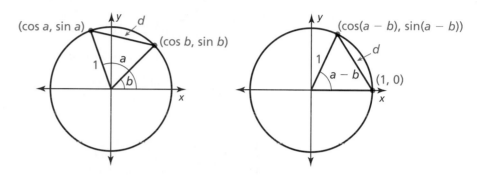

b. Use the Distance Formula to write an expression for d in the first unit circle.

c. Use the Distance Formula to write an expression for d in the second unit circle.

d. Write an equation that relates the expressions in parts (b) and (c). Then simplify this equation to obtain a formula for $\cos(a - b)$.

EXPLORATION 2 Deriving a Sum Formula

Work with a partner. Use the difference formula you derived in Exploration 1 to write a formula for $\cos(a + b)$ in terms of sine and cosine of a and b. *Hint*: Use the fact that

$$\cos(a + b) = \cos[a - (-b)].$$

EXPLORATION 3 Deriving Difference and Sum Formulas

Work with a partner. Use the formulas you derived in Explorations 1 and 2 to write formulas for $\sin(a - b)$ and $\sin(a + b)$ in terms of sine and cosine of a and b. *Hint*: Use the cofunction identities

$$\sin\left(\frac{\pi}{2} - a\right) = \cos a \text{ and } \cos\left(\frac{\pi}{2} - a\right) = \sin a$$

and the fact that

$$\cos\left[\left(\frac{\pi}{2} - a\right) + b\right] = \sin(a - b) \text{ and } \sin(a + b) = \sin[a - (-b)].$$

Communicate Your Answer

4. How can you evaluate trigonometric functions of the sum or difference of two angles?

5. a. Find the exact values of $\sin 75°$ and $\cos 75°$ using sum formulas. Explain your reasoning.

   b. Find the exact values of $\sin 75°$ and $\cos 75°$ using difference formulas. Compare your answers to those in part (a).

CONSTRUCTING VIABLE ARGUMENTS

To be proficient in math, you need to understand and use stated assumptions, definitions, and previously established results.

Core Vocabulary

Previous
ratio

What You Will Learn

▶ Use sum and difference formulas to evaluate and simplify trigonometric expressions.

▶ Use sum and difference formulas to solve trigonometric equations and rewrite real-life formulas.

Using Sum and Difference Formulas

In this lesson, you will study formulas that allow you to evaluate trigonometric functions of the sum or difference of two angles.

Core Concept

Sum and Difference Formulas

Sum Formulas	Difference Formulas
$\sin(a + b) = \sin a \cos b + \cos a \sin b$	$\sin(a - b) = \sin a \cos b - \cos a \sin b$
$\cos(a + b) = \cos a \cos b - \sin a \sin b$	$\cos(a - b) = \cos a \cos b + \sin a \sin b$
$\tan(a + b) = \dfrac{\tan a + \tan b}{1 - \tan a \tan b}$	$\tan(a - b) = \dfrac{\tan a - \tan b}{1 + \tan a \tan b}$

In general, $\sin(a + b) \neq \sin a + \sin b$. Similar statements can be made for the other trigonometric functions of sums and differences.

EXAMPLE 1 Evaluating Trigonometric Expressions

Find the exact value of (a) $\sin 15°$ and (b) $\tan \dfrac{7\pi}{12}$.

SOLUTION

Check

```
sin(15°)
            .2588190451
(√(6)-√(2))/4
            .2588190451
```

a. $\sin 15° = \sin(60° - 45°)$ ⟶ Substitute $60° - 45°$ for $15°$.

$\quad = \sin 60° \cos 45° - \cos 60° \sin 45°$ ⟶ Difference formula for sine

$\quad = \dfrac{\sqrt{3}}{2}\left(\dfrac{\sqrt{2}}{2}\right) - \dfrac{1}{2}\left(\dfrac{\sqrt{2}}{2}\right)$ ⟶ Evaluate.

$\quad = \dfrac{\sqrt{6} - \sqrt{2}}{4}$ ⟶ Simplify.

▶ The exact value of $\sin 15°$ is $\dfrac{\sqrt{6} - \sqrt{2}}{4}$. Check this with a calculator.

Check

```
tan(7π/12)
            -3.732050808
-2-√(3)
            -3.732050808
```

b. $\tan \dfrac{7\pi}{12} = \tan\left(\dfrac{\pi}{3} + \dfrac{\pi}{4}\right)$ ⟶ Substitute $\dfrac{\pi}{3} + \dfrac{\pi}{4}$ for $\dfrac{7\pi}{12}$.

$\quad = \dfrac{\tan \dfrac{\pi}{3} + \tan \dfrac{\pi}{4}}{1 - \tan \dfrac{\pi}{3} \tan \dfrac{\pi}{4}}$ ⟶ Sum formula for tangent

$\quad = \dfrac{\sqrt{3} + 1}{1 - \sqrt{3} \cdot 1}$ ⟶ Evaluate.

$\quad = -2 - \sqrt{3}$ ⟶ Simplify.

▶ The exact value of $\tan \dfrac{7\pi}{12}$ is $-2 - \sqrt{3}$. Check this with a calculator.

ANOTHER WAY

You can also use a Pythagorean identity and quadrant signs to find $\sin a$ and $\cos b$.

EXAMPLE 2 Using a Difference Formula

Find $\cos(a - b)$ given that $\cos a = -\dfrac{4}{5}$ with $\pi < a < \dfrac{3\pi}{2}$ and $\sin b = \dfrac{5}{13}$ with $0 < b < \dfrac{\pi}{2}$.

SOLUTION

Step 1 Find $\sin a$ and $\cos b$.

Because $\cos a = -\dfrac{4}{5}$ and a is in Quadrant III, $\sin a = -\dfrac{3}{5}$, as shown in the figure.

Because $\sin b = \dfrac{5}{13}$ and b is in Quadrant I, $\cos b = \dfrac{12}{13}$, as shown in the figure.

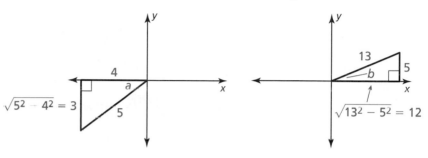

Step 2 Use the difference formula for cosine to find $\cos(a - b)$.

$$\cos(a - b) = \cos a \cos b + \sin a \sin b \qquad \text{Difference formula for cosine}$$

$$= -\frac{4}{5}\left(\frac{12}{13}\right) + \left(-\frac{3}{5}\right)\left(\frac{5}{13}\right) \qquad \text{Evaluate.}$$

$$= -\frac{63}{65} \qquad \text{Simplify.}$$

▶ The value of $\cos(a - b)$ is $-\dfrac{63}{65}$.

EXAMPLE 3 Simplifying an Expression

Simplify the expression $\cos(x + \pi)$.

SOLUTION

$$\cos(x + \pi) = \cos x \cos \pi - \sin x \sin \pi \qquad \text{Sum formula for cosine}$$

$$= (\cos x)(-1) - (\sin x)(0) \qquad \text{Evaluate.}$$

$$= -\cos x \qquad \text{Simplify.}$$

Monitoring Progress 🔊 Help in English and Spanish at *BigIdeasMath.com*

Find the exact value of the expression.

1. $\sin 105°$

2. $\cos 15°$

3. $\tan \dfrac{5\pi}{12}$

4. $\cos \dfrac{\pi}{12}$

5. Find $\sin(a - b)$ given that $\sin a = \dfrac{8}{17}$ with $0 < a < \dfrac{\pi}{2}$ and $\cos b = -\dfrac{24}{25}$ with $\pi < b < \dfrac{3\pi}{2}$.

Simplify the expression.

6. $\sin(x + \pi)$

7. $\cos(x - 2\pi)$

8. $\tan(x - \pi)$

Solving Equations and Rewriting Formulas

EXAMPLE 4   Solving a Trigonometric Equation

Solve $\sin\left(x + \dfrac{\pi}{3}\right) + \sin\left(x - \dfrac{\pi}{3}\right) = 1$ for $0 \le x < 2\pi$.

SOLUTION

$$\sin\left(x + \frac{\pi}{3}\right) + \sin\left(x - \frac{\pi}{3}\right) = 1 \qquad \text{Write equation.}$$

$$\sin x \cos\frac{\pi}{3} + \cos x \sin\frac{\pi}{3} + \sin x \cos\frac{\pi}{3} - \cos x \sin\frac{\pi}{3} = 1 \qquad \text{Use formulas.}$$

$$\frac{1}{2}\sin x + \frac{\sqrt{3}}{2}\cos x + \frac{1}{2}\sin x - \frac{\sqrt{3}}{2}\cos x = 1 \qquad \text{Evaluate.}$$

$$\sin x = 1 \qquad \text{Simplify.}$$

▶ In the interval $0 \le x < 2\pi$, the solution is $x = \dfrac{\pi}{2}$.

ANOTHER WAY

You can also solve the equation by using a graphing calculator. First, graph each side of the original equation. Then use the *intersect* feature to find the *x*-value(s) where the expressions are equal.

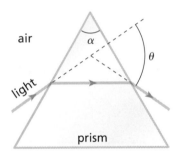

air

light

prism

α

θ

EXAMPLE 5   Rewriting a Real-Life Formula

The *index of refraction* of a transparent material is the ratio of the speed of light in a vacuum to the speed of light in the material. A triangular prism, like the one shown, can be used to measure the index of refraction using the formula

$$n = \frac{\sin\left(\dfrac{\theta}{2} + \dfrac{\alpha}{2}\right)}{\sin\dfrac{\theta}{2}}.$$

For $\alpha = 60°$, show that the formula can be rewritten as $n = \dfrac{\sqrt{3}}{2} + \dfrac{1}{2}\cot\dfrac{\theta}{2}$.

SOLUTION

$$n = \frac{\sin\left(\dfrac{\theta}{2} + 30°\right)}{\sin\dfrac{\theta}{2}} \qquad \text{Write formula with } \frac{\alpha}{2} = \frac{60°}{2} = 30°.$$

$$= \frac{\sin\dfrac{\theta}{2}\cos 30° + \cos\dfrac{\theta}{2}\sin 30°}{\sin\dfrac{\theta}{2}} \qquad \text{Sum formula for sine}$$

$$= \frac{\left(\sin\dfrac{\theta}{2}\right)\left(\dfrac{\sqrt{3}}{2}\right) + \left(\cos\dfrac{\theta}{2}\right)\left(\dfrac{1}{2}\right)}{\sin\dfrac{\theta}{2}} \qquad \text{Evaluate.}$$

$$= \frac{\dfrac{\sqrt{3}}{2}\sin\dfrac{\theta}{2}}{\sin\dfrac{\theta}{2}} + \frac{\dfrac{1}{2}\cos\dfrac{\theta}{2}}{\sin\dfrac{\theta}{2}} \qquad \text{Write as separate fractions.}$$

$$= \frac{\sqrt{3}}{2} + \frac{1}{2}\cot\frac{\theta}{2} \qquad \text{Simplify.}$$

Monitoring Progress    Help in English and Spanish at *BigIdeasMath.com*

9. Solve $\sin\left(\dfrac{\pi}{4} - x\right) - \sin\left(x + \dfrac{\pi}{4}\right) = 1$ for $0 \le x < 2\pi$.

Vocabulary and Core Concept Check

1. **COMPLETE THE SENTENCE** Write the expression $\cos 130° \cos 40° - \sin 130° \sin 40°$ as the cosine of an angle.

2. **WRITING** Explain how to evaluate $\tan 75°$ using either the sum or difference formula for tangent.

Monitoring Progress and Modeling with Mathematics

In Exercises 3–10, find the exact value of the expression. *(See Example 1.)*

3. $\tan(-15°)$

4. $\tan 195°$

5. $\sin \dfrac{23\pi}{12}$

6. $\sin(-165°)$

7. $\cos 105°$

8. $\cos \dfrac{11\pi}{12}$

9. $\tan \dfrac{17\pi}{12}$

10. $\sin\left(-\dfrac{7\pi}{12}\right)$

In Exercises 11–16, evaluate the expression given that $\cos a = \dfrac{4}{5}$ **with** $0 < a < \dfrac{\pi}{2}$ **and** $\sin b = -\dfrac{15}{17}$ **with** $\dfrac{3\pi}{2} < b < 2\pi.$ *(See Example 2.)*

11. $\sin(a + b)$

12. $\sin(a - b)$

13. $\cos(a - b)$

14. $\cos(a + b)$

15. $\tan(a + b)$

16. $\tan(a - b)$

In Exercises 17–22, simplify the expression. *(See Example 3.)*

17. $\tan(x + \pi)$

18. $\cos\left(x - \dfrac{\pi}{2}\right)$

19. $\cos(x + 2\pi)$

20. $\tan(x - 2\pi)$

21. $\sin\left(x - \dfrac{3\pi}{2}\right)$

22. $\tan\left(x + \dfrac{\pi}{2}\right)$

ERROR ANALYSIS In Exercises 23 and 24, describe and correct the error in simplifying the expression.

23.
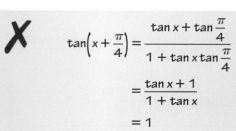

$$\tan\left(x + \dfrac{\pi}{4}\right) = \dfrac{\tan x + \tan \dfrac{\pi}{4}}{1 + \tan x \tan \dfrac{\pi}{4}}$$

$$= \dfrac{\tan x + 1}{1 + \tan x}$$

$$= 1$$

24.
$$\sin\left(x - \dfrac{\pi}{4}\right) = \sin \dfrac{\pi}{4} \cos x - \cos \dfrac{\pi}{4} \sin x$$

$$= \dfrac{\sqrt{2}}{2} \cos x - \dfrac{\sqrt{2}}{2} \sin x$$

$$= \dfrac{\sqrt{2}}{2}(\cos x - \sin x)$$

25. What are the solutions of the equation $2 \sin x - 1 = 0$ for $0 \le x < 2\pi$?

ⓐ $\dfrac{\pi}{3}$

Ⓑ $\dfrac{\pi}{6}$

Ⓒ $\dfrac{2\pi}{3}$

Ⓓ $\dfrac{5\pi}{6}$

26. What are the solutions of the equation $\tan x + 1 = 0$ for $0 \le x < 2\pi$?

ⓐ $\dfrac{\pi}{4}$

Ⓑ $\dfrac{3\pi}{4}$

Ⓒ $\dfrac{5\pi}{4}$

Ⓓ $\dfrac{7\pi}{4}$

In Exercises 27–32, solve the equation for $0 \le x < 2\pi.$ *(See Example 4.)*

27. $\sin\left(x + \dfrac{\pi}{2}\right) = \dfrac{1}{2}$

28. $\tan\left(x - \dfrac{\pi}{4}\right) = 0$

29. $\cos\left(x + \dfrac{\pi}{6}\right) - \cos\left(x - \dfrac{\pi}{6}\right) = 1$

30. $\sin\left(x + \dfrac{\pi}{4}\right) + \sin\left(x - \dfrac{\pi}{4}\right) = 0$

31. $\tan(x + \pi) - \tan(\pi - x) = 0$

32. $\sin(x + \pi) + \cos(x + \pi) = 0$

33. **USING EQUATIONS** Derive the cofunction identity $\sin\left(\dfrac{\pi}{2} - \theta\right) = \cos \theta$ using the difference formula for sine.

34. MAKING AN ARGUMENT Your friend claims it is possible to use the difference formula for tangent to derive the cofunction identity $\tan\left(\frac{\pi}{2} - \theta\right) = \cot\theta$. Is your friend correct? Explain your reasoning.

35. MODELING WITH MATHEMATICS A photographer is at a height h taking aerial photographs with a 35-millimeter camera. The ratio of the image length WQ to the length NA of the actual object is given by the formula

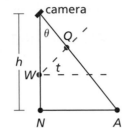

$$\frac{WQ}{NA} = \frac{35\tan(\theta - t) + 35\tan t}{h\tan\theta}$$

where θ is the angle between the vertical line perpendicular to the ground and the line from the camera to point A and t is the tilt angle of the film. When $t = 45°$, show that the formula can be rewritten as $\frac{WQ}{NA} = \frac{70}{h(1 + \tan\theta)}$. *(See Example 5.)*

36. MODELING WITH MATHEMATICS When a wave travels through a taut string, the displacement y of each point on the string depends on the time t and the point's position x. The equation of a *standing wave* can be obtained by adding the displacements of two waves traveling in opposite directions. Suppose a standing wave can be modeled by the formula

$$y = A\cos\left(\frac{2\pi t}{3} - \frac{2\pi x}{5}\right) + A\cos\left(\frac{2\pi t}{3} + \frac{2\pi x}{5}\right).$$

When $t = 1$, show that the formula can be rewritten as

$$y = -A\cos\frac{2\pi x}{5}.$$

37. MODELING WITH MATHEMATICS The busy signal on a touch-tone phone is a combination of two tones with frequencies of 480 hertz and 620 hertz. The individual tones can be modeled by the equations:

480 hertz: $y_1 = \cos 960\pi t$

620 hertz: $y_2 = \cos 1240\pi t$

The sound of the busy signal can be modeled by $y_1 + y_2$. Show that $y_1 + y_2 = 2\cos 1100\pi t \cos 140\pi t$.

38. HOW DO YOU SEE IT? Explain how to use the figure to solve the equation $\sin\left(x + \frac{\pi}{4}\right) - \sin\left(\frac{\pi}{4} - x\right) = 0$ for $0 \le x < 2\pi$.

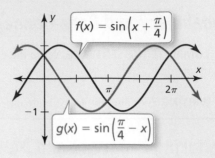

39. MATHEMATICAL CONNECTIONS The figure shows the acute angle of intersection, $\theta_2 - \theta_1$, of two lines with slopes m_1 and m_2.

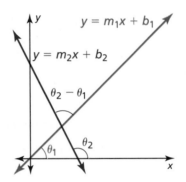

a. Use the difference formula for tangent to write an equation for $\tan(\theta_2 - \theta_1)$ in terms of m_1 and m_2.

b. Use the equation from part (a) to find the acute angle of intersection of the lines $y = x - 1$ and $y = \left(\frac{1}{\sqrt{3} - 2}\right)x + \frac{4 - \sqrt{3}}{2 - \sqrt{3}}$.

40. THOUGHT PROVOKING Rewrite each function. Justify your answers.

a. Write $\sin 3x$ as a function of $\sin x$.

b. Write $\cos 3x$ as a function of $\cos x$.

c. Write $\tan 3x$ as a function of $\tan x$.

Maintaining Mathematical Proficiency Reviewing what you learned in previous grades and lessons

Solve the equation. Check your solution(s). *(Section 6.5)*

41. $1 - \dfrac{9}{x - 2} = -\dfrac{7}{2}$

42. $\dfrac{12}{x} + \dfrac{3}{4} = \dfrac{8}{x}$

43. $\dfrac{2x - 3}{x + 1} = \dfrac{10}{x^2 - 1} + 5$

9.1–9.2 What Did You Learn?

Core Vocabulary

trigonometric identity, *p. 472*

Core Concepts

Section 9.1
Fundamental Trigonometric Identities, *p. 472*
Verifying Trigonometric Identities, *p. 474*

Section 9.2
Sum and Difference Formulas, *p. 478*

Mathematical Practices

1. How can you use tools to verify the identity in Exercise 32 on page 475.

2. How can you use definitions to relate the slope of a line with the tangent of an angle in Exercise 39 on page 482?

Reworking Your Notes

It's almost impossible to write down in your notes all the detailed information you are taught in class. A good way to reinforce the concepts and put them into your long-term memory is to rework your notes. When you take notes, leave extra space on the pages. You can go back after class and fill in:

- important definitions and rules

- additional examples

- questions you have about the material

STUDY SKILLS

Find the values of the other five trigonometric functions of θ**.** *(Section 9.1)*

1. $\sin \theta = -\dfrac{7}{25}, \pi < \theta < \dfrac{3\pi}{2}$ **2.** $\sec \theta = \dfrac{13}{5}, \dfrac{3\pi}{2} < \theta < 2\pi$ **3.** $\cot \theta = -\dfrac{5}{6}, \dfrac{\pi}{2} < \theta < \pi$

Simplify the expression. *(Section 9.1)*

4. $\cos\left(\dfrac{\pi}{2} - \theta\right) \csc \theta$

5. $\dfrac{\tan x \csc x}{\sec x}$

6. $\tan(-x) \sin\left(\dfrac{\pi}{2} - x\right)$

7. $\dfrac{(\csc x + 1)(\csc x - 1)}{\cot\left(\dfrac{\pi}{2} - x\right)}$

Verify the identity. *(Section 9.1)*

8. $\cos \theta \sec(-\theta) = 1$

9. $\sin x \csc(-x) = -1$

10. $\tan x \cot x - \sin^2 x = \cos^2 x$

11. $\dfrac{\sin x \csc x}{\sec^2 x - 1} = \cot^2 x$

12. $\sec\left(\dfrac{\pi}{2} - x\right) \tan x = \sec x$

13. $\dfrac{\tan \theta - 2 \tan\left(\dfrac{\pi}{2} - \theta\right)}{\tan(-\theta)} = 2 \cot^2 \theta - 1$

14. Describe two different ways you can verify the identity $\csc x + \csc x \cot^2 x = \csc^3 x$ algebraically. *(Section 9.1)*

15. Explain how to use trigonometric identities to verify that $\sec(-\theta) = \sec \theta$. *(Section 9.1)*

Find the exact value of the expression. *(Section 9.2)*

16. $\sin(-105°)$

17. $\cos\left(-\dfrac{13\pi}{12}\right)$

18. $\tan\left(\dfrac{13\pi}{12}\right)$

19. $\tan 255°$

20. Find $\sin(a - b)$ given that $\sin a = -\dfrac{3}{5}$ with $\pi < a < \dfrac{3\pi}{2}$ and $\cos b = -\dfrac{12}{13}$ with $\pi < b < \dfrac{3\pi}{2}$. *(Section 9.2)*

Simplify the expression. *(Section 9.2)*

21. $\cos(x - \pi)$

22. $\tan(x + 2\pi)$

23. $\sin\left(x + \dfrac{\pi}{2}\right)$

Solve the equation for $0 \le x < 2\pi$**.** *(Section 9.2)*

24. $\cos\left(x + \dfrac{\pi}{4}\right) - \cos\left(x - \dfrac{\pi}{4}\right) = 1$

25. $\sin\left(x + \dfrac{\pi}{2}\right) - \sin\left(x - \dfrac{\pi}{2}\right) = \sqrt{2}$

26. Derive the cofunction identity $\cos\left(\dfrac{\pi}{2} - \theta\right) = \sin \theta$ using the difference formula for cosine. *(Section 9.2)*

9.3 Law of Sines

Essential Question What is the Law of Sines?

EXPLORATION 1 **Discovering the Law of Sines**

Work with a partner.

a. Copy and complete the table for the triangle shown. What can you conclude?

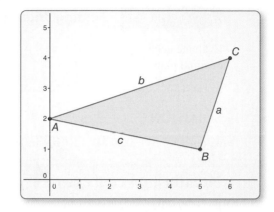

Sample
Segments
$a = 3.16$
$b = 6.32$
$c = 5.10$
Angles
$A = 29.74°$
$B = 97.13°$
$C = 53.13°$

USING TOOLS STRATEGICALLY

To be proficient in math, you need to use technology to compare predictions with data.

A	a	$\dfrac{\sin A}{a}$	B	b	$\dfrac{\sin B}{b}$	C	c	$\dfrac{\sin C}{c}$

b. Use dynamic geometry software to draw two other triangles. Copy and complete the table in part (a) for each triangle. Use your results to write a conjecture about the relationship between the sines of the angles and the lengths of the sides of a triangle.

EXPLORATION 2 **Discovering Cases of the Law of Sines**

Work with a partner.

a. Begin constructing $\triangle ABC$ by drawing side AC and acute angle A, as shown.

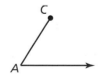

b. Set a compass to the distance from point C to the other side of the angle. How many triangles can you construct using this setting as the length of side BC? Explain your reasoning.

c. Repeat part (b) using a compass setting shorter than the setting in part (b).

d. Repeat part (b) using a compass setting longer than the setting in part (b).

Communicate Your Answer

3. What is the Law of Sines?

4. When would you use the Law of Sines to solve a triangle?

9.3 Lesson

Core Vocabulary

Law of Sines, *p. 487*

What You Will Learn

- Find areas of triangles.
- Use the Law of Sines to solve triangles.

Finding Areas of Triangles

Previously, you used trigonometric ratios to solve right triangles. In this lesson, you will learn how to solve any triangle. When the triangle is obtuse, you may need to find a trigonometric ratio for an obtuse angle.

EXAMPLE 1 Finding Trigonometric Ratios for Obtuse Angles

Evaluate each trigonometric function using a calculator. Round your answer to four decimal places.

a. $\tan 150°$ **b.** $\sin 120°$ **c.** $\cos 95°$

SOLUTION

a. $\tan 150° \approx -0.5774$ **b.** $\sin 120° \approx 0.8660$ **c.** $\cos 95° \approx -0.0872$

Monitoring Progress

Help in English and Spanish at *BigIdeasMath.com*

Evaluate the trigonometric function using a calculator. Round your answer to four decimal places.

1. $\tan 110°$ **2.** $\sin 97°$ **3.** $\cos 165°$

Core Concept

Area of a Triangle

The area of any triangle is given by one-half the product of the lengths of two sides times the sine of their included angle. For $\triangle ABC$ shown, there are three ways to calculate the area.

$\text{Area} = \frac{1}{2}bc \sin A$ $\text{Area} = \frac{1}{2}ac \sin B$ $\text{Area} = \frac{1}{2}ab \sin C$

EXAMPLE 2 Finding the Area of a Triangle

Find the area of the triangle. Round your answer to the nearest tenth.

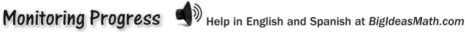

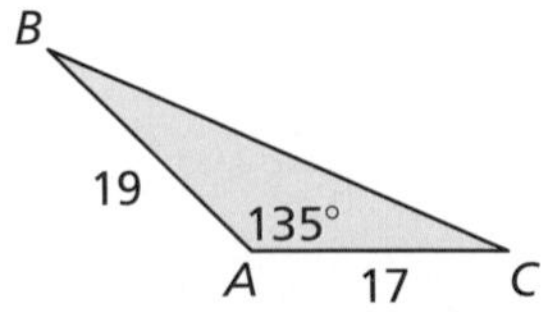

SOLUTION

$$\text{Area} = \frac{1}{2}bc \sin A = \frac{1}{2}(17)(19) \sin 135° \approx 114.2$$

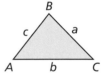

▶ The area of the triangle is about 114.2 square units.

Monitoring Progress

Help in English and Spanish at *BigIdeasMath.com*

Find the area of $\triangle ABC$. Round your answer to the nearest tenth.

4. $B = 60°, a = 19, c = 14$ **5.** $C = 29°, a = 38, b = 31$

Using the Law of Sines

You can use the **Law of Sines** to solve triangles when two angles and the length of any side are known (AAS or ASA cases), or when the lengths of two sides and an angle opposite one of the two sides are known (SSA case).

🌀 Theorem

Law of Sines

The Law of Sines can be written in either of the following forms for $\triangle ABC$ with sides of length a, b, and c.

$$\frac{\sin A}{a} = \frac{\sin B}{b} = \frac{\sin C}{c} \qquad \frac{a}{\sin A} = \frac{b}{\sin B} = \frac{c}{\sin C}$$

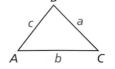

Proof Ex. 55, p. 492

EXAMPLE 3 Solving a Triangle for the AAS or ASA Case

Solve $\triangle ABC$. Round decimal answers to the nearest tenth.

  a. $B = 25°$, $C = 107°$, $b = 15$ **b.** $A = 71°$, $C = 60°$, $b = 21$

SOLUTION

a. By the Triangle Sum Theorem, $A = 180° - 107° - 25° = 48°$.

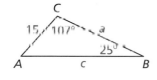

By the Law of Sines, you can write $\dfrac{a}{\sin 48°} = \dfrac{15}{\sin 25°} = \dfrac{c}{\sin 107°}$.

$\dfrac{a}{\sin 48°} = \dfrac{15}{\sin 25°}$ Write two equations, each with one variable.	$\dfrac{c}{\sin 107°} = \dfrac{15}{\sin 25°}$
$a = \dfrac{15\sin 48°}{\sin 25°}$ Solve for each variable.	$c = \dfrac{15\sin 107°}{\sin 25°}$
$a \approx 26.4$ Use a calculator.	$c \approx 33.9$

▶ In $\triangle ABC$, $A = 48°$, $a \approx 26.4$, and $c \approx 33.9$.

b. By the Triangle Sum Theorem, $B = 180° - 71° - 60° = 49°$.

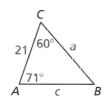

By the Law of Sines, you can write $\dfrac{a}{\sin 71°} = \dfrac{21}{\sin 49°} = \dfrac{c}{\sin 60°}$.

$\dfrac{a}{\sin 71°} = \dfrac{21}{\sin 49°}$ Write two equations, each with one variable.	$\dfrac{c}{\sin 60°} = \dfrac{21}{\sin 49°}$
$a = \dfrac{21\sin 71°}{\sin 49°}$ Solve for each variable.	$c = \dfrac{21\sin 60°}{\sin 49°}$
$a \approx 26.3$ Use a calculator.	$c \approx 24.1$

▶ In $\triangle ABC$, $B = 49°$, $a \approx 26.3$, and $c \approx 24.1$.

Monitoring Progress Help in English and Spanish at *BigIdeasMath.com*

STUDY TIP

Because the SSA case can result in 0, 1, or 2 triangles, it is called the *ambiguous case*.

Solve $\triangle ABC$. **Round decimal answers to the nearest tenth.**

  6. $A = 29°$, $B = 85°$, $b = 9$ **7.** $B = 70°$, $C = 81°$, $a = 10$

Two angles and one side (AAS or ASA) determine exactly one triangle. Two sides and an angle opposite one of the sides (SSA) may determine no triangle, one triangle, or two triangles.

Core Concept

Possible Triangles in the SSA Case

Consider $\triangle ABC$, where you are given a, b, and A. By fixing side b and angle A, you can sketch the possible positions of side a to figure out how many triangles can be formed. In the diagrams below, note that $h = b \sin A$.

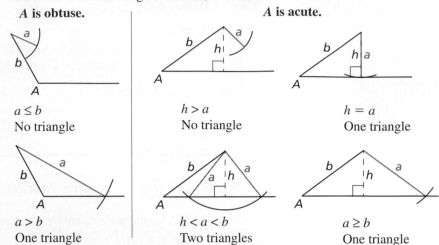

A is obtuse.	**A is acute.**	
$a \le b$ No triangle	$h > a$ No triangle	$h = a$ One triangle
$a > b$ One triangle	$h < a < b$ Two triangles	$a \ge b$ One triangle

---

EXAMPLE 4   **Solving the SSA Case with One Solution**

Solve $\triangle ABC$ with $A = 115°$, $a = 20$, and $b = 11$. Round decimal answers to the nearest tenth.

SOLUTION

First make a sketch. Because A is obtuse and the side opposite A is longer than the given adjacent side, you know that only one triangle can be formed. Use the Law of Sines to find B.

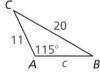

$$\frac{\sin B}{11} = \frac{\sin 115°}{20} \qquad \text{Law of Sines}$$

$$\sin B = \frac{11 \sin 115°}{20} \qquad \text{Multiply each side by 11.}$$

$$B \approx 29.9° \qquad \text{Use a calculator.}$$

By the Triangle Sum Theorem, $C \approx 180° - 115° - 29.9° = 35.1°$.

Use the Law of Sines again to find the remaining side length c of the triangle.

$$\frac{c}{\sin 35.1°} = \frac{20}{\sin 115°} \qquad \text{Law of Sines}$$

$$c = \frac{20 \sin 35.1°}{\sin 115°} \qquad \text{Multiply each side by } \sin 35.1°.$$

$$c \approx 12.7 \qquad \text{Use a calculator.}$$

▶ In $\triangle ABC$, $B \approx 29.9°$, $C \approx 35.1°$, and $c \approx 12.7$.

Monitoring Progress   🔊 Help in English and Spanish at *BigIdeasMath.com*

Solve $\triangle ABC$. Round decimal answers to the nearest tenth.

8. $A = 110°$, $a = 15$, $b = 10$ **9.** $B = 63°$, $a = 7$, $b = 12$

EXAMPLE 5 **Examining the SSA Case with No Solution**

Solve $\triangle ABC$ with $A = 51°$, $a = 3.5$, and $b = 5$. Round decimal answers to the nearest tenth.

SOLUTION

First make a sketch. Begin by drawing a horizontal line. On one end form a 51° angle (A) and draw a segment 5 units long ($\overline{AC}$, or b). At vertex C, draw a segment 3.5 units long (a). You can see that a needs to be at least $5 \sin 51° \approx 3.9$ units long to reach the horizontal side and form a triangle. So, it is not possible to draw the indicated triangle.

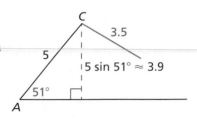

EXAMPLE 6 **Solving the SSA Case with Two Solutions**

Solve $\triangle ABC$ with $A = 40°$, $a = 13$, and $b = 16$. Round decimal answers to the nearest tenth.

SOLUTION

First make a sketch. Because $b \sin A = 16 \sin 40° \approx 10.3$, and $10.3 < 13 < 16$ ($h < a < b$), two triangles can be formed.

Use the Law of Sines to find the possible measures of B.

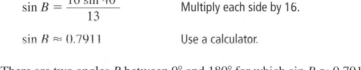

$\dfrac{\sin B}{16} = \dfrac{\sin 40°}{13}$	Law of Sines
$\sin B = \dfrac{16 \sin 40°}{13}$	Multiply each side by 16.
$\sin B \approx 0.7911$	Use a calculator.

There are two angles B between 0° and 180° for which $\sin B \approx 0.7911$. One is acute and the other is obtuse. Use your calculator to find the acute angle: $\sin^{-1} 0.7911 \approx 52.3°$.

The obtuse angle has 52.3° as a reference angle, so its measure is $180° - 52.3° = 127.7°$. So, $B \approx 52.3°$ or $B \approx 127.7°$.

Now find the remaining angle C and side length c for each triangle.

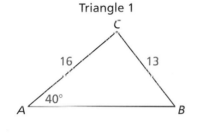

Triangle 1

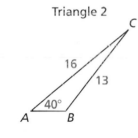

Triangle 2

Triangle 1	**Triangle 2**
$C \approx 180° - 40° - 52.3° = 87.7°$	$C \approx 180° - 40° - 127.7° = 12.3°$
$\dfrac{c}{\sin 87.7°} = \dfrac{13}{\sin 40°}$	$\dfrac{c}{\sin 12.3°} = \dfrac{13}{\sin 40°}$
$c = \dfrac{13 \sin 87.7°}{\sin 40°}$	$c = \dfrac{13 \sin 12.3°}{\sin 40°}$
$c \approx 20.2$	$c \approx 4.3$

▶ In Triangle 1, $B \approx 52.3°$, $C \approx 87.7°$, and $c \approx 20.2$.

▶ In Triangle 2, $B \approx 127.7°$, $C \approx 12.3°$, and $c \approx 4.3$.

Monitoring Progress  Help in English and Spanish at *BigIdeasMath.com*

Solve $\triangle ABC$, **if possible. Round decimal answers to the nearest tenth.**

10. $A = 44°$, $a = 11$, $b = 14$ **11.** $A = 65°$, $a = 6$, $b = 8$

Vocabulary and Core Concept Check

1. **VOCABULARY** What information do you need to use the Law of Sines?

2. **WRITING** Suppose a, b, and A are given for $\triangle ABC$ and $A < 90°$. Under what conditions would you have no triangle? one triangle? two triangles?

Monitoring Progress and Modeling with Mathematics

In Exercises 3–8, evaluate the trigonometric function using a calculator. Round your answer to four decimal places. *(See Example 1.)*

3. $\sin 127°$

4. $\sin 98°$

5. $\cos 139°$

6. $\cos 108°$

7. $\tan 165°$

8. $\tan 116°$

In Exercises 9–12, find the area of $\triangle ABC$. Round your answer to the nearest tenth. *(See Example 2.)*

9.

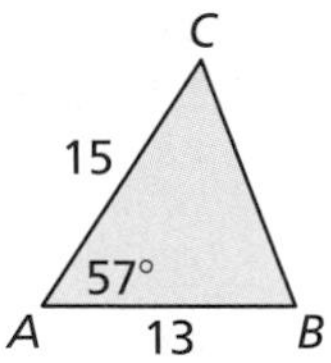

10.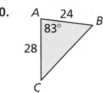

11.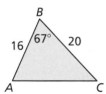

12.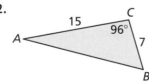

In Exercises 13–18, state the case (AAS, ASA, or SSA) applicable to the given measurements. Then decide whether the measurements determine *one triangle*, *two triangles*, or *no triangle*.

13. $A = 49°$, $a = 24$, $b = 22$

14. $A = 50°$, $B = 30°$, $b = 8$

15. $B = 65°$, $a = 21$, $b = 20$

16. $B = 95°$, $C = 46°$, $a = 14$

17. $C = 120°$, $b = 12$, $c = 11$

18. $C = 135°$, $b = 25$, $c = 30$

In Exercises 19–34, solve $\triangle ABC$, if possible. Round decimal answers to the nearest tenth. *(See Examples 3, 4, 5, and 6.)*

19.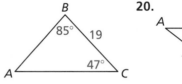

20.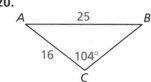

21.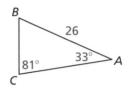

22.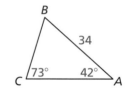

23.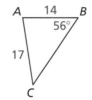

24.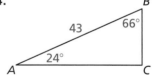

25. $A = 24°$, $B = 68°$, $b = 14$

26. $B = 35°$, $C = 92°$, $a = 15$

27. $A = 55°$, $a = 12$, $b = 8$

28. $C = 26°$, $b = 5$, $c = 5$

29. $A = 150°$, $a = 9$, $b = 16$

30. $B = 80°$, $b = 10$, $c = 20$

31. $A = 75°$, $a = 15$, $b = 15.5$

32. $B = 10°$, $b = 6$, $c = 6.5$

33. $A = 108°$, $a = 10.2$, $b = 7.8$

34. $C = 115°$, $b = 21.9$, $c = 17.8$

35. ERROR ANALYSIS Describe and correct the error in finding the area of △ABC.

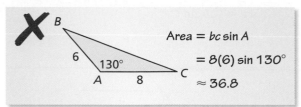

$$\text{Area} = bc \sin A$$
$$= 8(6) \sin 130°$$
$$\approx 36.8$$

36. ERROR ANALYSIS Describe and correct the error in finding C.

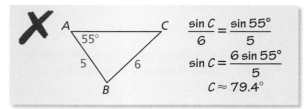

$$\frac{\sin C}{6} = \frac{\sin 55°}{5}$$
$$\sin C = \frac{6 \sin 55°}{5}$$
$$C \approx 79.4°$$

COMPARING METHODS In Exercises 37–44, tell whether you would use the Law of Sines or the Pythagorean Theorem and trigonometric functions to solve the triangle with the given information. Explain your reasoning. Then solve the triangle.

37. $A = 72°, B = 44°, b = 14$

38. $B = 98°, C = 37°, a = 18$

39. $B = 90°, a = 15, c = 6$

40. $C = 40°, b = 27, c = 36$

41. $B = 50°, C = 80°, c = 14$

42. $A = 110°, C = 48°, a = 26$

43. $A = 90°, b = 19, c = 35$

44. $C = 78°, b = 50, c = 49$

45. REASONING Use △XYZ.

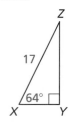

a. Can you use the Law of Sines to solve △XYZ? Explain your reasoning.

b. Can you use another method to solve △XYZ? Explain your reasoning.

46. MODELING WITH MATHEMATICS The Leaning Tower of Pisa in Italy has a height of 183 feet and is 4° off vertical. Find the horizontal distance d that the top of the tower is off vertical.

47. MODELING WITH MATHEMATICS You are on the observation deck of the Empire State Building looking at the Chrysler Building. When you turn 145° clockwise, you see the Statue of Liberty. You know that the Chrysler Building and the Empire State Building are about 0.6 mile apart and that the Chrysler Building and the Statue of Liberty are about 5.6 miles apart. Estimate the distance between the Empire State Building and the Statue of Liberty.

48. MAKING AN ARGUMENT Your friend calculates the area of the triangle using the formula $A = \frac{1}{2}qr \sin S$ and says that the area is approximately 208.6 square units. Is your friend correct? Explain your reasoning.

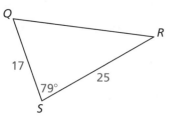

49. MODELING WITH MATHEMATICS You are fertilizing a triangular garden. One side of the garden is 62 feet long, and another side is 54 feet long. The angle opposite the 62-foot side is 58°.

   a. Draw a diagram to represent this situation.

   b. Use the Law of Sines to solve the triangle from part (a).

   c. One bag of fertilizer covers an area of 200 square feet. How many bags of fertilizer will you need to cover the entire garden?

50. HOW DO YOU SEE IT?
Can you use the Law of Sines to solve the triangle? Explain.

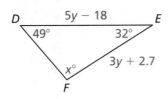

51. COMPARING METHODS A building is constructed on top of a cliff that is 300 meters high. A person standing on level ground below the cliff observes that the angle of elevation to the top of the building is 72° and the angle of elevation to the top of the cliff is 63°.

   a. How far away is the person from the base of the cliff?

   b. Describe two different methods you can use to find the height of the building. Use one of these methods to find the building's height.

52. THOUGHT PROVOKING Explain why there is no case for SSA where the angle is obtuse and two triangles are possible.

53. MATHEMATICAL CONNECTIONS
Find the values of x and y.

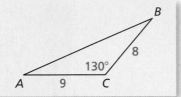

54. REWRITING A FORMULA Follow the steps to derive the formula for the area of a triangle, Area $= \frac{1}{2}ab \sin C$.

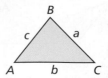

   a. Draw the altitude from vertex B to $\overline{AC}$. Label the altitude as h. Write a formula for the area of the triangle using h.

   b. Write an equation for $\sin C$.

   c. Use the results of parts (a) and (b) to write a formula for the area of a triangle that does not include h.

55. PROVING A THEOREM Follow the steps to use the formula for the area of a triangle to prove the Law of Sines.

   a. Use the derivation in Exercise 54 to explain how to derive the three related formulas for the area of a triangle.

$$\text{Area} = \frac{1}{2}bc \sin A,$$
$$\text{Area} = \frac{1}{2}ac \sin B,$$
$$\text{Area} = \frac{1}{2}ab \sin C$$

   b. Why can you use the formulas in part (a) to write the following statement?

$$\tfrac{1}{2}bc \sin A = \tfrac{1}{2}ac \sin B = \tfrac{1}{2}ab \sin C$$

   c. Show how to rewrite the statement in part (b) to prove the Law of Sines. Justify each step.

Maintaining Mathematical Proficiency
Reviewing what you learned in previous grades and lessons

Evaluate the trigonometric function using a calculator. *(Section 8.1)*

56. $\cos 25°$ **57.** $\sin 48°$ **58.** $\tan 20°$ **59.** $\sec 36°$

Find the value of x for the right triangle. *(Section 8.1)*

60.

61.

62.

63.

9.4 Law of Cosines

Essential Question What is the Law of Cosines?

EXPLORATION 1 **Discovering the Law of Cosines**

Work with a partner.

a. Copy and complete the table for the triangle shown. What can you conclude?

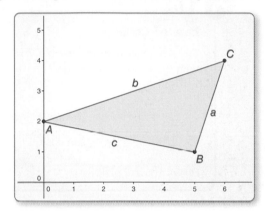

Sample
Segments
$a = 3.16$
$b = 6.32$
$c = 5.10$
Angles
$A = 29.74°$
$B - 97.13°$
$C = 53.13°$

USING TOOLS STRATEGICALLY

To be proficient in math, you need to use technology to compare predictions with data.

c	c^2	a	a^2	b	b^2	C	$a^2 + b^2 - 2ab \cos C$

b. Use dynamic geometry software to draw two other triangles. Copy and complete the table in part (a) for each triangle. Use your results to write a conjecture about what you observe in the completed tables.

EXPLORATION 2 **Discovering Heron's Area Formula**

Work with a partner.

a. Copy and complete the table for the triangle in Exploration 1(a). What can you conclude?

a	A	b	c	$s = \frac{1}{2}(a + b + c)$	$\sqrt{s(s - a)(s - b)(s - c)}$	Area $= \frac{1}{2}bc \sin A$

b. Use dynamic geometry software to draw two other triangles. Copy and complete the table in part (a) for each triangle. Use your results to write a conjecture about what you observe in the completed tables.

Communicate Your Answer

3. What is the Law of Cosines?

4. When would you use the Law of Cosines to solve a triangle?

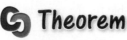
What You Will Learn

▶ Use the Law of Cosines to solve triangles.

▶ Find areas of triangles.

Using the Law of Cosines

You can use the **Law of Cosines** to solve triangles when two sides and the included angle are known (SAS case), or when all three sides are known (SSS case).

⟳ Theorem

Law of Cosines

If $\triangle ABC$ has sides of length a, b, and c, as shown, then the following are true.

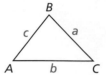

$$a^2 = b^2 + c^2 - 2bc \cos A$$

$$b^2 = a^2 + c^2 - 2ac \cos B$$

$$c^2 = a^2 + b^2 - 2ab \cos C$$

Proof Ex. 26, p. 498

EXAMPLE 1 **Using the Law of Cosines (SAS Case)**

Solve $\triangle ABC$. Round decimal answers to the nearest tenth.

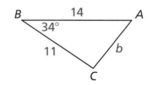

SOLUTION

Use the Law of Cosines to find side length b.

$b^2 = a^2 + c^2 - 2ac \cos B$	Law of Cosines
$b^2 = 11^2 + 14^2 - 2(11)(14) \cos 34°$	Substitute.
$b^2 = 317 - 308 \cos 34°$	Simplify.
$b = \sqrt{317 - 308 \cos 34°}$	Find the positive square root.
$b \approx 7.9$	Use a calculator.

ANOTHER WAY

When you know all three sides and one angle, you can use the Law of Cosines or the Law of Sines to find the measure of a second angle.

Use the Law of Sines to find A. You want to find the smaller remaining angle first because the inverse sine feature of a calculator only gives angle measures from $0°$ to $90°$.

$\dfrac{\sin A}{a} = \dfrac{\sin B}{b}$	Law of Sines
$\dfrac{\sin A}{11} = \dfrac{\sin 34°}{\sqrt{317 - 308 \cos 34°}}$	Substitute.
$\sin A = \dfrac{11 \sin 34°}{\sqrt{317 - 308 \cos 34°}}$	Multiply each side by 11.
$A \approx 51.6°$	Use a calculator.

By the Triangle Sum Theorem, $C \approx 180° - 34° - 51.6° = 94.4°$.

▶ In $\triangle ABC$, $b \approx 7.9$, $A \approx 51.6°$, and $C \approx 94.4°$.

Solve △*ABC*. Round decimal answers to the nearest tenth.

1.

2.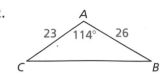

EXAMPLE 2 **Using the Law of Cosines (SSS Case)**

Solve △*ABC*. Round decimal answers to the nearest tenth.

SOLUTION

> **COMMON ERROR**
>
> In Example 2, the largest angle is found first to make sure that the other two angles are acute. This way, when you use the Law of Sines to find another angle measure, you will know that it is between 0° and 90°.

First, find the angle opposite the longest side, $\overline{AC}$. Use the Law of Cosines to find *B*.

$$b^2 = a^2 + c^2 - 2ac \cos B \qquad \text{Law of Cosines}$$

$$27^2 = 12^2 + 20^2 - 2(12)(20) \cos B \qquad \text{Substitute.}$$

$$\frac{27^2 - 12^2 - 20^2}{-2(12)(20)} = \cos B \qquad \text{Solve for } \cos B.$$

$$B \approx 112.7° \qquad \text{Use a calculator.}$$

Now, use the Law of Sines to find *A*.

$$\frac{\sin A}{a} = \frac{\sin B}{b} \qquad \text{Law of Sines}$$

$$\frac{\sin A}{12} = \frac{\sin 112.7°}{27} \qquad \text{Substitute.}$$

$$\sin A = \frac{12 \sin 112.7°}{27} \qquad \text{Multiply each side by 12.}$$

$$A \approx 24.2° \qquad \text{Use a calculator.}$$

By the Triangle Sum Theorem, $C \approx 180° - 24.2° - 112.7° = 43.1°$.

▶ In △*ABC*, $A \approx 24.2°$, $B \approx 112.7°$, and $C \approx 43.1°$.

EXAMPLE 3 **Solving a Real-Life Problem**

An organism's step angle is a measure of walking efficiency. The closer the step angle is to 180°, the more efficiently the organism walked. The diagram shows a set of footprints for a dinosaur. Find the step angle *B*.

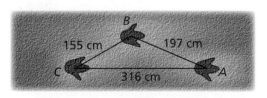

SOLUTION

$$b^2 = a^2 + c^2 - 2ac \cos B \qquad \text{Law of Cosines}$$

$$316^2 = 155^2 + 197^2 - 2(155)(197) \cos B \qquad \text{Substitute.}$$

$$\frac{316^2 - 155^2 - 197^2}{-2(155)(197)} = \cos B \qquad \text{Solve for } \cos B.$$

$$127.3° \approx B \qquad \text{Use a calculator.}$$

▶ The step angle *B* is about 127.3°.

Solve △*ABC*. Round decimal answers to the nearest tenth.

3.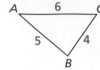

4.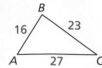

Finding Areas of Triangles

In the previous section, you used a formula involving sine to find the areas of triangles. Another formula for the area of a triangle is Heron's area formula, which can be derived using the Law of Cosines.

 **Core Concept**

Heron's Area Formula

The area of any triangle with sides of length a, b, and c is

$$\text{Area} = \sqrt{s(s-a)(s-b)(s-c)}$$

where $s = \frac{1}{2}(a+b+c)$. The variable s is called the *semiperimeter*, or half-perimeter, of the triangle.

EXAMPLE 4   **Finding the Area of a Triangle**

The intersection of three streets forms a piece of land called a traffic triangle. Find the area of the traffic triangle shown. Round your answer to the nearest tenth.

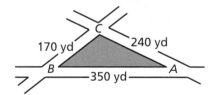

SOLUTION

Step 1   Find the semiperimeter s.

$$s = \frac{1}{2}(a+b+c)$$
$$= \frac{1}{2}(170 + 240 + 350)$$
$$= 380$$

Step 2   Use Heron's formula to find the area of △*ABC*.

$$\text{Area} = \sqrt{s(s-a)(s-b)(s-c)}$$
$$= \sqrt{380(380-170)(380-240)(380-350)}$$
$$\approx 18,307.4$$

▶   The area of the traffic triangle is about 18,307.4 square yards.

Find the area of △*ABC*. Round your answer to the nearest tenth.

5.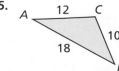

6.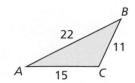

Vocabulary and Core Concept Check

1. **VOCABULARY** What information do you need to use the Law of Cosines?

2. **WRITING** After using the Law of Cosines for the SSS case to find the first angle measure, why can you use the Law of Sines to find the second angle measure?

Monitoring Progress and Modeling with Mathematics

In Exercises 3–12, solve △*ABC*. Round decimal answers to the nearest tenth. *(See Examples 1 and 2.)*

3.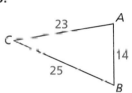

4.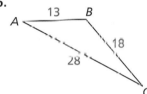

5.

6.

7. $B = 63°, a = 29, c = 38$

8. $a = 12, b = 5, c = 13$

9. $a = 8, b = 9, c = 12$

10. $A = 46°, b = 14, c = 16$

11. $B = 154°, a = 7, c = 10$

12. $a = 5, b = 11, c = 15$

13. **MODELING WITH MATHEMATICS** You and your friend are standing on the baseline of a basketball court. You bounce a basketball to your friend, as shown in the diagram. What is the distance between you and your friend? *(See Example 3.)*

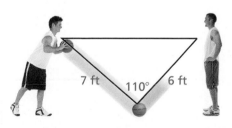

14. **MODELING WITH MATHEMATICS** A zip line is constructed across a valley, as shown in the diagram. What is the width *w* of the valley?

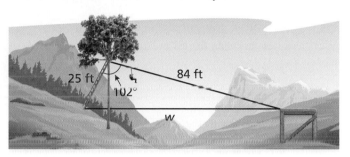

In Exercises 15–18, find the area of △*ABC*. Round your answer to the nearest tenth. *(See Example 4.)*

15.

16.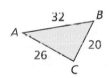

17.

18.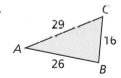

19. **ERROR ANALYSIS** Describe and correct the error in finding *A* in △*ABC* when $a = 19$, $b = 21$, and $c = 11$.

$$\cos A = \frac{19^2 - 21^2 - 11^2}{-2(19)(21)}$$

$$A \approx 75.4°$$

20. MODELING WITH MATHEMATICS A golfer hits a drive 260 yards on a hole that is 400 yards long. The shot is 15° off target.

Not drawn to scale

a. What is the distance x from the golfer's ball to the hole?

b. Assume the golfer is able to hit the ball precisely the distance found in part (a). What is the maximum angle θ by which the ball can be off target in order to land no more than 10 yards from the hole?

21. REWRITING A FORMULA Simplify the Law of Cosines for when the given angle is a right angle.

22. HOW DO YOU SEE IT? Would you use the Law of Sines or the Law of Cosines to solve the triangle? Explain.

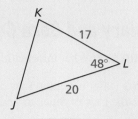

23. ABSTRACT REASONING Use the Law of Cosines to show that the measure of each angle of an equilateral triangle is 60°. Explain your reasoning.

24. THOUGHT PROVOKING How can you use the Law of Cosines to derive Heron's area formula?

25. CRITICAL THINKING An airplane flies 55° east of north from City A to City B, a distance of 470 miles. Another airplane flies 7° north of east from City A to City C, a distance of 890 miles. What is the distance between Cities B and C?

26. PROVING A THEOREM Use the given information to complete the two-column proof of the Law of Cosines.

Given $\overline{BD}$ is an altitude of $\triangle ABC$.

Prove $a^2 = b^2 + c^2 - 2bc \cos A$

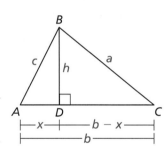

STATEMENTS	REASONS
1. $\overline{BD}$ is an altitude of $\triangle ABC$.	**1.** Given
2. $\triangle ADB$ and $\triangle CDB$ are right triangles.	**2.** _____
3. $a^2 = (b - x)^2 + h^2$	**3.** _____
4. _____	**4.** Expand binomial.
5. $x^2 + h^2 = c^2$	**5.** _____
6. _____	**6.** Substitution Property of Equality
7. $\cos A = \dfrac{x}{c}$	**7.** _____
8. $x = c \cos A$	**8.** _____
9. $a^2 = b^2 + c^2 - 2bc \cos A$	**9.** _____

Maintaining Mathematical Proficiency   Reviewing what you learned in previous grades and lessons

Write the first six terms of the sequence. *(Section 7.1)*

27. $a_n = n + 7$ **28.** $a_n = n^2 - 3$ **29.** $a_n = n^3 + 1$ **30.** $a_n = 2^{n-1}$

Core Vocabulary

Law of Sines, *p. 487*   Law of Cosines, *p. 494*

Core Concepts

Section 9.3

Area of a Triangle, *p. 486*
Law of Sines, *p. 487*
Possible Triangles in the SSA Case, *p. 488*

Section 9.4

Law of Cosines, *p. 494*
Heron's Area Formula, *p. 496*

Mathematical Practices

1. Describe the overall step-by-step process you used to solve Exercise 49 on page 492.

2. In Exercise 53 on page 492, explain how you started solving the problem and why you started that way.

3. Create a diagram to model Exercise 25 on page 498.

Performance Task:

Step Angles

As we walk, our footsteps make patterns that reveal the efficiency of our stride. The Law of Cosines helps analyze those patterns. Using this law, can you compare the strides of other bipeds?

To explore the answer to this question and more, check out the Performance Task and Real-Life STEM video at *BigIdeasMath.com*.

9 Chapter Review

Dynamic Solutions available at *BigIdeasMath.com*

9.1 Using Trigonometric Identities (pp. 471–476)

Verify the identity $\frac{\cot^2 \theta}{\csc \theta} = \csc \theta - \sin \theta$.

$\frac{\cot^2 \theta}{\csc \theta} = \frac{\csc^2 \theta - 1}{\csc \theta}$	Pythagorean identity
$= \frac{\csc^2 \theta}{\csc \theta} - \frac{1}{\csc \theta}$	Write as separate fractions.
$= \csc \theta - \frac{1}{\csc \theta}$	Simplify.
$= \csc \theta - \sin \theta$	Reciprocal identity

1. Given that $\cos \theta = -\frac{8}{17}$ and $\pi < \theta < \frac{3\pi}{2}$, find the values of the other five trigonometric functions of θ.

Simplify the expression.

2. $\cot^2 x - \cot^2 x \cos^2 x$

3. $\frac{(\sec x + 1)(\sec x - 1)}{\tan x}$

4. $\sin\left(\frac{\pi}{2} - x\right) \tan x$

Verify the identity.

5. $\frac{\cos x \sec x}{1 + \tan^2 x} = \cos^2 x$

6. $\tan\left(\frac{\pi}{2} - x\right) \cot x = \csc^2 x - 1$

9.2 Using Sum and Difference Formulas (pp. 477–482)

Find the exact value of sin 165°.

$\sin 165° = \sin(135° + 30°)$	Substitute 135° + 30° for 165°.
$= \sin 135° \cos 30° + \cos 135° \sin 30°$	Sum formula for sine
$= \frac{\sqrt{2}}{2} \cdot \frac{\sqrt{3}}{2} + \left(-\frac{\sqrt{2}}{2}\right) \cdot \frac{1}{2}$	Evaluate.
$= \frac{\sqrt{6} - \sqrt{2}}{4}$	Simplify.

▶ The exact value of sin 135° is $\frac{\sqrt{6} - \sqrt{2}}{4}$.

Find the exact value of the expression.

7. $\sin 195°$

8. $\tan(-105°)$

9. $\cos \frac{7\pi}{12}$

10. Find $\tan(a + b)$, given that $\tan a = \frac{1}{4}$ with $\pi < a < \frac{3\pi}{2}$ and $\tan b = \frac{3}{7}$ with $0 < b < \frac{\pi}{2}$.

Solve the equation for $0 \leq x < 2\pi$.

11. $\cos\left(x + \frac{3\pi}{4}\right) + \cos\left(x - \frac{3\pi}{4}\right) = 1$

12. $\tan(x + \pi) + \cos\left(x + \frac{\pi}{2}\right) = 0$

a. **Find the area of the triangle. Round your answer to the nearest tenth.**

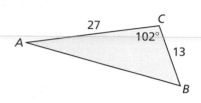

$$\text{Area} = \frac{1}{2}ab \sin C$$

$$= \frac{1}{2}(13)(27) \sin 102°$$

$$\approx 171.7$$

▶ The area of the triangle is about 171.7 square units.

b. **Solve △ABC. Round decimal answers to the nearest tenth.**

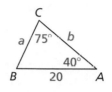

By the Triangle Sum Theorem,
$B = 180° - 40° - 75° = 65°$.

By the Law of Sines, you can write $\dfrac{a}{\sin 40°} = \dfrac{b}{\sin 65°} = \dfrac{20}{\sin 75°}$.

$\dfrac{a}{\sin 40°} = \dfrac{20}{\sin 75°}$	Write two equations, each with one variable.	$\dfrac{b}{\sin 65°} = \dfrac{20}{\sin 75°}$
$a = \dfrac{20 \sin 40°}{\sin 75°}$	Solve for each variable.	$b = \dfrac{20 \sin 65°}{\sin 75°}$
$a \approx 13.3$	Use a calculator.	$b \approx 18.8$

▶ In △ABC, $B = 65°$, $a \approx 13.3$, and $b \approx 18.8$.

Find the area of △ABC. Round your answer to the nearest tenth.

13.

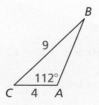

14.

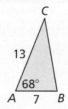

Solve △ABC. Round decimal answers to the nearest tenth.

15.

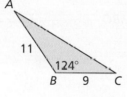

16.

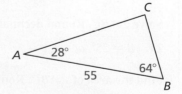

17. $C = 48°$, $b = 20$, $c = 28$

18. $B = 102°$, $C = 43°$, $b = 21$

19. $A = 50°$, $C = 56°$, $b = 5$

20. $B = 31°$, $a = 12$, $b = 10$

9.4 **Law of Cosines** *(pp. 493–498)*

a. **Solve △ABC. Round decimal answers to the nearest tenth.**

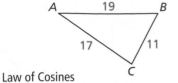

First, find the angle opposite the longest side, $\overline{AB}$.
Use the Law of Cosines to find C.

$$19^2 = 11^2 + 17^2 - 2(11)(17)\cos C \qquad \text{Law of Cosines}$$

$$\frac{19^2 - 11^2 - 17^2}{-2(11)(17)} = \cos C \qquad \text{Solve for cos } C.$$

$$C \approx 82.5° \qquad \text{Use a calculator.}$$

Now, use the Law of Sines to find A.

$$\frac{\sin A}{a} = \frac{\sin C}{c} \qquad \text{Law of Sines}$$

$$\frac{\sin A}{11} = \frac{\sin 82.5°}{19} \qquad \text{Substitute.}$$

$$\sin A = \frac{11 \sin 82.5°}{19} \qquad \text{Multiply each side by 11.}$$

$$A \approx 35.0° \qquad \text{Use a calculator.}$$

By the Triangle Sum Theorem, $B \approx 180° - 35.0° - 82.5° = 62.5°$.

▶ In △ABC, $A \approx 35.0°$, $B \approx 62.5°$, and $C \approx 82.5°$.

b. **Find the area of △ABC. Round your answer to the nearest tenth.**

Step 1 Find the semiperimeter s.

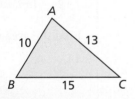

$$s = \frac{1}{2}(a + b + c) = \frac{1}{2}(15 + 13 + 10) = 19$$

Step 2 Use Heron's formula to find the area of △ABC.

$$\text{Area} = \sqrt{s(s - a)(s - b)(s - c)}$$

$$= \sqrt{19(19 - 15)(19 - 13)(19 - 10)}$$

$$\approx 64.1$$

▶ The area of the triangle is about 64.1 square units.

Solve △ABC. Round decimal answers to the nearest tenth.

21. $B = 25°$, $a = 8$, $c = 3$

22. $a = 10$, $b = 3$, $c = 12$

Find the area of △ABC. Round your answer to the nearest tenth.

23.

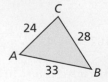

24.

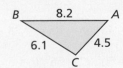

Verify the identity.

1. $\dfrac{\cos^2 x + \sin^2 x}{1 + \tan^2 x} = \cos^2 x$

2. $\dfrac{1 + \sin x}{\cos x} + \dfrac{\cos x}{1 + \sin x} = 2 \sec x$

3. $\cos\left(x + \dfrac{3\pi}{2}\right) = \sin x$

4. $\dfrac{\sin \theta \cot \theta - \cot(-\theta)}{\sin \theta + 1} = \cot \theta$

Solve $\triangle ABC$. Round decimal answers to the nearest tenth.

5.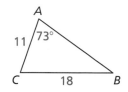

6.

7. $A = 26°$, $C = 35°$, $b = 13$

8. $a = 38$, $b = 31$, $c = 35$

9. $C = 44°$, $b = 15$, $c = 11$

10. $A = 103°$, $a = 24$, $b = 20$

11. Find the exact value of $\tan\left(-\dfrac{\pi}{12}\right)$.

12. Given that $\tan \theta = -\dfrac{2}{5}$, and $\dfrac{\pi}{2} < \theta < \pi$, find the values of the other five trigonometric functions of θ.

Simplify the expression.

13. $\sin x + \cot x \cos(-x)$

14. $\dfrac{\cot^2 x - \csc^2 x}{\sin(-x)}$

15. $\dfrac{\sin\left(\dfrac{\pi}{2} - \theta\right)}{\sec \theta} + \sin^2 \theta$

16. $\sin(x - \pi)$

17. Solve $\sin\left(x + \dfrac{\pi}{2}\right) + \sin\left(x - \dfrac{3\pi}{2}\right) = 1$ for $0 \le x < 2\pi$.

18. The Research Triangle in North Carolina is an area situated between the cities of Raleigh and Durham, and the town of Chapel Hill, as shown on the map. It is one of the most popular research and development centers in the United States.

   a. Find the area enclosed by Raleigh, Durham, and Chapel Hill.

   b. Solve the triangle formed by Raleigh, Durham, and Chapel Hill.

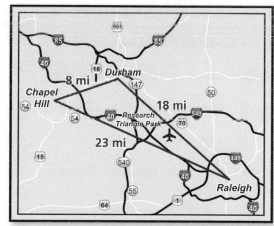

19. Use the diagram of the Bermuda Triangle shown.

   a. Find the area of the Bermuda Triangle.

   b. Solve the triangle formed by the Bermuda Triangle.

1. Which expressions are equivalent to 1?

$\tan x \sec x \cos x$	$\sin^2 x + \cos^2 x$	$\dfrac{\cos^2(-x)\tan^2 x}{\sin^2(-x)}$	$\cos\left(\dfrac{\pi}{2} - x\right)\csc x$

2. A surveyor makes the measurements shown. What is the width of the river?

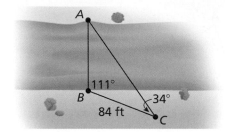

3. Order the acute angles from smallest to largest. Explain your reasoning.

$\tan \theta_1 = 1$	$\tan \theta_2 = \dfrac{1}{2}$	$\tan \theta_3 = \dfrac{\sqrt{3}}{3}$
$\tan \theta_4 = \dfrac{23}{4}$	$\tan \theta_5 = \dfrac{38}{5}$	$\tan \theta_6 = \sqrt{3}$

4. Which statements describe the transformation of the graph of $f(x) = x^3 - x$ represented by $g(x) = 4(x - 2)^3 - 4(x - 2)$?

(A) a vertical stretch by a factor of 4

(B) a vertical shrink by a factor of $\frac{1}{4}$

(C) a horizontal shrink by a factor of $\frac{1}{4}$

(D) a horizontal stretch by a factor of 4

(E) a horizontal translation 2 units to the right

(F) a horizontal translation 2 units to the left

5. About 105,000 people live in a circular region with a 9-mile diameter. Find the population density in people per square mile.

6. Let the graph of g represent a vertical stretch and a reflection in the x-axis, followed by a translation left and down of the graph of $f(x) = x^2$. Use the tiles to write a rule for g.

-3	-1	$-\dfrac{1}{2}$	0	$\dfrac{1}{2}$	1	3

x	$g(x)$	$+$	$-$	$\times$	$\div$	$=$

7. Order the triangles from smallest to largest according to their area.

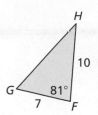

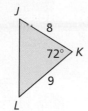

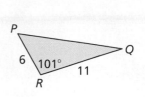

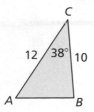

8. Two points in front of a cliff are 75 meters apart. The angles of elevation to the top of the cliff from the two points are 60° and 40°. What is the height of the cliff?

(A) about 35 meters

(B) about 70 meters

(C) about 91 meters

(D) about 122 meters

9. Match each trigonometric function with its correct value given that $\cos \theta = -\dfrac{5}{8}$ and $\dfrac{\pi}{2} < \theta < \pi$.

| $\sin \theta$ | $\tan \theta$ | $\csc \theta$ | $\sec \theta$ | $\cot \theta$ |

| $\dfrac{8\sqrt{39}}{39}$ | $\dfrac{\sqrt{39}}{5}$ | $-\dfrac{\sqrt{39}}{8}$ | $-\dfrac{8}{5}$ | $\dfrac{5\sqrt{39}}{39}$ |

| $\dfrac{8}{5}$ | $-\dfrac{\sqrt{39}}{5}$ | $\dfrac{\sqrt{39}}{8}$ | $-\dfrac{5\sqrt{39}}{39}$ | $-\dfrac{8\sqrt{39}}{39}$ |

10. What is the exact value of $\sin \dfrac{11\pi}{12}$?

(A) $-\dfrac{\sqrt{6} - \sqrt{2}}{4}$

(B) $\dfrac{\sqrt{6} - \sqrt{2}}{4}$

(C) $\dfrac{\sqrt{6} + \sqrt{2}}{4}$

(D) $\dfrac{3 - \sqrt{2}}{4}$

11. A right triangle with legs of length 7 and 12 is rotated about its shorter leg. What is the volume of the solid of revolution that is formed?

(A) about 615.75 cubic units

(B) about 976.12 cubic units

(C) about 1055.58 cubic units

(D) about 3166.73 cubic units

10 Data Analysis and Statistics

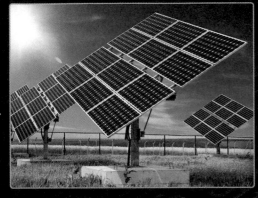

Solar Power *(p. 545)*

Reading *(p. 538)*

SEE the Big Idea

Volcano Damage *(p. 529)*

SAT Scores *(p. 519)*

Infant Weights *(p. 512)*

Maintaining Mathematical Proficiency

Comparing Measures of Center

Example 1 Find the mean, median, and mode of the data set 4, 11, 16, 8, 9, 40, 4, 12, 13, 5, and 10. Then determine which measure of center best represents the data. Explain.

Mean $\bar{x} = \dfrac{4 + 11 + 16 + 8 + 9 + 40 + 4 + 12 + 13 + 5 + 10}{11} = 12$

Median 4, 4, 5, 8, 9, 10, 11, 12, 13, 16, 40   Order the data. The middle value is 10.

Mode 4, 4, 5, 8, 9, 10, 11, 12, 13, 16, 40   4 occurs most often.

▶ The mean is 12, the median is 10, and the mode is 4. The median best represents the data. The mode is less than most of the data, and the mean is greater than most of the data.

Find the mean, median, and mode of the data set. Then determine which measure of center best represents the data. Explain.

1. 36, 82, 94, 83, 86, 82 **2.** 74, 89, 71, 70, 68, 70 **3.** 1, 18, 12, 16, 11, 15, 17, 44, 44

Finding a Standard Deviation

Example 2 Find and interpret the standard deviation of the data set 10, 2, 6, 8, 12, 15, 18, and 25. Use a table to organize your work.

x	$\bar{x}$	$x - \bar{x}$	$(x - \bar{x})^2$
10	12	−2	4
2	12	−10	100
6	12	−6	36
8	12	4	16
12	12	0	0
15	12	3	9
18	12	6	36
25	12	13	169

Step 1 Find the mean, $\bar{x}$.
$$\bar{x} = \frac{96}{8} = 12$$

Step 2 Find the deviation of each data value, $x - \bar{x}$, as shown in the table.

Step 3 Square each deviation, $(x - \bar{x})^2$, as shown in the table.

Step 4 Find the mean of the squared deviations.
$$\frac{(x_1 - \bar{x})^2 + (x_2 - \bar{x})^2 + \cdots + (x_n - \bar{x})^2}{n} =$$
$$\frac{4 + 100 + \cdots + 169}{8} = \frac{370}{8} = 46.25$$

Step 5 Use a calculator to take the square root of the mean of the squared deviations.

$$\sqrt{\frac{(x_1 - \bar{x})^2 + (x_2 - \bar{x})^2 + \cdots + (x_n - \bar{x})^2}{n}} = \sqrt{\frac{370}{8}} = \sqrt{46.25} \approx 6.80$$

▶ The standard deviation is about 6.80. This means that the typical data value differs from the mean by about 6.80 units.

Find and interpret the standard deviation of the data set.

4. 43, 48, 41, 51, 42 **5.** 28, 26, 21, 44, 29, 32 **6.** 65, 56, 49, 66, 62, 52, 53, 49

7. **ABSTRACT REASONING** Describe a data set that has a standard deviation of zero. Can a standard deviation be negative? Explain your reasoning.

Mathematical Practices

Mathematically proficient students use diagrams and graphs to show relationships between data. They also analyze data to draw conclusions.

Modeling with Mathematics

Core Concept

Information Design

Information design is the designing of data and information so it can be understood and used. Throughout this book, you have seen several types of information design. In the modern study of statistics, many types of designs require technology to analyze the data and organize the graphical design.

EXAMPLE 1   Comparing Age Pyramids

You can use an *age pyramid* to compare the ages of males and females in the population of a country. Compare the mean, median, and mode of each age pyramid.

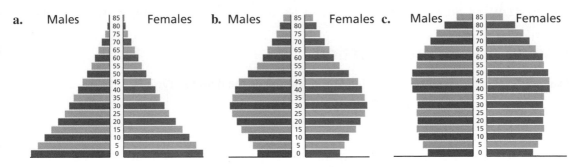

SOLUTION

a. The relative frequency of each successive age group (from 0–4 to 85+) is less than the preceding age group. The mean is roughly 25 years, the median is roughly 20 years, and the mode is the youngest age group, 0–4 years.

b. The mean, median, and mode are all roughly 32 years.

c. The mean, median, and mode are all roughly middle age, around 40 or 45 years.

Monitoring Progress

Use the Internet or some other reference to determine which age pyramid is that of Canada, Japan, and Mexico. Compare the mean, median, and mode of the three age pyramids.

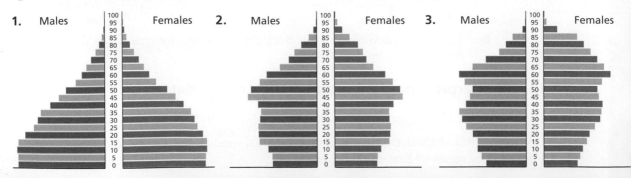

10.1 Using Normal Distributions

Essential Question
In a normal distribution, about what percent of the data lies within one, two, and three standard deviations of the mean?

Recall that the standard deviation σ of a numerical data set is given by

$$\sigma = \sqrt{\frac{(x_1 - \mu)^2 + (x_2 - \mu)^2 + \cdots + (x_n - \mu)^2}{n}}$$

where n is the number of values in the data set and μ is the mean of the data set.

EXPLORATION 1   Analyzing a Normal Distribution

Work with a partner. In many naturally occurring data sets, the histogram of the data is bell-shaped. In statistics, such data sets are said to have a *normal distribution*. For the normal distribution shown below, estimate the percent of the data that lies within one, two, and three standard deviations of the mean. Each square on the grid represents 1%.

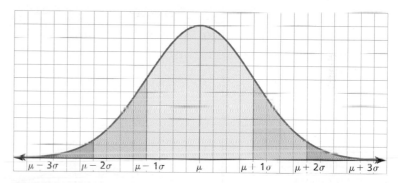

MODELING WITH MATHEMATICS

To be proficient in math, you need to analyze relationships mathematically to draw conclusions.

Chest size	Number of men
33	3
34	18
35	81
36	185
37	420
38	749
39	1073
40	1079
41	934
42	658
43	370
44	92
45	50
46	21
47	4
48	1

EXPLORATION 2   Analyzing a Data Set

Work with a partner. A famous data set was collected in Scotland in the mid-1800s. It contains the chest sizes (in inches) of 5738 men in the Scottish Militia. Do the data fit a normal distribution? Explain.

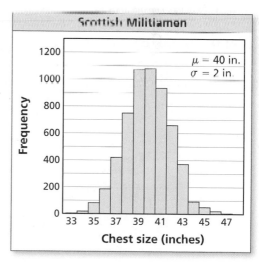

Communicate Your Answer

3. In a normal distribution, about what percent of the data lies within one, two, and three standard deviations of the mean?

4. Use the Internet or some other reference to find another data set that is normally distributed. Display your data in a histogram.

10.1 Lesson

Core Vocabulary

normal distribution, *p. 510*
normal curve, *p. 510*
standard normal distribution,
   p. 511
z-score, *p. 511*

Previous
probability distribution
symmetric
mean
standard deviation
skewed
median

What You Will Learn

▶ Calculate probabilities using normal distributions.

▶ Use *z*-scores and the standard normal table to find probabilities.

▶ Recognize data sets that are normal.

Normal Distributions

You have studied probability distributions. One type of probability distribution is a *normal distribution*. The graph of a **normal distribution** is a bell-shaped curve called a **normal curve** that is symmetric about the mean.

🔄 Core Concept

Areas Under a Normal Curve

A normal distribution with mean μ (the Greek letter *mu*) and standard deviation σ (the Greek letter *sigma*) has these properties.

- The total area under the related normal curve is 1.

- About 68% of the area lies within 1 standard deviation of the mean.

- About 95% of the area lies within 2 standard deviations of the mean.

- About 99.7% of the area lies within 3 standard deviations of the mean.

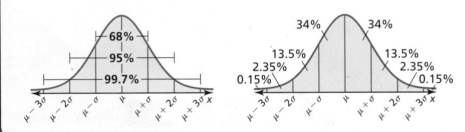

From the second bulleted statement above and the symmetry of a normal curve, you can deduce that 34% of the area lies within 1 standard deviation to the left of the mean, and 34% of the area lies within 1 standard deviation to the right of the mean. The second diagram above shows other partial areas based on the properties of a normal curve.

The areas under a normal curve can be interpreted as probabilities in a normal distribution. So, in a normal distribution, the probability that a randomly chosen *x*-value is between *a* and *b* is given by the area under the normal curve between *a* and *b*.

USING A GRAPHING CALCULATOR

A graphing calculator can be used to find areas under normal curves. For example, the normal distribution shown below has mean 0 and standard deviation 1. The graphing calculator screen shows that the area within 1 standard deviation of the mean is about 0.68, or 68%.

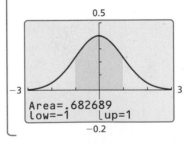

EXAMPLE 1   Finding a Normal Probability

A normal distribution has mean μ and standard deviation σ. An *x*-value is randomly selected from the distribution. Find $P(\mu - 2\sigma \le x \le \mu)$.

SOLUTION

The probability that a randomly selected
x-value lies between $\mu - 2\sigma$ and μ is the
shaded area under the normal curve shown.

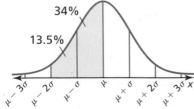

$$P(\mu - 2\sigma \le x \le \mu) = 0.135 + 0.34 = 0.475$$

EXAMPLE 2 **Interpreting Normally Distributed Data**

The scores for a state's peace officer standards and training test are normally distributed with a mean of 55 and a standard deviation of 12. The test scores range from 0 to 100.

a. About what percent of the people taking the test have scores between 43 and 67?

b. An agency in the state will only hire applicants with test scores of 67 or greater. About what percent of the people have test scores that make them eligible to be hired by the agency?

SOLUTION

Check

a.

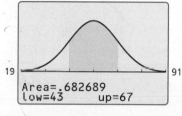

Area=.682689
low=43   up=67

b.

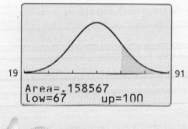

Area=.158567
Low=67   up=100

a. The scores of 43 and 67 represent one standard deviation on either side of the mean, as shown. So, about 68% of the people taking the test have scores between 43 and 67.

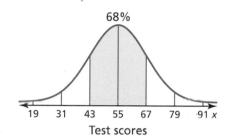

b. A score of 67 is one standard deviation to the right of the mean, as shown. So, the percent of the people who have test scores that make them eligible to be hired by the agency is about 13.5% + 2.35% + 0.15%, or 16%.

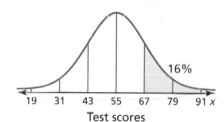

Monitoring Progress Help in English and Spanish at *BigIdeasMath.com*

A normal distribution has mean μ and standard deviation σ. Find the indicated probability for a randomly selected *x*-value from the distribution.

1. $P(x \le \mu)$

2. $P(x \ge \mu)$

3. $P(\mu \le x \le \mu + 2\sigma)$

4. $P(\mu - \sigma \le x \le \mu)$

5. $P(x \le \mu - 3\sigma)$

6. $P(x \ge \mu + \sigma)$

7. **WHAT IF?** In Example 2, about what percent of the people taking the test have scores between 43 and 79?

The Standard Normal Distribution

The **standard normal distribution** is the normal distribution with mean 0 and standard deviation 1. The formula below can be used to transform *x*-values from a normal distribution with mean μ and standard deviation σ into *z*-values having a standard normal distribution.

Formula $z = \dfrac{x - \mu}{\sigma}$ ← Subtract the mean from the given *x*-value, then divide by the standard deviation.

The *z*-value for a particular *x*-value is called the **z-score** for the *x*-value and is the number of standard deviations the *x*-value lies above or below the mean μ.

For a randomly selected z-value from a standard normal distribution, you can use the table below to find the probability that z is less than or equal to a given value. For example, the table shows that $P(z \le -0.4) = 0.3446$. You can find the value of $P(z \le -0.4)$ in the table by finding the value where row -0 and column .4 intersect.

Standard Normal Table

z	.0	.1	.2	.3	.4	.5	.6	.7	.8	.9
−3	.0013	.0010	.0007	.0005	.0003	.0002	.0002	.0001	.0001	.0000+
−2	.0228	.0179	.0139	.0107	.0082	.0062	.0047	.0035	.0026	.0019
−1	.1587	.1357	.1151	.0968	.0808	.0668	.0548	.0446	.0359	.0287
−0	.5000	.4602	.4207	.3821	(.3446)	.3085	.2743	.2420	.2119	.1841
0	.5000	.5398	.5793	.6179	.6554	.6915	.7257	.7580	.7881	.8159
1	.8413	.8643	.8849	.9032	.9192	.9332	.9452	.9554	.9641	.9713
2	.9772	.9821	.9861	.9893	.9918	.9938	.9953	.9965	.9974	.9981
3	.9987	.9990	.9993	.9995	.9997	.9998	.9998	.9999	.9999	1.0000−

You can also use the standard normal table to find probabilities for any normal distribution by first converting values from the distribution to z-scores.

EXAMPLE 3 Using a z-Score and the Standard Normal Table

A study finds that the weights of infants at birth are normally distributed with a mean of 3270 grams and a standard deviation of 600 grams. An infant is randomly chosen. What is the probability that the infant weighs 4170 grams or less?

SOLUTION

Step 1 Find the z-score corresponding to an x-value of 4170.

$$z = \frac{x - \mu}{\sigma} = \frac{4170 - 3270}{600} = 1.5$$

Step 2 Use the table to find $P(z \le 1.5)$. The table shows that $P(z \le 1.5) = 0.9332$.

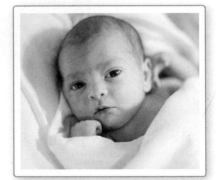

Standard Normal Table

z	.0	.1	.2	.3	.4	.5	.6	.7	.8	.9
−3	.0013	.0010	.0007	.0005	.0003	.0002	.0002	.0001	.0001	.0000+
−2	.0228	.0179	.0139	.0107	.0082	.0062	.0047	.0035	.0026	.0019
−1	.1587	.1357	.1151	.0968	.0808	.0668	.0548	.0446	.0359	.0287
−0	.5000	.4602	.4207	.3821	.3446	.3085	.2743	.2420	.2119	.1841
0	.5000	.5398	.5793	.6179	.6554	.6915	.7257	.7580	.7881	.8159
1	.8413	.8643	.8849	.9032	.9192	(.9332)	.9452	.9554	.9641	.9713

▶ So, the probability that the infant weighs 4170 grams or less is about 0.9332.

Monitoring Progress Help in English and Spanish at *BigIdeasMath.com*

8. **WHAT IF?** In Example 3, what is the probability that the infant weighs 3990 grams or more?

9. Explain why it makes sense that $P(z \le 0) = 0.5$.

Recognizing Normal Distributions

Not all distributions are normal. For instance, consider the histograms shown below. The first histogram has a normal distribution. Notice that it is bell-shaped and symmetric. Recall that a distribution is symmetric when you can draw a vertical line that divides the histogram into two parts that are mirror images. Some distributions are skewed. The second histogram is *skewed left* and the third histogram is *skewed right*. The second and third histograms do *not* have normal distributions.

UNDERSTANDING MATHEMATICAL TERMS

Be sure you understand that you cannot use a normal distribution to interpret skewed distributions. The areas under a normal curve do not correspond to the areas of a skewed distribution.

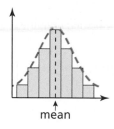

mean

Bell-shaped and symmetric
- histogram has a normal distribution
- mean = median

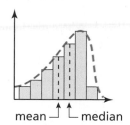

mean ⌐ ⌐ median

Skewed left
- histogram does not have a normal distribution
- mean < median

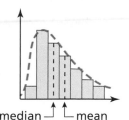

median ⌐ ⌐ mean

Skewed right
- histogram does not have a normal distribution
- mean > median

EXAMPLE 4 **Recognizing Normal Distributions**

Determine whether each histogram has a normal distribution.

a.

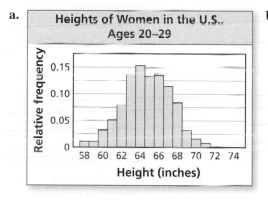

b.

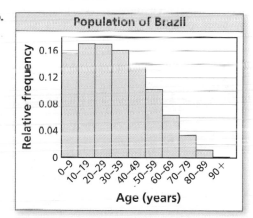

SOLUTION

a. The histogram is bell-shaped and fairly symmetric. So, the histogram has an approximately normal distribution.

b. The histogram is skewed right. So, the histogram does not have a normal distribution, and you cannot use a normal distribution to interpret the histogram.

Monitoring Progress

Help in English and Spanish at *BigIdeasMath.com*

10. Determine whether the histogram has a normal distribution.

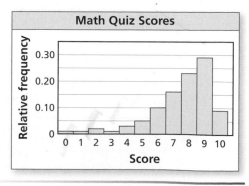

Vocabulary and Core Concept Check

1. **WRITING** Describe how to use the standard normal table to find $P(z \leq 1.4)$.

2. **WHICH ONE DOESN'T BELONG?** Which histogram does *not* belong with the other three? Explain your reasoning.

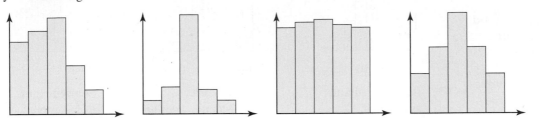

Monitoring Progress and Modeling with Mathematics

ATTENTING TO PRECISION In Exercises 3–6, give the percent of the area under the normal curve represented by the shaded region(s).

3.

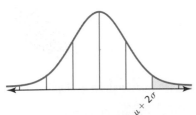

4.

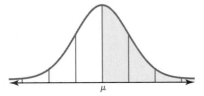

5.

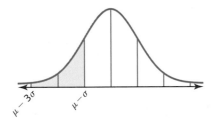

6.

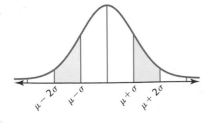

In Exercises 7–12, a normal distribution has mean μ and standard deviation σ. Find the indicated probability for a randomly selected x-value from the distribution. *(See Example 1.)*

7. $P(x \leq \mu - \sigma)$

8. $P(x \geq \mu - \sigma)$

9. $P(x \geq \mu + 2\sigma)$

10. $P(x \leq \mu + \sigma)$

11. $P(\mu - \sigma \leq x \leq \mu + \sigma)$

12. $P(\mu - 3\sigma \leq x \leq \mu)$

In Exercises 13–18, a normal distribution has a mean of 33 and a standard deviation of 4. Find the probability that a randomly selected x-value from the distribution is in the given interval.

13. between 29 and 37

14. between 33 and 45

15. at least 25

16. at least 29

17. at most 37

18. at most 21

19. **PROBLEM SOLVING** The wing lengths of houseflies are normally distributed with a mean of 4.6 millimeters and a standard deviation of 0.4 millimeter. *(See Example 2.)*

wing length

a. About what percent of houseflies have wing lengths between 3.8 millimeters and 5.0 millimeters?

b. About what percent of houseflies have wing lengths longer than 5.8 millimeters?

20. **PROBLEM SOLVING** The times a fire department takes to arrive at the scene of an emergency are normally distributed with a mean of 6 minutes and a standard deviation of 1 minute.

   a. For about what percent of emergencies does the fire department arrive at the scene in 8 minutes or less?

   b. The goal of the fire department is to reach the scene of an emergency in 5 minutes or less. About what percent of the time does the fire department achieve its goal?

   c. The fire department implements personnel changes that increase the standard deviation of the arrival times to 1.5 minutes. Discuss an advantage and a disadvantage of these changes.

ERROR ANALYSIS In Exercises 21 and 22, a normal distribution has a mean of 25 and a standard deviation of 2. Describe and correct the error in finding the probability that a randomly selected x-value is in the given interval.

21. between 23 and 27

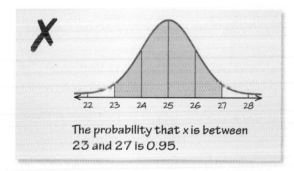

The probability that x is between 23 and 27 is 0.95.

22. at least 21

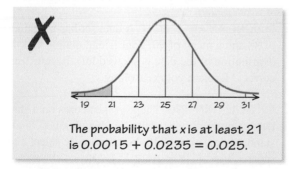

The probability that x is at least 21 is $0.0015 + 0.0235 = 0.025$.

23. **PROBLEM SOLVING** Scientists conducted aerial surveys of a seal sanctuary and recorded the number x of seals they observed during each survey. The numbers of seals observed were normally distributed with a mean of 73 seals and a standard deviation of 14.1 seals. Find the probability that at most 50 seals were observed during a randomly chosen survey. *(See Example 3.)*

24. **PROBLEM SOLVING** A busy time to visit a bank is during its Friday evening rush hours. For these hours, the waiting times at the drive-through window are normally distributed with a mean of 8 minutes and a standard deviation of 2 minutes. You have no more than 11 minutes to do your banking and still make it to your meeting on time. You want to do your banking as long as it is unlikely that it will cause you to be late for the meeting. Should you do your banking? Explain your reasoning.

In Exercises 25 and 26, determine whether the histogram has a normal distribution. *(See Example 4.)*

25.

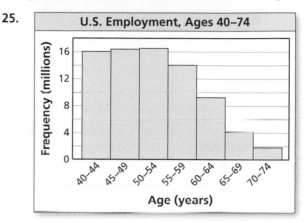

26.

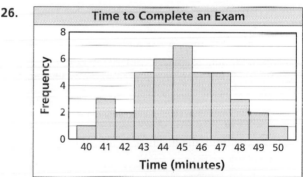

27. **ANALYZING RELATIONSHIPS** The table shows the numbers of tickets that are sold for various baseball games in a league over an entire season. Display the data in a histogram. Do the data fit a normal distribution? Explain.

Tickets sold	Frequency
150–189	1
190–229	2
230–269	4
270–309	8
310–349	8
350–389	7

28. PROBLEM SOLVING The guayule plant, which grows in the southwestern United States and in Mexico, is one of several plants that can be used as a source of rubber. In a large group of guayule plants, the heights of the plants are normally distributed with a mean of 12 inches and a standard deviation of 2 inches.

a. What percent of the plants are taller than 16 inches?

b. What percent of the plants are at most 13 inches?

c. What percent of the plants are between 7 inches and 14 inches?

d. What percent of the plants are at least 3 inches taller than or at least 3 inches shorter than the mean height?

29. REASONING Boxes of cereal are filled by a machine. Tests show that the amount of cereal in each box varies. The weights are normally distributed with a mean of 20 ounces and a standard deviation of 0.25 ounce. Four boxes of cereal are randomly chosen.

a. What is the probability that all four boxes contain no more than 19.4 ounces of cereal?

b. Do you think the machine is functioning properly? Explain.

30. THOUGHT PROVOKING Sketch the graph of the standard normal distribution function, given by

$$f(x) = \frac{1}{\sqrt{2\pi}} e^{-x^2/2}.$$

Estimate the area of the region bounded by the x-axis, the graph of f, and the vertical lines $x = -3$ and $x = 3$.

31. REASONING For normally distributed data, describe the value that represents the 84th percentile in terms of the mean and standard deviation.

32. HOW DO YOU SEE IT? In the figure, the shaded region represents 47.5% of the area under a normal curve. What are the mean and standard deviation of the normal distribution?

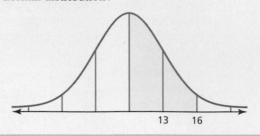

33. DRAWING CONCLUSIONS You take both the SAT (Scholastic Aptitude Test) and the ACT (American College Test). You score 650 on the mathematics section of the SAT and 29 on the mathematics section of the ACT. The SAT test scores and the ACT test scores are each normally distributed. For the SAT, the mean is 514 and the standard deviation is 118. For the ACT, the mean is 21.0 and the standard deviation is 5.3.

a. What percentile is your SAT math score?

b. What percentile is your ACT math score?

c. On which test did you perform better? Explain your reasoning.

34. WRITING Explain how you can convert ACT scores into corresponding SAT scores when you know the mean and standard deviation of each distribution.

35. MAKING AN ARGUMENT A data set has a median of 80 and a mean of 90. Your friend claims that the distribution of the data is skewed left. Is your friend correct? Explain your reasoning.

36. CRITICAL THINKING The average scores on a statistics test are normally distributed with a mean of 75 and a standard deviation of 10. You randomly select a test score x. Find $P(|x - \mu| \geq 15)$.

Maintaining Mathematical Proficiency
Reviewing what you learned in previous grades and lessons

Graph the function. Identify the x-intercepts and the points where the local maximums and local minimums occur. Determine the intervals for which the function is increasing or decreasing. *(Section 3.8)*

37. $f(x) = x^3 - 4x^2 + 5$

38. $g(x) = \frac{1}{4}x^4 - 2x^2 - x - 3$

39. $h(x) = -0.5x^2 + 3x + 7$

40. $f(x) = -x^4 + 6x^2 - 13$

10.2 Populations, Samples, and Hypotheses

Essential Question How can you test theoretical probability using sample data?

Work with a partner.

a. When two six-sided dice are rolled, what is the theoretical probability that you roll the same number on both dice?

b. Conduct an experiment to check your answer in part (a). What sample size did you use? Explain your reasoning.

c. Use the dice rolling simulator at *BigIdeasMath.com* to complete the table and check your answer to part (a). What happens as you increase the sample size?

> **USING TOOLS STRATEGICALLY**
>
> To be proficient in math, you need to use technology to visualize the results of varying assumptions, explore consequences, and compare predictions with data.

Number of Rolls	Number of Times Same Number Appears	Experimental Probability
100		
500		
1000		
5000		
10,000		

Work with a partner.

a. When three six-sided dice are rolled, what is the theoretical probability that you roll the same number on all three dice?

b. Compare the theoretical probability you found in part (a) with the theoretical probability you found in Exploration 1(a).

c. Conduct an experiment to check your answer in part (a). How does adding a die affect the sample size that you use? Explain your reasoning.

d. Use the dice rolling simulator at *BigIdeasMath.com* to check your answer to part (a). What happens as you increase the sample size?

Communicate Your Answer

3. How can you test theoretical probability using sample data?

4. Conduct an experiment to determine the probability of rolling a sum of 7 when two six-sided dice are rolled. Then find the theoretical probability and compare your answers.

Core Vocabulary

population, *p. 518*
sample, *p. 518*
parameter, *p. 519*
statistic, *p. 519*
hypothesis, *p. 519*

Previous
Venn diagram
proportion

What You Will Learn

▶ Distinguish between populations and samples.

▶ Analyze hypotheses.

Populations and Samples

A **population** is the collection of all data, such as responses, measurements, or counts, that you want information about. A **sample** is a subset of a population.

A *census* consists of data from an entire population. But, unless a population is small, it is usually impractical to obtain all the population data. In most studies, information must be obtained from a *random sample*. (You will learn more about random sampling and data collection in the next section.)

It is important for a sample to be representative of a population so that sample data can be used to draw conclusions about the population. When the sample is not representative of the population, the conclusions may not be valid. Drawing conclusions about populations is an important use of *statistics*. Recall that statistics is the science of collecting, organizing, and interpreting data.

EXAMPLE 1   Distinguishing Between Populations and Samples

Identify the population and the sample. Describe the sample.

a. In the United States, a survey of 2184 adults ages 18 and over found that 1328 of them own at least one pet.

b. To estimate the gasoline mileage of new cars sold in the United States, a consumer advocacy group tests 845 new cars and finds they have an average of 25.1 miles per gallon.

SOLUTION

a. The population consists of the responses of all adults ages 18 and over in the United States, and the sample consists of the responses of the 2184 adults in the survey. Notice in the diagram that the sample is a subset of the responses of all adults in the United States. The sample consists of 1328 adults who said they own at least one pet and 856 adults who said they do not own any pets.

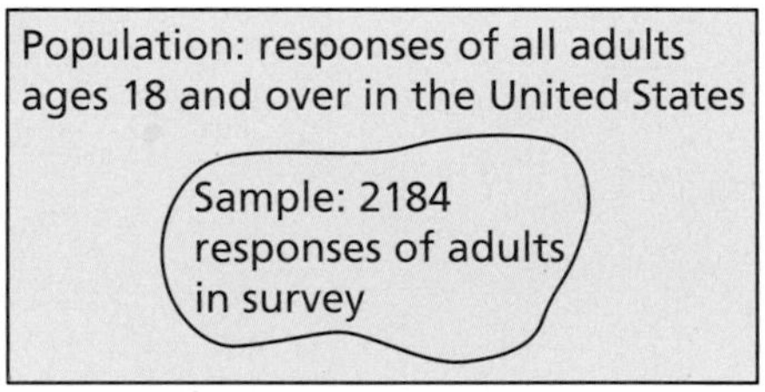

> Population: responses of all adults ages 18 and over in the United States
>
> Sample: 2184 responses of adults in survey

b. The population consists of the gasoline mileages of all new cars sold in the United States, and the sample consists of the gasoline mileages of the 845 new cars tested by the group. Notice in the diagram that the sample is a subset of the gasoline mileages of all new cars in the United States. The sample consists of 845 new cars with an average of 25.1 miles per gallon.

> Population: gasoline mileages of all new cars sold in the United States
>
> Sample: gasoline mileages of 845 new cars in test

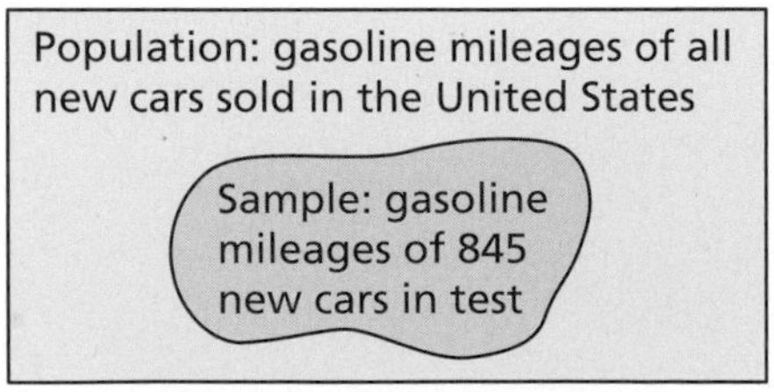

A numerical description of a population characteristic is called a **parameter**. A numerical description of a sample characteristic is called a **statistic**. Because some populations are too large to measure, a statistic, such as the sample mean, is used to estimate the parameter, such as the population mean. It is important that you are able to distinguish between a parameter and a statistic.

EXAMPLE 2 **Distinguishing Between Parameters and Statistics**

a. For all students taking the SAT in a recent year, the mean mathematics score was 514. Is the mean score a parameter or a statistic? Explain your reasoning.

b. A survey of 1060 women, ages 20–29 in the United States, found that the standard deviation of their heights is about 2.6 inches. Is the standard deviation of the heights a parameter or a statistic? Explain your reasoning.

SOLUTION

a. Because the mean score of 514 is based on all students who took the SAT in a recent year, it is a parameter.

b. Because there are more than 1060 women ages 20–29 in the United States, the survey is based on a subset of the population (all women ages 20–29 in the United States). So, the standard deviation of the heights is a statistic. Note that if the sample is representative of the population, then you can estimate that the standard deviation of the heights of all women ages 20–29 in the United States is about 2.6 inches.

Monitoring Progress Help in English and Spanish at *BigIdeasMath.com*

In Monitoring Progress Questions 1 and 2, identify the population and the sample.

1. To estimate the retail prices for three grades of gasoline sold in the United States, the Energy Information Association calls 800 retail gasoline outlets, records the prices, and then determines the average price for each grade.

2. A survey of 4464 shoppers in the United States found that they spent an average of $407.02 from Thursday through Sunday during a recent Thanksgiving holiday.

3. A survey found that the median salary of 1068 statisticians is about $72,800. Is the median salary a parameter or a statistic? Explain your reasoning.

4. The mean age of U.S. representatives at the start of the 113th Congress was about 57 years. Is the mean age a parameter or a statistic? Explain your reasoning.

Analyzing Hypotheses

In statistics, a **hypothesis** is a claim about a characteristic of a population. Here are some examples.

1. A drug company claims that patients using its weight-loss drug lose an average of 24 pounds in the first 3 months.

2. A medical researcher claims that the proportion of U.S. adults living with one or more chronic conditions, such as high blood pressure, is 0.45, or 45%.

To analyze a hypothesis, you need to distinguish between results that can easily occur by chance and results that are highly unlikely to occur by chance. One way to analyze a hypothesis is to perform a *simulation*. When the results are highly unlikely to occur, the hypothesis is probably false.

UNDERSTANDING MATHEMATICAL TERMS

A *population proportion* is the ratio of members of a population with a particular characteristic to the total members of the population. A *sample proportion* is the ratio of members of a sample of the population with a particular characteristic to the total members of the sample.

EXAMPLE 3   Analyzing a Hypothesis

INTERPRETING MATHEMATICAL RESULTS

Results of other simulations may have histograms different from the one shown, but the shape should be similar. Note that the histogram is fairly bell-shaped and symmetric, which means the distribution is approximately normal. By increasing the number of samples or the sample sizes (or both), you should get a histogram that more closely resembles a normal distribution.

You roll a six-sided die 5 times and do not get an even number. The probability of this happening is $\left(\frac{1}{2}\right)^5 = 0.03125$, so you suspect this die favors odd numbers. The die maker claims the die does not favor odd numbers or even numbers. What should you conclude when you roll the actual die 50 times and get (a) 26 odd numbers and (b) 35 odd numbers?

SOLUTION

The maker's claim, or hypothesis, is "the die does not favor odd numbers or even numbers." This is the same as saying that the proportion of odd numbers rolled, in the long run, is 0.50. So, assume the probability of rolling an odd number is 0.50. Simulate the rolling of the die by repeatedly drawing 200 random samples of size 50 from a population of 50% ones and 50% zeros. Let the population of ones represent the event of rolling an odd number and make a histogram of the distribution of the sample proportions.

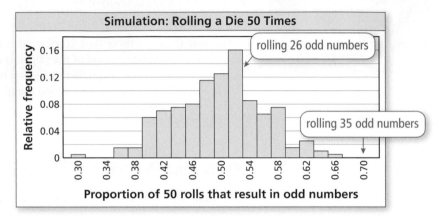

a. Getting 26 odd numbers in 50 rolls corresponds to a proportion of $\frac{26}{50} = 0.52$. In the simulation, this result had a relative frequency of 0.16. In fact, most of the results are close to 0.50. Because this result can easily occur by chance, you can conclude that the maker's claim is most likely true.

b. Getting 35 odd numbers in 50 rolls corresponds to a proportion of $\frac{35}{50} = 0.70$. In the simulation, this result did not occur. Because getting 35 odd numbers is highly unlikely to occur by chance, you can conclude that the maker's claim is most likely false.

JUSTIFYING CONCLUSIONS

In Example 3(b), the theoretical probability of getting 35 odd numbers in 50 rolls is about 0.002. So, while unlikely, it is possible that you incorrectly concluded that the die maker's claim is false.

Monitoring Progress Help in English and Spanish at *BigIdeasMath.com*

5. **WHAT IF?** In Example 3, what should you conclude when you roll the actual die 50 times and get (a) 24 odd numbers and (b) 31 odd numbers?

In Example 3(b), you concluded the maker's claim is probably false. In general, such conclusions may or may not be correct. The table summarizes the incorrect and correct decisions that can be made about a hypothesis.

		Truth of Hypothesis	
		Hypothesis is true.	Hypothesis is false.
Decision	You decide that the hypothesis is true.	correct decision	incorrect decision
	You decide that the hypothesis is false.	incorrect decision	correct decision

Vocabulary and Core Concept Check

1. **COMPLETE THE SENTENCE** A portion of a population that can be studied in order to make predictions about the entire population is a(n) _____.

2. **WRITING** Describe the difference between a parameter and a statistic. Give an example of each.

3. **VOCABULARY** What is a hypothesis in statistics?

4. **WRITING** Describe two ways you can make an incorrect decision when analyzing a hypothesis.

Monitoring Progress and Modeling with Mathematics

In Exercises 5–8, determine whether the data are collected from a population or a sample. Explain your reasoning.

5. the number of high school students in the United States

6. the color of every third car that passes your house

7. a survey of 100 spectators at a sporting event with 1800 spectators

8. the age of each dentist in the United States

In Exercises 9–12, identify the population and sample. Describe the sample. *(See Example 1.)*

9. In the United States, a survey of 1152 adults ages 18 and over found that 403 of them pretend to use their smartphones to avoid talking to someone.

10. In the United States, a survey of 1777 adults ages 18 and over found that 1279 of them do some kind of spring cleaning every year.

11. In a school district, a survey of 1300 high school students found that 1001 of them like the new, healthy cafeteria food choices.

12. In the United States, a survey of 2000 households with at least one child found that 1280 of them eat dinner together every night.

In Exercises 13–16, determine whether the numerical value is a parameter or a statistic. Explain your reasoning. *(See Example 2.)*

13. The average annual salary of some physical therapists in a state is $76,210.

14. In a recent year, 53% of the senators in the United States Senate were Democrats.

15. Seventy-three percent of all the students in a school would prefer to have school dances on Saturday.

16. A survey of U.S. adults found that 10% believe a cleaning product they use is not safe for the environment.

17. **ERROR ANALYSIS** A survey of 1270 high school students found that 965 students felt added stress because of their workload. Describe and correct the error in identifying the population and the sample.

> ✗ The population consists of all the students in the high school. The sample consists of the 965 students who felt added stress.

18. **ERROR ANALYSIS** Of all the players on a National Football League team, the mean age is 26 years. Describe and correct the error in determining whether the mean age represents a parameter or statistic.

> ✗ Because the mean age of 26 is based only on one football team, it is a statistic.

19. **MODELING WITH MATHEMATICS** You flip a coin 4 times and do not get a tails. You suspect this coin favors heads. The coin maker claims that the coin does not favor heads or tails. You simulate flipping the coin 50 times by repeatedly drawing 200 random samples of size 50. The histogram shows the results. What should you conclude when you flip the actual coin 50 times and get (a) 27 heads and (b) 33 heads? *(See Example 3.)*

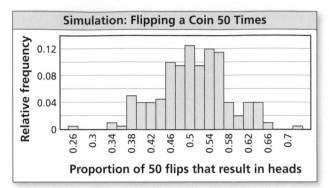

20. **MODELING WITH MATHEMATICS** Use the histogram in Exercise 19 to determine what you should conclude when you flip the actual coin 50 times and get (a) 17 heads and (b) 23 heads.

21. **MAKING AN ARGUMENT** A random sample of five people at a movie theater from a population of 200 people gave the film 4 out of 4 stars. Your friend concludes that everyone in the movie theater would give the film 4 stars. Is your friend correct? Explain your reasoning.

22. **HOW DO YOU SEE IT?** Use the Venn diagram to identify the population and sample. Explain your reasoning.

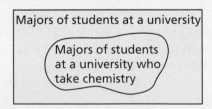

23. **OPEN-ENDED** Find a newspaper or magazine article that describes a survey. Identify the population and sample. Describe the sample.

24. **THOUGHT PROVOKING** You choose a random sample of 200 from a population of 2000. Each person in the sample is asked how many hours of sleep he or she gets each night. The mean of your sample is 8 hours. Is it possible that the mean of the entire population is only 7.5 hours of sleep each night? Explain.

25. **DRAWING CONCLUSIONS** You perform two simulations of repeatedly selecting a marble out of a bag with replacement that contains three red marbles and three blue marbles. The first simulation uses 20 random samples of size 10, and the second uses 400 random samples of size 10. The histograms show the results. Which simulation should you use to accurately analyze a hypothesis? Explain.

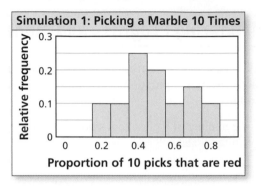

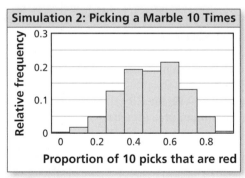

26. **PROBLEM SOLVING** You roll an eight-sided die five times and get a four every time. You suspect that the die favors the number four. The die maker claims that the die does not favor any number.

    a. Perform a simulation involving 50 trials of rolling the actual die and getting a four to test the die maker's claim. Display the results in a histogram.

    b. What should you conclude when you roll the actual die 50 times and get 20 fours? 7 fours?

Maintaining Mathematical Proficiency
Reviewing what you learned in previous grades and lessons

Solve the equation by completing the square. *(Skills Review Handbook)*

27. $x^2 - 10x - 4 = 0$

28. $3t^2 + 6t = 18$

29. $s^2 + 10s + 8 = 0$

Solve the equation using the Quadratic Formula. *(Skills Review Handbook)*

30. $n^2 + 2n + 2 = 0$

31. $4z^2 + 28z = 15$

32. $5w - w^2 = -11$

10.3 Collecting Data

Essential Question What are some considerations when undertaking a statistical study?

The goal of any statistical study is to collect data and then use the data to make a decision. Any decision you make using the results of a statistical study is only as reliable as the process used to obtain the data. If the process is flawed, then the resulting decision is questionable.

EXPLORATION 1 Analyzing Sampling Techniques

Work with a partner. Determine whether each sample is representative of the population. Explain your reasoning.

a. To determine the number of hours people exercise during a week, researchers use random-digit dialing and call 1500 people.

b. To determine how many text messages high school students send in a week, researchers post a survey on a website and receive 750 responses.

c. To determine how much money college students spend on clothes each semester, a researcher surveys 450 college students as they leave the university library.

d. To determine the quality of service customers receive, an airline sends an e-mail survey to each customer after the completion of a flight.

EXPLORATION 2 Analyzing Survey Questions

Work with a partner. Determine whether each survey question is biased. Explain your reasoning. If so, suggest an unbiased rewording of the question.

a. Does eating nutritious, whole-grain foods improve your health?

b. Do you ever attempt the dangerous activity of texting while driving?

c. How many hours do you sleep each night?

d. How can the mayor of your city improve his or her public image?

EXPLORATION 3 Analyzing Survey Randomness and Truthfulness

Work with a partner. Discuss each potential problem in obtaining a random survey of a population. Include suggestions for overcoming the problem.

a. The people selected might not be a random sample of the population.

b. The people selected might not be willing to participate in the survey.

c. The people selected might not be truthful when answering the question.

d. The people selected might not understand the survey question.

Communicate Your Answer

4. What are some considerations when undertaking a statistical study?

5. Find a real-life example of a biased survey question. Then suggest an unbiased rewording of the question.

JUSTIFYING CONCLUSIONS

To be proficient in math, you need to justify your conclusions and communicate them to others.

Core Vocabulary

random sample, *p. 524*
self-selected sample, *p. 524*
systematic sample, *p. 524*
stratified sample, *p. 524*
cluster sample, *p. 524*
convenience sample, *p. 524*
bias, *p. 525*
unbiased sample, *p. 525*
biased sample, *p. 525*
experiment, *p. 526*
observational study, *p. 526*
survey, *p. 526*
simulation, *p. 526*
biased question, *p. 527*

Previous
population
sample

What You Will Learn

▶ Identify types of sampling methods in statistical studies.
▶ Recognize bias in sampling.
▶ Analyze methods of collecting data.
▶ Recognize bias in survey questions.

Identifying Sampling Methods in Statistical Studies

The steps in a typical statistical study are shown below.

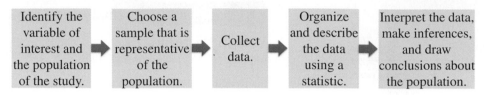

There are many different ways of sampling a population, but a *random sample* is preferred because it is most likely to be representative of a population. In a **random sample**, each member of a population has an equal chance of being selected.

The other types of samples given below are defined by the methods used to select members. Each sampling method has its advantages and disadvantages.

⑤ Core Concept

Types of Samples

For a **self-selected sample**, members of a population can volunteer to be in the sample.

For a **systematic sample**, a rule is used to select members of a population. For instance, selecting every other person.

For a **stratified sample**, a population is divided into smaller groups that share a similar characteristic. A sample is then randomly selected from each group.

STUDY TIP

A stratified sample ensures that every segment of a population is represented.

For a **cluster sample**, a population is divided into groups, called *clusters*. All of the members in one or more of the clusters are selected.

STUDY TIP

With cluster sampling, a member of a population cannot belong to more than one cluster.

For a **convenience sample**, only members of a population who are easy to reach are selected.

| | EXAMPLE 1 | Identifying Types of Samples |

You want to determine whether students in your school like the new design of the school's website. Identify the type of sample described.

a. You list all of the students alphabetically and choose every sixth student.

b. You mail questionnaires and use only the questionnaires that are returned.

c. You ask all of the students in your algebra class.

d. You randomly select two students from each classroom.

SOLUTION

a. You are using a rule to select students. So, the sample is a *systematic* sample.

b. The students can choose whether to respond. So, the sample is a *self-selected* sample.

c. You are selecting students who are readily available. So, the sample is a *convenience* sample.

d. The students are divided into similar groups by their classrooms, and two students are selected at random from each group. So, the sample is a *stratified* sample.

Monitoring Progress Help in English and Spanish at *BigIdeasMath.com*

1. **WHAT IF?** In Example 1, you divide the students in your school according to their zip codes, then select all of the students that live in one zip code. What type of sample are you using?

2. Describe another method you can use to obtain a stratified sample in Example 1.

Recognizing Bias in Sampling

STUDY TIP

All good sampling methods rely on random sampling.

A **bias** is an error that results in a misrepresentation of a population. In order to obtain reliable information and draw accurate conclusions about a population, it is important to select an *unbiased sample*. An **unbiased sample** is representative of the population that you want information about. A sample that overrepresents or under-represents part of the population is a **biased sample**. When a sample is biased, the data are invalid. A *random sample* can help reduce the possibility of a biased sample.

| | EXAMPLE 2 | Identifying Bias in Samples |

Identify the type of sample and explain why the sample is biased.

a. A news organization asks its viewers to participate in an online poll about bullying.

b. A computer science teacher wants to know how students at a school most often access the Internet. The teacher asks students in one of the computer science classes.

SOLUTION

a. The viewers can choose whether to participate in the poll. So, the sample is a *self-selected* sample. The sample is biased because people who go online and respond to the poll most likely have a strong opinion on the subject of bullying.

b. The teacher selects students who are readily available. So, the sample is a *convenience* sample. The sample is biased because other students in the school do not have an opportunity to be chosen.

Section 10.3   Collecting Data   **525**

EXAMPLE 3   Selecting an Unbiased Sample

You are a member of your school's yearbook committee. You want to poll members of the senior class to find out what the theme of the yearbook should be. There are 246 students in the senior class. Describe a method for selecting a random sample of 50 seniors to poll.

SOLUTION

Step 1   Make a list of all 246 seniors. Assign each senior a different integer from 1 to 246.

Step 2   Generate 50 unique random integers from 1 to 246 using the *randInt* feature of a graphing calculator.

Step 3   Choose the 50 students who correspond to the 50 integers you generated in Step 2.

```
randInt(1,246)
                84
               245
                50
               197
               235
                55
```

Monitoring Progress Help in English and Spanish at *BigIdeasMath.com*

3. The manager of a concert hall wants to know how often people in the community attend concerts. The manager asks 45 people standing in line for a rock concert how many concerts they attend per year. Identify the type of sample the manager is using and explain why the sample is biased.

4. In Example 3, what is another method you can use to generate a random sample of 50 students? Explain why your sampling method is random.

Analyzing Methods of Data Collection

There are several ways to collect data for a statistical study. The objective of the study often dictates the best method for collecting the data.

Core Concept

Methods of Collecting Data

An **experiment** imposes a treatment on individuals in order to collect data on their response to the treatment. The treatment may be a medical treatment, or it can be any action that might affect a variable in the experiment, such as adding methanol to gasoline and then measuring its effect on fuel efficiency.

An **observational study** observes individuals and measures variables without controlling the individuals or their environment. This type of study is used when it is difficult to control or isolate the variable being studied, or when it may be unethical to subject people to a certain treatment or to withhold it from them.

A **survey** is an investigation of one or more characteristics of a population. In a survey, every member of a sample is asked one or more questions.

A **simulation** uses a model to reproduce the conditions of a situation or process so that the simulated outcomes closely match the real-world outcomes. Simulations allow you to study situations that are impractical or dangerous to create in real life.

EXAMPLE 4 **Identifying Methods of Data Collection**

Identify the method of data collection each situation describes.

a. A researcher records whether people at a gas station use hand sanitizer.

b. A landscaper fertilizes 20 lawns with a regular fertilizer mix and 20 lawns with a new organic fertilizer. The landscaper then compares the lawns after 10 weeks and determines which fertilizer is better.

SOLUTION

a. The researcher is gathering data without controlling the individuals or applying a treatment. So, this situation is an *observational study*.

b. A treatment (organic fertilizer) is being applied to some of the individuals (lawns) in the study. So, this situation is an *experiment*.

Monitoring Progress Help in English and Spanish at *BigIdeasMath.com*

Identify the method of data collection the situation describes.

5. Members of a student council at your school ask every eighth student who enters the cafeteria whether they like the snacks in the school's vending machines.

6. A park ranger measures and records the heights of trees in a park as they grow.

7. A researcher uses a computer program to help determine how fast an influenza virus might spread within a city.

Recognizing Bias in Survey Questions

When designing a survey, it is important to word survey questions so they do not lead to biased results. Answers to poorly worded questions may not accurately reflect the opinions or actions of those being surveyed. Questions that are flawed in a way that leads to inaccurate results are called **biased questions**. Avoid questions that:

- encourage a particular response
- are too sensitive to answer truthfully
- do not provide enough information to give an accurate opinion
- address more than one issue

EXAMPLE 5 **Identify and Correct Bias in Survey Questioning**

A dentist surveys his patients by asking, "Do you brush your teeth at least twice per day and floss every day?" Explain why the question may be biased or otherwise introduce bias into the survey. Then describe a way to correct the flaw.

SOLUTION

Patients who brush less than twice per day or do not floss daily may be afraid to admit this because the dentist is asking the question. One improvement may be to have patients answer questions about dental hygiene on paper and then put the paper anonymously into a box.

Monitoring Progress Help in English and Spanish at *BigIdeasMath.com*

8. Explain why the survey question below may be biased or otherwise introduce bias into the survey. Then describe a way to correct the flaw.

"Do you agree that our school cafeteria should switch to a healthier menu?"

Vocabulary and Core Concept Check

1. **VOCABULARY** Describe the difference between a stratified sample and a cluster sample.

2. **COMPLETE THE SENTENCE** A sample for which each member of a population has an equal chance of being selected is a(n) _____ sample.

3. **WRITING** Describe a situation in which you would use a simulation to collect data.

4. **WRITING** Describe the difference between an unbiased sample and a biased sample. Give one example of each.

Monitoring Progress and Modeling with Mathematics

In Exercises 5–8, identify the type of sample described.
(See Example 1.)

5. The owners of a chain of 260 retail stores want to assess employee job satisfaction. Employees from 12 stores near the headquarters are surveyed.

6. Each employee in a company writes their name on a card and places it in a hat. The employees whose names are on the first two cards drawn each win a gift card.

7. A taxicab company wants to know whether its customers are satisfied with the service. Drivers survey every tenth customer during the day.

8. The owner of a community pool wants to ask patrons whether they think the water should be colder. Patrons are divided into four age groups, and a sample is randomly surveyed from each age group.

In Exercises 9–12, identify the type of sample and explain why the sample is biased. *(See Example 2.)*

9. A town council wants to know whether residents support having an off-leash area for dogs in the town park. Eighty dog owners are surveyed at the park.

10. A sportswriter wants to determine whether baseball coaches think wooden bats should be mandatory in collegiate baseball. The sportswriter mails surveys to all collegiate coaches and uses the surveys that are returned.

11. You want to find out whether booth holders at a convention were pleased with their booth locations. You divide the convention center into six sections and survey every booth holder in the fifth section.

12. Every tenth employee who arrives at a company health fair answers a survey that asks for opinions about new health-related programs.

13. **ERROR ANALYSIS** Surveys are mailed to every other household in a neighborhood. Each survey that is returned is used. Describe and correct the error in identifying the type of sample that is used.

> Because the surveys were mailed to every other household, the sample is a systematic sample.

14. **ERROR ANALYSIS** A researcher wants to know whether the U.S. workforce supports raising the minimum wage. Fifty high school students chosen at random are surveyed. Describe and correct the error in determining whether the sample is biased.

> Because the students were chosen at random, the sample is not biased.

In Exercises 15–18, determine whether the sample is biased. Explain your reasoning.

15. Every third person who enters an athletic event is asked whether he or she supports the use of instant replay in officiating the event.

16. A governor wants to know whether voters in the state support building a highway that will pass through a state forest. Business owners in a town near the proposed highway are randomly surveyed.

17. To assess customers' experiences making purchases online, a rating company e-mails purchasers and asks that they click on a link and complete a survey.

18. Your school principal randomly selects five students from each grade to complete a survey about classroom participation.

19. **WRITING** The staff of a student newsletter wants to conduct a survey of the students' favorite television shows. There are 1225 students in the school. Describe a method for selecting a random sample of 250 students to survey. *(See Example 3.)*

20. **WRITING** A national collegiate athletic association wants to survey 15 of the 120 head football coaches in a division about a proposed rules change. Describe a method for selecting a random sample of coaches to survey.

In Exercises 21–24, identify the method of data collection the situation describes. *(See Example 4.)*

21. A researcher uses technology to estimate the damage that will be done if a volcano erupts.

22. The owner of a restaurant asks 20 customers whether they are satisfied with the quality of their meals.

23. A researcher compares incomes of people who live in rural areas with those who live in large urban areas.

24. A researcher places bacteria samples in two different climates. The researcher then measures the bacteria growth in each sample after 3 days.

In Exercises 25–28, explain why the survey question may be biased or otherwise introduce bias into the survey. Then describe a way to correct the flaw. *(See Example 5.)*

25. "Do you agree that the budget of our city should be cut?"

26. "Would you rather watch the latest award-winning movie or just read some book?"

27. "The tap water coming from our western water supply contains twice the level of arsenic of water from our eastern supply. Do you think the government should address this health problem?"

28. A child asks, "Do you support the construction of a new children's hospital?"

In Exercises 29–32, determine whether the survey question may be biased or otherwise introduce bias into the survey. Explain your reasoning.

29. "Do you favor government funding to help prevent acid rain?"

30. "Do you think that renovating the old town hall would be a mistake?"

31. A police officer asks mall visitors, "Do you wear your seat belt regularly?"

32. "Do you agree with the amendments to the Clean Air Act?"

33. **REASONING** A researcher studies the effect of fiber supplements on heart disease. The researcher identified 175 people who take fiber supplements and 175 people who do not take fiber supplements. The study found that those who took the supplements had 19.6% fewer heart attacks. The researcher concludes that taking fiber supplements reduces the chance of heart attacks.

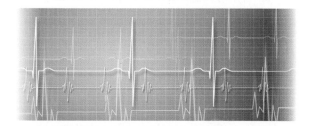

a. Explain why the researcher's conclusion may not be valid.

b. Describe how the researcher could have conducted the study differently to produce valid results.

34. HOW DO YOU SEE IT? A poll is conducted to predict the results of a statewide election in New Mexico before all the votes are counted. Fifty voters in each of the state's 33 counties are asked how they voted as they leave the polls.

a. Identify the type of sample described.

b. Explain how the diagram shows that the polling method could result in a biased sample.

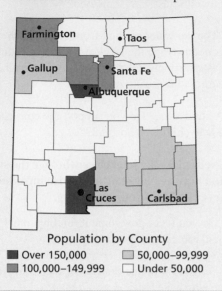

Population by County

- ■ Over 150,000
- ■ 100,000–149,999
- ▨ 50,000–99,999
- ☐ Under 50,000

35. WRITING Consider each type of sample listed on page 524. Which of the samples are most likely to lead to biased results? Explain.

36. THOUGHT PROVOKING What is the difference between a "blind experiment" and a "double-blind experiment?" Describe a possible advantage of the second type of experiment over the first.

37. WRITING A college wants to survey its graduating seniors to find out how many have already found jobs in their field of study after graduation.

a. What is the objective of the survey?

b. Describe the population for the survey.

c. Write two unbiased questions for the survey.

38. REASONING About 3.2% of U.S. adults follow a vegetarian-based diet. Two randomly selected groups of people were asked whether they follow such a diet. The first sample consists of 20 people and the second sample consists of 200 people. Which sample proportion is more likely to be representative of the national percentage? Explain.

39. MAKING AN ARGUMENT The U.S. Census is taken every 10 years to gather data from the population. Your friend claims that the sample cannot be biased. Is your friend correct? Explain.

40. OPEN-ENDED An airline wants to know whether travelers have enough leg room on its planes.

a. What method of data collection is appropriate for this situation?

b. Describe a sampling method that is likely to give biased results. Explain.

c. Describe a sampling method that is *not* likely to give biased results. Explain.

d. Write one biased question and one unbiased question for this situation.

41. REASONING A website contains a link to a survey that asks how much time each person spends on the Internet each week.

a. What type of sampling method is used in this situation?

b. Which population is likely to respond to the survey? What can you conclude?

Maintaining Mathematical Proficiency
Reviewing what you learned in previous grades and lessons

Evaluate the expression without using a calculator. *(Section 4.1)*

42. $4^{5/2}$ **43.** $27^{2/3}$ **44.** $-64^{1/3}$ **45.** $8^{-2/3}$

Simplify the expression. *(Section 4.2)*

46. $(4^{3/2} \cdot 4^{1/4})^4$ **47.** $(6^{1/3} \cdot 3^{1/3})^{-2}$ **48.** $\sqrt[3]{4} \cdot \sqrt[3]{16}$ **49.** $\dfrac{\sqrt[4]{405}}{\sqrt[4]{5}}$

Core Vocabulary

normal distribution, *p. 510*
normal curve, *p. 510*
standard normal distribution, *p. 511*
z-score, *p. 511*
population, *p. 518*
sample, *p. 518*
parameter, *p. 519*
statistic, *p. 519*

hypothesis, *p. 519*
random sample, *p. 524*
self-selected sample, *p. 524*
systematic sample, *p. 524*
stratified sample, *p. 524*
cluster sample, *p. 524*
convenience sample, *p. 524*
bias, *p. 525*

unbiased sample, *p. 525*
biased sample, *p. 525*
experiment, *p. 526*
observational study, *p. 526*
survey, *p. 526*
simulation, *p. 526*
biased question, *p. 527*

Core Concepts

Section 10.1

Areas Under a Normal Curve, *p. 510*
Using *z*-Scores and the Standard Normal Table, *p. 511*

Recognizing Normal Distributions, *p. 513*

Section 10.2

Distinguishing Between Populations and Samples, *p. 518*
Analyzing Hypotheses, *p. 519*

Section 10.3

Types of Samples, *p. 524*

Methods of Collecting Data, *p. 526*

Mathematical Practices

1. What previously established results, if any, did you use to solve Exercise 31 on page 516?

2. What external resources, if any, did you use to answer Exercise 36 on page 530?

Studying for Finals

- Form a study group of three or four students several weeks before the final exam.

- Find out what material you must know for the final exam, even if your teacher has not yet covered it.

- Ask for a practice final exam or create one yourself and have your teacher look at it.

- Have each group member take the practice final exam.

- Decide when the group is going to meet and what you will cover during each session.

- During the sessions, make sure you stay on track.

STUDY SKILLS

A normal distribution has a mean of 32 and a standard deviation of 4. Find the probability that a randomly selected *x*-value from the distribution is in the given interval. *(Section 10.1)*

1. at least 28   **2.** between 20 and 32   **3.** at most 26   **4.** at most 35

Determine whether the histogram has a normal distribution. *(Section 10.1)*

5.

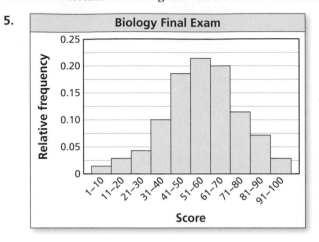

6.

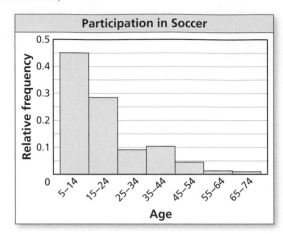

7. A survey of 1654 high school seniors determined that 1125 plan to attend college. Identify the population and the sample. Describe the sample. *(Section 10.2)*

8. A survey of all employees at a company found that the mean one-way daily commute to work of the employees is 25.5 minutes. Is the mean time a parameter or a statistic? Explain your reasoning. *(Section 10.2)*

9. A researcher records the number of bacteria present in several samples in a laboratory. Identify the method of data collection. *(Section 10.3)*

10. You spin a five-color spinner, which is divided into equal parts, five times and every time the spinner lands on red. You suspect the spinner favors red. The maker of the spinner claims that the spinner does not favor any color. You simulate spinning the spinner 50 times by repeatedly drawing 200 random samples of size 50. The histogram shows the results. Use the histogram to determine what you should conclude when you spin the actual spinner 50 times and the spinner lands on red (a) 9 times and (b) 19 times. *(Section 10.2)*

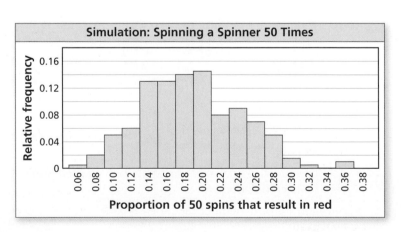

11. A local television station wants to find the number of hours per week people in the viewing area watch sporting events on television. The station surveys people at a nearby sports stadium. *(Section 10.3)*

a. Identify the type of sample described.   **b.** Is the sample biased? Explain your reasoning.

c. Describe a method for selecting a random sample of 200 people to survey.

10.4 Experimental Design

Essential Question How can you use an experiment to test a conjecture?

EXPLORATION 1   Using an Experiment

Work with a partner. Standard white playing dice are manufactured with black dots that are indentations, as shown. So, the side with six indentations is the lightest side and the side with one indentation is the heaviest side.

lightest side

You make a conjecture that when you roll a standard playing die, the number 6 will come up more often than the number 1 because 6 is the lightest side. To test your conjecture, roll a standard playing die 25 times. Record the results in the table. Does the experiment confirm your conjecture? Explain your reasoning.

Number						
Rolls						

EXPLORATION 2   Analyzing an Experiment

Work with a partner. To overcome the imbalance of standard playing dice, one of the authors of this book invented and patented 12-sided dice, on which each number from 1 through 6 appears twice (on opposing sides). See *BigIdeasMath.com*.

As part of the patent process, a standard playing die was rolled 27,090 times. The results are shown below.

Number	1	2	3	4	5	6
Rolls	4293	4524	4492	4397	4623	4761

What can you conclude from the results of this experiment? Explain your reasoning.

CONSTRUCTING VIABLE ARGUMENTS

To be proficient in math, you need to make conjectures and perform experiments to explore the truth of your conjectures.

Communicate Your Answer

3. How can you use an experiment to test a conjecture?

4. Exploration 2 shows the results of rolling a standard playing die 27,090 times to test the conjecture in Exploration 1. Why do you think the number of trials was so large?

5. Make a conjecture about the outcomes of rolling the 12-sided die in Exploration 2. Then design an experiment that could be used to test your conjecture. Be sure that your experiment is practical to complete and includes enough trials to give meaningful results.

What You Will Learn

▶ Describe experiments.

▶ Recognize how randomization applies to experiments and observational studies.

▶ Analyze experimental designs.

Core Vocabulary

controlled experiment, *p. 534*
control group, *p. 534*
treatment group, *p. 534*
randomization, *p. 534*
randomized comparative
  experiment, *p. 534*
placebo, *p. 534*
replication, *p. 536*

Previous
sample size

Describing Experiments

In a **controlled experiment**, two groups are studied under identical conditions with the exception of one variable. The group under ordinary conditions that is subjected to no treatment is the **control group**. The group that is subjected to the treatment is the **treatment group**.

Randomization is a process of randomly assigning subjects to different treatment groups. In a **randomized comparative experiment**, subjects are randomly assigned to the control group or the treatment group. In some cases, subjects in the control group are given a **placebo**, which is a harmless, unmedicated treatment that resembles the actual treatment. The comparison of the control group and the treatment group makes it possible to determine any effects of the treatment.

Randomization minimizes bias and produces groups of individuals who are theoretically similar in all ways before the treatment is applied. Conclusions drawn from an experiment that is not a randomized comparative experiment may not be valid.

EXAMPLE 1   Evaluating Published Reports

Determine whether each study is a randomized comparative experiment. If it is, describe the treatment, the treatment group, and the control group. If it is not, explain why not and discuss whether the conclusions drawn from the study are valid.

a.

Health Watch

Vitamin C Lowers Cholesterol

At a health clinic, patients were given the choice of whether to take a dietary supplement of 500 milligrams of vitamin C each day. Fifty patients who took the supplement were monitored for one year, as were 50 patients who did not take the supplement. At the end of one year, patients who took the supplement had 15% lower cholesterol levels than patients in the other group.

b.

Supermarket Checkout

Check Out Even Faster

To test the new design of its self checkout, a grocer gathered 142 customers and randomly divided them into two groups. One group used the new self checkout and one group used the old self checkout to buy the same groceries. Users of the new self checkout were able to complete their purchases 16% faster.

STUDY TIP

The study in part (a) is an *observational study* because the treatment is not being imposed.

SOLUTION

a. The study is not a randomized comparative experiment because the individuals were not randomly assigned to a control group and a treatment group. The conclusion that vitamin C lowers cholesterol may or may not be valid. There may be other reasons why patients who took the supplement had lower cholesterol levels. For instance, patients who voluntarily take the supplement may be more likely to have other healthy eating or lifestyle habits that could affect their cholesterol levels.

b. The study is a randomized comparative experiment. The treatment is the use of the new self checkout. The treatment group is the individuals who use the new self checkout. The control group is the individuals who use the old self checkout.

1. Determine whether the study is a randomized comparative experiment. If it is, describe the treatment, the treatment group, and the control group. If it is not, explain why not and discuss whether the conclusions drawn from the study are valid.

Motorist News

Early Birds Make Better Drivers

A recent study shows that adults who rise before 6:30 A.M. are better drivers than other adults. The study monitored the driving records of 140 volunteers who always wake up before 6:30 and 140 volunteers who never wake up before 6:30. The early risers had 12% fewer accidents.

Randomization in Experiments and Observational Studies

You have already learned about random sampling and its usefulness in surveys. Randomization applies to experiments and observational studies as shown below.

Experiment	Observational study
Individuals are assigned at random to the treatment group or the control group.	When possible, random samples can be selected for the groups being studied.

Good experiments and observational studies are designed to compare data from two or more groups and to show any relationship between variables. Only a well-designed *experiment*, however, can determine a cause-and-effect relationship.

Core Concept

Comparative Studies and Causality

- A rigorous randomized comparative experiment, by eliminating sources of variation other than the controlled variable, can make valid cause-and-effect conclusions possible.

- An observational study can identify *correlation* between variables, but not *causality*. Variables, other than what is being measured, may be affecting the results.

EXAMPLE 2 **Designing an Experiment or Observational Study**

Explain whether the following research topic is best investigated through an experiment or an observational study. Then describe the design of the experiment or observational study.

You want to know whether vigorous exercise in older people results in longer life.

SOLUTION

The treatment, vigorous exercise, is not possible for those people who are already unhealthy, so it is not ethical to assign individuals to a control or treatment group. Use an observational study. Randomly choose one group of individuals who already exercise vigorously. Then randomly choose one group of individuals who do not exercise vigorously. Monitor the ages of the individuals in both groups at regular intervals. Note that because you are using an observational study, you should be able to identify a *correlation* between vigorous exercise in older people and longevity, but not *causality*.

2. Determine whether the following research topic is best investigated through an experiment or an observational study. Then describe the design of the experiment or observational study.

   You want to know whether flowers sprayed twice per day with a mist of water stay fresh longer than flowers that are not sprayed.

Analyzing Experimental Designs

An important part of experimental design is *sample size*, or the number of subjects in the experiment. To improve the validity of the experiment, **replication** is required, which is repetition of the experiment under the same or similar conditions.

UNDERSTANDING
MATHEMATICAL
TERMS

The *validity* of an experiment refers to the reliability of the results. The results of a valid experiment are more likely to be accepted.

STUDY TIP

The experimental design described in part (c) is an example of *randomized block design*.

EXAMPLE 3 Analyzing Experimental Designs

A pharmaceutical company wants to test the effectiveness of a new chewing gum designed to help people lose weight. Identify a potential problem, if any, with each experimental design. Then describe how you can improve it.

a. The company identifies 10 people who are overweight. Five subjects are given the new chewing gum and the other 5 are given a placebo. After 3 months, each subject is evaluated and it is determined that the 5 subjects who have been using the new chewing gum have lost weight.

b. The company identifies 10,000 people who are overweight. The subjects are divided into groups according to gender. Females receive the new chewing gum and males receive the placebo. After 3 months, a significantly large number of the female subjects have lost weight.

c. The company identifies 10,000 people who are overweight. The subjects are divided into groups according to age. Within each age group, subjects are randomly assigned to receive the new chewing gum or the placebo. After 3 months, a significantly large number of the subjects who received the new chewing gum have lost weight.

SOLUTION

a. The sample size is not large enough to produce valid results. To improve the validity of the experiment, the sample size must be larger and the experiment must be replicated.

b. Because the subjects are divided into groups according to gender, the groups are not similar. The new chewing gum may have more of an effect on women than on men, or more of an effect on men than on women. It is not possible to see such an effect with the experiment the way it is designed. The subjects can be divided into groups according to gender, but within each group, they must be randomly assigned to the treatment group or the control group.

c. The subjects are divided into groups according to a similar characteristic (age). Because subjects within each age group are randomly assigned to receive the new chewing gum or the placebo, replication is possible. So, there are no potential problems with the experimental design.

Monitoring Progress Help in English and Spanish at *BigIdeasMath.com*

3. In Example 3, the company identifies 250 people who are overweight. The subjects are randomly assigned to a treatment group or a control group. In addition, each subject is given a DVD that documents the dangers of obesity. After 3 months, most of the subjects placed in the treatment group have lost weight. Identify a potential problem with the experimental design. Then describe how you can improve it.

4. You design an experiment to test the effectiveness of a vaccine against a strain of influenza. In the experiment, 100,000 people receive the vaccine and another 100,000 people receive a placebo. Identify a potential problem with the experimental design. Then describe how you can improve it.

10.4 Exercises

Vocabulary and Core Concept Check

1. **COMPLETE THE SENTENCE** Repetition of an experiment under the same or similar conditions is called _____.

2. **WRITING** Describe the difference between the control group and the treatment group in a controlled experiment.

Monitoring Progress and Modeling with Mathematics

In Exercises 3 and 4, determine whether the study is a randomized comparative experiment. If it is, describe the treatment, the treatment group, and the control group. If it is not, explain why not and discuss whether the conclusions drawn from the study are valid. *(See Example 1.)*

3.

Insomnia

New Drug Improves Sleep

To test a new drug for insomnia, a pharmaceutical company randomly divided 200 adult volunteers into two groups. One group received the drug and one group received a placebo. After one month, the adults who took the drug slept 18% longer, while those who took the placebo experienced no significant change.

4.

Dental Health

Milk Fights Cavities

At a middle school, students can choose to drink milk or other beverages at lunch. Seventy-five students who chose milk were monitored for one year, as were 75 students who chose other beverages. At the end of the year, students in the "milk" group had 25% fewer cavities than students in the other group.

ERROR ANALYSIS In Exercises 5 and 6, describe and correct the error in describing the study.

A company's researchers want to study the effects of adding shea butter to their existing hair conditioner. They monitor the hair quality of 30 randomly selected customers using the regular conditioner and 30 randomly selected customers using the new shea butter conditioner.

5.

 The control group is individuals who do not use either of the conditioners.

6.

 The study is an observational study.

In Exercises 7–10, explain whether the research topic is best investigated through an experiment or an observational study. Then describe the design of the experiment or observational study. *(See Example 2.)*

7. A researcher wants to compare the body mass index of smokers and nonsmokers.

8. A restaurant chef wants to know which pasta sauce recipe is preferred by more diners.

9. A farmer wants to know whether a new fertilizer affects the weight of the fruit produced by strawberry plants.

10. You want to know whether homes that are close to parks or schools have higher property values.

11. **DRAWING CONCLUSIONS** A company wants to test whether a nutritional supplement has an adverse effect on an athlete's heart rate while exercising. Identify a potential problem, if any, with each experimental design. Then describe how you can improve it. *(See Example 3.)*

    a. The company randomly selects 250 athletes. Half of the athletes receive the supplement and their heart rates are monitored while they run on a treadmill. The other half of the athletes are given a placebo and their heart rates are monitored while they lift weights. The heart rates of the athletes who took the supplement significantly increased while exercising.

    b. The company selects 1000 athletes. The athletes are divided into two groups based on age. Within each age group, the athletes are randomly assigned to receive the supplement or the placebo. The athletes' heart rates are monitored while they run on a treadmill. There was no significant difference in the increases in heart rates between the two groups.

12. DRAWING CONCLUSIONS A researcher wants to test the effectiveness of reading novels on raising intelligence quotient (IQ) scores. Identify a potential problem, if any, with each experimental design. Then describe how you can improve it.

    a. The researcher selects 500 adults and randomly divides them into two groups. One group reads novels daily and one group does not read novels. At the end of 1 year, each adult is evaluated and it is determined that neither group had an increase in IQ scores.

    b. Fifty adults volunteer to spend time reading novels every day for 1 year. Fifty other adults volunteer to refrain from reading novels for 1 year. Each adult is evaluated and it is determined that the adults who read novels raised their IQ scores by 3 points more than the other group.

13. DRAWING CONCLUSIONS A fitness company claims that its workout program will increase vertical jump heights in 6 weeks. To test the workout program, 10 athletes are divided into two groups. The double bar graph shows the results of the experiment. Identify the potential problems with the experimental design. Then describe how you can improve it.

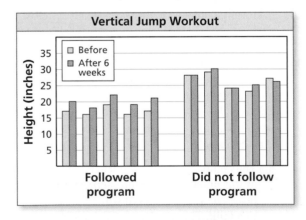

14. WRITING Explain why observational studies, rather than experiments, are usually used in astronomy.

15. MAKING AN ARGUMENT Your friend wants to determine whether the number of siblings has an effect on a student's grades. Your friend claims to be able to show causality between the number of siblings and grades. Is your friend correct? Explain.

16. HOW DO YOU SEE IT? To test the effect political advertisements have on voter preferences, a researcher selects 400 potential voters and randomly divides them into two groups. The circle graphs show the results of the study.

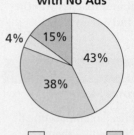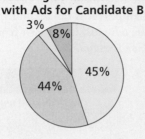

    a. Is the study a randomized comparative experiment? Explain.

    b. Describe the treatment.

    c. Can you conclude that the political advertisements were effective? Explain.

17. WRITING Describe the *placebo effect* and how it affects the results of an experiment. Explain how a researcher can minimize the placebo effect.

18. THOUGHT PROVOKING Make a hypothesis about something that interests you. Design an experiment that could show that your hypothesis is probably true.

19. REASONING Will replicating an experiment on many individuals produce data that are more likely to accurately represent a population than performing the experiment only once? Explain.

Maintaining Mathematical Proficiency
Reviewing what you learned in previous grades and lessons

Draw a dot plot that represents the data. Identify the shape of the distribution. *(Skills Review Handbook)*

20. Ages: 24, 21, 22, 26, 22, 23, 25, 23, 23, 24, 20, 25

21. Golf strokes: 4, 3, 4, 3, 3, 2, 7, 5, 3, 4

Tell whether the function represents *exponential growth* or *exponential decay*. Then graph the function. *(Section 5.1)*

22. $y = 5e^x$

23. $y = \frac{1}{2}e^{-x}$

24. $y = 0.4e^{-2x}$

25. $y = 1.5e^{0.5x}$

10.5 Making Inferences from Sample Surveys

Essential Question How can you use a sample survey to infer a conclusion about a population?

> ### EXPLORATION 1 Making an Inference from a Sample
>
> **Work with a partner.** You conduct a study to determine what percent of the high school students in your city would prefer an upgraded model of their current cell phone. Based on your intuition and talking with a few acquaintances, you think that 50% of high school students would prefer an upgrade. You survey 50 randomly chosen high school students and find that 20 of them prefer an upgraded model.

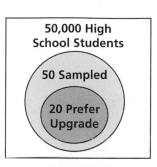

MODELING WITH MATHEMATICS

To be proficient in math, you need to apply the mathematics you know to solve problems arising in everyday life.

a. Based on your sample survey, what percent of the high school students in your city would prefer an upgraded model? Explain your reasoning.

b. In spite of your sample survey, is it still possible that 50% of the high school students in your city prefer an upgraded model? Explain your reasoning.

c. To investigate the likelihood that you could have selected a sample of 50 from a population in which 50% of the population does prefer an upgraded model, you create a binomial distribution as shown below. From the distribution, estimate the probability that exactly 20 students surveyed prefer an upgraded model. Is this event likely to occur? Explain your reasoning.

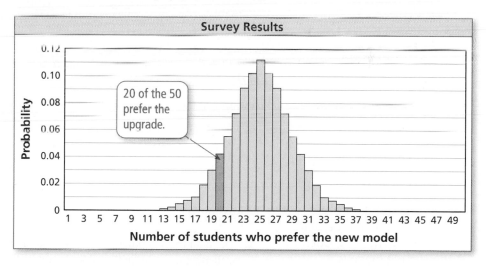

d. When making inferences from sample surveys, the sample must be random. In the situation described above, describe how you could design and conduct a survey using a random sample of 50 high school students who live in a large city.

Communicate Your Answer

2. How can you use a sample survey to infer a conclusion about a population?

3. In Exploration 1(c), what is the probability that exactly 25 students you survey prefer an upgraded model?

Core Vocabulary

descriptive statistics, *p. 540*
inferential statistics, *p. 540*
margin of error, *p. 543*

Previous
statistic
parameter

What You Will Learn

▶ Estimate population parameters.
▶ Analyze estimated population parameters.
▶ Find margins of error for surveys.

Estimating Population Parameters

The study of statistics has two major branches: *descriptive statistics* and *inferential statistics*. **Descriptive statistics** involves the organization, summarization, and display of data. So far, you have been using descriptive statistics in your studies of data analysis and statistics. **Inferential statistics** involves using a sample to draw conclusions about a population. You can use statistics to make reasonable predictions, or *inferences*, about an entire population when the sample is representative of the population.

EXAMPLE 1 **Estimating a Population Mean**

The numbers of friends for a random sample of 40 teen users of a social networking website are shown in the table. Estimate the population mean μ.

Number of Friends				
281	342	229	384	320
247	298	248	312	445
385	286	314	260	186
287	342	225	308	343
262	220	320	310	150
274	291	300	410	255
279	351	370	257	350
369	215	325	338	278

REMEMBER

Recall that $\bar{x}$ denotes the sample mean. It is read as "*x* bar."

STUDY TIP

The probability that the population mean is *exactly* 299.15 is virtually 0, but the sample mean is a good estimate of μ.

SOLUTION

To estimate the unknown population mean μ, find the sample mean $\bar{x}$.

$$\bar{x} = \frac{\Sigma x}{n} = \frac{11{,}966}{40} = 299.15$$

▶ So, the mean number of friends for all teen users of the website is about 299.

Monitoring Progress Help in English and Spanish at *BigIdeasMath.com*

1. The data from another random sample of 30 teen users of the social networking website are shown in the table. Estimate the population mean μ.

Number of Friends				
305	237	261	374	341
257	243	352	330	189
297	418	275	288	307
295	288	341	322	271
209	164	363	228	390
313	315	263	299	285

Not every random sample results in the same estimate of a population parameter; there will be some sampling variability. Larger sample sizes, however, tend to produce more accurate estimates.

EXAMPLE 2 **Estimating Population Proportions**

A student newspaper wants to predict the winner of a city's mayoral election. Two candidates, A and B, are running for office. Eight staff members conduct surveys of randomly selected residents. The residents are asked whether they will vote for Candidate A. The results are shown in the table.

Sample Size	Number of Votes for Candidate A in the Sample	Percent of Votes for Candidate A in the Sample
5	2	40%
12	4	33.3%
20	12	60%
30	17	56.7%
50	29	58%
125	73	58.4%
150	88	58.7%
200	118	59%

a. Based on the results of the first two sample surveys, do you think Candidate A will win the election? Explain.

b. Based on the results in the table, do you think Candidate A will win the election? Explain.

SOLUTION

a. The results of the first two surveys (sizes 5 and 12) show that fewer than 50% of the residents will vote for Candidate A. Because there are only two candidates, one candidate needs more than 50% of the votes to win.

▶ Based on these surveys, you can predict Candidate A will not win the election.

b. As the sample sizes increase, the estimated percent of votes approaches 59%. You can predict that 59% of the city residents will vote for Candidate A.

▶ Because 59% of the votes are more than the 50% needed to win, you should feel confident that Candidate A will win the election.

Monitoring Progress Help in English and Spanish at *BigIdeasMath.com*

2. Two candidates are running for class president. The table shows the results of four surveys of random students in the class. The students were asked whether they will vote for the incumbent. Do you think the incumbent will be reelected? Explain.

Sample Size	Number of "Yes" Responses	Percent of Votes for Incumbent
10	7	70%
20	11	55%
30	13	43.3%
40	17	42.5%

Analyzing Estimated Population Parameters

An estimated population parameter is a hypothesis. You learned in Section 10.2 that one way to analyze a hypothesis is to perform a simulation.

EXAMPLE 3 **Analyzing an Estimated Population Proportion**

A national polling company claims 34% of U.S. adults say mathematics is the most valuable school subject in their lives. You survey a random sample of 50 adults.

a. What can you conclude about the accuracy of the claim that the population proportion is 0.34 when 15 adults in your survey say mathematics is the most valuable subject?

b. What can you conclude about the accuracy of the claim when 25 adults in your survey say mathematics is the most valuable subject?

c. Assume that the true population proportion is 0.34. Estimate the variation among sample proportions using samples of size 50.

SOLUTION

The polling company's claim (hypothesis) is that the population proportion of U.S. adults who say mathematics is the most valuable school subject is 0.34. To analyze this claim, simulate choosing 80 random samples of size 50 using a random number generator on a graphing calculator. Generate 50 random numbers from 0 to 99 for each sample. Let numbers 1 through 34 represent adults who say math. Find the sample proportions and make a dot plot showing the distribution of the sample proportions.

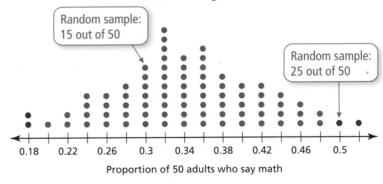

Simulation: Polling 50 Adults

Random sample: 15 out of 50

Random sample: 25 out of 50

Proportion of 50 adults who say math

STUDY TIP

The dot plot shows the results of one simulation. Results of other simulations may give slightly different results but the shape should be similar.

a. Note that 15 out of 50 corresponds to a sample proportion of $\frac{15}{50} = 0.3$. In the simulation, this result occurred in 7 of the 80 random samples. It is *likely* that 15 adults out of 50 would say math is the most valuable subject when the true population percentage is 34%. So, you can conclude the company's claim is probably accurate.

b. Note that 25 out of 50 corresponds to a sample proportion of $\frac{25}{50} = 0.5$. In the simulation, this result occurred in only 1 of the 80 random samples. So, it is *unlikely* that 25 adults out of 50 would say math is the most valuable subject when the true population percentage is 34%. So, you can conclude the company's claim is probably *not* accurate.

INTERPRETING MATHEMATICAL RESULTS

Note that the sample proportion 0.3 in part (a) lies in this interval, while the sample proportion 0.5 in part (b) falls outside this interval.

c. Note that the dot plot is fairly bell-shaped and symmetric, so the distribution is approximately normal. In a normal distribution, you know that about 95% of the possible sample proportions will lie within two standard deviations of 0.34. Excluding the two least and two greatest sample proportions, represented by red dots ● in the dot plot, leaves 76 of 80, or 95%, of the sample proportions. These 76 proportions range from 0.2 to 0.48. So, 95% of the time, a sample proportion should lie in the interval from 0.2 to 0.48.

3. **WHAT IF?** In Example 3, what can you conclude about the accuracy of the claim that the population proportion is 0.34 when 21 adults in your random sample say mathematics is the most valuable subject?

Finding Margins of Error for Surveys

When conducting a survey, you need to make the size of your sample large enough so that it accurately represents the population. As the sample size increases, the *margin of error* decreases.

The **margin of error** gives a limit on how much the responses of the sample would differ from the responses of the population. For example, if 40% of the people in a poll favor a new tax law, and the margin of error is ±4%, then it is likely that between 36% and 44% of the entire population favor a new tax law.

Core Concept

Margin of Error Formula

When a random sample of size n is taken from a large population, the margin of error is approximated by

$$\text{Margin of error} = \pm \frac{1}{\sqrt{n}}.$$

This means that if the percent of the sample responding a certain way is p (expressed as a decimal), then the percent of the population who would respond the same way is likely to be between $p - \frac{1}{\sqrt{n}}$ and $p + \frac{1}{\sqrt{n}}$.

EXAMPLE 4   Finding a Margin of Error

In a survey of 2048 people in the U.S., 55% said that television is their main source of news. (a) What is the margin of error for the survey? (b) Give an interval that is likely to contain the exact percent of all people who use television as their main source of news.

Americans' Main News Source

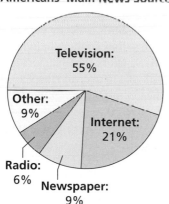

SOLUTION

a. Use the margin of error formula.

$$\text{Margin of error} = \pm \frac{1}{\sqrt{n}} = \pm \frac{1}{\sqrt{2048}} \approx \pm 0.022$$

▶ The margin of error for the survey is about ±2.2%.

b. To find the interval, subtract and add 2.2% to the percent of people surveyed who said television is their main source of news (55%).

$$55\% - 2.2\% = 52.8\% \qquad 55\% + 2.2\% = 57.2\%$$

▶ It is likely that the exact percent of all people in the U.S. who use television as their main source of news is between 52.8% and 57.2%.

Monitoring Progress Help in English and Spanish at *BigIdeasMath.com*

4. In a survey of 1028 people in the U.S., 87% reported using the Internet. Give an interval that is likely to contain the exact percent of all people in the U.S. who use the Internet.

Vocabulary and Core Concept Check

1. **COMPLETE THE SENTENCE** The _____ gives a limit on how much the responses of the sample would differ from the responses of the population.

2. **WRITING** What is the difference between descriptive and inferential statistics?

Monitoring Progress and Modeling with Mathematics

3. **PROBLEM SOLVING** The numbers of text messages sent each day by a random sample of 30 teen cellphone users are shown in the table. Estimate the population mean μ. *(See Example 1.)*

Number of Text Messages				
30	60	59	83	41
37	66	63	60	92
53	42	47	32	79
53	80	41	51	85
73	71	69	31	69
57	60	70	91	67

4. **PROBLEM SOLVING** The incomes for a random sample of 35 U.S. households are shown in the table. Estimate the population mean μ.

Income of U.S. Households				
14,300	52,100	74,800	51,000	91,500
72,800	50,500	15,000	37,600	22,100
40,000	65,400	50,000	81,100	99,800
43,300	32,500	76,300	83,400	24,600
30,800	62,100	32,800	21,900	64,400
73,100	20,000	49,700	71,000	45,900
53,200	45,500	55,300	19,100	63,100

5. **PROBLEM SOLVING** Use the data in Exercise 3 to answer each question.

   a. Estimate the population proportion ρ of teen cellphone users who send more than 70 text messages each day.

   b. Estimate the population proportion ρ of teen cellphone users who send fewer than 50 text messages each day.

6. **WRITING** A survey asks a random sample of U.S. teenagers how many hours of television they watch each night. The survey reveals that the sample mean is 3 hours per night. How confident are you that the average of all U.S. teenagers is exactly 3 hours per night? Explain your reasoning.

7. **DRAWING CONCLUSIONS** When the President of the United States vetoes a bill, the Congress can override the veto by a two-thirds majority vote in each House. Five news organizations conduct individual random surveys of U.S. Senators. The senators are asked whether they will vote to override the veto. The results are shown in the table. *(See Example 2.)*

Sample Size	Number of Votes to Override Veto	Percent of Votes to Override Veto
7	6	85.7%
22	16	72.7%
28	21	75%
31	17	54.8%
49	27	55.1%

   a. Based on the results of the first two surveys, do you think the Senate will vote to override the veto? Explain.

   b. Based on the results in the table, do you think the Senate will vote to override the veto? Explain.

8. **DRAWING CONCLUSIONS** Your teacher lets the students decide whether to have their test on Friday or Monday. The table shows the results from four surveys of randomly selected students in your grade who are taking the same class. The students are asked whether they want to have the test on Friday.

Sample Size	Number of "Yes" Responses	Percent of Votes
10	8	80%
20	12	60%
30	16	53.3%
40	18	45%

  a. Based on the results of the first two surveys, do you think the test will be on Friday? Explain.

  b. Based on the results in the table, do you think the test will be on Friday? Explain.

9. **MODELING WITH MATHEMATICS** A national polling company claims that 54% of U.S. adults are married. You survey a random sample of 50 adults. *(See Example 3.)*

  a. What can you conclude about the accuracy of the claim that the population proportion is 0.54 when 31 adults in your survey are married?

  b. What can you conclude about the accuracy of the claim that the population proportion is 0.54 when 19 adults in your survey are married?

  c. Assume that the true population proportion is 0.54. Estimate the variation among sample proportions for samples of size 50.

10. **MODELING WITH MATHEMATICS** Employee engagement is the level of commitment and involvement an employee has toward the company and its values. A national polling company claims that only 29% of U.S. employees feel engaged at work. You survey a random sample of 50 U.S. employees.

  a. What can you conclude about the accuracy of the claim that the population proportion is 0.29 when 16 employees feel engaged at work?

  b. What can you conclude about the accuracy of the claim that the population proportion is 0.29 when 23 employees feel engaged at work?

  c. Assume that the true population proportion is 0.29. Estimate the variation among sample proportions for samples of size 50.

In Exercises 11–16, find the margin of error for a survey that has the given sample size. Round your answer to the nearest tenth of a percent.

11. 260

12. 1000

13. 2024

14. 6400

15. 3275

16. 750

17. **ATTENDING TO PRECISION** In a survey of 900 U.S. adults, 41% said that their top priority for saving is retirement. *(See Example 4.)*

  a. What is the margin of error for the survey?

  b. Give an interval that is likely to contain the exact percent of all U.S. adults whose top priority for saving is retirement.

18. **ATTENDING TO PRECISION** In a survey of 1022 U.S. adults, 76% said that more emphasis should be placed on producing domestic energy from solar power.

  a. What is the margin of error for the survey?

  b. Give an interval that is likely to contain the exact percent of all U.S. adults who think more emphasis should be placed on producing domestic energy from solar power.

19. **ERROR ANALYSIS** In a survey, 8% of adult Internet users said they participate in sports fantasy leagues online. The margin of error is ±4%. Describe and correct the error in calculating the sample size.

$$\pm 0.08 = \pm \frac{1}{\sqrt{n}}$$
$$0.0064 = \frac{1}{n}$$
$$n \approx 156$$

20. **ERROR ANALYSIS** In a random sample of 2500 consumers, 61% prefer Game A over Game B. Describe and correct the error in giving an interval that is likely to contain the exact percent of all consumers who prefer Game A over Game B.

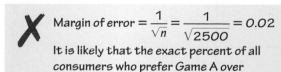

Margin of error $= \frac{1}{\sqrt{n}} = \frac{1}{\sqrt{2500}} = 0.02$

It is likely that the exact percent of all consumers who prefer Game A over Game B is between 60% and 62%.

21. MAKING AN ARGUMENT Your friend states that it is possible to have a margin of error between 0 and 100 percent, not including 0 or 100 percent. Is your friend correct? Explain your reasoning.

22. HOW DO YOU SEE IT? The figure shows the distribution of the sample proportions from three simulations using different sample sizes. Which simulation has the least margin of error? the greatest? Explain your reasoning.

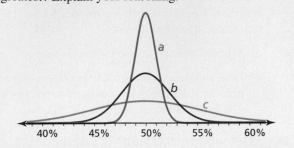

23. REASONING A developer claims that the percent of city residents who favor building a new football stadium is likely between 52.3% and 61.7%. How many residents were surveyed?

24. ABSTRACT REASONING Suppose a random sample of size n is required to produce a margin of error of $\pm E$. Write an expression in terms of n for the sample size needed to reduce the margin of error to $\pm \frac{1}{2}E$. How many times must the sample size be increased to cut the margin of error in half? Explain.

25. PROBLEM SOLVING A survey reported that 47% of the voters surveyed, or about 235 voters, said they voted for Candidate A and the remainder said they voted for Candidate B.

   a. How many voters were surveyed?

   b. What is the margin of error for the survey?

   c. For each candidate, find an interval that is likely to contain the exact percent of all voters who voted for the candidate.

   d. Based on your intervals in part (c), can you be confident that Candidate B won? If not, how many people in the sample would need to vote for Candidate B for you to be confident that Candidate B won? (*Hint:* Find the least number of voters for Candidate B so that the intervals do not overlap.)

26. THOUGHT PROVOKING Consider a large population in which ρ percent (in decimal form) have a certain characteristic. To be reasonably sure that you are choosing a sample that is representative of a population, you should choose a random sample of n people where

$$n > 9\left(\frac{1 - \rho}{\rho}\right).$$

   a. Suppose $\rho = 0.5$. How large does n need to be?

   b. Suppose $\rho = 0.01$. How large does n need to be?

   c. What can you conclude from parts (a) and (b)?

27. CRITICAL THINKING In a survey, 52% of the respondents said they prefer sports drink X and 48% said they prefer sports drink Y. How many people would have to be surveyed for you to be confident that sports drink X is truly preferred by more than half the population? Explain.

Maintaining Mathematical Proficiency
Reviewing what you learned in previous grades and lessons

Find the inverse of the function. *(Section 5.2)*

28. $y = 10^{x-3}$ **29.** $y = 2^x - 5$ **30.** $y = \ln(x + 5)$ **31.** $y = \log_6 x - 1$

Determine whether the graph represents an arithmetic sequence or a geometric sequence. Then write a rule for the nth term. *(Section 7.2 and Section 7.3)*

32.

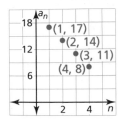

33.

34.

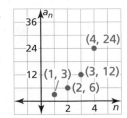

Making Inferences from Experiments

Essential Question How can you test a hypothesis about an experiment?

EXPLORATION 1   Resampling Data

Work with a partner. A randomized comparative experiment tests whether water with dissolved calcium affects the yields of yellow squash plants. The table shows the results.

a. Find the mean yield of the control group and the mean yield of the treatment group. Then find the difference of the two means. Record the results.

b. Write each yield measurement from the table on an equal-sized piece of paper. Place the pieces of paper in a bag, shake, and randomly choose 10 pieces of paper. Call this the "control" group, and call the 10 pieces in the bag the "treatment" group. Then repeat part (a) and return the pieces to the bag. Perform this resampling experiment five times.

c. How does the difference in the means of the control and treatment groups compare with the differences resulting from chance?

Yield (kilograms)	
Control Group	Treatment Group
1.0	1.1
1.2	1.3
1.5	1.4
0.9	1.2
1.1	1.0
1.4	1.7
0.8	1.8
0.9	1.1
1.3	1.1
1.6	1.8

EXPLORATION 2   Evaluating Results

Work as a class. To conclude that the treatment is responsible for the difference in yield, you need strong evidence to reject the hypothesis:

Water dissolved in calcium has no effect on the yields of yellow squash plants.

To evaluate this hypothesis, compare the experimental difference of means with the resampling differences.

a. Collect all the resampling differences of means found in Exploration 1(b) for the whole class and display these values in a histogram.

b. Draw a vertical line on your class histogram to represent the experimental difference of means found in Exploration 1(a).

c. Where on the histogram should the experimental difference of means lie to give evidence for rejecting the hypothesis?

d. Is your class able to reject the hypothesis? Explain your reasoning.

MODELING WITH MATHEMATICS

To be proficient in math, you need to identify important quantities in a practical situation, map their relationships using such tools as diagrams and graphs, and analyze those relationships mathematically to draw conclusions.

Communicate Your Answer

3. How can you test a hypothesis about an experiment?

4. The randomized comparative experiment described in Exploration 1 is replicated and the results are shown in the table. Repeat Explorations 1 and 2 using this data set. Explain any differences in your answers.

	Yield (kilograms)									
Control Group	0.9	0.9	1.4	0.6	1.0	1.1	0.7	0.6	1.2	1.3
Treatment Group	1.0	1.2	1.2	1.3	1.0	1.8	1.7	1.2	1.0	1.9

What You Will Learn

▶ Organize data from an experiment with two samples.

▶ Resample data using a simulation to analyze a hypothesis.

▶ Make inferences about a treatment.

Core Vocabulary

Previous
randomized comparative
    experiment
control group
treatment group
mean
dot plot
outlier
simulation
hypothesis

Experiments with Two Samples

In this lesson, you will compare data from two samples in an experiment to make inferences about a treatment using a method called *resampling*. Before learning about this method, consider the experiment described in Example 1.

EXAMPLE 1   Organizing Data from an Experiment

A randomized comparative experiment tests whether a soil supplement affects the total yield (in kilograms) of cherry tomato plants. The control group has 10 plants and the treatment group, which receives the soil supplement, has 10 plants. The table shows the results.

Total Yield of Tomato Plants (kilograms)										
Control Group	1.2	1.3	0.9	1.4	2.0	1.2	0.7	1.9	1.4	1.7
Treatment Group	1.4	0.9	1.5	1.8	1.6	1.8	2.4	1.9	1.9	1.7

a. Find the mean yield of the control group, $\overline{x}_{control}$.

b. Find the mean yield of the treatment group, $\overline{x}_{treatment}$.

c. Find the experimental difference of the means, $\overline{x}_{treatment} - \overline{x}_{control}$.

d. Display the data in a double dot plot.

e. What can you conclude?

SOLUTION

a. $\overline{x}_{control} = \dfrac{1.2 + 1.3 + 0.9 + 1.4 + 2.0 + 1.2 + 0.7 + 1.9 + 1.4 + 1.7}{10} = \dfrac{13.7}{10} = 1.37$

▶ The mean yield of the control group is 1.37 kilograms.

b. $\overline{x}_{treatment} = \dfrac{1.4 + 0.9 + 1.5 + 1.8 + 1.6 + 1.8 + 2.4 + 1.9 + 1.9 + 1.7}{10} = \dfrac{16.9}{10} = 1.69$

▶ The mean yield of the treatment group is 1.69 kilograms.

c. $\overline{x}_{treatment} - \overline{x}_{control} = 1.69 - 1.37 = 0.32$

▶ The experimental difference of the means is 0.32 kilogram.

d.

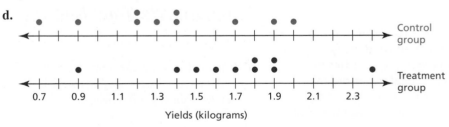

e. The plot of the data shows that the two data sets tend to be fairly symmetric and have no extreme values (outliers). So, the mean is a suitable measure of center. The mean yield of the treatment group is 0.32 kilogram more than the control group. It appears that the soil supplement might be slightly effective, but the sample size is small and the difference could be due to chance.

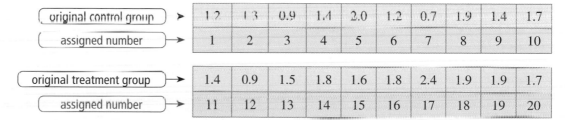

1. In Example 1, interpret the meaning of $\bar{x}_{\text{treatment}} - \bar{x}_{\text{control}}$ when the difference is (a) negative, (b) zero, and (c) positive.

Resampling Data Using a Simulation

The samples in Example 1 are too small to make inferences about the treatment. Statisticians have developed a method called resampling to overcome this problem. Here is one way to resample: combine the measurements from both groups, and repeatedly create new "control" and "treatment" groups at random from the measurements without repeats. Example 2 shows one resampling of the data in Example 1.

EXAMPLE 2   Resampling Data Using a Simulation

Resample the data in Example 1 using a simulation. Use the mean yields of the new control and treatment groups to calculate the difference of the means.

SOLUTION

Step 1   Combine the measurements from both groups and assign a number to each value. Let the numbers 1 through 10 represent the data in the original control group, and let the numbers 11 through 20 represent the data in the original treatment group, as shown.

original control group	1.2	1.3	0.9	1.4	2.0	1.2	0.7	1.9	1.4	1.7
assigned number	1	2	3	4	5	6	7	8	9	10

original treatment group	1.4	0.9	1.5	1.8	1.6	1.8	2.4	1.9	1.9	1.7
assigned number	11	12	13	14	15	16	17	18	19	20

Step 2   Use a random number generator. Randomly generate 20 numbers from 1 through 20 *without repeating a number*. The table shows the results.

```
randIntNoRep(1,20)
{14 19 4 3 18 9...
```

14	19	4	3	18	9	5	15	2	7
1	17	20	16	6	8	13	12	11	10

Use the first 10 numbers to make the new control group, and the next 10 to make the new treatment group. The results are shown in the next table.

Resample of Tomato Plant Yields (kilograms)										
New Control Group	1.8	1.9	1.4	0.9	1.9	1.4	2.0	1.6	1.3	0.7
New Treatment Group	1.2	2.4	1.7	1.8	1.2	1.9	1.5	0.9	1.4	1.7

Step 3   Find the mean yields of the new control and treatment groups.

$$\bar{x}_{\text{new control}} = \frac{1.8 + 1.9 + 1.4 + 0.9 + 1.9 + 1.4 + 2.0 + 1.6 + 1.3 + 0.7}{10} = \frac{14.9}{10} = 1.49$$

$$\bar{x}_{\text{new treatment}} = \frac{1.2 + 2.4 + 1.7 + 1.8 + 1.2 + 1.9 + 1.5 + 0.9 + 1.4 + 1.7}{10} = \frac{15.7}{10} = 1.57$$

▶ So, $\bar{x}_{\text{new treatment}} - \bar{x}_{\text{new control}} = 1.57 - 1.49 = 0.08$. This is less than the experimental difference found in Example 1.

Making Inferences About a Treatment

To perform an analysis of the data in Example 1, you will need to resample the data more than once. After resampling many times, you can see how often you get differences between the new groups that are at least as large as the one you measured.

EXAMPLE 3 **Making Inferences About a Treatment**

To conclude that the treatment in Example 1 is responsible for the difference in yield, you need to analyze this hypothesis:

The soil nutrient has no effect on the yield of the cherry tomato plants.

Simulate 200 resamplings of the data in Example 1. Compare the experimental difference of 0.32 from Example 1 with the resampling differences. What can you conclude about the hypothesis? Does the soil nutrient have an effect on the yield?

SOLUTION

The histogram shows the results of the simulation. The histogram is approximately bell-shaped and fairly symmetric, so the differences have an approximately normal distribution.

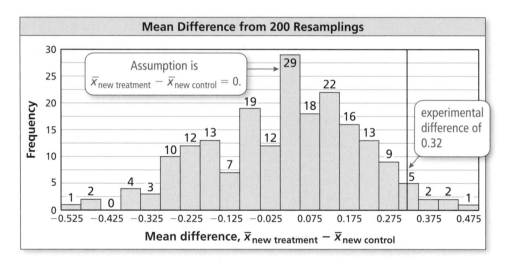

Note that the hypothesis assumes that the difference of the mean yields is 0. The experimental difference of 0.32, however, lies close to the right tail. From the graph, there are about 5 to 10 values out of 200 that are greater than 0.32, which is at most 5% of the values. Also, the experimental difference falls outside the middle 90% of the resampling differences. (The middle 90% is the area of the bars from -0.275 to 0.275, which contains 180 of the 200 values, or 90%.) This means it is unlikely to get a difference this large when you assume that the difference is 0, suggesting the control group and the treatment group differ.

INTERPRETING MATHEMATICAL RESULTS

With this conclusion, you can be 90% confident that the soil supplement does have an effect.

▶ You can conclude that the hypothesis is most likely false. So, the soil nutrient *does* have an effect on the yield of cherry tomato plants. Because the mean difference is positive, the treatment *increases* the yield.

Monitoring Progress Help in English and Spanish at *BigIdeasMath.com*

2. In Example 3, what are the consequences of concluding that the hypothesis is false when it is actually true?

Vocabulary and Core Concept Check

1. **COMPLETE THE SENTENCE** A method in which new samples are repeatedly drawn from the data set is called _____.

2. **DIFFERENT WORDS, SAME QUESTION** Which is different? Find "both" answers.

What is the experimental difference of the means?

What is $\overline{x}_{treatment} - \overline{x}_{control}$?

	Weight of Tumor (grams)					
Control Group	3.3	3.2	3.7	3.5	3.3	3.4
Treatment Group	0.4	0.6	0.5	0.6	0.7	0.5

What is the square root of the average of the squared differences from -2.85?

What is the difference between the mean of the treatment group and the mean of the control group?

Monitoring Progress and Modeling with Mathematics

3. **PROBLEM SOLVING** A randomized comparative experiment tests whether music therapy affects the depression scores of college students. The depression scores range from 20 to 80, with scores greater than 50 being associated with depression. The control group has eight students and the treatment group, which receives the music therapy, has eight students. The table shows the results. *(See Example 1.)*

	Depression Score			
Control Group	49	45	43	47
Treatment Group	39	40	39	37

Control Group	46	45	47	46
Treatment Group	41	40	42	43

   a. Find the mean score of the control group.

   b. Find the mean score of the treatment group.

   c. Find the experimental difference of the means.

   d. Display the data in a double dot plot.

   e. What can you conclude?

4. **PROBLEM SOLVING** A randomized comparative experiment tests whether low-level laser therapy affects the waist circumference of adults. The control group has eight adults and the treatment group, which receives the low-level laser therapy, has eight adults. The table shows the results.

	Circumference (inches)			
Control Group	34.6	35.4	33	34.6
Treatment Group	31.4	33	32.4	32.6

Control Group	35.2	35.2	36.2	35
Treatment Group	33.4	33.4	34.8	33

   a. Find the mean circumference of the control group.

   b. Find the mean circumference of the treatment group.

   c. Find the experimental difference of the means.

   d. Display the data in a double dot plot.

   e. What can you conclude?

5. **ERROR ANALYSIS** In a randomized comparative experiment, the mean score of the treatment group is 11 and the mean score of the control group is 16. Describe and correct the error in interpreting the experimental difference of the means.

    $\overline{x}_{control} - \overline{x}_{treatment} = 16 - 11 = 5$
   So, you can conclude the treatment increases the score.

6. REASONING In Exercise 4, interpret the meaning of $\bar{x}_{\text{treatment}} - \bar{x}_{\text{control}}$ when the difference is positive, negative, and zero.

7. MODELING WITH MATHEMATICS Resample the data in Exercise 3 using a simulation. Use the means of the new control and treatment groups to calculate the difference of the means. *(See Example 2.)*

8. MODELING WITH MATHEMATICS Resample the data in Exercise 4 using a simulation. Use the means of the new control and treatment groups to calculate the difference of the means.

9. DRAWING CONCLUSIONS To analyze the hypothesis below, use the histogram which shows the results from 200 resamplings of the data in Exercise 3.

Music therapy has no effect on the depression score.

Compare the experimental difference in Exercise 3 with the resampling differences. What can you conclude about the hypothesis? Does music therapy have an effect on the depression score? *(See Example 3.)*

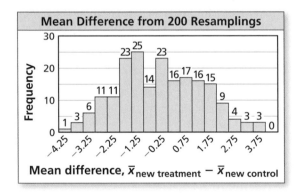

10. DRAWING CONCLUSIONS Suppose the experimental difference of the means in Exercise 3 had been -0.75. Compare this experimental difference of means with the resampling differences in the histogram in Exercise 9. What can you conclude about the hypothesis? Does music therapy have an effect on the depression score?

11. WRITING Compare the histogram in Exercise 9 to the histogram below. Determine which one provides stronger evidence against the hypothesis, *Music therapy has no effect on the depression score.* Explain.

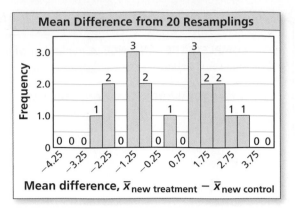

12. HOW DO YOU SEE IT? Without calculating, determine whether the experimental difference, $\bar{x}_{\text{treatment}} - \bar{x}_{\text{control}}$, is positive, negative, or zero. What can you conclude about the effect of the treatment? Explain.

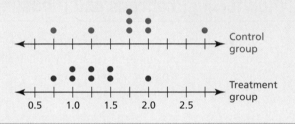

13. MAKING AN ARGUMENT Your friend states that the mean of the resampling differences of the means should be close to 0 as the number of resamplings increase. Is your friend correct? Explain your reasoning.

14. THOUGHT PROVOKING Describe an example of an observation that can be made from an experiment. Then give four possible inferences that could be made from the observation.

15. CRITICAL THINKING In Exercise 4, how many resamplings of the treatment and control groups are theoretically possible? Explain.

Maintaining Mathematical Proficiency   Reviewing what you learned in previous grades and lessons

Factor the polynomial completely. *(Section 3.4)*

16. $5x^3 - 15x^2$ **17.** $y^3 - 8$ **18.** $z^3 + 5z^2 - 9z - 45$ **19.** $81w^4 - 16$

Determine whether the inverse of f is a function. Then find the inverse. *(Section 6.5)*

20. $f(x) = \dfrac{3}{x + 5}$ **21.** $f(x) = \dfrac{1}{2x - 1}$ **22.** $f(x) = \dfrac{2}{x} - 4$ **23.** $f(x) = \dfrac{3}{x^2} + 1$

10.4–10.6 What Did You Learn?

Core Vocabulary

controlled experiment, *p. 534*

control group, *p. 534*

treatment group, *p. 534*

randomization, *p. 534*

randomized comparative experiment, *p. 534*

placebo, *p. 534*

replication, *p. 536*

descriptive statistics, *p. 540*

inferential statistics, *p. 540*

margin of error, *p. 543*

Core Concepts

Section 10.4

Randomization in Experiments and Observational Studies, *p. 535*

Comparative Studies and Causality, *p. 535*

Analyzing Experimental Designs, *p. 536*

Section 10.5

Estimating Population Parameters, *p. 540*

Analyzing Estimated Population Parameters, *p. 542*

Margin of Error Formula, *p. 543*

Section 10.6

Experiments with Two Samples, *p. 548*

Resampling Data Using Simulations, *p. 549*

Making Inferences About Treatments, *p. 550*

Mathematical Practices

1. In Exercise 7 on page 537, find a partner and discuss your answers. What questions should you ask your partner to determine whether an observational study or an experiment is more appropriate?

2. In Exercise 23 on page 546, how did you use the given interval to find the sample size?

Performance Task:

Volcano Damage

Scientists at the U.S. Geological Survey record and analyze data that describes potential damage due to volcano eruptions in the United States and abroad. Predictions for future damage are based on data from the past. Based on their analysis, where in the United States are you most likely to be affected by volcano damage?

To explore the answer to this question and more, check out the Performance Task and Real-Life STEM video at *BigIdeasMath.com*.

10.1 Using Normal Distributions *(pp. 509–516)*

A normal distribution has mean μ and standard deviation σ. An x-value is randomly selected from the distribution. Find $P(\mu - 2\sigma \le x \le \mu + 3\sigma)$.

The probability that a randomly selected x-value lies between $\mu - 2\sigma$ and $\mu + 3\sigma$ is the shaded area under the normal curve shown.

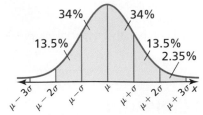

▶ $P(\mu - 2\sigma \le x \le \mu + 3\sigma) = 0.135 + 0.34 + 0.34 + 0.135 + 0.0235 = 0.9735$

1. A normal distribution has mean μ and standard deviation σ. An x-value is randomly selected from the distribution. Find $P(x \le \mu - 3\sigma)$.

2. The scores received by juniors on the math portion of the PSAT are normally distributed with a mean of 48.6 and a standard deviation of 11.4. What is the probability that a randomly selected score is at least 76?

10.2 Populations, Samples, and Hypotheses *(pp. 517–522)*

You suspect a die favors the number six. The die maker claims the die does not favor any number. What should you conclude when you roll the actual die 50 times and get a six 13 times?

The maker's claim, or hypothesis, is "the die does not favor any number." This is the same as saying that the proportion of sixes rolled, in the long run, is $\frac{1}{6}$. So, assume the probability of rolling a six is $\frac{1}{6}$. Simulate the rolling of the die by repeatedly drawing 200 random samples of size 50 from a population of numbers from one through six. Make a histogram of the distribution of the sample proportions.

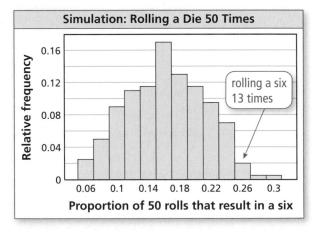

▶ Getting a six 13 times corresponds to a proportion of $\frac{13}{50} = 0.26$. In the simulation, this result had a relative frequency of 0.02. Because this result is unlikely to occur by chance, you can conclude that the maker's claim is most likely false.

3. To estimate the average number of miles driven by U.S. motorists each year, a researcher conducts a survey of 1000 drivers, records the number of miles they drive in a year, and then determines the average. Identify the population and the sample.

4. A pitcher throws 40 fastballs in a game. A baseball analyst records the speeds of 10 fastballs and finds that the mean speed is 92.4 miles per hour. Is the mean speed a parameter or a statistic? Explain.

5. A prize on a game show is placed behind either Door A or Door B. You suspect the prize is more often behind Door A. The show host claims the prize is randomly placed behind either door. What should you conclude when the prize is behind Door A for 32 out of 50 contestants?

Collecting Data *(pp. 523–530)*

You want to determine how many people in the senior class plan to study mathematics after high school. You survey every senior in your calculus class. Identify the type of sample described and determine whether the sample is biased.

▶ You select students who are readily available. So, the sample is a *convenience* sample. The sample is biased because students in a calculus class are more likely to study mathematics after high school.

6. A researcher wants to determine how many people in a city support the construction of a new road connecting the high school to the north side of the city. Fifty residents from each side of the city are surveyed. Identify the type of sample described and determine whether the sample is biased.

7. A researcher records the number of people who use a coupon when they dine at a certain restaurant. Identify the method of data collection.

8. Explain why the survey question below may be biased or otherwise introduce bias into the survey. Then describe a way to correct the flaw.

   "Do you think the city should replace the outdated police cars it is using?"

10.4 **Experimental Design** *(pp. 533–538)*

Determine whether the study is a randomized comparative experiment. If it is, describe the treatment, the treatment group, and the control group. If it is not, explain why not and discuss whether the conclusions drawn from the study are valid.

▶ The study is not a randomized comparative experiment because the individuals were not randomly assigned to a control group and a treatment group. The conclusion that headphone use impairs hearing ability may or may not be valid. For instance, people who listen to more than an hour of music per day may be more likely to attend loud concerts that are known to affect hearing.

Headphones Hurt Hearing
A study of 100 college and high school students compared their times spent listening to music using headphones with hearing loss. Twelve percent of people who listened to headphones more than one hour per day were found to have measurable hearing loss over the course of the three-year study.

9. A restaurant manager wants to know which type of sandwich bread attracts the most repeat customers. Is the topic best investigated through an experiment or an observational study? Describe how you would design the experiment or observational study.

10. A researcher wants to test the effectiveness of a sleeping pill. Identify a potential problem, if any, with the experimental design below. Then describe how you can improve it.

    The researcher asks for 16 volunteers who have insomnia. Eight volunteers are given the sleeping pill and the other 8 volunteers are given a placebo. Results are recorded for 1 month.

11. Determine whether the study is a randomized comparative experiment. If it is, describe the treatment, the treatment group, and the control group. If it is not, explain why not and discuss whether the conclusions drawn from the study are valid.

Cleaner Cars in Less Time!
To test the new design of a car wash, an engineer gathered 80 customers and randomly divided them into two groups. One group used the old design to wash their cars and one group used the new design to wash their cars. Users of the new car wash design were able to wash their cars 30% faster.

Before the Thanksgiving holiday, in a survey of 2368 people, 85% said they are thankful for the health of their family. What is the margin of error for the survey?

Use the margin of error formula.

$$\text{Margin of error} = \pm\frac{1}{\sqrt{n}} = \pm\frac{1}{\sqrt{2368}} \approx \pm0.021$$

▶ The margin of error for the survey is about $\pm2.1\%$.

12. In a survey of 1017 U.S. adults, 62% said that they prefer saving money over spending it. Give an interval that is likely to contain the exact percent of all U.S. adults who prefer saving money over spending it.

13. There are two candidates for homecoming king. The table shows the results from four random surveys of the students in the school. The students were asked whether they will vote for Candidate A. Do you think Candidate A will be the homecoming king? Explain.

Sample Size	Number of "Yes" Responses	Percent of Votes
8	6	75%
22	14	63.6%
34	16	47.1%
62	29	46.8%

10.6 Making Inferences from Experiments *(pp. 547–552)*

A randomized comparative experiment tests whether a new fertilizer affects the length (in inches) of grass after one week. The control group has 10 sections of land and the treatment group, which is fertilized, has 10 sections of land. The table shows the results.

	Grass Length (inches)									
Control Group	4.5	4.5	4.8	4.4	4.4	4.7	4.3	4.5	4.1	4.2
Treatment Group	4.6	4.8	5.0	4.8	4.7	4.6	4.9	4.9	4.8	4.4

a. Find the experimental difference of the means, $\bar{x}_{treatment} - \bar{x}_{control}$.

$$\bar{x}_{treatment} - \bar{x}_{control} = 4.75 - 4.44 = 0.31$$

▶ The experimental difference of the means is 0.31 inch.

b. What can you conclude?

▶ The two data sets tend to be fairly symmetric and have no extreme values. So, the mean is a suitable measure of center. The mean length of the treatment group is 0.31 inch longer than the control group. It appears that the fertilizer might be slightly effective, but the sample size is small and the difference could be due to chance.

14. Describe how to use a simulation to resample the data in the example above. Explain how this allows you to make inferences about the data when the sample size is small.

1. Market researchers want to know whether more men or women buy their product. Explain whether this research topic is best investigated through an experiment or an observational study. Then describe the design of the experiment or observational study.

2. You want to survey 100 of the 2774 four-year colleges in the United States about their tuition cost. Describe a method for selecting a random sample of colleges to survey.

3. The grade point averages of all the students in a high school are normally distributed with a mean of 2.95 and a standard deviation of 0.72. Are these numerical values parameters or statistics? Explain.

A normal distribution has a mean of 72 and a standard deviation of 5. Find the probability that a randomly selected *x*-value from the distribution is in the given interval.

4. between 67 and 77

5. at least 75

6. at most 82

7. A researcher wants to test the effectiveness of a new medication designed to lower blood pressure. Identify a potential problem, if any, with the experimental design. Then describe how you can improve it.

   The researcher identifies 30 people with high blood pressure. Fifteen people with the highest blood pressures are given the medication and the other 15 are given a placebo. After 1 month, the subjects are evaluated.

8. A randomized comparative experiment tests whether a vitamin supplement increases human bone density (in grams per square centimeter). The control group has eight people and the treatment group, which receives the vitamin supplement, has eight people. The table shows the results.

	Bone Density (g/cm²)							
Control Group	0.9	1.2	1.0	0.8	1.3	1.1	0.9	1.0
Treatment Group	1.2	1.0	0.9	1.3	1.2	0.9	1.3	1.2

   a. Find the mean yields of the control group, $\bar{x}_{control}$, and the treatment group, $\bar{x}_{treatment}$.

   b. Find the experimental difference of the means, $\bar{x}_{treatment} - \bar{x}_{control}$.

   c. Display the data in a double dot plot. What can you conclude?

   d. Five hundred resamplings of the data are simulated. Out of the 500 resampling differences, 231 are greater than the experimental difference in part (b). What can you conclude about the hypothesis, *The vitamin supplement has no effect on human bone density*? Explain your reasoning.

9. In a recent survey of 1600 randomly selected U.S. adults, 81% said they have purchased a product online.

   a. Identify the population and the sample. Describe the sample.

   b. Find the margin of error for the survey.

   c. Give an interval that is likely to contain the exact percent of all U.S. adults who have purchased a product online.

   d. You survey 75 teachers at your school. The results are shown in the graph. Would you use the recent survey or your survey to estimate the percent of U.S. adults who have purchased a product online? Explain.

Have You Purchased a Product Online?

No 8%

Yes 92%

1. Your friend claims any system formed by three of the following equations will have exactly one solution.

$$3x + y + 3z = 6$$

$$x + y + z = 2$$

$$4x - 2y + 4z = 8$$

$$x - y + z = 2$$

$$2x + y + z = 4$$

$$3x + y + 9z = 12$$

   a. Write a linear system that would support your friend's claim.

   b. Write a linear system that shows your friend's claim is incorrect.

2. Which of the following samples are biased? If the sample is biased, explain why it is biased.

   (A) A restaurant asks customers to participate in a survey about the food sold at the restaurant. The restaurant uses the surveys that are returned.

   (B) You want to know the favorite sport of students at your school. You randomly select athletes to survey at the winter sports banquet.

   (C) The owner of a store wants to know whether the store should stay open 1 hour later each night. Each cashier surveys every fifth customer.

   (D) The owner of a movie theater wants to know whether the volume of its movies is too loud. Patrons under the age of 18 are randomly surveyed.

3. A survey asks adults about their favorite way to eat ice cream. The results of the survey are displayed in the table shown.

Survey Results	
Cup	45%
Cone	29%
Sundae	18%
Other	8%
(margin of error ±2.11%)	

   a. How many people were surveyed?

   b. Why might the conclusion, "Adults generally do not prefer to eat their ice cream in a cone" be inaccurate to draw from this data?

   c. You decide to test the results of the poll by surveying adults chosen at random. Four of the six respondents in your survey said they prefer to eat their ice cream in a cone. You conclude that the other survey is inaccurate. Why might this conclusion be incorrect?

   d. What is the margin of error for your survey?

4. You are making a lampshade out of fabric for the lamp shown. The pattern for the lampshade is shown in the diagram on the left.

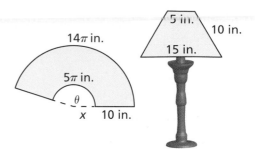

5 in.
10 in.
14π in.
15 in.
5π in.
θ
x   10 in.

    a. Use the smaller sector to write an equation that relates θ and x.

    b. Use the larger sector to write an equation that relates θ and $x + 10$.

    c. Solve the system of equations from parts (a) and (b) for x and θ.

    d. Find the amount of fabric (in square inches) that you will use to make the lampshade.

5. For all students taking the Medical College Admission Test over a period of 3 years, the mean score was 25.1. During the same 3 years, a group of 1000 students who took the test had a mean score of 25.3. Classify each mean as a parameter or a statistic. Explain.

6. Complete the table for the four functions. Explain your reasoning.

Function	Is the inverse a function?		Is the function its own inverse?	
	Yes	No	Yes	No
$y = -x$				
$y = 3 \ln x + 2$				
$y = \left(\dfrac{1}{x}\right)^2$				
$y = \dfrac{x}{x - 1}$				

7. The normal distribution shown has mean 63 and standard deviation 8. Find the percent of the area under the normal curve that is represented by the shaded region. Then describe another interval under the normal curve that has the same area.

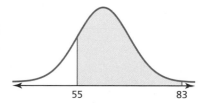

55   83

8. Which of the rational expressions *cannot* be simplified?

    (A) $\dfrac{2x^2 + 5x - 3}{x^2 - 7x + 12}$ (B) $\dfrac{3x^3 + 21x^2 + 30x}{x^2 - 25}$

    (C) $\dfrac{x^3 + 27}{x^2 - 3x + 9}$ (D) $\dfrac{x^3 + 2x^2 - 8x - 16}{2x^2 - 21x + 55}$

Selected Answers

Chapter 1

Chapter 1 Maintaining Mathematical Proficiency (p. 1)

1. **a.** about 265.9 cm²

   b. about 2002.96 in.²

2. 482.8 ft²

3. about 1993.34 ft², about 5725.55 ft³

4. about 2463.01 in.², about 11,494.04 in.³

5. 896 m², 1568 m³

6. yes; The box is a cube with side length $2r$, so the volume of the box is $8r^3$.

1.1 Vocabulary and Core Concept Check (p. 7)

1. *Sample answer:* The population of a state is the total number of people who live in that state. The population density of a state is the number of people per square mile in that state.

1.1 Monitoring Progress and Modeling with Mathematics (pp. 7–8)

3. about 34 people per mi²

5. about 5747 people per mi²

7. about 319,990 people

9. about 7 mi

11. The diameter was substituted into the formula instead of the radius; $1550 = \dfrac{x}{\pi \cdot 3.75^2}$; $1550 = \dfrac{x}{14.0625\pi}$; $x \approx 68,477$;

    The number of people who live in the region is about 68,477.

13. **a.** $160\ell - \ell^2$

    b. $\ell = 80$ yd, $w = 80$ yd; The field with the maximum area is a square.

15. The surface area is 4 times the original surface area.

17. **a.** no; The smaller ball needs $\frac{1}{16}$ times the amount of rubber coating.

    b. $4\sqrt{2}$ in.

19. no; California and Texas also have two of the greatest areas, so they may not have the greatest population densities.

1.1 Maintaining Mathematical Proficiency (p. 8)

21. 77

23. -7

25. about 929.9 ft³cm³

27. 7350 m³

1.2 Vocabulary and Core Concept Check (p. 13)

1. the object's mass

1.2 Monitoring Progress and Modeling with Mathematics (pp. 13–14)

3. copper

5. Density is $\dfrac{\text{mass}}{\text{volume}}$ not $\dfrac{\text{volume}}{\text{mass}}$; density $= \dfrac{24}{28.3} \approx 0.85$ g/cm³

7. The volume is 27 times the original volume.

9. **a.** The volume is $\frac{1}{27}$ times the original volume.

   b. about 23,900 lane miles; about 917 lane miles

11. **a.** 18,000 kg

    b. $\frac{4}{3}$ m

13. yes; A section of water that is deep in the ocean will have more water molecules, and therefore more mass than a section of water with the same volume that is on the surface. So, the density of water deeper in the ocean is greater than the density of water on the surface.

15. **a.** *Sample answer:* the average of the outside perimeter and the inside perimeter; Because different metals bend different ways, the average is a good estimate of the length; about 2926.92 g

    b. about 451.2 cm; The total length of 100 links is $100(1.5 + 2.7 + 1.5) = 570$ centimeters. However, when the links are connected to form a taut chain, the links overlap 99 times. So, you must subtract $99(0.6 + 0.6) = 118.8$ centimeters from the total length of the 100 links.

1.2 Maintaining Mathematical Proficiency (p. 14)

17. 42 in.

1.3 Vocabulary and Core Concept Check (p. 21)

1. cross section

1.3 Monitoring Progress and Modeling with Mathematics (pp. 21–22)

3. circle

5. triangle

7.

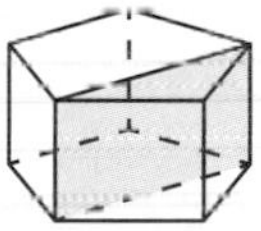

   rectangle

9.

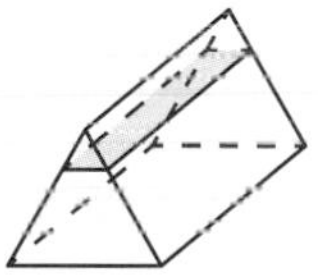

   rectangle

11. The cross section is not a trapezoid, it is a rectangle.

13. *Sample answer.*

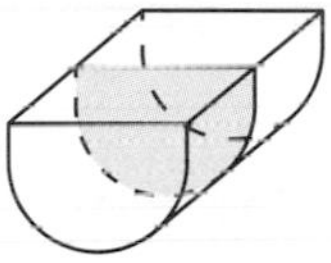

    yes; yes; The cross section can also be a rectangle.

15.

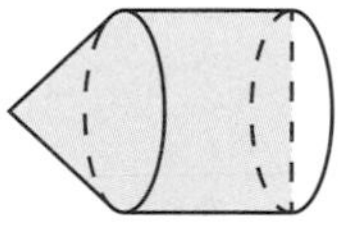

    no

17. *Sample answer:*

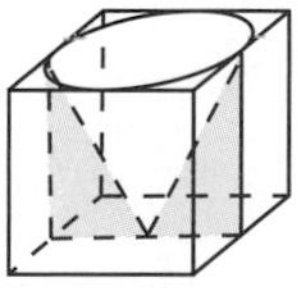

    yes; When the vertical plane used in the diagram shown is rotated 90°, the cross section does not change. When the vertical plane is rotated 45°, the cross section is two trapezoids.

19. **a.** 36.5 in., 59.5 in.²

    b. about 153.94 in.²; increases by 119 square inches

    c. yes; *Sample answer:* about 43.98 in., about 153.94 in.²

21. a. *Sample answer:*

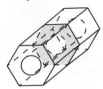

b. infinitely many ways; Any cut made lengthwise through the center of the hexagon will form two congruent parts.

23. no; The plane can intersect the sphere at a point.

25.

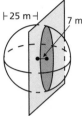

about 1809.6 m²

1.3 Maintaining Mathematical Proficiency *(p. 22)*

27. 4

29. 2

31.

33.

1.4 Vocabulary and Core Concept Check *(p. 27)*

1. cylinder

1.4 Monitoring Progress and Modeling with Mathematics *(pp. 27–28)*

3.

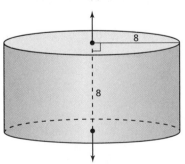

cylinder with a height of 8 units and a base radius of 8 units

5.

sphere with a radius of 3 units

7. The height and base radius are wrong; The solid is a cylinder with a height of 12 units and a base radius of 5 units.

9.

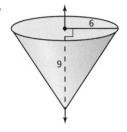

cylinder with a height of 4 units and a base radius of 4 units

11.

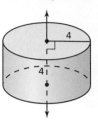

cone with a height of 9 units and a base radius of 6 units

13.

15.

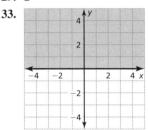

17.

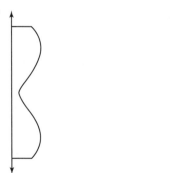

cone with a height of 12 units and a base radius of 10 units; about 804.89 square units, about 1256.64 cubic units

19.

cylinder with a height of 7.4 units and a base radius of 2.5 units; about 155.51 square units, about 145.3 cubic units

21.

two cones, both with a height of 3 units and a base radius of 2 units; about 45.31 square units, about 25.13 cubic units

23.

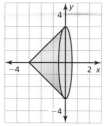

cone with a height of 3 units and a base radius of 3 units; about 28.27 cubic units

25.

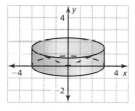

cylinder with a cone removed, both with a height of 1.5 units and a base radius of 3 units; about 28.27 cubic units

27. no; The solid produced by rotating the figure around the *x*-axis is a sphere and the solid produced by rotating the figure around the *y*-axis is a hemisphere.

29. cone with a height of 15 units and a base radius of 20 units, 2000π cubic units; cone with a height of 20 units and a base radius of 15 units, 1500π cubic units; two cones, one with a base radius of 12 units and a height of 9 units, the other with a base radius of 12 units and a height of 16 units, 1200π cubic units

31. a.

b. *Sample answer:* cylinder; Stretch the cylinder and connect the bases.

1.4 Maintaining Mathematical Proficiency (p. 28)

33. no   **35.** yes

37. about 9 mi

Chapter 1 Review (pp. 30–32)

1. about 9903 people per mi^2

2. about 2.5 km

3. a. $\frac{49}{64}$ times the amount of glaze

b. $\frac{25}{16}$ times the amount of glaze

4. about 94 mm

5. The volume is 2 times the original volume.

6. The volume is 4 times the original volume.

7. The volume is $\frac{1}{3}$ times the original volume.

8. a. about 32.4 cm³; The volume is approximately equal to the volume of the sphere minus the volume of the cylindrical hole.

b. no, yes; For the surface area, the lateral surface area of the cylinder is added, while the areas of the bases of the cylinder are subtracted. Because the lateral surface area is greater than the total area of the bases, the surface area of the wooden ball increases after the hole is made. The volume decreases because part of the sphere is removed.

9. rectangle

10. square

11. triangle

12.

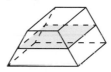

pentagon

13.

rectangle

14. *Sample answer:* rectangle, triangle

15.

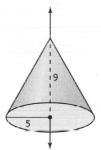

cone with a height of 9 units and a base radius of 5 units; about 240.26 square units, about 235.62 cubic units

16.

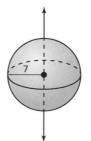

sphere with a radius of 7 units; about 615.75 square units, about 1436.76 cubic units

17.

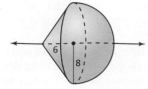

cone with a height of 6 units and a base radius of 8 units and a hemisphere with a radius of 8 units; about 653.45 square units, about 1474.45 cubic units

18.

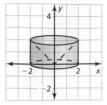

cylinder with a cone removed, both with a height of 2 units and a base radius of 2 units; about 16.76 cubic units

Chapter 2

Chapter 2 Maintaining Mathematical Proficiency *(p. 37)*

1. 47   **2.** -46

3. $3\frac{3}{5}$ **4.** 4

5. 13   **6.** 0

7.

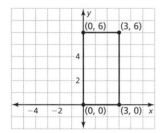

8.

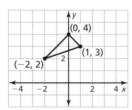

9.

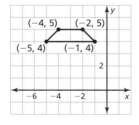

10. *Sample answer:* $12 + 18 \div 3$ equals 18 when division is performed first and 10 when addition is performed first; yes; If the point $(3, 2)$ is translated up 3 units then reflected in the x-axis, the new coordinate is $(3, -5)$. If it is reflected in the x-axis first then translated up 3, the new coordinate is $(3, 1)$.

2.1 Vocabulary and Core Concept Check *(p. 44)*

1. parent function

2.1 Monitoring Progress and Modeling with Mathematics *(pp. 44–46)*

3. absolute value; The graph is a vertical stretch with a translation 2 units left and 8 units down; The domain of each function is all real numbers, but the range of f is $y \geq -8$, and the range of the parent function is $y \geq 0$.

5. linear; The graph is a vertical stretch and a translation 2 units down; The domain and range of each function is all real numbers.

7.

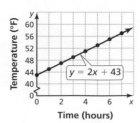

linear; The temperature is increasing by the same amount at each interval.

9.

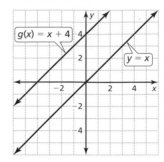

The graph of g is a vertical translation 4 units up of the parent linear function.

11.

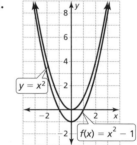

The graph of f is a vertical translation 1 unit down of the parent quadratic function.

13.

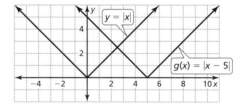

The graph of g is a horizontal translation 5 units right of the parent absolute value function.

15.

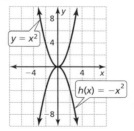

The graph of h is a reflection in the x-axis of the parent quadratic function.

17.

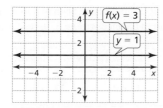

The graph of f is a vertical translation 2 units up of the parent constant function.

19.

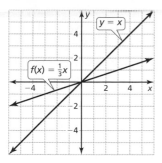

The graph of f is a vertical shrink of the parent linear function.

21.

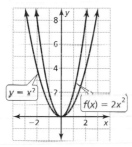

The graph of f is a vertical stretch of the parent quadratic function.

23.

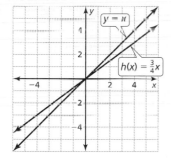

The graph of h is a vertical shrink of the parent linear function.

25.

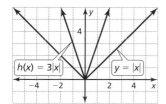

The graph of h is a vertical stretch of the parent absolute value function.

27.

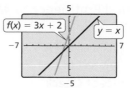

The graph of f is a vertical stretch followed by a translation 2 units up of the parent linear function.

29.

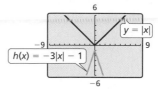

The graph of h is a vertical stretch and a reflection in the x-axis followed by a translation 1 unit down of the parent absolute value function.

31.

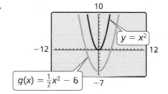

The graph of g is a vertical shrink followed by a translation 6 units down of the parent quadratic function.

33.

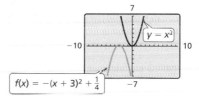

The graph of f is a reflection in the x-axis followed by a translation 3 units left and $\frac{1}{4}$ unit up of the parent quadratic function.

35. It is a vertical stretch, not shrink. The graph is a reflection in the x-axis followed by a vertical stretch of the parent quadratic function.

37. $(2, -1), (-1, -4), (2, -5)$

39. absolute value; domain is all real numbers; range is $y \geq -1$

41. linear; domain is all real numbers; range is all real numbers

43. quadratic; domain is all real numbers; range is $y \geq -2$

45. absolute value; 8 mi/h

47. no; f is shifted right and g is shifted down.

49. yes; Shifting the parent linear function down 2 units will create the same graph as shifting it 2 units right.

51. a. quadratic

b. 0; At the moment the ball is released, 0 seconds have passed.

c. 5.2; Because $f(t)$ represents the height of the ball, find $f(0)$.

53. a. vertical translation; The graph will have a vertical stretch and will be shifted 3 units down.

b. horizontal translation; The graph will be shifted 8 units right.

c. both; The graph will be shifted 2 units left and 4 units up.

d. neither; The graph will have a vertical stretch.

2.1 Maintaining Mathematical Proficiency (p. 46)

55. no   **57.** yes

59. x-intercept: 0; y-intercept: 0

61. x-intercept: $\frac{1}{3}$; y-intercept: 1

2.2 Vocabulary and Core Concept Check (p. 52)

1. shrink

2.2 Monitoring Progress and Modeling with Mathematics (pp. 52–54)

3. $g(x) = x - 1$ **5.** $g(x) = |4x + 3|$

7. $g(x) = 4 - |x - 2|$

9. f could be translated 3 units up or 3 units right.

11. $g(x) = 5x - 2$ **13.** $g(x) = |6x| - 2$

15. $g(x) = -3 + |-x - 11|$ **17.** $g(x) = 5x + 10$

19. $g(x) = |4x| + 4$ **21.** $g(x) = -|x - 4| + 1$

23. C; The graph has been translated left.

24. A; The graph has been stretched vertically.

25. D; The graph has been translated up.

26. B; The graph has been shrunk horizontally.

27. $g(x) = 2x + 1$ **29.** $g(x) = \left|\frac{1}{2}x - 2\right|$

31. $g(x) = -|x| - 8$

33. Translating a graph to the right requires subtraction, not addition; $g(x) = |x - 3| + 2$

35. no; Suppose a graph contains the point (3, 2) and is translated up 3 units then reflected in the x-axis. The new coordinate is $(3, -5)$. If it is reflected in the x-axis first then translated up 3, the new coordinate is $(3, 1)$.

37. The graph has been translated 6 units left; $A = 9$

39. The graph has been reflected in the x-axis; $A = 16$

41. **a.** $f(x) + (c - b)$

     b. $f\left(x + \dfrac{c - b}{m}\right)$

43. vertical stretch, translation, reflection; *Sample answer:* $-(4|x| - 2) = -4|x| + 2$

45. $a = -2$, $b = 1$, and $c = 0$; $g(x) = -2|x - 1|$ represents the transformation of $f(x)$.

2.2 Maintaining Mathematical Proficiency (p. 54)

47. -5 **49.** 0

51.

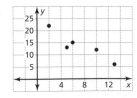

2.3 Vocabulary and Core Concept Check (p. 60)

1. slope-intercept

2.3 Monitoring Progress and Modeling with Mathematics (pp. 60–62)

3. $y = \frac{1}{5}x$; The tip increases $0.20 for each dollar spent on the meal.

5. $y = 50x + 100$; The balance increases $50 each week.

7. $y = 55x$; The number of words increases by 55 each minute.

9. Greenville Journal; 5 lines

11. The original balance of $100 should have been included; After 7 years, the increase in balance will be $70, resulting in a new balance of $170.

13. yes; *Sample answer:* $y = 4.25x + 1.75$; $y = 65.5$; After 15 minutes, you have burned 65.5 calories.

15. yes; *Sample answer:* $y = -4.6x + 96$; $y = 27$; After 15 hours, the battery will have 27% of life remaining.

17. $y = 380.03x + 11,290$; $16,990.45$; The annual tuition increases about $380 each year and the cost of tuition in 2005 is about $11,290.

19. $y = 0.42x + 1.44$; $r = 0.61$; weak positive correlation

21. $y = -0.45x + 4.26$; $r = -0.67$; weak negative correlation

23. $y = 0.61x + 0.10$; $r = 0.95$; strong positive correlation

25. **a.** *Sample answer:* height and weight; temperature and ice cream sales; Correlation is positive because as the first goes up, so does the second.

     b. *Sample answer:* miles driven and gas remaining; hours used and battery life remaining; Correlation is negative because as the first goes up, the second goes down.

     c. *Sample answer:* age and length of hair; typing speed and shoe size; There is no relationship between the first and second.

27. no; Because r is close to 0, the points do not lie close to the line.

29. It is negative; As x increases, y increases, so z decreases.

31. about 2.2 mi

2.3 Maintaining Mathematical Proficiency (p. 62)

33. $(16, -41)$ **35.** $\left(1, \frac{1}{2}\right)$

37. $\left(\frac{16}{17}, \frac{15}{17}\right)$

2.4 Vocabulary and Core Concept Check (p. 68)

1. ordered triple

2.4 Monitoring Progress and Modeling with Mathematics (pp. 68–70)

3. $(1, 2, -1)$ **5.** $(3, -1, -4)$

7. $\left(\frac{151}{64}, \frac{9}{8}, -\frac{51}{32}\right)$

9. The entire second equation should be multiplied by 4, not just the x-term.

$$4x - y + 2z = -18$$
$$-4x + 8y + 4z = 44$$
$$\overline{7y + 6z = 26}$$

11. no solution   **13.** $(z - 1, 1, z)$

15. no solution

17. A small pizza costs $5, a liter of soda costs $1, and a salad costs $3.

19. $(4, -3, 2)$ **21.** no solution

23. $(7, 3, 5)$ **25.** $(3, 2, 1)$

27. $\left(\dfrac{-3z + 3}{5}, \dfrac{-13z + 13}{5}, z\right)$ **29.** 1%

31. *Sample answer:* When one variable has the same coefficient or its opposite in each equation. The system

$$3x + 2y - 4z = -5$$
$$2x + 2y + 3z = 8$$
$$5x - 2y - 7z = -9$$

can be solved by eliminating y first.

33. $\ell + m + n = 65, n = \ell + m - 15, l = \frac{1}{3}m; \ell = 10$ ft,
$m = 30$ ft, $n = 25$ ft

35. **a.** *Sample answer:* $a = -1, b = -1, c = -1$; Use
elimination on equations 1 and 2.

   b. *Sample answer:* $a = 4, b = 4, c = 5$; The solution is
$\left(\frac{2}{3}, -\frac{2}{3}, 2\right)$.

   c. *Sample answer:* $a = 5, b = 5, c = 5$; Use elimination on
equations 1 and 2.

37. 350 ft^2

39. **a.** $r + l + i = 12, 2.50r + 4l + 2i = 32, r = 2l + 2i$

   b. 8 roses, 2 lilies, 2 irises

   c. no; *Sample answer:* 8 roses, 4 lilies, 0 irises; 8 roses,
0 lilies, 4 irises; 8 roses, 3 lilies, 1 iris

41. $a = 12, b = -4, c = 10$; These are the values you obtain
when you substitute -1 for x, 2 for y, and -3 for z.

43. $t + a = g, t + b = a, 2g = 3b$; 5 tangerines

2.4 Maintaining Mathematical Proficiency *(p. 70)*

45. $9m^2 + 6m + 1$ **47.** $16 - 8y + y^2$

49. $g(x) = -|x| + 5$ **51.** $g(x) = 3|x| - 15$

2.5 Vocabulary and Core Concept Check *(p. 78)*

1. parabola

2.5 Monitoring Progress and Modeling with Mathematics *(pp. 78–80)*

3. The graph of g is a translation 3 units down of the graph of f.

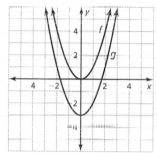

5. The graph of g is a translation 2 units left of the graph of f.

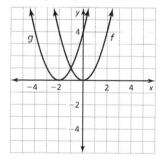

7. The graph of g is a translation 1 unit right of the graph of f.

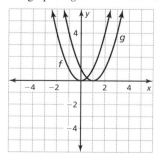

9. The graph of g is a translation 6 units left and 2 units down
of the graph of f.

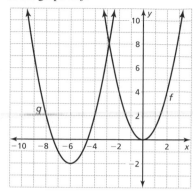

11. The graph of g is a translation 7 units right and 1 unit up of
the graph of f.

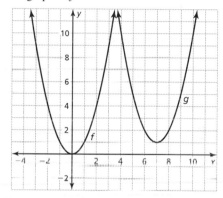

13. A; The graph has been translated 1 unit right.

14. D; The graph has been translated 1 unit up.

15. C; The graph has been translated 1 unit right and 1 unit up.

16. B; The graph has been translated 1 unit left and 1 unit down.

17. The graph of g is a reflection in the x-axis of the graph of f.

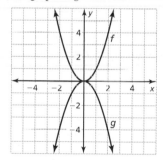

19. The graph of g is a vertical stretch by a factor of 3 of the
graph of f.

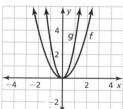

21. The graph of g is a horizontal shrink by a factor of $\frac{1}{2}$ of the graph of f.

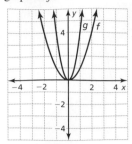

23. The graph of g is a vertical shrink by a factor of $\frac{1}{5}$ followed by a translation 4 units down.

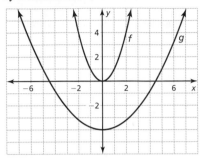

25. The graph is a reflection in the x-axis, not y-axis; The graph is a reflection in the x-axis and a vertical stretch by a factor of 6, followed by a translation 4 units up of the graph of the parent quadratic function.

27. The graph of f is a vertical stretch by a factor of 3 followed by a translation 2 units left and 1 unit up of the graph of the parent quadratic function; $(-2, 1)$

29. The graph of f is a vertical stretch by a factor of 2 followed by a reflection in the x-axis and a translation 5 units up of the graph of the parent quadratic function; $(0, 5)$

31. $g(x) = -4x^2 + 2$; $(0, 2)$

33. $g(x) = 8\left(\frac{1}{2}x\right)^2 - 4$; $(0, -4)$

35. C; The graph is a vertical stretch by a factor of 2 followed by a translation 1 unit right and 2 units down of the parent quadratic function.

36. B; The graph is a vertical shrink by a factor of $\frac{1}{2}$ followed by a translation 1 unit left and 2 units down of the parent quadratic function.

37. D; The graph is a vertical stretch by a factor of 2 and a reflection in the x-axis, followed by a translation 1 unit right and 2 units up of the parent quadratic function.

38. E; The graph is a vertical stretch by a factor of 2 followed by a translation 1 unit left and 2 units up of the parent quadratic function.

39. F; The graph is a vertical stretch by a factor of 2 and a reflection in the x-axis followed by a translation 1 unit left and 2 units down of the parent quadratic function.

40. A; The graph is a vertical stretch by a factor of 2 followed by a translation 1 unit right and 2 units up of the parent quadratic function.

41. Subtract 6 from the output; Substitute $2x^2 + 6x$ for $f(x)$; Multiply the output by -1; Substitute $2x^2 + 6x - 6$ for $h(x)$; Simplify.

43. $h(x) = -0.03(x - 14)^2 + 10.99$

45. a. $y = \dfrac{-5}{1089}(x - 33)^2 + 5$

 b. The domain is $0 \le x \le 66$ and the range is $0 \le y \le 5$; The domain represents the horizontal distance and the range represents the height of the fish.

 c. yes; The value changes to $-\frac{1}{225}$; The vertex has changed but it still goes through the point $(0, 0)$, so there has been a horizontal stretch or shrink which changes the value of a.

47. a. $a = 2$, $h = 1$, $k = 6$; $g(x) = 2(x - 1)^2 + 6$

 b. $g(x) = 2f(x - 1) + 6$; For each function, a, h, and k are the same but the second function does not indicate the type of function that is being translated.

 c. $a = 2$, $h = 1$, $k = 3$; $g(x) = 2(x - 1)^2 + 3$; $g(x) = 2f(x - 1) + 3$; For each function, a, h, and k are the same, but the answer in part (b) does not indicate the type of function that is being translated.

 d. *Sample answer:* vertex form; Writing a transformed function using function notation requires an extra step of substituting $f(x)$ into the newly transformed function.

49. a vertical shrink by a factor of $\frac{7}{16}$

2.5 Maintaining Mathematical Proficiency *(p. 80)*

51. $(4, 4)$

2.6 Vocabulary and Core Concept Check *(p. 87)*

1. If a is positive, then the quadratic function will have a minimum. If a is negative, then the quadratic function will have a maximum.

2.6 Monitoring Progress and Modeling with Mathematics *(pp. 87–90)*

3.

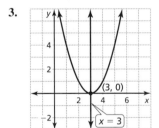

5.

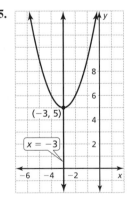

7.

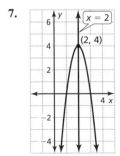

9.

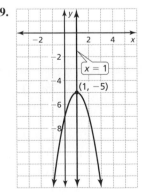

11.

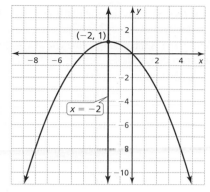

13.

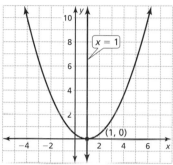

15. C

16. D

17. B

18. A

19.

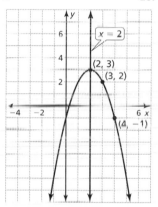

21.

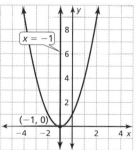

23.

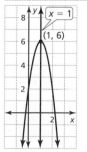

25.

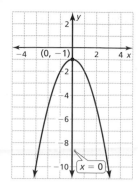

27.

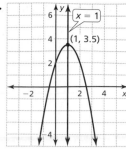

29.

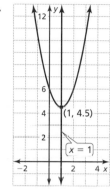

31. Both functions have an axis of symmetry of $x = 2$.

33. The formula is missing the negative sign; The x-coordinate of the vertex is
$$x = -\frac{b}{2a} = -\frac{24}{2(4)} = -3.$$

35. (25, 18.5); When the basketball is at its highest point, it is 25 feet from its starting point and 18.5 feet off the ground.

37. B

39. The minimum value is -1. The domain is all real numbers and the range is $y \geq -1$. The function is decreasing to the left of $x = 0$ and increasing to the right of $x = 0$.

41. The maximum value is 2. The domain is all real numbers and the range is $y < 2$. The function is increasing to the left of $x = -2$ and decreasing to the right of $x = -2$.

43. The maximum value is 15. The domain is all real numbers and the range is $y \leq 15$. The function is increasing to the left of $x = 2$ and decreasing to the right of $x = 2$.

45. The minimum value is -18. The domain is all real numbers and the range is $y \geq -18$. The function is decreasing to the left of $x = 3$ and increasing to the right of $x = 3$.

47. The minimum value is -7. The domain is all real numbers and the range is $y \geq -7$. The function is decreasing to the left of $x = 6$ and increasing to the right of $x = 6$.

49. a. 1 m

 b. 3.25 m

 c. The diver is ascending from 0 meters to 0.5 meter and descending from 0.5 meter until hitting the water after approximately 1.1 meters.

51. $A = w(20 - w) = -w^2 + 20w$; The maximum area is 100 square units.

53.

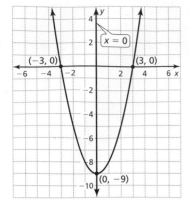

55.

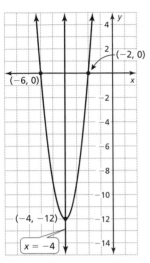

57.

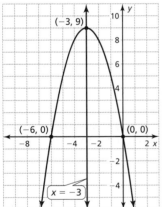

59.

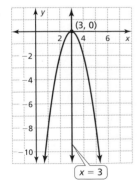

61. $p = 2$, $q = -6$; The graph is decreasing to the left of $x = -2$ and increasing to the right of $x = -2$.

63. $p = 4$, $q = 2$; The graph is increasing to the left of $x = 3$ and decreasing to the right of $x = 3$.

65. the second kick; the first kick

67. *Sample answer:* $y = 2(x - 2)(x - 4)$ and $y = 2(x + 1)(x - 7)$

69. $(-1, -5)$

71. center: $(0, -6)$, radius: 7

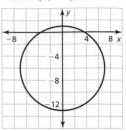

73. focus: $(2, 4)$, directrix: $x = 0$, vertex: $(1, 4)$

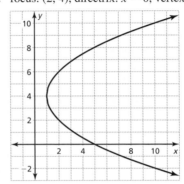

75. \$1.75

77. no; The vertex of the graph is $(3.25, 2.1125)$, which means the mouse cannot jump over a fence that is higher than 2.1125 feet.

79.

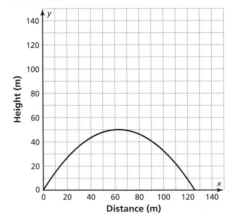

The domain is $0 \le x \le 126$ and the range is $0 \le y \le 50$; The domain represents the distance from the start of the bridge on one side of the river, and the range represents the height of the bridge.

81. no; The vertex must lie on the axis of symmetry, and $(0, 5)$ does not lie on $x = -1$.

83. a. about 14.1%; about 55.5 cm³/g

b. about 13.6%; about 44.1 cm³/g

c. The domain for hot-air popping is $5.52 \le x \le 22.6$, and the range is $0 \le y \le 55.5$. The domain for hot-oil popping is $5.35 \le x \le 21.8$, and the range is $0 \le y \le 44.1$. This means that the moisture content for the kernels can range from 5.52% to 22.6% and 5.35% to 21.8%, while the popping volume can range from 0 to 55.5 cubic centimeters per gram and 0 to 44.11 cubic centimeters per gram.

2.6 Maintaining Mathematical Proficiency (p. 90)

85.

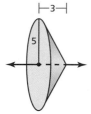

87. $y = 3.98x + 0.92$

2.7 Vocabulary and Core Concept Check (p. 96)

1. A quadratic model is appropriate when the second differences are constant.

2.7 Monitoring Progress and Modeling with Mathematics (pp. 96–98)

3. $y = -3(x + 2)^2 + 6$

5. $y = 0.06(x - 3)^2 + 2$

7. $y = -\frac{1}{3}(x + 6)^2 - 12$

9. $y = -4(x - 2)(x - 4)$

11. $y = \frac{1}{10}(x - 12)(x + 6)$

13. $y = 2.25(x + 16)(x + 2)$

15. If given the x-intercepts, it is easier to write the equation in intercept form. If given the vertex, it is easier to write the equation in vertex form.

17. $y = -16(x - 3)^2 + 150$

19. $y = -0.75x(x - 4)$

21. The x-intercepts were substituted incorrectly.
$y = a(x - p)(x - q)$
$4 = a(3 + 1)(3 - 2)$
$a = 1$
$y = (x + 1)(x - 2)$

23. $S(C) = 180C^2$; 18,000 lbs

25. intercept form; The three points can be substituted into the intercept form of a quadratic equation to solve for a, and then the equation can be written. This method is much shorter than writing and solving a system of three equations, although it can only be used when given the intercepts.

27. a. parabola; not a constant rate of change

b. $h = -16t^2 + 280$

c. about 4.18 sec

d. The domain is $0 \le t \le 4.18$ and represents the time the sponge was in the air. The range is $0 \le h \le 280$ and represents the height of the sponge.

29. quadratic; The second differences are constant;
$y = -2x^2 + 42x + 470$

31. neither; The first and second differences are not constant.

33. a. The vertex indicates that on the 6th day, 19 people were absent, more than any other day.

b. $y = -0.5(10 - 6)^2 + 19$; 11 students

c. From 0 to 6 days, the average rate of change was 3 students per day. From 6 to 11 days, the average rate of change was -2.5 students per day. The rate at which students were missing school was changing more rapidly as more became ill, in comparison to when the students were becoming well.

35. $y = -16x^2 + 6x + 22$; after about 1.24 sec; 1.375 sec

37. 155 tiles

2.7 Maintaining Mathematical Proficiency (p. 98)

39. $(x - 2)(x - 1)$

41. $5(x + 3)(x - 2)$

Chapter 2 Review (pp. 100–104)

1.

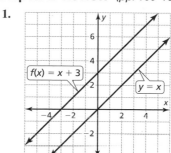

The graph of f is a translation 3 units up of the parent linear function.

2.

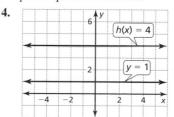

The graph of g is a translation 1 unit down of the parent absolute value function.

3.

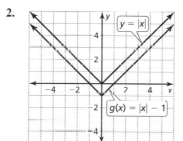

The graph of h is a vertical shrink by a factor of $\frac{1}{2}$ of the parent quadratic function.

4.

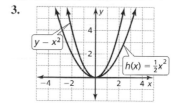

The graph of h is a translation 3 units up of the parent constant function.

5.

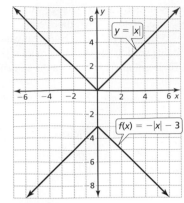

The graph of f is a reflection in the x-axis followed by a translation 3 units down of the parent absolute value function.

6.

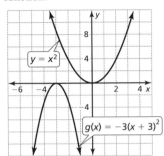

The graph of g is a vertical stretch by a factor of 3 followed by a reflection in the x-axis and a translation 3 units left of the parent quadratic function.

7. $g(x) = -|x + 4|$

8. $g(x) = \frac{1}{2}|x| + 2$

9. $g(x) = -x - 3$

10. $y = 0.03x + 1.23$

11. $y = 0.35x$; 15.75 mi

12. $(4, -2, 1)$

13. $\left(-\frac{4}{3}, -\frac{17}{3}, \frac{26}{3}\right)$

14. $(9 + 4y, y, -7 - 5y)$

15. no solution

16. $(-11, -8, 3)$

17. $(-16, 12, 10)$

18. 200 student tickets, 350 adult tickets, and 50 children under 12 tickets

19. The graph is a translation 4 units left of the parent quadratic function.

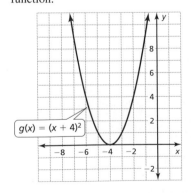

20. The graph is a translation 7 units right and 2 units up of the parent quadratic function.

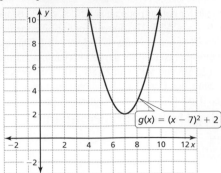

21. The graph is a vertical stretch by a factor of 3 followed by a reflection in the x-axis and a translation 2 units left and 1 unit down of the parent quadratic function.

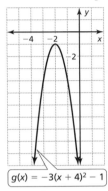

22. $g(x) = \frac{9}{4}(x + 5)^2 - 2$

23. $g(x) = (-x + 2)^2 - 2(-x + 2) + 3 = x^2 - 2x + 3$

24. The minimum value is -4; The function is decreasing to the left of $x = 1$ and increasing to the right of $x = 1$.

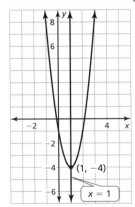

25. The maximum value is 35; The function is increasing to the left of $x = 4$ and decreasing to the right of $x = 4$.

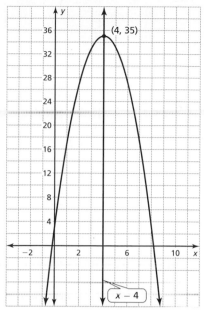

26. The minimum value is -25; The function is decreasing to the left of $x = -2$ and increasing to the right of $x = -2$.

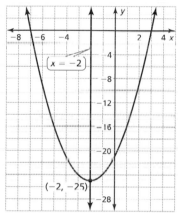

27. $y = \frac{16}{81}(x - 10)^2 - 4$ **28.** $y = -\frac{3}{5}(x + 1)(x - 5)$

29. $y = 4x^2 + 5x + 1$

30. $y = -16x^2 + 150$; about 3.06 sec

Chapter 3

Chapter 3 Maintaining Mathematical Proficiency (p. 109)

1. $2x$ **2.** $4m + 3$

3. $-y + 6$ **4.** $x + 4$

5. $z - 4$ **6.** $5x$

7. $x = -2, x = -1$ **8.** $x = 2, x = 4$

9. $x = -5$ **10.** $x = -6, x = 7$

11. $x = \frac{3}{2}$ **12.** $x = -3, x = \frac{1}{3}$

13. Set each factor equal to zero by the Zero Product Property and solve for x.

3.1 Vocabulary and Core Concept Check (p. 116)

1. The end behavior describes the behavior of a graph as x approaches positive infinity and negative infinity.

3.1 Monitoring Progress and Modeling with Mathematics (pp. 116–118)

3. polynomial function; $f(x) = 5x^3 - 6x^2 - 3x + 2$; degree: 3 (cubic), leading coefficient: 5

5. not a polynomial function

7. polynomial function; $h(x) = -\sqrt{7}x^4 + 8x^3 + \frac{5}{3}x^2 + x - \frac{1}{2}$; degree 4: (quartic), leading coefficient: $-\sqrt{7}$

9. The function is not in standard form so the wrong term was used to classify the function; f is a polynomial function. The degree is 4 and f is a quartic function. The leading coefficient is -7.

11. $h(-2) = -46$ **13.** $g(8) = -43$

15. $p\left(\frac{1}{2}\right) = \frac{45}{4}$

17. $h(x) \to -\infty$ as $x \to -\infty$ and $h(x) \to -\infty$ as $x \to \infty$

19. $f(x) \to \infty$ as $x \to -\infty$ and $f(x) \to \infty$ as $x \to \infty$

21. The degree of the function is odd and the leading coefficient is negative.

23. polynomial function; $f(x) = -4x^4 + \frac{5}{2}x^3 + \sqrt{2}x^2 + 4x - 6$; degree: 4 (quartic), leading coefficient: -4.

25.
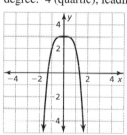
27.
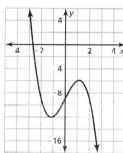

29.
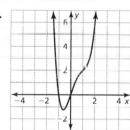
31.
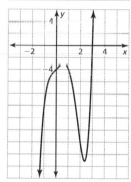

33. a. The function is increasing when $x > 4$ and decreasing when $x < 4$.

  b. $x < 3$ and $x > 5$

  c. $3 < x < 5$

35. a. The function is increasing when $x < 0$ and $x > 2$ and decreasing when $0 < x < 2$.

  b. $-1 < x < 2$ and $x > 2$

  c. $x < -1$

37. The degree is even and the leading coefficient is positive.

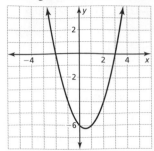

39. The degree is even and the leading coefficient is positive.

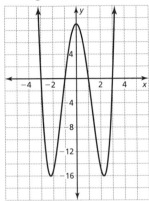

41. a.

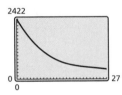

From 1980 to 2007 the number of open drive-in theaters decreased. Around the year 1995, the rate of decrease began to level off.

b. 1980 to 1995: about -119.6, 1995 to 2007: about -19.2; About 120 drive-in movie theaters closed each year on average from 1980 to 1995. From 1995 to 2007, drive-in movie theaters were closing at a much lower rate, with about 20 theaters closing each year.

c. Because the graph declines so sharply in the years leading up to 1980, it is most likely not accurate. The model may be valid for a few years before 1980, but in the long run, decline may not be reasonable. After 2007, the number of drive-in movie theaters declines sharply and soon becomes negative. Because negative values do not make sense given the context, the model cannot be used for years after 2007.

43. Because the graph of g is a reflection of the graph of f in the y-axis, the end behavior would be opposite; $g(x) \to -\infty$ as $x \to -\infty$ and $g(x) \to \infty$ as $x \to \infty$.

45.

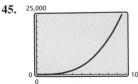

about 27.14%; *Sample answer:* yes; r only increased by about 8% but caused the volume to increase by more.

47. a.

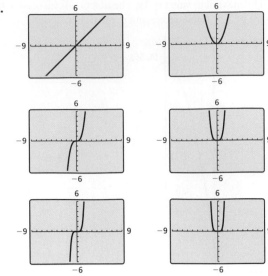

$y = x$, $y = x^3$, and $y = x^5$ are all symmetric with respect to the origin.

$y = x^2$, $y = x^4$, and $y = x^6$ are all symmetric with respect to the y-axis.

b. The graph of $y = x^{10}$ will be symmetric with respect to the y-axis. The graph of $y = x^{11}$ will be symmetric with respect to the origin; The exponent is even. The exponent is odd.

49. $f(-5) = -480$; Substituting the two given points into the function results in the system of equations $2 + b + c - 5 = 0$ and $16 + 4b + 2c - 5 = 3$. Solving for b and c gives $f(x) = 2x^3 - 7x^2 + 10x - 5$.

3.1 Maintaining Mathematical Proficiency *(p. 118)*

51. $-2x^2 + 3xy + y^2$ **53.** $12kz - 4kw$

55. $-x^3y^2 + 3x^2y + 13xy - 12x + 9$

3.2 Vocabulary and Core Concept Check *(p. 125)*

1. *Sample answer:* Multiply horizontally or vertically; Pascal's Triangle; Binomial Theorem.

3.2 Monitoring Progress and Modeling with Mathematics *(pp. 125–128)*

3. $x^2 + x + 1$ **5.** $12x^5 + 5x^4 - 3x^3 + 6x - 4$

7. $7x^6 + 7x^5 + 8x^3 - 9x^2 + 11x - 5$

9. $-2x^3 - 14x^2 + 7x - 4$ **11.** $5x^6 - 7x^5 + 6x^4 + 9x^3 + 7$

13. $-x^5 + 7x^3 + 11x^2 + 10x - 4$

15. $P = 47.7t^2 + 678.5t + 17{,}667.4$; The constant term represents the total number of people attending degree-granting institutions at time $t = 0$.

17. $35x^5 + 21x^4 + 7x^3$ **19.** $-10x^3 + 23x^2 - 24x + 18$

21. $x^4 - 5x^3 - 3x^2 + 22x + 20$

23. $3x^5 - 6x^4 - 6x^3 + 25x^2 - 23x + 7$

25. The negative was not distributed through the entire second set of parenthesis;
$(x^2 - 3x + 4) - (x^3 + 7x - 2) = x^2 - 3x + 4 - x^3 - 7x + 2$
$= -x^3 + x^2 - 10x + 6$

27. $x^3 + 3x^2 - 10x - 24$ **29.** $12x^3 - 29x^2 + 7x + 6$

31. $-24x^3 + 86x^2 - 57x - 20$

33. $(a + b)(a - b) = a^2 - ab + ab - b^2 = a^2 - b^2$;
Sample answer: $24 \cdot 16 = (20 + 4)(20 - 4)$
$$= 20^2 - 4^2$$
$$= 400 - 16$$
$$= 384$$

35. $x^2 - 81$ **37.** $9c^2 - 30c + 25$

39. $49h^2 + 56h + 16$ **41.** $8k^3 + 72k^2 + 216k + 216$

43. $8t^3 + 48t^2 + 96t + 64$

45. $16q^4 - 96q^3 + 216q^2 - 216q + 81$

47. $y^5z^5 + 5y^4z^4 + 10y^3z^3 + 10y^2z^2 + 5yz + 1$

49. 1, 6, 15, 20, 15, 6, 1;
$x^6 + 18x^5 + 135x^4 + 540x^3 + 1215x^2 + 1458x + 729$

51. 1, 9, 36, 84, 126, 126, 84, 36, 9, 1;
$a^9 + 9a^8b^2 + 36a^7b^4 + 84a^6b^6 + 126a^5b^8 + 126a^4b^{10}$
$\quad + 84a^3b^{12} + 36a^2b^{14} + 9ab^{16} + b^{18}$

53. row 0 : 1, row 1 : 2, row 2 : 4, row 3 : 8, row 4 : 16, row n : 2^n

55. $x^3 + 6x^2 + 12x + 8$

57. $a^4 + 12a^3b + 54a^2b^2 + 108ab^3 + 81b^4$

59. $w^{12} - 12w^9 + 54w^6 - 108w^3 + 81$

61. $729u^6 + 1458u^5v^2 + 1215u^4v^4 + 540u^3v^6 + 135u^2v^8$
$\quad + 18uv^{10} + v^{12}$

63. -8064 **65.** $-13{,}608$

67. $316{,}800{,}000$ **69.** $-337{,}920$

71. $_8C_0$, $_8C_1$, $_8C_2$, $_8C_3$, $_8C_4$, $_8C_5$, $_8C_6$, $_8C_7$, $_8C_8$; 1, 8, 28, 56, 70, 56, 28, 8, 1

73. about 11,391   **75.** about 6388.068

77. $9a^8 + 66a^6b^2 + 97a^4b^4 - 88a^2b^6 + 16b^8$; Sample answer: Pascal's Triangle; Use Pascal's Triangle to expand the two binomials. Multiply the results vertically to find your final product.

79. $2x^3 + 10x^2 + 14x + 6$

81. a. $5000(1 + r)^3 + 1000(1 + r)^2 + 4000(1 + r)$

   b. $7000r^3 + 25{,}000r^2 + 34{,}000r + 16{,}000$; 7000 is the total amount of money that gained interest for three years, 25,000 is the total amount of money that gained interest for two years, 34,000 is the total amount of money that gained interest for one year, and 16,000 is the total amount of money invested.

   c. about \$17,763.38

83. $\left(\frac{2}{3}\right)^8 + 8\left(\frac{2}{3}\right)^7\left(\frac{1}{3}\right)^1 + 28\left(\frac{2}{3}\right)^6\left(\frac{1}{3}\right)^2 + 56\left(\frac{2}{3}\right)^5\left(\frac{1}{3}\right)^3 + 70\left(\frac{2}{3}\right)^4\left(\frac{1}{3}\right)^4$
$+ 56\left(\frac{2}{3}\right)^3\left(\frac{1}{3}\right)^5 + 28\left(\frac{2}{3}\right)^2\left(\frac{1}{3}\right)^6 + 8\left(\frac{2}{3}\right)^1\left(\frac{1}{3}\right)^7 + \left(\frac{1}{3}\right)^8$
The xth term in the sum is the probability of rolling exactly $x - 1$ multiples of 3 in 8 rolls.

85. no; The sum of $(x + 3)$ and $(x - 3)$ is $2x$, a monomial. The product of $(x + 3)$ and $(x - 3)$ is $x^2 - 9$, a binomial.

87. equivalent; They produce the same graph.

89. not equivalent; Although they appear to produce the same graph, the table of values shows they are off by a constant of 1.

91. a. $1 + 5i + 10i^2 + 10i^3 + 5i^4 + i^5$; $-4 - 4i$

   b. $729 - 1458i + 1215i^2 - 540i^3 + 135i^4 - 18i^5 + i^6$; $-352 - 936i$

93. a. 5   **b.** 5

   c. 9

   d. $g(x) + h(x)$ has degree m. $g(x) - h(x)$ has degree m. $g(x) \cdot h(x)$ has degree $(m + n)$.

95. a. $(x^2 - y^2)^2 + (2xy)^2 = (x^2 + y^2)^2$
$(x^4 - 2x^2y^2 + y^4) + (4x^2y^2) = x^4 + 2x^2y^2 + y^4$
$x^4 + 2x^2y^2 + y^4 = x^4 + 2x^2y^2 + y^4$

   b. The Pythagorean triple is 11, 60, and 61.

   c. $121 + 3600 = 3721$
$3721 = 3721$

3.2 Maintaining Mathematical Proficiency (p. 128)

97. $5 + 11i$ **99.** $9 - 2i$

3.3 Vocabulary and Core Concept Check (p. 133)

1. To evaluate the function $f(x) = x^3 - 2x + 4$ when $x = 3$, synthetic division can be used to divide $f(x)$ by the factor $x - 3$. The remainder is the value of $f(3)$. So, $f(3) = 25$.

Sample answer:

$$3 \,\big|\, \begin{array}{cccc} 1 & 0 & -2 & 4 \\ & 3 & 9 & 21 \\ \hline 1 & 3 & 7 & 25 \end{array}$$

3. $(x^3 - 2x^2 - 9x + 18) \div (x + 3) = x^2 - 5x + 6$

3.3 Monitoring Progress and Modeling with Mathematics (pp. 133–134)

5. $x + 5 + \dfrac{3}{x - 4}$ **7.** $x + 1 + \dfrac{2x + 3}{x^2 - 1}$

9. $5x^2 - 12x + 37 + \dfrac{-122x + 109}{x^2 + 2x - 4}$

11. $x + 12 + \dfrac{49}{x - 4}$ **13.** $2x - 11 + \dfrac{62}{x + 5}$

15. $x + 3 + \dfrac{18}{x - 3}$ **17.** $x^3 + x^2 - 2x + 1 - \dfrac{6}{x - 6}$

19. D; $(2)^2 + (2) - 3 - 3$ so the remainder must be 3.

20. A; $(2)^2 - (2) - 3 = -1$ so the remainder must be -1.

21. C; $(2)^2 - (2) + 3 = 5$ so the remainder must be 5.

22. B; $(2)^2 + (2) + 3 = 9$ so the remainder must be 9.

23. The quotient should be one degree less than the dividend.
$$\frac{x^3 - 5x + 3}{x - 2} = x^2 + 2x - 1 + \frac{1}{x - 2}$$

25. $f(-1) = 37$ **27.** $f(2) = 11$

29. $f(6) = 181$ **31.** $f(3) = 115$

33. no; The Remainder Theorem states that $f(a) = 15$.

35. $\dfrac{A}{T} = \dfrac{-1.95x^3 + 70.1x^2 - 188x + 2150}{14.8x + 725}$
$= 0.13x^2 + 11.19x - 560.90 + \dfrac{408{,}563.25}{14.8x + 725}$, $0 < x < 18$

37. A   **39.** $2x + 5$

3.3 Maintaining Mathematical Proficiency (p. 134)

41. $x = 3$ **43.** $x = -7$

3.4 Vocabulary and Core Concept Check (p. 140)

1. quadratic; $3x^2$

3. It is written as a product of unfactorable polynomials with integer coefficients.

3.4 Monitoring Progress and Modeling with Mathematics (pp. 140–142)

5. $x(x - 6)(x + 4)$ **7.** $3p^3(p - 8)(p + 8)$

9. $q^2(2q - 3)(q + 6)$ **11.** $w^8(5w - 2)(2w - 3)$

13. $(x + 4)(x^2 - 4x + 16)$ **15.** $(g - 7)(g^2 + 7g + 49)$

17. $3h^6(h - 4)(h^2 + 4h + 16)$

19. $2t^4(2t + 5)(4t^2 - 10t + 125)$

21. $x^2 + 9$ is not a factorable binomial because it is not the difference of two squares; $3x^3 + 27x = 3x(x^2 + 9)$

23. $(y^2 + 6)(y - 5)$ **25.** $(3a^2 + 8)(a + 6)$

27. $(x - 2)(x + 2)(x - 8)$ **29.** $(2q + 3)(2q - 3)(q - 4)$

31. $(7k^2 + 3)(7k^2 - 3)$ **33.** $(c^2 + 5)(c^2 + 4)$

35. $(4z^2 + 9)(2z + 3)(2z - 3)$ **37.** $3r^2(r^3 + 5)(r^3 - 4)$

39. factor   **41.** not a factor

43. factor

45.
$$\begin{array}{r|rrrr} -4 & 1 & -1 & -20 & 0 \\ & & -4 & 20 & 0 \\ \hline & 1 & -5 & 0 & 0 \end{array}$$
$f(x) = x(x + 4)(x - 5)$

47.
$$\begin{array}{r|rrrrr} 6 & 1 & -6 & 0 & -8 & 48 \\ & & 6 & 0 & 0 & -48 \\ \hline & 1 & 0 & 0 & -8 & 0 \end{array}$$
$f(x) = (x - 6)(x - 2)(x^2 + 2x + 4)$

49.
$$\begin{array}{r|rrrr} -7 & 1 & 0 & -37 & 84 \\ & & -7 & 49 & -84 \\ \hline & 1 & -7 & 12 & 0 \end{array}$$
$f(x) = (x + 7)(x - 3)(x - 4)$

51. D; The x-intercepts of the graph are 2, 3, and -1.

52. C; The x-intercepts of the graph are 0, -2, -1, and 2.

53. A; The x-intercepts of the graph are -2, -3, and 1.

54. B; The x-intercepts of the graph are 0, 2, 1, and -2.

55. The model makes sense for $x > 6.5$; When factored completely, the volume is $V = x(2x - 13)(x - 3)$. For all three dimensions of the box to have positive lengths, the value of x must be greater than 6.5.

57. $a^4(a + 6)(a - 5)$; A common monomial can be factored out to obtain a factorable trinomial in quadratic form.

59. $(z - 3)(z + 3)(z - 7)$; Factoring by grouping can be used because the expression contains pairs of monomials that have a common factor. Difference of two squares can be used to factor one of the resulting binomials.

61. $(4r + 9)(16r^2 - 36r + 81)$; The sum of two cubes pattern can be used because the expression is of the form $a^3 + b^3$.

63. $(4n^2 + 1)(2n - 1)(2n + 1)$; The difference of two squares pattern can be used to factor the original expression and one of the resulting binomials.

65. **a.** no; $7z^4(2z + 3)(z - 2)$

     b. no; $n(2 - n)(n + 6)(3n - 11)$

     c. yes

67. 0.7 million

69. *Sample answer:* Factor Theorem and synthetic division; Calculations without a calculator are easier with this method because the values are lesser.

71. $k = 22$
$$\begin{array}{r|rrrr} 7 & 2 & -13 & -22 & 105 \\ & & 14 & 7 & -105 \\ \hline & 2 & 1 & -15 & 0 \end{array}$$

73. **a.** $(c - d)(c + d)(7a + b)$

     b. $(x^n - 1)(x^n - 1)$

     c. $(a^3 - b^2)(ab + 1)^2$

75. **a.** $\dfrac{(x - 1)^2}{4} + \dfrac{y^2}{12} = 1$; center: $(1, 0)$

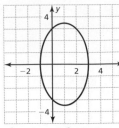

     b. $\dfrac{x^2}{6} + \dfrac{(y - 1)^2}{3} = 1$; center: $(0, 1)$

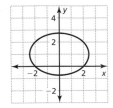

     c. *Sample answer:* The graph of an ellipse is an elongated circle with two vertices and two co-vertices. The major axis connects the vertices and the minor axis connects the co-vertices. The major and minor axes are perpendicular and intersect in the center of the ellipse.

3.4 Maintaining Mathematical Proficiency *(p. 142)*

77. $x = 6$ and $x = -5$ **79.** $x = \frac{5}{3}$ and $x = 2$

81. $x = 18$ and $x = -6$ **83.** $x = -3$ and $x = -7$

3.5 Vocabulary and Core Concept Check *(p. 150)*

1. constant term; leading coefficient

3.5 Monitoring Progress and Modeling with Mathematics *(pp. 150–152)*

3. $z = -3$, $z = 0$, and $z = 4$ **5.** $x = 0$ and $x = 1$

7. $w = 0$ and $w = \pm\sqrt{10} \approx \pm 3.16$

9. $c = 0$, $c = 3$, and $c = \pm\sqrt{6} \approx \pm 2.45$

11. $n = -4$

13. $x = -3$, $x = 0$, and $x = 2$

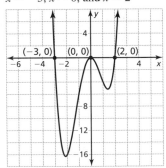

15. $x = 0$, $x = 5$, and $x = 6$

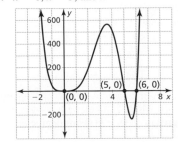

17. $x = -3$, $x = 0$, and $x = 5$

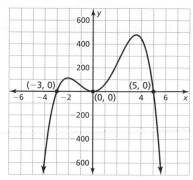

19. $x = -3$, $x = -1$, and $x = 3$

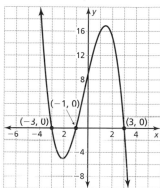

21. C

23. The $\pm$ was not included with each factor; ± 1, ± 3, ± 5, ± 9, ± 15, ± 45

25. $x = -5$, $x = 1$, and $x = 3$ **27.** $x = -1$, $x = 5$, and $x = 6$

29. $x = -3$, $x = 4$, and $x = 5$

31. $x = -4$, $x = -0.5$, and $x = 6$

33. -5, 3, and 4 **35.** -5, -3, and -2

37. -4, 1.5, and 3

39. $1, \dfrac{-1 + \sqrt{17}}{2} \approx 1.56$, and $\dfrac{-1 - \sqrt{17}}{2} \approx -2.56$

41. $f(x) = x^3 - 7x^2 + 36$ **43.** $f(x) = x^3 - 10x - 12$

45. $f(x) = x^4 - 32x^2 + 24x$

47. $x = -3$, $x = 3$, and $x = 4$; *Sample answer:* graphing; The equation has three real solutions, all of which can be found by graphing to find the x-intercepts.

49. 4 cm by 4 cm by 7 cm

51. The block is 3 meters high, 21 meters long, and 15 meters wide.

53. a. $-20t^3 + 252t^2 - 280t - 2400 = 0$
  b. 1, 2, 3, 4, 5, 6, 8, 10
  c. $t = 5$ years and $t = 10$ years

55. The length should be 8 feet, the width should be 4 feet, and the height should be 4 feet.

57. a. $k = 60$
  b. $k = 33$
  c. $k = 6$

59. $x = 1$ **61.** $x = 2$

63. The height of each ramp is $\frac{5}{3}$ feet and the width of each ramp is 5 feet. The left ramp is to be 24 feet in length while the right ramp is to be 12 feet in length.

65. rs; Each factor of a_0 can be written as the numerator with each factor of a_n as the denominator, creating $r \times s$ factors.

3.5 Maintaining Mathematical Proficiency *(p. 152)*

67. not a polynomial function

69. not a polynomial function; The term $\sqrt[4]{x}$ has an exponent that is not a whole number.

71. $x = \pm 3i$ **73.** $x = \pm \dfrac{\sqrt{2}}{4}$

3.6 Vocabulary and Core Concept Check *(p. 158)*

1. complex conjugates

3.6 Monitoring Progress and Modeling with Mathematics *(pp. 158–160)*

3. 3; -4, $2 - 2i\sqrt{3}$, and $2 + 2i\sqrt{3}$

5. 6; -1, 0, 0, 1, i, and $-i$

7. 5; -1, 1, 1, $\dfrac{-1 - i\sqrt{3}}{2}$, and $\dfrac{-1 + i\sqrt{3}}{2}$

9. -1, 1, 2, and 4 **11.** -2, -2, 1, and 3

13. -3, -1, $2i$, and $-2i$ **15.** -4, -1, 2, $i\sqrt{2}$, and $-i\sqrt{2}$

17. 2; The graph shows 2 real zeros, so the remaining zeros must be imaginary.

19. 2; The graph shows no real zeros, so all of the zeros must be imaginary

21. $f(x) = x^3 + 4x^2 - 7x - 10$

23. $f(x) = x^3 - 11x^2 + 41x - 51$

25. $f(x) = x^3 - 4x^2 - 5x + 20$

27. $f(x) = x^6 - 8x^4 + 23x^0 - 32x^7 + 22x - 4$

29. The conjugate of the given imaginary zeros was not included.

$f(x) = (x - 2)[x - (1 + i)][x - (1 - i)]$
$\quad = (x - 2)[(x - 1) - i][(x - 1) + i]$
$\quad = (x - 2)[(x - 1)^2 - i^2]$
$\quad = (x - 2)[(x^2 - 2x + 1) - (-1)]$
$\quad = (x - 2)(x^2 - 2x + 2)$
$\quad = x^3 - 2x^2 + 2x - 2x^2 + 4x - 4$
$\quad = x^3 - 4x^2 + 6x - 4$

31. *Sample answer:* $y = x^6 - 4x^4 - x^2 + 4$;
$y = (x - 1)(x + 1)(x - 2)(x + 2)(x - i)(x + i)$
$\quad = (x^2 - 1)(x^2 - 4)(x^2 + 1)$
$\quad = (x^4 - 5x^2 + 4)(x^2 + 1)$
$\quad = x^6 + x^4 - 5x^4 - 5x^2 + 4x^2 + 4$
$\quad = x^6 - 4x^4 - x^2 + 4$

33.

Positive real zeros	Negative real zeros	Imaginary zeros	Total zeros
1	1	2	4

35.

Positive real zeros	Negative real zeros	Imaginary zeros	Total zeros
2	1	0	3
0	1	2	3

37.

Positive real zeros	Negative real zeros	Imaginary zeros	Total zeros
3	2	0	5
3	0	2	5
1	2	2	5
1	0	4	5

39.

Positive real zeros	Negative real zeros	Imaginary zeros	Total zeros
3	3	0	6
3	1	2	6
1	3	2	6
1	1	4	6

41. C; There are two sign changes in the coefficients of $f(-x)$. So, the number of negative real zeros is two or zero, not four.

43. in the year 1958

45. in the 3rd year and the 9th year

47. $x = 4.2577$

49. no; The Fundamental Theorem of Algebra applies to functions of degree greater than zero. Because the function $f(x) = 2$ is equivalent to $f(x) = 2x^0$, it has degree 0, and does not fall under the Fundamental Theorem of Algebra.

51.

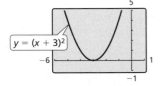

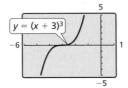

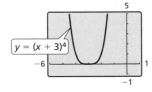

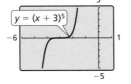

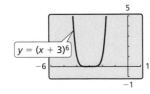

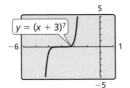

a. For all functions, $f(x) \to \infty$ as $x \to \infty$. When n is even, $f(x) \to \infty$ as $x \to -\infty$, but when n is odd, $f(x) \to -\infty$ as $x \to -\infty$.

b. As n increases, the graph becomes more flat near the zero $x = -3$.

c. The graph of g becomes more vertical and straight near $x = 4$.

53. a.

Deposit	Year 1	Year 2	Year 3	Year 4
1st Deposit	1000	$1000g$	$1000g^2$	$1000g^3$
2nd Deposit		1000	$1000g$	$1000g^2$
3rd Deposit			1000	$1000g$
4th Deposit				1000

b. $v = 1000g^3 + 1000g^2 + 1000g + 1000$

c. about 1.0484; about 4.84%

3.6 Maintaining Mathematical Proficiency (p. 160)

55. The function is a translation 4 units right and 6 units up of the parent quadratic function.

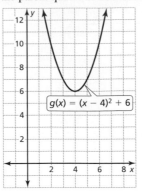

57. The function is a vertical stretch by a factor of 5 followed by a translation 4 units left of the parent quadratic function.

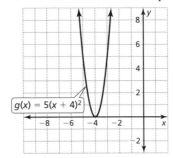

59. $g(x) = \left| \frac{1}{9}x + 1 \right| - 3$

3.7 Vocabulary and Core Concept Check (p. 165)

1. horizontal

3.7 Monitoring Progress and Modeling with Mathematics (pp. 165–166)

3. The graph of g is a translation 3 units up of the graph of f.

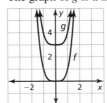

5. The graph of g is a translation 2 units right and 1 unit down of the graph of f.

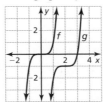

7. B; The graph has been translated 2 units right.

8. C; The graph has been translated 2 units left and 2 units up.

9. D; The graph has been translated 2 units right and 2 units up.

10. A; The graph has been translated 2 units down.

11. The graph of g is a vertical stretch by a factor of 2 followed by a reflection in the x-axis of the graph of f.

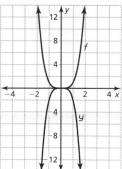

13. The graph of g is a vertical stretch by a factor of 5 followed by a translation 1 unit up of the graph of f.

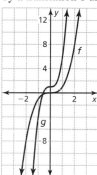

15. The graph of g is a vertical shrink by a factor of $\frac{3}{4}$ followed by a translation 4 units left of the graph of f.

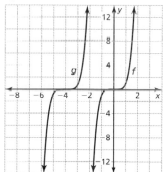

17. $g(x) = (x + 2)^4 + 1$

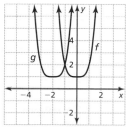

The graph of g is a translation 2 units left of the graph of f.

19. $g(x) = -x^3 + x^2 - 3$

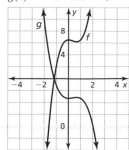

The graph of g is a vertical shrink by a factor of $\frac{1}{2}$ followed by a reflection in the x-axis of the graph of f.

21. The graph has been translated horizontally to the right 2 units instead of to the left 2 units.

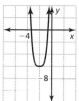

23. $g(x) = -x^3 + 9x^2 - 27x + 21$

25. $g(x) = 27x^3 - 18x^2 + 7$

27. $W(x) = 27x^3 - 12x$; $W(5) = 3315$; When x is 5 yards, the volume of the pyramid is 3315 cubic feet.

29. *Sample answer:* If the function is translated up and then reflected in the x-axis, the order is important; If the function is translated left and then reflected in the x-axis, the order is not important; Reflecting a graph in the x-axis does not affect its x-coordinate, but it does affect its y-coordinate. So, the order is only important if the other translation is in the y.

31. a. 0 m, 4 m, and 7 m
   b. $g(x) = -\frac{2}{5}(x - 2)(x - 6)^2(x - 9)$

33. $V(x) = 3\pi x^2(x + 3)$; $W(x) = \frac{\pi}{3}x^2\left(\frac{1}{3}x + 3\right)$;

$W(3) = 12\pi \approx 37.70$; When x is 3 feet, the volume of the cone is about 37.70 cubic yards.

3.7 Maintaining Mathematical Proficiency *(p. 166)*

35. The maximum value is 4; The domain is all real numbers and the range is $y \leq 4$. The function is increasing to the left of $x = 0$ and decreasing to the right of $x = 0$.

37. The maximum value is 9; The domain is all real numbers and the range is $y \leq 9$. The function is increasing to the left of $x = -5$ and decreasing to the right of $x = -5$.

39. The maximum value is 1; The domain is all real numbers and the range is $y \leq 1$. The function is increasing to the left of $x = 1$ and decreasing to the right of $x = 1$.

3.8 Vocabulary and Core Concept Check *(p. 172)*

1. turning

3.8 Monitoring Progress and Modeling with Mathematics *(pp. 172–174)*

3. A   **4.** C

5. B   **6.** D

7.

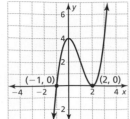

9.

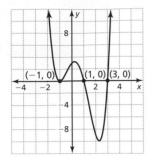

11.

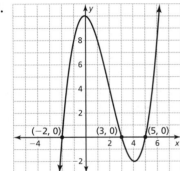

13.

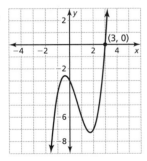

15. The *x*-intercepts should be -2 and 1.

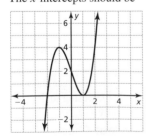

17. -1, 1, and 4 **19.** -4, $-\frac{1}{2}$, and 1

21. -4, $\frac{3}{4}$, and 3

23.

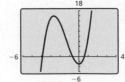

The *x*-intercepts of the graph are $x \approx -3.90$, $x \approx -0.67$, and $x \approx 0.57$. The function has a local maximum at $(-2.67, 15.96)$ and a local minimum at $(0, -3)$; The function is increasing when $x < -2.67$ and $x > 0$ and is decreasing when $-2.67 < x < 0$.

25.

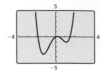

The *x*-intercepts of the graph are $x \approx -1.88$, $x = 0$, $x \approx 0.35$, and $x \approx 1.53$. The function has a local maximum at $(0.17, 0.08)$ and local minimums at $(-1.30, -3.51)$ and $(1.13, -1.07)$; The function is increasing when $-1.30 < x < 0.17$ and $x > 1.13$ and is decreasing when $x < -1.30$ and $0.17 < x < 1.13$.

27.

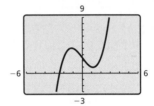

The *x*-intercept of the graph is $x \approx -2.46$. The function has a local maximum at $(-1.15, 4.04)$ and a local minimum at $(1.15, 0.96)$; The function is increasing when $x < -1.15$ and $x > 1.15$ and is decreasing when $-1.15 < x < 1.15$.

29.

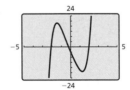

The *x*-intercepts of the graph are $x \approx -2.10$, $x \approx -0.23$, and $x \approx 1.97$. The function has a local maximum at $(-1.46, 18.45)$ and a local minimum at $(1.25, -19.07)$; The function is increasing when $x < -1.46$ and $x > 1.25$ and is decreasing when $-1.46 < x < 1.25$.

31. $(-0.29, 0.48)$ and $(0.29, -0.48)$; $(-0.29, 0.48)$ corresponds to a local maximum and $(0.29, -0.48)$ corresponds to a local minimum; The real zeros are -0.5, 0, and 0.5. The function is of at least degree 3.

33. $(1, 0)$, $(3, 0)$, and $(2, -2)$; $(1, 0)$ and $(3, 0)$ correspond to local maximums, and $(2, -2)$ corresponds to a local minimum; The real zeros are 1 and 3. The function is of at least degree 4.

35. $(-1.25, -10.65)$; $(-1.25, -10.65)$ corresponds to a local minimum; The real zeros are -2.07 and 1.78. The function is of at least degree 4.

37.

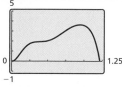

39. odd   **41.** even

43 neither   **45** even

47.

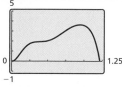

about 1 sec into the stroke

49. A quadratic function only has one turning point, and it is always the maximum or minimum value of the function.

51. no; When multiplying two odd functions, the exponents of each term will be added, creating an even exponent. So, the product will not be an odd function.

53. **a.** $\dfrac{1100 - \pi r^2}{\pi r}$

     b. $V = 550r - \dfrac{\pi}{2}r^3$

     c. about 10.8 ft

55. $V(h) = 64\pi h - \dfrac{\pi}{4}h^3$; about 9.24 in.; about 1238.22 in.^{3}

3.8 Maintaining Mathematical Proficiency *(p. 174)*

57. quadratic; The second differences are constant.

3.9 Vocabulary and Core Concept Check *(p. 179)*

1. finite differences

3.9 Monitoring Progress and Modeling with Mathematics *(pp. 179–180)*

3. $f(x) = (x + 1)(x - 1)(x - 2)$

5. $f(x) = \dfrac{1}{7}(x + 5)(x - 1)(x - 4)$

7. $3; f(x) = \dfrac{2}{3}x^3 + 4x^2 - \dfrac{1}{3}x - 4$

9. $4; f(x) = -3x^4 - 5x^3 + 9x^2 + 3x - 1$

11. $4; f(x) = x^4 - 15x^3 + 81x^2 - 183x + 142$

13. The sign in each parentheses is wrong. The x-intercepts should have been subtracted from zero, not added.

$(-6, 0), (1, 0), (3, 0), (0, 54)$
$54 = a(0 + 6)(0 - 1)(0 - 3)$
$54 = 18a$
$a = 3$
$f(x) = 3(x + 6)(x - 1)(x - 3)$

15. *Sample answer:*

$y = (x - 3)(x - 4)(x + 1),$
$y = 3(x - 3)(x - 4)(x - 1),$
$y = \dfrac{1}{2}(x - 3)(x - 4)(x + 4);$
$y = a(x - 3)(x - 4)(x - c)$
$6 = a(2 - 3)(2 - 4)(2 - c)$
$6 = 2a(2 - c)$
$3 = a(2 - c)$

$\dfrac{3}{2 - c} = a$

Any combination of a and c that fit the equation will contain these points.

17. $y = 0.002x^2 + 0.60x - 2.5$; about 15.9 mph

19. $d = \dfrac{1}{2}n^2 - \dfrac{3}{2}n$; 35

21. With real-life data sets, the numbers rarely fit a model perfectly. Because of this, the differences are rarely constant.

23. C, A, B, D

3.9 Maintaining Mathematical Proficiency *(p. 180)*

25. $x = \pm 6$ **27.** $x = 3 \pm 2\sqrt{3}$

29. $x = 1$ and $x = -2.5$ **31.** $x = \dfrac{-3 \pm \sqrt{29}}{10}$

Chapter 3 Review *(pp. 182–186)*

1. polynomial function; $h(x) = -15x^7 - x^3 + 2x^2$; It has degree 7 and has a leading coefficient of -15.

2. not a polynomial

3.

4.

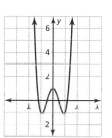

5.

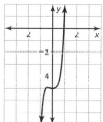

6. $4x^3 - 4x^2 - 4x - 8$ **7.** $3x^4 + 3x^3 - x^2 - 3x + 15$

8. $2x^2 + 11x + 1$ **9.** $2y^3 + 10y^2 + 5y - 21$

10. $8m^3 + 12m^2n + 6mn^2 + n^3$

11. $s^3 + 3s^2 - 10s - 24$

12. $m^4 + 16m^3 + 96m^2 + 256m + 256$

13. $243s^5 + 810s^4 + 1080s^3 + 720s^2 + 240s + 32$

14. $z^6 + 6z^5 + 15z^4 + 20z^3 + 15z^2 + 6z + 1$

15. $x - 1 + \dfrac{4x - 3}{x^2 + 2x + 1}$ **16.** $x^2 + 2x - 10 + \dfrac{7x + 43}{x^2 + x + 4}$

17. $x^3 - 4x^2 + 15x - 60 + \dfrac{233}{x + 4}$

18. $g(5) = 546$ **19.** $8(2x - 1)(4x^2 + 2x + 1)$

20. $2z(z^2 - 5)(z - 1)(z + 1)$ **21.** $(a - 2)(a + 2)(2a - 7)$

22.

$$
\begin{array}{r|rrrrr}
-2 & 1 & 2 & 0 & -27 & -54 \\
   &   & -2 & 0 & 0 & 54 \\
\hline
   & 1 & 0 & 0 & -27 & 0
\end{array}
$$

$f(x) = (x + 2)(x - 3)(x^2 + 3x + 9)$

23. $x = -4$, $x = -2$, and $x = 3$

24. $x = -4$, $x = -3$, and $x = 2$

25. $f(x) = x^3 - 5x^2 + 5x - 1$

26. $f(x) = x^4 - 5x^3 + x^2 + 25x - 30$

27. $f(x) = x^4 - 9x^3 + 11x^2 + 51x - 30$

28. The length is 6 inches, the width is 2 inches, and the height is 20 inches; When $\ell(\ell - 4)(3\ell + 2) = 240$, $\ell = 6$

29. $f(x) = x^3 - 5x^2 + 11x - 15$

30. $f(x) = x^4 - x^3 + 14x^2 - 16x - 32$

31. $f(x) = x^4 + 7x^3 + 6x^2 - 4x + 80$

32.

Positive real zeros	Negative real zeros	Imaginary zeros	Total zeros
2	0	2	4
0	0	4	4

33.

Positive real zeros	Negative real zeros	Imaginary zeros	Total zeros
1	3	0	4
1	1	2	4

34. The graph of g is a reflection in the y-axis followed by a translation 2 units up of the graph of f.

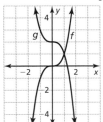

35. The graph of g is a reflection in the x-axis followed by a translation 9 units left of the graph of f.

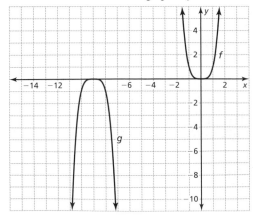

36. $g(x) = \frac{1}{1024}(x - 3)^5 + \frac{3}{4}(x - 3) - 5$

37. $g(x) = x^4 + 2x^3 - 7$

38.

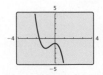

The x-intercept of the graph is $x \approx -1.68$. The function has a local maximum at $(0, -1)$ and a local minimum at $(-1, -2)$; The function is increasing when $-1 < x < 0$ and decreasing when $x < -1$ and $x > 0$.

39.

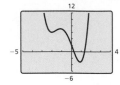

The x-intercepts of the graph are $x \approx 0.25$ and $x \approx 1.34$. The function has a local maximum at $(-1.13, 7.06)$ and local minimums at $(-2, 6)$ and $(0.88, -3.17)$; The function is increasing when $-2 < x < -1.13$ and $x > 0.88$ and is decreasing when $x < -2$ and $-1.13 < x < 0.88$.

40. odd   **41.** even

42. neither

43. $f(x) = \frac{3}{16}(x + 4)(x - 4)(x - 2)$

44. $3; f(x) = 2x^3 - 7x^2 - 6x$

Chapter 4

Chapter 4 Maintaining Mathematical Proficiency (p. 191)

1. y^7 **2.** n

3. $\dfrac{1}{x^3}$ **4.** $3x^3$

5. $\dfrac{8w^9}{z^6}$ **6.** $\dfrac{m^{10}}{z^4}$

7. $y = 2 - 4x$ **8.** $y = 3 + 3x$

9. $y = \dfrac{13}{2}x + \dfrac{9}{2}$ **10.** $y = \dfrac{5}{x + 3}$

11. $y = \dfrac{8x - 3}{4x}$ **12.** $y = \dfrac{15 - 6x}{7x}$

13. yes; *Sample answer:* When simplifying $x^3 \cdot (x^2)^2$, you must first apply the Power of a Power Property and then apply the Product of Powers Property.

4.1 Vocabulary and Core Concept Check (p. 197)

1. $\dfrac{1}{(\sqrt[t]{a})^s}; t$

3. When a is positive, it has two real fourth roots, $\pm\sqrt[4]{a}$, and one real fifth root $\sqrt[5]{a}$. When a is negative, it has no real fourth roots and one real fifth root, $\sqrt[5]{a}$.

4.1 Monitoring Progress and Modeling with Mathematics (pp. 197–198)

5. 2

7. 0

9. -2

11. 2

13. 125

15. -3

17. $\frac{1}{4}$

19. The cube root of 27 was calculated incorrectly;
$27^{2/3} = (27^{1/3})^2 = 3^2 = 9$

21. B; The denominator of the exponent is 3 and the numerator is 4.

22. D; The denominator of the exponent is 4 and the numerator is 3.

23. A; The denominator of the exponent is 4 and the exponent is negative.

24. C; The denominator of the exponent is 4 and the expression is negative.

25. 8

27. 0.34

29. 2840.40

31. 50.57

33. $r \approx 3.72$ ft

35. $x = 5$

37. $x \approx -7.66$

39. $x \approx -2.17$

41. $x = \pm 2$

43. $x = \pm 3$

45. potatoes: 2.4%; ham: 3.7%; eggs: 1.7%

47. 3, 4; $\sqrt[4]{81} = 3$ and $\sqrt[4]{256} = 4$

49. about 753 ft³/sec

4.1 Maintaining Mathematical Proficiency (p. 198)

51. 5^5

53. $\dfrac{1}{z^6}$

55. 5000

57. 0.82

4.2 Vocabulary and Core Concept Check (p. 204)

1. No radicands have perfect *n*th powers as factors other than 1, no radicands contain fractions, and no radicals appear in the denominator of a fraction.

4.2 Monitoring Progress and Modeling with Mathematics (pp. 204–206)

3. $9^{2/3}$

5. $6^{3/4}$

7. $\dfrac{5}{4}$

9. $3^{1/3}$

11. 4

13. 12

15. $2\sqrt[4]{3}$

17. 3

19. 6

21. $3\sqrt[4]{7}$

23. $\dfrac{\sqrt[3]{10}}{2}$

25. $\dfrac{\sqrt{6}}{4}$

27. $\dfrac{4\sqrt[3]{7}}{7}$

29. $\dfrac{1 - \sqrt{3}}{-2}$

31. $\dfrac{15 + 5\sqrt{2}}{7}$

33. $\dfrac{9\sqrt{3} - 9\sqrt{7}}{-4}$

35. $\dfrac{3\sqrt{2} + \sqrt{30}}{-2}$

37. $12\sqrt[3]{11}$

39. $12(11^{1/4})$

41. $-9\sqrt{3}$

43. $5\sqrt[5]{7}$

45. $6(3^{1/3})$

47. The radicand should not change when the expression is factored;
$3\sqrt[3]{12} + 5\sqrt[3]{12} = (3 + 5)\sqrt[3]{12} = 8\sqrt[3]{12}$

49. $3y^2$

51. $\dfrac{m^2}{n}$

53. $\dfrac{|g|}{|h|}$

55. Absolute value was not used to ensure that all variables are positive;
$\dfrac{\sqrt[6]{2^6 (h^2)^6}}{\sqrt[6]{g^6}} = \dfrac{2h^2}{|g|}$

57. $9a^3 b^6 c^4 \sqrt{ac}$

59. $\dfrac{2m\sqrt[5]{5mn^3}}{n^2}$

61. $\dfrac{\sqrt[6]{w^5}}{5w^6}$

63. $\dfrac{2v^{3/4}}{3w}, v \neq 0$

65. $21\sqrt[3]{y}$

67. $-2x^{7/2}$

69. $4w^2\sqrt{w}$

71. $P = 2x^3 + 4x^{2/3}$
$A = 2x^{11/3}$

73. about 0.45 mm

75. no; The second radical can be simplified to $18\sqrt{11}$. The difference is $-11\sqrt{11}$.

77. $10 + 6\sqrt{5}$

79. a. $r = \sqrt[3]{\dfrac{3V}{4\pi}}$

b. $S = 4\pi\left(\sqrt[3]{\dfrac{3V}{4\pi}}\right)^2$

$S = \dfrac{4\pi(3V)^{2/3}}{(4\pi)^{2/3}}$

$S = (4\pi)^{3/3 \,-\, 2/3}(3V)^{2/3}$

$S = (4\pi)^{1/3}(3V)^{2/3}$

c. The surface area of the larger balloon is $2^{2/3} \approx 1.59$ times as large as the surface area of the smaller balloon.

81. when *n* is even and *m/n* is odd

4.2 Maintaining Mathematical Proficiency (p. 206)

83.
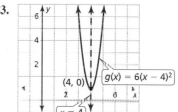

85.
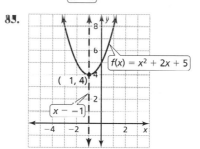

87. $g(x) = x^3 - x - 3$; The graph of *g* is a translation 3 units down of the graph of *f*.

89. $g(x) = 16x^4 + 16x^3 - 16x^2$; The graph of *g* is a horizontal shrink by a factor of $\frac{1}{2}$ of the graph of *f*.

4.3 Vocabulary and Core Concept Check (p.212)

1. radical

4.3 Monitoring Progress and Modeling with Mathematics (pp. 212–214)

3. B

4. D

5. F

6. A

7. E

8. C

9.

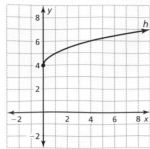

The domain is $x \geq 0$. The range is $y \geq 4$.

11.

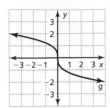

The domain and range are all real numbers.

13.

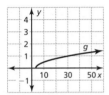

The domain is $x \geq 3$. The range is $y \geq 0$.

15.

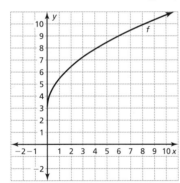

The domain is $x \geq 0$. The range is $y \geq 3$.

17.

The domain is $x \geq 0$. The range is $y \leq 0$.

19. The graph of g is a translation 1 unit left and 8 units up of the graph of f.

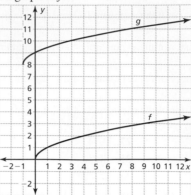

21. The graph of g is a reflection in the x-axis followed by a translation 1 unit down of the graph of f.

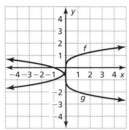

23. The graph of g is a vertical shrink by a factor of $\frac{1}{4}$ followed by a reflection in the y-axis of the graph of f.

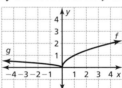

25. The graph of g is a vertical stretch by a factor of 2 followed by a translation 5 units left and 4 units down of the graph of f.

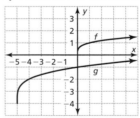

27. The graph was translated 2 units left but it should be translated 2 units right.

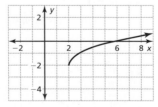

29. The domain is $x \leq -1$ and $x \geq 0$. The range is $y \geq 0$.

31. The domain is all real numbers. The range is $y \geq -\dfrac{\sqrt[3]{2}}{2}$.

33. The domain is all real numbers. The range is $y \geq \dfrac{\sqrt{14}}{4}$.

35. always **37.** always

39. $M(n) = 0.915\sqrt{n}$; about 91.5 mi

41. $g(x) = 2\sqrt{x} + 8$ **43.** $g(x) = \sqrt{9x + 36}$

45. $g(x) = 2\sqrt{x + 1}$ **47.** $g(x) = 2\sqrt{x} + 3$

49. $g(x) = 2\sqrt{(x + 5)^2} - 2$

51. 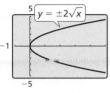 **53.**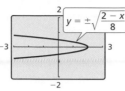

(0, 0), right (2, 0), left

55.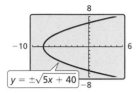

(8, 0), right

57.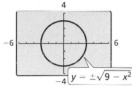

The center is (0, 0). The radius is 3 units. The x-intercepts are ± 3. The y-intercepts are ± 3.

59.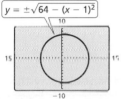

The center is (1, 0). The radius is 8 units. The x-intercepts are -7 and 9. The y-intercepts are $\pm\sqrt{63}$.

61.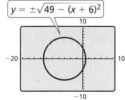

The center is $(-6, 0)$. The radius is 7 units. The x-intercepts are -13 and 1. The y-intercepts are $\pm\sqrt{13}$.

63.

about 3 ft; *Sample answer:* Locate the T-value 2 on the graph and estimate the ℓ-value.

65.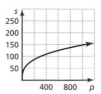

a. about 2468 hp

b. about 0.04 mph/hp

67. a. the 165-lb skydiver

b. When $A = 1$, the diver is most likely vertical. When $A = 7$, the diver is most likely horizontal.

4.3 Maintaining Mathematical Proficiency (p. 214)

69. $x = 1$ and $x = -\frac{7}{3}$ **71.** $x = 2$ and $x = 6$

73. $x > 3$

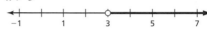

75. $x \leq -4$

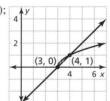

4.4 Vocabulary and Core Concept Check (p. 222)

1. no; The radicand does not contain a variable.

4.4 Monitoring Progress and Modeling with Mathematics (pp. 222–224)

3. $x = 7$ **5.** $x - 24$

7. $x = 6$ **9.** $x = -\dfrac{1000}{3}$

11. $x - 1024$ **13.** about 21.7 yr

15. $x = 12$ **17.** $x = 14$

19. $x = 0$ and $x = \frac{1}{2}$ **21.** $x - 3$

23. $x = -1$ **25.** $x - 4$

27. $x = \pm 8$ **29.** no real solution

31. $x = 3$ **33.** $x = 5$

35. Only one side of the equation was cubed;
$$\sqrt[3]{3x - 8} = 4$$
$$\left(\sqrt[3]{3x - 8}\right)^3 = 4^3$$
$$3x - 8 = 64$$
$$x = 24$$

37. $x \geq 64$ **39.** $x > 27$

41. $0 \leq x \leq \frac{25}{4}$ **43.** $x > -220$

45. about 0.15 in.

47. (3, 0) and (4, 1);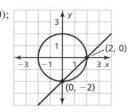

49. (0, −2) and (2, 0);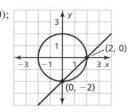

Selected Answers

51. $(0, -1)$;

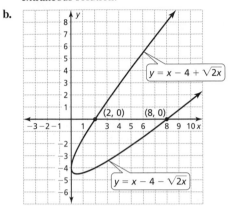

53. a. The greatest stopping distance is 450 feet on ice. On wet asphalt and snow, the stopping distance is 225 feet. The least stopping distance is 90 feet on dry asphalt.

   b. about 272.2 ft; When $s = 35$ and $f = 0.15$, $d \approx 272.2$.

55. a. When solving the first equation, the solution is $x = 8$ with $x = 2$ as an extraneous solution. When solving the second equation, the solution is $x = 2$ with $x = 8$ as an extraneous solution.

   b.

57. The square root of a quantity cannot be negative.

59. Raising the price would decrease demand.

61. $36\pi \approx 113.1 \text{ ft}^2$

63. a. $h = h_0 - \dfrac{kt}{\pi r^2}$

   b. about 5.75 in.

4.4 Maintaining Mathematical Proficiency (p. 224)

65. $x^5 + x^4 - 4x^2 + 3$ **67.** $x^3 + 11x - 8$

69. $g(x) = \frac{1}{2}x^3 - 2x^2$; The graph of g is a vertical shrink by a factor of $\frac{1}{2}$ followed by a translation 3 units down of the graph of f.

4.5 Vocabulary and Core Concept Check (p. 229)

1. You can add, subtract, multiply, or divide f and g.

4.5 Monitoring Progress and Modeling with Mathematics (pp. 229–230)

3. $(f + g)(x) = 14\sqrt[4]{x}$ and the domain is $x \geq 0$;
$(f - g)(x) = -24\sqrt[4]{x}$ and the domain is $x \geq 0$;
$(f + g)(16) = 28$; $(f - g)(16) = -48$

5. $(f + g)(x) = -7x^3 + 5x^2 + x$ and the domain is all real numbers; $(f - g)(x) = -7x^3 - 13x^2 + 11x$ and the domain is all real numbers; $(f + g)(-1) = 11$; $(f - g)(-1) = -17$

7. $(fg)(x) = 2x^{10/3}$ and the domain is all real numbers; $\left(\dfrac{f}{g}\right)(x) = 2x^{8/3}$ and the domain is $x \neq 0$; $(fg)(-27) = 118{,}098$; $\left(\dfrac{f}{g}\right)(-27) = 13{,}122$

9. $(fg)(x) = 36x^{3/2}$ and the domain is $x \geq 0$; $\left(\dfrac{f}{g}\right)(x) = \dfrac{4}{9}x^{1/2}$ and the domain is $x > 0$; $(fg)(9) = 972$; $\left(\dfrac{f}{g}\right)(9) = \dfrac{4}{3}$

11. $(fg)(x) = -98x^{11/6}$ and the domain is $x \geq 0$; $\left(\dfrac{f}{g}\right)(x) = -\dfrac{1}{2}x^{7/6}$; and the domain is $x > 0$; $(fg)(64) = -200{,}704$; $\left(\dfrac{f}{g}\right)(64) = -64$

13. 2541.04; 2458.96; 102,598.56; 60.92

15. 7.76; -14.60; -38.24; -0.31

17. Because the functions have an even index, the domain is restricted; The domain of $(fg)(x)$ is $x \geq 0$.

19. a. $(F + M)(t) = 0.0001t^3 - 0.016t^2 + 0.21t + 7.4$

   b. the total number of employees from the ages of 16 to 19 in the United States

21. yes; When adding or multiplying functions, the order in which they appear does not matter.

23. $(f + g)(3) = -21$; $(f - g)(1) = -1$; $(fg)(2) = 0$; $\left(\dfrac{f}{g}\right)(0) = 2$

25. $r(x) = x^2 - \frac{1}{2}x^2 = \frac{1}{2}x^2$

27. a. $r(x) = \dfrac{20 - x}{6.4}$; $s(x) = \dfrac{\sqrt{x^2 + 144}}{0.9}$

   b. $t(x) = \dfrac{20 - x}{6.4} + \dfrac{\sqrt{x^2 + 144}}{0.9}$

   c. $x \approx 1.7$; If Elvis runs along the shore until he is about 1.7 meters from point C then swims to point B, the time taken to get there will be a minimum.

4.5 Maintaining Mathematical Proficiency (p. 230)

29. $n = \dfrac{5z}{7 + 8z}$ **31.** $n = \dfrac{3}{7b - 4}$

33. no; -1 has two outputs.   **35.** no; 2 has two outputs.

4.6 Vocabulary and Core Concept Check (p. 237)

1. Inverse functions are functions that undo each other.

3. x; x

4.6 Monitoring Progress and Modeling with Mathematics (pp. 237–240)

5. $x = \dfrac{y - 5}{3}$; $-\dfrac{8}{3}$ **7.** $x = 2y + 6$; 0

9. $x = \sqrt[3]{\dfrac{y}{3}}$; -1 **11.** $x = 2 \pm \sqrt{y + 7}$; 0, 4

13. $g(x) = \frac{1}{6}x$;

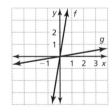

15. $g(x) = \dfrac{x - 5}{-2}$;

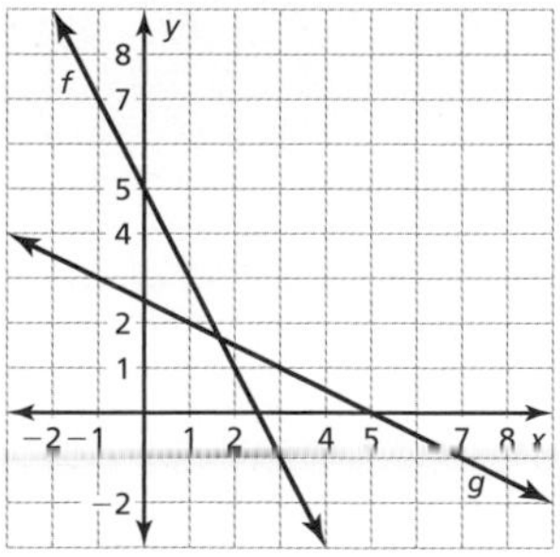

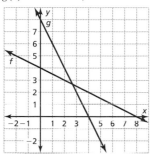

17. $g(x) = -2x + 8$;

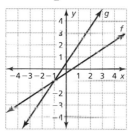

19. $g(x) = \dfrac{3x + 1}{2}$;

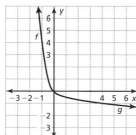

21. $g(x) = \dfrac{x - 4}{-3}$; *Sample answer:* switching x and y; You can graph the inverse to check your answer.

23. $g(x) = -\dfrac{\sqrt{x}}{2}$;

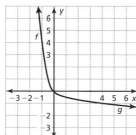

25. $g(x) = \sqrt[3]{x} + 3$

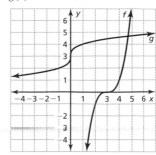

27. $g(x) = \sqrt[4]{\dfrac{x}{2}}$;

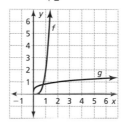

29. When switching x and y, the negative should not be switched with the variables;

$$y = -x + 3$$
$$x = -y + 3$$
$$-x + 3 = y$$

31. no; The function does not pass the horizontal line test.

33. no; The function does not pass the horizontal line test.

35. yes; $g(x) = \sqrt[3]{x} + 1$

37. yes; $g(x) = x^2 - 4$, where $x \geq 0$

39. yes; $g(x) = \dfrac{x^3}{8} + 5$ **41.** no; $y = \pm\sqrt[4]{x} - 2$

43. yes; $g(x) = \dfrac{x^3}{27} - 1$ **45.** yes; $g(x) = \sqrt[5]{2x}$

47. B

49. The functions are not inverses.

51. The functions are inverses.

53. $\ell = \left(\dfrac{v}{1.34}\right)^2$; about 31.3 ft

55. B   **56.** C

57. A   **58.** D

59. 5; When $x = 5$, $2x^2 + 3 = 53$.

61. a. $w = 2\ell - 6$; the weight of an object on a stretched spring of length ℓ

   b. 5 lb

   c. $0.5(2\ell - 6) + 3 = \ell$; $2(0.5w + 3) - 6 = w$

63. a. $F = \dfrac{9}{5}C + 32$; The equation converts temperatures in Celsius to Fahrenheit.

   b. start: 41° F; end: 14° F

   c. −40°

65. B   **66.** C

67. A   **68.** D

69. a. false; All functions of the form $f(x) = x^n$, where n is an even integer, fail the horizontal line test.

   b. true; All functions of the form $f(x) = x^n$, where n is an odd integer, pass the horizontal line test.

71. The inverse $y = \dfrac{1}{m}x - \dfrac{b}{m}$ has a slope of $\dfrac{1}{m}$ and a y-intercept

of $-\dfrac{b}{m}$.

4.6 Maintaining Mathematical Proficiency (p. 240)

73. $-\dfrac{1}{3^3}$

75. 4^2

77. The function is increasing when $x > 1$ and decreasing when $x < 1$. The function is positive when $x < 0$ and when $x > 2$, and negative when $0 < x < 2$.

79. The function is increasing when $-2.89 < x < 2.89$ and decreasing when $x < -2.89$ and $x > 2.89$. The function is positive when $x < -5$ and $0 < x < 5$ and negative when $-5 < x < 0$ and $x > 5$.

Chapter 4 Review (pp. 242–244)

1. 128

2. 243

3. $\dfrac{1}{9}$

4. $x \approx 1.78$

5. $x = 3$

6. $x = -10$ and $x = -6$

7. $\dfrac{1}{6^{3/5}}$

8. 4

9. $2 + \sqrt{3}$

10. $7\sqrt[5]{8}$

11. $7\sqrt{3}$

12. $5^{1/3} \cdot 2^{3/4}$

13. $5z^3$

14. $\dfrac{\sqrt[4]{2z}}{6}$

15. $-z^2\sqrt{10z}$

16. The graph of g is a vertical stretch by a factor of 2 followed by a reflection in the x-axis of the graph of f;

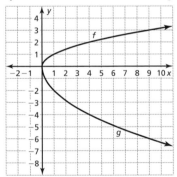

17. The graph of g is a reflection in the y-axis followed by a translation 6 units down of the graph of f.

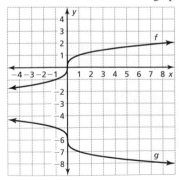

18. $g(x) = \sqrt[3]{-x + 7}$

19.

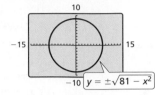

$(8, 0)$; right

20.

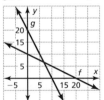

The center is $(0, 0)$. The radius is 9. The x-intercepts are ± 9. The y-intercepts are ± 9.

21. $x = 62$

22. $x = 2$ and $x = 10$

23. $x = \pm 36$

24. $x > 9$

25. $8 \le x < 152$

26. $x \ge 30$

27. about 4082 m

28. $(fg)(x) = 8(3 - x)^{5/6}$ and the domain is $x \le 3$;

$\left(\dfrac{f}{g}\right)(x) = \dfrac{1}{2}(3 - x)^{1/6}$ and the domain is $x < 3$; $(fg)(2) = 8$;

$\left(\dfrac{f}{g}\right)(2) = \dfrac{1}{2}$

29. $(f + g)(x) = 3x^2 + x + 5$ and the domain is all real numbers; $(f - g)(x) = 3x^2 - x - 3$ and the domain is all real numbers; $(f + g)(-5) = 75$; $(f - g)(-5) = 77$

30. $g(x) = -2x + 20$;

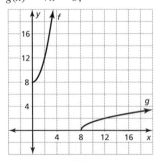

31. $g(x) = \sqrt{x - 8}$;

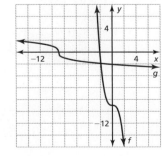

32. $g(x) = \sqrt[3]{-x - 9}$;

33. $g(x) = \frac{1}{9}(x - 5)^2$, $x \geq 5$;

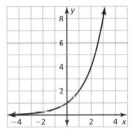

34. no   **35.** yes

36. $p = \dfrac{d}{1.587}$; about 63£

Chapter 5

Chapter 5 Maintaining Mathematical Proficiency *(p. 249)*

1. 48   **2.** -32
3. $-\dfrac{25}{36}$ **4.** $\dfrac{27}{64}$
5. exponential growth   **6.** exponential growth

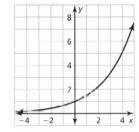

7. exponential decay

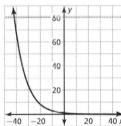

8. all values, odd values; no values, even values; The exponent of -4^n is evaluated first, then the result is multiplied by -1, so the value will always remain negative. The product of an odd number of negative values is negative. After the exponent of -4^n is evaluated, the result is multiplied by -1, so it will never be positive. The product of an even number of negative values is positive.

5.1 Vocabulary and Core Concept Check *(p. 255)*

1. an irrational number that is approximately 2.718281828

5.1 Monitoring Progress and Modeling with Mathematics *(pp. 255–256)*

3. e^8 **5.** $\dfrac{1}{2e}$

7. $625e^{28x}$ **9.** $3e^{3x}$

11. $e^{-5x + 8}$

13. The 4 was not squared; $(4e^{3x})^2 = 4^2 e^{(3x)(2)} = 16e^{6x}$

15. exponential growth

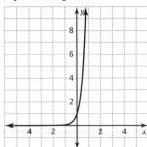

17. exponential decay

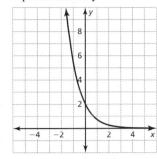

19. exponential growth

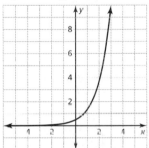

21. exponential decay

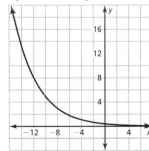

23. D; The graph shows growth and has a y-intercept of 1.
24. A; The graph shows decay and has a y-intercept of 1.
25. B; The graph shows decay and has a y-intercept of 4.
26. C; The graph shows growth and has a y-intercept of 0.75.
27. $y = (1 - 0.221)^t$; 22.1% decay
29. $y = 2(1 + 0.492)^t$; 49.2% growth

31.

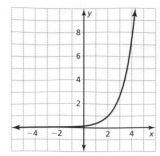

domain: all real numbers, range: $y > 0$

33.

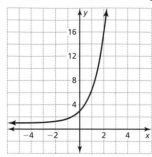

domain: all real numbers, range: $y > 1$

35. the education fund; the education fund

37. *Sample answer:* $a = 6, b = 2, r = -0.2, q = -0.7$

39. no; e is an irrational number. Irrational numbers cannot be expressed as a ratio of two integers.

41. account 1; With account 1, the balance would be

$A = 2500\left(1 + \dfrac{0.06}{4}\right)^{4\,\cdot\,10} \approx \$4535.05$. With account 2, the

balance would be $A = 2500e^{0.04\,\cdot\,10} \approx \$3729.56$.

43. a. $N(t) = 30e^{0.166t}$

b.

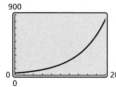

c. At 3:45 P.M., it has been 2 hours and 45 minutes, or 2.75 hours, since 1:00 P.M. Using the *trace* feature of the calculator, type 2.75 to find the point (2.75, 47.356183). At 3:45 P.M., there are about 47 cells.

5.1 Maintaining Mathematical Proficiency *(p. 256)*

45. 5×10^3 **47.** 4.7×10^{-8}

49. $y = -\sqrt{x + 1}$

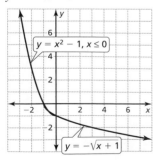

51. $y = \sqrt[3]{x} + 2$

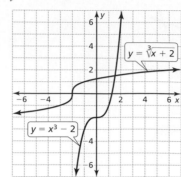

5.2 Vocabulary and Core Concept Check *(p. 262)*

1. common   **3.** They are inverse equations.

5.2 Monitoring Progress and Modeling with Mathematics *(pp. 262–264)*

5. $3^2 = 9$ **7.** $6^0 = 1$

9. $\left(\tfrac{1}{2}\right)^{-4} = 16$ **11.** $\log_6 36 = 2$

13. $\log_{16} \tfrac{1}{16} = -1$ **15.** $\log_{125} 25 = \tfrac{2}{3}$

17. 4   **19.** 1

21. -4 **23.** -1

25. $\log_7 8, \log_5 23, \log_6 38, \log_2 10$

27. 0.778   **29.** -1.099

31. -2.079 **33.** 4603 m

35. x **37.** 4

39. $2x$

41. -3 and $\tfrac{1}{64}$ are in the wrong position; $\log_4 \tfrac{1}{64} = -3$

43. $y = \log_{0.3} x$ **45.** $y = 2^x$

47. $y = e^x + 1$ **49.** $y = \tfrac{1}{3} \ln x$

51. $y = \log_5(x + 9)$

53. a. about 283 mi/h

b. $d = 10^{(s\,-\,65)/93}$; The inverse gives the distance a tornado will travel given the wind speed, s.

55.

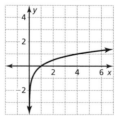

57.

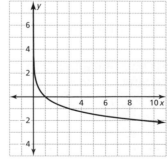

59.

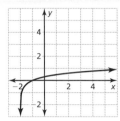

61.

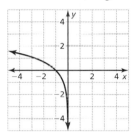

domain: $x > -2$, range: all real numbers, asymptote: $x = -2$

63.

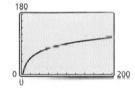

domain: $x < 0$, range: all real numbers, asymptote: $x = 0$

65. yes; $\log_b 1 = 0$ for any positive real number $b \neq 1$

67. a.

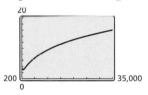

b. about 281 lb

c. (3.4, 0); no; The x-intercept shows that an alligator with a weight of 3.4 pounds has no length. If an object has weight, it must have length.

69. a.

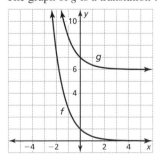

b. 15 species

c. about 3918 m²

d. The number of species of fish increases; *Sample answer:* This makes sense because in a smaller pool or lake, one species could dominate another more easily and feed on the weaker species until it became extinct.

71. a. $\frac{2}{3}$ **b.** $\frac{5}{3}$ **c.** $\frac{4}{3}$ **d.** $\frac{7}{2}$

5.2 Maintaining Mathematical Proficiency (p. 264)

73. $g(x) = \sqrt[3]{\frac{1}{2}x}$ **75.** $g(x) = \sqrt[3]{x + 2}$

77. quadratic; The graph is a translation 2 units left and 1 unit down of the parent quadratic function.

5.3 Vocabulary and Core Concept Check (p. 270)

1. Positive values of a vertically stretch ($a > 1$) or shrink ($a < 1$) the graph of f, h translates the graph of f left ($h < 0$) or right ($h > 0$), and k translates the graph of f up ($k > 0$) or down ($k < 0$). When a is negative, the graph of f is reflected in the x-axis.

5.3 Monitoring Progress and Modeling with Mathematics (pp. 270–272)

3. C; The graph of f is a translation 2 units left and 2 units down of the graph of the parent function $y = 2^x$.

5. A; The graph of h is a translation 2 units right and 2 units down of the graph of the parent function $y = 2^x$.

7. The graph of g is a translation 5 units up of the graph of f.

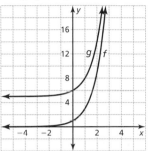

9. The graph of g is a translation 1 unit down of the graph of f.

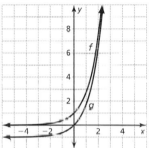

11. The graph of g is a translation 7 units right of the graph of f.

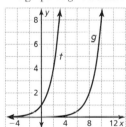

13. The graph of g is a translation 6 units up of the graph of f.

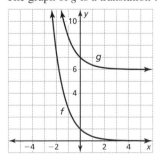

15. The graph of g is a translation 3 units right and 12 units up of the graph of f.

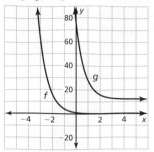

17. The graph of g is a horizontal shrink by a factor of $\frac{1}{2}$ of the graph of f.

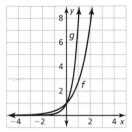

19. The graph of g is reflection in the x-axis followed by a translation 3 units right of the graph of f.

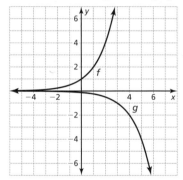

21. The graph of g is a horizontal shrink by a factor of $\frac{1}{6}$ followed by a vertical stretch by a factor of 3 of the graph of f.

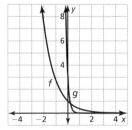

23. The graph of g is a vertical stretch by a factor of 6 followed by a translation 5 units left and 2 units down of the graph of f.

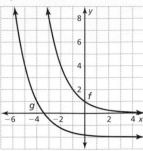

25. The graph of the parent function $f(x) = 2^x$ was translated 3 units left instead of up.

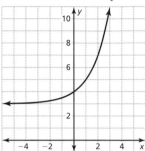

27. The graph of g is a vertical stretch by a factor of 3 followed by a translation 5 units down of the graph of f.

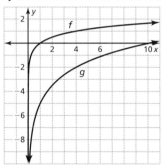

29. The graph of g is a reflection in the x-axis followed by a translation 7 units right of the graph of f.

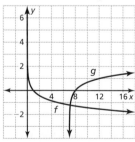

31. A; The graph of f has been translated 2 units right.

32. D; The graph of f has been translated 2 units left.

33. C; The graph of f has been stretched vertically by a factor of 2.

34. B; The graph of f has been shrunk horizontally by a factor of $\frac{1}{2}$.

35. $g(x) = 5^{-x} - 2$ **37.** $g(x) = e^{2x} + 5$

39. $g(x) = 6 \log_6 x - 5$ **41.** $g(x) = \log_{1/2}(-x + 3) + 2$

43. Multiply the output by -1; Substitute $\log_7 x$ for $f(x)$. Subtract 6 from the output; Substitute $-\log_7 x$ for $h(x)$.

45. The graph of g is a translation 4 units up of the graph of f; $y = 4$

47. The graph of g is a translation 6 units left of the graph of f; $x = -6$

49. The graph of S is a vertical shrink by a factor of 0.118 followed by a translation 0.159 unit up of the graph of f; For fine sand, the slope of the beach is about 0.05. For medium sand, the slope of the beach is about 0.09. For coarse sand, the slope of the beach is about 0.12. For very coarse sand, the slope of the beach is about 0.16.

51. yes; *Sample answer:* If the graph is reflected in the y-axis, the graphs will never intersect because there are no values of x where $\log x = \log(-x)$.

53. **a.** never; The asymptote of $f(x) = \log x$ is a vertical line and would not change by shifting the graph vertically.

   b. always; The asymptote of $f(x) = e^x$ is a horizontal line and would be changed by shifting the graph vertically.

   c. always; The domain of $f(x) = \log x$ is $x > 0$ and would not be changed by a horizontal shrink.

   d. sometimes; The graph of the parent exponential function does not intersect the x-axis, but if it is shifted down, the graph would intersect the x-axis.

55. The graph of h is a translation 2 units left of the graph of f; The graph of h is a reflection in the y-axis followed by a translation 2 units left of the graph of g; x has been replaced with $x + 2$. x has been replaced with $-(x + 2)$.

5.3 Maintaining Mathematical Proficiency (p. 272)

57. $(fg)(x) = x^6$; $(fg)(3) = 729$

59. $(f + g)(x) = 14x^3$; $(f + g)(2) = 112$

5.4 Vocabulary and Core Concept Check (p. 279)

1. Product

5.4 Monitoring Progress and Modeling with Mathematics (pp. 279–280)

3. 0.565

5. 1.424

7. -0.712

9. B; Quotient Property

10. D; Power Property

11. A; Power Property

12. C; Product Property

13. $\log_3 4 + \log_3 x$

15. $1 + 5 \log x$

17. $\ln x - \ln 3 - \ln y$

19. $\log_7 5 + \frac{1}{2}\log_7 x$

21. The two expressions should be added, not multiplied; $\log_2 5x = \log_2 5 + \log_2 x$

23. $\log_4 \frac{7}{10}$

25. $\ln x^6 y^4$

27. $\log_5 4\sqrt[3]{x}$

29. $\ln 32x^7 y^4$

31. B;

$$\log_5 \frac{y^4}{3x} = \log_5 y^4 - \log_5 3x \quad \text{Quotient Property}$$

$$= 4\log_5 y - (\log_5 3 + \log_5 x) \quad \text{Power and Product Properties}$$

$$= 4\log_5 y - \log_5 3 - \log_5 x \quad \text{Distributive Property}$$

33. 1.404

35. 1.232

37. 1.581

39. -0.860

41. yes; Using the change-of-base formula, the equation can be graphed as $y = \dfrac{\log x}{\log 3}$.

43. 60 decibels

45. **a.** $2 \ln 2 \approx 1.39$ knots

   b. $s(h) = 2 \ln 100h$

$$s(h) = \ln(100h)^2$$

$$e^{s(h)} = e^{\ln(100h)^2}$$

$$e^{s(h)} = (100h)^2$$

$$\log e^{s(h)} = \log(100h)^2$$

$$s(h) \log e = 2 \log(100h)$$

$$s(h) \log e = 2(\log 100 + \log h)$$

$$s(h) \log e = 2(2 + \log h)$$

$$s(h) = \frac{2}{\log e}(\log h + 2)$$

47. Rewrite each logarithm in exponential form to obtain $a = b^x$, $c = b^y$, and $a = c^z$. So,

$$\frac{\log_b a}{\log_b c} = \frac{\log_b c^z}{\log_b c} = \frac{z \log_b c}{\log_b c} = z = \log_c a.$$

5.4 Maintaining Mathematical Proficiency (p. 280)

49. $x = -2, x = -4$; *Sample answer:* The equation is of the form $x^2 = d$ where x is a binomial, so solve using square roots.

51. $x = -3 \pm \sqrt{2}$; *Sample answer:* $a = 1$ and b is even, so solve by completing the square.

53. $x < 4$

55. $n > -15$

5.5 Vocabulary and Core Concept Check (p. 286)

1. exponential

3. The domain of a logarithmic function is positive numbers only, so any quantity that results in taking the log of a non-positive number will be an extraneous solution.

5.5 Monitoring Progress and Modeling with Mathematics (pp. 286–288)

5. $x = -1$

7. $x = 7$

9. $x \approx 1.771$

11. $x = -\frac{5}{3}$

13. $x \approx 0.255$

15. $x \approx 0.173$

17. about 17.6 years old

19. about 50 min

21. $x = 6$

23. $x = 3$

25. $x = 6$

27. $x = 10$

29. $x = 1$

31. $x = \dfrac{1 + \sqrt{41}}{2} \approx 3.7$ and $x = \dfrac{1 - \sqrt{41}}{2} \approx -2.7$

33. $x = 4$

35. $x \approx 6.04$

37. $x = \pm 1$

39. $x \approx 10.24$

41. 3 should be the base on both sides of the equation;

$$\log_3(5x - 1) = 4$$

$$3^{\log_3(5x - 1)} = 3^4$$

$$5x - 1 = 81$$

$$5x = 82$$

$$x = 16.4$$

43. **a.** 39.52 years

   b. 38.66 years

   c. 38.38 years

   d. 38.38 years

45. a. $x \approx 3.57$
 b. $x = 0.8$

47. $x > 1.815$ **49.** $x \geq 20.086$

51. $x < 1.723$ **53.** $x \geq \frac{1}{5}$

55. $0 < x < 25$; *Sample answer:* algebraically; Converting the equation to exponential form is the easiest method because it isolates the variable.

57. $r > 0.0718$ or $r > 7.18\%$ **59.** $x \approx 1.78$

61. no solution

63. a. $a = -\dfrac{1}{0.09} \ln\!\left(\dfrac{45 - \ell}{25.7}\right)$

 b. 36 cm footprint: 11.7 years old; 32 cm footprint: 7.6 years old; 28 cm footprint: 4.6 years old; 24 cm footprint: 2.2 years old

65. *Sample answer:* $2^x = 16$; $\log_3(-x) = 1$

67. $x \approx 0.89$ **69.** $x \approx 10.61$

71. $x = 2$ and $x = 3$

73. To solve exponential equations with different bases, take a logarithm of each side. Then use the Power Property to move the exponent to the front of the logarithm, and solve for x. To solve logarithmic equations of different bases, find a common multiple of the bases, and exponentiate each side with this common multiple as the base. Rewrite the base as a power that will cancel out the given logarithm and solve the resulting equation.

5.5 Maintaining Mathematical Proficiency *(p. 288)*

75. $y + 2 = 4(x - 1)$ **77.** $y + 8 = -\frac{1}{3}(x - 3)$

79. 3; $y = 2x^3 - x + 1$

81. 4; $y = -3x^4 + 2x^3 - x^2 + 5x - 6$

5.6 Vocabulary and Core Concept Check *(p. 294)*

1. exponential

5.6 Monitoring Progress and Modeling with Mathematics *(pp. 294–296)*

3. exponential; The data have a common ratio of 4.

5. quadratic; The second differences are constant.

7. $y = 0.75(4)^x$ **9.** $y = \frac{1}{8}(2)^x$

11. $y = \frac{2}{5}(5)^x$ **13.** $y = 5(0.5)^x$

15. $y = 0.25(2)^x$

17. Data are linear when the first differences are constant; The outputs have a common ratio of 3, so the data represents an exponential function.

19. *Sample answer:* $y = 7.20(1.39)^x$

21. yes; *Sample answer:* $y = 8.88(1.21)^x$

23. no; *Sample answer:* $y = -0.8x + 66$

25.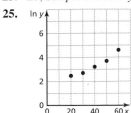
Sample answer: $y = 3.25(1.052)^x$

27.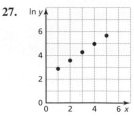
yes; $y = 9.14(1.99)^x$

29.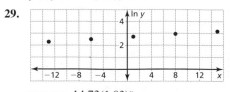
yes; $y = 14.73(1.03)^x$

31. $y = 6.70(1.41)^x$; about 208 scooters

33. $t = 12.59 - 2.55 \ln d$; 2.6 h

35. a.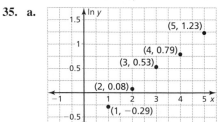
Sample answer: $y = 0.50(1.47)^x$

 b. about 47%; The base is 1.47 which means that the function shows 47% growth.

37. no; When d is the independent variable and t is the dependent variable, the data can be modeled with a logarithmic function. When the variables are switched, the data can be modeled with an exponential function.

39. a. 5.9 weeks
 b.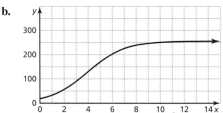
The asymptote is the line $y = 256$ and represents the maximum height of the sunflower.

5.6 Maintaining Mathematical Proficiency *(p. 296)*

41. no; When one variable is increased by a factor, the other variable does not increase by the same factor.

43. yes; When one variable is increased by a factor, the other variable increases by the same factor.

45. $x = 6$ **47.** $x = -8$

Chapter 5 Review *(pp. 298–300)*

1. e^{15} **2.** $\dfrac{2}{e^3}$

3. $\dfrac{9}{e^{10x}}$

4. exponential growth

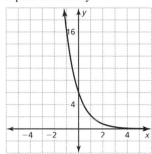

5. exponential decay

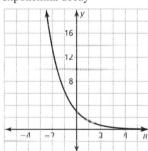

6. exponential decay

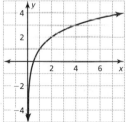

7. 3

8. −2

9. 0

10. $g(x) = \log_8 x$

11. $y = e^x + 4$

12. $y = 10^x - 9$

13.

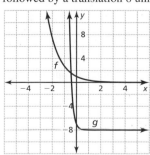

14. The graph of g is a horizontal shrink by a factor of $\frac{1}{5}$ followed by a translation 8 units down of the graph of f.

15. The graph of g is a vertical shrink by a factor of $\frac{1}{2}$ followed by a translation 5 units left of the graph of f.

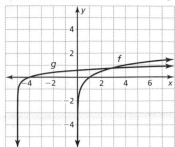

16. $g(x) = 3e^{x+6} + 3$

17. $g(x) = \log(-x) - 2$

18. $\log_8 3 + \log_8 x + \log_8 y$

19. $1 + 3 \log x + \log y$

20. $\ln 3 + \ln y - 5 \ln x$

21. $\log_7 384$

22. $\log_2 \dfrac{12}{x^2}$

23. $\ln 4x^2$

24. about 3.32

25. about 1.13

26. about 1.19

27. $x \approx 1.29$

28. $x = 7$

29. $x \approx 3.59$

30. $x > 1.39$

31. $0 < x \leq 8103.08$

32. $x \geq 1.19$

33. $y = 6(2)^x$

34. $y = 64\left(\frac{1}{2}\right)^x$

35. $y = 0.04(5)^x$

36. $s = 3.95 + 27.48 \ln t$; 53 pairs

Chapter 6

Chapter 6 Maintaining Mathematical Proficiency (p. 305)

1. $\frac{19}{15}$, or $1\frac{4}{15}$

2. $-\frac{17}{42}$

3. $\frac{1}{3}$

4. $\frac{11}{12}$

5. $-\frac{3}{7}$

6. $-\frac{1}{20}$

7. $\frac{9}{20}$

8. $-\frac{7}{20}$

9. $\frac{8}{11}$

10. 0; Division by zero is not possible.

6.1 Vocabulary and Core Concept Check (p. 311)

1. The ratio of the variables is constant in a direct variation equation, and the product of the variables is constant in an inverse variation equation.

6.1 Monitoring Progress and Modeling with Mathematics (pp. 311–312)

3. inverse variation

5. direct variation

7. neither

9. direct variation

11. direct variation

13. inverse variation

15. $y = -\dfrac{20}{x}; y = -\dfrac{20}{3}$

17. $y = -\dfrac{24}{x}; y = -8$

19. $y = \dfrac{21}{x}; y = 7$

21. $y = \dfrac{2}{x}; y = \dfrac{2}{3}$

23. The equation for direct variation was used; Because $5 = \dfrac{a}{8}$, $a = 40$. So, $y = \dfrac{40}{x}$.

25. a.

Size	2	2.5	3	5
Number of songs	5000	4000	3333	2000

    b. The number of songs decreases.

27. $A = \dfrac{26,000}{c}$; about 321 chips per wafer

29. yes; The product of the number of hats and the price per hat is \$50, which is constant.

31. *Sample answer:* As the speed of your car increases, the number of minutes per mile decreases.

33. cat: 4 ft, dog: 2 ft; The inverse equations are $d = \dfrac{a}{7}$ and $6 - d = \dfrac{a}{14}$. Because the constant is the same, solve the equation $7d = 14(6 - d)$ for d.

6.1 Maintaining Mathematical Proficiency (p. 312)

35. $x^2 - 6$

37.

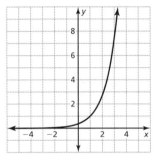

    domain: all real numbers, range: $y > 0$

39.

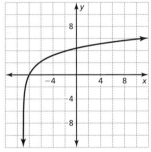

    domain: $x > -9$, range: all real numbers

6.2 Vocabulary and Core Concept Check (p. 318)

1. range; domain

6.2 Monitoring Progress and Modeling with Mathematics (pp. 318–320)

3.

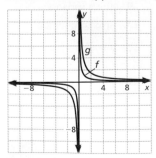

    The graph of g lies farther from the axes. Both graphs lie in the first and third quadrants and have the same asymptotes, domain, and range.

5.

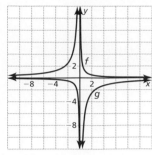

The graph of g lies farther from the axes and is reflected in the x-axis. Both graphs have the same asymptotes, domain, and range.

7.

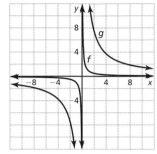

The graph of g lies farther from the axes. Both graphs lie in the first and third quadrants and have the same asymptotes, domain, and range.

9.

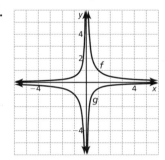

The graph of g lies closer to the axes and is reflected in the x-axis. Both graphs have the same asymptotes, domain, and range.

11.

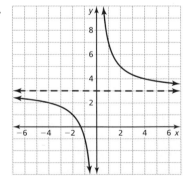

domain: all real numbers except 0; range: all real numbers except 3

13.

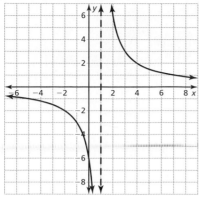

domain: all real numbers except 1; range: all real numbers except 0

15.

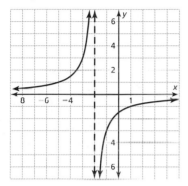

domain: all real numbers except −2; range: all real numbers except 0

17.

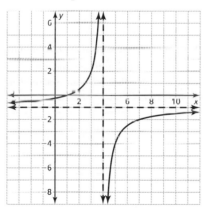

domain: all real numbers except 4; range: all real numbers except −1

19. The graph should lie in the second and fourth quadrants instead of the first and third quadrants;

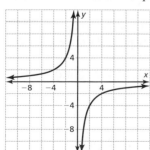

21. A; The asymptotes are $x = 3$ and $y = 1$.

22. C; The asymptotes are $x = -3$ and $y = 1$.

23. B; The asymptotes are $x = 3$ and $y = -1$.

24. D; The asymptotes are $x = -3$ and $y = -1$.

25.

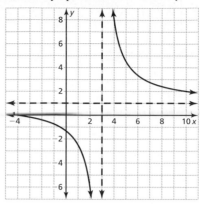

domain: all real numbers except 3; range: all real numbers except 1

27.

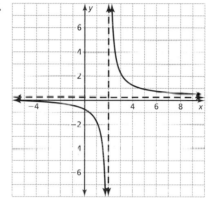

domain: all real numbers except 2; range: all real numbers except $\frac{1}{4}$

29.

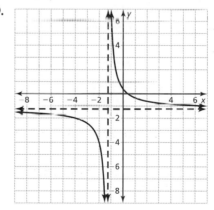

domain: all real numbers except $-\frac{5}{4}$; range: all real numbers except $-\frac{5}{4}$

31.

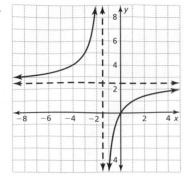

domain: all real numbers except $-\frac{3}{2}$; range: all real numbers except $\frac{5}{2}$

33. $g(x) = \dfrac{1}{x+1} + 5$

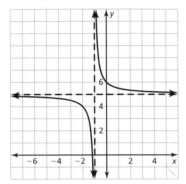

translation 1 unit left and 5 units up

35. $g(x) = \dfrac{6}{x-5} + 2$

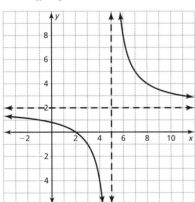

translation 5 units right and 2 units up

37. $g(x) = \dfrac{24}{x-6} + 1$

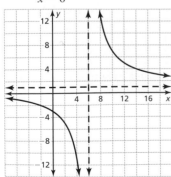

translation 6 units right and 1 unit up

39. $g(x) = \dfrac{-111}{x+13} + 7$

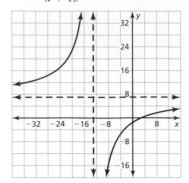

translation 13 units left and 7 units up

41. a. 50 students

　　b. The average cost per student approaches $20.

43. B

45. a. about 23°C

　　b. -0.005 sec/°C

47.

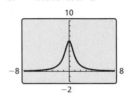

even

49.

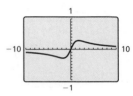

odd

51. yes; A rational function can have more than one vertical asymptote when the denominator is zero for more than one value of x, such as $y = \dfrac{3}{(x+1)(x-1)}$.

53. $y = x$, $y = -x$; The function and its inverse are the same.

55. $(4, 3)$; The point $(2, 1)$ is one unit left and one unit down from $(3, 2)$, so a point on the other branch is one unit right and one unit up from $(3, 2)$.

57. The competitor is a better choice for less than 18 months of service; The cost of Internet service is modeled by $C = \dfrac{50 + 43x}{x}$. The competitor's cost is lesser when $x = 6$ and $x = 12$, and greater when $x = 18$ and $x = 24$.

6.2 Maintaining Mathematical Proficiency (p. 320)

59. $4(x-5)(x+4)$ **61.** $2(x-3)(x+2)$

63. 3^6 **65.** $6^{2/3}$

6.3 Vocabulary and Core Concept Check (p. 328)

1. To multiply rational expressions, multiply numerators, then multiply denominators, and write the new fraction in simplified form. To divide one rational expression by another, multiply the first rational expression by the reciprocal of the second rational expression.

6.3 Monitoring Progress and Modeling with Mathematics (pp. 328–330)

3. $\dfrac{2x}{3x-4}$, $x \neq 0$ **5.** $\dfrac{x+3}{x-1}$, $x \neq 6$

7. $\dfrac{x+9}{x^2-2x+4}$, $x \neq -2$ **9.** $\dfrac{2(4x^2+5)}{x-3}$, $x \neq \pm\sqrt{\dfrac{5}{4}}$

11. $\dfrac{y^3}{2x^2}$, $y \neq 0$ **13.** $\dfrac{(x-4)(x+6)}{x}$, $x \neq 3$

15. $(x - 3)(x + 3), x \neq 0, x \neq 2$

17. $\dfrac{2x(x + 4)}{(x + 2)(x - 3)}, x \neq 1$ 　　**19.** $\dfrac{(x + 9)(x - 4)^2}{(x + 7)}, x \neq 7$

21. The polynomials need to be factored first, and then the common factors can divide out; $\dfrac{x + 12}{x + 4}$

23. B

25. The expressions have the same simplified form, but the domain of f is all real numbers except $x \neq \frac{7}{3}$, and the domain of g is all real numbers.

27. $\dfrac{256x^7}{y^{14}}, x \neq 0$ 　　**29.** $2, x \neq -2, x \neq 0, x \neq 3$

31. $\dfrac{(x + 2)}{(x + 4)(x - 3)}$

33. $\dfrac{(x + 6)(x - 2)}{(x + 2)(x - 6)}, x \neq -4, x \neq -3$

35. **a.** $\dfrac{2(r + h)}{rh}$

　　b. soup: about 0.784, coffee: about 0.382, paint: about 0.341; from most efficient to least efficient: paint can, coffee can, soup can

37. $M = \dfrac{171{,}000t + 1{,}361{,}000}{(1 + 0.018t)(2.96t + 278.649)}; \$8443$

39. **a.** The population is increasing by 2,960,000 people each year.

　　b. The population was 278,649,000 people in 2000.

41.

x	y
−3.5	−0.1333
−3.8	0.1282
−3.9	−0.1266
−4.1	−0.1235
−4.2	−0.1220

The graph does not have a value for y when $x = -4$ and approaches $y = -0.125$.

43. $\dfrac{4}{7x}$

45. $9(x + 3), x \neq -\frac{3}{2}, x \neq \frac{5}{2}, x \neq 7$

47. Galapagos: about 0.371, King: about 0.203; King; The King penguin has a smaller surface area to volume ratio, so it is better equipped to live in a colder environment.

49. $f(x) = \dfrac{x(x - 1)}{x + 2}, g(x) = \dfrac{x(x + 2)}{x - 1}$

6.3 Maintaining Mathematical Proficiency (p. 330)

51. $x = -\frac{24}{5}$ 　　**53.** $x = \frac{32}{15}$

55. $7 \cdot 13$ 　　**57.** prime

6.4 Vocabulary and Core Concept Check (p. 336)

1. complex fraction

6.4 Monitoring Progress and Modeling with Mathematics (pp. 336–338)

3. $\dfrac{5}{x}$ 　　**5.** $\dfrac{9 - 2x}{x + 1}$

7. $5, x \neq -3$ 　　**9.** $3x(x - 2)$

11. $2x(x - 5)$ 　　**13.** $(x + 5)(x - 5)$

15. $(x - 5)(x + 8)(x - 8)$

17. The LCM of $5x$ and x^2 is $5x^2$, so multiply the first term by $\dfrac{x}{x}$ and the second term by $\dfrac{5}{5}$ before adding the numerators; $\dfrac{2(x + 10)}{5x^2}$

19. $\dfrac{37}{30x}$ 　　**21.** $\dfrac{2(x + 7)}{(x + 4)(x + 6)}$

23. $\dfrac{3(x + 12)}{(x + 8)(x - 3)}$ 　　**25.** $\dfrac{8x^3 - 9x^2 - 28x + 8}{x(x - 4)(3x - 1)}$

27. sometimes; When the denominators have no common factors, the product of the denominators is the LCD. When the denominators have common factors, use the LCM to find the LCD.

29. A

31. $g(x) = \dfrac{-2}{x - 1} + 5$

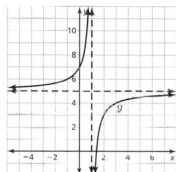

The graph of g is a translation 1 unit right and 5 units up of the graph of $f(x) = \dfrac{-2}{x}$.

33. $g(x) = \dfrac{60}{x - 5} + 12$

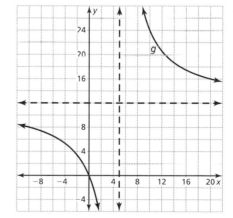

The graph of g is a translation 5 units right and 12 units up of the graph of $f(x) = \dfrac{60}{x}$.

35. $g(x) = \dfrac{3}{x} + 2$

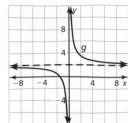

The graph of g is a translation 2 units up of the graph of $f(x) = \dfrac{3}{x}$.

37. $g(x) = \dfrac{20}{x - 3} + 3$

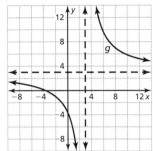

The graph of g is a translation 3 units right and 3 units up of the graph of $f(x) = \dfrac{20}{x}$.

39. $\dfrac{x(x - 18)}{6(5x + 2)}, x \neq 0$ **41.** $-\dfrac{3}{4x}, x \neq \dfrac{5}{2}$

43. $\dfrac{x - 4}{12(x - 6)(x - 1)}, x \neq -1, x \neq 4$

45. $T = \dfrac{2ad}{(a + j)(a - j)}$; about 10.2 h

47. $y = \dfrac{20(7x + 60)}{x(x + 30)}$

49. no; The LCM of 2 and 4 is 4, which is greater than one number and equal to the other number.

51. a. $M = \dfrac{Pi}{1 - \left(\dfrac{1}{1 + i}\right)^{12t}}$

$= \dfrac{Pi}{1 - \dfrac{1}{(1 + i)^{12t}}} \cdot \dfrac{(1 + i)^{12t}}{(1 + i)^{12t}}$

$= \dfrac{Pi(1 + i)^{12t}}{(1 + i)^{12t} - 1}$

b. \$364.02

53. $g(x) = \dfrac{2.3058}{x + 12.2} + 0.003$; translation 12.2 units left and 0.003 unit up of the graph of f

55. a. $R = \dfrac{x^2 + 90x + 400}{40x(x + 10)}$

b. about 0.0758 car/min; about 4.5 cars/h; Multiply the number of cars washed per minute by the rate 60 min/h to obtain an answer in cars per hour.

57. a. $A = \dfrac{391(t - 1)^2 + 0.112}{0.218(t - 1)^4 + 0.991(t - 1)^2 + 1}$

b. $A = \dfrac{391t^2 + 0.112}{0.218t^4 + 0.991t^2 + 1}$
$+ \dfrac{391(t - 1)^2 + 0.112}{0.218(t - 1)^4 + 0.991(t - 1)^2 + 1}$

6.4 Maintaining Mathematical Proficiency (p. 338)

59. $x = -2$ **61.** $x = -2, x = 0, x = 2$

6.5 Vocabulary and Core Concept Check (p. 344)

1. when each side of the equation is a single rational expression; *Sample answer:* The equation is a proportion.

6.5 Monitoring Progress and Modeling with Mathematics (pp. 344–346)

3. $x = 4$ **5.** $x = 5$

7. $x = -5, x = 7$ **9.** $x = -1, x = 0$

11. 26 serves   **13.** 20.5 oz

15. $x(x + 3)$ **17.** $2(x + 1)(x + 4)$

19. $x = 2$ **21.** $x = \dfrac{7}{2}$

23. $x = -\dfrac{3}{2}, x = 2$ **25.** no solution

27. $x = -2, x = 3$ **29.** $x = \dfrac{-3 \pm \sqrt{129}}{4}$

31. Both sides of the equation should be multiplied by the same expression;

$$3x^3 \cdot \dfrac{5}{3x} + 3x^3 \cdot \dfrac{2}{x^2} = 3x^3 \cdot 1$$

33. a.

	Work rate	Time	Work done
You	$\dfrac{1 \text{ room}}{8 \text{ hours}}$	5 hours	$\dfrac{5}{8}$ room
Friend	$\dfrac{1 \text{ room}}{t \text{ hours}}$	5 hours	$\dfrac{5}{t}$ room

b. The sum is the amount of time it would take for you and your friend to paint the room together; $\dfrac{5}{8} + \dfrac{5}{t} = 1$,

$t = 13.\overline{3}$ h = 13 h 20 min

35. *Sample answer:* $\dfrac{x + 1}{x + 2} = \dfrac{3}{x + 4}$, Cross multiplication can be used when each side of the equation is a single rational expression; *Sample answer:* $\dfrac{x + 1}{x + 2} + \dfrac{3}{x + 4} = \dfrac{1}{x + 3}$; Multiplying by the LCD can be used when there is more than one rational expression on one side of the equation.

37. yes; $y = \dfrac{2}{x} + 4$ **39.** yes; $y = \dfrac{3}{x + 2}$

41. yes; $y = \dfrac{-2}{x} + \dfrac{11}{2}$ **43.** no; $y = \pm\sqrt{\dfrac{1}{x - 4}}$

45. a. about 190.6 ft
b. about 190.6 ft

47. $x \approx \pm 0.8165$ **49.** $x \approx 1.3247$

51. $\dfrac{1 + \sqrt{5}}{2}$ **53.** $g(x) = \dfrac{4x + 1}{x - 3}$

55. $y = \dfrac{b - xd}{xc - a}$

57. a. always true; When $x = a$, the denominators of the fractions are both zero.

   b. sometimes true; The equation will have exactly one solution except when $a = 3$.

   c. always true; $x = a$ is an extraneous solution, so the equation has no solution.

6.5 Maintaining Mathematical Proficiency (p. 346)

59. discrete; The number of quarters in your pocket is an integer.

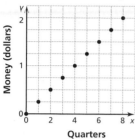

61. 3   **63.** 15

Chapter 6 Review (pp. 348–350)

1. inverse variation   **2.** direct variation

3. direct variation   **4.** neither

5. direct variation   **6.** inverse variation

7. $y = \dfrac{5}{x}$; $y = -\dfrac{5}{3}$ **8.** $y = \dfrac{24}{x}$; $y = -8$

9. $y = \dfrac{45}{x}$; $y = -15$ **10.** $y = \dfrac{-8}{x}$; $y = \dfrac{8}{3}$

11.

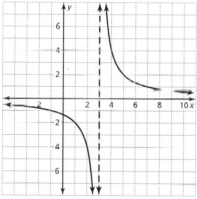

domain: all real numbers except 3; range: all real numbers except 0

12.

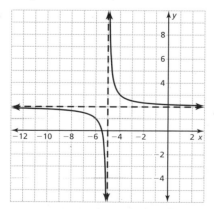

domain: all real numbers except -5; range: all real numbers except 2

13.

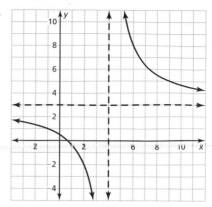

domain: all real numbers except 4; range: all real numbers except 3

14. $\dfrac{16x^3}{y^2}$, $x \neq 0$ **15.** $\dfrac{3(x + 4)}{x + 3}$, $x \neq 3$, $x \neq 4$

16. $\dfrac{3x(4x - 1)}{(x - 4)(x - 3)}$, $x \neq 0$, $x \neq \dfrac{1}{4}$

17. $\dfrac{1}{(x + 3)^2}$, $x \neq 5$, $x \neq 8$ **18.** $\dfrac{3x^2 + 26x + 36}{6x(x + 3)}$

19. $\dfrac{5x^2 - 11x - 9}{(x + 8)(x - 3)}$ **20.** $\dfrac{-2(2x^2 + 3x + 3)}{(x - 3)(x + 3)(x + 1)}$

21. $g(x) = \dfrac{16}{x - 3} + 5$

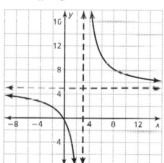

translation 3 units right and 5 units up of the graph of f

22. $g(x) = \dfrac{-26}{x + 7} + 4$

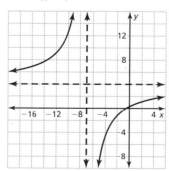

translation 7 units left and 4 units up of the graph of f

23. $g(x) = \dfrac{-1}{x - 1} + 9$

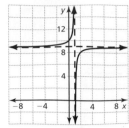

translation 1 unit right and 9 units up of the graph of f

24. $\dfrac{pq}{p + q}, p \neq 0, q \neq 0$

25. $x = 5$

26. $x = 0$

27. no solution

28. yes; $g(x) = \dfrac{3}{x} - 6$

29. yes; $g(x) = \dfrac{10}{x} + 7$

30. yes; $g(x) = \dfrac{1}{x - 8}$

31. a. 4 games

 b. 4 games

Chapter 7

Chapter 7 Maintaining Mathematical Proficiency *(p. 355)*

1.

x	y
1	1
2	-1
3	-5

2.

x	y
2	21
3	46
4	81

3.

x	y
5	4
10	-16
15	-36

4. $x = 4$

5. $x = 6$

6. $x = 66$

7. $x = 7$

8. $x = 100$

9. $x = 3$

10. *Sample answer:* The points on the scatterplot are increasing and f is decreasing; Both level off as x increases.

7.1 Vocabulary and Core Concept Check *(p. 362)*

1. sigma notation

3. A sequence is an ordered list of numbers and a series is the sum of the terms of a sequence.

7.1 Monitoring Progress and Modeling with Mathematics *(pp. 362–364)*

5. 3, 4, 5, 6, 7, 8

7. 1, 4, 9, 16, 25, 36

9. 1, 4, 16, 64, 256, 1024

11. $-4, -1, 4, 11, 20, 31$

13. $\dfrac{2}{3}, 1, \dfrac{6}{5}, \dfrac{4}{3}, \dfrac{10}{7}, \dfrac{3}{2}$

15. arithmetic; $a_5 = 5(5) - 4 = 21; a_n = 5n - 4$

17. arithmetic; $a_5 = 0.7(5) + 2.4 = 5.9; a_n = 0.7n + 2.4$

19. arithmetic; $a_5 = -1.6(6) + 7.4 = -2.2; a_n = -1.6n + 7.4$

21. arithmetic; $a_5 = \dfrac{1}{4}(5) = \dfrac{5}{4}; a_n = \dfrac{n}{4}$

23. $\dfrac{2}{3(1)}, \dfrac{2}{3(2)}, \dfrac{2}{3(3)}, \dfrac{2}{3(4)}; a_5 = \dfrac{2}{3(5)} = \dfrac{2}{15}; a_n = \dfrac{2}{3n}$

25. $(1)^3 + 1, (2)^3 + 1, (3)^3 + 1, (4)^3 + 1; a_5 = 5^3 + 1 = 126;$ $a_n = n^3 + 1$

27. D; The number of squares in the nth figure is equal to the sum of the first positive n integers which is equal to the equation shown in D.

29. $a_n = 4n + 2$

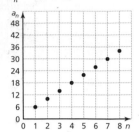

31. $\displaystyle\sum_{i=1}^{5} (3i + 4)$

33. $\displaystyle\sum_{i=1}^{\infty} (i^2 + 3)$

35. $\displaystyle\sum_{i=1}^{\infty} \dfrac{1}{3i}$

37. $\displaystyle\sum_{i=1}^{5} (-1)^i (i + 2)$

39. 42

41. 100

43. 82

45. $\dfrac{481}{140}$

47. 35

49. 280

51. There should be ten terms in the series;

$$\sum_{n=1}^{10} (3n - 5) = -2 + 1 + 4 + 7 + 10 + 13 + 16 + 19$$

$$+ 22 + 25 = 115$$

53. a. \$50.50

 b. 316 days

55. $a_n = \dfrac{1}{2}(n)(n + 1)$

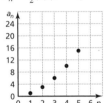

57. yes; Subtract 3 from the sum.

59. a. true;

$$\sum_{i=1}^{n} ca_i = ca_1 + ca_2 + ca_3 + \cdots + ca_n$$

$$= c(a_1 + a_2 + a_3 + \cdots + a_n)$$

$$= c\sum_{i=1}^{n} a_i$$

 b. true;

$$\sum_{i=1}^{n} (a_i + b_i) = (a_1 + b_1) + (a_2 + b_2) + \cdots + (a_n + b_n)$$

$$= a_1 + a_2 + \cdots + a_n + b_1 + b_2 + \cdots + b_n$$

$$= \sum_{i=1}^{n} a_i + \sum_{i=1}^{n} b_i$$

 c. false; $\displaystyle\sum_{i=1}^{2} (2i)(3i) = 30, \left(\sum_{i=1}^{2} 2i\right)\left(\sum_{i=1}^{2} 3i\right) = 54$

 d. false; $\displaystyle\sum_{i=1}^{2} (2i)^2 = 20, \left(\sum_{i=1}^{2} 2i\right)^2 = 36$

61. **a.** $a_n = 2^n - 1$
  b. 63; 127; 255

7.1 Maintaining Mathematical Proficiency (p. 364)

63. $(3, 1, 1)$

7.2 Vocabulary and Core Concept Check (p. 370)

1. common difference

7.2 Monitoring Progess and Modeling with Mathematics (pp. 370–372)

3. arithmetic; The common difference is -2.

5. not arithmetic; The differences are not constant.

7. not arithmetic; The differences are not constant.

9. arithmetic; The common difference is $\frac{1}{4}$.

11. **a.** $a_n = -6n + 3$
  b. $a_n = 5n + 2$

13. $a_n = 8n + 4$; 164

15. $a_n = -3n + 54$; -6

17. $a_n = \frac{2}{3}n - \frac{5}{3}$; $\frac{35}{3}$

19. $a_n = -0.8n + 3.1$; -12.9

21. The formula should be $a_n = a_1 + (n - 1)d$; $a_n = 35 - 13n$

23. $a_n = 5n - 12$

25. $a_n = -2n + 13$

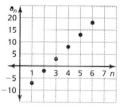

27. $a_n = -\frac{1}{2}n + \frac{7}{2}$

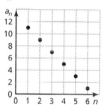

29. C

31. $a_n = 11n - 14$

33. $a_n = -6n + 28$

35. $a_n = -4n + 13$

37. $a_n = \frac{5}{4}n + 2$

39. $a_n = -3n + 12$

41. $a_n = 3n - 7$

43. $a_n = 4n + 9$

45. The graph of a_n consists of discrete points and the graph of f consists of a continuous line.

47. 360

49. -924

51. -8.2

53. -1026

55. **a.** $a_n = 2n + 1$
  b. 63 band members

57. $1 + \sum\limits_{i=1}^{4} 8i$; 81

59. no; Doubling the difference does not necessarily double the terms.

61. $22{,}500$; $\sum\limits_{i=1}^{150} (2i - 1) = 150\left(\dfrac{1 + 299}{2}\right)$

63. $\left(\dfrac{2y}{n} - x\right)$ seats

65. $\frac{7}{16}, \frac{9}{16}, \frac{11}{16}, \frac{13}{16}, \frac{15}{16}, \frac{17}{16}, \frac{19}{16}, \frac{21}{16}, \frac{23}{16},$ and $\frac{25}{16}$

7.2 Maintaining Mathematical Proficiency (p. 372)

67. 3^2

69. $5^{3/4}$

71. exponential decay

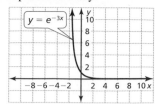

73. exponential growth

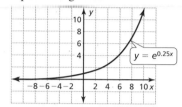

7.3 Vocabulary and Core Concept Check (p. 378)

1. common ratio

3. $a_1 r^{n-1}$

7.3 Monitoring Progress and Modeling with Mathematics (pp. 378–380)

5. geometric; The common ratio is $\frac{1}{2}$.

7. not geometric; The ratios are not constant.

9. not geometric; The ratios are not constant.

11. geometric; The common ratio is $\frac{1}{3}$.

13. **a.** $a_n = -3(5)^{n-1}$
  b. $a_n = 72\left(\frac{1}{3}\right)^{n-1}$

15. $a_n = 4(5)^{n-1}$; $a_7 = 62{,}500$

17. $a_n = 112\left(\frac{1}{2}\right)^{n-1}$; $a_7 = \frac{7}{4}$

19. $a_n = 4\left(\frac{3}{2}\right)^{n-1}$; $a_7 = \frac{729}{16}$

21. $a_n = 1.3(-3)^{n-1}$; $a_7 = 947.7$

23. $a_n = 2^{n-1}$

25. $a_n = 60\left(\frac{1}{2}\right)^{n-1}$

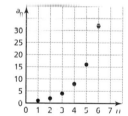

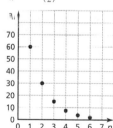

27. $a_n = -3(4)^{n-1}$

29. $a_n = 243\left(-\frac{1}{3}\right)^{n-1}$

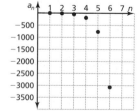

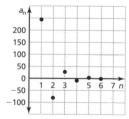

31. The formula should be $a_n = a_1 r^{n-1}$; $a_n = 8(6)^{n-1}$

33. $a_n = 7(4)^{n-1}$

35. $a_n = -6(3)^{n-1}$ or $a_n = -6(-3)^{n-1}$

37. $a_n = 512\left(\frac{1}{8}\right)^{n-1}$ or $a_n = -512\left(-\frac{1}{8}\right)^{n-1}$

39. $a_n = -432\left(\frac{1}{6}\right)^{n-1}$ or $a_n = 432\left(-\frac{1}{6}\right)^{n-1}$

41. $a_n = 4(2)^{n-1}$

43. $a_n = 5\left(\frac{1}{2}\right)^{n-1}$

45. $a_n = 6(-2)^{n-1}$

47. 40,353,606

49. $\dfrac{989{,}527}{65{,}536}$

51. $\dfrac{32{,}312}{6561}$

53. $-262{,}140$

55. The graph of a_n consists of discrete points and the graph of f is continuous.

57. \$276.25

59. a. $a_n = 32\left(\dfrac{1}{2}\right)^{n-1}$; $1 \le n \le 6$; The number of games must be a whole number.

    b. 63 games

61. a. $a_n = 8^{n-1}$; 2,396,745 squares

    b. $b_n = \left(\dfrac{8}{9}\right)^n$; about 0.243 square units

63. \$141,521.58

65. no; The total amount repaid for loan 1 is about \$205,000 and the total amount repaid for loan 2 is about \$284,000.

7.3 Maintaining Mathematical Proficiency (p. 380)

67. domain: all real numbers except 3; range: all real numbers except 0

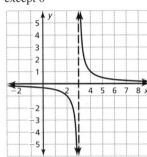

69. domain: all real numbers except 2; range: all real numbers except 1

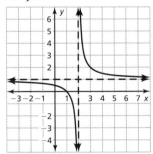

7.4 Vocabulary and Core Concept Check (p. 387)

1. partial sum

7.4 Monitoring Progress and Modeling with Mathematics (pp. 387–388)

3. $S_1 = 0.5$, $S_2 = 0.67$, $S_3 \approx 0.72$, $S_4 \approx 0.74$, $S_5 \approx 0.75$; S_n appears to approach 0.75.

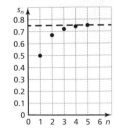

5. $S_1 = 4$, $S_2 = 6.4$, $S_3 = 7.84$, $S_4 \approx 8.70$, $S_5 \approx 9.22$; S_n appears to approach 10.

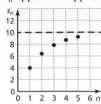

7. 10

9. $\dfrac{88}{15}$

11. 8

13. 18

15. Because $\left|\dfrac{7}{2}\right| > 1$, the sum does not exist.

17. 56 ft

19. $\dfrac{2}{9}$

21. $\dfrac{16}{99}$

23. $\dfrac{3200}{99} = 32\dfrac{32}{99}$

25. *Sample answer:* $\displaystyle\sum_{i=1}^{\infty} 3\left(\dfrac{1}{2}\right)^{i-1}$; $\displaystyle\sum_{i=1}^{\infty} 2\left(\dfrac{2}{3}\right)^{i-1}$; $\dfrac{3}{1-\dfrac{1}{2}} = 6$

and $\dfrac{2}{1-\dfrac{2}{3}} = 6$

27. \$5000

29. yes; At 2 seconds, both distances are 40 feet.

31. a. $a_n = \dfrac{1}{4}\left(\dfrac{3}{4}\right)^{n-1}$

    b. $1\ \text{ft}^2$; As n increases, the area of the removed triangles gets closer to the area of the original triangle.

7.4 Maintaining Mathematical Proficiency (p. 388)

33. quadratic

35. neither

7.5 Vocabulary and Core Concept Check (p. 395)

1. equation

7.5 Monitoring Progress and Modeling with Mathematics (pp. 395–398)

3. $a_1 = 1$, $a_2 = 4$, $a_3 = 7$, $a_4 = 10$, $a_5 = 13$, $a_6 = 16$

5. $f(0) = 4$, $f(1) = 8$, $f(2) = 16$, $f(3) = 32$, $f(4) = 64$, $f(5) = 128$

7. $a_1 = 2$, $a_2 = 5$, $a_3 = 26$, $a_4 = 677$, $a_5 = 458{,}330$, $a_6 = 210{,}066{,}388{,}901$

9. $f(0) = 2$, $f(1) = 4$, $f(2) = 2$, $f(3) = -2$, $f(4) = -4$, $f(5) = -2$

11. $a_1 = 21$, $a_n = a_{n-1} - 7$

13. $a_1 = 3$, $a_n = 4a_{n-1}$

15. $a_1 = 44$, $a_n = \dfrac{a_{n-1}}{4}$

17. $a_1 = 2$, $a_2 = 5$, $a_n = a_{n-2} \cdot a_{n-1}$

19. $a_1 = 1$, $a_2 = 4$, $a_n = a_{n-2} + a_{n-1}$

21. $a_1 = 6$, $a_n = n \cdot a_{n-1}$

23. $f(1) = 1$, $f(n) = f(n-1) + 1$

25. $f(1) = -2$, $f(n) = f(n-1) + 3$

27. A recursive rule needs to include the values of the first terms; $a_1 = 5$, $a_2 = 2$, $a_n = a_{n-2} - a_{n-1}$

29. $a_1 = 7$, $a_n = a_{n-1} + 4$

31. $a_1 = 2$, $a_n = a_{n-1} - 10$

33. $a_1 = 12$, $a_n = 11a_{n-1}$

35. $a_1 = 1.9$, $a_n = a_{n-1} - 0.6$

37. $a_1 = -\dfrac{1}{2}$, $a_n = \dfrac{1}{4}a_{n-1}$

39. $a_1 = 112$, $a_n = a_{n-1} + 30$

41. $a_n = -6n + 9$

43. $a_n = -2(3)^{n-1}$

45. $a_n = 9.1n - 21.1$

47. $a_n = -\dfrac{1}{3}n + \dfrac{16}{3}$

49. $a_n = -2n + 22$

51. B; An explicit rule is $a_n = 6n - 2$.

53. a. $a_1 = 50{,}000, a_n = 0.8a_{n-1} + 5000$

b. 35,240 members

c. The number stabilizes at about 25,000 people.

55. *Sample answer:* You have saved $100 for a vacation. Each week, you save $5 more. $a_1 = 100, a_n = a_{n-1} + 5$

57. a. $1612.38

b. $91.39

59. 144 rabbits; When $n = 12$, each formula produces 144.

61. a. $a_1 = 9000, a_n = 0.9a_{n-1} + 800$

b. The number stabilizes at 8000 trees.

63. a. 1, 2, 4, 8, 16, 32, 64; geometric

b. $a_n = 2^{n-1}; a_1 = 1, a_n = 2a_{n-1}$

65. 15 months; $213.60; $a_1 = 3000$,

$$a_n = \left(1 + \frac{0.1}{12}\right)a_{n-1} - 213.59$$

67. a. 3, 10, 21, 36, 55

b. quadratic

c. $a_n = 2n^2 + n$

69. a. $T_n = \frac{1}{2}n^2 + \frac{1}{2}n; S_n = n^2$

b. $T_1 = 1, T_n = T_{n-1} + n; S_1 = 1, S_n = S_{n-1} + 2n - 1$

c. $S_n = T_{n-1} + T_n$

7.5 Maintaining Mathematical Proficiency (p. 398)

71. $x = 25$

73. $x = 27$

75. $y = \frac{18}{x}; y = \frac{9}{2}$

77. $y = \frac{320}{x}; y = 80$

Chapter 7 Review (pp. 400–402)

1. $a_n = n^2 + n$

2. $\sum_{i=1}^{12}(3i + 4)$

3. $\sum_{i=0}^{\infty}(i^2 + i)$

4. -729

5. 1081

6. 650

7. 15

8. yes; The terms have a common difference of -8.

9. $a_n = 6n - 4$

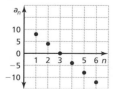

10. $a_n = 3n$

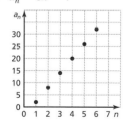

11. $a_n = -4n + 12$

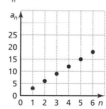

12. 2070

13. $a_n = 1500n + 35{,}500;$ $244,500

14. yes; The terms have a common ratio of 2.

15. $a_n = 25\left(\frac{2}{5}\right)^{n-1}$

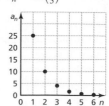

16. $a_n = 2(-3)^{n-1}$

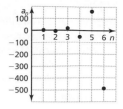

17. $a_n = 4^{n-1}$ or $a_n = (-4)^{n-1}$

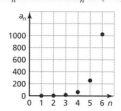
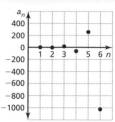

18. 855

19. $S_1 = 1, S_2 = 0.75, S_3 \approx 0.81, S_4 \approx 0.80, S_5 \approx 0.80;$ S_n approaches 0.80.

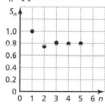

20. -16

21. $\frac{4}{33}$

22. $a_1 = 7, a_2 = 18, a_3 = 29, a_4 = 40, a_5 = 51, a_6 = 62$

23. $a_1 = 6, a_2 = 24, a_3 = 96, a_4 = 384, a_5 = 1536, a_6 = 6144$

24. $f(0) = 4, f(1) = 6, f(2) = 10, f(3) = 16, f(4) = 24, f(5) = 34$

25. $a_1 = 9, a_n = \frac{2}{3}a_{n-1}$

26. $a_1 = 2, a_n = a_{n-1}(n - 1)$

27. $a_1 = 7, a_2 = 3, a_n = a_{n-2} - a_{n-1}$

28. $a_1 = 105, a_n = \frac{3}{5}a_{n-1}$

29. $a_n = 26n - 30$

30. $a_n = 8(-5)^{n-1}$

31. $a_n = 26\left(\frac{2}{5}\right)^{n-1}$

32. $P_1 = 11{,}120, P_n = 1.04P_{n-1}$

33. $a_1 = 1, a_n = a_{n-1} + 4n - 3$

Chapter 8

Chapter 8 Maintaining Mathematical Proficiency (p. 407)

1.

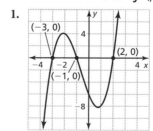

2.

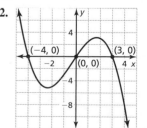

3.

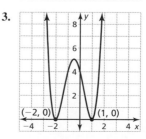

4. 13 m

5. 28 km

6. $11\frac{2}{3}$ in.

7. 0.4 yd

8. yes; The line passing through the points (x_1, y_1) and (x_2, y_1) is horizontal. The line passing through the points (x_2, y_1) and (x_2, y_2) is vertical. Horizontal and vertical lines are perpendicular, so the triangle formed by the line segments connecting (x_1, y_1), (x_2, y_1), and (x_2, y_2) contains a right angle.

8.1 Vocabulary and Core Concept Check *(p. 414)*

1. cosine and secant

3. To solve a right triangle, the missing angles and side lengths must be found.

8.1 Monitoring Progress and Modeling with Mathematics *(pp. 414–416)*

5. $\sin \theta = \frac{4}{5}$, $\cos \theta = \frac{3}{5}$, $\tan \theta = \frac{4}{3}$, $\csc \theta = \frac{5}{4}$, $\sec \theta = \frac{5}{3}$, $\cot \theta = \frac{3}{4}$

7. $\sin \theta = \frac{5}{7}$, $\cos \theta = \frac{2\sqrt{6}}{7}$, $\tan \theta = \frac{5\sqrt{6}}{12}$, $\csc \theta = \frac{7}{5}$, $\sec \theta = \frac{7\sqrt{6}}{12}$, $\cot \theta = \frac{2\sqrt{6}}{5}$

9. $\sin \theta = \frac{2\sqrt{14}}{9}$, $\cos \theta = \frac{5}{9}$, $\tan \theta = \frac{2\sqrt{14}}{5}$, $\csc \theta = \frac{9\sqrt{14}}{28}$, $\sec \theta = \frac{9}{5}$, $\cot \theta = \frac{5\sqrt{14}}{28}$

11. $\sin \theta = \frac{4\sqrt{97}}{97}$, $\cos \theta = \frac{9\sqrt{97}}{97}$, $\csc \theta = \frac{\sqrt{97}}{4}$, $\cot \theta = \frac{9}{4}$

13. $\cos \theta = \frac{6\sqrt{2}}{11}$, $\tan \theta = \frac{7\sqrt{2}}{12}$, $\csc \theta = \frac{11}{7}$, $\sec \theta = \frac{11\sqrt{2}}{12}$, $\cot \theta = \frac{6\sqrt{2}}{7}$

15. $\sin \theta = \frac{7\sqrt{85}}{85}$, $\cos \theta = \frac{6\sqrt{85}}{85}$, $\csc \theta = \frac{\sqrt{85}}{7}$, $\sec \theta = \frac{\sqrt{85}}{6}$, $\cot \theta = \frac{6}{7}$

17. $\sin \theta = \frac{\sqrt{115}}{14}$, $\cos \theta = \frac{9}{14}$, $\tan \theta = \frac{\sqrt{115}}{9}$, $\csc \theta = \frac{14\sqrt{115}}{115}$, $\cot \theta = \frac{9\sqrt{115}}{115}$

19. The adjacent side was used instead of the opposite; $\sin \theta = \frac{\text{opp}}{\text{hyp}} = \frac{8}{17}$

21. $x = 4.5$

23. $x = 6$

25. $x = 8$

27. 0.9703

29. 1.1666

31. 9.5144

33. $A = 54°$, $b \approx 16.71$, $c \approx 28.43$

35. $B = 35°$, $b \approx 11.90$, $c \approx 20.75$

37. $B = 47°$, $a \approx 28.91$, $c \approx 42.39$

39. $A = 18°$, $a \approx 3.96$, $b \approx 12.17$

41. $w \approx 514$ m

43. about 427 m

45. **a.** about 451 ft
b. about 5731 ft

47. **a.** about 22,818 mi
b. about 7263 mi

49. **a.** about 59,155 ft
b. about 53,613 ft
c. about 39,688 ft; Use the tangent function to find the horizontal distance, $x + y$, from the airplane to the second town to be about 93,301 ft. Subtract 53,613 ft to find the distance between the two towns.

51. yes; The triangle must be a 45-45-90 triangle because both acute angles would be the same and have the same cosine value.

53. **a.** $x = 0.5$; 6 units
b. *Sample answer:* Each side is part of two right triangles, with opposing angles $\left(\dfrac{180°}{n}\right)$. So, each side length is $2\sin\left(\dfrac{180°}{n}\right)$, and there are n sides.
c. $n \cdot \sin\left(\dfrac{180°}{n}\right)$; about 3.14

8.1 Maintaining Mathematical Proficiency *(p. 416)*

55. $\frac{19}{33}$

57. $\frac{112{,}000}{999}$

59. $C \approx 69.1$ in., $A \approx 380.1$ in.^{2}

8.2 Vocabulary and Core Concept Check *(p. 422)*

1. origin; initial side

3. *Sample answer:* A radian is a measure of an angle that is approximately equal to 57.3° and there are 2π radians in a circle.

8.2 Monitoring Progress and Modeling with Mathematics *(pp. 422–424)*

5.

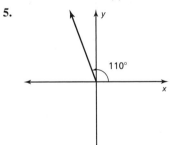

7.

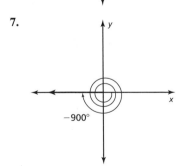

9. 430°; −290°

11. 235°; −485°

13. $\dfrac{2\pi}{9}$

15. $-\dfrac{13\pi}{9}$

17. 20°

19. about −286.5°

21. A full revolution is 360° or 2π radians. The terminal side rotates one-sixth of a revolution from the positive x-axis, so multiply by $\frac{1}{6}$ to get $\frac{1}{6} \cdot 360° = 60°$ and $\frac{1}{6} \cdot 2\pi = \frac{\pi}{3}$.

23. B   **24.** D

25. A   **26.** C

27. about 15.7 yd, about 78.5 yd²

29. The wrong conversion was used;

$$24° = 24 \text{ degrees}\left(\frac{\pi \text{ radians}}{180 \text{ degrees}}\right)$$

$$= \frac{24\pi}{180} \text{ radians}$$

$$\approx 0.42 \text{ radians}$$

31. $72{,}000°, 400\pi$ **33.** -0.5

35. 3.549   **37.** -0.138

39. 528 in.²   **41.** $60°, \frac{\pi}{3}$

43. about 6.89 in.², about 0.76 in.², about 0.46 in.²

45. yes; When the arc length is equal to the radius, the equation $s = r\theta$ shows that $\theta = 1$ and $A = \frac{1}{2}r^2\theta$ is equivalent to $A = \frac{s^2}{2}$ for $r = s$ and $\theta = 1$.

47. a. $70°33'$

    b. $110.76°$; $110 + \frac{45}{60} + \frac{30}{3600} \approx 110.76°$

8.2 Maintaining Mathematical Proficiency (p. 424)

49. about 27.02   **51.** about 18.68

8.3 Vocabulary and Core Concept Check (p. 430)

1. quadrantal angle

8.3 Monitoring Progress and Modeling with Mathematics (pp. 430–432)

3. $\sin\theta = -\frac{3}{5}$, $\cos\theta = \frac{4}{5}$, $\tan\theta = -\frac{3}{4}$, $\csc\theta = -\frac{5}{3}$, $\sec\theta = \frac{5}{4}$, $\cot\theta = -\frac{4}{3}$

5. $\sin\theta = -\frac{4}{5}$, $\cos\theta = -\frac{3}{5}$, $\tan\theta = \frac{4}{3}$, $\csc\theta = -\frac{5}{4}$, $\sec\theta = -\frac{5}{3}$, $\cot\theta = \frac{3}{4}$

7. $\sin\theta = -\frac{3}{5}$, $\cos\theta = -\frac{4}{5}$, $\tan\theta = \frac{3}{4}$, $\csc\theta = -\frac{5}{3}$, $\sec\theta = -\frac{5}{4}$, $\cot\theta = \frac{4}{3}$

9. $\sin\theta = 0$, $\cos\theta = 1$, $\tan\theta = 0$, $\csc\theta = $ undefined, $\sec\theta = 1$, $\cot\theta = $ undefined

11. $\sin\theta = 1$, $\cos\theta = 0$, $\tan\theta = $ undefined, $\csc\theta = 1$, $\sec\theta = $ undefined, $\cot\theta = 0$

13. $\sin\theta = 1$, $\cos\theta = 0$, $\tan\theta = $ undefined, $\csc\theta = 1$, $\sec\theta = $ undefined, $\cot\theta = 0$

15.
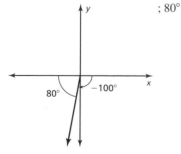
; 80°

17.
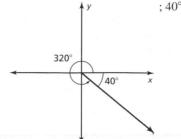
; 40°

19.
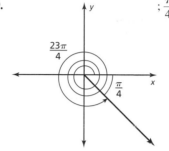
; $\frac{\pi}{4}$

21.
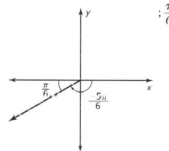
; $\frac{\pi}{6}$

23. The equation for tangent is $\tan\theta = \frac{y}{x}$; $\tan\theta = \frac{y}{x} = -\frac{2}{3}$

25. $-\sqrt{2}$ **27.** $-\frac{1}{2}$

29. 1   **31.** $\frac{\sqrt{2}}{2}$

33. 65 ft   **35.** about 16.5 ft/sec

37. about 10.7 ft

39. a.

Angle of sprinkler, θ	Horizontal distance water travels, d
30°	16.9
35°	18.4
40°	19.2
45°	19.5
50°	19.2
55°	18.4
60°	16.9

    b. 45°; Because $\frac{v^2}{32}$ is constant in this situation, the maximum distance traveled will occur when $\sin 2\theta$ is as large as possible. The maximum value of $\sin 2\theta$ occurs when $2\theta = 90°$, that is, when $\theta = 45°$.

    c. The distances are the same.

41.

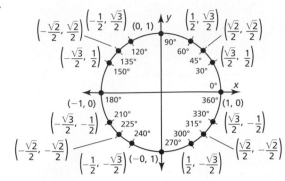

43. $\tan \theta = \dfrac{\sin \theta}{\cos \theta}$; $\sin 90° = 1$ and $\cos 90° = 0$, so $\tan 90°$ is

undefined because you cannot divide by 0, but

$\cot 90° = \dfrac{0}{1} = 0$.

45. $m = \tan \theta$

47. **a.** $(-58.1, 114)$

   b. about 218 pm

8.3 Maintaining Mathematical Proficiency *(p. 432)*

49. $x = -3$ and $x = 1$

51.

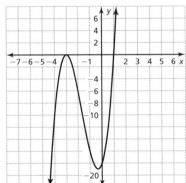

53.

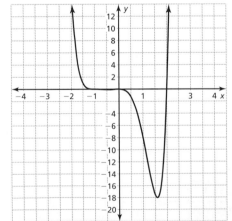

8.4 Vocabulary and Core Concept Check *(p. 441)*

1. cycle

3. A phase shift is a horizontal translation of a periodic

function; *Sample answer:* $y = \sin\left(x - \dfrac{\pi}{2}\right)$

8.4 Monitoring Progress and Modeling with Mathematics *(pp. 441–444)*

5. yes; 2   **7.** no

9. $1, 6\pi$ **11.** $4, \pi$

13. $3, 2\pi$; The graph of g is a vertical stretch by a factor of 3 of
the graph of $f(x) = \sin x$.

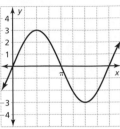

15. $1, \dfrac{2\pi}{3}$; The graph of g is a horizontal shrink by a factor of $\dfrac{1}{3}$
of the graph of $f(x) = \cos x$.

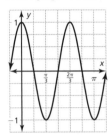

17. $1, 1$; The graph of g is a horizontal shrink by a factor of $\dfrac{1}{2\pi}$

of the graph of $f(x) = \sin x$.

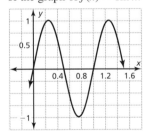

19. $\dfrac{1}{3}, \dfrac{\pi}{2}$; The graph of g is a horizontal shrink by a factor of $\dfrac{1}{4}$

and a vertical shrink by a factor of $\dfrac{1}{3}$ of the graph of
$f(x) = \cos x$.

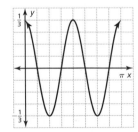

21. B, D

23. The period is $\frac{1}{4}$ and represents the amount of time, in seconds, that it takes for the pendulum to go back and forth and return to the same position. The amplitude is 4 and represents the maximum distance, in inches, the pendulum will be from its resting position.

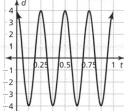

25.

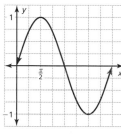

27.

29.

31.

33.

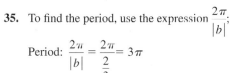

35. To find the period, use the expression $\frac{2\pi}{|b|}$;

Period: $\frac{2\pi}{|b|} = \frac{2\pi}{\frac{2}{3}} = 3\pi$

37. The graph of g is a vertical stretch by a factor of 2 followed by a translation $\frac{\pi}{2}$ units right and 1 unit up of the graph of f.

39. The graph of g is a horizontal shrink by a factor of $\frac{1}{3}$ followed by a translation 3π units left and 5 units down of the graph of f.

41.

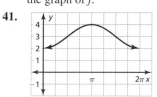

43.

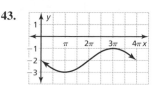

45.

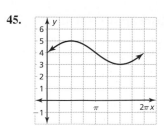

47.

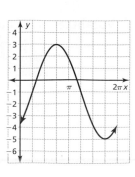

49. A

51. $g(x) = 3\sin(x - \pi) + 2$

53. $g(x) = -\frac{1}{3}\cos \pi x - 1$

55.

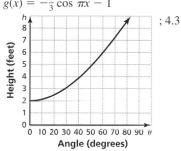

; 4.3

57. days 205 and 328; When the function is graphed with the line $y = 10$, the two points of intersection are (205.5, 10) and (328.7, 10).

59. **a.** about -1.27

b. about 0.64

c. about 0.64

61. **a.**

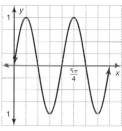

b. 4.5

c. 175 ft, 5 ft

63. The x-intercepts occur when $x = \pm\frac{\pi}{4}, \pm\frac{3\pi}{4}, \pm\frac{5\pi}{4}, \dots$

Sample answer: The x-intercepts can be represented by the expression $(2n + 1)\frac{\pi}{4}$, where n is an integer.

65. The graph of $g(x) = \cos x$ is a translation $\frac{\pi}{2}$ units to the right of the graph of $f(x) = \sin x$.

67. 80 beats per minute

8.4 Maintaining Mathematical Proficiency (p. 444)

69. $x - 2, x \neq -3$

71. $\frac{(x - 5)(x + 1)}{(x + 5)(x - 1)}$

73. $2x(x - 5)$

75. $(x + 6)(x + 2)$

8.5 Vocabulary and Core Concept Check (p. 450)

1. The graphs of the tangent, cotangent, secant and cosecant functions have no amplitude because the ranges do not have minimum or maximum values.

3. $2\pi; \pi$

8.5 Monitoring Progress and Modeling with Mathematics (pp. 450–452)

5.

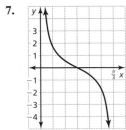

The graph of g is a vertical stretch by a factor of 2 of the graph of $f(x) = \tan x$.

7.

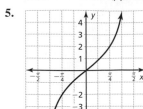

The graph of g is a horizontal shrink by a factor of $\frac{1}{3}$ of the graph of $f(x) = \cot x$.

9.

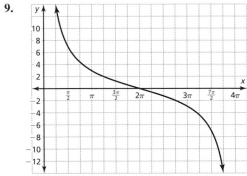

The graph of g is a horizontal stretch by a factor of 4 and a vertical stretch by a factor of 3 of the graph of $f(x) = \cot x$.

11.

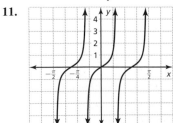

The graph of g is a horizontal shrink by a factor of $\frac{1}{\pi}$ and a vertical shrink by a factor of $\frac{1}{2}$ of the graph of $f(x) = \tan x$.

13. To find the period, use the expression $\frac{\pi}{|b|}$; Period: $\frac{\pi}{|b|} = \frac{\pi}{3}$

15. a.

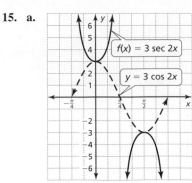

b.

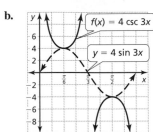

17.

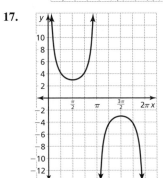

The graph of g is a vertical stretch by a factor of 3 of the graph of $f(x) = \csc x$.

19.

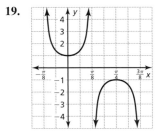

The graph of g is a horizontal shrink by a factor of $\frac{1}{4}$ of the graph of $f(x) = \sec x$.

21.

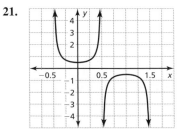

The graph of g is a horizontal shrink by a factor of $\frac{1}{\pi}$ and a vertical shrink by a factor of $\frac{1}{2}$ of the graph of $f(x) = \sec x$.

23.

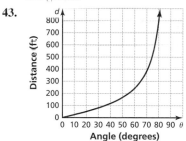

The graph of g is a horizontal stretch by a factor of $\frac{2}{\pi}$ of the graph of $f(x) = \csc x$.

25. $y = 6 \tan x$ **27.** $y = 2 \tan \pi x$

29. B; The parent function is the tangent function and the graph has an asymptote at $x = \frac{\pi}{2}$.

30. C; The parent function is the cotangent function and the graph has an asymptote at $x = 0$.

31. D; The parent function is the cosecant function and the graph has an asymptote at $x = 1$.

32. F; The parent function is the secant function and the graph has an asymptote at $x = -\frac{1}{2}$.

33. A; The parent function is the secant function and the graph has an asymptote at $x = \frac{\pi}{4}$.

34. E; The parent function is the cosecant function and the graph has an asymptote at $x = \frac{\pi}{2}$.

35. The tangent function that passes through the origin and has asymptotes at $x = \pi$ and $x = -\pi$ can be stretched or shrunk vertically to create more tangent functions with the same characteristics.

37. $g(x) = \cot\left(2x + \frac{\pi}{2}\right) + 3$ **39.** $g(x) = -5 \sec(x - \pi) + 2$

41. Function B has a local maximum value of -5 so Function A's local maximum value of $-\frac{1}{4}$ is greater. Function A has a local minimum of $\frac{1}{4}$ so Function B's local minimum value of 5 is greater.

43.

As d increases, θ increases because, as the car gets farther away, the angle required to see the car gets larger.

45. a. $d = 260 - 120 \tan \theta$

b.

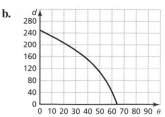

The graph shows a negative correlation meaning that as the angle gets larger, the distance from your friend to the top of the building gets smaller. As the angle gets smaller, the distance from your friend to the top of the building gets larger.

47. no; The graph of cosecant can be translated $\frac{\pi}{2}$ units right to create the same graph as $y = \sec x$.

49. $a \sec bx = \dfrac{a}{\cos bx}$

Because the cosine function is at most 1, $y = a \cos bx$ will produce a maximum when $\cos bx = 1$ and $y = a \sec bx$ will produce a minimum. When $\cos bx = -1$, $y = a \cos bx$ will produce a minimum and $y = a \sec bx$ will produce a maximum.

51. *Sample answer:* $y = 5 \tan\left(\frac{1}{2}x - \frac{3\pi}{4}\right)$

8.5 Maintaining Mathematical Proficiency *(p. 452)*

53. $y = -x^3 + 2x^2 + 5x - 6$ **55.** $y = \frac{1}{5}x^3 + \frac{1}{5}x^2 - \frac{9}{5}x - \frac{9}{5}$

57. $3, \pi$

8.6 Vocabulary and Core Concept Check *(p. 458)*

1. sinusoids

8.6 Monitoring Progress and Modeling with Mathematics *(pp. 458–460)*

3. $\dfrac{1}{2\pi}$ **5.** $\dfrac{2}{\pi}$

7. $\dfrac{3}{2}$ **9.** $\dfrac{3}{8\pi}$

11. $P = 0.02 \sin 40\pi t$

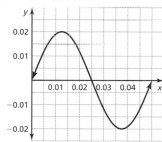

13. $y = 3 \sin 2x$ **15.** $y = -2 \cos \frac{\pi}{2}(x + 4)$

17. To find the amplitude, take half of the difference between the maximum and the minimum; $\dfrac{10 - (-6)}{2} = 8$

19. $h = -2.5 \cos \pi t + 6.5$

21. $D = 19.81 \sin(0.549t - 2.40) + 79.8$; The period of the graph represents the amount of time it takes for the weather to repeat its cycle, which is about 11.4 months.

23. $V = 100 \sin 4\pi t$

25. a. $N = 3.68 \sin(0.776t - 0.70) + 20.4$

    b. about 23,100 employees

27. a. and b. A cosine function because it does not require determining a horizontal shift.

    c. A sine function because it does not require determining a horizontal shift.

29. $y = 2.5 \sin 4\left(x - \dfrac{\pi}{8}\right) + 5.5,\ y = -2.5 \cos 4x + 5.5$

31. a. $d = -6.5 \cos \dfrac{\pi}{6}t + 10$

    b. low tide: 12:00 A.M., 12:00 P.M., high tide: 6:00 A.M., 6:00 P.M.

    c. It is a horizontal shift to the left by 3.

8.6 Maintaining Mathematical Proficiency (p. 460)

33. $\dfrac{6 + 3\sqrt{6}}{2}$

35. $\dfrac{13\sqrt{11} - 13\sqrt{3}}{8}$

37. $\ln 2 + \ln x$

39. $\ln 4 + 6 \ln x - \ln y$

Chapter 8 Review (pp. 462–464)

1. $\sin \theta = \dfrac{\sqrt{85}}{11},\ \tan \theta = \dfrac{\sqrt{85}}{6},\ \csc \theta = \dfrac{11\sqrt{85}}{85},\ \sec \theta = \dfrac{11}{6},$

    $\cot \theta = \dfrac{6\sqrt{85}}{85}$

2. about 15 ft

3. $22°;\ -338°$

4. $\dfrac{\pi}{6}$

5. $\dfrac{5\pi}{4}$

6. $135°$

7. $300°$

8.

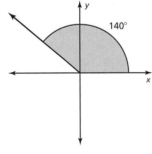

    about 1497 m²

9. $\sin \theta = 1,\ \cos \theta = 0,\ \tan \theta =$ undefined, $\csc \theta = 1,$ $\sec \theta =$ undefined, $\cot \theta = 0$

10. $\sin \theta = -\dfrac{7}{25},\ \cos \theta = \dfrac{24}{25},\ \tan \theta = -\dfrac{7}{24},\ \csc \theta = -\dfrac{25}{7},$ $\sec \theta = \dfrac{25}{24},\ \cot \theta = -\dfrac{24}{7}$

11. $\sin \theta = \dfrac{3\sqrt{13}}{13},\ \cos \theta = -\dfrac{2\sqrt{13}}{13},\ \tan \theta = -\dfrac{3}{2},\ \csc \theta = \dfrac{\sqrt{13}}{3},$ $\sec \theta = -\dfrac{\sqrt{13}}{2},\ \cot \theta = -\dfrac{2}{3}$

12. $-\dfrac{\sqrt{3}}{3}$

13. $\sqrt{2}$

14. $\dfrac{1}{2}$

15. 2

16. $8, 2\pi$; The graph of g is a vertical stretch by a factor of 8 of the graph of $f(x) = \cos x$;

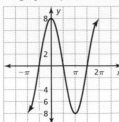

17. $6, 2$; The graph of g is a horizontal shrink by a factor of $\dfrac{1}{\pi}$ and a vertical stretch by a factor of 6 of the graph of $f(x) = \sin x$;

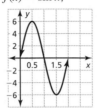

18. $\dfrac{1}{4}, \dfrac{\pi}{2}$; The graph of g is a horizontal shrink by a factor of $\dfrac{1}{4}$ and a vertical shrink by a factor of $\dfrac{1}{4}$ of the graph of $f(x) = \cos x$;

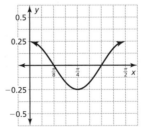

19.

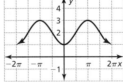

20.

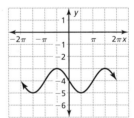

21.

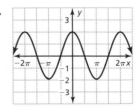

22.

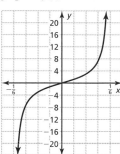

The graph of g is a vertical stretch by a factor of 2 of the graph of $f(x) = \cot x$.

23.

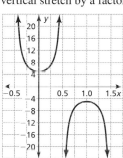

The graph of g is a horizontal shrink by a factor of $\dfrac{1}{3\pi}$ and a vertical stretch by a factor of 4 of the graph of $f(x) = \tan x$.

24.

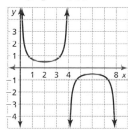

25.

26. *Sample answer:* $y = -\sin \frac{1}{2}x$

27. *Sample answer:* $y = \cos \pi x - 2$

Chapter 9

Chapter 9 Maintaining Mathematical Proficiency *(p. 469)*

1. $x = 3.4$
2. $x = 0.25$
3. $x = 9.625$
4. $x = -\dfrac{19}{12}$
5. $x = -6$ and $x = 6$
6. $x = -20$ and $x = 20$
7. $A = 17°$, $a \approx 2.63$, and $b \approx 8.61$
8. $A = 55°$, $b \approx 8.40$, and $c \approx 14.65$
9. $B = 48°$, $a \approx 10.71$, and $b \approx 11.89$
10. $B = 61°$, $a \approx 22.45$, and $c \approx 46.31$
11. yes; *Sample answer:* Draw a right triangle with acute angle A, opposite leg x, and adjacent leg y. The hypotenuse is $\sqrt{x^2 + y^2}$, so $\sec A = \dfrac{\sqrt{x^2 + y^2}}{y}$.

9.1 Vocabulary and Core Concept Check *(p. 475)*

1. A trigonometric equation is true for some values of a variable but a trigonometric identity is true for all values of the variable for which both sides of the equation are defined.

9.1 Monitoring Progress and Modeling with Mathematics *(pp. 475–476)*

3. $\cos \theta = \dfrac{2\sqrt{2}}{3}$, $\tan \theta = \dfrac{\sqrt{2}}{4}$, $\csc \theta = 3$, $\sec \theta = \dfrac{3\sqrt{2}}{4}$, $\cot \theta = 2\sqrt{2}$

5. $\sin \theta = \dfrac{3\sqrt{58}}{58}$, $\cos \theta = -\dfrac{7\sqrt{58}}{58}$, $\csc \theta = \dfrac{\sqrt{58}}{3}$, $\sec \theta = -\dfrac{\sqrt{58}}{7}$, $\cot \theta = -\dfrac{7}{3}$

7. $\sin \theta = -\dfrac{\sqrt{11}}{6}$, $\tan \theta = \dfrac{\sqrt{11}}{5}$, $\csc \theta = -\dfrac{6\sqrt{11}}{11}$, $\sec \theta = -\dfrac{6}{5}$, $\cot \theta = \dfrac{5\sqrt{11}}{11}$

9. $\sin \theta = -\dfrac{\sqrt{10}}{10}$, $\cos \theta = \dfrac{3\sqrt{10}}{10}$, $\tan \theta = -\dfrac{1}{3}$, $\csc \theta = -\sqrt{10}$, $\sec \theta = \dfrac{\sqrt{10}}{3}$

11. $\cos x$
13. $-\tan \theta$
15. $\cos x$
17. $-\csc x$
19. $-\sec x$
21. 1
23. $\sin^2 \theta = 1 - \cos^2 \theta$;
$1 - \sin^2 \theta = 1 - (1 - \cos^2 \theta) = 1 - 1 + \cos^2 \theta = \cos^2 \theta$

25. $\sin x \csc x = \sin x \cdot \dfrac{1}{\sin x}$
$= 1$

27. $\cos\left(\dfrac{\pi}{2} - x\right) \cot x = \sin x \cdot \dfrac{\cos x}{\sin x}$
$= \cos x$

29. $\dfrac{\cos\left(\dfrac{\pi}{2} - \theta\right) + 1}{1 - \sin(-\theta)} = \dfrac{\sin \theta + 1}{1 - \sin(-\theta)}$
$= \dfrac{\sin \theta + 1}{1 - (-\sin \theta)}$
$= \dfrac{\sin \theta + 1}{1 + \sin \theta}$
$= 1$

31. $\dfrac{1 + \cos x}{\sin x} + \dfrac{\sin x}{1 + \cos x} = \dfrac{1 + \cos x}{\sin x} + \dfrac{\sin x(1 - \cos x)}{(1 + \cos x)(1 - \cos x)}$
$= \dfrac{1 + \cos x}{\sin x} + \dfrac{\sin x(1 - \cos x)}{1 - \cos^2 x}$
$= \dfrac{1 + \cos x}{\sin x} + \dfrac{\sin x(1 - \cos x)}{\sin^2 x}$
$= \dfrac{\sin x(1 + \cos x)}{\sin^2 x} + \dfrac{\sin x(1 - \cos x)}{\sin^2 x}$
$= \dfrac{\sin x(1 + \cos x) + \sin x(1 - \cos x)}{\sin^2 x}$
$= \dfrac{\sin x(1 + \cos x + 1 - \cos x)}{\sin^2 x}$
$= \dfrac{\sin x(2)}{\sin^2 x}$
$= \dfrac{2}{\sin x}$
$= 2 \csc x$

33. $\dfrac{2 \sin \theta + \csc(-\theta)}{1 - \cot^2 \theta} = \dfrac{2 \sin \theta - \dfrac{1}{\sin \theta}}{1 - \dfrac{\cos^2 \theta}{\sin^2 \theta}}$

$= \dfrac{2 \sin \theta - \dfrac{1}{\sin \theta}}{1 - \dfrac{\cos^2 \theta}{\sin^2 \theta}} \cdot \dfrac{\sin^2 \theta}{\sin^2 \theta}$

$= \dfrac{2 \sin^3 \theta - \sin \theta}{\sin^2 \theta - \cos^2 \theta}$

$= \dfrac{2 \sin^3 \theta - \sin \theta}{\sin^2 \theta - (1 - \sin^2 \theta)}$

$= \dfrac{\sin \theta(2 \sin^2 \theta - 1)}{2 \sin^2 \theta - 1}$

$= \sin \theta$

35. $\sin x, \csc x, \tan x, \cot x; \cos x, \sec x;$

$\sin(-\theta) = -\sin \theta$

$\csc(-\theta) = \dfrac{1}{\sin(-\theta)} = -\dfrac{1}{\sin \theta} = -\csc \theta$

$\tan(-\theta) = -\tan \theta$

$\cot(-\theta) = \dfrac{1}{\tan(-\theta)} = -\dfrac{1}{\tan \theta} = -\cot \theta$

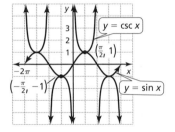

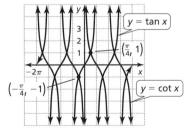

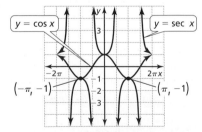

37. yes; $\sec x \tan x - \sin x = \dfrac{1}{\cos x} \cdot \dfrac{\sin x}{\cos x} - \sin x$

$= \dfrac{\sin x}{\cos^2 x} - \sin x$

$= \sec^2 x \sin x - \sin x$

$= \sin x(\sec^2 x - 1)$

$= \sin x \tan^2 x$

39. $s = \dfrac{h \sin(90° - \theta)}{\sin \theta}$

$s = \dfrac{h \cos \theta}{\sin \theta}$

$s = h \cot \theta$

41. a. $u = \tan \theta$

   b. u starts at 0 and increases without bound.

43. You can obtain the graph of $y = \cos x$ by reflecting the graph of $f(x) = \sin x$ in the y-axis and translating it $\dfrac{\pi}{2}$ units right.

9.1 Maintaining Mathematical Proficiency *(p. 476)*

45. $\frac{1}{2}$ **47.** $\sqrt{2}$

49. The graph of g is a vertical stretch by a factor of 3 and a horizontal shrink by a factor of $\frac{1}{4}$ followed by a translation 1 unit down of the graph of f.

9.2 Vocabulary and Core Concept Check *(p. 481)*

1. $\cos 170°$

9.2 Monitoring Progress and Modeling with Mathematics *(pp. 481–482)*

3. $\sqrt{3} - 2$ **5.** $\dfrac{\sqrt{2} - \sqrt{6}}{4}$

7. $\dfrac{\sqrt{2} - \sqrt{6}}{4}$ **9.** $\sqrt{3} + 2$

11. $-\dfrac{36}{85}$ **13.** $-\dfrac{13}{85}$

15. $-\dfrac{36}{77}$ **17.** $\tan x$

19. $\cos x$ **21.** $\cos x$

23. The sign in the denominator should be negative when using the sum formula;

$\dfrac{\tan x + \tan \dfrac{\pi}{4}}{1 - \tan x \tan \dfrac{\pi}{4}} = \dfrac{\tan x + 1}{1 - \tan x}$

25. B, D   **27.** $x = \dfrac{\pi}{3}, \dfrac{5\pi}{3}$

29. $x = \dfrac{3\pi}{2}$ **31.** $x = 0, \pi$

33. $\sin\left(\dfrac{\pi}{2} - \theta\right) = \sin \dfrac{\pi}{2} \cos \theta - \cos \dfrac{\pi}{2} \sin \theta$

$= (1) \cos \theta - (0) \sin \theta$

$= \cos \theta$

35. $\dfrac{35 \tan(\theta - 45°) + 35 \tan 45°}{h \tan \theta}$

$= \dfrac{35\left(\dfrac{\tan \theta - \tan 45°}{1 + \tan \theta \tan 45°}\right) + 35 \tan 45°}{h \tan \theta}$

$= \dfrac{35\left(\dfrac{\tan \theta - 1}{1 + \tan \theta}\right) + 35}{h \tan \theta}$

$= \dfrac{35(\tan \theta - 1) + 35(1 + \tan \theta)}{h \tan \theta(1 + \tan \theta)}$

$= \dfrac{35 \tan \theta - 35 + 35 + 35 \tan \theta}{h \tan \theta(1 + \tan \theta)}$

$= \dfrac{70 \tan \theta}{h \tan \theta(1 + \tan \theta)}$

$= \dfrac{70}{h(1 + \tan \theta)}$

37. $y_1 + y_2 = \cos 960\pi t + \cos 1240\pi t$

$= \cos(1100\pi t - 140\pi t) + \cos(1100\pi t + 140\pi t)$

$= \cos 1100\pi t \cos 140\pi t + \sin 1100\pi t \sin 140\pi t$

$\quad + \cos 1100\pi t \cos 140\pi t - \sin 1100\pi t \sin 140\pi t$

$= \cos 1100\pi t \cos 140\pi t + \cos 1100\pi t \cos 140\pi t$

$= 2 \cos 1100\pi t \cos 140\pi t$

39. a. $\tan(\theta_2 - \theta_1) = \dfrac{m_2 - m_1}{1 + m_2 m_1}$

   b. $60°$

9.2 Maintaining Mathematical Proficiency *(p. 482)*

41. $x = 4$ **43.** $x = -\frac{2}{3}$

9.3 Vocabulary and Core Concept Check *(p. 490)*

1. the measures of two angles and the length of any side (AAS or ASA cases), or the lengths of two sides and the measure of an angle opposite one of the two sides (SSA case)

9.3 Monitoring Progress and Modeling with Mathematics *(pp. 490–492)*

3. about 0.7986   **5.** about -0.7547

7. about -0.2679 **9.** about 81.8 square units

11. about 147.3 square units   **13.** SSA; one triangle

15. SSA; two triangles   **17.** SSA; no triangle

19. $A = 48°, b = 25.5, c = 18.7$

21. $B = 66°, a \approx 14.3, b \approx 24.0$

23. $A \approx 80.9°, C \approx 43.1°, a \approx 20.2$

25. $C = 88°, a \approx 6.1, c \approx 15.1$

27. $B \approx 33.1°, C \approx 91.9°, c \approx 14.6$

29. no solution

31. Two solutions:

$B \approx 86.5°, C \approx 18.5°, c \approx 4.9$

$B \approx 93.5°, C \approx 11.5°, c \approx 3.1$

33. $B \approx 46.7°, C \approx 25.3°, c \approx 4.6$

35. The area should be multiplied by $\frac{1}{2}$; Area $= \frac{1}{2}bc \sin A \approx 18.4$

37. Law of Sines; given two angle measures and the length of a side; $C = 64°, a \approx 19.2, c \approx 18.1$

39. Pythagorean Theorem and trigonometric functions; given the length of the legs of a right triangle; $b \approx 16.2, A \approx 68.2°, C \approx 21.8°$

41. Law of Sines; given two angle measures and the length of a side; $A = 50°, a \approx 10.9, b \approx 10.9$

43. Pythagorean Theorem and trigonometric functions; given the length of the legs of a right triangle; $a \approx 39.8, B \approx 28.5°, C \approx 61.5°$

45. a. yes; You are given the measure of two angles and the length of a side.

   b. yes; You can also use the Pythagorean Theorem and trigonometric functions to solve the triangle, because $\triangle XYZ$ is a right triangle.

47. about 5.1 mi

49. a.

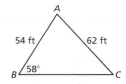

   b. $C \approx 47.6°, A \approx 74.4°, a \approx 70.4$ ft

   c. 9 bags

51. a. about 152.9 m

   b. Use the tangent function to find the distance from the ground to the top of the building, and then subtract the height of the cliff from this distance. Or, use the Pythagorean Theorem to find the hypotenuse of the triangle used in part (a). Then, subtract 63° from 72° to find the measure of the angle between the two lines of sight. Find the angle of this triangle opposite of the hypotenuse using the rules of supplementary angles, and use the Law of Sines to solve the triangle formed by the building and the two lines of sight; about 170.4 ft

53. $x = 99, y \approx 20.1$

55. a.

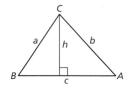

The formula for the area of $\triangle ABC$ with altitude h drawn from C to $\overline{AB}$ as shown is Area $= \frac{1}{2}ch$. Because $\sin A = \dfrac{h}{b}, h = b \sin A$. By substituting, you get

Area $= \frac{1}{2}c(b \sin A) = \frac{1}{2}bc \sin A$.

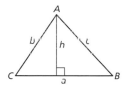

The formula for the area of $\triangle ABC$ with altitude h drawn from A to $\overline{BC}$ as shown is Area $= \frac{1}{2}ah$. Because $\sin B = \dfrac{h}{c}, h = c \sin B$. By substituting, you get

Area $= \frac{1}{2}a(c \sin B) = \frac{1}{2}ac \sin B$. See Exercise 54 for

Area $= \frac{1}{2}ab \sin C$.

   b. They are all expressions for the area of the same triangle, so they are all equal to each other by the Transitive Property.

   c. By the Multiplication Property of Equality, multiply all three expressions by 2 to get $bc \sin A = ac \sin B = ab \sin C$. By the Division Property of Equality, divide all three expressions by abc to get $\dfrac{\sin A}{a} = \dfrac{\sin B}{b} = \dfrac{\sin C}{c}$.

9.3 Maintaining Mathematical Proficiency *(p. 492)*

57. about 0.7431   **59.** about 1.2361

61. $x = 8$ **63.** $x = 31$

9.4 Vocabulary and Core Concept Check *(p. 497)*

1. the lengths of two sides and the measure of the included angle (SAS case), or the lengths of all three sides (SSS case)

9.4 Monitoring Progress and Modeling with Mathematics (pp. 497–498)

3. $a \approx 5.2$, $B \approx 50.5°$, $C \approx 94.5°$

5. $A \approx 81.1°$, $B \approx 65.3°$, $C \approx 33.6°$

7. $b \approx 35.8$, $A \approx 46.2°$, $C \approx 70.8°$

9. $A \approx 41.8°$, $B \approx 48.6°$, $C \approx 89.6°$

11. $b \approx 16.6$, $A \approx 10.7°$, $C \approx 15.3°$

13. about 10.7 ft   **15.** about 89.0 square units

17. about 189.9 square units

19. The denominator of the fraction should be $-2bc$, not $-2ab$;

$$\cos A = \frac{19^2 - 21^2 - 11^2}{-2(21)(11)}, A \approx 64.2°$$

21. $c^2 = a^2 + b^2$

23. Because the triangle is equilateral, we can say $a = b = c = x$. So, the Law of Cosines is $x^2 = x^2 + x^2 - 2(x)(x) \cos X$ for all of the angles. By the Subtraction Property of Equality, $0 = x^2 - 2x^2 \cos X$. Then, by the Addition Property of Equality, $2x^2 \cos X = x^2$. By the Division Property of Equality, $2 \cos X = 1$, or $\cos X = \frac{1}{2}$. So, $X = \cos^{-1} \frac{1}{2} = 60°$. So, the measure of each angle of an equilateral triangle is 60°.

25. about 523.8 mi

9.4 Maintaining Mathematical Proficiency (p. 498)

27. 8, 9, 10, 11, 12, 13   **29.** 2, 9, 28, 65, 126, 217

Chapter 9 Review (pp. 500–502)

1. $\sin \theta = -\frac{15}{17}$, $\tan \theta = \frac{15}{8}$, $\csc \theta = -\frac{17}{15}$, $\sec \theta = -\frac{17}{8}$, $\cot \theta = \frac{8}{15}$

2. $\cos^2 x$ **3.** $\tan x$

4. $\sin x$

5. $\dfrac{\cos x \sec x}{1 + \tan^2 x} = \dfrac{\cos x \sec x}{\sec^2 x}$

$= \dfrac{\cos x}{\sec x}$

$= \cos x \cos x$

$= \cos^2 x$

6. $\tan\left(\dfrac{\pi}{2} - x\right) \cot x = \cot x \cot x$

$= \cot^2 x$

$= \csc^2 x - 1$

7. $-\dfrac{\sqrt{6} - \sqrt{2}}{4}$ **8.** $2 + \sqrt{3}$

9. $-\dfrac{\sqrt{6} - \sqrt{2}}{4}$ **10.** $\dfrac{19}{25}$

11. $x = \dfrac{3\pi}{4}, -\dfrac{5\pi}{4}$ **12.** $x = 0, \pi$

13. about 41.0 square units   **14.** about 42.2 square units

15. $B \approx 24.3°$, $C \approx 43.7°$, $c \approx 6.7$

16. $C = 88°$, $a \approx 25.8$, $b \approx 49.5$

17. $A \approx 99.9°$, $B \approx 32.1°$, $a \approx 37.1$

18. $A = 35°$, $a \approx 12.3$, $c \approx 14.6$

19. $B = 74°$, $a \approx 4.0$, $c \approx 4.3$

20. Two solutions:

$A \approx 38.2°$, $C \approx 110.8°$, $c \approx 18.2$

$A \approx 141.8°$, $C \approx 7.2°$, $c \approx 2.4$

21. $b \approx 5.4$, $A \approx 141.4°$, $C \approx 13.6°$

22. $A \approx 42.6°$, $B \approx 11.7°$, $C \approx 125.7°$

23. about 329.1 square units   **24.** about 13.5 square units

Chapter 10

Chapter 10 Maintaining Mathematical Proficiency (p. 507)

1. about 77.2, 82.5, 82; median or mode; The mean is less than most of the data.

2. about 73.7, 70.5, 70; median or mode; The mean is greater than most of the data.

3. about 19.8, 16, 44; median; The mean and mode are both greater than most of the data.

4. about 3.85; The typical data value differs from the mean by about 3.85 units.

5. about 7.09; The typical data value differs from the mean by about 7.09 units.

6. 6.5; The typical data value differs from the mean by 6.5 units.

7. All the data values are the same; no; The formula for standard deviation includes taking only the positive square root.

10.1 Vocabulary and Core Concept Check (p. 514)

1. Find the value where row 1 and column 4 intersect.

10.1 Monitoring Progress and Modeling with Mathematics (pp. 514–516)

3. 50%   **5.** 2.5%

7. 0.16   **9.** 0.025

11. 0.68   **13.** 0.68

15. 0.975   **17.** 0.84

19. a. 81.5%

b. 0.15%

21. The values on the horizontal axis show a standard deviation of 1 instead of 2.

19 21 23 25 27 29 31

The probability that x is between 23 and 27 is 0.68.

23. 0.0548   **25.** no

27.

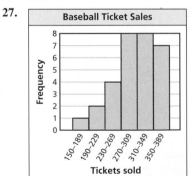

no; The histogram is skewed left, not bell-shaped.

29. a. about 4.52×10^{-9}

b. yes; The probability that a box contains an amount of cereal significantly less than the mean is very small.

31. one standard deviation above the mean

33. a. 88th percentile

b. 93rd percentile

c. ACT; Your percentile on the ACT was higher than your percentile on the SAT.

35. no; When the mean is greater than the median, the distribution is skewed right.

10.1 Maintaining Mathematical Proficiency (p. 516)

37.

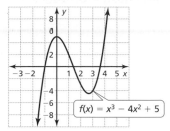

$f(x) = x^3 - 4x^2 + 5$

x-intercepts: -1, about 1.4, and about 3.6; local maximum: $(0, 5)$; local minimum: $(2.67, -4.48)$; increasing when $x < 0$ and $x > 2.67$; decreasing when $0 < x < 2.67$

39.

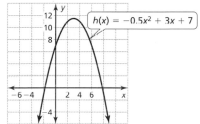

$h(x) = -0.5x^2 + 3x + 7$

x-intercepts: about -1.8 and about 7.8; maximum: $(3, 11.5)$; no local minimum; increasing when $x < 3$; decreasing when $x > 3$

10.2 Vocabulary and Core Concept Check (p. 521)

1. sample

3. a claim about a characteristic of a population

10.2 Monitoring Progress and Modeling with Mathematics (pp. 521–522)

5. population; Every high school student is counted.

7. sample; The survey is given to a subset of the population of spectators.

9. population: every adult age 18 and over in the United States, sample: the 1152 adults age 18 and over who were surveyed; The sample consists of 403 adults who pretend to use their smartphone to avoid talking to someone, and 749 adults who do not.

11. population: every high school student in the district, sample: the 1300 high school students in the district who were surveyed; The sample consists of 1001 high school students who like the new healthy cafeteria food choices, and 299 high school students who do not.

13. statistic; The average annual salary of a subset of the population was calculated.

15. parameter; The percentage of every student in the school was calculated.

17. The sample number in the statement is not the size of the entire sample; The population consists of all the students in the high school. The sample consists of the 1270 students that were surveyed.

19. a. The maker's claim is most likely true.

b. The maker's claim is most likely false.

21. possibly, but extremely unlikely; The result is unlikely to occur by chance. The sample size of the population is too small to make such a conclusion.

23. *Sample answer:* population: all American adults, sample: the 801 American adults surveyed; The sample consists of 606 American adults who say the world's temperature will go up over the next 100 years, 174 American adults who say it will go down, and 21 American adults who have no opinion.

25. simulation 2; Simulation 2 gives a better indication of outcomes that are not likely to occur by chance.

10.2 Maintaining Mathematical Proficiency (p. 522)

27. $x = 5 \pm \sqrt{29}$ or $x \approx 10.39$, $x \approx -0.39$

29. $s = -5 \pm \sqrt{17}$ or $s \approx -0.88$, $s \approx -9.12$

31. $z = \frac{1}{2}$, $z = -\frac{15}{2}$

10.3 Vocabulary and Core Concept Check (p. 528)

1. In a stratified sample, after the groups are formed, a random sample is selected from each group. In a cluster sample, after the groups are formed, all the members of one or more groups are randomly selected.

3. *Sample answer:* to determine how quickly an oil spill would spread through a lake

10.3 Monitoring Progress and Modeling with Mathematics (pp. 528–530)

5. convenience sample

7. systematic sample

9. convenience sample; Dog owners probably have a strong opinion about an off-leash area for dogs.

11. cluster sample; Booth holders in section 5 are likely to have a different opinion than booth holders in other sections about the location of their booth.

13. Not every survey that was mailed out will be returned, so it is not a systematic sample; Because households in the neighborhood can choose whether or not to return the survey, the sample is a self-selected sample.

15. no; The sample represents the population.

17. yes; Only customers with a strong opinion about their experience are likely to complete the survey.

19. *Sample answer:* Assign each student in the school a different integer from 1 to 1225. Generate 250 unique random integers from 1 to 1225 using the random number function in a spreadsheet program. Choose the 250 students who correspond to the 250 integers generated.

21. simulation   **23.** observational study

25. encourages a yes response; *Sample answer:* Reword the question, for example: Should the budget of our city be cut?

27. implies that the arsenic level is a health risk; *Sample answer:* Reword the question, for example: Do you think the government should address the issue of arsenic in tap water?

29. no; Responses to the question will accurately reflect the opinions of those being surveyed.

31. yes; Visitors are unlikely to admit to a police officer that they do not wear their seatbelt.

33. a. *Sample answer:* The researcher did not take into account previous heart conditions.

b. *Sample answer:* Divide the population into groups based on past heart conditions and whether or not they take fiber supplements. Select a random sample from each group.

35. self-selected sample and convenience sample; In a self-selected sample, only people with strong opinions are likely to respond. In a convenience sample, parts of the population have no chance of being selected for the survey.

37. a. to determine the employment rate of graduates in their field of study

b. all graduating seniors of the college

c. *Sample answer:* Are you employed? If yes, is your job in your field of study?

39. no; *Sample answer:* Some groups in the population, like the homeless, are difficult to contact.

41. a. self-selected sample

b. people who spend a lot of time on the Internet and visit that particular site; The survey is probably biased.

10.3 Maintaining Mathematical Proficiency *(p. 530)*

43. 9

45. $\frac{1}{4}$

47. $\dfrac{\sqrt[3]{18}}{18}$

49. 3

10.4 Vocabulary and Core Concept Check *(p. 537)*

1. replication

10.4 Monitoring Progress and Modeling with Mathematics *(pp. 537–538)*

3. The study is a randomized comparative experiment; The treatment is the drug for insomnia. The treatment group is the individuals who received the drug. The control group is the individuals who received the placebo.

5. The individuals who do not use either of the conditioners were not monitored; The control group is the individuals who use the regular conditioner.

7. observational study; *Sample answer:* Randomly choose one group of individuals who smoke. Then, randomly choose one group of individuals who do not smoke. Find the body mass index of the individuals in each group.

9. experiment; *Sample answer:* Randomly select the same number of strawberry plants to be put in each of two groups. Use the new fertilizer on the plants in one group, and use the regular fertilizer on plants in the other group. Keep all other variables constant and record the weight of the fruit produced by each plant.

11. a. *Sample answer:* Because the heart rates are monitored for two different types of exercise, the groups cannot be compared. Running on a treadmill may have a different effect on heart rate than lifting weights; Check the heart rates of all the athletes after the same type of exercise.

b. no potential problems

13. *Sample answer:* The sample size is not large enough to provide valid results; Increase the sample size.

15. no; Your friend would have to perform an observational study, and an observational study can show correlation, but not causality.

17. *Sample answer:* The placebo effect is response to a dummy treatment that may result from the trust in the researcher or the expectation of a cure; It can be minimized by comparing two groups so the placebo effect has the same effect on both groups.

19. yes; Repetition reduces the effect of unusual results that may occur by chance.

10.4 Maintaining Mathematical Proficiency *(p. 538)*

21.

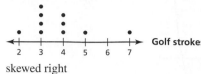

skewed right

23. exponential decay;

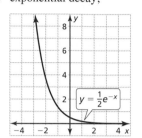

25. exponential growth;

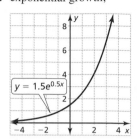

10.5 Vocabulary and Core Concept Check *(p. 544)*

1. margin of error

10.5 Monitoring Progress and Modeling with Mathematics *(pp. 544–546)*

3. 60.4

5. a. about 0.267

b. about 0.267

7. a. yes; The first 2 surveys show more than the 66.7% of votes needed to override the veto.

b. no; As the sample size increases, the percent of votes approaches 55.1%, which is not enough to override the veto.

9. a. The company's claim is probably accurate.

b. The company's claim is probably not accurate.

c. *Sample answer:* 0.42 to 0.68

11. about $\pm 6.2\%$

13. about $\pm 2.2\%$

15. about $\pm 1.7\%$

17. a. about $\pm 3.3\%$

b. between 37.7% and 44.3%

19. The wrong percentage was substituted in the formula; $\pm 0.04 = \pm \dfrac{1}{\sqrt{n}}$; $0.0016 = \dfrac{1}{n}$; $n = 625$

21. no; A sample size of 1 would have a margin of error of 100%.

23. about 453 residents

25. a. 500 voters

b. about $\pm 4.5\%$

c. candidate A: between 42.5% and 51.5%, candidate B: between 48.5% and 57.5%

d. no; 273 voters

27. more than 2500; To be confident that sports drink X is preferred, the margin of error would need to be less than 2%.

10.5 Maintaining Mathematical Proficiency (p. 546)

29. $y = \log_2(x + 5)$ **31.** $y = 6^{x+1}$

33. geometric; $a_n = 3(2)^{n-1}$

10.6 Vocabulary and Core Concept Check (p. 551)

1. resampling

10.6 Monitoring Progress and Modeling with Mathematics (pp. 551–552)

3. a. 46

   b. 40.125

   c. -5.875

   d.

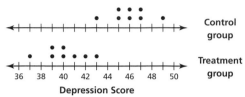

Depression Score

   e. The music therapy may be effective in reducing depression scores of college students.

5. The order of the subtraction is reversed;
$\bar{x}_{\text{treatment}} - \bar{x}_{\text{control}} = 11 - 16 = -5$; So, you can conclude the treatment decreases the score.

7. *Sample answer:* -1.75

9. The hypothesis is most likely false; Music therapy decreases depression scores.

11. The histogram in Exercise 9 has a roughly normal distribution and shows the mean differences from 200 resamplings. The histogram in Exercise 11 is random and shows the mean differences from 20 resamplings; the histogram in Exercise 9 because it uses a large number of resamplings and the roughly normal distribution suggests music therapy decreases depression scores

13. yes; As the number of samplings increase, the individual values should end up in each group approximately the same number of times, so the positive and negative differences in the means should balance out to 0.

15. 12,870; The number of combinations of 16 items in groups of 8 amounts to 12,870.

10.6 Maintaining Mathematical Proficiency (p. 552)

17. $(y - 2)(y^2 + 2y + 4)$

19. $(9w^2 + 4)(3w + 2)(3w - 2)$

21. yes; $g(x) = \dfrac{1}{2x} + \dfrac{1}{2}$ **23.** no; $y = \pm\sqrt{\dfrac{3}{x-1}}$

Chapter 10 Review (pp. 554–556)

1. 0.0015   **2.** 0.0082

3. population: all U.S. motorists, sample: the 1000 drivers surveyed

4. statistic; The mean was calculated from a sample.

5. The host's claim is most likely false.

6. stratified sample; not biased **7.** observational study

8. It encourages a yes response; *Sample answer:* Reword the question, for example: Should the city replace the police cars it is currently using?

9. experiment; *Sample answer:* Randomly select the same number of customers to give each type of bread to. Record how many customers from each group return.

10. *Sample answer:* The volunteers may not be representative of the population; Randomly select from members of the population for the study.

11. The study is a randomized comparative experiment; The treatment is using the new design of the car wash. The treatment group is the individuals who use the new design of the car wash. The control group is the individuals who use the old design of the car wash.

12. between 58.9% and 65.1%

13. no; As the sample size increases, the percent of votes approaches 46.8%, which is not enough to win.

14. *Sample answer:* Combine the measurements from both groups and assign a number to each value. Let the numbers 1 through 10 represent the data in the original control group, and let the numbers 11 through 20 represent the data in the original treatment group. Use a random number generator. Randomly generate 20 numbers from 1 through 20 without repeating a number. Use the first 10 numbers to make the new control group, and the next 10 to make the new treatment group; Repeatedly make new control and treatment groups and see how often you get differences between the new groups that are at least as large as the one you measured.

English-Spanish Glossary

English

Spanish

amplitude *(p. 436)* One-half the difference of the maximum value and the minimum value of the graph of a trigonometric function

amplitud *(p. 436)* La mitad de la diferencia del valor máximo y el valor mínimo del gráfico de una función trigonométrica

arithmetic sequence *(p. 366)* A sequence in which the difference of consecutive terms is constant

secuencia aritmética *(p. 366)* Una secuencia en la que la diferencia de términos consecutivos es constante

arithmetic series *(p. 368)* An expression formed by adding the terms of an arithmetic sequence

serie aritmética *(p. 368)* Una expresión formada al sumar los términos de una secuencia aritmética

axis of revolution *(p. 24)* The line around which a two-dimensional shape is rotated to form a three-dimensional figure

eje de revolución *(p. 24)* La recta alrededor de la cual una forma bidimensional rota para formar una figura tridimensional

axis of symmetry *(p. 82)* A line that divides a parabola into mirror images and passes through the vertex

eje de simetría *(p. 82)* Una recta que divide una parábola en imágenes reflejo y que pasa a través del vértice

bias *(p. 525)* An error that results in a misrepresentation of a population

sesgo *(p. 525)* Un error que da como resultado una representación errónea de una población

biased question *(p. 527)* A question that is flawed in a way that leads to inaccurate results

pregunta sesgada *(p. 527)* Una pregunta imperfecta que lleva a obtener resultados inexactos

biased sample *(p. 525)* A sample that overrepresents or underrepresents part of the population

muestra sesgada *(p. 525)* Una muestra que representa excesiva o insuficientemente parte de la población

Binomial Theorem *(p. 124)* For any positive integer n, the binomial expansion of $(a + b)^n$ is
$$(a + b)^n = {_nC_0}a^nb^0 + {_nC_1}a^{n-1}b^1 + {_nC_2}a^{n-2}b^2 + \cdots + {_nC_n}a^0b^n.$$

teorema del binomio *(p. 124)* Por cada número entero positivo n, la expansión del binomio de $(a + b)^n$ es
$$(a + b)^n = {_nC_0}a^nb^0 + {_nC_1}a^{n-1}b^1 + {_nC_2}a^{n-2}b^2 + \cdots + {_nC_n}a^0b^n.$$

central angle *(p. 420)* The angle measure of a sector of a circle formed by two radii

ángulo central *(p. 420)* La medida del ángulo de un sector de un círculo formado por dos radios

cluster sample *(p. 524)* A sample in which a population is divided into groups, called clusters, and all of the members in one or more of the clusters are randomly selected

muestra de cluster *(p. 524)* Una muestra en la que una población se divide en grupos, llamados cluster en inglés, y todos los miembros de uno o más de los cluster son seleccionados en forma aleatoria

common difference *(p. 366)* The constant difference d between consecutive terms of an arithmetic sequence

diferencia común *(p. 366)* La diferencia constante d entre términos consecutivos de una secuencia aritmética

common logarithm *(p. 259)* A logarithm with base 10, denoted as $\log_{10}$ or simply by log

logaritmo común *(p. 259)* Un logaritmo de base 10, denotado como $\log_{10}$ o simplemente como log

common ratio *(p. 374)* The constant ratio r between consecutive terms of a geometric sequence

complex conjugates *(p. 155)* Pairs of complex numbers of the forms $a + bi$ and $a - bi$, where $b \neq 0$

complex fraction *(p. 335)* A fraction that contains a fraction in its numerator or denominator

composite figure *(p. 2)* A figure that consists of triangles, squares, rectangles, and other two-dimensional figures

conjugate *(p. 202)* Binomials of the form $a\sqrt{b} + c\sqrt{d}$ and $a\sqrt{b} - c\sqrt{d}$, where a, b, c, and d are rational numbers

constant of variation *(p. 308)* The constant a in the inverse variation equation $y = \dfrac{a}{x}$, where $a \neq 0$

control group *(p. 534)* The group under ordinary conditions that is subjected to no treatment during an experiment

controlled experiment *(p. 534)* An experiment in which two groups are studied under identical conditions with the exception of one variable

convenience sample *(p. 524)* A sample in which only members of a population who are easy to reach are selected

correlation coefficient *(p. 59)* A number r from -1 to 1 that measures how well a line fits a set of data pairs (x, y)

cosecant *(p. 410)* A trigonometric function for an acute angle θ of a right triangle, denoted by
$$\csc \theta = \frac{\text{hypotenuse}}{\text{opposite}}$$

cosine *(p. 410)* A trigonometric function for an acute angle θ of a right triangle, denoted by
$$\cos \theta = \frac{\text{adjacent}}{\text{hypotenuse}}$$

cotangent *(p. 410)* A trigonometric function for an acute angle θ of a right triangle, denoted by
$$\cot \theta = \frac{\text{adjacent}}{\text{opposite}}$$

coterminal *(p. 419)* Two angles whose terminal sides coincide

cross multiplying *(p. 340)* A method used to solve a rational equation when each side of the equation is a single rational expression

razón común *(p. 374)* La razón constante r entre términos consecutivos de una secuencia geométrica

conjugados complejos *(p. 155)* Pares de números complejos de las formas $a + bi$ y $a - bi$, donde $b \neq 0$

fracción compleja *(p. 335)* Una fracción que contiene una fracción en su numerador o denominador

figura compuesta *(p. 2)* Una figura que se compone de triángulos, cuadrados, rectángulos, y otras figureas de dos dimensiones

conjugado *(p. 202)* Binomios de la forma $a\sqrt{b} + c\sqrt{d}$ y $a\sqrt{b} - c\sqrt{d}$, donde a, b, c y d son números racionales

constante de variación *(p. 308)* La constante a en la ecuación de variación inversa $y = \dfrac{a}{x}$, donde $a \neq 0$

grupo de control *(p. 534)* El grupo bajo condiciones ordinarias, que no se ve sometido a tratamiento durante un experimento

experimento controlado *(p. 534)* Un experimento en el que dos grupos son estudiados bajo condiciones idénticas, con la excepción de una variable

muestra de conveniencia *(p. 524)* Una muestra en la que únicamente se seleccionan los miembros de una población a los que es fácil de llegar

coeficiente de correlación *(p. 59)* Un número r de -1 a 1 que mide cuán bien ajusta una recta a un conjunto de pares de datos (x, y)

cosecante *(p. 410)* Una ecuación trigonométrica de un ángulo agudo θ de un triángulo recto, denotado por
$$\csc \theta = \frac{\text{hipotenusa}}{\text{opuesto}}$$

coseno *(p. 410)* Una ecuación trigonométrica de un ángulo agudo θ de un triángulo recto, denotado por
$$\cos \theta = \frac{\text{adyacente}}{\text{hipotenusa}}$$

cotangente *(p. 410)* Una ecuación trigonométrica de un ángulo agudo θ de un triángulo recto, denotado por
$$\cot \theta = \frac{\text{adyacente}}{\text{opuesto}}$$

coterminal *(p. 419)* Dos ángulos cuyos lados terminales coinciden

multiplicación cruzada *(p. 340)* Un método utilizado para resolver una ecuación racional cuando cada lado de la ecuación es una sola expresión racional

cross section *(p. 18)* The intersection of a plane and a solid

cycle *(p. 436)* The shortest repeating portion of the graph of a periodic function

sección transversal *(p. 18)* La intersección de un plano y un sólido

ciclo *(p. 436)* La porción más corta que se repite en el gráfico de una función periódica

D

density *(p. 10)* The amount of matter that an object has in a given unit of volume

descriptive statistics *(p. 540)* The branch of statistics that involves the organization, summarization, and display of data

densidad *(p. 10)* La cantidad de materia que tiene un objeto en una unidad de volumen dada

estadística descriptiva *(p. 540)* La rama de la estadística que implica la organización, resumen y presentación de datos

E

end behavior *(p. 113)* The behavior of the graph of a function as x approaches positive infinity or negative infinity

even function *(p. 171)* For a function f, $f(-x) = f(x)$ for all x in its domain

experiment *(p. 526)* A method that imposes a treatment on individuals in order to collect data on their response to the treatment

explicit rule *(p. 390)* A rule that gives a_n as a function of the term's position number n in the sequence

exponential equations *(p. 282)* Equations in which variable expressions occur as exponents

extraneous solutions *(p. 219)* Solutions that are not solutions of the original equation

comportamiento final *(p. 113)* El comportamiento del gráfico de una función a medida que x se aproxima al infinito positivo o negativo

función par *(p. 171)* Para una función f, $f(-x) = f(x)$ para toda x en su dominio

experimento *(p. 526)* Un método que impone un tratamiento a individuos para recoger datos con respecto a su respuesta al tratamiento

regla explícita *(p. 390)* Una regla que da a_n como una función del número de posición n del término en la secuencia

ecuaciones exponenciales *(p. 282)* Ecuaciones en donde las expresiones de una variable ocurren como exponentes

soluciones externas *(p. 219)* Soluciones que no son soluciones de la ecuación original

F

factor by grouping *(p. 137)* A method of factoring a polynomial by grouping pairs of terms that have a common monomial factor

factored completely *(p. 136)* A polynomial written as a product of unfactorable polynomials with integer coefficients

finite differences *(p. 176)* The differences of consecutive y-values in a data set when the x-values are equally spaced

frequency *(p. 454)* The number of cycles per unit of time, which is the reciprocal of the period

factorización por agrupación *(p. 137)* Un método de factorización de un polinomio al agrupar pares de términos que tienen un factor monomio común

factorizado completamente *(p. 136)* Un polinomio escrito como un producto de polinomios no factorizables con coeficientes de números enteros

diferencias finitas *(p. 176)* Las diferencias de valores consecutivos y en un conjunto de datos cuando los valores x están igualmente espaciados

frecuencia *(p. 454)* El número de ciclos por unidad de tiempo, que es el recíproco del período

geometric sequence (p. 374) A sequence in which the ratio of any term to the previous term is constant

secuencia geométrica (p. 374) Una secuencia en donde la razón de cualquier término con respecto al término anterior es constante

geometric series (p. 376) The expression formed by adding the terms of a geometric sequence

serie geométrica (p. 376) La expresión formada al sumar los términos de una secuencia geométrica

hypothesis (p. 519) A claim about a characteristic of a population

hipótesis (p. 519) Una declaración acerca de una característica de una población

index of a radical (p. 194) The value of n in the radical $\sqrt[n]{a}$

índice de un radical (p. 194) El valor de n en el radical $\sqrt[n]{a}$

inferential statistics (p. 540) The branch of statistics that involves using a sample to draw conclusions about a population

estadística inferencial (p. 540) La rama de la estadística que implica el uso de una muestra para sacar conclusiones acerca de una población

initial side (p. 418) The fixed ray of an angle in standard position in a coordinate plane

lado inicial (p. 418) El rayo fijo de un ángulo en posición normal en un plano coordenado

intercept form (p. 85) A quadratic function written in the form $f(x) = a(x - p)(x - q)$, where $a \neq 0$

forma de intersección (p. 85) Una ecuación cuadrática escrita en la forma $f(x) = a(x - p)(x - q)$, donde $a \neq 0$

inverse functions (p. 233) Functions that undo each other

funciones inversas (p. 233) Funciones que se anulan entre sí

inverse variation (p. 308) Two variables x and y show inverse variation when $y = \dfrac{a}{x}$, where $a \neq 0$.

variación inversa (p. 308) Dos variables x e y muestran variación inversa cuando $y = \dfrac{a}{x}$, donde $a \neq 0$.

Law of Cosines (p. 494) For $\triangle ABC$ with side lengths of a, b, and c,

$$a^2 = b^2 + c^2 - 2bc \cos A,$$
$$b^2 = a^2 + c^2 - 2ac \cos B, \text{ and}$$
$$c^2 = a^2 + b^2 - 2ab \cos C.$$

Ley de cosenos (p. 494) Para $\triangle ABC$ con longitudes de lados de a, b, y c,

$$a^2 = b^2 + c^2 - 2bc \cos A,$$
$$b^2 = a^2 + c^2 - 2ac \cos B, \text{ y}$$
$$c^2 = a^2 + b^2 - 2ab \cos C.$$

Law of Sines (p. 487) For $\triangle ABC$ with side lengths of a, b, and c,

$$\frac{\sin A}{a} = \frac{\sin B}{b} = \frac{\sin C}{c} \text{ and}$$
$$\frac{a}{\sin A} = \frac{b}{\sin B} = \frac{c}{\sin C}.$$

Ley de senos (p. 487) Para $\triangle ABC$ con longitudes de lados de a, b, y c,

$$\frac{\sin A}{a} = \frac{\sin B}{b} = \frac{\sin C}{c} \text{ y}$$
$$\frac{a}{\sin A} = \frac{b}{\sin B} = \frac{c}{\sin C}.$$

like radicals (p. 202) Radical expressions with the same index and radicand

radicales semejantes (p. 202) Expresiones radicales con el mismo índice y radicando

line of best fit *(p. 59)* A line that lies as close as possible to all of the data points in a scatter plot

recta de mejor ajuste *(p. 59)* Una recta que se acerca lo más posible a todos los puntos de datos en un diagrama de dispersión

line of fit *(p. 58)* A line that models data in a scatter plot

recta de ajuste *(p. 58)* Una recta que modela datos en un diagrama de dispersión

linear equation in three variables *(p. 64)* An equation of the form $ax + by + cz = d$, where x, y, and z are variables and a, b, and c are not all zero

ecuación lineal en tres variables *(p. 64)* Una ecuación de la forma $ax + by + cz = d$, donde x, y, y z son variables y a, b, y c no son todas cero

local maximum *(p. 170)* The y-coordinate of a turning point of a function when the point is higher than all nearby points

máximo local *(p. 170)* La coordenada y de un punto de inflexión de una función cuando el punto es mayor que todos los puntos cercanos

local minimum *(p. 170)* The y-coordinate of a turning point of a function when the point is lower than all nearby points

mínimo local *(p. 170)* La coordenada y de un punto de inflexión de una función cuando el punto es menor que todos los puntos cercanos

logarithm of *y* with base *b* *(p. 258)* The function $\log_b y = x$ if and only if $b^x = y$, where $b > 0$, $y > 0$, and $b \neq 1$

logaritmo de *y* con base *b* *(p. 258)* La función $\log_b y = x$ si y solo si $b^x = y$, donde $b > 0$, $y > 0$, y $b \neq 1$

logarithmic equations *(p. 283)* Equations that involve logarithms of variable expressions

ecuaciones logarítmicas *(p. 283)* Ecuaciones que implican logaritmos de expresiones variables

--- **M** ---

margin of error *(p. 543)* The limit on how much the responses of the sample would differ from the responses of the population

margen de error *(p. 543)* El límite de cuánto habrían de diferir las respuestas de la muestra de las respuestas de la población

maximum value *(p. 84)* The y-coordinate of the vertex of the quadratic function $f(x) = ax^2 + bx + c$, when $a < 0$

valor máximo *(p. 84)* La coordenada y del vértice de la función cuadrática $f(x) = ax^2 + bx + c$, cuando $a < 0$

midline *(p. 438)* The horizontal line $y = k$ in which the graph of a periodic function oscillates

línea media *(p. 438)* La línea horizontal $y = k$ en la que oscila el gráfico de una función periódica

minimum value *(p. 84)* The y-coordinate of the vertex of the quadratic function $f(x) = ax^2 + bx + c$, when $a > 0$

valor mínimo *(p. 84)* La coordenada y del vértice de la función cuadrática $f(x) = ax^2 + bx + c$, cuando $a > 0$

--- **N** ---

natural base *e* *(p. 252)* An irrational number approximately equal to 2.71828…

base natural *e* *(p. 252)* Un número irracional aproximadamente equivalente a 2.71828…

natural logarithm *(p. 259)* A logarithm with base e, denoted by $\log_e$ or ln

logaritmo natural *(p. 259)* Un logaritmo con base e, denotado como $\log_e$ o ln

normal curve *(p. 510)* The graph of a normal distribution that is bell-shaped and is symmetric about the mean

curva normal *(p. 510)* El gráfico de una distribución normal con forma acampanada y es simétrica con respecto a la media

normal distribution *(p. 510)* A type of probability distribution in which the graph is a bell-shaped curve that is symmetric about the mean

distribución normal *(p. 510)* Un tipo de distribución de probabilidades en la que el gráfico es una curva acampanada que es simétrica con respecto a la media

n*th root of *a *(p. 194)* For an integer n greater than 1, if $b^n = a$, then b is an nth root of a.

raíz de orden *n* de *a* *(p. 194)* Para un número entero n mayor que 1, si $b^n = a$, entonces b es una raíz de orden n de a.

observational study *(p. 526)* Individuals are observed and variables are measured without controlling the individuals or their environment.

estudio de observación *(p. 526)* Se observan individuos y se miden variables sin controlar a los individuos o a su entorno.

odd function *(p. 171)* For a function f, $f(-x) = -f(x)$ for all x in its domain

función impar *(p. 171)* Para una función f, $f(-x) = -f(x)$ para toda x en su dominio

ordered triple *(p. 64)* A solution of a system of three linear equations represented by (x, y, z)

triple ordenado *(p. 64)* Un solución de un sistema de tres ecuaciones lineales representadas por (x, y, z)

parabola *(p. 74)* The U-shaped graph of a quadratic function

parábola *(p. 74)* El gráfico con forma de "U" de una función cuadrática

parameter *(p. 519)* A numerical description of a population characteristic

parámetro *(p. 519)* Una descripción numérica de una característica de la población

parent function *(p. 40)* The most basic function in a family of functions

función principal *(p. 40)* La función más básica en una familia de funciones

partial sum *(p. 384)* The sum S_n of the first n terms of an infinite series

sumatoria parcial *(p. 384)* La sumatoria parcial S_n de los primeros términos n de una serie infinita

Pascal's Triangle *(p. 123)* A triangular array of numbers such that the numbers in the nth row are the coefficients of the terms in the expansion of $(a + b)^n$ for whole number values of n

triángulo de Pascal *(p. 123)* Una disposición triangular de números, de tal manera que los números en la fila n son los coeficientes de los términos en la expansión de $(a + b)^n$ para los valores de números enteros de n

period *(p. 436)* The horizontal length of each cycle of a periodic function

período *(p. 436)* La longitud horizontal de cada ciclo de una función periódica

periodic function *(p. 436)* A function whose graph has a repeating pattern

función periódica *(p. 436)* Una función cuyo gráfico tiene un patrón de repetición

phase shift *(p. 438)* A horizontal translation of a periodic function

desplazamiento de fase *(p. 438)* Una traslación horizontal de una función periódica

placebo *(p. 534)* A harmless, unmedicated treatment that resembles the actual treatment

placebo *(p. 534)* Un tratamiento no medicado e inofensivo que se asemeja al tratamiento real

polynomial *(p. 112)* A monomial or a sum of monomials

polinomio *(p. 112)* Un monomio o una suma de monomios

polynomial function *(p. 112)* A function of the form $f(x) = a_n x^n + a_{n-1} x^{n-1} + \cdots + a_1 x + a_0$, where $a_n \neq 0$, the exponents are all whole numbers, and the coefficients are all real numbers

función polinómica *(p. 112)* Una función de la forma $f(x) = a_n x^n + a_{n-1} x^{n-1} + \cdots + a_1 x + a_0$, donde $a_n \neq 0$, todos los exponentes son números enteros y todos los coeficientes son números reales

polynomial long division *(p. 130)* A method to divide a polynomial $f(x)$ by a nonzero divisor $d(x)$ to yield a quotient polynomial $q(x)$ and a remainder polynomial $r(x)$

división larga de polinomios *(p. 130)* Un método para dividir un polinomio $f(x)$ por un divisor distinto de cero $d(x)$ para obtener un polinomio de cociente $q(x)$ y un polinomio de resto $r(x)$

population *(p. 518)* The collection of all data, such as responses, measurements, or counts, that you want information about

población *(p. 518)* La recolección de datos, tales como respuestas, medidas o conteos, sobre los que se quiere información

population density *(p. 4)* A measure of how many people live within a given area

densidad de población *(p. 4)* Medición de la cantidad de personas que habitan un área dada

quadrantal angle *(p. 427)* An angle in standard position whose terminal side lies on an axis

ángulo cuadrantal *(p. 427)* Un ángulo en posición estándar cuyo lado terminal descansa en un eje

quadratic form *(p. 137)* An expression of the form $au^2 + bu + c$, where u is an algebraic expression

forma cuadrática *(p. 137)* Una expresión de la forma $au^2 + bu + c$, donde u es una expresión algebraica

quadratic function *(p. 74)* A function that can be written in the form $f(x) = a(x - h)^2 + k$, where $a \neq 0$

función cuadrática *(p. 74)* Una función que puede escribirse en la forma $f(x) = a(x - h)^2 + k$, donde $a \neq 0$

radian *(p. 419)* For a circle with radius r, the measure of an angle in standard position whose terminal side intercepts an arc of length r is one radian.

radián *(p. 419)* Para un círculo con radio r, la medida de un ángulo en posición estándar cuyo lado terminal intercepta un arco de longitud r es un radián.

radical equation *(p. 218)* An equation with a radical that has a variable in the radicand

ecuación radical *(p. 218)* Una ecuación con un radical que tiene una variable en el radicando

radical function *(p. 208)* A function that contains a radical expression with the independent variable in the radicand

función radical *(p. 208)* Una función que contiene una expresión radical con la variable independiente en el radicando

random sample *(p. 524)* A sample in which each member of a population has an equal chance of being selected

muestra aleatoria *(p. 524)* Una muestra en la que cada miembro de una población tiene igual posibilidad de ser seleccionado

randomization *(p. 534)* A process of randomly assigning subjects to different treatment groups

aleatorización *(p. 534)* Un proceso de asignación aleatoria de sujetos a distintos grupos de tratamiento

randomized comparative experiment *(p. 534)* An experiment in which subjects are randomly assigned to the control group or the treatment group

experimento comparativo aleatorizado *(p. 534)* Un experimento en el que los sujetos son asignados aleatoriamente al grupo de control o al grupo de tratamiento

rational expression *(p. 324)* A fraction whose numerator and denominator are nonzero polynomials

expresión racional *(p. 324)* Una fracción cuyo numerador y denominador son polinomios distintos a cero

rational function *(p. 314)* A function that has the form $f(x) = \dfrac{p(x)}{q(x)}$, where $p(x)$ and $q(x)$ are polynomials and $q(x) \neq 0$

función racional *(p. 314)* Una función que tiene la forma $f(x) = \dfrac{p(x)}{q(x)}$, donde $p(x)$ y $q(x)$ son polinomios y $q(x) \neq 0$

recursive rule *(p. 390)* A rule that gives the beginning term(s) of a sequence and a recursive equation that tells how a_n is related to one or more preceding terms

regla recursiva *(p. 390)* Una regla para definir el(los) primer(os) término(s) de una secuencia y una ecuación recursiva que indica cómo se relaciona a_n a uno o más términos precedentes

reference angle *(p. 428)* The acute angle formed by the terminal side of an angle in standard position and the x-axis

ángulo de referencia *(p. 428)* El ángulo agudo formado por el lado terminal de un ángulo en posición normal y el eje x

reflection *(p. 41)* A transformation that flips a graph over the line of reflection

reflexión *(p. 41)* Una transformación que voltea un gráfico sobre una recta de reflexión

repeated solution *(p. 146)* A solution of an equation that appears more than once

replication *(p. 536)* The repetition of an experiment under the same or similar conditions to improve the validity of the experiment

solución repetida *(p. 146)* Una solución de una ecuación que aparece más de una vez

réplica *(p. 536)* La repetición de un experimento bajo las mismas o similares condiciones para mejorar la validez del experimento

S

sample *(p. 518)* A subset of a population

muestra *(p. 518)* Un subconjunto de una población

secant *(p. 410)* A trigonometric function for an acute angle θ of a right triangle, denoted by

$$\sec \theta = \frac{\text{hypotenuse}}{\text{adjacent}}$$

secante *(p. 410)* Una ecuación trigonométrica de un ángulo agudo θ de un triángulo recto, denatado por

$$\sec \theta = \frac{\text{hipotenusa}}{\text{adyacente}}$$

sector *(p. 420)* A region of a circle that is bounded by two radii and an arc of the circle

sector *(p. 420)* Una región de un círculo conformada por dos radios y un arco del círculo

self-selected sample *(p. 524)* A sample in which members of a population can volunteer to be in the sample

muestra autoseleccionada *(p. 524)* Una muestra en la que los miembros de una población pueden ofrecerse voluntariamente para formar parte de la misma

sequence *(p. 358)* An ordered list of numbers

secuencia *(p. 358)* Una lista ordenada de números

series *(p. 360)* The sum of the terms of a sequence

serie *(p. 360)* La suma de los términos de una secuencia

sigma notation *(p. 360)* For any sequence $a_1, a_2, a_3, \ldots,$ the sum of the first k terms may be written as

$$\sum_{n=1}^{k} a_n = a_1 + a_2 + a_3 + \cdots + a_k, \text{ where } k \text{ is an integer.}$$

notación sigma *(p. 360)* Para cualquier secuencia $a_1, a_2, a_3, \ldots,$ la suma de los primeros términos k puede escribirse como $\sum_{n=1}^{k} a_n = a_1 + a_2 + a_3 + \cdots + a_k,$ donde k es un número entero.

simplest form of a radical *(p. 201)* An expression involving a radical with index n that has no radicands with perfect nth powers as factors other than 1, no radicands that contain fractions, and no radicals that appear in the denominator of a fraction

mínima expresión de un radical *(p. 201)* Una expresión que conlleva un radical con índice n que no tiene radicandos con potencias perfectas de orden n como factores distintos a 1, que no tiene radicandos que contengan fracciones y que no tiene radicales que aparezcan en el denominador de una fracción

simplified form of a rational expression *(p. 324)* A rational expression whose numerator and denominator have no common factors (other than ± 1)

forma simplificada de una expresión racional *(p. 324)* Una expresión racional cuyo numerador y denominador no tienen factores comunes (distintos a ± 1)

simulation *(p. 526)* The use of a model to reproduce the conditions of a situation or process so that the simulated outcomes closely match the real-world outcomes

simulación *(p. 526)* El uso de un modelo para reproducir las condiciones de una situación o proceso, de tal manera que los resultados posibles simulados coincidan en gran medida con los resultados del mundo real

sine *(p. 410)* A trigonometric function for an acute angle θ of a right triangle, denoted by

$$\sin \theta = \frac{\text{opposite}}{\text{hypotenuse}}$$

seno *(p. 410)* Una ecuación trigonométrica de un ángulo agudo θ de un triángulo recto, denotado por

$$\sin \theta = \frac{\text{opuesto}}{\text{hipotenusa}}$$

sinusoid *(p. 455)* The graph of a sine or cosine function

sinusoide *(p. 455)* El gráfico de una función seno o coseno

solid of revolution (p. 24) A three-dimensional figure that is formed by rotating a two-dimensional shape around an axis

sólido de revolución (p. 24) Una figura tridimensional que se forma por la rotación de una forma bidimensional alrededor de un eje

solution of a system of three linear equations (p. 64) An ordered triple (x, y, z) whose coordinates make each equation true

solución de un sistema de tres ecuaciones lineales (p. 64) Un triple ordenado (x, y, z) cuyas coordenadas hacen verdadera cada ecuación

standard form (p. 82) A quadratic function written in the form $f(x) = ax^2 + bx + c$, where $a \neq 0$

forma estándar (p. 82) Una función cuadrática escrita en la forma $f(x) = ax^2 + bx + c$, donde $a \neq 0$

standard normal distribution (p. 511) The normal distribution with mean 0 and standard deviation 1

distribución normal estándar (p. 511) La distribución normal con una media de 0 y desviación estándar 1

standard position (p. 418) An angle in a coordinate plane such that its vertex is at the origin and its initial side lies on the positive x-axis

posición estándar (p. 418) Un ángulo en un plano coordenado de tal manera que su vértice esté en el origen y que su lado inicial descanse en el eje x positivo

statistic (p. 519) A numerical description of a sample characteristic

estadística (p. 519) Una descripción numérica de una característica de la muestra

stratified sample (p. 524) A sample in which a population is divided into smaller groups that share a similar characteristic and a sample is then randomly selected from each group

muestra estratificada (p. 524) Una muestra en la que una población se divide en grupos más pequeños que comparten una característica similar, y una muestra se selecciona en forma aleatoria de cada grupo

summation notation (p. 360) For any sequence $a_1, a_2, a_3, \ldots$, the sum of the first k terms may be written as

$$\sum_{n=1}^{k} a_n = a_1 + a_2 + a_3 + \cdots + a_k, \text{ where } k \text{ is an integer.}$$

notación de sumatoria (p. 360) Para cualquier secuencia $a_1, a_2, a_3, \ldots$, la sumatoria de los primeros términos k puede escribirse como $\sum_{n=1}^{k} a_n = a_1 + a_2 + a_3 + \cdots + a_k$, donde k es un número entero.

survey (p. 526) An investigation of one or more characteristics of a population

encuesta (p. 526) Una investigación de una o más características de una población

synthetic division (p. 131) A shortcut method to divide a polynomial by a binomial of the form $x - k$

división sintética (p. 131) Un método abreviado para dividir un polinomio por un binomio de la forma $x - k$

system of three linear equations (p. 64) A set of three equations of the form $ax + by + cz = d$, where x, y, and z are variables and a, b, and c are not all zero

sistema de tres ecuaciones lineales (p. 64) Un conjunto de tres ecuaciones de la forma $ax + by + cz = d$, donde x, y, y z son variables y a, b, y c no son todos cero

systematic sample (p. 524) A sample in which a rule is used to select members of a population

muestra sistemática (p. 524) Una muestra en la que se usa una regla para seleccionar miembros de una población

tangent (p. 410) A trigonometric function for an acute angle θ of a right triangle, denoted by

$$\tan \theta = \frac{\text{opposite}}{\text{adjacent}}$$

tangente (p. 410) Una ecuación trigonométrica de un ángulo agudo θ de un triángulo recto, denotado por

$$\tan \theta = \frac{\text{opuesto}}{\text{adyacente}}$$

terminal side (p. 418) A ray of an angle in standard position that has been rotated about the vertex in a coordinate plane

lado terminal (p. 418) Un rayo de un ángulo en posición normal que ha sido rotado con respecto al vértice en un plano coordenado

terms of a sequence *(p. 358)* The values in the range of a sequence

transformation *(p. 41)* A change in the size, shape, position, or orientation of a graph

translation *(p. 41)* A transformation that shifts a graph horizontally and/or vertically but does not change its size, shape, or orientation

treatment group *(p. 534)* The group that is subjected to the treatment in an experiment

trigonometric identity *(p. 472)* A trigonometric equation that is true for all values of the variable for which both sides of the equation are defined

término de una secuencia *(p. 358)* Los valores en el rango de una secuencia

transformación *(p. 41)* Un cambio en el tamaño, forma, posición u orientación de un gráfico

traslación *(p. 41)* Una transformación que desplaza un gráfico horizontal y/o verticalmente, pero no cambia su tamaño, forma u orientación

grupo de tratamiento *(p. 534)* El grupo que está sometido al tratamiento en un experimento

identidad trigonométrica *(p. 472)* Una ecuación trigonométrica verdadera para todos los valores de la variable por la cual se definen ambos lados de la ecuación

---

U

---

unbiased sample *(p. 525)* A sample that is representative of the population that you want information about

unit circle *(p. 427)* The circle $x^2 + y^2 = 1$, which has center (0, 0) and radius 1

muestra no sesgada *(p. 525)* Una muestra que es representativa de la población de la que se quiere información

círculo unitario *(p. 427)* El círculo $x^2 + y^2 = 1$, que tiene como centro (0, 0) y radio 1

V

---

vertex form *(p. 76)* A quadratic function written in the form $f(x) = a(x - h)^2 + k$, where $a \neq 0$

vertex of a parabola *(p. 76)* The lowest point on a parabola that opens up or the highest point on a parabola that opens down

vertical shrink *(p. 42)* A transformation that causes the graph of a function to shrink toward the x-axis when all the y-coordinates are multiplied by a factor a, where $0 < a < 1$

vertical stretch *(p. 42)* A transformation that causes the graph of a function to stretch away from the x-axis when all the y-coordinates are multiplied by a factor a, where $a > 1$

fórmula de vértice *(p. 76)* Una función cuadrática escrita en la forma $f(x) = a(x - h)^2 + k$, donde $a \neq 0$

vértice de una parábola *(p. 76)* El punto más bajo de una parábola que se abre hacia arriba o el punto más alto de una parábola que se abre hacia abajo

reducción vertical *(p. 42)* Una transformación que hace que el gráfico de una función se reduzca hacia el eje x cuando todas las coordenadas y se multiplican por un factor a, donde $0 < a < 1$

ampliación vertical *(p. 42)* Una transformación que hace que el gráfico de una función se amplíe desde el eje x cuando todas las coordenadas y se multiplican por un factor a, donde $a > 1$

Z

---

z-score *(p. 511)* The z-value for a particular x-value which is the number of standard deviations the x-value lies above or below the mean

puntaje z *(p. 511)* El valor z para un valor particular x que es el número de desviaciones estándar que el valor x tiene por encima o por debajo de la media

Index

evaluating, 259
Common ratio, 374, 375
Comparative studies and causality, 535
Complex conjugates, 155–156
Complex fractions
  defined, 335
  simplifying, 305, 335
Composite figures, areas of, 2
Compound interest, 254
Concept Summary, degree and radian measures of special angles, 420
Cones
  surface areas of, 1
  volumes of, 1, 12
Conjectures, on infinite geometric series, 383
Conjugates, defined, 202
Connections to Geometry, volume of a pyramid, 164
Consecutive ratio test for exponential models, 250
Constant function, 40
Constant of variation, 308
Constant term of a polynomial, 112
Continued fractions, 424
Continuous functions, 110
Continuously compounded interest, 254
Control group
  defined, 534
  resampling data using simulation, 549
Controlled experiment, 534
Convenience sample, 524
Coordinate (of point), on unit circle, 408
Coordinate plane, solids of revolution in, 26
Corollary to the Fundamental Theorem of Algebra, 154
Correlation coefficient, 59
Cosecant function
  characteristics of, 448
  defined, 409, 410
  graphing, 448–449
Cosine function
  amplitude of, 437–438
  characteristics of, 436
  defined, 409, 410
  graphing, 435–440, 463
  period of, 437–438
  reflecting, 440
  stretching and shrinking, 437–438
  translating, 438–439
Cosines, Law of, *See* Law of Cosines

Cotangent function
  characteristics of, 446
  defined, 409, 410
  graphing, 446–448, 464
  period of, 447
  vertical asymptotes of, 447
Cotangent identity, 472
Coterminal angles, 419
Cross multiplying, to solve rational equations, 340
Cross sections of solids, 17–20, 31
  defined, 17
  describing, 17, 18
  drawing, 19
  real-life applications of, 20
Cube(s)
  Difference of Two, 136–137
  Sum of Two, 136–137
Cube of a binomial, 119, 121
Cube root function, parent function for, 208
Cubic equations
  and imaginary solutions, 153
  and repeated solutions, 145
Cubic functions
  inverse of, 235
  transforming graphs of, 161
  writing for set of points, 176
Cylinders
  surface areas of, 6
  volumes of, 11

Data
  organizing, 548–549
  resampling, 547
    using simulation, 549
Data analysis and statistics
  data collection, 523–527, 555
  experimental design, 533–536, 555
  inferences from experiments, 547–550, 555
  inferences from sample surveys, 539–543, 555
  normal distributions, 509–513, 554
  populations, samples, and hypotheses, 517–520, 554
Data collection, 523–527, 555
  bias in sampling, 525–526
  bias in survey questions, 527
  methods of, 526–527
  sampling methods in statistical studies, 524–525
Data sets
  analyzing, 509
  classifying, 290
Decay factor, *See* Exponential decay functions

Degree measure of angles
  converting to radians, 419–421
  of special angles, 420
Degree of a polynomial, 112
Denominators, *See also* Least common denominator (LCD)
  like and unlike, adding or subtracting rational expressions, 331–335
Density
  defined, 10
  finding, 9–10
Descartes, René, 156
Descartes's Rule of Signs, 156–157
Descriptive statistics, 540
Difference formulas for trigonometric functions, 477–480, 500
Difference of Two Cubes, 136–137
Differences of outputs, 94
Direct variation, 307–308
Dirichlet Prime Number Theorem, 372
Division
  of polynomials, 129–132, 183
    by long division, 130
    Remainder Theorem, 132
    synthetic division, 131
  of rational expressions, 323, 326–327, 349
  of two functions, 226–228
Domain
  of parent functions, 40
  of sequences, 358

End behavior, of polynomial functions, 113
Equations
  literal, rewriting, 191
  solving, 355
Even functions, 171, 470
Exactly one solution, *See* One solution
Experiment(s)
  defined, 526
  describing, 534–535
  making inferences (*See* Inferences from experiments)
  randomization in, 535
  with two samples, 548–549
Experimental design, 533–536, 555
  analyzing, 536
  describing experiments, 534–535
  randomization in experiments and observational studies, 535
Explicit rule
  defined, 390

Index

Postulates

Integrated Mathematics I

Ruler Postulate (p. 388)

The points on a line can be matched one to one with the real numbers. The real number that corresponds to a point is the coordinate of the point. The distance between points A and B, written as AB, is the absolute value of the difference of the coordinates of A and B.

Segment Addition Postulate (p. 390)

If B is between A and C, then $AB + BC = AC$.
If $AB + BC = AC$, then B is between A and C.

Protractor Postulate (p. 415)

Consider $\overleftrightarrow{OB}$ and a point A on one side of $\overleftrightarrow{OB}$. The rays of the form $\overrightarrow{OA}$ can be matched one to one with the real numbers from 0 to 180. The measure of $\angle AOB$, which can be written as $m\angle AOB$, is equal to the absolute value of the difference between the real numbers matched with $\overrightarrow{OA}$ and $\overrightarrow{OB}$ on a protractor.

Angle Addition Postulate (p. 417)

If P is in the interior of $\angle RST$, then the measure of $\angle RST$ is equal to the sum of the measures of $\angle RSP$ and $\angle PST$.

Two Point Postulate (p. 460)

Through any two points, there exists exactly one line.

Line-Point Postulate (p. 460)

A line contains at least two points.

Line Intersection Postulate (p. 460)

If two lines intersect, then their intersection is exactly one point.

Three Point Postulate (p. 460)

Through any three noncollinear points, there exists exactly one plane.

Plane-Point Postulate (p. 460)

A plane contains at least three noncollinear points.

Plane-Line Postulate (p. 460)

If two points lie in a plane, then the line containing them lies in the plane.

Plane Intersection Postulate (p. 460)

If two planes intersect, then their intersection is a line.

Linear Pair Postulate (p. 480)

If two angles form a linear pair, then they are supplementary.

Parallel Postulate (p. 499)

If there is a line and a point not on the line, then there is exactly one line through the point parallel to the given line.

Perpendicular Postulate (p. 499)

If there is a line and a point not on the line, then there is exactly one line through the point perpendicular to the given line.

Translation Postulate (p. 546)

A translation is a rigid motion.

Reflection Postulate (p. 554)

A reflection is a rigid motion.

Rotation Postulate (p. 564)

A rotation is a rigid motion.

Integrated Mathematics II

Arc Addition Postulate (p. 583)

The measure of an arc formed by two adjacent arcs is the sum of the measures of the two arcs.

Theorems

Integrated Mathematics I

Properties of Segment Congruence *(p. 471)*

Segment congruence is reflexive, symmetric, and transitive.

Reflexive   For any segment AB, $\overline{AB} \cong \overline{AB}$.

Symmetric   If $\overline{AB} \cong \overline{CD}$, then $\overline{CD} \cong \overline{AB}$.

Transitive   If $\overline{AB} \cong \overline{CD}$ and $\overline{CD} \cong \overline{EF}$, then $\overline{AB} \cong \overline{EF}$.

Properties of Angle Congruence *(p. 471)*

Angle congruence is reflexive, symmetric, and transitive.

Reflexive   For any angle A, $\angle A \cong \angle A$.

Symmetric   If $\angle A \cong \angle B$, then $\angle B \cong \angle A$.

Transitive   If $\angle A \cong \angle B$ and $\angle B \cong \angle C$, then $\angle A \cong \angle C$.

Right Angles Congruence Theorem *(p. 478)*

All right angles are congruent.

Congruent Supplements Theorem *(p. 479)*

If two angles are supplementary to the same angle (or to congruent angles), then they are congruent.

Congruent Complements Theorem *(p. 479)*

If two angles are complementary to the same angle (or to congruent angles), then they are congruent.

Vertical Angles Congruence Theorem *(p. 480)*

Vertical angles are congruent.

Corresponding Angles Theorem *(p. 504)*

If two parallel lines are cut by a transversal, then the pairs of corresponding angles are congruent.

Alternate Interior Angles Theorem *(p. 504)*

If two parallel lines are cut by a transversal, then the pairs of alternate interior angles are congruent.

Alternate Exterior Angles Theorem *(p. 504)*

If two parallel lines are cut by a transversal, then the pairs of alternate exterior angles are congruent.

Consecutive Interior Angles Theorem *(p. 504)*

If two parallel lines are cut by a transversal, then the pairs of consecutive interior angles are supplementary.

Corresponding Angles Converse *(p. 510)*

If two lines are cut by a transversal so the corresponding angles are congruent, then the lines are parallel.

Alternate Interior Angles Converse *(p. 511)*

If two lines are cut by a transversal so the alternate interior angles are congruent, then the lines are parallel.

Alternate Exterior Angles Converse *(p. 511)*

If two lines are cut by a transversal so the alternate exterior angles are congruent, then the lines are parallel.

Consecutive Interior Angles Converse *(p. 511)*

If two lines are cut by a transversal so the consecutive interior angles are supplementary, then the lines are parallel.

Transitive Property of Parallel Lines *(p. 513)*

If two lines are parallel to the same line, then they are parallel to each other.

Linear Pair Perpendicular Theorem *(p. 522)*

If two lines intersect to form a linear pair of congruent angles, then the lines are perpendicular.

Perpendicular Transversal Theorem *(p. 522)*

In a plane, if a transversal is perpendicular to one of two parallel lines, then it is perpendicular to the other line.

Lines Perpendicular to a Transversal Theorem *(p. 522)*

In a plane, if two lines are perpendicular to the same line, then they are parallel to each other.

Slopes of Parallel Lines *(p. 528)*

In a coordinate plane, two distinct nonvertical lines are parallel if and only if they have the same slope. Any two vertical lines are parallel.

Slopes of Perpendicular Lines *(p. 528)*

In a coordinate plane, two nonvertical lines are perpendicular if and only if the product of their slopes is -1. Horizontal lines are perpendicular to vertical lines.

Composition Theorem *(p. 546)*

The composition of two (or more) rigid motions is a rigid motion.

Reflections in Parallel Lines Theorem *(p. 572)*

If lines k and m are parallel, then a reflection in line k followed by a reflection in line m is the same as a translation. If A'' is the image of A, then

1. $\overline{AA''}$ is perpendicular to k and m, and
2. $AA'' = 2d$, where d is the distance between k and m.

Reflections in Intersecting Lines Theorem (p. 573)

If lines k and m intersect at point P, then a reflection in line k followed by a reflection in line m is the same as a rotation about point P. The angle of rotation is $2x°$, where $x°$ is the measure of the acute or right angle formed by lines k and m.

Triangle Sum Theorem (p. 589)

The sum of the measures of the interior angles of a triangle is $180°$.

Exterior Angle Theorem (p. 590)

The measure of an exterior angle of a triangle is equal to the sum of the measures of the two nonadjacent interior angles.

Corollary to the Triangle Sum Theorem (p. 591)

The acute angles of a right triangle are complementary.

Properties of Triangle Congruence (p. 597)

Triangle congruence is reflexive, symmetric, and transitive.

Reflexive For any triangle $\triangle ABC$, $\triangle ABC \cong \triangle ABC$.

Symmetric If $\triangle ABC \cong \triangle DEF$, then $\triangle DEF \cong \triangle ABC$.

Transitive If $\triangle ABC \cong \triangle DEF$ and $\triangle DEF \cong \triangle JKL$, then $\triangle ABC \cong \triangle JKL$.

Third Angles Theorem (p. 598)

If two angles of one triangle are congruent to two angles of another triangle, then the third angles are also congruent.

Side-Angle-Side (SAS) Congruence Theorem (p. 602)

If two sides and the included angle of one triangle are congruent to two sides and the included angle of a second triangle, then the two triangles are congruent.

Base Angles Theorem (p. 608)

If two sides of a triangle are congruent, then the angles opposite them are congruent.

Converse of the Base Angles Theorem (p. 608)

If two angles of a triangle are congruent, then the sides opposite them are congruent.

Corollary to the Base Angles Theorem (p. 609)

If a triangle is equilateral, then it is equiangular.

Corollary to the Converse of the Base Angles Theorem (p. 609)

If a triangle is equiangular, then it is equilateral.

Side-Side-Side (SSS) Congruence Theorem (p. 618)

If three sides of one triangle are congruent to three sides of a second triangle, then the two triangles are congruent.

Hypotenuse-Leg (HL) Congruence Theorem (p. 620)

If the hypotenuse and a leg of a right triangle are congruent to the hypotenuse and a leg of a second right triangle, then the two triangles are congruent.

Angle-Side-Angle (ASA) Congruence Theorem (p. 626)

If two angles and the included side of one triangle are congruent to two angles and the included side of a second triangle, then the two triangles are congruent.

Angle-Angle-Side (AAS) Congruence Theorem (p. 627)

If two angles and a non-included side of one triangle are congruent to two angles and the corresponding non-included side of a second triangle, then the two triangles are congruent.

Integrated Mathematics II

Perpendicular Bisector Theorem (p. 344)

In a plane, if a point lies on the perpendicular bisector of a segment, then it is equidistant from the endpoints of the segment.

Converse of the Perpendicular Bisector Theorem (p. 344)

In a plane, if a point is equidistant from the endpoints of a segment, then it lies on the perpendicular bisector of the segment.

Angle Bisector Theorem (p. 346)

If a point lies on the bisector of an angle, then it is equidistant from the two sides of the angle.

Converse of the Angle Bisector Theorem (p. 346)

If a point is in the interior of an angle and is equidistant from the two sides of the angle, then it lies on the bisector of the angle.

Circumcenter Theorem (p. 352)

The circumcenter of a triangle is equidistant from the vertices of the triangle.

Incenter Theorem (p. 355)

The incenter of a triangle is equidistant from the sides of the triangle.

Centroid Theorem (p. 362)

The centroid of a triangle is two-thirds of the distance from each vertex to the midpoint of the opposite side.

Triangle Midsegment Theorem (p. 373)

The segment connecting the midpoints of two sides of a triangle is parallel to the third side and is half as long as that side.

Triangle Longer Side Theorem (p. 379)

If one side of a triangle is longer than another side, then the angle opposite the longer side is larger than the angle opposite the shorter side.

Triangle Larger Angle Theorem (p. 379)

If one angle of a triangle is larger than another angle, then the side opposite the larger angle is longer than the side opposite the smaller angle.

Triangle Inequality Theorem (p. 381)

The sum of the lengths of any two sides of a triangle is greater than the length of the third side.

Hinge Theorem (p. 386)

If two sides of one triangle are congruent to two sides of another triangle, and the included angle of the first is larger than the included angle of the second, then the third side of the first is longer than the third side of the second.

Converse of the Hinge Theorem (p. 386)

If two sides of one triangle are congruent to two sides of another triangle, and the third side of the first is longer than the third side of the second, then the included angle of the first is larger than the included angle of the second.

Polygon Interior Angles Theorem (p. 404)

The sum of the measures of the interior angles of a convex n-gon is $(n - 2) \cdot 180°$.

Corollary to the Polygon Interior Angles Theorem (p. 405)

The sum of the measures of the interior angles of a quadrilateral is $360°$.

Polygon Exterior Angles Theorem (p. 406)

The sum of the measures of the exterior angles of a convex polygon, one angle at each vertex, is $360°$.

Parallelogram Opposite Sides Theorem (p. 412)

If a quadrilateral is a parallelogram, then its opposite sides are congruent.

Parallelogram Opposite Angles Theorem (p. 412)

If a quadrilateral is a parallelogram, then its opposite angles are congruent.

Parallelogram Consecutive Angles Theorem (p. 413)

If a quadrilateral is a parallelogram, then its consecutive angles are supplementary.

Parallelogram Diagonals Theorem (p. 413)

If a quadrilateral is a parallelogram, then its diagonals bisect each other.

Parallelogram Opposite Sides Converse (p. 420)

If both pairs of opposite sides of a quadrilateral are congruent, then the quadrilateral is a parallelogram.

Parallelogram Opposite Angles Converse (p. 420)

If both pairs of opposite angles of a quadrilateral are congruent, then the quadrilateral is a parallelogram.

Opposite Sides Parallel and Congruent Theorem (p. 422)

If one pair of opposite sides of a quadrilateral are congruent and parallel, then the quadrilateral is a parallelogram.

Parallelogram Diagonals Converse (p. 422)

If the diagonals of a quadrilateral bisect each other, then the quadrilateral is a parallelogram.

Rhombus Corollary (p. 432)

A quadrilateral is a rhombus if and only if it has four congruent sides.

Rectangle Corollary (p. 432)

A quadrilateral is a rectangle if and only if it has four right angles.

Square Corollary (p. 432)

A quadrilateral is a square if and only if it is a rhombus and a rectangle.

Rhombus Diagonals Theorem (p. 434)

A parallelogram is a rhombus if and only if its diagonals are perpendicular.

Rhombus Opposite Angles Theorem (p. 434)

A parallelogram is a rhombus if and only if each diagonal bisects a pair of opposite angles.

Rectangle Diagonals Theorem (p. 435)

A parallelogram is a rectangle if and only if its diagonals are congruent.

Isosceles Trapezoid Base Angles Theorem (p. 443)

If a trapezoid is isosceles, then each pair of base angles is congruent.

Isosceles Trapezoid Base Angles Converse (p. 443)

If a trapezoid has a pair of congruent base angles, then it is an isosceles trapezoid.

Isosceles Trapezoid Diagonals Theorem (p. 443)

A trapezoid is isosceles if and only if its diagonals are congruent.

Trapezoid Midsegment Theorem (p. 444)

The midsegment of a trapezoid is parallel to each base, and its length is one-half the sum of the lengths of the bases.

Kite Diagonals Theorem (p. 445)

If a quadrilateral is a kite, then its diagonals are perpendicular.

Kite Opposite Angles Theorem (p. 445)

If a quadrilateral is a kite, then exactly one pair of opposite angles are congruent.

Perimeters of Similar Polygons (p. 478)

If two polygons are similar, then the ratio of their perimeters is equal to the ratios of their corresponding side lengths.

Areas of Similar Polygons (p. 479)

If two polygons are similar, then the ratio of their areas is equal to the squares of the ratios of their corresponding side lengths.

Angle-Angle (AA) Similarity Theorem (p. 486)

If two angles of one triangle are congruent to two angles of another triangle, then the two triangles are similar.

Side-Side-Side (SSS) Similarity Theorem (p. 494)

If the corresponding side lengths of two triangles are proportional, then the triangles are similar.

Side-Angle-Side (SAS) Similarity Theorem (p. 496)

If an angle of one triangle is congruent to an angle of a second triangle and the lengths of the sides including these angles are proportional, then the triangles are similar.

Triangle Proportionality Theorem (p. 500)

If a line parallel to one side of a triangle intersects the other two sides, then it divides the two sides proportionally.

Converse of the Triangle Proportionality Theorem (p. 500)

If a line divides two sides of a triangle proportionally, then it is parallel to the third side.

Three Parallel Lines Theorem (p. 501)

If three parallel lines intersect two transversals, then they divide the transversals proportionally.

Triangle Angle Bisector Theorem (p. 502)

If a ray bisects an angle of a triangle, then it divides the opposite side into segments whose lengths are proportional to the lengths of the other two sides.

Pythagorean Theorem (p. 518)

In a right triangle, the square of the length of the hypotenuse is equal to the sum of the squares of the lengths of the legs.

Converse of the Pythagorean Theorem (p. 520)

If the square of the length of the longest side of a triangle is equal to the sum of the squares of the lengths of the other two sides, then the triangle is a right triangle.

Pythagorean Inequalities Theorem (p. 521)

For any $\triangle ABC$, where c is the length of the longest side, the following statements are true.
If $c^2 < a^2 + b^2$, then $\triangle ABC$ is acute.
If $c^2 > a^2 + b^2$, then $\triangle ABC$ is obtuse.

45°-45°-90° Triangle Theorem (p. 526)

In a 45°-45°-90° triangle, the hypotenuse is $\sqrt{2}$ times as long as each leg.

30°-60°-90° Triangle Theorem (p. 527)

In a 30°-60°-90° triangle, the hypotenuse is twice as long as the shorter leg, and the longer leg is $\sqrt{3}$ times as long as the shorter leg.

Right Triangle Similarity Theorem (p. 532)

If the altitude is drawn to the hypotenuse of a right triangle, then the two triangles formed are similar to the original triangle and to each other.

Geometric Mean (Altitude) Theorem (p. 534)

In a right triangle, the altitude from the right angle to the hypotenuse divides the hypotenuse into two segments. The length of the altitude is the geometric mean of the lengths of the two segments of the hypotenuse.

Geometric Mean (Leg) Theorem (p. 534)

In a right triangle, the altitude from the right angle to the hypotenuse divides the hypotenuse into two segments. The length of each leg of the right triangle is the geometric mean of the lengths of the hypotenuse and the segment of the hypotenuse that is adjacent to the leg.

Tangent Line to Circle Theorem (p. 576)

In a plane, a line is tangent to a circle if and only if the line is perpendicular to a radius of the circle at its endpoint on the circle.

External Tangent Congruence Theorem (p. 576)

Tangent segments from a common external point are congruent.

Congruent Circles Theorem (p. 584)

Two circles are congruent circles if and only if they have the same radius.

Congruent Central Angles Theorem (p. 584)

In the same circle, or in congruent circles, two minor arcs are congruent if and only if their corresponding central angles are congruent.

Similar Circles Theorem (p. 585)

All circles are similar.

Congruent Corresponding Chords Theorem (p. 590)

In the same circle, or in congruent circles, two minor arcs are congruent if and only if their corresponding chords are congruent.

Perpendicular Chord Bisector Theorem (p. 590)

If a diameter of a circle is perpendicular to a chord, then the diameter bisects the chord and its arc.

Perpendicular Chord Bisector Converse (p. 590)

If one chord of a circle is a perpendicular bisector of another chord, then the first chord is a diameter.

Equidistant Chords Theorem (p. 592)

In the same circle, or in congruent circles, two chords are congruent if and only if they are equidistant from the center.

Measure of an Inscribed Angle Theorem (p. 598)

The measure of an inscribed angle is one-half the measure of its intercepted arc.

Inscribed Angles of a Circle Theorem (p. 599)

If two inscribed angles of a circle intercept the same arc, then the angles are congruent.

Inscribed Right Triangle Theorem (p. 600)

If a right triangle is inscribed in a circle, then the hypotenuse is a diameter of the circle. Conversely, if one side of an inscribed triangle is a diameter of the circle, then the triangle is a right triangle and the angle opposite the diameter is the right angle.

Inscribed Quadrilateral Theorem (p. 600)

A quadrilateral can be inscribed in a circle if and only if its opposite angles are supplementary.

Tangent and Intersected Chord Theorem (p. 606)

If a tangent and a chord intersect at a point on a circle, then the measure of each angle formed is one-half the measure of its intercepted arc.

Angles Inside the Circle Theorem (p. 607)

If two chords intersect inside a circle, then the measure of each angle is one-half the sum of the measures of the arcs intercepted by the angle and its vertical angle.

Angles Outside the Circle Theorem (p. 607)

If a tangent and a secant, two tangents, or two secants intersect outside a circle, then the measure of the angle formed is one-half the difference of the measures of the intercepted arcs.

Circumscribed Angle Theorem (p. 608)

The measure of a circumscribed angle is equal to $180°$ minus the measure of the central angle that intercepts the same arc.

Segments of Chords Theorem (p. 614)

If two chords intersect in the interior of a circle, then the product of the lengths of the segments of one chord is equal to the product of the lengths of the segments of the other chord.

Segments of Secants Theorem (p. 615)

If two secant segments share the same endpoint outside a circle, then the product of the lengths of one secant segment and its external segment equals the product of the lengths of the other secant segment and its external segment.

Segments of Secants and Tangents Theorem (p. 616)

If a secant segment and a tangent segment share an endpoint outside a circle, then the product of the lengths of the secant segment and its external segment equals the square of the length of the tangent segment.

Integrated Mathematics III

Law of Sines (p. 487)

The Law of Sines can be written in either of the following forms for $\triangle ABC$ with sides of length a, b, and c.

$$\frac{\sin A}{a} = \frac{\sin B}{b} = \frac{\sin C}{c}$$

$$\frac{a}{\sin A} = \frac{b}{\sin B} = \frac{c}{\sin C}$$

Law of Cosines (p. 494)

If $\triangle ABC$ has sides of length a, b, and c, then the following are true.

$$a^2 = b^2 + c^2 - 2bc \cos A$$
$$b^2 = a^2 + c^2 - 2ac \cos B$$
$$c^2 = a^2 + b^2 - 2ab \cos C$$

Reference

Properties

Properties of Equality

Let a, b, and c be real numbers.

Addition Property of Equality
If $a = b$, then $a + c = b + c$.

Subtraction Property of Equality
If $a = b$, then $a - c = b - c$.

Multiplication Property of Equality
If $a = b$, then $a \cdot c = b \cdot c$, $c \neq 0$.

Division Property of Equality
If $a = b$, then $a \div c = b \div c$, $c \neq 0$.

Reflexive Property of Equality
$a = a$

Symmetric Property of Equality
If $a = b$, then $b = a$.

Transitive Property of Equality
If $a = b$ and $b = c$, then $a = c$.

Substitution Property of Equality
If $a = b$, then a can be substituted for b (or b for a) in any equation or expression.

Properties of Inequality

Let a, b, and c be real numbers.

Addition Property of Inequality
If $a > b$, then $a + c > b + c$.
If $a < b$, then $a + c < b + c$.

Subtraction Property of Inequality
If $a > b$, then $a - c > b - c$.
If $a < b$, then $a - c < b - c$.

Multiplication Property of Inequality ($c > 0$)
If $a > b$ and $c > 0$, then $ac > bc$.
If $a < b$ and $c > 0$, then $ac < bc$.

Division Property of Inequality ($c > 0$)
If $a > b$ and $c > 0$, then $\dfrac{a}{c} > \dfrac{b}{c}$.

If $a < b$ and $c > 0$, then $\dfrac{a}{c} < \dfrac{b}{c}$.

Multiplication Property of Inequality ($c < 0$)
If $a > b$ and $c < 0$, then $ac < bc$.
If $a < b$ and $c < 0$, then $ac > bc$.

Division Property of Inequality ($c < 0$)
If $a > b$ and $c < 0$, then $\dfrac{a}{c} < \dfrac{b}{c}$.

If $a < b$ and $c < 0$, then $\dfrac{a}{c} > \dfrac{b}{c}$.

* The Properties of Inequality are also true for $\geq$ and $\leq$.

Properties of Exponents

Let a and b be real numbers and let m and n be rational numbers.

Zero Exponent
$a^0 = 1$, where $a \neq 0$

Negative Exponent
$a^{-n} = \dfrac{1}{a^n}$, where $a \neq 0$

Product of Powers Property
$a^m \cdot a^n = a^{m+n}$

Quotient of Powers Property
$\dfrac{a^m}{a^n} = a^{m-n}$, where $a \neq 0$

Power of a Power Property
$(a^m)^n = a^{mn}$

Power of a Product Property
$(ab)^m = a^m b^m$

Power of a Quotient Property
$\left(\dfrac{a}{b}\right)^m = \dfrac{a^m}{b^m}$, where $b \neq 0$

Rational Exponents
$a^{m/n} = (a^{1/n})^m = (\sqrt[n]{a})^m$

Rational Exponents
$a^{-m/n} = \dfrac{1}{a^{m/n}} = \dfrac{1}{(a^{1/n})^m} = \dfrac{1}{(\sqrt[n]{a})^m}$,
where $a \neq 0$

Properties of Absolute Value

Let a and b be real numbers.

$|a| \geq 0$

$|-a| = |a|$

$|ab| = |a||b|$

$\left|\dfrac{a}{b}\right| = \dfrac{|a|}{|b|}$, $b \neq 0$

Properties of Radicals

Let a and b be real numbers and let n be an integer greater than 1.

Product Property of Square Roots

$\sqrt{ab} = \sqrt{a} \cdot \sqrt{b}$, where $a, b \geq 0$

Product Property of Radicals

$\sqrt[n]{ab} = \sqrt[n]{a} \cdot \sqrt[n]{b}$

Quotient Property of Square Roots

$\sqrt{\dfrac{a}{b}} = \dfrac{\sqrt{a}}{\sqrt{b}}$, where $a \geq 0$ and $b > 0$

Quotient Property of Radicals

$\sqrt[n]{\dfrac{a}{b}} = \dfrac{\sqrt[n]{a}}{\sqrt[n]{b}}$, where $b \neq 0$

Square Root of a Negative Number

1. If r is a positive real number, then $\sqrt{-r} = i\sqrt{r}$.
2. By the first property, it follows that $(i\sqrt{r})^2 = -r$.

Properties of Logarithms

Let b, m, and n be positive real numbers with $b \neq 1$.

Product Property

$\log_b mn = \log_b m + \log_b n$

Quotient Property

$\log_b \dfrac{m}{n} = \log_b m - \log_b n$

Power Property

$\log_b m^n = n \log_b m$

Properties of Segment and Angle Congruence

Reflexive Property of Congruence

For any segment AB, $\overline{AB} \cong \overline{AB}$.

For any angle A, $\angle A \cong \angle A$.

Symmetric Property of Congruence

If $\overline{AB} \cong \overline{CD}$, then $\overline{CD} \cong \overline{AB}$.

If $\angle A \cong \angle B$, then $\angle B \cong \angle A$.

Transitive Property of Congruence

If $\overline{AB} \cong \overline{CD}$ and $\overline{CD} \cong \overline{EF}$, then $\overline{AB} \cong \overline{EF}$.

If $\angle A \cong \angle B$ and $\angle B \cong \angle C$, then $\angle A \cong \angle C$.

Other Properties

Property of Equality for Exponential Equations

If $b > 0$ and $b \neq 1$, then $b^x = b^y$ if and only if $x = y$.

Property of Equality for Logarithmic Equations

If b, x, and y are positive real numbers with $b \neq 1$, then $\log_b x = \log_b y$ if and only if $x = y$.

Distributive Property

Sum

$a(b + c) = ab + ac$

Difference

$a(b - c) = ab - ac$

Zero-Product Property

If a and b are real numbers and $ab = 0$, then $a = 0$ or $b = 0$.

Transitive Property of Parallel Lines

If $p \parallel q$ and $q \parallel r$, then $p \parallel r$.

Triangle Inequalities

Triangle Inequality Theorem

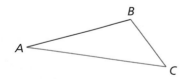

$AB + BC > AC$
$AC + BC > AB$
$AB + AC > BC$

Pythagorean Inequalities Theorem

If $c^2 < a^2 + b^2$, then $\triangle ABC$ is acute.

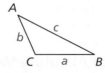

If $c^2 > a^2 + b^2$, then $\triangle ABC$ is obtuse.

Patterns

Square of a Binomial Pattern
$(a + b)^2 = a^2 + 2ab + b^2$
$(a - b)^2 = a^2 - 2ab + b^2$

Sum and Difference Pattern
$(a + b)(a - b) = a^2 - b^2$

Cube of a Binomial Pattern
$(a + b)^3 = a^3 + 3a^2b + 3ab^2 + b^3$
$(a - b)^3 = a^3 - 3a^2b + 3ab^2 - b^3$

Completing the Square
$x^2 + bx + \left(\dfrac{b}{2}\right)^2 = \left(x + \dfrac{b}{2}\right)^2$

Difference of Two Squares Pattern
$a^2 - b^2 = (a + b)(a - b)$

Perfect Square Trinomial Pattern
$a^2 + 2ab + b^2 = (a + b)^2$
$a^2 - 2ab + b^2 = (a - b)^2$

Sum of Two Cubes Pattern
$a^3 + b^3 = (a + b)(a^2 - ab + b^2)$

Difference of Two Cubes Pattern
$a^3 - b^3 = (a - b)(a^2 + ab + b^2)$

Algebra Theorems

The Remainder Theorem
If a polynomial $f(x)$ is divided by $x - k$, then the remainder is $r = f(k)$.

The Factor Theorem
A polynomial $f(x)$ has a factor $x - k$ if and only if $f(k) = 0$.

The Rational Root Theorem
If $f(x) = a_n x^n + \cdots + a_1 x + a_0$ has *integer* coefficients, then every rational solution of $f(x) = 0$ has the form

$\dfrac{p}{q} = \dfrac{\text{factor of constant term } a_0}{\text{factor of leading coefficient } a_n}.$

The Irrational Conjugates Theorem
Let f be a polynomial function with rational coefficients, and let a and b be rational numbers such that $\sqrt{b}$ is irrational. If $a + \sqrt{b}$ is a zero of f, then $a - \sqrt{b}$ is also a zero of f.

The Fundamental Theorem of Algebra

Theorem   If $f(x)$ is a polynomial of degree n where $n > 0$, then the equation $f(x) = 0$ has at least one solution in the set of complex numbers.

Corollary   If $f(x)$ is a polynomial of degree n where $n > 0$, then the equation $f(x) = 0$ has exactly n solutions provided each solution repeated twice is counted as two solutions, each solution repeated three times is counted as three solutions, and so on.

The Complex Conjugates Theorem
If f is a polynomial function with real coefficients, and $a + bi$ is an imaginary zero of f, then $a - bi$ is also a zero of f.

Descartes's Rule of Signs
Let $f(x) = a_n x^n + a_{n-1} x^{n-1} + \cdots + a_2 x^2 + a_1 x + a_0$ be a polynomial function with real coefficients.

- The number of positive real zeros of f is equal to the number of changes in sign of the coefficients of $f(x)$ or is less than this by an even number.

- The number of negative real zeros of f is equal to the number of changes in sign of the coefficients of $f(-x)$ or is less than this by an even number.

Formulas

Algebra

Slope

$$m = \frac{y_2 - y_1}{x_2 - x_1}$$

Slope-intercept form

$$y = mx + b$$

Point-slope form

$$y - y_1 = m(x - x_1)$$

Standard form of a linear equation

$Ax + By = C$, where A and B are not both 0

Vertex form of an absolute value function

$f(x) = a|x - h| + k$, where $a \neq 0$

Standard form of a quadratic function

$f(x) = ax^2 + bx + c$, where $a \neq 0$

Vertex form of a quadratic function

$f(x) = a(x - h)^2 + k$, where $a \neq 0$

Intercept form of a quadratic function

$f(x) = a(x - p)(x - q)$, where $a \neq 0$

Quadratic Formula

$$x = \frac{-b \pm \sqrt{b^2 - 4ac}}{2a}, \text{ where } a \neq 0$$

Standard equation of a circle

$(x - h)^2 + (y - k)^2 = r^2$

Standard form of a polynomial function

$f(x) = a_n x^n + a_{n-1} x^{n-1} + \cdots + a_1 x + a_0$

Exponential growth function

$y = a(1 + r)^t$, where $a > 0$ and $r > 0$

or

$y = ab^x$, where $a > 0$ and $b > 1$

Exponential decay function

$y = a(1 - r)^t$, where $a > 0$ and $0 < r < 1$

or

$y = ab^x$, where $a > 0$ and $0 < b < 1$

Logarithm of y with base b

$\log_b y = x$ if and only if $b^x = y$

Change-of-base formula

$\log_c a = \dfrac{\log_b a}{\log_b c}$, where a, b, and c are positive real numbers

with $b \neq 1$ and $c \neq 1$.

Explicit rule for an arithmetic sequence

$a_n = a_1 + (n - 1)d$

Explicit rule for a geometric sequence

$a_n = a_1 r^{n-1}$

Recursive equation for an arithmetic sequence

$a_n = a_{n-1} + d$

Recursive equation for a geometric sequence

$a_n = r \cdot a_{n-1}$

Sum of n terms of 1

$$\sum_{i=1}^{n} 1 = n$$

Sum of first n positive integers

$$\sum_{i=1}^{n} i = \frac{n(n + 1)}{2}$$

Sum of squares of first n positive integers

$$\sum_{i=1}^{n} i^2 = \frac{n(n + 1)(2n + 1)}{6}$$

Sum of first n terms of an arithmetic series

$$S_n = n\left(\frac{a_1 + a_n}{2}\right)$$

Sum of first n terms of a geometric series

$S_n = a_1\left(\dfrac{1 - r^n}{1 - r}\right)$, where $r \neq 1$

Sum of an infinite geometric series

$S = \dfrac{a_1}{1 - r}$ provided $|r| < 1$

Statistics

Sample mean

$$\bar{x} = \frac{\Sigma x}{n}$$

Standard deviation

$$\sigma = \sqrt{\frac{(x_1 - \bar{x})^2 + (x_2 - \bar{x})^2 + \cdots + (x_n - \bar{x})^2}{n}}$$

z-Score

$$z = \frac{x - \mu}{\sigma}$$

Margin of error for sample proportions

$$\pm \frac{1}{\sqrt{n}}$$

Probability and Combinatorics

Theoretical Probability $= \dfrac{\text{Number of favorable outcomes}}{\text{Total number of outcomes}}$

Experimental Probability $= \dfrac{\text{Number of successes}}{\text{Number of trials}}$

Probability of the complement of an event
$P(\overline{A}) = 1 - P(A)$

Probability of independent events
$P(A \text{ and } B) = P(A) \cdot P(B)$

Probability of dependent events
$P(A \text{ and } B) = P(A) \cdot P(B \mid A)$

Probability of compound events
$P(A \text{ or } B) = P(A) + P(B) - P(A \text{ and } B)$

Odds

Odds in favor $= \dfrac{\text{Number of favorable outcomes}}{\text{Number of unfavorable outcomes}}$

Odds against $= \dfrac{\text{Number of unfavorable outcomes}}{\text{Number of favorable outcomes}}$

Permutations

$_nP_r = \dfrac{n!}{(n - r)!}$

Combinations

$_nC_r = \dfrac{n!}{(n - r)! \cdot r!}$

Binomial experiments

$P(k \text{ successes}) = \,_nC_k p^k (1 - p)^{n - k}$

The Binomial Theorem

$(a + b)^n = \,_nC_0 a^n b^0 + \,_nC_1 a^{n - 1} b^1 + \,_nC_2 a^{n - 2} b^2 + \cdots + \,_nC_n a^0 b^n$, where n is a positive integer.

Coordinate Geometry

Midpoint Formula
$\left(\dfrac{x_1 + x_2}{2}, \dfrac{y_1 + y_2}{2} \right)$

Distance Formula
$d = \sqrt{(x_2 - x_1)^2 + (y_2 - y_1)^2}$

Right Triangles

Pythagorean Theorem

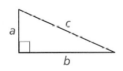

$a^2 + b^2 = c^2$

45°-45°-90° Triangles

hypotenuse $= \text{leg} \cdot \sqrt{2}$

30°-60°-90° Triangles

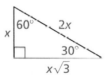

hypotenuse $= \text{shorter leg} \cdot 2$
longer leg $= \text{shorter leg} \cdot \sqrt{3}$

Trigonometric Ratios

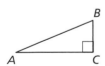

$\sin A = \dfrac{BC}{AB}$

$\sin^{-1} \dfrac{BC}{AB} = m\angle A$

$\cos A = \dfrac{AC}{AB}$

$\cos^{-1} \dfrac{AC}{AB} = m\angle A$

$\tan A = \dfrac{BC}{AC}$

$\tan^{-1} \dfrac{BC}{AC} = m\angle A$

Sine and cosine of complementary angles
Let A and B be complementary angles. Then the following statements are true.

$\sin A = \cos(90° - A) = \cos B$

$\cos A = \sin(90° - A) = \sin B$

$\sin B = \cos(90° - B) = \cos A$

$\cos B = \sin(90° - B) = \sin A$

Trigonometry

General definitions of trigonometric functions

Let θ be an angle in standard position, and let (x, y) be the point where the terminal side of θ intersects the circle $x^2 + y^2 = r^2$. The six trigonometric functions of θ are defined as shown.

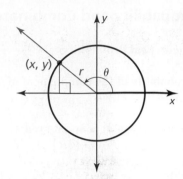

$$\sin \theta = \frac{y}{r} \qquad \cos \theta = \frac{x}{r} \qquad \tan \theta = \frac{y}{x}, x \neq 0$$

$$\csc \theta = \frac{r}{y}, y \neq 0 \qquad \sec \theta = \frac{r}{x}, x \neq 0 \qquad \cot \theta = \frac{x}{y}, y \neq 0$$

Conversion between degrees and radians
$180° = \pi$ radians

Arc length of a sector
$s = r\theta$

Area of a sector
$A = \frac{1}{2}r^2\theta$

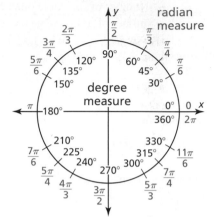

Reciprocal Identities

$$\sin \theta = \frac{1}{\csc \theta} \qquad \cos \theta = \frac{1}{\sec \theta} \qquad \tan \theta = \frac{1}{\cot \theta}$$

$$\csc \theta = \frac{1}{\sin \theta} \qquad \sec \theta = \frac{1}{\cos \theta} \qquad \cot \theta = \frac{1}{\tan \theta}$$

Tangent and Cotangent Identities

$$\tan \theta = \frac{\sin \theta}{\cos \theta} \qquad \cot \theta = \frac{\cos \theta}{\sin \theta}$$

Pythagorean Identities
$\sin^2 \theta + \cos^2 \theta = 1$
$1 + \tan^2 \theta = \sec^2 \theta$
$1 + \cot^2 \theta = \csc^2 \theta$

Negative Angle Identities
$\sin(-\theta) = -\sin \theta$
$\cos(-\theta) = \cos \theta$
$\tan(-\theta) = -\tan \theta$
$\csc(-\theta) = -\csc \theta$
$\sec(-\theta) = \sec \theta$
$\cot(-\theta) = -\cot \theta$

Cofunction Identites

$$\sin\left(\frac{\pi}{2} - \theta\right) = \cos \theta \qquad \csc\left(\frac{\pi}{2} - \theta\right) = \sec \theta$$

$$\cos\left(\frac{\pi}{2} - \theta\right) = \sin \theta \qquad \sec\left(\frac{\pi}{2} - \theta\right) = \csc \theta$$

$$\tan\left(\frac{\pi}{2} - \theta\right) = \cot \theta \qquad \cot\left(\frac{\pi}{2} - \theta\right) = \tan \theta$$

Sum Formulas
$\sin(a + b) = \sin a \cos b + \cos a \sin b$
$\cos(a + b) = \cos a \cos b - \sin a \sin b$

$$\tan(a + b) = \frac{\tan a + \tan b}{1 - \tan a \tan b}$$

Difference Formulas
$\sin(a - b) = \sin a \cos b - \cos a \sin b$
$\cos(a - b) = \cos a \cos b + \sin a \sin b$

$$\tan(a - b) = \frac{\tan a - \tan b}{1 + \tan a \tan b}$$

Any Triangle

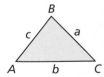

Area

$$\text{Area} = \frac{1}{2}bc \sin A$$

$$\text{Area} = \frac{1}{2}ac \sin B$$

$$\text{Area} = \frac{1}{2}ab \sin C$$

Law of Sines

$$\frac{\sin A}{a} = \frac{\sin B}{b} = \frac{\sin C}{c}$$

$$\frac{a}{\sin A} = \frac{b}{\sin B} = \frac{c}{\sin C}$$

Law of Cosines
$a^2 = b^2 + c^2 - 2bc \cos A$
$b^2 = a^2 + c^2 - 2ac \cos B$
$c^2 = a^2 + b^2 - 2ab \cos C$

Polygons

Triangle Sum Theorem

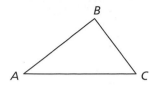

$$m\angle A + m\angle B + m\angle C = 180°$$

Exterior Angle Theorem

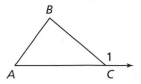

$$m\angle 1 = m\angle A + m\angle B$$

Triangle Midsegment Theorem

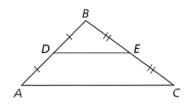

$$\overline{DE} \parallel \overline{AC}$$
$$DE = \tfrac{1}{2}AC$$

Trapezoid Midsegment Theorem

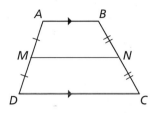

$$\overline{MN} \parallel \overline{AB}$$
$$\overline{MN} \parallel \overline{DC}$$
$$MN = \tfrac{1}{2}(AB + CD)$$

Polygon Interior Angles Theorem

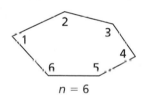

$$m\angle 1 + m\angle 2 + \cdots + m\angle n = (n - 2) \cdot 180°$$

Polygon Exterior Angles Theorem

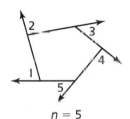

$$m\angle 1 + m\angle 2 + \cdots + m\angle n = 360°$$

Geometric Mean (Altitude) Theorem

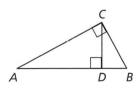

$$CD^2 = AD \cdot BD$$

Geometric Mean (Leg) Theorem

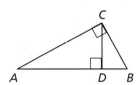

$$CB^2 = DB \cdot AB$$
$$AC^2 = AD \cdot AB$$

Circles

Arc length

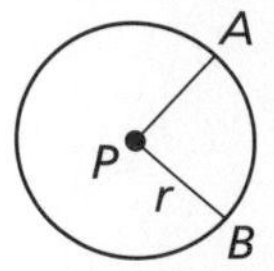

Arc length of $\overset{\frown}{AB} = \dfrac{m\overset{\frown}{AB}}{360°} \cdot 2\pi r$

Area of a sector

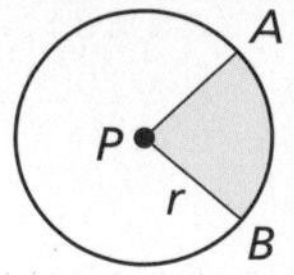

Area of sector $APB = \dfrac{m\overset{\frown}{AB}}{360°} \cdot \pi r^2$

Central angles

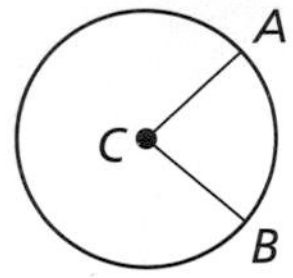

$m\angle ACB = m\overset{\frown}{AB}$

Inscribed angles

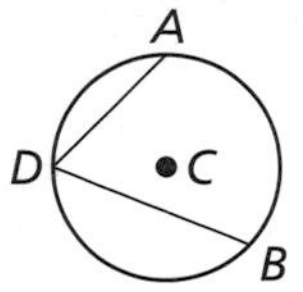

$m\angle ADB = \frac{1}{2}m\overset{\frown}{AB}$

Tangent and intersected chord

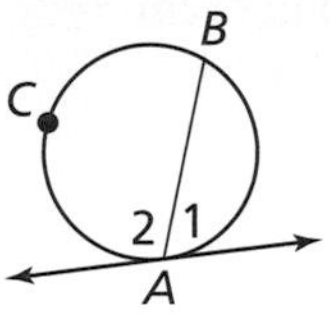

$m\angle 1 = \frac{1}{2}m\overset{\frown}{AB}$

$m\angle 2 = \frac{1}{2}m\overset{\frown}{BCA}$

Angles and Segments of Circles

Two chords

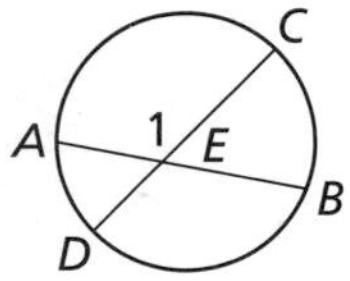

$m\angle 1 = \frac{1}{2}\left(m\overset{\frown}{AC} + m\overset{\frown}{DB}\right)$

$EA \cdot EB = EC \cdot ED$

Two secants

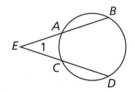

$m\angle 1 = \frac{1}{2}\left(m\overset{\frown}{BD} - m\overset{\frown}{AC}\right)$

$EA \cdot EB = EC \cdot ED$

Tangent and secant

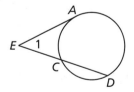

$m\angle 1 = \frac{1}{2}\left(m\overset{\frown}{AD} - m\overset{\frown}{AC}\right)$

$EA^2 = EC \cdot ED$

Two tangents

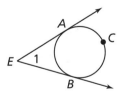

$m\angle 1 = \frac{1}{2}\left(m\overset{\frown}{ACB} - m\overset{\frown}{AB}\right)$

$EA = EB$

Other Formulas

Simple Interest
$I = Prt$

Compound Interest
$A = P\left(1 + \dfrac{r}{n}\right)^{nt}$

Continuously Compounded Interest
$A = Pe^{rt}$

Distance
$d = rt$

Geometric mean
$x = \sqrt{a \cdot b}$

Density
$\text{Density} = \dfrac{\text{Mass}}{\text{Volume}}$

Similar polygons or similar solids with scale factor k
Ratio of perimeters $= k$
Ratio of areas $= k^2$
Ratio of volumes $= k^3$

Reference

Perimeter, Area, and Volume Formulas

Square

$P = 4s$
$A = s^2$

Rectangle

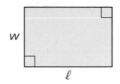

$P = 2\ell + 2w$
$A = \ell w$

Triangle

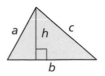

$P = a + b + c$
$A = \frac{1}{2}bh$

Circle

$C = \pi d$ or $C = 2\pi r$
$A = \pi r^2$

Parallelogram

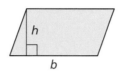

$A = bh$

Trapezoid

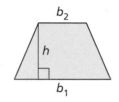

$A = \frac{1}{2}h(b_1 + b_2)$

Rhombus/Kite

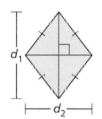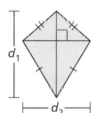

$A = \frac{1}{2}d_1 d_2$

Regular *n*-gon

$A = \frac{1}{2}aP$ or $A = \frac{1}{2}a \cdot ns$

Prism

$L = Ph$
$S = 2B + Ph$
$V = Bh$

Cylinder

$L = 2\pi rh$
$S = 2\pi r^2 + 2\pi rh$
$V = \pi r^2 h$

Pyramid

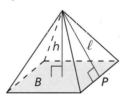

$L = \frac{1}{2}P\ell$
$S = B + \frac{1}{2}P\ell$
$V = \frac{1}{3}Bh$

Cone

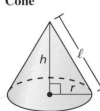

$L = \pi r \ell$
$S = \pi r^2 + \pi r \ell$
$V = \frac{1}{3}\pi r^2 h$

Sphere

$S = 4\pi r^2$
$V = \frac{4}{3}\pi r^3$

Conversions

U.S. Customary

1 foot = 12 inches
1 yard = 3 feet
1 mile = 5280 feet
1 mile = 1760 yards
1 acre = 43,560 square feet
1 cup = 8 fluid ounces
1 pint = 2 cups
1 quart = 2 pints
1 gallon = 4 quarts
1 gallon = 231 cubic inches
1 pound = 16 ounces
1 ton = 2000 pounds

U.S. Customary to Metric

1 inch = 2.54 centimeters
1 foot $\approx$ 0.3 meter
1 mile $\approx$ 1.61 kilometers
1 quart $\approx$ 0.95 liter
1 gallon $\approx$ 3.79 liters
1 cup $\approx$ 237 milliliters
1 pound $\approx$ 0.45 kilogram
1 ounce $\approx$ 28.3 grams
1 gallon $\approx$ 3785 cubic centimeters

Time

1 minute = 60 seconds
1 hour = 60 minutes
1 hour = 3600 seconds
1 year = 52 weeks

Temperature

$$C = \frac{5}{9}(F - 32)$$

$$F = \frac{9}{5}C + 32$$

Metric

1 centimeter = 10 millimeters
1 meter = 100 centimeters
1 kilometer = 1000 meters
1 liter = 1000 milliliters
1 kiloliter = 1000 liters
1 milliliter = 1 cubic centimeter
1 liter = 1000 cubic centimeters
1 cubic millimeter = 0.001 milliliter
1 gram = 1000 milligrams
1 kilogram = 1000 grams

Metric to U.S. Customary

1 centimeter $\approx$ 0.39 inch
1 meter $\approx$ 3.28 feet
1 meter $\approx$ 39.37 inches
1 kilometer $\approx$ 0.62 mile
1 liter $\approx$ 1.06 quarts
1 liter $\approx$ 0.26 gallon
1 kilogram $\approx$ 2.2 pounds
1 gram $\approx$ 0.035 ounce
1 cubic meter $\approx$ 264 gallons

Credits

Front Matter

vii ©iStockphoto.com/Christopher Futcher; **viii** CristinaMuraca/Shutterstock.com; **ix** Rodrigo Garrido/Shutterstock.com; **x** Doug Matthews/Shutterstock.com; **xi** Reinhold Leitner/Shutterstock.com; **xii** Ariwasabi/Shutterstock.com; **xiii** Miguel Navarro; **xiv** Charles Knowles/Shutterstock.com; **xv** Guy Shapira/Shutterstock.com; **xvii** mark higgins/Shutterstock.com; **xix** © Pniesen | Dreamstime.com

Chapter 1

0 *top left* Jorg Hackemann/Shutterstock.com; *top right* TFoxFoto/Shutterstock.com; *center left* Bronwyn Photo/Shutterstock.com; *bottom right* Bohbeh/Shutterstock.com; *bottom left* CristinaMuraca/Shutterstock.com; **4** CristinaMuraca/Shutterstock.com; **5** Bohbeh/Shutterstock.com; **6** kai4107/Shutterstock.com; **9** *top left* Mega Pixel/Shutterstock.com; *top right* JIANG HONGYAN/Shutterstock.com; *bottom left* forest_strider/Shutterstock.com; *bottom right* Mario Savoia/Shutterstock.com; **11** Sahani Photography/Shutterstock.com, Adapted from Slice of millennial tree. Marked annual rings corresponding to important events - the discovery of America , etc., by Vovchar (*http://commons.wikimedia.org/wiki/File:Srez_sequoia.jpg*), CC BY SA-3.0.; **13** *top right* Only Fabrizio/Shutterstock.com; *exercise 3 left* Zelenskaya/Shutterstock.com; *exercise 3 right* Kompaniets Taras/Shutterstock.com; *bottom left* Patryk Kosmider/Shutterstock.com; **14** *exercise 10 left* Gyvafoto/Shutterstock.com; *exercise 10 right* ©iStockphoto.com/DonNichols; *top right* ©iStockphoto.com/Prill Mediendesign & Fotografie, Natykach Nataliia/Shutterstock.com; **15** Nattika/Shutterstock.com; **16** *exercise 7* Hurst Photo/Shutterstock.com; *exercise 8* rangizzz/Shutterstock.com; **17** *exploration 1 a.* Coprid/Shutterstock.com; *exploration 1 b.* HomeArt/Shutterstock.com; *exploration 1 c.* Svetlana Foote/Shutterstock.com; *exploration 1 d.* indigolotos/Shutterstock.com; *bottom right* PaulPaladin/Shutterstock.com; **20** TFoxFoto/Shutterstock.com; **22** topnatthapon/Shutterstock.com; **25** Ferenz/Shutterstock.com; **27** *exercise 2 from left to right* GeorgeMPhotography/Shutterstock.com, Givaga/Shutterstock.com, bitt24/Shutterstock.com, ©iStockphoto.com/kedsanee; *exercise 13* Carlos E. Santa Maria/Shutterstock.com; *exercise 14* ravl/Shutterstock.com; *exercise 15* Sashkin/Shutterstock.com; *exercise 16* Jorg Hackemann/Shutterstock.com; **29** tuulijumala/Shutterstock.com, luminaimages/Shutterstock.com; **31** ©iStockphoto.com/mlevy; **33** *top right* Bryan Solomon/Shutterstock.com; *bottom left* Tarasyuk Igor/Shutterstock.com; **34** *top right* neelsky/Shutterstock.com; *center left* Pavel L Photo and Video/Shutterstock.com; **35** MaxyM/Shutterstock.com

Chapter 2

36 *top left* Lisa F. Young/Shutterstock.com; *top right* Fotokostic/Shutterstock.com; *center left* ©iStockphoto.com/Dirk Freder; *bottom right* bikeriderlondon/Shutterstock.com; *bottom left* Rodrigo Garrido/Shutterstock.com; **43** Rodrigo Garrido/Shutterstock.com; **46** bikeriderlondon/Shutterstock.com; **52** © Farang | Dreamstime.com; **57** bikeriderlondon/Shutterstock.com; **59** Potapov Alexander/Shutterstock.com; **62** iPortret/Shutterstock.com; **68** Daniel Korzeniewski/Shutterstock.com; **69** Gemenacom/Shutterstock.com; **71** Nattika/Shutterstock.com; **77** Mike Brake/Shutterstock.com; **79** ©iStockphoto.com/Dirk Freder; **80** feathercollector/Shutterstock.com; **88** Mitch Gunn/Shutterstock.com; **89** Fotokostic/Shutterstock.com; **90** *center left* © Redeyed | Dreamstime.com; *center right* Garsya/Shutterstock.com; **93** Lisa F. Young/Shutterstock.com; **99** tuulijumala/Shutterstock.com, Marco Govel/Shutterstock.com; **104** KID_A/Shutterstock.com, Adam Fahey Designs/Shutterstock.com; **105** Steve Mann/Shutterstock.com

Chapter 3

108 *top left* Doug Matthews/Shutterstock.com; *top right* © Oseland | Dreamstime.com; *center left* Anton_Ivanov/Shutterstock.com; *bottom right* Aspen Photo/Shutterstock.com; *bottom left* clean_fotos/Shutterstock.com; **115** clean_fotos/Shutterstock.com; **117** *center right* © Lightvision | Dreamstime.com; *bottom right* tawan/Shutterstock.com; **118** JRB67/Shutterstock.com; **125** Flashon Studio/Shutterstock.com; **126** balein/Shutterstock.com; **134** Aspen Photo/Shutterstock.com; **139** Xavier Pironet/Shutterstock.com; **141** GoodMood Photo/Shutterstock.com; **143** Nattika/Shutterstock.com; **151** Anton_Ivanov/Shutterstock.com; **159** *top right* © Oseland | Dreamstime.com; *center right* Tyler Olson/Shutterstock.com; **164** d3images/Shutterstock.com; **166** Steve Byland/Shutterstock.com; **173** bikeriderlondon/Shutterstock.com; **174** Doug Matthews/Shutterstock.com; **178** nostal6ie/Shutterstock.com; **181** tuulijumala/Shutterstock.com, Anthony Ricci/Shutterstock.com; **187** Sergio Bertino/Shutterstock.com

Chapter 4

190 *top left* © Irur | Dreamstime.com; *top right* Reinhold Leitner/Shutterstock.com; *center left* katatonia82/Shutterstock.com; *bottom right* Courtesy NASA/JPL-Caltech; *bottom left* Sarun T/Shutterstock.com; **196** Nerthuz/Shutterstock.com; **206** Sarun T/Shutterstock.com; **210** Courtesy NASA/JPL-Caltech; **214** Krzysztof Gorski/Shutterstock.com; **215** Nattika/Shutterstock.com; **219** Glynnis Jones/Shutterstock.com; **222** Xiebiyun/Shutterstock.com; **223** *exercise 46 left* Christopher Meder/Shutterstock.com; *exercise 46 right* Samot/Shutterstock.com; **224** katatonia82/Shutterstock.com; **228** Reinhold Leitner/Shutterstock.com; **238** © Irur | Dreamstime.com; **239** *top left* Piotr Marcinski/Shutterstock.com; *bottom right* Dmitry Kalinovsky/Shutterstock.com; **241** tuulijumala/Shutterstock.com, Bartosz Budrewicz/Shutterstock.com; **245** Aspen Photo/Shutterstock.com

Chapter 5

248 *top left* NASA; *top right* Ariwasabi/Shutterstock.com; *center left* UnaPhoto/Shutterstock.com; *bottom right* Minerva Studio/Shutterstock.com; *bottom left* ©iStockphoto.com/slobo; **256** ©iStockphoto.com/slobo; **262** Joggie Botma/Shutterstock.com, Germanskydiver/Shutterstock.com; **263** *bottom left* Minerva Studio/Shutterstock.com; *top right* Lightspring/Shutterstock.com; **264** *top left* Richard A McMillin/Shutterstock.com; *top right* Arkorn/Shutterstock.com; **273** Nattika/Shutterstock.com; **278** UnaPhoto/Shutterstock.com; **280** *bottom left* Johan_R/Shutterstock.com; *top right* vasabii/Shutterstock.com, Suat Gursozlu/Shutterstock.com, ©iStockphoto.com/claudiaveja; **283** Ariwasabi/Shutterstock.com; **286** *bottom left* Ian Scott/Shutterstock.com; *center right* ©iStockphoto.com/joebelanger; **293** Edward Haylan/Shutterstock.com; **294** bikeriderlondon/Shutterstock.com; **295** *bottom left* Anton Zabielskyi/Shutterstock.com, photobank.ch/Shutterstock.com, Markus Gann/Shutterstock.com, Gladskikh Tatiana/Shutterstock.com, VladGavriloff/Shutterstock.com, Vasilyev Alexandr/Shutterstock.com; *bottom right* NASA; **296** rawcaptured/Shutterstock.com; **297** tuulijumala/Shutterstock.com, Dragon Images/Shutterstock.com; **301** escova/Shutterstock.com, Inna Petyakina/Shutterstock.com